KINGS AND QUEENS

800–1000

802	839	856	860	866	871	899	924	940	946	955	959	975	978

Egbert — Ethelwulf — Ethelbald — Ethelbert — Ethelred — Alfred — Edward the Elder — Athelstan — Edmund the Elder — Edred — Edwyn the Fair — Edgar the Peaceful — Edward the Martyr — Ethelred the Unready

1000–1200

April-Nov 1016 · 1035 · 1037 · 1040 · 1042 · Jan-Oct 1066 · 1087 · 1100 · 1135 · 1154 · 1189 · 1199

Ethelred — Edmund Ironside — Canute the Great — No monarch — Harold Harefoot — Hardicanute — St. Edward the Confessor — Harold II — William I (the Conqueror) — William II (Rufus) — Henry I — Stephen — Henry II — Richard I (the Lionheart) — John

1200–1400

1216 · 1272 · 1307 · 1327 · 1377 · 1399

John — Henry III — Edward I — Edward II — Edward III — Richard II — Henry IV

1400–1600

1413 · 1422 · 1461 · April-June 1483 · 1485 · 1509 · 1547 · 1553 · 1558

Henry IV — Henry V — Henry VI — Edward IV — Edward V — Richard III — Henry VII — Henry VIII — Edward VI — Mary I — Elizabeth I

1600–1800

1603 · 1625 · 1649 · 1660 · 1685 · 1688 · 1702 · 1714 · 1727 · 1760

Elizabeth I — James I — Charles I — Oliver Cromwell (Protectorate) — Charles II — James II — William III and Mary II — Anne — George I — George II — George III

1800–

1820 · 1830 · 1837 · 1901 · 1910 · Jan-Dec 1936 · 1952–

George III — George IV — William IV — Victoria — Edward VII — George V — Edward VIII — George VI — Elizabeth II

©

Stone Age Britain

The first men and women settled in Britain around 250,000BC. For tens of thousands of years only about 250 human beings lived in our country at any one time. They roamed the land in groups of about 15, hunting animals, snaring birds, fishing, and eating nuts and berries. They lived in caves and used rough stone tools. Gradually, people came from Europe, across the land that then joined Britain to the continent.

They brought with them better stone tools, and they lived in huts or skin tents. By this time they were growing crops of wheat and barley, domesticating pigs, sheep and cattle, and using bows and arrows.

ice sheet   *land bridge*

During early times, ice covered Britain north of the Thames. Until 6000BC Britain was joined to France across the Channel.

Man's first method of hunting was to dig a pit and cover it with branches and grass. When an animal fell into it, like a great mammoth - a creature now extinct - they hurled rocks at it and speared it to death.

250000BC

250,000BC First human being known to have lived in Britain - a young woman, whose remains have been found at Swanscombe, near Gravesend, Kent.

250,000BC - 3500BC This period is known as the Old Stone Age. Very few humans inhabit Britain - possibly only about 250 in all, living in small groups of 12-15 individuals.

10,000BC The ice cap retreats towards the Arctic at the end of the last Ice Age.

1. **A pick** for digging, made from the antler of a deer.
2. **A handaxe.** This was early man's basic tool. With it he could cut undergrowth, shape wood, scrape skins and cut meat.
3. **A flint arrowhead**
4. **A stone axe.** This was a later development.
5. **Chipping** a flint tool with a piece of bone.

By about 3000BC people were beginning to grow crops of corn in Britain. As in the drawing, they used sharp stone sickles to cut their crop. A woman followed the harvester and tied the corn into a sheaf. Families lived in thatched huts whose walls were made of woven twigs, plastered with mud. The huts were defended with a wooden stockade.

2000BC

3000BC First development at hill top camp of Maiden Castle, Dorset. Britons trade with Europe and Ireland and mine copper and tin.

2000BC The Stone Age village of Skara Brae is built in the Orkneys. It still survives intact to this day.

3500BC New Stone age settlers arrive from Europe. Using sharp stone tools, they sow and harvest crops, herd goats, pigs, sheep and cattle, and plough the land with wooden ploughs.

6,000BC The Land Bridge between Britain and Europe is covered by the waters of the English Channel, and Britain becomes an island.

With so much demand for flint or stone tools, flint mining became a specialist job. Flint mines 7m deep, dated about 2000BC, have been found at a place called Grimes Graves, in Norfolk.

The miners dug tunnels along the seams of flint, and worked by the light of lamps made of chalk cups in which a rush wick burnt in animal fat.

Bronze Age

About 2000BC, new settlers arrived in Britain, having travelled from Spain and Northern Europe. They wanted British copper, tin and gold. They made weapons and tools of bronze, which is a mixture of nine parts copper to one part tin. These people built great religious monuments, the best known being at Stonehenge, on Salisbury Plain; they also observed the sun, moon and stars. They imported wine and pottery from Europe, and exported slaves, gold and bronze ornaments and jewellery. Horses were used on farms and in warfare. When their chiefs died they were buried separately from the rest of the tribe.

2000BC

To protect themselves from their enemies, some people lived on islands in marshes and lakes. They drove tree-trunks into the mud and piled earth up, to make a firm base for their round wattle huts.

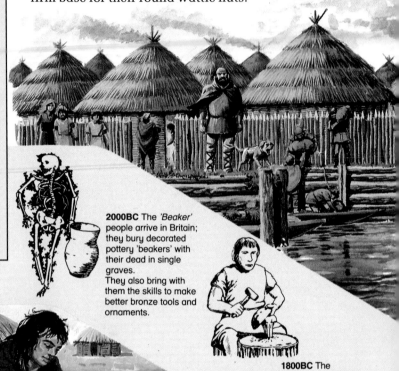

2000BC The *'Beaker'* people arrive in Britain; they bury decorated pottery 'beakers' with their dead in single graves.
They also bring with them the skills to make better bronze tools and ornaments.

1800BC The Beginnings of the Bronze Age in Britain. The 'Beaker' people settle in Ireland and work with copper, and bronze (copper and tin).

Many of the most ornate bronze tools, weapons, and ornaments belonged to the chiefs of the tribe and were buried with them. Above are a sword, axeheads, shield, flagon and mirror.

When men first became farmers they grew corn, particularly wheat. They rubbed the wheat seeds between stone querns to grind it into flour, which was then mixed with water.

Early men made long sea journeys in coracles, which are still used today by fishermen in Ireland and Wales. They were made of wicker-work, covered with skins, and were light enough to carry over land.

Wool from sheep was wrapped around a distaff, spun into a thread with a spindle and woven into cloth on a simple loom.

1600BC The Great Stonehenge temple is completed. Settlers arrive in Wessex from across the Channel; they trade with Europe, and use horses.

776BC First recorded Olympic Games in Greece.

600BC Celts begin to settle in Britain from Europe and introduce the use of iron.

600-400BC *'Halstadt'* people of Europe spread the use of iron.

500BC

Stonehenge was built from stones cut in South Wales. They were carried by sea and river, and finally dragged overland on wooden rollers. Thousands of people were employed in this feat of engineering.

500BC People start using wheeled carts. They also begin to observe the seasons, the Sun, the Moon and stars.

5

Around 600BC the Celts landed in Britain from Europe. They had stronger tools, and weapons made from iron. They spoke a language from which modern Welsh, Irish, Gaelic and Cornish are descended.

Celts were skilled farmers, fencing their villages and building barns and pens for their animals, and storage pits for grain.

Their ploughs had iron blades, and with them they could plough the heavy soils of the valleys, instead of settling only on the lighter soils of the hills.

They traded with the peoples of Europe and made beautiful pottery on potter's wheels, spun by heavy stone flywheels.

Some of the Celtic tribes lived in forts built on the tops of hills, surrounded by ditches and defended by wooden palisades at the top of steep banks. The most famous of these Celtic hill forts is Maiden Castle in Dorset, where the outlines of the ditches and banks can still be seen today.

Druids were the priests of the British tribes. They often lived away from the tribe in holy places in the forest. They put spells on the tribe's enemies and made human sacrifices.

100BC Gold coins are first introduced to Britain.

500BC

500BC More Celts arrive in Britain, using iron axes, sickles and saws to clear land for farming and growing crops of barley and wheat. The languages they speak are early forms of Welsh, Irish and Gaelic.

300BC Further development of Maiden Castle. It is now 1200 metres long by 600 metres wide, with earthworks 30 metres high. Herds of sheep and cattle are kept inside.

The first chariots were heavy, with solid wheels. Their sides were often basket-work, covered with a layer of ox-hide.

"The Celts are madly fond of war", wrote a visitor to Britain. They used double-edged bronze and iron swords, wore elaborate horned and decorated helmets and carried beautiful, ornate shields.

100 - 55BC Belgae Celts arrive in Britain from Europe, bringing heavier ploughs which can plough heavy soils. They cremate their dead, elect their chieftains, 'throw' pottery on a wheel, and are skilled doctors and horsemen. Celtic women are highly respected, and some become chiefs.

55BC Julius Caesar leads the first Roman raids on Britain. He explores Southern England, defeats the Celtic armies, but then returns to France. Julius Caesar's accounts of his raids are the very first recorded details of British life.

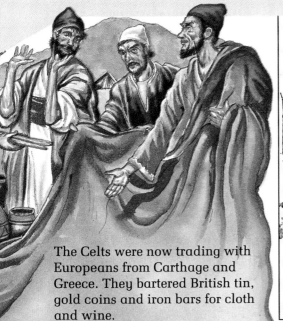

The Celts were now trading with Europeans from Carthage and Greece. They bartered British tin, gold coins and iron bars for cloth and wine.

Celts wore hand-woven woollen clothes. The dyed wool was woven into a checked pattern.

These iron fire dogs supported a spit for roasting meat. The iron pot was used for cooking meat, vegetables and cereal porridge over a slow-burning peat fire.

The Roman Invasion

In 55BC, the Roman General, Julius Caesar, whose armies had already conquered France, raided Southern England. He wanted to see how strong the Celtic (or British) tribes were, and whether Britain was worth including in the great Roman Empire.

The Romans did not return, and British life continued unchanged, although trade with Roman-occupied Europe increased.

Finally, in 43AD, the Roman General Aulus Plautius landed in Kent, determined to colonise Britain. Within a few years almost all of England had been conquered, but parts of Wales, Cornwall, Scotland and all of Ireland remained independent.

Women played many important roles in British life. The most famous of them was Boudicca, the elected Queen of the Iceni tribe, in Norfolk. She led a revolt against the Romans which very nearly brought about their withdrawal from Britain. Her troops burnt London, Colchester and St Albans to the ground. She killed herself when she was finally defeated.

55BC

54BC Caesar leads a second expedition to the South coast of Britain.
He conquers many chiefs, who promise to pay a tribute to Rome. The Roman forces then return to France.

44BC Julius Caesar is murdered on the Ides (15th) of March.

43AD Roman general Aulus Plautius conquers Britain for the Emperor Claudius. British tribal chief Caractacus is sent as a prisoner to Rome, but is released for his bravery. The Roman colonisation of Britain is based on the construction of towns and the use of British labour at all levels of importance.

44AD The Romans defeat the Britons at the siege of Maiden Castle.

Roman clothes were also worn by leading Britons. Men wore togas, women had elaborate hair styles, used make-up and jewellery.

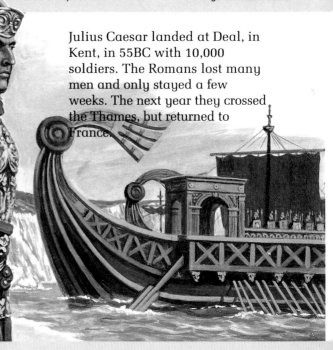

Julius Caesar landed at Deal, in Kent, in 55BC with 10,000 soldiers. The Romans lost many men and only stayed a few weeks. The next year they crossed the Thames, but returned to France.

The Romans were experts at destroying the forts of their enemies. Walls could not withstand their battering rams, nor the rocks thrown by their slings.

The Romans introduced glass bottles, jars and vases into Britain. They used oil lamps and pottery wine jars and were fond of gold and silver jewellery.

60AD First Roman villas appear in Britain.

60AD Boudicca, Queen of the Iceni tribe, leads a rebellion against the Romans.

75AD Fishbourne Palace is built in Sussex.

78AD Julius Agricola, Roman General, continues the conquest of Britain by conquering Wales.

80AD Agricola attacks Scotland, but is soon recalled to Rome.

100AD

The Romans and the leading Britons who adopted their ways, loved good food and wine. They were very fond of mutton, bacon, olives and fruit.

Roman officials and leading Britons lived in villas. In the country the villa was the centre of a big estate. In the town it was similarly designed, around a central open courtyard.

Roman Britain

For nearly 400 years Britain was a part of the Roman Empire, enjoying the security of *Pax Romana* – the peace of Rome. The mighty Roman army kept the constantly warring British tribes under control and Roman roads improved communications and trade.

The people of Britain learned many of the Roman ways, draining marshlands and clearing woodland to improve farming. They saw Roman towns with shops, schools, clean running water, public baths and theatres.

Unfortunately, when the Romans left our shores they had not taught the British to rule themselves and their civilisation was swept away by the peoples that succeeded them.

In Roman Britain, the public baths (thermae) were the centre of life in the towns. There were cold baths and steam rooms, heated by furnaces. The bathers would first be massaged with oil, which was scraped off with a strigil.

209AD A Roman army officer named Alban changed clothes with a Christian to save him from arrest. He was then arrested himself and executed in Verulamium (later to be renamed St Albans). For this he became the first Christian martyr in Britain.

100 AD

122AD The Roman Emperor Hadrian's visit to Britain is commemorated by the minting of a coin. He begin's his construction of Hadrian's Wall which was designed to hold back the Picts in the north and protect Roman Britain.

142AD A wall is built between the Forth and the Clyde for the Emperor Antoninus Pius. The wall was unsuccessful in keeping the Picts out of Roman Britain.

The Romans brought their love of circuses to Britain. Many towns had amphitheatres where the gladiators fought. As in Rome, the crowd decided if the loser would live or die.

The Romans worshipped many gods and goddesses such as Jupiter, Mars and Minerva. These Roman gods often had temples next to the shrines of Celtic gods.

In 122AD, the Emperor Hadrian began the construction of a great wall to protect Roman Britain from the Picts. It took 8,500 men eight years to complete the 117km wall from the Tyne to the Solway.

Mosaics were made by setting tiny pieces of coloured stone into a concrete base. They were used to decorate the villas of the wealthy with patterns and scenes from Roman mythology.

Many children of British tribal chiefs were taught to write Latin on a wax-covered board with a pointed bronze scriber.

306AD Constantine is proclaimed Emperor of Rome, in Eboracum (York). And later becomes a Christian.

360AD The first books of pages sewn together appear. Before this all writings were produced on scrolls of vellum.

367AD Saxons attack the east coast and Picts swarm over Hadrian's Wall. Count Theodosius restores Roman rule in the following year.

383AD Hadrian's Wall is again overrun by Picts and finally abandoned, ending full Roman control of Britain.

407AD Roman forces are withdrawn from Britain to defend Rome itself.

410AD The Emperor Honorius tells the Britains 'to provide for their own defence'. As the Roman legions leave Britain, the Saxon raids begin.

407AD

The Anglo-Saxons

Tribes from Northern Germany had been raiding Britain long before the Romans left our shores. Now that the country was undefended, Angles (after whom the country is named), Saxons, Jutes and many other tribes settled in England. The British were forced into Cornwall, Wales and Cumberland.

The Anglo-Saxons spoke different languages, and it is from these that the English language came. They cleared vast areas of land for farming, using their heavy ploughs to turn the soil.

Life was very hard; few adults lived past the age of forty, and few mothers had more than two surviving children.

In 596AD, Pope Gregory sent Augustine to Britain to spread Christianity. When Augustine met King Ethelbert, he converted him to the Christian faith.

407AD

410AD The invasion of the English, comprising Jutes, Angles and Saxons.

449AD The Jutes form the Kingdom of Kent.

470AD Cadbury Castle in Somerset is built. It is believed to be the site of the legendary King Arthur's Camelot.

477AD The Saxons form the Kingdom of Sussex, followed by the Kingdoms of Wessex (495AD) and Essex (527AD).

547AD The Angles form the Kingdom of Northumbria, followed by the Kingdoms of East Anglia (575AD) and Mercia (586AD).

The Saxons arrived on our shores as fierce raiders, but they soon settled as farmers and brought with them many new ideas that changed our countryside.

The monks established the first schools in England since Roman times. Here Bede, famous for writing the first English history, is teaching children in his monastery in Jarrow.

Saxon Chiefs loved to hold great banquets in their high, wooden halls. They often held them at Christmas time. This was when they slaughtered many of their animals, having no winter food for them. The Chief's family and servants all slept in the hall.

At Sutton Hoo, in Suffolk, an amazing discovery was made. Inside a burial mound, a Saxon ship, complete with weapons and treasure was unearthed.

The monks produced the first books in Britain. These were hand written and beautifully decorated in gold and enamel paint on vellum (animal skin).

597AD St Augustine's mission to Britain. Augustine, an emissary of Pope Gregory, spreads Christianity amongst the 'heathen' English. Ireland, Wales, Scotland and parts of Northern England had already been converted by the Celtic Christian Church.

664AD The Catholic and Celtic Churches combine at the Synod of Whitby.

779AD Offa the Mighty, King of Mercia, builds the 193 km long Offa's Dyke to keep out the Welsh tribes.

793AD First great Danish raid against Lindisfarne monastery, Northumbria.

796AD King Offa dies and the Kings of Wessex take control of England.

800AD

A Saxon noble, or Thane, with his lady. They were skilled weavers, and their long cloaks were often fastened with fine brooches.

The Saxons cleared vast areas of England for farming. Their iron ploughs, drawn by oxen, turned the heavy earth of the valleys, so that settlements no longer had to be on the light soil of hilltops. The tools they used are shown in early manuscripts.

The Danes

About 800AD pirates from Denmark began raids all along the British coasts. Like their brothers from Norway and Sweden, these Northmen or Vikings were some of the greatest sailors and explorers that there have ever been.

They sent their expeditions all over Europe, including Ireland and Russia, and settled in Iceland, from where they sailed to America. After raiding and looting many English towns, the Danes occupied Eastern England, which became called the Danelaw.

There they settled down to farm and also to trade. From York their merchants traded throughout Northern Europe.

The Danes (or Vikings) were fine sailors and great explorers. They raided the coasts of Britain for many years, but eventually settled as peaceful farmers.

839AD Norwegian chief Turgeis founds the city of Dublin and proclaims himself King of Ireland.

800AD

871AD-901AD The reign of Alfred the Great, who saves England from the Danes.

878AD Alfred defeats the Danes at the Battle of Ethandun.

886AD 'Alfred and Guthrum's Peace' divides England between the English and the Danes. The East of England is known as the Danelaw.

Edward the Confessor (or saint) was the last English King. He rebuilt Westminster Abbey, the monastery next to the royal palace of Westminster. He was buried at Westminster Abbey, and his funeral appeared later in the Bayeux tapestry (above).

Canute the Great was the first Danish King of England. The famous tale of him commanding the tide to turn, is believed by some that he was proving that even a king cannot control nature.

King Alfred of Wessex divided England with the Danes along Roman Watling Street.

Wessex
Danelaw

When King Alfred was hiding from the Danes he is said to have stayed with a poor Saxon peasant woman, who scolded him because he allowed her cakes to burn.

897AD King Alfred builds a navy and defeats the Danes at sea.

900AD-950AD The English recapture the Danelaw. Danes settle in Britain as peaceful farmers.

979AD-1016 The reign of Ethelred the Unready, who was unprepared for the further Danish raids which led to their victory over the English.

1017-1035 Reign of Danish King Canute.

1042-1066 Reign of Edward the Confessor, who restores the Royal House of Alfred.

1066

The Vikings placed wood carvings like this on the prows of their ships. They later made similar stone carvings in churches.

These Viking longships sailed around Europe and beyond.

They were often built of oak with animal hair between each plank.

The Norman Invasion

In the autumn of 1066, the French Duke William of Normandy, landed in Sussex with a strong army, many of whom were mounted knights. He claimed the English crown, which he said the late King, Edward the Confessor, had promised him. However, Harold of Wessex had been crowned King, having defeated a Norwegian invading army at Stamford Bridge, near York. His men marched for over a fortnight, and were exhausted when they met William's army 15 kms from Hastings. William won a decisive victory and Harold was killed. On Christmas Day in 1066 William was crowned King of England in Westminster Abbey.

Duke William's army met King Harold's on the 14th October 1066 at Senlac Hill, where the Sussex village of Battle now stands. Harold's army was larger and stood at the top of the hill, but William had more cavalry. The Normans won when they pretended to retreat and the English followed them down the hill.

The last English stand against the Normans was led by Hereward the Wake (watchful). He and his men held out at Ely, surrounded by marshes. Finally, in 1071, the Normans found a way through.

1066

1066 Harold II becomes King of England.
1066 Battle of Stamford Bridge. Harold defeats invaders led by his brother Tostig and Harold Hardrada, King of Norway. He then marches South and is defeated at the Battle of Hastings by the Norman Duke, William.

1066-1087 Reign of William I - William the Conqueror - the first Norman King of England.

1067 Work begins on the Bayeux Tapestry.

The story of the Norman invasion of England, from the dispute about the English crown, through to William's great victory at the Battle of Hastings, was recorded at the time, in the greatest detail, on the Bayeux Tapestry. These long sections of tapestry were embroidered in many colours, and can still be seen at Bayeux, in Normandy.

When the Normans took control of England, they started the feudal system. King William gave land to his barons and bishops, who allotted land to their knights. This was divided into manors and the work done by Saxon peasants.

1067 First revolt of the Saxons is subdued by King William.

1068-1069 A great rising of the Saxons, under Edwin and Morcar, assisted by the Danes, is defeated by William. He gives the Saxon lands to his Norman Barons.

1071 The last Saxon uprising is led by Morcar and Hereward (the Wake) from their stronghold, the *'Camp of Refuge'* in the Fens of East Anglia. By building a causeway 3kms long, William finally defeats them to complete his conquest of England.

1071

In this thatched hut a woman is cooking over an open hearth, without a chimney, while a man sleeps on a wooden bunk. The animals also lived in the hut.

Saxon Kings were advised by meetings of the Witan or Council of Wise Men. They were composed of nobles and were like an early House of Lords.

Norman Britain

When the Norman Kings conquered England there were only about a million people living in the country. Most of the countryside was waste land or forest. The Norman feudal system gave great estates and power to the barons. In return they had to serve the King whenever they were asked, especially in war. One percent of the people were barons. The remainder were soldiers, knights, churchmen, craftsmen, merchants, and finally peasants and their families who worked on the land and depended entirely on their lord. The Kings of England at that time also ruled much of France and fought endless wars there.

The castle of a Norman baron was both a home and a fortress, with walls several metres thick. The central keep was protected by both a wall and a moat.

1. Drawbridge 2. Gatehouse 3. Moat 4. Towers with arrow slits 5. Outer wall 6. Dovecote 7. Storerooms 8. Well 9. Stables and smithy 10. Barracks 11. Chapel 12. Lord's apartments 13. Great hall 14. Passages 15. Guard room 16. Buttery (for storing casks or butts)

1071

1086 Much of England is surveyed for tax purposes, and the information is compiled into the Domesday Book.

1096 The First Crusade is started with the preaching of Peter the Hermit. Many Crusading Knights die in their attempt to cross Europe and fight the Turks who were persecuting Christian pilgrims in the Holy land. The Holy Crusades lasted for 200 years.

1100-1135 Reign of Henry I.

1135 Henry I dies after a meal of lampreys (a type of fish).

William I ordered his officials to survey England, for taxes. The book - Domesday meaning Judgement Day - took two years to complete and is in the Public Record Office in London.

The man wears a clasped cloak and the woman's head is covered. Both of them wear long skirts.

The cook is rolling and cutting pastry, while a girl is turning meat on a spit. Above the fire a cauldron is simmering. The kitchen is lit by a small window.

William II, called Rufus (or red-faced), ruled after his father, William I. Like most Kings and nobles he enjoyed hunting, and was killed in the New Forest by an arrow, which was supposed to be an accident.

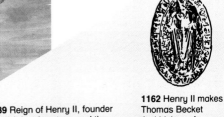

1162 Henry II makes Thomas Becket Archbishop of Canterbury.

1164 Henry II tries to reduce the power of the church. Thomas Becket is accused of treason and flees to France, disguised as a monk.

1170

1154-1189 Reign of Henry II, founder of the English legal system, and the first Plantagenet king.

1135-1154 Reign of Stephen, nephew of Henry I. Stephen takes the throne despite having promised to support Matilda, daughter of Henry I, in her claim to be Queen.

1139-1154 Civil War, as Matilda's supporters fight against Stephen for the throne.

The first plays were based on Bible stories, especially from the life of Christ, and were performed by wandering actors or mummers in town squares.

Hawking was very popular in Norman times. The sharp-eyed hawks were trained by falconers to catch birds like wild ducks in flight. The hawks would perch on the falconer's wrist, wearing a leather hood, until a suitable prey was sighted.

The Middle Ages

The life of a baron or knight was built around horses and warfare. Their idea of good manners was known as chivalry, which means knights or horsemen. The tournament at which good horsemen could show their skill, was the main sport of noblemen.

If there were no wars in England or France, the barons went to Palestine (now Israel) to fight in the Holy Crusades. The Church was a great landowner, and had power over the people, who had strong religious beliefs. The only man who could challenge the power of the King was the Archbishop of Canterbury, who spoke on behalf of the Church of God.

1170

1170 Thomas Becket is murdered in Canterbury Cathedral. Henry II is thought to have been involved in the plot.

1172 Henry II begins the conquest of Ireland.

1173–1189 Henry's sons, Henry, Richard, Geoffrey and John, join their mother in a rebellion against him.

1189-1199 Reign of Richard I, Richard the Lionheart, son of Henry II, who spends much of his life fighting abroad in the Crusades.

1199-1216 Reign of King John, fourth son of Henry II, a bad and unpopular king who plotted to take his brother's crown whilst he was away at the Crusades.

1204 King Philip II of France recaptures Normandy from the English.

Archbishop of Canterbury, Thomas Becket, claimed the Church was independent of the King's power. Henry II insisted that churchmen owed him allegiance, as much as any other of his subjects. Four knights murdered Becket in Canterbury Cathedral, claiming that it was the King's order, but Henry later denied it.

Most peasants worked on the land and covered their whole bodies and their heads to protect them from the summer sun.

Robin Hood was supposed to have been outlawed in the 13th century, and to have hidden with a band of followers in Sherwood Forest, Nottingham. He is said to have robbed the rich and given the money to the poor.

When the Muslim Turks captured Jerusalem, they stopped the Christians visiting the places where Christ taught and died. Crusaders who left Britain with crosses on their shields, fought to free Jerusalem, but failed.

The joust was a fight between two armoured, mounted knights, each wielding a blunted lance. Their helmets weighed almost 10kgs and carried colourful crests and emblems. The winner was the knight who knocked the other from his mount.

1215 The Magna Carta or Great Charter is signed by King John at Runnymede. This establishes the rights of the Barons, forms the basis of the British Constitution, and starts her people's fight for their liberties.

1216-1272 Reign of Henry III, son of John, who is only nine years old when crowned. He is protected by the Earl of Pembroke, as Regent.

1258 The rebellion of the Barons, led by Simon de Montfort, forces Henry III to meet with the *'Mad Parliament'* at Oxford, and accept new rules.

1264 Henry III defies the Barons once more, but is defeated and captured by Simon de Montfort at the Battle of Lewes.

1265

Each lord had his coat of arms shown on his shield, displayed at his castle and worn by his servants. The choice of arms and the entitlement to use them was decided by the herald.

Life in the Middle Ages

Though trade and towns grew steadily, the great majority of English men and women still lived off the land, Christian monasteries were to be found even in the wildest parts of the country, organising schools and hospitals and helping the poor. The monks were also skilled farmers and ran some of the best farms in Britain.

During this time many of the King's lands in France were lost and the country endured long periods of civil war, with the barons fighting among themselves and against the King. Wales was conquered by English troops, but when English armies tried to occupy Scotland they were defeated.

A windmill stands in the background, where the wheat will be ground into flour. Men cut the crop with sickles and the women bind it into sheaves. Others load the sheaves onto a cart pulled by oxen.

1298 Edward I, 'Hammer of the Scots', puts down another Scots rebellion, led by Sir William Wallace at Falkirk. Sir William is then hung, drawn and quartered.

1296 Edward defeats the Scots under Baliol at Dunbar. Scotland becomes a dependency of England, and the coronation Stone of Scone, or Stone of Destiny, is placed in Westminster Abbey.

Trials were often decided by physical tests (ordeals) such as carrying red-hot iron. If the wounds healed, it was thought that the accused was innocent.

1265 Simon de Montfort summons the first House of Commons.

1272-1307 Reign of Edward I, the only son of Henry III.

1265

1282 At Builth, Edward defeats the Welsh, led by Llywelyn, to complete his conquest of Wales. Here he builds a series of magnificent castles.

In the middle ages football was played with a pig's bladder in the streets. The goals were the open doors of two public houses and the teams were unlimited.

A large monastery was completely self-supporting. The monks were such skilful farmers that they sold their produce as well. They cared for the sick, gave hospitality to travellers in the guest house. The almoner gave money and food to the local poor, and the monks ran the only schools. About 100 monks and 100 lay brothers inhabited a large monastery.

1. Cloister (covered walk) 2. Monk's refectory (dining hall) 3. Infirmary (hospital) 4. Kitchens 5. Almoner's house 6. Guest house 7. Carpenter's workshop 8. Chapel 9. Chapter house

When Robert I of Scotland was on the run from the English, he wondered whether to give himself up. He is supposed to have seen a spider, trying to climb a web and eventually succeeding. This gave him the hope to carry on and lead the Scots to victory.

Wealthier people wore clothes with simple, but flowing lines. The man has a cloak, instead of a coat, and soft leather shoes.

In the days before newspapers and television, information was spread by the town crier, who shouted the news in the streets.

1307-1327 Reign of Edward II, son of Edward I, who inherits the throne when his father dies whilst marching once more against the Scots.

1314 The English army is defeated by Robert Bruce's Scots at Bannockburn, near Stirling Castle. This victory secures Scotland's independence.

1327 Edward is overthrown by his wife, Queen Isabella of France, and Roger of Mortimer. Edward is imprisoned in Berkeley Castle, Gloucestershire and is then murdered.

1337

1327-1377 Reign of Edward III, son of Edward II, who executes Roger of Mortimer and imprisons his mother.

The Hundred Years War

Although there was a lot of disease and many plagues during these times, the worst by far was the Black Death of 1349. About one-third of the entire English population was killed by this terrible plague.

The Black Death left England without enough workers, so for a time working people were treated much better by their lords. However, they soon began to be treated badly again. In 1381, thousands of peasants revolted against their masters, and for a while this revolt shook the power of the King and barons, but it was eventually put down.

Under Edward III, the English resumed the wars in France, and won important battles.

The peasants, who were already furious over their treatment by their masters, were further annoyed by the King's poll tax. Men from Kent and Essex marched to London, led by John Ball and Wat Tyler. Young King Richard II promised to help them, but his promises were not kept. Tyler was killed by the Lord Mayor, and many were executed, including John Ball.

1337

1337 King Edward III claims the French throne, as his mother Isabella is the daughter of French King Philip IV. This marks the beginning of the Hundred Years War between England and France.

1340 The French fleet is destroyed at Sluys, giving England mastery of the seas.

1347 Calais is captured by the English after an eleven month siege. It remains an English town for the next 210 years.

1349 A bubonic plague spread by rat's fleas, known as the Black Death, kills about one third of all English people.

English longbow

French crossbow

The English longbow could kill an armoured knight at 200m. It could also be fired at a faster rate than the French crossbow.

Edward III's claim to the French throne started a series of wars with France – the Hundred Years War. His son, the Black Prince, led English troops at the Battle of Crecy in 1346. Victory was mainly due to the rapid firing rate of the English longbow.

Knights underwent careful training in horsemanship, good manners and the arts of war. Boys in training were called pages, and young men squires.

1356 The Black Prince, Edward - the eldest son of Edward III - defeats the French at Poitiers against heavy odds. The French King John II is captured and paraded through London.

1374 The English lose all their lands in France, except Bordeaux, Bayonne and Calais.

The symptoms of The Black Death were swellings, black spots, and a high fever. Three-quarters of those who caught it died within five days, and were buried in the plague pits.

1377-1399 Edward the Black Prince died before he could become King. His son Richard II was only ten years old when he came to the throne. Richard II's early rule was in the hands of his uncle John of Gaunt, Duke of Lancaster. Richard is deposed in 1399 and dies in Pontefract Castle.

1384 The death of John Wycliffe, the first English Protestant.

1381 The Peasant's Revolt, which was led by Wat Tyler and John Ball.

1400

The main English export trade was wool. The Lord Chancellor still sits on a sack of wool in the House of Lords, to show the importance of the wool trade.

At a lord's banquet, roast swan was a popular dish. After it was cooked, the feathers were then stuck back onto the bird.

The Wars of the Roses

Two of Edward III's sons founded the Houses of York and Lancaster. Their subsequent rivalries led to a battle for the English throne.

After the heroic Henry V led England to victory at Agincourt, the rule of Henry VI plunged the country into crisis. His loss of our lands in France, the end of the Hundred Years War and the fall in income of the nobility led to the Wars of the Roses, between the white rose of York and the red rose of Lancaster.

Some eighty nobles of royal blood died in the confused struggle that followed, leaving Henry Tudor to claim the throne unopposed after his victory at Bosworth Field.

Before William Caxton observed the printing press in Europe and established his own press in 1476, all books in Britain were copied by hand in monasteries.

1431 Joan of Arc is burned at the stake in Rouen, accused of witchcraft.

1422–1461 Reign of Henry VI, son of Henry V. As the young Henry is only 9 months old, his uncles the Dukes of Bedford and Gloucester are made Protectors.

1400

1400 The deposed King Richard II is imprisoned in Pontefract Castle, where he is murdered by his jailer.

1415 Henry V declares the resumption of the Hundred Year's War. He invades France and is victorious at Agincourt.

Music was becoming more popular and minstrels toured castles, manor houses and fairs.

The instrument in the foreground is a gittern. It is the oldest surviving musical instrument.

While the clothes of the peasants remained simple, the costume of the wealthy became elaborate.

On the 25th October 1415, Henry V's army of 5,000 men faced 25,000 Frenchmen on the rain-soaked field of Agincourt. The heavily-armoured French knights floundered to defeat in the mud as the English archers filled the air with arrows.

When peace came after the Wars of the Roses, houses no longer needed to be fortified. The first windows of small panes of glass set in wooden frames appeared.

King Henry VI had a great love of learning and religion. He started the great school of Eton in 1440 and founded Kings College, Cambridge in 1441.

 1453 The Wars of the Roses begin. Due to Henry VI's insanity the Duke of York becomes Protector. On Henry's recovery, the Duke of York is dismissed in favour of the Lancastrian Duke of Somerset. This caused a struggle for the throne that lasted thirty years.

 1460 Richard Duke of York is executed, and his head, adorned with a paper crown, is displayed on the gates of York.

 1461–1483 Edward IV, son of Richard of York, claims the throne after defeating the Lancastrians at Towton.

 1483–1485 Twelve year old Edward V is king, with Richard of Gloucester as Protector. He imprisons the young king and his brother and takes the throne as Richard III. In 1485 he is killed at Bosworth Field by Henry Tudor.

1485

On 22nd August 1485 at Market Bosworth, Richard III faced Henry Tudor's army. The desertion of Richard's nobles led to his defeat and the crowning of Henry VII.

When appointed Protector, Richard of Gloucester imprisoned the twelve year old King Edward V and his younger brother Richard in the Tower of London. After he had declared himself King Richard III, the two brothers were never seen again.

The Tudors

After the years of civil war - The Wars of the Roses - people wanted a strong government to rule the country again. The early Tudor Kings, Henry VII and Henry VIII provided this. Henry VIII also cut England off from the Roman Catholic Church, after nearly a thousand years of membership.

He closed down the monasteries and established the Church of England, with himself as its head. He began to wage war on France again, but nothing was gained and many lives were lost. Later, during Mary Tudor's short reign, England became Roman Catholic once more. The merchants and gentry prospered during these years.

After years of war, Henry VIII and Francis I of France met near Calais in 1520. Huge pavilions were erected for the courtiers, made of gold cloth. This meeting is known as the Field of the Cloth of Gold. Despite the meeting they were soon at war again.

1485

1485-1509 Reign of Henry VII, the first Tudor King, who united the Houses of York and Lancaster by marrying Elizabeth of York, daughter of Edward IV.

1492 Christopher Columbus discovers the New World, the continent of America.

1509-1547 Reign of Henry VIII, son of Henry VII.

1515 Thomas Wolsey is made Archbishop of York, Lord Chancellor and in the next year Papal Legate (ambassador of the Pope).

1530-1540 Thomas Cromwell succeeds the disgraced Wolsey, and guides the rise of Protestantism or Reformation of England. He is beheaded in 1540.

Most people accepted Henry VIII's new Church of England, but the Lord Chancellor, Sir Thomas More would not. He and Bishop Fisher along with leading monks, were executed publicly. Their courageous act did nothing to change Henry's determination.

Now that the country was more peaceful, wealthy men - many of whom had bought land taken from the Church - began to build country houses. Many of their timbered, tile roofed houses with stately gardens are still standing in parts of England.

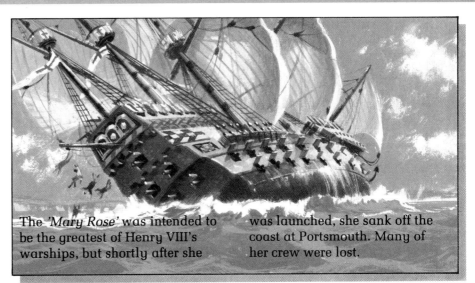

The *'Mary Rose'* was intended to be the greatest of Henry VIII's warships, but shortly after she was launched, she sank off the coast at Portsmouth. Many of her crew were lost.

Henry VII strictly controlled his barons. If they defied him or formed private armies, he prosecuted them in his own Court. This was called the Star Chamber because of the painted stars on the courtroom ceiling.

In Mary's reign 300 people were burnt for refusing to become Roman Catholic. A similar number of Catholics were burnt by Elizabeth I for refusing to accept the Church of England.

1535 The Act of Supremacy declares Henry, and not the Pope, to be the Supreme head of the Church of England. Pope Pius excommunicates (cuts off) Henry from the Church in Rome.

1539 Henry dissolves the monasteries, and the Abbot of Glastonbury is hanged for resisting. Henry then claims their lands and treasures for himself.

1547-1553 Reign of the boy-king Edward VI, son of Henry VIII. His reign is guided by his Protectors the Duke of Somerset (1547-9), and later the Duke of Northumberland (1549-53). England becomes fully Protestant.

1553-1558 The unpopular reign of Queen Mary, eldest daughter of Henry VIII. She marries Philip II of Spain and re-introduces the Roman Catholic Church.

1558 France recaptures England's last foothold on the continent, Calais.

1558

"Divorced, beheaded, died, divorced, beheaded, survived" – This rhyme tells of the fate of Henry VIII's six wives. From left to right - Catherine of Aragon, Anne Boleyn, Jane Seymour, Anne of Cleves, Catherine Howard and Catherine Parr. Henry's first divorce was due to his desire for a male heir.

The Elizabethan Era

When Elizabeth I became Queen she was surrounded by so many enemies that people feared she would not survive very long. In fact she re-established the Church of England, and withstood opposition from Roman Catholics, Puritans and MP's. The Spanish attempt to invade England in their Armada of 1588 failed, and English seamen began to explore the whole world.

During these times poor people were treated very badly, English sailors joined in the slave trade, and the English continued to colonise Ireland.

Elizabeth became a very popular Queen, enjoying journeys around the country.

The Roman Catholic Queen Mary claimed the English throne. Expelled to England by the Scots, she was imprisoned and eventually executed.

The most famous Elizabethan voyage was by the *'Golden Hind'* around the world, commanded by Francis Drake. He looted over £1.5 million from the Spaniards, and was knighted for his deeds by Elizabeth I.

1570 Pope Pius excommunicates Elizabeth and many Catholics plot to support Mary Queen of Scot's claim to the English throne. Elizabeth finally signs her death warrant in 1587.

1558-1603 Reign of Elizabeth I, youngest daughter of Henry VIII.

1558

1559 Under the Protestant rule of Elizabeth I, the Reformation continues and the Church of England is gradually established.

1567 The Dutch War of Independence from Spain begins.

1568 Mary Queen of Scots is expelled by the people of Scotland. She takes refuge in England, where she is imprisoned by Elizabeth I for 19 years.

William Shakespeare was one of many popular actor-playwrights, whose plays were performed at the Globe Theatre, Southwark. In those days the parts of women were played by young boys.

In 1588 the Armada left Spain with 132 ships. They planned to pick up troops in Belgium, land in Kent, and march to London. Bad weather and the British Navy prevented this, and only 79 ships returned.

1587 Sir Francis Drake attacks and burns the Spanish fleet in Cadiz harbour and delays the Armada's invasion of England

1588 The Spanish Armada is defeated.

1599 Hugh O'Neill, Earl of Tyrone, leads an Irish rebellion, defeating Sir Henry Bagenal at Blackwater.

1601 Essex, the Queen's favourite, is executed for raising a rebellion in London against her.

1603 Lord Mountjoy defeats O'Neill's rebellion in Ireland.

1603

With peace in the land, the rich contented themselves by building beautiful houses and furnishing them with carved furniture like the table, chair and bed above.

⇨ *Hawkins – 1566*
⇨ *Hawkins – 1567/69*
⇨ *Drake – 1572/73*
⇨ *Drake – 1579*
⇨ *Raleigh – 1585/86*

The greatest voyage was Drake's circumnavigation, via South America and across the Pacific. Raleigh made two unsuccessful voyages to try to establish an English colony in Virginia, USA. Hawkins carried slaves from West Africa to the West Indies.

Gunpowder was introduced in the 14th century and the first firearms began to be used. They were very heavy and had to be rested on a pole. The powder which fired the ball was lit with a smouldering match.

King and Parliament

During these years relations between the English Parliament and the Kings James I and Charles I grew worse. In 1642 civil war started. Most MP's (Members of Parliament) wanted the country ruled by a combination of Royal and Parliamentary power.

They were Puritan in religion and thought the Church of England was too much like the Roman Catholics. The Kings, particularly Charles I, believed their duty was to rule the country on their own, only consulting Parliament when it pleased them. MP's only granted taxes when they agreed with Royal policies, so the country became impossible either to govern or to defend.

Charles I's doctor, William Harvey is seen here showing the King his discovery of the circulation of blood. He showed that blood travels from one part of the heart to the lungs and then back to another part, before being pumped all around the body.

1603 **1603-1625** Reign of James I, James Stuart, son of Mary Queen of Scots and the first Stuart King. He was also James VI of Scotland.

1611 The colonisation of Ulster (Northern Ireland) begins, with English and Scottish Protestants given lands seized from the defeated Irish rebels.

 1625-1649 Reign of Charles I, the only son of James I.

1628 Placed in severe financial difficulty by the wars in France and Spain, King Charles is forced to accept Parliament's Petition of Right. This forbids: the King demanding taxes, imprisonment without trial, billeting of troops in private houses and the use of martial (military) law in peacetime.

In 1620 one hundred English Puritans left to settle in North America, on a ship called *'The Mayflower'*.

The Puritans who sailed in *'The Mayflower'*, landed at Cape Cod, in Massachusetts. During their first winter many of them starved, and half of them died. Although they were helped by local Indians, they began to quarrel with them later on.

The translation of the Bible from Greek and Hebrew was authorised by King James and is known as the King James Bible or Authorised Version.

1629-1640 Charles I dissolves Parliament, and rules without it.

1639 16,000 Scottish 'covenanters' rise against Charles' attempt to force Scotland's churches to use the English Prayer Book. Charles is forced to make peace at Berwick.

Guy Fawkes rented a cellar under the Houses of Parliament, where he secretly stored barrels of gunpowder. He was plotting with English Roman Catholics to blow up James I and his government, when Parliament opened on 5th November, 1605.

1640 The Scots defeat the English at Newburn. In the Treaty of Ripon, Charles agrees to pay £850 a day to maintain the Scots' army until their grievances are settled.

1640 Threatened with a new Scottish rebellion, and short of money, Charles is forced to recall Parliament.

1640 Charles calls his 5th Parliament, which forces him to execute his chief minister, the Earl of Strafford in 1641.
This Parliament lasts for 20 years, and is known as the Long Parliament.

1642

1641 Numbers of English and Scottish Protestant settlers are massacred in Ulster by Irish Roman Catholics.

The Puritans dressed as they lived and worshipped God - simply. They wore black and starched white linen.

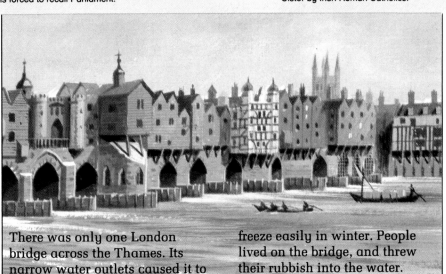

There was only one London bridge across the Thames. Its narrow water outlets caused it to freeze easily in winter. People lived on the bridge, and threw their rubbish into the water.

The Civil Wars

Parliament's control of London, and its creation and support of the first British professional army, the red-coated New Model Army, gave it victory over King Charles I. But the winners could not agree amongst themselves about how to govern the country, and Charles would not sign any agreement with them. Finally the army took control of the situation, and arranged the trial and execution of Charles I.

Its leader, Oliver Cromwell, became Lord Protector of the country, but when he died his supporters were again divided. In 1660 Charles I's eldest son, Charles II, was invited to become King again.

One of the main battles of the civil war was fought at Marston Moor, near York, in 1644. Two powerful forces dominated the battle, commanded by Oliver Cromwell for Parliament, and by Prince Rupert for the King. Scottish troops fought for the victorious Parliamentarians.

1642

JAN 1642 Charles I tries to arrest five leading MPs while they are sitting in the House of Commons. When he arrives with 50 guards, he finds they are gone, and leaves London with his court to prepare for war.

AUG 1642 The First Civil War starts between the Parliamentarians (Roundheads) and the King's Royalists (Cavaliers).

1643 The Scots enter the civil war on the side of Parliament.

1645 The New Model Army is formed under Oliver Cromwell and Sir Thomas Fairfax. It is England's first professional army and its infantry wears scarlet tunics. This new army defeats the Royalists at Naseby and ends the First Civil War.

1648 The Second Civil Wars begins when the Scots change sides and support the King, but they are defeated by Cromwell at Preston.

1649 Irish opposition is quickly stamped out by Cromwell's troops.

People loved sweet foods at this time. They ate candied fruit and elaborate pastry cases with sweet fillings, baked by skilled pastry cooks.

The outstanding Parliamentary general was Oliver Cromwell. He became Protector of England, controlling the country with the army. He allowed Jews to become citizens and made England widely respected abroad.

Charles II tried to recapture the throne with Scottish troops. Defeated at Worcester, he went on the run, once hiding in a tree to escape his enemies.

The Puritans believed that pleasure was wicked. They banned theatres, betting and dancing. They also publicly burned books that they did not approve of.

1653-1658 Oliver Cromwell rules England as Lord Protector. The country lives under a stern Puritan, military dictatorship, but is widely respected abroad.

JAN 1649 The trial and execution of Charles I, at the order of a small number of MPs, dominated by Oliver Cromwell. Britain abolishes the monarchy and the House of Lords and becomes the Commonwealth.

1658 The death of Oliver Cromwell. Richard, his son, succeeds him for a short time as Lord Protector, but is soon forced to abdicate.

MAY 1660 The Restoration of Charles II as King of England and the return to a monarchy.

1660

The Royalists loved grand and colourful clothes. The men wore floppy hats with plumes and high leather boots. Their hair was long and curled. Women wore long gowns with low-cut necklines.

After the second civil war the army put Charles I on trial. The charge was treason, and the court voted to execute him. The sentence was carried out on a cold winter's afternoon outside

Charles' own Whitehall Palace. When the executioner's axe fell, an observer wrote that he heard *"a groan, as I have never heard before, and desire I may never hear again"*.

Fire and Plague

The newly returned King Charles II made no attempt to govern as his father had done. But bitter disputes with Parliament continued, and our modern system of political parties began to appear.

The King's supporters were called Tories, and Parliamentarians were known as Whigs.

Charles II's brother James II became King. He tried to rule without Parliament and favoured the Roman Catholics. In the Revolution of 1688, he made his escape to France. England, and her main trading rival, the Netherlands, twice went to war during these years, and the English expanded their colonies in North America.

Samuel Pepys was an eminent and hard working civil servant in charge of supplying the navy. He kept a detailed diary of London life. His accounts of the Plague and the Fire of London are very vivid.

1660

1666 After the Great Fire of London, Sir Christopher Wren begins the rebuilding of St Paul's Cathedral.

1673 The Test Act is passed by Parliament, barring Roman Catholics from holding positions in public office.

1675 The Royal Greenwich Observatory, in London, is established.

1678 The Popish Plot. The lies of Titus Oates, who claims knowledge of a Roman Catholic plot (supported by the Pope) against the King, cause widespread panic. After the murder of Sir Edmund Berry Godfrey, over 2,000 Roman Catholics are imprisoned, and many executed, as the Protestants fear a Catholic uprising.

1679 The Habeas Corpus Act forbids any illegal or indefinite imprisonment.

When James II was King, the Duke of Monmouth led a rebellion. When the rebels were defeated, Judge Jeffreys' special courts tried them. They were hanged or transported to the West Indies.

The streets of London were very narrow, filthy and infested with rats. This led to the spread of the plague of 1665, causing the deaths of about 70,000 people.

King Charles II was involved in many scandals. One of his mistresses was Nell Gwynn, an actress of humble background.

Isaac Newton established the theory of gravity. He was made President of the Royal British Scientific Society.

Stage coaches began to travel all over England, but the bad roads made journeys slow and expensive. It took four days to travel from London to Exeter and cost £2 - which a farm labourer earned in 8 weeks. Travellers were often stopped by highwaymen who stole their valuables.

The fire of London started in a baker's shop and was fanned by strong winds. 80% of the old city of London was destroyed, including St Pauls Cathedral. Over 100,000 people were made homeless by the fire.

1679-1681 A Parliamentary battle takes place between the Whigs - who support a bill to prevent the Roman Catholic Duke of York from becoming King - and the Tories who support James.

1685 The Battle of Sedgemoor, Somerset. The uprising of the Duke of Monmouth, the illegitimate son of Charles II, is put down by a small Royal army.

1685- 1688 Reign of King James II, the second son of Charles I.

1688 The Glorious Revolution - When James II's wife produces a Roman Catholic heir, leading Whigs and Tories invite his daughter Mary and her Dutch Protestant husband William of Orange to invade England. They land at Torbay with 15,000 men and King James flees to France, flinging the Great Seal which symbolises his office into the River Thames.

1689

James II was succeeded by one of his daughters, Mary, who married the Dutch King William. The Dutch had long been fighting for their independence against the French, and English troops were now fighting alongside them. The battles continued in the reign of James' younger daughter Anne (1701-14) when, for the first time since Agincourt, British troops fought long campaigns in Europe.

Another Irish rebellion, which was supported by French troops, was repressed, and the lands of Catholic farmers, particularly in Ulster, were given to English Protestant settlers.

After the fire of London, Christopher Wren rebuilt St Paul's Cathedral. His model for the new domed building was St Peter's in Rome. It took forty years to build and although he planned for large open spaces around the cathedral, they were not allowed.

The mother wears a tall head-dress over her hair. Like her daughter, she wears both under and overskirts with lace and ruffles. Her son is in a long coat, stockings and breeches.

The Duke of Marlborough led German, Dutch and English troops against the French army of Louis XIV. His men defeated the French near the banks of the Danube, at the Battle of Blenheim and saved Europe from French control.

1689

1689 A new Parliament pronounces William and Mary joint rulers, and introduces a Bill of Rights to establish the supremacy of Parliament and end the monarch's Divine Right to Rule.

1689-1702 Reign of William III and Queen Mary II.

1690 Battle of the Boyne. William defeats the Irish, who had risen in support of the deposed James II. The English soldiers act with great savagery on this day - which is now remembered as Orangeman's Day.

1694 The Bank of England is established.

1701 The Act of Settlement secures the English throne for a Protestant, so excluding James II's son.

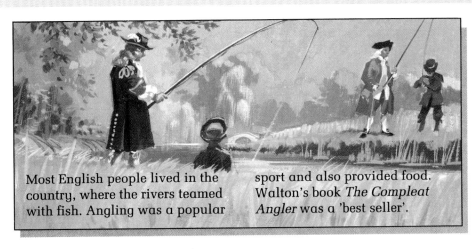

Most English people lived in the country, where the rivers teamed with fish. Angling was a popular sport and also provided food. Walton's book *The Compleat Angler* was a 'best seller'.

For years men had wanted union of England with Scotland, a common currency and a united parliament. In 1707 Queen Anne signed the Act of Union.

Highland Scottish chiefs had to swear loyalty to William, but Macdonald arrived late. As a result, 38 Macdonald's were massacred at Glencoe by British soldiers.

1704 In England's long war against Louis XIV's France, the French are defeated at Blenheim, losing 26,000 dead and 15,000 captured. John Churchill, the Duke of Marlborough, is rewarded for his victory with a pension and the magnificent Blenheim Palace in Oxfordshire.

1705 Edmund Halley correctly predicts that Halley's Comet will return in 1758.

1713 The Treaty of Utrecht ends England's wars with France and Spain, which had lasted for eleven years.

1714

1702-1714 Reign of Queen Anne, Protestant daughter of James II, whose 17 pregnancies left her in poor health, but with no living heir.

1702 The first newspaper, The *Daily Courant*, is produced.

The British East India Company had opened up trade with India and tea and coffee were becoming popular among weathly people. Fashionable people would meet in coffee houses to gossip, drink and smoke tobacco.

The Georgians

The new kings, who came from the German state of Hanover, willingly accepted the power of Parliament, but MP's were elected only by wealthy voters. Many of them were country squires, and very keen on improving their own farms. Others were merchants who encouraged the further expansion of the British Empire.

British armies won Canada and most of India from the French. The Church of England seemed to become less active and was challenged by the great Christian preacher John Wesley. There were two further uprisings in Scotland, but both were defeated.

In 1745, a Scottish army under James II's grandson, Charles (Bonnie Prince Charlie), reached Derby, and threatened London. But they were driven back to defeat at Culloden. The English went on to occupy the highlands, but their cruelties were never forgotten.

General Wolfe died whilst commanding the attack on Quebec, in 1759, which led to our victory over the French, in the dispute over the control of Canada.

1721 After resolving the South Sea Bubble crisis, Sir Robert Walpole becomes Britain's first Prime Minister.

1720 The South Sea Bubble. When the South Sea Trading Company paid off the national debt, many people flocked to buy shares, but the *'bubble'* burst when the share price dropped. Many people were ruined.

1714

1708 Abraham Darby opens his first iron smelting works at Coalbrookdale, in Shropshire.

1714-1727 Reign of George I, the first English King from the German House of Hanover. He was the son of Sophia, grand-daughter of James I, and the nearest Protestant heir to the throne. At first he speaks no English - so the importance of Parliament in ruling the country grows.

1715-1716 The Jacobite Rebellion begins when the Earl of Mar raises an army to support James II in Scotland. The rebellion is defeated at Sherriffmuir by the Duke of Argyle.

For over 50 years, John Wesley travelled all over the country preaching. He eventually set up his own church - the Methodists.

In 1755, Doctor Samuel Johnson published his *Dictionary*. It was the first one in English. In it he defined 40,000 words.

Wealthy people wore wigs, made from other peoples hair. They shaved their own heads to avoid catching head lice.

Robert Clive arrived in India aged nineteen, as a clerk. Just thirteen years later he led the troops at the Battle of Plessey winning control of India.

Wood for making charcoal to smelt iron was getting scarcer. At Coalbrookdale in Shropshire, Abraham Darby found out how coke could be used instead and his idea began to spread.

1727-1760 Reign of George II, the only son of George I.

1730 The British Army uses 65,000 tons of flour, in one year, for powdering wigs.

1731 Jethro Tull develops the first practical seed drill.

1745 Roused by England's war with France, a new Jacobite Rebellion is led by Bonnie Prince Charlie, the grandson of James II.

1745 When the Scottish rebels reach Derby, the actors at Drury Lane theatre add ' God Save the King ' to the end of their show. It becomes the National Anthem.

1756-1763 The Seven Years War between France and England is caused by competition for colonies in India and America. Clive's victories in India establish British rule.

1760

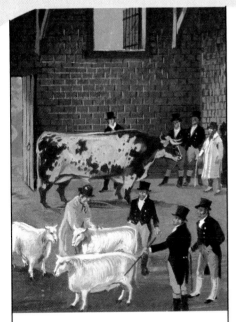

Farmers began to grow crops of turnips and swedes to feed their livestock in the winter. This improved their quality, with the average weight of cattle doubling in the eighteenth century.

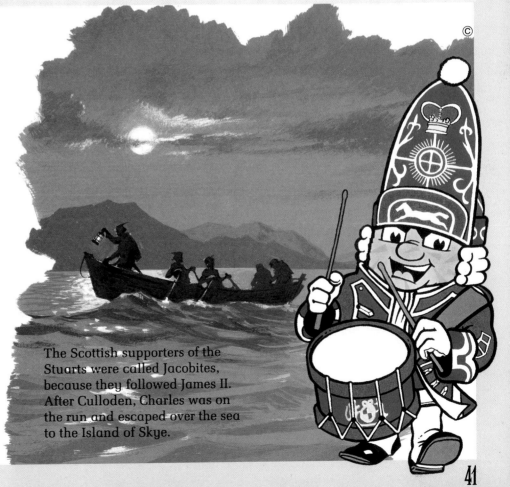

The Scottish supporters of the Stuarts were called Jacobites, because they followed James II. After Culloden, Charles was on the run and escaped over the sea to the Island of Skye.

Revolution

Some of the greatest changes since stone age men and women turned from hunting and gathering to farming, now occurred in Britain, as we began to mechanise our industries. Great towns grew up, and with them terrible slums. The population more than doubled in a hundred years. The roads were improved and canals were built. All this is called the Industrial Revolution.

The British pioneered these changes and, for a while, were the world's leading industrial power. The Americans later broke British control after they won the American War of Independence and established the United States of America.

James Cook made three voyages of discovery. He explored the coasts of New Zealand and Australia, made important discoveries in the South Pacific and, in 1773, was the first to cross the Antarctic Circle.

1760

1760-1820 Reign of George III, grandson of George II. The first British-born monarch since 1714, he tried to re- establish the King's right to rule over Parliament.

1763 The First Treaty of Paris ends the Seven Years War. It awarded Canada to Britain, but restored many other colonies to France.

1768 Rioters crying 'Wilkes and Liberty' force the release of John Wilkes MP who had been imprisoned for writing newspaper articles mocking the King. Wilkes returned to Parliament in 1774, having established the Freedom of the Press and the right of the press to print Parliamentary debates.

1775-1783 The American War of Independence. British colonists in America fight for their independence from British rule.

1776 The Declaration of Independence is signed by delegates from all the thirteen States of America on 4th July.

British roast beef, puddings and beer may have been famous, as this caricature shows, but in fact, ordinary people would have rarely seen meat on their table.

James Watt was not the inventor of the steam engine. He was a Glasgow instrument-maker, who was asked to repair an early steam engine. Seeing how the machine could be improved, he set about building them with his partner Matthew Boulton.

Josiah Wedgwood's works at Stoke-on-Trent produced china. He was the first to make plates of uniform size and teapots with lids that fitted properly.

1777 Abraham Darby, grandson of the first Abraham Darby, erects the World's first cast-iron bridge over the River Severn, at Ironbridge. The First Industrial Revolution is marked by increasing mechanisation and the rapid growth of new industrial towns.

1778 France joins with The United States in the war against Britain. Spain joins them in 1779.

1780 Anti-Catholic rioters, led by Lord George Gordon, besiege London and burn Newgate Prison. 10,000 troops are brought in, and 500 of the rioters are killed or wounded.

1781 After a long siege, the British under Lord Cornwallis surrender at Yorktown, giving the United States victory in the War of Independence.

1783 In the Treaty of Versailles, Britain recognises the independence of the United States of America.

1783

Britain had removed all taxes on goods for its American colony, except tea. In 1773, a ship arrived in Boston, USA, loaded with a cargo of tea. Americans, dressed as Indians, dumped the tea into the harbour. This is known as the *'Boston Tea Party'*.

Machines and structures began to be made of cast iron, like this bridge over the River Severn, at Ironbridge in Shropshire.

Some of the first machines were used in the cotton industry. Hargreaves' *Spinning Jenny* was worked by women in their homes, but Arkwright's *Water Frames*, powered by running water, were installed in factories, as were Crompton's *Mules*.

water frame   **spinning Jenny**   **mule**

Britain at War

When the French Revolution started, many Britons sympathised with its aim to remove dictator Kings and arrogant nobles. But when the French began to take over lands in Europe, and challenge British seapower, the two countries went to war.

At Trafalgar, Britain secured the control of the sea that made possible the world-wide British Empire; and Napoleon's defeats in Russia ended French hopes of controlling Europe. After the war there was so much poverty in Britain, and resentment that ordinary people were denied a vote in Parliamentary elections, that it seemed that Britain too might have a Revolution.

During Britain's war with France, it was feared that the Emperor Napoleon would invade England. After Admiral Horatio Nelson's defeat of the French fleet at Trafalgar, in 1805, the fear of invasion faded.

1783

1788 First British penal settlement in Australia.

1789 The French people overthrow the monarchy, storm the great prison - the Bastille - and declare a Republic. King Louis XVI and his Queen, Marie Antoinette, are beheaded by the guillotine.

1793-1815 England and France at war.

1803 The French under Napoleon plan an invasion of England, but it is not carried out.

1807 The slave trade, in which Africans were cruelly transported to work on American plantations, is abolished.

For many years the British fought Napoleon's army in Europe, and eventually drove them out of Spain. Napoleon's final defeat, at the hands of the Duke of Wellington, took place in 1815, at the battle of Waterloo, in Belgium.

The British were leading slave traders from West Africa to the West Indies and the United States. In 1807 they banned the trade and later banned slavery.

Humphrey Davy invented a lamp whose flame was shielded. Now miners could work without the risk of exploding gases.

1816 Riots of the Luddites, who break the new machines of the Industrial Revolution because they fear that they will steal their jobs.

1811 When his father George III goes mad, George, Prince of Wales, becomes Prince Regent. This period of history is known as the Regency.

1819 At the Peterloo massacre, 11 people are killed by soldiers when a crowd of over 50,000 gather at a meeting in St Peter's Fields, Manchester, to try to reform Parliament.

1820 The Cato Street Conspiracy. 'Radicals' plotting to blow up the cabinet are discovered in a loft in Cato Street, London. Their leader, Thistlewood, and four others are executed.

1825 The Combination Acts are repealed (cancelled), allowing workers to form Trades Unions.

1829

In 1804, Richard Trevithick's locomotive pulled five coal wagons and 70 passengers along a 15 km track.

The Brighton Pavilion was built for George IV, when he was Prince Regent, by the architect John Nash.

Invention and Discovery

The growing division between rich and poor had begun to cause unrest amongst the working classes of Georgian Britain. Despite the example of the French Revolution of 1830, there was no similar uprising by the workers of Britain. The Reform Bills of the following years began a new era of democracy, with a fairer voting system.

A revolution of a different kind was inspired by George Stephenson's *Rocket*, as the railway age brought new prosperity to Britain. Many new inventions and industries followed and the wealthy indulged themselves in fashion, gambling, sport and the pursuit of pleasure.

Sir Robert Peel formed the first Metropolitan police force, known as 'bobbies' or 'peelers', in 1829.

In 1834, when six farm workers formed the first trade union, they were transported to Australia for seven years and became known as the Tolpuddle Martyrs.

1834 The new Poor Laws establish the hated workhouses, where able-bodied paupers were put to work. Only the sick or aged were paid dole.

1829

1829 Oxford beat Cambridge at Henley, in the first University Boat Race.

1830 The opening of the first great railway, the Liverpool & Manchester is marred by the death of Cabinet Minister William Huskisson, killed by a locomotive.

1830–1837 Reign of William IV, son of George III. He was crowned at the age of 64 and known as 'silly Billy'.

1832 The Great Reform Act is passed by Parliament, allowing the middle classes a vote, as well as the landed aristocracy.

In 1829, the first horse-drawn omnibus service was introduced in London by George Shillibeer. It carried 22 passengers.

Bare-fist boxing or prize-fighting was popular in Regency times.

In October 1829, the Rainhill Trials were set up to choose a locomotive to run on the new Liverpool & Manchester Railway. The winner was *Rocket* with a top speed of 56kph, designed by George Stephenson and built by his son Robert.

1834 Charles Babbage, English mathematician, invents the computer–his 'Analytical Engine.

1835 Danish writer Hans Christian Andersen publishes the first four of his 168 children's stories.

1835 William Fox Talbot takes the first ever negative photograph. It is of a window in Lacock Abbey, Wiltshire.

1837 William IV dies and is succeeded by Queen Victoria.

1837

Although duelling had been made illegal in 1828, Regency gentlemen would still meet with pistols at dawn, to settle an affair of honour. Hyde Park was the fashionable location.

The streets of Regency Britain were thronged with street traders. They sold a huge variety of goods and services, like knife-grinding, rat-catching and chair-mending.

Michael Faraday made many discoveries about electricity. Here he shows his electric motor.

When French Chef Carème visited Russia, he brought back the idea of serving meals in courses.

Victoria — The Early Years

By the middle of the nineteenth century, Britain was at the height of her industrial power and wealth. The use of child labour in factories and mines had been ended. In 1840, following Edward Jenner's discoveries, free vaccination was introduced, which virtually eliminated smallpox. A start had been made on providing sewers and clean water supplies in the vast industrial cities.

But in a terrible famine in Ireland many thousands starved to death. In the ten years 1845-55, 1.5 million people - out of a population of 8.5 million - left Ireland, mostly to start a new life in the United States of America.

In the Crimean War 40% of soldiers in hospitals were dying when Florence Nightingale arrived with a small team of nurses. They scrubbed the wards and improved the care of patients. When she returned home she devoted herself to the new nursing profession.

1837

1837-1901 The reign of Queen Victoria, daughter of Edward, Duke of Kent, who was the son of George III. Britain's longest reigning monarch, she married Prince Albert of Saxe-Coburg in 1840.

1838-1848 the Chartists demand a vote for all men in a secret ballot.

1839-1841 The Opium War with the Chinese started when the Chinese tried to stop the British from importing opium into China from India. In 1841, Hong Kong is given to Great Britain.

1840 Doctor David Livingstone, a Scots missionary embarks on his first expedition to Bechuanaland, in Africa.

1842 Child labour in factories and mines is abolished.

Prince Albert, the husband of Queen Victoria, was responsible for the *Great Exhibition,* which was held in the Crystal Palace, in Hyde Park in 1851. It was intended to demonstrate Britain's technological achievements and advances in the sciences.

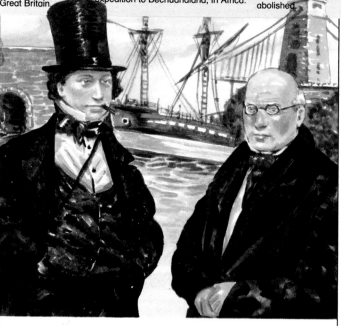

"*Railway mania*" now gripped Britain. Within twenty years railways covered much of the country, designed by world-famous engineers and built by "*navvies*" (navigators). The best known of all was Brunel, who designed a tunnel under the Thames, the *Great Western Railway,* and the iron ship, *The Great Eastern.*

When Britain and France fought Russia in the Crimean War (1854- 6), a military disaster occured. Due to misunderstood orders, 247 men of the Light Brigade's 637 men were killed or wounded in their famous charge.

1845 The failure of the potato crop in Ireland causes a famine, and Prime Minister Robert Peel abolishes the Corn Laws, which imposed a tax on imported corn.

1845-1850 Almost 1 million people die from the famine in Ireland.

1848-1849 After the Second Sikh War, the Punjab becomes part of the British Indian Empire.

1851 The Great Exhibition is held at the Crystal Palace, in London.

1853-1856 The Crimean War. Britain, France and Turkey land troops in the Crimea to attack the Russian naval base at Sebastapol. A surprise Russian attack at Balaclava is held back by the famous 'thin red line' of Highlanders, but after the disastrous Charge of the Light Brigade, the war continues through the terrible winter of 1854. Peace is achieved with the Third Treaty of Paris, signed in 1856.

1857

The man wears a top hat, long coat and tapered trousers. The woman wears a crinoline skirt and a hat with feathers.

Charles Dickens was the most popular of all English writers. His stories first appeared in magazines, and readers waited impatiently for the next issue.

Before Roland Hill's Penny Post, letters were charged by weight and distance. After 1840 they cost a penny to send anywhere.

The Victorian Empire

During this time it was possible to sail all around the world, protected by British ships from nearby naval bases, so large had the British Empire grown.

Huge areas of Africa had become a part of the Empire. From India, British colonists also took over Burma, Ceylon (now called Sri Lanka), Singapore and Malaysia.

At home, voting in elections became secret, and by the end of the century most men had a vote. Education was compulsary for all children, and parents did not have to pay fees. But abroad, British businesses were facing increased competition from Germany and the United States.

Much of East Africa was explored by the Scotsman David Livingstone, who discovered the Victoria Falls in Zambia. When he disappeared, the *New York Herald* sent the explorer H M Stanley to find him.

In 1865, Joseph Lister made surgery much safer by his use of antiseptic. He discovered that carbolic acid killed the germs that caused infection.

1870 The Education Act lays the foundations of compulsory schooling for children. The introduction of the ballot box makes voting at elections secret.

1860 The first horse-drawn trams run in the streets of London.

1857

1861-1865 The American Civil War, between the Northern 'Union' States and the Southern 'Confederate' States.

1867 The Second Great Reform Act allows all male rate-payers to vote.

The British controlled Egypt and the Suez Canal, but did not intend to colonise the Sudan, to the South. They ordered General Gordon to withdraw from its capital city Khartoum. He was surrounded and killed before a relief expedition could arrive.

The British East India Company controlled India. Its company officials and their wives lived in style, waited on by servants.

When Indian troops mutinied, the British only regained control after fierce fighting and India became a British colony.

1875 Prime Minister Disraeli buys a controlling interest in the Suez Canal, and so secures the route to India.

1879 The powerful Zulu tribe wages war against English settlers in southern Africa, many of whom are massacred before the Zulus are defeated at Ulundi.

1884 The Third Great Reform Act further extends British men's right to vote.

1885 The first bicycles appear on British roads.

1886 Prime Minister William Gladstone's Home Rule Bill for Ireland is defeated in the House of Commons.

1887

Wealthy gentlemen wore top hats, frock-coats and high winged collars. Women wore crinoline skirts, tight bodices, high necks and long sleeves.

After thirty years research, Charles Darwin published his *Origin of the Species*. He

showed that man had not just suddenly been created, but had changed over millions of years.

Although child labour in mines and factories was banned in 1842, children still acted as

sweeps, climbing up chimneys. It was dangerous work and they often got stuck in the flues.

The Victorian Age

At the end of Queen Victoria's reign, working men began to organise themselves into trade unions. London dock workers won improvements in their pay and working conditions after they had closed the docks by striking for six weeks.

Many ordinary people could now afford to visit the seaside sometimes, travelling on the railways. The new bicycles also enabled men and women to travel away from their home, whenever they pleased.

British seapower was now being challenged by the German Navy, and although Britain eventually won the Boer War, several early defeats shocked the national pride.

For years British settlers in South Africa had quarrelled with the Afrikaners, the first European settlers (the British insultingly called them Boers, meaning peasants). The two lived separately and eventually went to war (1899–1902). The British finally won and the two areas combined to form South Africa.

1887

1887 Queen Victoria's Golden Jubilee celebrates her 50 years of rule. She refuses to wear the royal crown and robes, appearing instead in her usual black bonnet.

1889 London dock workers win an extra sixpence (2.5p) an hour pay-rise in the country's first major strike.

1892 Keir Hardie, the first Independent Socialist (Labour) MP, arrives at the House of Commons, wearing a tweed jacket and cloth cap, and accompanied by a brass band.

1892 New Zealand gives women the vote, and is the first country to do so.

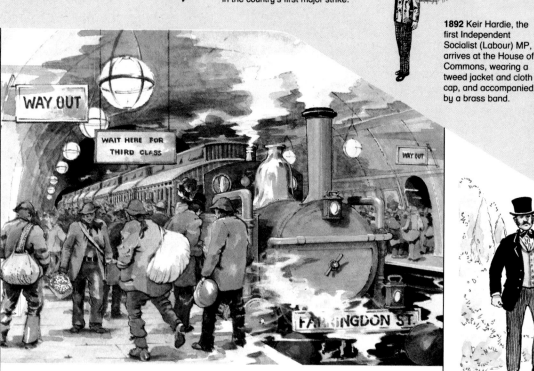

WAY OUT

WAIT HERE FOR THIRD CLASS

WAY OUT

FARRINGDON ST.

The first London Underground - from Paddington to the City - ran only a few feet below the surface. The engines were steam powered and the smoke was sucked out by fans. The first 'deep' tube was 12m down and was opened in 1890, using electric trains.

A wealthy Victorian family walk in the park. The man has side-whiskers and a moustache, his wife wears a large picture hat.

Lord Kitchener commanded the victorious British forces at Omdurman, which brought the Sudan into the British Empire. He later became Commander-in-Chief during the Boer War.

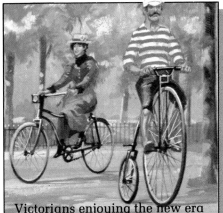

Victorians enjoying the new era of bicycles. Here, a man on a penny-farthing and a lady on a safety, chain-driven bicycle, explore the countryside.

During Queen Victoria's reign the Royal Navy was the pride of Britain. Each year at Spithead, off the coast of Portsmouth, the great battleships and cruisers were displayed to the public.

In 1897, Britain celebrated Queen Victoria's Diamond Jubilee, marking her 60 years of reign.

During her long reign Britain was the richest and most powerful nation in the world.

1895 The *'Daily Mail'*, the first mass circulation newspaper is published.

1896 Motor cars begin to appear on Britain's roads, as the Red Flag Act, which required a man to walk ahead of a moving motorcar with a red flag, is repealed by Parliament.

1898 The Germans begin to rebuild their navy, and to challenge Britain at sea.

1900 The Labour Party is formed.

1901

In 1914 the terrible First World War started. Germany and Austria fought Britain, France, Russia and, later, the United States of America.

Women gained the vote after a bitter struggle. Most of Ireland achieved independence, although Ulster remained a part of Britain. The worst slums were rebuilt, but millions of people were out of work, especially in Wales and the North, where the Industrial Revolution had started. Yet many ordinary people's lives became more comfortable. Radios were found in almost every home, and more people began to own their own cars.

The liner *Titanic* was thought to be unsinkable, and a marvel of engineering. Yet on the night of April 14th 1912, on her maiden voyage, she hit an iceberg and sank. Of 2340 people on board, only 745 survived.

The opposing armies lived in trenches, dug within a few hundred metres of each other and protected by razor-sharp barbed wire. Fighting started when soldiers charged out of their trenches with bayonets fixed to their rifles, while great field guns behind them hurled shells at the enemy's trenches.

The British explored both the Arctic and the Antarctic. Captain Robert Scott reached the South Pole in 1912, but died on his return journey. After months of toil, he had discovered that Roald Amundsen had reached the pole just before him.

1901

1901-1910 The reign of Edward VII, eldest son of Queen Victoria, who was sixty years old when he came to the throne.

1903 The Wright Brothers make the world's first powered flight, at Kittyhawk, in the USA.

1905-1916 The Liberal Government introduces the Old Age Pension and National Insurance.

1910-1936 The Reign of George V, second son of Edward VII, the first King of the House of Windsor.

1911 The Parliament Act limits the power of the House of Lords.

1914 The murder of the Archduke Franz Ferdinand of Austria and his wife, at Sarajevo in Bosnia, leads to the Great War in which Britain, France and Russia fought Germany and Austria.

In 1926 millions of workers went on strike in support of the coal miners. After nine days, the trade unions called off the strike, having gained nothing.

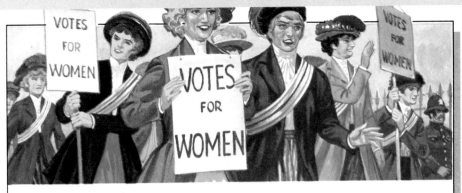

Led by Emmeline Pankhurst, the Suffragettes demanded votes for women. After the failure of peaceful methods, they went on hunger strike in prison, and smashed shop windows in Oxford Street. At the end of the war they gained the right to vote.

The Boy Scouts were formed by Lord Baden-Powell, and later followed by the Girl Guides. His idea was to teach children to be independent and practical.

1928 Movies with sound - 'talkies', first appear.

1931 Three million people are unemployed in the Great Slump.

1931 Canada, Australia, and New Zealand become Dominions - independent, but associated with Britain.

1919 The Treaty of Versailles establishes peace after the Great War, and the League of Nations is formed.

1933 Adolf Hitler becomes Dictator in Germany, as leader of the Nazi Party.

1936 The reign and abdication of Edward VIII, eldest son of George V.

1917 The US enters the war against Germany.

1916 The Easter Rising of the Sinn Fein proclaims Ireland to be a Republic. Southern Ireland gains Independence in 1922, but Northern Ireland remains British.

1936

The wealthy were very fond of parties and dancing during the *'jazz age'* of the nineteen twenties. Women wore short skirts and had short hairstyles. Men wore evening dress or blazers and straw boaters.

The World at War

In 1939 Britain and France again went to war with Germany, whose leader Adolf Hitler, head of the Nazi Party, was out to conquer the world. The Germans soon occupied most of Europe, but not Britain.

When they invaded Russia, and their ally Japan attacked the USA at Pearl Harbour, the war became world-wide. Finally, Germany was occupied and Japan surrendered when atomic bombs were dropped.

After the war the Labour Government was determined to end unemployment and to make ordinary people's lives better. India and Pakistan became independent, and soon other British colonies followed them.

In 1940, Germany defeated France. However, without the control of the air, they could not invade Britain. In the Battle of Britain they tried to destroy the Royal Air Force, and bomb its airfields. But Britain eventually won the war for the skies.

Gandhi spent most of his life working peacefully for the independence of India from Britain. After he succeeded many other countries became independent.

1939 Germany invades Poland, forcing Britain and France to join World War II (1939-1945).

1938 Prime Minister Neville Chamberlain, trying to maintain peace with the armed aggression of Hitler's Germany, signs the Munich Agreement. He returns to Britain waving his famous *'piece of paper'* and promising *"Peace with honour- Peace in our time"*.

1936

1936 The first Weetabix appears on a British breakfast table.

1936-1952 The reign of George VI, second son of George V, married to Lady Elizabeth Bowes-Lyon, Queen Elizabeth the Queen Mother.

Edward VIII could not marry the American Mrs Simpson, because she was divorced. He announced his abdication on the radio.

Alexander Fleming discovered a mould called Penicillin, which kills bacteria without harming people, and saved many lives.

After failing to win the Battle of Britain, the Germans began to bomb London and other cities. Each night from 1940-41, wailing sirens alerted the people, who took refuge in air-raid shelters or underground stations. The British people, under Churchill, grew more determined and in the summer of 1941, the Germans changed to attacking Russia.

During and just after the Second World War, only the wealthy could afford to wear fashionable clothes. Most ordinary people wore simple *'utility'* clothes, which were rather plain, but cheap and easy to manufacture.

From the beginning of the Second World War, until 1954, food was rationed. Ration books contained coupons for each person's ration.

1945 Germany surrenders on May 7th. The Labour Government establishes the Welfare State.

1948 The National Health Service is established, giving free medical care to all.

1949 The North Atlantic Treaty Organisation (NATO) in which the USA, Canada, Great Britain and nine other European countries join together for mutual defence, is formed.

1941 Entry of Russia and USA on the side of Britain in World War II, against Germany, Italy and Japan.

1945 The USA drop the first atomic bombs on Nagasaki and Hiroshima, forcing Japan to surrender.

1947 The Indian sub-continent is granted independence, and divided into India and Pakistan.

1951 Britain returns to a Conservative Government, under Winston Churchill.

1951

The New Age

After the rationing of food and clothes and the shortages of wartime, British life became much more comfortable for most people. More and more people bought their own homes and owned cars and refrigerators.

Watching television became the main national pastime, but poverty remained, especially amongst the old. British industry lost many of its foreign markets, and the failure of Britain and France to occupy Egypt's Suez Canal, in the emergency of 1956, shocked the nation's pride.

Britain ended conscripting men into its armed forces, and the country began to rely on nuclear weapons for its defence.

One hundred years after the Great Exhibition of 1851, King George VI and Queen Elizabeth opened a great national exhibition at London's South Bank. It was called the *Festival of Britain* and celebrated Britain's recovery from the Second World War.

1951

1952 - The reign of Elizabeth II, eldest daughter of George VI, married to Prince Philip, the Duke of Edinburgh.

1954 Food-rationing ends, after almost 15 years.

1954 The ITA (Independent Television Authority) is allowed by Government to finance its programmes by selling advertising time.

1955 The Queen opens the world's first Nuclear Power Station, at Calder Hall.

The Hovercraft was invented by Sir Christopher Cockerell. To develop his idea for an air-cushion vehicle, he used two tin cans and a vacuum cleaner.

In 1953, John Hunt led the first successful expedition to climb Mount Everest. On May 29th, the New Zealander, Edmund Hillary and the Sherpa, Tenzing Norgay reached the summit – a height of 8848m (8,85 kms).

In 1956, Egypt seized the Suez Canal. Britain and France both protested and sent troops, but it was settled by the UN.

1956 British troops occupy the Suez Canal Zone during the Suez crisis, but are forced to withdraw.

1958 The RAF takes delivery of *THOR*, the first American Ballistic Missile.

1958 Britain's first section of motorway, the M6 Preston By-pass, is opened at a cost of £3,750.000.

When the young Queen Elizabeth II was crowned in Westminster Abbey, vast crowds crammed London. Although the monarchy has little power now, it is more popular than ever before.

1959 The British Motor Corporation launches the *Mini* car, designed by Alec Issigonis, and costing £500.

1960

In the nineteen fifties, television became a national craze. Everywhere thousands of aerials sprouted up on rooftops.

Young people's attitude to clothes was beginning to change. *'Teddy boys'* wore clothes that were like their grandfathers.

In October 1952, the first British atomic bomb was tested. In 1955, the world's first nuclear power-station opened at Calder Hall in Britain.

The European Connection

Under the threat of nuclear war, relations between Europe and Russia were at their worst. As Russia formed her satellite countries into the Soviet '*Bloc*', Europe formed the European Economic Community, with Britain joining in 1973.

During this time the '*Swinging Sixties*' were born, with the Beatles leading a revolution in music that established Britain as the centre of pop culture.

Throughout the sixties the consumer society grew with huge increases of mass-produced goods. Concorde carried passengers faster than the speed of sound and man took his first steps on the surface of the moon.

From a small club in Liverpool, the Beatles emerged to world stardom in the early 60's. John Lennon, Paul McCartney, Ringo Starr and George Harrison received M.B.E's in 1965 for their services to music.

The woman's role in family life has changed, with many more women beginning to have full-time jobs, both in the professions and in industry.

1960

1963 The world is shocked by the news of the assassination of US President John F Kennedy, who was shot in Dallas, Texas.

1963 Britain, USA and USSR sign a Nuclear Test Ban Treaty banning further testing of nuclear weapons.

1965 Sir Winston Churchill, Britain's wartime leader, dies and is given a state funeral.

1968 Riots in Northern Ireland between Catholics who want a united Ireland and Protestants who want to stay British.

In 1980, for the first time this century, Sebastian Coe – a British athlete – held four World Records in middle-distance running in 1980.

☐ *EEC members in 1973.*

After being blocked by France since 1957 because of our Commonwealth connections, Prime Minister Edward Heath took Britain into the European Economic Community in 1973.

In 1969, Prince Charles, heir to the throne, was invested as Prince of Wales, in a ceremony at Caernarvon Castle.

The discovery of oil and natural gas beneath the North Sea in the early 1960's provided Britain with a vital new industry. In 1976 our oil reserves reached a level where Britain could export.

Many of the ideas that have influenced the British way of life have come to us from the USA. One arrival that has changed our lives is the 'fast food' chain, which first appeared in the 60's.

The spread of television allowed millions of people to see England beat West Germany, to win the World Cup at Wembley in 1966.

1969 Neil Armstrong steps from Apollo 11 to become the first man to set foot on the surface of the Moon.

1971 Britain introduces decimal coinage.

1977 Britain celebrates Queen Elizabeth II's Silver Jubilee.

1978 Louise Brown, the world's first 'test-tube' baby is born.

1979 Margaret Thatcher becomes Britain's first woman Prime Minister.

1980

The Anglo-French supersonic airliner Concorde, made her maiden flight in 1969 and went in to service in 1977.

Flying at twice the speed of sound, the journey from London to New York takes her just 3hrs 42mins.

History in the Making

Conservative governments of the nineteen eighties, led by Britain's first woman Prime Minister, Margaret Thatcher, set out to reduce inflation and weaken the power of the Trade Unions. Unemployment rose to over three million, and there was bitter poverty in many Northern towns. Inflation did come down, however, and for many men and women - for in most homes women were as likely to go out to work as men - times were prosperous, especially in the South.

In the Falklands War the British army defeated the Argentinians, who tried to take over the Falkland Islands, but there is continued unrest in Ulster.

The raising of the *'Mary Rose'*, Henry VIII's great ship, sunk off Portsmouth, revealed many details about Tudor life - hundreds of items, including thimbles, coins, tools and weapons were found.

1980

1983 American Cruise missiles arrive at Greenham Common military base.

1985 The Anglo-Irish Agreement on Ulster is signed for a closer co-operation between the British and Irish Governments.

1986 Britain and France agree to construct the Channel Tunnel, due to open in 1993.

The first London Marathon took place on 29th March 1981. Of the 7,055 entrants, 6,418 completed the 39 km course to Constitution Hill. Since then it has been extended to 42 km, ending at Westminster Bridge.

The wedding of the Prince of Wales to the Lady Diana in 1981 was celebrated by the Archbishop of Canterbury, in St Paul's Cathedral. Although huge crowds gathered in London, the wedding was also seen by 700 million people worldwide, on television.

The Thames Barrier, completed in 1982, to prevent the River Thames from flooding London. The huge steel shutters can be raised to control the water level.

After 100 years of discussion, Britain and France have agreed to build a Channel tunnel. Two rail tunnels and a central maintenance shaft will be built.

One of the few British colonies left, the Falkland Islands, were seized by nearby Argentina. The British sent an expeditionary force to the South Atlantic and recaptured the Islands in 1982.

1986 A nuclear power station at Chernobyl, in the USSR, is seriously damaged in an explosion. High levels of radiation were recorded in Britain.

1987–8 Russian leader Mikhail Gorbachev introduces a new era of *glasnost* (openness) and *perestroika* (restructuring) into Russian politics.

1988 The Americans begin to withdraw Cruise missiles from Britain.

EEC

1992 All trade barriers between EEC countries will be removed.

1997 Britain has promised to hand control of Hong Kong back to the Chinese.

2000

During the 80's, concern about the environment is growing, with demands for an end to pollution of the sea, inland waters, and the damage to our atmosphere.

In 1985, pop-star Bob Geldof formed Band Aid, and raised many millions of pounds for victims of the famine in Africa.

In 1989, Margaret Thatcher MP became our longest serving Prime Minister, this century.

Index

Personality, Individual Differences and Intelligence

Personality, Individual Differences and Intelligence

Third Edition

John Maltby
University of Leicester

Liz Day
Sheffield Hallam University

Ann Macaskill
Sheffield Hallam University

PEARSON

Harlow, England • London • New York • Boston • San Francisco • Toronto • Sydney • Auckland • Singapore • Hong Kong
Tokyo • Seoul • Taipei • New Delhi • Cape Town • São Paulo • Mexico City • Madrid • Amsterdam • Munich • Paris • Milan

Pearson Education Limited
Edinburgh Gate
Harlow CM20 2JE
United Kingdom
Tel: +44(0)1279 623623
Fax: +44(0)1279 431059
Web: www.pearson.com/uk

First published 2007 (print)
Second edition published 2010 (print)
Third edition published 2013 (print and electronic)

ISBN: 978-0-273-75116-8 (print)
         978-0-273-75117-5 (PDF)
         978-0-273-79497-4 (eText)

British Library Cataloguing-in-Publication Data
A catalogue record for the print edition is available from the British Library

Library of Congress Cataloging-in-Publication Data
A catalog record for the print edition is available from the Library of Congress

10 9 8 7 6 5 4 3 2 1
16 15 14 13

Print edition typeset in Minion Pro Regular 9.5/12
Print edition printed and bound by L.E.G.O. S.p.A., Italy

NOTE THAT ANY PAGE CROSS REFERENCES REFER TO THE PRINT EDITION

BRIEF CONTENTS

The following additional material can be found on the website (www.pearsoned.co.uk/maltby)

CONTENTS

8 Biological Basis of Personality I: Genetic Heritability of Personality and Biological and Physiological Models of Personality 175

9 Biological Basis of Personality II: Evolutionary Psychology and Animal Studies of Personality 205

10 Further Ideas and Debates in Personality: Personality and Culture 230

PART 2 Intelligence 261

11 An Introduction to Intelligence 262

12 Theories and Measurement of Intelligence 278

13 The Use of Intelligence Tests: What Questions Emerge from the Measurement of Intelligence? 305

14 Heritability and Socially Defined Race Differences in Intelligence 336

**The following additional material
can be found on the website
(www.pearsoned.co.uk/maltby)**

Companion Website

For open-access **student resources** specifically written
to complement this textbook and support your learning,
including three additional web-only chapters, please
visit **www.pearsoned.co.uk/maltby**

Lecturer Resources

For password-protected online resources tailored to support
the use of this textbook in teaching, please visit
www.pearsoned.co.uk/maltby

GUIDED TOUR

Navigation and Setting the Scene

Part opener identifies the chapters and topics covered within each part. ▶

PART 1
Personality

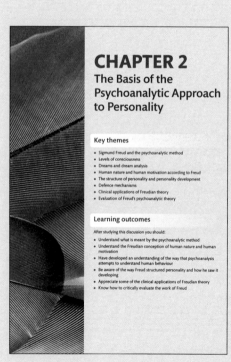

CHAPTER 2
The Basis of the Psychoanalytic Approach to Personality

Key themes

- Sigmund Freud and the psychoanalytic method
- Levels of consciousness
- Dreams and dream analysis
- Human nature and human motivation according to Freud
- The structure of personality and personality development
- Defence mechanisms
- Clinical applications of Freudian theory
- Evaluation of Freud's psychoanalytic theory

Learning outcomes

After studying this discussion you should:

- Understand what is meant by the psychoanalytic method
- Understand the Freudian conception of human nature and human motivation
- Have developed an understanding of the way that psychoanalysis attempts to understand human behaviour
- Be aware of the way Freud structured personality and how he saw it developing
- Appreciate some of the clinical applications of Freudian theory
- Know how to critically evaluate the work of Freud

Chapter opener page

◀ • **Key themes** give you an immediate idea of the general themes and topics covered in the chapter.

◀ • **Learning outcomes** are a list of learning objectives so that you can check that you have understood all the major areas by the end of the chapter.

• **Chapter introductions** give you an overview of the topics covered in the chapter by drawing on interesting real-life examples to show you how they relate to your everyday experiences. ▶

Introduction

Sigmund Freud was a major intellectual figure of the twentieth century and founded the psychoanalytic approach to personality. At the core of the psychoanalytic approach is the belief that most of our behaviour is driven by motives of which we are unaware. These motives are conceptualised as unconscious forces that make it difficult for us to truly know ourselves. This may lead us occasionally to behave in ways that we have difficulty explaining. In our everyday life, for example, people frequently refer to factors in their unconscious having influenced their behaviour. A colleague might forget to go to a meeting, despite having it in his diary and being reminded about it earlier in the day. When thinking about it, he admits that he was likely to be a boring meeting; consequently, Freud would have suggested that he was unconsciously motivated to forget about it.

The psychoanalytic approach, as we shall see, explains how much of our psychological energy is taken up with suppressing our unconscious urges or finding socially acceptable ways of expressing them. Freud's theory is controversial, and some current psychologists are keen to dismiss him as merely a historical figure, albeit an important one. Freud is a central figure in the development of the clinical strand of personality theorising discussed previously (Chapter 1). Freud's work is important historically, but Freud and related psychoanalytic theories are included here because of the continuing influence that his concepts have, not just on psychology but in many other disciplines also. Many psychoanalytic concepts provide such useful descriptions of human behaviour that they have been incorporated into our everyday language. By the end of the text, you will have come across many of these examples.

We begin by exploring in some detail the work of Sigmund Freud. Biographical details of Freud are included in the next Profile box to help us understand how his life

Source: Pearson Education Ltd, Jules Selmes

experiences have helped shape the theory that he produced (Chapter 1). The discussion of Freud reflects on the importance and extent of his contribution to personality theory. At the end of the discussion, the criteria described earlier (Chapter 1) are used to evaluate the theory.

Description of Freud's theory of personality

We will first describe Freud's theory of personality that comprises:

- levels of consciousness;
- the nature of human beings and the source of human motivation;
- the structure of personality;
- the development of personality.

Levels of consciousness

When Freud began theorising, there was a strong tradition within intellectual circles of regarding human beings

as basically rational creatures whose behaviour is determined by will or the seeking of goals in a conscious manner. Human beings were conceptualised as being in control of their lives and exercising free will in their behaviour to the extent that their social circumstances allowed. Freud did not create the idea of unconscious mind. Philosophers had been discussing the idea of unconscious mind for hundreds of years. However, the predominant view, as popularised by the German philosopher Johann Friedrich (1776–1841) in his two-volume book, *Psychology as Knowledge Newly Founded on Experience, Metaphysics and Mathematics* (1824–1825), was that unconscious ideas were weaker ideas that had been pushed from consciousness by the stronger conscious ideas. Freud (1940/1969) disagreed strongly both with the rational view of human beings and with the suggestion

Aiding your Understanding

Stop and think looks at topics in more depth to inspire critical thinking about the areas you have just read. ▶

Key terms are highlighted in the text when they first appear and are also included in the Glossary at the end of the book. ▶

◀ **Profile boxes** outline the biographies of key thinkers or researchers so you can learn more about these psychologists.

Chapter summaries succinctly recap and reinforce the key points to take away from the chapter. ▶

Stop and think

Treating classically conditioned emotional responses

Systematic desensitisation

This can be used to treat phobias, for example, someone with a phobia of birds. The aim is to replace the old association between the feared stimulus (bird) and the feared response (panic symptoms) with a new association of relaxation. The client and therapist begin by ranking bird-related fears from most to the least feared. Holding a bird might be most feared; a picture of a bird might be least feared. Next, the client is taught how to relax. The response of relaxation is incompatible with the feared response. The client and therapist move through the list of fears, ensuring that at each

level the feared response becomes conditioned to the relaxation response, until the client can comfortably face their worst fear of birds. Many phobias and other anxieties have been successfully treated with systematic desensitisation.

Alcoholism

Aversion therapy has been used to treat people with alcohol addictions. Here, the image of a drink could be paired with images of being sick or other negative images. This therapy has also been used to assist individuals stop smoking.

---

ego and superego, or problems in personality development of some other kind. The learning theorists rejected this as an explanation for the cause of mental problems, seeing it as unscientific to refer to what they saw as unobservable inner mental processes and/or structures to explain observed differences in behaviour. For these learning theorists, psychopathology was a learnt maladaptive response to a situation that may have generalised to other situations or similar stimuli, and, as such, it could be unlearnt. Normal development was about learning adaptive responses in a variety of situations, while abnormal development resulted from acquiring maladaptive responses.

Pavlov (1927) began this line of research by inducing what he called experimental neuroses in one of his laboratory dogs. The dog was conditioned so that he would salivate to the shape of a circle. He then learnt to distinguish between circles and ellipses, only salivating to circles. However, when the distinctions between circles and ellipses became harder to distinguish, the dog became very distressed; his behaviour was disorganised, with a preponderance of neurotic symptoms. The dog barked when taken into the laboratory, shivered in his harness and tried to bite the restraining straps. Pavlov interpreted this as demonstrating that when the dog could no longer cope with what was being asked of him, he developed neurotic symptoms.

Watson and his colleague Rayner (1920) went on to demonstrate that human emotional responses could also be manipulated using classical conditioning. This is the famous classical conditioning experiment carried out on an 11-month-old infant called Albert. This has come to be known as the 'Little Albert' study and is still regarded as a classic in psychology. Albert initially did not display any fear of laboratory rats, but he did produce a startle and fear response to a loud noise made by banging a hammer on a

metal bar. As Albert began to reach for a rat, the noise was made behind his head. After a few repetitions, he had been conditioned to fear the rat in the absence of any noise. This demonstrates how a child can learn an emotional response. This conditioned fear of white rats then generalised to other white, furry objects like a mask of Father Christmas and even Watson's own white hair. This work led to other psychologists exploring ways in which negative emotional reactions could be unlearned, and a great deal of work was carried out in this area from the 1920s until the 1980s. A summary of some of this work on classical conditioning is given in the Stop and think box: Treating classically conditioned emotional responses, for those of you with a clinical bent. The principles are still applied in some contexts; however, our next theorist, Skinner, developed this work further.

The radical behaviourism of B. F. Skinner

Skinner had been influenced by the research of Pavlov and Watson, among others, and developed it further. (See the Profiles box.) He did not claim that unconscious processes or inner states did not exist, but he strongly felt that it was unscientific and unnecessary to rely on these unobservable processes to explain behaviour. He did not deny that we had ideas and thoughts, but he strongly believed that these inner thoughts did not cause our behaviour. Suppose you do not turn up to do a seminar presentation; you may say that you were so anxious at the thought of doing it that you could not make yourself attend. For you, the explanation is that your anxiety prevented you from attending. You are

---

Theory of personal constructs of George A. Kelly

In this part of the text we are going to describe the theory of personal constructs of George A. Kelly (see Profile: George Alexander Kelly). We are going to outline:

- the view of the person in Kelly's theory;
- concepts within Kelly's theory;
- personality development according to Kelly;
- assessing personality in personal construct theory;
- clinical applications of personal construct theory.

The view of the person in Kelly's theory

Kelly's (1955) theory is based on a radically different view of the individual from the theories we have considered so far. He suggested that individuals act as *scientists*, each trying to understand and control the world around them. However, he was careful to stress that, unlike true scientists, we do not have objective data to work with; rather, we use our own very personal interpretations of the world. He denied the possibility of an agreed, objective reality that we all tuned into. Instead, Kelly (1955) saw us all as

interpreting events in the world according to our own theories of human behaviour. We construct hypotheses to try to explain events, and then we test these hypotheses and change them if necessary to make sense of what is happening. These are mainly private observations that we do not attempt to share with others. These are essentially our private perceptions of individuals and situations, but we perceive them as representing how the individuals or situations are in reality. Indeed, it is often only when we share our perceptions with others that we become aware that others do not always share our perception of the world.

Imagine a group of friends in trying to decide who is going to get the biggest room in the new house they are going to share. Tom suggests that he should get the biggest room as he found the house. Annabel disagrees, saying she found the house last year but did not get the biggest room. Mark agrees that Tom should not get the biggest room as several people had worked to find a suitable house and Tom had simply been lucky to find the house. Jenny thought that individuals' contribution to the rent should depend on the size of room they had. The others felt that the room sizes were not sufficiently different for this to work and that the furniture was better in some rooms and this needed to be factored into the equation. Louise was adamant that they should draw lots as she had done this in a previous house.

Profile

George Alexander Kelly

George Kelly was born in Perth, a small farming town in Kansas, United States, in 1905. He was the only son of a Presbyterian minister and received some of his early education at home. His first degree, awarded in 1926, was in physics and mathematics, and his intention was to become an engineer. He had undertaken an introductory psychology course and found it very dull (Kelly, 1966). He then undertook a part-time masters course in educational sociology while working in various engineering and educational jobs. In 1929, he was awarded a scholarship to study for an educational degree at Edinburgh University in Scotland. It was there that he developed an interest in psychology, undertaking a dissertation on factors that might predict teaching success. Returning to the States, Kelly undertook doctoral studies in psychology at Iowa State University, graduating in 1931. His interest was in the physiological aspects of speech and reading difficulties; however, as jobs in physiological psychology were scarce, he developed a career in clinical psychology. He inaugurated clinical psychology services for the State of Kansas, with mobile assessment and treatment centres for schoolchildren. At the same time, he taught at a state college. During the Second World War he enlisted

in the US Navy, working as a psychologist on training programmes. Throughout this period, Kelly had experimented with different approaches to treatment, and he concluded that none of the existing approaches really met the needs of his clients. In his work in schools, he observed that teachers would sometimes describe children as being lazy, but that this was not a helpful description for him to use when approaching the child. He would try to understand how the child saw school and then examine how the child's perception compared with the teacher's. From this work, he came to appreciate that problems often arose because teacher and pupil were construing the situation differently. The child had perhaps fallen behind and did not understand what was being taught, so had stopped trying to learn. This observation played a crucial part in the later development of his theory of personal constructs.

Kelly did not publish very much in his lifetime, but he lectured extensively and taught for 20 years at Ohio State University, followed by an appointment at Brandeis University to do research. Unfortunately, 2 years into that appointment, he died. While Kelly's theory was developed purely in the United States, it has been more influential and is more widely applied in the United Kingdom and mainland Europe.

United Kingdom and in Holland, Canada and Israel. There are still large numbers of therapists using personal construct theory. Similarly, for a long time REBT was more popular in the United Kingdom and the rest of the world than it was in the United States, although this is beginning to change. As we discussed earlier, cognitive theories are the fastest-growing and most researched approach currently.

Applied value

Kelly's work, as we have seen, is utilised in clinical psychology and has provided useful insights into disordered thinking in schizophrenia and other conditions. More recently, it has been applied in occupational psychology, where the rep grid is used to explore relationships within organisations or consumers'

perceptions of a company's products. Kelly's theory has also been used to help people identify their ideal jobs. Ellis' work is used in an even wider context, from clinical psychology, business and education to personal growth.

Final comments

By now, you should understand Kelly's personal construct theory and its constituent parts. You should appreciate what is meant by subjective perception of the world, be aware of different views on the effects of development on personality and be familiar with the repertory grid as an assessment tool. You should now also understand the basic model of REBT, have an appreciation of the clinical applications of cognitive theories and be able to broadly evaluate cognitive approaches to personality.

Summary

- Cognitive theories challenge both the psychoanalytic and learning theory approaches to personality.
- Kelly conceives individuals acting as scientists, each trying to understand and control the world around them.
- The criteria that we each use to perceive and interpret events are labelled our personal constructs. Within our construct system, we have overarching constructs known as superordinate constructs. Within the superordinate concepts are subordinate constructs.
- Central to Kelly's theory is the concept of constructive alternativism.
- Kelly sees free will and determinism as interrelated. He assumes that we all have free will in selecting our goals, but once we have selected a goal, it may determine our subsequent behaviour.
- Kelly suggests that our motivation to act comes from our future aims, not from our past learning or early experiences or innate drives. This is termed the fundamental postulate of his theory.
- In Kelly's theory, personal constructs are organised in terms of similarities and contrasts.
- Kelly's fundamental postulate is expanded on by the addition of 11 corollaries outlining how the interpretative processes operate to allow us to create our personal constructs.
- Kelly's constructs have two opposing properties: permeability and impermeability.
- Kelly believes that predicting behaviour is very complex. The individual's 'cognitive world', which will include inconsistent as well as logical subsystems, has to be assessed.
- Kelly proposes three types of constructs: pre-emptive, constellatory and propositional.

- In personal construct theory, the aim of development was for the individual to maximise their knowledge of the world via the development of their personal construct systems.
- The assessment technique that Kelly is best known for is the role construct repertory test (rep grid).
- People with psychological problems were using personal constructs that were invalid and unhelpful. To bring about change in his clients' personal constructs, Kelly used several techniques, including controlled elaboration, self-characterisation sketches and fixed-role therapy.
- Ellis' REBT theory also comes from the clinical tradition and was influenced by learning theory and the psychoanalytic approaches of Horney and Adler.
- Ellis suggests that human beings are uniquely rational and uniquely irrational in our thinking and the ways we attempt to reach our goals in life.
- Irrational thought is recognised by its demanding nature. We make demands on ourselves, other people or the world in general.
- REBT and theory adopts a logico-empirical approach, stressing the importance of having evidence for your beliefs. It also stresses the subjective nature of our perception of the world. We use perception, sensing, thinking and emotion to interpret the world.
- Ellis asserts that we have free will as individuals, but that also makes us responsible for our actions.
- The theory of REBT sees being fallible as an innate quality of human beings.
- Ellis asserts that 80 per cent of individual differences are genetic, but he does talk about the role of developmental experiences in encouraging human beings to think irrationally.

Critical Thinking and Going Further

Connecting up identifies and directs you to related topics in other chapters.

Critical thinking provides interesting and stimulating **Discussion questions** that may be suitable for discussion or seminar work, and **Essay questions** which provide a basis to practise the type of essay questions you may encounter in your exams.

Career focus provides an insight into what it's like to work in different areas of psychology. Find out firsthand from professional psychologists how they got into their field and how studying personality helped.

---

148   PART 1 PERSONALITY

- How parents relate to their children will be heavily influenced by the adequacy of the parents' own self-concepts and the number of conditions of worth that they themselves have.
- Rogers felt that individuals intuitively know what is good for them, but there is no evidence to support this contention.
- The fully functioning person emerges as a result of self-actualisation, and Rogers provided descriptions of such individuals.
- Rogers' theory originated in his clinical work, and a lot of his writing related to the development of his approach to counselling and therapy.
- The aim of therapy was to facilitate a reintegration of the self-concept. Most clients have many conditions of worth, so they have an idealised self and their

current self falls very short of this ideal. The aim of therapy is to reduce this gap and to reintegrate the self-concept with the real self.
- Rogers stressed that the relationship between the therapist and the client is crucial. He outlined the core conditions of counselling to describe the nature of the relationship. Rogers claimed that all that is required for positive change to occur is that these core conditions of counselling be met.
- Rogers was very aware of the importance of trying to provide research evidence to evaluate his approach, and he endeavoured to do this. While there is some support, the methodologies he used tend to rely very heavily on self-report measures.
- Finally, guidelines for evaluating both theories are provided.

Connecting up

You might wish to look back at Chapter 3 and Jung's discussion of individuation and compare and contrast these ideas with Maslow's ideas of self-actualisation.

Critical thinking

Discussion questions

- Is the distinction between B-love and D-love a valuable one in helping us to understand human relationships?
- How do you feel about the concept of peak or optimal experiences? Does it seem a useful concept and a description of the ultimate human experience?
- What would you see as the strengths and weaknesses of self-actualisers?
- Is it as difficult to find your goals in life and life satisfaction as Maslow and Rogers imply?
- Compare the conceptualisations of human nature posited by Maslow, Rogers and Freud. Is there anything in the biographical experiences of the three theorists that might help explain these differences?
- Do you consider conditions of worth to be a valuable concept? Can you identify any of your own conditions of worth? Do they play a useful role in your psyche?
- Is there any evidence to support Rogers' organismic valuing process?
- Is Rogers' distinction between what is generally termed 'love' and unconditional positive regard a valid one? If so, is it an important distinction in your view?

- How realistic is it to describe Rogers' approach to therapy as non-directive?
- Rogers is adamant that all self-evaluation is bad, even positive evaluations. Can you explain why he takes this view? Do you agree?
- How adequately do humanistic theorists explain human motivation?

Essay questions

- Critically discuss Rogers' theory and practice of person-centred therapy.
- Critically discuss Maslow's theory of self-actualisation.
- Discuss how developmental experiences influenced the theorising of Rogers.
- Compare and contrast Maslow's and Rogers' theory of self-actualisation.
- Critically discuss Rogers' contribution to our understanding of human personality.
- Critically discuss Maslow's contribution to our understanding of human personality.

---

118   PART 1 PERSONALITY

Contentious issues

Some researchers suggest that the relationship between cognitions and emotions does not always hold (Bower, 1981). There are sometimes chicken-and-egg arguments put forward about whether the depression causes negative thoughts or the negative thoughts cause the depression. With depressed individuals, their negative mood may produce negative cognitions. However, in support of cognitive approaches, it is clear from the case study literature that negative cognitions may maintain depression once it is started and that helping individuals change their negative thinking improves their depression.

REBT and other cognitive approaches are sometimes criticised for trying to adjust the individual to fit in with social reality, whereas it may be that social changes are needed. This is an argument that is sometimes made about

stress management training, for example. Instead of tackling the sources of stress, institutions may simply help individuals cope better with it. Therapists generally respond to these sorts of criticisms by saying that their aim is to reduce the suffering of the individual as that is generally within their power while societal changes are not.

Meehl (1981) accuses Ellis of using logical positivism when asking for proof of values from clients. He points out that many of our human values cannot be empirically verified by data. The suggestion he makes is that in REBT and other cognitive approaches, clients substitute one set of values for another more socially acceptable or socially convenient set, and that it has nothing to do with rationality. This point reminds us that, as we discussed previously (Chapter 1), all theorising occurs within a cultural context; it does involve value judgements about what is 'acceptable' behaviour, and therapists are expected to work within an ethical framework.

Career focus: Working in clinical psychology

According to the British Psychological Society website, the main role of clinical psychologists is to alleviate psychological distress and support psychological well-being among their clients. The sort of problems that clinical psychologists cover include, but are not exclusive to,

mental illness, depression, anxiety and child and family problems. Clinical psychologists work in a variety of settings and with a variety of individuals and agencies. This includes hospitals, mental health teams and health and social services.

Professor Susan Llewelyn

1. **Why did you choose to pursue the area of clinical psychology?**
   I found clinical questions were the most interesting to explore; for example, why do some people have such different experiences (especially psychosis) and how could psychology help to reduce distress.

2. **In what way do the skills and/or knowledge you learned when studying personality and individual differences apply to your work/research today?**
   My clinical work has mainly involved working therapeutically with people who have difficulties in personal relationships and psychological self-care, such as those often following the experience of childhood sexual abuse. I have also worked extensively with health care teams, especially in the mental health sector, helping them to work constructively together to improve the care of their patients, by being clear about their purpose and structure, and through effective communication processes. Knowing about how people work in teams and groups has helped me to improve mental health care services. Knowing how to provide a safe and encouraging environment (see attachment theories in Chapter 21) has helped me to help others work out a way of resolving their distress.

For further advice on becoming a clinical psychologist, including guidance on the necessary qualifications and experience, visit the British Psychological Society website at **http://www.bps.org.uk/careers-education-training /how-become-psychologist/types-psychologists/becoming-clinical-psychologis**

Going further provides a list of other books, journals and websites you may wish to explore to find out more about the areas discussed in the chapter.

▶

Film and literature introduces chapter-relevant classic novels, films and television programmes to add interest.

▶

Three extra chapters online on Academic Argument and Thinking, Statistical Terms, and Research Ethics provide a framework for academic and technical terms used throughout the book. These chapters can be used as a reference to help you in your studies and to help you develop your own skills in these areas. Please access them at www.pearsoned.co.uk/maltby

▶

ABOUT THE AUTHORS

Dr John Maltby is a Senior Lecturer in Psychology at the University of Leicester. He has over 100 publications in the area of personality and individual differences.

Dr Liz Day is a Senior Lecturer in Psychology at Sheffield Hallam University. She has over 40 publications in the area of individual differences. She has also trained as a Clinical Hypnotherapist.

Professor Ann Macaskill is at Sheffield Hallam University and is a Chartered Health Psychologist and trained in cognitive behaviour therapy. She has published extensively, with current research in individual differences, health and well-being.

PREFACE

Introduction

How would you describe your personality? Are you outgoing? Do you make friends easily? Do you worry too much? Think of two or three words that best describe how you generally behave, think and feel. How would you describe your general level of intelligence? Are you particularly good at some things and not so good at others?

Now think of your brothers or sisters (if you have them). Compared to everyone else you know, how similar are your brothers and sisters to your personality and level of intelligence? How like your parents are you? Are you more like your mother or your father? Would you say you and your friends have similar personalities, or very different ones?

Do you respond to situations in the same way that your family and friends respond? Do you hold similar views about the world, or very different ones? When it comes to general approaches to life, how different are you to everyone around you? Do you generally have a happy disposition or find life difficult a lot of the time? Can you name people who are similar in your approach to life, and people who are very different? In psychology, personality, individual differences and intelligence are all topics that examine how people are similar and how they differ in their behaviour, the way they think and how they feel. In this text we provide an overview of major theories, methods, research findings and debates in personality, individual differences and intelligence. Although the areas of personality, individual differences and intelligence cover a multitude of subjects, ranging from psychophysiology to socially learnt behaviour, you will see how these three main topics come together by using several similar approaches.

Our aim is to cover the topic areas that meet the requirements of the British Psychological Society qualifying exam and the Quality Assurance Agency Benchmarks for Psychology under their heading of 'Individual Differences'. The contents of this examination help to define the curriculum that is taught in psychology undergraduate degrees accredited by the British Psychological Society. With the British Psychological Society and Quality Assurance Agency Benchmarks for Psychology curriculum requirements in mind, this text also covers aspects of the history of various theories and approaches. This information will be useful for courses that teach history of psychology in an integrated fashion within specific modules.

Consequently, the overall aim of the text is to include substantial coverage of personality, individual differences and intelligence, as well as their integration, that is applicable to United Kingdom/European students. We have discussed historical material and viewpoints as well as including contemporary and newer debates to make the material accessible and interesting to read.

We have written text with the novice in mind, and we guide you through the material, from the foundations to the more advanced material, so you can constantly build on previously acquired knowledge and build up a critical understanding of each topic.

To help you do this, we include opportunities to reflect on the material and test your own understanding.

Structure of the text

While writing this text, we consulted over 30 academics in the United Kingdom and Europe over what it should cover. We now know that people have many different ideas about what constitutes personality, intelligence and individual differences. We know that some courses teach all three topics as an Individual Differences course. Other courses see large distinctions between the different areas covered; for example, personality and intelligence. With this in mind, we have not assumed that there is a typical route through the text. Instead, we have sought to make the material in each chapter self-contained so that it may be taught separately. That said, you can divide the text's contents in the following three ways: parts, levels and themes.

Parts of the text

The first way that this text is organised is into three parts: (1) personality, (2) intelligence and (3) further debates and applications in individual differences. It is easy to see how these three sections might be taught separately as topic areas. Each part also has its own introduction, which serves as a guide and helps you structure your learning.

Part 1: Personality

The aim of this part is to provide a parsimonious account of personality theories and approaches to individual differences. We cover the major schools of psychology (psychoanalytic, learning, cognitive, humanistic, trait theorists and biological). Theories are set in a historical context and issues and debates are highlighted, always bearing in mind the key questions that the theories are designed to address. Topics covered include the nature of human beings, the basis of human motivation, the generation of emotions and cognitions and conceptions of psychological health and illness within the various models. Where appropriate, clinical applications of the various theories are also examined, not only to complement your learning in abnormal psychology but also to appeal to those of you with an interest in clinical psychology. Consistent criteria are used throughout to help you to evaluate, compare and contrast the various theoretical approaches. By the end of Part 1, readers will have a theoretical and a research-based appreciation of the sources of individual differences in behaviour, thinking and feeling.

Part 2: Intelligence

This part of the text covers theory, research, measurement and the application of intelligence. This is a controversial area of psychology, where there is a lot of debate. Indeed, you may already have some feelings about theories and measurement of intelligence. For example, what is your view of intelligence tests? If you haven't a view now, you will have by the end of Part 2. We have given full consideration to the theories and controversies in the topic of intelligence, and we highlight classical and modern approaches to how intelligence is defined, debated and applied, all within the historical context of intelligence.

Part 3: Further debates and applications in individual differences

The aim of this part is to cover a series of subjects that are commonly covered in the personality and individual differences journals, but much less so in personality and individual differences textbooks. The rationale for the topics chosen is to draw on influential subjects in individual differences that are contemporary and that we know excite students.

Individual differences in optimism, irrational beliefs, social anxiety, personal relationships, health, well-being and the social attitudes are important when applied in the individual differences literature to explain a wealth of human behaviours, feelings, thinking and reactions. These include explanations of our mental health, how we succeed and fail in interpersonal relationships and how we understand the social world. We have also structured these chapters to develop your 'individual differences' thinking by drawing on different aspects of theory and methodology. For example, in the optimism chapter we will show you how it is useful to unfold a single concept to allow a number of different considerations. In the irrational beliefs chapter we will present the central idea of irrational beliefs and show you how to assess the strength of this concept through to a conclusion by exploring how well it applies to a number of situations. In the social anxiety chapter,

we consider two subject areas (shyness and embarrassment) and show you how sometimes it is useful to provide a general context to ideas. In the interpersonal relationships chapter, we show you how useful it can be to take a series of topics and try to link them together, so that you can present an overall process and identify recurring themes.

Level of study

The second way that this text is organised is through level of study. We are aware that some psychology courses teach different topic areas in personality, intelligence and individual differences in different years (ranging from first year to final year). Therefore, we have organised each of the three parts of the text so that the later chapters in each part may be considered as more advanced topics of study. In this way, there is a developmental progression in the learning. This also means that the text should be useful across all the years of your degree.

- **Personality** – This topic area is presented mainly in historical order. Therefore, you will see how approaches and theories in individuals have developed over time. In this part you can compare the classical psychoanalytic, learning, cognitive and humanistic approaches (Chapters 2–6) to understanding the self with modern-day humanistic, trait and biological approaches (Chapters 7–10) in individual differences.
- **Intelligence** – In this topic area the development of learning focuses on a historical overview but is also a comparison in terms of the complexity of arguments. We contrast everyday notions of intelligence and a historical overview of classical and modern theories and applications of intelligence (Chapters 11–13) with controversial and modern-day considerations and applications of intelligence (Chapters 14–16).
- **Further Debates and Applications in Individual Differences** – In this topic area the development is based on the number of subjects covered in the chapter. Therefore, the chapters that look at single concepts, such as optimism and irrational beliefs (Chapters 18 and 19), compare with the chapters that look at several topic areas surrounding social anxiety, interpersonal relationships and social attitudes and health well-being (Chapters 20–24).

Themes within the text

The main themes within the text reflect the British Psychological Society qualifying exam. In line with the exam, we have outlined the assumptions, evidence and main approaches to emotion, motivation, the self and personality and abnormal development. We consider the psychoanalytic, behavioural, cultural, social learning, social-cognitive, radical behaviourist, humanistic-existential, phenomenological, lexical-trait, neo-Darwinist, biological and behavioural genetic approaches to personality. These approaches can be found definitively in Chapters 1–9, but topics covering biological, cognitive and social learning aspects to emotion, motivation, the self, personality and abnormal development are also covered in Chapters 17, 18 and 19.

The influence of genetic, biological, environmental and cultural factors on individual differences, as well as the temporal and situational consistency of individual differences, is addressed throughout the text from Chapter 1 to Chapter 25. The controversies and debates regarding the interaction of genetic, environmental and cultural factors on personality and intelligence are focused on in Chapters 8 and 14.

The influence of personality, intelligence and individual differences on other behaviours, including health, education, culture, relationships, occupational choice and competency, again, is a focus throughout the text from Chapters 1 to 25. For specific examples, you may want to concentrate on Chapters 5 and 6 as well as Chapters 13 through to 25.

The history of mental and psychological testing, the nature of intelligence, contemporary approaches to intelligence and their implications for educational and social policy are covered in Chapters 11–16.

We would also like to draw your attention to other themes that might reflect emerging interests of students in individual differences and provide the basis of material for option modules. For example, those interested in following a theme on well-being might focus on the latter part of the book (Chapters 18–24) in addition to the chapters covering Freud (Chapter 2), Jung, Adler and Horney (Chapter 3), Ellis (Chapter 5), humanistic psychology (Chapter 6) and self-determination theory (Chapter 10). Those interested in statistical applications in psychology would be able to show the uses of factor analysis in intelligence testing (Chapter 12), meta-analysis and effect sizes in comparing sex differences in intelligence (Chapter 15) and the use of psychometrics in developing psychological tests (Chapter 25). Those interested in developing a positive psychology theme should note that there is material on theories within humanistic psychology (Chapter 6), self-determination theory (Chapter 10), wisdom and creativity (Chapter 16), optimism and hope (Chapter 18), love (Chapter 21), forgiveness (Chapter 21), positive aspects of religiosity (Chapter 22), subjective and psychological well-being (Chapter 23) and positive psychology and health (Chapter 24).

Finally, for this third edition of the text, there are some changes and additions since the last edition. As the literature is constantly updating, we have revised all chapters to include recent and key papers. We have also provided substantial new sections in the biologically focused chapters (Chapters 8 and 9), outlining the adaptive personality and behavioural ecology and debates around the general factor of personality, and introduced some further discussion (e.g. the Dickens/Flynn Model) around the Flynn effect that is covered in Chapter 13.

Additionally, in each chapter we have referred the reader to related discussions in other areas of the text.

Features of the text

There are features to the text, including within-chapter features and supplementary material provided on a website.

Within-chapter features

Each chapter has these features:

- **Key themes**, so you know the general areas that are covered in each chapter.
- Clear chapter objectives, put in the form of **learning outcomes**, so you can check that you have covered all the major areas.
- A series called **Stop and think** that asks you to think about the areas a little more, or gives you some further information to think about. These features are provided to spur you on and to start thinking critically about the area you have just read.
- **Profiles** that outline biographies of key thinkers or researchers in the topic area, so you get to know more about these psychologists.
- A number of chapters feature **Career focus** interviews, which explore the roles of different psychologists, such as clinical psychologist, neuropsychologist and organisational psychologist, and ask how skills and knowledge learned when studying personality and individual differences apply in these areas.
- **Summary** boxes at the end of each chapter to outline the main points that you should take forward.
- **Discussion questions** containing material that might be suitable for discussion or seminar work.
- **Essay questions** that address the core material in the chapter, allowing you to test your own knowledge and practise essays in the area.
- **Going further** material via key texts, journals and established web resources. This is to get you reading more around the topic areas.
- References to **film and literature** that reflect some of the ideas explored in the chapter.
- **Connecting up** points that references material elsewhere in the text that links with the themes explored in the chapter.

Personality, Individual Differences and Intelligence Companion Website (www.pearsoned.co.uk/maltby)

In addition to the features integrated into the text, there are also a variety of valuable resources on the website for both students and lecturers.

The Companion Website for students includes:

- **Multiple choice questions** – You will be able to access over 200 multiple choice questions so you can test your knowledge of the topics covered in the book.
- **Essay questions** – In addition to those in the text there are over 100 essay questions covering a range of topics so you can practise for your essay and examination assessment.
- **Advanced reading** – There are over 20 additional topic areas and recent readings that can be used to supplement or advance your study and act as a source for ideas for your independent projects.
- **Web links** – Annotated links to a variety of relevant personality, individual differences and intelligence sites on the web.

For lecturers there are:

- **PowerPoint slides** – These slides contain details of the main areas and figures provided in each chapter.
- **Additional essay and discussion questions** – There are over 300 essay and discussion questions covering topics to facilitate group work and assessment.
- **Multiple choice questions** – You will be able to access over 400 multiple choice questions so you are able to set your own multiple choice test for students.
- **Advanced reading** – There are over 20 additional topic areas and readings that can be used to supplement or advance students' study or be used for tutorials or seminars.

Also online are three supplementary chapters. These provide a framework for many of the academic and technical terms that are commonly used in the text and should be used as reference material to support your learning. One might expect to find a chapter early in the text outlining these terms; however, we found that it distracted from the content. We also didn't wish to dictate certain areas of study if the lecturer did not feel they were needed or taught these aspects in different ways.

The three chapters are on the following topics:

- **Academic argument (Chapter 26)** – In this chapter we discuss acceptable and unacceptable forms of academic argument. At points within the text, you will come across academic arguments that form the basis of discussion and debate in chapters. So this chapter on academic argument can be helpful to you to appreciate many aspects of the debate fully. There are many controversies and arguments in personality, individual differences and intelligence, and it is important that you are able to use argument effectively. This chapter can be used to inform what constitutes effective and valid argument and what comprises poor argument. It will also give you advice on the key ideas in critical thinking that can be used to improve your academic work.

- **Statistical analysis (Chapter 27)** – This chapter describes the statistical ideas that lie behind simple inferential statistics (i.e. correlations and t-tests); multivariate statistics, such as factor analysis and multiple regression; and advanced considerations in statistics, including meta-analysis and effect size. This material is needed because throughout the text we use statistical terms and concepts to outline, illustrate and support the topics we discuss. The use of statistical terms is common in psychology, and through your research methods and statistics classes you will already be aware of, or become familiar with, many of the terms we mention. However, there may be some statistical concepts with which you are less familiar. Whatever your knowledge or experience of statistical terms, we have included some supplementary material that will give you an easy understanding of many of the statistical terms to build your confidence with using these concepts in the material.

- **Ethics (Chapter 28)** – This chapter deals with ethics. Several times in the text, we touch on issues of ethics; for example, when considering psychoanalytic and humanistic personality or psychology or psychological testing in education and the workplace. This chapter, which outlines ethical guidelines alongside those suggested for research participants by the British Psychological Society, might prove useful in supplementing these discussions.

All these chapters refer to core academic skills or approaches in psychology. You might want to read through these chapters or you might like to use them as a resource that you can draw upon when required.

Final prefatorial comments

When we first started this text we thought that the topics of personality, individual differences and intelligence were important in modern-day psychology. Today we are convinced that they are crucial. Not only do they serve modern-day psychology well, but the past and the future of psychology are bound up in these three areas. No other topic area in psychology has provided so many commonly used concepts and applications to psychology. No other area of psychology can provide such controversy and emotion (for example, IQ testing, socially defined race differences in intelligence) while also providing such simple and eloquent answers to complicated questions (for example, the five-factor model of personality). Most of all, no other area starts with the construction of the first intelligence test and invention of statistical tests, dabbles in the psycho-physiological properties of the brain and finishes by explaining how we love and forgive.

ACKNOWLEDGEMENTS

Authors' acknowledgements

Liz would like to thank her mother, Norma, and Ann would like to thank her family, Norman, Sean and Fiona, all for their patience and high levels of support.

Our appreciation goes to the whole editorial and production team at Pearson Education who have been involved in producing this third edition, including Philippa Fiszzon, Kelly Miller and Sarah Beanland. In particular a big thank you to Neha Sharma, Jane Lawes, and also to Janey Webb, as always fantastic, and for whom no question is too big or too small; also not forgetting Emma Travis, who oversaw the first edition of the book.

Our thanks to Rajvinder Lally for allowing us to use her initial work on the concept of academic vindictiveness in Chapter 25.

Also, special thanks must go to Steven Muncer, who kindly and unselfishly wrote an additional 'Stop and think' for the psychometrics chapter. This is a real asset to the book for which we are deeply grateful.

Last, and by no means least, we would also like to thank the reviewers, of this and the previous editions. We would like to thank them especially for devoting their valuable time, incredible patience and superb guidance, and, not least, for always going beyond the call of duty in their help and advice.

John Maltby
Liz Day
Ann Macaskill

Publisher's acknowledgements

Our grateful thanks go to the reviewers of this third edition of the book for their time and valuable help:

Emma Barkus – University of Wollongong, Australia
Caroline Bettenay – London South Bank University
Philip Corr – University of East Anglia
Filip De Fruyt – Ghent University
Peter Hancock – University of Stirling
Wendy Johnson – University of Edinburgh
Lars Penke – University of Edinburgh
Susan Rasmussen – University of Strathclyde

We are very grateful to the following reviewers for their helpful comments and suggestions on the second edition of the book:

Tom Buchanan – University of Westminster
Stephen Fisher – formerly University of Strathclyde
Melanie Mitchell – Northumbria University
Simon Moore – London Metropolitan University
Marcus Munafò – University of Bristol
Steven Muncer – Teesside University
Paddy O'Donnell – University of Glasgow
Leif Edward Ottesen Kennair – Norwegian University of Science and Technology
Susan Rasmussen – University of Strathclyde
Jeremy Ray – University of Gothenburg
Teresa Rushe – University of Ulster
Maria Sandgren – Södertörn University

And a continued thanks to the following for all their help in developing the first edition:

Martin Bäckström – Lund University
Geoff Bunn – Manchester Metropolitan University
Martin Eisemann – University of Tromsø
Henrik Høgh-Olesen – Aarhus University
Val Tuck – Newcastle University

Thanks also to those reviewers who we were unable to contact for permission to print their names – their comments have been very helpful.

We are grateful to the following for permission to reproduce copyright material:

Figures

Figure 4.4 Copyright © 1966 by the American Psychological Association, adapted with permission, from Table 1 (adapted) pp. 11–12, from Generalised expectancies for internal versus external control of reinforcement, *Psychological Monographs: General and Applied*, Vol. 80 (1), pp. 1–28 (Rotter, Julian B. 1966), doi: 10.1037/h0092976. No further reproduction or distribution is permitted without written permission from the American Psychological Association; Figure 5.2 from *The Psychology of Personal Constructs*, Vol. 1, Routledge (Kelly, G.A. 1955) p. 270, Thomson

Publishing Services; Figure 7.2 adapted from *The Biological Basis of Personality*, Charles C. Thomas, Springfield, IL (Eysenck, H.J. 1967) p. 36, Figure 14, reproduced with permission of Charles C. Thomas, publisher, via Copyright Clearance Center; Figure 12.1 from *Weschler Adult Intelligence Scale, Third Edition (WAIS-III)*, Copyright © 1997 NCS Pearson, Inc., reproduced with permission, all rights reserved, "Wechsler Adult Intelligence Scale" and "WAIS" are trademarks, in the US and/or other countries, of Pearson Education, Inc. or its affiliates(s); Figure 12.4 from Raven's Progressive Matrices (Coloured, Parallel, Sets A, AB, B). Copyright © 1998 NCS Pearson, Inc. Raven's Progressive Matrices (Standard, Sets A-E). Copyright © 1976, 1958, 1938 NCS Pearson, Inc. Raven's Progressive Matrices (Advanced). Copyright © 1976, 1947, 1943 NCS Pearson, Inc. Reproduced with permission, all rights reserved. "Raven's Progressive Matrices" is a trademark, in the US and/or other countries, of Pearson Education, Inc. or its affiliates(s); Figure 12.5 from *The Analysis of Intelligence*, New York: McGraw-Hill (Guilford, J.P. and Hoepfner, R. 1971) Copyright © 1971, The McGraw-Hill Companies, Inc.; Figure 13.2 from *Kaufman Assessment Battery for Children, Second Edition (KABC-II)*, Copyright © 2004 NCS Pearson, Inc., reproduced with permission, all rights reserved. 'KABC' and 'Vineland' are trademarks, in the US and/or other countries, of Pearson Education, Inc. or its affiliate(s); Figure 13.3 adapted from Premorbid (early life) IQ and later mortality risk: systematic review, *Annals of Epidemiology*, Vol. 17 (4), pp. 278–88 (Batty, G.D., Deary, I.J. and Gottfredson, L.S. 2007), Figure 1, p. 284, with permission from Elsevier; Figure 14.7 adapted from *The Bell Curve: Intelligence and Class Structure in American Life*, The Free Press, A Division of Simon and Schuster, Inc. (Herrnstein, R.J. and Murray, C. 1994) p. 279, Copyright © 1994 by Richard J. Herrnstein and Charles Murray. All rights reserved, with the permission of The Free Press, a Division of Simon & Schuster, Inc.; Figure 15.4 adapted from J.D. Mayer, P. Salovey and D.R. Caruso, Models of Emotional Intelligence, in *The Handbook of Intelligence*, pp. 398, 404, 415 (Sternberg, R.J. (Ed.) 2000), Cambridge University Press; Figure 15.5 from *Mayer-Salovey-Caruso Emotional Intelligence Test (MSCEIT) V.20* (Mayer, J.D., Salovey, P. and Caruso, D.R. 2002) Copyright © 1999, 2000, 2002 Multi-Health Systems, Inc., all rights reserved; Figure 15.6 from D. Goleman, An EI-based theory of performance, in *The Emotionally Intelligent Workplace: How to select for, measure, and improve emotional intelligence in individuals, groups, and organizations* p. 28 (Cherniss, C. and Goleman, D. (Eds.) 2001), New York: Jossey Bass Wiley. Copyright © 2001 Cary Cherniss and Daniel Goleman, reproduced with permission of John Wiley & Sons, Inc.; Figure 16.7 from J.S. Renzulli, The three-ring conception of giftedness: a developmental model for promoting creative productivity, in *Conceptions of Giftedness* (Sternberg. R.J. and Davidson, J.

(Eds) 1986), Cambridge University Press; Figure 20.3 from L. Henderson and P.G. Zimbardo, Shyness, in *The Encyclopedia of Mental Health*, Vol. 7, pp. 497–509 (Friedman, H.S. (Ed.) 1998), Copyright © 1998 Elsevier Science, reprinted with permission; Figure 21.2 from R.J. Sternberg, Triangulating love, in *The Psychology of Love* (Sternberg, R.J. and Barnes, M.L. (Eds.) 1998), New Haven, CT: Yale University Press, Copyright © 1998 by Yale University; Figure 23.1 adapted from Toward a consensual structure of mood, *Psychological Bulletin*, Vol. 98, pp. 219–235 (Watson, D. and Tellegen, A. 1985), American Psychological Association, adapted with permission; Figures 25.1, 25.2, 25.4, 25.5, 25.6, 25.8, 25.13 screenshots from SPSS for Windows, Microsoft product screen shots are printed with permission from Microsoft Corporation; Figure 25.7 screenshot from Monte Carlo PCA for Parallel Analysis, Version 2.0.5, reprinted with permission from Marley W. Watkins; Figures 25.11, 25.12 from WINSTEPS(R) Rasch measurement computer program, Chicago: Winsteps.com (Linacre, J. M. 2009), John M. Linacre.

Tables

Table 14.1 adapted from Why g matters: the complexity of everyday life, *Intelligence*, Vol. 24, pp. 79–132 (Gottfredson, L.S. 1997), Copyright © 1997, with permission from Elsevier; Table 23.1 from 1989 Psychological Well-Being Scales, Carol Ryff, reprinted with permission from Carol Ryff; Table 25.11 from Monte Carlo PCA for Parallel Analysis, Version 2.0.5, reprinted with permission from Marley W. Watkins.

Text

General Displayed Text on page 118 from Professor Susan Llewelyn, Clinical Psychologist, Warneford Hospital; General Displayed Text on page 141 from Dr Jo Nowill, Chartered Counselling Psychologist, Cheltenham Trauma Clinic; General Displayed Text on page 191 from Dr Camilla Herbert, Consultant in Neuropsychology and Rehabilitation at the Brain Injury Rehabilitation Trust, West Sussex; General Displayed Text on pages 391 and 406 from *The Relevance of Science Education Project (ROSE) in England: a Summary of Findings*, CSSME (Jenkins, E.W. and Pell, R.G. 2006), with permission from E.W. Jenkins; General Displayed Text on page 423 from Professor Ivan Robertson, Managing Director of Robertson Cooper Ltd. and Professor of Organisational Psychology, Leeds University Business School; Extract on pages 462–3 and Exhibit 25.10 Copyright © 1994 by the American Psychological Association, reproduced with permission, from Distinguishing optimism from neuroticism (and trait anxiety, self-mastery, and self esteem): a re-evaluation of the Life Orientation Test, *Journal of Personality and Social Psychology*, Vol. 67

(6), pp. 1063–1078 (Scheier, M.F., Carver, C.S. and Bridges, M.W, 1994), doi:10.1037/0022-3514.67.6.1063. No further reproduction or distribution is permitted without written permission from the American Psychological Association; Extract on pages 486–7 from *The Essence of Rational Emotive Behavior Therapy: A Comprehensive Approach to Treatment* (Ellis, A. 1994, 2006), permission granted by the Albert Ellis Institute; Extract on page 533 from The love attitudes scale: short form, *Journal of Social and Personal Relationships*, Vol. 15 (2), pp. 147–159 (Hendrick, C., Hendrick, S.S. and Dicke, A. 1998), Copyright © 1998, Sage Publications, reprinted by permission of Sage and the authors; Extract on page 587 from 1989 Psychological Well-Being Scales, Carol Ryff, reprinted with permission from Carol Ryff; General Displayed Text on page 627 from Dr Heather Buchanan, Registered Health Psychologist and Lecturer in Health Psychology at the University of Nottingham; Extract on page 649 from Detection of postnatal depression: development of the 10-item Edinburgh Postnatal Depression Scale, *British Journal of Psychiatry*, Vol. 150, pp. 782–786 (Cox, J.L., Holden, J.M. and Sagovsky, R. 1987), Copyright © The Royal College of Psychiatrists; General Displayed Text on pages 664–7 from Stop and Think: Rasch Analysis and Item Response Theory by Dr Steven Muncer; Exhibit 25.4 extract from 'Yes, Prime Minister', © Anthony Jay and Jonathan Lynn. Copyright agent: Alan Brodie Representation Ltd., Fairgate House, 78 New Oxford Street, London WC1A 1HB, www.alanbrodie.com; Exhibits 25.9 and 25.16 Copyright © 1989 by the American Psychological Association, adapted with permission from Assessing coping strategies: a theoretically based approach, *Journal of Personality and Social Psychology*, Vol. 56 (2), pp. 267–83 (Carver, Charles S., Scheier, Michael F. and Weintraub, Jagdish K. 1989), doi: 10.1037/0022-3514.56.2.267. No further reproduction or distribution is permitted without written permission from the American Psychological Association; Exhibits 25.11 and 25.14 from *Assessment of Dispositional Embarassability, Anxiety, Stress and Coping*, 10th ed. (Kelly, K. M. and Jones, W. H. 1997) pp. 307–333, reprinted by permission of the publisher (Taylor & Francis Ltd., http://www.tandf.co.uk/journals); Exhibits 25.12 and 25.15 Copyright © 1988 by the American Psychological Association, adapted with permission from Development and validation of brief measures of positive and negative affect: The PANAS Scales, *Journal of Personality and Social Psychology*, Vol. 54 (6), pp. 1063–1070 (Watson, David, Clark, Lee A. and Tellegen, Auke 1988), doi: 10.1037/0022-3514.54.6.1063. No further reproduction or distribution is permitted without written permission from the American Psychological Association.

Photographs

(Key: b-bottom; c-centre; l-left; r-right; t-top)

Alamy Images: Ace Stock Ltd 395, Adrian Sherratt 536, Asperra Images 54, BananaStock 298, Blend Images 503, Chris Howes / Wild Places Photograhy 43, Christoph & Friends / Das Fotoarchiv 424, Comstock Images 114, Danita Delimont 263, Dave Watts 206, David Hancock 615, David R. Frazier Photolibrary, Inc. 84, imac 464, Image Source Black 124, Image Source Pink 445, Imagebroker 11, Janine Wiedel Photolibrary 562, Mark Eveleigh 382, Network Photographers 581, Pat Behnke 190, Photofusion Picture Library 31, Picture Partners 622, Radius Images 447b, Steve Bloom Images 496, Thinkstock 186, Tina Manley 314; **BBC Photo Library:** 45; **Corbis:** 610, Grace / Zefa 410, John Henley 306, Scott Barrow 3, Tom Stewart 632; **Digital Vision:** 481, Digital Vision 223, Digital Vision / Rob van Petten 7; **Dr Camilla Herbert** (Consultant in Neuropsychology and Rehabilitation, Kerwin Court, Brain Injury Rehabilitation Trust, West Sussex): 191; **Dr Heather Buchanan PhD, CPsychol:** 627; **Dr Jo Nowill:** 141; **Getty Images:** Chris Jackson 231, Daniel Berehulak 353, Erik Dreyer 375, Hulton Archive 24, Laurence Dutton 520, Nina Leen / Time Life Pictures 75, Oppenheim Bernhard 548, Photodisc 152, 272, Photodisc 152, 272, Tim Platt 337, White Packert 446; **Grand Canyon National Park:** 104; **Ingram:** Ingram Image Library - Diamond Edition, Vol. 1 100, 482; **Ivan Robertson:** 423; **Panos Pictures:** Dieter Telemans 472; **Pearson Education:** 157, 457, 157, 457; **Pearson Education Ltd:** 394, Carlos Reyes-Manzo 215, Image Source 329, Jules Selmes 21, 70, 133, 386, 588; Lisa Payne Photography 280, Tudor Photography 140; **PhotoDisc:** M Freeman / Photolink / Photodisc 570, Photodisc / Ingo Jezierski 556; **Rex Features:** Brian Rasic 655, Image Source 637, KeystoneUSA-Zuma 450, Nick Kane / Arcaid 279, OJO Images 614, Stuart Atkins 517; **Ronald Grant Archive:** 241; **Science Photo Library Ltd:** Pasieka 176; **Shutterstock.com:** Simon Burchell / Featureflash 339; **Susan Llewelyn:** 118; **The Kobal Collection:** COLUMBIA TRISTAR / THE KOBAL COLLECTION / Suzanne Tener 594, Discover Films / BBC 162, FILM 4 / CELADOR FILMS / PATHÉ INTERNATIONAL 527, Workin' Man Films / FilmFour 267; **www.imagesource.com:** Image Source Ltd 232.

In some instances we have been unable to trace the owners of copyright material, and we would appreciate any information that would enable us to do so.

PART 1
Personality

CHAPTER 1
Personality Theory in Context

Key themes

- Nature of personality
- Implicit personality theories
- Definitions of personality
- Aims of studying personality
- Approaches to studying personality
- Describing personality
- Distinctions made in personality research
- Measurement issues
- Strands of theorising
- Reading critically and evaluating theory

Learning outcomes

After studying this discussion you should:

- Appreciate why psychologists study personality
- Be aware of a variety of definitions of personality
- Understand the components of psychological definitions of personality
- Have developed an understanding of the historical roots of personality theory
- Understand the major questions that personality theories aim to address
- Understand the criteria that can be used to evaluate personality theories

Introduction

One of us recently overheard two female students who were discussing the merits of their friend's boyfriend. One student concluded, 'I don't know what she sees in him; he has no personality whatsoever.' The other agreed vehemently with this statement. What is this poor guy actually like? This is not an unusual comment, and you may have used it yourself. Can an individual have no personality? How do you visualise someone who is described as having 'no personality'? Take a minute to think about it. We tried this out on a group of students and asked them what they thought someone was like who could be described as having no personality. They easily produced descriptions such as quiet, not a lot of fun, unassuming, geeky, not very sociable, no sense of humour and dull.

A few students even suggested that such people are unhappy looking, and others suggested that they dress in dull clothes.

Clearly the description of 'no personality' does not literally mean that the individual does not have personal characteristics of the type that we normally think of as being part of a person's personality; rather, it implies a certain sort of person. This then raises the issue of what we mean by personality. Firstly, following from our example, we will begin by looking at how non-psychologists, as opposed to psychologists, deal with personality. Then we will explore what psychologists mean by personality. At that point, some of the complexities of the topic area will become apparent.

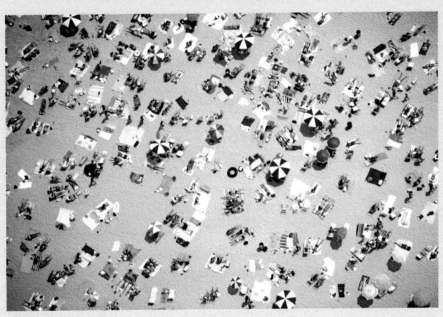

Source: Corbis/Scott Barrow

General population perspectives: implicit personality theories

It is clear from the opening example that describing someone as having 'no personality' conveys meaning to most people; and, for my students at least, there was a fairly good consensus about exactly what it meant. This is an example of what psychologists call **implicit personality theories**. These are intuitively based theories of human behaviour that we all construct to help us to understand both others and ourselves. We hear descriptions of individuals and we observe people going about their business, chatting with us and with others, and then we use this information to help us decide what sort of person we think they are. Most of the time we are not even consciously aware that we are doing this; it happens so frequently that it becomes an automatic response. In this way, we are all psychologists collecting data based on our observations of social situations. Human beings seem to have a natural curiosity about why people behave as they do. We use our observations to construct our implicit personality theories. These implicit theories are then used to explain behaviour.

For example, what about the student in your seminar group who never contributes to the discussion? Is it because of shyness, stupidity or laziness? How would you decide? We make observations and then we infer cause and effect. We see the student in the bar surrounded by a large group of people, obviously the centre of attention, chatting and laughing; and we may conclude that this person is not shy. Sometimes we discuss it with our friends to compare their observations with ours. Someone may tell you that the silent seminar student won a business sponsorship to come to university. You may conclude that this rules out stupidity as a motivator for their behaviour. Are they lazy? Perhaps we think they are too arrogant to join in the discussion, that they find the level of debate beneath them intellectually. Therefore, we may have them down as either lazy or arrogant, and we look for confirmation in their subsequent behaviour in seminars. In this way, we make what are called causal inferences about behaviour. This means we assume that people behave the way they do because of the sort of people they are; it is down to their personality. Most people find it difficult to identify how they make these judgements. Think about how you do it if you find this hard to believe.

Problems with implicit theories

Judging what other people are like is a skill that is valued. Think how often you hear people saying, 'I am a good judge of character'. We all like to think that we know about people, and most of the time our implicit theories of personality appear to work quite well in our everyday life – however, they are flawed in several ways. You may notice that we said implicit theories *appear* to work well, but a major difficulty with them is that we seldom have the opportunity to check them out properly. We decide to share our flat with Sarah and not Joanne, and therefore we never have the opportunity to see if Joanne is a good flatmate. If it turns out that we get along well with Sarah as a flatmate, we congratulate ourselves on being a good judge of character. Joanne might have been even better, but we will never know. In this way, our evaluation of the situation is flawed.

Implicit theories are also based on casual and non-random observations of individuals. By this, we mean that they are not based on observations of behaviour that have been systematically selected to portray accurately how that person spends his or her life. Instead, we have chance observations of other people. We can see this from the student seminar example. With most people, we sample only a tiny fraction of their behaviour; yet, based on this, we have to make decisions about whether we are going to pursue a friendship with them, give them a job or go out of our way to avoid them in future. If we decide not to pursue further contact with the individual, that is usually the end of the story. Implicit theories are not scientific theories of personality. Exactly what constitutes a scientific theory will be discussed later in the chapter. However, it should be

clear from these examples that some more reliable way of understanding individual behaviour and classifying people would be useful. Psychologists have set out to do this; and, as we shall see, they have developed a range of theories, all attempting to meet this need.

How is personality defined?

Psychologists need to be very clear about exactly what they are studying and define it precisely if they are going to measure it effectively. One difficulty that frequently arises is that many of the words used by psychologists are already part of our everyday language or have been adopted into normal language use. However, it is still important to consider what the public (as opposed to psychologists) think that a term means so that accurate communication can occur. In most instances public, or lay, definitions tend to be very wide and not specific enough for psychologists to use for research purposes to define precisely what they are examining. However, lay definitions provide a good starting point for developing psychological definitions.

Lay definitions of personality

Lay definitions of personality frequently involve value judgements in terms of the social attractiveness of individuals. Sometimes the emphasis is on aspects of the individual's physical appearance, perhaps with some comments on their social style. This view produces the following personality description: 'Richard is tall and fairly attractive, but never has much to say for himself although he can be very funny with people he knows well.' Such definitions are essentially evaluations of individuals and include relative judgements, in this instance about height and attractiveness. This definition also includes some judgements about how Richard interacts with others: 'never has much to say for himself although he can be very funny with people he knows well'. The elements of descriptions or judgements made about the person when they are in social settings are common elements. These lay definitions are commonly linked to the implicit personality theories that we discussed earlier. Sometimes they include elements of folklore within particular cultures. This may be an assumed match between a physical attribute and a personality attribute. Common examples are that people with red hair also have fiery tempers or that fat people are jolly.

From lay definitions of personality, it seems that personality is judged in a social context; that is, it has elements about how well people get on with others and their style of interacting as well as comments on their appearance. Does this mean that our personality is apparent only in social situations? This is obviously not the case. When people are alone, they still display individual differences in terms of how they cope with solitude and their attitude towards it. For most people their personality is an integral part of their being, which exists whether they are alone or with others.

Psychological definitions of personality

Psychological definitions of personality differ from lay definitions in that they define personality in terms of characteristics, or the qualities typical of that individual. Gordon Allport, a prominent early figure in personality psychology, popularised the term 'personality' and provided a definition in 1961. He defined personality as 'a dynamic organisation, inside the person, of psychophysical systems that create the person's characteristic patterns of behaviour, thoughts and feelings' (Allport, 1961, p. 11).

This dense definition requires some unpacking. *Dynamic organisation, inside the person* refers to a process that is continually adjusting, adapting to the experiences we have, changes in our lives, ageing and the like. In other words, personality is conceptualised as being an active, responsive system. It is conceptualised as being organised in some sort of internal structural system, the details of which are not yet quite clear – although hypotheses abound, as you will see in later chapters. *Psychophysical systems* refer to the inclusion of both our minds and our bodies in what we refer to as personality. In somewhat crude terms, the psychological elements in the mind interact with the body sometimes in complex ways to produce behaviour. *The person's characteristic patterns* suggest that something relatively stable is being produced that becomes typical of that individual. The implied stability is important; without it, all attempts at measuring personality would be futile. *Behaviour, thoughts and feelings* refer to the fact that personality is a central component influencing, and being discernible in, a wide range of human experiences and activities.

While this is only one of a multitude of definitions, it includes some important elements and is reasonably comprehensive. Personality theorists are still struggling to produce a universally acceptable definition of personality. Part of the problem arises from the concept being so wide, which makes it difficult to conceptualise succinctly. It has to embrace and account for individual differences between people, their genetic inheritance, and the internal processing that occurs within individuals, leading them to behave in the ways that are characteristic of them. Despite the lack of a single agreed-upon definition, some agreement has emerged about what constitutes personality. There is consensus that the term 'personality', as now used, describes a **psychological construct**; that is, a mental concept that influences behaviour via the mind–body interaction. As an understanding of what constitutes a psychological construct and how it is identified is important for your understanding of psychological theory, a fuller description is given in Stop and think: Defining and testing psychological constructs.

The aims of studying personality

Psychologists are interested in what people are like, why they behave as they do and how they became that way. Underlying these apparently simple issues are more profound questions about human beings as a species, as we shall see when we address these issues later in this text. To put it in more academic language, personality theorists seek to explain the **motivational basis** of behaviour. Why do individuals behave as they do? What gets us up every morning? Why are you studying for a degree? Basically, personality theorists have to address the question of what drives our behaviour. This question of motivation necessarily touches on crucial issues about the *basic nature* of human beings. Do we behave in certain ways because we have little choice? As a species, are we innately aggressive and self-destructive? What are the basic human drives? Some personality theorists, such as the psychoanalyst Sigmund Freud (Chapter 2), adopt the view that human nature is essentially, innately self-destructive and aggressive. Other theorists such as Carl Rogers, an American who is often seen as one of the founding figures of counselling psychology (Chapter 6), see human nature as being benign. Rogers claims that human beings are driven by positive motives towards growth and self-acceptance. We shall explore this in more detail later and see that there is a range of views. The quality of human nature, however, is a fundamental question that has to be addressed by personality theorists. Are we benign or malevolent as a species? As yet there appears to be no definitive answer.

As well as addressing issues of human motivation and the nature of human beings, personality theorists aim to *provide descriptions or categorisations of how individuals behave*. This is addressed in different ways, but the aim is to understand why individuals behave as they do. Implicit here is some level of acceptance in most, but not all, theories that there is a finite range of possible behaviour and that some patterns of behaviour are shared by individuals with similar personalities. Hence types or categories of personalities are outlined as part of many theories. Linked to the idea of classifying types of personality is the issue of **measuring personality**.

Closely linked to this question of what people are like is the issue of how they become that way. Theories pay different attention to this issue, with some theoretical approaches encompassing detailed **developmental theories** while others are much more schematic in their treatment of how personality develops. Within developmental theories there are diverse views about the age at which personality becomes fixed. Is your personality fixed at age 2, or is it age 5 or older, or is change always possible?

Stop and think

Defining and testing psychological constructs

Psychological constructs refer to concepts that are not directly observable but are hypothesised to be influential in determining or explaining behaviour. We do not directly observe personality, for example, but our theory is that personality plays an important role in determining behaviour. Our observations are of behaviour; and from these observations, we infer that the individual has a certain personality characteristic or type of personality. In this way personality is a psychological construct. To determine that a particular phenomenon is a psychological construct and not merely a chance observation, it is necessary to demonstrate that it can be reliably measured and is relatively stable across time, amongst other things.

Lee J. Cronbach (1916–2001), Professor of Education at Stanford University in the United States, spent most of his long career examining issues related to the identification and measurement of psychological concepts. In 1955 he published, with Paul Meehl, what has come to be seen as a classic seminal paper in psychology. The authors propose a method for establishing the validity of psychological constructs in personality tests. Paul Meehl (1920–2003) was a Professor of Psychology at the University of Minnesota in the United States and, like Lee Cronbach, he was concerned with investigating how reliably psychologists could predict behaviour. The joint paper by Cronbach and Meehl is heavily quoted within the psychological literature. The following are the authors' three essential steps for establishing the validity of a psychological construct.

- Describe the characteristics that make up the construct and suggest how they may be related to each other based on some underlying theoretical speculation. For example, take the construct of extraversion. Extraverted individuals are described as being outgoing, friendly and warm. These are all characteristics that are hypothesised to promote social interaction. The theoretical speculation is that extraverts like and need higher levels of social interaction.
- Ways of measuring the suggested characteristics of the construct are then developed. For our example this would involve developing measures of 'outgoingness', friendliness and warmth.
- Finally, the hypothesised relationships are tested. In our example we would expect to find that individuals who scored highly on outgoingness also scored highly on friendliness and warmth and that these individuals all liked interacting with other people. Finding these relationships would result in a valid concept. Cronbach and Meehl were keen to emphasise that establishing the validity of psychological concepts is an ongoing process that may have to be revisited as our knowledge within psychology expands.

There are diverse views on this aspect. Even within some of the clinically derived theories, like the psychoanalytic ones that see personality development as occurring in early childhood, change is considered to be possible but is assumed to be difficult to achieve. Some theorists, as you will see, suggest that interventions such as psychotherapy or counselling can facilitate this change. Conceptualising therapeutic interventions in this way makes it easier to understand why so many personality theories have been produced by psychologists and psychotherapists who are in clinical practice. Their interest is in understanding individuals so that interventions to assist in behaviour change can be developed.

Closely related to the development of personality is the issue of **heritability versus environment**. Is personality development determined more by genetic inheritance or environmental influences, or is it some sort of interactional effect? Theories differ, as we shall see in this text, in terms of the role they give to each, and some theories do not really address this issue. Trait theorists and biological theorists tend to have more to say on genetic influences on personality.

Personality theory developed within psychology originally to help us understand mental illness and abnormal behaviour. We will examine the details of this effort later, when different theorists are presented. At this point it is enough to know that to study and classify the experiences of psychologically disturbed people, it is necessary to have a concept of what is normal in human behaviour. Without some idea of what constitutes the normal range of human behaviour, it is impossible to make judgements about what is abnormal. From this early work, it soon became apparent that there are huge individual differences in human behaviour. However, some of the early personality theorists began to see that there are patterns in human behaviour and that it is possible to classify types of human personality. This led to the measurement of personality and the development of personality questionnaires. This will be examined in detail in later chapters. As you are now aware, psychologists have many reasons for studying personality;

- Explain the motivational basis of behaviour
- Ascertain the basic nature of human beings
- Provide descriptions/categorisations of how individuals behave
- Measure personality
- Understand how personality develops
- Foster a deeper understanding of human beings to assist in the development of interventions to facilitate behaviour change
- Assess the effects of heredity versus environment

Figure 1.1 Summary of the aims of studying personality.

we have summarised these aims in Figure 1.1 to help you remember them.

What we have not yet considered is where the term 'personality' originated. In many courses, historical aspects of psychology are addressed within individual modules. To facilitate this approach, we will include some relevant material such as the history of core terms.

The source of the term 'personality'

The word 'personality' derives from the Latin *persona*, meaning 'mask' (Kassin, 2003). It was the famous, pioneering, American psychologist Gordon Allport who popularised the term with the publication in 1937 of *Personality: A Psychological Interpretation*. Prior to this a variety of terms, such as 'character' or 'temperament', were commonly used. Allport carried out a survey of the ways in which the concept of personality has been defined; he identified over 50 different ways. These varied from lay commonsense understandings to sociological, philosophical, ethical and legal definitions. Allport argued that many of the existing terms were value-laden in the way that they were used. Examples would be a description of a woman of good character or a man of bad character. Within a particular cultural setting, this description would take on a specific meaning that was generally shared. Allport felt it was necessary to develop a consensus on the use of a word that would describe individual uniqueness without implying an evaluation of that uniqueness. As a result of Allport's influence, 'personality' increasingly became the term used across the discipline to describe individual differences. A few – theorists, mainly – psychometricians, used the label of 'individual differences', and this usage continues to some extent. Psychometricians are concerned with the development of good, accurate measures of individual differences. In these instances of 'individual differences', it is frequently really an abbreviated form of 'individual differences in personality' or variables related to personality. You will already be getting the idea that there are a variety of approaches to studying and researching personality; we will now look at some of them.

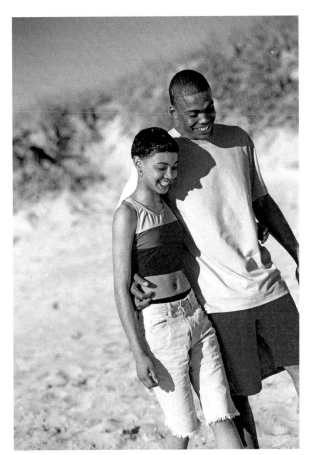

Is it important to understand the basic nature of human beings?
Source: Digital Vision, Rob van Petten

Approaches to studying personality: idiographic versus nomothetic

An important distinction made by Allport in his early work on personality was between **idiographic** and **nomothetic** approaches to personality. The idiographic approach focuses on the individual and describes the personality variables within that individual. The term comes from the ancient Greek *idios*, meaning 'private or personal'. Theorists, who adopt this approach in the main, are only interested in studying individuals one at a time. They see each person as having a unique personality structure. Differences between individuals are seen to be much greater than the similarities. The possible differences are infinite. Idiographic approaches produce a *unique understanding* of that individual's personality.

The single case study method is generally the research method of choice for idiographic approaches to personality theorising. The aim is to develop an in-depth understanding of a single individual. For example, Freud used the idiographic approach to study his patients. He developed a detailed description of each patient based on his observations of that patient during treatment. He would make notes on the patient after each treatment session, reviewing and revising his previous notes as his knowledge of the patient increased. He then wrote up the session notes as a clinical case study describing that particular patient.

Idiographic approaches mainly use qualitative research methodologies, such as interviews, diaries, therapeutic sessions or narratives, to collect data on an individual. Some personality theorists do not go beyond this focus on the individual, as they truly consider each person to be unique and deny the existence of types of personality. Others will make some generalisations about human behaviour based on studying a number of case studies. They may observe from a series of case studies that there are similarities in the way that some individuals behave. Freud, for example, produced his personality theory based on his observations of dozens of patient case studies. The clinical case study approach has been used mainly by idiographic personality researchers.

In contrast, the nomothetic approach comes from the ancient Greek term for '*law*' and is based on the assumption that there exists a finite set of variables that can be used to describe human personality. The aim is to identify these personality variables or traits that occur consistently across groups of people. Each individual can then be located within this set of variables. By studying large groups of people on a particular variable, we can establish the average levels of that variable in particular age groups, or in men and women, and in this way produce group averages – generally called **norms** for variables. Individuals can then be described as being above or below the average or norm on a particular variable. Thus, when a friend who is very outgoing and friendly is rated as being an extravert on a personality test, it means that her score was higher than the average on the variable called extraversion. The variable 'extraversion' is measured by asking questions about how sociable and assertive she is. This approach, while acknowledging that each person will possess different degrees of particular personality traits, concentrates on the similarities in human personality. One aim of the nomothetic approach is to identify a universal set of variables that will underpin the basic structure of human personality. We will visit this concept in considerably more detail when we look at trait theorists (Chapter 7).

There are advantages and drawbacks to each approach, and we have summarised these in Figure 1.2.

There is a long-standing debate about the relative merits of idiographic versus nomothetic approaches; it applies to many subject areas within psychology, not just to personality theorising. A common issue for students, however,

Feature	Idiographic	Nomothetic
Strategy	Emphasises the uniqueness of individuals	Focuses on similarities between groups of individuals. Individuals are unique only in the way their traits combine
Goal	To develop an in-depth understanding of the individual	To identify the basic structure of personality and the minimum number of traits required to describe personality universally
Research methodology	Qualitative methodologies to produce case studies mainly. Some generalisation across series of case studies is possible	Quantitative methods to: • explore the structures of personality • produce measures of personality • explore the relationships between variables across groups
Data collection	Interviews, diaries, narratives, treatment of session data	Self-report personality questionnaires
Advantages	Depth of understanding of the individual	Discovery of general principles that have a predictive function
Disadvantages	Can be difficult to make generalisations from the data	Can lead to a fairly superficial understanding of any one person. Training needed to analyse personality profiles accurately

Figure 1.2 Comparison of idiographic and nomothetic approaches to the study of personality.

is remembering which is which. You may find it useful to remember 'I' for Idiographic and Individual.

Two celebrated personality researchers, Charles Carver and Michael Scheier, have discussed this issue at some length. Carver and Scheier (2000) argue that within personality theorising, the distinction between idiographic and nomothetic is not clear-cut. They argue that psychologists adopting the nomothetic approach still accept the uniqueness of individuals. However, they do not accept that there is an infinite number of personality variables. They see that there is an underlying common structure of personality with an associated finite number of personality variables. The uniqueness of the individual comes from their particular mix of variables from the finite set. It is how these personality variables are combined that makes each individual unique. Some idiographic researchers also go beyond the focus purely on the individual. They collect sets of case studies, for example, and then identify common themes across these case studies. In this way, they can generate theories and make predictions that can be tested, often by using nomothetic approaches.

Describing personality

Individuals are described as having certain degrees of happiness, activity, assertiveness, neurosis, warmth, impulsiveness and so on. Physical descriptions, unlike lay definitions, are rarely included in psychological definitions. The focus is on identifying psychological as opposed to physical characteristics on which people differ. These characteristics are measured in specific populations, and the mean (average) levels of occurrence are calculated. This might be done separately for men and women and for different age groups. A study might, for example, give a mean level of anxiety separately for men and women aged between 20 and 29, another for men and women aged between 30 and 39 and so on. These calculations give the **population norms** for that particular characteristic.

Population norms represent the mean scores that particular groups of individuals score on a specific test. For example, they allow you to compare the test score on anxiety for a woman between ages 20 and 29 with the mean levels for her age group of women. You can then conclude that her anxiety score was either above or below the average for her age group as well as comparing her with other individuals in your sample. This information gives profiles of individual differences that are then frequently used to define types of personalities. As we shall see (Chapter 7), trait theorists frequently develop population norms.

Distinctions and assertions in personality research

Personality is perceived to be a **relatively stable, enduring,** important aspect of the self. People may act differently in different situations, but personality will have a major influence on their behaviour. For example, someone who is classified as being extravert will behave in a more outgoing fashion than a person who is introverted, regardless of the social situation. The differences in social behaviour between the two will be observable whether they are at a party or a funeral tea. Personality characteristics in this way are thought to exert a relatively consistent influence on behaviour in different situations. Personality characteristics in this way are **enduring** across different social contexts.

While it is accepted that individuals can and do change over time, there is a contention that personality is **relatively stable** over time. People may learn from their mistakes and change their behaviour; but the more profound the change, the longer it generally takes. Changing aspects of ourselves is typically not easy, as counsellors and therapists will attest. It tends to take considerable time and effort for individuals to change aspects of themselves, if indeed they are successful. Expert help is frequently needed from counsellors or therapists before change is achieved.

Related to this contention is the fact that *not all differences between individuals are considered to be equally important* by personality theorists. The English language allows us to make fine distinctions between individuals. Another contribution made by Gordon Allport was to identify the number of words in an English dictionary that describe areas where individual differences are possible. In 1936, Allport and his colleague Odbert listed 18,000 such words, suggesting that over 4,500 of these appeared to describe aspects of personality. Of course, many of these were synonyms. Psychologists, through their research over time, have identified the personality characteristics that can be reliably assessed, where differences make most impact on behaviour and are most consistent over time. These are considered to be the *important* personality characteristics, and they are listed in Figure 1.3. The figure includes what are considered to be the major structures of personality and the main subdivisions within each. Observant readers may note that the first letters of major structures make up the word 'OCEAN', a useful mnemonic. You will learn more about these characteristics and the structure of personality later (Chapter 7).

Personality theorists make a further distinction between the overt, **observable** aspects of personality and the **unobservable** aspects of personality such as thoughts, memories and dreams. This distinction was mentioned earlier. The psychoanalytic theoretical school goes further, making a distinction between the **conscious** and **unconscious** aspects of personality. Specific drives or mechanisms of which the individual is unaware are thought to be influential in determining personality. From specific examples of behaviour or habitual styles of behaving, the existence of these personality characteristics in the individual are inferred. For example, the young woman who always seems to have boyfriends who are very much older

Openness to new experience: Feelings, Ideas, Values, Actions, Fantasy, Aesthetics	**Conscientiousness:** Competence, Achievement striving, Self-discipline, Orderliness, Dutifulness, Deliberation
Extraversion: Gregariousness, Activity level, Assertiveness, Excitement seeking, Positive emotions, Warmth	**Agreeableness:** Trust, Altruism, Straightforwardness, Compliance, Modesty, Tender-mindedness
Neuroticism: Anxiety, Self-consciousness, Depression, Vulnerability, Impulsiveness, Angry hostility	

Figure 1.3 Major and subdivisions of personality that can be reliably assessed.

than her would be described, in Freudian terms, as being motivated by an unconscious wish for a father figure – or at least the properties in a boyfriend that she associates with father figures. She wants someone to look after her. In terms of her personality, she is seen to be lacking in independence. In this way some theories focus much more on the unobservable influences of personality, as will become apparent as you progress through the text.

A further distinction is often made between what is called the individual's **private persona** and their **public persona.** The private persona is conceptualised as being the 'real' inner person, while the public persona is the way that the individual presents themselves to the outside world. Measures of personality and theoretical explanations are considered to define the persona. That is, they describe the kind of person that the individual really is, despite the social pressures on them to behave in particular ways in various social settings. It is this social pressure that involves the public persona. Personality goes beyond physical appearance and behaviour (public persona) and refers to what we see as the essence of the individual.

Effects of personality versus situational effects

This is an appropriate point to alert you to a lack of consensus among psychologists about the concept of personality. Some social psychologists, especially social deconstructionists, claim that it is the situation that largely dictates how we behave, whereas personality theorists argue that individual personality plays a crucial role in shaping our behaviour whatever the situation. Individuals do behave differently in different situations. We may be confident and outgoing in some situations and less sure of ourselves and

more retiring in other situations, but it is not simply the situation that influences our behaviour. Even in what are described as highly socially proscribed situations – that is, situations where the behavioural choices open to individuals are limited as there are rules that have to be followed – individual differences in behaviour can be observed. A good example here is a student graduation ceremony.

The university largely dictates the dress code, and students are instructed to follow well-rehearsed procedures. They mount the platform when their name is called, cross the platform, shake hands with the university chancellor and so on. There seems to be little opportunity for individual differences in behaviour to emerge, but emerge they do. One student rushes eagerly onto the platform, turns to the audience and waves at her family and friends, smiles at the chancellor and acknowledges the staff on the stage. The next student hesitantly mounts the stage, keeps his head down and scuttles across the stage, barely stopping to shake the chancellor's hand, and so on. We observe the first student to be outgoing, confident, someone who enjoys the limelight. The second student is seen as less confident, shy and somewhat anxious in social situations. These differences in behaviour, even in such a highly structured situation, are seen to be due to differences in the personalities of the two individuals. Most psychologists would accept that most behaviour results from an interaction between the effects of personality and the dictates of the situation. We will return to this debate in some detail when we consider the work of Walter Mischel (Chapter 4).

Measurement issues

The methods of measuring important personality characteristics have to be reliable. This is obviously important if you are going to use personality tests to assess individuals

Though we know we are all unique, personality suggests we share common characteristics.
Source: Alamy Images/Imagebroker

for training or further education or as a tool to aid staff recruitment in an organisation. With the organisational example, you need to identify which factors are relevant to performance within the specific organisational context, whether these can be consistently and reliably measured, and whether they are relatively enduring over time. It is not a simple exercise, as the example on occupational testing in Stop and think: Occupational testing demonstrates. We shall return to issues of assessment later, as it is a critical area for psychologists to get right.

Stop and think

Occupational testing

Many organisations now use psychometric testing as part of employee selection. The underlying principles are simple. If we know the demands made by a job in terms of personality and abilities, then we can test individuals and match them against the job requirements. It is estimated that somewhere between 50 and 70 per cent of companies use some form of testing to select their employees. Testing should help to improve job selection, but there are dangers. Consider the following example.

An old private hospital is being closed down. Patients are being transferred to a new purpose-built private hospital nearby. Unfortunately, there are not enough jobs in the new hospital for all the nurses at the old hospital to be offered employment. A senior manager is asked to decide which nurses should be offered jobs in the new hospital and which will be made redundant. In order to ensure a fair process, and recruitment of the best staff, he decides to use psychometric testing. He himself has recently undergone psychometric testing when he was promoted. He locates a test on the Internet that claims to measure positive emotions, assertiveness, warmth, activity level and gregariousness. These seem to him to be admirable qualities for nurses. Administering the test proves to be complex but, as he lives quite near the hospital,

he drops in on several mornings. He manages to test the night-shift workers when they finish their shift and the day workers just before they start their shift. A few staff have been missed, however, so he sends them the questionnaire to complete at home and return to him by post.

Based on their high scores on the questionnaire, some nurses are offered jobs in the new hospital and others are made redundant. Some of the redundancy nurses then raise the issue with their union, which seeks advice from an occupational psychologist and a lawyer. Complaints are made on the grounds that the manager is not a trained tester, the test is extremely inappropriate as it does not assess the required characteristics, and the testing conditions were different for different nurses. Some nurses were tested when tired, at the end of a night shift, while other tests were administered at the start of the shift. Other nurses received the test by post and completed it unsupervised.

The hospital also has no idea whether they have chosen to retain the most able staff. The test that the manager used is a measure of the personality trait of extraversion, and its relevance to the role of nurse has not been established. The repercussions from badly conceived personality testing can be very serious.

Stop and think

Personality theorising of the Ancient Greeks

The Ancient Greek philosopher and teacher Aristotle (384–23 BC) was the first person to write about individual differences in character and how these relate to behaviour. He suggested that personality characteristics, such as modesty, vanity and cowardice, determined how moral or immoral individuals were.

A student of Aristotle's called Theophrastus (371–287 BC) went further in his description of personality characteristics by describing 30 personality types.

One of the Greek Stoic philosophers, Epictetus (AC 55–135), wrote extensively on the characteristics and actions that lead to achieving a happy life. He wrote about the importance of characteristics like imperturbability, not having a passionate nature, being motivated by virtue not vice and so on. He was very interested in how human beings become upset, and he concluded that 'Men are disturbed not by things, but by their perception of things'. This quotation is still relevant in current clinical personality theorising, as we shall see.

Strands of personality theorising

There are two distinct strands to theorising about personality, stemming from the original research on the topic. The first is the clinical strand that has developed from studies of the mentally ill. The second is the individual differences strand, focusing initially on documenting differences. Later this approach led to the statistical analyses of individual differences.

The clinical approach and its history

Freud is frequently credited as the founding father of the clinical strand of personality theory. However, interest in studying human personality predates Freud. The Ancient Greeks produced the first recorded discourses on human personality characteristics in the fourth century BC. Some of the major contributions from these philosophers are described in Stop and think: Personality theorising of the Ancient Greeks.

This early work was based largely on philosophers' reflections on their own behaviour and thought processes, the method of introspection outlined in the Stop and think box. Philosophers continued to speculate on human nature and man's relationship with God throughout the Middle Ages.

In terms of the *psychological* study of personality, it was in the clinical area that the first developments occurred. As a result of the scientific revolution of the late seventeenth and eighteenth centuries, great advances in our knowledge of physiology occurred with parallel advances in medicine. There was enormous interest in the study of what was described as madness, and different treatment methods were being tried.

Franz Anton Mesmer (1734–1815), a Viennese physician, developed a treatment based initially on the power of magnets. He believed that all living beings have a magnetic fluid flowing through them and that from time to time the flow gets disturbed. Blockages of the flow could be apparent in physical or mental illnesses. Applying magnets to different parts of the body, Mesmer claimed, would unblock the flow and return the individual to good health.

Later, while still using magnets, Mesmer claimed that some individuals have greater natural magnetism than others and that this magnetism itself could be used to cure other people. He treated people in groups in a dimly lit, carpeted room. His patients held hands in a circle around a tub of magnetised water, called a *baquet*. Mesmer, wearing a long cloak, would enter the room dramatically waving a sword. He claimed that his animal magnetism was enough to cure his patients. Many patients reported that his treatment worked. What we now know is that Mesmer was using the drama of the setting, and his own powers of suggestion, in complex ways to *psychologically* influence his patients. This was, in fact, a forerunner of hypnosis, and Mesmer is seen as an important figure in the history of hypnosis. To him we owe the term 'mesmerised'. He also acknowledged that there were individual differences in animal magnetism as well as in the ability of individuals to be mesmerised.

In the course of these developments in mental illness, a new, more technical language of mind began to develop. The physiologists and the medics, by labelling the phenomena they were identifying, began to create some of what later became the language of psychology as we know it today. They also created the culture that made the scientific study of the human mind increasingly acceptable and even desirable.

The developments in mental health also created a demand to know more about how to define individuals so that they could be managed better in institutional settings such as mental asylums and prisons. It is from this tradition that Freud and the psychoanalytic school emerged. We will continue with this strand of theorising later in the text (Chapter 2).

Individual differences' emphasis on personality and its history

The developments in medicine linked to the scientific revolution again provided the impetus for research on individual differences in personality. A Swiss priest called Johann Casper Lavater, working in the second half of the eighteenth century, described a theory linking facial features with character traits. He termed his theory **physiognomy**. He made some detailed predictions, including 'as are the lips so is the character' and 'the more the chin, the more the man'. Dr Gall, a Viennese physician, further developed Lavater's ideas. During the 1790s Dr Gall carried out research in the hospitals and mental asylums in Vienna, where he developed what he called **craniology** (later labelled **phrenology**). The theory hypothesised that different human functions were located in different structures within the brain. It was suggested that the relative size of these structures or areas was reflected in the shape of the cranium. Gall claimed that an individual's character could be determined from the shape of their cranium.

This can be conceptualised as the first personality theory of the scientific revolution, although the term 'personality' was not yet in vogue. The theory became extremely popular in Victorian England. There were many public lectures and demonstrations, which served to introduce many sections of British society to these new psychological ideas about character differences. However, developments in physiology did not lend support to phrenology, although the approach remained popular for a long time, especially with the public. The British Phrenological Society was only disbanded in 1967, owing to a lack of interest.

The major advance in psychological research in individual differences was caused by the work of Francis Galton at the end of the nineteenth century; his work is outlined in the Profile box below. Galton is acknowledged as being the founder of research on individual differences. He developed a range of measures of intelligence, aptitudes and attitudes and, most crucially, the statistical techniques that could be used to analyse this data. Galton also developed the first questionnaires and outlined statistical methods for ensuring their reliability. By collecting very large data sets from general population samples, he produced standardised normative values for a range of measures. Galton's work provided the statistical tools of analysis that allowed the scientific investigation and analysis of individual differences. From this early work, the modern study of individual differences developed.

These two historical strands of personality research continue to be reflected in current approaches to personality. The range of personality theories can seem confusing as well as lacking much sense of developmental continuity, but awareness of this division between clinically derived theories and more statistically based research on individual differences in personality is helpful in categorising theories.

A further consequence arising from the early influence of medicine on the development of psychology is the focus on the individual. The clinically derived theories, as we have seen, used mainly individual case study methods as the basis for theory development. Hand in hand with theory development went the development of treatments. This encouraged concentration on the individual. Capitalist western societies also tend to encourage this individualistic perspective. It is often difficult for those who have grown up within a western culture to conceptualise societies where there is not a preoccupation with the individual and their psyche. This focus on the individual and individual needs largely continues today in psychology. It is for this reason that sociologists frequently criticise psychologists for ignoring the social context within which individuals function. This focus on individualism is prevalent in the development of personality theory.

Studying personality as a personal experience

As we mentioned earlier, in studying personality we are interested in what people are like, why they behave as they do and how they became that way. Our first point of comparison in

Profile

Francis Galton

Francis Galton was born in Birmingham in 1822, into an affluent middle-class family. He trained initially as a doctor in Birmingham and London and then went on to Cambridge University for further study. He excelled in many areas, spending some years as an explorer in Africa and developing an interest in anthropology as well as geography. Next he developed an interest in meteorology which he maintained throughout his life. He introduced graphical charts for mapping the weather, a forerunner of the system still in use today, and introduced the term 'anticyclone'. He also published research on genetics, developing statistical techniques that he then applied to the study of individual differences. To him we owe percentiles, median, quartiles and other methods of measuring and describing the distribution of data. He invented the correlational method, which is frequently used to explore the relationships between characteristics in personality research. From this he developed regression analysis, which is used to explore the relationships between personality variables in more detail.

He applied the principles of measurement to a variety of areas, carrying out groundbreaking work on developing a system of fingerprinting and fingerprint recognition.

this study will be ourselves. Does what theorist A writes ring true in our experience of life? Students commonly tell me that they really like the theory of Jung or that Adler makes so much sense to them or that they don't like a particular theory. While it is important to point out that psychology is about testing theories, not intuitively being attracted to or disliking particular theories, it is helpful to think about what is happening in these situations.

Many texts, including this one, include biographical details about the theorists they cover, to provide insights into that theorist's own developmental experiences. You may wonder why this is relevant, as generally when you are writing essays for your lecturers, you are told not to include biographical detail. However, if you think about the processes involved in theory development, then biographical material about the author of the theory is relevant to our understanding of that theory. Within psychology, personality theorists are researching themselves at the same time as they are collecting data from others. One of the first judgements likely to be made is whether the theory fits one's own experience. By examining the biographies of each theorist, it is often possible to see why they have chosen to study particular characteristics.

The same thing seems to happen when individuals are introduced to a new personality theorist. We tend to judge whether a theory makes sense, at least initially, by assessing whether it fits our experience. A good example of this response occurs when students are introduced to the psychoanalyst Alfred Adler's theorising about birth order. Basically, Adler suggests that first-born children are different from second-born children, who are different from the third child and so on, for the family dynamics change as each new child is added. We will examine this idea in detail later (Chapter 3). When students first meet this theory, the instructor frequently hears references to whether it fits with their experience. You may learn quite a lot about yourself by noting your initial responses to each theory after you first read it. Reflecting on the theorists who initially appeal to us can help us to explore our implicit theories of personality that were discussed in the introduction to this chapter.

It is this possibility of reflecting on your own and others' life experiences that makes personality theory a fascinating area of study. You may well find that your explanations for behaviour will change or expand. Remember that theories of personality are attempting to answer the 'why' of behaviour. As you assimilate different theories, you are actually increasing your knowledge of the possible causes of behaviour. This is what social psychologists term causal attribution. Your pool of causal attributions for particular behaviours will be much larger. (See Stop and think: Reflective exercise on causal attribution.)

The inclusion of many psychological concepts derived from personality theory in our everyday language attests to the success of personality theorists in identifying and labelling these common experiences.

Reading critically and evaluating theories

To get the most out of studying personality, you have to be able to move on from the position where you initially like or dislike a theory, in terms of whether it fits your personal experience. You must be able to distance yourself from the theory. Having a set of criteria against which you can judge the theory will allow you to do this. Knowing how to evaluate theories also allows you to become a critical reader as you are absorbing the information about each theory. It also makes it much easier to compare and contrast theories, as you are clear about the criteria to use. By adopting this approach, you are far less likely to fall into the trap of producing purely descriptive essays on personality theories.

Evaluation of personality theory raises particular difficulties compared with most other areas of psychology. One reason for the difficulties is that much of the literature on personality does not include critical appraisal of the work being presented. Individual theorists or their followers have produced books describing their approaches. These

Stop and think

Reflective exercise on causal attribution

Your flatmate forgets to send his mother a Mother's Day card and claims it was a genuine lapse in memory. You may think the genuine mistake unlikely given all the publicity about Mother's Day and the fact that all the rest of you were sending cards. Your flatmate claims to have a good relationship with his mother.

How do you explain his behaviour?

Keep a record of your answers, and repeat this exercise once you have finished your personality course. You are likely to find that your list of possible causes has grown considerably.

are often very interesting to read, particularly if they come from the clinical tradition and include lots of case material. Convincing arguments are made that appear to be supported by the case study material presented. It all seems to make perfect sense. You can feel unable to challenge such apparent expertise and may not know where to start. Textbooks on personality theory are also often of little help, as they frequently present personality theories in chronological order with little evaluation of any of the theories. You read the first theory and it seems to make sense, but so does the second theory, and the third and so on.

The traditional approach to evaluating theory by examining the weight of research evidence to support it is often difficult in the area of personality. Many influential concepts that have emerged from personality theorising have not been evaluated, often because the concepts are difficult to define and measure accurately. Where research evidence is available to support or refute aspects of the theories presented in this text, guidance through this literature will be given. However, when it comes to evaluating personality theories as totalities, research evidence is sadly lacking. In what follows, we present some of the general criteria that can be used to evaluate theories.

It is useful to begin by thinking about what a theory aims to do, as this can then help us to specify the basic criteria that a theory of personality should satisfy (Figure 1.4). These criteria are outlined here in no particular order of importance as evaluation will inevitably be influenced by the nature of the theory being evaluated, and different criteria may assume greater or lesser importance.

- **Description** – A theory should bring order into the complexity of behaviours that have been observed and/or measured. It should help to simplify, identify

and clarify the important issues that need to be addressed.

- **Explanation** – A theory should help in understanding the 'why' of behaviour. Does the theory provide a convincing explanation of typical commonly observed instances of that category of behaviour? Does the theory explain how and why individual differences in commonly observed instances of behaviour occur?

- **Empirical validity** – A good theory will generate predictions so that it can be empirically tested and shown to be valid. Can it predict future events or behaviour in particular situations?

- **Testable concepts** – Linked to prediction is the question of whether the concepts included within the theory can be *operationalised* so that they can be tested. By 'operationalised', we mean can the concept be defined precisely enough to enable it to be reliably measured? As you will discover in the succeeding text, some key concepts in personality theories have proved to be difficult, if not impossible, to operationalise as they are poorly defined.

- **Comprehensiveness** – A good theory should be able to encompass and explain a wide variety of both normal and abnormal behaviour. However, owing to the huge variety of human behaviour, it is unlikely that a personality theory will emerge that can explain all behaviour. In this respect, decisions have to be made about the importance of behaviour so that the limits are set. Making decisions about what constitutes important behaviour does of course necessitate value judgements being made, and ethical issues could well arise about the nature of the decisions made. What tends to happen in practice is that a consensus emerges within researchers, and it is often

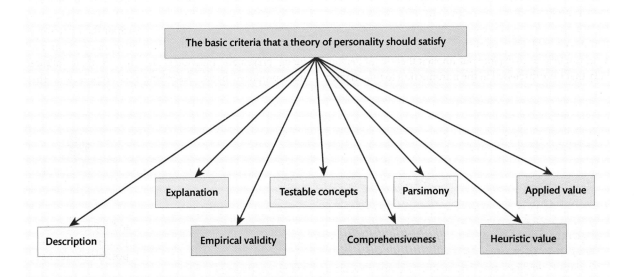

Figure 1.4 The basic criteria that a theory of personality should satisfy.

supported by statistical judgements about how common a particular behaviour is.

- **Parsimony** – A good theory should be economical in terms of the number of explanatory concepts it includes. All concepts included should be demonstrated to be necessary to explain the phenomena under study. A theory may also be too parsimonious if too few concepts are included to explain the data adequately.

- **Heuristic value** – A good theory stimulates interest and research in an area. This criterion does need to be qualified, however. Sometimes, as we saw with mesmerism, a theory may create enormous interest but have little scientific substance. Occasionally a theory may be so inadequate that it also stimulates a great deal of research, as investigators are eager to refute it. This happened with research in America in the 1970s and 1980s on race and intelligence. The psychologist A. R. Jensen (1973) suggested that there was a genetic difference in intelligence between black African Americans and white Americans. Other psychologists were keen to refute what appeared to be a racist position, and this response stimulated a great deal of research.

- **Applied value** – This criterion sets the theory in a wider context. Under this criterion, the practical usefulness of a theory is judged. Does it lead to beneficial changes in the environment, for example, or better control of unwanted behaviours? Or, does it provide a qualitative leap in knowledge in a particular area? Does the theory lead to new approaches to solving problems? For example, the greater understanding of the mentally ill that came from the work of Freud and others was influential in bringing about changes in the conditions under which mental patients were treated. Prior to that, mental patients were locked away from society, usually on the outskirts of towns, where they were kept in appalling conditions. In many such places, the public could pay to enter and observe the behaviour of the 'insane'. With better understanding of the mentally ill came calls for more humane treatment; the reform movement created much better environments for patients in mental asylums. These were brighter buildings with proper provision for the needs of patients, and activities and entertainments were laid on for them. Freud's work also led to new treatments and introduced new ideas, as we shall see later (Chapter 2).

One proviso is perhaps necessary in relation to the evaluation of theories and comparisons of theories. Not all parts of each theory may be equally valid. Various theories may provide convincing explanations of parts of the totality of personality, which makes comparisons and evaluations of competing theories difficult. For these reasons, disputes among theorists may also be difficult

to resolve. For example, if we revisit Mesmer's theory, it would be false to say that his work was of no value as it proved to be a forerunner of hypnosis. The magnetised water and the idea of animal magnetism appear to have been unsupported by any evidence and of no value. However, Mesmer himself, in the way that he presented himself and in his charismatic charm, did have an effect on individuals. He made them more suggestible. By displaying that human beings could be psychologically influenced and could be put into trancelike states, he provided the spur for others to explore this phenomenon more systematically. From this further study, hypnosis has emerged.

Evaluations of personality theory also need to consider the philosophical view of human beings inherent in any theory. Does the theory conceptualise human beings as aggressive and destructive by nature, or as loving and kind? We also need to consider whether there is any evidence for this particular view of human nature.

Another consideration is the relative influence of internal and external determinants of behaviour within the theory. Does the unconscious figure in the theory serve as an internal determinant, or is it more concerned with the here and now as external determinants? This is an important distinction, for, if we think that much of our motivation to behave in certain ways is unconscious, does it then mean there are limits to the conscious control we have over our behaviour? A very simple example would be someone who wants to stop smoking. Freud would see one explanation of why people choose to smoke as being that the individual has a need for oral stimulation, caused by lack of oral stimulation as an infant. The individual as a baby was deprived of a dummy, or not allowed other opportunities to suck their thumb or the like. The individual is not aware that this is the real reason they smoke; their true motivation is unconscious.

Questions need to be asked about how well the theory deals with the influence of the past, the present and the future on behaviour. Some theories, as, you will see, consider that the past is irrelevant as, although it undoubtedly influenced who we are, we cannot change it. An example would be of a woman who was sexually abused as a child. One set of theories would see it as important for this woman to explore her past abuse in the hope that, by understanding it better, she can come to cope with it. Another theoretical approach would suggest that having the woman relive her early experiences by telling you about them is futile and is only likely to disturb her further. This second approach would instead help the woman to cope with her current distress and try to put the past behind her.

An assessment also needs to be made about how well the theory explains the integration or apparent integration of behaviour. As individuals we do not always appear to behave consistently. Therefore, we need to assess whether a theory can cope with such inconsistencies. For example, we may have as our long-term goal the achievement of a really good degree. To do this, we know that we need to focus on our studies and work hard. Despite having this goal, we skip lectures when we have had a late night previously, or we avoid going to the library to prepare for assessments yet worry about not getting the assessment done in time. As we shall see, theories vary according to how well they can explain such apparent inconsistencies in behaviour.

The cultural context of personality theories

Another important issue in the evaluation of personality theories is rarely raised; it concerns the cultural context of most theories. One cross-cultural study by Curt Hoffman, Ivy Lau and David Johnson (1986) compared the types of personality that can be identified by name in western cultures with those in Chinese culture. In the west there is a recognised artistic personality. This describes someone who is creative, temperamental and intense. However, there is no label in Chinese to describe such an individual, although there are words equivalent to the characteristics that make up the western artistic temperament. The Chinese also have personality types, such as a *shi gú* individual, which do not exist in western cultures. A *shi gú* individual is described as being worldly, socially skilful, devoted to their family and fairly reserved. We see from this example that, while the same characteristics of personality are identifiable across the cultures, it is the way that these are then expressed as personality types that is influenced by culture. Culture will also influence which personality types are valued within a particular culture. In western capitalist cultures the driving, ambitious individualist is often valued, while in a more cooperative society the team player type is likely to be valued more.

The individualistic perspective of western psychology was discussed earlier in this chapter, and this perspective permeates the study of personality. Western psychology has sometimes been termed the 'cult of the individual'. The theories of personality that constitute western psychology all focus on individual functioning. There is an assumption that individuals will behave, or at least wish to behave, in ways that put their needs first. Most of us will have experienced this attitude directly. How often have we said or heard someone else say, 'It's my life and I'll do what I want with it'? Words to this effect are not unusual in family disputes between parents and their children. Similarly, in the clinical treatments linked to some of the personality theories, the focus is on treating the individual and meeting that individual's needs. The concept of self is at the core of this theorising. There is often no real consideration of what might be appropriate for the family, especially if this is at odds with what appears to be best for the individual.

There is virtually no acknowledgement that the personality theories we are about to study are culturally bound. Many of these theories will have limited applicability in collectivist cultures, where decisions are made at the group or community level to promote the welfare of the groups as opposed to the constituent individuals. One example might be of a student who is thinking of doing a PhD after completing her first degree. She is very able, very motivated and funding is available. However, she doesn't make the application. On being asked about it, she says that, after discussion with her family, she has decided that it is not the right thing to do at this time. She is philosophical about it and does not seem at all upset. She says that she could have gone against her family, but it would not make her happy to do this. She feels that to do so would have been very selfish. She adds that some of her friends had tried to persuade her, talking about it being her right to decide what she does with her future; however, she does not see it this way, as her family is more important to her.

There is a lot to consider if you are going to develop a truly critical appreciation of personality theories. In the following discussions, you will be introduced to a range of personality theorists. It is impossible to cover in depth every theorist; rather, we have included theorists in order to reflect their contribution to the discipline and to ensure that all the major approaches are covered. There is a huge literature on personality theory, and we offer guidance on further reading for each theorist. The concepts within each theory that have been researched are identified and examples of the major studies included. After debating how to order the theories, we have grouped similar types of theoretical approaches together and have begun with the earliest theories chronologically. This is no reflection on the importance of the theory. With this said, we hope you enjoy the experience as we know other students do.

Final comments

In summary, you should now appreciate why psychologists study personality and be aware of a variety of definitions of personality. You should understand the components of psychological definitions of personality and have developed an understanding of the historical roots of personality theory. Finally, you should understand the major questions that personality theories aim to address and understand the criteria that can be used to evaluate personality theories.

Summary

- The difficulties associated with defining personality have been examined. A range of definitions have been presented, including lay definitions and psychological definitions. Lay definitions frequently include physical attributes.
- The emphasis in psychological definitions is on individual differences. Allport (1961) developed one of the earliest definitions, describing personality as a 'dynamic organisation, inside the person, of psycho-physical systems that create the person's characteristic patterns of behaviour, thoughts and feelings'. Characteristics that usefully and reliably distinguish between individuals are identified, and individuals are then compared with each other or with population norms. There is still no consensus on a definition of personality within psychology.
- Criteria of psychological definitions include the following: relatively stable, enduring, important aspect of the self. A distinction is sometimes made between observable and unobservable aspects of personality as well as between conscious and unconscious aspects.
- The origins of personality theory in the scientific developments of physiology and medicine have been examined. The division between clinically derived and the more statistically based individual differences approach are also examined.
- Personality theories aim to explain the motivational basis of behaviour, the basic nature of human beings,

the developmental experiences that help to shape personality and categorisations of types of human personality that can be used to predict behaviour. The traditional question of heredity versus environment is also addressed. In all these areas, there are diverse views among theorists. The question of how to bring about changes in behaviour is addressed by some of the more clinical theorists, while others are more descriptive.
- The idiographic approach to studying personality adopts case study types of methodology, studying individuals and stressing the uniqueness of each individual. The alternative nomothetic approach studies groups of individuals aiming to identify similarities. The distinction is not always clear-cut in personality research.
- A further distinction is made between research-based theories and clinically derived theories for which there may be a dearth of supporting research evidence.
- Personality theories can be difficult to evaluate owing to the absence of research on particular theories or concepts within theories. Suggestions for the evaluation of theories are presented. These include empirical validity, testable concepts, comprehensiveness, parsimony, heuristic value and applied value. The importance of citing theories within a cultural and historical context is also emphasised.

Connecting up

This chapter serves as the introduction to the first part of the book (Chapters 2–10), though many of the themes discussed are explored throughout the book.

Critical thinking

Discussion questions

- What are the strengths and weaknesses of everyday ideas of personality compared with formal theories of personality?
- What do you think determines or influences your personality?
- How easy is it to get to really know someone who has grown up in a different culture? Are the similarities greater than the differences?

Essay questions

- Critically discuss the origins of personality theory.
- Describe the different techniques used to study personality. What are the strengths and weaknesses of each?
- What are the major aims of studying personality?
- Describe the criteria that can be used for the evaluation of personality theories.
- Compare the idiographic versus nomothetic approaches to studying personality.

Going further

Books

- Deese, J. (1972). *Psychology as science and art*. New York: Harcourt Brace. A short book but a classic of its kind. Sets current approaches to psychology in context and addresses the nature of theories.
- Miles, J. (2008). *Research methods and statistics: Success in your psychology degree*. Exeter: Crucial. Chapter 1 of this book, *The role of theory in psychology*, gives a practical approach to linking theory and research with lots of useful tips presented in a reader-friendly way. This book is now available as a wiki at **www.researchmethodsinpsychology.com/wiki/index.php**
- King, D., Viney, W. and Woody, W. (2009). *A history of psychology: Ideas and Context*. Harlow: Pearson Education.
- Lawson, R., Graham, J. and Baker, K. (2006). *A history of psychology*. Harlow: Pearson Education.
- Leahy, T. (2003) *A history of modern psychology* (6th edn). London: Prentice Hall. Chapter 1 is useful as it covers material on psychology as science and the nature of theory in quite an accessible style.
- Richards, G. (2010). *Putting psychology in its place: Critical historical perspectives* (3rd edn). London: Routledge. Chapter 12 covers personality theory in particular.

Journals

We would also encourage you at this stage to start looking at what personality journals you have access to via your library or online resources. It might be worth checking to see if you have access to the following journals, as they could be used to supplement your further reading:

- *European Journal of Personality*. Published by Wiley. Available online via Wiley InterScience.

- *Journal of Personality*. Published by Blackwell Publishing. Available online via Blackwell Synergy, SwetsWise and Ingenta.
- *Journal of Personality and Social Psychology*. Published by the American Psychological Association. Available online via PsycARTICLES.
- *Journal of Personality Assessment*. Published by the Society for Personality Assessment. Available online via Business Source Premier.
- *Journal of Research in Personality*. Published by Academic Press. Available online via Ingenta Journals.
- *Personality and Social Psychology Bulletin*. Published by Sage Publications for the Society for Personality and Social Psychology. Available online via SwetsWise, Sage Online, Ingenta and Expanded Academic ASAP.
- *Personality and Social Psychology Review*. Published by the Society for Personality and Social Psychology, Inc. Available online via Business Source Premier.
- *Personality and Individual Differences*. Published by Pergamon Press. Available online via Science Direct.

A specific journal relating to this text is the *History of Psychology* journal published by the American Psychology Association. Available online via PsycARTICLES.

Web links

- A good website outlining many of the personality theories covered in this part of the book is at **www.personalityresearch.org**.
- A website about the historical and philosophical background of psychology written by Dr C. George Boeree is at **http://webspace.ship.edu/cgboer/historyofpsych.html**.
- Links on the history of psychology, including timelines and online archives, can be found at the Social Psychology Network at **www.socialpsychology.org/history.htm**.

Explore the website accompanying this text at **www.pearsoned.co.uk/maltby** for further resources to help you with your studies. These include multiple-choice questions, essay questions, web links and ideas for advanced reading.

CHAPTER 2
The Basis of the Psychoanalytic Approach to Personality

Key themes

- Sigmund Freud and the psychoanalytic method
- Levels of consciousness
- Dreams and dream analysis
- Human nature and human motivation according to Freud
- The structure of personality and personality development
- Defence mechanisms
- Clinical applications of Freudian theory
- Evaluation of Freud's psychoanalytic theory

Learning outcomes

After studying this discussion you should:

- Understand what is meant by the psychoanalytic method
- Understand the Freudian conception of human nature and human motivation
- Have developed an understanding of the way that psychoanalysis attempts to understand human behaviour
- Be aware of the way Freud structured personality and how he saw it developing
- Appreciate some of the clinical applications of Freudian theory
- Know how to critically evaluate the work of Freud

Introduction

Sigmund Freud was a major intellectual figure of the twentieth century and founded the psychoanalytic approach to personality. At the core of the psychoanalytic approach is the belief that most of our behaviour is driven by motives of which we are unaware. These motives are conceptualised as unconscious forces that make it difficult for us to truly know ourselves. This may lead us occasionally to behave in ways that we have difficulty explaining. In our everyday life, for example, people frequently refer to factors in their unconscious having influenced their behaviour. A colleague might forget to go to a meeting, despite having it in his diary and being reminded about it earlier in the day. When thinking about it, he admits that he knew it was likely to be a boring meeting; consequently, Freud would have suggested that he was unconsciously motivated to forget about it.

The psychoanalytic approach, as we shall see, explains how much of our psychological energy is taken up with suppressing our unconscious urges or finding socially acceptable ways of expressing them. Freud's theory is controversial, and some current psychologists are keen to dismiss him as merely a historical figure, albeit an important one. Freud is a central figure in the development of the clinical strand of personality theorising discussed previously (Chapter 1). Freud's work is important historically, but Freud and related psychoanalytic theories are included here because of the continuing influence that his concepts have, not just on psychology but in many other disciplines also. Many psychoanalytic concepts provide such useful descriptions of human behaviour that they have been incorporated into our everyday language. By the end of the text, you will have come across many of these examples.

We begin by exploring in some detail the work of Sigmund Freud. Biographical details of Freud are included in the next Profile box to help us understand how his life

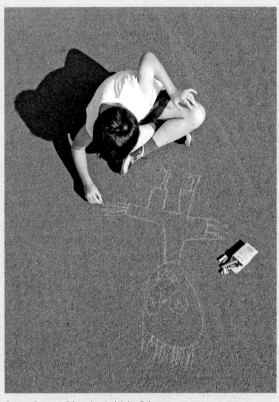

Source: Pearson Education Ltd. Jules Selmes

experiences have helped shape the theory that he produced (Chapter 1). The discussion of Freud reflects on the importance and extent of his contribution to personality theory. At the end of the discussion, the criteria described earlier (Chapter 1) are used to evaluate the theory.

Description of Freud's theory of personality

We will first describe Freud's theory of personality that comprises:

- levels of consciousness;
- the nature of human beings and the source of human motivation;
- the structure of personality;
- the development of personality.

Levels of consciousness

When Freud began theorising, there was a strong tradition within intellectual circles of regarding human beings as basically rational creatures whose behaviour is determined by will or the seeking of goals in a conscious manner. Human beings were conceptualised as being in control of their lives and exercising free will in their behaviour to the extent that their social circumstances allowed. Freud did not create the idea of unconscious mind. Philosophers had been discussing the idea of unconscious mind for hundreds of years. However, the predominant view, as popularised by the German philosopher Johann Friedrich (1776–1841) in his two-volume book, *Psychology as Knowledge Newly Founded on Experience, Metaphysics and Mathematics* (1824–1825), was that unconscious ideas were weaker ideas that had been pushed from consciousness by the stronger conscious ideas. Freud (1940/1969) disagreed strongly both with the rational view of human beings and with the suggestion that unconscious ideas were weaker than conscious ones. Instead, Freud (1940/1969) suggested that there were levels of consciousness and unconsciousness.

Firstly, there is the level of **conscious** thought. This consists of material of which we are actively aware at any given time. For example, as I am writing this I am aware of trying to think of an example of conscious thought; indeed, what to write next is my conscious thought at this moment. Next to this is what Freud termed **preconscious** mind. This consists of thoughts that are unconscious at this instant, but which can be easily recalled into our conscious mind. An example might be the colour of your car or what you did last evening. Preconscious material can easily be brought to mind when required. The final level is the **unconscious** mind. It consists of thoughts, memories, feelings, urges or fantasies that we are unaware of because they are being actively kept in our unconscious. Freud argued that they were kept in our unconscious because of their unacceptable nature. They may be sexual urges that we would find unacceptable, or aggressive instincts that frighten us, so they are kept repressed in our unconscious. The term he used for this process of keeping material unconscious was **repression**. He saw it as an active, continuous process and described repressed material as being dynamically unconscious to reflect this sense of activity.

Although three levels of thought are described, there are no clear-cut divisions between conscious, preconscious and unconscious thought; rather, there are different degrees or levels within each. For example, at times repression may weaken, so that previously unconscious material becomes conscious. This unconscious material is usually in a modified form, such as in dreams when we are asleep, at stressful times in symptoms of illness or psychological disturbance, or in the emergence of apparently alien impulses under the influence of drugs or alcohol. An example might be the quiet student who appears easygoing and unassertive, but under the influence of alcohol becomes ready to argue with her shadow and is loud and quite aggressive. Drugs like alcohol are disinhibitors, and unconscious urges are more likely to emerge into our consciousness. Freud compared the content of mind to an iceberg, describing conscious and preconscious thought as the small sections above the surface.

Related to these levels of consciousness, Freud suggested that different thought processes are at work within the various levels. Dreams exemplify this well. Freud (1901/1953) suggested that the function of dreams is to preserve sleep by representing wishes as fulfilled. Worries that we have may disappear in the dream, or problems may be represented as solved. Or desires that are unacceptable to our conscious mind may find expression in our dreams. Freud argued that representing these desires as fulfilled in our dreams helps to preserve sleep, as we are no longer trying to solve our problems or worrying about a situation as it is fixed in the dream.

Freud believed that dreams were a direct route into the patient's unconscious. He considered that there were two important elements to dreams – the manifest content and the latent content. The **manifest content** is the description of the dream as recalled by the dreamer. However, he felt that this was not a true representation of the unconscious mind, as the dreamer unconsciously censors some of the true meaning of the dream or uses symbols to represent key elements to avoid becoming too disturbed by their recall of the dream. The task of the analyst was to identify what Freud called the **latent content** of the dream. He felt that skilled interpretation was often necessary to get at the real meaning of the dream. In line with the thrust of his theory, as we shall see later, he suggested that much of the unconscious content of dreams was sexual in nature. While most symbols used in dreams have a personal meaning for the dreamer, Freud (1901/1953) identified some commonly occurring dream symbols. He suggested that snakes and knives symbolise the penis; a staircase or ladder, sexual intercourse; baldness or tooth extraction, castration fears; robbers, a father figure; and so on. Hence, a dream with a manifest content of climbing a ladder is actually about sexual intercourse (latent content). Freud used dreams as a way to explore the patient's unconscious conflicts. He would get patients to keep dream diaries. During treatment sessions, the patient would report the manifest content of the dream, and Freud would analyse this material to uncover the latent content. In this way, he could access the patient's unconscious mind.

Freud (1940/1969) claimed that different styles of thinking were associated with different levels of consciousness. Dreams, for example, represented what he called **primary process thinking**. This is essentially irrational mental activity. Dreams exemplify this activity by the way in which events are often oblivious to the categories of time and space, extreme contradiction is tolerated and events are displaced and condensed in impossible ways. The logically impossible becomes possible in our dreams. Freud claimed that it was a result of our being governed partly by what he called the **pleasure principle** – an urge to have our drives met. This is not a desire to actively seek pleasure, but rather an instinct to avoid displeasure, pain and upset. It is about preserving equilibrium within the organism in the face of internal and/or external attacks. Thus, the irrational thinking of dreams (primary process thinking) serves the function of keeping us asleep by presenting our unconscious desires as being fulfilled (pleasure principle).

Primary process thinking is contrasted with **secondary process thinking**. This is rational thought, which is logical and organised. Secondary process thinking is governed by the **reality principle**. This means that we operate according to the actual situation in the external world and the facts as we see them. Secondary process thinking is characteristic of conscious and preconscious thought. Freud suggests that the pleasure principle is an innate, primitive instinct driving our behaviour while the reality principle is learnt as we grow up. Daydreaming, imaginative thought, creative activities and emotional thinking are claimed to involve a mixture of both primary and secondary process thinking (Freud, 1940/1969).

The nature of human beings and the source of human motivation

As discussed previously (Chapter 1), personality theory aims to address several questions about human nature; the biggest of these is arguably what motivates us as human beings? For Freud (1901/1965), the answer to this question lies in the way that personality is structured and in how it develops. When Freud began his work on the development of personality, it was within a scientific culture in which Darwin's evolutionary theory was dominant. The human infant was seen to be somewhere between apes and human adults in terms of development, hence it was assumed that the same basic biological drives would be shared by human infants and other animals. Hunger and sexuality were seen to be the most important drives for animals and for human infants also.

Linked to Darwinism, there was great interest in explaining how specific behaviour arose and in explaining how behaviour was energised. Freud (1901/1965) assumed

that each child was born with a fixed amount of mental energy. He called this energy the **libido**. This libido, after development, will in time become the basis of the adult sexual drives. We will examine this concept in more detail later. In his approach to development, Freud emphasised not only the child's biological inheritance in terms of instinctual drives – libido and the pleasure principle, for example – but also the child's environmental factors, such as developmental experiences. All behaviour was energised by fundamental instinctual drives. Freud initially described two types of drives or instincts. There were the sexual drives energised by the libido, as we have just discussed. Then there were life-preserving drives, including hunger and pain. Both of these drives can be conceptualised as being positive and leading to prolongation of life and renewal of life. Later in the 1920s Freud introduced the death instinct, sometimes termed Thanatos, which is thought to be a response to the First World War. He suggests that human beings also possess a self-destructive instinct. It is different from an aggressive instinct, as the emphasis is not on destroying another but on wiping out oneself. Hence, to Freud (1920/1977), the human species appeared to possess a death instinct. It could be observed both at the group and the individual level. Human motivation is explained by our attempts throughout our lives to satisfy these basic instinctual drives. The form taken by this gratification of our instinctual needs typically changes with age, as we shall see.

Profile

Sigmund Freud

Sigmund Freud was born in 1856 to a Jewish family in Freiberg, Moravia, now the Czech Republic. He was his mother's first child. His mother had seven more children, the youngest of whom died aged 8 months. Later in life, Freud reported experiencing great guilt over the death of this sibling as he had resented having to share his mother with his baby brother. He was his mother's favourite, and they had a very close relationship, while relations with his father were colder and sometimes hostile. Freud reported having guilt feelings about his relationship with his father. Shortly after his father died, he began to psychoanalyse himself to deepen his understanding of his own unconscious feelings.

When Freud was 3 years old, his family moved to Vienna. He was very able and studied physiology and medicine at the University of Vienna. As a medical student, he went to work for Ernst Brücke, one of the greatest physiologists of the nineteenth century. Brücke was the first physiologist to suggest that the laws of physics and chemistry applied to human beings and to

describe living organisms as dynamic systems. By this, he meant that organisms were constantly in a state of movement and change, constantly energised. Freud was greatly taken with this conceptualisation of human beings. He graduated from medicine in 1881, but he never intended to become a doctor; instead, he specialised in research on the nervous system. However, this work was not well paid, and financial pressures created by the wish to marry and support a family resulted in him beginning to practise medicine. Given his interests, Freud decided to specialise in nervous disorders in his practice. At this time, there was little treatment available for the mentally ill, as we saw previously.

Freud heard of the work of Jean Charcot, a French doctor who was using hypnosis as a treatment method with some success, particularly with patients with hysteria. Hysteria is a condition where the patient reports physical symptoms of illness, but no evidence of a physical condition is present; the cause of the condition is therefore thought to be psychological. Nowadays we call these psychosomatic conditions. Charcot would hypnotise patients; when they were under hypnosis, he would tell them that they no longer suffered from their symptoms and that they had overcome their illness. Freud studied hypnosis with Charcot in Paris between 1885 and 1886. Although initially enthusiastic about hypnosis, Freud came to feel that its effects were only short-lived and did not address the roots of the individual's problem. He was more interested in what drove patients to develop hysterical symptoms in the first place. Returning to Vienna, he met a Viennese doctor, Joseph Breuer, who had developed a system of encouraging his psychiatric patients to talk about their problems while the doctor listened. Freud adopted this approach, and it is from this time that he truly became a psychological researcher and began to develop his own theory.

Freud spent much of the 1890s undertaking what he termed a self-analysis of his own unconscious process. He studied his own dreams and got his patients to report their dreams to him. He developed Breuer's approach of encouraging patients to talk about their problems, expanding it to embrace what is termed free association. Free associations are thoughts that come spontaneously into one's mind. Freud encouraged patients to report these thoughts to him as they occurred. He examined his own free associations and compared them with those of his patients. From this emerged his theory of how the personality was created and functioned.

Freud was a prolific writer; he produced 21 books between 1900 and 1931 and hundreds of journal articles and lectures. These books mainly chronicled his scientific theorising about how the mind worked. His extensive writing resulted in him becoming the most frequently cited psychologist of the twentieth century. He was invited to lecture in the United States in 1909. His books attracted great interest and provoked many debates amongst intellectuals both outside and within medical and psychological circles. He was careful to write for a lay audience as well as the scientific community. His books – *The Psychopathology of Everyday Life, Three Essays on Sexuality and The Interpretation of Dreams* – contributed to his fame, and it became fashionable for the rich to be psychoanalysed.

Freud spent almost 80 years in Austria, only being driven out by the increasing power of the Nazis. His books were publicly burnt in Berlin in 1933. In 1938, when Hitler invaded Austria, Freud fled to London with his family. For the last 16 years of his life he suffered from cancer of the jaw and was frequently in great pain, but he continued to work. He died in London in 1939, aged 83. Freud had six children, the youngest of whom, Anna Freud, continued her father's work by becoming a psychoanalyst working extensively with children. There are conflicting opinions about Freud's own personality. He was essentially a very private person. In appearance,

he was neat and well turned out, describing himself as having an obsessive personality that required routine and dedication to work. He smoked compulsively and, despite his diagnosis with cancer, could not give up smoking. He was obstinate and intolerant of those who disagreed with his ideas, and this helps to explain his numerous splits from colleagues. As a doctor, his professional life was not beyond reproach. In 1884, Ernst Fleiss, a friend of Freud's, had become addicted to morphine to help him cope with a painful illness. Freud recommended that Fleiss use cocaine instead to control his pain, describing it as a harmless substitute and writing an article proposing cocaine for the management of chronic pain.

Freud regularly treated patients for 8 or 9 hours each day, then wrote each evening and on Sundays. Although offered opportunities to become rich, he had simple tastes, never owning more than three sets of clothes. In 1924, he turned down a contract worth $100,000 to advise on a project to make films about famous love stories for Samuel Goldwyn. He also turned down lucrative deals to write for and be interviewed by popular magazines, claiming no wish for celebrity for himself but only wishing to be known for his ideas – something he certainly achieved.

Freud's thinking was influenced by events going on in the world at the time of his writings.
Source: Hulton Archive/Getty Images

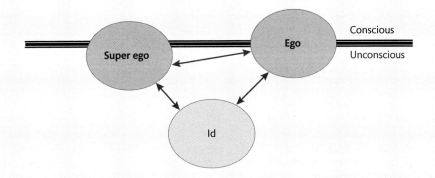

Figure 2.1 Freud's structural model of the mind.

The structure of the personality

Freud's theory includes a concept of a mental apparatus consisting of three basic structures of personality that assist us in gratifying our instincts. This apparatus can be thought of as the anatomy of the personality and consists of the id, the ego and the superego (Freud, 1901/1965; 1923/1960). They develop in the order stated, and we shall discuss each one in turn (also see Figure 2.1).

The **id** can be thought of as the basic storehouse of raw, uninhibited, instinctual energy. It is the source of all cravings, of all impulses and of all mental energy. All our survival drives for food, warmth and safety, plus our sexual drives for satisfaction and reproduction, our aggressive drives for domination and our self-destructive instincts originate in the id. Freud thought that only the id was present in the baby at birth and that, because of this, infants try to gratify their needs very directly. The pleasure principle with related primary process thinking operates in the id. Babies cry loudly when they are hungry, uncomfortable or in pain. They want to be seen to immediately. Any delay in feeding hungry babies, and they

will simply cry more lustily. Infants have no sense of what is termed **delayed gratification**; that is, the notion that if you wait patiently your needs will be met. Delayed gratification is something that the child has to acquire as they develop. (See Stop and think: Id instincts and advertising.)

These instinctual demands from the id become socialised during development as the expression of id impulses often runs counter to the wishes of the outside world. We also learn that gratification of our id impulses can frequently be achieved more successfully by planning, requesting, delaying gratification and other techniques.

As the child develops, libido energy transfers from the id and the part of the personality called the **ego** develops. The ego can be thought of as the executive part of the personality. In Freud's model, it is the planning, thinking and organising part of the personality. The ego operates according to the reality principle with related secondary process thinking. The ego becomes the mediator between the child and the outside world. The child is still trying to get what they want, but now they are taking into account social realities in achieving this. Mummy will not give them

---

Stop and think

Id instincts and advertising

The id instinct demanding immediate gratification does remain with us throughout our lives, and advertisements are often directed at this instinct. Walk around any shopping mall or along any high street and notice the number of stores that advertise instant credit.

> 'Buy what you like! £500 instant credit with our new store card.'
> 'Buy now, pay nothing till 2020.'

The whole concept of credit cards plays to our instinctual need for immediate gratification. Why save up for something if you can have it now? It encourages primary process thinking. When the time comes to pay, somehow we believe the money will be there. Reality is distanced and postponed for our immediate gratification. In this way, we can see how the instinctual needs of the id continue to shape our behaviour even in adulthood. I am sure you can recall other examples.

a drink if they simply shout that they are thirsty; but if they ask nicely and remember to say please and add a smile, they are more likely to get it.

Finally, the third structure of personality develops, the **superego**. This can roughly be conceived of as being the conscience of the child. It helps the child make judgements about what is right or wrong and which behaviours are permissible. It is thought to be composed of internalised parental attitudes and evaluations. The superego acts in opposition to the id, helping the ego to rechannel immoral id impulses. Also, if the ego is seen to allow the expression of bad instinctual demands, the superego turns against the ego. As Freud describes it, these three parts of the personality can be seen as being in conflict with each other. The id says, 'I want it now.' The ego says, 'You can have it later; or do a, b and c, and then you can have it.' The superego says, 'You can't have it' or 'That way's wrong, you must find another way.' There will be elements of social prescription contained within the superego, as what is internalised from parents will depend on the values of the family. Similarly, different societies will promote different values, as will religious and educational institutions.

These interactions between the three structures of personality create what is termed intra-psychic conflict (Freud, 1965). The outcome of this conflict can be observed as symptoms of mental upset or disturbance. The basic symptom, which we are all thought to experience, is anxiety. An example will help to clarify this. Suppose you really want to go to an old school friend's party on Friday night, but the friend lives a 2-hour train journey away. When you check the train times, you realise that you will have to miss a laboratory class on Friday afternoon to get there in time. You already missed a class this semester; and besides, the lab is on a topic that really interests you. You are really torn and don't know what to do. The id instinct is saying, 'Go to the party, have a good time.' The ego is saying, 'Perhaps we can find a way round it, you can download the notes and get the results from a friend.' Your superego is saying, 'That is wrong, you can't go. You already skipped a practical for no good reason. You want to do well at this, and it is a topic that interests you.' The competing demands have made it difficult to decide; and whatever the decision, there will be some anxiety about the path you take. This is the basic anxiety that Freud talks about. If you do go, you will feel guilty about missing the practical; if you don't go, you will feel guilty about disappointing your friend and so on. We will see later how we attempt to deal with this basic anxiety, but first we will look at how the personality develops.

The development of personality

Freud (1940/1969) described the personality as developing through five distinct stages (see Figure 2.2). His theory is described as a theory of psychosexual development, as he is concerned primarily with the development of the sexual drives. He suggested that at each stage the libido or energy source is invested in a single part of the body, which he called the **erogenous zone**. The areas of the body selected at any one stage are supposedly determined by the child's biological development. It is argued that the erogenous zone, at any time, is the area that is most sensitive to stimulation and the focus of pleasure and the source of gratification. Freud believed that biological factors were the main influence in development and paid little attention to social factors. We will look at each stage in turn, with examples to clarify the process.

Oral stage – birth to 1 year

Freud (1901/1965) argued that during infancy the earliest pleasure is focused on feeding, so that the baby's energies or libidos are centred on satisfying their needs for nourishment. The baby's mouth, lips and tongue are said to be the erogenous zones. Events around feeding are the most important sources of gratification, meeting the drive for self-preservation and thus providing sensual pleasure to the infant. All of the events around feeding are said to be pleasurable, even thumb sucking in the absence of food. Thus, Freud conceptualised babies as deriving pleasure from stimulation of the erogenous zone even without food.

According to Freud, when babies are being fed and cared for, some of their libidinal energy becomes focused on the person providing the gratification, frequently the mother. This is claimed to be the source of their first human attachment. This process of investing libidinal energy in the mother is an example of what Freud (1901/1965) called **cathexis**. It describes how some of the infant's libidinal energy becomes invested in the pleasure provider. For normal development, infants must receive sufficient oral stimulation so that their needs are met. Having their needs met in this first relationship allows the child to develop trust in the adult caregiver. This basic trust is a necessary prerequisite for all relationships. Every time you meet someone new, you trust that what they tell you is true, that they are not setting out to deceive or hurt you. The infant whose needs are met develops this basic trust in others, while the child whose needs are not met develops a sense of mistrust.

While the amount of oral stimulation required for normal development is not specified, the results of under- or over-stimulation are clearly described. In either case the baby will be fixated on oral gratification and continue to seek oral stimulation in later life. Freud describes fixation as an internal resistance to transferring the libidinal energy to a new set of objects and activities. Fixation can occur at any of the stages of psychosexual development and is an indication that the child has failed to progress satisfactorily

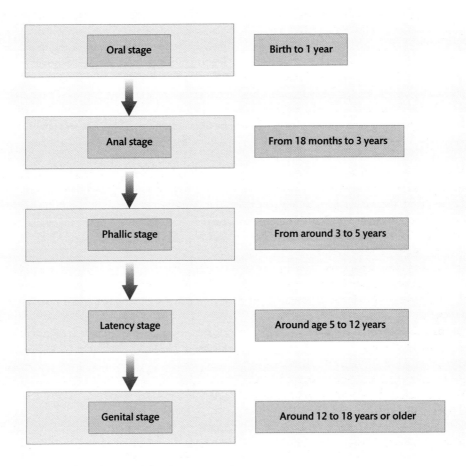

Oral stage	Birth to 1 year
Anal stage	From 18 months to 3 years
Phallic stage	From around 3 to 5 years
Latency stage	Around age 5 to 12 years
Genital stage	Around 12 to 18 years or older

Figure 2.2 Freud's theory of psychosexual development.

through that stage. Evidence of fixation can be observed in the personality and behaviour of affected adults, according to Freud (1901/1965). It is claimed that fixation at the oral stage is linked to the seeking of excessive oral stimulation in adulthood, such as smoking, chewing gum or excessive eating. The adult who was over-indulged at the oral stage is described as having an **oral receptive character**, being overly dependent on other people for gratification of their needs, being trusting, accepting and gullible (Blum, 1953). Oral under-indulgence can lead to the **oral aggressive personality**, where the individual has an exploitative attitude towards others and tries to get as much as possible from them. In extreme cases they have sadistic attitudes, envying others and always trying to dominate (Fenichel, 1945). Freud argues that the child who has received sufficient oral stimulation will transfer their libidinal energy to the next stage.

Anal stage – 18 months to 3 years

As the child matures, the lower trunk becomes physiologically more developed and comes under increased voluntary control. Freud (1901/1965) suggests that the baby comes to receive sensual pleasure from bowel movements. At the same time, parents begin to emphasise toilet training and reward the child when they demonstrate control of their bladder and bowel. These two developments come together and help to shift the child's attention from oral stimulation and the mouth area to the anal region, and this becomes the new erogenous zone. At this stage, toilet training is the issue that has to be handled appropriately by parents; otherwise, fixation may result. Toilet training can involve the child and the parent in interpersonal conflict, if the parents make demands on the child to become toilet trained. The child may resist these demands and a battle of wills can commence. Freud suggested that this experience of conflict with demanding carers may lead individuals to rebel against authority figures throughout their lives.

When toilet training is handled badly, fixation at the anal stage can occur, resulting in the anal-retentive personality. This personality type is described as having a constipated orientation, in that they are very orderly, stingy, stubborn, with a tendency to hoard things and to delay gratification until the last possible moment (Freud, 1901/1965). These behaviour patterns are thought to come from meeting parental exhortations and delaying their bowel movements until their parents deemed it appropriate. The opposing type resulting from anal fixation is the anal-expulsive personality. These individuals resist others' attempts to control them, in the same way that they resisted their parents' attempts at toilet training. They are untidy, disorganised and disregard accepted rules about cleanliness and appropriate behaviour. The appropriate approach for the parents to adopt is to be relaxed about the child's preferences and positively reward successes. This is thought to foster positive self-esteem and encourages the child to move on smoothly to the next psychosexual stage.

Phallic stage – from around 3 to 5 years

As the child's genitals become more sensitive as a result of physiological maturity, the libidinal energy moves from the anal region to the genital area as the genitals are now the source of pleasure for the child. Freud (1920/1977) claimed that gratification at this stage is gained from masturbation. This stage is thought to be particularly difficult for girls as they become aware that while boys have penises they do not. This realisation of their deficiency is thought to make girls jealous of boys, experiencing what Freud calls **penis envy**. This leads to feelings of deficiency in girls and a wish to possess a penis. Boys respond to the girls' lack of a penis by becoming anxious about the thought of losing their own penis, and Freud terms this **castration anxiety**. These developments are accompanied by changes in the children's relationships with their parents. Boys are thought to intuitively become aware of their mothers as sexual objects (Rapaport, 1960). This leads to the boy developing a sort of sexual attachment to his mother and to regard his father as a sexual rival. This is termed the **Oedipal complex** after the mythical Ancient Greek, Oedipus Rex, who killed his father and married his mother. The boy is envious of the father as he has access to the mother that the boy is denied in that he sleeps with her and so on. The boy also perceives the father to be a powerful, threatening figure, someone with the power to castrate the boy. The boy is thus trapped between his desire for his mother and his fear of his father. This causes the boy to experience anxiety. To resolve his anxiety, the boy begins to identify with his father. The suggestion is that, by trying to become as like his father as possible, the boy not only reduces the likelihood of attack by his father but also takes on some of his father's power. This 'inner father' comes to serve as the core of the child's superego.

A parallel process, the Electra complex, is thought to occur in girls, but Freud did not spell this out in quite so much detail, reflecting the lesser importance of women within his theory. Girls are thought to develop the same intuitive awareness of the father as a sex object as boys do for the mother. For girls, the mother is seen as a rival for the father's love; the mother is also seen to possess some power, although not as much as the father. The wish for the father and the fear of the mother creates anxiety in the girl, although at a lower level as the mother is less powerful, having already lost her penis. Girls resolve this conflict by identifying with their mother, although less strongly than boys identify with their father. The girl also wishes to identify with her father in the hope of obtaining the missing penis from him. Thus, for girls, the Electra complex cannot be satisfactorily resolved. According to Freud (1901/1965), this conflict results in girls having weaker ego functioning, which makes it more difficult for them to balance the competing demands of the id and reality.

Fixation at this stage again is thought to result in problems that will be apparent in adulthood. The male may become promiscuous, seeking the sexual gratification that was refused him when he was a child. The other alternative is that the male fails to adopt masculine characteristics; he develops feminine characteristics and may become attracted to men. Similarly, women who are fixated at this stage may develop masculine traits and be attracted to women. This then is how Freud explains the process of children being socialised into male and female roles. Boys, by identifying with their father, become like him; and similarly, girls become like their mothers. Freud also saw the root cause of homosexuality in the unsatisfactory resolution of the phallic stage.

Latency stage – around age 5 to 12 years

This stage is described as a resting period in the child's psychosexual development. The child's energies are taken up in socialisation and learning. Freud (1901/1965) suggested that peer group interaction during this phase was predominantly with same-sexed children. Identification with same-sexed parents was followed by identification with same-sexed peers. As children learn more about the world and become more involved in social interactions, they develop defence mechanisms during this period to help them cope with the basic anxiety caused by the conflicts between the id, ego and superego that we discussed earlier. The nature of defence mechanisms will be discussed later.

Genital stage – from around 12 to 18 years or older

Changes in the child's body brought on by puberty are thought to reawaken the child's sexual energy or libido, and a more mature form of sexual attachment occurs. Freud (1901/1965) claimed that from the beginning of this period, the sexual objects chosen were always members of the opposite sex in normal development. However, he pointed out that not everyone works through this period to the point of achieving mature heterosexual love. Some may have conflicts left from the Oedipal or Electra stage, so they do not cope well with

Stop and think

Observational example

Try to observe a toddler having a temper tantrum. This can often be observed in a supermarket, or you may see it on some of the reality television shows about bringing up children. The toddler wants something, and the parent or carer says that they can't have it. The ferocity of the child's emotions is truly amazing when their wishes are frustrated. In Freudian terms, the child's id instincts are being denied. They want whatever it is with a passion, and they want it now. The role of the parent or carer is to socialise the child so that they learn not only that they cannot have everything they want exactly when they want it but also that there might be better ways of trying

to get what they want. In psychoanalytic terms, this is about encouraging the development of the child's ego, so that they learn to moderate their instinctual demands. They may initially demand sweets in the supermarket and have a tantrum when sweets are refused and they ultimately do not get the sweets, being told that being naughty (tantrum) means that they do not get sweets. The child learns that if they are good in the supermarket and then ask for sweets at the end, they are more likely to get them.

Can you think of alternative explanations for the child's behaviour?

the resurgence of sexual energies in adolescence. Others may not have had a satisfactory oral stage and so do not have the basic foundation of trust for a love relationship, as described earlier.

Freud sees the child's personality emerging as a result of these developmental processes. The crucial stages are the earliest ones – the oral, anal and phallic – so Freud sees that, by age 5, the basic adult personality is formed in the child. It is also at these ages that the process of containing the id begins, first with the development of the ego as the child learns about the world and parental discipline is applied to frustrate the child's id impulses. The young child has to learn how to increase the chances of getting their own way. (See Stop and think: Observational example for an illustration of this process.)

Defence mechanisms

We discussed earlier how the conflicting demands of the id, ego and superego create anxiety in the individual at every age and that in the latency stage, the child is thought to develop **defence mechanisms**. Freud is somewhat vague about how this development occurs, seeing defence mechanisms as emerging from the socialisation that occurs at this stage. The purpose of defence mechanisms is to make us feel better about ourselves and to protect us from pain – in psychological terms, to protect our self-esteem. It may be something upsetting that happens to us or aspects of ourselves that we find disturbing, so we push those aspects from our conscious minds and then employ defence mechanisms to keep them in our unconscious. It is important to stress that everyone needs and uses defence mechanisms at some time. It is psychologically healthy to do so. The question is, to what extent is their use healthy and adaptive, and when

is it problematic? The simple answer given by Freud is that defence mechanisms become unhelpful when they are used inappropriately or indiscriminately. Examples will make this statement clearer as each defence mechanism is described.

The first defence mechanism that Freud described was repression. He observed this being used when he was studying patients suffering from hysteria. Freud continued to identify defence mechanisms being used by patients in his clinical practice, so that by 1936 his daughter, Anna Freud, who had also become a psychoanalyst, described 11 defence mechanisms identified by her father: repression, denial, projection, reaction formation, rationalisation, conversion reaction, phobic avoidance, displacement, regression, isolation and undoing (see Figure 2.3). Anna Freud (1966) added a twelfth defence mechanism, sublimation, and others have been added since then by later psychoanalysts, as we shall see. Although each defence is described separately, the examples included will illustrate how frequently several defence mechanisms may operate together.

Repression

As discussed previously, at times we all suppress inconvenient or disagreeable feelings. We push unacceptable thoughts, feelings or impulses into our unconscious. We act as if what we can't recall can't hurt us. An American research study by Morokoff (1985) measured levels of sexual guilt in women, identifying a group high in guilt and a group low in guilt. The women were then shown an erotic video while physiological measures of their levels of sexual arousal were taken and verbal self-reports of arousal level were given. In women high in sexual guilt, the reported levels of arousal were significantly less than their physiological levels of arousal, while in women low in sexual guilt, the two measures were closely matched. In the high sexual

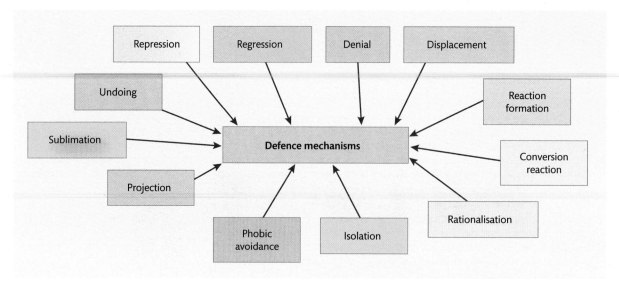

Figure 2.3 Common defence mechanisms.

guilt group, the guilt associated with sexual arousal was causing the women to repress their experienced arousal.

There is nothing pathological about repression unless it is carried to extremes such as, for example, the person who claims never to be angry. Anger is a natural human response on occasions for everyone, so what is likely to be happening is that the individual is not allowing themselves to be angry for some reason; their anger is repressed. Repression can be compared to a dam holding back the flow of a river. If the volume of water becomes too great, a problem arises, and similarly with repression. Excess use of repression results in individuals being out of touch with their true feelings, and this makes honest relationships with others impossible (Freud, 1901/1965).

Denial

We deny unpleasant events or the reality of a situation. Consider the individual who refuses to open the bank statement month after month, even though they know they should keep track of their finances. They suspect it may be bad news, so the letter always goes unopened to the bottom of the pile. An extreme form of denial is seen in the phenomenon of experiencing a phantom limb after amputation, especially as the experience is most common after unexpected amputation. The most extreme form is seen in amnesia (loss of memory) following traumatic events. This has been observed quite frequently in troops in times of war.

Projection

The defence known as **projection** involves us blaming our friends, neighbours, other nations and so on for our own shortcomings. We externalise unacceptable feelings and then attribute them to others. In an argument with a partner, for example, we deny that we are jealous. Instead, we claim that it is our partner who is jealous or angry. We project our jealousy or anger onto the other person. We are saying, 'I am not the problem – you are.' Regrettably, projection is a normal human defence; however, in extreme forms, it can lead to the individual becoming paranoid.

Reaction formation

We use **reaction formation** to overcome impulses that are unacceptable to us, gaining mastery over the initial impulse by exaggerating the opposing tendency. A good example of this is the character Monica in the television programme *Friends*. Monica comes across as obsessionally tidy and organised. However, it is revealed that she keeps a locked cupboard that is incredibly messy and disorganised. This mess is hidden from her friends. In Freudian terms, she deals with her impulses to be untidy by becoming obsessionally tidy, but her reaction formation is not totally successful, as the impulse is expressed via her untidy cupboard. In its extreme form, reaction formation can develop into obsessional neurosis (Freud, 1901/1965). In this condition, the individual may become obsessed with cleanliness, for example, and be unable to function normally because of all the cleaning rituals they have to follow. They may have to wash everything they touch and so on.

Rationalisation

Rationalisation is the process whereby the reasons for a course of action are given after it has happened. The reasons given not only justify the action but also conceal its true meaning. Someone may go eagerly for a job interview

To what extent are attempts to ban smoking in the workplace and public places a repression of the oral stage?
Source: Photofusion Picture Library/Alamy Images

and seem to really want the position. However, they are not appointed; and then they say that they did not really want the job and/or that it was not a very good position. This example shows that denial can be useful in helping us to save face and, in so doing, it can protect our self-esteem. Much easier to say that you did not want the job than to say that you really wanted it but you were not good enough. Denial in these situations is useful in protecting us from disappointments, and it can give us the courage to try again at things we may not have succeeded at first time round.

Conversion reaction

A **conversion reaction** is observed when unacceptable thoughts or emotions are converted into physical symptoms, as in hysterical symptoms or psychosomatic symptoms. Many of Freud's patients presented with hysterical symptoms – as in the famous case of Anna O, who presented with paralysis of her arms, for which no physical cause could be found (Freud and Breuer, 1966). Anna O had unconsciously converted her psychological distress into paralysis of her arms, which also meant that she could do nothing. Nowadays hysterical conversion reactions are rarer, as people have become more psychologically sophisticated; but psychosomatic disorders are on the increase. These are conditions in which no physical illness is identified, although the patient presents with physical symptoms. Back pain is reported in many cases to be psychosomatic in origin. The person who hates their job but does not admit it instead has

to have large amounts of time off work because of back pain. The wish not to go to work has been converted into a physical symptom that then prevents the individual working.

Phobic avoidance

To some extent, we all try to avoid places and situations that arouse unpleasant emotions in us. This may be public speaking, the site of an accident and so on. **Phobic avoidance** is an extreme form of this. Situations or events that arouse anxiety or other unpleasant emotions are avoided at all costs. The intensity of the anxiety experienced even at the thought of an encounter is totally out of proportion to the situation. Phobic avoidance is different from phobias of spiders or other animals; such phobias are relatively common and can be explained on the basis of learning theory.

Displacement

Displacement is a defence mechanism that occurs when we are too afraid to express our feelings directly to the person who provoked them, so we deflect them elsewhere. It is summarised by the common expression of 'kicking the cat' when we come home annoyed by our boss, for example. We take our frustration out on someone lower down the pecking order or less likely to complain. This defence mechanism can be useful in preventing unwise conflict with powerful others; but, when heavily used, it is not conducive to good interpersonal relationships (Freud, 1901/1965).

Regression

The defence mechanism called **regression** occurs when we are trying to avoid anxiety by returning to an earlier, generally simpler, stage of our life. Where individuals regress to is determined by the existence of fixation points in their development. We have discussed this previously. At times, regression is normal and a healthy response. For example, going on holiday can be conceptualised as a form of regression. You leave the normal cares of everyday living behind. You play games, are often looked after, give up your daily responsibilities and generally enjoy yourself in a way that is more reminiscent of the carefree days of childhood. More seriously, a young child who has achieved toilet training may start wetting the bed after the birth of a new sibling. This is seen as regression to an earlier age before the birth of the other child, when the elder child felt no anxiety about competing for attention with the new sibling. Often, when they are traumatised, adults become much more dependent and helpless in a similar way.

Isolation

Isolation occurs when the anxiety associated with an event or threat is dealt with by recalling the event without the emotion associated with it. The feelings that would normally be associated with the event are separated and denied. Freud (1965) called this intellectualisation, where thoughts and emotions are separated into watertight compartments. Such individuals come across as extremely unemotional, merely reporting facts with no feeling.

Undoing

The defence mechanism called **undoing** frequently accompanies isolation. It has an almost magic appeal to it, as ritualistic behaviours are adopted that symbolically negate the thoughts or actions that the person had earlier, and felt guilty about having (Freud, 1901/1965). Children sometimes indulge in such ritualistic behaviour, and childhood incidences are good examples. Where I grew up, there was a commonly held belief among young children that seeing an ambulance was associated with bad luck; but this bad luck was avoided if you then held your collar until you saw a dog. The negative emotion associated with anticipating 'bad luck' was neutralised by the collar holding, and seeing the dog negated the whole incident. Very anxious, disturbed individuals may adopt all sorts of rituals to protect themselves in this way.

Sublimation

Anna Freud (1966) described **sublimation** as the most advanced and mature defence mechanism, as it allows partial expression of unconscious drives in a modified, socially acceptable and even desirable way. The instinctual drives are diverted from their original aim and channelled into something seemingly socially desirable. For example, individuals who set themselves up to protect society from pornography in films or television may actually spend quite a lot of their time watching pornography so that they can then protest about the decisions made by the official censors. In Freudian terms, they have sublimated their strong desire to watch pornography, sexual voyeuristic drives, and expressed them in what can be perceived as a socially desirable form. Some of the psychoanalytic examples here are amusing, such as firemen conceptualised as having sublimated their urethral drives (i.e. the urge to urinate publicly) and gastroenterologists (surgeons who deal with digestion and the bowel) as sublimating their anal fixations. Art and music are often cited as examples of successful sublimations of the instinctual drives. These will help you remember sublimation. Both Freud and his daughter Anna saw healthy levels of sublimation as enriching society.

Stop and think

Psychoanalytic explanation of mental illness

Within the psychoanalytic model, it is suggested that we all have unresolved conflicts left over from our childhood. For the most part, we use our defence mechanisms to keep these conflicts in our unconscious. However, situations may arise in life that reactivate the early conflict. The individual who had dependency/independence conflicts with parents may find that leaving home raises the feelings associated with these earlier conflicts. The anxiety is such that the defence mechanism can no longer keep the worries out of consciousness. The individual may then become very anxious and psychologically unwell. Mental illness then results from a breakdown of defence mechanisms. In these situations, the defence mechanisms come to be used inappropriately and/or applied rigidly. This causes more problems, as we saw in the discussion of the various defences.

Clinical applications of Freudian theory

By now you will have gathered that Freud was interested in exploring the patient's unconscious, as this was where the root of the patient's problems lay. The traditional analytic approach developed by Freud (1940/1969) involved the patient lying on a couch while the psychoanalyst sat in a chair behind the patient. The treatment was not about a social relationship between patient and analyst. The analyst sat behind the patient so he was not visible to the patient; the patient thus received no non-verbal cues from the analyst, and any possible social interactions were minimised. The consulting room should be relatively impersonal for the same reason.

The analyst aims to locate where fixations have occurred in the individual's development and to help the individual understand these issues and resolve the emotional conflicts associated with them within the therapy session. The physical expression of emotion is termed **catharsis** and is a crucial, if not the crucial, element of the psychoanalytic method of treatment. The term 'catharsis' literally means purging. Patients were encouraged to discharge the emotions associated with their conflicts within the therapy session, and this was called an **abreaction**. Initially, abreaction was thought to be sufficient for a cure; but Freud was later convinced that patients also needed to understand the nature of their conflicts.

We have seen that, to access the unconscious, Freud used free association and recounts of patients' dreams.

There are three assumptions underlying free association (see Figure 2.4).

- All the patient's thoughts lead to material in the unconscious that is significant in some way.
- The patient's therapeutic needs and the knowledge that they are in therapy will lead their associations towards what is psychologically significant except so far as resistance operates. Resistance is the reluctance of the patient to allow unconscious material to become conscious. It may also be demonstrated when the patient refuses to accept the analyst's interpretation of their conflicts.
- Resistance is minimised by relaxation, hence the patients had to lie down on a couch; and it is maximised by concentration, so they had only the ceiling to distract them.

The analyst would listen uncritically to the patient and then offer interpretations of the patient's problems to help the patient gain insight to their problems. The essential characteristic of the relationship between the patient and the analyst is its emotionality, although the relationship is considered one-sided as the analyst is expected to remain detached from the patient. The key concept in this relationship is **transference**. This is the process where a patient displaces onto his analyst feelings that derive from previous figures in his life. Freud (1913/1950) saw it as an essential part of therapy. The relationship that the patient has with the analyst becomes a central phenomenon that has to be analysed. To put it simply, within the analysis the patient projects their needs and desires onto the analyst. At times, the analyst may be receiving projections as if they were the

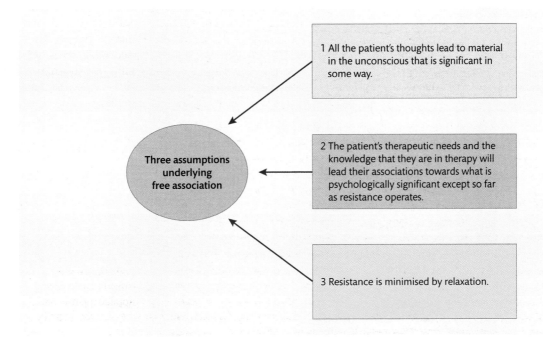

Figure 2.4 Three assumptions underlying free association.

patient's mother, father, hated sibling and so on. Within the therapy session, the patient then resolves these conflicts by discharging the emotion associated with them (abreaction). This is thought to be possible as the therapist provides a more articulate, insightful, yet emotionally detached encounter than was possible in the original relationship.

A related phenomenon termed **counter-transference** may also occur. This is where the analyst transfers some of their own emotional reactions onto the patient. It may be that the analyst gets annoyed with the patient at a particular point. The patient may have 'touched a raw nerve' in the analyst and reawakened some of the analyst's conflicts. All analysts will have undergone their own psychoanalysis as part of their training, to make them aware of and help them to resolve their own unfinished conflicts. This training will help them to recognise when counter-transference is occurring, and they will have been trained to use it to further their understanding of the patient. Analysts also have to be supervised regularly to ensure that they are operating effectively and that they will bring any counter-transference issues to discuss with their supervisor. Analytic sessions typically last for 50 minutes, the 'therapy hour', to allow a break between patients. Treatment tends to be open-ended, and it is not unusual for analysis to continue for several years.

Evaluation of Freudian theory

We will now evaluate Freud's theory using the eight criteria identified previously (Chapter 1): description, explanation, empirical validity, testable concepts, comprehensiveness, parsimony, heuristic value and applied value (though in this section we combine empirical validity and testable concepts).

Description

Freud's theory is based on evidence gathered from his patients. However, to protect the anonymity of his patients, he published very few actual case studies. Rather, he presented arguments for his theorising accompanied by clinical illustrations from his patients. He did not annotate most of his case studies in very much detail, rather focusing on what he felt were interesting aspects of the case and often writing up his case notes retrospectively from memory (Storr, 1989). This does not constitute good qualitative data as currently understood within psychology, and it raises questions about the validity of some of the data underpinning his descriptions.

Freud addressed a wide range of phenomena, as evidenced in his collected works. However, he often revised his ideas, which can make his work difficult to follow. He provides good descriptions of his conceptualisation

of personality developing, how it is structured and the complexity of its functioning in terms of unconscious motivation, defence mechanisms and basic anxiety. However, we can query whether it is appropriate to produce descriptions of normal behaviour and normal development based on observations of mainly neurotic individuals.

He did address the complexity of human behaviour, demonstrating that similar motives may lead to different behaviour and that similar motives may underpin quite different behaviour. His theorising led psychologists to debate what are the important issues for the development of personality. His work on defence mechanisms, continued by his daughter Anna, provides us with some excellent descriptions of how we function psychologically. There is some debate about the originality of Freud's ideas; many of his concepts came from his teachers or had been around previously but were popularised by Freud (Sulloway, 1992).

Explanation

Although Freud produced theories of normal development, there is some vagueness in his theory of psychosexual development about exactly what is required for normal development. He talks about sufficient oral stimulation, for example, without detailing what that might be. He is stronger on the explanation of the development of pathology. This is perhaps understandable given that most of his data came from patients with psychological disturbance. For many, including some of his fellow psychoanalysts, his theory of psychosexual development seems to overly stress sexual drives as being at the heart of human development. We will return to this issue when considering the empirical validity of Freud's theorising.

Regarding Freud's model of the structure of personality, it has face validity in that we are all aware of the conflicts that making choices creates in our lives and the anxiety that this can cause. Even with things we want to do, by enjoying doing *a*, we may feel guilty about not doing *b*. However, the notion of these conflicts providing the psychic energy to help motivate our behaviour is questioned by current cognitive theorists (Dalgleish and Power, 1999). The concept of defence mechanisms is one of Freud's most valuable contributions. They appear to offer good explanations of commonly observed behaviour, as evidenced by their common use as descriptors of behaviour (Brewin and Andrews, 2000).

Empirical validity and testable concepts

For over 90 years, researchers have attempted to evaluate some of the various concepts described by Freud. Some of the areas that have been addressed are outlined in the following subsections. However, as we have already discussed, for traditional Freudian analysts, the only evidence they require comes from their treatment of patients (Power, 2000). We will now examine some of the psychological research that has been undertaken to assess the theory.

Research on the unconscious

Research has examined subliminal perception, suggesting that it provides evidence for the existence of a dynamic unconscious. Subliminal perception occurs when participants register stimuli without being consciously aware of them. The subliminal stimuli are shown to affect subsequent behaviour, thus demonstrating the existence of unconscious motivational effects on the behaviour produced. Erdelyi (1984) showed participants emotionally threatening words and neutral words and measured their anxiety levels. Participants showed physiological anxiety responses to the emotionally toned words before they could identify what the stimulus word was. This demonstrated that individuals defend themselves against the anxiety associated with emotional stimuli without being aware of it. Silverman (1976) presented participants with upsetting messages relating to emotional wishes or conflicts subliminally, and this stimulus was shown to affect their subsequent behaviour. For example, women with eating disorders were presented with neutral and emotionally upsetting subliminal messages and were shown to eat more after the upsetting subliminal messages (Patton, 1992). Weinberger and Silverman (1990)

reported on a series of experimental studies undertaken in their laboratory which provide some empirical basis for subliminal perception and other aspects of the unconscious.

There is also a body of research on parapraxes; that is, slips of the tongue, forgetting names and misreading words. Freud felt that these were all unconsciously motivated. However, cognitive psychologists such as Norman (1981) and Reason (1990, 1979; Reason and Lucas, 1984), while acknowledging that so-called Freudian slips occur, suggest that they are caused by cognitive and attentional errors. It may be because of a lack of attention or emotional arousal, resulting in a word that the individual more commonly uses or has recently used being produced rather than the correct word (see the Stop and think box on Parapraxes). However, Reason (2000) concludes that Freud was correct in conceptualising Freudian slips as representing unconscious processing that interrupts our conscious processing. For Reason (2000), the unconscious refers to our automatic mental processing rather than Freud's dynamic unconscious, although he acknowledges that they can reveal suppressed emotions. As part of the current debate about the precise nature of the unconscious, Kihlstrom (1999) suggests that a cognitive unconscious exists that links more closely with our thought processes and is not qualitatively different from conscious thought in terms of how it functions. Reason (2000) concludes that Freud was almost correct when he makes these links between cognitions and emotions and the unconscious. Norman (2010), in a

Stop and think

Parapraxes (Freudian slips)

Freud (1901/1965) believed that we do not make unintentional mistakes in our lives; rather, errors are the result of mainly unconscious motivators. One example of this is parapraxes – in everyday language we call them Freudian slips. An American psychologist, Motley (1985, 1987), designed studies to investigate the effects that unconscious forces have on our behaviour and produced empirical examples of parapraxes (Freudian slips). Pairs of words were flashed on a screen, and male participants had to say them aloud. Three conditions were compared. In the first, participants were told that they might receive electric shocks during the experiment. In the second condition, the researcher was a provocatively dressed woman. The third condition, the control condition, had no threat of electric shocks and the researcher was dressed sedately. In the electric shock threat group, participants made specific types of errors, saying, 'cursed wattage' instead of 'worst cottage' and 'damn shock' instead of 'sham dock'. The group with

the provocatively dressed researcher reported mistakes like 'nude breasts' instead of 'brood nests' and 'fast passion' instead of 'past fashion'. The control group did not make errors related to electricity or that were sexual in nature. Motley (1985, 1987) suggested that these systematic errors demonstrated the effects of unconscious motivation. Individuals threatened with electric shocks displayed their anxiety in the errors that they made (e.g. making references to the electric shock threat). Participants with the sexually provocative researcher demonstrated unconscious expression of sexual thoughts (e.g. by making sexual references).

To what extent do you think the findings from this study present support for Freudian theory of the unconscious? Or do you think that a possible explanation of the findings is that these parapraxes are the result of lack of attention or emotional arousal, resulting in a word that the individual more commonly uses or has recently used being produced rather than the correct word?

review of evidence of empirical research on emotion, motivation, decision-making and attitudes, concludes that there is evidence for the operation of unconscious processes as conceptualised by Freud.

Research on the component structures of personality

The one aspect of Freud's personality structures that has been systematically investigated is the ego. There are many studies focused on the functioning of the ego, and several measures of ego functioning have been created. The argument here appears to be that if you can consistently measure something called ego functioning, then it must exist. Loevinger developed a Sentence Completion Test (Loevinger and Wessler, 1970), which measures the development of the ego in individuals and individual differences in development in adults. Barron (1953) developed a scale to measure individual differences in ego strength. Block and his colleagues developed measures of ego control and ego resiliency (Block, 1993; Block and Block, 1980; Funder and Block, 1989). They have identified common characteristics typical of individuals with high ego strength. Qualities such as high stress tolerance, the ability to delay gratification of needs, to tolerate frustration, the skill to have good personal relationships and a solid sense of self are common to all the measures.

Fisher and Greenberg (1996) conducted a detailed review of existing research on Freudian concepts, concluding that there is empirical evidence to support the concepts of oral and anal personalities. However, they found only weak evidence to support Oedipal conflicts and no evidence to support any differential impact on the development of women from the Electra complex. Hunt (1979) reviews research on the psychosexual stages and concludes that, while anal characteristics could be observed in adults, their development did not seem to be related to toilet-training practices.

Research on defence mechanisms

There are over 70 years of research on aspects of defence mechanisms (Madison, 1961). Significant research evidence has accrued for projection (Newman *et al.*, 1997), denial (Steiner, 1966; Taylor and Armor, 1996) and many others (Madison, 1961). Of particular interest and relevance is the research on repression as it is assumed that traumatic memories that have been repressed can be recovered in therapy or under hypnosis. Cognitive psychologists agree that there are mechanisms for excluding unwanted material from consciousness (Conway, 1997). Myers (2000) has identified a group of individuals who have a repressive coping style. Such individuals consistently underreport feelings of anxiety even when physiological measures indicate that they are very anxious. The contention that traumatic memories can be repressed has led to court cases with adult children accusing parents and others of sexual abuse, based on memories recovered in therapy. Brewin and Andrews (1998) reviewed the research in this area and concluded that between 20 and 60 per cent of therapy clients who had suffered sexual abuse in childhood reported not being able to recall the abuse for considerable periods of their lives. Brewin and Andrews (2000) point out that current cognitive therapies (Borkovec and Lyonfields, 1993; Salkovskis, 1985) have identified a concept that they label cognitive avoidance, which appears to be very similar to Freud's concept of defence mechanism and to operate in a similar way to protect individuals from anxiety.

Evidence for dream content

Solms (1997) outlines current research on the neuropsychology of dreaming, showing that activation of instinctual and emotional mechanisms in the centre of the brain initiates dreaming. The manifest content of the dream is then projected backwards onto the perceptual areas of the brain. Solms (2000) claims that this evidence is compatible with many aspects of Freudian dream theory. Dreaming becomes impossible only if the cognitive and visuospatial areas of the brain are destroyed. Panksepp (1999) has identified a system in the brain that initiates goal-seeking behaviour and is involved in behavioural cravings and in dreaming. Solms (2000) points out that this involvement of instinctual mechanisms in dreaming was originally described by Freud, although the detail of the structures was unknown. Solms (2000) concludes his review by suggesting that Freud's dream theory is on the right track according to current findings in neuropsychology; even the idea of censorship in dreaming may be compatible with current research (Hobson, 1999).

Concluding comments on the research evidence

There are undoubtedly methodological difficulties with some studies, but the conclusion is that there is support for some of the main concepts that it has been possible to operationalise and that others need to be modified in the light of this research (Brewin and Andrews, 2000). However, large areas of Freud's work remain untested and there has been little attempt in recent years to address this.

Comprehensiveness

Freud's theory is fairly comprehensive. The theory addresses both normal and abnormal behaviour, and demonstrates that the psychological processes underlying both are fundamentally the same. In addition to the material covered here, Freud addressed a wealth of other topics. He did groundbreaking work on the importance of slips of the tongue, humour, marriage, death, friendship, suicide, creativity, competition, importance of culture, society, war and many others.

Parsimony

Given the range of behaviour – both normal and abnormal – that Freud attempts to cover, his theory is relatively parsimonious. There are not huge numbers of concepts within the various theories, and all seem to have relevance in terms of explaining commonly observed normal and abnormal behaviour. Where the theory does not meet the parsimony criteria is in terms of its explanation of the motivational basis of behaviour. Sexual and aggressive instincts are identified as the sole motivators underlying all behaviour, and this view is too restricted to account for the complexity of human behaviour.

Heuristic value

Undoubtedly Freud's work has had an enormous impact, and it still provokes debate and research over 70 years after his death. Freud introduced exciting, novel ideas about the psychology of human beings. Studying Freud's theory has led theorists to develop their own theories or modifications of Freud's theory, and this work continues. In terms of approaches to treatment, Freud's work has provoked enormous interest and debate. It has led to breakaway schools of psychoanalysis and has motivated other therapists to develop alternative approaches to psychoanalysis, as you will see in this text. His work has also influenced many other disciplines, such as literature and art.

Applied value

As regards applied value, Freud's work has again resulted in huge advances in treatment of mental patients. It was at the forefront of developments to treat mental patients more humanely. It stressed the importance of allowing patients to talk and then really listening to what they had to say; it is the forerunner of all the current approaches to counselling and therapy. Debates about the effectiveness of psychoanalysis as a treatment still rage. The most famous of these was led by Hans Eysenck, the British psychologist, who carried out a sustained attack on psychoanalysis (Eysenck, 1952, 1963, 1965b, 1986). Eysenck savagely attacked the effectiveness of all therapies, claiming that the only effective therapy was behaviour therapy. However, Eysenck's statistics were queried, and it was claimed that he was overstating the case to provoke debate. More recently, the International Psychoanalytic Society undertook a review of research on the efficacy of psychoanalysis (Fonagy *et al.*, 1999). This review concluded that, while there were methodological problems with some of the studies, there was some support for the effectiveness of psychoanalysis, but it was not unequivocal. Psychoanalysis is shown to be beneficial to patients with mild neurotic disorders but to be less so for patients with more serious conditions. It is agreed that traditional psychoanalysis as practised by Freud is time-consuming and consequently very expensive. However, key concepts from his theory are still at the core of many of the newer, briefer versions of psychoanalytic therapy.

Final comments

Freud is rightly criticised for having a narrow motivational basis to explain behaviour. Does it seem feasible that sexual and aggressive drives are the major motivators of human behaviour? Freud totally ignores the social world in which individuals operate. He was not particularly interested in the current life problems of his patients, except in relation to the way they reflected their earlier fixations. He also presents a very pessimistic, one-sided view of human nature, with his concept of Thanatos (Freud, 1901/1965). Although he acknowledged that human beings could act rationally, he then appeared to focus almost exclusively on the irrational side of human nature in his writing (Blum, 1953). The status accorded to women in Freudian theory is also problematic (Fisher and Greenberg, 1996). We will examine some of the theorists who challenged aspects of Freud's theorising.

Stop and think

Experimental research and Freudian theory: 'It can do no harm'?

There is some controversy about how psychoanalytic theory is conceptualised and therefore how it should be evaluated. Psychoanalysts suggest that the only valid evidence is the clinical experience of practitioners (Grünbaum, 1993). Freud himself devalued the experimental examination of his theory and methods with some disdain. One well known example is that when Saul Rosenzweig, an experimenter, presented studies testing Freud's assertions, Freud wrote back, saying 'I have examined your experimental studies for the verification of the psychoanalytic assertions with interest. I cannot put much value on the confirmations because the wealth of reliable observations on which these assertions rest makes them independent of experimental verification. Still, it can do no harm' (quoted in Grünbaum, 1993, p. 101).

Psychoanalysts who suggest that the only valid evidence is the clinical experience of practitioners present a somewhat circular argument. To truly understand psychoanalysis you need to be an analyst, according to this argument. These analysts see the traditional empirical and experimental evidence of psychology as being irrelevant. To put it bluntly, they demonstrate a total commitment to the psychoanalytic approach and see no real need for empirical evidence other than the experiences of their patients while they are undergoing therapy. Criticisms from the wider psychology and psychotherapy community are put down to a lack of understanding of psychoanalysis due to the critics not having been trained as analysts. Despite these attitudes, empirical evidence in support of psychoanalytic theory does exist in many areas.

What do you think? Is the experimental testing of Freud's ideas important? Why?

Stop and think

Objectivity

When reviewing this research, pay careful attention to the measures employed and the samples used, as these are not always directly comparable across studies. The objectivity of some of the psychoanalytic studies is sometimes questioned, as studies sometimes seem designed to collect evidence that confirms Freud's theory, rather than seeking to assess a process.

Summary

- The psychoanalytic approach to personality was developed by Sigmund Freud. It is a clinically derived theory based on case studies of patients and Freud's introspection about his own behaviour. The theory postulates that most of our behaviour is driven by unconscious motives.
- Mind is conceptualised as being composed of three levels: conscious thought, preconscious thought and the unconscious. The unconscious is the largest part of the mind and exerts the strongest influence on our behaviour. Material is kept in our unconscious (repressed) as it causes us anxiety.
- Dreams are seen as a direct route into the unconscious mind. A distinction is made between the manifest content, what the dreamer recalls, and the latent content, which is the true meaning that becomes apparent only after it has been interpreted by the psychoanalyst.
- Freud claimed that different styles of thinking were associated with the different levels of consciousness. Primary process thinking is driven by the pleasure principle. This contrasts with secondary process thinking, defined as rational thought governed by the demands of the external world and termed the reality principle.
- Freud held that biological drives were the primary motivators of human behaviour, namely the sexual drive for reproduction and life-preserving drives, including hunger and pain. Later he added a self-destructive instinct, the death instinct (Thanatos).
- The personality is composed of three structures that we use to gratify our instincts: the id, ego and superego.

- Behaviour is energised by the conflicts created by the interaction of the id, ego and superego. These conflicts create anxiety, and we all use defence mechanisms to help deal with this anxiety.
- A number of defence mechanisms were identified by Freud and his daughter, Anna Freud. These are repression, denial, projection, reaction formation, rationalisation, conversion reaction, phobic avoidance, displacement, regression, isolation, undoing and sublimation.
- Personality develops through five distinct stages, sometimes called psychosexual stages. The stages are the oral stage, anal stage, phallic stage, latency stage and genital stage.
- Children require sufficient appropriate satisfaction of their instinctual needs at each stage of their psychosexual development, or fixation occurs. Fixation can lead to distortions in personality development and may also lead to problems in later life.
- Freud outlined a clear method of treatment, termed psychoanalysis. It involved using free association, dream analysis and psychoanalytic interpretation by the analyst to uncover the problems located in the patient's unconscious.
- An evaluation of the theory is provided, demonstrating that there is significant support for many aspects of Freud's theory and that a considerable amount of work is still being undertaken in this area. There are methodological weaknesses in some studies, particularly in the older evaluations of psychoanalysis.

Connecting up

Chapter 3 outlines the work of a number of psychoanalytic theorists who follow chronologically on from Freud. These theorists are Adler, Jung and Horney.

Critical thinking

Discussion questions

- How well do you think Freud's theory explains your own behaviour or that of your friends?
- How valid was the evidence that Freud used when developing his theory?
- Does Freud's theory go any way towards addressing gender differences?
- Would you like to be psychoanalysed?
- Had Freud's mother not been young and beautiful, would he have described the Oedipal complex or the Electra complex?
- How important do you think unconscious motivation is in explaining our behaviour?
- How does Freud account for mental illness? Does his conceptualisation seem adequate?
- Critically discuss Freud's conception of women.
- How adequately does Freud explain human motivation?

Essay questions

- Critically discuss Freud's theory of personality.
- Critically discuss the contribution made by Sigmund Freud to our understanding of personality.
- Discuss the major influences on Freud's theory of development.
- Discuss whether there is any evidence for Freud's theory of development.
- Critically examine Freud's theory of defence mechanisms.
- 'We all carry elements of neurosis from our developmental experiences.' Critically discuss with reference to our use of defence mechanisms.
- Outline the crucial elements of psychoanalysis and comment on its effectiveness as a therapy.

Going further

Books

- Freud, S. (1986). *The essentials of psychoanalysis.* Harmondsworth: Pelican Books or Freud, S. (2005) (edited by Anna Freud). *The essentials of psychoanalysis.* New York: Vintage. This book provides an excellent, relatively short introduction to a selection of Freud's major works. It includes an introduction by his daughter Anna, setting the work in context. I would always advise you to read some of the Freud's actual writing to get a flavour of his style.
- Rycroft, C. (1972). *A critical dictionary of psychoanalysis.* Harmondsworth: Penguin Books. This short dictionary is invaluable as it provides definitions for the complex terminology employed in psychoanalytic theory.
- Storr, A. (2001). *Freud: a very short introduction.* Oxford: Oxford University Press. This is an easily accessible, concise overview of Freud by a prominent psychoanalyst.
- Chessick, R. D. (1980). *Freud teaches psychotherapy.* Cambridge: Hackett Publishing Company. Read this book

if you are keen to explore the art of psychoanalysis further. It is written by a clinician and teacher and provides an excellent introduction to the theory as it is applied.
- Hall, C. S. (1999). *A primer of Freudian psychology.* New York: Meridian. This is a classic text written by a psychologist who studied Freud for 30 years. It is short and presents an accurate but concise summary of Freud's work.
- Eysenck, H. J. (1992). *Decline and fall of the Freudian empire.* London: Penguin. Eysenck's critique of psychoanalysis.

Journals

A good place to start may be with two special issues of *The Psychologist* on Freudian theory in the light of modern research and reading. You can find *The Psychologist* on the British Psychological Society website (**www.bps.org.uk**). *The Psychologist* (2000), Vol. 13, No. 12 (guest editors

Bernice Andrews and Chris R. Brewin). This is an issue dedicated to evaluating the status of Freudian theory in the light of current knowledge in psychology. It makes interesting reading. Moreover, it is freely available online. Most recently a series of articles in September 2006, *The Psychologist* (2006), Vol. 19, No. 9, discuss Freud's influence in terms of personal and professional perspectives, particularly in the domains of neuropsychology, social psychology and memory.

Also worth looking at is Silverman, L. H. (1976). Psychoanalytic theory: The reports of my death are greatly exaggerated. *American Psychologist, 31*, 621–637. This article gives a balanced view of the influence of psychoanalytic thought.

Relevant research studies can be found in a range of journals, including the normal personality and individual differences journals, psychotherapy and counselling journals. Good terms to use in any online library database (e.g. Web of Science; PsyclNFO) are 'ego' and 'defence mechanisms' (or 'defense mechanism').

One journal that your university is likely to hold and that deals with Freudian and psychoanalytic themes is *Psychology and Psychotherapy – Theory Research and Practice*, which is published by the British Psychological Society, Leicester. It is available online via IngentaConnect and SwetsWise.

If you really want to delve into the world of psychoanalysis, there are some dedicated journals to psychoanalytic theory. It is less likely that you will be able to gain access to these articles unless your university subscribes to the print or online edition because they fall outside of mainstream psychology. However, if your university does have subscriptions, it is worth looking at these journals:

- *The International Journal of Psychoanalysis*. Publishes contributions on methodology, psychoanalytic theory and technique, the history of psychoanalysis, clinical contributions, research and life-cycle development, education and professional issues, psychoanalytic psychotherapy and interdisciplinary studies (**www.ijpa.org, http://onlinelibrary.wiley.com/journal/10.1111/(ISSN)1745-8315**).
- *The Psychoanalytic Quarterly*. Represents all contemporary psychoanalytic perspectives on the theories, practices, research endeavours and applications of adult and child psychoanalysis (**www.psaq.org/journal.html**).
- *Journal of the American Psychoanalytic Association*. Publishes original articles, plenary presentations, panel reports, abstracts, commentaries, editorials and correspondence in psychoanalysis. There is a special issue on Freudian theory in the 2005 Vol. 53, No. 2 edition (**www.apsa.org/japa/index.htm**).

Web links

- The Freud museum in Vienna can be accessed online (**www.freud-museum.at**). This site includes pictures of Freud's consulting room as well as material relating to his practice in Vienna.
- The London house where Freud lived and his daughter Anna continued to practise after his death is now a museum and can be accessed online (**www.freud-museum.at/cms/index.php/en_home.htm**).
- Information on the International Psychoanalytic Society is located online (**www.ipa.org**).
- The British Psychoanalytic Society is online (**www.psychoanalysis.org.uk**).

Film and literature

Freud's ideas have also influenced many areas of western life, including drama, theatre, literature, political campaigning, advertising and even religion (Fisher, 1995). Some examples of Freudian influences on films and literature are included here.

- *A Dangerous Method* (2011, directed by David Cronenberg). A film exploring how the intense relationship between Carl Jung and Sigmund Freud gives birth to psychoanalysis.
- Pinocchio is a character that first appeared in the book *The Adventures of Pinocchio* published in 1833 by Carlo Collodi. However, Pinocchio is best known for the portrayal in Walt Disney's second animated feature **Pinocchio** (1940, directed by Hamilton Luske and Ben Sharpsteen). Pinocchio, a living puppet, must prove himself worthy to become a real boy. There are

many Freudian themes presented in the film. The most obvious Freudian theme is that of the superego, which is represented as a cricket who acts as his conscience in guiding Pinocchio through his life.
- Director Alfred Hitchcock's films are full of Freudian themes; notably the Oedipus complex in **Psycho** (1960), repressed memory in **Marnie** (1964) and psychoanalysis in **Spellbound** (1945).
- **Bram Stoker's *Dracula***. If you are looking for a story of the time which mirrors many aspects of Freudian theory, Bram Stoker's *Dracula* is that novel. Written in 1897, the story of *Dracula* deals with the intertwining themes of sex, sexual taboos and repression, life and death. *Dracula* has been the basis for countless films. The two films that most closely follow the plot of the original novel are **Nosferatu** (1922, directed

by F. W. Murnau) and ***Bram Stoker's Dracula*** (1992, produced and directed by Francis Ford Coppola and starring Gary Oldman, Winona Ryder, Keanu Reeves and Anthony Hopkins).

- ***Pollock*** (2002, directed by Ed Harris). We mentioned, in the section on defence mechanisms, the defence mechanism termed sublimation. Anna Freud (1966) described this as the most advanced and mature defence mechanism; it allows partial expression of unconscious drives in a modified, socially acceptable and even desirable way. Art and music are often cited as examples of sublimations of the instinctual drives. One film that shows how inner conflicts might make their way into art is *Pollock*, the biopic about Jackson Pollock.

- ***Neurotic Behaviour*** (Educational Resource Film). Illustrates several varieties of neurotic behaviour and classical defence mechanisms. McGraw-Hill, USA. Concord Video and Film Council, United Kingdom.

Explore the website accompanying this text at **www.pearsoned.co.uk/maltby** for further resources to help you with your studies. These include multiple-choice questions, essay questions, web links and ideas for advanced reading.

CHAPTER 3
Developments of Freudian Theorising

Key themes

- Disagreements between Freud and some of his followers
- Adler's individual psychology, the inferiority complex and birth order
- Carl Jung's analytic psychology and structures within the psyche
- The psychology of Karen Horney
- Approaches to treatment adopted by Adler, Jung and Horney
- Evaluation of Adler, Jung and Horney

Learning outcomes

After studying this discussion you should be able to:

- Outline and critically evaluate Adler's individual psychology
- Outline and critically evaluate Carl Jung's analytic psychology
- Outline and critically evaluate Karen Horney's approach to personality
- Consider why splits occurred between Freud and his followers

Introduction

The common strand in this discussion is that all three theorists accept the importance of unconscious motivation in explaining behaviour. We begin by examining the two major dissenters from Freud and conclude with the first feminist challenge to Freud. No unifying theory emerges from this discussion; rather, you will become aware of how ideas in personality theory and approaches to treatment develop. Significant aspects of the work of the three theorists covered here have influenced current theorists and practitioners, as we shall see later.

As we saw earlier (Chapter 2), the groundbreaking nature of Freud's early work attracted great attention both from the medical profession and the popular press. Freud was an obstinate individual who was intolerant of others' views, especially when they posed a challenge to his own work. These qualities appear to have been responsible for the disagreements that he had with colleagues. When other clinicians disagreed with him, he ceased to collaborate with them. Two of the most famous of Freud's early collaborators who split with him were Alfred Adler and Carl Jung (Stern, 1977). Adler was a Viennese doctor who had written a spirited defence of Freud's theory of dreams when the local press attacked it in 1902. Freud contacted him and invited him to join the Vienna Psychoanalytic Society. This was a discussion forum for Freud's new psychoanalysis. In 1902, Adler was elected president of the Vienna Psychoanalytic Society, but resigned in 1911 as he had grown tired of Freud's intolerance of others' opinions and his dictatorial manner. Adler appears always to have found Freud difficult personally and never had a particularly close relationship with him, but his rejection of Freud's emphasis on the sexual instinct finally ended their relationship. Jung was a Swiss doctor and in 1906 he sent Freud a copy of a book he had written on the psychoanalytic treatment of schizophrenia. They corresponded, and Jung went to visit Freud in Vienna in 1906. Jung and Freud were close and maintained a collaboration until 1913. Again, Jung disagreed with Freud about the sexual instinct being the major motivator in human behaviour. Jung had also become tired of Freud's emphasis on psychopathology as he himself was much more interested in examining what human beings could achieve, their aspirations and their spiritual needs. Both Jung and Adler have made significant and lasting contributions to personality theory, hence their inclusion here.

In the previous discussion (Chapter 2), we became aware that Freud's theorising about women is problematic. He appears to adopt extremely chauvinistic views about women and their psychology. Karen Horney was a German doctor who trained as a Freudian psychoanalyst. She corresponded with Freud and collaborated with him. Eventually she too came to disagree with Freud, largely over the treatment of women in his theory. Horney is sometimes described as the first feminist voice in psychoanalysis, hence her inclusion here. While she did not develop a comprehensive theory of personality, her work was a major influence on Albert Ellis' rational-emotive behaviour therapy (Chapter 5), one of the most popular cognitive therapies utilised currently.

Source: Alamy Images/Chris Howes/Wild Places Photography

Individual psychology of Alfred Adler

Have you heard of the **inferiority complex**? Most people have, but few people know where it originates. This is one of the major concepts that we owe to Alfred Adler.

Adler (1979) disagreed with Freud's negative view of human motivation. He could not accept the Freudian model of the personality as being composed of competing structures; rather, he perceived an essential unity in the personality. He felt that there was a consistency in individuals' behaviour and that individuals worked towards maintaining it. We each know ourselves as a certain kind of person, and we act accordingly. To reflect this unity, Adler termed his approach individual psychology. One of the meanings of 'individual' is total or indivisible entity, and this is what he meant – not the study of individuals. (See Adler's Profile box.)

Adler stressed the importance of what he termed **social context** in personality development and in the current functioning of the individual. He felt that the social world that we live in plays a crucial part in determining who we become and the problems we have in living. He placed great emphasis on the concept of community and regarded 'events in the lives of individuals as having no meaning except as participating in a collective whole' (Adler, 1964). His aim was to develop a scientific knowledge of human beings that would be accessible to all and that would, above all, provide a treatment guide; hence, he wrote simply so that lay readers could follow his work. He is conceptualised as a healer rather than a theorist.

Inferiority feelings

The term 'inferiority' was borrowed from Darwinism. It was used initially to label biological disabilities, termed organ inferiorities, that are apparent at birth or in early childhood. Adler, based on his observations in his medical practice, noted that what happened to an inferior organ always depended on the individual. He observed that, frequently, individuals worked hard to compensate for their weakness in some way.

Adler maintained that the fate of an inferior organ would always depend on the individual and their attitude towards it. He suggested that the central nervous system participated in this compensation, with increases in growth or specialised function. As examples he cites the one-armed man who develops superior muscular power in his remaining arm, the blind person's acute hearing and sense of touch. Adler began by focusing purely on biological inferiorities; but through his studies of children he widened the concept to include what he described as purely imaginary inferiorities, which resulted from social convention. He quoted left-handedness

and having red hair as examples. He suggested that mind and body constituted a single entity and that these purely social prescribed inferiorities would bring the need for compensation. Later he widened the concept further and argued that we all experience inferiority feelings both psychological and social beginning at birth and continuing throughout our childhood, owing initially to the helplessness of the human infant (Adler, 1979). Our parents, siblings and so on are all bigger and more competent than we are, and this is the basis for our inferiority feelings. In this way, Adler widened the scope of organ inferiority, claiming that feelings of inferiority are widespread and that, as a way of compensating for it, we all strive for superiority. We are all striving for mastery in the world, trying to fulfil our potential. He describes us all as struggling from a minus to a plus situation, whether it be learning to ride a bike like our older brother or gaining a degree. He firmly asserted that the person's attitude towards their inferiority is crucial, as is how significant others in our lives treat us, as the two are thought to interact in complex ways. If we acknowledge our inferiority, it can serve as the basis for mutual help and cooperation in overcoming problems in living. Adler argues that we all have inferiority feelings, and they allow us to empathise with others who admit to having difficulties and ask for help. However, if we become preoccupied with our inferiorities, we become defensive and develop an **inferiority complex**. Our energies go into disguising our inferiority, and it makes us less likely to trust others or ourselves. He suggests that, consequently, individuals with inferiority complexes will not contribute much to life, as they are too afraid to take risks and reveal themselves to others for fear of failing (Adler, 1979). Others may respond to their inferiorities by relying on overcompensation to make up for their deficiencies. This then leads them to develop an exaggerated sense of their own superiority that others find difficult. This act of acting superior to compensate was termed **masculine protest** and could apply to men or women. This represented the individual's decision to reject the stereotypical female role of weakness associated with femininity.

Adler believed that we all have this goal of superiority or mastery motivating us to achieve and maximise our potential at each stage of our lives. This belief that goals direct our current behaviour is described as **teleology**. It contrasts with the **deterministic** view exemplified by Freud, which suggests that behaviour does not occur freely but is the result of other events. Adler emphasised that our goal of superiority was fictitious, as we could never realistically achieve it; at each stage of our lives, there are new tasks to master and challenges to meet. How we approach our inferiority determines what Adler (1958) termed our fundamental attitude towards life, labelled our **style of life**, the attitude that guides all our behaviour. To understand an individual, he said, you needed to know what their goals were in life. We will now look at how one's style of life is said to develop.

Profile

Alfred Adler

Adler was born in Vienna in 1870, the second son and third child in a fairly affluent middle-class family. He was a delicate, sickly child and suffered from rickets. He had some unfortunate experiences as a child, including having a brother die in the bed next to him and being run over twice in the streets. While not initially excelling at school, he worked hard and overcame his difficulties and went on to study medicine in Vienna. In his first practice he treated circus performers, who impressed him with their physical abilities. Many of them seemed to have overcome significant physical problems to achieve their success. We know already about how Adler met Freud through defending the latter's work in 1902, but their allegiance was relatively short-lived. After splitting from Freud in 1911, Adler set up a rival organisation named The Society for Free Psychoanalytic Research, reflecting his view of Freud's group. During the First World War, Adler worked in military hospitals. As a result of those experiences, he came to be interested in persuading ordinary people about the need for trust, cooperation, love and respect within a society. He travelled widely, giving lecture tours as well as continuing his clinical work. He died in Aberdeen, Scotland, while on a lecture tour in the United Kingdom in 1937.

Personality development in Adlerian terms

Adler (1917, 1963) claimed that feelings of inferiority in the child develop initially because of the basic helplessness of the human infant. Both parents play key roles in the child's development of a distinctive style of life. Style of life is not an easy concept to grasp; initially it was translated from the German as 'life plan' or 'guiding image', and it refers to the unique ways in which people pursue their goals. The style of life is established in early childhood between the ages of 3 and 5.

For Adler, feelings of superiority and inferiority are crucial to our personality.
Source: BBC Photo Library

Adler concluded that there are three basic concerns that we all have to address in life – work, friendship and love. The major role of parents is to provide the child with accurate conceptions of all three. Adler was the first theorist to stress the interactional nature of all relationships, pointing out that, while babies need their mothers, the mothers also need their babies. The mother has to introduce her baby to what Adler (1964) terms the **social life**. The mother's attitude towards her role is crucial. If the child is loved and wanted, the mother will concentrate on teaching the child the social skills he/she needs for the future. However, if the mother is dissatisfied with her role, she may be more concerned with proving her own superiority; and to this end, she will place competitive demands on her child. Her child will have to sleep better, walk earlier, be more intelligent, etc. than other children. This pressure on the child may result in the child developing an inferiority complex if they find these targets hard to achieve.

Adler (1964) also saw fathers as having an important role to play. He said the main task of the father is to contribute to the welfare of his family and society. The father has to provide a good role model of a worthwhile human being. Adler stressed that, for optimum development, the father must be seen to treat his wife as an equal and cooperate with her. Adler (1927), despite developing concepts like masculine protest, was no chauvinist and argued vigorously against treating anyone, male or female, as inferior. Mothers should also treat their husbands as equals and value them. Adler condemned the common practice of mothers requiring fathers to discipline their children. He said that such mothers are exploitative, in allocating the difficult tasks to their husbands. Good parenting from good role models is critical for the child to develop an appropriate style of life.

Birth order

Another factor that Adler (1927) emphasised was the effect of **birth order**, claiming that it contributed significantly to the development of an individual's style of life. Each child is treated uniquely within the family depending on their order of birth. Adler was the first theorist to point out that the family is not experienced in the same way by every member within it. Family relationships change with each additional child. He suggested that how each new addition is handled is crucial. His views on birth order are summarised in Table 3.1.

Adler (1958) claimed that out of the wealth of family experience and the individual's interpretation of it, a distinctive guiding goal or style of life emerges for that person. He believed that three conditions could be particularly damaging in development and lead to the development of a neurotic personality. These are perceived inferiorities that are not compensated for but rather serve as excuses for the child not to compete in life. An example of this would be the asthmatic child who uses their condition to avoid all sport and outdoor activity. The compensating asthmatic child, on the other hand, might be driven to excel at sports; examples of these individuals abound in athletes like Paula Radcliffe or the winner of nine Olympic gold medals, Mark Spitz, and countless professional footballers. The other conditions that damage children are neglect or rejection, and pampering. As a result, Adler claimed, such children are likely to develop what he described as a neurotic personality.

Characteristics of the neurotic personality

Neurotic individuals feel their own inferiority very acutely and try to compensate with varying success. They are grossly inaccurate in their own self-evaluations, either under- or over-evaluating themselves. They are continually tense and fearful, especially of decision-making, tests and any situation where failure is possible. Adler (1917, 1963) described such individuals as not being 'socially courageous'. They adapt defensive strategies to cover themselves and are primarily interested in themselves. When such individuals are unable to obtain their goals of superiority by legitimate means, they develop psychologically based symptoms as either an excuse to avoid situations where they might fail or to gain control of others using their symptoms as a sort of emotional blackmail. We are sure that many of you are familiar with the individual who cannot be challenged in case it upsets them. They are treated as partial invalids, although no one really knows what is wrong with them, but allowances are made.

Healthy development, on the other hand, demands what Adler (1964) called **social interest**. This is quite a difficult concept as there is no directly equivalent word in English. It is variously translated as social feeling, community feeling, fellow feeling, community interest or social sense. Adler claimed that it is innate and leads us to help each other and work together to build better communities. He is saying that we are born as social beings with a need to cooperate with others. In many ways, Adler is an early humanistic psychologist, predating Maslow and Rogers (who are presented in Chapter 6). He emphasised the personal worth of all individuals, their drive to achieve their potential, their innate need to be social and cooperate with others and their ability to make choices in their lives, including making the choice to change. Adler (1973) stressed that cooperation is required to solve the major problems in life: work, friendship and love.

The individual with a healthy lifestyle will have had role models in their family who have fostered the development of these healthy goals in accord with social interest. However, the exact nature of these healthy goals is not clearly

Table 3.1 Adler's conceptualisation of the effects of birth order

Family position	Description of personality characteristics
Eldest children	These children are the centre of attention, but with the birth of a sibling they may become what Adler called the 'dethroned monarch'. This child best understands the importance of power and authority, having experienced it and then lost it. Adult characteristics: conservative, support authority, maintain the status quo, excel in intellectual activities and attain high levels of eminence.
Second children	These children are likely to view the elder child as a competitor to be overcome. Their development is highly dependent on how the elder child treated them. If the older child is supportive, then healthy development is more probable. However, if the older child is resentful, problems arise. Adult characteristics: demanding of themselves, sometimes setting unrealistically high goals to ensure their own failure, as then they did not run the risk of upsetting their older sibling.
Youngest children	Remains to some extent the baby of the family, getting most attention, pampering and spoiling by parents. Adult characteristics: high dependency needs, a great need to excel and a need for praise.
Only children	With no sibling rivals and no sibling models, these children are likely to be pampered, especially by the mother. Adult characteristics: have a high need for approval, have great difficulty handling criticism and dislike, intellectually able and high achievers.

Table 3.2 Adlerian personality types

Type	Description
The ruling type	This type lacks social interest and courage and is typified by an intense striving for personal superiority and power. They typically exploit others to accomplish their goals. They are also emotionally manipulative. Adler suggested that drug addicts and juvenile delinquents were examples of this type but also suggested that many domineering, apparently successful individuals fitted this profile as they grossly exploit others, never giving credit where it is due and always taking centre stage.
The avoiding type	Lacking the necessary confidence to solve their problems, these individuals typically try to pretend that the problem does not exist, using the well-known ostrich head in the sand manoeuvre. Alternatively, they may claim that it is not their problem, someone else is to blame, and therefore they cannot be held accountable.
The getting type	These individuals are relatively passive, making little effort to solve their problems. They will use their charm to get others to do things for them. Adler felt such parasitism was very unhealthy.
The socially useful type	This is the healthy option. Such an individual faces life confidently, with positive social interest, prepared to cooperate with others and to contribute to the welfare of others.

specified. To assist readers in understanding the differences between healthy and unhealthy individuals, Adler (1973) provided descriptors of personality types, summarised in Table 3.2. He did stress that each individual was unique, but said that the types were indicative of tendencies displayed by groups of individuals.

A measure of social interest has been developed (Crandall, 1975). Based on this, it was reported that individuals with high positive social interest are less self-centred, less hostile and aggressive and more cooperative and helpful than those with low social interest. Crandall (1980) found individuals with high social interest to be better adjusted psychologically. There has been some resurgence of interest in the concept of social interest; for example, Nikelly (2005), quoting data from a range of disciplines, suggests that it plays a key role in attaining optimal well-being. However, the personality types have not been tested, although some clinicians have reported their usefulness (Ellenberger, 1970).

Adlerian treatment approaches

Adler, like Freud, felt that an understanding of the individual's personality would come from an examination and analysis of their childhood experiences as these had shaped their social interest and style of life, as we have seen. There were clear aims underpinning his approach to treatment. These were, firstly, to understand the specific unique lifestyle of the individual. Secondly, the therapist had to enable patients to understand their own lifestyles and the mistakes that are contained in them. Finally, the therapist had to strengthen, via the therapeutic relationship between patient and therapist, the rudiments of social interest – which Adler assumed would still be present in all patients, as we are all born with social interest. Adler (1964) claimed that as their social interest increased, patients gained courage, understood their mistakes and stopped making them. To uncover the patient's style of life, Adler (1973) used several sources of information that were the focus of therapy sessions (see Figure 3.1). These were as follows.

Figure 3.1 Adler's sources of information that were the focus of therapy sessions.

- **Earliest childhood recollection** – Adler believed that patients' earliest memories provide useful insights into their style of life. This memory is thought to provide the prototype for later development of the style of life. It could be a real memory or a fantasy, but that was not important. What was important was that individuals report what they remember, and it is significant because they have remembered it.
- **Position of the child in the birth order** – As discussed previously, it was not just birth-order position that was important, but how other members of the family had treated the arrival of the new child.
- **Childhood disorders** – This links to Adler's notion of the importance of organ inferiority and his belief that the style of life is adopted during the first 5 years of life. He was interested in fears, stuttering, aggression, daydreaming, social habits, lying, stealing and so on to try to build up an in-depth picture of the early years as experienced by the patient.
- **Day and night dreams** – Here Adler acknowledged a debt to Freud, as he followed the same procedures for dream analysis without Freud's emphasis on dreams as expressions of sexual needs. He was particularly interested in recurrent dreams, seeing them as the individual's unconscious attempts to achieve their personal goals or solve their problems. Adler gives the example of a student who dreams of climbing mountains and enjoying the view from the top. He interprets this as indicating that the individual is courageous and unafraid of their approaching exams. Students who dream of falling, on the other hand, are not so courageous, want to postpone their exams and have a fear of failing.
- **The nature of the exogenous (external) factor that caused the illness** – Adler (1973) explored the nature of the problems that patients were currently experiencing in their lives. This was a real break from traditional psychoanalysis, for which the individual's current life problems are of limited interest.

In the course of therapy, patients would recognise and correct their faulty lifestyles and become concerned for others. This might mean that they had to reorganise their mistaken beliefs about themselves and others and eliminate any goals that were unhelpful to the achievement of a socially useful and therefore healthy style of life. Adler also relied on his own intuition and empathy for the patient as well as on the attitude that the patient had towards him. He did not encourage dependency in his patients. Patients were encouraged to see that they were responsible for their own choices in life and had to take responsibility for their own treatment. This approach predates the focus on choice and responsibility that is a central feature of current approaches to cognitive therapy. We will examine this topic further when we cover the work of Albert Ellis (in Chapter 5).

Evaluation of Adler's individual psychology theory

We will now evaluate Adler's theory using the eight criteria identified previously (Chapter 1): description, explanation, empirical validity, testable concepts, comprehensiveness, parsimony, heuristic value and applied value (though in this section we combine empirical validity and testable concepts).

Description

Adler provides a good description of personality development, normal and abnormal behaviour. His account is relatively uncomplicated and easy to follow. This was because Adler saw himself as an educator as well as a clinician, so he ensured his writings and his lectures could be understood by the general public, not just by psychologists and psychiatrists.

Explanation

Adler has provided us with some useful explanations that fit with our experience in some areas. The inferiority and superiority complexes describe psychological phenomena that are so familiar to us that they have become part of our everyday language in western cultures. His work on explaining the potential influence of parents and siblings and the interactional nature of child–parent relationships was groundbreaking. Many developmental psychology texts still talk about family styles and types of family, ignoring the fact that each child must experience the dynamic of the family differently depending on their role within it. However, Adler's explanations of development and psychopathology are not very detailed.

Testable concepts and their empirical validity

There has been interest in attempting to test aspects of Adler's theory. We have already seen work on style of life, measuring social interest and cooperation (Crandall, 1975; Leak et al., 1985; Leak and Williams, 1989). Leak and Gardner (1990) found that students high in social interest endorsed more mature concepts of love, involving sharing and cooperation, while those low in social interest endorsed egocentric game playing in relationships. There is some empirical support for birth order, although, in smaller and more complex families than Adler dealt with, some of the issues are different. Two early reviews of this theory by Schooler (1972) and Falbo and Polit (1986) provide evidence of birth-order effects. A more recent review aims to separate myth from reality in terms of birth order and includes some new approaches to research (Herrera et al., 2003). Research in this area continues. Zajonc (1976) caused controversy among psychologists by claiming that family size and position in the family affected intelligence. Sulloway (1997) pointed out that 21 of the first 23 American astronauts were first-born or only children. There has been much discussion, and birth-order research continues (Paulhaus *et al.*, 1999; Sulloway, 1997, 2001, 2002).

There has also been a significant amount of research on the relationship between early recollections (ERs) and individuals' conceptions of themselves. Watkins (1992) reviewed 30 studies of ERs, concluding that there was a relationship between ERs and current interpersonal behaviour, emotionality and perceived control. Therapy patients produced more positive ERs as they got better.

Comprehensiveness

In terms of coverage of topics, Adler's is a very comprehensive theory; but, like Freud's theory, the motivational basis for explaining behaviour is very limited, with social interest as the sole motivator. The theory does cover both normal and abnormal behaviour and the process of development of personality. Adler (1958) also wrote extensively about political, educational and religious institutions within society and the way that they influenced the development of the individual. He was interested in how they could be restructured to promote individual well-being.

Parsimony

As we have seen, Adler's aim was to construct an explanation that would make sense to the 'ordinary' person. Consequently, he uses relatively few constructs, which then have to be applied in highly generalised and imprecise ways. It is a global theory, and the actual detail is sparse. He talks about the need for good role models, for example, without specifying exactly what these are. Similarly, with parenting, his descriptions are not very specific; rather, he provides vague general principles. The reduction of motivation to one single motivator, striving for superiority, also appears untenable.

Heuristic value

Adler's work provoked a great deal of interest and attention. He was the first theorist to emphasise the importance of the self, although he used the term 'individual' instead of self. As we have seen, he was an early humanistic psychologist, predating Maslow and Rogers – two theorists that we will examine later (Chapter 6) – both of whom acknowledged a debt to his individual psychology. Adler became very well known and undertook extensive lecture tours in Europe and the United States.

Applied value

Undoubtedly, Adler's work has made an impact. It has influenced subsequent theorists, as we shall see, and his ideas about the influence of the family and the need for parenting skills have led to moves to develop effective parenting training such as the American STEP: Systematic Training for Effective Parenting (Dinkmeyer *et al.*, 1997), which has been widely implemented. Its effectiveness has been reviewed by Robinson *et al.* (2003). His concept of the inferiority complex does seem to address a crucial issue in highly competitive western societies, and its adoption into everyday language attests to its usefulness in labelling a common experience. (See Stop and think: Adler's model of personality.) Adler (1973) was an early proponent of treating individuals within community settings and, as such, is sometimes considered the first community psychiatrist. Adler also founded the first child guidance clinics in Vienna. This move reflected his concern that problems should be tackled early to give children the best chance of a healthy adulthood (Adler, 1963). There are many Adlerian therapists, mainly in the United States; and they continue to publish their own research journal, *Individual Psychology*. They have developed brief therapies that have been shown to be effective (Carlson, 1989) and adopted Adlerian techniques for counselling individuals (Kern and Watts, 1993).

Stop and think

Adler's model of personality

We pointed out earlier (Chapter 1) that, when developing a model of personality, theorists will inevitably test their theory against their own experiences. This is easy to see from Adler's biographical details. In his early life, Adler experienced serious illness, accidents and the traumatic loss of a sibling who died in the bed next to him. He also experienced lack of academic success, although this was important to him; but through repeating a year at school and working very hard, he overcame his scholastic difficulties and went on to excel. It is not difficult to see how the concepts of inferiority and

striving for superiority fit within his experience. He was the second son and the third child in the family. His older brother appears to have been a more successful child than Adler was, being fitter and initially doing better at school. Adler also felt that because of his illnesses, his mother tried to pamper him; he felt that he had to work very hard to counteract this.

You may find it useful to carry out this exercise by considering other theorists. It may help you to examine why some theories are intuitively more appealing to you than others.

Carl Jung and analytic psychology

Are you an extravert? Are you outgoing and sociable, adapting easily to new situations, making friends easily and boldly striding through life? Perhaps you are more of an introvert; quieter and more reflective, enjoying your own company and less of a bold spirit. These personality descriptors were identified by Carl Jung. (See Profile: Carl Jung.) Here again, we have psychoanalytically based concepts that have become part of our everyday language.

Jung's model of the personality is quite unique, covering a wide range of behaviour and incorporating material from many other disciplines. Jung (1965) saw the psyche as a complex network of opposing forces in which the aim of development is to create harmony with the structures of the personality. He called the total personality the **psyche**. Jung adopted Freud's idea of psychic energy or libido as the motivating force behind our behaviour but used it in a much broader sense. He suggested that it was some hypothetical sort of life force that was much wider than purely sexual or aggressive drives. This **life-process energy** resulted from the conflicts between the different forces within the psyche. Every choice

we make involves some possible conflict, as we have previously discussed, and Jung felt that the number of potential conflicts within the structures of the psyche was infinite (Bennett, 1983). He termed this system of creating life-process energy within the psyche the **principle of opposites**. For example, he suggested that conscious and unconscious forces are continually opposed to each other and thereby create energy. He talked about love and hatred for the same person co-existing within the psyche. This theory may help account for the majority of murders being committed within relationships.

While he did not write much about the development of personality in childhood, he strongly believed that personality development continues throughout life. In this way he was an early proponent of lifespan development. He did not believe that only the past affected an individual's behaviour, seeing us as being influenced also by our future goals. This emphasis on understanding the future goals or purpose of behaviour is termed **teleology**. The endpoint of our development was thought by Jung to be **self-realisation**. He saw us as continuously working towards achieving our potential, our own unique nature; and in doing so, we come to accept ourselves. This sense of accepting oneself and feeling

Profile

Carl Jung

Carl Gustav Jung was born in 1875 in Switzerland. He was the only surviving son of a Protestant country pastor who had lost his faith and found life difficult. Jung was a solitary child, spending a lot of time on his own, thinking and reading. He appears to have had quite an emotionally deprived childhood. When he was 3, his mother went into hospital for several months, and Jung reported that this separation affected him profoundly. He said that it left him with a fundamental distrust of women, which was further reinforced by his mother's inconsistent attitudes towards him (Storr, 1973). Initially, he was lazy in school and used to pretend to faint in order to get out of doing things that he disliked. However, after overhearing his father say that he was worried that his son would achieve nothing in life, he made himself stop his fainting fits and engage with schoolwork. Later in life, he used this experience as an example of how the knowledge of the realities of life can help people overcome their neurotic behaviour. He went on to take a medical degree at the University of Basel and then trained as a psychiatrist with Eugen Bleuler, who specialised in working with patients suffering from schizophrenia and who actually invented the term 'schizophrenia'. In 1903, Jung married and eventually he and his wife had four sons and a daughter. His

wife trained as a Jungian therapist. In middle age, Jung had a long-lasting affair with a former patient, but his wife accepted the other woman, even having her as a regular guest for Sunday lunch.

Jung first wrote to Freud in 1906; they met in 1907 and spent 13 hours in discussion. Freud came to see Jung as his successor. However, Jung could not accept the Oedipus complex and other aspects of psychosexual development, and the two parted company in 1913. After his split with Freud, Jung went through a deep psychological crisis, withdrawing to his home in Zurich. He spent the next 6 years there, exploring his own unconscious in an extensive self-analysis. He still saw patients throughout this period and became well known as a psychoanalyst, with patients travelling from all over the world to visit him. By 1919, he had completed his own analysis, recovered from the break with Freud and was concentrating on developing his own theory. Jung travelled extensively, being very interested in the effects of culture on mental life. He was very well read in a huge range of subjects and continued to be interested in the occult and things spiritual. He remained based in Switzerland and died there at age 85 in 1961.

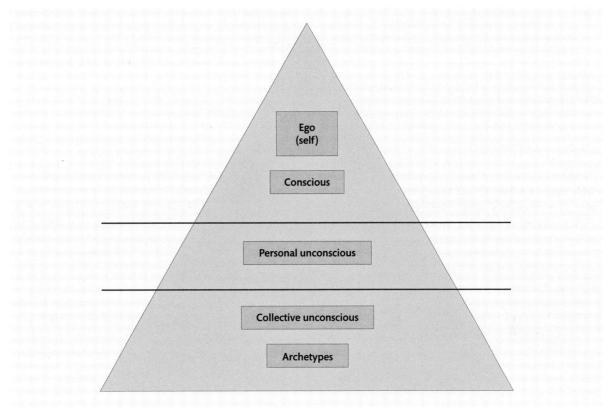

Figure 3.2 Jung's model of the psyche.

at peace with oneself is the endpoint of our development. Jung (1954) believed that this self-realisation could only be achieved later in life, as a considerable amount of life experience was required for its achievement.

Psychic energy could move in all directions within the psyche and might find expression in bizarre forms, such as hallucinations or unpredictable moods or even delusions. Borrowing terms from physics, Jung suggested that the psyche operates according to the **principle of equivalence**. Put simply, this means that if the activity increased in one part of the psyche it would decrease correspondingly in another part, and vice versa. If you become more focused on achieving success at work, you might become less focused on enjoying your social life. He also claimed that the **principle of entropy** operates in the psyche. This is a drive to create balanced energies across the psyche so that we express more of ourselves in our behaviour. An example might be of the party-loving student who starts to get bored by the constant social whirl and looks for some more meaningful, serious things to do. This example typifies Jung's idea that the development of our personality needs to be balanced to allow all the disparate parts that make up our psyche to come into harmony. One-sided development was thought to be very unhealthy. In current terms, Jung would

be a proponent of work–life balances, for example, seeing this as healthy.

Structures within the psyche

In outlining Jung's description of the psyche we are going to concentrate on four main aspects: the ego, the personal unconscious, the collective unconscious and archetypes (Figure 3.2).

Ego

The ego is described by Jung as being a unifying force in the psyche at the centre of our consciousness. Later writers sometimes call this structure the self. It contains the conscious thoughts and feelings related to our own behaviour and feelings, and memories of our previous experiences. The ego is responsible for our feelings of identity and continuity as human beings (Jung, 1965). By this we mean that you are aware that as a child, you were different in many ways, but there is still a sense of being uniquely you. In the future, you know that you may change, but there will still be an inner sense of your own identity.

Personal unconscious

The personal unconscious is next to the ego and contains all our personal experiences that have been blocked from our awareness because they are unacceptable in some way. This is the same conceptualisation of the unconscious that Freud outlined, containing repressed material that can be brought into our consciousness in psychoanalysis or hypnosis.

Collective unconscious

The collective unconscious lies deeper within the psyche (Jung, 1965). Jung observed that the delusions, hallucinations, fantasies, dreams and drawings of patients with schizophrenia were very similar. They were also similar to the myths and fantasies that appear in ancient cultures and in contemporary culture. They contained images of good versus evil as well as various conceptualisations of human fears, like fear of fire, falling, darkness and so on. Jung pointed out that every culture from the ancient Egyptians onwards has folklore consisting of good conquering evil, of devils and demons. Based on these observed similarities, he suggested that the collective unconscious is not a personal acquisition, that it goes beyond personal experience and has its origins in human evolutionary development. In other words, Jung suggested that the collective unconscious is innate. It is a repository of inherited instincts and what he termed archetypes or universal symbols or themes, going beyond personal experience. He suggested that we are born with fears of the unknown, fears of the dark, knowing about death and so on. He suggested that only some hereditary factor like the collective unconscious could adequately explain the phenomena. It is the stored memories of our human and even pre-human ancestry. No matter how unique each mind may be, Jung suggested that it still has striking similarities to other minds because of our shared collective unconscious. More significantly, he suggested that these innate ideas in our collective unconscious result in human beings as a species tending to organise their worlds in innately predetermined ways. He stressed the similarities in organisational structures and ideas in what appear to be very different cultures. Jung (1959) called these universal ideas that we are born with archetypes.

Archetypes

Archetypes are universal themes or symbols that lie with the collective unconscious in the psyche and under certain conditions may be projected onto our current experiences. Examples will make this easier to follow. Jung (1959) cites the concept of God as an archetype. He points out that in every culture, when individuals are placed in threatening or ambiguous situations with a lot of stressful uncertainty, they respond by appealing to some form of all-powerful being or God. The heightened levels of fear activate the archetype of God in the collective unconscious. We witness examples of this when there are modern disasters and many people lose their lives. We usually see thousands of people turning up to religious services, including many who do not normally go to church; when faced with this frightening and unexpected disaster, they somehow felt the need to attend some sort of religious ceremony. Jung would see this as a prime example of the God archetype. To quote Jung:

> **God is an absolute, necessary function of an irrational nature, which has nothing whatever to do with the question of God's existence. The human intellect can never answer this question, for the idea of an all-powerful divine being is present everywhere unconsciously if not consciously because it is an archetype.**
>
> (Jung, 1964, p. 68)

Jung (1964) described many other archetypes, and some examples are given in Table 3.3. Jung (1959) suggested

Table 3.3 Examples of archetypes (Jung, 1954, 1964)

Archetype	Description
Persona	The mask or role that we adopt to help us deal with other people. It helps us to disguise our inner feelings and respond in socially appropriate ways to others. We have personas for all our roles. It is largely an adaptive function but, when used to extremes, it may result in stereotypical behaviour.
Shadow	The dark sinister side of our nature, consisting of repressed material in our personal unconscious and universal images of evil from our collective unconscious. We never truly know the shadow side of ourselves, as it is too frightening for us to explore our potential to do harm or to think evil thoughts. It is expressed in unexplained moods such as uncontrollable anger, psychosomatic pain and desires to harm others and ourselves. Example: Dr Jekyll (persona) and Mr Hyde (shadow).
Anima	The feminine element in the male psyche, consisting of inherited ideas of what constitutes woman, derived from man's experience of women throughout evolution and their experience of their mother, the prototype for their female relationships. It consists of feminine qualities – emotionality, sensitivity, irrationality, vanity and moodiness.
Animus	The male element within the female psyche, which is similarly primarily derived from women's evolutionary experience and their experience of their father. These archetypes help males and females understand each other better. The animus has masculine qualities – reason, logic and social insensitivity.
Self	The potential that we all have to achieve the unique individuality that is within us, like Adler's goal of perfection. We reach it through a process of individuation, which entails creating balance within the psyche and of coming to accept oneself as one really is (Jung, 1959).

that these archetypes exert their influences not only in dreams and fantasies but also in real-life situations. For example, a man may project his anima archetype onto his relationship with a woman. He may need to see her as the universal mother or the ultimate expression of caring femininity, regardless of how she actually is. This results in him perceiving her initially as he would wish her to be rather than as she is. When experience leads to his misperceptions being uncovered, the relationship breaks down. The same argument would hold for a woman projecting her animus onto a male. (See Stop and think: Reflection on Jung.) Archetypes include the mother, the father, the child, the wise old man, the wife, the husband, the hero and many others. Jung argues that different archetypes exert their influence on us in different situations, leading us to having predetermined ways of thinking about situations and dealing with objects and events. Jung claimed that the self is somewhat different, as it may not be achieved by everyone and never occurs until middle age, although analysis could help. He gave the example of a man who, through analysis, comes to see that he always has to idealise his girlfriend and to ignore her faults. This realisation helps him to understand his relationship and to deal better with conflicts. He then begins to live more productively and to cope better, as he is more in touch with his own feelings and can consciously acknowledge these previously unconscious impulses. In this way his psyche is more in balance, and individuation of the self comes closer. Jung (1965) felt that there are individual differences in how people approach the development of selfhood, as reflected in their very different attitudes to life. This view resulted in his theory of personality types.

Jungian personality types

As we see in Jung's biography (Jung, 1971), he was initially very close to Freud and was thus upset by their split. In an attempt to understand the root of their interpersonal difficulties, he set himself the task of understanding the fundamental disagreement between Freud and Adler to see if this would shed some light on his differences with Freud. He took a patient's case history and analysed it from Freudian and Adlerian perspectives, thus producing two explanations.

These explanations, while being incompatible, both made some sort of sense in terms of explaining the underlying pathology of the patient. It seemed as if a neurosis could be understood in two different ways, depending on the theorist's perspective. Jung (1971) concluded that parts of both explanations were sound, and all the observations made by Freud and Adler were valid; however, they resulted because the two men saw the world differently as they had very different personalities. From this and clinical observations, Jung concluded that there must be at least two different personality types – one that focuses more on the external world, extraversion, and one that is more internally oriented, introversion.

Extraversion (though Jung spelled this *extroversion*) refers to 'an outgoing, candid and accommodating nature that adapts easily to a given situation, quickly forms attachments, and, setting aside any possible misgivings, often ventures forth with careless confidence into an unknown situation'. **Introversion** in contrast signifies 'a hesitant, reflective retiring nature that keeps itself to itself, shrinks from objects, is always slightly on the defensive and prefers to hide behind mistrustful scrutiny' (Jung, 1964).

He was careful to point out that individuals are never wholly one or the other but incorporate aspects of both, although usually one type predominates in certain aspects of an individual's functioning. Freud was predominantly an extravert while Adler was an introvert. Jung considered himself to be an introvert, although he was very different from Adler; hence he concluded that there must be significant differences within extraverts and introverts. In extraversion, Jung said, the flow of psychic energy is outward; that is, the contents of consciousness refer mainly to external objects in the world. In introversion, the contents of consciousness refer more to the individual themselves; that is, to what is within the person. Hence, an introvert and an extravert observing the same situation may form very different views. His feeling was that the dominant attitude was conscious and the inferior attitude was unconscious, so that the principle of opposites still holds. Neither personality type is thought to be healthier than the other, just different. To address the differences that he felt existed within groups of introverts and extraverts, Jung classified the ways in which people can relate to the world, suggesting that four approaches were possible.

(See Stop and think: Reflection on Jung.)

Stop and think

Reflection on Jung

Much is written in the popular press currently about the 'new man'. This is the male who is caring, sensitive, kind and not afraid to appear vulnerable at times and to express his finer emotions. How do you feel that this description relates to Jung's conception of anima? Could it be that current conceptions of the 'new man' are about allowing expression of the anima in male adult life? Is there anything similar relating to women?

- **Sensing** – This is where we experience stimuli without any evaluation. We register that it is light, for example, or that a man is walking up to our front door. We simply register that something is present.
- **Thinking** – This is interpreting stimuli using reason and logic, something we hope you are doing as you read this text, to develop your understanding of the material.
- **Feeling** – This involves evaluating the desirability or worth of what has been presented. For example, we might feel happy and full of anticipation as we now recognise that the man coming up the path is a postman bringing us a parcel.
- **Intuitive** – This is when we relate to the world with a minimum of interpretation and reasoning; instead we form hunches or have premonitions.

To quote from Jung, '*Sensation* tells you that something exists; *thinking* tells you what it is; *feeling* tells you whether it is agreeable or not; and *intuition* tells you whence it comes and where it is going' (Jung, 1968, p. 49). Jung describes thinking and feeling as being opposites, but he calls them both rational functions, as they both involve the cognitive processes we use to form conclusions or make judgements. Thinkers use logic and analysis, while feelers use values, attitudes and beliefs. Similarly, sensation and intuition are described as being irrational opposites. These are less planned activities but tend to happen more reflexively. Sensors respond reflexively to situations based on what they perceive to be happening with little reflection or evaluation, while the intuitor also responds reflexively, looking for meaning in terms of past or future events. From these two major attitudes, introversion and extraversion, and the four functions – sensing, thinking, feeling and intuiting – Jung developed a classification of 16 possible psychological types, but he focused on 8 types, as outlined in Table 3.4.

The shadow is a very important concept in a Jungian theory.
Source: Alamy Images/Asperra Images

There is some research evidence for Jung's personality types. A personality test, the Myers–Briggs Type Indicator (MBTI; Myers and McCaulley, 1985) was developed to measure Jungian personality types. It is used frequently in

Table 3.4 Jung's theory of psychological types

Extraverted types	Introverted types
Sensing type: Reality-oriented and typically shun thinking and contemplation. Act rather than think. Pleasure-seeking and very sociable. Keen to enjoy the good things in life, food, painting, literature, etc. Thought to be more typical of men.	**Sensing type:** Tend to be very sensitive and may often seem to overact to outside stimuli. May take innocuous comments from others and turn them into something sinister. Tend to be calm and quite passive. May be artistic.
Thinking type: Tries always to be objective and guided by the facts of the situation, repressing emotional responses and being guided by rules. These individuals may neglect the more spiritual and aesthetic side of their natures and neglect friendships.	**Thinking type:** Are very private people, often ill at ease socially. Tend to be intellectual and repress their feelings. Often find it difficult to express their ideas and feelings. They are very involved in their inner world and may appear cold and aloof.
Feeling type: Tend to be conventional. The expectations of other people strongly influence their feelings and behaviour. They are sociable, respecting authority and tradition. Jung suggested that women were more likely to be this type than men are.	**Feeling type:** Tend to be quiet, thoughtful and difficult to get to know. May seem quite mysterious. Not very involved with others but feel things very intensely. Jung felt this type was most common in women. Often better with animals than with people.
Intuitive type: Very creative individuals excited by what is new. Keen to exploit all opportunities. Tendency to follow their hunches rather than decide on the basis of facts. Politicians, speculators and wheeler-dealers thought to typify this type.	**Intuitive type:** May seem very withdrawn from the world and uninterested in it, appearing to be dreamers. May come up with unusual new ideas. Communicate poorly since their judgement functions (thinking and feeling) are relatively repressed.

occupational settings and in research studies, demonstrating that different personality types pursue different interests, report different memories and have different job preferences among other things (DeVito, 1985; Kuipers *et al.*, 2009).

Jung's conception of mental illness and its treatment

Jung saw mental illness as resulting from one-sided development in the psyche. He gave little detail about how this development might occur, rather providing clinical examples of adult problems. From examples, we have seen that this could be the male who has problems in relationships because of repressing his anima. This results in him being extremely insensitive to the feelings of other people. The extremely chauvinistic man would be an example of this, or the sort of person who never shows any emotion and considers the display of emotions to be unmanly.

Treatment methods

Like Freud, Jung used dream analysis and word association tests to help him to explore his patients' unconscious to locate where the imbalances were. While his use of word association was similar to Freud's, his understanding of the function of dreams and his style of analysis were different. Jung (1965) felt that dreams stem from both our personal unconscious and our collective unconscious and represent material that we have repressed as it is upsetting in some way. However, he claimed that dreams often represent the dreamer's attempt at solving problems in their lives and finding psychologically healthy ways forward. Dreams could also be compensatory in nature, with the fearful person dreaming that they are skydiving or climbing a cliff. Jung would analyse a series of dreams for any one patient to identify repeated themes. He made a distinction between everyday and archetypal dreams, being particularly interested in the latter. Archetypal dreams come from the collective unconscious. These are the more bizarre dreams that we have, often with strange symbolism. These tend to be very intense dreams, and sometimes the same dream may reoccur throughout a person's life, at times when they are stressed. Jung believed that interpreting these dreams helped uncover the patient's underlying fears. He used a **method of amplification** in his dream analysis. This involved the analyst and the patient identifying the significant symbols in the dream and focusing in on them to explore their possible meaning in ever-greater depth.

Jung (1964) also got his patients to produce paintings for him. He was not interested in the paintings as art but rather saw them as a way that patients could express their unconscious thoughts and feelings. Along with the patients, he would interpret the symbolism and the emotional content in the paintings. This was the first form of art therapy for patients and is still practised.

For Jung (1968), there were four stages in therapy: confession, elucidation, education and transformation. Firstly, the patient working with the therapist comes to admit to having problems, termed confession; then they come to understand the nature of their problems (elucidation). Next, the patient becomes educated about their problems and possible ways forward to develop their personality and gain more satisfaction from life (education). Finally, the patient comes to achieve balance between the opposing forces within their psyche; and they may achieve self-realisation, which, as we saw earlier, is the final goal of personality development for Jung.

Once Jung became established as an analyst, he took as his patients people who were not typically mentally ill as the term is normally understood. Rather, he concentrated on treating middle-aged people who were often very successful (his services were not cheap), but who were unsatisfied by their success and searching for something more in their lives. His aim was to get them in touch with their inner self, and know and accept their psyche with its conflicts, to achieve selfhood.

Evaluation of Jung's theory

We will now evaluate Jung's theory using the eight criteria identified previously (Chapter 1): description, explanation, empirical validity, testable concepts, comprehensiveness, parsimony, heuristic value and applied value.

Description

As a theory of personality, Jung's work does not describe how personality develops in any real detail. He was most interested in development of the personality in middle age; and his therapy aimed to assist his patients to achieve self-realisation, the final stage of personality development. The descriptions of behaviour provided by Jung are complex, as are the potential explanations for this behaviour. A lot of his work, like the collective unconscious and its related archetypes, is quite mystical. Rather than bringing order and simplicity to our understanding of behaviour so that the important issues are easily identified, Jung's theory is frequently confusing and very complex. Part of this complexity in description stems from his writing style, as it is often confused and difficult to follow, lacking a logical flow and almost resembling his free associations. In addition, he was extremely well read in a variety of disciplines, from Ancient Greek to eastern culture, and his work contains many obscure references.

Explanation

At times, Jung's work does seem to provide good explanations of behaviour. The concept of persona, for example, is a useful one, being broadly equivalent to the roles that we all have to play in different parts of our lives. As behaviour becomes more complex, however, the explanation is often less clear-cut. The concept of the shadow is another interesting idea, acknowledging the possibility for wrongdoing and dark thoughts within all of us. This is something that is rarely addressed by other theories – the human ability to perform evil deeds. However, the complexity of the psyche does mean that it is difficult to identify precisely why certain behaviours occur. In most instances, there can be multiple causes. Take the concept of love as an example. A man may be instantly attracted to a woman because of his anima – she fulfils his archetypal idea of woman – but the attraction could also be due to the influence of other archetypes, like the mother, wife, good woman and so on. As we saw with the example of religion and religious belief, Jung concluded that the whole concept of explanation was pointless. This is a rather circular argument. If behaviour is difficult to explain and/or commonly observed, it is simply because of the way we are wired. While this has some truth, it cannot adequately explain all individual differences in behaviour. Also, Jung claimed that the forces in the collective unconscious sometimes lead us to behave in very unpredictable ways, that behaviour is not deterministic, in that current behaviour is caused by previous behaviour; rather, some behaviour is produced by a **principle of synchronicity**. This means that two events may occur at the same time without one causing the other. For example, a woman dreams of her mother's death and then hears the next day that her mother has died. Clearly, dreaming about her mother's death did not cause the death, neither did the death cause her to dream about it. Jung did not feel that such an event is purely coincidence. The two events are related in a meaningful way. He suggested that somehow the archetypal death image in the woman's collective unconscious had knowledge of the mother's impending death and made this known in the woman's dream. The principle of synchronicity certainly adds a mystical element to psychological theorising that many have found attractive both within and outside psychology.

Empirical validity

From what we have discussed, it is clear that Jung's theory is difficult to test. Most research has concentrated on his theory of types (Carlson and Levy, 1973; Kilmann and Taylor, 1974; McPeek, 2008). The work on the MBTI (Myers and McCaulley, 1985) is long established and is still heavily used, particularly in organisational research, although it has been modified to improve its psychometric qualities. Two new functions, judging and perceiving, have been added to Jung's original 4, resulting in 16 possible personality types (Thorne and Gough, 1991).

Testable concepts

In terms of testable concepts, many of the concepts employed are difficult to define precisely and therefore impossible to

measure. Jung (1959) himself admitted that archetypes were impossible to define precisely as they were always changing over time and always had to be interpreted anew. As we have seen, Jung's personality types have been operationalised and measured with some success. This is particularly true of the concepts of introversion and extraversion, which Eysenck, a British personality psychologist, has examined with considerable success (as shown in Chapters 7 and 8).

Comprehensiveness

While Jung did address a huge range of phenomena, including religion, education, relationships, cultural issues, and even the occult, coverage was often quite superficial. Jung's work runs to 20 volumes, much of which has not been studied in detail by other psychologists.

Parsimony

Jung's theory is certainly not parsimonious. He describes a huge range of structures within the personality, many with overlapping functions, and it is unclear how they relate to observed behaviour. He uses a lot of different concepts to explain similar behaviour. If you become really angry and quite aggressive at something that seems quite innocuous, it could be the influence of your shadow, the unpredictable forces within your collective unconscious, the influence of one of many archetypes and so on. Jung makes no attempt to describe exactly how the archetypes exert their influence on behaviour and in what order. Are some more influential than others? He does not make this clear.

Heuristic value

Jung's theory has been influential in many disciplines – especially his work on spiritual concerns and religion, as he felt that spiritual concerns were the highest human values. He was popular with hippies in the last century as he advocated that individuals should strive to get in touch with their true selves. He felt that, in the west, we have focused too much on developing our rational powers and that we need to develop our spiritual side more and use techniques like meditation to assist us in this. Many of his ideas, such as the concept of and importance of balance within the individual, are more in line with eastern conceptions of personality and with eastern philosophies. While Jung's work has not stimulated a great deal of psychological research, in other disciplines like literature, history, art, anthropology and religious studies it has been and is still very influential. Jung has posed big questions – such as the nature of religion, religious belief, the concept of evil and the evolutionary influences – which psychology has not had the tools to address empirically, although this is changing as the discipline develops further.

Applied value

In relation to applied value, Jung's theory has been very influential. We have already discussed how it continues to provoke interesting debate in many disciplines other than psychology. For evidence of this, if you consult the Internet, you will find that Jung is very well represented across a range of disciplines. Practically, there is the development of the MBTI and its continued use in occupational testing. Eysenck adopted Jung's concepts of introversion and extraversion, as previously mentioned. Clinically, aspects of Jung's work have been influential. Many therapists still train and practise as Jungian analysts. His word association test has proved to be a useful tool for exploring the unconscious. He popularised discussion of the concept of self in psychology, and this was taken up by many subsequent theorists, as we shall see. His emphasis on a positive conceptualisation of human nature was in contrast to Freud and influenced many later theorists. He was the first to introduce a form of art therapy, as we have seen, and he was influential in developing Alcoholics Anonymous.

In therapy, Jung introduced the idea of shorter treatments – or brief therapies, as they have come to be called. His idea of complexes appears to provide such a valid description of an aspect of human personality that it has been incorporated into our everyday language, as have introversion and extraversion.

The psychology of Karen Horney

We discussed previously the ways in which Freud's conceptualisation of women is problematic. This issue led to our next theorist, Karen Horney, breaking from Freud and modifying aspects of his theory. Perhaps you know the term

'penis envy'? Horney devised this term in her attempt to develop a more female-friendly version of psychoanalysis, as we shall see; but she also developed her own description of personality types based on her critique of Freud and her experiences as a clinician. (See Profile: Karen Horney.)

Essentials of Horney's theoretical position

Horney (1950) found her own psychoanalysis disappointing, and this led her to question Freud's conception of neuroses. As we have seen, for Freud neurosis was an outgrowth of a person's inability to cope with their sexual impulses and strivings. Horney could not accept this as a valid explanation of her own or her patients' neurosis. It seemed to her that neurosis was based primarily upon disturbed human relationships and that these frequently originated in disturbed relationships between parents and their children. She suggested that poor parenting resulted in the child's personality not developing healthily, and this resulted in the child having problems later in their life. She strongly believed that Freud's psychosexual theory was too limited to account for all human psychological disturbance. She felt that cultural and social relationship factors played a crucial role in personality development. Horney believed, on the basis of her clinical observations, that sexual disturbance and neurosis were often linked, but that neurosis, based upon faulty personality development, produced the sexual disturbance. For Freud, it was the impaired sexual functioning that produced the neurosis.

Horney agreed with Freud that anxiety was produced by conflicts within individuals and that anxiety-provoking

Profile

Karen Horney

Karen Horney was born in Eilbek, Germany, in 1885. Her father was a Norwegian sea captain and her mother was Dutch. Her father was very strict and believed that women were innately inferior; hence, he opposed her wish to pursue higher education. He was at sea a great deal, so her mother was able to support Horney's wish to be educated. Horney felt that she was unattractive, although her mother and grandmother were acknowledged beauties; so, to compensate, she threw herself into her studies. She was the only woman in her medical class and excelled, but she felt that she had to be more competent than her male colleagues to be accepted. She married a very successful businessman. Horney had three daughters, but, unusually for the time, she continued to work and to study. The stresses of this and the death of her mother resulted in

her developing what was called neurosis and becoming depressed. (The term 'neurosis' is used to describe disorders of the personality within psychoanalysis.) This led her to enter psychoanalysis with Dr Karl Abraham, a disciple of Freud. She found psychoanalysis disappointing but was intrigued by the process. She went on to train as a psychoanalyst and began to question both Freud's emphasis on the sexual instincts and his lack of focus on the social relationships of his patients and the cultural conditions within which they lived. In 1932, Horney emigrated to the United States and lived there until her death from cancer in 1952. She did not have an easy time in the States, being rejected by many other psychoanalysts because of her criticisms of Freud. She was a founding editor of the *American Journal of Psychoanalysis*.

experiences in childhood could result in maladjustment within the personality. Horney (1977) also felt that each culture produces its own unique set of fears in its people. This might be a fear of nature in societies prone to natural disasters such as volcanoes, hurricanes and the like, or it might be culturally produced fears. She suggested that western cultures, with their emphasis on competition and success, produce fear of failure and inferiority feelings to which all the members of the culture are susceptible. In some eastern cultures the fear might be of losing face or of bringing dishonour to the family. Horney suggests that the healthy person can adjust to these fears associated with their culture and make the best of it by using the defence mechanisms that Freud described along with some additional ones that Horney identified. However, the neurotic individual cannot adjust to these fears, as they cannot use their defence mechanisms adaptively. This view fits in with Freudian theory to this point. Horney (1945) suggested that, in addition, problems and fears are created by the way we interact with each other in our social lives. She placed a heavy emphasis on the role of socialisation and culture in our development and de-emphasised the more biological instinctual approach of Freud. Much of Horney's work focuses on the development of the abnormal personality, and from this the requirements for healthy development are inferred.

The development of the personality and the neurotic personality

For Horney (1977), healthy personality development is the result of warm, loving, consistent parenting, where the child is respected and supported. Each child is considered to be special with a unique potential to become what Horney called its **real self**. She had a positive view of human nature, seeing the real self as the ultimate expression of the individual's abilities and talents. She also saw humans as a social species and believed that part of the expression of the real self involves being able to relate easily to others and feel comfortable in the world with a real sense of belonging (Horney, 1950). However, many children do not experience this ideal parenting and go on to become psychologically disturbed, developing what Horney called neurotic personalities or neurosis.

For Horney, neurosis typically originates in disturbed relationships between parents and their children. Horney (1945) suggested that inconsistencies in parenting, over-permissive or extremely strict parenting styles, a lack of respect for the needs of the child, indifference or too much attention, or having to take sides in parental disputes, hostile atmospheres, too much or too little responsibility, broken promises and isolation from other children and lack of a social life were all very damaging to a child, and promoted the development of neurosis. She strongly

believed that behaviour was multiply determined, so that several factors combined to produce psychological disturbance (neurosis). When the child experiences some of these negative circumstances, what Horney termed **basic anxiety** is created in the child. Basic anxiety is described as a feeling of being isolated and helpless in a potentially hostile world. Such children feel their social environment is unfair, unpredictable, begrudging and merciless. They see themselves as having no power to influence situations and tend to have low self-esteem. When basic anxiety develops, it is accompanied by feelings of *insecurity*, as the child's world is a very unpredictable place lacking consistent behaviour from adult carers. Such children also tend to feel *isolated*, as their needs are not being met. They feel that no one understands them, making the world seem a lonely place. These feelings are frequently accompanied by feelings of *distrust* and *hostility* towards others. To help them cope, such children use **defensive attitudes**. These are protective devices that temporarily help alleviate pain and make the child feel safer. Hence they are used to survive these feelings of insecurity, loneliness, distrust and hostility (Horney, 1945). Horney described these defensive attitudes as neurotic needs designed to make the individual's environment a safer place. Neurotic needs can be distinguished from normal needs by their **compulsiveness**, their **rigidity**, their **indiscriminate usage** and the fact that they are **unconscious** (Horney, 1945). It is the last criterion that is sometimes difficult for observers to comprehend fully. The individual with neurotic needs is unaware that they have these needs, although it may be very apparent to observers. The observer may find it hard to comprehend that such individuals are truly unaware of how they interact with others and of the choices they make as they continue to repeat the same mistakes.

The child's energies are focused on the fulfilment of their neurotic needs as a defence against their basic anxiety, so they become less and less in touch with their real feelings and thoughts, becoming alienated from their true selves. Although they are driven by their neurotic needs, they still need to develop a sense of identity and worth as a person to be able to function. Horney (1977) suggests that they create **idealised selves**. These images portray them as powerful and successful, perfect human beings. They are driven to become these idealised images, feeling that they should be successful, should have a loving relationship, should always be treated fairly, should not be dependent on anyone, should like everyone, should not need anyone and so on. Horney calls these compulsions originating in the idealised self the **tyranny of the shoulds**. If only the person could attain these ideals, then all their inner conflicts with their related pain and anxiety would disappear. This belief explains why neurotic individuals cling onto their idealised selves. Horney (1945) described 10 neurotic needs and outlining these will help to make it clearer (Figure 3.3).

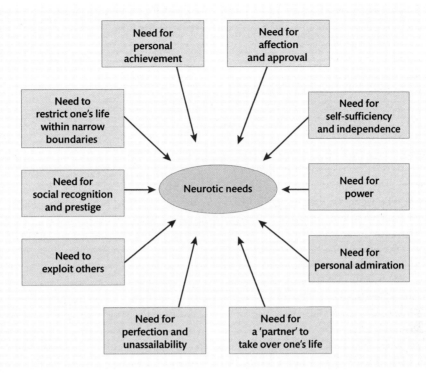

Figure 3.3 Horney's (1945) 10 'neurotic needs'.

The neurotic need for affection and approval

Horney observed that we all prefer to be liked and approved of, especially by people whose opinions we value. However, neurotic individuals show an indiscriminate hunger for affection, regardless of whether the other person cares for them or not. They need everyone to like them and approve of them. This makes them very sensitive to criticism. The neurotic individual cannot say no to anyone, for fear of being criticised. They find it difficult to express their wishes or ask a favour in case they are refused or thought badly of. They *should* be loved by everyone.

The neurotic need for a 'partner' to take over one's life

Many neurotic individuals are overly dependent on others. They feel lonely and inadequate without a partner in their life. They need to be looked after and cannot function happily on their own. These individuals are incapable of a normal relationship that involves mutual caring, sharing and unconditional love, as they are too dependent. Women seem to be more prone to developing this condition in western cultures. They *should*/must have a partner to feel complete.

The neurotic need to restrict one's life within narrow boundaries

Neurotic individuals seldom take risks. Basically, they are afraid of failure, so they stick to that of which they know

they are capable. They may feel safe only when they are living a highly circumscribed life, where routine and orderliness are paramount. With such individuals, you can perhaps tell the days of the week by the food they eat as their routine never changes, they holiday in the same place and so on. They may say that it is because they like it, but their resistance to trying anything else suggests that they like it because it is predictable and therefore safe. Things *should* always be the same and therefore safe.

The neurotic need for power

Horney saw ambition and striving to better oneself as normal; however, she suggested that, in healthy individuals, the pursuit of power tended to be associated with improving the lot of their family, professional group, country or some worthy cause. She identified a striving for power in neurotic individuals that was different from normal ambition. Power-oriented neurotics need power to protect themselves from their own underlying feeling of helplessness. This leads them to behave in very predictable ways. They do not ask others for help, in case they appear weak. They believe that they should be able to master any situation and control all their relationships, as they are superior to others. They are extremely manipulative, although they may disguise these tendencies by pretending to be generous. They have to be right all the time in their interactions with others and in any conflict situations. They also avoid unpredictable situations. They *should* always be in control and on top.

The neurotic need to exploit others

Exploitative neurotic individuals are hostile and distrustful. They assume that other people are also out to exploit them, so they feel safe only if they have got in first and are exploiting the other. Such individuals lead a parasitic existence, going through life expecting others to do them favours, share ideas and so on but never reciprocating. They believe that they deserve good things to happen to them. If things go wrong, other people are always to blame (Horney, 1950). The neurotic individual *should* get what they want and stay ahead of the game.

The neurotic need for social recognition and prestige

The healthy person likes to be popular and have their accomplishments recognised; but it is not the main focus of their lives, in the way it is for the neurotic individual. Everything from their friendships to their houses, cars, jobs, etc. is judged in terms of its prestige value. Here the neurotic individual's primary fear is loss of status. We can see how advertisers play to this neurotic need. The recent mobile phone advert that suggested that your old-model handset was a social embarrassment, 'letting you down', is a prime example of this. The neurotic individual *should* be admired and treated as a person of importance.

The neurotic need for personal admiration

Horney suggested that many neurotics are full of self-contempt and self-loathing; to avoid these feelings, they are driven to create an ideal image of themselves. They deny any faults in themselves and are unconsciously striving to seem perfect. The character Bree in the television series *Desperate Housewives* is a prime example. She sees herself as the perfect housewife, mother, wife and so on, yet it is apparent to viewers that this is far from the case. The neurotic individual *should* be admired as they are perfect.

The neurotic need for personal achievement

Horney (1977) suggests that it is normal to want to strive to be the best in one's chosen occupation or in sport, but that neurotic individuals of this type are characterised by indiscriminate ambition. They strive to excel in too many areas, as they want and need to be best at everything. As this goal is unrealistic, they develop a hostile attitude towards others, and they unconsciously wish to prevent others from being successful. Their own success is important; but if they cannot excel, they can at least feel superior to others by 'bringing down' their opponents. They put their energies into undermining others and trying secretly to sabotage their chances of success. Such individuals have a hostile attitude to others. It is not so much that they must succeed, but that others *should* not succeed.

The neurotic need for self-sufficiency and independence

Horney recognised that most healthy people have periodic needs for privacy and solitude. However, some neurotic individuals are permanently estranged from others. They seek solitude and resist becoming close to anyone and thus keep their aura of personal superiority. They *should* not need anyone.

The neurotic need for perfection and unassailability

This neurotic need originates in childhood, with authoritarian parents who apply excessively high standards to their children's behaviour. The children claim to adopt their parents' values, but there is a gap, of which they appear to be unconscious, between their values and how they actually behave. Horney (1950) suggested that, for such individuals, knowing about moral values is enough for them to see themselves as 'good' people. They are very sensitive to any criticism (for example, 'I know about morals and I *should* be judged as a moral person').

However, the gap between their idealised selves and their **actual selves** becomes more apparent as adults. They should be a success at work, but they have failed to get the last two promotions and so on. This discrepancy between the idealised and the real self leads the individual to experience self-hate with accompanying feelings of inferiority and guilt. Horney (1950) explains that, while the individual is aware of the outward results of their self-hate, the inferiority feelings and the guilt, they are not aware that they themselves have caused these feelings by their unconscious comparisons of the actual and idealised selves. Self-hate is an unconscious process, and rather than examine their unconscious motivations, neurotic individuals tend to blame other people, fate or situational factors for their failings. Horney describes neurosis as being relatively common in western cultures but in varying degrees. She described how neurotic needs are combined within individuals to form personality types. These are summarised in Table 3.5.

Defence mechanisms

Horney (1977) agreed with Freud about the way that all individuals use defence mechanisms to protect themselves from anxiety and to maintain their self-esteem. However, based on her clinical work, she felt that neurotic individuals developed additional defences to help them cope with their inner conflicts and disturbed relationships. She described the following seven additional defence mechanisms, which she felt that neurotic personalities used to project their feelings and shortcomings onto others. She called this defensive

Table 3.5 Horney's personality types and their style of dealing with people

Personality type	Description	People style
Compliant types	Desperately need other people – self-effacing, submissive and devalue their own abilities; cannot tolerate any criticism; need to fit in, live within restricted boundaries to feel safe.	Moving towards people
Aggressive types	Need power, social recognition, prestige, admiration and to achieve. Believe that others are essentially hostile and untrustworthy. Believe in the survival of the fittest. Seem tough and unemotional but poor at relationships.	Moving against people
Detached types	Need self-sufficiency, perfection and unassailability. Very secretive, solitary, feel that others do not understand them and keep themselves aloof.	Move away from people
Healthy personality	The other three personality trends are present, but they complement each other as healthy individuals are flexible. Have confidence in their abilities, trust other people, are secure in their selfhood.	Adopt all three styles when appropriate – adaptable and flexible

process **externalisation**, and all of its mechanisms are used for self-deception to protect the individual from their basic anxiety (see Figure 3.4).

Blind spots

The blind spot defence mechanism allows painful experiences to be denied or ignored because they are at odds with the person's idealised self. The neurotic individual remains completely unaware of the contradictions in their behaviour – between what they say they believe in and what they do. An example might be the individual who presents themselves as honest and upright and is very critical of individuals' wrongdoing, but who regularly takes stationery from work to meet his family's needs. He condemns stealing but does not see what he is doing as theft from his employer.

Compartmentalisation

In using compartmentalisation, the neurotic individual copes with their anxiety by separating incompatible needs within themselves. For example, they separate their beliefs and actions into categories so that they do not appear inconsistent with each other. A historical example was that of the many white South Africans who were devout Christians, yet were also supporters of apartheid without appearing to see any inconsistency there. The white South African frequently achieved this compartmentalisation by believing that black South Africans were different from them: they were childlike, or they needed to be ruled; they could not be trusted with power and so on. Their Christian charity was in one box, reserved for people like them, and black South Africans were in another.

Rationalisation

Rationalisation is the defence where individuals ward off the anxiety associated with a particular situation by offering plausible but inaccurate excuses for their conduct. The extremely unemotional, tough individual caught with suspiciously watery eyes at a colleague's retirement presentation

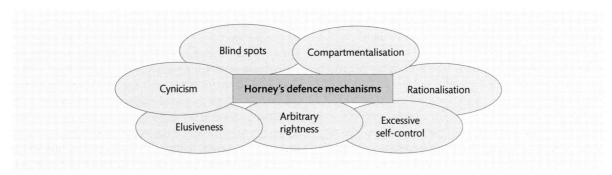

Figure 3.4 Horney's (1977) defence mechanisms.

Stop and think

Exploration of our own neurotic needs

Horney (1950) suggested that we all have some degree of neurotic needs. She felt that taking the opportunity to explore these needs was one way of coming to understand ourselves better and developing our real selves. She suggested that we focus on one of the following scenarios and write down how we felt in the situation. This exercise is purely for you, so try to be honest about how you felt and what you said to yourself about the other people involved.

1   Recall a time when you asked for something that was really unrealistic to expect to get or to be allowed to do and you became upset when you did not get it or it did not happen.

2   Recall how you felt when you agreed to do something that you really did not want to do.

3   Recall a time when you were very critical of someone else because they violated your standards of right and wrong.

4   Recall a time when your pride was hurt.

When you have finished, reflect on what you have written. Are you displaying some features of the tyranny of the shoulds? I know that I do if I complete this exercise honestly. It can tell us a lot about how we see the world.

---

who claims to have something in his eye might be one example of this.

Excessive self-control

The mechanism termed excessive self-control is used by individuals who will not allow their emotions free expression. They have to keep their emotions in check at all times. They use their willpower either consciously or unconsciously to keep conflicting emotions under control. Such an individual may proudly say that they never get angry. The reality is that they do not allow themselves to express their anger; it does not fit with their idealised image of themselves, so it is suppressed. Horney (1945) describes the way that such individuals seek to remove all spontaneity from their lives. They are wary of drinking alcohol for fear of losing control, and many have a profound fear of having anaesthetics for operations as this implies the ultimate loss of control.

Arbitrary rightness

Arbitrary rightness is a protective mechanism whereby individuals are convinced that they are invariably correct in all their judgements. The reality is that they are full of self-doubt and indecision but cannot tolerate these feelings, so they dogmatically assert that they are right in all situations and cannot be swayed by rational argument. This person always has to be right and always has to have the last word.

Elusiveness

The defence mechanism termed elusiveness involves the person refusing to take a view on anything or express a definite opinion. In this way, they can never be shown to be wrong and criticised by others. They always sit on the fence and often attempt to confuse the truth of the situation. They are impossible to pin down to a statement; they either deny having said it, or say that they have been misinterpreted. They also do not report things clearly; there is always some confusion and lack of detail. Some politicians seem prone to using this defence mechanism.

Cynicism

Cynicism is the defence in which the person believes in nothing. They have no positive expectations of others or situations, so therefore they cannot be disappointed. Such individuals deny the worth of moral values and mock others who uphold these values.

Penis envy and female masochism

Horney's work was important historically, as it marked the start of the orientation of social values towards the equality of women. Horney (1993) pointed out that psychoanalysis was the creation of a male mind, Freud's, and that almost all of the subsequent theorists developing his ideas have also been male; as a result, she felt that their understanding of women was likely to be limited. She took particular umbrage with Freud's conception of penis envy and the related concept of female masochism.

Freud (1913/1950) claimed that the most upsetting discovery for little girls was that boys have a penis while they do not. He claimed that this was a turning point in the girl's life. The girl who is developing normally eventually accepts that she will never have a penis and transfers this wish into the wish to have a child, although she is still left with a sense of loss and inferiority compared with males

(Abrahams, 1927). Her body is deficient, and therefore she has a sense of being a lesser being and envies those who possess a penis; hence, the term **penis envy**. Freud claims that the woman's penis envy becomes apparent through her wish to have a child, particularly a son; her happiness during pregnancy is seen as the symbolic gratification of the possession of a penis. Delays in producing the child are said to be due to the mother's reluctance to be separated from the penis (child). Further, when women are experiencing conflicts with males or seen to be in competition with men, these are interpreted as being the ultimate results of penis envy. What Freud is claiming is that women basically envy men. Many female character traits are attributed to penis envy. For example, women's inferiority feelings are interpreted as an expression of contempt for their own sex because of their lack of a penis. Modesty in women in Freud's time was seen as a wish to hide their deficiency. Freud (1901/1965) claimed that, as a result of lacking a penis, women were envious and jealous of men. Women might display this by trying to do better than men or by striving to be independent of men. Freud pointed out that young girls sometimes wish to be boys or to be able to urinate like boys and often display tomboyish behaviour.

Horney (1993) vehemently argues against this Freudian interpretation. She asserts that what girls and women want is not the literal penis, but the attributes that go along with the male identity in our society: freedom, independence, respect and so on. She points out that the psychoanalytic view was developed by men and, crucially, that they were basing their assumptions and deductions on neurotic women. She felt that the characteristics that were true of neurotic women were also true of neurotic men. Further, she suggested that explanations like penis envy allow neurotic women to avoid taking any responsibility for their disturbed behaviour. It is much easier for a woman to think that she is nasty to her husband because unfortunately she was born without a penis and envies him for having one rather than to think that she has some nasty personality traits. For Horney (1993), culture primarily provides the explanation for wishes by women to possess so-called masculine traits. Here, she agreed with Adler that the apparent wish to be a man, as sometimes expressed by women, is most likely to be a wish for the qualities and privileges that men have in society. Women actually want some of the power that men traditionally have had.

Freud (1907/1961) also claimed that women are masochistic by nature and even when masochism occurs in males that it is associated with female fantasies. By female masochism, he meant that women are biologically programmed to get satisfaction from enduring pain. As evidence, he cited menstruation and the pain of childbirth as being satisfying experiences for women. Women were also seen to tolerate sex passively and even to get some pleasure from it though they are not sexual creatures. This masochism was thought to generalise to all aspects of women's lives, as it was suggested that women gain pleasure from self-denial and submissiveness.

Horney (1993) did not deny that there are instances of what might appear to some as female masochism, where women may appear to get pleasure from pain or from self-denial generally, but she did deny that it is biologically determined. She suggested that it is largely cultural. Social attitudes assume that males are superior, and social convention requires women to be more dependent and compliant than males. Women undertake caring roles within the family, which often means that they demonstrate altruistic behaviour, putting the needs of their children or partners before their own. This is the behaviour that Horney said Freudians define as masochistic. Horney denied that any woman enjoys the pain of childbirth; she asserted that women do not dwell on the pain, but rather focus on the joy of the new child. It is the latter that gives them pleasure, and the pain is merely an unavoidable accompaniment. The current popularity of elective Caesarean sections and epidural anaesthetics might attest to women's lack of enjoyment of labour pains. Horney suggested that males might in fact envy women because of their ability to have children and their nurturing roles but that this envy is disguised and appears in a devalued form in labelling females masochistic. (See Stop and think: Horney's treatment approach.)

Evaluation of Horney's theory

We will now evaluate Horney's theory using the eight criteria identified previously (Chapter 1): description, explanation, empirical validity, testable concepts, comprehensiveness, parsimony, heuristic value and applied value.

Description

Horney's theory provides only a general description of normal personality development. Horney is one of the easiest personality theorists to read. She writes very clearly and describes the various concepts very well. Her description of the types of neurotic needs and the types of adult personality, including neurotic personalities, is very clear and easy to follow and intuitively makes sense. Her clinical examples are also clear and easy to follow. Her descriptions of additional defence mechanisms add significantly to Freud's work and have gained fairly wide acceptance among psychotherapists.

Explanation

While real attempts are made to explain the development of both the healthy and the problematic personality types, the explanation tends to be at a very general level. It is imprecise about exactly what constitutes effective parenting, for example, providing only general descriptions that are of limited value. The details provided about neurotic personality development are again fairly general. While Horney provides good detailed explanations of what constitutes neurotic needs, she does not explain how the individual needs relate specifically to particular developmental experiences. Perhaps the most original part of her theory is the explanation of the idealised and actual self and the discrepancy between the two. This is something that later theorists have developed further. Her defence mechanisms also provide good explanations of some commonly observed behaviour styles. The way that she presented alternative explanations to the Freudian conception of women and the nature of female masochism provided useful challenges to male-dominated psychoanalytic theorising and provoked a debate that still continues. For further discussion of the feminist perspective, see Caplan (1984), Westkott (1986) and Minsky (1996).

Empirical validity

There is very little research designed to test Horney's theorising, although some supportive evidence has come from other areas. The tyranny of the shoulds has been adopted by the American cognitive therapist, Albert Ellis, and we will consider his work on this in detail later (Chapter 5). There is some supporting evidence in cognitive therapy for this concept, as we shall see later, and for Horney's description of the nature of neurotic needs. Similarly, other theorists, such as the American Carl Rogers, have adopted her concepts of idealised and actual self, and tools have been developed to measure the discrepancy between the two, as we shall see (Chapter 6) when we look at Rogers' work.

A measure of extreme competitiveness has been developed and linked to some of the characteristics that Horney suggested are linked to it (Ryckman *et al.*, 1994; 1997; Houston *et al.*, 2002).

Testable concepts

In terms of testable concepts, with the exception of extreme competitiveness, Horney's concepts are generally too difficult to measure precisely. Horney – like Freud, Jung and Adler – was trained as a clinician and did not have the training to conduct the research that might have supported her theorising. If concepts made clinical sense, then they were deemed to be useful, although, as we have seen, other theorists have adopted some of her theoretical concepts and begun to test them empirically.

Comprehensiveness

In terms of normal personality development, Horney's is not a very comprehensive theory as it focuses more on abnormal development. It is a more comprehensive theory than Freud's in terms of defining different types of neurotic personality, and she added to Freud's defence mechanisms. Her theorising also incorporated social and cultural factors, and introduced the concepts of actual and idealised self.

Parsimony

Horney's is a fairly complex theory and covers a lot of material, particularly about the development of the neurotic personality and how it operates; the theory is parsimonious in this respect. However, in terms of the development of the normal personality, some of the detail and complexity is missing, and it is perhaps too parsimonious here.

Heuristic value

Horney's work has been and continues to be of great interest to other theorists and clinicians, although she does not always receive the credit that her theorising would seem to merit. She was an early contributor to the humanistic

Stop and think

Horney's treatment approach

Horney believed that the root of her patients' problems lay in disturbed interpersonal relationships caused by difficulties in their developmental experiences. Like Freud, she utilised free association and dream analysis, but she interpreted them in terms of the disturbed interpersonal relationships that her patients were currently experiencing. She felt that the patient, when interacting with the psychoanalyst, would display the difficulties they had with other relationships, and she used this knowledge to help patients to understand their problems. For her the relationship between patient and therapist was thus a

crucial part of therapy, something acknowledged in most of the current therapeutic approaches. She felt that it was important to be honest with patients, so she would confront them when she did not approve of their behaviour or when she thought they were being dishonest. For her the patients needed to learn what was unacceptable in relationships, and in this way they could come to understand the nature of their neurotic conflicts. Only when the patient gave up their illusions about themselves could they come to find their true selves. This approach is very different to the detached approach advocated by Freud.

psychology movement, with her emphasis on the uniqueness and value of each individual and her focus on the development of the self. Later feminist theorists found her challenges to Freud about the nature of women valuable, and debate on this issue continues, as mentioned previously.

Applied value

Again here, the applied value of Horney's work was considerable – although not always acknowledged by those who followed her and adopted her ideas. Modern cognitive therapy owes a great debt to her, as does Rogers' person-centred therapy, as we shall see (Chapter 6). She also provoked debate within psychotherapy about treatment approaches with her emphasis on the importance of the relationship between patient and therapist and her focus on problems in the patient's life.

Final comments

Freud worked with a number of people, and some of these people disagreed with his theories and sought to develop their own. In this chapter you have been introduced to Adler's individual psychology, Carl Jung's analytic psychology and Karen Horney's approach to personality. You should also be able to evaluate each of these theories critically.

Summary

- Adler developed a theory called individual psychology to reflect the essential unity that he felt was in the individual's personality, as total or indivisible entity is one of the meanings of 'individual'.
- Adler suggested that all human beings suffer both psychological and social inferiority feelings, beginning at birth and continuing throughout our childhood, owing to the helplessness of the human infant. To compensate for it, we all strive for superiority. If the adjustment is unsuccessful, we may end up with either an inferiority complex or a superiority complex.
- Within Adler's theory, the attitude of parents, siblings and our birth order all contribute to the ways in which our personality develops. They provide us with role models for the main tasks in life, work, friendship and love. From this, we develop our attitude towards life. Adler termed this our style of life.
- According to Adler, the neurotic personality is associated with the development of inferiority or superiority complexes.
- Adler maintained that healthy development requires social interest. This is defined as social feeling or community feeling that motivates individuals to help others.
- Adler outlined four personality types: the ruling type, the avoiding type, the getting type and the socially useful type. This last one was the healthy option.
- Adler modified Freud's treatment approach. For Adler, psychological illness occurred as a result of the patients' pursuing a faulty lifestyle. Once patients understood their faulty lifestyle, they could be helped to rekindle their social interest and develop a healthy lifestyle.
- Carl Jung developed a model of the personality that he called the psyche. It was a complex structure of opposing forces (principle of opposites), which created the life-process energy that motivates our behaviour.
- Jung believed that development continues throughout adulthood but did not pay much attention to personality development in childhood, stating that the endpoint of personality development is the achievement of self-realisation and that this demands considerable life experience so cannot occur before middle age.
- Jung argued that our behaviour is motivated by our future goals (teleology) as well as by our past experiences.
- Jung argued that our psyche operates according to the principle of equivalence and the principle of entropy.
- Jung described the psyche as complex and including the ego, personal unconscious, collective unconscious and a range of archetypes. Archetypes include gods, the persona, the shadow, anima and the animus and the self.
- Jung developed a theory of personality types based on two fundamental personality types: extraversion and introversion. He suggested that these two personality types interact with the world in four ways: sensing, thinking, feeling and intuition. The Myers–Briggs Type Indicator measures Jung's personality types.
- Mental illness, according to Jung, is caused by imbalance within the psyche. To treat mental illness, Jung used word association tests, dream analysis and painting to explore the patient's unconscious. There were four stages in therapy: confession, elucidation, education and transformation.
- Karen Horney developed her own version of psychoanalytic theory that included emphasis on the role played by cultural and social factors in personality development. She suggested that as well as the conflicts created within our personality as described by Freud, each society has its own specific fears (fear of failure in western culture).
- Horney maintained that the endpoint of personality development is the creation of the real self. For normal development, warm, consistent parenting is necessary so that the child can then become their real self.
- Horney's main focus was on the development of neurotic personalities. The origin of neurosis is disturbed

relationships with the parents, which creates basic anxiety in the child and is accompanied by feelings of insecurity. To protect themselves, children develop neurotic needs that are compulsive, rigid and used indiscriminately and are unconscious. These needs use up the child's energies, and they become distanced from their real selves. To further protect themselves, they develop an idealised self. They are driven to try to become their idealised self (tyranny of the shoulds).

- Horney outlined 10 neurotic needs that form the basis for three unhealthy (neurotic) personality types: compliant types, aggressive types and detached types.
- Horney suggested that in healthy personality development, the three trends in the neurotic personality types are present, but healthy individuals can respond flexibly to situations.

- Horney outlined seven new defence mechanisms to add to Freud's. These were used by neurotic individuals to project their shortcomings onto other people (externalise). These were blind spots, compartmentalisation, rationalisation, excessive self-control, arbitrary rightness, elusiveness and cynicism.
- Horney challenged Freud's view of penis envy and attacked Freud's conception of female masochism.
- Horney's treatment approach was very different from traditional psychoanalysis in that she felt the patient's problem was caused by disturbed relationships; consequently, she used her relationship with the patient over time to explore their interpersonal difficulties.
- Outline evaluations of all the theories are provided to guide your study using the same criteria as described previously (Chapter 1).

Connecting up

This chapter outlines the work of a number of psychoanalytic theorists who followed on chronologically from the Freudian theory outlined in Chapter 2.

We discuss the influence of birth order and of family size on intelligence in Chapter 13.

Critical thinking

Discussion questions

- Based on your own family position and your life experiences, what is your assessment of Adler's theories of birth order? Is there research evidence to support Adler's views?
- Adler (1927) emphasised the effect of birth order, claiming that it contributed significantly to the development of an individual's style of life. Consider these famous people. How well does Adler's theory reflect what we know about these people?

  - First-borns: Bill Clinton, Hillary Clinton, Winston Churchill, Oprah Winfrey, Mikhail Gorbachev, Albert Einstein, Steven Spielberg, J. K. Rowling, Bruce Willis, Richard Branson.
  - Youngest children: Jim Carrey, Cameron Diaz, Rosie O'Donnell, Dannii Minogue, Eddie Murphy.
  - Only children: Frank Sinatra, Elvis Presley, Robert De Niro, Robin Williams, Natalie Portman, Leonardo da Vinci, Tiger Woods.

- How adequate an explanation for human motivation is the concept of striving for superiority? Would you say that competition within a society is bad?

- Is there any evidence for the existence of the collective unconscious?
- Keep a dream diary for several nights. This involves keeping pen and paper by your bedside and making a point of noting down your dreams as soon as you awaken. Is there any pattern to your dreams? Can you identify any archetypal dreams?
- Can you identify which attitude is dominant in your personality? Do you think Jung's model gives a realistic description of personality types, or do you think that our personality is more determined by the situations in which we find ourselves?
- How realistic do Horney's personality types seem to be, based on the people that you know?
- What do you feel about the validity of the concept of penis envy? Can Horney be criticised for not being radical enough in her critique of psychoanalysis?
- Based on your own behaviour and the results of your self-reflection on the tyranny of the shoulds, how valid do you feel this concept is?
- How valid is Jung's approach to religion?
- How adequately do Jung, Adler and Horney explain human motivation?

Essay questions

- Critically examine the contribution made by one of the following psychologists to our understanding of personality:

  - Adler
  - Jung
  - Horney.

- Discuss the role and contents of the collective unconscious in Jung's theory of personality.
- Describe Jung's five major archetypes.
- According to Jung, how is the process of self-realisation achieved?

- Discuss how Adler explains problems in adult functioning. How adequate is his explanation?
- According to Adler, what motivates behaviour and what constitutes personality?
- Assess the validity of Jung's approach to the unconscious.
- Outline how Horney's neurotic needs form the basis for three unhealthy personality types.
- Critically compare two of the three following theorists:

  - Adler
  - Jung
  - Horney.

Going further

Books

Adler

- Adler, A. (2009). *What life could mean to you*. Oxford: Oneworld. An easily read, fairly short book that provides a good introduction to the man and his theory.
- Ansbacher, H. L. and Ansbacher, R. R. (eds) (1956). *The individual psychology of Alfred Adler*. New York: Basic Books. Perhaps the classic translation and interpretation of Adler's work.
- Leman, K. (2007). *The new birth order*. Grand Rapids, MI: Fleming Revell. This sets birth-order theory and research in a modern context, examining how modern family structures impact on birth order amongst other things.

Jung

- Jung, C. G. (1961/1965). *Memories, dreams, reflections*. Princeton, NJ: Princeton University Press. This is Jung's autobiography, and it gives a good overview of the man and his work.
- Bennett, E. A. (1995). *What Jung really said*. New York: Schocken Books. A fairly short paperback that provides an easily read overview.
- Storr, A. (1999). *Jung: Selected writings. Introduced by Anthony Storr*. New York: Princeton University Press. A very authoritative account overviewed by a prominent analyst.

Horney

- Horney, K. (1950). *Neurosis and human growth*. London: Norton. An easily read, in-depth presentation of Horney's

work in her own words. She writes very well and uses interesting clinical examples to illustrate her concepts.
- Horney, K. (1993). *Feminine psychology*. London: Norton. In this book Horney gives the full details of her disagreements with the Freudian position on women.
- Westkott, M. (1986). *The feminist legacy of Karen Horney*. New York: Yale Books. Provides an overview and evaluation of Horney's contribution to the debate about the treatment of women within psychoanalytic theory.

Journals

An article by Overholser, J. C. (2010). Psychotherapy that strives to encourage social interest: A simulated interview with Alfred Adler. *Journal of Psychotherapy Integration, 20(4)*, 347–363 provides an excellent overview of his theory. It uses quotes from his writings to answer questions about his theory.

The following research-based article demonstrates the differences between Freudian and Jungian theory as applied to the analysis of case study dreams: Fischer, C., Kächele, H. (2009). Comparative analysis of patients' dreams in Freudian and Jungian treatment. *International Journal of Psychotherapy, 13(3)*, 34–40.

One article that looks at Horney's theory is by Caplan, P. J. (1984). The myth of women's masochism. *American Psychologist, 39*, 130–139. It may be hard to find other relevant theory and research studies for all these theories, so you will have to search a little. Examples of good terms to use in any online library database (e.g. Web of Science; PsychINFO) are 'archetypes', 'social interest', 'birth order' and 'masochism'.

More clinically based articles and evaluations can be found in the specialist psychotherapy journals, such as:

- *The Journal of Individual Psychology*. Provides a forum for work relating to Adlerian practices, principles and theoretical development (**www.utexas.edu/utpress/journals/jip.html**).
- *The International Journal of Psychoanalysis*. Publishes contributions on methodology, psychoanalytic theory and technique, the history of psychoanalysis, clinical contributions, research and life-cycle development, education and professional issues, psychoanalytic psychotherapy and interdisciplinary studies (**http://onlinelibrary.wiley.com/journal/10.1111/(ISSN)1745-8315**).
- *The Psychoanalytic Quarterly*. Represents all contemporary psychoanalytic perspectives on the theories, practices, research endeavours and applications of adult and child psychoanalysis (**www.psaq.org/journal.html**).
- *Journal of the American Psychoanalytic Association*. Publishes original articles, plenary presentations, panel reports, abstracts, commentaries, editorials and correspondence in psychoanalysis. There is a special issue on Freudian theory in the 2005 Vol. 53, No. 2 edition (**www.apsa.org/japa/index.htm**).

Web links

- The Kristine Mann Library is a well-known resource for Jungian studies. The library collects and catalogues books, papers, journals, audiovisuals and other materials by and about C. G. Jung and others in the field of Jungian psychology, as well as materials in related areas such as eastern and western religions, alchemy, mythology, symbolism, the arts, anthropology, psychoanalysis and general psychology. (**www.junglibrary.org**).
- Drawing upon Carl Jung's work on the *archetype* is the Archive for Research in Archetypal Symbolism (ARAS), a pictorial and written archive of mythological, ritualistic and symbolic images from all over the world and from all epochs of human history (**http://aras.org**).
- The Alfred Adler Institutes of San Francisco and Northwestern University web pages have a number of articles on Adler's theory. (**www.adlerian.us**).

Film and literature

- *A Dangerous Method* (2011, directed by David Cronenberg). A film exploring how the intense relationship between Carl Jung and Sigmund Freud gives birth to psychoanalysis.
- *Strange Case of Dr Jekyll and Mr Hyde* (1886, Robert Louis Stevenson). We have dealt with ideas surrounding the shadow. In this book Stevenson deals with the duality of human nature and the inner conflict.
- *Citizen Kane* (1941, directed by Orson Welles). We have dealt with issues of self-actualisation. Multimillionaire newspaper tycoon Charles Foster Kane dies alone in his extravagant mansion, Xanadu. He speaks a single word: 'Rosebud'. Despite Kane's realising all possible dreams and ambitions in his life, the film deals with the attempts to figure out the meaning of this word and why it remains so important to his life.
- We have described Adler's suggestion that all human beings suffer inferiority feelings and, to compensate for these, we all strive for superiority. There are many films about characters overcoming adversity, but a notable one is *Born on the 4th of July* (1989, directed by Oliver Stone), which tells the story of a disabled Vietnam War veteran who became an anti-war activist.
- *Fight Club* (1999, directed by David Fincher). In the section on Jung, we discussed the shadow. This is the dark, sinister side of our nature, consisting of repressed material in our personal unconscious and universal images of evil from our collective unconscious. We never truly know the shadow side of ourselves, as it is too frightening for us to explore our potential to do harm or to think evil thoughts. It is expressed in unexplained moods such as uncontrollable anger, psychosomatic pain and desires to harm others and ourselves. We also discussed the animus and masculinity, including social insensitivity. *Fight Club*, in which an office employee and a soap salesman build a global organisation to help vent male aggression, explore the shadow and the animus in terms of the male psyche.
- *An Introduction to Carl Jung* (Educational Resource Video). This video introduces the major concepts of Jung's theory, his continuing influences on current practice and theory and his significance to the recent widespread emphasis on the spiritual component of psychotherapy. Publisher: Insight Media.

Explore the website accompanying this text at **www.pearsoned.co.uk/maltby** for further resources to help you with your studies. These include multiple-choice questions, essay questions, web links and ideas for advanced reading.

CHAPTER 4
Learning Theory Perspectives on Personality

Key themes

- Historical learning theory approaches to personality
- Pavlov and classical conditioning
- Watson and behaviourism
- Skinner and operant conditioning
- Integrative personality theory of Dollard and Miller
- Social cognitive approaches of Bandura
- The concept of self-efficacy
- Rotter and the locus of control
- Mischel and social learning theory

Learning outcomes

After studying this dicussion you should:

- Understand the principles underlying the learning theory approach to personality
- Be aware of the opposing views about whether differences in behaviour are learnt or result from differences in personality
- Be able to identify the learning theorists who have contributed to personality theory
- Understand the principles of classical conditioning and some of its applications
- Appreciate Skinner's approach to psychology
- Understand the principles underlying operant conditioning
- Be aware of the work of Dollard and Miller, who attempted to integrate psychodynamic and behavioural concepts within a learning theory framework
- Understand Bandura's social learning approach to personality
- Appreciate the concept of self-efficacy
- Have developed an understanding of the concept of locus of control
- Understand the contribution that Mischel has made to personality research
- Appreciate the person-situation debate in personality
- Know how to critically evaluate learning theory approaches to explaining personality

Introduction

Do you love parties and never miss one, or do parties make you anxious so that you avoid them if possible? What causes these differences? The concept of personality, as we have seen, is used to help explain such differences in behaviour between individuals. The theories that we have previously examined suggest that differences in the personality structures that are said to exist within each individual interact to produce differences in behaviour. Our behaviour is driven by inner motives such as instincts, unconscious drives, feelings of inferiority and so on, that all shape our personality. Based on what we have read so far, we might well claim that the person who enjoys parties and interacting with others does so because they have an outgoing, sociable personality. They are driven by an inner need to be with other people and are not so comfortable in their own company. There are alternative explanations for personality, and this discussion is about a series of theoretical approaches that adopt a radically different view. These theories reject the idea of our behaviour being directed by inner motives, suggesting instead that all our behaviour is learned. Individual differences in behaviour are the result of the different learning experiences that people have had and the situations in which they find themselves. To understand why someone behaves in a particular way, you need to examine carefully the situation they are in and to explore their past experiences in similar situations, rather than explain differences in behaviour as resulting from differences in personality. No underlying personality structure like Jung's psyche is thought necessary; rather, individuals have learnt to behave in certain ways because in the past they have been rewarded or they have avoided discomfort or punishment by doing so.

These approaches to understanding the individual are based on theories of how we learn. The learning theory explanation of the happy party-goer would suggest that such individuals have learnt to enjoy parties. Their first experience of a party as a child was wonderful. They were given presents, everything went well and they had a good time. This initial positive party experience has been followed by others, so that the individual looks forward to parties as pleasant experiences because of their learning history of parties. By contrast, the individual who dreads parties will have had some initial bad experiences of parties. Perhaps they were made to share their special toys with other children, or the other children broke their presents, or they did not get what they wanted or they were punished for being rude and so on. Learning theory would suggest that this negative experience can lead the individual to dread parties, especially if the negative experience is repeated. These examples are somewhat simplified, but we hope they have got the point across. The contention is that your attitudes to events like socialising are dictated not by your personality but by the past experiences of parties and similar events that you have had. As we mentioned earlier, these approaches are based on learning theory, and they vary in terms of how radical they are. We shall begin by looking briefly at the history of learning theory and outlining the major concepts that you need to understand.

Source: Pearson Education Ltd. Jules Selmes

Early learning theory developed primarily in the United States. The roots of the psychoanalytic schools of personality were firmly based in the European tradition of psychology, as we have seen, although they later became established in North America. We shall examine some of the major approaches to learning theory in the United States, from the radical approach of B. F. Skinner to the more moderate views of John Dollard and Neal Miller. Next, we will examine the work of Albert Bandura. While still maintaining a learning theory approach, Bandura introduces cognitive and emotional variables as factors influencing behaviour. Next, we will look at

two learning theory concepts that have stimulated enormous amounts of research. These are Bandura's concept of self-efficacy and Rotter's locus of control. Finally, we will examine the work of Walter Mischel. Mischel has not developed a full-blown theory of personality, but his critique of existing approaches has been enormously influential in personality psychology, as you will see.

The focus for much of the discussion is the question of whether you behave as you do because of an inner personality that drives your behaviour, or whether it is purely that you have learnt to behave in certain ways in particular situations.

Introduction to learning theory

We take a slight detour here and look at the history of learning theory, as many of the crucial concepts that underpin more current developments emerged early in the development of psychology as a discipline. You need to understand these core concepts as they have heavily influenced many later developments.

Although learning theory developed mainly in the United States, a major influence was the work of a Russian physiologist, Ivan Pavlov. At the beginning of the last century, Pavlov was exploring the digestive system in humans and other animals. While he was undertaking research examining the salivary response of dogs, he observed what appeared to him to be ways in which dogs learnt to respond to objects and people. When it is given food, a dog will automatically salivate. This is a naturally occurring response. In the terminology of learning theory, the food is called the **unconditioned stimulus** and the response of salivating is called the **unconditioned response**. Pavlov observed that if a light went on or a bell rang (**neutral stimulus**) before the dog received food, after a few trials the dog would salivate when the light went on or the bell rang. The dog had learnt to associate what had been a neutral unconditioned stimulus (bell or light) with the food and salivated at the neutral stimulus even in the absence of food. This is the basis of what is known as **classical conditioning**, and the basic process is summarised in Figure 4.1. Pavlov (1906; 1927; 1928) carried out extensive research on the learning associated with classical conditioning.

Classical conditioning also accounts for some learning in humans. For example, suppose a parental goal was to bring up their young child to enjoy books. One scenario for achieving this, according to classical conditioning, would be to start with the child being cuddled on a parent's lap – an experience that makes the child feel good. This is an unconditioned response (naturally occurring). Reading

a book across a room to a young child will initially be a neutral stimulus. However, if the parent reads the book to the child while cuddling the child on their lap, after a few repeated sessions, being read to will produce pleasant feelings in the child even when they are not being cuddled by their parent. In this way, reading books has become a conditioned stimulus that produces pleasure in the child. Once reading the book has become a conditioned response, reading to the child across the room will induce the same pleasurable response in the child.

Pavlov demonstrated that the conditioned response could *generalise* to similar stimuli. In the dog example, it could be changes in brightness or colour or the light that would evoke the same response. Similarly, with children, reading while on their parent's knee may generalise to being read to across a room and eventually to reading anywhere, even on their own, and finding it a pleasant experience. Pavlov showed that there are limits to generalisation. In the dog example, if the food is delivered to some sounds but not to others, the dog will learn to discriminate between the sounds and will only salivate to the 'food' sounds. Finally, Pavlov demonstrated that the conditioning process could be reversed. If the light is presented repeatedly with no food following, then the dog's salivary response gets weaker and weaker, until eventually what is termed **extinction** is achieved.

At this point, you may wonder what all of this has to do with personality, but Pavlov went on to show that classical conditioning could explain many of our emotional reactions. It could be that I am an anxious person because I have had experiences where I learnt to be anxious; it is not simply that I possess a neurotic personality. The crucial difference is that if you have learnt to be anxious, then you can unlearn; or, in learning theory terminology, the anxiety response can be extinguished as it is not a part of your personality. We will return to this shortly with a detailed example once we have understood how Pavlov's work came to be so influential within psychology.

1 Natural response (before conditioning occurs)

Food presented to dog [Food = Unconditioned stimulus]	Dog salivates [Salivation = Unconditioned response]
Light is switched on [Light = Neutral stimulus]	No response from the dog

2 Conditioning procedure for several trials

Light is switched on and food is presented to dog Neutral stimulus + Unconditioned stimulus	Dog salivates Unconditioned response

3 After the conditioning trials

Light alone is presented to dog Conditioned stimulus	Dog salivates Conditioned response

Figure 4.1 Summary of classical conditioning.

John B. Watson, an American psychologist, read the early work of Pavlov and was very impressed by it. He began to apply some of Pavlov's observational techniques in his own research and replicated some of his work in the United States. As he became established within psychology, Watson began to call for a change in the direction of American psychology so that it could become a true science. He wanted to reject the methods of introspection and interpretation of patients' reminiscences that Freud and the other psychoanalysts had employed. He saw these methods as unscientific and argued instead for a psychology that considered only observable aspects of behaviour. In practice, this means that no assumptions or hypotheses can be made about what is going on inside someone's mind. Stimuli and their effect on behaviour are the subject matter of the behavioural approach, and rigorous scientific methods, mainly based in laboratories, are used to collect data. Watson published his views in 1914 in a book entitled *Behavior.* In 1919, he published *Psychology from the Standpoint of a Behaviorist.* This book was influential in American psychology. It included summaries of Pavlov's work on classical conditioning, thereby introducing Pavlov's work to a wider audience. Watson is generally credited as being the founding figure of the School of Behaviourism, but his career as a psychologist ended with his withdrawal from academia in 1920 to enter business. Behaviourism and the popularising of Pavlov's work had set the scene

for developments in personality theorising and research. From this perspective variables are manipulated, ideally in a controlled laboratory setting, and then the effects of these manipulations on the subject of the research are carefully observed.

The clinical perspective within classical conditioning

If you recall, earlier in the text (Chapter 1) a distinction was made between the *clinical* and *individual differences* approaches to the study of personality. Although the behavioural approach is a radical departure from the psychoanalytic approaches discussed previously, it still maintained a heavy focus on behaviour change, particularly within a clinical context. Put simply, if your hypothesis is that behaviour is learnt, then it is necessary to show that it can be unlearnt. The behavioural approaches, like the psychoanalytic approaches, focused on demonstrating that mental health problems (psychopathology) could be cured using behavioural interventions. A crucial difference between the psychoanalysts and the early learning theorists concerns how psychopathology arises. For the psychoanalysts, as we have seen, psychopathology arises because of inner causes such as unresolved developmental crises, or conflict between the structures within the personality such as the id,

Stop and think

Treating classically conditioned emotional responses

Systematic desensitisation

This can be used to treat phobias, for example, someone with a phobia of birds. The aim is to replace the old association between the feared stimulus (bird) and the feared response (panic symptoms) with a new association of relaxation. The client and therapist begin by ranking bird-related fears from most to the least feared. Holding a bird might be most feared; a picture of a bird might be least feared. Next, the client is taught how to relax. The response of relaxation is incompatible with the feared response. The client and therapist move through the list of fears, ensuring that at each level the feared response becomes conditioned to the relaxation response, until the client can comfortably face their worst fear of birds. Many phobias and other anxieties have been successfully treated with systematic desensitisation.

Alcoholism

Aversion therapy has been used to treat people with alcohol addictions. Here, the image of a drink could be paired with images of being sick or other negative images. This therapy has also been used to assist individuals stop smoking.

ego and superego, or problems in personality development of some other kind. The learning theorists rejected this as an explanation for the cause of mental problems, seeing it as unscientific to refer to what they saw as unobservable inner mental processes and/or structures to explain observed differences in behaviour. For these learning theorists, psychopathology was a learnt maladaptive response to a situation that may have generalised to other situations or similar stimuli, and, as such, it could be unlearnt. Normal development was about learning adaptive responses in a variety of situations, while abnormal development resulted from acquiring maladaptive responses.

Pavlov (1927) began this line of research by inducing what he called **experimental neuroses** in one of his laboratory dogs. The dog was conditioned so that he would salivate to the shape of a circle. He then learnt to distinguish between circles and ellipses, only salivating to circles. However, when the distinctions between circles and ellipses became harder to distinguish, the dog became very distressed; his behaviour was disorganised, with a preponderance of neurotic symptoms. The dog barked when taken into the laboratory, shivered in his harness and tried to bite the restraining straps. Pavlov interpreted this as demonstrating that when the dog could no longer cope with what was being asked of him, he developed neurotic symptoms.

Watson and his colleague Rayner (1920) went on to demonstrate that human emotional responses could also be manipulated using classical conditioning. This is the famous classical conditioning experiment carried out on an 11-month-old infant called Albert. This has come to be known as the 'Little Albert' study and is still regarded as a classic in psychology. Albert initially did not display any fear of laboratory rats, but he did produce a startle and fear response to a loud noise made by banging a hammer on a metal bar. As Albert began to reach for a rat, the noise was made behind his head. After a few repetitions, he had been conditioned to fear the rat in the absence of any noise. This demonstrates how a child can learn an emotional response. This conditioned fear of white rats then generalised to other white, furry objects like a mask of Father Christmas and even Watson's own white hair. This work led to other psychologists exploring ways in which negative emotional reactions could be unlearned, and a great deal of work was carried out in this area from the 1920s until the 1980s. A summary of some of this work on classical conditioning is given in the Stop and think box: Treating classically conditioned emotional responses, for those of you with a clinical bent. The principles are still applied in some contexts; however, our next theorist, Skinner, developed this work further.

The radical behaviourism of B. F. Skinner

Skinner had been influenced by the research of Pavlov and Watson, among others, and developed it further. (See the Profiles box.) He did not claim that unconscious processes or inner states did not exist, but he strongly felt that it was unscientific and unnecessary to rely on these unobservable processes to explain behaviour. He did not deny that we had ideas and thoughts, but he strongly believed that these inner thoughts did not cause our behaviour. Suppose you do not turn up to do a seminar presentation; you may say that you were so anxious at the thought of doing it that you could not make yourself attend. For you, the explanation is that your anxiety prevented you from attending. You are claiming anxiety as the inner cause of your not attending behaviour. You may even go as far as to claim a neurotic personality. Skinner would not agree with this interpretation. This inner state of anxiety is not the cause of your non-attendance. He would argue that you experienced certain aversive behaviours when preparing to attend; you may have felt nauseous, had palpitations, sweated and so on, perhaps at the sight of your presentation or while packing your bag. This resulted in you altering your preparatory behaviour. The change in your behaviour and the change in your feelings have the same cause. Saying that you are an anxious person does not explain the cause of the anxiety. For Skinner the cause of your anxiety was located somewhere in your developmental learning history where you have learned maladaptive responses. Skinner felt that much of the time, we do not know the real causes of our behaviour, in terms of what stimuli in the environment trigger specific behaviour; and he rejected completely the notion of behaviour being motivated by inner states. So if you say you feel happy, something in the environment has triggered a response that you have previously learnt to label as happiness; it is not some internally generated feeling for Skinner, but is stimulated by something in the environment.

Skinner (1948) did not accept the concept of personality, seeing it as unnecessary and unscientific to postulate unobservable, inner psychological, personality-generating structures. He accepted that our genetic inheritance would have some influence on how we interacted with the environment, but he played it down, claiming instead that the situational determinants were crucial in explaining the cause of behaviour. He made reference to Charles Darwin's principles of natural selection, suggesting that over many generations human beings have evolved particular characteristics to meet the demands of their particular environment, and he believed this had led to some genetically based individual differences. Perhaps being agile had a survival value for a particular group of people; then these individuals would have opportunities to express their agility in their environment, and these responses would be reinforced. The more agile you were, the greater the reinforcement and so on.

This then would explain observed individual differences in behaviour. Heredity would only impose limits on behaviour. For Skinner, it is not the kind of person you are, but the learning history you have had and the current demands of your environment that dictate how you behave.

Skinner accepted the principles of classical conditioning but felt that it applied to a limited range of learning situations. He argued that what happened after particular ways of behaving was a crucially important aspect of learning that applied to most situations where we learn. He suggested that the classical conditioning paradigm, consisting of a stimulus followed by a response, is too simplistic for most learning situations. He demonstrated that what happens after the response – the *consequences* of the response – is what is crucial, as it affects the probability of the response being repeated. If you are praised for your seminar presentation, then you are more likely to volunteer to do a seminar presentation in future; if you are heavily criticised, then you are more likely to want to avoid future presentations.

Skinner refers to this learning process as **operant conditioning**. If the consequence of a piece of behaviour is to encourage the repetition of that behaviour, this is termed **positive reinforcement**. Consequences that discourage repetition of the behaviour are termed **negative reinforcement**. Although Skinner's primary interest was in human behaviour, most of his research was on animals in laboratory situations in the now famous Skinner box. This is illustrated in the photograph.

There were slightly different versions of the box for different animals; however, essentially there is a lever of some sort that the animal in the course of exploring the box will press at some point. When this happens, the animal is rewarded with food. There is an electronic device attached to the lever to record the animal's rate of pressing. What Skinner demonstrated was that, after the bar pressing had resulted in the animal being reinforced with food, the rate at which the animal pressed the bar increased. The animal did not have to be reinforced every time for learning to occur, and Skinner studied the effects of different schedules of reinforcement. Much of the detail of this work is not

Stop and think

Ethical reflection on the 'Little Albert' study

Do you consider it ethical to carry out experiments in which you make a young child fearful and upset to the point where the child cries? For most of us, this research is unethical, as modern codes of ethical conduct would make clear. The aim is to cause distress in a very young child. Ethical issues are complex, however, and you may want to reflect on the following:

- Watson carried out much of his conditioning research on his own children. Does this make any difference?
- Was his research worthwhile? Have we gained useful knowledge from his work?

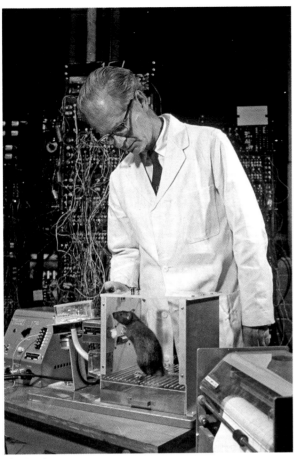

Skinner box.
Source: Getty Images/Nina Leen/Time Life Pictures

particularly relevant in the context of personality theory, and we will cover only the relevant concepts.

Skinner demonstrated that **random or partial reinforcement schedules** produce behaviours that are very resistant to change, as an example will show. In one family, the teenage son was told that his weekend curfew was 11 p.m. However, every Friday night, Tim (the teenage son) would plead with his mother to be allowed to stay out later, and an argument would often ensue. The mother could not understand why Tim always had to argue and could not just accept that 11 p.m. was the curfew. She said he was stubborn and argumentative like his dad. In other words, it was down to his personality. When asked if she ever did allow Tim to stay out later than 11 p.m. on a Friday, she said that sometimes he just wore her down or, if she was in a good mood, she sometimes let him have another hour. In Skinnerian terms, Tim was on a random/partial reinforcement schedule. The rule was that his curfew was 11 p.m. However, Tim had learnt that it was always worth challenging this as sometimes his mother gave in and he was rewarded with a later curfew. So, for Skinner it was unnecessary and unscientific to refer to internal personality attributes to explain this behaviour, as learning theory provided an adequate

explanation based on observable events. We are sure that if you reflect on some of the conflicts that you have experienced over family rules when you were growing up, you will find that operant conditioning provides a good explanation.

Another relevant Skinnerian concept is **shaping**. Skinner observed that when pigeons first entered a Skinner box, it might take them some time before they found the lever and pressed it. To speed up the process, he would deliver a food reward when they were facing in the direction of the lever, another reward when they came close to the lever and so on until the pigeon had actually achieved the desired response of pressing the lever. Shaping is applied to many aspects of behaviour where individuals are initially rewarded for behaviour that approximates the desired goal, and once that behaviour is established they are rewarded only for behaviour that comes closer to the goal and so on. Many of the current television programmes that help parents develop parenting skills areas are based on principles of operant conditioning where desired behaviours are gradually shaped. The children have a star chart. They are rewarded for 'good' behaviour with a star, and earning stars 'buys' treats. Gradually, as the initial good behaviour becomes established, the parents up the ante for the child to earn stars. Skinner's contention is that eventually the children's good behaviour will become self-reinforcing as their relationships will be better, and this is rewarding in itself.

As we have seen, one of the big questions for personality theory is the nature of human motivation. For Skinner (1971; 1972; 1976) the issue was straightforward. He believed that human beings aim to produce pleasant events and to avoid painful events, if possible. All our emotional states can be understood by analysing the behavioural events in the environment that preceded them. He does accept that some behaviour is private, but he refuses to accept that internal private behaviour causes our emotions. You don't get anxious because you have an anxious personality, but because something in your environment stimulates the anxious behaviour.

Skinner devoted a lot of his writing to examining Freudian concepts and dismissed most of them as unscientific, constructs for which there was no observable evidence. He agreed with Freud that the early experiences of the child had long-lasting effects, which could even continue into adulthood. However, he contended that it was the early conditioning experiences of the child that shaped their later behaviour, not the influence of inner conflicts between hypothesised personality structures. For Skinner, demanding individuals are not governed by their id impulses, as Freud would claim; rather, they have in the past been rewarded for displaying demanding behaviour by having their demands met and have therefore learnt to behave in a demanding way. Skinner (1953) agreed that personality trait names do convey useful information describing the individual, like how friendly

Profiles

Major figures in learning theory: Ivan Petrovich Pavlov, John Broadus Watson and Burrhus Frederic Skinner

Ivan Petrovich Pavlov

Pavlov was born in Ryazan, a small village in central Russia, in 1849. He was educated at a church school followed by a seminary and seemed destined to enter the priesthood. However, in 1870 he changed direction and studied chemistry and physiology, followed by medicine at St Petersburg, becoming a skilful surgeon. After working for 2 years in Germany, he returned to St Petersburg and was made professor of physiology in 1890 at the Imperial Medical Academy. In 1904, he was awarded the Nobel Prize for his work on digestion. Pavlov was an independent, outspoken man; yet, despite this, he managed to survive the Russian revolution and was allowed to continue his research although never becoming communist and openly criticising aspects of the regime. In 1922, at a time of famine in the Soviet Union, he asked Stalin for permission to take his laboratory overseas. This was denied as Stalin felt that the Soviet Union needed scientists like Pavlov. However, Stalin did allow Pavlov to visit America, first in 1923 and then in 1929. Although Pavlov was a physiologist, his research on learning and the methods associated with it have had, and continue to have, a major influence on the development of psychology.

John Broadus Watson

Watson was born in 1878, the first son of a poor family in Greenville, South Carolina. His father was a womaniser and abandoned his family when Watson was 13 years old. Watson found this difficult and rebelled against his mother and school. With the support of one of his teachers, he returned to study and eventually studied for a doctorate in psychology at the University of Chicago. In 1902, in the last year of his doctoral studies, he suffered an emotional breakdown. In his autobiography (Watson, 1936) he discusses how, after his breakdown, he could accept the validity of much of Freud's work. This seems at odds with the individual who, as we have seen, founded the school of psychology known as **behaviourism**. In 1913 Watson lectured and published the seminal paper on behaviourism, *Psychology as the Behaviorist Views It*. In 1915, while professor of psychology at Johns Hopkins University, he became president of the American Psychological Association and seemed set for a career as an eminent psychologist. However, in his private life, like his father, he had a great number of affairs with women and, in 1920, he was forced to resign from Johns Hopkins University over a sexual scandal involving his research assistant. His academic career was over, although he continued to publish for a few years. He went into the advertising business and became a successful businessman. However, his relationships with his family were poor; after his retirement from business in 1945 and the death of his second wife, he lived as a recluse on a farm in Connecticut until his death in 1958.

Burrhus Frederic Skinner

Skinner was born in Susquehanna, a small town in Pennsylvania, in 1904. He had a middle-class upbringing in a warm, supportive family. His initial interest was in literature, and he wanted to become a writer. While working in a bookstore to support himself, he read books by Pavlov and Watson. Wanting to know more about psychology, at age 24 he enrolled at Harvard for a research degree. This was supposedly jointly supervised by the physiology and psychology departments but, in reality, Skinner was allowed a great deal of freedom to develop his own research and experiment with equipment, developing the Skinner box (illustrated). In 1936 he married and left Harvard for a lecturing post in Minnesota. During the Second World War, he was funded by the American government to carry out a project to train pigeons to guide bombs. The pigeons would keep pecking at a target that kept the missile on course. A parallel secret project was on the development of radar and, when that was successful, Skinner's research was discontinued. However, he had discovered that pigeons learnt more quickly than rats, and from this point onwards he used only pigeons in his research. In 1945, Skinner became professor of psychology at the University of Indiana; the following year, the Society for the Experimental Analysis of Behavior was set up. This development reflected the growing influence of behaviourism in the United States. In 1948, Skinner was given a chair at Harvard. In the same year, he wrote his only novel, *Walden Two*. This describes a community governed by the principles of learning theory. It describes a utopian society, which provided a wealth of experience for individuals to fulfil their potential. Although the book was fictional, a group of young people set up a community based on the book in Virginia (Kinkade, 1973). Skinner continued to work until his death from leukaemia in 1990. He focused on developing effective ways of teaching and learning, being an early proponent of programmed learning. In later life he became interested in philosophical issues, but he continued to be upset by the misrepresentation of his work by sections of psychology. However, the huge number of publications related to his work testifies to his influence. Indeed, the *Journal of Experimental Analysis of Behavior*, set up in 1958, is still dedicated to research in the Skinnerian tradition.

or enthusiastic they are; however, they do not explain, in any empirical way, how they came to be friendly or enthusiastic. For him the friendly person has been reinforced more for being friendly than has the unfriendly person and so on.

Skinner also denies that human beings are purposeful. He claims that what we label 'intentions' are really responses to internal stimuli. For example, when you say that you want to go for a picnic in the park, for Skinner, you are not setting some mental future goal; rather, you are responding to some observations – perhaps internal and external – that in the past were associated with you having a picnic. It could be that the sun is shining; you observe that you have nothing else to do, you catch sight of a Thermos flask in your kitchen, or you drive past a park and perhaps a previous memory of a picnic is triggered. For Skinner these, or variations of them, are the stimuli that you are responding to when you make a statement of intent to have a picnic.

Attempts to apply learning theory approaches to personality

All learning theorists are not as radical as Skinner is, and the theorists that we will explore now all made serious attempts to apply concepts derived from learning theory to personality. John Dollard and Neal Miller, two of the earliest of these theorists, both worked at Yale University. They are somewhat unique in that their aim was to try to integrate learning theory principles with Freud's psychoanalytic approach. Both Dollard and Miller had trained as Freudian analysts, Dollard at the Berlin Institute and Miller at the Vienna Institute. By background, Dollard was a social scientist, teaching anthropology, sociology and psychology and only specialising in psychology later in his career. Miller had trained as an academic psychologist before his analytic training. Both men were impressed with the work of the learning theorists while also influenced by Freud's theory. They sought to develop a synthesis of the two concepts to create a theory of personality.

Dollard and Miller collaborated on animal laboratory studies, mainly using rats, sharing Skinner's view that animal learning could be generalised to humans. However, unlike Skinner, they allowed for inner causation in behaviour. They believed that, because of the higher mental processes of humans, our behaviour does not consist merely of responding to stimuli in our environment; instead, we can also respond to inner stimuli, and thoughts can be reinforcing for us. This is the first attempt to allow cognitive processing within a primarily learning theory model. The principles of learning demonstrated in lower species in the laboratory still applied to human learning but, because

of their superior mental processes, humans were capable of more complexity. Thoughts and memories could cue behaviour within their model. This also allowed humans to plan ahead and anticipate events. There was even a role for the unconscious.

Dollard and Miller acknowledged the importance of unconscious processes in human behaviour, but their definition of the unconscious is different from Freud's; he saw the unconscious as comprising the sex and death instincts, which were inherited from birth. Dollard and Miller suggest that we are unaware of some processes because we acquired our drives and the cues before we learnt to talk and consequently they are not labelled. Examples might be some of our secondary drives for social contact, love and so on that we learnt as infants from our initial contacts with our parents. We have learnt to associate a particular smell, perhaps with the good feeling of being fed, but are unconscious of it. In future when we are exposed to the smell, it will affect our behaviour at an unconscious level. Other cues may be unconscious, as they are not labelled in our society. For example, in Japanese society to lose face (to be embarrassed or humiliated, especially publicly) is an important concept, and there is a richer vocabulary in Japanese for labelling the experience than is the case in English, where the concept is not so important. Whether labels are readily available also affects how we perceive cues. The well-known example always cited here is that of the Inuit people (people who live on the arctic coasts, including Siberia, Alaska and Greenland) and their wealth of labels for different types of snow. Consequently, they make discriminations between types of snow that English speakers would find difficult or even impossible to do. This then accounts for material being in the unconscious because it is **unlabelled**.

Cues may also be unconscious because they have been repressed. Dollard and Miller suggest that the defence mechanism of repression is a learned response, like the rest of our behaviour. When we discussed repression previously, as a Freudian defence mechanism, we saw that it involves suppressing inconvenient or disagreeable feelings or thoughts. If we cannot remember something, it cannot upset us. For Dollard and Miller, repression is about a failure to label the upsetting thoughts or memories so that they are not easy to recall and making a decision not to think about it. When you recall unpleasant events, this reinforces the negative experience you originally had. Repression avoids this, and not labelling the feelings makes it harder for them to be recalled to conscious thought. Dollard and Miller accepted the importance of the effects of unconscious motivation and Freudian defence mechanism on behaviour, but they expressed defence mechanisms in learning theory terminology. The interested reader can find a very readable account in their book, *Personality and Psychotherapy*, published in 1950.

The stimulus–response model of personality of Dollard and Miller

As expected in a stimulus–response (S–R) theory, the emphasis was on how behaviour is learnt. From Hull, another early American learning theory researcher, Dollard and Miller borrowed the term **habit** to label the association between stimulus and response. Within their model, personality is composed largely of learned habits, and they go on to explain how these habits are acquired and maintained.

They agreed with Freud that the infant is born with some innate drives, which they termed **primary drives**, but disagreed with Freud about the nature of these drives. These innate primitive drives are physiological drives associated with ensuring survival for the individual. They include hunger, thirst, the need for sleep and the avoidance of pain. Reduction of these drives provides the most powerful reinforcement for the individual. Dollard and Miller (1950) claim that this reinforcement occurs automatically and unconsciously, and, to be maximally effective, it should immediately follow the response. Like many other personality theorists with a clinical background, Dollard and Miller focus mainly on psychopathology in the development of their theory and then extrapolate from this to normal development. For example, if an infant is left to become extremely hungry (primary drive), then it cries very loudly for attention (response). If the mother then feeds the infant, what the infant is said to have learnt is that making a fuss is rewarded. Such a child might then go on to make an excessive fuss every time they have a drive that requires satisfaction. In this terminology, making a fuss has become a habit. The baby whose primary drive of hunger was quickly met would not have this habit of over-reacting and would develop normal levels of response, in this case distress. In most western societies, primary drives are rarely directly observed, apart from in infant feeding, as societies have developed means of reducing them before they become pressing. The process for doing this involves the acquisition of what Dollard and Miller termed **secondary drives**. These secondary drives are learned mainly to help us cope with our primary drives. An example would be of setting regular mealtimes so that you are motivated to eat at particular times before the primary drive of hunger becomes overwhelming and therefore distressing. Associated with these primary and secondary drives are different types of reinforcement. For the innate primary drives, **primary reinforcers** are food, water, sleep and so on. Secondary drives similarly have **secondary reinforcers**. These secondary reinforcers are items or events that were originally neutral but have acquired a value as a reinforcer through being associated with primary drive reduction. A mother smiling at her child is a secondary reinforcer as it is associated with physical well-being. Money is also a

secondary reinforcer as it is associated with being able to buy food, provide shelter and so on.

Dollard and Miller describe the learning of habits as being composed of four constituent parts: the initial drive, the cue to act, the response and reinforcement of the response. As discussed earlier, the drive stimulates the person to act. It does not guide them how to act but simply lets the person know that they want something. A drive might be hunger. Cues provide guidance about how to act or respond in S–R terminology. You notice a billboard advertising a new Chinese takeaway. This might be the cue for you to respond, by taking a detour past the takeaway to get something to eat. If you then pick up a delicious meal that you enjoy hugely, you will no longer be hungry; your drive will have been satisfied. In this situation, the Chinese meal constitutes reinforcement. Reinforcement refers to the effect that a response has. As the meal was good, it reinforced your action of going to get it; next time you are in a similar position, hungry when walking home, you may be tempted to repeat the experience. In S–R terms, a habit has been formed. If, on the other hand, the meal was disgusting and the portions were tiny, the experience of visiting the takeaway would not have been reinforcing and you are unlikely to visit it again. In S–R terms, if the response does not satisfy the drive, it will undergo extinction. It does not mean that you will never again visit the takeaway, but you are less likely to do so. Remember that habits can be both positive and negative. They are simply associations between stimuli and responses.

Dollard and Miller (1941, 1950) were particularly interested in what happened when we became frustrated in our attempts to satisfy our drives. They described four types of conflict situations that we could face. The conflict is caused by our tendencies to wish to obtain (termed 'approach') certain goals or objects. They developed a simple diagrammatic system to illustrate these conflicts, as they felt that this helped them to understand exactly what was going on in any situation (see Figure 4.2).

- **Approach–approach conflict** – This describes the situation where there are two equally desirable goals, but they are incompatible. This could be when you are asked to choose between two equally desirable objects to have as a gift. You really want both but can only have one. Both goals are positive but incompatible.
- **Avoidance–avoidance conflict** – This is the situation where you are faced with what you perceive as two equally undesirable alternatives. You have a spare hour, and your partner asks you to go jogging, which you hate; or you could offer to do the ironing as an excuse not to go jogging, but you equally hate ironing. Here, for you, both goals are undesirable and incompatible in terms of having neither the wish nor the time to do both.
- **Approach–avoidance conflict** – Here there is one goal, but while an element of it is attractive, an aspect of it

Figure 4.2 The Dollard and Miller system for analysing conflicts.

is equally unattractive. For example, you are offered a place in what seems an ideal house; however, one of your housemates would be someone you really do not like.

- **Double approach-avoidance conflict** – Here there may be multiple goals, some desirable and some undesirable. This is more like most situations, where there are a variety of factors, positives and negatives, to take into consideration before being able to make a decision.

Although we have used human examples to illustrate the analysis of conflict situations, Dollard and Miller used laboratory animals rather than humans to demonstrate that this system was accurate at predicting behaviour.

For Dollard and Miller, therefore, behaviour is motivated by the need to reduce our primary or secondary drives, and we learn new behaviours in the process. It is a deterministic account of human development. It is more complex than

the early learning theory models as it allows for the inner influence of human cognitive processes and, in this, it is a forerunner of the cognitive models of personality that we will examine later (Chapter 5).

One aspect of Dollard and Miller's model that is subject to criticism from behaviourists as not being radical enough is their approach to the treatment of mental disorder. For them, as with the other learning theorists, psychopathology consists of learned, unproductive, unhelpful habits or responses. In their integrative approach, they suggested that some of these habits might be unconscious because of the reasons we have discussed earlier and that this factor added to the complexity. The aim of treatment is to remove these ineffective habits and replace them with new, more effective habits. Unlike the earlier behaviourists, Dollard and Miller did not adopt a purely deconditioning approach to treatment; they maintain significant elements of psychotherapy, the 'talking cure', in their approach. There are two phases to their treatment: first is a **talking phase**, where the problem habits are identified, explored and labelled. In the second phase, the patient is encouraged to learn more adaptive habits and apply them in their life. They call this phase the **performance phase**. They departed from their Freudian psychoanalytic training in not attending to the problems that patients had experienced in the past. They felt that past emotional issues do not have to be relived in therapy for them to be resolved. The past is only helpful sometimes in helping patients understand the source of their problems. Their focus was on current problems in living and future strategies. This predates the current treatment practice in cognitive therapy (examined in Chapter 5).

One other significant contribution made by Dollard and Miller (1941) was to recognise and outline the process of observational learning. They demonstrated how performance on a novel task can be improved by seeing someone else perform the task. This increases the speed of the learning process. They suggested that observational learning is important in development as children learn from observing adults and other children in situations that are novel to them. They stressed that observational learning could explain how both adaptive and maladaptive habits are learned.

We will now examine the contributions of theorists Albert Bandura and Michael Rotter, who have further developed this concept of social and observational learning in ways that can be usefully applied within personality theorising.

Albert Bandura and social learning theory

One of the major questions in personality theorising is whether inner or outer forces control our behaviour. As we have seen, the psychoanalysts would have us believe that inner forces determine who we are and how we behave. The learning theorists that we have examined so far conceptualise human beings as being at the mercy of outer forces. The environment determines your opportunities for learning new behaviour, the interests you are likely to develop and your history of learning. Dollard and Miller allowed for some inner influence from the higher cognitive functioning possessed by humans but said that principles of reinforcement external to the individual are thought mainly to control human behaviour. Bandura challenges this view, as we shall see. (For background on Bandura, see the Profile box.)

Bandura's work is grounded in the learning theory tradition, but his focus is on human problems in living. He moved from animal studies to focusing on purely human behaviour, although he kept the methodology of undertaking mainly laboratory-based research. His laboratory techniques are much more sophisticated, emphasising observation in situations designed to simulate real-life experiences. He is interested in developing theory and applying it to behavioural problems to facilitate positive change in individuals and groups.

The model of the individual in his approach is of an active player responding both to inner stimuli and the external environment and moving back and forward in a dynamic system. Individuals are seen to be influential in determining their own motivation, development and behaviour. Bandura (1978; 1989) uses the term **reciprocal determinism** to label the processes that drive behaviour. He sees an individual as being influenced by personal factors, behaviour and environmental factors. All three factors interact with one another to influence how individuals behave. The direction of these interactions is displayed in Figure 4.3.

Personal factors include the individual's cognitions, emotions and biological variables that contribute to their inner state. This is a major break from the traditional learning theory approaches that we have examined previously. These personal factors can impact on both an individual's

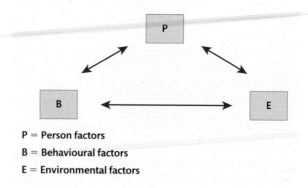

P = Person factors
B = Behavioural factors
E = Environmental factors

Figure 4.3 The interacting factors in reciprocal determinism.

behaviour and on their environment. If you truly think you will fail at a task in a specific setting, Bandura (1995) has shown that this greatly increases the likelihood of failure, as you approach the task differently. Your cognitions are affecting your behaviour. If you do not like opera, then you are unlikely to choose to go to an opera. Here your cognitions are influencing the environments you experience. Similarly, if you hate smoking, you may avoid bars that you know will be smoky. Here, environmental factors and personal cognitions are impacting on your behaviour.

Bandura also suggests that **behavioural factors** can affect the individual's cognitions, feelings and emotions. Supposing you go skiing for the first time with some friends, and you prove to be good at it. You get your balance quickly, and the instructor is complimentary. You now have the cognition that 'This is something I can do.' Your feelings may also change from apprehension about whether you could do it, to feeling positive about skiing. The converse might also be true if your initial experience of skiing was awful. Your behaviour with regard to the skiing experience has influenced your cognitions and

Profile

Albert Bandura

Albert Bandura was born in 1925 in Mundare, a small Canadian town in the province of Alberta. He was an only son with five older sisters. His parents were farmers of Polish descent. Bandura went to a small school with a shortage of teachers. To combat this, the pupils formed groups to educate themselves in subjects where no teacher was available. This led to his interest in self-motivation and group effects in the process of learning and motivation. As a young man, he worked with a gang of labourers repairing the Alaskan highway. He met a diverse range of individuals, many escaping from the

law and others on the fringes of society, and this is said to have sparked his interest in psychology and how it could address the real problems of living (Stokes, 1986). Bandura studied psychology at the University of British Columbia and the University of Iowa. Here he was introduced to researchers working on learning theory. He was appointed to a teaching post at Stanford University in 1954 and is still there. Bandura is one of the most distinguished living American psychologists. He received the American Psychological Association's award for Distinguished Scientific Contributions in 1980.

your feelings, and both are likely to influence whether you choose to ski in future. If you take up skiing, you may even become an expert and your body will develop neurological networks reflecting your expertise. In this way, Bandura (2001) demonstrated how our behaviour affects our cognitions, feelings, emotions and even our neurobiology in some instances.

With regard to the environment, we have seen from the earlier examples how **environmental factors** like polluted environments may affect our behavioural choices. The hole in the ozone layer is another good example that has resulted in us having to take more care to avoid burning when it is sunny. We may have to spend time and money buying sunscreens or we may avoid sunbathing (behavioural factors). In addition, we may also worry about sunburn and plan ways to avoid it (personal factors). We hope that these examples give you an idea of Bandura's model of **reciprocal causation** in action. You surely can think of other examples. Doing this makes you aware of the complexity of learned behaviour that, unlike the earlier models, Bandura's model can handle.

Unlike Skinner, Bandura (1995; 1998) believes that individuals do possess free will and are not at the mercy of their drives and reinforcement schedules in their learning environment. For Bandura, our cognitive processes allow us some control in selecting the situations we operate in and in creating or transforming situations. We may have to work, but we can choose what we do in our leisure; or we may work towards changing a work situation to make it more amenable to us. We can start businesses or interest groups or throw parties to provide the experiences and environments that we need. Bandura has labelled this **personal agency**: the belief that you can change things to make them better for yourself or others. Bandura (1999) has extended the concept to include **proxy agency**, where the individual enlists other people to help change some of the factors impacting on their life. They may ask a family member to look after their child so that they can get a job, or so that they can change their life in some other way. Bandura points out that there can be a downside to proxy agency in that people may in the process surrender their power to the other, who may not have their best interests at heart, and/or they may become subservient and give up control of their lives. He prefers the idea of **collective agency**, which is where a group of individuals come together believing that they can make a difference to their own and/or others' life circumstances. An example might be the recent emergence of farmers' markets. Here, groups of like-minded people who want to be able to continue earning a living from farming by getting a fair price for their produce and who share a commitment to fresh local produce have joined together to sell their produce directly to the public for a fair price. There are many other examples of collective agency in community and national groups and charities.

Learning within Bandura's model

Within Bandura's model, personality development is about how we learn to become the person we are, and this then explains why we behave as we do. Bandura (1977) suggests that, for learning to be effective, individuals have to be aware of the consequences of their behaviour. He demonstrated that people think about the consequences of their behaviour in learning situations. We think beyond the immediate situation and anticipate possible outcomes with an eye to the future. Being aware of the consequences of our behaviour also allows us **forethought**, in that we can anticipate what possible outcomes may follow our behaviour, and this knowledge can affect how we choose to behave and what we learn in the situation. Bandura (1995; 1999) sees awareness of the consequences of our behaviour and foresight as being human attributes as we possess language and symbolic thought which make it easier to record the consequences of our actions.

One of the most well-known aspects of Bandura's work is **observational learning**. He points out that more of our learning occurs by watching and following what other people do and imitating their behaviour than occurs by classical or operant conditioning. What happens is that an individual watches someone perform a novel behaviour, and, when they are required to perform the same behaviour, they copy what they have previously seen. This is termed modelling by Bandura.

Bandura and Walters (1963) undertook a series of famous studies with a doll (Bobo); you may have covered these studies in your social psychology courses. To summarise, nursery school children were divided into two groups. One group, the experimental group, watched an adult playing aggressively with a plastic doll called 'Bobo'. The adult hit and kicked the doll, shouting things like 'Throw him in the air.' The second group of children, the control group, did not see the aggressive play. Later, both groups of children were allowed to play with the doll. Children in the experimental group displayed twice as much aggression towards the doll as did those in the control group.

From variations of this study, Bandura (1977) concluded that three factors are important in modelling. Firstly, the **characteristics of the model** influence how likely we are to imitate them. The more similar to ourselves the model is, the more likely we are to imitate them. Models undertaking simple behaviour are more likely to be copied than they are if the behaviour is complex. The type of behaviour being modelled also has an effect, with hostile and aggressive behaviour more likely to be modelled. Secondly, the **attributes of the observer** exert an influence. Less confident individuals and those with low self-esteem or those who feel incompetent in the situation are more likely to imitate the model. Individuals with a learning history of being rewarded for conforming behaviour or who are highly dependent also imitate models more. Finally, Bandura showed that the **consequences of imitating a behaviour** are the most influential factor. If individuals believe that imitating a behaviour will bring positive results, then they are more likely to do so.

While we have talked about modelling using the term 'imitation', Bandura is insistent that modelling involves more than passive imitation. It is an active process of learning through observation, where the observer makes judgements and constructs symbolic representations of the behaviours observed. These symbolic representations may be verbal descriptions or visual images, and they are used to guide the individuals' future behaviour in similar situations. Bandura has studied the factors that may influence these processes in great detail; interested readers can refer to the further reading provided at the end of the discussion. Here we will restrict ourselves to a more aerial view of his theory as it relates to aspects of personality and its development. It is sufficient for us to be aware that modelling is not a passive process of observation, but an active process where the observer reviews what they have learnt and makes judgements about it and may decide to keep or discard parts of the behaviour. A distinction is also made between what we have learned (knowledge acquired) and what we can do (performance). Performance is seen to involve trial and error as we gradually shape our behaviour into the desired format. We may also acquire knowledge that we do not use, like learning about ways to murder someone from watching television; fortunately, few of us ever put this knowledge to use.

While reinforcement is crucial for learning in classical and operant conditioning, Bandura demonstrates that it is not always necessary in observational learning. You notice vivid billboard adverts, or loud noises, because they command your attention. You may not think about the information at the time; however, when faced with an array of soap powder at the supermarket, you recognise the one from the billboard. Bandura also demonstrates that we can, and frequently do, reinforce our own behaviour. This **self-reinforcement** is where we evaluate our own behaviour; we may stop doing something we are getting no pleasure from, or that we judge as harming us in some way, while continuing to do things that bring positive reinforcement. The other crucial element for learning that Bandura identifies is an **incentive** so that we are motivated to learn. Here, **forethought** plays an important part, as well as the more traditional cues for learning. Forethought can allow us to anticipate reinforcements and thus motivate our behaviour. He suggests that motivation is crucial with observational learning, as it requires practice for the skills to be perfected. Motivation and reinforcement are much more dynamic complex processes in this model.

Bandura (2002) is keen to encourage the application of his social learning theory to address global problems such as the AIDS pandemic, population growth and gender inequalities. He sees social modelling and observational learning as being core components of behavioural change. The modelling principles in his famous Bobo study were incorporated into serial dramas and soap operas by a well-known writer (Sabido, 1981; 2002). These dramas incorporate positive role models demonstrating beneficial lifestyles, negative role models displaying detrimental lifestyles and individuals who are making the transition from negative to more positive life roles. Bandura (2002) reports that these dramas provide individuals with positive role models. They also provide the inspiration for viewers to make positive changes in their own lives. To assist in the change process, supporting resources on linked websites or in post-programme information slots are made available to the viewers. These dramas are tailored for different cultures and are delivered in Africa, Asia and Latin America (Bandura, 2000; Brown and Cody, 1991; Singhal and Rogers, 1989; Vaughan et al., 1995). You see examples of post-programme information slots closer to home, with helpline details being provided after popular soap operas when particular social issues are included in the programme.

Personality development in social learning theory

It is this emphasis on observational learning that has led to the term 'social' being included in the theory, to stress that it is about how people learn from other individuals. In terms of how children develop their personalities, it is a learning process where parents, peers and others provide role models for children to learn from through observational learning mainly. The children learn to model their behaviour on successful models in their environment. This might be a sibling who manages to avoid trouble in one situation and a friend who gets on well in another and so on. Unfortunately, parents and others are not always consistent in their reinforcement, as we have seen, so the picture is more complicated than it might seem at first. Role models will be more or less effective, as will individual children's learning. Children will be exposed to different experiences, different environments and different cultures, and all of these influences help account for the observed diversity of human beings. The child is at the centre of these learning experiences and actively shaping the process. It is a truly dynamic, complex process.

Identifying goals to achieve is a crucial part of this process, and obtaining external feedback from relevant others on progress made towards achieving these goals plays an important part in maintaining motivation and ultimate success (Bandura, 1991). Bandura also demonstrated that goal achievement depends heavily on self-regulatory processes (Bandura, 1990; 1991; 1994; 1999; 2002). These **internal self-regulatory processes** include self-criticism, self-praise, valuation of own personal standards, re-evaluation of own personal standards if necessary, self-persuasion, evaluation of attainment and acceptance of challenges. Bandura (1990) describes these processes as being attempts at self-influence, and he has shown that the more of these factors involved in achieving a goal, the higher the levels of motivation to succeed. He identified self-efficacy as one of the most powerful of the self-regulatory processes, and we shall examine it next.

Self-efficacy as a self-regulatory process

Self-efficacy is defined as being your belief that if you perform some behaviour, it will get you a desired positive outcome (Bandura, 1989; 1994). It has become a really hot topic in psychology during the past 10 or so years and has stimulated a great deal of research, especially in health. Individuals have been shown to vary greatly in their levels of self-efficacy related to specific tasks. If we take smokers who wish to stop smoking as an example, they will vary greatly in whether they believe that they can achieve their goal. It is a special kind of confidence in your ability to perform. In the smoking example, it might be that the smoker felt that not smoking at home and at work was achievable (high self-efficacy) but that not smoking when out with friends would be more difficult (low self-efficacy). Their overall judgement would depend on the relative amount of time they spent in each activity, and perhaps on their past experiences of similar success in a relevant area and so on. Bandura (1997) has shown that high self-efficacy significantly increases the likelihood of achieving success. Self-efficacy will influence whether a task will be attempted as well as the effort put into it and the persistence with which it is pursued in the face of difficulties or apparent lack of progress. For example, one recent study of the factors that affected the likelihood of relapse in a smoking cessation programme found that low levels of self-efficacy in individuals were a significant predictor (Segan et al., 2006). Another study looked at factors that predicted heavy drinking in anxiety-provoking social situations for a student population in the United States (Gilles et al., 2006). The students most likely to drink heavily in these situations had low self-efficacy for avoiding heavy drinking in social situations and a correspondingly high belief that alcohol facilitated social interactions. Halkitis et al., (2005) looked at adherence with HIV antiretroviral treatment in 300 HIV-positive men. They found that poorer adherence

was associated with low self-efficacy towards adherence, amongst other factors. Having confidence in your ability to succeed at something is consistently shown to be a significant factor in a wide range of scenarios (Bandura, 1997).

An example will help to clarify the application of self-efficacy. Let us compare two students, Dan and Stuart, who have to give assessed seminar presentations.

One student, Dan, is quite looking forward to his presentation. He knows that if he does well he will get a good mark, and he really wants to do well this year to get a good degree. He knows from experience that, although he will be anxious initially, once he gets started he likes public speaking and will enjoy it. He is interested in the topic, and he is already quite well informed about it. He knows that he can organise his work effectively as he has received good marks previously when he has given himself sufficient time to undertake the preparatory work well. Not surprisingly then, his self-efficacy is high with regard to the seminar presentation; he feels confident about all the component parts that go into producing a good seminar presentation, and he has some positive experiences to reinforce this. The one proviso he has is about ensuring that he has enough time to complete the task. As his motivation to succeed is high and his self-efficacy is high, he is more likely to devote the time to the work. The chances of Dan succeeding in delivering a good presentation are also correspondingly high.

Stuart dreads the event. He hates public speaking, and he has no confidence in his ability to master the constituent parts of the task. He knows that he has to do it, but his self-efficacy in relation to the task is low. As a result, thinking about it makes him anxious. He tries to put it out of his mind, and he avoids cues that remind him about it, like going to the library to prepare and so on. He indulges in ostrich-like behaviour and, consequently, his chances of success are reduced. His initial low self-efficacy rating has resulted in him not being motivated to perform the task. Self-efficacy has been shown to be an important variable in predicting educational achievement. Lane and Lane (2001) showed that self-efficacy was a good predictor of British students' achievement on sports science courses. Hoy and Davis (2006) demonstrated that, in school situations, teachers' ratings of their own self-efficacy in teaching are associated with the levels of achievement attained by their pupils.

Increasing self-efficacy ratings

The good news is that Bandura (1997) has demonstrated that self-efficacy can be modified by several different methods. Bandura (1999) has shown that the most straightforward way to improve self-efficacy is to get the person to 'perform the dreaded task'. If someone can be encouraged and supported to do something they fear, it has a dramatic effect on their self-efficacy. If the level of their performance is an issue, then further self-regulatory processes may be called into play so that the individual sees it as a gradual process. The first goal will be to perform, and subsequent goals may be about making improvements to their performance. **Vicarious experience** has also been shown to have an effect (Bandura, 1994). This is where the individual sees someone, whom they know shares the same fears as theirs, actually performing the task. Their cognitions become more positive, and they may say something like, 'If they can learn to do it, then so can I.' This then changes their self-efficacy directly. The final method is termed **participant modelling**. In this method, the person with low self-efficacy shadows a person who is successfully completing the task. Even this imitative behaviour has been shown to lower anxiety.

Returning to the student seminar example discussed earlier, Bandura's model outlines three possible courses of action for the student low in self-efficacy. He would suggest that observing another anxious student perform successfully and discussing how they prepared for the seminar would be very helpful in raising self-efficacy. Taking this action allows the student to change their cognitions, to see that they can learn to deliver a good presentation as well. Another technique would be to pair up the anxious student with someone less anxious. The anxious student would follow the confident student through the preparation and performance. Any possibility for feedback in the process would increase the chances of success by increasing the anxious student's confidence that they were progressing in the right direction. So, obtaining feedback on the content is valuable, as is rehearsing the presentation with a friendly audience of family or friends. Once this rehearsal has

been achieved, it again increases confidence. Any steps to improve confidence will improve the chances of a successful outcome.

Self-efficacy and the other self-regulatory processes help us to maintain our motivation and to be resilient even when faced with setbacks to our progress. Bandura (1990) quotes interesting examples of such resilience, including that displayed by the author James Joyce, whose book *Dubliners* was rejected by 22 publishers before becoming a success. Similarly, the artist Van Gogh died a pauper, having only ever sold one of his many paintings that are now worth a fortune. There are many more examples of amazing resilience shown by individuals in the face of rejection and apparent failure. Bandura sees the self-regulatory processes such as self-efficacy as being important in helping us to survive hard knocks and continue to strive to achieve our goals. Benight and Bandura (2004) published an extensive review of research undertaken on the role of self-efficacy in helping individuals recover from traumatic experiences. They looked at natural disasters, war, terrorist attacks, loss of a spouse and other interpersonal traumas. They concluded that individuals who believe that they can overcome their difficulties (high in self-efficacy) are consistently shown in all the studies they examined to make a better recovery.

Measuring self-efficacy

There are psychometric tests that have developed to measure General Self-Efficacy: Sherer *et al.*'s (1982) General Self-Efficacy Scale, Schwarzer and Jerusalem's (1995) General Perceived Self-Efficacy Scale, and Chen *et al.*'s (2001)

Children copy adults' behaviour in many different and subtle ways.
Source: Alamy Images/David R. Frazier Photolibrary, Inc.

New General Self-Efficacy Scale. Sherer *et al*.'s General Self-Efficacy Scale aims to measure self-efficacy via items that measure a general set of expectations that the respondent brings into new situations that they face. An example item from this scale is 'If I can't do a job the first time, I keep trying until I can'. Schwarzer and Jerusalem's General Perceived Self-Efficacy Scale is designed to measure general self-efficacy by examining the participant's beliefs around their own capability to handle new and difficult tasks in a variety of different domains. An example item from this measure is 'I can handle whatever comes my way'. Chen *et al*.'s New General Self-Efficacy Scale is designed to measure the respondent's belief in their overall competence at being able to produce a necessary performance across a variety of possible 'achievement' situations. An example item from this scale is 'I will be able to achieve most of the goals that I have set for myself'.

However, Bandura is critical of attempts to measure self-efficacy with global scales. He points out that few people are confident about every aspect of their lives and the tasks they have to perform. Hence, self-efficacy is measured in relation to specific tasks. It demands confidence judgements to be made about the constituent skills or knowledge elements that make up a task. Researchers need to undertake this analysis systematically to ensure that all the relevant components are assessed. Bandura (2006) provides detailed guidance on measuring self-efficacy. Consequently, Bandura suggests that new and separate scales need to be developed for each self-efficacy domain. So, for example, Bandura (2006) suggests the following.

- **Children's Self-Efficacy Scale**, which measures children's self-efficacy around a number of learning situations that students may experience at school, e.g. Self-Efficacy for Academic Achievement ('Learn reading, writing and language skills'), Self-Efficacy for Self-Regulated Learning ('Organise my schoolwork') and Social Self-Efficacy ('Carry on conversations with others').
- **Teacher Self-Efficacy Scale**, which measures teachers' self-efficacy around a number of teaching situations in which teachers may face challenges, e.g. Efficacy to Influence Decision-Making ('Get the instructional materials and equipment I need'), Disciplinary Self-Efficacy ('Get children to follow classroom rules') and Efficacy to Create a Positive School Climate ('Make students enjoy coming to school').
- **Parental Self-Efficacy**, which measure parents' self-efficacy around a number of situations in which parents may face challenges, e.g. Efficacy in Setting Limits, Monitoring Activities and Influencing Peer Affiliations ('Keep track of what your children are doing when they are outside the home'), Efficacy to Exercise Control over High-Risk Behaviour ('Prevent your children from doing things you do not want them to do outside the

home') and Resiliency of Self-Efficacy ('Keep up your spirits when you suffer hardships').

Julian Rotter and locus of control

We now want to introduce you to an important concept, **locus of control**, that has been and is still used extensively in research in personality and individual differences. This concept was first described by Julian Rotter (1966), another American learning theory researcher, who carried out most of his research at the University of Connecticut, where he still works. We will begin by examining the theoretical background to the concept of locus of control before going on to explore how locus of control is measured. There is a wealth of research on locus of control, as it has been and continues to be as popular a research tool as are measures of self-efficacy. For this reason, we present only a brief taste of some of the research findings here, with an indication of the areas of research where it has been applied.

Like Bandura, Rotter felt that animal studies were too simplistic to address the complexity of human behaviour. Rotter was interested in how you might predict how individuals would respond in particular situations. Supposing someone makes a nasty remark about you in front of other people. You could respond angrily; you could mock them for doing it; you could get upset; you could go quiet; or you could walk away. There are a variety of possibilities. Rotter (1966) aimed to predict which option an individual might choose in a particular situation. He termed this the **behaviour potential**; that is, the likelihood of a specific behaviour occurring in a particular situation. The response that you choose will be the one with the strongest behaviour potential in that situation. However, the crucial question is, how is the strength of the behaviour potential determined? Rotter developed a formula to answer this question:

Behaviour potential = Reinforcement value × Expectancy

In this formula, **expectancy** is our subjective estimate of the likely outcome of a course of behaviour. It is what we *expect* will happen. In learning theory terminology, it is our estimate of probability of our behaviour receiving a particular reinforcement in that situation. This is generally based on our experience of the same or similar situations. In the nasty insult example, it is your estimate of what you expect will happen if, for example, you mock the person. You may estimate that they will blush and feel ashamed of having made the nasty remark. Each option will have a different expectancy associated with it. This expectancy influences how you choose to behave in that situation. The final variable that contributes to predicting our behaviour is **reinforcement value**. This refers to our preferences amongst the possible reinforcements available. You may be more

Stop and think

Your own General Self-Efficacy?

Take the three statements from the three General Self-Efficacy Scales described above in the text.

- If I can't do a job the first time, I keep trying until I can.
- I can handle whatever comes my way.
- I will be able to achieve most of the goals that I have set for myself.

    Rate yourself on each statement using the scale 1 to 5, with 1 being 'disagree strongly', 2 being 'disagree', 3 being 'not certain', 4 being 'agree' and 5 being 'agree strongly'. Total up your scores and look at your individual score for each statement. Though this is not necessarily an accurate measurement of General Self-Efficacy, what do your total score and your answers to each statement tell you about your level of General Self-Efficacy? Remember each statement refers to a different definition of General Self-Efficacy.

---

inclined to help someone move some furniture if you know they will buy you a drink as a thank you.

To summarise, Rotter suggests that to predict behaviour in a particular situation, we need to know what the options are and what the individual sees as being the possible outcomes for each option. The individual then assesses the likely outcome of each option (expectancy). Next, they assess how much they value this outcome. The behaviour that is likely to occur (behaviour potential) will be the behaviour that gets the highest rating. A summary of this decision-making process for our hypothetical example is shown in Table 4.1.

In novel situations, where by definition we have no experience to guide us, Rotter (1966) suggests that we rely on what he calls **generalised expectancies**. What he showed to be important about this concept is that individuals come to believe on the basis of their other learning experiences that either reinforcement is controlled by outside forces or that their behaviour controls reinforcement (Rotter, 1966). The question he was interested in was whether it makes a difference if people believe that the reinforcement they receive is linked to how they perform, compared to individuals who believe that the reinforcement they receive is unrelated to their own behaviour. He labelled individuals who believe that reinforcement depends on external forces as **externals**. The external forces may include powerful others in the

person's world, luck, God, fate, the State and so on. What is crucial is that externals believe that the locus of control is external to them. What they do does not influence the outcomes. Individuals who believe that their behaviour does make a difference to the outcome are labelled **internals**. Rotter (1966) demonstrated that locus of control is a relatively stable personality characteristic and developed a scale to assess it, the IE Scale. It is assessed via a 30-item forced-choice scale. Scores are on a continuum of I–E, and Rotter does not suggest a cut-off point to separate externals from internals. He has published normative scores for particular groups to allow comparisons to be made. Although other assessment tools to measure locus of control have been developed since Rotter's scale was published, his IE Scale is still the most widely used in research. Some sample items from the scale are shown in Figure 4.4.

The impact of locus of control on behaviour

Rotter (1982) demonstrated that people with an internal locus of control are more likely to feel in control of their lives and to feel empowered to try to change things in their environment. Individuals with an external locus of control are more likely to feel powerless and helpless to change

---

Table 4.1 Application of Rotter's equation for predicting behaviour to an insult. **Stimulus:** Someone you know, Angela, makes a nasty remark about you in front of other people.

Behavioural option	Possible outcome	Rating of expectancy of outcome	Value of the outcome to the individual	Behaviour potential (probability that option will occur)
Angry reply	Argument	High	Low	Low
Mocking comment	Angela is embarrassed	High	High	High
Get upset	Angela feels remorse	Low	High	Low
Say nothing	Feel silly	High	Low	Low
Walk away	Feel silly	High	Low	Low

Respondents are asked to circle either of the two statements to indicate which statement they agree with.

Item 2
- Many of the unhappy things in people's lives are partly due to bad luck. (external locus of control)
- People's misfortunes result from the mistakes they make. (internal locus of control)

Item 9
- I have often found that what is going to happen will happen. (external locus of control)
- Trusting to fate has never turned out as well for me as making a decision to take a definite course of action. (internal locus of control)

Item 29
- What happens to me is my own doing. (internal locus of control)
- Sometimes I feel that I don't have enough control over the direction my life is taking. (external locus of control)

Figure 4.4 Sample items from Rotter's Locus of Control Scale.
Source: Rotter (1966).

things and to be dependent on others. Research has shown that internality increases with age. Children become more internal as they develop into adulthood. Internality becomes stable in middle age and does not decrease in old age. Warm, supportive parents who encourage independence in their offspring have been shown to foster the development of internality in their children (de Mann *et al.*, 1992).

Locus of control scores tend to correlate with anxiety, and there tend be more externals than internals among people with mental health problems (Lefcourt, 1992). A major review of studies on depression and locus of control concluded that external scores correlate positively with higher levels of depression (Benassi *et al*, 1988). This link with externality and depression is still reported currently, and it also links with suicidal behaviour. Cvengros *et al.* (2005) examined relationships between locus of control and levels of depression in patients suffering chronic kidney disease. They compared patient scores on health, locus of control, depression and progression of the illness over a 22-month period. Results demonstrated that patients who experienced an increase in their locus of control scores, demonstrating that they felt that they had more control over aspects of their condition, were less likely to be depressed. Liu *et al.* (2005) surveyed 1,362 adolescents in five schools in rural China and examined the relationships between locus of control, suicidal behaviours, life stressors, depression and family characteristics. They reported that high scores on the external locus of control were a risk factor for suicidal ideation and suicide attempts, along with high life stress, increasing age and depression.

A similar pattern is found for physical health, with internals becoming better informed about their illness and coping better with physical illness. Externals are more likely to adopt a passive patient role, while internals are more likely to get involved in their treatment by adopting healthier behaviour (Powell, 1992). Internal locus of control has been shown to be associated with improved quality of life in patients undergoing treatment for HIV (Préau and the APROCO study group, 2005). The study assessed quality of life, locus of control and demographic and health factors in 309 HIV-infected patients at the start of their treatment programme and then monitored the sample over 44 months of treatment. After 44 months of treatment, internal locus of control was a determinant of higher quality of both physical and mental health. Similar results, demonstrating better quality of life for internals, have been reported for individuals suffering from chronic illnesses such as epilepsy (Amir *et al.*, 1999), diabetes (Aalto *et al.*, 1997) and migraines (Allen *et al.*, 2000).

Locus of control has also been shown to impact on behaviour in many other situations. Lerner *et al.* (2005) carried out a study examining risk and protective factors in psychological distress experienced by 6,000 immigrants who had come to Israel from Russia. In a survey taken 5 years after the immigration, the researchers showed that psychological distress levels in the participants were linked with having an external locus of control as well as with other negative health and social factors. Locus of control is also applied in organisational research. For example, Allen *et al.* (2005) looked at the role of locus of control among other variables in predicting whether employees acted on their intention to change jobs, or whether they simply talked about it. They found that individuals with an internal locus of control were more likely to translate their intention to change jobs into action and change their job.

Locus of control has also been applied in educational contexts. Martinez (1994) showed that internals tend to achieve greater academic success than externals do. It is suggested that when internals do well in examinations or essays, they tend to attribute their success to their own abilities or to having worked hard. Externals, on the other hand, are more likely to put their success down to luck or an easy test. These differences in causal attribution will affect the confidence with which internals and externals approach academic assessment. Bender (1995) has suggested that the experience of continued failure despite trying at school leads to the development of an external locus of control in schoolchildren. They see that trying hard brings no reward, so they give up and may come to see failure as their destiny. Anderman and Midgley (1997) suggest that in the circumstances of repeated failure, having an external locus of control protects the individual's self-esteem. It is then not their fault that they fail. Internals, on the other hand, will be more confident and have higher expectations of themselves, both of which increase their probability of success. With very few exceptions, it appears that internals are more successful than externals in most situations. However, remember that the IE Scale is a continuum, and scores tend to cluster around the middle of the scale with few very extreme scores.

Walter Mischel

We debated whether to place Mischel's theory in the section on cognitive theories (Chapter 5); however, we decided to include it here because of its focus on the importance of situations and as it is frequently described as a social-cognitive approach to personality. Mischel was also heavily influenced by Bandura's work on self-efficacy and Rotter's approach to personality measurement. Mischel's theory could equally well sit in the section on cognitive theories.

In 1968 Walter Mischel published *Personality and Assessment*, a book that created enormous controversy in personality psychology. As outlined in the Profile box, Mischel's own research on the efficacy of global personality traits to predict performance led him to question the stability of personality traits across situations. This became known as the person–situation debate, or the 'personality paradox'. The question to be addressed was, do you behave as you do because of the situation you are in or because of your personality? Mischel (1968) was concerned about the way psychologists interpreted personality test scores and then used them to make decisions about individuals. He pointed

out that traits and other measures of personality are not good enough as predictive measures of how an individual will behave in different situations that they can be used to make important judgements about that individual, such as whether they are the right person for the job or whether they are likely to violate the conditions of their parole. He pointed out that there was little evidence that individuals' behaviour is consistent in different situations. Mischel (1973; 1979; 1983a; 1983b) makes it clear that, despite what some critics said, he was not questioning the existence of personality traits but simply the way that they were interpreted.

Mischel (1968) claimed that the correlation between personality trait self-report measures and behaviour was between 0.2 and 0.3, meaning that the trait was accounting for under 10 per cent of the variance in behaviour. He termed this correlation between traits measures and behaviour the **personality coefficient**. Other researchers questioned the size he claimed for the personality coefficient, demonstrating that a more realistic figure is 0.4 (Nisbett and Ross, 1980), which is still low.

Personality researchers tried to combat Mischel's argument by comparing how well situations and traits predict behaviour (Endler and Hunt, 1966; 1968). The conclusion was that knowing about both the situation and the personality was better than knowing about either one on their own. However, this approach is impractical as there are so many possibilities, and researchers have to make decisions about which traits are likely to be relevant in particular situations. Mischel (2004) cites a study undertaken by Newcombe (1929) where 51 boys were measured on the personality characteristics of extraversion and introversion and then studied in 21 situations in a summer camp on a daily basis. Systematic recordings were made of the amount of time each boy talked at meals and of how much time he played alone or with others. Much to his dismay, Newcombe found that the average correlation of behaviour across situations based on these daily observations was 0.14. Mischel and others have continued to examine the consistency in behaviour that individuals display across situations and have concluded that there is substantial variation (Mischel, 1968; 1973; Mischel and Peake, 1982; Moskowitz, 1994; Ross and Nisbett, 1991).

Epstein (1979; 1980) argues that most personality researchers do not measure the relationships between personality traits and behaviour correctly. They take a personality score and then take one measure of behaviour, such as the likelihood of offering to donate blood, rated on a Likert Scale. This violates the principles of good measurement (Epstein, 1980). You need multiple measures to ensure reliability. For example, if we wanted to compare the different amounts of time that introverts and extraverts spent studying, a reliable measure would not be obtained by asking them how long they studied the previous evening. We would have to measure their study habits over some more extended time to get a true picture. This is what researchers have done to address this issue of the variability across situations and the associated measurement error. Behaviour measures from individuals are aggregated. Using this approach, researchers have demonstrated that there are stable individual differences between individuals on almost every dimension studied (Epstein, 1979; 1980; Mischel and Peake, 1982; Pervin, 1994). Epstein (1979) compared extraversion–introversion scores in students with the number of social contacts they made, where the contacts were recorded in daily diaries over a 2-week period. They found a personality coefficient of 0.52, which is a major improvement on previous figures. What aggregation does is to minimise the effect of the situation so that the stable underlying characteristics of the individual become apparent.

Mischel (2004) points out that the person versus situation debate caused real divisions between personality psychologists looking to show consistent differences in individuals that are independent of the situations they are in, while social psychologists stressed the importance of the situation (Nisbett and Ross, 1980; Ross and Nisbett, 1991). Some personality psychologists did examine the person–situation interaction in more detail (e.g. Fleeson, 2001; Moskowitz, 1994; Vansteelandt and Van Mechelen, 1998), but, as Mischel (2004) points out, these were rare exceptions.

For Mischel, the way forward was to incorporate the findings from developments in cognitive psychology about how the mind works. Mischel (1973) outlined a set of social-cognitive person variables, as opposed to trait descriptors, to describe individual differences. These variables described processes that were important in describing how individuals construed situations (encoding and appraisal), variables relating to the situation (people and the self) and the beliefs, behavioural expectancies, goals and processes

of self-regulation. The aim was to discover the psychological processes to determine how individuals characteristically interpreted the world and how particular situations produced characteristic behaviour in individuals. It is an interactional approach that still aims to uncover individual personality differences; however, in Mischel's approach, these differences are not encapsulated in situation-free personality trait terms like 'optimistic', 'considerate', 'sociable', but in situation-related descriptions of how individuals characteristically behave. Examining some of the research undertaken by Mischel and his colleagues will make it clearer.

Mischel and Peake (1982) examined what they called 'college conscientiousness' and friendliness in college students. To begin with, the students themselves specified the behaviours and situational contexts that they considered relevant to the traits being examined. This ensured that the behaviours and situations being measured were personally meaningful for the college students' definitions of 'college conscientiousness' and friendliness. While the researchers found behavioural variability across different situations, so that one person might be very friendly in one situation but low in another, they also found temporal stability in an individual's behaviour *within* similar situations. Mischel suggested that some situations were perceived as being highly similar, forming what he describes as a **functional equivalence class of situations**. Individuals perceived themselves as having the personality characteristic of friendliness, for example, based on how consistently they behaved within a particular situation rather than on how they behaved across situations. In other words, you might well see yourself as being high in the characteristic of friendliness even though you do not act in a friendly way in every situation. From this study, Mischel and Peake (1982) concluded that there was consistency in how individuals

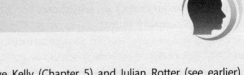

Profile

Walter Mischel

Walter Mischel was born in Vienna in 1930, in a house that was a short walk away from where Freud lived. His family moved to New York when he was 10 years old to escape from the Nazis. He studied psychology but qualified as a social worker. He suggested that the early link with Freud led him to begin his career as an advocate of Freud and psychoanalysis. However, he found that the psychoanalytic approach was of little help in his work with inner-city aggressive youngsters. This led him to undertake a PhD in psychology at Ohio State University. Here he worked with

George Kelly (Chapter 5) and Julian Rotter (see earlier). After graduation he worked at Harvard and then Stanford Universities before moving to his present post at Columbia University in 1984. While at Harvard he worked on a project assessing performance for the Peace Corps and found that global trait measures of personality were not good predictors of performance. This led him to question existing approaches to personality, as we shall see. He received the Distinguished Scientist Award from the Clinical Division of the American Psychological Association in 1978.

behaved within a situation, and there appeared to be consistent differences between types of situations that were worth exploring further.

While acknowledging that some of the differences between situations might be random noise, Mischel and his colleagues were convinced that there were also systematic differences in the perception of situations. They set out to look for some underlying structure that would help explain where these differences came from. An example may help your understanding here. Mischel (2004) compares two individuals who have the same score on a personality trait measure of aggressiveness. However, observation of their behaviour shows that they behave aggressively in very different situations and that these differences in their behaviour patterns are stable. One is aggressive to his junior colleagues at work but very friendly to his superiors, while the other is very friendly with colleagues but aggressive to his superiors. In this example, simply describing them as equally aggressive based on a trait measure does not give a real description of how they differ in terms of their personality characteristics.

Searching for invariance in an individual's behaviour across situations is a massive undertaking; but Mischel and his colleagues ran a replication of the Newcombe (1929) study, using a residential summer camp set up to treat children with behavioural problems, particularly aggression (Mischel *et al.*, 2002; Shoda *et al.*, 1993; 1994). The children were filmed over many weeks and for many hours. Mischel *et al.* reported that aggressive behaviour observed in one type of situation was not a good predictor of how that individual would behave in another type of situation. This in itself is not surprising, but Mischel *et al.* demonstrated that an individual's rank-order position on aggression relative to others in the group changes predictably and dramatically in different situations. The conclusion was that individuals might have a similar mean level of aggression but that there are predictable differences in terms of which situations they behave aggressively in, and these provide much more insight into the kind of person they are. It might be that one child is aggressive to his peers when asked for anything, but another child with the same aggression trait score might characteristically only be aggressive to adults when they are chastising him. Mischel and his colleagues helpfully characterise these stable situation-behaviour relationships with the phrase, 'if … then … ', and describe them as providing a **behavioural signature of personality** (Shoda *et al.*, 1993; 1994). These behavioural signatures represent our characteristic reactions to situations. Other researchers have confirmed the existence of behavioural signatures of personality that provide distinctive characterisations of individuals (Andersen and Chen, 2002; Cervone and Shoda, 1999; Morf and Rodewalt, 2001; Shoda and LeeTiernan, 2002). To summarise, Mischel and his colleagues have

described the two types of behavioural consistencies. The first is behavioural consistency, called type 1 consistency, and it represents the trait ratings describing what individuals are generally like. Type 2 consistency represents the behavioural signatures of personality which show distinctive patterns of behaviour across similar situations, the if … then … propositions that encapsulate patterns of situational effects on personality.

Mischel argues the need for a dynamic personality system that will incorporate developments from cognitive science and genetics that are relevant to personality. He suggests that a dynamic personality system will go beyond mere descriptions of personality and give us more information about how the individual mind functions and personality is organised. He suggests that information about the individual's mental and emotional processes is an essential component of any model of personality. Mischel and Shoda (1995) outlined a model of a **cognitive-affective processing system (CAPS)** that fulfils some of these criteria. The aim was to demonstrate how the CAPS model can predict the type 1 and type 2 consistencies in personality that are described earlier. CAPS is composed of various mental representations, labelled **cognitive-affective units (CAUs)**. These CAUs include the individual's representations of self, others, situations, expectations, beliefs, long-term goals, values, emotional states, competencies, self-regulatory systems and memories of people and past events. Mischel and Shoda (1995) propose that the CAUs are organised in an interrelated system within the individual's stable networks of cognitions and emotions. A diagram showing how the CAPS model operates is shown in Figure 4.5. The yellow box contains developmental influences, and the green arrows indicate how these influences affect the system. All the other interactions, indicated by purple lines and arrows, are envisaged to happen concurrently.

Higgins (1996) has demonstrated that, within one individual, some representations are more accessible than others.

This differential accessibility of CAUs, and the differences in the ways that they are interrelated within each individual, both contribute to the observed differences in personality between individuals. Different CAUs will be activated in different situations and at different times, but the way that change occurs does not vary, reflecting the stability of structures within the individual's CAPS (Mischel and Shoda, 1995; Shoda and Mischel, 1998). The CAPS model has been shown to generate type 1 and type 2 behavioural consistencies in computer simulations (Mischel and Shoda, 1998; Shoda *et al.*, 2002).

The CAPS model produces descriptions of personality types based on how individuals organise their CAUs and how they process situational features. Downey *et al.* (2000)

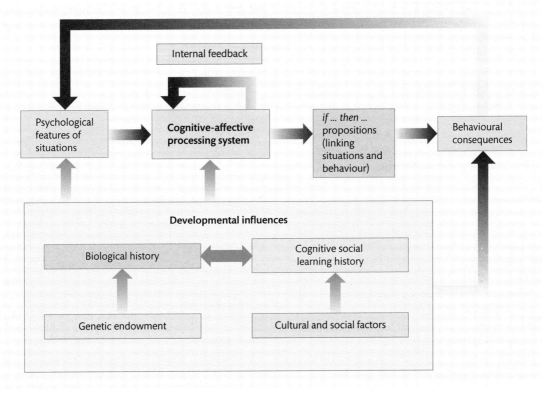

Figure 4.5 Mischel and Shoda's (1995) cognitive-affective processing system (CAPS).

have provided an example describing the way that individuals who fear rejection respond to perceived uncaring behaviour in their partners, such as when their partner is paying attention to another person. Rejection-fearful individuals perceive, interpret and evaluate their partners' behaviour in terms of potential rejection. They ruminate about it, and these ruminations instigate the emotional responses of anger and fear as the individual becomes more fearful of being abandoned. They then respond to their partners by activating controlling, coercive behaviours and blaming their partner for this. This then creates a self-fulfilling prophecy as their partner in turn gets angry and may respond with threats of rejection. This response from the partner then reinforces the rejection-fearful individual's feeling that they are right to fear rejection, oblivious to the role that they themselves played in generating the rejection threat. From these observations, the personality signature of a rejection-fearing individual is apparent. When appraising interpersonal situations, they anxiously look for evidence of potential rejection, any evidence of rejection threat is magnified and they overreact to it with anger and blame (Downey *et al.*, 2000).

This analysis demonstrates how personality signatures provide a more in-depth analysis of individual differences by incorporating situation-specific information or, in this

instance, relation-specific information. Shoda *et al.* (2002) point out that, in interpersonal situations, the 'situation' is another person, and they have demonstrated that the CAPS model deals equally well with this case. A great deal of work has already been accomplished on classifying different types of situations. Kelley *et al.* (2003) have published an *Atlas of Interpersonal Situations*. The aim was to go beyond a superficial description of situations and identify the psychologically important aspects of situations that play a functional role in generating behaviour. It is about the way that types of individuals characteristically perceive a situation, as demonstrated in the rejection-fearful example. More work is needed to develop a better understanding of how situation-behaviour signatures work and to link them with types of individuals.

What Mischel (2004) is arguing for is an approach to personality research that integrates research findings from other areas of psychology; he is arguing that cognitions, memories, emotions, perceptual processes, genetic influences, regulatory systems and memories all play a part in generating individual differences. As we have seen, Mischel and his colleagues have already demonstrated, with their CAPS model, that there is a complex interaction between situations and enduring individual personality differences. There are still debates about the details, and the effects of many variables still have to be examined. Carver and Scheier (2003) have been examining the self-regulatory process by looking at the relationships between behavioural goals and the effects of feedback on goals. It is a complex undertaking.

The impact of Mischel

Mischel (2004) relates an amusing incident where one of his students reports to him that, according to a multiple-choice question in a state licensing exam for psychologists, he does not believe in personality. After reflection, Mischel suggests that, if personality is defined purely by trait and state measures (Chapter 7), the answer is true. However, he now believes that personality research is moving on; a new era is emerging as researchers are returning to the original aim of personality theorising, which was to understand the systems that produce individual differences in behaviour. Mischel's work has been a major stimulus in these developments, bringing closer the possibility of an overarching explanatory theory of personality.

Mischel's original paper in 1968 has had a major effect on personality research. Swann and Seyle (2005) conclude that initially it led to a decline in research in personality for about 10 years and that social psychologists began to focus on the impact of situations and de-emphasise any personality effects in their research. However, Mischel's paper did lead to significant improvements in personality research. There have been many rebuttals of Mischel's views that involved researchers looking very critically at their methodologies, admitting that measures were often weak and the selection of which traits to study was sometimes inappropriate (Baumeister and Tice, 1988; Bem and Allen, 1974; Funder, 1999; 2001).

The concern about the validity of personality tests led Cronbach and Meehl (1955) to develop a clear procedure for establishing the construct validity of psychological tests. There is now widespread adherence to these procedures in personality test construction, resulting in improved validity of tests, and more care is taken in the interpretation of test scores (Swann and Seyle, 2005). Meyer *et al.* (2001) have demonstrated that personality tests now share the same high levels of validity as seen in medical tests. More attention has also been paid to the design of studies, with variables being more carefully selected and operationalised (Block, 1977; Funder, 1999; 2001; 2002).

The grand explanatory theory of personality that Mischel envisages has not yet emerged, but considerable progress has been made in resolving the person-situation debate and in developing our understanding of how the two interact to produce both consistency and change in behaviour. Situations affect individuals, but individuals also act to change situations, often in complex ways (Magnusson, 2001). Swann and Seyle (2005), in their review of the effects of Mischel's attack on traditional approaches to personality,

conclude that, while the new integrative approach is likely to be fruitful, there are still instances where it is helpful to make distinctions between personal and situational determinants of behaviour.

Evaluation of learning theory approaches

We will now evaluate learning theory approaches using the eight criteria identified previously (Chapter 1): description, explanation, empirical validity, testable concepts, comprehensiveness, parsimony, heuristic value and applied value.

Description

Both classical and operant conditioning provide useful descriptions of relatively simple behaviour. However, Pavlov, Skinner and Dollard and Miller all based their research on observations of pigeons, rats and dogs; the more developed and unique qualities of human beings, such as the effects of language on our behaviour, are largely ignored. Skinner (1963) did address this criticism by agreeing that human behaviour was very complex and therefore difficult to study. However, he strongly felt that the basic principles governing the way we learn behaviour are the same for humans and other animals. It was simpler to study animals in the laboratory and, as the testing conditions could be controlled very rigorously with animals, it was better science, as far as Skinner was concerned. These views of Skinner's were contentious and generated as much debate as Freud's theory. Opponents argued that people are capable of higher cognitive processing, resulting in more complex learning *than observed in rats and pigeons*, and that the principles of classical and operant conditioning do not really address that complexity (Bailey and Bailey, 1993; Garcia, 1993).

Bandura and Rotter addressed this issue by abandoning animal studies and by allowing for the effects of inner mental processes on human behaviour. In this way, they both provided a more comprehensive description of human behaviour, although it was nothing like the complexity of Freud's work. By examining the importance of self-efficacy and locus of control, they have provided descriptions of valuable personality processes. Mischel's work follows in the tradition of Bandura and Rotter, but his ultimate aim is for an overarching, integrative theory of personality.

Explanation

The principles of learning theory do provide valid explanations of observed behaviour in specific situations. However, human beings have a rich mental life, which is ignored in the behavioural approaches. We are all capable of thinking and feeling, and these inner mental processes are ignored. As we have seen, many of the psychoanalytic theorists suggest that we are not always conscious of the reasons for our behaviour. Ruling out any idea of unconscious motivation as it cannot be directly observed seems absurd to such theorists. Dollard and Miller allowed for a concept of the unconscious, but they did not explain the role these processes play in determining behaviour.

These approaches can be criticised as being as deterministic as Freud's. The individual has no free will; our behaviour is determined by how others react to us. With the exception of the more recent work of Bandura, Rotter and Mischel, learning theory cannot explain intentional behaviour. We may have long-term goals that are unconnected with our prior learning history. An example will help to illustrate this. Imagine that an individual grows up in a family where her mother and father were both doctors. The parents had a burning ambition for their daughter to follow in their footsteps, and she was certainly intelligent enough to achieve the necessary academic qualifications. According to the learning theorists, this example should result in the daughter becoming a doctor as she was brought up in an environment that fostered this, and her academic ability did not provide a bar. However, in this instance the daughter became a librarian. This is just one case history, but we are sure that if you ask around among your friends, you will come across other examples where children do not follow the paths that parents have wished for.

Sometimes we all do the unexpected in situations, and learning theory principles cannot easily explain this creativity in behaviour. Skinner (1972) rejected this criticism and said that it applies to classical conditioning with its emphasis purely on the stimulus and the response. In operant conditioning, we may behave in new and creative ways, but whether we repeat the behaviour is determined by its consequences. If we are rewarded in some way for the behaviour, then it should occur again, whereas if we are not rewarded, it should extinguish. I am sure you will agree that this is certainly not the case for much of human behaviour. Many would-be novelists continue to write, yet no one will publish their work; similarly, musicians continue to compose although no one plays their work, inventors continue to invent despite a lack of success and so on. We can still maintain goal-directed behaviour in the absence of positive consequences. Other personality theorists here might talk to inner drives that motivate us to behave in certain ways.

Bandura is the only learning theorist who addresses this issue with his concept of self-regulatory processes and self-reinforcement. These concepts allow for intentional behaviour and for behaviour to continue in the absence of any external reinforcement. The recognition of the role of cognitive processes and social factors in behaviour results in Bandura and Rotter's theories being very different from the earlier theories, although they still have the same emphasis on learning being a sufficient explanation for the development of personality. Mischel's position goes beyond that of Bandura and Rotter, although their approaches would be included as constituent components of an integrative theory as the effects of learning still need to be explained within such a theory. Rotter included the effects of memories of previous situations (prior learning) explicitly in the description of his theoretical approach.

For these learning theorists, any similarities in the way that people respond in different situations are down to environmental factors and prior learning. The environment that the person occupies is similar to a previous situation they had experienced; hence, they are responding in a similar fashion, rather than expressing a particular character trait that they possess. This rejection of the idea that people possess individual characteristics that influence how they behave in different situations flies in the face of all the empirical studies of stable measured individual differences in behaviour that are evidenced in this text. Again, Bandura, Rotter and Mischel are exceptions in that they have each identified individual personality characteristics. Both Bandura and Rotter see these differences resulting from learning experiences. At no point do Bandura and Rotter acknowledge a role for any possible genetic inheritance of personality traits, unlike Mischel, who is clear that biological factors have a part to play.

Empirical validity

One strength of the learning theorists is that their work is based on empirical data collected under controlled laboratory conditions. However, researchers such as Black (1973) have suggested that these theorists sometimes go beyond the data they have collected and make assumptions. This is especially the case with regard to complex human behaviour. Much of the empirical data is about animal behaviour, but the assumption is that the principles uncovered with animals will apply to human beings. They have examined very simple learning situations in animals and then go on to assume that somehow, some combination of the same learning principles can be used to explain much more complex behaviour in human beings (Skinner, 1973). There is no empirical evidence for these claims. Bandura and Rotter do not use animal studies, but even in their human studies, they too are sometimes guilty of making assumptions that go beyond their data. The same cannot be said about Mischel, although the early critiques of his position claimed that he did. He successfully refuted these claims, as overviews by Snyder and Ickes (1985) and Swann and Seyle (2005) make clear.

Certainly the concepts of classical and operant conditioning can be, and have been, tested quite exhaustively. The argument is not that we cannot demonstrate the occurrence of both classical and operant conditioning; rather, that the concepts are not sufficient in themselves as an explanation of human behaviour. The animal explanation applies here also. The concepts may have been adequately tested in regard to rats, pigeons and dogs; however, this is not the case for much of human behaviour, especially the more complex human behaviour.

Testable concepts

With regard to Bandura, Rotter and Mischel's work, the concepts they have developed have been extensively tested in a variety of psychological disciplines, and there is a great deal of supporting evidence. They have provided useful conceptualisations of elements of the process of acquiring personality. Mischel has gone further and caused personality psychologists to improve their methodologies and measurement tools.

Comprehensiveness

Skinner rejected the idea of personality and did not see himself as creating any theory; rather, he tackled specific problems in learning and behaviour. Taken at this level, he has provided a sound explanation of some aspects of learning and some specific behaviour, although most of the emphasis has been on lower animals, not humans. Within his research, Skinner focused on simple behaviours as they were easy to control, but this has resulted in his work failing to address adequately the complexity of human behaviour. This was also true of Pavlov, who was purely interested in learning mechanisms.

Dollard and Miller, Bandura and Rotter were interested in personality and in developing relevant theories. Dollard and Miller's attempts were not very comprehensive. They did provide learning theory descriptions for how some Freudian defence mechanisms could be acquired. However, they fell short of developing a comprehensive theory of personality. Bandura's theory is probably the most comprehensive, but the lack of any discussion of genetic influences on personality development is a weakness in all the learning theory approaches. While Rotter has not yet produced a detailed comprehensive theory of personality, he has outlined the major components of such a theory.

Parsimony

From what we have discussed so far, it is apparent that learning theories can be criticised for being too parsimonious to explain all of human behaviour and human motivation adequately. The approaches are very parsimonious; they assume a small number of principles will apply to all situations, sometimes without empirical evidence. Towards

the end of his life, Skinner did accept that additional concepts might be necessary to explain the more complex learning that occurs in humans. This criticism cannot be applied to Rotter's work as it aims to incorporate relevant explanatory and organisational concepts from all areas of psychology relevant to personality.

Heuristic value

As we have seen, both classical and operant conditioning have had an enormous impact on the discipline of psychology. Firstly, by emphasising the importance of empirical research evidence in theory development and hypothesis testing, the learning theorists played a major role in shaping psychology as an empirical science. They also demonstrated the importance of attending to situational and environmental variables that may affect behaviour in any situation and led to an early emphasis on laboratory studies where such variables can be more readily controlled. This early work has generated and continues to stimulate research within psychology, as evidenced by the continuation of the *Journal of Experimental Analysis of Behavior*, which is devoted to learning theory approaches to research. Skinner himself has been a controversial figure, and his work has created great debates within psychology, psychiatry, education, philosophy, politics and the general public.

Bandura and Rotter, with their concepts of self-efficacy and locus of control in particular, have stimulated a huge amount of research. Mischel has also stimulated a great deal of controversy and research in both personality and social psychology, and it may well be that Rotter's work has created major changes in the discipline, some of which are yet to become apparent.

Applied value

In terms of applications of psychology, all the learning theorists have advocated the adoption of very pragmatic approaches to disturbed behaviour, and this has led to many new treatments for mental illness. By focusing on the detail of the ill person's behaviour, they have provided unique understanding of how such behaviour may have arisen in the individual's previous learning. The concept of disturbed behaviour as a maladaptive response that has previously been reinforced immediately opens up the possibility of that behaviour being extinguished and new responses being acquired. This concept also helps to demystify mental illness and, consequently, it can be presented as a positive approach to mental illness.

The concepts of self-efficacy and locus of control have both been valuable additional factors to consider in behavioural change programmes. Programmes have been developed to improve self-efficacy in treatment programmes ranging from smoking cessation to safe sex campaigns. Similarly, locus of control has proved a useful tool in understanding treatment compliance issues in a variety of areas. Mischel too has always been interested in clinical aspects of psychology, and his work has led to better understanding of how personality attributes interact in situations to amplify disturbed behaviour, as in our example of the rejection-fearful individual.

This very idea of changing behaviour also leads to concerns about the potential to apply learning theory in unethical ways to mould both individual behaviour and that of societies. One example that we have already examined is the development of experimental neuroses in the Little Albert case study. As we have seen in his novel, *Walden Two*, Skinner also acknowledged this concern. Behavioural approaches need to be applied ethically, as with all attempts to change behaviour, hence the importance of research ethics. Ethical issues in relation to personality research are discussed further later (see online Chapter 28; www.pearsoned.co.uk/maltby).

Final comments

In this discussion you were introduced to the learning theory approach to personality, notably Pavlov and classical conditioning, Watson and behaviourism, Skinner and operant conditioning, the integrative personality theory of Dollard and Miller and the social-cognitive approaches of Bandura. You were also introduced to the concept of self-efficacy, Rotter and the locus of control and Mischel and social learning theory. You should be able to critically evaluate each of these theories. You should be able to broadly evaluate learning approaches to personality.

Summary

- The early learning theories reject the idea of our behaviour being directed by inner motives. All our behaviour is learned. Individual differences in behaviour are the result of the different learning experiences that people have had and the situations that they have experienced rather than being caused by differences in personality.
- Pavlov demonstrated how behaviour is learnt via classical conditioning. The process begins with an unconditioned stimulus (e.g. food), which is something that automatically produces the response you are interested in, called unconditioned response (salivating).
- Pavlov demonstrated that the acquisition of many of our emotional responses can be explained by classical conditioning.
- Watson, influenced by Pavlov's work, called for the adoption of rigorous scientific method in psychology and for theory building to be based on empirical evidence rather than the introspection, reflection and anecdotal case study methodologies of the psychoanalytic school.
- For the learning theorists, psychopathology is caused by faulty learning. Normal development is about learning responses that are adaptive in the individual's environment. Abnormal development occurs when maladaptive responses are learned.
- Skinner was a radical behaviourist, and he did not allow for inner experiences in his account of learning. As inner experiences could not be observed, he therefore considered them unscientific. Only behaviour that could be observed was included in his model of learning. For the same reason, he rejected the concept of personality as being produced by the interaction of inner forces. All behaviour was learnt. He demonstrated three key concepts important for learning: operant conditioning, positive reinforcement and negative reinforcement.
- Skinner's theory is deterministic. He rejects the concept of free will and the idea of intention or creativity in human behaviour. We merely respond to stimuli in our environment, and the consequences of our responding determine our learning.
- A strength of all the learning theory approaches is their emphasis on the application of rigorous methodologies to collect data and the underpinning of all theory with empirical data. Criticisms are that they fail to address the complexity of human behaviour. They are too heavily grounded in animal studies and have a very limited conceptual basis.
- Dollard and Miller made the first attempt to allow for cognitive processing in learning theory. They allow for unconscious influences on motivation but strictly define what they mean by the unconscious.
- Dollard and Miller outlined a stimulus–response (S–R) theory of learning. This includes the consideration of primary drives and secondary drives.
- Dollard and Miller demonstrated that observational learning played an important role in learning. Role models are observed, and their performance is imitated.
- Bandura was the first learning theorist to allocate a significant role in learning to inner cognitive processes. Bandura uses the term reciprocal determinism to label the processes that drive behaviour. He sees an individual as being influenced by three interacting factors: personal factors, behaviour and environmental factors.
- Bandura further develops Dollard and Miller's concept of observational learning and has demonstrated its

importance in the acquisition of aggressive behaviour, in particular with the Bobo doll study. He demonstrated that the characteristics of the model, attributes of the observer and the consequences of imitating behaviour are all influential factors in the learning process.

- For Bandura, modelling behaviour was an active process of learning through observation where the observer makes judgements and constructs symbolic representations.
- Bandura demonstrated that humans use self-reinforcement to control our behaviour via internal self-regulatory processes.
- Self-efficacy is identified as one of the most powerful of the self-regulatory processes.
- Rotter demonstrated that the likelihood of a behaviour occurring, termed behaviour potential, is predicted by our expectancy and reinforcement value.

- Rotter termed our generalised expectancies in new situations as locus of control.
- Mischel began his major work by criticising traditional trait and state approaches to measuring personality, claiming that not enough attention was paid to situational factors.
- Mischel and his colleagues carried out extensive research to examine the interactions between personality dispositions and situations. This work produced behavioural signatures of personality.
- Mischel and Shoda (1995) outlined and tested a model of the cognitive-affective processing system (CAPS). Individual differences in this system result from differential accessibility of cognitive-affective units (CAUs) and differences in their interrelationships.
- Evaluative criteria are applied to all the theories covered here.

Connecting up

In this chapter we started to introduce some cognitive ideas that overlapped with learning theories. You will learn more on cognitive ideas of personality in the next chapter in this book.

In this chapter we emphasised how behaviours are learnt. Chapter 18 demonstrates a further consideration of learning theories when we outline the theory of learned optimism.

Critical thinking

Discussion questions

- A child is having a problem at school. When it comes to taking her turn in class, rather than raising her hand and waiting to speak, she shouts out answers to questions and interrupts other students when they are talking. What would a behaviourist recommend to solve this problem? How might they explain how the problem arose?
- A friend of yours is having a problem with their university work. They are unmotivated, fail to turn up to lectures and leave doing their coursework to the last minute, often leading to them getting very low marks. What would a behaviourist recommend to solve this problem?
- How adequately do learning theorists explain human motivation?
- Skinner argues that humans do not have free will. Critically discuss.
- How necessary is external reinforcement for behaviour? Can you think of examples where either positive or negative reinforcement is ineffectual?

- Discuss the contribution that learning theories have made to the treatment of mental illness.
- 'Behavioural treatments need to be applied within an ethical framework'. Critically discuss.
- Discuss whether the concept of personality is necessary.
- Has the person-situation debate been adequately resolved?
- Earlier in this chapter, we asked you to make some ethical reflections on the Little Albert study. Nowadays carrying out such research on your own children would be likely to bring you into conflict with social services. It could be construed as child abuse. While we have gained useful knowledge from this study, it would be very unlikely to get ethical approval currently. Would this be a loss to psychology? You may want to reflect on current ethical codes and consider whether we have become too stringent to the detriment of scientific knowledge (for more, see online Chapter 28). The situation may be straightforward when children are involved, but how about if it were adults old enough to consent freely?
- Are learning theories only about forms of reward and punishment?

Essay questions

- Critically examine the contribution made by one of the following psychologists to our understanding of personality:

  – Skinner
  – Bandura
  – Mischel.

- Compare the differences between classical and operant conditioning.
- Critically discuss how Skinner's and Watson's behaviourisms differ.

- 'Personality is no more than the sum of our learning experiences.' Discuss in reference to learning theories.
- How adequately does learning theory explain the development of personality?
- Discuss the concept of reward and punishment within learning theory.
- Critically compare two of the following three theorists:

  – Skinner
  – Bandura
  – Mischel.

Going further

Books

- Skinner, B. F. (1971). *Beyond freedom and dignity*. London: Prentice Hall. This is a controversial book that sparks debate. Skinner argues in this book that human beings do not have free will, so there is no real concept of choice in human behaviour.
- Nye, R. (1992). *The legacy of B. F. Skinner. Concepts and perspectives, controversies and misunderstandings*. Belmont, CA: Brooks/Cole. This book provides an excellent, fair evaluation of Skinner's work.
- Skinner, B. F. (1978). *Reflections on behaviourism and society*. Englewood Cliffs, NJ: Prentice Hall. In this book, Skinner discusses the development of his ideas and their application in the real world.
- The classic source for Dollard and Miller is *Personality and psychotherapy: An analysis in terms of learning, thinking, and culture* (1950, McGraw-Hill).
- Bandura, A. (1996). *Self-efficacy: The exercise of control*. New York: Freeman. This is the most recent publication by Bandura specifically on self-efficacy.
- Rotter, J. B., Chance, J. and Phares, E. J. (eds) (1972). *Application of a social learning theory of personality*. New York: Holt, Rinehart & Winston. This is the book where Rotter, in collaboration with Chance and Phares, described a general theory of social learning.
- Lefcourt, H. M. (1981; 1983; 1984) has edited three volumes of the early work on locus of control. These volumes are titled *Research with the locus of control construct* (New York: Academic Press).

Journals

- Bandura, A. (1974). Behaviour theory and models of man. *American Psychologist*, 29, 859–869. In this article,

Bandura discusses his concept of personality. Published by the American Psychological Association and available online via PsycARTICLES.
- Bandura, A. (1977). Self-efficacy: Toward a unifying theory of behavioural change. *Psychological Review*, 84, 191–215. This is the classic account of self-efficacy. Published by the American Psychological Association and available online via PsycARTICLES.
- Bandura, A. (2002). Swimming against the mainstream: The early years from chilly tributary to transformative mainstream. *Behaviour Research and Therapy*, 42, 613–630. This is Bandura's account of the development of his ideas and their application in therapeutic contexts. *Behaviour Research and Therapy*, an international multidisciplinary journal, is published by Oxford Elsevier and is available online via Science Direct.
- Bandura, A. (2012). On the functional properties of perceived self-efficacy revisited. *Journal of Management, 38(1)*, 9–44. In this recent article Bandura reviews some of the research on self-efficacy that has produced negative or null effects. He puts these down to badly conceived measures and/or lack of understanding of contextual factors that influence self-efficacy. He explains how self-efficacy should not be treated as simple personality trait but needs to be understood within specific contexts and conditions. This is a challenging but worthwhile read and is available online via PsycARTICLES.
- If you are interested in examining applications of locus of control in health, *Journal of Health Psychology* (2005), Vol. 10, No. 5, is a special edition devoted to the measure, including a short version, and to its new applications in health.
- Mischel, W. (2004). Toward an integrative science of the person. *Annual Review of Psychology*, 55, 1–22.

This article by Mischel gives an excellent overview of his current position and the progress that personality theory has made in addressing the person-situation controversy. *Annual Review of Psychology* is published by Annual Reviews of Palo Alto, California, and is available online via Business Source Premier.

- Overskeid, G. (2007). Looking for Skinner and finding Freud. *American Psychologist, 62,* 590–595. Published by the American Psychological Association and available online via PsycARTICLES. In this article Overskeid suggests that, though Sigmund Freud (whose theory we outline in Chapter 2) and B. F. Skinner are often seen as opposing theorists, they had many things in common, including basic assumptions shaped by positivism and determinism. The article discusses how many of Skinner's views may have been influenced by Freud.
- Skinner, B. F. (1990). Can psychology be a science of mind? *American Psychologist, 45,* 1206–1210. Again this article is available online via PsycARTICLES. It presents Skinner's views on the role of cognitions in behaviour.
- If you would like to look through some journals related to behavioural analysis, there are:

  - *Journal of Applied Behavior Analysis.* A journal primarily for the original publication of experimental

research involving applications of the experimental analysis of behaviour to problems of social importance.
  - *Journal of the Experimental Analysis of Behavior.* A journal primarily for the original publication of experiments relevant to the behavior of individual organisms; it also publishes review articles and theoretical contributions.

Web links

- The Cambridge Center for Behavioral Studies is a resource for those interested in behaviour analysis and its role in education, health and the workplace. Also provides a comprehensive list of links to other behaviour analysis resources (**www.behavior.org**).
- This site has a wealth of material on self-efficacy, including contributions from Bandura himself. It also has an extensive reference list of research on self-efficacy (**http://p20motivationlab.org**).
- This is the link to Walter Mischel's website. Here you will get an idea of the work he is currently undertaking and a list of his most recent publications (**www.columbia .edu/cu/psychology/indiv_pages/mischel.html**).

Film and literature

- *Nineteen Eighty-Four* (1949, George Orwell, Penguin). Primarily concerned with the prospect of state control by behaviourist means. In *Nineteen Eighty-Four*, rats are used as a means of shaping Winston's behaviour to produce the required response. A summary of the book is also available online (**www.online-literature.com/ orwell/1984**) and was made into a film in 1984 (directed by Michael Radford).
- *Brave New World* (1932, Aldous Huxley, Penguin). Also a book primarily concerned with the prospect of state control by behaviourist means.
- Two films that depict the principles of learning, reward and positive and negative reinforcement very strongly are **The Village** (2004, directed by M. Night Shyamalan) and **The Island** (2005, directed by Michael Bay). We

have not gone into too much detail of these films so as not to give the plots away.
- *Token Economy: Behaviourism Applied* (Educational Resource Film; McGraw-Hill, 1972). Outlines B. F. Skinner's ideas on behaviourism and rewards. Concord Video and Film Council.
- *Classical and Operant Conditioning* (Educational Resource Film, 1996). The work of Ivan Pavlov and B. F. Skinner is outlined. The two types of conditioning are illustrated, including examples of historical laboratory work and Skinner boxes. Uniview WorldWide.
- *Discovering Psychology* video (Educational Resource Film, 1990). The theory of self-efficacy. WGBH/ Annenberg-PCB-Project/CS.

Explore the website accompanying this text at **www.pearsoned.co.uk/maltby** for further resources to help you with your studies. These include multiple-choice questions, essay questions, web links and ideas for advanced reading.

CHAPTER 5
Cognitive Personality Theories

Key themes

- Kelly's personal construct theory
- Clinical applications of Kelly's theory
- Ellis' rational-emotive behaviour therapy and theory
- Applications of rational-emotive behaviour therapy and theory
- Critical perspectives on cognitive models
- Evaluation of cognitive approaches

Learning outcomes

After studying this discussion you should:

- Understand Kelly's personal construct theory and its constituent parts
- Appreciate what is meant by subjective perception of the world
- Be aware of different views of the effects of development on personality
- Be familiar with the repertory grid as an assessment tool
- Understand the theory that surrounds rational-emotive behaviour therapy
- Understand the basic model of rational-emotive behaviour therapy
- Have an appreciation of the clinical applications of cognitive theories
- Be able to broadly evaluate cognitive approaches to personality

Introduction

What makes you the person you are? Is this a crucial question for personality theories to address? The psycho-analytic theories described previously (Chapters 2 and 3) suggest that your early experiences are crucial in deter-mining your personality, but claim that you are largely unconscious of how these experiences impact on your behaviour. The learning theorists discussed previously (Chapter 4) rejected the idea of unconscious motivation and suggested instead that you are who you are because of the learning experiences you have had and the environ-ments within which you operate. Both of these approaches allocate a relatively passive role to the individual. For the psychoanalysts the focus is mainly on inner processes, while the learning theorists emphasise external environ-mental events as driving behaviour. An example will help.

Suppose we are introduced to a stranger who is going to become one of our new flatmates. To begin a new relationship requires that we trust the other person. We operate on the basis that if we treat the other person well, then they will reciprocate. The psychoanalysts would suggest that we behave in this way because we are trusting individuals. We have become trusting individuals because we have experienced sufficiently high, consistent levels of good caring from our parents or other carers at an early age in our development when our prototypes of relationships were formed with our carers. Failure for this issue of trust to be resolved in infancy, because of deficiencies in the caring provided to the infant, results in an individual who has difficulty trusting others. The untrusting individual is likely to experience great diffi-culty with new relationships. With the flatmate example, they will be extremely suspicious of the new flatmate and expect to find them unreliable, so they may insist on many rules and regulations to try to protect their inter-ests. According to the analysts, unless the flatmate has had therapy, they are unlikely to be aware of why they find new relationships difficult or how the difficulty has come about, as it is all unconsciously motivated.

For learning theorists, there is no such concept as the untrusting individual; instead, there is an individual who displays a particular response when put into a situation that might require interactions with new people. The new person is a stimulus that through prior learning has become associated with particular responses in certain situations. The processes are similar in some ways, and both approaches are equally deterministic about human behaviour. For the psychoanalyst, being untrusting is treated as a characteristic of the individual, while for the learning theorist it is simply the way that the individual responds in a particular situation.

We are now going to examine two theoretical approaches that challenge both these views and assign more creative, active roles to individuals in determining who they are and how they behave. Firstly, we will focus on George A. Kelly's theory of personal constructs and then on Albert Ellis' theory of rational-emotive behav-iour. Nowadays both these approaches are conceptual-ised as cognitive theories of personality, although Kelly (1955) resisted this classification, for reasons we shall discuss later. These theories assign a role to our 'inner' processes and to the external environment in which we operate. These inner psychological processes are our conscious thoughts (cognitions) about ourselves, other people and situations that influence how we perceive the world and how we choose to behave. These models, while still having an important role for environmental factors and prior experience, allow for internal moti-vational influences on behaviour that are not deeply embedded in our unconscious. To return to the question of what makes you the person you are: these theories, while acknowledging that past experience has had a role in determining our current behaviour, emphasise the potential for creativity and change in our behaviour. Put simply, you are the person you are because of the way you see the world. By the end of the discussion, all will become clear.

Source: Ingram Image Library – Diamond Edition, Vol. 1

Theory of personal constructs of George A. Kelly

In this part of the text we are going to describe the theory of personal constructs of George A. Kelly (see Profile: George Alexander Kelly). We are going to outline:

- the view of the person in Kelly's theory;
- concepts within Kelly's theory;
- personality development according to Kelly;
- assessing personality in personal construct theory;
- clinical applications of personal construct theory.

The view of the person in Kelly's theory

Kelly's (1955) theory is based on a radically different view of the individual from the theories we have considered so far. He suggested that individuals act as *scientists*, each trying to understand and control the world around them. However, he was careful to stress that, unlike true scientists, we do not have objective data to work with; rather, we use our own very personal interpretations of the world. He denied the possibility of an agreed, objective reality that we all tuned into. Instead, Kelly (1955) saw us all as interpreting events in the world according to our own theories of human behaviour. We construct hypotheses to try to explain events, and then we test these hypotheses and change them if necessary to make sense of what is happening. These are mainly private observations that we do not attempt to share with others. These are essentially our private perceptions of individuals and situations, but we perceive them as representing how the individuals or situations are in reality. Indeed, it is often only when we share our perceptions with others that we become aware that others do not always share our perception of the world.

Imagine a group of friends is trying to decide who is going to get the biggest room in the new house they are going to share. Tom suggests that he should get the biggest room as he found the house. Annabel disagrees, saying she found the house last year but did not get the biggest room. Mark agrees that Tom should not get the biggest room as several people had worked to find a suitable house and Tom had simply been lucky to find the house. Jenny thought that individuals' contribution to the rent should depend on the size of room they had. The others felt that the room sizes were not sufficiently different for this to work and that the furniture was better in some rooms and this needed to be factored into the equation. Louise was adamant that they should draw lots as she had done this in a previous house.

Profile

George Alexander Kelly

George Kelly was born in Perth, a small farming town in Kansas, United States, in 1905. He was the only son of a Presbyterian minister and received some of his early education at home. His first degree, awarded in 1926, was in physics and mathematics, and his intention was to become an engineer. He had undertaken an introductory psychology course and found it very dull (Kelly, 1966). He then undertook a part-time masters course in educational sociology while working in various engineering and educational jobs. In 1929, he was awarded a scholarship to study for an educational degree at Edinburgh University in Scotland. It was there that he developed an interest in psychology, undertaking a dissertation on factors that might predict teaching success. Returning to the States, Kelly undertook doctoral studies in psychology at Iowa State University, graduating in 1931. His interest was in the physiological aspects of speech and reading difficulties; however, as jobs in physiological psychology were scarce, he developed a specialism in clinical psychology. He inaugurated clinical psychology services for the State of Kansas, with mobile assessment and treatment centres for schoolchildren. At the same time, he taught at a state college. During the Second World War he enlisted in the US Navy, working as a psychologist on training programmes. Throughout this period, Kelly had experimented with different approaches to treatment, and he concluded that none of the existing approaches really met the needs of his clients. In his work in schools, he observed that teachers would sometimes describe children as being lazy, but that this was not a helpful description for him to use when approaching the child. He would try to understand how the child saw school and then examine how the child's perception compared with the teacher's. From this work, he came to appreciate that problems often arose because teacher and pupil were construing the situation differently. The child had perhaps fallen behind and did not understand what was being taught, so had stopped trying to learn. This observation played a crucial part in the later development of his theory of personal constructs.

Kelly did not publish very much in his lifetime, but he lectured extensively and taught for 20 years at Ohio State University, followed by an appointment at Brandeis University to do research. Unfortunately, 2 years into that appointment, he died. While Kelly's theory was developed purely in the United States, it has been more influential and is more widely applied in the United Kingdom and mainland Europe.

Tom and Mark did not agree as it meant that someone who had made no effort to find the house could end up with the best room. This example illustrates how each individual was construing the situation differently. For some, there was a sense of earning the privilege of the large room by house searching or payment; for others, room size was not the only or indeed the major influence on the decision; for another, leaving it to chance seemed the fairest option. Each person was convinced that his or her solution was the most appropriate. They were all perceiving aspects of the situation differently. This exemplifies what Kelly means by personal constructs. Tom and Mark share a personal construct that rewards have to be earned, but they have different concepts about how success is rewarded. Tom believes that the successful outcome of finding the house should be rewarded, while Mark feels that the effort individuals made, regardless of whether they were successful, should be rewarded. As you will see later, a system has been devised for measuring an individual's personal constructs more systematically; but examining the basis for decision-making, as in this example, can give you a good idea of the constructs that people are using. **Personal constructs** are the criteria that we each use to perceive and interpret events. What Kelly is saying is that we all create our own view of the world, and we then act according to our perceptions.

To illustrate how personal constructs are said to operate, consider the following somewhat oversimplified example. Supposing you meet a new person; you are likely to make judgements about their degree of friendliness (friendly/unfriendly personal construct). Within the friendly/unfriendly **superordinate construct**, you will have some **subordinate constructs** that you use to judge the person. What these are will vary between individuals and will reflect your personality and interests. So you might have a subordinate construct of chatty/quiet, and you make a decision here and so on through the relevant subordinate constructs in your system of personal constructs. The possibilities are limitless. However, through experience we tend to develop structures within our construct system to help us deal with this complexity, as we shall explore in some detail in the rest of this section.

Kelly then sees us operating as scientists in our attempts to understand the world. This process of employing personal constructs explains why individual differences in behaviour arise. It also allows for creativity in behaviour; we are free to take on alternative interpretations, as often happens when we begin to discuss a problematic situation with friends. We listen to their interpretations and the constructs they are using, and sometimes we adopt them if we think they are more likely to be successful. This process also allows us to respond creatively in situations rather than our response being dictated purely by our past experiences.

Concepts within Kelly's theory

Because of the processes just outlined, we are also free to change our perception of situations or individuals. This ability that people have to change their minds about situations is central to Kelly's theorising. This is what Kelly (1955) refers to as **constructive alternativism**. As we have said, it simply refers to Kelly's assumption that we are all capable of altering our present interpretation of events or even adopting entirely new interpretations. This ability has further implications for Kelly's conception of the individual. He assumes that we all have free will, but that our thoughts and behaviour are sometimes determined by such things as our goals or the views of others and so on. Kelly thus sees free will and determinism as being interrelated. For example, suppose your long-term goal is to get a first-class degree. You may decide to take third-year options that involve a lot of coursework, as you do not perform as well in examinations, rather than do the options that interest you most. More of your time may be devoted to studying and less to social activities and enjoying yourself. Your long-term goal of success determines some of the other choices you make. In Kelly's terminology, your long-term goal is labelled the **superordinate construct**. The superordinate construct is freely chosen, but it then determines subsequent choices. In this way, the initial exercise of free will determines subsequent behaviour. (See Stop and think: Reflection on Kelly's conception of free will.)

Stop and think

Reflection on Kelly's conception of free will

In the argument presented in this section, do you think that it is sufficient for Kelly to state that the superordinate concept (goal of obtaining a first-class degree) is determined by free will?

Learning theorists, for example, would argue that all behaviour is determined. This would mean that the goal of a first-class degree was chosen because of a wish for positive reinforcement from significant others or something similar. Some psychoanalysts might suggest that it is motivated by an unconscious wish to prove their superiority over others, for example. The idea of unconscious motivation is at odds with the idea of free will.

Can you think of examples where free will is demonstrated in the choices that individuals make?

Kelly emphasises that people are future-oriented. We identify goals and use our personal constructs to interpret current events and then to make behavioural choices to help in the achievement of these goals. If our strategies are unsuccessful we may change our interpretation of events, which will involve changes in the personal constructs we are using. From this analysis it becomes apparent that Kelly sees human beings as future-oriented. A lot of the time we are trying to anticipate future events. If we do A now, then in the future B and C will occur. This is exemplified in what Kelly terms the *fundamental postulate* of his theory; namely, that 'A person's processes are psychologically channelized by the ways in which he anticipates events' (1955, p. 46).

This is a crucial difference from previous theories we have explored. According to Kelly our motivation to act comes from our future aims, not from our past learning or early experiences or innate drives. For example, we do not challenge a colleague's abruptness, as we don't want an argument and we know from past experiences that she can be prickly and argumentative if challenged. We are in a good mood and don't want to lose the feeling and get annoyed, so we let it pass. So future aims are not simply long-term goals but also include our current short-term goals.

Kelly's theory is presented in a structured way. When using personal constructs, we are organising our experiences in terms of similarities and contrasts. Constructs must consist of at least three elements, two of which are similar and which contrast with the third element. To say that Joanne and Sarah are extraverts is to imply that someone else is introverted. Identifying similarities necessitates identifying differences with some other person or situation. If it is A, then it cannot be X. Kelly expanded on the fundamental postulate with 11 **corollaries** describing how the interpretative processes operate to allow us to create our personal constructs. The content of each corollary is summarised in the label he selected for it. They begin by addressing the basic processes employed to interpret events and become more complex. We will examine each corollary in turn (see Figure 5.1).

Construction corollary

The **construction corollary** simply refers to the processes we use to understand what is going on in any situation. We construct meaning for what is going on, and then we use this construction to help us understand and deal with future situations. Kelly did not see the constructions we make as being simply equivalent to the verbal labels that we may use to describe them. He pointed out that infants and young children construct meaning in their worlds before they have language. They respond appropriately to others and act in purposeful ways. Older children and adults sometimes formulate concepts that they then have difficulty verbalising. You have a feeling or a thought that is difficult to put into words. For Kelly, constructs actually represent the discriminations that we make when we perceive events. Individuals suffering psychological distress are sometimes unsure of how to construe situations and may need therapeutic help to help them make sense of the situation. Various factors will influence the creation of personal constructs, as illustrated in the corollaries that follow.

Individuality corollary

The **individuality corollary** embodies the observation that there are individual differences in behaviour. Kelly stresses that our constructions of events are personal to us. As we have seen previously, we do not all interpret a situation in the same way, but we all have to make sense of the world. For one person behaviour may be labelled as 'aggressive', while someone else observing the same incident may label the behaviour as 'assertive'. How you construe the

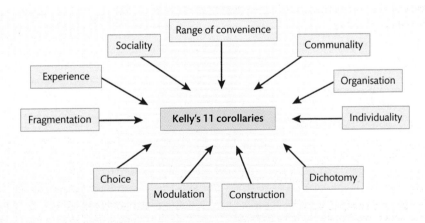

Figure 5.1 Kelly's 11 corollaries outlining how the interpretative processes operate to allow us to create our personal constructs.

The aim of development for Kelly was for the individual to maximise their knowledge of the world. (Hiker in Grand Canyon National Park, Arizona, USA.)
Source: Grand Canyon National Park

event will obviously influence how you behave in the situation. Someone interested in fashion may closely observe what someone wears, while a psychologist might be more interested in what they say. Our interests and our existing personal constructs will all play a part in determining how we see the world. For Kelly there is no objective reality; rather, each individual has their own subjective view of events.

Organisation corollary

In his **organisation corollary**, Kelly suggests that each individual's construct system is organised hierarchically. For some people, some constructs will be more important than others and will therefore be applied earlier in the process. For example, a religious person may have an overarching concept of good versus evil that they then use to organise their other concepts. A 'good' person might be honest, truthful, just and considerate of others, while an 'evil' individual is dishonest, untruthful, unjust and exploitative of others. In this way, the concept of the 'good' person subsumes all these other positive values. In this way, the individual's cognitions used to interpret events are in ordered relationships. It is an ordered process, reflecting that we do not interpret events in the world in a haphazard fashion. In Kelly's terms, we operate as scientists with a system of constructs that we employ to help us understand the world. We may prioritise some constructs over others to help us make decisions. In the student example

we considered earlier, studying was prioritised over social activities. Conflicts can result when individuals in relationships have prioritised their concepts differently. The businessperson who has prioritised building up his business over spending time with his family may find life difficult if his partner has different priorities.

Dichotomy corollary

The **dichotomy corollary** relates specifically to the nature of our personal constructs and how we organise them. Kelly suggests that all concepts are based on dichotomies. When we say that something is 'good', we are also asserting that it is not 'bad'. If we say we are 'happy', it implies that we are not 'sad' and so on. In this way, all our constructs are bipolar. This bipolarity of personal constructs then allows for constructive alternativism, which is the possibility of changing your mind about how you see things.

Choice corollary

Kelly's **choice corollary** says that individuals are free to choose the alternative in the dichotomised concept that best fits their purpose or makes most sense in any particular situation. This is essentially the process whereby people make judgements about their reality, choosing the alternative that in their view best fits the situation. Kelly claimed that people generally make choices that increase their understanding of the world, and in this way they grow as individuals.

Range of convenience corollary

Kelly outlined how some constructs were widely applied while some others made sense only when applied more narrowly. This is the **range of convenience** of a construct. The good–bad construct may be applied to a wide range of objects and situations, ranging from the state of your hairstyle on a particular day to exam marks or behavioural judgements. However, concepts such as spiritual/non-spiritual will apply to a much narrower range of constructs. Kelly (1955) suggested that there are large individual differences in terms of how broadly or narrowly individuals apply their personal constructs.

Experience corollary

Kelly's **experience corollary** refers to the way that we are able to change the personal constructs we use in the light of our later experience. For example, we may construe a new acquaintance as a pleasant individual on the basis of an initial meeting; however, after witnessing them aggressively confronting another friend, our 'pleasant' construct is likely to change.

Modulation corollary

The **modulation corollary** refers to how fixed constructs are and how much change is possible within an individual's personal construct system. Constructs that easily allow additions to be made are termed *permeable*. An individual's concept of acceptable manners may be open to change as they experience new cultures if they have a permeable personal construct of manners. The converse is also true. Individuals with rigid (*impermeable*) personal constructs of manners cannot do this and will be more likely to condemn violations of their construct of manners. From this example it becomes clearer how the nature of our personal constructs defines how we are as individuals. Permeability allows for change and personal growth in individuals.

Fragmentation corollary

So far the corollaries have implied that an individual's personal construct system is organised, but this does not mean that it is logically coherent. People may employ subsystems with their constructs that are apparently incompatible with each other. The **fragmentation corollary** explains the inconsistencies that we can sometimes observe in individuals' behaviour. An individual may be an upstanding citizen and publicly assert that honesty is always the best policy, yet they may cheat on their income tax return. The cheating, the declaration of honesty and being an upstanding citizen appear to be incompatible construct systems. However, inquiries reveal that the individual runs a company with several hundred people dependent on him for work. He is experiencing some cash flow problems, so to keep his business going he lies on his tax return to save money. Here the superordinate construct of upstanding citizen may have been widened to include the construct of keeping people in work. This then explains how the previously unpredictable behaviour of lying to the taxman occurs. Predicting behaviour is very complex, and Kelly stresses that what is required is an assessment of the individual's 'cognitive world', which will include inconsistent as well as logical subsystems.

Communality corollary

Kelly suggests, in the **communality corollary**, that people who share similar constructions of their experience are alike psychologically. This means that they will behave in similar ways. He stresses that individual differences in behaviour will still manifest themselves, but if people have similar personal constructs, then they are likely to behave in similar ways and share similar views. If two people share a particular view of a situation, then they are much more likely to propose similar actions in that situation.

Sociality corollary

The **sociality corollary** helps to explain the process of social interaction. Kelly (1955) claimed that some understanding of a person's construct system is necessary for us to be able to predict their behaviour and interact satisfactorily with them. In social interaction, he suggests that we then use the knowledge of the other's personal constructs to modify our behaviour to fit the situation. We also use social interaction to test out our own personal constructs. Kelly suggested that much of our social behaviour involves mutual adjustment of our personal construct systems to produce mutual understandings of our experiences. It is these mutual understandings that are crucial for the smooth operation of society.

In addition, Kelly (1955) described three types of constructs: pre-emptive, constellatory and propositional. **Pre-emptive constructs** are very specialised and contain only their own elements. Kelly gives an example of an individual who claims that a ball can only be a ball. It cannot be anything related, like a sphere. Individuals sometimes display this type of rigid thinking. They may have very narrow views that they stick to dogmatically. They may claim dogmatically, for example, that 'property is theft' or that 'women cannot be priests' and their personal construct is not open to change.

Constellatory constructs explain how we sometimes cluster information within our personal construct system. If we take stereotypes as an example of constellatory constructs, it should make the process clear. Once an individual has been identified as belonging to a particular group or category, then we attribute other characteristics to them that are part of the stereotype. The characteristics we attribute to the stereotype may be part of other constructs, but their use tends to be fixed in the stereotype and not open to change.

Propositional constructs represent flexible thinking. With a propositional construct, every element of the construct is open to change. When using propositional constructs, the individual is open to new experiences, change and development. However, Kelly is keen to point out that if we were to use only propositional thinking, we would find life almost impossible. To cope effectively and interact with others we need to have some certainty, to feel that we know how to behave in certain situations and that we can predict how others will behave. Overuse of propositional thinking makes us indecisive, as we are continually interpreting and evaluating our experiences. Kelly suggests that the individual who copes best with the world is the one who knows when to use pre-emptive or propositional thinking.

Personality development according to Kelly

The aim of development for Kelly (1963) was for the individual to maximise their knowledge of the world. This was achieved via the development of their personal construct systems. Kelly did not directly address where the motivation for this came from, but he appears to have assumed that, as human beings, we have an innate need to know about our world. He also assumes that we have a wish to develop as accurate a perception of our world as possible. As we have seen, the more our personal constructs are similar to others', the more like them we are psychologically. This is the communality corollary that we have examined previously. The more communality there is in our personal constructs, the easier it is to understand each other and predict our behaviour – all factors that facilitate social interactions and increase the accuracy of our perceptions. Kelly thus seems to see human development as being motivated by an innate need to maximise our accurate knowledge of the world. He suggests that, while the environment is obviously an important factor in the process of development, our behaviour is not determined by environmental factors in the way that the learning theorists had assumed. Within his system, individuals actively construe the environment through a process of interpretation and reinterpretation of situations. We then use these constructs to help us anticipate what will happen in the future. This is where the scientist analogy comes in, as Kelly (1963) suggests that we then use our experiences to create hypotheses about future events and courses of actions.

If we consider the developing child within Kelly's system, as they grow the range of experiences open to them increases. They are provided with feedback about the accuracy and effectiveness of their personal constructs by family and wider society as part of the learning experience. There is more tolerance for young people being uncertain in situations than there is for adults, acknowledging that young people are less experienced players. Kelly (1958) describes the way

that we behave when we are faced with a situation; we engage in what he calls a **circumspection-pre-emption-control (CPC) cycle**. Firstly, we consider all the ways of construing the situation. This involves us examining the propositional constructs that we already possess that might be appropriate in this situation, based on our experience or based on what we already know in a novel situation. At the pre-emptive phase, we weed out the constructs that seem less likely to succeed, thereby reducing the number of constructs available. We then seriously consider the remaining constructs in terms of which one is most likely to produce the solution we want. Finally, we take control and make the choice of alternative within a construct that we hope will maximise our chances of solving the problem.

For Kelly (1963), development is a dynamic constructive process between the individual and their environment. Healthy development results in the individual developing an accurate system of personal constructs that allows them to view the world flexibly. Such an individual is open to new experiences and is able to modify and adapt their personal constructs to meet new challenges. They demonstrate the ability to grow in positive ways. For Kelly (1963), your personal construct system is in essence your personality. Your construct system determines how you construe the world and ultimately how you behave. Kelly did not write a great deal about the specifics of development in childhood. Instead, he appears to have assumed that the same process of construct testing, modification and growth continues throughout life.

Assessing personality in personal construct theory

Kelly's theory was based on research he undertook with students in schools and universities. Unlike the psychoanalytic theories, his work is based on normally functioning samples. Initially he used interviews to assess students' personal constructs. Kelly (1958) was very clear that the most obvious way of obtaining an individual's perception of their world was simply to ask them about it. He would sometimes also ask his participants to write character sketches describing themselves. They had to write in the third person about themselves, as if a very close friend was writing the sketch.

The assessment technique that Kelly is best known for is the role construct repertory test, more commonly known as the rep grid test. Kelly was above all else a practising therapist, and he developed the rep grid test to help him assess clients in his clinical work. It can appear to be a complex system. Here we will outline the principles, and you can refer to the completed rep grid example in Figure 5.2 to help you follow the procedure. Clients are presented with a grid and are asked to list the important people in their lives by name. They then have to consider these people in sets

Important people in client's life									Constructs	
Self	Father	Mother	Sister	Brother	Boss	Friend	Popular person	Caring person	Similarity	Contrast
⊗	◯	⊗							Sense of humour	Humourless
			◯	⊗	⊗				Both male	Female
◯	⊗				⊗				Successful	Unsuccessful
				◯			⊗	⊗	Sociable	Unsociable
	⊗			⊗		◯			Religious	Not religious
◯			⊗	⊗					Likes sport	Does not like sport
			◯	⊗	⊗				Good listener	Poor listener
			⊗	⊗	◯				Same age	Different ages
⊗		◯	⊗						Tolerant	Intolerant
	⊗	⊗	◯						Contented	Discontented
			◯			⊗	⊗		Happy	Sad

Figure 5.2 Completed role construct repertory test (rep grid).
Source: Kelly (1955) p. 270.

of three. They put a circle under the three they are considering, and then in the 'Constructs' columns at the right of the grid, they write the way in which two are similar and the way in which the third person differs from the other two. They put an 'x' in the circle to show which two are similar. These two rows give the similarity and the contrast parts of the personal construct that we considered previously when we examined the corollaries of personal constructs. So, in the example in Figure 5.2, 'having a sense of humour' is the similarity and 'no sense of humour' is the contrast. The clients then consider the other people listed and, if they consider them to have a sense of humour, they would add a tick under the person's name on the same line.

Clients then begin a new comparison, in this case comparing sister, brother and boss. Two are similar because they are male, and the contrast is female. Similarly, males amongst the other names are identified with an additional tick on the same row. The clients themselves dictate the number of constructs to be used. It depends on the number of contrasts they see as relevant and the comparison they wish to make.

There is no standard way to score rep grids. They are intended to give an insight into a client's personal construct system. From examining the grid, the number of constructs used is apparent, and the nature of the constructs used is also of interest. Remember that clients will spontaneously generate the constructs to be used. They are simply asked to compare groups of three and identify how two are similar and the other different. If you have the same or very similar patterns for some constructs, it may be that you do not really differentiate between them, as with content/discontent and happy/sad in this example. For some people these distinctions will be meaningful, and here we have identified one source of individual differences in terms of how even labels may be interpreted. In the example shown, most of the similarities were positive attributes; the contrasts were more negative, which is interesting. From studying the rep grid, it also becomes very clear which constructs the individual applies to describe themselves. From Figure 5.2 we see that the client perceives herself as having a keen sense of humour, being unsuccessful, sociable, not religious, not liking sport, being tolerant, discontented and unhappy.

One American psychologist, James Bieri, suggested that by examining the patterns across rows, an assessment of the individual's cognitive complexity could be made. Bieri (1955) assumed that where the patterns are similar, there was a lack of differentiation in the way that the client perceived others. He termed this cognitive simplicity and contrasted it with cognitive complexity where many different patterns emerge. Based on a series of experiments reviewed by Bonarius (1965), individuals demonstrating cognitive complexity are better at predicting behaviour outcomes and more sensitive to others' views. Cognitively simple individuals tend to be much more egocentric.

Stop and think

Applying the role construct repertory test (rep grid)

This is a self-reflective exercise, which will help you to explore your own personal construct system. This will help you understand Kelly's theory. The rep grid has proved to be a useful tool for exploring various cognitive structures.

1   You need to construct a grid similar to the example given in Figure 5.2.
2   Begin by creating a list of the important people in your life, by name, beginning with yourself in the first column. There are a variety of people you could choose, or you may want to restrict it to family or friends.
3   Next, consider these people in sets of three.
4   Put a circle under the three you are considering, then, in the construct space at the end of the line, write the way in which two are similar and the way in which the third person differs from the other two.
5   Put an 'x' in the circles to show which two are similar.
6   Consider the other people listed, and if you think the construct applies to them, place a tick under the person's name on the same line.

7   Now begin the next comparison of three. You are free to make the comparisons that most interest you. You may be interested in the qualities that people in your life share, or you may be more interested in how they differ.
8   Continue making comparisons until you have completed the grid. You may find that you need more space than that provided in Figure 5.2.

Interpretation of the rep grid

As mentioned in the text, rep grids provide a lot of information about how individuals construe their worlds. You may want to examine the constructs you use, both the number and their nature. It will give you some insights into the common qualities that you share with important people in your life, as well as about the ways you differ. You may also want to examine how complex your construct system appears to be. More suggestions for interpretation are given in the text.

When Kelly was alive, there was not a great deal of interest in this cognitive aspect of his theory. This may in part be due to his reluctance to classify his theory as being a cognitive theory. He also did not produce much written work, as we have seen, and only moved into a post that would have provided him with time to do research shortly before his untimely death. However, since the 1980s there has been more interest in using the rep grid in particular, and computerised versions have been developed (Bringmann, 1992; Ford and Adams-Webber, 1991).

To really get an understanding of the rep grid, we suggest that you try completing one yourself. Instructions are given in Stop and think: Applying the role construct repertory test.

Clinical applications of personal construct theory

Kelly was primarily a clinician, and he suggested that clients who are suffering psychological problems are using personal constructs that are invalid and unhelpful. They are having problems because they are construing events inaccurately and/or unhelpfully. The therapist's role is to help clients become aware of their faulty personal constructs and prepare them for the possibility of changing these concepts. However, Kelly was careful to stress that the therapist has

to be very aware of the client's view of therapy. The client enters therapy with a conception of what is involved in therapy, and the therapist needs to explore the conception. The client's idea of therapy and what they wish to gain from it may be very different from that of the therapist, and this situation has to be negotiated.

Kelly (1966) suggests that the therapist will begin with the client's view of therapy and, if necessary, demonstrate to the client that they need to make more changes than they had initially envisaged. This is in line with Kelly's notion of each individual having their own subjective worldview. The therapist initially seeks to understand the client's worldview and works with it. Kelly listened carefully to clients, and once he understood where they were coming from, he would challenge their maladaptive constructs in several ways. He would demonstrate to clients how their present system was not working and suggest changes. He believed it was essential that clients feel accepted by the therapist if major changes are going to occur. Kelly's method encouraged clients to think through their problems with the therapist and to reach a conclusion. Kelly (1958) called this process **controlled elaboration**. During this procedure, the therapist would help the client to revise unhelpful constructs or discard them and replace them with new constructs, thus opening up the possibility of change. Therapists need to be aware of their own construct systems but also need to be open and flexible, so that they can accept differences in their clients' construing without feeling threatened by it. Clients would often become anxious during this process of change, but Kelly viewed this anxiety as a useful motivator for change. The therapist needs to be verbally skilled, creative and energetic in pursuing the goal of getting the client well.

Kelly felt that, while the client's past could be important, therapists should not dwell exclusively on the past. He would explore the client's past to explore the origins of their constructs and to examine the effect of the individual's social and cultural experiences on the development of their personal construct system. He would also use the rep grid to explore the client's personal construct system and how they saw themselves.

Other techniques that Kelly (1955) developed to bring out change were **self-characterisation sketches** and **fixed-role therapy**. For self-characterisation sketches, clients are asked to write about themselves in the third person. The therapist interprets the sketch and then writes a role-play exercise that the client has to re-enact. This technique is called fixed-role therapy. According to Kelly, writing in the third person and using fictitious names leads the client to believe that it is a fictitious character role that they are undertaking. This makes them more comfortable, and they feel safe trying out the new role. Only afterwards do they see that it can apply to them, and they make the changes with the encouragement of the therapist. Clients would rehearse the role in the therapist's office and then be asked to implement it in their lives. Kelly made no attempt to research the effectiveness of his therapy. He was a charismatic lecturer and teacher who felt that his successful case studies provided sufficient evidence of the worth of his approach.

The one technique that found a wider application clinically was the rep grid test, as mentioned earlier. Bannister and Fransella (1966), in a classic study, measured the personal construct systems of patients with schizophrenia and compared their thought patterns with non-psychotic patients such as patients suffering from depression, neuroses and mild organic disorders as well as with a healthy sample of individuals. This, and a subsequent seminal study by Bannister, Fransella and Agnew (1971), demonstrated the nature of thought disturbance

in patients with schizophrenia. Bannister died in 1986, but his colleague Fay Fransella continued to work in construct theory until her death in 2011. She published a book in 2004 that includes work by Kelly and Bannister and also has a useful section illustrating how personal construct theory has been applied in business (Fransella *et al.*, 2004). Applications have included using rep grids to improve group understanding (Robertson, 2003), to help organisations deal with change (Cornelius, 2003) and to improve relationships with customers (Lemke *et al.*, 2011).

Albert Ellis and rational-emotive behaviour therapy

Another early advocate of cognitive approaches is the American psychologist Albert Ellis. Like many of the other theories of personality we have examined, Ellis' approach has come from the clinical tradition. He did not set out to develop a theory of personality; rather, his conceptualisation of personality emerged from his approach to therapy. He was interested in understanding behaviour so that he could develop effective programmes for change in therapy clients. His approach is now called **rational-emotive behaviour therapy (REBT)** although previously it had other names, as indicated in Profile: Albert Ellis.

Origins of the theory of rational-emotive behaviour therapy

Ellis was impressed by the learning theorists' approaches to changing behaviour. From his psychoanalytic practice, he had become aware that, for most individuals, understanding why you are fearful is not enough to stop your fears. All the insight in the world about the origin of your fears does not actually get rid of them. Deconditioning, as outlined by the learning theorists, struck him as a valuable tool for bringing about behaviour change. For example, if you repeatedly make people do things that they are afraid of, then eventually their fear disappears. This approach does raise ethical issues in treatment, and clients may be reluctant to participate. Ellis (1958a) also found that a

Profile

Albert Ellis

Albert Ellis was born in 1913 in Pittsburgh, of Jewish parents, and grew up in a poor inner-city neighbourhood. He was the eldest of three children. Ellis describes

his parents as providing little emotional support for their children, although they always had enough to eat. His mother was preoccupied with her own mental health and found it difficult to look after children. His father travelled a great deal and played a minor role in his life. Later his parents divorced. Ellis was a sickly child and was often hospitalised. He grew up shy and introverted, but he was always, on his own admission, a cheerful child. He responded to his mother's neglect of the family by taking on responsibility for his siblings, getting them up and dressed for school each day and generally looking after them. His early ambition was to be a businessman, and his first degree was in business studies. He had a short career in business, but the Great Depression in the 1930s put an end to his ambitions in business. He then tried to become a novelist, keeping himself by doing odd jobs. When he failed to get any of his six novels published, Ellis turned to further study. He enrolled in a psychology course in 1942, becoming a clinical psychologist. His doctoral research was on approaches to designing personality questionnaires. Once qualified, he undertook psychoanalytic training in the Horney Institute for Psychoanalysis. This is the institute established in the United States by Karen Horney (as mentioned in Chapter 3). Ellis found psychoanalysis frustrating and in 1947 he published the first of a series of articles critical of the approach and highlighting the need for research to produce scientific evaluation of the therapy. He felt that, while he obtained results and his patients recovered, it took a long time; he thus began to look for a more efficient way to deliver therapy. He also continued to undertake research on aspects of sexual behaviour and began to publish and counsel in this area. His research on sex was not well received in New Jersey, where he had become a senior psychologist in the clinical psychology service, so in 1952 he resigned. He moved to New York to set up practice. He produced some well-received books on sexual issues, *The Folklore of Sex* (1951), *The American Sexual Tragedy* (1954) and *Sex without Guilt* (1958b). However, his growing reputation as a sexologist and as an outspoken advocate for sexual freedom and gay rights came at a cost. He could not get a university or college in New York to employ him as a lecturer in the 1950s. He supported himself with a large therapy practice and continued to read widely.

In 1953 he broke totally from psychoanalysis. He had read the work of Dollard and Miller (1950) and had profoundly disagreed with their attempts to integrate psychoanalysis with learning theory. He felt that their conception of unconscious repression causing clients to have neurotic problems was fundamentally wrong (see Chapter 4). In his experience, clients were conscious of their irrational beliefs and clung onto them despite the fact that they were causing them grief. In 1955, Ellis published an outline of his new approach, entitled rational psychotherapy. As a response to critics who claimed that this new approach ignored the emotions, Ellis quickly changed the name to rational-emotive therapy. Ellis had continued to work on his ideas, reframing his theory several times and exploring more applications. Ellis had been impressed by the systematic approach of the learning theorists and saw the usefulness of learning theory techniques. In the application of his theory, he always emphasises the importance of learning; in acknowledgement of this, in 1991 he changed the name of his approach to rational-emotive behaviour therapy (REBT). From the outset, Ellis was interested in attempting to evaluate his theory and provide a scientific basis to underpin it.

Ellis set up the Institute for REBT in New York. It is a charitable institute that, as well as running training courses for therapists and treating patients, also runs some free therapy projects in poor areas of New York. Ellis was a prolific writer and still continued to work despite having severe diabetes and poor eyesight. Before his death in 2007, he had become the most published living psychologist. His work, like that of Kelly, has received more acclaim in the rest of the world than it did in his native America. Examining recent American texts on personality, we found that Ellis was only included in one text and received a passing reference in two others. Despite this, he received awards from the American Psychological Association for his contribution to psychology. He toured extensively, giving lectures and workshops to promote his cognitive approach. He was married twice and had many relationships, only one of which lasted any time. He had no children and dedicated his life to his work and to addressing a variety of human problems.

purely learning theory explanation of behaviour was too simplistic to account for most human behaviour. He was interested in the fact that individuals often maintain their own disturbance by thinking about it and telling themselves how upset they are. In learning theory terms, we sometimes reinforce our own distress. In other words, our cognitions can reinforce our distress. Imagine that you are angry with a friend for something they did. Every time you think about it, you tell yourself that they had no right to do it, and you keep telling yourself how angry you are. Ellis was interested in how our cognitions impacted on our emotions and our behaviour in situations such as these.

Rational and irrational thoughts

Many of the ideas in the theory of REBT are not new. Ellis was influenced by the ideas of the Ancient Greek and Roman philosophers and some of the ancient Taoist and Buddhist thinkers (Ellis, 1958a; 1958b). Central to his theory is the conceptualisation of humankind as a uniquely rational as well as a uniquely irrational species. From his observations, Ellis (1958a; 1958b) concluded that individual emotional or psychological disturbances are largely the result of illogical or irrational thinking. He suggested that individuals could rid themselves of most of their emotional distress, ineffectual behaviour and unhappiness if they would learn to maximise their rational thinking and minimise their irrational thinking. He found this dichotomy of rationality/ irrationality present in the descriptions of human nature in the writings of many of the ancient philosophers and was gratified and reassured by this knowledge, concluding that rationality/irrationality is an innate characteristic of human beings.

At this point, we need to examine exactly what Ellis meant by rationality and its converse, irrationality. Ellis (1976) assumed that as human beings we have two basic goals; the first is to stay alive and the second is to be happy. However, he suggested that people often pursue happiness in idiosyncratic ways. This then relates to his definition of rationality. **Rational behaviour** in the theory of REBT means that which helps individuals to achieve their basic goals and purposes. Consequently, **irrational behaviour** is that which prevents people from achieving their basic goals. In other words, if your goal is to pass your course on individual differences, then you are behaving rationally by reading this book, especially if the exam is imminent. There are no absolute criteria of rationality. Like Kelly, Ellis stresses the subjective nature of our experience, which is reflected in the personal nature of our goals. For example, you might think that the rational goal is to want to succeed whenever possible. However, we can think of one instance where the goal of the individual was to enjoy not being good at something. This woman had parents with high expectations of her. As a child she was introduced to many activities and sports but was only allowed to continue in ones where she showed aptitude. This had become a habit, and she felt that her goal in everything was to be successful. She placed enormous expectations on herself and could never properly enjoy her activities, as she worried about her performance. Her goal was to take up painting as a hobby, although she had no artistic talent. She knew she could never be a good artist, but she wanted to be able to enjoy the process of painting badly. Hence, her goal was to be happy about doing something badly. Stated baldly, it does not seem a rational goal but, in the context of her life, it is a perfectly rational goal. Perhaps you can think of other instances.

Ellis (1976) hypothesises that all humans have biological tendencies to think irrationally as well as rationally. He cites as evidence many examples of observed human irrational behaviour. Some examples are included in Table 5.1.

Irrational thought is recognised by its *demanding nature*. Ellis (2001) explains that we escalate our preferences in a situation into absolutist demands. These may be demands on *ourselves* or on *other people* or *the world* more generally.

In this aspect of his theory development, Ellis acknowledges a debt to the work of Karen Horney (Chapter 3) and her 'tyranny of the shoulds'. He says that people who are angry do not simply wish or prefer something to happen,

Table 5.1 Examples of human irrationality (Ellis, 1985a)

- Virtually all individuals, including intelligent and competent people, show evidence of major human irrationalities.
- Almost all the disturbance-creating irrationalities (tyranny of the shoulds) that are found in our society are also found in other cultures and throughout history.
- We indulge in irrational behaviours such as procrastination and lack of self-discipline despite what we have been taught by parents, schoolteachers and so on.
- Individuals may work to overcome some of their irrational behaviour only to adopt new irrationalities.
- Having insight into irrational thought and behaviours helps only partially to change them. For example, people can acknowledge that binge drinking is harmful, yet this knowledge does not necessarily help them abstain from heavy drinking.
- Individuals often find it easier to learn self-defeating rather than self-enhancing behaviours. For example, it can be very easy to overeat but much more difficult to follow a sensible diet.
- Ellis points out that cognitive therapists, who presumably should be good role models of rationality, often act irrationally in their personal and professional lives.
- Individuals demand that the world is fair and just when all the evidence suggests otherwise.

but demand that it must happen. Yet, as we have seen earlier, logically we do not have the power to make other people do things if they do not want to do them. When the thing they want to happen does not happen, the angry person gets even more upset. Similarly, we may insist that people treat us fairly and consistently, and we become very angry when it does not happen. Here again, Ellis, following the logico-empirical approach, would ask the individual whether they had evidence to suggest that the world is a fair and just place.

Patently, the world is not always a fair place, yet Ellis (1985a) suggests that the human *demand* for fairness is evidence of our irrationality. In the theory of REBT, the rational response is to prefer to be treated fairly and to accept that you cannot demand to be treated fairly. If being treated fairly is a preference and not an absolute demand, when it does not happen, you are disappointed rather than furiously angry. If we thought rationally, then being treated fairly would be a cause for celebration and being treated unfairly would be the norm. Many people question this example, but Ellis would suggest that few, if any, of us are brought up rationally, and this encourages the development of irrational thought. We assume you accept that the world is an unfair place. Undeserving people thrive and good people become ill, suffer accidents and so on. Despite this, most parents go out of their way to treat their children fairly. Treats are shared between siblings. A bar of chocolate will be divided up so that everyone gets the same-sized piece and so on. In this way, we raise children who have an expectation that the world will treat them fairly and get angry when it does not happen. This is further evidence to support Ellis' contention that human beings think irrationally as well as rationally.

This belief in the world as a fair and just place where people get what they deserve is so widespread that social psychologists such as Lerner (1977; 1980) have described it as a fundamental attributional error. Lerner (1977) suggests that individuals have a personal contract with their social world, where the expectation is that, if they behave well, then they will be treated justly. Put simply, it is a belief that good things happen to good people and bad things happen to bad people. There is a well-established body of research in this area, going back over 30 years (Furnham, 1985; Furnham and Proctor, 1989; Lerner, 1977; Lerner and Miller, 1978). Dalbert (1996) presents a detailed review of this research area and the implications it has for our social interactions. Violations of just world beliefs have been shown to negatively affect the health and psychological well-being of individuals (Dalbert, 1998; Dalbert *et al.*, 2001). The existence of this body of research provides further support for human irrationality within Ellis' model.

By now, you may be asking what is wrong with getting angry. Ellis (1985a) suggests that when we get very angry or very anxious or upset, our emotional state frequently prevents us from behaving effectively, and this makes us more distressed. We are sure you have had the experience of being so angry that you find yourself speechless, and only afterwards, when you have calmed down a bit, can you think of things to say. Had you not been so angry, you would have dealt with the situation more effectively. In addition, prolonged extreme anger is bad for our health. Ellis does not say that we should not get upset; rather, he believes that we can learn to avoid levels of distress that are so extreme that they are dysfunctional. In this way, we can also learn to reduce the length of time for which we experience such extreme emotions. Ellis (1958a, 1978, 2001) suggests that we can minimise our distress and thereby maximise our happiness by thinking rationally and stopping the escalation of our preferences into demands of ourselves, others and the world.

The importance of perception and the subjective worldview

Like Kelly, Ellis (1955, 1958a) was impressed by the way that people develop hypotheses about the nature of the world. Having read philosophers such as Popper (1969/2002) and Russell (1949), Ellis adopted their approach, which stresses the importance of testing out the validity of your hypotheses rather than assuming they are true. This has led to what is called the logico-empirical approach of REBT and theory. Exactly how this operates will become clear

shortly. Ellis, like Kelly, also believed that we each create our own perception of the world, and we then assume that our subjective view is factually accurate. He linked this belief very neatly to the way that we respond emotionally to events, quoting Epictetus, a Stoic philosopher from the first century AD. Epictetus famously stated that, 'Men are disturbed not by things but by their view of things'. This principle underlies all the theory of REBT. Ellis (1958a) is suggesting that we all create our emotions and our behavioural responses, and their nature depends on how we have interpreted the world. Human beings use four fundamental, interrelated processes to interpret the world: *perception*, *sensing*, *thinking* and *emotion*. We perceive events and think about them, and this then produces emotional and behavioural responses. There are similarities with Kelly's conception of how we construe the world, but Ellis goes further in elucidating how our emotional responses are generated. An example will make it clearer.

Supposing you are out shopping and you see Harry, a student you know from your seminar group, coming towards you. You get ready to acknowledge him, but he walks right past you as if he has not seen you. There are several possible interpretations of this event, as follows:

- You shrug and smile, saying to yourself, 'He has not seen me. He is really distracted. I will joke with him about it next time I see him.' You are quite amused by the event.
- You frown and look thoughtful, saying to yourself, 'He is ignoring me. Did I say something to offend him in the last seminar?' You are a little anxious about the event.
- You look indignant and think, 'He is ignoring me. The conceited sod, how dare he?' This time you are angry.

Here there is one situation, yet different interpretations are possible – each generating different emotional responses. Ellis was the first theorist to present such a simple yet feasible explanation of our emotional responses. He pointed out that we tend to talk about our emotions as if they are caused by other people. Your mother makes you angry, a film makes you sad and so on. We talk about our emotions as if we have no control over them, yet the reality is that we create our own emotional responses inside our own brains. The emotion we experience depends on how we interpret events. Obviously, our current emotional state will also influence the interpretations we make of new events. So, someone who is depressed will pick up on the negatives in a situation and vice versa.

Individuals generally find it difficult to accept that other people do not cause their emotions and that their feelings are caused mainly by what they think. Ellis (2001) uses the example where he asks you to imagine that just now, you found out that someone you know called Joe made a very unkind remark about you several weeks ago. As you walk home, you begin to get angry about it. Ellis asks why you are angry. It cannot be Joe's behaviour, as that happened ages ago and you did not even know about it. It cannot simply be knowing about it, as when you were told you were not immediately angry. It is thinking about it that has resulted in your anger. You are telling yourself, 'How dare he say that about me. He has no right.' Other interpretations are also possible. You could have thought something like, 'Oh well, it happened a long time ago. I am disappointed but so what.' REBT is interested in the nature of the self-talk that we indulge in when we are interpreting events such as these. We do it very quickly and almost automatically, and it can be quite difficult at first to observe the process.

Free will, responsibility and control

Ellis (1958a, 1978) sees human beings as having free will to choose how they behave in particular situations. Sometimes we might like to think that we do not have free will, but Ellis suggests that this is because the choices may be too difficult or painful for us to contemplate at times. An extreme example of this situation comes from work with the terminally ill. REBT is sometimes used with people who have been diagnosed with incurable cancer. Such individuals will only have a short time to live. It is harder to imagine a more distressing situation. Yet even here, Ellis points out that there are choices to be made. The individual may choose to spend all the time they have left being upset, or they may choose to use the time in more constructive ways as their illness allows. We have known individuals who have used the time to resolve family conflicts, thus ensuring that the situation was better for the family they were leaving. Others have gone travelling to places they have always wanted to see; one person bought a luxury car that he had always wanted and so on. Ellis suggests that, while few of us will ever be happy at the thought of dying, we can still choose how we use our remaining time and get some pleasure from it. Terminal illness is an extreme example. There are many less drastic situations where we feel that we are being forced to do something. Here Ellis says we need to undertake a costs–benefits analysis. You have tickets for a festival that you really want to go to, but you are told that it is your great aunt's ninetieth birthday, and your parents make it clear that you are expected to attend the party. You feel resentful about being forced into attending. The reality is that you could still say no, but it might be too costly. Your parents would be upset, your aunt too, and the rest of your extended family would be critical of you. You do care what they think of you, and it would be good to see some of them again. Also, you think that perhaps your aunt may not have too many more birthdays, while you can attend other festivals. After undertaking this costs–benefits analysis, you decide to go to the party. According to Ellis (2001), what is crucial in these difficult situations is that individuals are made aware that they have a choice and they are not trapped. The person who has decided to do something feels much better about it than does the person who feels they have no choice. The consequence of our free will is that we are responsible for our actions. Ellis sees acceptance of responsibility for the creation of our emotional and behavioural choice as being crucial for psychological health.

Related to this concept is the issue of the control we have over other people. If we have free will, this also means that other people have it also. They are free to make their own choices, and we cannot *demand* that people behave in certain ways. Ellis (1976) points out that quite often when we get upset at other people, we demand that they should not behave in certain ways or should not say certain things. Yet, we do not have the power to do this. We are free to ask and to negotiate with the other, but we have not got the right to dictate how they behave. However, we do have control over how we interpret their behaviour. As we saw in the last example with Joe, who had made nasty comments about us, we cannot control what he says, but we have some control over how we respond to being told about it. We can get angry or disappointed, but we cannot demand the comment to be unsaid or that he apologises. After all, perhaps he even thinks it is a fair comment.

Within REBT and theory, each individual is seen as being at the centre of their own universe and having considerable power of choice in their emotional life. This lends an existential bent to the theory. Like the existential philosophers, Ellis also puts considerable emphasis on the language that we use, as it influences our thoughts. We will see examples of this when we examine developmental influences.

Hedonism

As mentioned earlier, the assumption is that our basic goals in life are hedonistic. We want to stay alive and to be happy. Ellis (1985b) makes a distinction between long-term and short-term hedonism. We often opt for short-term hedonism at the expense of achieving our longer-term goals. In therapy, clients are encouraged to identify both their long-term and short-term goals and find an acceptable balance between the two. Perhaps you want to save for a holiday next year but, in the meantime, you also want to go out and have some fun, so you decide on an appropriate amount to save that will still allow you to go out sometimes. Ellis would see this as rational, in that it is goal-oriented, behaviour.

Enlightened self-interest

The concept of self-interest is sometimes seen as contentious. Ellis (1979) advocates that individuals should put themselves first most of the time, while putting significant others a close second. He stresses that this is not selfishness. He stresses that, for your own long-term happiness,

We can choose whether we are angry, responsible or in control or not in certain situations.
Source: Alamy Images/Comstock Images

you need to ensure that your choices will contribute to your achievement of your goals in life. The complexities of making decisions about whose interests to serve are acknowledged, and your choices will depend on the context, the importance of your goals versus the importance that others attribute to their goals and the likely consequences of the decision. What the theory of REBT says is crucial is that the individual is free to make a decision and makes a decision rather than feeling that they have no choice. We saw this exemplified earlier in the terminally ill and the festival attendance examples. Ellis points out that people who are 'doormats' are not happy. They frequently complain that no one thinks about their needs. They have always put others first, but this is at a cost to themselves. The message in the theory of REBT is clear that, while others' needs are important, individuals also have to pay attention to the achievement of their own needs.

Other values in the theory of rational-emotive behaviour therapy

Although Ellis himself did not practise any religion, he advocated a theory of human value similar to a Christian one; namely, condemn the sin but forgive the sinner. Underpinning this is an assumption that human nature is good. People can do bad things, but they are not bad people. Ellis (1962) follows the humanism of the philosopher Bertrand Russell in this and in condemning all forms of self-rating. There is good in everyone, and each person is valued as a human being. Rational-emotive behavioural therapists will criticise bad behaviour in their clients but

will still value the client themselves. It is important to make a distinction between the behaviour and the person. Behaviour is condemned but not the person. Ellis describes his theory as pursuing an ethical humanism. In this he requires therapists to have high ethical standards and sees it as part of their role to point out to clients when their choices are unethical. He advocates self-acceptance, with an acceptance of responsibility for the choices you make as the way to work towards happiness. This philosophical stance perhaps goes some way towards explaining the popularity of REBT as a treatment approach within the prison and probation services in the United Kingdom and North America. While stressing the complexity of human beings, it also emphasises that we all have the potential to change, if we want to change. We are responsible for what we do, but we always have the potential to change our behaviour.

Ellis (1962) observes that as human beings we have an innate tendency to evaluate our own and others' behaviour. He sees this tendency for evaluation of self and others as being very unhealthy, as it leads to constant insecurity. If your aim is to be the cleverest, most caring, most successful, most admired, best looking or whatever, you may succeed in getting the highest mark for one assignment, but you will constantly be worrying about someone else overtaking you. In line with the logico-empirical approach of REBT, Ellis poses the question of when is the right time to make judgements about your life or the life of others. The logical response is, of course, when all the evidence is in; by that time, the object of the evaluation will be dead. In REBT, the rational goal is to want to do as well as you can, rather than feeling that you have to be best. This means that individuals focus on their own performance and are less interested in rating themselves against others. Ellis does not suggest that it is wrong to set high goals for ourselves, rather that we must not elevate such goals into irrational demands. This would mean that we would like to do well, but we realise that it is not the end of the world if we mess up from time to time.

This last example leads us on to another important conceptualisation of the individual within REBT. Ellis (1979) is at pains to stress that as human beings we are all fallible, yet we have a tendency to be self-critical. He sees **fallibility** as a property of the human species. It goes along with our innate ability to be irrational as well as rational. The world is complex, and social relationships can be difficult to manage. Everyone gets things wrong and makes mistakes sometimes. However, we tend to condemn ourselves when we make these mistakes and, according to the theory of REBT, a lot of our psychological distress is caused by our failure to accept that we are fallible by nature. We irrationally demand that we should always get things right; therefore, when we mess up, it is very upsetting and we roundly condemn ourselves for doing it. Ellis suggests that we can minimise our distress if only we would accept ourselves as fallible human beings who will mess things up from time to time. It is unfortunate that this is the case, but this is the way that things are. Ellis suggests that we can be sad about it and learn from our mistakes, but that we should not condemn ourselves for making mistakes. We are simply being human.

Development of the individual

To recap, Ellis (1976) sees the human child as having innate abilities to think rationally, but also an innate tendency to think irrationally. Children are brought up by adults who also have a tendency to think irrationally. This means that individuals are unlikely to have been lucky enough to experience a totally rational upbringing. As a result of our upbringing we all carry with us irrational tendencies, the nature of which will differ depending on the experiences we have had. In this, Ellis, like the psychoanalysts who preceded him, sees us as having emotional baggage originating in our childhood family experiences. Our different developmental experiences plus our innate differences account for differences in personality. Ellis (1978) suggests that about 80 per cent of individual differences in personality are probably biological and 20 per cent are down to the environment.

While he does not provide a detailed theory of development, Ellis does outline some of the ways that we are encouraged to think irrationally. We have already mentioned the way that parental socialisation practices tend to encourage belief in a just world and the problems that this then causes

us when we are treated unfairly. Ellis points out that our tendency to use language imprecisely leads to further problems. We frequently forget that young children take what is said to them literally. The exasperated parent, whose child has been misbehaving, finally, with a very angry face, tells the child that they are a very naughty little girl or a bad little girl. The child gets the message that they are 'bad' and therefore less loved or loveable for behaving in that way. The parent does not actually mean that the child herself is bad, but rather that her behaviour in this instance is bad. We take shortcuts with our language; in doing so, we convey the wrong message. Ellis (1979) sees us as learning to rate ourselves through experiences like these and suggests that it is detrimental to our mental health in the long term, as we have already discussed in the last section.

Ellis (2001) is clear that growth and change are always a possibility if the individual chooses to work at it. Mental health and happiness are conceptualised in terms of aiming to maximise your rational behaviour and minimise your irrational behaviour in an endeavour to attain the human goals of staying alive and being happy. Growth of the individual is not achieved by a specific age; rather, it is an ongoing process of change.

The basic model of rational-emotive behaviour therapy

Ellis (1979) outlines a simple-sounding ABC model to describe how emotional and behavioural responses occur. The notation is as follows:

A represents the **Activating event**;
B represents the clients' **Belief system**;
C represents the emotional and behavioural **Consequences** that occur as a result.

Most people assume that *A* causes *C*. For example, your flatmate uses all the milk and you get angry because there is no milk for your breakfast. The flatmate's inconsiderate behaviour is the *A*, and your anger at it is the *C*. A typical understanding is that the flatmate's behaviour made you angry (*A* caused *C*). The first task in therapy is to convince clients that *B* causes *C*, not *A*. Our emotions result largely from what we tell ourselves at *B*. Different personalities will have different belief systems, and this variation helps to explain why we may interpret situations differently. Our current mood and the importance of the situation will also be contributory factors. All should become clear when we return to the inconsiderate flatmate example. You may be telling yourself that he/she is selfish and never thinks of others. If you have a hangover and are desperate for coffee, you may feel even more annoyed at him/her. This is your *B* causing the *C*. (See Stop and think: What would you do?)

Stop and think

What would you do?

Think about yourself as being the victim in the flat-mate scenario. What would you be saying to yourself to feel angry? What sort of thing would you have to say to yourself to feel mildly irritated, as opposed to angry? Can you think what you would have to say to actually feel good about their having used the milk? It can be interesting to compare responses with your friends.

Ellis (1962) calls this stage 'developing insights' into the causation of emotions and behaviour. He uses several techniques to help clients accept the insight that emotions result largely from what we tell ourselves. This is very different from the psychoanalytic models we have considered earlier (Chapters 2 and 3). There, our psychological disturbance was firmly rooted in our past, and we had to revisit our past via the process of psychoanalysis to resolve the conflicts. Ellis chooses not to focus on the past. Past events may have been important in contributing to the distress that you experienced in the past, but they are a problem in the present only if you *continue* to think about them in the same way. Past beliefs only continue to be a problem because patients continually re-indoctrinate themselves with these beliefs. If you think you are bad at relationships because you had bad relationships with your parents, this becomes a self-fulfilling prophecy. For Ellis (1962), the relationships you had with your parents are irrelevant other than in that you believe they have left you with a problem. Ellis' approach is pragmatic. He points out that you cannot change the past, you have to accept it, but you can change how you *think* about it. He would explore how the individual deals with their relationships and what they are telling themselves. To do this involves the next stage of his model, labelled **D** for **Disputation**.

Disputation is firmly embedded in the logico-empirical approach. Clients are continually asked what the evidence for their beliefs is. The therapist undertakes to challenge the clients' irrational beliefs and discusses with them alternative beliefs that they could hold. Ellis gets individuals to recognise the voice in their head that tells them what they are thinking at stage *B*. This can sometimes be difficult for people to do, as many of our responses at *B* are so highly practised that they are virtually automatic. Imagine the situation where you are really angry with someone. You might be asked to rate on a scale of 1–10 how angry you are. You say you are feeling 10 and it is really upsetting you; you can't cope with it. Your sleep is affected; you are tearful and generally distraught. The therapist would then ask what level of distress you think is appropriate, using the same 1–10 scale. You might say 6 or 7, as then you would feel more in control and more able to do something about

it. The therapist would then explore, with you, your current self-talk about the anger incident and discuss what you would have to be saying to yourself to change your level of anger to 6 or 7. Rational-emotive behaviour therapists might use paper and pencil to help the client unpick their thoughts at *B*.

The concept of irrational beliefs is sometimes quite difficult for individuals to grasp. Ellis (1996) acknowledged that it was not the best label he could have chosen for self-defeating beliefs and later preferred the term **dysfunctional beliefs**. However, generations of rational-emotive behaviour therapists have been trained in the old terminology, so change may take some time. What is important to remember is that rational beliefs are unproblematic as they help you to attain your goals, while irrational or dysfunctional beliefs do not.

Unlike psychoanalysis, where all the therapeutic work occurs in the therapeutic hour, REBT begins from the premise that behaviour change is difficult. We may develop insight about our behaviour in therapy, but changing our behaviour has to happen in the real world. To assist them with this change, clients are sent homework assignments that they are required to do to begin the process of behaviour change. Rational-emotive behaviour therapists may use learning theory techniques to try to encourage clients to carry out their homework tasks.

Homework is part of the final component of Ellis' approach, which is labelled **E** for **Education**. In line with individuals taking responsibility for their behaviour, Ellis' approach aims to teach them the ABCDE model so that they can then utilise it in their lives. Clients may be asked to read articles and books on aspects of the therapy as well as to practise the new cognitions and related behaviour that they have learned in therapy. As we have outlined the model, it may have appeared as a linear process; Ellis (1996) points out that it is really much more complex. Clients seldom have one clear-cut problem, and our perception, thinking, emotions and behaviour all interact in several directions. It is a bidirectional, interactive theory. In common with the psychoanalytic theories, the personality theory has emerged from what was originally a therapy designed to elicit personality change.

Sources of psychological disturbance

Ellis (1979; 1984) claims that most psychological disturbance results from irrational thinking. He classifies the disturbance as one of two types, either ego disturbance or discomfort disturbance (see Figure 5.3):

- **Ego disturbance** – the person makes demands on themselves, other individuals and the world; when these demands are not met, the person becomes upset and damns himself or herself. If you think you must get an A grade for your next assignment and you fail to do so, then you might respond by feeling really bad about yourself, thinking that you are a useless student, cannot get your act together and so on. You would be giving yourself a negative global rating. The rational response is to stress one's fallibility and refuse to rate oneself globally. In this case you have failed to meet your target. But it is only one assignment, and what can you learn from the experience? The aim is to use your energy by learning from the experience rather than putting your energy into continuing to damn yourself.

- **Discomfort disturbance** – again, the person makes demands on self, others and the world that are related to dogmatic commands that life should be comfortable and things should not be too difficult to achieve. If these demands are not met, the person becomes disturbed. Tolerating discomfort to achieve goals and long-term happiness is the healthy, rational alternative to demands for immediate gratification. This concept refers also to tolerance of delayed gratification. When we discussed Freud (Chapter 2), we saw that id instincts work against delayed gratification. In the Freudian model we saw that the id is extremely demanding; it wants to be rewarded instantaneously. Ellis, whatever the source of our demandingness as human beings, classifies this response as irrational behaviour and describes us as having **low frustration tolerance**. He sees the ability to tolerate frustration and delay gratification as being signs of the mature personality.

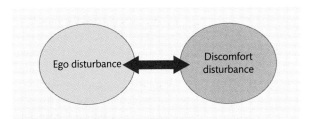

Figure 5.3 Ellis' two forms of disturbance resulting from irrational thinking.

Applications of rational-emotive behaviour therapy

Ellis' therapy is used to treat people with a wide range of clinical and non-clinical problems and also for personal growth. It can be practised as an individual or group therapy. The advantages of REBT are that it provides therapists with powerful, effective and fast-acting methodologies. The constructs used are less esoteric than those of psychoanalysis and are therefore easier to understand for clients, who thus get a better appreciation of what is occurring. Like the behaviour therapies we discussed earlier, REBT is systematic, planned and structured but much more flexible than the former. It can also allow integration of different approaches to therapy to fit the needs of the individual client. It encourages clients to adopt a more flexible approach to life and not fit into a rigid worldview. Finally, it is cost-effective as it is a brief therapy. It is not unusual for psychoanalysis to continue for several years, while cognitive therapy achieves results generally within 10–16 sessions of treatment, sometimes less. It can also be delivered effectively online to patients with moderate levels of psychological disturbance (Cavanagh *et al.*, 2004).

Research evidence for effectiveness of rational-emotive behaviour therapy

As with all the theories we have examined so far, there are a large number of publications on Ellis' theory, but far fewer on evaluation. DiGiuseppe *et al.* (1979) reviewed research evidence for the early years of application and found support for REBT as an effective therapy. Since then, a large number of studies have evaluated the effectiveness of REBT for particular conditions; only a sample of these studies will be provided here. Macaskill and Macaskill (1997) found that a combination of REBT and antidepressants is more effective in treating severely depressed patients than is medication alone, and relapse was significantly less. In 1999, a survey of over 30 studies evaluating the effectiveness of REBT in treating post-traumatic stress disorder (PTSD) concluded that it was an effective treatment resulting in significant reductions in symptoms (Bryant *et al.*, 1999). Rector and Beck (2001) demonstrated that cognitive therapy could be used effectively with patients suffering from schizophrenia. Brown *et al.* (2005) demonstrated that cognitive therapy was effective in preventing clients who had already attempted suicide undertaking further attempts. An excellent overview of the state of cognitive approaches is provided by Beck (2005). Aaron Beck is a well-known American cognitive therapist who developed a variation of cognitive therapy, initially for the treatment of depression. This therapy developed from the early work of both Kelly and Ellis.

Contentious issues

Some researchers suggest that the relationship between cognitions and emotions does not always hold (Bower, 1981). There are sometimes chicken-and-egg arguments put forward about whether the depression causes negative thoughts or the negative thoughts cause the depression. With depressed individuals, their negative mood may produce negative cognitions. However, in support of cognitive approaches, it is clear from the case study literature that negative cognitions may maintain depression once it is started and that helping individuals change their negative thinking improves their depression.

REBT and other cognitive approaches are sometimes criticised for trying to adjust the individual to fit in with social reality, whereas it may be that social changes are needed. This is an argument that is sometimes made about stress management training, for example. Instead of tackling the sources of stress, institutions may simply help individuals cope better with it. Therapists generally respond to these sorts of criticisms by saying that their aim is to reduce the suffering of the individual as that is generally within their power while societal changes are not.

Meehl (1981) accuses Ellis of using logical positivism when asking for proof of values from clients. He points out that many of our human values cannot be empirically verified by data. The suggestion he makes is that in REBT and other cognitive approaches, clients substitute one set of values for another more socially acceptable or socially convenient set, and that it has nothing to do with rationality. This point reminds us that, as we discussed previously (Chapter 1), all theorising occurs within a cultural context; it does involve value judgements about what is 'acceptable' behaviour, and therapists are expected to work within an ethical framework.

Career focus: Working in clinical psychology

According to the British Psychological Society website, the main role of clinical psychologists is to alleviate psychological distress and support psychological well-being among their clients. The sort of problems that clinical psychologists cover include, but are not exclusive to, mental illness, depression, anxiety and child and family problems. Clinical psychologists work in a variety of settings and with a variety of individuals and agencies. This includes hospitals, mental health teams and health and social services.

Professor Susan Llewelyn

1. **Why did you choose to pursue the area of clinical psychology?**

    I found clinical questions were the most interesting to explore; for example, why do some people have such different experiences (especially psychosis) and how could psychology help to reduce distress.

2. **In what way do the skills and/or knowledge you learned when studying personality and individual differences apply to your work/research today?**

    My clinical work has mainly involved working therapeutically with people who have difficulties in personal relationships and psychological self-care, such as those often following the experience of childhood sexual abuse. I have also worked extensively with health care teams, especially in the mental health sector, helping them to work constructively together to improve the care of their patients, by being clear about their purpose and structure, and through effective communication processes. Knowing about how people work in teams and groups has helped me to improve mental health care services. Knowing how to provide a safe and encouraging environment (see attachment theories in Chapter 21) has helped me to help others work out a way of resolving their distress.

For further advice on becoming a clinical psychologist, including guidance on the necessary qualifications and experience, visit the British Psychological Society website at **http://www.bps.org.uk/careers-education-training/how-become-psychologist/types-psychologists/becoming-clinical-psychologis**.

Overall evaluation of cognitive approaches

We will now evaluate the cognitive approaches using the eight criteria identified previously (Chapter 1): description, explanation, empirical validity, testable concepts, comprehensiveness, parsimony, heuristic value and applied value.

Description

Kelly is criticised for the difficulty of some of the descriptions he provides. Some of his descriptions of the 11 corollaries in his theory are not always easy to follow. He uses complex language, and his meaning is not always clear. Ellis, on the other hand, provides very clear descriptions. For both theorists, however, their descriptions are very focused in the present, in providing systems to uncover the cognitive and belief structures of individuals.

Explanation

Kelly and Ellis have both described clear systems for understanding and exploring the way that an individual's cognitions are structured. Both Kelly's rep grid and Ellis' ABC model provide valuable insights into the way we perceive our world, how we organise our attitudes and beliefs, how we generate our emotional responses and how these influence our behaviour. Both approaches can be criticised for concentrating too much on the individual's thought processes and ignoring other aspects of their personality. Both theories focus on the uniqueness of individuals yet conceptualise us all as operating within the same framework, and this is a real strength of these theories.

Empirical validity

Kelly himself was not a researcher as such and did not provide empirical evidence for the effectiveness of his model or therapy. Many others, however, have shown the efficacy of the rep grid as a tool for exploring an individual's cognitions, attitudes and beliefs. One of the most influential applications has been in the area of schizophrenia, as we have seen. It does need to be stressed, however, that much of the research involves self-report and is correlational in nature. There are virtually no well-designed experimental studies testing Kelly's theory. The interpretation of the rep grid test is also not systematic. It relies on the expertise of the therapist or researcher to interpret it effectively. While it undoubtedly produces useful material, it is not an objective research measure. Ellis' work, on the other hand, is now the most heavily researched theory in contemporary psychology. The review of 40 years of cognitive therapy carried out by Beck (2005) shows the evidence for this research.

Testable concepts

Both theories are very easy to test. It is relatively easy to derive hypotheses for testing based on the theories, and this has been done. The rep grid also provides a precise, valid way of measuring personal constructs.

Comprehensiveness

In the general scheme of things, Kelly's theory is not very comprehensive. It focuses almost exclusively on what is going on within the individual. Situational factors that may determine behaviour are largely ignored in favour of cognitions. This theory also presents a somewhat oversimplified view of individuals' thought processes in assuming that human thought processes are always rational. It plays down the irrational tendencies of human beings that are so clearly displayed in Ellis' theoretical approach. In this respect, Ellis' theory is more comprehensive. It allows for the effects of the individual's belief system, emotional state, history of learning and genetic influences on personality as well as of their cognitions in producing both rational and irrational behaviour.

Parsimony

Kelly's theory is too parsimonious. It employs few concepts. It talks about the processes of healthy personality development, for example, only in the most general of terms, and it is not clear from this description exactly what would be involved. Similarly, with maladjustment, only a global picture is presented. No real detail is provided about the kinds of experiences necessary to create the flexible personal construct systems that are seen to be desirable. Ellis' theory has sometimes been described as being simplistic, as it too utilises relatively few concepts. The response that Ellis (1996) gives is that many groundbreaking ideas appear simple. He quotes the wheel as an example of a development that, once it was invented, seemed simple and obvious, yet it transformed the way that individuals do things. While Ellis' theory seems simple with relatively few concepts, in practice it is more complex.

Heuristic value

Personal construct theory has been and continues to be more popular in the United Kingdom than in the United States where it originated. It challenged the mainstream learning theory perspective in America and, as such, it may have been too radical for psychologists to take up. One British clinical psychologist, David Bannister, has done much to promote Kelly's work (Bannister, 1977; 1985). It has provided a lot of interest clinically in the

United Kingdom and in Holland, Canada and Israel. There are still large numbers of therapists using personal construct theory. Similarly, for a long time REBT was more popular in the United Kingdom and the rest of the world than it was in the United States, although this is beginning to change. As we discussed earlier, cognitive theories are the fastest-growing and most researched approach currently.

Applied value

Kelly's work, as we have seen, is utilised in clinical psychology and has provided useful insights into disordered thinking in schizophrenia and other conditions. More recently, it has been applied in occupational psychology, where the rep grid is used to explore relationships within organisations or consumers'

perceptions of a company's products. Kelly's theory has also been used to help people identify their ideal jobs. Ellis' work is used in an even wider context, from clinical psychology, business and education to personal growth.

Final comments

By now, you should understand Kelly's personal construct theory and its constituent parts. You should appreciate what is meant by subjective perception of the world, be aware of different views on the effects of development on personality and be familiar with the repertory grid as an assessment tool. You should now also understand the basic model of REBT, have an appreciation of the clinical applications of cognitive theories and be able to broadly evaluate cognitive approaches to personality.

Summary

- Cognitive theories challenge both the psychoanalytic and learning theory approaches to personality.
- Kelly conceives individuals acting as scientists, each trying to understand and control the world around them.
- The criteria that we each use to perceive and interpret events are labelled our personal constructs. Within our construct system, we have overarching constructs known as superordinate constructs. Within the superordinate concepts are subordinate constructs.
- Central to Kelly's theory is the concept of constructive alternativism.
- Kelly sees free will and determinism as interrelated. He assumes that we all have free will in selecting our goals, but once we have selected a goal, it may determine our subsequent behaviour.
- Kelly suggests that our motivation to act comes from our future aims, not from our past learning or early experiences or innate drives. This is termed the fundamental postulate of his theory.
- In Kelly's theory, personal constructs are organised in terms of similarities and contrasts.
- Kelly's fundamental postulate is expanded on by the addition of 11 corollaries outlining how the interpretative processes operate to allow us to create our personal constructs.
- Kelly's constructs have two opposing properties: permeability and impermeability.
- Kelly believes that predicting behaviour is very complex. The individual's 'cognitive world', which will include inconsistent as well as logical subsystems, has to be assessed.
- Kelly proposes three types of constructs: pre-emptive, constellatory and propositional.

- In personal construct theory, the aim of development was for the individual to maximise their knowledge of the world via the development of their personal construct systems.
- The assessment technique that Kelly is best known for is the role construct repertory test (rep grid).
- People with psychological problems were using personal constructs that were invalid and unhelpful. To bring about change in his clients' personal constructs, Kelly used several techniques, including controlled elaboration, self-characterisation sketches and fixed-role therapy.
- Ellis' REBT and theory also comes from the clinical tradition and was influenced by learning theory and the psychoanalytic approaches of Horney and Adler.
- Ellis suggests that human beings are uniquely rational and uniquely irrational in our thinking and the ways we attempt to reach our goals in life.
- Irrational thought is recognised by its demanding nature. We make demands on ourselves, other people or the world in general.
- REBT and theory adopts a logico-empirical approach, stressing the importance of having evidence for your beliefs. It also stresses the subjective nature of our perception of the world. We use perception, sensing, thinking and emotion to interpret the world.
- Ellis asserts that we have free will as individuals, but that also makes us responsible for our actions.
- The theory of REBT sees being fallible as an innate quality of human beings.
- Ellis asserts that 80 per cent of individual differences are genetic, but he does talk about the role of developmental experiences in encouraging human beings to think irrationally.

- The ABC model he outlines explains how we generate our emotional responses and how this impacts on our behaviour and our subsequent cognitions.
- Two main forms of disturbance are described: ego disturbance and discomfort disturbance.

- REBT is currently the most researched therapy. There is a lot of evidence to support its effectiveness in many areas, although it is not without its critics, as we have seen.
- Finally, both theories are evaluated using the criteria outlined previously (Chapter 1).

Connecting up

You can read more on the application of Ellis' theory of irrational beliefs in Chapter 19, Irrational Beliefs.

Critical thinking

Discussion questions

- Do you agree with Kelly that we see ourselves as scientists when we are trying to understand the world?
- How easy is it to identify your own personal constructs?
- Is the repertory grid a useful tool for understanding individuals?
- Can you identify similarities between the cognitive approaches of Kelly and Ellis?
- Ellis maintains that how an individual thinks largely determines how they feel and behave. Do you think that there is evidence to support this view?
- Do you agree with Ellis that human beings have a biological tendency to think irrationally as well as rationally?
- Do you think that it is possible to bring up a child according to the principles of REBT? Would it be desirable?

- How adequately do cognitive theorists explain human motivation?

Essay questions

- Critically examine Kelly's personal construct approach.
- Critically examine Kelly's theory of personality development.
- Critically examine the theory and research that surrounds Ellis' REBT.
- Does the theory of REBT really provide us with a good model of personality?
- Ellis maintains that how an individual thinks largely determines how they feel and behave. Critically discuss.
- Critically discuss the contribution made by Ellis to our understanding of personality.

Going further

Books

Kelly

- Bannister, D. and Fransella, F. (1989). *Inquiring man: The psychology of personal constructs*. London: Croom Helm. This is a very readable account of Kelly's theory; the book is still widely available.
- Bannister, D. (1985). *New perspectives on personal construct theory*. London: Academic Press. This book contains a number of contributions from a variety of well-known authors in the world of personal construct theory and measurement.

- Kelly, G. A. (1963). *A theory of personality: The psychology of personal constructs*. New York: Norton. This is the first three chapters of Kelly's seminal work, published in 1955 and included in the references at the end of this book. Kelly is not easy to read, but this book is easier than his 1955 works.

Ellis

- Ellis, by contrast, is very easy to read. He is an amusing and entertaining writer, so almost any of his books are worth recommending as they give a real flavour of the individual. He was a very prolific writer, as a visit to

Amazon.com will confirm. You can also buy tapes of Ellis in therapy sessions and hear him talking about his theory; see the Institute for Rational-Emotive Behaviour Therapy at the website listed in Web links.

- Ellis, A. (1986). *The handbook of rational-emotive therapy*. New York: Springer.
- Harper, R. and Ellis, A. (1975). *A guide to rational living*. New York: Image Book Company.
- Ellis, A. (1991). *Hold your head up high (Overcoming common problems)*. London: Sheldon Press.
- Ellis, A. and Dryden, W. (2007). *The practice of rational-emotive behaviour therapy* (2nd edn). New York: Springer.

Journals

- Raskin, J. D. (2001). The modern, the postmodern, and George Kelly's personal construct psychology. *American Psychologist, 56*, 368–369. The *American Psychologist* is published by the American Psychological Association and is available online via PsycARTICLES.
- Walker, B. M. and Winter, D. A. (2007). The elaboration of personal construct psychology. *Annual Review of Psychology, 58*, 453–477. This article provides a good overview. *Annual Review of Psychology* is published by Annual Reviews (Palo Alto, California) and is available online via Business Source Premier.
- If you are interested, you can also read an original George Kelly article: Kelly, G. A. (1958). The theory and technique of assessment. *Annual Review of Psychology, 9*, 323–353. *Annual Review of Psychology* is published by Annual Reviews (Palo Alto, California) and is available online via Business Source Premier.

If you would like to read some more about how cognitive theories are applied to therapy situations, the journal *Behaviour Research and Therapy* may be of interest to you. Today the journal concentrates on theory and research using cognitive therapies in application to traditional clinical disorders. It is published by Elsevier Science and is available online via Science-Direct. There is also the *Journal of Rational-Emotive and Cognitive-Behaviour Therapy*, a publication that has theory and research articles on REBT. It is published by Springer/Kluwer and available online via SwetsWISE.

Web links

- This is the link to the British Centre for Personal Construct Theory. It is now a virtual centre at the University of Hertfordshire (**www.centrepcp.co.uk**).
- This site gives a useful introduction to completing rep grids. Atherton, J. S. (2005). *Learning and teaching: Personal construct theory*. Available online (**www.learningandteaching.info/learning/personal.htm**).
- This is the link to the Institute for RBT in New York. It contains information about Albert Ellis and his therapy (**www.rebt.org**).
- A more comprehensive source of information about Ellis and his work and links to other websites can be found at (**www.rebtnetwork.org**). This site was set up in 2006 to celebrate Ellis' lifetime achievements.

Film and literature

- *Three Approaches to Psychotherapy: Gloria* (Educational Resource Film). Therapists Carl Rogers and Albert Ellis are two of the three psychotherapists who demonstrate their different techniques on the same client. Concord Video and Film Council.
- *Confessions of a Dangerous Mind*. There are several films that ask you to consider the way the lead character constructs his personal world. However, the best example

is *Confessions of a Dangerous Mind* (2002, directed by George Clooney), based on the autobiography of Chuck Barris – television producer by day; at the height of his TV career, he was recruited by the CIA and trained to become a covert operative. Or so Barris said. Also see the *Matrix* series (1999, May and November, 2003; written and directed by Andy and Larry Wachowski) and *The Truman Show* (1998, directed by Peter Weir).

Explore the website accompanying this text at **www.pearsoned.co.uk/maltby** for further resources to help you with your studies. These include multiple-choice questions, essay questions, web links and ideas for advanced reading.

CHAPTER 6
Humanistic Personality Theories

Key themes

- Humanistic personality theories
- Maslow's theory of self-actualisation
- Carl Rogers and person-centred therapy
- Evaluation of the humanistic theories of Maslow and Rogers

Learning outcomes

After studying this discussion you should:

- Understand what is meant by humanistic theories in psychology and how they evolved
- Be familiar with the developmental experiences that influenced the theorising of Maslow and Rogers
- Appreciate the Maslow and Rogers' conceptualisations of human nature
- Be familiar with Maslow's hierarchy of needs and the motives related to it
- Understand the principles of personality development and the causes of mental illness as described by Maslow and Rogers
- Be familiar with Rogers' conceptualisation of self-actualisation and its importance in development
- Understand the principles of Rogerian counselling, including the importance of the core conditions of counselling
- Be aware of an approach to measuring the self-concept and the ideal self
- Know how to critically evaluate the work of Maslow and Rogers

Introduction

What was your school like? Were you allowed to const-ruct your timetable, decide which subjects to study, have no obligatory assessment? Were the teachers concerned that you had enough time to play and enjoy yourself? This was probably not your experience of school. It is most likely to have had a set curriculum, obligatory coursework, tests and examinations. The theorists that we examine here suggest that such educa-tional conformity frequently stifles our individuality and creativity as human beings and encourages competition rather than cooperation. There is one school in England that defies this educational conformity. Summerhill was set up by the famous educationalist A. S. Neil in 1923, in Lyme Regis. In 1927 the school was moved to Suffolk, where it still operates today, run by Neil's son.

Neil believed that children must live their own lives, not the lives that their parents or school teachers think they should live. Neil believed that our aim in life is to find happiness. By living different experiences, Neil felt, we will find things that interest us; and this will make us happy and provide us with the motivation to work at these things. He strongly believed that traditional education stifles creativity in most children, and that they lose their love of learning and exploring new ideas. He established Summerhill to provide the ideal learning environment, giving children freedom to choose their interests and to develop their personalities freely within a democratically run community. The Summerhill philos-ophy exemplifies many of the ideas expounded by the personality theorists who are discussed here. There are scheduled lessons at Summerhill; however, each child

is given a blank timetable, and they are free to attend lessons as they choose. Many new pupils say they have no intention of ever going to lessons again, but such is the culture of the school that they are drawn to partici-pate in learning because the experiences are fun. The basic belief in Summerhill, shared by the theorists who we discuss here, is that as a species we are inquisitive and want to learn – and that if we are given the freedom to learn, then we will learn. There is no compulsory coursework; there are no tests or examinations. Neil believed that education must be a preparation for life and that children will learn what they want to learn and be happier as a result. He felt that only by giving chil-dren the freedom to develop as they choose will their true personalities develop. He believed that assess-ment, examinations and prizes sidetrack proper person-ality development. Children in conventional education, he claimed, are socialised into developing in ways that meet the expectations of others, such as parents and teachers, and the children's true selves can often be lost in the process.

This is obviously a very contentious stance and one that you may want to discuss further with your fellow students. Do you think it would have been a good experience for you? We have included the web address for Summerhill School at the end of the discussion for those of you who want to know more. In 1999 the school received an unfavourable Office for Stand-ards in Education (Ofsted) report from the govern-ment school inspectors. The school was in danger of being closed, but it took the government to court and

Source: Alamy Images/Image Source Black

actually won the case. From the site you can access the Ofsted report and details of the court case. Summerhill is of interest to us as it practises many of the principles outlined by Abraham Maslow and Carl Rogers, the two personality theorists presented here, and we will return to it later.

Both Maslow and Rogers were American psychologists, but European psychology and philosophy heavily influenced their ideas. In this discussion, we will examine the historical roots of the approach that influenced both theorists and helped define the key principles. Each theorist is presented in turn and then the overall approach is evaluated.

Historical roots and key elements of the humanistic approach

In early twentieth-century American psychology, the two main influences were the psychoanalytic tradition and the learning theory approaches that we have covered previously. Maslow and Rogers were initially educated in the psychoanalytic tradition, and the dominant learning theory approaches played a significant part in their early education as psychologists. However, as neither theorist was comfortable with these approaches, they developed alternative approaches. These approaches drew on the European tradition of existential philosophy, epitomised in the writings of Friedrich Nietzsche, Søren Kierkegaard and Jean-Paul Sartre. There is no one agreed-upon definition of existential philosophy. It addresses what is called ontology, defined as 'the science of being'. Existential philosophers are concerned with how we find meaning for our existence, what motivates us to keep on living. They emphasise the uniqueness of human beings and focus on issues of free will and human responsibility. These existential themes are incorporated into the work of both Maslow and Rogers.

Maslow and Rogers' theories are often described as humanistic personality theories. Several characteristics define humanistic approaches. There is always an emphasis on *personal growth*. Human beings are seen to be motivated by a need to grow and develop in a positive way. Human nature is conceptualised as being positive, unlike the Freudian conception of human nature as innately aggressive and destructive. The focus in humanistic theories is on the here and now. Individuals are discouraged from focusing on the past. While the past may have helped to shape the person you are, you are seen as being able to change. Within humanistic approaches, individuals are encouraged to savour the moment

without worrying overly about the past or the future. There is also an emphasis on personal responsibility. Borrowing from the existential philosophers, there is an emphasis on human beings having free will in terms of the choices they make in their lives; and consequently, they are responsible for these choices. Sometimes we assume that we do not have a choice, but the humanists would suggest that this is because we find the alternatives too hard to undertake. We saw some examples of this when we discussed Albert Ellis' rational-emotive behaviour therapy (in Chapter 5). Ellis' theory, although classified as a cognitive theory, also shares this humanistic bent.

The final defining feature of humanistic theories is an emphasis on the phenomenology of the individual person. Phenomenological approaches focus on trying to understand individual experience and consciousness. The concept of the uniqueness of each individual and their experience is stressed. Individuals are conceptualised as being the experts on themselves, and humanistic therapists aim merely to help their clients understand what their problems are and not to provide solutions. We will return to this concept in more detail later as we consider the work of Maslow and then Rogers in detail.

Abraham Maslow and self-actualisation

The first area we are going to concentrate on in Maslow's work is his view of human nature and human motivation.

Human nature and human motivation

An explanation of the influences that led Maslow to want to focus on what human beings could achieve and what would make them happy is given in the Profile box for Maslow.

Profile

Abraham Maslow

Abraham Maslow was born in Brooklyn, New York, in 1908, the first of seven children. His parents were Russian-Jewish immigrants. He describes his childhood as being very lonely, and he had a strong sense of not belonging in his environment. He attributes this to his family being the only Jewish family in the neighbourhood. His parents, although uneducated themselves, were keen for their children to be successful educationally and pushed him hard. He describes himself as having turned to books for solace, having few friends. He initially studied law at the behest of his parents, but soon dropped out as he found law uninteresting. He was attracted to study psychology after reading about behaviourism and the learning theory approach (Chapter 4), and his doctoral studies were on the sexuality of monkeys. However, the birth of his first child led Maslow to question the behaviourist approach, feeling that it was too simplistic to provide a real understanding of the complexity of human life. This need to understand human personality became his goal and remained so throughout his life. He first turned to the psychoanalytic tradition (see Chapters 2 and 3), reading widely, undergoing psychoanalysis and interacting with many of the major psychoanalysts such as Adler and Horney, many of whom had emigrated to the United States to escape Nazism. While finding aspects of psychoanalysis to be interesting, Maslow found the negative view of humanity emanating from Freud's work to be unacceptable. He was increasingly interested in showing that the human race was capable of achieving great feats, and he began his study of what he described as remarkable human beings who had achieved much and were content with their lives (Maslow, 1970). He began by studying two individuals he had met who were high achievers and seemed to have achieved a high level of satisfaction with their lives. The first individual was the Jewish German psychologist Max Wertheimer, who had come to the States to escape the Nazis. Wertheimer had achieved breakthroughs in our understanding of perception and learning. The second object of study was Ruth Benedict, an American anthropologist who had become famous for her work on the influence of culture on individuals. Maslow described these individuals as being self-actualised, and we will explore exactly what he meant by this elsewhere in this text. He published a major study of such self-actualised people in 1970, shortly before he died from a heart attack.

Maslow wanted to move from the early focus of psychology on clinical populations and the related psychopathology to explore how to make the average human being happier and healthier. He began with the assumption that human nature is basically good, as opposed to the negative conceptualisation of humans provided by Freud. Maslow described human beings as having innate tendencies towards healthy growth and development that he labelled **instinctoid tendencies** (Maslow, 1954). These positive instinctoid tendencies were conceptualised by Maslow as being weak and easily overcome by negative environmental influences. If the instinctoid tendencies in children are fostered, they will have the capacity to display honesty, trust, kindness, love and generosity and will develop constructively into healthy individuals. Conversely, if children grow up in an unhealthy environment they can easily lose their positive instinctoid tendencies and grow up to become destructive, aggressive and unloving individuals, engaging in self-destructive and self-defeating behaviour (Maslow, 1954; 1965; 1968; 1970). Maslow suggests that such individuals feature among Freud's case studies, and he acknowledges that psychoanalytic theories and therapies provide useful tools for psychologists having to deal with this disturbed population. However, his wish was to focus on the positive possibilities in human development; he felt that this approach, alongside the work of the psychoanalysts, would then provide a complete theory of human personality (Maslow, 1968).

Maslow's interest was in trying to understand what motivates us to go about our lives and make the choices that we do. As we saw previously (Chapter 1), this is a fundamental area for personality theories to address. In his early doctoral studies, Maslow had become interested in the needs that animals display, and he demonstrated that it was possible to organise these needs into a hierarchy. The needs lower in the hierarchy must be satisfied before we address higher-level needs. From his observations, he suggested that a similar system existed for human beings. He described two distinct types of human motivations. The first are **deficiency motives**; that is, basic needs that we are driven to fulfil. These include drives like hunger, thirst and the need for safety and to be loved by someone. Maslow conceptualises these needs as representing something that we lack and are motivated to get. If we are hungry, once we have obtained sufficient food, this need is met. The need then ceases to be a motivator. Maslow gave examples of the economic depression in America in the 1930s, when thousands of people lost their jobs. Feeding their family became the dominant need for many people, so they were happy to get any job that would allow them to achieve their goal. He compares this situation with economically affluent times and suggests that, when people are wealthier, their motivational needs change. Hunger is no longer a threat, so they are motivated to get a better house or car, or a more interesting job and so on.

The second type of needs Maslow outlines are **growth motives**, sometimes called **being motives** or **B-motives**. These needs are unique to each individual and are conceptualised as gaining intensity as they are met. He suggests that these needs are about developing the individual's potential. They include things like giving love unselfishly; increases in drive, like curiosity and the thirst for knowledge; developing skills and having new experiences. Maslow felt that the personal growth involved in these B-motives was exciting and rewarding for the individuals and served to stimulate them further. This is a crucial difference between deficiency motives and growth motives. Deficiency motives create a negative motivational state that can be changed only by satisfying the need; in contrast, growth motives can be enjoyable, and satisfying these needs can act as further motivation to achieve personal goals and ambitions. In this way, deficiency motives are seen to ensure our survival, while growth needs represent a higher level of functioning that can result in us becoming happier, healthier and more fulfilled as individuals. Maslow suggested that the psychoanalysts had overemphasised drive reduction as a motivator for human behaviour because this tended to be true of the clinical populations that were their focus. He acknowledged that human motives were complex and that behaviour could be motivated by several needs. For example, an apparently simple behaviour like eating might be motivated by hunger, the need to be with others or by the need for emotional comfort when a love affair goes wrong; we are sure you can think of other motives. If we ate only to fulfil our hunger needs, obesity would not be such a health problem in western societies.

Hierarchy of needs

Maslow (1970) felt that it would be difficult to produce lists of human needs given the complexity of human motivation and the way that behaviour could be motivated by several needs. However, he argued that needs vary significantly in terms of their importance for ensuring our survival. To this end, he developed what has become his famous hierarchy of needs. Some needs have to be met before other needs are acknowledged and begin to motivate our behaviour. We saw this earlier in the economic depression example. Maslow's hierarchy of needs is displayed in Figure 6.1. It begins with lower-level or survival needs, which have to be satisfied first before we seek gratification of our higher-order needs.

Figure 6.1 Maslow's hierarchy of needs.

The physiological needs

Our physiological needs include hunger, thirst, sleep, oxygen, the elimination of bodily waste and sex. Most of these are deficiency needs, and once they are satisfied, the motivation to pursue the activity ceases. If we are thirsty we have a drink of water, and the need is satisfied. The exceptions are sexual drive, the need for elimination and sleep; these are considered to be growth needs (Maslow, 1968). Sexual needs, for example, do not decrease with gratification but frequently increase. Rarely in western cultures are individuals in the position of being motivated only by their physiological needs; however, we can imagine that if you were starving, food would be your number one priority and all your other needs for respect, love and the like would be of little importance. Once our physiological needs are satisfied, we then turn our attention to the next level of needs as a source of motivation.

The safety needs

Needs at the next level of Maslow's hierarchy include needs for security, safe circumstances to live within, self-protection, law-abiding communities and a sense of order. Although Maslow tended to focus on the positive aspects of these drives, what emerges at this level are your fears and anxieties about your own safety – and these motivate your behaviour. If you live in a large estate where violence and crime are rife, you can imagine being motivated to work either at getting a house in a safer place or at changing the environment to make it safer. Which you would choose is likely to be influenced by other personality factors, such as your levels of altruism and political and situational factors. For others, the choice might be getting securer locks on their doors or altering their behaviour to minimise the risk of being harmed. All of these behaviours Maslow would conceptualise as being motivated by our need for security.

Maslow (1970) pointed out that the safety needs can be clearly observed in infants and young children where they are upset by loud unexplained noises, rough handling or major changes in their daily routine. He strongly believed that children need routines, consistently enforced rules and limits imposed on their behaviour to meet their safety needs. The absence of this safe, relatively predictable environment would impact badly on a child's development, although Maslow did not specify the specific negative effects likely to occur.

His contention was that we all prefer to live in stable societies, where we feel safe and are not continually at risk of being robbed or mugged or our homes burgled. This may be one of the reasons that, in general elections, voters always seem to be interested in issues of law and order. Maslow would say that such prospective voters are being motivated by their safety needs to take an interest in such things. Our safety needs also motivate us to buy insurance and save for a pension or a rainy day, and they may motivate us to train for a secure job where we feel our skills will always be in demand and we are unlikely to be made redundant. Maslow (1968) pointed out that the downside of safety needs is that they can stifle our growth by encouraging us always to opt for the safe choice and thereby minimise risk in our life.

Belongingness and love needs

Once our physiological and safety needs are largely taken care of, Maslow states that our needs for belongingness and love become more important motivators of our behaviour. He is saying that we all need to feel that we are needed and accepted by others. Human beings are conceptualised as social beings, and we need to feel that we are rooted in communities, with ties to family and friends. Our need for belongingness motivates us to make friends, to join clubs and other organisations where we can meet people and socialise. Once our more basic needs have been met, we become more aware of our loneliness, absence of companions and friends, and we become motivated to do something about it. Maslow defined two distinct types of love that were based on different needs, D-love and B-love. The first is **D-love**, which is based on a deficiency need, hence the label. It is the love that we seek to meet the emptiness inside ourselves. We want it for ourselves; the loved one is there to meet our needs. In this way, it is a relatively selfish deficiency need. Maslow defines this love as consisting of individual yearning for affection, tenderness, feelings of elation and sexual arousal. It does not always bring out the best in individuals, as they may display all sorts of manipulative behaviour to try to get the attention of the person they desire. It can sometimes be observed in the young child competing for their mother's attention with their younger sibling. Maslow contrasts this need for love and belongingness for ourselves with the ability we have to love others. He calls this latter type of love **B-love** and suggests that, once our basic needs for D-love have been met, we become capable of attaining B-love. B-love or Being-love is about being able to love others in a non-possessive, unconditional way, simply loving them for being. It involves showing respect for the other, accepting their individuality, putting their needs before your own on occasion and valuing them. B-love is a growth need, and Maslow sees it as representing an emotionally mature type of love. It is possible only when the basic needs have been sufficiently gratified. At this stage, Maslow (1970) considers that the person is moving towards **self-actualisation**. Maslow was concerned about the high numbers of individuals living alone in western cultures and felt that, while this lifestyle is valued by some individuals, for most it creates loneliness as belongingness and love needs may not be met sufficiently.

The esteem needs

Esteem needs are the last of our basic needs. Maslow (1970) divided these into two types of needs. The first type of esteem need is based on our need to see ourselves as competent, achieving individuals. Secondly, there is the need for esteem based on the evaluation of others. He claimed that we have a need for respect and admiration from other people but advises that this must be deserved. He suggests that the incompetent individual who lies, cheats or buys their way into a position of authority will still feel inferior and will not enjoy their position, as their real esteem needs – especially their need to see themselves as competent and achieving – are not being met (Maslow, 1970).

The need for self-actualisation

The highest level of need is for self-actualisation. Maslow (1968; 1970) argues that once our basic needs have been met, we start to focus on what we want from life. Individuals may be very successful financially and have enough power and success that all their lower-level needs are being met, but they may still not be happy and contented. They are still searching for something. This restlessness comes from their need for self-actualisation. Self-actualisation demands that individuals develop themselves so that they achieve their full potential. It is about maximising their talents and finding meaning in life, so that they are at peace with themselves. Maslow is eager to stress that this process will be different for everyone depending on the individual's talents and interests. It is a growth need that emerges only after the other basic needs have been addressed. For this reason, Maslow (1968; 1970) describes it as coming to prominence only in older people. This idea is similar to Jung's concept of individuation that we discussed earlier (Chapter 3). Young adults are seen as being taken up with addressing their basic needs, such as getting an education and finding work, somewhere to live, love and relationships. Maslow (1964) is clear that not all individuals achieve self-actualisation, although many strive to do so. Self-actualised individuals are thought to be rare. He suggests that the model of motivation we have just described does not fit these self-actualised individuals. He suggests that the needs of self-actualisers are qualitatively different; he describes them as **metaneeds**. The foci of metaneeds are very different, being concerned with higher aesthetic and moral values such as beauty, truth, justice and ethics. We shall be looking in some more detail shortly at the qualities of self-actualised individuals after we have concluded the discussion of Maslow's model of motivation.

Discussion of basic needs

Maslow's model appears very neat and simple at one level, but he stressed that his hierarchical model is an oversimplification of the actual relationship between needs and behaviour. The reality is that, while the order makes sense for most people, there will be individual exceptions. The priority of our needs will vary depending on our personal circumstances across time, so that it is not a static model. At any level, a need does not have to be totally gratified for us to be motivated by higher-order needs. Maslow estimated some average figures for need fulfilment in the average American, suggesting that on average around 85 per cent of individual physical needs are met, 70 per cent of safety needs, 50 per cent of belongingness and love, 40 per cent of self-esteem needs and 10 per cent of self-actualisation needs. Thinking about percentage need in this way helps to get across Maslow's idea that the degree to which a need is unfulfilled will influence the impact it has on the individual's behaviour. For example, if a long-term relationship ends, the belongingness and love needs are likely to be much less satisfied than they were previously. This results in the individual becoming more motivated to seek solace with others, and the person will derive some comfort from being with friends and other relatives as this helps increase their sense of belonging.

Maslow (1968; 1970) claimed that his model had universal applicability, but that the means of gratification might change within cultures. He felt that we share many of the basic needs, such as physiological and safety needs, with other animals, but the higher-order needs are distinctly human. The higher apes display a need for love and belongingness, but Maslow felt that self-actualisation is a uniquely human pursuit.

He stressed that the motivation for behaviour is frequently immensely complex and that many behaviours are motivated by a variety of needs. Using the example of sexual behaviour, Maslow pointed out that it can be motivated by a physiological need for sexual release, or it can be a need for love and affection, a wish to feel masculine or feminine or to express a sense of mastery in a situation and so on. Thus, the activities we engage in may also satisfy more than one set of needs at any one time. Maslow (1970) also acknowledges the importance of unconscious motivation. He perceives the instinctoid tendencies as being quite weak and easily overcome by situational factors, and consequently we may often not be consciously aware of how they affect our motivation. However, unlike Freud, who claims that unconscious motives originating in our past experiences cause our behaviour and also determine our goals, Maslow sees human beings as being future-oriented. For Maslow, our ultimate goal is self-actualisation driven on by our motivational needs. It is the instinctoid needs that he conceptualises as frequently influencing us unconsciously. There is some inconsistency in Maslow's theorising here as he also accepts the validity of the Freudian defence mechanisms (see Chapter 2). He accepted that they play a crucial role in preventing individuals knowing themselves and yet the individual is unconscious of their effect. So, here

we have further evidence of unconscious motivation based on past experiences influencing behaviour. In Maslow's defence, he wanted his focus to be on healthy individuals. He was clear that the psychologically healthy individual needs to use defence mechanisms much less, and therefore the role of unconscious motivation based on past experiences is also less.

Characteristics of self-actualisers

Maslow wanted his theory to be about human aspirations and abilities. He did not want to focus on clinical populations and their psychopathology, as is the case with so many other personality theories. To meet this aim, he undertook interview studies of individuals who appeared to him to be self-actualised; he also conducted studies of famous historical figures, using any documents about them that he could find. Among those he studied were Albert Einstein, Eleanor Roosevelt, William James, Thomas Jefferson, Albert Schweitzer, Jane Addams and Baruch Spinoza (Maslow, 1968). He described this research as undertaking a holistic analysis, the aim of which was to understand individuals in some depth. From this study, he outlined the characteristics of self-actualising individuals. At the outset we need to acknowledge, as Maslow (1970) did, that this data was impressionistic and did not meet conventional scientific standards in terms of reliability and validity. However, Maslow published these studies as he felt that the topic was so important.

Every healthy person studied was described by Maslow as being creative. The creativity of the self-actualised was a way of approaching life. It did not necessarily mean that they painted pictures or produced poetry and so on, which is how we tend to think conventionally about creativity. Rather, they approached everyday tasks in novel ways. They might be a conventionally creative person as well, but an example he gave was of a woman who expressed her creativity in producing very interesting meals and presenting them beautifully in quite novel ways. Self-actualisers found little everyday things interesting, and Maslow compares them with young children who take such pleasure from small discoveries. Self-actualisers have not lost their awe of the world and their interest in the minutiae.

Self-actualisers also think differently, according to Maslow (1962). He claimed that self-actualisers engage more often in what he termed **being cognition (B-cognition)**. This is a non-judgemental form of thought. It is about accepting oneself and the world and just being and feeling at one with the world. Maslow referred to B-cognition occurring at moments of experiencing self-actualisation in what he termed **peak experiences**; and obviously, self-actualisers have more of these peak experiences. More recently, Csikszentmihalyi (1999) has defined this concept of peak experiences in some detail, although he has renamed them optimal experiences. The characteristics that Csikszentmihalyi describes as defining such experiences are summarised in Table 6.1. This list will give you a much better understanding of Maslow's concept of peak experience.

B-cognition is contrasted with the more normally occurring **deficiency cognition (D-cognition)**. D-cognition is judgemental, and in it we see ourselves as distinct from the world around us. It is about making judgements about how well our experiences are meeting our deficiency needs. Maslow (1962) stresses that B-cognition states are transient even for self-actualisers. He points out that it is dangerous to exist continually in a passive, non-judgemental, non-intervening state.

In terms of their personal characteristics, self-actualisers tend to have higher levels of self-acceptance. They also accept others more easily, being less judgemental and more tolerant of others. Maslow also claimed that they perceive reality more accurately with fewer distortions. This is linked to them being more in touch with themselves and being less psychologically defended. The use of a defence mechanism tends to distort reality. For example, if you failed to get a job you really wanted, the defended individual might say that the process was unfair, or deny that they wanted the job, while the self-actualiser is more likely to be truthful.

Self-actualisers tend to have well-developed ethical and moral standards and are more likely to accept responsibility for their actions. They have greater self-knowledge and tend to follow their codes of ethics. They also have a strong wish to help others and are concerned about the welfare of the communities in which they live. This quality is the same as Adler's concept of social interest (discussed in Chapter 3), and Maslow acknowledges a debt to Adler for this concept. Self-actualisers are good at focusing on problems and seeing them through to resolution. They are often more interested in the big picture than the minor details. In their working lives, they are more likely to be motivated by a desire to fulfil their inner potential than by promises of more wealth or other trappings of success. They do things because they want to rather than it being a way to get on at work. In this way, they are more independent and less influenced by cultural norms and much more likely to make up their own minds about issues and act accordingly.

In their personalities, self-actualisers tend to have deeper personal relationships, preferring to have a few close friends rather than a wide circle of acquaintances. Maslow also claimed that they are more likely to demonstrate the non-possessive B-love. Their sense of humour is also different. They find jokes based on superiority or aggressive hostility offensive and prefer more philosophically based humour.

Maslow's description of self-actualising individuals makes them sound like absolute paragons of virtue. However, as Maslow (1968; 1970) points out, this is far from the case. No one is a self-actualising individual all the time in all their activities. Similarly, peak experiences come and go. At times, self-actualising individuals can be as annoying and irritating as anyone. Like Albert Ellis (as we saw in Chapter 5), Maslow strongly believed that there are no perfect human beings, but some are happier than others.

Personality development

Maslow did not provide a great deal of detailed information about personality development; rather, he outlined some core principles. Firstly, he conceptualised children as having an innate drive to develop. This is a positive drive fuelled by the motivational needs outlined in his hierarchy of needs. Maslow felt that, as children become socialised, there is a crucial time for their development. This is when they decide whether they are going to listen to what he terms 'their inner voice' and develop according to their own instinctoid needs or whether they are going to follow their parental dictates. Maslow concluded that parental expectations and cultural expectations influence most children, but this is because children are seldom given real choices. If you cast your mind back to the material you read about Summerhill School in the introduction to this discussion, Summerhill exemplifies the sort of learning experience that Maslow felt was the ideal for creating happy, fulfilled individuals. Children are not coerced but are given choices, and Maslow assumed that their natural desire to grow will direct them towards engaging in learning experiences. This is the reported Summerhill experience. There are rules – indeed, quite a large number of them – but they are formulated with the pupils and enforced

Table 6.1 The characteristics of peak experiences

1   The individual's attention is totally absorbed by the activity.
2   The activity has clear objectives so that the person has a clear goal to work towards.
3   It is a challenging activity that requires the person's full attention but is not so difficult that they cannot make meaningful progress.
4   The person is able to concentrate fully on the task at hand, and other parts of their life do not impinge on what they are doing.
5   The individual feels in control of the activity.
6   The activity is so personally engrossing that the individual does not think about themselves while engaging in it.
7   All sense of time is lost while the person is engaged. Most commonly, time passes very quickly.
8   The activity tends to be one where feedback is clearly available, so that the person is aware of making progress even though it may be based on only a personal evaluation.

by the whole community. Maslow is clear that children need rules and limits to meet their safety needs. Like Adler, he felt that pampering is very bad for children and that having some rules to come up against is beneficial. Children need to be given considerable freedom of choice but they also need to be given responsibilities. In this way, they are encouraged always to take responsibility for their behaviour. The satisfaction of a child's needs, as specified in Maslow's hierarchy, is the best way to encourage healthy development; as long as this is done in a disciplined way and the child is not pampered.

Mental illness and its treatment in Maslow's approach

For Maslow (1970) there was one underlying cause for all mental illness and psychological disturbance, and that was the failure to satisfy the individual's fundamental needs as outlined in the hierarchy. He felt the lower the level of need that is not being satisfied, the more profound the disturbance. For example, someone who has failed to find any place in the world and in relationships that make them feel safe is more disturbed than someone who is still searching for love and respect. In this conceptualisation, it is clear that the basic needs have a psychological aspect to them and are not merely physical needs. Safety is not just about a safe environment, although it is part of it. If you feel unsafe where you live, you are more likely to be anxious and it will impact your psychological health. Similarly, if you do not have any family or close relationships that you feel secure in, you are going to be very anxious and upset as your needs are not being met.

In terms of treatment, Maslow adopted an eclectic approach. He was against all diagnostic labels and the medical model that they implied. To improve their health, individuals needed to be assisted towards self-actualisation. Maslow was a trained psychoanalyst, and he used psychoanalysis on occasion for severe problems following the method described previously (Chapter 2). For less disturbed individuals, he would use briefer therapies, including behaviour therapy. He was also a fan of group therapy and encounter groups for healthy individuals to help them to self-actualise further. We will discuss encounter groups in more detail later in the discussion, when we look at the work of Carl Rogers. Thus Maslow is seen as adopting an eclectic approach to therapy – even utilising psychoanalysis, which is somewhat at odds with his rejection of the medical model and his conceptualisation of the causes of psychological disturbance. This inconsistency did not appear to concern him.

Evaluation of Maslow's theory

We will now evaluate Maslow's theory using the eight criteria identified previously (Chapter 1): description,

explanation, empirical validity, testable concepts, comprehensiveness, parsimony, heuristic value and applied value.

Description

Maslow provides a reasonable, if somewhat simplified, description of human behaviour. The theory therefore is high on face validity. However, he does present an extremely positive and almost simplistic view of human nature and human beings. This is somewhat at odds with his acceptance of many Freudian defence mechanisms, as we have discussed earlier in this discussion. Defence mechanisms (as we saw in Chapter 2) refer to the complexity of human motivation and the difficulties in explaining behaviour even to ourselves. Maslow does not acknowledge these inconsistencies in his theorising.

It seems somewhat simplistic to claim that blocks to self-actualisation are at the root of all human behavioural problems. There is no mention of genetic susceptibilities to mental illness and sociopathic conditions, for example. To put so much emphasis on environmental influences is untenable, as you will see from the biological evidence reviewed later (Chapters 8 and 9).

Explanation

While Maslow's theory seems to present a neat, rational explanation of human motivation, it does appear to suggest that motivation is more clear-cut than it generally is, and that the link between our needs and our behaviour is obvious. The reality is that behaviour is frequently the result of many different motivators. For example, if you take the case of someone doing a menial job that is poorly paid, the assumption from Maslow is that they are working to earn money to meet their physiological and safety needs. The job itself is not inherently satisfying; however, they may work with a good set of colleagues, and this may meet their belongingness needs and compensate for the nature of the work, so they are not motivated to seek more conducive or better paid work. An example of this might be where a member of a company cleaning staff shows a marked reluctance to become a supervisor even though it paid more. Although the job might bring extra money and be physically easier, they might not consider this compensation for the loss of comradeship from the other cleaners. Maslow has provided useful insights into human motivational needs, but perhaps not the whole picture.

Maslow's work on defining types of needs and types of love is interesting. It was a new, very creative approach to these topics. In his work on general needs and types of love, he presents a less positive perspective on human beings, seeing us as capable of being manipulative, disrespectful of others and very demanding in the way that we treat others. This is somewhat at odds with his generally positive view of human beings, but he does not really acknowledge these inconsistencies in his theory.

Empirical validity

While self-actualisation is at the core of Maslow's theory, the research on which it is based is dubious. He selected a very small sample of participants to investigate the concept. These were not randomly selected; rather, Maslow chose to examine individuals whom he believed to be self-actualisers. He did not use any objective measures to assess these individuals, and there was a lack of consistency in assessment between individuals. In all, it was an extremely subjective process, more descriptive than evaluative.

Testable concepts

Many of Maslow's other concepts are also difficult to define precisely and therefore difficult to test empirically. Examples include peak experiences where it is unclear exactly what is meant. Self-actualisers are thought to be rare individuals, yet researchers such as Leiby (1997) report that drug-induced peak experiences are common. This raises the issue of whether and how these artificially induced experiences relate to self-actualisation. Ravizza (1977) reported that many athletes report peak experiences but are not self-actualisers in any other aspects of their lives. Thus, questions are raised about the relationship between peak experiences and self-actualisation.

The basis for Maslow's selection of the five basic needs is also unclear. He does not provide a rationale for their selection, and many other human needs can be identified. His theorising embraces many assumptions about human behaviour that are stated authoritatively, but the supporting evidence is either absent or weak. He did argue against the empiricism of existing psychological methodologies, but this does not excuse his lack of attention to providing objective support for this theory (Maslow, 1970).

Most of the concepts in Maslow's theory are imprecisely defined, so they are difficult to research. There have been more systematic attempts to measure self-actualisation. Shostrum (1966) developed a measure called the personal orientation inventory (POI). It is a self-report questionnaire with 150 items that are answered positively or negatively. It measures the degree to which individuals are inner-directed on one major scale and whether they use their time effectively on the second major scale, both of which are thought to relate to self-actualisation, as we have seen. There are 10 subscales measuring self-actualising values, feeling reactivity, existentiality, self-regard, spontaneity, self-acceptance, nature of humankind, synergy, acceptance of aggression and capacity for intimate contact. While the validity and the usefulness of the measure was established using several samples (Dosamantes-Alperson and Merrill, 1980; Knapp, 1976), there are problems with it. Participants do not like the forced-choice response mode, feeling that it does not give an accurate reflection of their views, and other researchers have reported that it correlates poorly with other related measures such as the purpose in life test (PIL) devised by Crumbaugh and Maholick (1969). Mittleman (1991) reviews much of this work on self-actualisation and concludes that self-actualisation is difficult to measure, but the most reliable aspect of it relates only to possessing openness to experience.

Comprehensiveness

Maslow's theory is really focused on positive growth and, as such, it is not a comprehensive theory. His approach was new and creative, making a welcome change to the previous theories with their emphasis on psychopathology. He did attempt some discussion of psychopathology and adopted aspects of Freud's model, but this was not done in a systematic or comprehensive fashion. The explanation of human motivation is also limited. There is much more emphasis on self-actualisation, but even here the precise detail is missing. Maslow does not spell out exactly how self-actualisation can be achieved. Similarly, he talks only in very general terms about the development of personality.

Parsimony

Maslow's theory is very concise for a theory of human personality. We have already discussed how his concept of motivation is limited and how the selection of five basic needs is somewhat arbitrary. The description of personality development is lacking in detail. We have also discussed the limitations of Maslow's treatment of psychopathology and how the adoption of Freudian concepts such as defence mechanisms is inconsistent with the rest of his theory. As a general theory, the conclusion must be that it is too parsimonious.

Heuristic value

Although Maslow's theory has many limitations, it undoubtedly has had a major impact on many researchers, both in psychology and other disciplines. He was one of the first theorists to focus on the healthy side of human psychological development. His focus on human achievement and human values introduced new foci for psychologists. By vehemently questioning the dominant laboratory study approach to psychology, he caused psychologists to review their research methodologies (Maslow, 1970). He stressed the need to ask meaningful questions rather than pursue more trivial research that could easily be addressed by the existing laboratory-based practices. He wanted researchers to think creatively about developing methodologies that could address important real-life issues, although it might mean losing some control of the laboratory-based studies. He also influenced subsequent theorists such as Rogers, as we shall see.

Applied value

The area where Maslow's work has had most impact is in business. His theory of motivation became and is still popular with managers. It led to an increasing emphasis on the need to offer development opportunities to employees. Maslow stressed the importance of consulting with employees and fostering a sense of belonging within companies, and this concept has been embraced by generations of business managers (Maslow, 1967). His influence also extended to counselling and healthcare professional training, as it provided a neat system for examining human motivational needs. Maslow's work also had a major impact on educational programmes. He emphasised the importance of student-centred learning, suggesting that individuals want to learn and that the role of educators is to provide the environment to facilitate such learning. As discussed in the introduction, he saw schools like Summerhill as offering this learning environment.

Carl Rogers and person-centred therapy

In our review of Carl Rogers' theory, we are first going to outline the basic principles underlying the theory.

Basic principles underlying the theory

Carl Rogers, like most of the personality theorists we have studied, based his theory on disturbed clinical populations. His initial work was based mainly on his experience of working with disturbed adolescents, as detailed in the

Profile box. Many of the therapists that Rogers worked with initially at the American equivalent of the National Society for the Prevention of Cruelty to Children (NSPCC) were psychoanalytically trained, but he increasingly felt uncomfortable working psychoanalytically. His personality theory grew out of his theory of therapy. He acknowledged that experience plays an important part in personality development, but he could not accept the Freudian notion that the early years largely dictate adult development. He felt that individuals can play an active role in shaping their own lives. He, like Maslow, saw human beings as being future-oriented and believed that our future goals influence our current behaviour. In this way, he saw individuals as having the power to shape their own lives.

This focus on the power of the individual to change their lives is reflected in the title of his approach. He first named it client-centred therapy. The term 'patient' was the norm at the time among therapists and is very much associated with the medical model of illness where the doctor/therapist is the expert who provides treatment and hopefully a cure to the patient. In this relationship, the therapist is the expert and the patient is less powerful and receives the expert's knowledge. Therefore the medical model has traditionally assigned a relatively passive role to the patient. Adopting an existential humanistic stance, as we discussed in the introduction, Rogers (1951) felt that individuals are the best experts on themselves, not the therapist. He selected the term 'client' to suggest a more equal role, similar to that of customer and provider. The term 'client-centred' reflects Rogers' view that clients are the experts on themselves and that the role of the therapist is to help the client to better recognise their problems and formulate their issues. In this way, the therapist acts more as a facilitator. Once clients understood what the

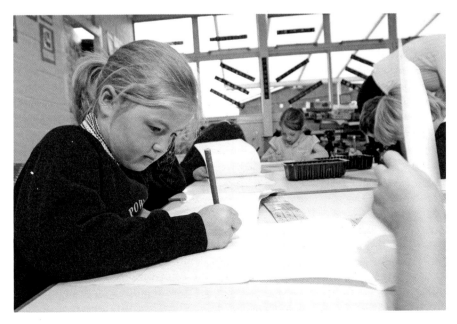

Rogers believed that we are the best experts on ourselves and that people are capable of working out their own solutions to their own problems.
Source: Pearson Education Ltd. Jules Selmes

Profile

Carl Rogers

Carl Ransom Rogers was born in 1902 into a very religious family in Oak Park, Illinois, a suburb of Chicago in the United States. He was the fourth child of six and described his upbringing as warm and caring although the family adhered to very strict religious principles, where the work ethic and taking responsibility for your actions were stressed. His father was a successful civil engineer who also owned a farm. As a child, Rogers was encouraged to breed animals on the farm, and he reported that studying how to do this effectively introduced him to the world of science and scientific method and later influenced his approach to psychology. Rogers first set out to study agriculture, but after graduating from agricultural college, he enrolled in a seminary to study religion. He became somewhat disillusioned with the religious course in the seminary and enrolled instead at Columbia University Teacher's College to study psychology as he had previously studied some psychology and enjoyed it. While still a student, he married his childhood sweetheart and had to take a job to support his family before he had completed his doctoral studies. He then spent 12 years working for the American

equivalent of the National Society for the Prevention of Cruelty to Children (NSPPC) dealing with very disturbed children. During that time, he published a book entitled *Measuring Personality Adjustment in Children* in 1931, followed by *The Clinical Treatment of the Problem Child* in 1939. It was while working with disturbed children that Rogers developed his approach to personality and his unique approach to treatment, client-centred therapy. Following the publication of his books, he obtained a professorship at Ohio State University in the psychology department. The next year, 1940, he first outlined his full theory of client-centred therapy at a conference in Minnesota. He went on to work at several other American universities, setting up counselling centres, before finally setting up his own Centre for the Study of the Person in La Jolla, California. Rogers was a productive writer, producing 16 books and over 200 journal articles. He died of a heart attack at age 85. His books continue to be published; several were reissued with new introductions by Rogerian scholars, all attesting to the popularity of the man and the lasting contribution he has made to psychology.

problem was, Rogers felt that they would know how to solve it in a way that suited their particular life situation. Later he changed the term to 'person-centred', feeling that the term 'person' is more power-neutral than the word 'client'.

Rogers adopted a phenomenological position about the nature of reality. He stressed that we all function within a perceptual or subjective frame of reference (Rogers, 1956). He denied the possibility of an objective reality that we all share. Instead, we all perceive our own reality. Sometimes students have a problem with this idea, as you may be having. However, if you think about the unreliability of eyewitness testimony, something that social psychologists have spent some time studying (Kassin *et at.*, 1989; Loftus, 1979), the meaning will become clearer. We know that even in experimental situations, there are significant individual differences in terms of the interpretation of events and the details seen by different observers. Rogers points out that how we perceive a situation depends on our mood, the type of person we are, our beliefs, our past experiences and so on. We discussed this in some detail when we explored the ABC model (Chapter 5), used in rational-emotive behaviour therapy, to conceptualise our perceptual processes. Rogers, like Ellis, accepts that everyone perceives situations differently; therefore, to understand an individual, you have to try to understand how they see the world. We will return to this later when we discuss Rogers' approach to counselling and therapy.

Self-actualisation

Rogers (1961) stressed the uniqueness of each individual. He felt that clients are the best experts on themselves and that people are capable of working out their own solutions to their own problems. He believed that each person has a natural tendency towards growth and self-actualisation. His definition of **self-actualisation** is the same as Maslow's, discussed earlier: it is an innate, positive drive to develop and realise our potential. Individuals are described as having an innate actualising tendency. It is our single basic motivating drive, and it is a positive drive towards growth. From birth, Rogers suggested we all have a drive towards actualising our potential, to become what we are capable of becoming.

Rogers (1959; 1977) claimed that we can all cope with our lives and remain psychologically healthy as long as our actualising potential is not blocked. Blocks in our actualising tendency are the cause of all psychological problems. This role for the actualising tendency differs from Maslow's conception. You will recall that, for Maslow, psychological problems result from an individual's needs not being met, and he is specific about these needs. The role that Rogers ascribed to self-actualisation is less specific. It is a general positive motivator; indeed, our only motivator. There are two aspects to it. The biological aspect includes the *drive for satisfaction* of our basic needs such as food, water, sleep, safety and sexual reproduction. The psychological aspect involves the development of our potential and the qualities that make us more worthwhile human beings (Rogers, 1959). Rogers paid most attention to the psychological aspect, self-actualisation, as he conceptualised it as being crucial for our psychological health. It is a positive drive towards growth for Rogers, just as it was for Maslow. Rogers (1977) suggested that we develop our capacity for self-destructive, aggressive and harmful behaviour only under perverse circumstances, such as growing up in a difficult environment with few opportunities for self-actualisation or not being given the freedom to develop according to our true nature. In these circumstances, our self-actualisation is blocked and problems occur. Individuals may become psychologically distressed and/or demonstrate antisocial behaviour.

Effect of society on self-actualisation

To understand fully the process of self-actualisation, we need to examine Rogers' conception of the self. Rogers made a distinction between our real self and our self-concept (see Figure 6.2). The real self is defined as being our underlying organismic self. This is, if you like, the genetic blueprint for the person we are capable of becoming if our development occurs within totally favourable circumstances. If we had these ideal developmental experiences, Rogers suggested, our behavioural choices would be guided purely by our actualising tendency. Self-actualisation would then be within everyone's reach once you had lived long enough to accrue sufficient life experiences to discover what truly made you fulfilled. However, Rogers argued that this is rarely, if ever, the case. The explanation for this is quite complex, and we will go through it in stages.

He asserted that human beings as a species are social animals. We all need to be liked/loved by other people. Rogers was very clear about the nature of the emotional experience that is necessary for optimum development, and he termed it **unconditional positive regard**. He preferred this to the term 'love' as he asserted that love is seldom truly unconditional. Unconditional positive regard means

accepting someone for who they are and valuing them just for being. The term 'regard' means seeing oneself as making a positive difference in someone else's life. It is about knowing that someone would truly miss you were you to die tomorrow. They would feel that they had a gap in their life that would always be there. It is an unselfish love, like Maslow's Being-love (B-love). You want what is best for the other above what is best for you. However, Rogers suggested that unconditional positive regard is rare and that mostly what we experience is conditional positive regard. As part of the socialisation process, we learn that we are loved/liked more when we do what others want us to do. When we behave in ways that please our parents, for example, they reward us with praise and this makes us feel good. We have obtained positive regard from them. For the most part, the positive regard we experience is not unconditional. When we misbehave, or fail an examination or refuse to do something that our parents desperately want us to do, we are likely to have experienced a sense of having disappointed our parents and being less loved and loveable as a result. These experiences help us to learn what we need to do to get positive regard from other people.

Even more crucially, we develop what Rogers called **conditions of worth** related to these experiences. We learn that we are loved more when we do things that make our parents or other people in our social world happy. This need for positive regard leads to us acquiring conditions of worth, which we use to evaluate the impact that our behaviour is likely to have on others. What is important about conditions of worth is that they can distort the natural direction of our actualising tendency. For example, if one of my conditions of worth is that I am loved more when I am helpful and agree to do things that my friends want, I am going to find it difficult to say no to these friends when they ask for my help. I may well find myself doing lots of things that I do not really want to do. This is often the case with individuals who lack assertiveness, for example. They always agree to do things for others because their condition of worth dictates that, by doing so, they will be liked and that, conversely, if they refuse, they will be disliked. Conditions of worth are important as they can keep us doing things that do not meet our real needs, and this makes it difficult for us ever to achieve self-actualisation.

We began this section by referring to two aspects of the self: the real organismic self and the self-concept. Conditions of worth, as we shall now see, impact on our self-concept. As children grow and become socialised, they develop a sense of who they are as people. Rogers termed this their **self-concept**. It is our perception of who we are based largely on how other people have described us and evaluated us. You may have been told in your family that you are the clever one or the good-looking one, and you will have internalised this description as part of who you are. The easiest way to access your self-concept

Figure 6.2 Rogers' two aspects of the self.

is to answer the question, 'Who am I?' Most of us find it relatively easy to produce a list of adjectives to describe ourselves, and this is our self-concept. We use the conditions of worth that we have acquired as our self-concept has developed, to evaluate our own behaviour and to help us make choices in our lives. We are conscious of the contents of our self-concept, whereas our real organismic self may have become obscured as a result of our developmental experiences of socialisation. As we saw in our discussion of conditions of worth, we may end up making choices that make other people happy but do not meet the needs of our real self. In the longer term, we are unlikely to be able to self-actualise; if this is the case, we will experience feelings of being discontented at least and perhaps even psychological illnesses such as depression.

The conditions of worth linked to our self-concept can be problematic as they keep us doing things that do not meet our real needs. We also tend to perceive things so that they fit our self-concept. For example, suppose you do not think you are a very able student and then, in an assignment, you get an A-grade. You are unlikely to say, 'I did that piece of work well and I deserved that mark'. Instead, you are more likely to explain your mark to your friends by saying that you were lucky or that the instructor was a soft marker and so on. This is because getting an A-grade does not fit with your concept of yourself as a poor student academically. In this way, our self-concept can serve to lower our own levels of self-regard.

You may ask, why do we maintain a self-concept if aspects of it are ineffective? There are several reasons, as follows. Firstly, we use it and our related conditions of worth to judge our own personal adequacy. This is potentially problematic, as our self-concept will contain conditions of worth that were applicable to us at an earlier age. These conditions of worth are very deeply embedded and are therefore more resistant to change. As you will know from learning theory, knowledge that we acquire early is more resistant to change. Say, for example, you met an eminent businessman who, from a modest start, had become wealthy and successful. All the evidence is that he is an able man and obviously very bright to have achieved all that he had achieved. On learning that you were at university, he comments that he has always been 'thick'. He tells you that he failed the grammar school entrance examination and was always useless at learning. He goes on to say that this was a great disappointment to his parents. Obviously, he had learnt a great deal to be as successful as he was, but still he judged himself according to a condition of worth he had acquired as a child. Rogers felt that conditions of worth have the effect of lowering our sense of worth and make it less likely that we will have the confidence to attempt change. If we believe that we are uncoordinated, for example, then we are unlikely to enrol for a dancing class or take up gymnastics. In

these ways, our self-concept and conditions of worth are important; they dictate the way in which we interact with people to meet our own needs, and they influence the choices we make in our lives.

Thus we can see that our self-concept is socially constructed. To summarise, we tend to judge ourselves according to what others think of us rather than on what we ourselves feel. We behave this way because of our high need for positive regard. This may result in us relying more on other people's judgements about our personal worth than on our own views. Rogers (1959) suggested that, because of our high need for positive regard, our organismic valuing processes may be overwhelmed. We are out of touch with our real needs. Only if we are raised with sufficient unconditional positive regard is there likely to be congruence between the self and the self-concept, and the better the match between the two, the more psychologically healthy we will be as adults. Rogers believed that parents and educational establishments can create helpful environments. These are environments that foster creativity, with democratic rules that enable us to be curious, self-reliant and respectful of others and ourselves within safe limits. This is very much the environment that is provided at Summerhill, the school we discussed in the introduction. Harrington, Block and Block (1987) used data from a longitudinal study, set up by Block and Block in 1968 at the University of California, to show that children raised in such environments were more creative in later life than were children in a matched control group that did not experience a creative environment. This is a major study documenting around 100 young people from age 3. The longitudinal study concluded after the retirement of the main researcher, but an overview of 30 years of research on the participants has been published (Block and Block, 2006). We have included the web address at the end of the discussion for anyone wanting to know more about this research.

Developmental impact on the child of their parents' self-concept

For Rogers, one important way that parents impacted on their children related to the adequacy of the parents' self-concepts. In his model, the healthy individual has experienced significant amounts of unconditional positive regard and consequently has relatively few conditions of worth. Here two points are worth noting. Firstly, Rogers did not specify precisely how much unconditional positive regard qualifies as a significant amount. He is always very vague about this, but the assumption is that none of us get enough. Secondly, as a consequence, we all have some conditions of worth. Individuals with fewer conditions of worth are classified as high-functioning adults, while those with more conditions of worth are classified as low-functioning.

High-functioning adults are more accepting of themselves and of others and therefore impose fewer conditions of worth on their children, for example. Low-functioning individuals have many more conditions of worth, are consequently less accepting and more judgemental, and impose more conditions of worth on their children. The ways that the adequacy of parents' self-concept affects how they relate to their own children are summarised in Figure 6.3.

From this discussion, you can see that having conditions of worth makes us judgemental of both others and ourselves. Being self-accepting means that you are less judgemental of yourself and others. In psychological terms, self-accepting individuals are less psychologically defended, so that Rogers claimed they perceive the world more accurately and have less need to distort situations to fit with their self-concept. Take the example of someone who is interviewed for a job that they really want. Although they prepared well and thought that they performed well at interview, they did not get the job. In Rogers' view, the self-accepting person will accept that they were not right for the position in some way. On the other hand, the individual with low self-acceptance will defend their self-esteem by asserting that they really did not want the job and had only applied for the experience of being interviewed or something similar. This exemplifies what Rogers meant by distorting their perception of reality.

Rogers was keen that his ideas were tested, and Wylie (1979) and Swann (1984) found some support among students for this idea, although it is not completely clear how well the measures they used actually assessed perceptual distortions. They asked individuals to report how they would react to various scenarios involving failure and then asked a friend of the participant to assess how honest they thought the person's judgement was. Perceptual distortions of this type are notoriously difficult to measure. You may also recall from our discussion of Freudian defence mechanisms (Chapter 2) that Freud suggested that distorting our perception so that we rationalise our failures is a psychologically adaptive response, as it serves to protect our self-esteem. It is problematic only if it is taken to extreme in the Freudian model.

Given Rogers' emphasis on the importance of the subjective worldview, it is quite strange to find him discussing individual perceptual distortions of reality. His emphasis in therapy, as we shall see, was to accept the individual's perceptions – distorted or otherwise. The point he made was that the healthy individual has fewer distortions, and they are more accepting of themselves. In the course of therapy, Rogers would expect perceptual distortions to decrease as the individual became more in touch with

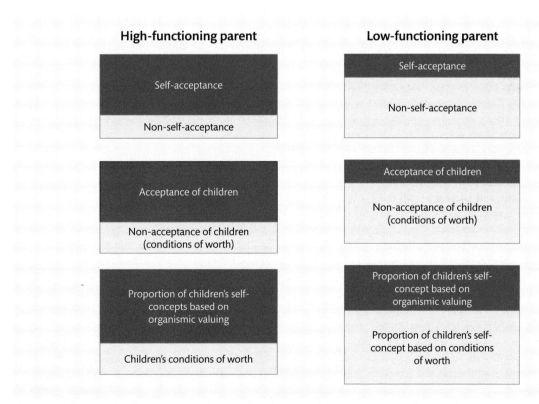

Figure 6.3 Degree of self-acceptance of parents in relation to their acceptance of their children, and the extent of conditions of worth imposed on their children.

their organismic values that can lead to self-actualisation. We will return to this in more detail when we discuss Rogers' approach to therapy.

The role of the actualising tendency in development

From infancy, Rogers claimed, we interact with the world in terms of our self-actualising tendency. Towards this end, infants are seen as engaging in an **organismic valuing** process. This is defined as an innate bodily process for evaluating which experiences are 'right' or 'wrong' for the person. Infants will value food when hungry and reject it when full. Rogers (1959) and Rogers and Stevens (1967) went further and suggested that infants 'know' instinctively which foods are good for them and which are bad. As evidence, Rogers quoted a study by Davis (1928). Davis studied three infants aged between 8 and 10 months. Two of the babies were on a particular diet for 6 months, and one was on it for 1 year. Nurses interpreted the babies pointing to various foods, and the babies were given this food. All the babies remained healthy, and Rogers quoted this study as supporting his hypothesis that even babies know what is good for them. However, examination of the choices of food available showed that all the food choices were healthy. It would not have been ethical to present infants with a totally unhealthy diet. There is now well-established evidence showing that babies prefer sweet substances to nutritious substances (Lipsitt, 1977). In Lipsitt's study, infants under 4 months were shown to suck longer and to have shorter pauses between sucking when fed sugar-and-water solutions then they did when fed nutritious, non-sweet solutions. This finding lends no support to Rogers' notion that human beings instinctively always know what is good for them. Rogers (1980) admitted that the valuing process is more complex than he initially envisaged; but he still insisted that if adults are to grow constructively, they must trust their own bodies and their own intuitions. The idea is that our sole motivator is the drive for self-actualisation. We may lose sight of our real needs because of our need to please others and meet our conditions of worth.

For Rogers (1961), as we have seen, parents play a significant role in determining how in touch the child ultimately is with their self-actualising tendency. To maximise the chances of self-actualisation, the child needs to grow up with relatively few conditions of worth. Rogers (1977) saw schools and the wider society as having a crucial role to play here also, as we have seen (Rogers, 1951; 1969; 1983; Rogers and Freiberg, 1993). He advocated student-centred teaching, where the role of the educational establishment is to provide the conditions that facilitate the child's learning. As we have previously discussed, educational establishments such as Summerhill meet Rogers' principles. These schools do not encourage competition and are relatively non-judgemental. The rules that are enforced are democratically agreed ones that ensure the children are in a safe, humane environment. Rogers felt that if conditions of trust develop, it is easier for individuals to work towards self-actualisation guided by their actualising tendency (Rogers and Freiberg, 1993). In a trusting, non-judgemental environment, it is easier for children to evaluate their experiences and have the confidence to select those that they enjoy and find worthwhile. Rogers stated that such children will be more in touch with their true selves and, as such, will instinctively know which experiences are good for them. Traditional schooling, in Rogers' view, encouraged the development of conditions of worth in the child and stifled creativity. Children need to be respected and to have freedom to make choices in their lives. This freedom also brings with it responsibilities, and Rogers suggested that children must also respect others and acknowledge that others too have the right to make their own decisions. This position is very similar to the rights and responsibilities that Albert Ellis saw as the corollary of human free will. (We discussed these in Chapter 5.)

There are no stages in the development of self-actualisation in Rogers' theory. The emphasis is on providing the right environment for optimum growth to occur. Rogers was keen to promote the development of what he termed person-centred families, where his principles would be applied, as well as person-centred educational establishments. Personality development can be a lifelong process, Rogers felt. Unlike Freud and many of the other psychoanalysts that we have studied, Rogers does not see childhood as determining the adult personality. Individuals are always open to change in his model, and personality growth can occur at any age.

The endpoint of self-actualisation for Rogers was what he called the **fully functioning person**. Such an individual is described as being very open to experience and high in self-acceptance, with few, if any, conditions of worth. As a result, they have a positive self-concept and high self-esteem. Their organismic valuing process guides the choices they make in life, and other people's expectations and judgements of them do not influence them. If they make mistakes, they are able to acknowledge them openly and learn from them. Rogers suggested that such individuals are true to their inner selves. He gave examples of artists like El Greco, who painted in a style that was not accepted at the time; even so, he did not deviate from it to gain social acceptance or to make money, being convinced that it was right for him and it was art. A summary of the attributes of the fully functioning person is given in Table 6.2. Rogers saw individuals as continually growing, and he suggested

Table 6.2 Rogers' goals for counselling and for living

Overall goal The fully functioning (mature) person	**Overall goals for development throughout life** What Rogers terms the person of tomorrow
Personal qualities ● Open to experience and able to perceive realistically ● Rational and not defensive ● Engaged in existential process of living ● Trusts in their own organismic valuing process ● Construes experience in an existential manner ● Accepts responsibility for being different from others ● Accepts responsibility for own behaviour ● Relates creatively towards the environment ● Accepts others as unique individuals ● Prizes herself or himself ● Prizes others ● Relates openly and freely on the basis of immediate experiencing ● Communicates rich self-awareness when desired	**Personal qualities** ● Openness to the world, both inner and outer ● Desire for authenticity ● Scepticism regarding science and technology ● Desire for wholeness as a human being ● The wish for intimacy ● Accepts other people as they are ● Cares for others ● Attitude of closeness towards nature ● Anti-institutional in approach ● Trusts their own internal authority ● Material things are unimportant ● A yearning for spiritual values and experiences

that we have a concept of how we wish to grow; this description is also included in Table 6.2.

In terms of personal relationships, the fully functioning individual respects the rights of others and cares deeply for them. Such individuals display high levels of unconditional positive regard for the other people in their lives and are capable of forming deep relationships. Self-actualisation is not conceptualised as the endpoint of development but rather as a journey that the individual is on. It is a process that the individual is continually engaged in, seeking out satisfying experiences and discarding unsatisfying ones whenever possible or compensating for them in other ways. For example, the individual who undertakes a job that they find dull and boring may continue to do the job as no other option is readily available and they need money to live, but they may experience self-actualisation in other ways. Such an individual may find activities such as gardening or other hobbies, or voluntary work in the community or close relationships within their family that fulfil their needs for self-actualisation. The self-actualising individual is described as being *congruent* with the totality of their lives. They feel satisfied with their life and believe that they fit within it. From this it is clear that self-actualisation is about an attitude to life, to oneself and to others. It is part of an ongoing process of living.

Rogers' conceptualisation of psychological problems

The fully functioning person, as we have seen, is the ideal and is rarely achieved as most of us have conditions of worth associated with our self-concept. The greater the conditions of worth associated with an individual's

self-concept, the less psychologically healthy they are in Rogers' model. The individual is alienated from their true self, and this situation is expressed either in feelings of discontent, symptoms of psychological illness or antisocial behaviour or combinations of all three. Rogers avoided using diagnostic labels to describe his clients as he felt that using labels served to stress the expertise of the therapist and consequently disempowered the client. We discussed this approach in some detail, you will remember, in the introduction when we covered Rogers' objections to the medical model of illness and treatment. Clients simply need to be provided with an empowering environment that will allow them to get in touch with their true selves. This will then provide the guidance necessary for them to make helpful changes in the way that they run their lives. This environment is provided through an empowering relationship with the therapist, and we shall examine this concept next.

The principles of Rogerian counselling

You may recall that, like all the theories we have examined so far, Rogers' theory of personality originated in his clinical work with disturbed clients. His aim was to develop a more effective method of helping individuals, and through this his conceptualisation of what human beings are like emerged. He believed that human nature is positive and that we are motivated towards positive growth and continual development. The disturbed individual has deviated from this positive path, as they have not had sufficiently growth-enhancing relationships, experiences and environments. The aim of therapy is to provide the client with the experience of a good relationship in a safe environment. This focus becomes even more apparent when we examine Rogers' goals for counselling in Table 6.2 and see that the goals for counselling are identical to his goals for living. The aim in counselling is to provide a safe environment and experience of a good relationship as Rogers believed that this will be sufficient to allow the individual to get in touch with their true organismic self and rediscover their way to self-actualisation. It is about finding their true selves. This may sound like 'hippie' sentiments, and Rogerian counselling and derivatives of it were very popular in the 1960s and 1970s with the general public, especially the young. Group sessions based on Rogerian principles were common and led to what became known as the encounter group experience. These were groups set up to allow people to explore aspects of themselves in a psychologically safe environment. Through these encounters with themselves and others, they would find their true selves (Rogers, 1970). We will now examine in more detail Rogers' approach to therapy and the provision of a psychologically safe, empowering environment.

The aim of therapy was to facilitate a reintegration of the self-concept. To understand what this means, we need to return to conditions of worth and what they imply. If you have many conditions of worth, you are very aware of having imperfections as you have an image of the ideal person that you should be. If you were this ideal, then you would be more loveable and more admired than you currently are. It might involve being smarter, kinder, more organised, healthier or whatever. This would be our **ideal self**. We use this ideal self to judge ourselves. When we do not meet the criteria in our ideal self, our self-esteem is lowered, making us feel even worse about

ourselves. To put it simply, the individual with few conditions of worth accepts themselves as they are, and the gap between their ideal self and real self is a narrow one. The person with many conditions of worth has a much wider perceptual gap between how they see themselves and how they would like to be; their ideal self. The existence of this gap leads to unhappiness and discontent and, in extreme conditions, depression. The aim of therapy is to reduce this gap and to reintegrate the self-concept with the real self. The individual then becomes more accepting of who they are and are happier consequently. At this point, many students then ask, 'But what if the client appears to be a thoroughly rotten individual? Does Rogerian therapy still involve helping the person feel good about themselves?' The answer to this question lies in Rogers' conception of human nature and the source of human motivation. If you recall from earlier in the discussion, Rogers asserted that human nature is basically benign. As a species, we want to do good things, and our actualising tendency, the sole source of motivational energy, is a positive drive towards growth. So, to return to the question posed, Rogers did not accept the idea that individuals are rotten. The apparently rotten individual had their actualising tendency blocked at some point because of poor relationship and/or environmental experiences. Counselling aims to allow the individual to rediscover their actualising tendency, and, in doing so, they will be able to solve their problems and choose a more constructive way forward. This will then maximise their chances of happiness. Rogers, like Ellis, saw human beings as a hedonistic species, with happiness/contentment as our ultimate goal.

Ideas of how we see and reflect on ourselves are very important in Rogers' theory.
Source: Pearson Education Ltd. Tudor Photography

Stop and think

Rogers' approach to treatment

It may have registered that, when discussing Rogers' approach to treatment, sometimes we talk about the treatment as counselling and sometimes as therapy. Rogers himself does this also in places in his writing; when he talks about the core conditions of counselling, for example, and then when he talks about client-centred therapy. To clarify, both counselling and therapy refer to very similar processes and there is a huge overlap in terms of what actually happens in treatment sessions. However, counselling tends to deal with less severe psychological problems than does therapy. Consequently, counselling generally takes less time than therapy. Many therapists begin their training as counsellors, and we believe that this practice has added to the confusion. Therapy is about utilising additional theory-based techniques that go beyond core counselling skills. For example, the psychoanalytic therapist may use dream analysis, free association or interpretation in addition.

Career focus: Working in counselling psychology

According to the British Psychological Society website, a counselling psychologist works with people across a range of issues, including mental health issues, disorders and stressful life events, such as bereavement and relationship issues. Specific roles or jobs might be assessing individuals' mental health, planning and implementing therapy, working with teams and supervising and training other psychologists. Counselling psychologists work in a number of settings, including education, industry, commerce, the prison service and health and social care settings.

Dr Jo Nowill, Chartered Counselling Psychologist, Cheltenham Trauma Clinic

1. **How/why did you choose to pursue the area of psychology that you did?**

   I chose counselling psychology because I liked the idea of treating a person holistically, not just using the medical model. In addition, counselling psychology offers a great deal of scope in terms of working environments – I have worked in prisons and the NHS, for example.

2. **In what way do the skills and/or knowledge you learned when studying personality and individual differences apply to your work/research today?**

   I see clients for one-to-one therapy and they are often victims of road accidents, domestic abuse, or suffering from depression and anxiety, phobia and so on. The goals of therapy are set out in the first session with the client – for example, 'to be rid of flashbacks', 'to be able to socialise without anxiety' or 'to feel like a worthwhile person'. There are also aims for the individual sessions, which might range from helping the client to understand the 'fight/flight' system so that they can understand their anxiety and how to manage it, or it might be to help them look at a particular issue from other perspectives; for example, 'my boss ignored me so she does not like me' to 'my boss is busy and might have been worrying about her own problems'. I also work for a private hospital as part of their bariatric team (weight loss) to make sure patients are entering surgery without irrational expectations.

   In my work it is essential to understand the client's personality and how their traits may impact on the way that they deal with trauma and other challenges. A client may present with classical symptoms of OCD, for example, but the way that the symptoms are experienced by that client is unique to them, so we cannot use a 'textbook' approach to working with them.

You can read more on becoming a counselling psychologist at the British Psychological Society website at **http://www.bps.org.uk/careers-education-training/how-become-psychologist/types-psychologists/becoming-counselling-psycholo**.

The role of the therapist or counsellor

To achieve successful counselling, Rogers emphasised that the relationship between client and therapist is crucial. The clients have the ability to change within themselves, and the counsellor's role is to facilitate the process. To achieve a successful outcome, the counsellor needs to possess certain qualities and the client needs to be in a certain psychological state so that a relationship that facilitates growth in the client is created. These conditions have come to be labelled the **core conditions of counselling** and will now be described in turn. None of the conditions are considered more important than the others; Rogers (1959) stated that all need to be present.

The core conditions of counselling which facilitate personal growth

a   Both the *client and the therapist must be in psychological contact*. By this condition, Rogers meant that counselling is about more than simply chatting to someone. It is not about exchanging pleasantries, although counsellors may do so initially to help put clients at their ease. It is about discussing inner feelings focused on the self. Rogers (1961) suggested that clients frequently go through stages in their conversations with their therapist before they are making true deep psychological contact (Figure 6.4). These stages are described as follows:

- **Stage 1** – The client's talk is about other people mostly, not themselves. Clients may make general statements or discuss their children or work colleagues and so on.
- **Stage 2** – Although the client begins to talk about feelings, they do not refer these feelings to themselves. They are still general statements about how people feel.
- **Stage 3** – Now the client begins to talk about themselves, usually about things they have done in the past. At this point, psychological contact is becoming properly established.

- **Stage 4** – Here the client begins to express how they feel now, but very tentatively. Clients still express their feelings at a fairly descriptive level.
- **Stage 5** – At this point, the client begins to live their feelings within the counselling session. Emotions are expressed spontaneously, and the client is focused on the present. They may still be a little tentative in recognising fully how they feel.
- **Stage 6** – Now the client can accept their feelings fully and explores them freely.
- **Stage 7** – This is the final stage, where the client has come to accept their own feelings and is also more open to the feelings of others. The person is in touch with themself psychologically and can also relate to others in the same way.

Obviously, there will be individual differences in how long this process takes. Some individuals may establish psychological contact within the first session, while for others it will take longer as they adjust to the process.

b   *The client is in a state of incongruence* and feels anxious about it. By this condition, Rogers meant that the client is emotionally upset. It is this emotional upset that provides the motivation for clients to come for counselling. If you are happy and your life is going well, you are unlikely to feel the need to seek out a counsellor.

c   *The counsellor is congruent in the relationship*. Rogers said that the counsellor must be genuine and not simply role-playing. Counsellors must be aware of their own feelings and be at ease with them. They must also be able to communicate their feelings if this is appropriate. To facilitate this congruence, most schools of counselling now require trainee counsellors to undertake personal counselling or therapy as part of their training. Counsellors are also required to have their work supervised regularly by another trained counsellor. This is a further check that they are dealing honestly with any feelings that the clients may provoke in them.

d   The therapist experiences **unconditional positive regard** for the client. This is one of the crucial qualities required

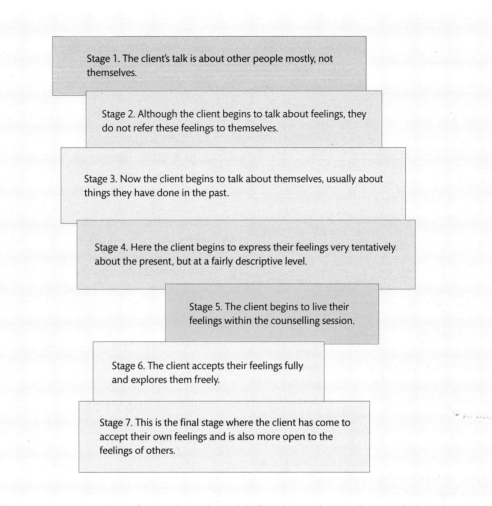

Stage 1. The client's talk is about other people mostly, not themselves.

Stage 2. Although the client begins to talk about feelings, they do not refer these feelings to themselves.

Stage 3. Now the client begins to talk about themselves, usually about things they have done in the past.

Stage 4. Here the client begins to express their feelings very tentatively about the present, but at a fairly descriptive level.

Stage 5. The client begins to live their feelings within the counselling session.

Stage 6. The client accepts their feelings fully and explores them freely.

Stage 7. This is the final stage where the client has come to accept their own feelings and is also more open to the feelings of others.

Figure 6.4 The seven stages that clients frequently go through before they make true deep psychological contact with their therapist.

by counsellors, according to Rogers (1951; 1961). Experiencing unconditional positive regard requires the therapist not to judge the client, but to value them as another human being. They have worth simply because they exist within Rogers' humanistic perspective, and all human beings should be treated with respect and dignity.

e   The therapist experiences an **empathic understanding** of the client's internal frame of reference. This condition is about accepting that there is no external reality, but that we all have a subjective view of the world. We discussed taking this phenomenological perspective in the introduction to humanistic theories at the start of the discussion. The role of the therapist is to try to understand the client's view of the world, so that they can better understand why the client feels as they do. Empathy is a concept that is often misunderstood and is frequently confused with sympathy. Comparing the two concepts is a useful way of increasing our

understanding of them. Sympathy is what we usually give to our friends when they are having problems. We agree that what has happened to them is awful, and we say that we understand how they are feeling. What we are actually doing is saying that we know what they are going through, yet Rogers would say that we can never truly understand what someone else is going through. Further, when expressing sympathy we are agreeing with the individual's negative interpretation of the event. We are reinforcing their perception of the event as awful. However, the role of the counsellor is to help the client feel better about what has happened, so reinforcing the client's negative worldview of the event is not a good starting point. To be empathic, the counsellor is required simply to try to understand what the client is experiencing and feeling and not to judge or evaluate the experience. The counsellor, by listening carefully and asking questions to help them really understand what has happened, also helps the client to become clearer in their own mind about their situation. In this way, the counsellor is facilitating the client's understanding of their situation.

By not judging the client, the therapist also introduces the client to the idea of not judging themselves. Rogers believes that continually judging oneself is unhelpful. It implies that you are comparing yourself with an ideal self, as we have already discussed. Self-acceptance is the goal for counselling and for living in Rogers' model. It is accepted that, as human beings, we will make mistakes, but the aim is to help people learn from their mistakes. This position is very similar to that advocated by Albert Ellis in his rational-emotive behaviour therapy that we discussed previously (Chapter 5). Rogers went further in that he felt that, if individuals are in touch with their real organismic self, then they are less likely to make mistakes in their lives (Rogers, 1961).

f   The *client perceives the counsellor's unconditional positive regard for them and the counsellor's empathic understanding of their difficulties.* Rogers (1959) emphasised that it is crucial for the counsellor to be able to convey their empathy and unconditional positive regard to the client. The client needs to experience this feeling of being valued and of someone really trying to understand them, accepting them and valuing them as another human being. This is the positive emotional environment that Rogers said we all need to optimise our chances of self-actualising. It is acceptance and valuing with no conditions of worth attached. For many clients, it may be their first experience of such a relationship where they feel valued and understood. This then is the relationship that Roger claimed will facilitate change and growth.

Rogers (1959) claimed that, if a good therapeutic relationship is established, which involves meeting all the six core conditions of counselling, then clients will change in the following ways:

- Clients will have *more realistic perceptions of their world.* They will also be more open to new experiences.
- Clients will *behave more rationally.* They will be more in touch with their actualising tendency, which guides them to grow in positive ways. They will engage more in developing themselves.
- The level of *personal responsibility* that they take for their own behavioural choices will increase. They will trust their own organismic valuing process. They will have learnt how to help themselves, and they will have a clearer understanding of the nature of the choices they make.
- Clients' *levels of self-regard will increase.* They will have lost many of their conditions of worth and have a much higher degree of unconditional self-acceptance. Their feelings about themselves are now based on their own values

rather than on the praise and needs of others in their lives. Fundamentally, they will know that as people they are sound although sometimes they may behave in mistaken ways. This is similar to the distinction Ellis made between judging behaviour, but not the person (Chapter 5).

- Clients will also have an *increased capacity for good personal relations.* If you are self-accepting, as we saw earlier in the discussion of conditions of worth and parenting, then you are more likely to accept others without conditions of worth attached. Rogers (1959) clearly defined what he meant by good personal relationships. He felt that such relationships involve accepting others as unique individuals, prizing them, relating openly and freely to them, communicating appropriately and being genuine in your feelings.
- Rogers believed that self-actualisation resulted in the individual *living ethically.* The individual is seen as a trustworthy person who does not infringe on the rights of others and can distinguish between good and evil. Rogers suggested that the following qualities within the individual contribute to this change:

  - They trust in their own internal feelings rather than relying on external authority to do what is right. This is based on Rogers' positive view of human nature and human motivation.
  - Their value system will focus more on people and relationships, and they will be fairly indifferent to material things.
  - They will develop more of a closeness and a reverence for nature. They will feel more at one with the world.
  - Rogers suggests that they will also have a yearning for values to guide their lives and for spiritual experiences.

These were very substantial claims to make about the benefits of Rogerian counselling, and Rogers was keen to provide research to assess its validity. Much of his early research involved the case study approach, where he would provide a detailed account of a client's progress (Rogers, 1954). To improve on the evaluation of the effects of counselling, Rogers adopted the Q-sort to measure clients' self-concepts. The detail of the Q-sort is outlined in Stop and think: Q-sort measurement of the self-concept.

At the start of counselling, the correlation between the client's current self-concept and ideal self is low. What this means is that the individual does not accept themselves as they are; they may wish to be cleverer, more reliable or whatever. After counselling, the correlation between the self and the ideal self tends to be much higher. What this means in practice is that individuals are selecting the same items to describe how they are and how they would like to be. Rogers and his colleagues carried out ambitious research projects to assess the effectiveness of client-centred therapy. Truax and Carkhuff (1967) provide a detailed review of this work. The studies quoted provide some support for the effectiveness of Rogerian counselling, but not all the studies are unproblematic. Many of the measures of improvement are not objectively based; rather, they are self-report ratings completed by the client and/or therapist. Obviously, if clients and therapists have invested significant amounts of time and perhaps money on therapy, they are unlikely to rate the experience as having been worthless. More objective measures of changes in the client's behaviour would be preferable for measuring the effectiveness of therapy. There is also a lack of long-term follow-up studies to assess how lasting any changes obtained are.

Evaluation of Rogers' theory

We will now evaluate Rogers' theory using the eight criteria identified previously (Chapter 1): description, explanation, empirical validity, testable concepts, comprehensiveness, parsimony, heuristic value and applied value.

Description

Rogers, like Maslow, is criticised for his overly optimistic conceptualisation of human beings. As a total description of human behaviour, Rogers' theory is limited. His initial focus is on abnormal development and psychopathology and its treatment. However, his concept of conditions of worth provides a very valuable way of describing the mechanisms that we use to evaluate our own behaviour. His description of how the self is construed is innovative, and his comparison of self and ideal self is valuable. Intuitively, these concepts seem to provide useful descriptions and are therefore high in face validity.

His phenomenological approach represents a real attempt to engage with the world as individuals experience it. However, such an approach, with its focus on conscious experience, excludes what many will conceptualise as the rich world of the unconscious. We have explored this concept already (Chapters 2 and 3). Another danger of Rogers' approach is that it may rely so much on individual

Stop and think

Q-sort measurement of the self-concept

The Q-sort technique is used to measure an individual's self-concept. It was developed by an American psychologist, Stephenson, and published in 1953. It is administered in many formats, depending on the approach of the psychologist using it; however, the basic principles remain the same (Block, 1961; Rogers and Dymond, 1954). A list of around 100 adjectives or short statements describing personality attributes of individuals is generated. Each statement is printed on a separate card. Some typical examples are given here:

I am ambitious.	I am enthusiastic.
I am generally happy.	I am pessimistic.
I am a worrier.	I am careless.
I am a weak person.	I am a procrastinator.

Individuals are asked to sort the cards into nine categories, according to how well the phrase on the card describes who they are. Category 1 includes the descriptions that are most like the individual, and category 9 includes those that are least like the individual. The scale looks as follows:

At the start of therapy, clients do the task described earlier, which gives a measure of their *current self-concept*. It is not an easy task to complete, and clients normally begin by putting the cards into piles that are like them or not like them or not applicable to them. Then they make finer distinctions within each pile, comparing attributes to determine what represents them best. Stephenson argued that the effort involved adds to the reliability of the method as a representation of an individual's self-concept. Once this step is completed and recorded, the pack of cards is shuffled and clients are asked to sort the pack again to match their **ideal self**.

The hypothesis is that an individual's self-concept should change over the course of therapy. Individuals should be more in touch with their organismic self and more accepting of themselves. Used in the manner described, the Q-sort allows measurement of the discrepancy between a client's actual and ideal selves. This was the way that Rogers used it. However, it can be used with a range of personality variables or to measure preferences of any sort. Variations of the Q-sort technique, as it has become labelled, are still utilised quite widely within psychology.

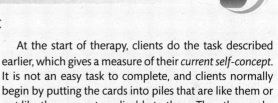

1	2	3	4	5	6	7	8	9
Most like me								Least like me

observations that objective measurement is ignored and no knowledge is generated that is applicable to the wider science of psychology. Rogers was very aware of this, and his utilisation of measures such as the Q-sort was his attempt to overcome this shortcoming.

Explanation

Rogers attempted to explain a vast range of human behaviour, ranging from what we require for optimum individual development to the nature of the society that would promote psychological health. However, he used the same principles that he developed for counselling troubled individuals to propose solutions for societies and indeed for the world's problems. This ignores the social, historical and political factors that play a crucial role in developing and maintaining these problems and leads to his explanations being limited in scope and somewhat reductionist in nature. His underlying thesis was that, if individuals communicated better, then society's problems would be solved. While good communication is helpful, it is unrealistic and overly optimistic to see it as the solution to what are very complex problems.

Empirical validity

Rogers was very aware of the need to provide empirical evidence to validate his theory. There is a lot of research on his therapy in particular. The results are generally positive, but all of this research is heavily reliant on self-report measures. Clients self-assess their progress, but this is hardly objective evidence given that they have invested considerable time and frequently money in their treatment, so are unlikely to evaluate it as a negative undertaking. Similarly, therapists provide reports of clients' progress, and here the tendency must surely be to provide a positive assessment. There is a need for more objective measures of therapeutic progress using standardised instruments and/or involving significant others of the client in the assessment of progress.

As we saw earlier, Rogers' idea about human beings knowing intuitively what is good for them received little research support. We know from work on the relationship between attitudes and behaviour that knowing some behaviour is harmful is not a good predictor of whether we practise that behaviour. If this were not so, we would not currently be having problems with binge drinking, obesity, smoking and many other health issues in our society.

Testable concepts

As mentioned already, Rogers was keen to construct a testable theory, and he did encourage research on his concepts. Despite this, some of his concepts are not easy to define. The concept of empathy has been researched, and reliable measures are available. However, concepts like unconditional positive regard and genuineness are more difficult to define and have proved difficult to measure. Rogers does need to be commended for his attempts to produce a testable theory and a therapy that can be evaluated. Traditionally, his counselling approach has been described as being non-directive, in that the therapist does not claim to know what is best for the client. Clients produce their own solutions. This idea that Rogerian therapists are somehow less directive than other therapists is contentious. As videos of his therapy sessions show, Rogers himself made considerable use of non-verbal signals when interacting with his clients. In this way he is likely to have influenced clients. This claim of non-directiveness can thus be seen to be difficult to assess objectively.

Comprehensiveness

Most of Rogers' work focuses on understanding psychopathology and developing an intervention that could be used as an effective treatment. This meant that his early work was not very comprehensive. Later in his life, he expanded his interests to look in more detail at development, education and the effect of culture and society's institutions on mental health. In this way, his approach became more comprehensive. His work on social and political structures, while interesting, is very speculative.

Parsimony

Rogers has chosen to take a broad approach to human behaviour; despite this, his theory utilises very few concepts. He fails the parsimony criteria by using too few concepts and assumptions. This results in imprecision, as his concepts are applied very widely to explain very different phenomena. A good example is his explanation of psychopathology. This is too simplistic to explain the full range of psychopathologies that have been documented and results in a reductionist approach.

Heuristic value

Rogers' work has provoked a great deal of controversy within psychology and continues to provoke debate. This in itself is a valuable contribution to make to a science. His humanistic and phenomenological stance has led to a re-evaluation of the importance of the individual and their subjective worldview. His emphasis on the concepts of self and ideal self also led to more attention being paid to these concepts and significant amounts of research being undertaken. His ideas about the core conditions of counselling also led therapy and counselling trainers to reflect on the educational training of counsellors, and useful debates ensued.

Applied value

Rogers' theory has been applied widely. This is certainly one of its strengths. His views of therapy have helped define the training of most counsellors. The recent trend, to encourage counselling psychologists to be trained in several schools of counselling, generally results in trainee counsellors beginning their education with Rogerian therapy. This means that most counsellors are familiar with the core conditions and develop active listening skills and empathy for their clients.

Rogers was also extremely influential in the development of group approaches to psychological treatments. The development of encounter groups in the 1960s and 1970s was attributable to Rogers' influence. These were group experiences designed to help individuals explore their true inner selves and thereby set them on the road to self-actualisation.

Final comments

Now you should understand what is meant by humanistic theories in psychology and how they evolved. You should be familiar with the developmental experiences that influenced the theorising of Maslow and Rogers and appreciate Maslow and Rogers' conceptualisations of human nature. You should also be familiar with Maslow's hierarchy of needs and the motives related to it, understand the principles of personality development and the causes of mental illness as described by Maslow and Rogers, be familiar with Rogers' conceptualisation of self-actualisation and its importance in development and understand the principles of Rogerian counselling, including the importance of the core conditions of counselling. You should also be able to outline the Q-sort method of measuring the self-concept and the ideal self. You should be able to critically evaluate the work of Maslow and Rogers.

Summary

- Maslow and Rogers' theories were based upon the European tradition of existential philosophy. Existential philosophy is concerned with ontology, defined as 'the science of being'.
- Maslow and Rogers' theories are humanistic personality theories. They emphasise **personal growth**. Human nature is conceptualised as being positive; the focus is on the here and now, not the past.
- Both theorists adopt a phenomenological approach focusing on the uniqueness of each individual and aiming to understand their experience. Humanistic therapists aim merely to help their clients understand what their problems are and do not provide solutions.
- Human beings have innate tendencies towards healthy growth and development that Maslow labelled **instinctoid tendencies**. These are weak positive tendencies that can easily be overcome by negative environmental influences. Healthy development depends on the fostering of the instinctoid tendencies in children.
- Maslow described two types of human motives: deficiency motives (D-motives) that are needs we are driven to fulfil; and growth motives, called being motives (B-motives). Satisfaction of B-motives brings pleasure and acts as further motivation to achieve and develop.
- Maslow outlined a hierarchy of needs to describe human motivation. These begin with physiological needs, then safety needs, belongingness and love needs, esteem needs and the need for self-actualisation. Individuals require that their lower-level needs be met before higher-level needs come into play.

- Self-actualisation is the ultimate goal that is not achieved by everyone. Self-actualisers are unique individuals with metaneeds that are different from the normal hierarchy of needs. Self-actualisers think differently, engaging more in being cognitions (B-cognitions), and are distinguished by having peak experiences linked to their B-cognitions.
- Maslow does not produce much detail about development in childhood other than to stress the importance of children being given the freedom to develop according to their inner selves.
- Maslow argued that mental illness was the result of the individual's inner needs not being met.
- Client-centred therapy refers to Rogers' feeling that clients are the best experts on themselves and have the power to solve their own problems. The therapist merely facilitates the process by providing a good relationship experience for the client in an empowering environment.
- Individuals have an innate drive to self-actualise. This is our sole motivating drive in Rogers' model. As long as our actualising tendency is not blocked, healthy development is assured. Blocks to self-actualising result in psychopathology.
- The concept of self is crucial in Rogers' model. He distinguishes between the real organismic self and the self-concept.
- In ideal circumstances, Rogers suggested, individuals receive unconditional positive regard. This is being valued simply for existing, with no conditions. Few individuals experience just this. Most parents and educational experiences impose conditions of worth. This results in us developing conceptualisations of our ideal selves that we compare with our real selves.

- How parents relate to their children will be heavily influenced by the adequacy of the parents' own self-concepts and the number of conditions of worth that they themselves have.
- Rogers felt that individuals intuitively know what is good for them, but there is no evidence to support this contention.
- The fully functioning person emerges as a result of self-actualisation, and Rogers provided descriptions of such individuals.
- Rogers' theory originated in his clinical work, and a lot of his writing related to the development of his approach to counselling and therapy.
- The aim of therapy was to facilitate a reintegration of the self-concept. Most clients have many conditions of worth, so they have an idealised self and their current self falls very short of this ideal. The aim of therapy is to reduce this gap and to reintegrate the self-concept with the real self.
- Rogers stressed that the relationship between the therapist and the client is crucial. He outlined the core conditions of counselling to describe the nature of the relationship. Rogers claimed that all that is required for positive change to occur is that these core conditions of counselling be met.
- Rogers was very aware of the importance of trying to provide research evidence to evaluate his approach, and he endeavoured to do this. While there is some support, the methodologies he used tend to rely very heavily on self-report measures.
- Finally, guidelines for evaluating both theories are provided.

Connecting up

You might wish to look back at Chapter 3 and Jung's discussion of individuation and compare and contrast these ideas with Maslow's ideas of self-actualisation.

Critical thinking

Discussion questions

- Is the distinction between B-love and D-love a valuable one in helping us to understand human relationships?
- How do you feel about the concept of peak or optimal experiences? Does it seem a useful concept and a description of the ultimate human experience?
- What would you see as the strengths and weaknesses of self-actualisers?
- Is it as difficult to find your goals in life and life satisfaction as Maslow and Rogers imply?
- Compare the conceptualisations of human nature posited by Maslow, Rogers and Freud. Is there anything in the biographical experiences of the three theorists that might help explain these differences?
- Do you consider conditions of worth to be a valuable concept? Can you identify any of your own conditions of worth? Do they play a useful role in your psyche?
- Is there any evidence to support Rogers' organismic valuing process?
- Is Rogers' distinction between what is generally termed 'love' and unconditional positive regard a valid one? If so, is it an important distinction in your view?

- How realistic is it to describe Rogers' approach to therapy as non-directive?
- Rogers is adamant that all self-evaluation is bad, even positive evaluations. Can you explain why he takes this view? Do you agree?
- How adequately do humanistic theorists explain human motivation?

Essay questions

- Critically discuss Rogers' theory and practice of person-centred therapy.
- Critically discuss Maslow's theory of self-actualisation.
- Discuss how developmental experiences influenced the theorising of Rogers.
- Compare and contrast Maslow's and Rogers' theory of self-actualisation.
- Critically discuss Rogers' contribution to our understanding of human personality.
- Critically discuss Maslow's contribution to our understanding of human personality.

Going further

Books

- Maslow, A. (1987). *Motivation and personality* (3rd edn). New York: Harper & Row. This book presents an easily readable account of the main aspects of his theory. It is Maslow's most comprehensive description of his theory and his research on healthy individuals.
- Maslow, A. (1968). *Toward a psychology of being.* Princeton, NJ: Van Nostrand. In this book, Maslow addresses the concept of self-actualisation and offers strategies for personal growth.
- Thorne, B. (1992). *Carl Rogers.* London: Sage. This book is an excellent introduction to Rogers' work and life. It is written in an accessible style. Thorne is a Rogerian therapist and adds a useful clinical perspective to the theory.
- Rogers, C. R. (1980). *A way of being.* Boston: Houghton Mifflin. This book, written by Rogers, covers a lot of material. It includes personal reflections on his own life, his professional work and a final section on education. This latter section includes his thoughts about the changes needed in society to create psychologically enhancing cultures.
- Barrett-Lennard, G. T. (1998). *Carl Rogers' helping system: Journey and substance.* London: Sage. This text presents a fairly comprehensive coverage of Rogers' ideas with a useful review and discussion of research on Rogerian concepts.
- Rogers, C. R. (1961). *On becoming a person: A therapist's view of psychotherapy.* Boston: Houghton Mifflin. This is perhaps Rogers' classic book on his theory. It is easy to read and thought-provoking. He addresses the topic of personal growth and how it can be facilitated in some detail. The role of research in his theory and in therapy generally is addressed as well as reflections on society and how it impacts on our lives. Recent editions can be found, e.g. Rogers, C. R. (2004). *On becoming a person.* London: Constable and even a Kindle edition in 2011.
- Rogers, C. R. and Freiberg, H. J. (1993). *Freedom to learn* (3rd edn). New York: Merrill. As current consumers of the mainstream western educational system, you

may well find this text relevant and thought-provoking. It is a re-edit of Rogers' 1983 text, *Freedom to learn for the 80s* (Columbus, OH: Merrill). Unless an author has a difficult writing style, our preference is for you to read the text by the original author. This is our advice here, as Rogers is easy to read. However, you may find it easier to access the later re-edited text, and this is why we include it here.

Journals

The Journal of Humanistic Psychology is published by Sage Journals and is an interdisciplinary publication for contributions, controversies and diverse statements pertaining to humanistic psychology. Apart from the journal being available online, with subscription, at **http://www.sagepub.com** you may find that your library subscribes to the online database Expanded Academic ASAP and you may find many articles from the journal there.

Web links

- A site on Rogers written by his daughter, Natalie Rogers, is available online (**www.nrogers.com/carlrogers.html**).
- A site that lists all Maslow's publications is available online (**www.maslow.com**).
- Summerhill School (**www.summerhillschool.co.uk**), which we mention in the text. If you follow the links, you can also get the Ofsted report on the school and a report on the legal case that the school won when it looked as if the government were trying to close the school in 2000.
- The Block and Block longitudinal study is available online (**http://review.ucsc.edu/summer.97/29_years.html**).

Film and literature

- *A Christmas Carol* (or, to give its full title, *A Christmas Carol in Prose, Being a Ghost Story of Christmas*) by Charles Dickens (1843) tells a story of self-actualisation. The story tells of Mr Scrooge, who is a financier who has devoted his life to the accumulation of wealth and has a disregard for friendship and love. Over the

course of Christmas Eve, he has a number of ghostly visitations, and Scrooge finds out that he will end up walking the Earth forever as an invisible and lonely ghost. Following this experience, Scrooge changes his life and reverts to being generous, kindhearted and finding joy in others.

- *Shirley Valentine* and *Educating Rita*, both powerful plays by Willy Russell, outline a woman's self-actualisation. Both plays were made into films (*Educating Rita*, 1983; *Shirley Valentine*, 1989) and were directed by Lewis Gilbert.
- Other films that depict elements of self-actualisation, but with slightly different overtones, are *Thelma and Louise* (1991, directed by Ridley Scott) and *Vanilla Sky* (2001, directed by Cameron Crowe). Both films portray emerging aspects of personality and strengths.
- *Carl Rogers on Empathy* (Educational Resource Film; British Association for Counselling). Carl Rogers discusses the concept of empathy. Central for understanding the person-centred therapy process. Concord Video and Film Council.

Explore the website accompanying this text at **www.pearsoned.co.uk/maltby** for further resources to help you with your studies. These include multiple-choice questions, essay questions, web links and ideas for advanced reading.

CHAPTER 7
The Trait Approach to Personality

Key themes

- The history of trait approaches to personality
- Defining traits
- Lexical hypothesis approach to personality traits
- The contribution of Gordon Allport
- Raymond Cattell and the Sixteen Personality Factor Inventory
- Hans Eysenck and the three-factor structure
- The Big Five
- Evaluating trait approaches

Learning outcomes

After studying this discussion you should:

- Be able to describe the nomothetic approach to personality research
- Appreciate the long history of attempts to describe and explain differences in personality
- Understand what is meant by the lexical hypothesis
- Be familiar with the approach to data analysis employed by trait theorists
- Be aware of the contribution of Gordon Allport to the trait approach
- Appreciate the contribution of Raymond Cattell to the trait approach
- Know about Hans Eysenck's attempts to uncover the basic structure of personality
- Understand the approaches that have resulted in the identification of the Big Five personality traits

Introduction

Easygoing, intelligent, funny, caring, professional man, aged 44, **good in a crisis,** seeks **warm, friendly, intelligent** woman of a similar age. Enjoys good food, wine, cinema and theatre.

Vibrant, charismatic, passionate, energetic sportswoman, aged 32, **loves all outdoor activities, foreign travel,** cooking, reading and gardening, seeks country-dwelling male with similar interests.

At this point, you may be wondering what lonely-hearts advertisements are doing in a textbook on personality. However, we want you to think about the image of the individuals that these advertisements convey. Most of us are good at doing this; from a short description of an individual, we can build up a mental picture of them and make decisions about which individuals we are attracted to and might like to meet and which hold no appeal for us. What we are doing is using our knowledge of personality traits to build up an image of the person from their description. We have highlighted the words that label personality traits in the advertisements above,

and it is worth taking a moment to reflect on what you understand by each of them and how you value them. Is the picture of a vibrant, charismatic, passionate, energetic woman one you value you positively or one you find unappealing?

What these types of adverts suggest is that from a few personality traits and statements about interests, we may be able to build up an image of the individual. This in effect is what trait personality theorists aim to do, but in a more rigorous, scientific way. Trait theorists employ the **nomothetic** approach to personality that we covered previously (Chapter 1). The aim is to identify those personality variables or traits that occur consistently across groups of people. Each individual can then be located within this set of variables. The aim is to identify the main traits that usefully distinguish between types of people. In achieving this, they hope to uncover the basic structure of personality. As you may recall (from Chapter 1), this is one of the major aims of studying human personality. It is a major undertaking, and we will now explore the progress that has been made, starting with the Ancient Greeks.

Source: Getty Images/Photodisc

Emergence of personality traits

The Ancient Greek philosopher, Aristotle (384–322 BC), provides the first written description of personality traits, or dispositions, as he preferred to call them. He described individual differences in traits such as modesty, bravery and vanity, seeing them as important determinants of whether a person behaved ethically. One of his students, Theophrastus (371–287 BC), published an account of 30 personality characters or types. These were early attempts to describe the commonly acknowledged differences between individuals and to identify individuals with similar dispositions. The task can be thought of as putting some order or structure into our everyday observations so that they are easier to conceptualise and discuss.

Another Ancient Greek philosopher, Hippocrates (460–377 BC), described physical illness as being caused by the balance of bodily fluids, or humours, as he labelled them. These fluids included blood, black bile, yellow bile and phlegm. Another Ancient Greek, a physician named Galen (AD 130–200), expanded on Hippocrates' theory of the humours and applied it to describe human temperament or personality (Stelmack and Stalikas, 1991). When the humours were in balance, an equitable temperament was the result. If the humours were out of balance, then physical illness and mental disturbance occurred. The terms Galen used to describe these mental disturbances are still part of the English language. An excess of black bile resulted in a **melancholic temperament**, associated with depressed mood and feelings of anxiety. Strong activity in the body fluids resulted in an individual with strong emotions described as being of **choleric temperament**, meaning that they had a tendency to become angry easily. Individuals of **phlegmatic temperament** were calm, as there was low humorous activity, while individuals of **sanguine temperament** were confident and optimistic.

In the Middle Ages the German philosopher Immanuel Kant (1724–1804) revisited the humoural temperaments and produced a description of four personality types. These were based on the strength of the individual's feelings and how active the person was. Melancholic individuals had weak feelings, while sanguine individuals had strong feelings. Phlegmatic individuals had low levels of activity, while choleric individuals had much higher levels of activity.

These early writers all described types of personality rather than personality traits. This is an important distinction. Personality types describe discrete categories into which individuals can be placed. Personality traits are continuous dimensions, and individuals can be positioned along the dimension depending on how much of the trait they possess.

It was Wilhelm Wundt, the founding father of modern-day psychology, who changed the categorical types of personality into trait dimensions. He revisited the humoural terms in his description of personality, reclassifying the old types in two dimensions based on their mood stability and the strength of their emotions. Individuals could then be placed along the dimensions of mood stability and strength of emotions rather than being simply placed in one category. Wundt's classification system is displayed in Figure 7.1.

It is true to say that little progress was made in terms of classifying personality traits from the time of the Ancient Greeks to the middle of the nineteenth century, when the clinical theories emerged – as we have already seen in (Chapter 1). The reason for the delay in the emergence of trait theories is easily understandable. There are a huge number of terms in all languages to describe personality traits. For

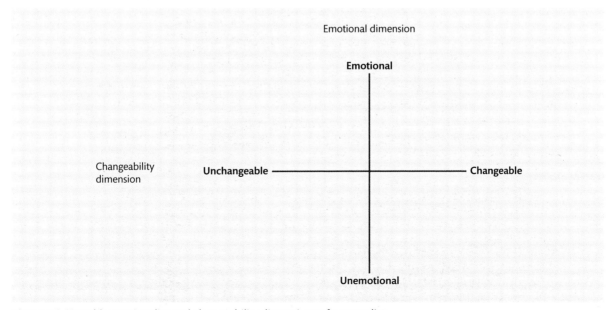

Figure 7.1 Wundt's emotionality and changeability dimensions of personality.

trait approaches to personality to develop scientifically, some systematic way of structuring these terms and identifying the common dimensions underlying them was necessary. It was the invention of statistical techniques such as correlation and factor analysis that made this possible, as we shall see.

Defining personality traits

Up until now, we have used the term 'trait' to describe personality. We are sure you have understood what we have been saying, but we should begin this section with a definition of exactly what psychologists mean by a personality trait. Frequently, terms that have a very specific meaning in psychology are also part of our everyday language. This can result in some confusion about the precise meaning of terms; hence psychology's obsession with defining the terms that we use. According to Burger (1997), 'A trait is a dimension of personality used to categorise people according to the degree to which they manifest a particular characteristic.'

Two assumptions underlie trait theory. The first assumption is that personality characteristics are relatively stable over time; the second is that traits show stability across situations. A person's behaviour may alter on different occasions, but the assumption is that there is some internal consistency in the ways that individuals behave. For example, someone who is described as an extravert may be very outgoing and chatty at a party but less so in a psychology seminar. In both situations, this person is likely to be more sociable than an introverted individual. We also assume that personality traits influence behaviour. The person is outgoing and chatty because they are an extravert. These are somewhat circular arguments, and the psychologist has to move beyond them. Trait theorists have to be able to make a distinction between the internal qualities of the individual and the way they behave. The causal relationship between the two then has to be explained if we are to avoid circular arguments. To say that individuals become angry easily because they have an angry disposition does not get us very far. We need to know where their angry disposition has come from and how it influences their day-to-day behaviour.

It follows logically from the trait approach that trait theorists are more interested in general descriptions of behaviour than in understanding the individual and making predictions about individual behaviour. They take the trait continuum and provide descriptions of how groups of people at different points on the continuum might be expected to behave. For example, they might compare a group high in aggression with a group with low scores on the same trait and observe how they behave in a debate. They are interested in typical group behaviour. It is frequently a descriptive rather than an explanatory approach. Some trait theorists are more interested in describing personality

and predicting behaviour than in identifying what caused the behaviour. This can lead to circular reasoning. An individual is said to behave in a certain way because they are an anxious person. When asked to explain why an individual is anxious, the response is that they are anxious because they have behaved in a certain way.

Increasingly, however, the identification processes are only the first stage. Trait theorists are becoming more interested in providing explanations for behaviour. Trait approaches make it relatively easy to make comparisons among people; individuals can be placed on a continuum relative to others, and groups can also be compared. However, trait theorists have little to say about personality change. The theorists with an interest in personality change have come from a clinical background, while trait theorists are more likely to be academic psychologists.

To recap, within psychology, traits are considered the fundamental units of personality. They represent dispositions to respond in certain ways. For a long time, there were arguments about how much the situation influenced the individual's behaviour and how much was down to their personality traits. It is now generally accepted that, while situational factors will affect behaviour, dispositional effects on that behaviour will still be observable. Mischel (1999) has produced an elegant definition of a personality trait that incorporates this. He suggests that a trait is the 'conditional probability of a category of behaviours in a category of contexts'. Hence, if a person is an extravert, then degrees of extraverted behaviour will be observable from that person in a variety of situations.

The development of trait theories within psychology

During the rest of this discussion we are going to take you through the development and establishment of the core trait theories of personality in psychology. These include the work of:

- Sheldon
- early lexical approaches
- Allport
- Cattell
- Eysenck
- the five-factor model.

Sheldon and somatotypes

Although the psychoanalyst Jung (Chapter 3) introduced the terms 'extraversion' and 'introversion', the real founding figure of trait psychology is considered to be an American psychologist, William Sheldon (1899–1977). He outlined what came to be a very well-known description of personality called somatotypes, which is based on physique and temperament. From his surveys of thousands of individuals, he concluded that there are three basic types of physique: endomorphy, mesomorphy and ectomorphy (Sheldon, 1970). Using correlational techniques, he demonstrated that each body type was associated with a particular temperament. A summary of his theory is displayed in Table 7.1.

While accepting that everyone had the same internal organs, Sheldon felt that individuals were different in terms of which organs were most prominent in their bodies and thus where their body's focus lay. Table 7.1 represents the extremes of each type, but Sheldon produced a detailed atlas of male body types where bodies were matched against these extremes using a seven-point grading scale. He planned a similar female body atlas, but this was never produced. You may still come across descriptions of Sheldon's body types in popular texts. In terms of personality theorising, Sheldon's work was important as it marked the start of the utilisation of psychometric approaches to the study of personality. He carried out extensive surveys of large populations, collected different measures from individuals using questionnaires and applied statistical techniques to the analysis of his data.

Early lexical approaches to personality and the lexical hypothesis

Several of the early researchers used dictionaries or *Roget's Thesaurus* to try to identify and count the number of words that describe personality traits. Sir Francis Galton (1822–1911) was an Englishman who is best known for his early studies on genetic influences on intelligence, but he was also interested in the relationships between language and personality. He suggested that the most meaningful personality descriptors will tend to become encoded in language as single words. Galton (1884) provides the first documented source of a dictionary and/or thesaurus being used to elicit words describing personality.

This approach has come to be known as the lexical hypothesis. It suggests that it is the individual differences between people that are important that become encoded as single terms. This appears to be a sensible assumption. Two additional criteria are included in the lexical hypothesis. First, frequency of use is also assumed to correspond with importance. Again, it seems logical that the words we use most to describe personality will be labelling the aspects of personality that we think are most important. Secondly, the number of words in a language that refer to each trait will be related to how important that trait is in describing human personality. An example from a thesaurus is included in Table 7.2 to help clarify what we mean. From the table, you can see that the personality descriptor 'honest' has 31 synonyms listed, suggesting that it is a more important descriptor of personality than the word 'aberrant', which is not listed in the *Oxford Concise Thesaurus* (2007). Similarly, the word 'warm' describes a more useful descriptor of personality than 'pedantic' does.

While most of the early work was conducted on the English language, it is assumed that, if the lexical hypothesis is a valid theory, then it should apply cross-culturally (Norman, 1963). This is the final assumption of the lexical hypothesis. We will return to the cross-cultural question later in the discussion. To summarise, it states that, if individual differences between people are important, there will be words to describe them; the more frequently a personality descriptor is used, the more important the personality characteristic; finally, the more synonyms of the word there are, the more important the difference.

Table 7.1 Sheldon's theory of physique and temperament

	Physique		Temperament	
	Focus on part of body	Physique	Temperament	Description
Ectomorph	Nervous system and the brain	Light-boned with a slight musculature	**Cerebrotonia**	A need for privacy, restrained, inhibited
Mesomorph	Musculature and the circulatory system	Large, bony with well-defined muscles	**Somatotonia**	Physically assertive, competitive, keen on physical activity
Endomorph	Digestive system, particularly the stomach	Rounded body tending towards fatness	**Viscerotonia**	Associated with a love of relaxation and comfort; like food and are sociable

Table 7.2 Evidence for the lexical hypothesis

Personality descriptor	Synonyms	Number
honest	trustworthy, truthful, veracious, trusty, honourable, creditable, decent, law-abiding, uncorrupted, uncorrupt, incorruptible, ethical, moral, virtuous, principled, upright, high-minded, dependable, reliable, reputable, above-board, straight, square-dealing, fair, just, candid, frank, sincere, direct, ingenuous, sound	31
warm	amiable, friendly, cheerful, cordial, affable, pleasant, genial, kindly, hospitable, hearty, affectionate, mellow, loving	13
pedantic	perfectionistic, scrupulous, finicky, fussy, punctilious, fastidious, meticulous, exact, quibbling	9
aberrant – meaning odd or peculiar	not included	

Source: Oxford Concise Thesaurus, Oxford, UK: Oxford University Press, 2007.

Gordon Allport

Initially, lexical researchers were limited to counting the terms used, identifying synonyms and producing lists of these words. One of the first psychologists to produce such a list was the American Gordon Allport (1897–1967). With a colleague, he identified 18,000 words, of which 4,500 described personality traits (Allport and Odbert, 1936). Allport published the first psychology text on personality traits, *Personality Traits: Their Classification and Measurement* (1921), and he is believed to have taught the first course on personality in the United States in 1924. While promoting the concept of personality traits, Allport (1961) was quite clear about the limitations of the trait approach. He felt that it was almost impossible to use an individual's

personality traits to predict how they will behave in a specific situation. He acknowledged that there is variability in everyone's behaviour, but that there is also some constancy. Personality traits constitute this constant portion of behaviour. He suggested that personality traits have a physical presence in our nervous systems. He suggested that advances in technology would one day enable psychologists to identify personality traits from inspection of the nervous system.

Although interested in traits, Allport adopted a unified approach to personality, suggesting that it is the way that the component traits come together that is important. It is how the traits come together that produces the uniqueness of all individuals, which he was keen to stress. Together, these traits produce a unified personality that is capable of

Stop and think

Nomothetic and idiographic approach

The **nomothetic** approach comes from the ancient Greek term for 'law' and is based on the assumption that there is a finite set of variables in existence that can be used to describe human personality. The aim is to identify these personality variables or traits that occur consistently across groups of people. Each individual can then be located within this set of variables. By studying large groups of people on a particular variable, we can establish the average levels of that variable in particular age groups, or in men and women, and in this way produce group averages, generally called **norms**, for variables. Individuals can then be described as being above or below the average or norm on a particular variable. The

nomothetic approach concentrates on the similarities between individuals.

The **idiographic** approach focuses on the individual and describes the personality variables within that individual. The term comes from the ancient Greek *idios*, meaning 'private or personal'. Theorists, who adopt this approach in the main, are only interested in studying individuals one at a time. They see each person as having a unique personality structure. Differences between individuals are seen to be much greater than the similarities. The possible differences are infinite. Idiographic approaches produce a *unique understanding* of that individual's personality. These approaches are usually based on case studies of individuals.

constant evolution and change. Allport felt that change is a component part of the personality system that is necessary to allow us to adapt to new situations and grow to cope with them. He adopted a very positive conceptualisation of human nature. He suggested that human beings are normally rational, creative, active and self-reliant. This was a very different view of human nature from the Freudian one that was dominant at the time.

Allport made the distinction between nomothetic and idiographic approaches to the study of personality. We covered this distinction earlier (Chapter 1), but we have included a reminder of these terms in Stop and think: Nomothetic and idiographic approach, as this is an important distinction with which you need to be familiar. Allport felt that both approaches bring unique insights into our understanding of personality. He felt that the nomothetic approach allows the identification of **common personality traits** (Allport, 1961). He saw these common traits as ways of classifying groups of individuals, with one group being classified as being more dominant, happier or whatever than another comparable group. He felt that such comparisons based on common traits are not particularly useful. Of more use is what he termed the **personal disposition** of the individual. The personal disposition represents the unique characteristics of the individual. This approach emphasises the uniqueness of each person, and Allport (1961) felt that this was potentially a more fruitful approach towards developing a real understanding of personality.

Personality traits were further classified into cardinal, central and secondary traits. **Cardinal traits** are single traits that may dominate an individual's personality and heavily influence their behaviour. These may be thought of as obsessions or ruling passions that produce a need that demands to be fulfilled. For example, someone may have a cardinal trait of competitiveness that permeates virtually every aspect of their behaviour. They strive to be best at everything they do. **Central traits** are the five to ten traits that Allport felt best describe an individual's personality. **Secondary traits** are more concerned with an individual's preferences and are not a core constituent of their personality. Secondary traits may only become apparent in particular situations – unlike central traits, which have a more general applicability.

The other major contribution that Allport made to personality theorising relates to the concept of self. He emphasised the importance of the concept to any theory of personality as he felt it is crucial to the development of identity and individuality. He hypothesised that children are not born with a concept of self, but that it gradually develops. He felt that it is a lifelong process of development. The child first becomes aware of the separateness of themselves from others in their environment and from this comes their sense of self-identity. As a result of their experiences while becoming integrated into their family and wider society, they develop self-esteem. Allport felt that the concept of self presented a challenge to psychologists as it is difficult

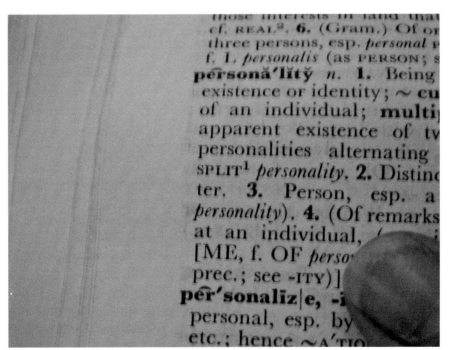

The aim of lexical approaches is to find underlying dimensions to the many ways we describe our personality.
Source: Pearson Education Ltd

to define precisely, consisting as it does of several component parts. He used the term **proprium** as a synonym for the self, suggesting that the term represented all the constituent parts that go to make up the concept of self.

Allport's major impact on personality theory was in terms of stressing the limitations of the trait approaches as they were currently adopted. He raised the issue about the relative influence of personality and situation in determining behaviour, something still of concern to psychologists. His inclusion of the concept of self as a legitimate and central concern of personality theorists was also important in the trait tradition of personality research. His distinction between nomothetic and idiographic approaches to the study of personality is an important one. He did not develop any standardised measures of personality traits as such; this was left to other theorists, as we shall see. His list of 4,500 personality traits is too long to be of much practical use in assessing personality.

Raymond Cattell and the emergence of the factor analytic approach

The real advances in trait approaches were only possible after the invention of the technique of factor analysis. A detailed description of the principles underlying factor analysis is given later (Chapter 25). You may find it helpful to read that section so that you can fully understand the rest of this discussion. Allport did not engage with factor analysis; however, the next theorist that we examine, Raymond Cattell, made full use of the technique, having been instructed in it by Spearman, the inventor of factor anal-

ysis. (See Profile: Raymond Cattell.) Following from this early scientific training, Cattell was keen to apply empirical methods to discover the basic structure of personality. From the lists of personality traits, he noted that many traits are very similar, and he argued that the existing lists could be reduced to a much smaller number of traits. This smaller number of traits would represent the basic components of personality. Cattell's work thus marks the beginning of the search for the structure of personality using factor analysis. Put simply, the procedure involves identifying lists of the most frequently used sets of words that seem to describe aspects of personality; large samples of individuals are then asked to rate the degree to which the attributes apply to them. This data set is then factor-analysed to identify which attributes cluster together. Clusters are composed of items that correlate with each other. So, for example, you might have the variables 'determined', 'persistent', 'productive' and 'goal-directed' that turn out to be highly correlated with each other and thus form a cluster or factor that you could perhaps call achievement-oriented. What this method gives you is a general measure of some ability – in this instance, achievement orientation – that you obtain by measuring the individual's ratings of their determination, persistence, productivity and goal-directedness.

Types of traits

Cattell (1965) defined personality as being the characteristics of the individual that allow prediction of how they will behave in a given situation. His approach to personality was a broad one, and he identified a range of traits, as we shall see. Later in his career, he became interested in the ways

Profile

Raymond Cattell

Raymond Bernard Cattell was born in a village just outside Birmingham, UK, in 1905. His first degree was in chemistry and physics at the University of London. He had become interested in psychology and undertook a PhD in psychology at the same university. His supervisor was the inventor of factor analysis, Charles Spearman. This resulted in Cattell being very well trained in the new statistical technique of factor analysis and adopting it as an analysis tool. Sir Cyril Burt, the psychologist who specialised in intelligence, was also in the same department; Cattell was influenced by his apparently rigorous approach to research. You will find out more about Burt later (Chapter 14) when you examine intelligence. Cattell undertook some studies

on personality and worked in a child guidance clinic to get clinical experience. In 1937, he emigrated to the United States and to a position at Columbia University. He has worked at Clark University, Harvard, and the University of Illinois, where he was director of the Laboratory of Personality Assessment. Cattell is not always easy to read in the original. A lot of his work deals with mathematical issues involved in factor analysis. He was a prolific writer, publishing 35 books and over 400 journal articles. In addition, he produced a variety of personality tests, including the Culture Fair Intelligence Tests, Motivation Analysis Test and the much-used Sixteen Personality Factor questionnaire (16PF test). Cattell died in February 1998.

that personality traits and situational variables interact to affect the way that individuals behave. Traits are conceptualised as being relatively stable, long-lasting building blocks of personality.

Cattell makes distinctions between types of traits. The first distinction relates to whether traits are genetically determined or the result of environmental experiences. The genetically determined traits are called **constitutional traits** while the environmentally induced traits are called **environmental-mold traits**. This distinction represents the nature versus nurture debate that occurs repeatedly in every area of psychology. In this application, it asks whether individual differences are caused by inherited aspects of our personality, or are they explained by how we have been treated and the environmental experiences we have had? Cattell (1982) was keen to try to establish the relative contribution of genetics and environment to various personality traits. He developed a statistical procedure called **multiple abstract variance analysis (MAVA)** to accomplish this. He administered personality tests to assess a particular trait in relation to complex samples consisting of family members raised together, family members raised apart, identical twins raised together, identical twins raised apart, unrelated children raised together and unrelated children raised apart. Using complex statistical procedures, the test allows the researcher to calculate the precise degree of influence that genetic and environmental factors have in the development of a particular personality trait.

Next, Cattell defines three different types of traits: ability, temperament and dynamic traits. **Ability traits** determine how well you deal with a particular situation and how well you reach whatever your goal is in that situation. For example, the various aspects of intelligence are good examples of ability traits. He also identifies individual differences in the styles that people adopt when they are pursuing their goals. These are labelled **temperament traits**. Some people may be laidback and easygoing, or irritable, or anxious and so on, in the way that they typically approach life. These then are examples of temperament traits.

Cattell, like many of the other theorists we have examined, was interested in what motivates human behaviour. You will recall (from Chapter 1) that this is a core area for personality theories to explain. He suggested that we have **dynamic traits** that motivate us and energise our behaviour (Cattell, 1965). For example, an individual may be motivated to succeed and be very competitive, or they may be ambitious, or driven to care for others, be artistic and so on. As Cattell (1965) considered the question of motivation to be at the heart of personality theorising, the dynamic traits were heavily researched. He concluded that there are three types of dynamic traits: **attitudes**, **sentiments** and **ergs**. Attitudes are defined as hypothetical constructs that express our particular interests in people or objects in specific situations. Attitudes help to predict how we will behave in a particular situation. Cattell (1950) defined sentiments as complex attitudes that include our opinions and interests that help determine how we feel about people or situations. Cattell (1979) considered ergs to be innate motivators. He suggested that ergs are innate drives. They cause us to recognise and attend to some stimuli more readily than others, and to seek satisfaction of our drives.

Cattell suggests that all these types of dynamic traits are organised in very complex and interrelated ways to produce the **dynamic lattice**. The aim is to explain how we have to acquire particular traits to achieve our goals. For example, if your goal is learning to ski, you need to learn to copy the instructor. You have to demonstrate patience and perseverance in practising. You have to tolerate being a figure of fun when you fall over, and you may have to conquer fear to go on the drag lift and so on. How others react to you will also affect the lattice as will your attitudes towards others and the mood you are in. This then gives a hint of the complexity involved. It is fair to say that this system certainly does not simplify the explanation of behaviour in any real way, and other psychologists have not followed up this work.

A further distinction is between **common traits** and **unique traits**. Common traits are those shared by many people. They would include intelligence, sociability, dependency and so on. Unique traits are rarer and specific to individuals. A unique trait might be an interest in collecting fishing reels by a particular maker or an interest in a particular entertainer or the like. They are specialised interests, if you like, that motivate individuals to pursue certain related activities. While Cattell's work is concerned almost exclusively with common traits, he includes the concept of unique traits to emphasise the uniqueness of human beings. He also stressed that the uniqueness of individuals is also because of the unique ways that common traits come together in different individuals. Different individuals will have different mixtures of common traits making up their personalities, thus making them unique.

Cattell (1950) suggested an important distinction between **surface traits** and **source traits**. Surface traits are collections of traits descriptors that cluster together in many individuals and situations. For example, individuals who are sociable also tend to be carefree, hopeful and contented. These are all surface traits; when you measure individuals on each of these surface traits, you find that their scores on each one are correlated with all the others. That is, if an individual scores highly on sociability, they also score highly on the carefree trait, the hopefulness trait and the contentedness trait. The technique of factor analysis suggests that there is an underlying trait, what Cattell calls a **source trait**, that is responsible for the observed variance in the surface traits. In this case, it is the source trait of extraversion. Extraversion is measured by the scores of the surface traits of sociability, carefreeness, hopefulness and contentedness. The surface traits relate to the overt behaviours that individuals display. The source trait, on the other hand, is the major difference in personality that is responsible for all these related differences in observed behaviour. In simple terms, being high in the source trait of extraversion causes you to display behaviour that is more sociable, to have more hopeful attitudes and so on.

The source traits are identified using the statistical technique of factor analysis, as we have previously discussed. Source traits are important as they represent the actual underlying structure of personality. If psychologists can identify the basic structure of personality, then they will be better able to predict behaviour. This has become the main quest for trait theorists. As we have seen, there are an enormous number of personality traits; identifying the source traits will reduce this number. By using a smaller number of source traits, psychologists can then construct personality tests that include only measures of surface traits that relate to the source traits. Personality tests produced in this way will provide better measures of individual differences in personality.

Cattell (1957) makes it clear that it is necessary to use a broad range of personality descriptors to ensure that the appropriate source traits are discovered. He began his quest for the underlying structure of personality with the list of 4,500 trait names as identified by Allport and Odbert (1936). You may recall that we mentioned this list earlier in the section on Allport. Firstly, using teams of raters, Cattell removed all the synonyms. This left him with a list of 171 trait names. By getting raters to assess individuals on these traits, he reduced the list further to produce 36 surface traits. Ten other surface traits were identified in further studies on personality assessment and from a review of the psychiatric literature. Thus, Cattell concluded that 46 surface traits are sufficient to describe individual differences in personality (Cattell and Kline, 1977).

Beginning with these 46 surface traits, Cattell used a variety of approaches to uncover the source traits of personality. The aim was to factor-analyse measures of all the 46 surface traits collected from large samples of individuals. As you will see in the material on factor analysis (Chapter 25), large numbers of participants are required for factor analysis. Cattell used different data collection procedures to obtain his data sets. One source of data he called **L-data**, short for 'life record data'. These are measurements of behaviour taken from the person's actual life. Ideally it might be things like the A-level grades the person got, the degree they were awarded, the number of car accidents they had and so on. Such data could be difficult to obtain, so Cattell settled for ratings of the individual's behaviour by individuals who knew them well in a particular situation. In a school setting it might be teacher's ratings of aspects of the individual's ability, sociability, conscientiousness, and/or fellow students' ratings. In a work setting, it might be ratings by colleagues

or managers, for example. These individuals would rate aspects of their target colleague's behaviour using a 10-point Likert Scale.

A second type of data collection involved using personality questionnaires. Cattell called this **Q-data**. This is the paper-and-pencil questionnaire that is widely used as an assessment tool in psychology.

Cattell's final method of generating data involved getting participants to complete tests under standardised testing conditions, but the tests are such that the responses cannot be faked. He called the data collected **T-data** and claimed that it represents truly objective test data. In normal questionnaires, respondents may lie about some of their answers to create a good impression, for example. However, participants completing the objective tests that produce T-data do not know what is being measured, so they cannot distort their answers. Cattell (1965) gives the Rorschach inkblot test as an example of such a test. Participants are presented with a series of different inkblots and have to report what they see. Clinical psychologists then interpret this information.

From the factor analyses of huge data sets gathered using these different procedures, Cattell identified 16 major source factors (Cattell, 1971; Cattell and Kline, 1977). Further research identified another 7 factors; however, his best-known measure of personality, the Sixteen Personality Factor (16PF) questionnaire uses the original 16 factors as they are the most robust measures. Cattell and his co-researchers have identified these 16 source traits as representing the basic structure of personality. He also ranked the traits in terms of how important they were in predicting an individual's behaviour. In the following list, we will present the 16 factors in this order, so that the most predictive items come first. Each factor represents a continuum along which individuals are ranked. At one end, individuals possess extremely high levels of the factor; at the other end, their levels are extremely low. Cattell (1965) was at pains to point out that almost all of the source traits have positive and negative aspects at each end of the continuum. We will highlight an example as we go through the trait descriptions. In labelling the source traits, we will use the factor letters that Cattell used to describe each factor, followed by what the scales measure (which has come to be the popular name for each of the scales) and then by the technical labels that Cattell has assigned to each factor (in parentheses). By doing this, we want to ensure that you will recognise the traits in other texts, where any of these names may be used.

- **Factor A, Outgoing–Reserved (affectothymia–schizothymia).** This factor measures whether individuals are outgoing or reserved. It is the largest factor. The technical labels Cattell chose for the endpoints of this factor, affectothymia (outgoing) and schizothymia (reserved), reflect the history of the employment of this trait in psychiatry. The outgoing–reserved dimension was shown to be important in determining which individuals were hospitalised for mental illness (Cattell, 1965).

- **Factor B, Intelligence (High '8'–Low '8').** Cattell was the first to include intelligence as an ability trait. He rated it as the second best predictor of behaviour in his initial analysis of the factors that best predict actual behaviour.

- **Factor C, Stable–Emotional (high ego strength–low ego strength).** This source trait measures emotional stability and the ability an individual has to control their impulses and solve problems effectively (Cattell, 1965). At the positive end, individuals are rated as being stable individuals who cope well in their lives and are realistic in their approach to life. At the negative end, individuals are emotionally labile. They are more neurotic and highly anxious.

- **Factor E, Assertive–Humble (dominance–submissiveness).** At the dominant end individuals display the surface traits of boastfulness, aggression, self-assertiveness, conceit, forcefulness, wilfulness, egotism and vigour. Humble or submissive individuals are seen to be modest, unsure, quiet, obedient, meek and retiring. This trait is the first to display a mixture of positive and negative attributes at each end of the scale. Dominant individuals have positive qualities of vigour and forcefulness but are boastful and egotistical.

- **Factor F, Happy-go-lucky–Sober (surgency–desurgency).** When discussing this term, Cattell defended his creation of new terms like surgency to describe his source traits. He suggests that the common names for traits often do not accurately represent what psychologists mean, so it is better to use a technical term that can be defined more precisely. High surgency individuals are cheerful, sociable, responsive, joyous, witty, humorous, talkative and energetic. He suggests that this is more than simply happy-go-lucky, the popular name for the term. Desurgent individuals are pessimistic, inclined to depression, reclusive, introspective, given to worrying, retiring and subdued. Cattell (1980) stated that this is the most important single predictive factor in children's personalities. He explored the influence of genetic factors on this trait and suggested that 55 per cent of the variance on this trait is due to heredity.

- **Factor G, Conscientious–Expedient (high superego–low superego).** Cattell (1965) compares this factor to Freud's concept of the superego. Individuals high in conscientiousness are persistent and reliable and exercise good self-control. At the other end of the continuum, expedient individuals tend to take the line of least resistance rather than be guided by their principles.

- **Factor H, Venturesome–Shy (parmia–threctia).** Here Cattell contrasts the bold, genial, adventurous, gregarious, individual (venturesome) with the shy, aloof, self-contained, timid individual (shy). Cattell's technical labels for these terms are not as obscure as they seem at first sight. The terms relate to the autonomic nervous system, specifically the sympathetic and parasympathetic systems. The sympathetic nervous system produces the body's fight-or-flight response in the presence of a stressor of some sort. Put simply, the parasympathetic system is involved in maintaining more normal, relaxed functioning. *Parmia* is an abbreviation of 'parasympathetic immunity', meaning that the individual remains calm under potentially threatening circumstances. They are immune to the effects of the sympathetic system. Similarly, *threctia* stands for 'threat reactivity' and hence is used to label an individual who has a reactive sympathetic system. Cattell (1982) undertook studies on the heritability of this trait and concluded that the genetic factor accounted for approximately 40 per cent of the variance.

- **Factor I, Tender-minded–Tough-minded (premsia–harria).** The popular name describes this trait well. Tough-minded individuals are mature, independent-minded, self-sufficient and realistic. Tender-minded individuals are gentle, imaginative, anxious, impatient, demanding, immature, creative, neurotic and sentimental. The technical terms are derived from the phrases 'protected emotional sensitivity' (*premsia*) and 'hard realism' (*harria*).

- **Factor L, Suspicious–Trusting (protension–alaxia).** Individuals high in factor L are at the suspicious end of the continuum and, as well as being suspicious, are jealous and withdrawn from others. Those scoring low on factor L are trusting, composed and understanding. Cattell (1957) explains that the technical term *protension* is derived from the words 'projection' and 'tension'. *Alaxia* is from the term 'relaxation'.

- **Factor M, Imaginative–Practical (autia–praxernia).** The individual high in factor M is unconventional, intellectual and imaginative. They may often be unconcerned with the practicalities of life. The technical term *autia* comes from the word 'autistic'. *Praxernia* is derived from 'practical and concerned'. Such individuals are conventional, practical, logical, with a tendency to worry, and conscientious.

- **Factor N, Shrewd–Forthright (shrewdness–artlessness).** Here the descriptors fit the labels well. The shrewd individual is astute, worldly, smart and insightful (Cattell and Kline, 1977). The forthright individual is spontaneous, unpretentious and somewhat naïve.

- **Factor O, Apprehensive–Placid (guilt-proneness–assurance).** High levels of guilt-proneness are conceptualised as a purely negative trait by Cattell and Kline (1977). It is seen to be typical of criminals, alcoholics, other drug abusers and individuals suffering from manic depression. Individuals low in factor O are placid, resilient and self-confident (Cattell and Kline, 1977).

Which one of Cattell's 16 personality factors might describe this man: outgoing–reserved, stable–emotional, happy-go-lucky–sober, venturesome–shy, apprehensive–placid, experimenting–conservative?
Source: The Kobal Collection/Discover Films/BBC

If you recall, at the beginning of this section you were told that the factors are presented in their order of importance in explaining individual differences in behaviour. The remaining four Q factors, therefore, are not particularly good predictors of behaviour; however, some of them have been researched extensively.

- **Factor Q$_1$, Experimenting–Conservative (radicalism–conservatism).** It is suggested that conservatives have a general fear of uncertainty and thus opt for the known and the well established. Radicals, on the other hand, prefer the non-conventional and conform less to the rules of society than conservatives do (Cattell, 1957).
- **Factor Q$_2$, Self-sufficiency–Group-tied (self-sufficiency–group adherence).** This factor is self-explanatory. It describes the individual's preference to go it alone or their need to be part of a group.
- **Factor Q$_3$, Controlled–Casual (high self-concept–low integration).** Individuals high in factor Q$_3$ are compulsive individuals. They crave a controlled environment that is highly predictable. Individuals low in factor Q$_3$ are undisciplined, lax individuals who have a preference for disorganisation in their surroundings.
- **Factor Q$_4$, Tense–Relaxed (high ergic tension–low ergic tension).** Again, this factor is largely self-explanatory. Those high in factor Q$_4$ are tense, driven individuals, while at the other end of the continuum, individuals are relaxed and easygoing (Cattell, 1973).

Contribution of Cattell

As we have seen, Cattell was keen to develop a comprehensive, empirically based trait theory of personality. He acknowledged the complexity of factors that all contribute to explain human behaviour, including genetics and environmental factors as well as ability and personality characteristics. Cattell (1965, 1980) was adamant that the test of any good personality theory was its ability to predict behaviour; he even produced an extremely complex mathematical equation that he suggested could do this. He wrote about the effect of learning on personality development and even turned his attention to classifying abnormal behaviour. While he produced vast amounts of empirically based work and attempted to develop a truly comprehensive theory of personality, he is best known in psychology for the 16PF (Cattell *et al.*, 1970).

The Sixteen Personality Factor (16PF) questionnaire has become a standard measure of personality and has been used consistently since its publication. However, the internal consistencies of some of the scales were quite low, and it has been revised and improved (Conn and Rieke, 1994). To do this, the questionnaire has been changed substantially, with over 50 per cent of the items being new or significantly modified.

Although these revisions have produced a better measure psychometrically, it does mean that studies using the 16PF cannot be directly compared with the work that uses the earlier measure. The earlier measure had good predictability. Studies were undertaken that linked participation in church activities to differences in personality characteristics (Cattell, 1973; Cattell and Child, 1975). Other researchers demonstrated that the 16PF was a good predictor of success in different school subjects (Barton *et al.*, 1971).

Given the amount that Cattell published, it is perhaps surprising that this work has not had more impact. Part of the reason for this is that much of his work is difficult to understand. His use of obscure labels for his factors and the complex systems that he postulated are not reader-friendly. He put great emphasis on the objectivity of his approach and did not acknowledge the inherent subjectivity involved in factor analysis, linked to the initial selection of traits the researcher chooses to measure and the explanatory labels they select for their underlying factors. Trait approaches generally will be evaluated at the end of the discussion so are not repeated here. What we need to remember at this point is that Cattell suggested that the underlying structure of personality consists of 16 factors.

Hans Eysenck's trait theory of personality

When Hans Eysenck began to work in the area of personality, he observed that there were two schools within psychology. The first consisted of personality theorists whose main focus was on the development of theories,

Profile

Hans Eysenck

Hans J. Eysenck was born in Berlin in 1916 during the First World War, to parents who were both actors. His parents divorced when he was only 2 years old and, as his mother was a silent film star, he went to live with his grandmother. Aged 6 years old, Eysenck appeared in a film alongside his mother. His father would have liked him to pursue an acting career, but his mother discouraged it. As a young man he was opposed to Hitler and the Nazi party and left Germany in 1934. He had been told that he could not go to university unless he joined the Nazi Party, and he was unwilling to do this. He went first to France before finally settling in England. In London, he studied for his undergraduate degree at the University of London, and it is said that he only specialised in psychology as he did not have the prerequisite subjects to study physics. He obtained his PhD in 1940 and tried to join the Royal Air Force to fight in the Second World War, but he was not accepted, as he was German and considered to be an enemy alien. Instead he went to work at a mental hospital and continued with his research career. After the war, he went to work at the Maudsley Hospital in London, where he soon established the first training course in clinical psychology. Eysenck continued to work at the Maudsley, where he was a prolific researcher. He published around 45 books and hundreds of research papers and edited chapters. He continued working up until his death from cancer in 1997.

with little, if any, emphasis on evaluating these theories with empirical evidence. The second group was made up of experimental psychologists who had little interest in individual differences. Eysenck (1947) stressed the need for an integration of these two approaches. He outlined his goals as being to identify the main dimensions of personality, devise means of measuring them and test them using experimental, quantitative procedures. He felt that these steps would lead to the development of sound personality theory. (See Profile: Hans Eysenck.)

Eysenck (1947; 1952) accepted the conventional wisdom that assumed that children inherit personality characteristics from their parents and other members of their family. At the time he was writing, the main theoretical slant in psychology was that babies were relatively blank slates and that, while development was limited by differences in intelligence or physical skills, it was environmental experiences, particularly parenting styles, that largely influenced the development of personality. This was a legacy from the strong tradition of behaviourism. Over 50 years ago, Eysenck was stressing the importance of genetic inheritance, a view that has gained ground within psychology. We know from physiology that there are differences in physiological functioning between individuals and that these biological differences often translate into different behaviour. Eysenck's early claim that there is a large biological determinant to personality was originally met with scepticism, but, as you will read later (Chapter 8), it has become accepted as supporting evidence has emerged from biological research.

Eysenck began by examining historical approaches to personality, including the work of Hippocrates and Galen that we covered earlier. His aim was to uncover the underlying structure of personality. The historical evidence suggested to him that there are different personality types, and the definition of personality that he adopted incorporates this concept. Eysenck (1970) defines personality as being the way that an individual's character, temperament, intelligence, physique and nervous system are organised. He suggests that this organisation is relatively stable and long-lasting. Traits are the relatively stable, long-lasting characteristics of the individual. In common with other trait researchers, Eysenck utilised factor analysis. He collected measurements of personality traits from large samples of individuals and factor-analysed them. After many years of research, he concluded that there are three basic personality dimensions, which he called types, and that all traits can be subsumed within these three types. Before we examine the three types, we need to become familiar with Eysenck's model of personality.

Eysenck's structure of personality

Beginning with observations of individual behaviour that he calls **specific responses**, Eysenck developed a hierarchical typology. An example of the methodology he used will make this clearer. For example, you would watch someone talking with their friends one evening and carefully observe their specific responses. If this person spends a great deal of their time talking with friends, you can begin to observe some of what Eysenck calls their **habitual responses**. Thus, habitual responses are the ways that individuals typically behave in a situation. From continued observations of the same individual, you might observe that this person seeks out occasions to interact with others and really enjoys social events. The conclusion would be

Figure 7.2 Eysenck's hierarchical model of personality.

Source: Adapted from Eysenck, H. J. (1967). *The Biological Basis of Personality*. Springfield, IL: Charles C. Thomas, p. 36. Reprinted courtesy of Charles C. Thomas Publisher, Ltd.

that this person is very sociable or, in personality terms, they possess the trait of sociability. This structure of personality is shown in Figure 7.2. From the figure, you can see that specific responses that are found together in the individual make up habitual responses, and collections of habitual responses that the individual produces make up the next level of personality traits. Using factor analyses, Eysenck argued that traits such as sociability, liveliness, activity, assertiveness and sensation-seeking are highly correlated. This means that an individual's scores on each of these traits are likely to be very similar. This collection of traits then forms a **supertrait** or **personality type**. Each supertrait represents a continuum along which individuals can be placed, depending on the degree of the attribute they possess.

Eysenck originally suggested that there are two super-traits. The first is a measure of sociability with **extraversion** at one end of the continuum and **introversion** at the other. **Extraverts** are sociable and impulsive people who like excitement and whose orientation is towards external reality. **Introverts** are quiet, introspective individuals who are oriented towards inner reality and who prefer a well-ordered life. The personality traits that make up extraversion are shown in Figure 7.3.

The second personality type or supertrait is **neuroticism**. Individuals can be placed on this dimension according to the degree of neuroticism they possess. Eysenck (1965b) defines neurotics as emotionally unstable individuals. He describes several types of neurotic behaviour. Some individuals high in neuroticism may have unreasonable fears

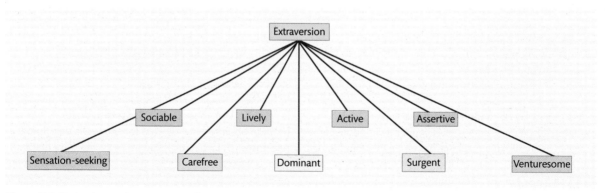

Figure 7.3 Traits that make up extraversion.

Source: Based on Eysenck and Eysenck (1985a).

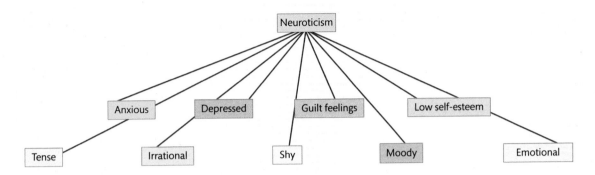

Figure 7.4 Traits that make up neuroticism.
Source: Based on Eysenck and Eysenck (1985a).

(phobias) of certain objects, places, animals or people. Others may have obsessional or impulsive symptoms. The distinguishing feature of neurotic behaviour is that the individual displays an anxiety or fear level that is disproportionate to the realities of the situation. The traits that make up neuroticism are shown in Figure 7.4. Eysenck does separate out one group of neurotics who are free from anxiety and fear, and he labels this group **psychopaths**. These are individuals who behave in an antisocial manner and seem unable to appreciate the consequences of their actions despite any punishment meted out (Eysenck, 1965b). Such individuals are described as acting as if they have no conscience and showing no remorse for things they have done. Psychopathic personalities are likely to be found within the prison population.

The recognition of this group of psychopaths by Eysenck led to the identification of a third personality factor. As the two personality types (extraversion and neuroticism) did not adequately explain all of Eysenck's data, he added a third type, **psychoticism**. It is the severity of the disorder that differentiates psychotics from neurotics. Psychotics display the most severe type of psychopathology, frequently being insensitive to others, hostile, cruel and inhumane with a strong need to ridicule and upset others. The traits that come together to form psychoticism are shown in Figure 7.5.

Eysenck and Eysenck (1985a) stated that, despite having all these undesirable traits, psychotics still tend to be creative individuals. Eysenck quoted several sources of evidence to support his hypothesis. First, he provided historical examples of individuals he felt were geniuses and who had all displayed personality traits typical of psychoticism. He defined geniuses as being extremely creative individuals, and he suggested that many of the traits associated with psychoticism could be perceived as aiding a creative career. Traits such as being egocentric, so you always put yourself first; being tough-minded, so that you pursue your own goals regardless of others or circumstances; being unempathic, so that you are not affected by other people's emotions and problems. Psychological studies of great individuals have demonstrated that they have needed to be self-centred and persistent to overcome the obstacles that they faced in their lives and that they also possess the ability to think in unusual, almost bizarre, ways (Simonton, 1994). Eysenck (1995) cited evidence that psychotic individuals perform well on tests of creativity that require divergent

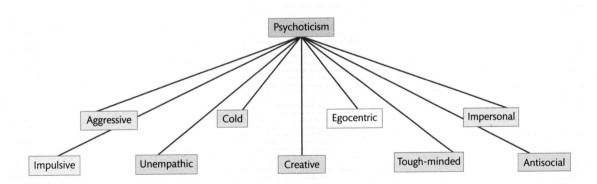

Figure 7.5 Traits that make up psychoticism.
Source: Based on Eysenck and Eysenck (1985a).

thinking. By divergent thinking, he meant the ability to produce novel ideas that are different from those that most people produce. He claimed that psychotics and geniuses have an overinclusive cognitive style that allows them to consider divergent solutions to problems. These views of Eysenck's are not universally accepted. As Simonton (1994) points out, humanistic psychologists such as Maslow and Rogers asserted that creativity is the result of optimum mental health, which implies balanced personalities. Eysenck (1995) did admit that more research is required in this area.

Eysenck (1967) claimed that these three types or super-traits make up the basic structure of personality, and he developed an instrument to measure the three types and their supporting traits. This is called the Eysenck Personality Questionnaire (EPQ; H. Eysenck and S. Eysenck, 1975). He suggested that there is a link between the clinical conditions of neurosis and psychoses and his scales of neuroticism and psychoticism. Individuals who score highly on neuroticism or psychoticism are not necessarily neurotic or psychotic, but he argued that they are at risk of developing these disorders. High scores indicate a predisposition, which may develop under adverse circumstances.

Eysenck's next task was to explain why individuals who differed along the supertrait dimensions should behave differently. His theoretical exposition, while not ignoring environmental influences, was heavily biological. Indeed, Eysenck (1982a) claimed that about two-thirds of the variance in personality development can be attributed to biological factors. Environment plays a part, particularly in influencing how traits are expressed, but Eysenck would argue that biology has imposed limits on how much an individual personality can change. A full account of Eysenck's biological explanation of personality differences is provided later (Chapter 8), with the other biological theories.

Research evidence for Eysenck's types

Many predictions have been made from this theory, and there is a high level of support over a period of 40 years. For example, Eysenck (1965b) reported that extraverts compared with introverts prefer to socialise. They like louder music and brighter colours, and they are more likely to smoke, drink more alcohol and engage in more varied sexual activities. These differences generally continue to be reported in the literature. Amirkham *et al.* (1995) found that extraverts are more likely than introverts to attract and maintain networks of friends and to approach others for help when they are undergoing a crisis. Eysenck and Eysenck (1975) reported that extraverts, because of their need for variety in their lives, have more career changes or job changes. Extraverts are also more likely to change relationship partners more frequently. Campbell and

Hawley (1982) looked at the study habits and the preferred location for studying of students and found that introverts prefer to study in quiet areas, while extraverts study in areas where there are other people and opportunities to socialise. Extraverts also took more study breaks than introverts did, indicating that they have a higher need for change in their activities and environment. Davies and Parasuraman (1992) reported that extraverts tire more easily than introverts on tasks requiring vigilance and are more likely to make errors. While there continues to be a significant amount of research utilising versions of the EPQ (H. Eysenck and S. Eysenck, 1975; 1991), the neuroticism and the extraversion scales have proved to be good reliable measures psychometrically; the psychoticism scale is more problematic, with much lower internal reliability statistics. (You can refer to Chapter 25 for a detailed explanation of reliability statistics). Eysenck (1967) admitted that this scale is less robust and did refine it somewhat (Eysenck, 1992) but, despite this, it remains the weakest measure.

If the three-factor solution represents the basic structure of personality, it should be found cross-culturally. Eysenck and Eysenck undertook a considerable programme of cross-cultural research to explore whether the theory held. His EPQ was carefully translated into many different languages. This research is summarised in Eysenck and Eysenck (1982). He reported that the primary factors were found in at least 24 nations in both males and females. His sample included African, Asian, North American and many European cultures. From this data and from twin studies (described in Chapter 8), Eysenck concluded that the three-factor structure has a genetic basis and represents the basic structure of personality.

Sybil Eysenck produced a child's version of the EPQ, called the Junior Eysenck Personality Questionnaire (S. Eysenck, 1965). It was also translated into many languages, and again the cross-cultural evidence was consistent. Studies of children found the same three factors cross-culturally. This provided additional evidence for the theory. H. Eysenck followed up this research with longitudinal studies to demonstrate that the structure was stable across time (H. Eysenck, 1967, 1982a, 1990b, 1993; S. Eysenck *et al.*, 1993; 1994). S. Eysenck concluded that all this research provided confirmatory evidence that there is a genetic basis for the primary personality types. They are all found cross-culturally, despite social pressures within different cultures to develop in specific ways. The same structures are found in children as in adults. Reviews of studies of identical and fraternal twins, raised together and raised apart, found the same structures and personality similarities between individual biological relatives and lend considerable support for a significant genetic component to personality. As mentioned previously, details of genetic studies of personality are included later (Chapter 8).

Eysenck (1990b) does still see a role for the environment in the development of personality. He suggested that, while individuals' genes provide a strong tendency to become a certain type of person, some modification is possible. He suggested that the way that children are socialised was crucial here. However, he did not provide a detailed developmental theory to explain how the environment might intervene in development or to specify the environment that would promote healthy development.

Psychopathology and Eysenck's therapeutic approach

Eysenck was a behaviourist, and therefore he placed a lot of emphasis on how learned behaviour was acquired. Thus, healthy and abnormal behaviour is the result of the way that individuals respond to the stimuli in their environment. Some individuals are more susceptible to developing psychopathology because of their inherited vulnerabilities. For example, Eysenck suggested that individuals who score highly on the personality trait neurosis are more likely to develop clinical neuroses than are those with low scores.

Eysenck's approach to treatment involved behaviour therapy. You may recall that we covered this previously (Chapter 4). He was extremely hostile to all other therapies but particularly targeted psychoanalytic approaches. Indeed, Eysenck (1965a) claimed that the only effective therapy was behaviour therapy. As mentioned in the Profile box, Eysenck developed clinical psychology training in the United Kingdom and was an active clinician as well as a personality researcher for much of his life.

Eysenck's contribution to trait theorising

Eysenck's theorising is fairly comprehensive, although not all aspects of it are equally well developed. This is particularly true of the developmental aspects and the biological basis, as you will see later (Chapter 8). He also focuses heavily on genetic factors and pays much less attention to the social context within which much behaviour occurs and that may affect personality and behaviour in particular situations. He would argue that personality determines to some degree the situations that individuals choose to be in, but that is debatable to some extent. In terms of heuristic value, Eysenck has been very influential. His critique of all therapies, apart from behaviour therapy, stimulated therapists to evaluate their work and led to a large increase in evaluative research on therapies. His work also has significant applied value. He demonstrated a rigorous approach to personality theorising. He moved beyond many personality trait researchers in that he tried to provide not merely a description of personality structure but also an explanation of what caused differences in personality, with his genetic studies and his biological theory. He also provided a fairly robust measure of personality. His work has stimulated an enormous amount of research. Eysenck founded the journal *Personality and Individual Differences*, and its continued growth and development attests to his influence over many years.

In one other aspect, his theory can perhaps be criticised for being too parsimonious, having only three factors. Do three factors really represent the basic structure of personality? This question of the number of factors necessary to describe personality structure is what we shall discuss next. There has been considerable debate in the psychological literature about the number of factors required for an adequate description of personality and, as we shall see, before his death Eysenck contributed to this discussion (Eysenck, 1991).

The five-factor model

Psychologists increasingly agree that five supertraits may adequately describe the structure of personality. The evidence to support this contention has come from several sources. There is still some debate, as we shall see, about how to label these factors; but this is perhaps unsurprising given that assigning labels is the most subjective aspect of factor analysis. Researchers are likely to have different opinions about which words best describe the constituent traits that make up a supertrait. We shall begin by examining the evidence for five factors, and then we will look at where this leaves Eysenck's three-factor model and Cattell's 16-factor model. Finally, we will evaluate the trait approach to personality.

Evidential sources for the five-factor model

There are three evidential sources for the five-factor model:

- the lexical approach;
- factor analysis evidence for the five-factor model;
- other evidence in support of the five-factor model of personality.

The lexical approach

You will recall that earlier in this discussion, we discussed the lexical hypothesis. This is the hypothesis that it is the differences in personality that are important for social interaction, and human societies have labelled these differences as single terms. Several detailed accounts of the lexical approach and its history are available if you want to explore this theory further (De Raad, 2000; Saucier and Goldberg, 2001).

You will recall that Cattell's 16PF came from the factor analysis of the list of 4,500 trait names identified by Allport and Odbert (1936). Cattell produced a 16-factor solution. Fiske (1949) reanalysed the same data but could not reproduce the 16 factors; he published instead a five-factor solution. This work was ignored for a long time. Tupes and Christal (1961/1992) reported five factors from analyses of trait words in eight different samples. Norman (1963) revisited the earlier research and reproduced the same five-factor structure using personality ratings of individuals given by their peers. Digman and Takemoto-Chock (1981) carried out further analyses and confirmed Norman's five-factor solution. Goldberg (1981) reviewed all the research and made a convincing argument for the Big Five. Since then, Goldberg and his team have carried out an extensive research programme investigating personality traits, and Goldberg (1990) concluded that in the English language trait descriptors are versions of five major features of personality: love, work, affect, power and intellect. Since then, the research has spread to other languages. Saucier and Ostendorf (1999) used a set of 500 personality traits and found a five-factor structure in the German language, for example.

Saucier and Goldberg (2001) have described the lexical approach to investigating whether the five-factor structure is universally applicable as an **emic approach** to research. (See Stop and think: Lexical approaches produce descriptive models of personality traits, below.) Basically, what the researchers do is to use the personality terms that are found in the native language of the country. They contrast this with what they call the **etic approach**, which uses personality questionnaires translated from another language that in practice tends to be English. Saucier and Goldberg (2001) report that etic approaches tend to replicate the five-factor structure while there is more variability reported in studies using emic approaches. Perugini and Di-Blas (2002) discuss this issue further in relation to emic and etic data that they collected on Italian samples. They point out that in the etic approach, the questionnaires being translated are based on five-factor structures found in the original language. Goldberg and his research team make a case for the necessity of further study of cultural differences in personality trait use that are being found using emic approaches as a core part of the search for the universal structure of personality. Goldberg's research team has made available copyrighted free adjective scales that can be used to measure the five factors and personality scales for measuring them. These can be accessed from his website and the address is included at the end of the discussion.

Factor analysis evidence for the five-factor model of personality

This is the second source of evidence for the existence of a structure of five factors. Costa and McCrae (1985; 1989; 1992; 1997) are arguably the most influential researchers in this area, and their factor solution has come to be called the Big Five model. This approach requires large samples of participants to complete at least two personality questionnaires. The resultant data set is then factor-analysed to uncover clusters of traits. The consistent finding is the emergence of five factors or dimensions of personality.

It is important to stress that it is the analysis of data that has produced the factors, not exploration of a theory about the number of factors necessary in a model. This is not the usual approach in psychology. Usually researchers begin with a theoretically based hypothesis about some aspect of behaviour. They then collect their data, and their results either support or refute their original theory-driven hypothesis. In contrast, with the five-factor research, the hypothesis that five factors represent the basic structure of personality has come from the data that was collected. In other words, the Big Five model is a data-derived hypothesis as opposed to a theoretically based one.

These are the factors described by the American personality researchers Costa and McCrae (1992), who measured personality with their well-known Neuroticism, Extraversion, Openness Personality Inventory (NEO-PI-R). The Big Five factors are **Openness, Conscientiousness, Extraversion, Agreeableness** and

---

Stop and think

Lexical approaches produce descriptive models of personality traits

You may recall from our early discussion that lexical approaches produce descriptive models of personality traits, and you need to bear this fact in mind. At this stage in their development, the lexical approaches do not explain why this structure is found, other than to refer to the lexical hypothesis. There are no explanatory models offered. However, they are a valuable source of confirmatory evidence for the existence of the five-factor model. If Saucier and Goldberg's suggestion to explore the differences uncovered by emic studies is followed up, this then might lead to explanatory models linking differences to cultural practices.

Neuroticism. You can use the acronym **OCEAN** to help you remember what the factors are called. More detailed descriptions of each factor are now provided. Each factor represents a continuum along which individuals can be placed according to their scores.

- **Openness** – This factor refers to the individual having an openness to new experiences. It includes the characteristics of showing intellectual curiosity, divergent thinking and a willingness to consider new ideas and an active imagination. Individuals scoring highly on openness are unconventional and independent thinkers. Individuals with low scores are more conventional and prefer the familiar to the new.
- **Conscientiousness** – This factor describes our degree of self-discipline and control. Individuals with high scores on this factor are determined, organised and plan for events in their lives. Individuals with low scores tend to be careless, easily distracted from their goals or the tasks that they are undertaking and undependable. If you look closely at the trait descriptors included in conscientiousness, you will see that they are all attributes likely to become apparent in work situations. For this reason, they are sometimes referred to as the **will to achieve** or **work dimension**.
- **Extraversion** – This factor is a measure of the individual's sociability. It is the same factor as described by Eysenck earlier in this discussion and by the psychoanalyst Jung (Chapter 3). Individuals who score highly on extraversion are very sociable, energetic, optimistic, friendly and assertive. Individuals with high scores are labelled extraverts. As with the Eysenck and Jung descriptions, individuals with low scores are labelled introverts. Introverts are described as being reserved and independent rather than followers socially and even-paced rather than sluggish in terms of their pace of work.
- **Agreeableness** – This factor relates very much to characteristics of the individual that are relevent for social interaction. Individuals with high scores are trusting, helpful, soft-hearted and sympathetic. Those with low scores are suspicious, antagonistic, unhelpful, sceptical and uncooperative.

- **Neuroticism** – This factor measures an individual's emotional stability and personal adjustment. Costa and McCrae (1992) suggest that, although a range of emotions exists, individuals who score highly on one also rate highly on others. In psychological terms, the various emotional states are highly correlated. Thus, the individual who scores highly on neuroticism experiences wide swings in their mood and they are volatile in their emotions. Individuals with low scores on the neuroticism factor are calm, well adjusted and not prone to extreme maladaptive emotional states. (Indeed, in some five-factor models of personality, this dimension is referred to as emotional stability.)

These are the five main dimensions popularly known as the Big Five. Within each of the main dimensions there are more specific personality attributes that cluster together, and all contribute to the category score. These subordinate traits are sometimes called facets (Costa and McCrae, 1992). The Big Five model is a hierarchical model similar in concept to Eysenck's model. Each of the Big Five factors consists of six facets or subordinate traits. The facets included in the NEO-PI-R (Costa and McCrae, 1992) are shown in Table 7.3. Thus, an individual's scores on the traits of fantasy, aesthetics, feelings, actions, ideas and values combine to produce their scores on the openness factor. The NEO-PI-R then allows measurement at a general factor level or on more specific factors. Obviously, the more specific the measure, the greater the likelihood of using it to actually predict behaviour.

Other evidence in support of the Big Five

There is too much research supporting the Big Five for us to review it all here. Instead, we will cite some examples from the main areas. In terms of how well this model fits with other measures of personality, the evidence is largely positive. McCrae and Costa (1989) factor-analysed scores on the Myers–Briggs Type Inventory and found that it supports a five-factor structure. Boyle (1989) reported that the five-factor model is also broadly compatible with

Table 7.3 The constituent facets of the Big Five factors

Openness	Conscientiousness	Extraversion	Agreeableness	Neuroticism
Fantasy	Competence	Warmth	Trust	Anxiety
Aesthetics	Order	Gregariousness	Straightforwardness	Angry hostility
Feelings	Dutifulness	Assertiveness	Altruism	Depressions
Actions	Achievement-striving	Activity	Compliance	Self-consciousness
Ideas	Self-discipline	Excitement-seeking	Modesty	Impulsiveness
Values	Deliberation	Positive emotions	Tender-mindedness	Vulnerability

Source: Based on Costa and McCrae (1985).

Cattell's fourteen-factor measure and Eysenck's three-factor measure. The latest measure of the 16PFI allows scoring on the Big Five (Conn and Rieke, 1994). Goldberg (1993) compared the five-factor model with Eysenck's three-factor model and concluded that two of the factors – extraversion and neuroticism – are very similar, and that psychoticism can be subsumed under agreeableness and conscientiousness.

The NEO-PI-R has also been translated into several other languages, and the same factor structure has been replicated (McCrae and Costa, 1997; McCrae et al., 1998; 2000). If you recall, this evidence is not uncontentious, based as it is on the etic approach to personality research that we discussed earlier. These researchers (McCrae and Costa, 1997; McCrae et al., 1998; 2000) have also demonstrated that the observed personality differences are stable over time and have a genetic basis. To summarise, Costa and McCrae (1992) claim that the five factors represent the universal structure of personality based on all the evidence we have discussed. The factors are found in different languages, ages of people and races.

Evaluation of the Big Five and trait approaches

Can we conclude then that the Big Five represent the structure of personality? Unfortunately, it is premature to say that there is total consensus on the model. Increasingly, there is debate about a six-factor model and the existence of higher order factors. We have included this material later (Chapter 10) as these are still contentious issues. Among researchers who agree that there are five factors, there is still some level of disagreement about the exact nature of each of the five factors. Indeed, Saucier and Goldberg (1998) and Saucier (1995) argue that research should look for solutions beyond the current five-factor models. This is the scientific approach – to search for contradictory evidence instead of purely focusing on searching for confirmation, as the present research does.

There is some debate about how the factors should be labelled. Labelling factors depends on the researcher's judgement about the best descriptor for the cluster of correlated traits. For example, the agreeableness factor has also been labelled conformity (Fiske, 1949) and likeability (Norman, 1963). The same debate applies for all the other factors.

Peabody and Goldberg (1989) have also demonstrated that the measures that are included in a questionnaire crucially affect the final factors produced. If a questionnaire does not have many items that measure openness, for example, then the description of openness that is produced will be narrower. There is still some argument

about the number of traits, with studies reporting different numbers between Eysenck's three and seven (Ashton and Lee, 2001, 2007; Briggs, 1989; Church and Burke, 1994; Zuckerman et al., 1993). McCrae and Costa (1995) suggest that the number depends on the nature of the trait measures that are included. They point out that five-factor models tend not to include evaluative traits like moral/immoral. If evaluative traits are included, Almagor et al., (1995) have suggested that a seven-factor solution emerges.

There has been some debate about what exactly some of the factors mean (Digman 1990). Are they perhaps linguistic categories that do not actually represent the underlying structure of personality? Is it that the five factors represent our ability to describe personality traits in language and are nothing to do with underlying structures? There is no easy answer to this question, although the accumulating weight of research evidence would seem to negate it. Is it perhaps that our cognitive abilities only allow for a five-factor structure but the reality is more complex and subtle?

Briggs (1989) has criticised the model for being atheoretical. As we have discussed earlier, the model is data-driven and was not derived from a theoretical base. There are currently some attempts to address this with genetic studies and the search for a physiological basis for the observed differences, as you will see later (Chapter 8). This criticism applies more generally to the trait approach, although theorists such as Eysenck saw theory building as being crucial within his approach.

One of the more general criticisms of trait approaches to personality is related to how the various measures are interpreted and used. For example, Mischel (1968; 1983a; 1990) has pointed out that many of these measures are largely descriptive and do not predict behaviour particularly well. Despite this claim, many of these measures are widely used to make important decisions about individuals' lives, and in workplace situations are often blindly interpreted by people who are not psychologists. Mischel (1968) demonstrates that, on average, personality trait measures statistically account for only around 10 per cent of the variance observed in behaviour. In other words, 90 per cent of the variance in behaviour is down to something other than the effect of personality. However, Kraus (1995) has shown that the variance figure is not insignificant and is similar to that found in studies measuring the relationship between attitudes and behaviour. Mischel's criticism of the overreliance on trait measures to assess individuals has had beneficial effects in work settings. The practice currently is to use multiple measures of personality assessment in work settings. Psychometric assessments, individual and group tasks and interviews are frequently used together as an assessment package, and this prevents overreliance on the psychometric tool.

Final comments

In summary, we have described the nomothetic approach to personality research. You should now appreciate the long history of attempts to describe and explain differences in personality. You should understand what is meant by the lexical hypothesis and be familiar with the approach to data analysis employed by trait theorists. You should also be aware of the contributions of Allport, Cattell and Eysenck to understanding personality, as well as the approaches that have resulted in the identification of the Big Five personality traits.

Summary

- Two assumptions underlie trait theory. The first is that personality characteristics are relatively stable over time. The second is that traits show stability across situations.
- Trait theorists are aiming to find the basic structure of personality and to produce reliable ways of measuring personality differences.
- William Sheldon outlined a description of personality, called somatotypes, based on physique and temperament. He described three basic types of physique – endomorphy, mesomorphy and ectomorphy – and demonstrated that each body type was associated with a particular temperament.
- The lexical hypothesis was first put forth by Sir Francis Galton. It suggests that it is the important individual differences between people that come to be encoded as single word terms (trait descriptors). The lexical hypothesis led to attempts to categorise the important personality traits. With the advent of factor analysis, these trait lists were analysed to try to uncover the underlying structure.
- Gordon Allport identified 18,000 words, of which 4,500 described personality traits.
- Allport conceptualised human nature as normally being rational, creative, active and self-reliant. He used the idiographic approach to discover personal dispositions. He described three types of personality traits: cardinal, central and secondary.
- Allport emphasised the importance of the concept of self to any theory of personality. He hypothesised that children were not born with a concept of self but that it gradually developed, and it was a lifelong process. Allport was a pioneer in trait theory, and one of his important contributions was to alert psychologists to the limitations of trait approaches.
- Cattell's work marks the beginning of the search for the structure of personality using factor analysis. He made a distinction between traits that are genetically determined and those that are the result of environmental experiences. He defined three different types of traits: ability, temperament and dynamic. He subdivided dynamic traits into three types: attributes, sentiments and ergs. All these types of dynamic traits are organised in complex and interrelated ways to produce a dynamic lattice. He makes a further distinction between common traits and unique traits. The latter account for the uniqueness of human beings.
- Cattell made an important distinction between surface traits and source traits. Surface traits are collections of trait descriptors that cluster together in many individuals and situations. Using factor analysis, he uncovered underlying traits that he called source traits. These are responsible for the observed variance in the surface traits.
- Cattell used a variety of approaches to uncover the source traits of personality. He finally produced 16 factors and claimed that they represent the basic structure of personality. He developed the 16PF as a measurement tool.
- Eysenck's goals were to identify the main dimensions of personality, devise means of measuring them and test them using experimental, quantitative procedures. He defined personality as being the way that an individual's character, temperament, intelligence, physique and nervous system are organised. Traits are the relatively stable, long-lasting characteristics of the individual.
- Eysenck developed a hierarchical model of personality types. At the bottom level are specific behavioural responses called habitual responses. These come together to make up personality traits. Clusters of traits come together to make up personality types. Using factor analysis, Eysenck identified three types or supertraits that he hypothesised made up the basic structure of personality. He developed the Eysenck Personality Questionnaire (EPQ) to measure these three types and their underlying traits.
- Eysenck claimed that about two-thirds of the variance in personality development can be attributed to biological factors. Environment influences how traits are expressed, but Eysenck argues that biology has imposed limits on how much an individual personality can change.
- There is good support for neuroticism and extraversion, including cross-cultural, developmental and longitudinal stability data. Psychoticism is the least reliable dimension.

- Eysenck provided not merely a description of personality structure but also an explanation of what causes differences in personality, with his genetic studies and his biological theory. His work has stimulated an enormous amount of research.
- There is a growing consensus that five supertraits make up the basic structure of personality. While there are arguments about the names accorded to these factors, those chosen by Costa and McCrae are the most popular. The Big Five factors are Openness, Conscientiousness, Extraversion, Agreeableness and Neuroticism (OCEAN).
- There are several sources of evidence underpinning the Big Five structure of personality. The first of these uses the lexical approach to uncover the struc-

tures. The second approach uses the factor analysis of personality questionnaires.
- The Big Five model is hierarchical, similar in concept to Eysenck's model. Each of the Big Five factors consists of six facets or subordinate traits. Costa and Macrae's NEO-PI-R measures both the subordinate traits and the supertraits.
- There is increasing agreement that there are five factors, but there is still some level of disagreement about the exact nature of each of the five factors. Debate continues about how the factors should be labelled.
- The lack of an underpinning theory is problematic for some psychologists. This trait approach is data-driven, not theoretically driven, although theoretical support is now developing.

Connecting up

- The personality theories covered in this chapter represent some of the most commonly used theories in the literature regarding main personality and individual differences. We go on to discuss the biological aspects of Eysenck's personality in the next chapter (Chapter 8), alongside other biological models of personality. In Chapter 10 we also explore an additional model of personality based on the lexical hypothesis, the

HEXACO model of personality, which is an extension of the five-factor model of personality.
- You may also want to return to Chapter 3 to look at the origins of extraversion in Jung's theory of personality.
- Throughout the rest of the book, when we consider personality variables in a number of chapters, we generally refer to the three- and five-factor models of personality.

Critical thinking

Discussion questions

- Can you identify any traits that Allport would classify as unique?
- How useful are Allport's categorisations of types of traits? Can you identify examples of each type of trait?
- Compare and contrast Cattell's concept of ergs to Freud's categories of instincts.
- Does Eysenck make a convincing case for his three-factor structure of personality?
- Have psychologists finally uncovered the basic structure of personality?
- Can you identify any problems with the current approaches to determining the structure of personality?
- 'The five-factor model of personality is now dominant in the research literature.' Evaluate the validity of this statement.

Essay questions

- Three, five or sixteen? Critically examine how many personality factors there are.
- Evaluate Eysenck's claim that his three factors are universal.
- Critically evaluate the evidence for the five-factor structure of personality.
- Discuss the contribution of Gordon Allport to the trait approach of personality.
- Discuss the contribution of Raymond Cattell to the trait approach.
- Compare and contrast two of the following three theories of personality:
  - three-factor
  - five-factor
  - sixteen-factor.
- Evaluate the five-factor model of personality and discuss its relationship to Cattell's theory of personality.

Going further

Books

- Allport, G. W. (1961) *Pattern and growth in personality*. New York: Holt, Rinehart & Winston. This is one of Allport's later texts, and it is written in an accessible style. It gives a comprehensive account of his position.
- Cattell, R. B. and Kline, P. (1977). *The scientific analysis of personality and motivation*. New York: Academic Press. This book provides a fairly detailed account of Cattell's theory, methodology and research.
- Costa, P. T. Jr and McCrae, R. R. (2003). *Personality in adulthood, a five-factor theory*. London: Guilford Press.
- Eysenck, H. J. (1970). *The structure of human personality* (3rd edn). London: Methuen. This text goes into more detail about Eysenck's model and is presented in an accessible format.
- Eysenck, H. J. and Eysenck, M. W. (1985). *Personality and individual differences: A natural science approach*. New York: Plenum Press. This book provides an excellent overview of Eysenck's work.
- De Raad, B. (2000). *The Big Five personality factors: The psycholexical approach to personality*. Seattle, WA: Hogrefe and Huber. This book provides an excellent summary of lexical approaches.
- Gregory, R. J. (2011). *Psychological testing: History, principles, and applications* (6th edn). New York: Pearson. This provides a very good overview of the problems.
- McCrae, R. R. (2009). The Five-Factor model of personality traits: Consensus and controversy. In: P. Corr and G. Matthews (eds) *The Cambridge University Press handbook of personality*. Cambridge: Cambridge University Press. This article provides a useful summary of the debate around the Big Five, and the book as a whole is a useful additional resource.
- Saucier, G., Hampson, S. E. and Goldberg, L. R. (2000). Cross-language studies of lexical personality factors. In: S. E. Hampson (ed.) *Advances in personality psychology*. London: The Psychology Press. This reading is an excellent summary of the lexical approach applied cross-culturally.

Journals

- Armon, G., Shirom, A. and Melamed, S. (2012). The Big Five personality factors as predictors of changes across time in burnout and its facets. *Journal of Personality, 20*(2), 403–427. This paper provides a good example of current research using the Big Five. *Journal of Personality* is published by Blackwell Publishing and is available online via PsycARTICLES.

- Ashton, M. C., Lee, K., Goldberg, L. R. and de Vries, R. E. (2009). Higher order factors of personality: Do they exist? *Personality and Social Psychology Review, 13, (2),* 79–91.
- McCrae, R. R., Costa, P. T., Ostendorf, F. *et al.* (2000). Nature over nurture: Temperament, personality, and life span development. *Journal of Personality and Social Psychology, 78,* 173–186. This paper begins to outline a theoretical underpinning for the Big Five. *Journal of Personality and Social Psychology* is published by the American Psychological Association and is available online via PsycARTICLES.
- Saucier, G. and Goldberg, L. R. (1998). What is beyond the Big Five? *Journal of Personality, 66,* 495–524. This paper includes a critique of much of the current research effort and some timely warnings about future directions. *Journal of Personality* is published by Blackwell Publishing and is available online with Blackwell Synergy, Swets Wise and Ingenta.

You will regularly find research articles relating to the personality theories described in this chapter in the following journals:

- *European Journal of Personality*. Published by Wiley. Available online via Wiley InterScience.
- *Journal of Personality*. Published by Blackwell Publishing. Available online via Blackwell Synergy, SwetsWise and Ingenta.
- *Personality Assessment*. Published by the Society for Personality Assessment. Available online via Business Source Premier.
- *Journal of Research in Personality*. Published by Academic Press. Available online via IngentaJournals.
- *Personality and Social Psychology Bulletin*. Published by Sage Publications for the Society for Personality and Social Psychology. Available online via SwetsWise, Sage Online, Ingenta and Expanded Academic ASAP.
- *Personality and Social Psychology Review*. Published by the Society for Personality and Social Psychology, Inc. Available online via Business Source Premier.
- *Personality and Individual Differences*. Published by Pergamon Press. Available online via Science Direct.

Web links

- **Goldberg's International Personality Item Pool (IPIP).** A scientific computer-supported system for the development of advanced measures of personality and other individual differences. The IPIP website is intended to provide rapid access to measures of individual differences, all in the public domain, to be developed conjointly among scientists worldwide (**http://ipip.ori .org/ipip/**).

- A good website outlining many of the personality theories covered in this discussion is at **www.personalityresearch .org**.

Film and literature

- *Abigail's Party* (1970, BBC Play for Today). If you want to see a film example of the contrast between an extraverted individual and an introverted individual, then the BBC Television film of the play *Abigail's Party* is a great example. The contrasts between the two main female characters typify these two personality traits. This is perhaps a little dated, but well worth viewing if you can get a copy or the opportunity to see the play. Other films that may be easier to get hold of that depict stories around introverted individuals include *Amélie* (2001, directed by Jean-Pierre Jeunet) and *Edward Scissorhands* (1990, directed by Tim Burton).

- *Cruel Intentions* (1999, directed by Roger Kumble), *Dangerous Liaisons* (1988, directed by Stephen Frears) and *Collateral* (2004, directed by Michael Mann). In this discussion we outlined the concept of psychoticism, a personality that emphasises hostile, cruel and inhumane traits with a strong need to ridicule and upset others. All these films have lead characters who clearly show these traits.

Explore the website accompanying this text at **www.pearsoned.co.uk/maltby** for further resources to help you with your studies. These include multiple-choice questions, essay questions, web links and ideas for advanced reading.

CHAPTER 8
Biological Basis
of Personality I:
Genetic Heritability of
Personality and Biological
and Physiological Models
of Personality

Key themes

- Behavioural genetics
- Heritability estimates
- Genetic and environmental effects on personality
- Neuropsychology and psychophysiology
- Eysenck, Gray and Cloninger's models of personality

Learning outcomes

After studying this discussion you should:

- Understand how psychologists have applied the ideas that surround behavioural genetics and heritability estimates to understand influences on personality
- Be aware of theoretical and research evidence surrounding genetic and environmental influences on personality that can be used to assess the value of heritability estimates
- Know how Eysenck, Gray and Cloninger have used neuropsychology and psychophysiology to develop biological models of personality
- Be familiar with evidence that assesses the strengths and weaknesses of biological models of personality

Introduction

Across certain cultures, superstition and amazement surround twins; Native American tribes and aboriginals in Japan and Australia used to kill twins, as many people used to fear them. Sometimes the mother was also killed as it was believed she must have had sex with two men for two children to be conceived. Although in the modern day less mysticism surrounds twins, findings such as that of Dr Tom Bouchard still attract interest. He found that two identical twins, who had been separated at birth, when reunited after 34 years, wore jewellery in the same way, had named their sons in a similar way, and had even left the same days blank during the year in their diaries.

We are not going to ponder on explanations of similarities between twins separated at birth and then reunited. (How many reunited twins do we hear about who don't share anything in common?) Instead, in this discussion we will look at an area of psychological research called behavioural genetics that uses the findings of twins, among other things, to explore how genes and the environment are thought to influence personality. We are then going to expand this view to look at psychophysiological and neurological explanations of personality, and in particular we are going to outline three theories of personality that suggest there are biological roots to personality.

Source: Science Photo Library/Pasieka

Behavioural genetics

The world of behavioural genetics is an exciting one. In the first section we are going to outline the main findings regarding how much our genes influence our personality, but we will also introduce you to a much wider debate. You will see that, over time, the way in which research has considered how genes influence our personality has gone from a very simple model that compared genes with the environments, to a much more comprehensive model that incorporates a number of genetic and environmental aspects thought to be working together.

Behavioural genetics: basic ideas

In very basic terms, behavioural genetics looks at the relationships between genes, environment and behaviour. Before we start exploring the theory and research that surrounds behavioural genetics, there are two important terms you need to know: genotype and phenotype.

The **genotype** is the internal genetic code or blueprint for constructing and maintaining a living individual. Your genotype is made up of a number of genes. Genes are made up of DNA, and DNA contains the instructions for building proteins in the body. Proteins control the structure and function of all the cells that make up your body. The genotype is a genetic code that is biologically inherited and is found within all the cells, tissues and organs of

the individual because it has helped design and build all of these structures. This genetic code also underlies all the biological functions, such as your heart rate and your metabolism. What is important to behavioural genetics is that the genotype influences the phenotype.

The **phenotype** is the outward manifestation of the individual: that is, the sum of all the atoms, molecules, cells, tissues and organs. The most obvious example of a phenotype is our physical appearance. The information in our genotype determines what we look like; for example, many children share the physical characteristics of their parents. What is really important to this discussion is that the phenotype can be our personality. In the next section we are going to show you how behavioural geneticists have explored and considered how our genotype – more commonly known as genes – influences our personality.

How the influence of genes is assessed in behavioural genetics

Behavioural geneticists such as Robert Plomin (see Profile: Robert Plomin) have written extensively about behavioural genetics (Plomin, 2004; Plomin *et al.* 2000). Behavioural genetics begins with the fact that genes are biologically transmitted from biological parents to the child. Children inherit 50 per cent of their father's genes and 50 per cent of their mother's genes. We can use this information as a starting point to explore how genes influence personality.

Profile

Robert Plomin

Robert Plomin is one of the leading researchers in the world of behavioural genetics, and he is one of the few researchers to have studied genetic influences on human behaviour both in the United States and in Europe. Robert Plomin is a Medical Research Council Professor in Behavioural Genetics, and Deputy Director of Social, Genetic, and Developmental Psychiatry at the Institute of Psychiatry, King's College London. In 1974, he received his psychology doctorate from the University of Texas, Austin, and then worked at the Institute for Behavioral Genetics at the University of Colorado. In 1994, he started work at Pennsylvania State University studying elderly twins. Plomin's current interest is examining the power of molecular genetics to identify genes for psychological traits. He has been president of the Behavior Genetics Association. He has over 550 publications, including *Behavioral Genetics in the Postgenomic Era* (Washington, DC: APA Books, 2003) and *Behavioral Genetics* (4th edn, New York: Worth Publishers, 2001). Plomin is currently conducting the Twins Early Development Study of all twins born in England during the period 1994 to 1996, focusing on developmental delays in early childhood and their association with behavioural problems.

The assessment of the extent to which any phenotype (physical attractiveness, personality and behaviours) is passed on from parents to children, from the results of their genes, is termed its genetic heritability. The genetic heritability of any phenotype is assessed according to variability (i.e. how much they differ) between the parents and the child. This variability is often assessed within the *proportion of shared variance* of that behaviour between the parent and child. Proportion of shared variance is presented as a percentage (i.e. out of 100 per cent). When a parent and child are very similar in a particular characteristic, there is thought to be a low variability between parent and child, and the proportion of shared variance of that behaviour is high (nearer 100 per cent). In other words, the parent and child are not very different in this characteristic. Conversely, when a parent and child are very different in a particular characteristic, there is thought to be a high variability between parent and child, and the proportion of shared variance of that behaviour is zero (0 per cent).

The heritability of a human physical characteristic, such as having a nose, is entirely genetic. It is not in any way influenced by factors such as the environment; in fact, the environment is seen as having zero variability, or a proportion of shared variance of 100 per cent. However, with some aspects of human behaviour (including personality) in which the environment is thought to have an influence there are greater amounts of heritable variability and lower shared variance. For example, choosing which football team to support would be heavily determined by environmental factors such as where you are born, your parents' football team, your friends and the first football team you see. Choosing a favourite football team has high variability between parent and child, but the proportion of shared variance of football team caused by genetic heritability would be much lower (i.e. approaching 0 per cent).

In behavioural genetics, researchers are primarily interested in: (1) *estimating* the extent of genetic heritability of behaviour across a population; and (2) stating the genetic heritability of that behaviour in terms of shared variance. This estimate of genetic heritability is known as h^2. The quantity h^2 is the *estimate* of the *average* proportion of variance for any behaviour thought to be accounted for by genetic factors across a population.

You may have noticed that we emphasised *estimating*, *estimate* (estimate meaning 'to calculate approximately') and *average* there. This is because, for a long time in psychology, for any phenotype (in our case, personality) the estimates of the strength of genetics factors was done and interpreted within a process called the *additive assumption*. This additive assumption suggests that there are only two dimensions that determine heritability of any phenotype (e.g. personality): (1) the genetic part (which we've just outlined); and (2) the environment. Consequently, overall, heritability of any phenotype is estimated in terms of the relative average strength of both dimensions. Therefore, the influence of genetic (G) and environmental (E) components in this theory will always add together to account for 100 per cent of the variance of any behaviour. On the basis of this assumption, the heritability coefficient (h^2) can be subtracted from 100 per cent to calculate the environmental contribution to any phenotype. If researchers computed that genetics accounted for an estimated average of 25 per cent of the variance for a particular phenotype (e.g. aggressiveness), they would assume that environmental factors account for an estimated average of 75 per cent of the variance in that particular phenotype. However, it is important to note that the additive assumption is now considered a starting point for calculating heritability of personality and for estimating the amount of genes that people are expected to share (e.g. brother and sisters are expected to share 50 per cent). We will see later in this discussion that this view of assessing heritability has advanced a lot. The idea of determining the relative strength of genetics and environmental factors by simply adding together genetic and environmental factors is more complicated than once thought, and we will see that psychologists really now emphasise the words 'estimate' and 'average' when referring to heritability.

Methods for assessing genetic heritability of personality

So, how might we assess genetic influences on personality? Well, within behavioural genetics of personality, the relationship between genes and personality has traditionally been made by concentrating on the similarities and differences between populations of individuals to assess the relative influence of their shared genes in personality.

Plomin (2004) identifies three main types of studies that use this technique: **family studies**, **twin studies** and **adoption studies**.

As children share 50 per cent of their genes with each of their parents and with their brothers and sisters, it is of interest to behavioural genetics researchers to examine possible associations between parental and child behaviours within a family. This leads to the first type of study, **family studies**. However, family studies on their own potentially tell us very little, because all children share an estimated average of 50 per cent of their genes with each of their parents and their brothers and sisters. As well as this, using observation, interview or questionnaire measures also presents a problem because similarities between personalities might be because of environmental influence (e.g. an extraverted son might be like his extraverted father because he copies his father's behaviour). These are real concerns until we consider the occasions when families don't typically share genes in this way. There are two main examples: twin studies and adoption studies.

Twin studies provide an interesting area of research, as there is a possibility of comparing different types of genetic makeup to compare genetic influences. Different types of twins are thought to share a different proportion of genes with each other. The term 'twin' refers to two individuals who have shared the same uterus (the uterus or womb is the major female reproductive organ). Identical (or monozygotic) twins happen when a single egg is fertilised to form one zygote (they are monozygotic), but then the zygote divides into two separate embryos. The two embryos develop into fetuses sharing the same womb. Identical twins are always of the same sex and have the same arrangement of genes and chromosomes (which contain the heritability information necessary for cell life). These twins share 100 per cent of genes with each other. Fraternal (or non-identical or dizygotic) twins usually occur when two

fertilised eggs are implanted in the uterine wall at the same time. The two eggs form two zygotes (hence the 'dizygotic'). These twins share an estimated average of 50 per cent of their genetic makeup. Therefore, some researchers compare behaviours across non-twins, identical twins and fraternal twins to examine the relative influence of genetics.

The influence of the environment and genetics is often compared in **adoption studies**. Personality can be compared between parents and adopted children as there is no genetic heritability. Variables are often compared between siblings, or twins, reared apart to examine the extent of genetic and environmental effects. For example, if two twins show similar behaviours, despite being raised in different environments, this suggests that genes may be important in that behaviour.

Once you consider all these types of studies together – in which personality is compared between parents and children, and siblings, that share between 0 and 100 per cent genetic similarity – you can begin to make assessments of the extent of genetic heritability.

It is important to remember that there is no physiological procedure in these sorts of studies. Behaviour geneticists don't have the ability to assess the genetic heritability of personality using advanced biological measures or a complex scientific genetic analysis (well, not yet). Rather, researchers look for similarities and differences in personality (using personality measures) among individual people by using observation, interview or questionnaire measures. They look for similarities between parents' and children's personalities to determine the extent of genetic influence on personality. What is also important to remember is that, when we deal with heritability estimates, we don't talk about heritability estimates in particular individuals. Rather, researchers estimate the average heritability estimates among certain populations of people; that is, monozygotic (MZ, identical) twins, dizygotic (DZ, fraternal) twins, family members, parents and children. Therefore, across a population there will be a range of scores of concordance between people (e.g. two twins), and heritability estimates represent the average score across the population. So, a heritability estimate of 50 per cent for a personality trait does not mean that we all inherit 50 per cent of our personality from our genes; it means that, across the population, the genetic heritability has been estimated at an average of 50 per cent.

Genetic heritability estimates and personality

There is a lot of evidence to suggest that there is a genetic influence on personality among human populations. To break down this evidence for you, we will look first at some specific studies and then some general findings and major studies that have examined genetic heritability based on the three-factor and five-factor theories of personality.

We covered both these personality theories in detail in the previous discussion (Chapter 7). However, for this section, all you need to know is that, within Eysenck's theory, there are three personality dimensions:

- psychoticism (solitary, troublesome, cruel and inhumane traits);
- extraversion (sociable, sensation-seeking, carefree and optimistic traits);
- neuroticism (anxious, worrying and moody traits).

You also need to know that the five-factor model comprises five personality dimensions (Costa and McCrae, 1992):

- openness (perceptive, sophisticated, knowledgeable, cultured, artistic, curious, analytical, liberal traits);
- conscientiousness (practical, cautious, serious, reliable, organised, careful, dependable, hardworking, ambitious traits);
- extraversion (sociable, talkative, active, spontaneous, adventurous, enthusiastic, person-oriented, assertive traits);
- agreeableness (warm, trustful, courteous, agreeable, cooperative traits);
- neuroticism (emotional, anxiety, depressive, self-conscious, worrying traits).

Genetic heritability estimates and personality: heritability estimates from twin studies

To illustrate the evidence on the genetic heritability of personality, we will first concentrate on the different ways in which twin studies can be used to show heritability. Researchers have compared two different types of twins to examine genetic influences on personality: monozygotic (MZ, identical) twins, who share 100 per cent of their genes, and dizygotic (DZ, fraternal) twins, who share 50 per cent of their genes.

The first common way in which this research has been done is to compare identical twins (MZ) who have been reared apart. For example, there have been a number of findings from the Minnesota Study of Twins Reared Apart, which involves the medical and psychological assessment of identical (MZ) and fraternal (DZ) twins separated early in life and

reared apart. This study is overseen by the US behavioural geneticist Thomas Bouchard. In one study from this data, Thomas Bouchard and his colleague Matt McGue (Bouchard and McGue, 1981) found a large correlation ($r = 0.70$) for neuroticism between MZ twins who were reared apart.

Within this model, researchers tend to have to assume that twins reared together have generally similar environmental influences on their personality. Consequently, researchers suggest that any difference between the heritability is caused by the difference in the estimated percentage of genes shared by MZ (100 per cent) and DZ (50 per cent) twins. Therefore, if MZ twins are more similar than DZ twins are, this is considered as evidence of heritability. For example, let us use the findings of German behavioural geneticist Rainer Riemann and his colleagues (Riemann et al., 1997), who looked at over 1,000 pairs of German and Polish twins and compared MZ and DZ twins on the five-factor model of personality. These findings are summarised in Table 8.1. Within this table you will see that the correlations between MZ twins for the five factors of personality range from 0.42 to 0.56, and the correlations between DZ twins for the five factors of personality are smaller and range from 0.13 to 0.35. This type of finding is evidence for the genetic heritability of personality.

You will see that these types of results are replicated across samples and apply to different models of personality. Table 8.2 provides a summary of results presented by US behaviour geneticist John Loehlin (1989), regarding Eysenck's measures of extraversion and neuroticism among

Table 8.1 Correlations on the five-factor model of personality between monozygotic and dizygotic twins reared together

Personality dimension	Monozygotic (MZ; identical) twins	Dizygotic (DZ; fraternal) twins
Extraversion	0.56	0.28
Neuroticism	0.53	0.13
Agreeableness	0.42	0.19
Conscientiousness	0.54	0.18
Openness	0.54	0.35

Source: Based on Riemann et al. (1997).

Table 8.2 Correlations on extraversion and neuroticism personality measures between monozygotic and dizygotic twins reared together in three countries

Sample	Extraversion				Neuroticism			
	Monozygotic males	Monozygotic females	Dizygotic males	Dizygotic females	Monozygotic males	Monozygotic females	Dizygotic males	Dizygotic females
Sweden	0.47	0.54	0.20	0.21	0.46	0.54	0.21	0.25
Finland	0.50	0.53	0.13	0.19	0.46	0.52	0.18	0.26
Australia	0.46	0.49	0.15	0.14	0.33	0.43	0.12	0.18

Source: Based on Loehlin (1989).

Table 8.3 Correlations on the five-factor model of personality between monozygotic and dizygotic twins reared together, with heritability statistics

Personality dimension	Monozygotic (MZ; identical) twins	Dizygotic (DZ; fraternal) twins	Heritability estimate $h^2 = 2$ $(r_{mz} - r_{dz})$
Extraversion	0.56	0.28	56%
Neuroticism	0.53	0.13	80%
Agreeableness	0.42	0.19	46%
Conscientiousness	0.54	0.18	72%
Openness	0.54	0.35	38%

Source: Based on Riemann *et al.* (1997).

10,000 Swedish, 3,000 Australian and 7,000 Finnish adult twins for both males and females. Again, you will see that the correlations between MZ twins for the five factors of personality are much larger than the correlations for DZ twins. In fact, correlations between MZ twins on measures of personality are frequently twice the size of the correlations found between DZ twins. Heritability estimates are subsequently derived from this type of study by doubling the difference in correlations between MZ and DZ twins. A heritability estimate for a twin study that compares MZ and DZ twins will be the correlation statistic for MZ twins (r_{mz}), minus the correlation statistic for dizygotic twins (r_{dz}) and then doubled $[h^2 = 2 (r_{mz} - r_{dz})]$, and then expressed in percentage terms. To show how this works, let us return to Riemann's findings among German and Polish twins (see Table 8.3). In this table, in addition to the correlation statistics, we have computed the heritability statistics. For example, for agreeableness, we have taken 0.19 (correlation for DZ twins) away from 0.42 (correlation for MZ twins), which is 0.23 and doubled it; which is 0.46. Expressed as a percentage, this is 46 per cent.

To help you in your study, we will summarise some more of the evidence regarding the genetic influence on personality from overviews and recent papers using twin studies (see Table 8.4).

Following numerous studies using measures of Eysenck's personality dimensions, in which genetic effects were found for all three of Eysenck's personality factors, Lindon J. Eaves, a US behavioural geneticist, Hans J. Eysenck and an Australian behavioural geneticist, Nick Martin, provided a meta-analysis of early twin studies (Eaves *et al.*, 1989). They found that heritability estimates (h^2) for extraversion were 0.58 (58%), for neuroticism 0.44 (44%) and for psychoticism 0.46 (46%). More recently, the US behavioural geneticists John C. Loehlin and Nick Martin (2001) compared Eysenck personality scales that had been given to 5,400 pairs of twins from the Australian Twin Registry. The heritability estimates for extraversion, neuroticism and psychoticism were 0.47, 0.40 and 0.28, respectively. Table 8.4 shows that similar sized heritability statistics have been computed from twin studies using the five-factor model of personality in the United States and Canada; results range from 0.33 to 0.58.

These types of findings suggest that personality is influenced by genetic factors. Towards the end of the last century, commentators on behavioural genetics, including the US academics Saudino and Plomin (1996) and the

Table 8.4 Examples from heritability estimates of the main personality factors from major twin studies

Personality dimension	Three-factor model of personality	
	Meta-analysis study (Eaves *et al.*, 1989)	Australian twin study (Loehlin and Martin, 2001)
Extraversion	0.58	0.47
Neuroticism	0.44	0.40
Psychoticism	0.46	0.28
	Five-factor model of personality	
	USA twin study (Waller, 1999)	Canadian twin study (Jang *et al.*, 1996)
Extraversion	0.49	0.56
Neuroticism	0.42	0.52
Agreeableness	0.33	0.42
Conscientiousness	0.48	0.53
Openness	0.58	0.51

European academics Riemann and De Raad (1998), estimated, from studies looking at early infancy through to old age and across a number of American, Australian and European samples, that there is a moderate heritability of personality from genetic factors, accounting for between 20 and 50 per cent of phenotypic variance.

Behaviour genetics and personality: heritability estimates from adoption studies

Furthermore, when researchers have been able to obtain measures from both biological and adoptive parents, children have been found to be more similar to their biological parents than to their adoptive parents in personality. A frequently cited study of this was done on a Texas sample by US psychologists Loehlin, Willerman and Horn (1985). The authors didn't use a direct measure of extraversion as measured with the three- and five-factor models of personality, but included measures such as sociability and activity from two personality measures called the California Psychological Inventory (Gough, 1987) and the Thurstone Temperament Schedule (Thurstone, 1953), which measure extraversion traits. Table 8.5 shows a summary of the strength of correlations between the adopted children and their adoptive and biological parents. As you can see, the correlations between biological parent and child are much larger than the correlations between adoptive parent and child. This finding suggests evidence of genetic influence between genetic parents and adopted children in their personality.

Other authors have looked at differences between identical (MZ) and fraternal (DZ) twins reared together and reared apart to look for genetic influence on personality. Some findings for the genetic influence on the major personality dimensions have been found from the Swedish Twin Registry by Swedish and US psychologists Nancy Pedersen, Robert Plomin, Gary McClearn and Lars Friberg (1988). In this study Pedersen and her colleagues looked at two dimensions from the three-factor model (and five-factor model) of personality – extraversion and neuroticism. This sample comprised 160 pairs of identical twins reared together, 99 pairs of identical twins reared apart, 212 pairs of fraternal twins reared together and 229 pairs of fraternal twins reared apart. As you can see from Table 8.6, the correlations for identical twins reared together and apart are larger than for fraternal twins reared together and apart. Most importantly, in terms of the evidence derived from adoption studies, the fact that the correlations for identical twins reared apart are greater than for fraternal twins reared together and apart suggests a genetic influence on personality for both extraversion and neuroticism.

US psychologists Scott L. Hershberger and Robert Plomin and Swedish psychologist Nancy Pedersen returned to the same sample and, in 1995, examined it for genetic influence on 24 personality traits from the same twin registry. Among this study, findings from using 58 pairs of identical twins reared together, 35 pairs of identical twins reared apart, 81 pairs of fraternal twins reared together and 68 pairs of fraternal twins reared apart were obtained from

Table 8.5 Correlations between adopted child and their biological and adoptive parent

Personality dimension: Indices of extraversion	Biological parent	Adoptive parent
Social presence (California Psychological Index)	0.34	0.12
Vigorous (Thurstone Temperament Schedule)	0.33	0.06
Sociable (Thurstone Temperament Schedule)	0.18	0.02
Sociability (California Psychological Index)	0.17	0.04
Active (Thurstone Temperament Schedule)	0.16	0.02

Source: Based on Loehlin *et al.* (1985).

Table 8.6 Correlations in personality variables for identical twins reared together, identical twins reared apart, fraternal twins reared together and fraternal twins reared apart

	Identical twins (MZ) reared together	Identical twins (MZ) reared apart	Fraternal twins (DZ) reared together	Fraternal twins (DZ) reared apart
Pedersen *et al.* (1988)				
Extraversion	0.54	0.30	0.06	0.04
Neuroticism	0.41	0.25	0.28	0.24
Hershberger *et al.* (1995)				
Extraversion	0.20	0.36	−0.04	0.09
Neuroticism	0.39	0.31	0.09	0.09
Openness	0.18	−0.08	0.15	0.05

the Swedish Adoption/Twin Study of Aging (Pedersen *et al.*, 1991). This time the researchers looked at a number of personality traits, and Table 8.6 shows three personality traits we are familiar with from the three-factor and five-factor model: neuroticism, extraversion (Pedersen *et al.*, 1988; Hershberger *et al.*, 1995) and openness (Hershberger *et al.*, 1995). Again, the correlations show evidence for the genetic influence on extraversion and neuroticism, but perhaps not for openness.

Finally, to complete the picture in terms of the five-factor model, US psychologist Cindy S. Bergeman, with a number of European and US psychologists – given the genetic influence on extraversion and neuroticism – assessed the genetic influence on the other three components of the five-factor model of personality: openness to experience, agreeableness and conscientiousness. In this study an abbreviated version of the NEO Personality Inventory (NEO-PI-R) was administered to 132 pairs of identical twins and 167 pairs of fraternal twins reared together and 82 pairs of identical twins and 171 pairs of fraternal twins reared apart. Estimates of genetic and environmental effects for openness and conscientiousness were similar to those found in other studies of personality for extraversion and neuroticism. However, these researchers found a much weaker relationship for agreeableness. None the less, these series of adoption studies suggest a genetic influence on personality for most aspects of personality.

In general, the studies summarised here suggest substantial heritability for genetic influence on personality. Genetic factors can sometimes explain as much as 40 to 50 per cent of the variance within the main personality dimensions.

Considerations within behavioural genetics and personality

However, it may not surprise you to learn that things are not quite as simple as they first seem in behavioural genetics. The idea of how genes and the environment are viewed and used to predict the heritability of personality (or any phenotype) has changed over recent years.

Authors such as US psychologists E. E. Maccoby (2000) and Plomin (2004) suggest that the additive principle of determining heritability of personality (or any phenotype) is not applicable any more. The validity of the additive assumption in computing the relative strength of genetics and environment in determining behaviour has been widely challenged. The first problem is that estimating the environment (E) is usually done without utilising any direct measures of environmental factors. For example, researchers often compute genetic heritability, and then subtract that from 100 per cent. Obviously, if the estimates of heritability are indeterminate or prone to error, so are the estimates

of E derived by subtracting from 100 per cent. A further problem with the additive assumption of computing heritability is that, when genetic heritability is large, it assumes that all environmental factors associated with that behaviour must be small. It is better to see human personality as a joint result of an interaction between the individual's genes and their environmental factors. Consequently, personality should not be seen as the result of 'Genetics + Environment' but rather 'Genetics × Environment'. For example, it is better to view the relative influences of genes and environment on personality as the result of a long-term interaction, with environmental factors triggering certain genetic behaviours and the effects of the environment differing between individuals because of their genetic makeup.

What is important for you to note is that these changes and developments in research and thinking have been suggested, encouraged and developed by both theorists and researchers, many of whom we have already mentioned, who support and criticise the idea of genetic inheritability in personality. So what has brought about, and resulted from, such a general shift in thinking, from the additive principle of 'Genetics + Environment' to the later, more integrative, idea of 'Genetics × Environment'? Well, there are six considerations surrounding modern-day thinking in behavioural genetics that are important when considering any phenotype, particularly personality:

- conceptions of heritability and the environment;
- different types of genetic variance;
- shared versus non-shared environmental influences;
- the representativeness of twin and adoption studies;
- assortative mating;
- the changing world of genetics.

Conceptions of genetic heritability and the environment

Gregory Carey (2002) suggests that there are two important contexts within which to consider heritability and environmental influence on personality. Carey notes that genetic heritability and the influence of the environment are largely:

- **Abstract concepts** – That is, they are generally theoretical (not applied or practical) concepts. As Carey explains, whatever the numerical estimates of either genetic or environmental influences, they provide us with little information about the specific genes or specific environmental variables that influence personality.
- **Population concepts** – We covered this topic earlier, but it is worth remembering that all these estimates refer to is any group of people that is considered a population; they tell us very little about any single individual. For example, just because personality may have a genetic heritability of around 40 per cent, it does not mean that

for any one individual 40 per cent of their personality is due to genes and 60 per cent of their personality is due to the environment. Rather, it is estimated across the population that genetic heritability of personality is an average of 40 per cent, and individuals will vary around that estimate.

Different types of genetic variance

So far in this discussion we've just treated genetic influence on personality as a single entity, namely the influence of your genes on your personality. However, behavioural genetics researchers such as Thomas Bouchard and M. McGue (1981) note that genetic influence does not simply comprise one aspect, but in fact three aspects:

- additive genetic variance;
- dominant genetic variance;
- epistatic genetic variance.

Additive genetic variance, which we have previously described in this discussion, is genetic variation in behaviour that is the total of the individual's genes inherited from their parents.

However, the two other types of genetic variation are known as non-additive genetic variance. **Dominant genetic variance** is part of a process by which certain genes are expressed (dominant genes) and other genes are not expressed (recessive genes). Every person has two copies of every gene, one inherited from their mother and one from their father. Sometimes the two genes, which determine a particular trait (for example, eye colour) will actually code for two types of characteristics (for example, blue eyes and brown eyes). If one of these genes is dominant, then only its character is expressed and not that of the other gene. For example, if blue eyes were a dominant gene, then if your mother had brown eyes and your father had blue eyes, you would be likely to inherit blue eyes.

The second non-additive type of genetic variation, **epistatic genetic variance** (also known as interactive genetic variance), refers to a process by which genes interact. It is now known that several different genes not only influence physical characteristics and behaviour on their own, but work and interact together. Unlike dominant genetic variance, which just applies to one gene replacing another, epistatic genetic variance is the result of the way certain genes that we inherit determine whether other genes we inherit will be expressed or suppressed (this process is epistasis).

It is difficult to measure dominant genetic variance and epistatic genetic variance when it comes to personality. However, it is now accepted that all three aspects – additive genetic variance, dominant genetic variance and epistatic genetic variance – are thought to make up *total genetic variance of personality*.

You can see that understanding the genetic side of things is a lot more complicated than viewing genes as a single entity; genes themselves interact and suppress other genes. You will see in the literature that behavioural geneticists refer to terms such as 'narrow heritability' and 'broad heritability'. Narrow heritability is just additive genetic variance. Broad genetic heritability is all three aspects of genetic heritability (additive genetic variance + dominant genetic variance + epistatic genetic variance).

Because of the complexity of genetics, authors such as Thomas Bouchard and M. McGue (1981) and US psychologists Heather Chipeur, Michael Rovine and Robert Plomin (1990) have suggested that original estimates of the percentage of parental genes that children inherit and siblings share may have been oversimplified. For example, these authors suggest that genetic variations in heritability of phenotypes should be made in the following terms:

- identical (MZ) twins = additive genetic variance + non-additive genetic variance (where previously it was presumed to be just additive genetic variance);
- fraternal (DZ) twins = 0.5 of additive genetic variance + 0.25 of non-additive genetic variance (rather than just 0.5 of additive genetic variance).

As you can see, computing levels of genetic variance may be more complicated than previously thought, and today behavioural geneticists take these factors into account when suggesting the strength of heritability estimates.

Shared and non-shared environments

We saw in the last section that the conception of genetics as simply a single dimension has changed. The same could be said of environmental factors. Within behavioural genetics, the conception of how the environment influences personality is based on two sets of experiences: shared and non-shared. When growing up, siblings (brothers and sisters) are thought to experience both shared and unique environments. **Shared environments** are environments that are shared between two individuals, while **non-shared environments** are environments that are *not* shared between two individuals. Siblings growing up within the same family will share many environments. These environments may range from very small experiences to larger ones. Two siblings having the same parents, living within the same house, going to the same school, experiencing particular times together (e.g. same family relatives, home environment, chaotic mornings before school, dad's awful jokes) are shared environments. A unique environment is an environment that has not been shared by siblings. Again, these environments may range from very small experiences to larger ones. Examples of unique environments might be when two siblings have been raised by different families. However, siblings raised in the same family might also have unique environments from each other. Siblings may have different sets of friends, go to different schools, have different types of relationships with their parents and have different interactions with teachers.

What is important in this area is that the theory and research around the differences between environmental influences on personality have grown in complexity. To begin with, researchers tend to concentrate on comparing how shared and non-shared environmental factors influence personality. Early consideration by reviewers such as Bouchard (1994) and Eysenck (1990a) suggested that environmental influences shared by siblings or twins contribute only marginally to personality differences. However, one interesting point to emerge from the literature, carried out by such researchers as US behavioural geneticists Braungart *et al.* (1992b), is that those environmental factors that are unique (non-shared) to family members are influential, over *shared* environmental factors. Consequently, non-shared environmental factors, such as different peer friendships, are important mechanisms that explain why members of the same family may differ in their personalities. This idea is supported by two pieces of research suggesting that the extent of differences in the experiences during childhood among siblings has been found to

be related to personality differences in adulthood (Baker and Daniels, 1990; Plomin and Daniels, 1987). Such a finding has developed whole areas of research that have emphasised how important non-shared environmental factors are to personality. The majority of research in this area considers how non-shared environmental factors develop: (1) within the family; and (2) outside the family.

Within-family factors

US behavioural geneticist David Reiss (1997) identifies three ways in which inherited genes form phenotypes (behaviours) based on the family environment (see Figure 8.1). These are:

- the passive model;
- the child-effects model;
- the parent-effects model.

On the left of the figure is the **passive model**. This model suggests that personality is generally explained by the 50 per cent overlap between a child and their parent. Consequently, behaviour may occur in the child as the result of the child and parent sharing the same genes that influence a

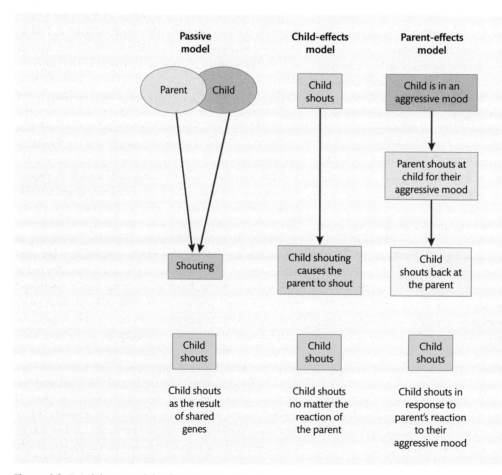

Figure 8.1 Reiss' three models of genetic transmission.

particular type of behaviour. For example, if a child is aggressive because of genetic influences, they are so because one of their biological parents had the genes that cause aggressiveness. The model very much assumes just a general genetic overlap and inheritance of behaviour, without considering possible other factors and interactions within the family, and this is why it is called the passive model. The other two models very much emphasise other dynamics occurrences.

In the **child-effects model**, the genes cause a behaviour in the child, which in turn causes the same or similar behaviour in the parent. Within this model, the parent does not matter in the development of the behaviour, as the child's development of the behaviour is the result of genes. An example of this is that the shared genes cause the child to be aggressive to the parent (because of their genetic makeup), which in turn causes the parent to be aggressive back to the child (because of their genetic makeup). The parent's own aggressiveness does not matter in the development of the behaviour, as the child's shouting is a consequence of the genetic makeup of the child rather than the parent.

US psychologist Judith Harris (1995) has expanded this viewpoint to *child-driven effects* that influence family circumstances that then influence the child's personality. Harris documents studies showing that adults do not behave in the same way to a child who shows different tendencies. They will treat a very attractive child differently to one of their children who is less attractive; they react differently to the one child who shows bad behaviour than they do to the one who is well behaved. They treat children who are healthy and ill differently, and they treat children who are active and quiet differently. Imagine a family with two twin children, one who is active and one who is quiet. These differences in the children will cause different reactions in the parents. The parents will begin to treat their children differently. The active one may be encouraged to be more active and be allowed to go out and play, while the quiet one will be allowed to read their books. Harris suggests that these reactions by parents to their children's natural personality tendencies can be viewed in two ways: as *positive feedback loops* and *negative feedback loops*. Positive feedback loops arise from parents reinforcing children's natural tendencies, as in the example just described, so that children's natural personalities are encouraged and these personalities will come out. Any differences between children in their personalities will also be developed – the active child is encouraged and allowed to be active, while the quiet child is encouraged and allowed to be quiet. Negative feedback loops occur when children are stopped from behaving in ways consistent with their natural tendencies. A quiet child might be encouraged to get out of the house more; an active child might be encouraged to spend less time outside playing but more time in their bedroom reading.

In the **parent-effects model**, the behaviour of the child is responded to by the parent, which in turn brings out the behaviour in the child. Within this model, how the parent responds does have an effect in the development of the behaviour. For example, the child may be being noisy; this then leads the parent to be aggressive (as it is part of their genetic makeup) with the child, which, in turn, causes the child to become aggressive also (as it is part of their genetic makeup). Within this model, how the parent acts leads to the development of aggression, which then leads to the development of shouting.

Again, Harris extends this idea to within-family situations. In these situations, children might be treated in a particular way by parents, not because of that child's own characteristics, but because of the parents' own beliefs or the characteristics of a child's siblings (brothers or sisters). Let us first look at the example of how a parent's own beliefs shape natural tendencies of children. Again, take our family with the one active twin and the one quiet twin. Our parents of the family may have certain beliefs about behaviour, such as 'children should be seen and not heard', and consequently the children will be encouraged and directed to behave in such ways. In our case of the active and quiet twin, the active child who is noisy will be encouraged to be quieter, and the quiet child will be encouraged to be more visible by coming out of their bedroom; thus both children have had their new behaviour (being seen and not heard) driven by their parents' behaviour. Secondly, let us look at how parents might influence children's behaviours in terms of a child's siblings. Harris notes research that suggests parents who consider their first child to be 'difficult' tend to label their second-born 'easy'. We can also see how active children might be asked or encouraged to calm down and be more like their quieter sibling. Equally, the quiet sibling might be encouraged to go out and play more like their brothers and sisters.

What Reiss and Harris' commentaries do is to suggest that **within-family effects** pose problems when considering genetic heritability. That is, child effects and parent effects can lead to overestimations and underestimations of heritability. Remember, behavioural geneticists looking at personality are only looking at the concordance between sets of children based on their scores on a personality test at some point. However, let us return to the family mentioned earlier, the one with one active twin and one quiet twin. Let us imagine that the parents of these twin children have been engaged in a negative feedback loop and have been trying to encourage both children to be similar; that is, somewhat active and somewhat quiet. The active child has been discouraged from being active all the time, and the quiet child has been discouraged from being too quiet. If we then compared these two children, we would find that these twin children have similar personalities; but this is, in fact, not because of genetic tendencies at all, but simply because of the parents trying to encourage similar behaviour in both children (i.e. not too active or not too quiet).

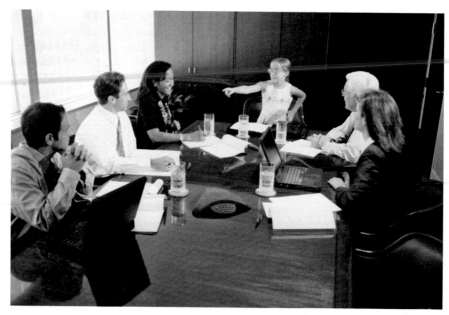

Reiss identifies three ways in which inherited genes form phenotypes; some are parent-led, some are child-led.
Source: Alamy Images/Thinkstock

Therefore, any estimation of similarities in personality being caused by genetic heritability of the twins would be an overestimation.

However, if the same pair of twins had been reared differently and both been in a positive feedback loop (that is, the active child had been encouraged to be more and more active, and the quiet child had been encouraged to be more and more quiet), then any estimation of the similarities in personality being caused by genetic heritability would be an underestimation. As Harris concludes, children's within-family situations not only play an important role in shaping of personality but are also an important consideration in estimating the genetic heritability of personality.

Outside-family factors

Harris has suggested that non-shared factors outside the family may in fact be more important in developing people's personalities. Harris presents the **group socialisation theory** to explain the importance of non-shared environmental factors in determining personality.

Group socialisation theory is based largely on the ideas surrounding social identity theory and social categorisation (Tajfel and Turner, 1986). Social psychologists have provided a lot of theoretical and empirical research work looking at how individuals perceive their social world as comprising in-groups and out-groups and suggesting that these categories help us form our social identity. Social psychologists argue that one mechanism humans use for understanding the complex social world is social categorisation. In social categorisation, individuals are thought to place other individuals into social groups on the basis of their similarities

and differences to the individual. Put simply, individuals who are viewed as similar to the person tend to be placed within their in-group. Individuals who are viewed as different to the person tend to be placed within an out-group. As a consequence, the individual's identity (social identity) is based on and derived from the groups we feel we belong to and our understanding of our similarities and differences in relation to different social groups. Social groups can be based on anything; however, common groups could be sex group, ethnic group, your religion, your peers, your interests, your educational status and so on. As such, your identity is based to a greater or lesser extent on how much you identify with different social groups. What is also important to our identity is that, when we attach ourselves to certain groups, we also try to fit in with those groups, and our personality might begin to reflect the characteristics of the group (i.e. you might make friends with people who are outgoing, and you may do more outgoing activities than you used to, and consequently become more active in your life).

Harris uses this theoretical basis to show how social groups can influence people's personalities and how these non-shared environments that occur in children of the same family can have a huge effect on personality. As part of this theory, Harris lists five aspects that are important to consider in how non-shared characteristics might influence our personality (see Figure 8.2).

1   **Context-specific socialisation**. This aspect refers to the fact that children learn behaviours not only at home but also outside the home, and that, as children get older, they become less influenced by their family life and more influenced by their life outside the family

Figure 8.2 Non-shared characteristics that influence our personality (Harris, 1995).

home. Possible influences include friends, your friends' parents, your extended family, teachers and even celebrities. What is also important is that contexts for behaviour of a child shift between environments. For example, one child might be very quiet. Let us consider the possible different contexts in which the child's quietness is considered, and responded to, by other people.

- Parents might not say anything to the child about being quiet because they believe in not criticising or praising their child over their personality.
- The child's friends might encourage this behaviour because they are also quiet and enjoy doing the same quiet activities.
- At school the child's teachers might try to encourage them to be less quiet by getting them to speak up more and get involved in class more.
- Other children at school might tease the child for being quiet.

Thus, we can see that there are many influences, both from inside the home and outside the home, that affect how a child learns behaviour.

2 **Outside the home socialisation.** In this aspect, Harris makes the point that children may identify with a number of social groups, based on people's age, gender, ethnicity, abilities, interests and personality. In other words, we have a range of groups that we identify with and share norms with (attitudes, interests, personality), and these groups have different influences on our personality. For example, compare the sort of person you are with the friends you made at school and with the friends you made at university. Are there differences in the sort of personality you have in these two groups?

3 **Transmission of culture via group processes.** In this aspect, Harris makes two points about the transmission of culture via group processes that establish norms in our social world and in turn influence our personality.

The first point is that the shared norms that might influence a child's personality aren't necessarily the result of parents sharing them with their children. They are really the result of shared norms among the parents' peers and social groups being passed on to the children. That is, your parents' values, abilities and personality are not the result of their parents' norms, but rather of their social identity, their identification with their own social groups. Your parents' identity isn't isolated to them on their own; it is a result of their interactions with their friends and others. For example, we're sure your parents don't agree on everything; in many cases, your father's personality might be closer to those of some of his friends, while your mother's personality might be closer to those of some of her friends. Therefore, influences on our personalities are not the result of interactions with our parents' personalities, but actually an interaction with our parents' social identities.

The second point considers that our individual norms, which we have developed from our family, are shared with other people only if they are accepted. For example, an individual might be quiet and enjoy listening to classical music and going to classical concerts. However, when they mention it to their friends, they are laughed at because the others are all into dance music and like clubbing. You can imagine how the individual will cover up this norm and may actually make an extra effort to like dance music and go clubbing; they may stop listening to classical music and going to classical music concerts.

4 **Group processes that widen differences between social groups.** It is important to note that within your personality norms are based not just on how you identify with your in-group but also on how you do not identify with, or reject, the out-groups. For example, consider sex roles; your personality as a male or female isn't just

based on your identification with people of your own sex, but on your rejection of characteristics of the opposite sex. For example, some young men develop their identity not just based on what it means to be a young man but also in terms of trying not to adopt behaviours associated with being a young woman (and vice versa for women). Your personality is influenced by what you identify with as well as by what you don't wish to identify with. This principle applies across the whole range of social groups; young women rarely want to adopt characteristics and personality traits associated with old women, men from ethnic minorities sometimes don't want to adopt behaviours or personality traits that are associated with men from ethnic majorities and so on.

5 **Group processes that widen differences among individuals within the group.** So far we have assumed that all the groups we are involved in basically share the same structure. However, we know that within all our social circles we play different roles that might influence, or bring out, different aspects of our personality. In our family, as a child, we take a less senior role; however, with our friends we might be more of a leader and allowed to be more like ourselves. On the other hand, the opposite may be true; we might not feel that we lead a group of friends, but tend to do what others say. It may even be possible that, among one group of friends, you feel more comfortable than you do among others. Harris' point is that our position in groups changes, and that our personality – and influences on our personality – change as a result of the hierarchies within a group. For example, if you are in a group of friends and they all look up to you, your personality will be influenced because you might think there is an expectation to come up with ideas for things to do, to become more dominant; also, you might become more and more active in the group because you are the one who holds the group together and organises things and so on.

What is important to consider in both within-family and outside-family factors is that these aspects can influence personality of children to a much wider extent than previously thought. It is not Harris' point that behavioural genetics is wrong and that environmental factors are more important, but rather that behavioural geneticists may have previously oversimplified family influences. By ignoring these variables, behavioural geneticists might be underestimating or overestimating the heritability effects of either genetics or the environment.

Problems with the representativeness of twin and adoption studies

One of the considerations put forward by psychologists such as Eleanor Maccoby and Leon Kamin and Arthur Goldberger (Kamin and Goldberger, 2002) concerns adoption and twin studies. A significant portion of studies examining heritability effects is devoted to twin and adoption studies. Twin studies are important because they allow the comparison of different types of twins to study genetic influences: monozygotic (MZ, identical) twins, who share 100 per cent of their genes, and dizygotic (DZ, fraternal) twins, who share 50 per cent of their genes. Adoption studies are important because they include two sets of factors that may account for differences in behaviour: biological parents and environmental parents. It is argued that, because these families are not necessarily representative of the general population, this natural bias in sampling may lead researchers to underestimate or overestimate the genetic heritability across the whole population.

This issue is particularly important when considering research that assesses heritability of personality using twin and adoption studies. Kamin and Goldberger (2002) suggest that twin studies might overestimate the role of genetics, particularly because identical twins have more similar environments than do same-sex fraternal twins. Also, research shows that identical twins are treated more similarly by their parents, spend more time together and have the same friends more often. Therefore, their environmental experience comprises a greater proportion of each other's social environment than does that of fraternal siblings. Consequently, if genetic heritability estimates are usually larger in twin studies than in adoption studies, then some of the estimated similarity that is attributed to genetic influence might not be correct. Stoolmiller (1998) has suggested that adoption studies also lead to a similar restriction in the measurement of environmental factors. Stoolmiller argues that the placement strategies of adoption agencies might influence heritability estimates. For example, adoption agencies might always place children in affluent or middle- to high-income families; thus the effects of economic status are never fully explored in these studies, because an adopted child would very rarely be placed into a household suffering from poverty.

Assortative mating

Nicholas Mackintosh (Mackintosh, 1998), animal-learning theorist at the University of Cambridge, raises the issue that assortative mating can have an effect on genetic variance and, consequently, on estimates of heritability. Assortative mating is a complicated name for the simple concept that, when couples mate, they either have traits in common or contrast widely in their traits. A lot of the understanding of human genetic variation is based on the assumption that two individuals mate quite randomly with random people, and therefore any genetic similarity between them occurs by chance. But we know that this is not true. We know that people mate with people who they perceive are similar to them. For example, we tend to see people mating with people who are of a similar size or similar in their 'good-lookingness' (you rarely see one partner who is very tall and one who is very short, or one who is very beautiful and one who is ugly). This is called positive assortative mating. Though, equally, we find people mating who are completely the opposite; that is, 'opposites attract'. This is called negative assortative mating.

There is evidence that people do engage in assortative mating, though usually it is positive assortative mating. Israeli human geneticists at Tel Aviv University (Ginsburg *et al.*, 1998) found that body height was positively correlated between spouses in four ethnically and geographically different populations: Kirghizians, Turkmenians, Chuvashians and Israelis. German psychologists Wirth and Luttinger (1998) found, by examining German national data from the German census between 1970 and 1993, that men and women were very similar in their social class. Whitbeck and Hoyt (1994) found that students' assortative mating was related to prestige. In much the same way, the assortative mating principle can be applied to personality. That is, individuals may seek to mate with people who are of similar personality, or of a particularly different personality. Think about your boyfriend or girlfriend, or an ideal mate. Do you think they are of a similar personality level to you?

What the theory of assortative mating suggests is that people don't tend to mate with people randomly. People make choices about their potential mate based on physical and behavioural characteristics that are influenced by genes. This genetic similarity (or dissimilarity) has an effect of reducing and expanding the range of genetic variation found between two mates. Consequently, assortative mating is a factor that may have influence on genetic heritability estimates in populations.

Changing world of genetics

You are reading this at an exciting time in biology. The Human Genome Project, a 13-year effort, was completed in 2003. The project has involved thousands of scientists. It was coordinated by the US Department of Energy and the National Institutes of Health, with the United Kingdom, Japan, France, Germany and China all making major contributions. The largest international collaboration ever undertaken in biology, it had the immense task of determining the three billion bases of genetic information residing in every human cell to identify all the approximately 20,000–25,000 genes in human DNA. Since then, researchers have been investigating each gene. Even though the functions are unknown for over 50 per cent of discovered genes, over 30 genes have been associated with breast cancer, muscle disease, blindness and deafness. However, what is an exciting time is also a

revealing time for scientists. A number of projects stemming from the Human Genome Project, such as the Encyclopedia of DNA Elements (ENCODE), have suggested that the innermost workings of genes are more complex than was previously thought, with what was thought to be redundant DNA actually being active and important to our functioning. Ewan Birney and his colleagues (Birney *et al.*, 2007 (The ENCODE Project Consortium)) carried out an analysis on just 1 per cent of our DNA code and found that DNA, which had previously been described as 'junk DNA' as it was thought to have no biological function, but makes up 97 per cent of the genome, was indeed active in an intricate control network of our physiological and biological functioning. Therefore, for researchers such as Birney, the future research is much more complex than previously imagined, but also potentially much more insightful.

What you should first remember about this area is that, as scientific advancements are made in what is known about the genes of humans, so will theoretical perspectives and research evidence regarding behavioural genetics and personality. For example, the mapping of the human genome (i.e. the complete set of genes found in mankind's 23 pairs of chromosomes) is an exciting and important development, which is still in its earliest stages and may uncover more about human potentials. Because this is a theoretical and research area in which knowledge is growing and changing all the time, critical assessment should be placed within the context of an ever-changing knowledge base.

One such advance in behavioural genetic research is in molecular genetics. So far we have talked about genes as single entities, but molecular genetics are concerned with the structure, makeup and activity of genes. Consequently, where there was a reliance on using twin and adoption studies to guess the strength of genetic influence on the genetic resemblance between individuals (e.g. identical and fraternal twins, biological parents and adoptive parents), US psychologists Saudino and Plomin (1996) explain that molecular genetics techniques can now identify thousands of DNA markers of genetic differences among individuals. This process will allow researchers to examine differences between individuals in their DNA related directly to behavioural variation, rather than assessing it simply through the genetic resemblance of relatives. Although it is accepted that there is no major gene for personality, research has suggested that multiple genes (rather than a single one) are related to traits. These multiple genes are referred to as quantitative trait loci (QTL). Within molecular genetics, a QTL (multiple genes) might be considered to be associated with personality if there is a higher frequency among affected versus unaffected individuals. Dina *et al.* (2004) found that a chromosome (this structure contains the heritability information necessary for building the human body and behaviour) called 8P gives evidence for a QTL (multiple

Genetics, family and environmental factors can all have influences on our personality.
Source: Alamy Images/Pat Behnke

genes) contributing to individual differences in an anxiety-related personality trait. Fullerton *et al.* (2003) found a QTL that influences neuroticism. As Saudino and Plomin (1996) emphasise, researchers are entering a new era in which molecular genetics techniques will revolutionise genetics research on personality by identifying specific genes that contribute to genetic variation in behavioural dimensions.

A framework for considering heritability in personality

As you can see, the area of behavioural genetics presents substantial findings and considerations and certainly would seriously challenge any academic who felt that all human behaviour and personality was solely down to just genes or the environment. Instead we have gained, through family, twin and adoption studies that have compared genetic heritability estimates, an interesting insight into how genetic factors influence personality. However, we have also seen how consideration of different influences on personality is important (e.g. dominance and interactive genetic variance, shared and non-shared environmental influences, assortative mating).

Bouchard and Loehlin (2001) suggest a framework regarding sources of population variance in personality (see Figure 8.3).

Bouchard and Loehlin not only provide a good overview of the debate but also set some prudent criteria in terms of assessing factors such as genetic effects (such as heritability)

and environmental effects. So, in all, Bouchard and Loehlin (2001) suggest that we must consider these factors:

- **Genetic influences** – what gene is involved; which aspects of molecular genetics; what type of genetic variation (for example, additive or non-additive); is there a sex limitation on personality?
- **Environmental influences** – to what extent does environment influence the personality; why are types of environments involved; are there gender effects?
- **Interaction between genetic and environmental influences** – what type are the interactions between genes and the environment that influence the personality?
- **Developmental influences** – do different genes influence the personality during development, and do different environmental factors influence the personality during development?
- **Assortative mating** – is assortative mating present in personality, and are there sex differences in mate preference for personality?
- **Evolution** – what sort of selective factors were at work during the original evolution of the personality behaviour? Are there current selective factors at work? (You may need to also refer to later discussion (Chapter 9) on evolutionary psychology to grasp some of these ideas fully.)

Clearly some of these areas are easier to identify than others when it comes to personality. However, many of the areas – assessing the level of genetic influence, the types of environmental influence and the possible interactions between genes and the environment – are known, or at least are sources of debate (see Stop and think: Crime and

Genetic

1 To what extent is the trait influenced by genes?
2 What type of genes are involved?
3 How many loci are involved?
4 Is there a sex limitation or sex linkage?
5 Are chromosomal effects involved?

Environmental

1 To what extent is the trait influenced by the environment?
2 What type of environment is involved?
3 Are there gender effects?
4 Is transmission horizontal, or is it vertical?

Genetic and environmental influence

1 Are there any genetic x environmental interactions?
2 What type are the interactions between genes and the environment?

Phenotype

Developmental

1 Do different genes influence during development?
2 Do different environmental factors influence during development?

Assortative mating

1 Is assortative mating present?
2 Are there sex differences in mate preference for the trait?

Evolution

1 What sort of selective factors were at work during the original evolution of the trait?
2 Are there current selective factors at work?
3 Is the trait an adaptation?

Figure 8.3 Framework and questions regarding sources of population variance in behaviour.
Source: Based on Bouchard and Loehlin (2001).

genes). By applying Bouchard and Loehlin's model, we can provide a focus to an area that comprises speculation and debates over the influences on the personality of: (1) genes; (2) the environment; and (3) the interactions between genes and the environment. But, as Thomas Bouchard and John Loehlin summarised in 2001, 'The behavior genetics of personality is alive and flourishing but there remains ample scope for new growth and much social science research is seriously compromised if it does not incorporate genetic variation in its explanatory models.'

Career focus: Working in neuropsychology

According to the British Psychological Society website, neuropsychologists work with people with brain injury or other neurological diseases. This would include people with neurological problems, which include brain injury, stroke, tumours and neurodegenerative diseases. Largely, a neuropsychologist will combine clinical and neurological relevant skills to work in the assessment and rehabilitation of people. A neuropsychologist will work in a variety of settings, including rehabilitation centres and with community services.

Dr Camilla Herbert, Consultant in Neuropsychology and Rehabilitation at the Brain Injury Rehabilitation Trust, West Sussex

1. **How/why did you choose to pursue the area of psychology that you did?**

   As an undergraduate I studied behavioural disorders on a course taught by a clinical psychologist. I was interested in what caused the various conditions and in the scientific approach to treatment. I came from a biological sciences background but was also interested in the philosophy of mind. Individual differences in personality, the interactions between nature and nurture, and between genetic predispositions and life experiences, have always interested me. I trained as a clinical psychologist, and went on to specialise in neuropsychology.

2. **In what way do the skills and/or knowledge you learned when studying personality and individual differences apply to your work/research today?**

My current role as a consultant neuropsychologist provides the perfect opportunity for me to draw on my academic and clinical interests. I work primarily with people who have sustained a brain injury and also in diagnostic work, i.e. identifying patterns of change in dementia and other neurological conditions. I need to understand the biology of the brain, the brain systems and how developmental issues and illnesses/injuries affect the brain functioning. I also need to understand how individuals respond to distress and life changes and the various coping mechanisms that the injured person and their families and friends draw upon. The concept of personality and how this can be affected by damage to the brain remains of everyday relevance to my work and a continuing source of fascination and interest.

You can read more on becoming a neuropsychologist at the British Psychological Society website at **http://www.bps.org .uk/careers-education-training/how-become-psychologist/types-psychologists/becoming-neuropsychologist/be**.

Psychophysiology, neuropsychology and personality

Your brain and your body are complicated and wonderful things. There are 10 billion nerve cells in your brain. Your brain is thought to send information messages at the rate of 240 miles a second. Your heart beats about 100,000 times a day. Placed end to end, all your body's blood vessels would measure about 62,000 miles. Neurons transmit messages from one part of your body to another. Your brain monitors and regulates unconscious body processes such as your digestion and your breathing to coordinate most movements

of your body. It controls your consciousness, allowing you to think, evaluate situations and react appropriately. It is not surprising then to find that your body can influence your behaviour. When your body is tired or hungry, it is likely to put you in a bad mood. The colder the room you sleep in, the better the chances are that you'll have a bad dream.

Psychophysiology and neuropsychology are both branches of psychology that are concerned with the physiological bases of psychological processes. Neuropsychology is predominantly concerned with how the brain influences psychological processes, while psychophysiology deals with all aspects of biological functioning and how it influences psychological processes. A common aim of both these areas of psychology

Stop and think

Crime and genes

1 Since the development of criminology in the 1700s, academics have speculated on the genetic explanation of criminal behaviour. The Human Genome Project and the mapping of human DNA research have again turned attention to whether criminality has a genetic influence. Indeed, there are some who support the notion of a genetic basis to criminal behaviour (Tehrani and Mednick, 2000). If there proves to be evidence suggesting that criminality is influenced by genes, consider:
   a What consequences does this have for understanding and treating criminals?
   b What role can psychology then play in the treatment and rehabilitation of criminals?
   c What consequences does this have for government policies towards criminal behaviour?

2 There is also evidence to suggest that addiction has a genetic basis (Crabbe, 2002). For example, four out of five twin studies report greater concordance for alcoholism in identical (MZ) than in fraternal (DZ) twins. If there is evidence that addiction has a genetic basis:
   a What are the consequences of this for understanding and treating criminals?
   b What consequence does this have for government policies towards addiction?

3 Drug use often begins in early teen years, is most prevalent in the late teens and early twenties and then generally declines substantially thereafter. In the United States, it is estimated that between 60 million and 70 million Americans have tried an illegal drug at some time in their lives. Does this mean nearly everyone inherits vulnerability for addiction?

is to use objective and scientific techniques to link behaviours to the biological functioning of the body; for example, activity levels of neural cells in the brain or heart rate. One of the assumptions underlying these research areas is that all behaviour, including personality and individual differences, can be influenced by physiological and neurological factors. Both psychophysiological and neuropsychological approaches suggest that human behaviour can be understood through exploring physiological factors.

Eysenck's biological model of personality and arousal

The German psychologist Hans Eysenck (1967; 1990a), though he lived all of his working life in London, was one of the first theorists to attempt to relate biology to personality. Eysenck suggested that the human brain has two sets of neural mechanisms, excitatory and inhibitory. The **excitatory mechanism** relates to keeping the individual alert, active and aroused, while the **inhibitory mechanism** relates to inactivity and lethargy.

Eysenck said that the individual seeks to maintain a balance between the excitatory and inhibitory mechanisms, and that this balance is regulated by something identified as the ascending reticular activating system (ARAS). The ARAS, which is located in the brain stem, connects to the areas of the brain such as the:

- **Thalamus** – manages and relays nerve impulses in the brain.
- **Hypothalamus** – regulates the body's metabolic processes, by which substances (i.e. food) are broken down to provide the energy necessary for life, and the autonomic process (heart rate, digestion, respiration and perspiration).
- **Cortex** – is responsible for sophisticated neural processing.

The ARAS manages the amount of information or stimulation that the brain receives and maintains individuals' waking and their sleep, and keeps individuals alert and active (Figure 8.4). Within Eysenck's theory, this information and stimulation process is known as arousal. Two circuits are thought to manage arousal within the individual: the reticulo-cortical and reticulo-limbic. The **reticulo-cortical** circuit controls the cortical arousal generated by incoming stimuli, whereas the **reticulo-limbic** circuit controls arousal to emotional stimuli. Eysenck suggests that arousal is a central variable allowing personality to be linked to a number of responses.

Eysenck linked arousal to two of his personality dimensions: extraversion and neuroticism. Neuroticism comprises personality traits such as anxiety, worry and moody traits. Extraversion comprises personality traits such as sociability, sensation-seeking and being carefree and optimistic.

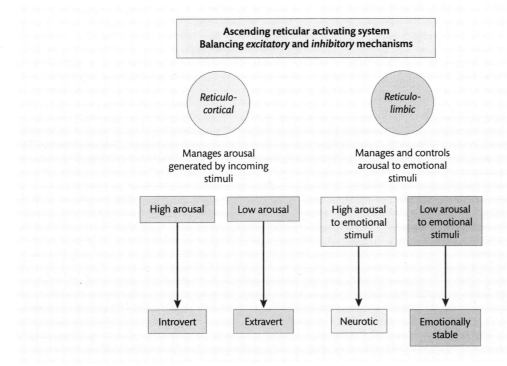

Figure 8.4 Eysenck's biological model of personality.

Extraversion and arousal

Eysenck proposes that extraversion–introversion personality traits are related with the arousal of the reticulo-cortical circuit (incoming stimuli), and that extraverts' and introverts' ARASs operate in different ways, particularly when aroused. Eysenck explained that an introvert would have an ARAS that provides a lot of arousal, while an extravert would have an ARAS that does not provide a lot of arousal. Although this seems the opposite way to what one might expect, Eysenck explains that, when an individual's ARAS continually makes them overly aroused, they will then attempt to avoid stimulation because they already have a lot of it. Consequently, this person will be introverted because they will avoid stimulation and exciting situations. On the other hand, when an individual's ARAS continually makes them under-aroused, they will seek stimulation. This person will be extraverted because they will always be seeking stimulation and exciting situations.

Let us work through an example of this theory to see how extraverts and introverts might differ in work situations. Suppose that our extravert and introvert both work as personal assistants in a company. They both have similar job descriptions; but for our extraverted personal assistant, their working life has to be full of excitement, chatting with co-workers, spending their time in meetings, contributing all the time in meetings, talking to people, enjoying the social aspects of work, and looking to be included in initiatives because they feel the need to be aroused all the time. However, for our introverted personal assistant, their working life is not full of these sorts of activities. Rather, we would find our introverted personal assistant preferring to get on with their own work rather than chatting to co-workers, attending meetings but rarely saying something, rarely engaging in office chat and tending to avoid social occasions, because they feel sufficiently aroused already by the job. What is crucial is that, although the two effectively do the same job, if the extravert and introvert are put into each other's situations, then they will find it difficult to manage. The extravert placed in a personal assistant's job where they simply have to get on with the work and not interact with people will become under-aroused and soon find the job boring; the introvert, when encouraged to interact more, contribute to meetings and organise social events, as they are already sufficiently aroused, will become over-aroused, find these aspects of the work unsatisfying and get upset by the demands of the job role.

A good research example is a well-cited experiment by US psychologist Geen (1984). Geen had two experimental groups: introverts and extraverts. He asked each group to choose the appropriate noise levels of some music to listen to while they were asked to do a difficult and boring task. As predicted, extraverts chose higher levels of music to listen to when working than introverts did. Geen found that both groups completed the task well under these chosen conditions. However, he then switched around the music level for the groups, so that introverts listened to the higher music level while working and extraverts listened to the lower levels of music while working. Under these conditions, extraverts very quickly got bored with the task while the introverts got upset, and both groups' performance at the task worsened.

Neuroticism and arousal

Neuroticism is related with the arousal of the reticulo-limbic circuit. Eysenck explains that neurotics become more aroused owing to emotional stimulation via the reticulo-limbic circuit, whereas people who are not neurotic (emotionally stable) will be less aroused. Eysenck suggested that this difference would be most obvious in stressful situations.

Let us take an example of two students: a neurotic university student and a non-neurotic university student who are about to take an exam. Clearly, taking an exam is a stressful situation – the build-up, the revising, the unseen questions, the actual day of the exam and the post-mortem of the event with one's friends on the course. Our neurotic student would be more aroused by the stress (emotional stimulation) surrounding the exam, and we would find this student worrying about the exam, fretting that they had not done enough revision, frantically searching for extra reading, having sleepless nights before the exam, feeling sick on the day; when the exam was finished, they would worry that they had done really badly and talk about it with their friends. However, in the case of our non-neurotic student, they are not aroused by the stress surrounding the exam. They would tend to worry less when doing their revision, not have sleepless nights before the exam and may prefer not to talk about the exam with their friends after it was over. What is important here is that there is no research to suggest that either personality type leads to better exam performance (we all know students who constantly worry and fret that they have done badly in an exam and end up always getting 100 per cent) but rather that the personality types and level of arousal lead to different reactions (individual differences) in their behaviour around the same stressful event.

Gray's BAS/BIS theory

UK psychologist Jeffrey A. Gray introduced reinforcement sensitivity theory (Gray, 1970; 1981; 1987). This theory began as a modification to Eysenck's theory but is now usually considered as an alternative theory. At the heart of this theory is the view that biological mechanisms move towards things they desire. Gray used the findings of research on animals to study human personality. Gray proposes that personality is based on the interaction between two basic

Profile

Jeffrey A. Gray

Jeffrey A. Gray was born in London and studied at Magdalen College, Oxford, for two degrees, the first in Modern Languages, the second in Psychology and Philosophy. In 1959–1960 he studied clinical psychology at the Institute of Psychiatry in London, after which he studied for a PhD which comprised experimental studies of environmental, genetic and hormonal influences on emotional behaviour in animals.

In 1964 Professor Gray was appointed to a university lectureship in experimental psychology at Oxford. He remained there until he retired from the chair of psychology in 1999, but continued his work as an emeritus professor. Professor Gray's work encompassed a wide area of topics, including neuroanatomical, neurochemical and molecular bases of behaviour in animals and the clinical investigation of abnormal human behaviour in a variety of psychiatric and neurological disorders. He published over 400 papers, comprising journal articles and book chapters, as well as writing seven books, including *Consciousness: Creeping Up on the Hard Problem* (Oxford University Press, 2004). His honours included Presidents' Award, British Psychological Society (1983); President, Experimental Psychology Society (1996); and Honorary Member, Experimental Psychology Society (2000).

We did say that originally Gray's model was seen as an alternative model to Eysenck's theory of arousal of personality. Whether Gray's model is a modification or an alternative to Eysenck's theory, it is worth noting how the two models go together. Figure 8.6 shows how Gray's model maps onto Eysenck's model of arousal and personality.

systems in the brain: the behavioural approach system (BAS) and the behavioural inhibition system (BIS).

The first system, the **behavioural approach system (BAS)**, comprises motivations to approach (Figure 8.5). This system causes the individual to be sensitive to potential rewards and to seek those rewards. Therefore, motivations arise from reward-seeking and are used to explain attractions to other people, certain objects and events, as they are seen by the individual as comprising rewards.

The second system, the **behavioural inhibition system (BIS)**, comprises motivations to avoid. Within this system are those motivations that make the individual sensitive to punishment or potential danger and inclined to avoid those consequences. Fear of certain things, such as animals or persons, are a result of this system.

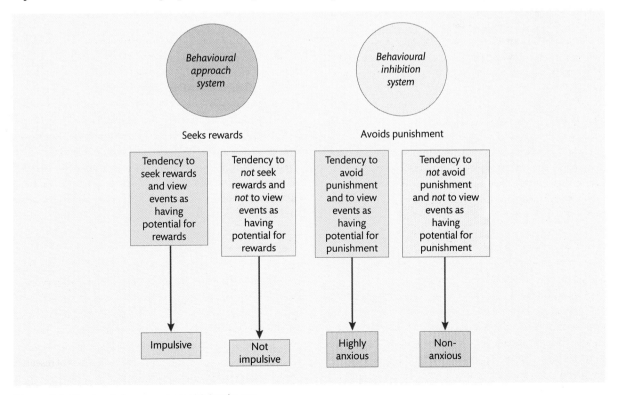

Figure 8.5 Gray's reinforcement sensitivity theory.

Gray linked this theory to two personality variables: impulsivity and anxiety. Those individuals with high levels of behavioural approach are described as impulsive, as they will be highly motivated to seek many rewards, and see the potential for rewards in many aspects of their lives. Individuals with low levels of behavioural approach are described as not impulsive. Individuals who have high levels of behavioural inhibition are described as anxious, as they are particularly responsive to potential punishment or danger. That is, they will tend to see many aspects of their lives as having the potential for possible punishment. Individuals with low levels of behavioural inhibition are described as not anxious.

Examples of how these systems can be measured were produced by US psychologists Charles Carver and Teri White (1994). Carver and White produced a 24-item questionnaire measure (BIS/BAS scales) of the behavioural approach system and the behavioural inhibition system. Questions that measure an individual's BAS include 'I go out of my way to get things I want [item 3]', 'I'm always willing to try something new if I think it will be fun [item 5]' and 'When good things happen to me, it affects me strongly [item 18]'. Questions that measure an individual's BIS include 'I feel pretty worried or upset when I think or know somebody is angry at me [item 13]', 'If I think something unpleasant is going to happen I usually get pretty "worked up" [item 16]' and 'I worry about making mistakes [item 24]'.

Again, let us consider our example of two personal assistants at work to illustrate these two systems. A worker who has high levels of behavioural approach will be impulsive in their work. They tend to seek rewards in their work, looking for opportunities for promotion, looking to contribute all the time, or looking for congratulations or appreciation from work colleagues. We might find our worker who has high levels of behavioural approach immediately volunteering for things and speaking out suddenly in work meetings. Meanwhile, our worker who has high levels of behavioural inhibition, who is particularly responsive to potential punishment or danger, will tend not to want to draw attention to themselves at work for fear of disapproval by managers and co-workers. They might worry and be anxious about talking at meetings, making mistakes at work and giving presentations in case they say the wrong thing or show themselves up.

The final point to highlight from Gray's theory is how the notions of reward and punishment relate to impulsive and anxious individuals. Impulsive people respond well to rewards, and not well to punishment. Anxious individuals respond well to punishment and not to rewards. If you are a manager in the workplace and you want to motivate impulsive people, you would do better to offer promotions and wage raises rather than suggest possible punishments, such as redundancies. Conversely, if you want to motivate anxious people, you would do better to indicate the possibilities of punishment rather than offer promotions and wage rises. For example, we can imagine how an impulsive person would spend their work days doing things looking for promotion, never concerning themselves with the possibility of losing their job. We can also imagine how an anxious person in work worries about the possibility of the sack, rather than potential promotion, thinking they would never be able to reach such heights.

A research example of how the BAS and the BIS work was carried out by Finnish psychologists Tarja Heponiemi, Liisa Keltikangas-Järvinen, Sampsa Puttonen and Niklas Ravaja (2003). This research concentrates on looking at the effects of reward and punishment on positive and negative feelings alongside measures of the BAS and the BIS. In this experiment, the researchers measured the BAS and the BIS using Carver and White's BIS/BAS scales. The researchers also asked participants in the experiment to complete a number of tasks, during which they were asked to indicate each time their own levels of positive and negative emotion. The tasks that participants were asked to complete included tasks designed to induce a negative experience (punishment tasks, such as being startled by a loud noise, and a reaction-time task where completion is done within a set time while loud noises are being played) and a task designed to induce a positive experience (reward) – a mental arithmetic task with a monetary prize ($40) for the best performance. Heponiemi and colleagues found that a greater degree of behavioural approach was related to more positive feelings during the appetitive math task. Additionally, they found that a greater degree of behaviour inhibition was related to more negative feelings during aversive tasks and especially during the startle task (Figure 8.6).

Cloninger's biological model of personality

C. Robert Cloninger, a US biological psychiatrist, proposed a psychobiological personality theory, including seven personality dimensions. His theory of personality is based on combining findings from a series of family, psychometric, neuropharmacologic (a branch of medical science dealing with the action of drugs on and in the nervous system) and neuroanatomical (a branch of anatomy that deals with the nervous system) studies of behavioural conditioning and learning in man (Cloninger et al., 1993).

To begin with, Cloninger's model included only three dimensions, but it has since been expanded to include seven domains of personality. The theory of personality is broken down into four *temperament* domains:

- novelty-seeking;
- harm avoidance;
- reward dependence;
- persistence,

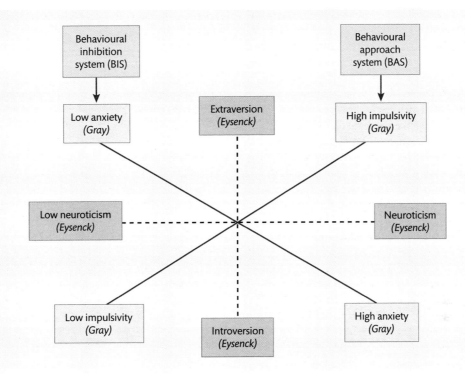

Figure 8.6 The relationship between Gray's model and Eysenck's model of personality and arousal.

and three *character* domains:

- self-directedness;
- cooperativeness;
- self-transcendence.

The temperament domains are the areas we are most interested in from a personality perspective. Like the theories of Eysenck and Gray, they are linked to biological systems and are thought to be inherited. The four temperaments are thought to be organised as independent brain systems aligned to specific nerve cells or fibres that transmit nerve impulses by neurotransmitters. Neurotransmitters are chemicals that are used to relay, amplify and modulate electrical signals in the brain. Cloninger links our personality to those neurotransmitters that are responsible for the activation and inhibition of our behaviour and the learning and responses to both real and perceived rewards and punishments. Cloninger's four temperament dimensions are:

- **Novelty-seeking** – This dimension reflects impulsive behaviour and activation of behaviour. The key term to describe novelty-seeking is 'behaviour activation'. Novelty-seeking is a tendency to like excitement, responding to novel stimuli. A person who scores high on novelty-seeking likes to explore, meet new people and find out about new things. Novelty-seeking is thought to be connected to the dopamine neurotransmitter. Dopamine is crucial to the parts of the brain that control our movements and is commonly associated with the pleasure

aspects of the brain, providing feelings of enjoyment and motivation to do things. In the frontal lobes of the brain, the part of the brain involved with planning, coordinating, controlling and executing behaviour, dopamine controls the flow of information from other areas of the brain. You can clearly see that Cloninger is using the brain's operations regarding motivation, enjoyment and planning to do things to define the temperament of novelty-seeking.

- **Harm avoidance** – This dimension reflects cautious and low-risk-taking behavioural traits. The key term to describe harm avoidance is 'behaviour inhibition'. Harm avoidance includes a tendency to respond intensely to aversive stimuli or to inhibit behaviour in order to avoid punishment or novelty. People who display harm avoidance traits are afraid to try out new things or are shy with people. Harm avoidance is thought to be connected to the serotonin (or 5-hydroxytryptamine, 5-HT) neurotransmitter that is known to modulate mood, emotion and sleep, and it is involved in the control of numerous behavioural and physiological functions.

- **Reward dependence** – This dimension reflects friendliness and a tendency for seeking rewards. People who are high on reward dependence respond well to reward, such as verbal signals of social approval or positive responses from other people. The key term to describe reward dependence is 'behaviour maintenance'. Reward dependence is thought to be connected to norepinephrine (also called noradrenaline). Norepinephrine is a stress hormone that affects parts of the human brain where attention and impulsivity are controlled. It is related to activation of the sympathetic nervous system, which regulates our responses to stress.

- **Persistence** – This dimension reflects a tendency to persevere in behaviour despite frustration and tiredness. Someone high in persistence would have the ability to stay with a task and not give up easily. Persistence wasn't in Cloninger's model originally but emerged from the reward dependence dimension. Cloninger had found, when trying to measure reward dependence, that certain items relating to persistence weren't associated with reward dependence. Persistence also represents behaviour maintenance. Similarly to reward dependence, this dimension is thought to be connected to norepinephrine.

The character traits in Cloninger's theory contrast to temperaments because they are not biological in origin, but rather refer to how individuals understand themselves in their social world. Character traits represent our emotions, habits, goals and intellectual abilities that we have formed in response to the outside world. Cloninger's three character traits are:

- **Self-directedness** – This trait reflects the individual's own concept of how autonomous a person is; for example, the extent to which they are independent in mind or judgement. In this dimension people show feelings such as self-esteem, personal integrity and leadership.
- **Cooperativeness** – This trait is based on the person's self-concept of how they fit into humanity or society. Feelings of morality, ethics, community and compassion are included in this dimension.
- **Self-transcendence** – This trait reflects individuals' self-concept in terms of their common beliefs about mystical experiences. Concepts such as religious faith and spirituality are formed within this dimension.

Although Cloninger separated out temperament and character traits, he did propose that the two interact. For example, individuals with the same temperament may behave differently as a result of character development. For example, one person might be high in novelty-seeking and also high in cooperativeness, and consequently, they might spend a lot of their time going out and seeking to raise money by doing a lot of charity work. Another person might be high in novelty-seeking and also high in self-transcendence, and therefore, they might travel the world exploring their spirituality by visiting a number of countries with different religious and spiritual backgrounds.

Cloninger's model of personality is measured by the Temperament and Character Inventory-Revised (TCI-R), which contains 240 items. Responses are scored on a 5-point scale (1, definitively false; 2, mostly or probably false; 3, neither true nor false, or about equally true or false;

4, mostly or probably true; 5, definitively true). These items reflect each of the temperament and character dimensions, for example:

- **Novelty-seeking** – These items ask the individual about how excitable, exploratory, impulsive and extravagant (high novelty-seeking) they are, as opposed to how reserved and reflective they are (low novelty-seeking).
- **Harm avoidance** – These items ask the individual about how much they worry and are pessimistic, fearful of uncertainty and shy (high harm avoidance) versus how optimistic they are (low harm avoidance).
- **Reward dependence** – These items ask the individual about how attached and dependent they are (high reward dependence) versus how detached and independent they are (low reward dependence).
- **Persistence** – These items ask the individual about their responses to potential rewards, their ambitiousness, their perfectionism (high persistence) versus their laziness, frustration when not achieving and their tendency to quit when faced with obstacles (low persistence).
- **Self-directedness** – These items ask the individual about their tendency to act and take responsibility, their purposefulness and resourcefulness (high self-direction) versus their tendency to blame people and have a lack of self-direction (low self-direction).
- **Cooperativeness** – These items ask the individual about their feeling of social acceptance, empathy and helpfulness (high cooperativeness) versus their social intolerance, social disinterestedness and tendency to want to take revenge (low cooperativeness).
- **Self-transcendence** – These items ask the individual about their tendencies to identify with transpersonal ideas and spiritual acceptance (high self-transcendence) versus a tendency to emphasise materialism (low self-transcendence).

Clearly there are links between Cloninger's model of personality and Eysenck's and Gray's models of personality. Novelty-seeking is thought to mirror Eysenck's extraversion, and harm avoidance is thought to mirror Gray's behavioural inhibition and Eysenck's neuroticism. Also, Cloninger's reward dependence seems to be equivalent to Gray's behavioural approach system.

Empirical evidence for biological theories of personality

In the last section, we introduced three theories that have linked personality variables to psychophysiological and neuropsychological processes. But how do researchers set about establishing such links? In this section we are going to give you a brief introduction to the types of physiological measures and studies that are used to examine whether these biological personality dimensions are related to psychophysiological and neuropsychological processes. What we are interested in most, here, is direct evidence that links physiological factors to personality dimensions, because then we would be able to show that there is a biological basis to the theories of Eysenck, Gray and Cloninger. There is a lot of research that looks at this area, so, to give you the best idea of the sort of physiological measures and physiological evidence for biological theories, we are going to use the 1999 summary of psychologists Matthews and Gilliland (1999), who looked at the biological personality theories of Eysenck and Gray.

Now, it is crucial to remember what we are looking for. With Eysenck's theory we are looking for extraversion being related to physiological measures of stimulation, and neuroticism being related to physiological measures of emotion. With Gray, we would expect to find that anxiety is associated with high sensitivity to signals of punishment and impulsivity, with high sensitivity to signals of reward.

UK psychologists Matthews and Gilliland (1999) suggest that two sets of measures have been used to examine these aspects of Eysenck's and Gray's theories: (1) measures of the central nervous system; and (2) measures of the autonomic nervous system.

The central nervous system and biological personality dimensions

The central nervous system comprises the brain and spinal cord; this system supervises and coordinates the activity of the entire nervous system and is the part of the body that transmits information to, and from, our senses or sensations. Measures of the central nervous system involve measuring brain activity.

A first measure of central nervous system activity is the **electroencephalogram (EEG)**. The EEG, a measure of the electrical activity produced by the brain, is obtained by placing electrodes on the scalp and is presented in waveform. The waveform can then be analysed and is broken down into four ranges: delta, theta, alpha and beta. Electrical activity that falls within the **beta range** is considered to reflect activity, while electrical activity that falls within the **alpha range** is considered to reflect low states of arousal.

Remember that, in Eysenck's theory, we are looking for extraversion being related to physiological measures of stimulation, and neuroticism being related to physiological measures of emotion. Gale (1973; 1983) reviewed a number of studies suggesting support for Eysenck's theory. In reviewing these studies, Gale shows that, when placed in aroused situations, introverts tend to show significantly higher levels of alpha activity (low

arousal) than extraverts do. However, Swedish psychologist George Stenberg (1992) found no significant relationship between a number of EEG measures and either extraversion or neuroticism.

A second measure of central nervous system activity suggested is the event-related potential (ERP). The ERP, like the EEG, measures electrical activity in the brain, but does so in response to stimuli in the environment. ERP is measured by responses within the first 100–500 milliseconds following stimuli, and Eysenck (1994) explains that waveforms of 300 milliseconds, something called P300, indicates when the cortical systems are showing arousal. Stelmack and Houlihan (1995) found higher levels of P300 amplitudes (arousal) in introverts and neurotics in response to stimuli, which suggests higher arousal and supports Eysenck's model. However, Matthews and Gilliland note that there are very few replications of this finding. In terms of extraversion and ERP, Fishman *et al.* (2011) found that higher scores on extraversion were found to be associated with higher amplitudes of the P300 component of the ERPs in response to human faces (i.e. a social based stimuli).

There is evidence to support Gray's theory of personality. With Gray we would expect to find that anxiety is associated with high sensitivity to signals of punishment and impulsivity with high sensitivity to signals of reward. Again, research has concentrated on similar measures of the central nervous system (i.e. EEG and ERP measures). For example, Stenberg (1992) found that impulsive participants showed signs of lower arousal, and more anxious participants showed higher levels of the beta waveform (remember that the beta range is considered to reflect activity) in response to negative emotional stimuli.

However, Matthews and Amelang (1993) and Matthews and Gilliland (1999) have suggested that the significant relationships between personality traits of both Eysenck and Gray and EEG and ERP measures are often very small, suggesting that the evidence supporting the predicted relationship between personality and brain activity is weak.

The autonomic nervous system and biological personality dimensions

The autonomic nervous system is the part of the brain that regulates unconscious or involuntary actions of the body, such as muscles, heart rate and glands (that produce secretions from the body, such as sweating). Measures of the autonomic nervous system measure those systems that are associated with regulating arousal (for example, the heart). Two further sets of measures tend to be used: cardiovascular and electromodal. Cardiovascular measures involve measuring the heart and the blood vessels. **Electromodal measures (EDA)** ascertain the electrical activity of the skin. There are two main ways of classifying EDA measures:

- **Baseline EDA measures** – are often obtained through a small electric current to the skin via an electrode leading to the measure of skin resistance or skin conductance.
- **Phasic EDA measures** – are skin responses to known stimuli, such as caffeine, noise or visual stimuli.

In applying Eysenck's theory, cardiovascular activity (e.g. heart rate) should be higher in neurotics and introverts as they both get upset by arousal and over-arousal, and EDA measures should be able to discriminate between introverts and extraverts. Some studies have explored the relationship between arousal and personality using cardiovascular activity. Richards and Eves (1991) found increased heart rate to arousal stimuli among introverts, though Naveteur and Roy (1990) did not. In terms of EDA measures, Matthews and Gilliland suggest that overall studies using baseline EDA measures have provided little information that supports Eysenck's theory, but studies using phasic EDA measures found general support for Eysenck's model. For example, Smith (1983) and Fowles *et al.* (1977) found evidence that introverts have higher levels of EDA than extraverts do where respondents are presented with arousal stimuli such as caffeine or stress. However, neuroticism is not generally found to be related to EDA measures (Matthews and Gilliland, 1999).

Biological personality dimensions and other biological and physiological systems

There are other studies that link biological personality dimensions to other biological and physiological systems. Dopamine is a neurotransmitter (it transmits signals from a neuron to cells) that regulates emotional responses and activity. Dopamine not only allows us to recognise rewards but also engage in behaviour that seeks out those rewards. Depue and Collins (1999) found that extraversion was related to higher sensitivity of the mesolimbic dopamine system (a pathway within the brain that carries dopamine from one part of the brain to another). Cohen *et al.* (2005) also found extraversion to be related to dopamine activation during a gambling task. This finding suggests that extraversion is associated with a physiological system that recognises and seeks out rewards.

Johnson *et al.* (1999) have found extraversion to be related to blood flow activity in the anterior cingulate cortex (thought to be related to reward anticipation, as well as regulating blood pressure and heart rate), temporal lobe

(contains the hippocampus and is important in the formation of long-term memories) and the posterior thalamus (relays sensory and motor signals to the cerebral cortex). Again, this finding suggests that extraversion is related to reward-sensitive regions of the brain.

A lot of research has concentrated on the effects of reward and punishment on physiological measures among impulsive and anxious people, as according to Gray's theory. Gray's theory asserts that anxiety is associated with high sensitivity to signals of punishment and impulsivity (best described as the behavioural approach system within his theory), with high sensitivity to signals of reward. One example is the study carried out by US psychologists Peter Arnett and Joseph Newman (2000). Arnett and Newman studied prison inmates at a minimum security prison in southern Wisconsin. These researchers measured a number of physiological responses while the prisoners took part in an experiment that involved positive and negative stimuli that were linked to gaining money or losing small amounts of money. Among this sample, there were increases in heart rate when participants were given a reward. This finding is consistent with predictions around the behavioural approach system and the theory that rewards are related to physiological responses. Arnett and Newman also found that participants showed significant increases in the electrical activity of the skin in response to punishment. This finding is consistent with predictions around the behavioural inhibition system regarding punishment and its relationship to physiological responses.

Consideration of biological theories of personality

The strength of biological theories of personality (Eysenck, Gray and Cloninger) is that they use important psychological mechanisms to explain the different dimensions of personality. Within these theories the concepts of arousal, activation and inhibition are important variables that allow personality to be linked to many different types of behaviours and responses to stimuli. Of particular note is Eysenck's theory of arousal and personality as this was the first modern attempt to examine personality within biological factors. The fact that it was developed before many modern physiological measures were developed certainly was an admirable attempt to try to understand human behaviour in relation to brain and body functioning. We can also see from some of the evidence that is outlined that personality dimensions are linked to physiological activity such as brain activity (EEG and ERP) and EDA measures (skin conductance or heart rate).

However, the main problem with biological theories of personality is the lack of consistent evidence supporting these theories. For example, Matthews and Gilliland (1999) suggest that, when you consider the EEG studies looking at Eysenck's personality dimensions, the relationships that are found to be consistent with Eysenck's theory tend to be weak. There is very little evidence to suggest that neuroticism is related to arousal. If Eysenck's theory should be deemed adequate, given that we are dealing with biological factors, the research evidence should perhaps be much stronger and much more consistent. Such a problem is found with research evidence across Eysenck's, Gray's and Cloninger's theories; although sometimes evidence is found to support the theory, sometimes it is not, and usually the results are not strong enough. Matthews and Gilliland (1999) suggest the reason for this might be that Eysenck's, Gray's and Cloninger's theories may have oversimplified a number of biological processes in their theory. For example, Zuckerman (1991) illustrates that the ascending reticular activating system (ARAS), thought to be a major system in Eysenck's theory, may not be as important to arousal as Eysenck thought. Arousal has been found to affect other aspects of the brain, and Eysenck's view that the ARAS regulates arousal by switching it on and off may represent an oversimplification of the brain. Furthermore, although Gray's and Cloninger's theories are more recent developments, they may also represent an oversimplification of complicated biological processes. As we noted before, there are links between Cloninger's model of personality and Eysenck's and Gray's models. Novelty-seeking is thought to mirror extraversion, and harm avoidance is thought to mirror Gray's behavioural inhibition and Eysenck's neuroticism. Also, Cloninger's reward dependence seems to be equivalent to Gray's behavioural approach system. However, there are differences between the personality theories in terms of which parts of the brain the theory emphasises. While Eysenck emphasises the ARAS and arousal, Gray emphasises two separate systems, the behavioural approach system (BAS) and the behavioural inhibition system (BIS), and Cloninger links the personality to dopamine, serotonin and norepinephrine. As evidence is found for each of the theories, it is probably likely that, on their own, each theory represents an oversimplification of the brain processes, and a combination of the different brain systems and activities identified by these theorists may best explain a biological basis to personality.

Together then, there does seem to be some biological evidence to support biological theories of personality. Reviews of the area, such as Matthews and Gilliland's (1999), suggest that further work needs to be done to explore such theories of personality fully. None the less, Eysenck's, Gray's and Cloninger's theories clearly link a number of personality and individual difference variables to neural processes, although their theories have had varying degrees of success in demonstrating this link empirically. Even so, these theories may produce important and dynamic foundations to expand our understanding of personality.

Final comments

The aim of this discussion was to introduce you to theories that explore biological bases of personality, behavioural genetics, neuropsychology and psychophysiology. We have shown you how psychologists have applied the ideas that surround behavioural genetics and heritability estimates to understand influences on personality. We have presented theoretical and research evidence surrounding genetic and environmental influence on personality that can be used to assess the value of heritability estimates. We have shown you how Eysenck, Gray and Cloninger have used neuropsychology and psychophysiology concepts to develop biological models of personality. We have also given you some evidence and general comments to assess the strengths and weaknesses of biological models of personality.

Stop and think

Personality and arousal, reward and punishment

1   Consider whether you are more an impulsive person or an anxious person. Do you generally respond well to reward or punishment?

2   Consider whether you are more an impulsive person or an anxious person in two situations: (1) when you are working or in university; or (2) when you are with your friends. Try to examine whether you respond well to reward or punishment in these situations.

3   Imagine you are a teacher trying to teach a class a new skill. Within this class some of the students are extraverted, some are impulsive, some are neurotic and some are anxious. Discuss how the issues of arousal, reward and punishment are going to influence how you teach the class this new skill.

Summary

- Two terms that are important to know in this area of study in behavioural genetics are genotype and phenotype.
- Three types of studies that you will regularly see in this research area are family studies, twin studies and adoption studies.
- These types of studies have been used to develop genetic heritability estimates of personality.
- A number of American, Australian and European samples consistently suggest that there is moderate heritability of personality from genetic factors accounting for from 20 to 50 per cent of phenotypic variance across a number of samples and cultures.
- Where previously researchers used the *additive assumption* to compare genetic versus environmental effects on personality, behaviour geneticists consider a number of genetic and environmental influences on personality.
- There are six general issues surrounding genetic heritability estimates of personality. These centre on conceptions of heritability and the environment, different types of genetic variance, shared versus non-shared environmental influences, the representativeness of twin and adoption studies, assortative mating and the changing world of genetics.
- Reiss outlines three models of genetic transmission in which inherited genes form phenotypes based on the family environment: the passive model, the child-effects model and the parent-effects model.
- Harris presents the group socialisation theory to explain the importance of non-shared environmental factors in personality. Harris lists five aspects that are important to consider: context-specific socialisation, outside the home socialisation, transmission of culture via group processes, group processes that widen differences between social groups and group processes that widen differences among individuals within the group.
- Eysenck proposes that extraversion–introversion personality traits are related to the arousal of the reticulo-cortical circuit, and that, for extraverts and introverts, the ascending reticular activating system (ARAS) operates in different ways, particularly in terms of arousal.
- Gray's reinforcement sensitivity theory proposes that personality is based on the interaction between two basic systems in the brain: the behavioural approach system (BAS) and the behavioural inhibition system (BIS). Gray linked this theory to two personality variables: impulsivity and anxiety.
- Cloninger identified four temperaments (novelty-seeking, harm avoidance, reward dependence and persistence) and three characters (self-directedness, cooperativeness and self-transcendence). Cloninger links the personality dimensions to dopamine, serotonin and norepinephrine.
- Physiological evidence for biological theories of personality is weak and inconsistent, but there is some evidence for these theories that may provide important and dynamic foundations to understanding personality.

Connecting up

You will want to look back at Chapter 7 (The Trait Approach to Personality) for more information on the three-factor and five-factor models of personality that are mentioned in this chapter.

We will revisit many of these issues regarding heritability estimates in Chapter 14 (Heritability and Socially Defined Race Differences in Intelligence) when we look at intelligence.

Critical thinking

Discussion questions

- How well do you think biological factors can predict personality?
- Think about the personality of three immediate family members. Try to assess them in terms of the five-factor model of personality (extraversion, neuroticism, openness, agreeableness and conscientiousness). Describe how similar, or different, the personality of each of these three family members is to your own personality. Speculate on reasons for this.

- Think about the personality of three of your closest friends. Again, try to assess them in terms of the five-factor model of personality. How similar or different is the personality of each of your friends to your own personality? Speculate on reasons for this.
- Consider Harris' list of outside-family factors that influence personality (see Figure 8.2). Have any of these factors influenced your own personality?
- What do you think is the most important predictor of personality: genetics or the environment?
- How useful do you think the concepts of arousal, reward and punishment are to understanding personality?

Essay questions

- Critically compare genetic versus environmental predictors of personality.
- Is personality purely a result of the environment? Critically discuss.
- Critically examine how biological factors influence personality.
- Critically compare Eysenck's, Gray's and Cloninger's biological models of personality.
- Critically evaluate the relationship between arousal and personality.

Going further

Books

- Plomin, R. (2004). *Nature and nurture: An introduction to human behavioral genetics*. London: Wadsworth.
- Plomin, R., DeFries, J. C., McClearn, G. E. and McGuffin, P. (2000). *Behavioral genetics: A primer*. London: Freeman.
- Eysenck, H. J. and Eysenck, M. W. (1985). The psychophysiology of personality. In: *Personality and individual differences: A natural science approach* (pp. 217–236). New York: Plenum.

Journals

- Maccoby, E. E. (2000). Parenting and its effects on children: On reading and misreading behavior genetics. *Annual Review of Psychology, 51*, 1–27. Published by Annual Reviews, Palo Alto, California. Available online via Business Source Premier.
- Baker, L. D. and Daniels, D. (1990). Nonshared environmental influences and personality differences in adult twins. *Journal of Personality and Social Psychology, 58*, 103–110. Published by the American Psychological Association. Available online via PsycARTICLES.
- Bouchard, T. J. Jr and Loehlin, J. C. (2001). Genes, personality, and evolution. *Behavioural Genetics, 31*, 243–273. Published by Kluwer Academic Publishers. Available online via Kluwer or SwetsWise.

- Harris, J. R. (1995). Where is the child's environment? A group socialization theory of development. *Psychological Review, 102*, 458–489. Published by the American Psychological Association. Available online via PsycARTICLES.

You may wish to search the following journals on an online library database (Web of Science; PsycINFO) with the search term 'Personality':

- *Behavioral and Brain Sciences.* Published by Cambridge University Press. Available online via Cambridge University Press and SwetsWise.
- *Behavioural Genetics.* Published by Kluwer Academic Publishers. Available online via Kluwer or SwetsWise.
- *Behavioural Brain Research.* Published by Elsevier. Available online via Science Direct.

Web links

- *Human Genome Project.* Completed in 2003, the Human Genome Project (HGP) was a 13-year effort coordinated by the US Department of Energy and the National Institutes of Health. During the early years of the HGP, the Wellcome Trust (UK) became a major partner; additional contributions came from Japan, France, Germany, China and others. (**www.ornl.gov/sci/techresources/Human_Genome/home.shtml** and **www.ornl.gov/sci/techresources/Human_Genome/elsi/ behavior.shtml**)

Film and literature

- *Eternal Sunshine of the Spotless Mind* (2004, directed by Michel Gondry). To what extent does knowledge of physiological aspects influence our behaviour? Joel is

stunned to discover that his girlfriend Clementine has had her memories of their relationship erased. Out of desperation, he contacts the inventor of the process to have Clementine removed from his own memory. But, as Joel's memories progressively disappear, he begins to rediscover their earlier passion. From deep within the recesses of his brain, Joel attempts to escape the procedure.

- In this discussion we looked at Harris' identification of a number of outside-family factors and their possible influence on personality. There is an excellent portrayal of how environmental factors interplay with personality in the film *The Departed* (2006, directed by Martin Scorsese).

- *Little Women* (1868–1869, Louisa M. Alcott). *Little Women* is the story of the March family. This is the story of five sisters, who share genetic similarities but, through their shared and non-shared environments, develop different personalities. Of course, this is a fictional story, but it shows you how non-shared environments can influence personality. Despite their efforts to be good, the girls show different personality traits through their own experiences. Meg becomes discontented, Jo becomes angry regularly, Amy becomes rather unnatural and artificial in her behaviour and Beth is always kind and gentle. The most recent adaptation to film was released in 1994 (directed by Gillian Armstrong and starring Winona Ryder, Kirsten Dunst, Claire Danes, Susan Sarandon and Christian Bale).

Explore the website accompanying this text at **www.pearsoned.co.uk/maltby** for further resources to help you with your studies. These include multiple-choice questions, essay questions, web links and ideas for advanced reading.

CHAPTER 9
Biological Basis of Personality II:
Evolutionary Psychology and Animal Studies of Personality

Key themes

- Evolutionary theory
- Adaptation
- Evolutionary theory, sexual strategies and altruism
- Evolutionary personality theory
- The evolution of individual differences
- Life history and personality
- Animal personality research
- Methods and measurement in animal personality research
- Animal personality and the five-factor model of personality

Learning outcomes

After studying this discussion you should:

- Be familiar with some key ideas and examples in evolutionary theory
- Understand the main elements of evolutionary personality and individual difference psychology
- Be able to describe methods and measurement in animal research
- Be able to describe how the five-factor model of personality has been used in animal personality research
- Understand the considerations of evolutionary personality and animal personality theory and research

Introduction

In September 2004, the Serbian education minister Ljiljana Colic resigned after causing public outrage by telling schools to restrict teaching of Charles Darwin's evolution theory. She had proposed banning the teaching of evolution theory in schools, until creationism (belief in the literal interpretation of the Bible) could be taught alongside the topic. The Serbian minister had said that Darwin's theory was no more legitimate than the idea that God created all the creatures in the world. Her policy was quickly reversed by the Serbian government after a storm of protests. Yet in 2005, in the town of Dover, Pennsylvania, in the United States, Darwin's theory was at the centre of another argument on the origins of mankind, as a local high school became the first school in the United States to discuss a creationism theory as an alternative to Darwin's theory of evolution in class. In this discussion we are going to outline how Darwin's theory of evolution has influenced personality and individual difference theory and research. We are also going to outline how the study of animals' personality and behaviour has informed our understanding of personality and individual differences.

Source: Alamy Images/Dave Watts

Evolutionary theory

Today, 150 years after Darwin published *The Origin of Species* in 1859, his ideas are still contentious. Before Darwin's publication there was a predominant belief in western culture that all species had been individually created by God and had not evolved, and that humans were quite separate from other animals. Darwin became stressed by the realisation that his theories would offend his family and friends (who were also scientists). It is thought that this stress eventually destroyed Darwin's health. As we can see from the examples in the introduction, Darwin's concerns were perhaps justified, as his ideas are still causing controversy today, not least in the United States and Europe.

Darwin's main theory was the theory of *natural selection*, and underlying Darwin's theory were four crucial ideas: variety, heritability, competition and adaptation. Behavioural ecologists J. R. Krebs and N. B. Davies (1993) provide a lovely example of Darwin's theory, presenting it in his original terms as well as showing how his ideas are applicable in modern genetic terms (although you will have had to have read the previous discussion (Chapter 8)

to appreciate this fully). Look at Table 9.1. In column 1 is Darwin's original theory of evolution as presented in his theory of natural selection. In column 2 is a description of how the theory of evolution fits in with our modern knowledge of genetics.

As you can see, there is a very complicated process occurring in terms of how certain genes (aspects of the genotype) and forms, functions and behaviour (aspects of the phenotype) survive within a population. Within the theory of evolution, the genes, the forms, their function and behaviour are undergoing a process of natural selection that includes variation, heritability, competition and adaptation.

In this discussion we are going to concentrate less on the biological side of these processes and instead look at how evolutionary theory has been used by some psychologists to inform our understanding of personality and individual differences. You will see how the themes and concepts of variation, heritability, competition and adaptation re-occur through the theory, research and application of evolutionary aspects to personality. However, we need first to consider evolutionary theory and its development into a psychological approach through the use of the concept of adaptation.

Table 9.1 Krebs and Davies' (1993) summary of Darwin's original theory of evolution as presented in his theory of natural selection and how it fits in with modern genetic knowledge

Column 1	Column 2
Summary of Darwin's original theory of evolution as presented in *The Origin of Species*	How the theory of evolution fits within modern genetic knowledge
First is the idea of *variation*: individuals within a species are variable in terms of their morphology (form and structure of animals and plants, especially with respect to the forms), physiology (functions of living organisms and their parts) and behaviour.	All individuals have a genotype (a composition of genes) that is the internal genetic code or blueprint for constructing and maintaining a living individual. This genetic code is biologically inherited and is found within the proteins that are fundamental components of all the atoms, molecules, cells, tissues and organs of the individual. This genetic code influences the form, functioning and behaviour of the individual.
Second is the idea of *heritability*. Some of the variation within a species is heritable (passed from one generation to the next). Darwin presented evidence for this idea by noting that, on average, offspring (the child) bore a closer resemblance to their parents than to other individuals in a population.	*Heritability and variability*: within a species, many of the genes are presented in a series or alternative forms on a chromosome (a linear strand of DNA and associated proteins). These are known as alleles. What is different about a set of alleles is that each allele codes for slightly different forms of the same protein. The different alleles will cause differences in the actual development of the individual, therefore producing individual differences in the population.
Third is the idea of *competition*. A species of individuals will increase in numbers. There are often more children than parents in a family, and this leads to an increase of numbers in the species. Therefore there is competition within a species for resources such as places to live, mates and food.	There is a process of *competition* between the different alleles of a gene to be on the chromosome.
Fourth is the central idea of *natural selection*. As the result of competition, some individuals of the species will leave more offspring than do others. These children will have inherited characteristics (form, functions and behaviour) from their parents, and so evolutionary change will have taken place. Darwin called this idea *natural selection*.	Any allele that is able to reproduce more than another allele does will become a dominant version of that gene. This is also a process of *natural selection*.
The final idea is *adaptation*. As a result of natural selection, the individuals within a species become adapted to the environment. These are the individuals who have genes of those parents who have done better in the competition within a species for resources such as places to live, mates and food.	Finally, there is also a process of *adaptation*. The selection of alleles and genes is mediated by the phenotype. The phenotype is the outward manifestation of the individual. It is the sum of all the atoms, molecules, cells, tissues and organs – namely, the form, functions and behaviour of any individual. By mediation, we mean that even if a particular allele becomes dominant, its survival depends on whether the phenotype interaction with the environment leads to its survival. That is, if a gene creates a particular form, function or behaviour, and the individual survives through natural selection with the environment, then that particular allele will survive. If the individual doesn't survive through natural selection with the environment, then that particular allele won't survive.

Source: Based on Krebs and Davies (1993).

Evolutionary psychology and adaptation

Evolutionary theory has spawned a number of schools of thought and investigation. One school of thought, sociobiology (E. O. Wilson, 1975), was influential in the literature examining how natural selection occurred within a species and how that species adapted. Many of the ideas explored and developed within sociobiology have been used to inform our next area of consideration, **evolutionary psychology**.

Evolutionary psychology attempts to explain behaviour within evolutionary terms. One of the key ideas for an evolutionary psychologist is that of 'adaptation'. Adaptation in general evolutionary psychology is a major part of the evolutionary natural selection process, and, within evolutionary theory, it is a way of explaining many biological characteristics. If we take the human body, we can see that many aspects of human biological functioning are adaptations. For example, muscles are an adaptation allowing us to move and lift things. Eyes are an adaptation allowing humans to see. In fact, it is possible to see a lot of body processes as adaptations. Indeed, there are three main ways of describing adaptations that allow us to identify and understand the evolutionary modifications that a species make: functionality, domain specificity and numerous.

- **Functional** – All adaptations need to be functionally related to survival or reproduction. That is, they must serve a purpose in the species' survival or reproduction. One of the characteristics most often identified as playing a role in human evolution is the opposable thumb. The evolution of opposable thumbs has allowed humans to do all sorts of tasks (use tools, build weapons, build homes) that have aided our development and helped us get round problems to enable our survival.
- **Domain-specific** – All adaptive processes are designed to solve a particular problem related to survival or reproduction. That is, adaptations evolve to solve problems in particular domains, and are often less well suited to solve problems occurring in other domains. For example, the biological mechanism, the heart, is responsible for pumping blood through the blood vessels of the body, but is not involved in many other biological functions of the body.
- **Numerous** – Often adaptations may involve numerous mechanisms. For example, the body has a number of biological mechanisms that allow humans to eat food, through consuming that food, digesting that food and getting rid of waste.

In a similar theme to the way that the concept of adaptation is used by evolutionary theorists to explain biological functions, evolutionary psychologists are concerned with studying and explaining how human *behaviour* can be described as adaptations. Therefore evolutionary psychologists will tend to examine a behaviour and explain it as being an adaptation, introducing concepts such as functionality, domain specificity and numerous others, to show how the behaviour can be understood in evolutionary terms. Let us now show you how evolutionary theory (with its theory of adaptation combined with elements of natural selection, variation, heritability and competition) is used by evolutionary psychologists to explain human behaviour. To do this we are going to look at two classic examples of how evolutionary psychologists explain:

- sexual and mating strategies;
- cooperation.

Using evolutionary psychology to understand sex differences in sexual mating strategies

One crucial idea within evolutionary psychology is how we, as a species, survive. Survival and reproduction of the species are the two main challenges of evolution, and how males and females ensure the survival of the species is a central focus for evolutionary psychology. One thing that evolutionary psychologists have focused on is the mating strategies of men and women.

Stop and think

Common misperceptions of evolutionary theory: the importance of individual differences in populations

One of the main misunderstandings is that evolutionary forces are moving in a particular direction or that individual species or populations choose to evolve or adapt to the environment. The main evolutionary force is that, if species fit the environment, they can continue to survive and reproduce. Those species and members of the species with the physical and behavioural traits that were fit to survive and reproduce, did survive and reproduce and therefore their physical and behavioural traits were carried forward. Those species and members of the species that were not fit to survive and reproduce did not survive and reproduce successfully and therefore those traits were not carried forward.

One example is particularly relevant in terms of understanding individual differences: the well-used example of the giraffe and its long neck. The long neck can be explained as an evolutionary adaptation, enabling it to feed from tall trees. However, giraffes as a species did not purposefully evolve a long neck. What would have happened is that, within the population of giraffes, the lengths of necks varied. Now imagine there was a drought and only food on the top of the trees was available. Those giraffes with the longer necks would have tended to survive and reproduce, while those with shorter necks, unable to reach food, would tended not to survive and reproduce. Therefore, within the giraffe population, those giraffes with longer necks would reproduce, and their offspring would tend to have longer necks.

You can see then that over (a very very long period of) time the physical characteristics of giraffes would have shifted toward longer necks. If this environmental condition continued for many generations, with those giraffes born with longer necks always having an advantage accessing resources (and therefore surviving and reproducing) over those giraffes born with shorter necks, you can see how the longer neck evolved with the giraffe population.

It is the variety in physical and behavioural characteristics in populations (i.e. individual differences among populations) that is interesting to evolutionary psychologists, because it, alongside concepts such as fit to the environment, allows them to explain evolutionary change.

Canadian evolutionary psychologists Martin Daly and Margo Wilson (1982) provide an explanation of men's and women's mating strategies. Evolutionary psychology argues that, in the pursuit of species survival and reproduction, men and women are interested in selecting partners who enhance the success of reproduction and continuation of that person's genes. Consequently, men and women have evolved sexual strategies to ensure this happens (i.e. adaptations). Within evolutionary psychology, it is argued that men and women have different sexual strategies. The reason for these separate strategies is borne out from the fact that, while men can potentially create huge numbers of children during their lifespan, women can have only one child at a time. Because of this reproductive distinction, evolutionary psychologists have argued that there are differences between male and female mating strategies.

Within an evolutionary perspective, women have been thought to evolve mechanisms that assess the potential male partner in many ways. One mechanism might be the assessment of the quality of genes. This might be good health and attractiveness. The second mechanism might be the assessment of whether the partner will protect her and her children from potential harm. A third mechanism is the assessment of whether the partner might devote resources to her and her children and have parental investment in their children. For example, will they spend time with their children and not leave to produce more children elsewhere?

Meanwhile, males are thought to have evolved mechanisms that enable them to detect whether their potential female partner will provide them with a rapid production of offspring and be faithful to them, thus providing them with more children.

Note how the mating strategies can be described within functional, domain-specific and numerous terms. First, the mating strategies are *functional* because they serve a purpose of obtaining a mate so that males and females can enhance their chances of, and success at, reproduction. The mating strategies are *domain-specific* because they are confined to reproduction and the continuation of that person's genes and not other aspects of life such as making friends or advancing oneself in society. Finally, there are *numerous* mechanisms surrounding mating strategies. For example, women have developed numerous mechanisms to assess the potential male partner, through various considerations and assessments of their potential partner's physical characteristics, their ability to protect and their potential parental investment.

The sexual strategies among men and women represent these different aims in reproduction. Whether or not such a concept seems dated to you, try to imagine how well this applies to your heterosexual friends and their strategies with the opposite sex. Does it explain why men are perceived as less faithful, and are there sex differences in the amount of time that men and women put into a relationship? There is evidence to support the evolutionary psychology view of sex differences in mating strategies. Buss *et al.* (1992) found that males are more concerned with the certainty that they are fathers of their children and are more upset by sexual infidelity of their partners, while females are more concerned with the long-term emotional investment of their partners and are more concerned about emotional infidelity by their partners.

In 1993, David Buss and David Schmitt from the Department of Psychology at the University of Michigan suggested nine main hypotheses that underlie men's and women's sexual strategies (see Table 9.2). The researchers found evidence to support each of these nine hypotheses that can be derived from the evolutionary psychology perspective of mating strategies (Buss and Schmitt, 1993).

Look at Table 9.2 and the Stop and think: Buss' nine hypotheses regarding sexual strategies. You may have thought that perhaps they are somewhat typical of men and women and gender relations. However, you may also have thought, in terms of your own experience and other people you know, men and women, that there is a lot of variability in terms of how well each of these people you can think of fit within the nine hypotheses. This variability is of great interest to individual difference psychologists, and in 2000 two USA evolutionary psychologists, Steven Gangestad and Jeffry Simpson, published a paper that explored some

Stop and think

Buss' nine hypotheses regarding sexual strategies

1 Look at Buss and Schmitt's (1993) nine hypotheses regarding sexual strategies. Compare them to your own personal experiences and what you know of your friends' personal relationships. Do the predictions and findings reflect your own personal experiences of gender relations?

2 Mother Teresa is often quoted as an example that questions the evolutionary role of altruism. She dedicated her adult life to caring for 'the dying, the crippled, the mentally ill, the unwanted, the unloved'. What do you think? Is any act truly unselfish?

Table 9.2 Nine main hypotheses and evidence that underlie men's and women's sexual strategies

	Hypothesis	Evidence presented by Buss and Schmitt
1	Because men have lower levels of parental investment, men will engage in shorter-term mating more often than women will.	Men seek short-term mates. Men desire a larger number of mates than women do. Men are willing to engage in sexual intercourse earlier in a relationship. Men impose less stringent standards on desired and undesired attributes of a potential mate.
2	Because men are interested in short-term mating, preference for short-term mates will solve the difficulty of identifying which women are sexually accessible.	Men value promiscuity or lots of sexual experience in short-term mates but do not value it in long-term mates. Men dislike prudishness, sexual inexperience and low sex drive in short-term mates.
3	Because men are interested in short-term mating, preference for short-term mates will solve the difficulty of minimising commitment and investment in the relationship.	Men find undesirable in short-term mates any signal that a woman wants a commitment.
4	Because men are interested in short-term mating, preference for short-term mates will solve the difficulty of identifying which women are fertile.	The most important cues of fertility and ability to reproduce are physical; men place a greater importance on physical attractiveness in both short-term and long-term mates.
5	When men pursue a long-term mate, they will use psychological mechanisms such as jealousy and specific mate preference that ensure paternal confidence.	Men focus on sexual jealousy (woman spending time with other men) while women focus on emotional jealousy (a man spending time with others). Men place greater value on faithfulness, sexual loyalty and chastity and shun promiscuity and sexual experience in long-term relationships.
6	When pursuing a long-term mate, men will express preferences that solve the problem of identifying women who are able to reproduce.	Men value youth in long-term mates because younger people are more likely to be able to reproduce, and reproduce more, over the length of the relationship.
7	With short-term mates, women will seek men who are willing to give immediate resources.	Women value men in short-term relationships who spend resources such as money or gifts and are viewed as having an extravagant lifestyle; women give low ratings to men in short-term relationships who don't expend resources.
8	Women, more than men, use short-term mating to evaluate long-term prospective mates. In a potential mate, women dislike characteristics that are detrimental to long-term prospects.	Women, more than men, dislike in a short-term mate that person being in another relationship. Women dislike promiscuity more than men do.
9	Women seeking a long-term mate will value the ability of a man to provide economic and other resources that can be used to invest in her children.	Women like men to show the potential resources; so ambition, good earning capacity and wealth are good indicators.

Source: Based on Buss and Schmitt (1993).

of Buss and Schmitt's ideas in terms of looking at individual differences among men and women and developed the strategic pluralism theory (Gangestad and Simpson, 2000).

Strategic pluralism theory suggests that men and women may use multiple, even sometimes seen as contradictory, reproductive strategies because these behaviours might be adaptive within certain environments, particularly when considered in terms of individual differences between men. For example, Gangestad and Simpson argue that men clearly show, and are aware, that there are individual differences in levels of attractiveness to women. Therefore, men have evolved reproductive strategies that depend on their own physical attractiveness. Gangestad and Simpson argue that, although physically attractive men may adopt reproductive strategies that are thought to be more typical of men (seeking multiple mating partners and spending less time investing in offspring), less attractive men are not able to generate the same

number of opportunities for mating. Therefore they engage in strategic pluralism. Less attractive men may initially seek a mate, but once they have found a potential mate, they adopt another evolutionary strategy. For example, they may invest in the long term in that mate and their eventual offspring for survival and reproduction. Strategic pluralism theory also applies to women. It may be, rather than simply seeking one long-term mate, that a woman may have a number of short-term mates so that she can maximise the number of possible good gene pools that her children may inherit. It may be only after they have mated that women seek a long-term mate to benefit from the parental investment.

We can see evidence for an evolutionary perspective to explain why men and women differ in their sexual mating strategies. Perhaps more importantly, strategic pluralism theory shows why there may be individual differences within populations of men and women in their sexual strategies.

Evolutionary psychology can help us to understand other human behaviours.

Evolutionary psychology and cooperation

One key aspect to evolutionary psychology is the concept of cooperation. The idea that people outside mating relationships cooperate, given that they are meant to be competing for mates, may seem counterintuitive. However, men and women do cooperate, and evolutionary psychologists have suggested this is for good evolutionary reasons.

US anthropologist Robert Trivers (1971) suggests that one reason for cooperation is through reciprocal altruism. Reciprocal altruism refers to acts that are exchanged between people to aid their continual survival (e.g. cooperation). For example, someone might help someone else out in a moment of crisis, and because of this there is a strengthened bond between two individuals. Consequently, if in the future that individual who originally helped was in crisis, the other person (who was helped) might in turn help them. Trivers suggests that being reciprocally altruistic helps individuals survive.

Other evolutionary psychologists, such as Oxford academic William Donald Hamilton (1964a; b), have suggested cooperation occurs due to *inclusive fitness*. Inclusive fitness focuses on altruism among family members. Hamilton's point was that an individual's family carries many of the same genes as the individual. Individuals may help their relatives because some of their genes will be passed on through their relatives' survival. So, for example, a mother may protect her young and risk death to ensure the survival of their group genes.

What is important about these speculations and findings is that evolutionary psychologists can provide explanations of different human behaviours. As personality and individual difference psychologists, we are also interested in these explanations because they can be used to explain differences between the sexes in their mating strategies and how differences in cooperation might occur because of the result of differences in genetic similarity. In the next section we are going to extend this particular consideration and outline how academics have tried to understand specific personality and individual differences variables in terms of evolutionary psychology.

Evolutionary personality and personality and individual differences psychology

In this section we're going to look at how evolutionary ideas such as adaptation and variation have been used to explain personality and individual differences. Using three examples, we are going to show you:

- how evolutionary personality psychology explains the five-factor model of personality;
- how individual differences arise. We shall show how individual differences arise by using the example of cooperation and leadership;
- how an evolutionary concept called life history is related to personality.

An introduction to evolutionary personality psychology: Buss' theory of personality and adaptation

Buss (1991) introduced the academic study of how evolutionary psychology, and particularly the concept of adaptation, can be used to explain human personality. Buss explains that evolutionary theory provides a framework for the central concepts of personality in three ways:

1 by providing an understanding of the major goals of humans and the problems that need to be addressed to enable reproductive success;
2 by describing the psychological mechanisms that have evolved to enable humans to reach these goals and solve these problems;
3 by identifying the personality and individual differences in behaviours that humans employ to reach goals and solve the problems that are obstacles to attaining those goals.

Buss suggests that goal-directed tactics and strategies employed by individuals are the building units of personality. Buss acknowledges that there is a huge amount of variance in individuals' goals and in how much effort they spend in achieving them. However, Buss maintains that an evolutionary theory of personality can provide us with an understanding of what human goals are, the strategies that exist for reaching the goals, and what behaviours exist for overcoming obstructions to these goals.

Buss states that all humans live in groups, and living in groups has a number of rewards and problems in terms of reaching a society's goals. For example, if we were to presume that societies' main goals are survival and the reproduction of the species, living in a group provides individuals with protection from predators, enhanced opportunities for collective hunting, the sharing of resources and more chances for meeting a mate. Therefore, these advantages of living in a group increase the members' chances of reaching these goals (survival and the reproduction of the species). However, living in a group also presents problems that hinder the goals. For example, conflict between members of the group and the spread of disease among group members may hinder the survival and reproduction of the species.

David Buss has used this social situation as a basis to explain how humans have developed certain personality traits to attain goals (for example, survival and reproduction of the species) and overcome obstacles to these goals (for example, conflict within the group and the spread of disease). To do so, Buss uses the five-factor model of personality. You will remember that the five-factor model comprises:

- openness (perceptive, sophisticated, knowledgeable, cultured, artistic, curious, analytical, liberal traits);
- conscientiousness (practical, cautious, serious, reliable, organised, careful, dependable, hardworking, ambitious traits);
- extraversion (sociable, talkative, active, spontaneous, adventurous, enthusiastic, person-oriented, assertive traits);
- agreeableness (warm, trustful, courteous, agreeable, cooperative traits);
- neuroticism (emotional, anxious, depressive, self-conscious, worrying traits).

According to Buss, personality traits such as being calm (low neuroticism), active, sociable, adventurous and person-oriented (extraversion), cooperative and trustful (agreeableness), practical, reliable, hardworking, ambitious and organised (conscientiousness) and sophisticated, knowledgeable, curious and analytical (openness) are all traits that would allow members of the species to cooperate to achieve goals (survival of the species) and overcome problems (conflict between members of the group). In more detail, Borkenau (1990) emphasised that conscientiousness traits are important; individuals must be reliable, hardworking and organised to meet goals. Graziano and Eisenberg (1990) emphasised agreeableness traits as important because, when a group works together, goals can be more easily accomplished if there is a willingness to cooperate. Buss himself emphasises the importance of extraversion traits, as these are traits relating to sociable, active and person-oriented behaviours, which are all important to the maintenance of a group.

When considering the adaptive landscape, Buss (2011) considers how the five-factor model of personality emerges within the relationships that people form. For example, Buss points to a range of studies that have found that the desirable qualities in a mate listed by people can be largely described within the five-factor model.

- High levels of extraversion, agreeableness, conscientiousness, emotional stability (low neuroticism) and intellectually open (openness to experience) (Botwin *et al.*, 1997).
- Considerate, affectionate, understanding, kind, dependable, loyal (agreeableness and conscientiousness traits) (Buss and Barnes, 1986).
- Dependable, emotionally stable, pleasing disposition (Buss *et al.*, 1990).

However, Buss also points to other social relationships that may seem less obviously related to evolutionary theory, but that have an adaptive function and can be understood within the five-factor model of personality. Buss points to *coalitions* between people. Coalitions are behaviours in which people may cooperate with other people for numerous reasons. For example, Buss suggests that individuals may form a coalition to compete for resources or against rivals (e.g. attacking other groups or accessing their resources) or to provide assistance in defending members of the group (sharing caring responsibilities for looking after or defending offspring). In terms of coalitions, Buss reports on an unpublished study (DeKay, Buss and Stone, unpublished manuscript; Buss, 2011) in which men and women were asked to rate the desired personality traits of people with whom individuals identified in terms of pursing a common goal (i.e. shared a coalition with). The common personality traits described as desirable in a coalition included high levels of agreeableness, conscientiousness, emotional stability and openness to experience. Buss and his colleagues also identified some sex differences between men and women in the traits they described, perhaps pointing to the possible different nature of coalitions for men and women. Buss describes how men in this study valued coalition members who were brave, physically strong and able to fight and defend themselves. However, women in this study value traits such as conscientiousness and being socially perceptive.

For Buss, the five factors of the personality sum up the most frequent dimensions of behaviour. He describes the five-factor model of personality emerging over the course and range of human behaviours to provide an 'adaptive landscape' resulting from, and ensuring that humans continue in, their adaptation to the environment to achieve their main goals of survival and reproduction. (See Profile: David M. Buss.)

Profile

David M. Buss

David Buss was born on 14 April 1953, in Indianapolis, Indiana. Both his mother and father were teachers. He left high school early to work at a truck stop before then going back to complete high school. He graduated from the University of Texas, and then attended the University of California at Berkeley where he gained his PhD in personality psychology in 1981. After completing his doctorate, Buss became an Assistant Professor at Harvard University, moving to the University of Michigan in 1985, and then moving to his current position at the University of Texas in 1996.

His primary research interests include the evolutionary psychology of human mating strategies. He has also published papers on conflict between the sexes; prestige, status and social reputation; the emotion of jealousy; homicide; anti-homicide defences; and stalking. His most notable book is *Evolutionary Psychology: The New Science of the Mind* (2000), which is viewed as a key text in the vibrant new discipline of evolutionary psychology and introduces many groundbreaking discoveries. In 2000 he was awarded the Robert W. Hamilton Book Award for this work.

In 1988 David Buss was awarded the American Psychological Association Distinguished Scientific Award for Early Career Contribution to Psychology, and in 1990 he received the Stanley Hall Award from the American Psychological Association.

How individual differences arise through cooperation: the example of leadership

So far, we have seen how personality factors may emerge in society to enable groups of people to achieve their main goals of survival and reproduction. However, how does evolutionary psychology explain individual differences in personality among species? Well, in 2003, a number of academics from the University of Cambridge and the Zoological Society of London, led by Professor Sean Rands, suggested how these individual differences in personality occur (Rands *et al.*, 2003).

The explanation they provide is based on a game called Prisoner's Dilemma. **Prisoner's Dilemma** got its name from a certain hypothetical situation (which you will have seen in any police drama or film). Imagine two people have been arrested because the police suspect they have committed a crime together. However, the police interviewing the suspects do not have sufficient evidence to enable a conviction. In an attempt to secure a conviction, the police separate the two prisoners and place them in separate cells. Then, in turn, the police visit each of the prisoners and offer them a deal. The police deal is a simple one: the prisoner who offers evidence against the other one will be freed. This sets up the Prisoner's Dilemma (see Figure 9.1).

- If neither of the prisoners accept the police deal, then they are in fact cooperating with each other; they may receive some punishment, but a smaller punishment (for example, 1 year) because of a lack of specific proof about who committed the crime. Both prisoners gain from this strategy.
- If one of the prisoners informs on the other prisoner by confessing to the police, the defector will gain more as they will be freed. The prisoner who remained silent will receive the full punishment (for example, life imprisonment: let's say more than 20 years) since they did not

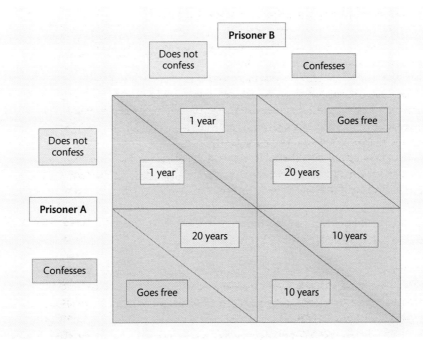

Figure 9.1 The Prisoner's Dilemma.

help the police, and there is now sufficient proof for this prisoner's conviction.

- If each prisoner betrays the other prisoner, both will be punished, but less severely than if one had refused to talk and the other had confessed (let's say they each get 10 years).

The Prisoner's Dilemma is that each prisoner has a choice between two options: confess or do not confess. However, although each prisoner has two choices, there are multiple outcomes dependent on the choices of each prisoner. What is important to this situation is that each prisoner cannot make the best decision for themselves without knowing what the other prisoner will do. For example, if prisoner A confesses and prisoner B doesn't, then prisoner A will go free. However, if prisoner A confesses and prisoner B also confesses, they will both receive a prison sentence of 10 years (hence the dilemma).

As you can see (and as the police know), there is a strong incentive for both prisoners to confess. If prisoner A does not confess, prisoner B is better off confessing because being set free is better than a year in jail. However, prisoner B would also be better off confessing if prisoner A confesses because 10 years is better than 20 years in prison. Therefore, prisoner B will tend to confess, regardless of what prisoner A will do. Prisoner A, using a similar thought process, will also tend to confess. However, the interesting point of the Prisoner's Dilemma is that it is actually better for them to cooperate by not confessing because they would each only get 1 year in prison, rather than 10 years in prison if they both confess.

This dilemma, and the issues around cooperation and non-cooperation in the Prisoner's Dilemma, is a game or rational choice process that has been studied by people in a variety of disciplines, ranging from biology through to sociology and including psychology. It is this process that Rands and his colleagues used to explain how individual differences occur in personality traits in species. Specifically, they used the Prisoner's Dilemma to explain how leadership and following behaviour might emerge among the same species.

Rands and his colleagues (2003) use the example of two foraging animals. Foraging animals are animals that look or search for food. So let us use the example of two rabbits living in the wild. Now, all foraging animals seek balance between eating enough to avoid starvation and avoiding being eaten by predators, such as foxes. The assumption is that a rabbit will forage only when it is hungry, and foraging will increase the rabbit's energy levels. Then, after eating, over time the rabbit's energy levels will fall until it is hungry again. Therefore, when the rabbit has high energy levels, it will not tend to forage because doing so is not worth the risk of being killed. A rabbit will forage only when it is hungry and its energy levels are low.

However, Rands *et al.* suggest that two foraging animals can reduce the risk of being killed by a predator if they forage together. Consequently, a similar scenario to that of the Prisoner's Dilemma would emerge between our two rabbits. Both rabbits have two choices, whether to forage or not, and there are several outcomes. Figure 9.2 illustrates the outcomes from cooperation and non-cooperation between the two rabbits.

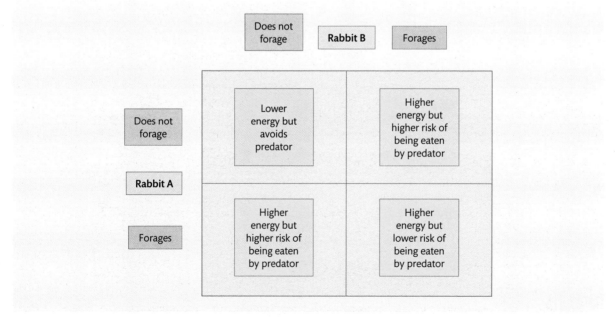

Figure 9.2 Illustration of the outcomes from cooperation and non-cooperation between the two rabbits in their foraging behaviour.

If both rabbits don't forage, then their energy levels decrease; but they don't get killed. If one or the other of the rabbits forages alone, then it will individually increase its energy levels but run a greater risk of being eaten. However, if both rabbits forage together, they will increase their energy levels but decrease their chances of being eaten by a predator. Clearly then, the optimum strategy for the rabbits will be to forage together. Consequently, there is a tendency for the rabbits to go out only when one of the animals is starving, to reduce the risk of being killed.

In terms of understanding how individual differences in leadership and following might occur, Rands and his colleagues postulated what would occur if two foraging animals met, where one had higher energy levels than the other (e.g. if one was fatter than the other). What the researchers argued is that, based on the model of cooperation detailed in Figure 9.2, the rabbits would go out only when one of the rabbits was hungry; that is, the rabbits would forage whenever the thinner of the two got hungry. When this happened they would both replenish their energy levels. However, as the fatter rabbit would also be topping up its energy levels, the rabbit that was thinnest to start with would always get hungry first. The rabbits would forage only when the thinner rabbit got hungry. In this situation the thinnest rabbit would make decisions about when to forage. Rands *et al.* argued that, in the case of the two rabbits, the thinner rabbit would become a leader and the fatter rabbit would become the follower. For Rands, this explains how individual differences, in this case leadership, emerge within species.

Life history and personality

Life history is an important concept in evolutionary psychology, and it has been developed by authors such as evolutionary sociobiologist E. O. Wilson (1975). In evolutionary theory, the term **life history** describes a schedule of growth, survival and reproduction throughout the individual's life that maximises reproduction and survival.

One simple example of how life history works is a trade-off between mating and parenting effort. Imagine an animal that is maximising the number of offspring it produces through its lifetime, thereby increasing the chances of its genes surviving into future generations (i.e. if it has no offspring, its genes won't survive). The animal can do this in two ways. The first is through mating as much as possible (**mating effort**) and enhancing its chances of greater reproduction (i.e. creating more offspring). The second is to spend more time with its existing offspring to ensure their survival, for example, by feeding them or protecting them from predators. This latter concept, spending more time with the existing offspring to ensure their survival, is called **parental investment**.

The important concept underlying life history is the trade-off between the number of offspring an individual creates and the number of its offspring that survive. Traditionally, this concept has been used to explain birth rates and the variation in the reproductive strategies between different species (i.e. cats compared to fish).

However, other authors have suggested that life history can be used to examine variation among individuals *within* a species – in particular, human personality and individual differences. US evolutionary psychologist Kevin

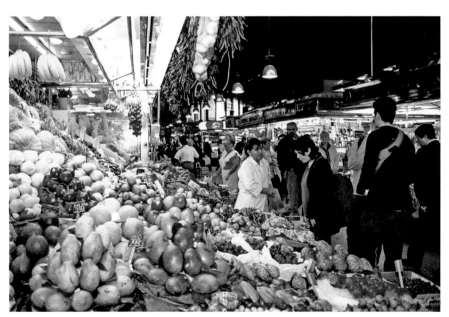

Clearly, in modern western society examples of foraging behaviour among humans are extremely rare.
Source: Pearson Education Ltd. Carlos Reyes-Manzo

Stop and think

Gossip – an evolutionary perspective

Professor Robin Dunbar (2004) at the University of Liverpool suggested that gossip can be viewed as an evolutionary behaviour. Gossip, which is conversation about social and personal topics of other people, is thought to be a core aspect of human behaviour. Dunbar suggests that there are positive aspects of gossip: it plays a number of roles in maintaining social relationships, from ensuring that a group of friends are kept up on the latest news and allowing them to bond, to helping the development of language through gossip by ensuring that people communicate with one another on several different levels. Dunbar argues that gossip was bound to evolve, as talking about what others are up to is not only of core interest to humans but also helps us to understand the problems faced by all individuals (for example, 'I can understand why person X has run off with person Y; they needed to be loved') and to show ourselves to be in a good light (for example, 'You'll never guess what X has done; I think it's terrible'). So next time you're having a good gossip, just remember that perhaps you are just taking part in an evolutionary process.

MacDonald (1997) suggests that the trade-off between mating effort and parental investment is a central dimension of reproductive strategies that range from a high parental investment/low mating effort to a low parental investment/high mating effort.

US psychologist Jean Philip Rushton (1985) used such an idea to develop his differential K theory. Within this theory, Ruston suggests that life history might be useful to understand human individual differences by looking at individual and group differences in life histories, social behaviour and physiological functioning. He referred to the central dimensions that represent the trade-off between parental investment and mating effort as K.

US psychologist Aurelio José Figueredo and his colleagues (Figueredo *et al.*, 2005) examined Rushton's idea of K and MacDonald's idea that K might be related to personality among a group of 222 university undergraduate students. First, Figueredo and colleagues had to measure K. They found that a number of variables correlate to measure an overall K-factor. These variables are as follows.

- **Childhood attachment to and parental investment from the biological father:** Emotional closeness a child feels towards either the biological father or surrogate father figure.
- **Adult attachment to romantic partners:** The security and emotional closeness a person *generally* experiences in their relationships.
- **Mating effort:** The amount of energy or resources an individual invests to attract potential sexual partners and/or maintain relationships with current sexual partners.
- **Machiavellianism:** A term used by personality psychologists to examine a person's tendency to deceive and manipulate others for personal gain.
- **Risk-taking attitudes:** A term regarding people's attitudes to, or abilities to take, risks.

In measuring this K-factor, lower scores represent a strategy of low parental investment/high mating effort and high scores represent high parental investment/low mating effort. In terms of how the individual variables fitted on this K-factor:

- Lower scores (low parental investment/high mating effort) meant *lower* levels of childhood attachment/parental investment and attachment to romantic partners and *higher* mating effort, higher Machiavellianism and higher risk-taking attitudes.
- Higher scores (high parental investment/low mating effort) meant *higher* levels of childhood attachment/parental investment and attachment to romantic partners and *lower* mating effort, lower Machiavellianism and lower risk-taking attitudes.

Next, Figueredo and his colleagues examined the relationship of the K-factor to sex. They found that females tended to score higher on the K-factor than males did, which is consistent with our earlier discussion that men and women have evolved different sexual strategies. In terms of the K-factor, the study's findings suggested that women are more likely to show high parental investment/low mating effort, and men are likely to show low parental investment/high mating effort.

Then the authors examined this K-factor against measures of personality (see Figure 9.3). Although they used measures of both the five-factor and three-factor personality model, they found that the scales were best represented by Eysenck's three-factor model comprising:

- psychoticism (solitary, troublesome, cruel and inhumane traits);
- extraversion (sociable, sensation-seeking, carefree and optimistic traits);
- neuroticism (anxious, worrying and moody traits).

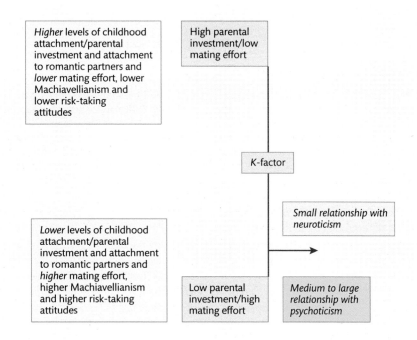

Figure 9.3 Visual summary of Figueredo *et al.*'s findings between life history (*K*-factor) and personality.

The authors found no relationship between the *K*-factor and extraversion, but they found that there was:

- a small significant negative relationship (*r* = −0.24) between neuroticism and the *K*-factor. This suggests that low parental investment/high mating effort is accompanied by anxious, worrying and moody traits.
- a medium to large significant negative relationship (*r* = −0.67) between psychoticism and the *K*-factor. This suggests that low parental investment/high mating effort is accompanied by antisocial, solitary, troublesome, cruel and inhumane traits.

This finding suggests that the evolutionary concept of life history is related to personality.

In all, we have given you three examples of how evolutionary theory has been used to inform and understand personality:

- Buss' theory of personality and adaptation;
- how individual differences arise through cooperation – the example of leadership;
- how the evolutionary concept of life history is related to personality.

In the next section we are going to consider some of the strengths and weaknesses of evolutionary personality and individual difference theory and its application to understanding personality and individual differences.

Consideration of the evolutionary theory of personality

Evolutionary personality psychology is an approach that bridges the gap between biology and personality. It provides a comprehensive analysis of the way that individuals and social groups behave within the goals of their society. However, there are some limitations to evolutionary personality psychology.

Lewontin (1991a) describes some reservations regarding evolutionary psychology that apply to Buss' evolutionary model of personality. First, Lewontin suggests that evolutionary theory provides little opportunity for empirical testing of the theory. Indeed, much of the basis for evolutionary theory involves speculations regarding behaviours across a number of generations. Ideas such as the nature of society's goals and the use of these goals to ensure the survival and reproduction of the species are difficult to test. Furthermore, many concepts referred to in evolutionary theory, such as dominant goals and active cooperation between groups, are routinely referred to; yet the group themselves are not consciously aware of them. For instance, we, as human beings, do not have discussions and agreements about our evolutionary goals.

Second, Lewontin has suggested that evolutionary psychology is open to reductionism. Reductionism is a tendency to explain a complex set of facts or ideas by using a

Stop and think

The evolutionary purpose of personality traits

List a number of personality traits or behaviours below. Perhaps include some traits that reflect your personality. Try to consider what the evolutionary purpose of each trait might be in ensuring a group's survival or survival of the species.

_____

_____

_____

simpler set of facts or ideas. For example, Lewontin suggests there may be a tendency for evolutionary psychology theorists to see collective social processes as arising from evolutionary processes. If economic cooperation occurs between two groups that were previously at war, it may be tempting to interpret this cooperation within an evolutionary psychology framework by suggesting that the newfound cooperation reflects group goals for survival. However, Lewontin notes that if this cooperation occurs within a very short time (for example, within a generation), the change is too rapid to be explained by evolutionary theory alone. Other explanations provided by evolutionary theory could also suffer from reductionism. For example, if we were to explain modern behaviour and the complex world of home, work, friends and family only in terms such as foraging, parental investment and adaptation, then that might be reductionism.

Despite such difficulties, it is important to consider a point made by Buss (1991). Buss acknowledges that evolutionary psychology and evolutionary personality psychology are attempts to understand a complicated social process, spread over generations. However, he emphasises

that the evolutionary theory of personality presents a constructive framework within which to consider and apply certain models of personality. He suggests that evolutionary psychology provides a heuristic (set of rules and principles) from which to link the effects of biology and the environment to understand common variability (personality dimensions) in human behaviour. (See Stop and think: The evolutionary purpose of personality traits.)

Animals and their personality

Apparently not just *any* animal can be an actor. Indeed, only ones with a certain personality are destined for the big time. So says James McKay in an interview with BBC Online (3 June 2005). McKay, a farmer and the owner of a company that supplies animals for TV and films, says that an animal that has an obedient personality and isn't going to be put off by being in a studio has a lot of potential.

A recent development in the world of personality research is the re-examination of whether animals have personality

Profile

Samuel Gosling

Although now living in the United States, Samuel Gosling went to a UK comprehensive school in Gloucestershire and received a BA in Philosophy and Psychology from Leeds University in 1991. He went on to receive a PhD in Psychology from the University of California at Berkeley in 1998 and started work at the University of Texas at Austin in 1999.

Although he also studies social perception and the history of psychology, Gosling is well known for his cross-species work, particularly on how animals can be used to inform theories of personality. He became interested in this area of study in his first year of graduate school, when he attended a seminar on the meaning of personality. Given his philosophy background, he started thinking about concepts and ideas by pushing their logic

until they no longer made sense. So, in thinking about personality, he thought of a context where it would make no sense to talk about personality: animals. As he began work on this exercise, the idea began to seem less absurd. At that point he started taking the idea more seriously and did some studies.

Samuel Gosling has published a number of papers in high-profile journals such as *Psychological Bulletin* and *Journal of Personality and Social Psychology*, which suggests that his area of research is now well established in academic psychology. In 2009 he published a book, *Snoop!: What your stuff says about you* (Profile Books, London), looking at how our personalities are expressed and judged in bedrooms, offices, websites and music collections.

traits. One of the leading modern day researchers is Samuel D. Gosling, a psychologist at the University of Texas at Austin (see the Profile box). Gosling (2001) suggests that there is no reason to assume that natural selection creates only physical traits in animals; it could also create emotional and behavioural traits. In reviewing over 200 studies and carrying out studies involving dogs, cats, fish and spotted hyenas, Gosling has shown that certain personality traits, such as extraversion and neuroticism, are evident in many animals. What we will outline now is this body of theory and research on animal personality.

Animals and personality: a historical context

The consideration of animals and their personality goes back to the early twentieth century. An early researcher in this field was M. P. Crawford, who looked at the personality and food-sharing behaviour of young chimpanzees (Crawford, 1938; Nissen and Crawford, 1936). Even earlier, a Japanese researcher was examining the effect of the environment on the character of young chickens (Hasuo, 1935). There are many other works from the 1940s to the 1970s linking personality and individual differences to animals, from neuroticism in rats (Billingslea, 1940) to individual differences in reactions among various species of fish in hostile environments (Huntingford, 1976; Shaklee, 1963). However, in the late 1970s and early 1980s there began a series of research studies by UK psychologist Dr Joan Stevenson-Hinde, who carried out a seminal piece of work. She began to measure and assess personality traits in rhesus monkeys over a number of years (Stevenson-Hinde and Zunz, 1978; Stevenson-Hinde et al., 1980a; b). What was important about Stevenson-Hinde's work was that she began to examine the stability of personality traits over time. To assess this stability, she introduced the idea of having humans who are familiar with the animals assess them using a number of personality statements. Stevenson-Hinde found that, in rhesus monkeys, three personality traits – excitability, sociability and confidence – were found to be consistent over 4 years of observation, even though different raters were used at different times.

However, not until relatively recently has there been a large-scale, organised examination of animals and their personality. Influenced by Stevenson-Hinde's work, US researcher Samuel Gosling has tried to bring all these ideas and research together.

Within-species versus cross-species comparisons

The first aspect Gosling notes about animal personality research is that, unlike human psychology research, there is a tendency to compare personality both within species and across species. Gosling notes that animal researchers do compare within species. For example, researchers will note that one dog is perhaps more aggressive than another dog, much the same as we do in human psychology when we say one person is more aggressive than another person. However, animal researchers also compare across species. For example, certain types of cats (lions and tigers) are considered more aggressive than other types of cats (domestic cats). Gosling states that this type of within-species versus cross-species comparison is important for us to understand research in animal personality. Imagine you are outside a room, and inside there is a lion, and outside is the lion's keeper. You want to go in the room. You might ask the keeper if the lion is dangerous. If the keeper takes a within-species approach to that question, they might suggest that the lion is not dangerous, because it has never attacked a human being, compared to other lions that might eat any human who comes into the same room. However, if the keeper takes an across-species approach and compares the lion to a whole range of animals (for example, dogs, rabbits and giraffes) they will probably reply that the lion is dangerous.

Gosling states that both approaches are useful for animal personality research. Variation within a species is important to personality psychologists because it holds clues to the nature of evolution of personality traits within a species and enables researchers to identify the adaptive nature of traits that allows the species to develop, evolve and survive. It is important to consider variations across species because this information can be used to examine the origins and adaptations of particular traits. Take the example of trait aggressiveness. Studying aggressiveness among different species of animals would help us to understand the different ways aggressiveness can be used – either to defend oneself and one's family or to ensure that members of the species get fed.

Overall, it seems that Gosling's within-species versus cross-species comparison provides a framework to examine and consider animals' behaviour and personality.

Methods in animal personality research

So, how do animal personality psychologists go about assessing the personality of animals? Gosling (2001) describes two main ways that this is done.

The first method is to assess the personality of animals through the use of coding. By coding, what we mean is that researchers have recorded how animals have responded to particular behavioural tests. This is the most widely used method for assessing animal personality. For example, if the researcher takes a set of dogs and throws a stick for them to chase, they will all act differently. Some might go bounding over to the stick and bring it back to the researcher, some might nervously approach it, bring it back but not release it, and some might just wander off in a different direction.

A research example of this method was carried out by animal personality psychologists Jennifer Mather and Roland Anderson (1993), who examined personality in octopuses. These psychologists put 44 octopuses in three simple situations and looked for differences in responses. The three situations presented to the octopuses were alerting (done by opening the tank lid), threat (by touching the octopus with a probe) and feeding (by giving them a crab). Overall, Mather and Anderson recorded 19 different behaviours in reaction to these three situations. Mather and Anderson also suggested that you can place octopuses on three personality dimensions: activity, reactivity and avoidance.

The second method for identifying the personality of animals involves rating traits within animals and having observers, with data recording instruments, rate the animals. For example, Gosling (1998) assessed the personality of hyenas by using four observers who knew the animals well. First, the observers, who had an average of nearly 10 years' experience of working with hyenas, were asked to select a number of traits – from a list of traits that had been used in previous research on animal personality – that they thought applied to hyenas. Next, the observers were asked to rate hyenas in terms of these traits. Gosling found that there was a high reliability of rating between observers (i.e. they all tended to agree in their ratings) and five dimensions of personality emerged to describe the personality of hyenas:

- assertiveness (for example, confident, jealous and strong);
- excitability (for example, nervous and fearful, excitable and highly strung);
- agreeableness with humans (for example, social, tame and warm);
- sociability (for example, friendly and less cold);
- curiosity (exploratory, impulsive and imaginative).

Reliability and validity of animal personality research

So, how accurate are these tests of animal personality? Well, if we were to treat these measures like any other measure, we would judge them by two criteria:

1   Reliability, of which there are two forms: internal reliability and reliability over time (test–retest reliability). (You can read more about these types of reliability in Chapter 25.)
2   Validity, which is concerned with assessing whether the test measures what it claims to measure. (You can read more about different types of validity in Chapter 25.)

Reliability of animal personality ratings

Gosling (2001) presents an overview of a number of studies that deal with the issues of internal reliability and reliability over time in animal personality studies.

Internal reliability refers to whether all the items used in the measure are measuring the same concept. Therefore, we would expect items of the same measure to be positively correlated with each other. Gosling states that there are two ways of establishing internal reliability in animal personality studies.

- **Inter-observer agreement** – The extent to which two or more observers agree in their personality rating between a number of animals. Two observers would agree that one animal being observed is different (for example, is the animal more aggressive?) from another animal being observed. An indicator of observer agreement is usually a correlation. These range from −1 to 1, and the closer the statistic is to 1, the more indicative it is of agreement between the raters.
- **Within-subject reliability** – The extent to which two or more observers agree in their personality rating for one animal; for example, is that animal more one type of personality than another personality (e.g. more extraverted than emotionally stable)? Again, the extent of this reliability is assessed via observer agreement (as in inter-observer agreement), a correlation statistic, and the closer the statistic is to 1, the more indicative it is of agreement between raters.

There is evidence that both forms of reliability occur in animal personality studies (Gosling, 2001). For example, for inter-observer studies, three studies (Crawford, 1938; Hebb, 1949; King and Figueredo, 1997) have found acceptable levels of inter-observer agreement in measuring dominance (observer correlation = 0.70), friendliness (observer correlation = 0.90) and dominance among chimpanzees (observer correlation = 0.61). Similarly, studies that have looked at curiosity among bears (Fagen and Fagen, 1996; observer correlation = 0.96), sociability among cats (Feaver et al., 1986; observer correlation = 0.91) and timidness in Gothic-arched squirrel monkeys (Martau et al., 1985; observer correlation = 0.92) have all found evidence that two or more observers agree in their personality ratings across animals.

Moreover, Gosling (2001) presents data to suggest that observer agreement occurs in within-subject studies. Gosling summarised data from 11 studies that looked at within-subject observer reliability across several different species of animals, including chimpanzees, baboons, cheetahs and rhinoceroses. He found that an average observer agreement across all the studies was a correlation of 0.64, with the correlations for the studies ranging from 0.48 for rhinoceroses to 0.81 for rhesus monkeys.

Test–retest reliability assesses reliability over time, so, for example, we might hope that two personality ratings for the same animal would be correlated on two or more occasions. This would also suggest some reliability in assessment of personality because on two separate occasions a similar personality assessment was given. Again, there does seem to be evidence for this type of reliability. Crawford

(1938) found a correlation statistic of 0.71 for confidence and 0.81 for cheerfulness for chimpanzees over a 4-week period. Stevenson-Hinde *et al.* (1980b) found that three personality traits in rhesus monkeys – excitability, sociability and confidence – were found to be consistent (above $r = 0.7$) over 4 years of observation, even though different raters were used at different times.

Validity of animal personality ratings

You will remember that validity is concerned with whether the test is measuring what we claim it is measuring. (You can get more information on the different types of validity in Chapter 25.) There is evidence to suggest that animal personality ratings do show validity.

- Capitanio (1999) tested the validity of animal personality measures on 42 rhesus monkeys. Within this study, Capitanio wanted to test the predictive validity (a type of validity that assesses whether a measure can accurately predict something in the future) of animal personality ratings. Capitanio found that ratings of sociability were found to be negatively associated with antagonistic behaviour 3 years later.
- Gosling (1998) found that female hyenas scored higher on an assertiveness dimension than male hyenas. This finding is consistent because hyenas live in a matriarchal society (where females rule the family).
- Feaver *et al.* (1986) found that cats who had been rated as aggressive previously spent more time in conflict situations (hitting or chasing) than other cats that had been previously rated as not aggressive.
- Stevenson-Hinde *et al.* (1980a; Stevenson-Hinde, 1983) found that monkeys who had been rated as confident were correlated to the amount of time they spent outside the reach of their mother.

Animal personality: the emergence of the five-factor model of personality

One important aspect of Gosling's work has been the finding that core personality dimensions among animals are similar to those of core personality dimensions that have been found among humans.

A huge number of traits, species and methods are used to study animal personality. However, Gosling and John (1999) suggest that the five-factor model of personality might provide an adequate context to consider animal personality. You may remember that the five-factor model of personality comprises:

- openness (perceptive, sophisticated, knowledgeable, cultured, artistic, curious, analytical, liberal traits);
- conscientiousness (practical, cautious, serious, reliable, organised, careful, dependable, hardworking, ambitious traits);

- extraversion (sociable, talkative, active, spontaneous, adventurous, enthusiastic, person-oriented, assertive traits);
- agreeableness (warm, trustful, courteous, agreeable, cooperative traits);
- neuroticism (emotional, anxiety, depressive, self-conscious, worrying traits).

Gosling and John (1999) researched 19 studies that have used a statistical technique called factor analysis to look at the data collected (you can read more about this statistical procedure in Chapter 25). These 19 studies covered 11 species of animals (chimpanzees, gorillas, monkeys, hyenas, dogs, cats, donkeys, pigs, rats, guppies and octopuses).

Gosling and John found that three of the five personality factors emerged in the majority of these 19 studies. These three factors were extraversion, neuroticism and agreeableness. Of the 19 studies reviewed, 17 found a behaviour that could be described as extraversion – whether it be a lively temperament in a dog, sociability in a pig or boldness in octopus.

In 15 of the studies, Gosling and John found behaviours that reflected a neuroticism factor. Examples of neurotic traits included fear in rhesus monkeys, nervousness in dogs and emotionality in rats.

In 14 of the studies reviewed, there was evidence of behaviours that reflected agreeableness. Examples of these behaviours included aggression and hostility (low agreeableness) in monkeys, affection in dogs and a tendency to fight (low agreeableness) in rats.

In terms of the other two five-factor personality dimensions, openness and conscientiousness, Gosling and John found some evidence that these personality dimensions occurred in animals. In terms of openness, in seven species studied, chimpanzees showed levels of openness and monkeys, hyenas and pigs all showed curiosity. Finally, in terms of conscientiousness, Gosling and John found evidence of conscientiousness personality traits, but only among chimpanzees.

Animal personality: informing evolutionary theories of personality?

Gosling and John's analysis of animal personality within the five-factor model of personality provides a constructive framework to consider animal personality across a number of species. However, it is worth noting that only three of the five factors emerged for most of the studies. While extraversion, neuroticism and agreeableness were found in most studies, openness and conscientiousness were found in the large minority of studies, with conscientiousness being found only among chimpanzees.

However, Gosling and John (1999) speculate how these differences between species might inform our understanding of how personality evolves. Conscientiousness comprises a number of advanced cognitive processes, such as following rules, establishing norms, creating and understanding values and acting, or refusing to act, on impulse. Gosling and John speculated that, as chimpanzees are humans' closest relatives, one reason for this is that conscientiousness as a personality factor might reflect evolutionary development among species. These authors suggest that this finding might be of interest to psychologists trying to examine the evolutionary development of personality.

Let us consider this. Different personality dimensions found in these species may reflect an evolutionary progression. If you remember back to the biological models of personality in the last discussion, you will recall that personality aspects such as neuroticism (or behavioural avoidance) and extraversion (behavioural activation) were basic dimensions of biological and physiological functioning. It is not surprising, then, to find that these aspects are seen as important in psychophysiological and neurological models of humans and may be at the lower end of evolutionary development. We also find among animal personality studies that agreeableness is a factor; this finding reflects low levels of aggression and hostility, which might also be considered as a basic personality trait.

However, the next two dimensions of personality might reflect higher stages in the evolution of personality. Openness might represent a species becoming more curious in its behaviours, tolerant of one another and increasingly engaged in new and different experiences. Finally, Gosling and John note that conscientiousness – which is the ability to follow rules; establish norms; create and understand values and act, or refuse to act, on impulses – also represents a further higher level of group evolutionary advancement (see Figure 9.4). This observation echoes one of the core ideas in evolutionary personality psychology: that species form groups and show adaptations in their personality to increase their chances of survival and reproduction.

Figure 9.4 A model of how personality might evolve from an evolutionary perspective.

Consideration of animal personality research

A lot of Gosling's research not only provides an understanding of animal personality but also may hold a key to understanding human personality from an evolutionary perspective. Clearly, if similar personality dimensions are found across a number of species in the animal kingdom, including humans, then this may suggest that not only is personality a strong feature to the world, but it also has biological roots.

However, Gosling (2001) suggests there are two critical considerations to be made of animal personality research. These are:

- problems with the reliability of assessing personality of animals;
- anthropomorphic projections – issues of attributing human characteristics to animals.

Problems with the reliability of assessing personality of animals

There are problems with the reliability of assessing personality of animals. Although we presented evidence to suggest that there was some reliability and validity to measure animal personality, there is also evidence that reliability estimates aren't always as high as reported in some studies (Gosling, 2001). For example, in inter-observer studies (where, for example, animals are compared to other animals on their personality) observer agreement on laziness in horses was $r = -0.11$ (Mills, 1998) and willingness in dogs was $r = 0.00$ (Goddard and Beilharz, 1983). In within-subject studies (where an animal is rated in terms of one type of personality over another personality), observer agreement was as low as $r = 0.20$ and $r = -0.14$ for chimpanzees and macaque monkeys, respectively (Buirski et al., 1978; Martau et al., 1985). Furthermore, test–retest correlation statistics of 0.21 for confidence and 0.12 for destructiveness have been reported for chimpanzees (Crawford, 1938).

As Gosling himself points out, there is some fluctuation in agreements among observers, ranging from excellent to unsatisfactory. Gosling suggests five factors that will affect the reliability of assessing the personality of animals:

- Observer agreement improves with the level of acquaintance with the animal. That is, the longer that two observers have known an animal, the more likely they are to agree on its personality.
- Prior communication between observers will increase the observer agreement. For example, if two zookeepers who look after a set of chimpanzees are asked to rate them in a psychology experiment, this might not be the first time that these zookeepers have discussed each of the chimpanzees' personality.

As brave as a lion. As strong as an ox. As loyal as a dog. As sly as a fox. Do we, and should we, associate personality characteristics with animals?
Source: Digital Vision

- Different types of interaction that observers have with animals might affect observer ratings. For example, the two zookeepers who look after the chimpanzees might have different roles; one zookeeper might feed the chimpanzees while the other zookeeper might clean out their living area. The zookeepers' previous experience might affect their ratings, as the first zookeeper might be clearer in rating the chimpanzees on their aggressiveness and sociability at feeding times, while the second zookeeper might be clearer in rating them on how clean and orderly they are.
- It is likely that the age of the animal will affect ratings, particularly when they are younger. The range of behaviours that young animals can engage in is limited, particularly among those animal species whose parents

are likely to spend a great deal of time caring for them. Consequently, the behaviour of such animals might be inhibited while around their parents.
- Some species of animal are more easily assessed than other species of animals. There is a huge amount of variability in trying to rate different animals from different species.
- Assessing the sociability of a domestic cat is slightly easier than assessing the sociability of an octopus.

Anthropomorphic projections: attributing human characteristics to animals

Some authors have argued that animal personality research has no bearing on understanding personality, particularly

Stop and think

The personality of animals

Consider the following five animals: dog, cat, monkey, elephant, giraffe.

The following five items are personality descriptors taken from a short 10-item measure of the five-factor model of personality (Gosling *et al.*, 2003b). What you are going to do is consider each animal in terms of each personality descriptor. Rate each of the animals on each of the items on a 5-point scale (1 = not at all, 2 = a little, 3 = somewhat, 4 = a lot, 5 = very much so).

1   ____Extraverted, enthusiastic (extraversion)

2   ____Dependable, self-disciplined (conscientiousness)

3   ____Sympathetic, warm (agreeableness)

4   ____Anxious, easily upset (neuroticism)

5   ____Open to new experiences, complex (openness)

- Now repeat the exercise for humans.
- Which exercise did you find easiest? Why do you think this is?
- Do you think these animals really have these different personality types? What experience have you had of each of these species of animals?

human personality. A first concern is that observers, when they are rating an animal's personality, might not be actually rating animal behaviours; rather, they are attributing human personality characteristics to animals (this is known as anthropomorphic projection). For example, our perception of the loyalty and friendliness of a dog around its mealtime might actually be a dog that is being self-serving and only being nice so it is fed. Mitchell and Hamm (1997) found that people were willing to label certain behaviours (e.g. that an animal was acting jealously) regardless of whether the behaviour described was by a human, dog, elephant or bear. Authors such as Nagel (1980) have suggested that it is impossible for humans to know what it is like to be an animal, and that it is impossible to measure or compare the two.

Gosling also points out that there are huge differences between animals and humans, and perhaps we should not consider animals as good models to understand complex human attitudes and behaviours. For example, humans have a unique ability for language, reasoning and forming complex social interactions that ultimately lead to culture, which in turn, influences their personality, attitudes and behaviours. Additionally, animals and humans have different anatomies. Humans have opposable thumbs and complex vocal potential. Some species can fly, some have beaks, some have amazing abilities to run, jump and kill. Consequently, the likely number of different behaviours that animals and humans engage in is not likely to lead to similar personality structures.

However, despite these concerns, Gosling's work suggests that some of these concerns may not be wholly appropriate. First, Gosling provides evidence suggesting that observers who know an animal, and observers who are independent of an animal, are able to arrive at similar assessments about the same animals. Secondly, Gosling uses the five-factor personality model to understand a wealth of literature on animal personality. This work with the five-factor model suggests not only that there are meaningful interpretations of animal behaviour but also that similar conclusions can be reached from observations of a variety of species that have been studied by different researchers.

Whatever your views of animal personality studies before reading this discussion, you can see that Gosling's research is important. It addresses the issue of animal personality in a systematic and exciting way. Gosling's work has helped psychologists to identify many similarities in personality across species and has led to further speculations regarding the evolution of personality traits.

Adaptive personality and behavioural ecology

We have, throughout this discussion, addressed the personality in the context of evolutionary psychology, and how it may represent successful adaptations. That is, that certain traits (e.g. agreeableness or conscientiousness) were part of the adaptive landscape and were linked to evolutionary approaches to the study of personality and that there were certain behaviours that were linked to survival and sexual strategies. In modern personality psychology, and certainly if you wanted to go on and study this further after your degree or in your dissertation or project work, then you would probably be interested in following it up within the area of behavioural ecology.

The concept that there are sets of personality traits that are adaptive has become an important topic for behavioural ecologists, ecology being the scientific study of the relations that living organisms have with respect to each other and their natural environment. You will have noted in the last section that one of the criticisms of evolutionary psychology was the notion of time, and that adaptation in traits in animals was likely to develop over long periods of time. However, within recent considerations of personality within behaviour ecology, psychologists have begun to consider how concepts such as time and consistency are important in understanding personality and individual differences, particularly in terms of adaptations.

In 2010 Canadian psychologist Denis Reale and Dutch psychologist Neils Dingemanse, with colleagues (Réale et al., 2010; Dingemanse et al., 2010), provided useful overall considerations of the study of adaptive personality. They suggest four main areas of considerations that need to be made when studying the adaptive personality. These are: (1) definition of adaptive personality; (2) behavioural consistency; (3) the conceptual nature and function of adaptive personality traits; and (4) possible models for studying the adaptive personality.

Definitions of personality: broad and narrow

The first area identified by Réale et al. is to suggest that, with behavioural ecologists, two general definitions of personality are used: those with a *broad-sense* and those with a *narrow-sense*. Within this area the broad-sense definition of personality is concerned with measuring any personality trait, or set of traits, within the context of evolutionary psychology. Here Réale et al. argue that the main concern is to understand patterns of behaviours within an adaptive framework. The behavioural ecologist would look at a single trait or a collection of traits and consider and describe them within an evolutionary framework. Therefore the work of Buss described earlier in the discussion regarding the adaptive landscape might fall into this category. A narrow-sense definition of personality in behavioural ecology recognises that there are many different traits that can be studied and will tend to focus on particular traits, and look at the particular physiology (i.e. the mechanical, physical and biochemical functions) that underlie a particular trait. This approach aims to see how a particular trait is linked to particular functions of the individual, such as physical reactions (e.g. stress) or emotions (e.g. anxiety) that are linked to evolutionary adaptations. Therefore, a trait (for example, those we studied with Eysenck's or Gray's models of personality; e.g. extraversion, neuroticism, behavioural activation or behavioural inhibition) that was linked to actual physical stress or physiological responses would be considered within an evolutionary framework as part of an adaptive coping response (e.g. fight or flight).

Behavioural consistency: short-term and long-term variation

Réale *et al.* (2010) also suggest that consideration of the adaptive personality has largely ignored the level of consistency of behaviour. We have considered that individuals may vary within a population in a particular trait, but Réale *et al.* also consider that the extent of behavioural consistency over time is important. These authors argue that individuals within a population may be consistent in their behaviour over a relatively short time period (e.g. a few days) or the consistency could be maintained across their life history (owing to genetic coding or experiencing the same environment). The importance of this point is that when we look at personality traits in terms of their adaptive value, there is very little consideration of how these traits may change or vary across the lifespan and of whether they may be traits that can be employed in the short-term for survival or need to be maintained over the lifespan.

The conceptual nature and function of adaptive personality traits: plasticity versus highly constrained

The issues of behavioural consistency and how this can change in both the relatively short term and the long term (in evolutionary terms) can be shown in the discussion of the conceptual nature and function of adaptive personality traits. Dingemanse *et al.* (2010) highlight that there are two contrasting conceptions in which adaptive personality traits are considered and how they are seen to function: the first is that personality traits are seen as very plastic; the second is that the personality traits are seen as highly constrained.

In the first consideration, personality trait behaviours are seen as being highly plastic; that is, having the potential to change rapidly in response to changes in the environment.

In this context much of the emphasis is on the environment as influencing behaviour, as variations in behaviour are influenced by changes in the environment.

So, for example, let's consider foraging behaviour and how it might show plasticity in traits in terms of a change in the environment and how this might then influence the level of a trait within a population. In this example, depending on the environment a population of animals may change their foraging behaviour in response to the number of predators in the environment. In the first instance this is done at an individual level, in which it is assumed that there is variation in behaviour across the population, but also that individuals can vary their behaviour. The presence of a lot of predators within an environment will immediately lead to an adaptive response by those foraging. In an environment where there are suddenly lots of predators, the animals foraging will either fight or flee a predator, and in all likelihood, over time, this is likely to lead to a decrease in the level of foraging among the population because those animals who forage a lot are likely to be scared off or killed. Réale and colleagues suggest that this would result in the long-term effect of selection of genes within that population. The tendency to forage behaviour traits may decrease in a high-predator environment because those who forage a lot are likely to have been killed. Therefore the traits relating to a tendency to forage are carried forward in the genes of the population that survived; these will be individuals that had a tendency to forage less or not to forage in the presence of predators. Equally, the converse may be true in an environment where there are few predators. Those who forage a lot may survive, owing to foraging more or being more likely to meet mates, and therefore these genes are carried forward within the population. Throughout this example there is a notion of plasticity. That is, at an individual level and at the population level the expression of the trait isn't closely aligned to the trait within the animal population (e.g. general level of foraging behaviour of the animal), but is more closely aligned to environmental conditions (i.e. level of predators within the population).

In the second consideration, personality traits can be viewed as highly constrained; that is, they are highly constrained to the characteristics of the population of the animal. Within any population the level of the personality trait is resilient to environmental changes and is seen as much more inflexible to the environment. So, any behavioural trait may be seen as a constant, with variation between individual members of species being seen at a minimum. Survival of the species or persistence of the trait doesn't depend on changes within, or in response to the environment, but rather on whether the existence of that trait has predisposed that animal for survival. So, for example, in the case of foraging, it may be that the level of foraging behaviour is relatively similar among individuals of a species, with the level of foraging based on eating enough to survive and not alter on the environment. Therefore, survival of that species or population of that species is dependent on the potential nature of that trait to fit to future environments. Where there is enough food in the environment, the population will continue to survive. However, when that food is no longer present in the environment, that population will have died out. In this approach the environment is less influential and the survival of the species is dependent on the behaviour trait. In this conceptualisation the focus is on the animal trait, not changes in the environment.

Models of adaptive personality

The ideas discussed above have led to the development of some key models to guide our understanding and summarise the study of adaptive personality. What is important about putting these ideas together as models is that they guide us systematically to identify key differences in levels of explanation of behaviours within an evolutionary or behaviour ecology framework. These models highlight very subtle differences but emphasise different parts of a process by which we can try to understand individual differences and behaviour. Dingemanse and Wolf (2010) identify three general models of adaptive personality models based on: (1) differences in state; (2) investigating the feedback between state and behaviour; and (3) models that are not based on state differences.

Models based on differences in state

These models are based on the idea that individual differences occur between members of a population based on a particular state (i.e. feature) related to that organism. This state could be physiological (e.g. physical, biochemical), neurobiological (biology of the nervous system) or environmental. However, it is this state that is central to understanding the adaptive personality of the species and that within any population there is variability among individuals in terms of the levels of this state.

Models focusing on the concept of feedback between state and behaviour: the role of feedback

This model of adaptive personality focuses on the stability of behaviours and the types of feedback that individuals receive around their behaviours. In these models the emphasis is on how state variables differ in their stability; that is, how much they are suitable for, or likely to change. Here Dingemanse and Wolf focus on the concept of

feedback as the explanatory framework for understanding change. They use the example of an animal's foraging behaviour under the threat of predators. In this example, there may be variation between animals in terms of their energy reserves. An animal with low energy reserves will tend to be bolder in their foraging behaviour than one with higher energy reserves because they need to obtain food. Over a short period of time, that individual animal has responded to feedback – in this instance the feedback is their own assessment of their energy reserves (i.e. how hungry they are feeling). Dingemanse and Wolf point to other examples in which individuals may receive feedback. Therefore, individual animals receive feedback for their behaviour at a number of points, and they will learn new behaviours or gain experience and this will increase or change the pattern of their behaviours.

Models that are not based on state differences

These models, identified by Dingemanse and Wolf, emphasise situations where there is limited variability between individuals in a population and the change is based on the current state of the environment. Within these models individual animals are largely seen as either responsive (can show plasticity) or unresponsive (highly constrained) to the environment, and the adaptive personality within a species is considered within the extent of this responsiveness. In this example, responsive individuals are responding to cues in the environment all the time (i.e. changes in the availability of food, presence of predators), while non-responsive individuals are ignoring these cues. Dingemanse and Wolf argue that responsive individuals are able to respond to environmental opportunities (e.g. the discovery of a more abundant patch) or dangers (e.g. the discovery of an area of predators), while non-responsive individuals do not react to such dangers or opportunities. As a result, the development of adaptive personalities is largely seen as the ability to respond (or not to respond) to environmental changes.

Final comments

The aim of this discussion was to introduce you to evolutionary psychology and animal personality research. We have outlined some key ideas in evolutionary theory. We have also shown how evolutionary theory can be applied to the five-factor model of personality, individual differences in behaviour and the relationship between life history and personality. We have described the main methods and measurement in animal research, and how the five-factor model of personality has been assessed in animal personality research.

Summary

- The roots of evolutionary psychology lie in the basics of evolutionary theory and theorists such as Darwin and the classical theory of natural selection.
- A central idea in evolutionary psychology is adaptation. Adaptation is defined as a biological structure, process or behaviour of a member of the species that enables that member's species to survive in response to the (changed) environment, not only over other species but also over other members of the same species.
- Three aspects exist to adaptations that allow us to understand the modifications that a species might make: functionality, domain specificity and numerous.
- Evolutionary theory creates a framework by providing an understanding of the major goals of humans and of those problems that need to be addressed to enable reproductive success, of the psychological mechanisms that have evolved to enable humans to reach these goals and solve these problems, and of typical and individual differences in behaviours that humans employ to reach goals and solve the problems that are obstacles to individuals attaining those goals.
- Buss uses the five-factor model of personality to understand the applicability of evolutionary theory to personality. Personality aspects such as being peaceful (emotionally stable), active, sociable, adventurous and person-oriented (extraversion), cooperative and trustful (agreeableness), practical, reliable, hard-working, ambitious and organised (conscientiousness), and sophisticated, knowledgeable, curious and analytical (openness) are all traits that would allow members of the species to cooperate to achieve goals (such as survival of the species) and to overcome problems (e.g. combating disease).
- In terms of understanding how individual differences in leadership might evolve, Rands and his colleagues postulated what would occur if two foraging animals met and fed together.
- Evolutionary concepts such as life history and parental investment are related to personality.
- Evolutionary psychology is another approach that bridges the gap between biology and personality. In the main it provides a comprehensive understanding of the way individuals and social groups behave within the goals for society.
- Evidence for evolutionary theory requires the measurement of behaviours across a number of generations and with regard to society's goals. These are ideas that are very difficult to test.
- Over 200 studies have looked at personality traits in animals; most notable is Stevenson-Hinde's work.
- Two dimensions exist in animal personality research: within-species versus cross-species comparison. Variation within a species is important to psychologists because it holds clues to the nature of evolution within a species and enables researchers to identify the adaptive nature of traits within a species to arrive at a better understanding of how a species develops, evolves and behaves. Variations across species are important because this information can be used to examine the origins and adaptations of particular traits.
- Gosling has identified two main ways that animal personality researchers rate animals on their personality: coding and observational studies. There are two ways of establishing internal reliability in animal personality studies: inter-observer agreement and within-subject reliability. Test–retest reliability assesses reliability over time, and there is evidence that animals show the same personality over time. Most studies have examined the reliability of the personality rating that animals receive, but less so the validity.
- Gosling and John (1999) suggest that the five-factor model of personality (extraversion, neuroticism, agreeableness, conscientiousness and openness) might provide an adequate context to consider animal personality.
- Problems with animal personality studies focus on the reliability of measurement and the issue of anthropomorphic projections.

Connecting up

If you need help with some of the statistical and psychometric terms used in this chapter, look ahead to the chapters on statistical and psychometric tests (Chapters 25 and 27 [online]). You would also benefit from reading Chapter 8 (biological and physiological theories of personality) before reading this chapter.

Critical thinking

Discussion questions

- Cavemen and evolutionary theory. Look critically at this news article: **http://news.bbc.co.uk/1/hi/uk/1184388 .stm**. If you can't, this article by Chris Horrie ('Did the cavemen teach us to queue?' BBC News Online, 23 February 2001) summarises some of the points made in a book called *Mean Genes*, by Terry Burnham and Jay Phelan. Some of this book is concerned with drawing analogies from basic human behaviour and the animal kingdom to explain how the basic impulses of human nature keep us alive in our natural environment. Horrie's article draws an example to the point made by the authors in the book:

  - 'Queuing may come from early humans who copied the behaviour of others who tended to live longer and, therefore, had a better chance of reproducing and passing on the behaviour to later generations. Those who [were not able to copy others] did not [and] died out.'
  - Overeating in modern western society occurs because 'as cavemen, we never knew where the next meal was coming from. Possibly there were Neanderthals who counted the calories, but the chances are they died out during the frequent famines of stone age life, having failed to build up enough fat.'
  - The authors also suggest biological roots to consumer behaviour in supermarkets, divorce, football and road rage.

- Critically discuss whether these sorts of modern behaviours can really be attributed to evolutionary forces.
- Earlier in the discussion we described that, when evolutionary theorists explain biological mechanisms as an adaptation, they describe them in terms of functionality, domain specificity and numerous. We then described how men and women's sexual strategies can be described within these three concepts. How can the following behaviours be described in terms of functionality, domain specificity and numerous?

  - altruism;
  - leadership;
  - five-factor model of personality (extraversion, neuroticism, agreeableness, conscientiousness, openness).

- Discuss whether Rands' explanation of how individual differences in leadership may occur in animals might be applied to humans.
- Evolutionary ideas have been applied to explain human sexual strategies in a number of areas. Think about and list other aspects of sexual relationships. How well does evolutionary theory explain these other aspects of sexual relationships?
- Do animals have a personality?

Essay questions

- Critically examine the idea that personality may be an evolutionary adaptive process.
- Critically outline how evolutionary theories inform our understanding of personality and individual differences.
- Critically discuss the view that the personality of animals can be assessed in a reliable and valid way.
- Critically discuss whether humans and animals can be compared in their personality.
- Critically examine the view that animals, much the same as humans, have personalities.
- Critically assess how well the five-factor model of personality explains animal personality.

Going further

Books

- Buss, D. M. (2008). *Evolutionary psychology: The new science of the mind* (3rd edn). Harlow: Pearson Education.
- Hawley, P. H. and Buss, D. M. (2011) *The evolution of personality and individual differences.* Oxford: Oxford University Press.
- Workman, L. and Reader, W. (2008). *Evolutionary psychology: An introduction* (2nd edn). Cambridge: Cambridge University Press.

Journals

- MacDonald, K. (1995). Evolution, the five-factor model, and levels of personality. *Journal of Personality, 63,* 525–567. Published by Blackwell Publishing. Available online via Blackwell Synergy, SwetsWise and Ingenta.
- Buss, D. M. (1991). Evolutionary personality psychology. *Annual Review of Psychology, 42,* 459–491. Published by Annual Reviews, Palo Alto, California. Available online via Business Source Premier.

- Gosling, S. D. (2001). From mice to men: What can we learn about personality from animal research? *Psychological Bulletin, 127*, 45–86. Published by the American Psychological Association. Available online at PsycARTICLES.
- Vazire, S. and Gosling, S. D. (2003). Bridging psychology and biology with animal research. *American Psychologist, 58*, 407. If you want to look further at some of the issues that surround using animal studies, then maybe a good place to start is this article. It discusses the combination of group-based research and individual differences research to illuminate the links between psychology and biology. This article will then link you with other recent articles. *American Psychologist* is published by the American Psychological Association. Available online via PsycARTICLES.

Also, you may wish to search the following journals on an online library database (Web of Science; PsycINFO) with the search term 'personality'.

- *Evolutionary Psychology.* This is an open access, peer-reviewed journal that aims to foster communication between experimental and theoretical work on the one hand and historical, conceptual and interdisciplinary writings across the whole range of the biological and human sciences on the other (**http://humannature.com**).
- *Evolution and Human Behaviour.* This is an interdisciplinary journal, presenting research reports and theory in which evolutionary perspectives are brought to bear on the study of human behaviour. It is primarily a scientific journal. Published by Elsevier Science. Available via Science Direct.

Web links

- A summary and links to Charles Darwin's work is here, including the origin of the species (**www.talkorigins.org/faqs/origin.html**).
- Dr Samuel Gosling maintains an online bibliography of research on animal personality at the University of Texas (**http://homepage.psy.utexas.edu/HomePage/Faculty/Gosling/bibliography.htm**).
- The Human Behavior and Evolution Society. The HBES is an interdisciplinary, international society of researchers, primarily from the social and biological sciences, who use modern evolutionary theory to help to discover human nature – including evolved emotional, cognitive and sexual adaptations (**http://hbes.com**).
- Evolutionary Psychology Frequently Asked Questions. This FAQ is written and maintained by Edward Hagen of the Centre for Evolutionary Psychology, University of California, Santa Barbara, and now at the Institute for Theoretical Biology in Berlin. The FAQ assumes a basic knowledge of genes and natural selection. Its purpose is to outline the foundations of evolutionary psychology (**www.anth.ucsb.edu/projects/human/evpsychfaq.html**).

Film and literature

- Dawkins, R. (1989). *The Selfish Gene*. Oxford: Oxford Paperbacks. Richard Dawkins suggested an enormous change in the way we see ourselves and the world with the publication of *The Selfish Gene*.
- Stinger, C. and Andrews, P. (2005). *The Complete World of Human Evolution*. London: Thames and Hudson. This compelling and authoritative account is essential reading for anyone interested in, or studying, the story of human origins.
- *Project Nim* (2011, directed by James Marsh). Tells the story of a chimpanzee taken from its mother at birth and raised like a human child. This film also tells you something about the nature of human behaviour and science.
- *Alien, Aliens, Alien 3* and *Alien Resurrection* (1979, directed by Ridley Scott; 1986, directed by James Cameron; 1992, directed by David Fincher; 1997, directed by Jean-Pierre Jeunet). These four films show how an alien species adapts to an ever-changing environment. We only get glimpses into their physiology, their behavioural patterns and their intelligence, but we do know that the main purpose of this species is to adapt and survive.
- *2001: A Space Odyssey* (1968, directed by Stanley Kubrick). Mankind finds a mysterious, obviously artificial, artefact buried on the moon and, with the intelligent computer HAL, sets off on a quest. The film begins with the 'Dawn of Man' segment, about the evolution of apes, and then ventures into the future. *2001: A Space Odyssey* is a story of birth and rebirth, human evolution and artificial intelligence.

Explore the website accompanying this text at **www.pearsoned.co.uk/maltby** for further resources to help you with your studies. These include multiple-choice questions, essay questions, web links and ideas for advanced reading.

CHAPTER 10
Further Ideas and Debates in Personality:
Personality and Culture

Key themes

- The sixth factor of personality
- The Big One
- The HEXACO model of personality
- Culture and personality
- The integrative model of personality
- Self-determination theory

Learning outcomes

After studying this discussion you should:

- Be able to present an overview of the HEXACO model of personality and outline why it is different from the five-factor model of personality
- Be able to evaluate the HEXACO model of personality and describe the biological and evolutionary theory that is thought to underpin this model of personality
- Be able to outline and criticise the main approaches to the study of culture and personality; psychological anthropology and the narrative approach to personality
- Be able to outline and evaluate the integrative model of personality
- Be able to outline the self-determination theory and its four mini theories

Introduction

In the UK newspaper, the *Guardian*, journalist John Kelly wrote an article entitled 'Binge drinking in Britain is just a side-effect of an endearing national trait: unbridled enthusiasm' (Kelly, 2008). In a light-hearted article Kelly wonders whether the much maligned characteristic of binge drinking in the UK is a reflection of a more national general personality trait, unbridled enthusiasm. He explores other national 'habits':

- Binge shopping – with an emphasis on the use of credit cards and going to the sales.
- Binge culture – via festivals such as the Edinburgh Festival or music festivals such as Glastonbury, Reading or Leeds where people jam in as many shows or as much music as possible.

On a more serious note we seem to give national traits to other events. The *Guardian* newspaper journalist Justin McCurry (McCurry, 2008) reported on the news that Japanese government measures had failed to cut their suicide rate, with suicide rates up 3 per cent from 2006. McCurry reported that almost 100 Japanese killed themselves every day in 2006 and that depression had been identified as the main factor in around a fifth of cases, followed by physical illness and debt. McCurry reported that Yuzo Kato, director of the Tokyo Suicide Prevention Centre, said that more should be done to encourage people to discuss their problems with their doctor, stating 'Japan's national character is such that people are socially conditioned to hide their pain, to avoid troubling others by opening up'. Similarly, Finnish reporter Jukka Huusko, for the *Independent* newspaper (Huusko, 2008), reported on gun crime in Finland following the tragic event when Pekka-Eric Auvinen, a high school student, used a gun to slaughter six classmates in a Finnish school. Huusko speculated on why Finland was viewed as quite a violent country when compared with its Scandinavian neighbours. He speculated that, as well as excessive alcohol consumption, family breakdown, isolation and loneliness, increasing wealth (making Finland a harsher, more competitive place), the increase in violent crime might also have something to do with 'Finnish national character traits, having problems with communication and expressing emotion'.

So far in this text we have looked at a number of psychological theories (psychoanalytic, behaviourist, cognitive, humanistic), and one of the themes of all these theories is how personality develops in terms of the self and how the self interacts with external influences and the social world. In this discussion we are going to continue with this emphasis as we introduce a number of new ideas. As you will see, underpinning many of the ideas and debates within this discussion is the role of culture; namely, how culture influences and interacts with personality, and how personality influences and interacts with culture.

Source: Getty Images/Chris Jackson

A sixth personality factor? Expanding on the five-factor model of personality

In an earlier discussion (Chapter 7) we outlined the history of trait approaches to personality and the models that accompanied them. This research is based on the lexical approach. This approach suggests that the important individual differences between people are encoded as single word terms (trait descriptors). The lexical hypothesis led to attempts to categorise the important personality traits. With the advent of factor analysis, these trait lists were statistically analysed to try to discover an underlying structure to all attitudes and behaviour.

As detailed previously (Chapter 7), Cattell used a lexical approach to uncover his theory of the source traits of personality. He finally found 16 factors and claimed that they represent the basic structure of personality. He developed the 16PF as a measurement tool. As we also outlined (Chapter 7), Eysenck identified three types or supertraits (extraversion, neuroticism and psychoticism) that he hypothesised made up the basic structure of personality. He developed a series of Eysenck Personality Questionnaires (EPQ) to measure these three types and their underlying traits. However, we also described (Chapter 7) how, using the lexical hypothesis, there was a growing consensus that five supertraits make up the basic structure of personality, largely attributed to Costa and McCrae (1992): these are openness, conscientiousness, extraversion, agreeableness and neuroticism (OCEAN):

- openness (perceptive, sophisticated, knowledgeable, cultured, artistic, curious, analytical, liberal traits);

- conscientiousness (practical, cautious, serious, reliable, organised, careful, dependable, hardworking, ambitious traits);
- extraversion (sociable, talkative, active, spontaneous, adventurous, enthusiastic, person-oriented, assertive traits);
- agreeableness (warm, trustful, courteous, agreeable, co-operative traits);
- neuroticism (emotional, anxious, depressive, self-conscious, worrying traits).

However, recent research has suggested that there is an additional factor to the five-factor model of personality. In this section we are going to tell you about the discovery and the research that surrounds this sixth factor.

The sixth factor of personality: honesty-humility? The introduction of the HEXACO model of personality

In 2000 Canadian personality psychologists Michael Ashton and Kibeom Lee and South Korean psychologist Chongnak Son began to compare more closely a number of lexical studies of personality (Ashton *et al.*, 2000). They found that among a number of studies in the USA, Germany, Hungary, Italy, Korea and Poland a sixth factor emerged. For example, Di Blas and Forzi (1998) found a sixth factor they called 'trustworthiness' in Italian, Peabody and Goldberg (1989) found a sixth factor which they named 'values' in the USA, and Hahn *et al.*, (1999) found a sixth factor they named 'trustworthiness'. Ashton *et al.* looked across these studies and compiled the sort of adjectives that loaded positively on this sixth factor and those adjectives

Being loyal, faithful and trustworthy is often proposed as the sixth factor of personality.
Source: Image Source Ltd

that loaded negatively (see Table 10.1). Considering these different adjectives, Ashton *et al.* (2000) suggested a sixth factor, 'honesty'.

Lee and Ashton developed from this a new model of personality that they called the HEXACO model. The personality traits within this approach comprise Honesty–humility (H), Emotionality (E; e.g. neuroticism), eXtraversion (X), Agreeableness versus anger (A), Conscientiousness (C), and Openness to experience (O), and these factors of personality can be identified across 12 different languages (Lee and Ashton, 2008).

Theory of the HEXACO model of personality structure

Ashton and Lee have continued to explore the HEXACO model of personality structure. One of the more recent developments is the theoretical context that surrounds this model of personality.

Ashton and Lee (2007) argue that the theoretical framework of the HEXACO involves two main contexts:

- First, the personality factors of honesty–humility, agreeableness and emotionality (i.e. neuroticism) are explained with biological theory of reciprocal and kin altruism.
- Second, that the personality factors of extraversion, conscientiousness and openness to experience factors are best understood as biologically driven concepts that relate to three separate areas of behaviour.

You may remember (from Chapter 9) that Buss (1991) used the five-factor model of personality to understand the applicability of evolutionary theory to personality. Evolutionary theory creates a framework by providing an understanding of the major goals of humans and of those problems that need to be addressed to enable reproduc-

tive success. Personality traits evolved to enable humans to reach these goals and solve the problems that are obstacles to individuals attaining these goals. Buss argued that personality aspects such as being peaceful (emotionally stable), active, sociable, adventurous and person-oriented (extraversion), cooperative and trustful (agreeableness), practical, reliable, hardworking, ambitious and organised (conscientiousness) and sophisticated, knowledgeable, curious and analytical (openness) are all traits that would allow members of the species to cooperate to achieve goals (such as survival of the species) and overcome problems (e.g. combating disease). Ashton and Lee (2007) use a similar approach but apply these ideas in terms of the HEXACO theory. We will now explain each of these contexts in turn.

Reciprocal and kin altruism

Ashton and Lee (2007) use the construct of reciprocal and kin altruism to explain the concepts of honesty–humility, agreeableness and emotionality.

Reciprocal altruism was a concept proposed by Robert L. Trivers, an American evolutionary biologist and sociobiologist. Reciprocal altruism (Trivers, 1971) is a form of altruism (practice of unselfish concern for, or devotion to, the welfare of others) in which an organism will make an altruistic act but will not expect any immediate benefit in return. However, such altruistic acts are usually carried out with two conditions. First of all, the act is made within a wider context, so that the act must benefit the recipient more than it costs the benefactor to make the act. For example, I might give you some money to keep you out of debt, so long as it does not put me in debt. Secondly, the *altruistic* act will only be carried out with the understanding that the recipient will return the act at some future date. For example, I will only give you some money if I know that you would give me some money if I was in debt at a future date.

Table 10.1 List of adjectives forming a sixth factor from lexical studies in the USA, Germany, Hungary, Italy and Korea

Positively loaded on a factor	Negatively loaded on a factor
Truthful (German, Hungarian, Italian, Korean)	Untruthful (German, Hungarian, Italian, Korean)
Truth-loving (German, Hungarian, Italian, Korean)	Dishonest (English, German, Korean)
Honest (English, German, Korean)	Arrogant (German, Hungarian, Italian, Korean)
Fair (English, German, Hungarian)	Conceited (German, Hungarian, Italian, Korean)
Just (English, German, Hungarian)	Pompous (German, Hungarian, Italian, Korean)
Sincere (German, Italian)	Greedy (German, Hungarian, Italian)
Faithful (German, Italian)	Grasping (German, Hungarian, Italian)
Loyal (German, Italian)	Sly (Italian, Korean)
Natural (Hungarian, Italian)	Corrupt (German, Italian)
Trustworthy (Hungarian, Italian)	Hypocritical (Hungarian, Italian)
Humane (German, Hungarian)	

Source: USA (Peabody and Goldberg, 1989), Germany (Angleitner and Ostendorf, 1989), Hungary (Szirmak and De Raad, 1994), Italy (Di Blas and Forzi, 1998) and Korea (Hahn *et al.*, 1999).

Therefore, reciprocal altruism is different to altruism where you wouldn't expect any return benefit at all.

Ashton and Lee (2007) ask us to look at honesty–humility and agreeableness factors within the concept of reciprocal altruism. For Ashton and Lee the distinction between honesty–humility and agreeableness is that honesty–humility is a reflection of reciprocal altruism in terms of fairness, and agreeableness is a reflection of reciprocal altruism in terms of tolerance. Within this context honesty–humility comprises a tendency to be fair and genuine in dealing with others when cooperating and not exploit them. Agreeableness represents the tendency to be tolerant and understanding of others when cooperating and not to act aggressively even when exploited by others. Ashton and Lee suggest that both these dimensions would increase reciprocal altruism because being honest in altruistic relationships will decrease the times that other people might withdraw from that relationship because they don't feel they have been exploited, and being agreeable in an altruistic relationship will lead to the individual putting more effort into maintaining the relationship even if being exploited.

Kin altruism is a concept developed by William Donald Hamilton, a British evolutionary biologist who evolved his ideas from Darwin's original theory of natural selection. Darwin's main theory was the theory of natural selection, and underlying Darwin's theory were four crucial ideas: variety, heritability, competition and adaptation. These ideas are outlined in previous discussion (Chapter 9). For example, adaptation is defined as a biological structure, process or behaviour of a member of the species that enables the member's species to survive in response to the (changed) environment, not only over other species but also over other members of the same species. However, Hamilton (1964a; 1964b) argued that natural selection is influenced by kin selection. That is, natural selection ensures the species survives and reproduces as a result of variety, heritability, competition and adaptation, but this is influenced by interactions between related individuals (be it a family or a species). Where a family or species help each other, then this is known as kin altruism. Ashton and Lee (2007) argue that the third dimension, emotionality, is relevant to kin altruism as emotions such as empathy (ability to appreciate the feelings, thoughts or attitudes of another) and attachment to others are important to kinship, as people are likely to support, protect and look after people whom they care about (likely to be members of one's own kin) and therefore ensure their survival.

Extraversion, conscientiousness and openness: three dimensions of engagement and behaviour

Here, Ashton and Lee suggest that the extraversion, conscientiousness and openness personality dimensions represent the ability and tendencies to engage in three different areas of behaviour (what Ashton and Lee called endeavours). Again, these ideas are linked to biology and the possible outcomes in terms of biological and evolutionary goals of humans, such as reproductive success, adaptation and survival.

They argue that extraversion represents engagement in social behaviours such as socialising, making friends, being positive. Therefore extraversion will promote social gains for the individual, for example, friends, allies or potential mates. They suggest that conscientiousness relates to proper and full engagement in tasks, such as working hard, planning, being organised. This leads to outcomes such as greater material gains or greater economic outcomes (money). Finally, openness to experience corresponds to engagements in learning, using one's imagination and thinking. Therefore, openness to experience promotes social and material gains via new discoveries and learning about new things.

Gains and losses as part of the theoretical interpretations of the HEXACO factors

However, there is an additional perspective to Ashton and Lee's theoretical framework. So far in our description we have discussed how each of the personality dimensions can aid evolutionary and biological goals of the individuals. However, what Ashton and Lee do is provide an additional context that discusses not only the gains but the possible costs to the individual of each of the personality dimensions.

What this part of the model emphasises is that there are potential losses from showing high levels of traits. In terms of honesty–humility, agreeableness and emotionality these are losses from:

- being too honest when the individual could have exploited someone because he/she is too fair (honesty–humility), or
- being exploited by others because the individual enters into relationships where he/she tends to be exploited, or continues relationships where he/she has been exploited but has forgiven the other person (agreeableness), or
- investing too much in others, such as family and friends, particularly in terms of potential personal gains (emotionality).

In terms of extraversion, conscientiousness and openness the main costs centre around energy in terms of continually engaging in social tasks and ideas and the potential risks from the environment of engaging in these ideas. The theoretical interpretation and the gains and losses associated with the HEXACO factors are summarised in Table 10.2.

Table 10.2 Gains and losses as part of the theoretical interpretations of the HEXACO factors (based on Ashton and Lee, 2007)

Factor	Theoretical interpretation	Examples of traits	Benefits of high levels of the traits	Costs of high levels of the traits
Honesty–humility	Reciprocal altruism (fairness)	Fairness, sincerity	Gains from cooperation	Loss of potential gains that would result from exploitation of others
Agreeableness	Reciprocal altruism (tolerance)	Tolerance, forgiveness	Gains from cooperation	Losses because of being exploited by others
Emotionality	Kin altruism	Empathy/attachment, help seeking	Survival of kin, personal survival	Loss of potential gains associated with risks to self and kin
Extraversion	Engagement in social behaviour	Sociability, leadership	Social gains (friends, mates)	Energy and time; risks from social environment
	Engagement in task behaviour	Work ethic, organisation, planning	Material gains	Energy and time
Openness to experience	Engagement in ideas	Curiosity, imaginativeness	Material and social gains	Energy and time; risks from social and natural environment

Criticisms of the choice of honesty–humility and HEXACO model of personality: 'gone too far?' or 'not gone far enough?'

So Ashton and Lee introduced a sixth dimension to create the HEXACO model because research suggested that this trait had been observed in a number of different countries. However, the introduction of this extra dimension of personality has caused some critical analysis. American psychologist Gerard Saucier (Saucier, 2002) provides a critical context to understand this work by examining the research within two questions: 'gone too far?' and 'not gone far enough?'

The first point Saucier makes is that definitive models of personality must provide completely independent factors. He explains that the five-factor model as a model of personality factors is most useful because they are independent of each other and allow us to conceptualise all behaviours, both theoretically and empirically, within these models. Saucier wonders how different the honesty factor is from the agreeableness factor of the five-factor model. He argues that in some of the findings, presented among French (Boies, Lee, Ashton, Pascal and Nicol, 2001) and Korean samples (Hahn *et al.*, 1999), their sixth factor correlated with agreeableness, and for Saucier this suggests that these factors are not independent of each other. Therefore this raises questions about the HEXACO representing six completely independent factors.

Another question that Saucier poses is, why honesty? He points out that over the years there are other constructs that could be added as the 'sixth' factor, particularly as they seem to be more independent of the big five personality factors. He points to other research that has suggested that

other constructs might form a sixth factor. For example, Saucier points to the work of Douglas A. MacDonald of the University of Detroit Mercy, USA. MacDonald (2000) has suggested that aspects of spirituality and religiosity might be the sixth factor. For example, MacDonald looked at 11 measures of spirituality that covered areas such as experiential spirituality (spirituality derived from experience), positive emotion and thoughts around spirituality and paranormal aspects of spirituality and religiosity. MacDonald found that, although he used 11 measures of spirituality, all of these aspects seemed unrelated to the big five personality factors.

Saucier also points to the work of American psychologists David P. Schmitt (Bradley University, USA) and David Buss (whose work we read about in Chapter 9). They suggested that behaviour related to sex, in terms of its link to evolutionary psychology, might be the sixth factor. In earlier discussion (Chapter 8) we outlined how evolutionary theory creates a framework by providing an understanding of the major goals of humans and of those problems that need to be addressed to enable reproductive success; for example, phenomena like mating strategies and life history, i.e. men can potentially create huge numbers of children during their lifespan whereas women can have only one child at a time. Consequently, they argue that these types of behaviour are important to understand basic ideas in individual differences. Schmitt and Buss (2000) used the lexical approach to start to look for personal dimensions relating to sexuality. You will remember from our earlier description (in Chapter 8) that one of the methods in the lexical approach is to generate a number of words in a language that refer to each trait and to see how important that trait is in describing human personality. Usually researchers will use a dictionary or thesaurus to get meaning and alternative wordings for a trait. Schmitt and Buss used such an approach by looking for all the adjectives that could be linked to sexuality from two thesauruses and two sexuality textbooks. Using an initial pool of 332 adjectives and the ratings of over 400 men and women, Schmitt and Buss found seven factors that defined sexuality. These were sexual attractiveness, relationship exclusivity, gender orientation, sexual restraint, erotophilic disposition (to what extent does a person have positive feelings about sex), emotional investment and sexual orientation. Importantly for our current study, and like MacDonald with his measures of spirituality, they found these dimensions to be largely independent of the five-factor personality dimensions.

Indeed, in 2000, Sampo V. Paunonen and Douglas N. Jackson considered what other factors exist outside of the big five by looking at some adjectives, identified by Saucier and Goldberg (1998), which they suspected didn't belong to the big five. Paunonen and Jackson suggest there is evidence for 10 possible dimensions that might lie outside the big five. These 10 dimensions are:

1 Religious, devout, reverent
2 Sly, deceptive, manipulative
3 Honest, ethical, moral
4 Sexy, sensual, erotic
5 Thrifty, frugal, miserly
6 Conservative, traditional, down to earth
7 Masculine–feminine
8 Egotistical, conceited, snobbish
9 Humorous, witty, amusing
10 Risk-taking and thrill-seeking.

As we can see, the third dimension – honest, ethical, moral – identified by Paunonen and Jackson is the sixth factor, honesty–humility. However, as Saucier argues, honesty–humility is one of many constructs that are independent of the big five and he asks why aren't any of these considered above the honesty–humility factor.

These different interpretations and findings emerging from the factor analysis of items across different cultures perhaps highlight limitations of the lexical/psychometric approach. There is a problem of rapidly increasing numbers of factors based on what is essentially a statistical procedure analysing self-report data. As we have seen, there can be much discussion over what the fifth factor is, and this variation in the sixth factor might be the result of cultural shifts or contexts, what items are actually presented to the respondents and the interpretations lent to the factor. Most importantly, these studies generally identify factors that emerge from self-report data. For some certainty, the validity of these factors must be further explored by providing external criteria (i.e. other people's ratings) and should have a theoretical basis, be it a biological, evolutionary or a learning theory.

An indicator of the ultimate outcome of the lexical/psychometric approach and where it could ultimately lead in terms of condensing attitudes and behaviours will be discussed in the next section; this is the idea and finding that there may be only one general factor of personality.

The big one? The general factor of personality

In 2007, Slovakian psychologist Janek Musek (Musek, 2007) examined the relationship between the five factors among three samples of Slovakian adults ($n = 301$, $n = 185$, $n = 285$). Using factor analysis, Musek found that a single factor of personality explained much of the variance in people's scores on the big five dimensions of personality. The finding suggests that when someone scored high on one of the factors (e.g. extraversion) they were likely to score high on one of the others. Therefore this finding suggested to Musek that there may be a further key trait underlying all these measures.

In developing this finding (see Figure 10.1) Musek found from the factor analysis that the five-factor model of personality first combined into two factors: stability (conformity [conforming and being stable]) and plasticity (non-conformity [or being open and having a capacity for

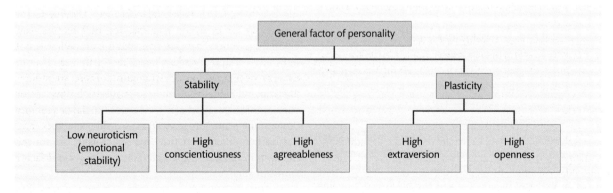

Figure 10.1 The general factor of personality (based on Musek, 2007).

change]), and that then these two factors reduced down to a single factor, the *general factor of personality*. So, what is the general factor of personality? Well, Musek suggests that it is simply a blend of all aspects of personality dimensions that are positively valued. In terms of stability and plasticity, it is those aspects of stability (conformity) and plasticity (non-conformity) that are positively valued. In terms of the five-factor model of personality, it is aspects of those personality factors that are highly valued, so, for example, high emotional stability (low neuroticism), higher conscientiousness, higher agreeableness, higher extraversion and higher openness.

J. Phillipe Rushton and Paul Irwing have found further evidence for the general factor of personality (Rushton and Irwing, 2008; 2009). They examined inter-scale correlations between the five-factor measure of personality from datasets compiled by researchers; 14 datasets totalling nearly 4,500 respondents (Digman, 1997), one large dataset of 4,000 respondents (Mount *et al.*, 2005), 16 datasets totalling 6,412 respondents (DeYoung *et al.*, 2002) and a survey of over 620,000 respondents carried out via the internet (Erdle *et al.*, 2010). Across each of these samples, Rushton and Irwing found evidence for the general factor of personality, a finding also replicated in a meta-analysis of 212 datasets containing over 140,000 respondents (Van der Linden *et al.*, 2010).

How do we understand these findings in terms of general psychological theory? Musek (2007) and Rushton and Irwing (2011) have argued that the big one may represent evolutionary, genetic and neurological accounts of personality. Although Musek doesn't provide any evidence for any of these theories, we can illustrate his explanation in terms of one of the aforementioned explanations: evolutionary theory. You may remember (Chapter 9) that we discussed Buss' evolutionary framework of the five-factor model as representing successful behaviours as an adaptation to:

- providing an understanding of the major goals of humans and the problems that need to be addressed to enable reproductive success;
- describing the psychological mechanisms that have evolved to enable humans to reach these goals and solve these problems;
- identifying the personality and individual differences in behaviours that humans employ to reach goals and solve the problems that are obstacles to attaining those goals.

According to Buss, personality traits such as being calm (low neuroticism), active, sociable, adventurous and person-oriented (extraversion), cooperative and trustful (agreeableness), practical, reliable, hardworking, ambitious and organised (conscientiousness) and sophisticated, knowledgeable, curious and analytical (openness) are all traits that would allow members of the species to cooperate to achieve goals (survival of the species) and overcome problems (conflict between members of the group). Therefore, for authors such as Musek (2007) and Rushton and Irwing (2011), from an evolutionary perspective, the existence of the big one would be explained in evolutionary terms, and the general factor of personality has evolved through the selection of desirable traits; that, is the general factor of personality comprises all those traits that led to successful adaptations.

However, University of Nottingham psychologist Eamonn Ferguson and colleagues (Ferguson *et al.*, 2011) have questioned the interpretation of the general factor of personality as representing evolutionary adaptations.

The first issue is that the correlations between the five-factor domains may be an *artefact* (spurious observation or occurrence arising from the techniques used to examine something) rather than a substantive (i.e. actual) finding. Ferguson suggests that the way personality is measured (that is, through self-report questionnaires) may be the result of an underlying factor producing the level of correlations between the factors that, when looked at on a large scale, produces the one factor. For example, if you imagine that you're answering a personality questionnaire that has lists of desirable and undesirable traits (e.g. friendly, agreeable, conscientious, emotionally stable, open) and you generally think of yourself as possessing desirable traits (perhaps with one or two exceptions), then you have the tendency over the course of the questionnaire to give weight to more desirable answers. Now that's not saying you would be lying, but you may tend to endorse more desirable aspects of your personality across at least some of the items (because, of course, on occasions you have been friendly, agreeable, conscientious, emotionally stable, open). Ferguson *et al.* (2011) call this social desirability, a term often used in psychology to describe when people might give answers that are seen as socially acceptable rather than answers that fully reflect reality. People are not lying, rather they are giving a slightly better impression of themselves. Imagine that everyone did this and had a tendency to give weight to desirable responses in their answers. You can see how, even if this was a very small effect, that, across a large population, it might be an underlying factor (the artefact) to why the five-factor personality scales would correlate together in this way. That is, the general factor of personality emerging is not result of evolutionary adaptations, rather it's the result of the way people answer questionnaires. There are studies that support this view. Evidence suggests the five-factor domains are associated with measures of social desirability (Viswesvaran and Ones, 1999; Li and Bagger, 2006), and Ferguson *et al.* suggest that this relationship across the five-factor domains could generalise to the general factor of personality.

The second issue that Ferguson *et al.* raise in regard to attributing the general factor of personality to evolutionary

Stop and think

1 From Paunonen and Jackson's list of the 10 possible dimensions that might lie outside the big five, what factor do you think should be the sixth factor of personality?

2 What are the advantages and disadvantages of having many factors of personality?

adaptations, is whether there is any evidence for linking the general factor of personality to behaviours that would reflect evolutionary adaptations; for example, is the general factor of personality related to fitness or mating success (e.g. longevity of life or reproductive attainment). However, when it comes to these relationships there is very little evidence that the general factor of personality is important, rather reported relationships being related to single aspects of personality, e.g. conscientiousness is related to longevity in life (Kern and Freidman, 2008), and emotional stability and extraversion are related to increased reproductive success (Jokela *et al.*, 2009).

Overall then, as Ferguson *et al.* (2011) note, the evidence for a general factor of personality is striking, but the evidence to suggest that it is the result of evolutionary adaptations is limited.

Culture and personality

So far in this discussion we have looked at the development of the sixth factor based on findings across a number of cultures. We have also looked at the general factor of personality and how that may be a response (in one way or another) to the world around us. Now we're going to look more directly at the study of culture and personality that seeks to understand the development of personality as part of the social world that surrounds the person. In this section, we are going to outline two areas that illustrate the major thinking and findings around culture and personality. These two areas are:

1 psychological anthropology;
2 narrative approach to personality.

Psychological anthropology

This area of study emerged at the beginning of the twentieth century and grew out of two disciplines, psychology and anthropology; psychology through the writings of Sigmund Freud on the structure of the mind and the development of personality (see Chapter 2), and the sociological discipline of anthropology, an approach that examines the origins, cultural development, social customs and beliefs of social groups. Consequently, this area is known as psychological anthropology.

Freud held that biological drives were the primary motivators of human behaviour, namely the sexual drive for reproduction and life-preserving drives, including hunger and pain and the self-destructive instinct, the death instinct (Thanatos). He argued that the personality comprises three structures that we use to gratify our instincts: the id, ego and superego. Personality develops through five distinct stages, sometimes called psychosexual stages. The stages are the oral stage, anal stage, phallic stage (comprising the oedipal complex), latency stage and genital stage (see Chapter 2).

In a number of papers, Freud used this theory to describe certain cultural aspects within society, the most notable of these papers being *Totem and Taboo* (Freud, 1913), 'Obsessive actions and religious practices' (Freud, 1907) and the 'Future of an illusion' (Freud, 1927–1961). Within these papers Freud drew on his key concepts of personality and development to provide explanations of cultural phenomena. For example, in *Totem and Taboo* he suggested that society was much like a person, as having to go through a number of traumatic stages before reaching civilisation. He went on to describe how primitive tribes, with all their savagery and neuroses, resembled the child going through the oedipal stage of psychosexual development, and that this was a process through which all societies had to go. In 'Obsessive actions and religious practices', Freud likened religious practices, which he saw as comprising guilt and containing numerous repeated rituals, to the person with an obsessional neurosis who also felt guilt and also performed repeated rituals. In 'Future of an illusion', Freud described religion as a way that societies dealt with the destructive force of the death instinct, repressing individuals' desire to be aggressive and destructive. Subsequently, anthropologists began to use psychological concepts to explore the origins, cultural development, social customs and beliefs of social groups. This has led to four approaches in understanding the relationship between culture and personality:

- the configurationalist approach;
- basic and modal personality approaches;
- national characteristic approach; and
- the work of the Netherlands cultural psychologist and sociologist Gerard Hendrik Hofstede.

Configurationalist approach

The configurationalist approach is the earliest school of thought in psychological anthropology. It was developed in the 1920s by anthropologists such as German-born Edward Sapir who was a close colleague of American academic Ruth Benedict, who in turn was the teacher of Margaret Mead. In the configurationalist approach it is argued that the culture takes on the character of all its members' personalities. That is, all members of society are thought to share similar characteristics through a culture that is linked by symbolism and interpretation of the world around them, and that, combined with the fact that they share common ideas and beliefs, a shared structure forms a 'culture type'. For researchers, such as Sapir, Benedict and Mead, personality is culture. They argue that the key to understanding the role of culture in personality from a configurationalist approach is to understand the individuals within that society, and from that you will understand that society as a whole. Each set of individuals represents a microcosm (a little world) of the culture in which they live. Therefore, differences between cultures were deemed to be the result of cultural personality types; that is, the differences between the personality of individuals within each society (see Figure 10.2a).

In Ruth Benedict's (1934) study of different tribal cultures, she identified the general culture of particular societies based on studying the personality of the individuals. So, for example, she studied the Pueblo Indians (American Indians, who lived in villages in north-western New Mexico – pueblo meaning village) who she characterised as a culture as being Apollonian (traits such as clarity, harmony and restraint) because she found the individuals within that culture avoided strong emotions, weren't allowed to show

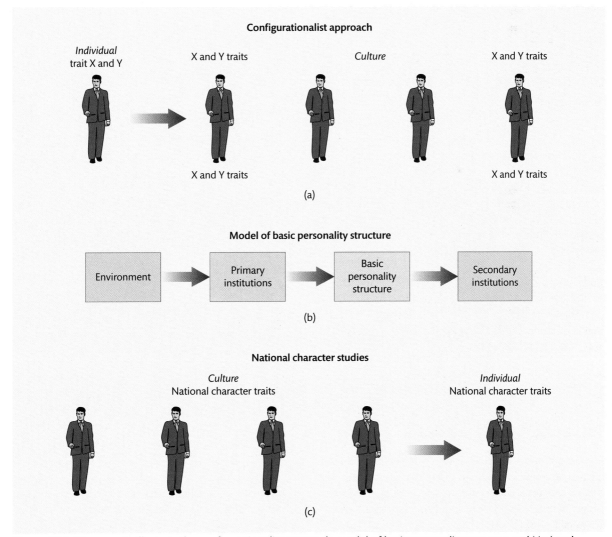

Figure 10.2 Diagrams to illustrate the configurationalist approach, model of basic personality structure and National Character Studies.

individual assertiveness and sought cooperation between members of the group, over personal gain, particularly in terms of the traditions of the group. Benedict also described the culture of the Dobuans (of Melanesia in New Guinea) as paranoid (tendency to be excessively suspicious of the motives of others). This was because she found that the individuals within that society were concerned with conflict and suspicious of others, looked to gain advantage over others at the other's loss, showed patterns of hostility, conflict and suspicion that flowed into aspects of marriage, economic exchanges and many other aspects of everyday life.

Basic and modal personality structure approach

The basic and modal personalities structure approaches are from two distinct but related ideas within culture and personality. The basic personality structure approach was developed by American anthropologists Abram Kardiner and Ralph Linton. Kardiner and Linton believed that the culture types identified by anthropologists such as Benedict were not adequate for identifying differences between societies. Instead, they suggested the model of basic personality structure, which compares the traits of the individuals of each society to achieve a basic personality for each culture. For example, Kardiner and Linton (1939) suggested that researchers need to:

- First, look at the primary institutions of any culture. A primary institution is a long-standing form of human association that serves a basic function to a culture. So, for example, the family is a primary institution.
- Second, look at aspects of a culture such as: family structure, the main form of subsistence (how a society made its living) or the type of child training that individuals went through. He argued that the analysis of these primary institutions would allow the researcher to look for basic personality characteristics of the culture; for example, what were their shared anxieties, what levels of cooperation existed within these institutions (for example, did extended family and friends involve themselves extensively in child training or not?).
- Third, see how these characteristics translated into secondary institutions (a social network that offers some expression of that culture's needs or desires) such as a society's religions, rituals or folklore.

This approach was seen as more dynamic than the configurationalist approach because it tried to explain how culture and personality interacted, in that all individuals within a society had shared experiences (within primary institutions) that produced this basic personality structure, which then, in turn, created and fed into other aspects of that culture (secondary institutions) (see Figure 10.2b).

This approach was developed into the modal personality theory by Cora DuBois, an American anthropologist. A criticism of the basic personality structure approach was that it identified personality traits that were most common to all members of society. This tended to mean that research only found those traits that were common to all members and therefore may have provided an over-simplification of the personality of a culture by identifying fewer traits. DuBois suggested that, rather than identifying traits that all of the members of a culture possessed, the characteristics of groups that were most frequently encountered within a society (i.e. modal, being a statistical term meaning the maximum occurring within any frequency of phenomena) were more apt. This then allowed a wider range of characteristics to be identified, because not all members of a society had to show the traits identified.

National character

A third approach to develop in culture and personality has emerged from studies on the national character. Ruth Benedict and Margaret Mead, who had done extensive work with the configurationalist approach to culture and personality, led the way to a new understanding of culture and personality. Early in their careers Benedict and Mead had used techniques to understand personality and culture in small-scale societies (e.g. small tribes); however, as their careers progressed they began to analyse the 'national character' of more complex societies (see also Figure 10.2). This work started during the Second World War (1939–1945), which involved many of the world's nations, either fighting each other or fighting together on the same side. Consequently, the differences between nations were highlighted and this led many anthropologists to describe and explain certain nations, such as Japan, Germany and the USA, in terms of their national character.

For example, Ruth Benedict (1946), in her book *Chrysanthemum and the Sword*, studied Japanese culture during wartime. Given that Japan was involved in a war at the time of the study she described the Japanese as comprising a contradiction between fanatical militarism (a strong military organisation) and restrained aestheticism (acceptance of artistic beauty and exaggerated devotion to art, music or poetry). Equally, much was made of the work of Erich Fromm (a German) (1941) *Escape From Freedom*. Fromm was an internationally renowned psychoanalyst and social psychologist. He speculated on the German national character and the question of why the German people submitted to Hitler. Here, Fromm described the German people as typical of an authoritarian personality (you can read more on this work in Chapter 22 of this book, Social Attitudes), obedient and subservient to superiors, and cruel to subordinates. Later, Margaret Mead with Rhoda Metraux, in their 1953 book *Themes in French Culture*, emphasised that the French national character comprised intellectual and emotional control.

These later studies are often criticised because of the method of research used. In their earlier work, using the configurationalist approach, Kardiner, Benedict and Mead provided ethnographic accounts (i.e. detailed fieldwork to provide a descriptive study of human groups). Clearly this work is more successful among small societies, producing a relatively straightforward analysis of small hunter–gatherer communities. Therefore, the work of these authors was often very powerful because it could provide a detailed account of the rituals, religious practices and child-rearing practices of a small group. However, later studies, such as those that looked at larger and more complex societies, i.e. capitalist and industrialised societies such as Japan, Germany and France, were problematic as an ethnographic approach did not suffice, as any modern society would be too complex to reduce down to a number of simple themes from fieldwork.

However, Robert R. McCrae and Antonio Terracciano of the National Institute on Aging in Maryland, USA, carried out a study on national character, seeking to explore whether perceptions of a nation's national character fitted the personality of individuals within that nation (McCrae and Terracciano, 2006). To explore the national character, McCrae and Terracciano (2006) used the personality characteristics of the five-factor model. You will remember that this personality model comprises five personality types:

- openness (perceptive, sophisticated, knowledgeable, cultured, artistic, curious, analytical, liberal traits);
- conscientiousness (practical, cautious, serious, reliable, organised, careful, dependable, hardworking, ambitious traits);
- extraversion (sociable, talkative, active, spontaneous, adventurous, enthusiastic, person-oriented, assertive traits);
- agreeableness (warm, trustful, courteous, agreeable, co-operative traits);
- neuroticism (emotional, anxious, depressive, self-conscious, worrying traits).

This research went through two stages. The first stage was to measure individuals' perceptions of their own national character; for example, Australian people's perceptions of the Australian national character or Spanish people's perceptions of the Spanish national character. The second stage was then to compare these perceptions to the individual participant's view of their own personality. To complete the first stage, the authors used the National Character Survey. The National Character Survey is a measure developed by Terracciano that asks respondents to make judgements about a hypothetical 'typical' member of a culture. It consists of a set of 30 bipolar scales intended to parallel the 30 facets (that then comprise the five factors, six facets each) of the main measure of the five-factor model of personality (NEO-PI-R; Costa and McCrae, 1992; you can see a list of all these traits in the Stop and think box: National characteristics of your country?). For example, a British respondent taking the test would be asked 'How extraverted is the typical British person?' The authors then also administered the NEO-PI-R (a measure of the five factors of personality) to individuals as well. Therefore the researchers had a measure of an individual impression of the national character that could be understood within the five-factor personality traits and an actual measure of each individual's personality within the five-factor personality traits. So, our British respondent mentioned above would be asked to fill in the NEO-PI-R themself.

Data was analysed from over 4,000 individuals from 49 countries (including Argentina, Australia, Brazil, Canada, China, UK, Germany, France, Spain, Italy, India, New Zealand, Russia and the USA) crossing six continents,

Japanese manga-style cartoon: often the personality of a culture is expressed through the art of that country.
Source: The Ronald Grant Archive

Stop and think

National characteristics of your country?

1   What is the national character of your country? Using the list of the main five-factor personality dimensions and their respective six facets, describe the national character of your country.

2   Now compare your national character against Hofstede's five dimensions of national culture. How would your national character be reflected in each of these five dimensions?

Openness	Conscientiousness	Extraversion	Agreeableness	Neuroticism
Fantasy	Competence	Warmth	Trust	Anxiety
Aesthetics	Order	Gregariousness	Straightforwardness	Angry hostility
Feelings	Dutifulness	Assertiveness	Altruism	Depression
Actions	Achievement striving	Activity	Compliance	Self-consciousness
Ideas	Self-discipline	Excitement-seeking	Modesty	Impulsiveness
Values	Deliberation	Positive emotions	Tender-mindedness	Vulnerability

with the scale translated into different languages when necessary. Terracciano and his colleagues then compared the data from the National Character Survey with the NEO-PI-R personality inventory for each country. Table 10.3 shows the average correlation between the dimensions that could be gained from the National Character Survey and NEO-PI-R. There were some significant relationships between the National Character Survey and NEO-PI-R; for example, there are medium- to large-sized significant positive correlations in Polish, Lebanese and Australian samples, and medium- to large-sized significant negative correlations in British, Danish and Belgian samples. However, across the large majority of the samples, the correlations were low. If you average out the correlations across these samples, the average correlation is –0.02. What this means is that personality profiles for individuals generally do not resemble profiles for what they believe to be typical culture members.

Table 10.3 Mean correlations (averaged across the five factors) between the five factors of personality and the National Character Survey (based on McCrae and Terracciano, 2006)

Country	Mean correlations between National Character Survey and the NEO-PI-R	Country	Mean correlations between National Character Survey and the NEO-PI-R	Country	Mean correlations between National Character Survey and the NEO-PI-R
Argentina	–0.08	Hong Kong	0.29	Portugal	–0.01
Australia	0.38	Iceland	–0.06	Puerto Rico	0.10
Belgium	–0.45	India	–0.06	Russia	–0.35
Botswana	–0.11	Indonesia	0.06	Serbia	0.08
Brazil	0.00	Italy	0.05	Slovakia	0.14
Burkina Faso	–0.16	Japan	0.05	Slovenia	0.25
Canada	–0.03	Kuwait	–0.07	South Korea	–0.09
Chile	–0.33	Lebanon	0.39	Spain	–0.10
China	–0.02	Malaysia	0.13	Switzerland (sample 1)	0.06
Croatia	–0.16	Malta	0.25	Switzerland (sample 2)	–0.29
Czech Republic	–0.16	Morocco	0.25	Turkey	0.00
Denmark	–0.40	New Zealand	0.36	Uganda	0.28
Estonia	–0.10	Nigeria	–0.12	UK: England	–0.57
Ethiopia	–0.09	Peru	0.13	UK: N. Ireland	0.29
France	0.27	Philippines	0.14	United States	0.23
Germany	–0.04	Poland	0.40		

McCrae and Terracciano have also provided more information on individual scores for some countries. For example, they found that USA respondents thought the typical US citizen was higher in neuroticism and lower in agreeableness. That is, they tended to be emotional, anxious, depressive, self-conscious and worrying and didn't tend to be warm, trustful, courteous, agreeable and cooperative. However, McCrae and Terracciano found that, when they rated themselves on these traits, US individuals, on average, tended to be much lower on neuroticism and much higher on agreeableness. Conversely, McCrae and Terracciano found that Canadians saw their own national character as being lower in neuroticism and higher in agreeableness. However, results from the NEO-PI-R revealed that Canadian individuals were higher in neuroticism and agreeableness.

What McCrae and Terracciano are keen to point out is that national character studies show reliability but not validity in terms of national character. Reliability regards consistency between the different aspects of any measurement, be it items of a questionnaire or different people rating certain behaviours, while validity refers to whether the phenomena you are measuring are accurate (see Chapter 25 for more on reliability and validity). That is, that individuals in many cultures are consistent in terms of identifying a national character for their own country (i.e. they are reliable); however, these national characters bear no relation to the actual personality types of individuals within these countries (they are not valid).

Personality and national culture: the work of Hofstede

One main investigator on the nature of personality and national culture was the Dutch cultural psychologist/sociologist Gerard Hendrik Hofstede. Hofstede has written on the interactions between national and organisational cultures (e.g. Hofstede, 1997; 2001; Hofstede and Hofstede, 2005). Hofstede carried out a huge research project into national culture differences across the multinational corporation of IBM (International Business Machines Corporation, an information technology company) in 64 countries, and in later work which looked at students in 23 countries, consumers in 15 countries, airline pilots in 23 countries and civil service managers in 14 countries. In this work he looked at national and regional cultural groups that influenced the behaviour of societies and organisations. Hofstede identified four independent dimensions of national culture differences, with a fifth dimension added later. These five dimensions are:

- *Low versus high power distance* – Low versus high power distance is the extent to which less powerful members of a culture, or institutions within that culture, accept and expect that power is distributed unequally throughout that culture. In low power distance cultures, people

relate to one another as they are equal, and will tend to ignore the formal position of the person. Within low power distance cultures individuals contribute more freely to decision-making processes. In higher power distance cultures those less powerful within a culture accept and expect aspects of that culture, such as decision-making, as more autocratic (a few people, or one person, having absolute rule). Hofstede found that places like Austria, Denmark and New Zealand were lower power distance cultures, while places like Malaysia and Slovakia were high power distance cultures.

- *Individualism versus collectivism* – Individualism is a social and cultural outlook that emphasises independence and self-reliance, and the promotion of the individuals' desires and goals. Collectivism is a social and cultural outlook that emphasises the communal aspects of the culture, emphasising community, group and cultural goals and values. Hofstede found that western cultures (i.e. USA, UK and Australia) were individualistic, while Latin American cultures were the most collectivist.

- *Masculinity versus femininity* – This is the extent to which a culture is understood in terms of masculinity and femininity (as understood in western cultures). Within Hofstede's findings masculine cultures are cultures that emphasise and value traits such as competitiveness, assertiveness, ambition, materialism, whereas feminine cultures are those that emphasise and value traits such as relationships and quality of life. Hofstede found that places like Japan could be considered masculine cultures, while countries like Sweden have feminine cultures. Later researchers have renamed this dimension as 'quantity' (masculine) versus 'quality' of life dimension (feminine).

- *Uncertainty avoidance* – This dimension reflects the extent to which the members of culture develop social mechanisms or rules to attempt to deal with the anxiety that surrounds their lives by minimising uncertainty. Cultural mechanisms in a culture that deal with uncertainty might be a tradition or a cultural rule or set of rules; for example, religion. Hofstede found that Japanese, Latin American and Mediterranean cultures scored high in uncertainty avoidance.

- *Long-term versus short-term orientation* – Long-term versus short-term orientation within a culture refers to the importance attached by that culture to the future versus the past and present. Here there is a distinction between the extent to which members of a culture expect immediate (short-term orientation) versus delayed (long-term orientation) gratification and realisation of goals and desires in society. This is sometimes known as the 'time horizon' or attitudes towards time. Within cultures with a short-term orientation, there is an emphasis and value on consumption or keeping up with competitors. Values within cultures with a long-term orientation include persistence and perseverance and being patient in achieving results and goals. Hofstede found that western nations are found to have short-term orientations, while China, Japan and the Asian cultures show long-term orientations.

Hofstede has developed a Values Survey Module, which is now in its third version (VSM 08; previous versions include the VSM 82 and the VSM 94), to measure these orientations. The Value Survey Module now measures the five dimensions mentioned above.

- Low versus high power distance is measured via the power distance index. Higher scores on this index indicate low power distance, a greater level of acceptance and expectation that power is distributed unequally within a culture (lower scores represent high power distance).
- Individualism versus collectivism is measured via the individualism subscale. Therefore higher scores on this measure indicate higher levels of individualism (lower scores indicate collectivism).
- Masculinity versus femininity is measured via the masculinity subscale, with higher scores representing higher

levels of masculinity and lower scores representing higher levels of femininity.
- Uncertainty avoidance is measured via the uncertainty avoidance index. Therefore higher scores on this measure indicate the greater extent to which a culture has cultural mechanisms or rules that attempt to deal with the anxiety, thereby minimising uncertainty.
- Long-term versus short-term orientation is measured via the long-term orientation subscale, with higher scores representing a greater tendency towards delayed gratification and realisation of goals and desires in society. This scale was developed later than the other scales.

Hofstede (1997; 2001; Hofstede and Hofstede, 2005) has published results on a number of countries for scores on this scale. We have listed these in Table 10.4. We highlighted some of the higher and lower scores in our descriptions of the dimensions above, but you might want to take some time looking at the different scores across different countries and continents. Note that there are fewer figures for the long-term orientation subscale because this was developed later in Hofstede's work.

Table 10.4 Hofstede's five dimensions of culture by country

	Low power distance	Individualism	Masculinity	Uncertainty avoidance	Long-term orientation
North America and Canada					
Canada	39	80	52	48	23
United States	40	91	62	46	29
Australasia					
Australia	36	90	61	51	31
New Zealand	22	79	58	49	30
Europe					
Austria	11	55	79	70	
Belgium	65	75	54	94	
Bulgaria	70	30	40	85	
Czech Republic	57	58	57	74	13
Denmark	18	74	16	23	
Estonia	40	60	30	60	
Finland	33	63	26	59	
France	68	71	43	86	
Germany	35	67	66	65	31
Greece	60	35	57	112	
Hungary	46	80	88	82	50
Ireland	28	70	68	35	
Italy	50	76	70	75	
Luxembourg	40	60	50	70	
Malta	56	59	47	96	
Netherlands	38	80	14	53	44
Norway	31	69	8	50	20
Poland	68	60	64	93	32
Portugal	63	27	31	104	
Romania	90	30	42	90	

	Low power distance	Individualism	Masculinity	Uncertainty avoidance	Long-term orientation
Russia	93	39	36	95	
Slovakia	104	52	110	51	38
Spain	57	51	42	86	
Sweden	31	71	5	29	33
Switzerland	34	68	70	58	
Turkey	66	37	45	85	
United Kingdom	35	89	66	35	25
Central and South America					
Argentina	49	46	56	86	
Brazil	69	38	49	76	65
Chile	63	23	28	86	
Colombia	67	13	64	80	
Costa Rica	35	15	21	86	
Ecuador	78	8	63	67	
El Salvador	66	19	40	94	
Guatemala	95	6	37	101	
Jamaica	45	39	68	13	
Mexico	81	30	69	82	
Panama	95	11	44	86	
Peru	64	16	42	87	
Uruguay	61	36	38	100	
Venezuela	81	12	73	76	
Asia					
China	80	20	66	30	118
Hong Kong	68	25	57	29	96
India	77	48	56	40	61
Japan	54	46	95	92	80
Malaysia	104	26	50	36	
Pakistan	55	14	50	70	0
Philippines	94	32	64	44	19
Singapore	74	20	48	8	48
South Korea	60	18	39	85	75
Taiwan	58	17	45	69	87
Thailand	64	20	34	64	56
Vietnam	70	20	40	30	80
Africa					
East Africa	64	27	41	52	25
South Africa	49	65	63	49	
West Africa	77	20	46	54	16
Middle East					
Iran	58	41	43	59	
Israel	13	54	47	81	

There are some criticisms of Hofstede's work. One of the main issues is that it tries to conceptualise cultures, when culture is something that is dynamic and is persistently changing. Therefore, for authors such as Mead (1994), the findings of Hofstede are likely to become outdated very quickly and therefore only offer a snapshot of a particular time within the culture that may not be relevant at a later time. Equally, some of Hofstede's work is not culturally sensitive; for example, a lot of his work is based on huge regions (e.g. East Africa, South Africa, West Africa), which themselves contain a multitude of different cultures.

A second criticism, put forward by academics such as Robinson (1983), is that the samples used by Hofstede are not representative of the wider population. He argues that IBM employees, students and airline pilots are from groups of individuals who tend to be of a higher socio-economic status and therefore aren't samples representative of the wider culture. Moreover, a lot of Hofstede's data is drawn from employees working at IBM, and therefore their answers or attitudes would have been influenced by a western organisational culture, which values western business ideals.

Finally, Tayeb (1996) has suggested that the methodology used by Hofstede, which is entirely questionnaire-based and focuses on attitudes, is a problematical way of studying culture and that some behavioural measures of culture would need to be used to aid such considerations.

Integrative model of personality

So far within this discussion, and throughout the rest of the text, we have looked at different explanations of personality. Some of these concentrate on the unconscious (psychoanalytic); some concentrate on how we learn (behaviourism); some theories use statistical techniques to define personality (e.g. the five-factor model of personality); some emphasise a biological approach (Gray's theory of personality) or an evolutionary basis (e.g. Buss and the five-factor theory as an adaptation); and some theories, as we have seen in this discussion, emphasise the role of culture. In 2006, two American psychologists, Dan P. McAdams and Jennifer L. Pals from Northwestern University, proposed an integrative science of personality.

With this integrative approach McAdams and Pals argued that there was a need to present a comprehensive framework for understanding the whole personality of the person. They suggested that personality theory was often viewed, as typified by personality textbooks, as fragmented and non-integrative. This means that, if you looked at your average personality textbook (much like this book), different theories are often segmented according to the originator of that theory; for example, Freud, Rogers, Maslow, the Big Five. They argue that, in current psychology, there

should be some progression from this fragmented view of the personality of the individual to a personality theory that combines these different aspects of personality theory – an integrative model of personality.

McAdams and Pals' paper outlined five main principles to establish a new model of personality that describes how culture and evolutionary aspects interact with basic traits, characters and life experiences that influence the roles and behaviours that we display (see Figure 10.3). The five main principles are:

- evolution and human behaviour;
- the dispositional signature;
- characteristic adaptations;
- life narratives and the challenge of modern identity;
- the differential role of culture.

We will now outline each of these five principles.

Evolution and human behaviour

One of the main problems, for McAdams and Pals, with the grand theories of personality, is that theories such as those of Freud (Chapter 2) or Maslow and Rogers (Chapter 6) start with 'unquestioned assumptions' about the basis of human nature. As a consequence, major parts of their theories have to be accepted at face value despite essentially being untested and untestable. For example, this might apply to Freud's 'assumptions' about the instincts (e.g. the pleasure principle), Maslow's descriptions of our basic physiological needs (e.g. hunger, thirst, sleep, sex), or Rogers' description of the need for all humans to self-actualise. McAdams and Pals argue that we have to take many of these theories 'on faith'. Consequently, the first idea that McAdams and Pals look for is the underlying motivation and assumptions of personality. To do this they turn to evolutionary psychology.

Figure 10.3 An integrative model of personality (based on McAdams and Pals, 2006).

The first principle that McAdams and Pals explore is the idea that human lives are the result of variations and adaptations from the evolution of human behaviour. You will remember (from Chapter 9 Biological Basis of Personality II) that evolutionary theory creates a framework by providing an understanding of:

- the major goals of humans and of those problems that need to be addressed to enable reproductive success;
- the psychological mechanisms that have evolved to enable humans to reach these goals and solve these problems; and
- the typical and individual differences in behaviours that humans employ to reach goals and solve the problems that are obstacles to individuals attaining those goals.

For example, Buss used the five-factor model of personality to understand the applicability of evolutionary theory to personality. Personality aspects such as being peaceful (emotionally stable), active, sociable, adventurous and person-oriented (extraversion), cooperative and trustful (agreeableness), practical, reliable, hardworking, ambitious and organised (conscientiousness), and sophisticated, knowledgeable, curious and analytical (openness) are all traits that would allow members of the species to cooperate to achieve goals (such as survival of the species) and overcome problems (e.g. combating disease). The existence of the five-factor traits across a number of cultures (McCrae and Costa, 1997; McCrae *et al.*, 1998; 2000), including German (Ostendorf, 1990) and Chinese (Trull and Geary, 1997) cultures, and evidence of the five-factor personality traits among animals (Gosling and John, 1999; see also Chapter 9 in this book) suggests support for the universality of the five-factor personality theory.

For McAdams and Pals, evolutionary theory provides an excellent explanation for why certain personality traits, such as the five-factor personality theory, emerge in human society across a number of cultures. That is, it explains why these traits exist in the first place, in that they ensure the survival and continuation of the species by providing humans with the necessary traits to adapt to their environment.

The dispositional signature

Secondly, McAdams and Pals point to the importance that dispositional trait theories of personality have placed on understanding the individual; for example, the trait theories of Allport, Eysenck and Costa and McCrae (see Chapter 7), who have outlined the broad dimensions of traits which demonstrate the main individual differences between people. Here, it is the identification of these traits that is crucial to understanding the human personality because:

- traits are seen as consistent aspects of our personality in that they characterise our personality over time (e.g. people who are extraverted at one time point in their life will tend to show similar levels of extraversion 6 months, 1 year … 30 years later);
- personality traits are consistent predictors of similar behaviour among individuals across a number of situations (e.g. people who are nervous in the workplace will tend to be nervous in social settings and nervous when they meet new people);
- personality is influenced by heritability factors and biological factors. We discussed this earlier (Chapter 8). For example, studies suggest that the heritability of certain personality traits is around 50 per cent and help us to understand differences between individuals in terms of genetics. Also, other research has linked personality to the functioning of the brain (see, for example, our description of Gray's theory in Chapter 8).

Characteristic adaptations

McAdams and Pals add that a huge range of individual differences emerge in motivations, social-cognitive factors and developmental experiences that occur during the course of an individual's life. McAdams and Pals refer to these as characteristic adaptations. There are a number of characteristic adaptations such as individual motives, personal goals, self-image, schemas and significant life experiences that have been identified as influences on personality. For example, a personal goal from beginning your degree would be to strive for a high final degree classification, which might need you to undertake the character adaptation of being hardworking and conscientious for a sustained period of time. Many of the theorists we have outlined earlier have identified characteristic adaptations made by individuals during the course of their lives. For example:

- Sigmund Freud noted how behaviour is energised by the conflicts created by the interaction of the id, ego and superego. These conflicts create anxiety, and defence mechanisms evolved to help deal with this anxiety (Chapter 2).
- Carl Jung described the psyche, a complex structure of opposing forces that created the life-process energy that motivates our behaviour, and believed that development continues throughout adulthood. He stated that the endpoint of personality development is the achievement of self-realisation and that this demands considerable life experience (Chapter 3).
- Horney emphasised the role played by cultural and social factors in personality development (Chapter 3).
- Rotter argued that the likelihood of a behaviour occurring, termed behaviour potential, is predicted by our expectancy and reinforcement value (Chapter 4).

- Bandura showed that our behaviour was an active process of learning through observation, where the observer makes judgements and constructs symbolic representations, and humans use self-reinforcement to control our behaviour via internal self-regulatory processes (Chapter 4).
- Kelly conceives individuals acting as scientists, each trying to understand and control the world around them, developing personal constructs, and that the motivation to act comes from our future aims, not from our past learning or early experiences or innate drives (Chapter 5).
- Rogers argued that individuals have an innate drive to self-actualise (Chapter 6).
- Maslow outlined a hierarchy of needs to describe human motivation. These begin with physiological needs, then safety needs, belongingness and love needs, esteem needs and the need for self-actualisation. Individuals require that their lower-level needs be met before higher-level needs come into play (Chapter 6).

Therefore McAdams and Pals argue that, although these different characteristic adaptations that cover motivations, social-cognitive factors and developmental experience have yet to be fully simplified, they are likely to fall outside what can be explained simply by the trait theories of personality, e.g. the five-factor model of personality, owing to there being so many aspects to consider.

Life narratives and the challenge of modern identity

Life narratives is an approach that has emerged from the psychological anthropology framework discussed earlier. This approach was developed by Cora DuBois, who developed the modal personality approach and emphasised documenting an individual's life experiences to understand personality. With personality theory this type of approach is known as the narrative approach to personality.

Kate McLean (McLean, 2008), from Western Washington University, is a researcher who uses the narrative approach to personality and has outlined the theory that lies behind the approach. McLean emphasises that within the theory it is recognised that, although children are able to talk about themselves very early on in their lives, it is in adolescence that a real sense of the self begins to develop. She explains that in adolescence the individual begins to interpret and understand themselves in terms of a story of their life. They begin to make connections between their own self in different settings (e.g. friends, families, education) and analyse themselves in terms of time (e.g. what has happened in the past, what might happen in the future, in terms of the directions they want to follow) and begin to construct a personal story of their life.

Dan P. McAdams, Professor of Psychology and Professor of Human Development and Social Policy at Northwestern University, USA, has written extensively on the narrative approach to personality. McAdams (e.g. McAdams, 1988, 1993) suggests that a life narrative is important for understanding personality. He describes a life narrative as comprising a personal and evolving life story, that helps individuals to understand the past and look forward to the future, and provides purpose and meaning that influences and shapes an individual's personality. What is also important is that people constantly revise their life story, and therefore the influence of an individual's narrative is lifelong with information from establishing oneself in the world through relationships, work and life events, feeding into this narrative. For example, as you move through life, different events and relationships will help you understand who you are. How you act in your first personal relationship will tell you something about your personality. If something happened to someone close to you, your reaction would tell you something about your personality. Therefore, your stories and explanations regarding your relationships, your experiences and important events in your life also shape your personality. What is also important about your life narrative is that it is something that you seek to maintain. So, for example, you may have decided that, because of past experiences and events, you are a 'fighter' who has had to confront and overcome obstacles in life as they presented themselves. Therefore this narrative, and your identification of yourself as a 'fighter', carries on into future events and you may act aggressively or with resilience as you enter new relationships or new experiences and encounter new events.

Within the narrative approach to personality, researchers have focused on how people understand and establish the meaning of past experiences and they have examined how this informs an individual's own identity and their personality. Research has shown that there is a link between the meaning individuals lend to past events and aspects of their personality. Pavel Blagov and Jefferson Singer examined four dimensions of autobiographical memory (specificity, meaning, content and affect) and their relationship to three possible personality types: self-restraint, distress and defensiveness (Blagov and Singer, 2004). In this study respondents were asked to generate 10 self-defining memories and then go back and rate each one of them in terms of vividness, importance and positive or negative emotions (e.g. happiness, sadness, anger, fear), and then rate themselves on the Weinberger Adjustment Inventory (WAI; Weinberger, 1997; 1998). This inventory measures long-term personality functioning such as distress (e.g. well-being such as self-esteem, depression), self-restraint (e.g. impulse control, suppression of aggression) and defensiveness (e.g. denial of distress and restraint). Overall, Blagov and Singer found that there was a link between self-defining memories and the measures of personality functioning and adjustment. Self-defining memories were related to the amount of emotional distress,

Two British personality psychologists, Alex Wood and Stephen Joseph, also wrote a response to the McAdams and Pals paper (Wood and Joseph, 2007). Like Epstein, the first point made by Wood and Joseph is to question McAdams and Pals' argument that the major theories describe the basis of human nature (i.e. Freud's descriptions of the instincts, Maslow's descriptions of our basic physiological needs) are problematic because we have to accept them at face value. Wood and Joseph argue that these theories have a major influence on therapeutic practice basis and so the basic assumptions of these theories clearly have some value. The second point they suggest is that McAdams and Pals make much of the suggestion of combining culture, life narratives and characteristic adaptations to existing models of personality. However, Wood and Joseph suggest that this is not a particularly new consideration, and many of the grand theories of personality actually deal with how human nature and personality interact with culture. For example, we saw earlier in our discussion of Freud's writings on religion and tribal traditions how his work influenced a whole discipline focusing on personality and culture. Further, Rogers' work focuses on how the individual balances the real self with influences on the self-concept from social factors such as parents and education.

Finally, Wood and Joseph suggest that different grand theories and theorists of personality disagree greatly on a number of issues and therefore can never be integrated. One example of these disagreements is the basic components of human nature. Freud argues that there are biological, even animalistic, instincts. Maslow argued that the basis of human nature was physiological. Rogers argued that it was a need to self-actualise. Ellis argued that being fallible is the innate quality of humans. Therefore, Wood and Joseph wonder whether it is ever possible to create an integrative model of personality.

Self-determination theory

In the last sections we looked at a number of areas regarding how personality factors across a number of cultures can inform our understanding of personality. We also looked at how some psychologists have looked to integrate some psychological approaches to provide an integrated model of personality. In this section we're going to look at another theory that has perhaps integrated different schools of thought more naturally in its development since the 1970s. This is of particular interest here because this theory also highlights the extent to which the individual is motivated by, and responds to, their cultural environment.

Self-determination theory (SDT) focuses on the motivation of the individual and looks at the development of personality within the context of the social world. The theory emphasises a number of approaches that reflect other theories of personality and psychology, including the following.

- Human needs, values and internal motivations that we have seen in the humanistic theories of personality (e.g. Maslow and Rogers' ideas around basic needs and self-actualisation; Chapter 6).
- Social learning models of behaviour and particularly the role of locus of control and rewards (e.g. behaviourism and Rotter's locus of control; Chapter 4).
- Aspects of cognitive psychology, particularly ideas around perception, evaluation and information processing.
- Aspects of social psychology: the study of how people and groups interact and how the thoughts, feelings and behaviours of individuals are influenced by other people.

This theory has been developed largely by American psychologists Edward L. Deci and Richard M. Ryan, who are professors in the Department of Clinical and Social Sciences in Psychology at the University of Rochester, USA. Deci and Ryan (1985, 2002) describe how SDT's main focus is to consider to what extent people's thinking, feeling and behaviour are the result of the choice they make of their own free will, without any influence from external forces. One of the main original ideas of SDT is the distinction between intrinsic and extrinsic motivations. Intrinsic motivations reflect reasons for doing things that are the result of factors internal to the person. They may reflect a person's internal desire to perform a particular task, or an event or activity that gives them pleasure, or develops something they want to improve about themselves, or they feel it is the right, or moral, thing to do. That is, it is something a person feels personally that they want to do. For example, an intrinsic motivation might be to be kind and gentle to all those around them. Extrinsic motivations are motivations that reflect reasons for doing things that are the result of factors external to the person. Therefore extrinsic motivations might involve doing things for money (i.e. rather than out of the goodness of your heart) or getting good marks in an exam (rather than feeling the satisfaction of doing a good piece of academic work for its own reward) or concerns about being punished by someone else (rather than doing something for yourself).

Deci and Ryan argue that both intrinsic and extrinsic motivations can lead to highly motivated individuals; for example, one can be highly motivated by values (intrinsic) or money (extrinsic). However, individuals are not always motivated. When this occurs this is called an amotivation. They argue that amotivations occur because people don't feel motivated to do something either because they feel unable to participate (i.e. things are beyond their control) or are unwilling to participate (i.e. because they don't feel they will receive either a reward or punishment) in a behaviour.

Deci and Ryan have suggested that intrinsic motivations are better than extrinsic motivations and that extrinsic motivations are better than amotivations (see Figure 10.4).

Amotivations   Extrinsic   Intrinsic
                    motivations   motivations

Figure 10.4 The self-determination theory continuum: intrinsic motivations, extrinsic motivations and amotivations.

Deci and Ryan have concentrated on how intrinsic motivations develop and used this idea to develop SDT.

In the rest of this section we will describe the main aspects of this theory, outline some of the ways it has been applied and look at some discussion points that exist around the theory.

The four theories of self-determination theory

Deci and Ryan (2002) suggest that there are four theories that underpin SDT. These are basic needs theory, cognitive evaluation theory, organismic integration theory and causality orientation theory (see Figure 10.5).

Basic needs theory

Within basic needs theory, Deci and Ryan (2002) proposed three main universal, innate and psychological intrinsic needs that influence an individual's self-determination (Deci and Ryan; 1991; 1995).

- *Need for competence* – The extent to which an individual sees himself/herself as a person who is capable of controlling their environment and external world, and how confident and accurate she/he is at reliably predicting outcomes in life.
- *Need for autonomy* (sometimes called self-determination) – The extent to which the person determines their own behaviours, how much they are in charge of the choices they make in life without the involvement of external factors.
- *Need for relatedness* – The extent to which a person feels the need to help and be involved with others; that is, a

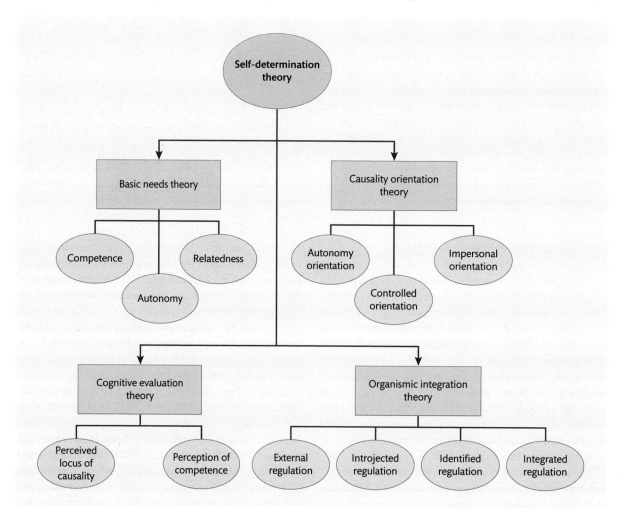

Figure 10.5 The four mini-theories of self-determination theory.

person who needs to feel satisfaction with the extent to which they participate, and are involved, with others socially.

Deci and Ryan suggest that these three basic intrinsic needs are central to the healthy development and functioning of an individual, and whether the individual will develop and function in a healthy or unhealthy manner is based on the extent to which these needs are satisfied (leading to healthy development and functioning) or thwarted (leading to unhealthy development and functioning).

Cognitive evaluation theory

Cognitive evaluation theory describes how intrinsic motivations are affected by social context and specifically influenced by external events. This part of SDT looks at how individuals perceive, make judgements and evaluate their motivations. Within this theory Deci and Ryan suggest that external events in the world affect intrinsic motivation via two routes:

- perceived locus of causality;
- perception of competence.

The **perceived locus of causality** separates into two aspects: (1) internal perceived locus of causality; and (2) external perceived locus of causality. An internal perceived locus of causality is when the individual feels they are engaging in a behaviour under their own free will and not being affected by any external influence. An external perceived locus of causality is when the individual feels they're engaging in a behaviour as a result of external influence.

The individual's **perception of competence** is the extent to which the individual believes they have the competence to carry out the behaviour. That is, if the individual does not believe themselves to be competent, this will have a detrimental effect on their intrinsic motivation, whereas if they believe themselves to be competent then this will have a positive effect on their intrinsic motivations. So, for example, if someone wants to help people and become a counselling psychologist (intrinsic motivation) but find they can't listen to people talking about their problems all day (do not believe themselves to be competent), then this may dampen their intrinsic motivation of becoming a counselling psychologist to help people. However, if they found they were good at listening to people, then this would have a positive effect on their intrinsic motivation of becoming a counselling psychologist because they would believe they were competent to undertake such a role.

The combined effects of perceived locus of causality and perception of competence may increase or decrease an individual's intrinsic motivation. Within this theory the role of rewards is central. Within psychology, a reward is typically thought to increase motivation towards what is being rewarded (e.g. if someone praises you [reward] for doing well in a piece of coursework, that may motivate you to work at least just as hard next time you do a piece of work, even if just to get the same reward next time). Within cognitive evaluation theory, rewards serve two main functions in terms of whether they increase or decrease an individual's intrinsic motivation.

- They may have an *information function*. That is, a reward provides information to the individual about their own competence, and therefore external rewards are likely to increase the intrinsic motivation. For example, if your intrinsic motivation is to do good, and you do something good for someone, and that person tells someone else that you are a good person and you hear about it, then it is likely to increase your view that you can do good. This doesn't make it an extrinsic motivation; rather, this praise is further reward for your intrinsic motivation.
- They may have a *controlling function*. The reward will have a positive effect, but if it is used as a way of controlling the behaviour of the individual (i.e. the behaviour or motivation is for the reward rather than for intrinsic motivation) then if the reward is at a later time absent (it may be withdrawn, taken away or not available any more) it is likely to lead to a decrease in the level of intrinsic motivation. So, using our example of coursework above, if someone stopped praising you for doing well on your coursework (even though you were still doing well), and the only reason you were trying at the coursework was to get the praise, not for the satisfaction of producing good work, then you might stop trying as hard at the work.

Organismic integration theory

Within organismic integration theory, Deci and Ryan propose that it is possible for some extrinsic motivations to become intrinsic to the individual. Organismic integration theory suggests that, when behaviours or motivations are endorsed by significant others (people who are important to the individual, such as close family or friends), then these too can be internalised by the individual. Internalisation is a process of the acceptance, by the individual, of norms (appropriate and inappropriate values, beliefs, attitudes and behaviours) that are established by people close to the individual. Internalisation is when the individual goes through a process of adopting these norms until they accept them as their own. Consequently, some extrinsic motivations can become internal to the individual. Deci and Ryan viewed these forms of extrinsic motivation as more autonomous (independent and not from control from outside) and regulated (more controlled), being somewhat similar in the way they operate, to intrinsically motivated behaviour.

Essentially, this theory is concerned with the way that individuals regulate external and social influences. As a result, Deci and Ryan suggested it was possible to divide extrinsic motivation into four different types based on the level of internalisation of the extrinsic motivation:

- **External regulation** – This is the behaviour that we have described so far as extrinsic motivations, as motivations controlled by rewards and threats from external influences.
- **Introjected regulation** – This is where the individual's behaviours and attitudes are motivated as a result of avoiding or trying to avoid negative feeling. For example, you may feel guilty about something and therefore regulate your behaviours based on this.
- **Identified regulation** – These are behaviours and attitudes that are motivated by having valued outcomes of engaging in a behaviour even though they may not be important motivations to the individual themselves.
- **Integrated regulation** – These are behaviours and attitudes that are motivated to satisfy personal goals that are consistent with the individual's self-identity (this is sometimes referred to as intrinsic motivations).

Ryan and Connell (1989) developed a number of self-regulation measures that can be used to differentiate types of extrinsic motivation with respect to the degree to which it has been internalised by the individual. Ryan and Connell suggest that each self-regulation measure has to be domain-specific; that is, it has developed to apply to the particular situation at which you are looking. So, Ryan and Connell originally developed seven questionnaires: academic, pro-social, treatment, learning, exercise, religion and friendship. For each questionnaire, the respondent is asked why they behave in a particular way and are then asked several questions that represent the different styles of regulation or motivation. In this questionnaire, integration regulation is called intrinsic motivation.

We will show you an example of one questionnaire that was developed, the Academic Self-Regulation Questionnaire. In the Academic Self-Regulation Questionnaire one set of questions is headed 'Why do I try to do well in school?' Then there are a number of statements to which respondents are asked whether each statement is 'Very true', 'Sort of true', 'Not very true' or 'Not at all true'. For these sets of questions, examples of each of the regulation styles include:

- External regulation: 'Because I will get in trouble if I don't do well' and 'Because I might get a reward if I do well'.
- Introjected regulation: 'Because I will feel really proud of myself if I do well' and 'Because I'll feel really bad about myself if I don't do well'.
- Identified regulation: 'Because it's important to me to try to do well in school'.

- Integrated regulation (intrinsic motivation): 'Because I enjoy doing my school work well'.

Causality orientation theory

Causality orientation theory looks at the role of individual differences in motivational orientations (Deci and Ryan, 2002). To some extent, this combines different aspects of the overall SDT and the three other mini-theories (basic needs theory, cognitive evaluation theory and organismic integration theory).

Deci and Ryan argued that there are individual differences in the orientation that people take in their motivations, that are shaped by both individual experiences of the external world and their inner self and resources that are developed as a result of interactions with the external world. This differs from other aspects of SDT because, rather than concentrating on social influence such as the cognitive evaluation theory, it concentrates on individual differences in personal motivational factors towards the environment. Deci and Ryan identified that there were three different motivational orientations: autonomy, controlled and impersonal, leading to individual differences between people.

- **Autonomy orientation** – This orientation reflects motivations towards aspects of the environment that stimulate the individual's intrinsic motivation. Within this orientation the environment also provides information that promotes the individual's self-endorsed values or well-integrated extrinsic motives that have been developed through integrated regulation (see organismic integration theory, behaviours and attitudes that are motivated to satisfy personal goals that are consistent with the individual's self-identity). Deci and Ryan describe a person who is high in autonomy orientation as someone who shows high levels of self-initiation, who will seek out activities that are interesting to them and provide them with a challenge and who takes responsibility for their own behaviour. This is the orientation that most reflects someone motivated by motivations intrinsic to the individual.
- **Controlled orientation** – This orientation assesses the extent to which a person is oriented toward extrinsic motivations, i.e. being controlled by rewards, deadlines and the directives of other people. Largely these are made up of extrinsic motivations and introjected regulation (see organismic integration theory, where the behaviours and attitudes are motivated and are the result of avoiding, or trying to avoid, negative feelings). A person high in a controlled orientation places importance on extrinsic factors, such as wealth, and is likely to be dependent on rewards, and pay attention to the demands and needs of others.
- **Impersonal orientation** – This orientation relates to amotivation (discussed at the beginning of this section) and assesses the extent to which there is a lack of

intentional (amotivated) behaviour in the individual and unintentional behaviour that lacks any motivation. People who are high in amotivation often believe that goals are beyond their control. They will often believe that any achievement is largely a matter of luck or fate rather than under their control.

To measure these orientations, Deci and Ryan (1985) developed the General Causality Orientation Scale (GCOS), which measures these three types of motivational orientations: autonomy, controlled and impersonal. The original scale comprises 12 vignettes and 36 items, and each vignette describes a typical social or achievement-oriented situation and is followed by three types of responses: an autonomous, a controlled and an impersonal type of response. Respondents indicate, on 7-point Likert-type scales (from 1 = very unlikely to 7 = very likely), the extent to which each response is typical for them. Higher scores indicate higher amounts of the particular orientation represented.

So, for example, one vignette on the scale is: 'You have been invited to a large party where you know very few people. As you look forward to the evening, you would likely expect that …'

Then the respondent would have to answer the likelihood of each of these behaviours.

The first statement is indicative of a *controlled orientation*.

(a) You'll try to fit in with whatever is happening in order to have a good time and not look bad.

The second statement is indicative of an *autonomy orientation*.

(b) You'll find some people with whom you can relate.

The third statement is indicative of an *impersonal orientation*.

(c) You'll probably feel somewhat isolated and unnoticed.

Applications of self-determination theory

For Deci and Ryan the key to well-being is the ability to satisfy all basic needs, to have and carry out behaviour that is intrinsically motivated, and these are essential for the psychological health and well-being of an individual. SDT and the concepts contained within the four mini-theories have been tested in a number of domains, including exercise, work, health, education, well-being and psychotherapeutic practice.

One example of the application of SDT was examined by Kennon M. Sheldon with Richard Ryan and Harry Reis (Sheldon *et al.*, 1996), who carried out a diary study to examine how two of the basic psychological needs, competence and autonomy, influenced everyday well-being. The authors collected, among 60 undergraduate students, measures of autonomy (an example item was 'I am free to do whatever I decide to do') and competence (an example item

was 'I am usually able to demonstrate my competence when I am being evaluated') alongside measures of well-being (e.g. positive and negative mood adjectives and vitality) over a 2-week period of study. Sheldon and his colleagues found that fulfilment of psychological needs for competence and autonomy was associated with greater daily well-being.

Another example of how SDT has been used is in work-related behaviour, more specifically job search behaviour. Belgian psychologist Maarten Vansteenkiste and his colleagues (Vansteenkiste *et al.*, 2004) used the self-regulation questionnaire format of Ryan and Connell (1989; see above) to assess unemployed individuals' autonomous, controlled and amotivation job search motivations. The authors found that autonomous motivations for a job search led to that person showing persistence in looking for a job.

SDT ideas have also been used in treatment settings. American psychologists Peter Britton, Geoffrey Williams and Kenneth Conner (Britton *et al.*, 2008) have suggested that SDT provides a framework for understanding the therapeutic relationship and clients' motivations for treatment, particularly when they are feeling suicidal. They argue that autonomy support may be critical to treating clients who have ideas of suicide by helping them to resolve their uncertainty about living by helping them access a motivation to live. Similarly, Canadian psychologists Luc Pelletier, Kim Tuson and Najwa Haddad (Pelletier *et al.*, 1997) developed a client motivation for therapy scale, which measures intrinsic motivation, extrinsic motivation and amotivation for therapy. Items included for motivation and regulations in response to why they attend therapy include:

- **Intrinsic motivation** – 'For the pleasure I experience when I feel completely absorbed in a therapy session.'
- **Integrated regulation** – 'Because through therapy I've come to see a way that I can continue to approach different aspects of my life.'
- **Identified regulation** – 'Because I believe that eventually it will allow me to feel better.'
- **Introjected regulation** – 'Because I would feel bad about myself if I didn't continue my therapy.'
- **External regulation** – 'Because other people think that it's a good idea for me to be in therapy.'

Pelletier *et al.* found that individuals with higher forms of self-determination (intrinsic motivation, integrated and identified regulation) for their therapy were more likely to consider therapy more important, experience less tension and more positive moods during therapy, and reported being more satisfied with the therapy, showing stronger intentions of continuing in therapy. Pelletier and colleagues also found that clients who perceived their motivation to be less self-determined (more extrinsic) experienced more tension and more negative moods during therapy, and reported being less satisfied with the therapy, showing weaker intentions of continuing in therapy.

Profiles

Edward L. Deci and Richard M. Ryan

Edward L. Deci is Professor of Psychology in the Social Sciences at the University of Rochester, USA. He received his PhD in Social Psychology from Carnegie-Mellon University in 1970 and has also studied at the University of Pennsylvania and the London School of Economics, as well as being post-doctoral fellow at Stanford University. He is a fellow of the American Psychological Association and the American Psychological Society. Deci has been engaged in a programme of research on human motivation for over 40 years that has focused around self-determination theory. He has published numerous research articles and books, including *Intrinsic Motivation and Self-Determination in Human Behavior* and *Why We Do What We Do*. He has received grants to aid his research from the National Institute of Mental Health, the National Institute of Child Health and Human Development, the National

Science Foundation and the Institute for Education Sciences. He also runs his own psychotherapy practice.

Richard M. Ryan is a Professor of Psychology in Psychiatry and Education at the University of Rochester, USA. He received his PhD from the University of Rochester in 1981 and has also studied at the University of Connecticut where he received a BA in philosophy in 1976. He is also a fellow of the American Psychological Association. He too has published numerous research articles and books and is a co-author of *Intrinsic Motivation and Self-Determination in Human Behavior*. He has received funding from the National Cancer Institute, Bill and Melinda Gates Foundation and the Institute of Education Sciences, US Department of Education. He has also won the Phi Delta Kappa award (which is an international association for professional educators) for Educational Research and Leadership in 1995 and 2005.

Finally, research using the General Causality Orientation Scale (GCOS), which measures three types of motivational orientations (autonomy, controlled and impersonal orientations), has found the following:

- *Autonomy orientations* are associated with:

  - Higher self-esteem and self-actualisation (Deci and Ryan, 1985)
  - Cardiac surgery patients viewing their surgery more as a challenge (King, 1984)
  - Positive experiences while studying at school (Wong, 2000)
  - Weight loss and weight-loss maintenance (Williams *et al.*, 1996).

- The *controlled orientations* are associated with:

  - Public self-consciousness (Deci and Ryan, 1985)
  - Poorer academic performance and commitment while studying at school (Wong, 2000).

- The *impersonal orientations* are associated with:

  - Higher levels of social anxiety, depression and self-derogation (Deci and Ryan, 1985).
  - Eating disorders (Strauss and Ryan, 1987).

Considerations of self-determination theory: the reward controversy and the eight criteria

One of the main debates to revolve around SDT results from a disagreement with the school of behaviourism

about the role of rewards and motivation. We covered the main ideas of behaviourism and the work of Skinner earlier (Chapter 4). To provide a re-cap, Skinner was a radical behaviourist, and he did not allow for inner experiences in his account of learning. As inner experiences could not be observed, he therefore considered them unscientific. Only behaviour that could be observed was included in his model of learning. For the same reason, he rejected the concept of personality as being produced by the interaction of inner forces. All behaviour was learnt. He demonstrated that three key concepts were important for learning: operant conditioning, positive reinforcement and negative reinforcement. Simply, within these learning models, extrinsic rewards (or reinforcements) are likely to increase the frequency of a behaviour, and when these rewards cease to be given, the behaviour is likely to return to the level of frequency that existed before the rewards started. Skinner's theory is deterministic. He rejects the concept of free will and the idea of intention or creativity in human behaviour. We merely respond to stimuli in our environment, and the consequences of our responding determine our learning. SDT, and particularly cognitive evaluation theory, proposes that extrinsic rewards such as monetary payments can undermine people's intrinsic motivation. This view seems to contradict the behaviourist approach, which maintains that the careful use of rewards (or reinforcements) is the most effective mechanism to promote motivation.

Throughout a number of decades (e.g. Scott, 1975; Deci, 1976; Rummel and Feinberg, 1988; Flora, 1990;

Cameron and Pierce, 1994; Deci *et al.*, 1999), supporters of behaviourism and SDT have debated the evidence for whether extrinsic rewards undermine people's intrinsic motivation. For example, Cameron and Pierce (1994) produced a meta-analysis of studies and concluded that rewards do *not* decrease intrinsic motivation, and suggested that the cognitive evaluation theory that had been formulated to explain reward effects on intrinsic motivation was problematic. However, Cameron and Pierce's findings have been rebutted by Deci *et al.* (1999), who presented their own meta-analysis and have argued that Cameron and Pierce made a number of errors and that their analysis is invalid. These authors also suggest that there is substantial evidence for cognitive evaluation theory in that rewards can decrease intrinsic motivation.

There are other considerations of SDT and we will do this using the eight criteria identified previously (Chapter 1): description, explanation, empirical validity, testable concepts, comprehensiveness, parsimony, heuristic value and applied value. In terms of **description**, self-determination does try to bring order into the complexity of behaviours by having a number of mini-theories to explain how motivation and resulting behaviours emerge from interactions within the environment. In terms of **explanation** the theory does attempt to explain the 'why' behaviour, arguing that attitudes and behaviour are the result of motivation or the lack of motivation (amotivation). However, it is the explanation of lack of motivation that may be a concern. There is very little explanation of why amotivations occur; rather it is attributed to feelings of a lack of control or unwillingness to be motivated. However, SDT lacks an explanation as to why these feelings regarding a lack of control or unwillingness occur.

In terms of **empirical validity** and **testable concepts**, there is a lot of empirical evidence for SDT and the fact that psychologists are able to measure many SDT concepts. We mentioned above a meta-analysis of studies relating to the cognitive evaluation theory. Equally, measures have been developed to examine key ideas within SDT. For example, the General Causality Orientation Scale (Deci and Ryan, 2002) has been developed to measure the three types of motivational orientations, and Ryan and Connell (1989) have developed a number of self-regulation measures that can be used to differentiate types of extrinsic motivation in respect of the degree to which it has been internalised by the individual. There is also evidence of the **applied value** of SDT, with many of the concepts being used in education, healthcare, parenting, organisations, sport and exercise and mental health. However, in terms of **comprehensiveness**, SDT may have a weakness. A good theory should be able to encompass and explain a wide variety of both normal and abnormal behaviour. However, how SDT relates to many areas of abnormal psychology and functioning is not clear.

In terms of **parsimony** a good theory should be economical in terms of the number of explanatory concepts it includes. One of the strengths of SDT is that it integrates a number of areas of psychology. We noted at the beginning of this section that SDT was based on ideas around human needs, values and internal motivations, combined with the social learning model of behaviours, as well as aspects of cognitive and social psychology. To what extent is this a parsimonious account of human personality and motivation? Currently, SDT lends itself to many different aspects of psychology, and therefore, with each overlap with a different area of psychology, brings a number of further ideas to consider. We saw with the reward controversy described above that the use of social learning principles, such as reward, brought in many more considerations than the theory might allow. For example, SDT uses cognitive ideas of perception and information processing and social psychological ideas of social influence. Cognitive and social psychologists would emphasise that these concepts are very complicated ideas which incorporate different theories. Consequently, using multiple concepts from different areas of psychology may lead to an unparsimonious account of human personality.

Finally, there is some evidence of the **heuristic value** (i.e. the ability to stimulate interest and research in an area) in SDT. Although there is successful empirical and applied research exploring the value of different aspects of SDT, and much of this work is in prestigious journals, this theory is still not considered to be a major theory of personality, with the main publications being limited to relatively few researchers. This may change, as it is considered by many to be a new and exciting personality theory. However, given that Deci began publishing work in the area in the 1970s, the fact that it is still considered as a new theory suggests that the growth of interest and research in the area has been slow and its heuristic value may be relatively low.

Final comments

In this discussion we have introduced you to a number of ideas. We have introduced the sixth dimension of personality, presented an overview of the HEXACO model of personality and also the general factor of personality. We have also outlined some of the main approaches to the study of culture and personality, including psychological anthropology ranging from the study of small cultures to the comparison of large cultures. We have introduced an integrative model of personality and outlined some of the criticisms of this approach and outlined the biological and evolutionary theory that is thought to underpin this model of personality. We have outlined another theory that sought to extend existing ideas of personality, that of self-determination theory.

Stop and think

What are your motivations?

1   Think about your academic work. Imagine you did a really good piece of university coursework. List the sort of feelings you would expect to have and rewards you would expect for doing a really good piece of university coursework.

2   Think about your friendships. Imagine you did something good for a friend. List the sort of feelings you would expect to have and rewards you would expect for doing something good for your friend.

3   Look at your answers to the last two questions. From these answers are you intrinsically or extrinsically motivated in these areas?

4   What are your intrinsic motivations?

5   What are your extrinsic motivations?

Summary

- Recent research in a number of studies, including the USA, Germany, Hungary, Italy, Korea and Poland, has suggested that there is an additional factor to the five-factor model of personality: honesty–humility.

- Ashton and Lee introduced the HEXACO model of personality structure comprising Honesty–humility (H), Emotionality (E; e.g. neuroticism), eXtraversion (X), Agreeableness versus anger (A), Conscientiousness (C), and Openness to experience (O), and asserted that these factors of personality can be identified across 12 different languages.

- Ashton and Lee (2007) argue that the theoretical framework of the HEXACO involves two main contexts. First, the personality factors of honesty–humility, agreeableness and emotionality (i.e. neuroticism) are explained within a biological theory of reciprocal and kin altruism. Second, that the personality factors of extraversion, conscientiousness and openness to experience factors are best understood within the concepts that they are involved in, describing engagement or investment in three separate areas of endeavours that are related to biology.

- Criticisms of the choice of honesty–humility and the HEXACO model of personality question how different the honesty–humility factor is from the agreeableness factor of the five-factor model and whether honesty–humility is one of many constructs that are independent of the Big Five.

- Musek found from the factor analysis of the five factors of personality that they first combined into two factors – stability and plasticity – and that these two factors then reduced down to a single factor, the general factor of personality, which is a blend of all aspects of personality dimensions that are positively valued.

- Within the area of psychological anthropology are the configurationalist approach, basic and modal personality approaches and national characteristic approaches. International research by Hofstede identified five dimensions of national culture differences: low versus high power distance, individualism versus collectivism, masculinity versus femininity, uncertainty avoidance and long-term versus short-term orientation.

- McAdams and Pals' paper outlined five main principles that establish a new model of personality that describes how culture and evolutionary aspects interact with basic traits, characters and life experiences which then influence the roles and behaviours we display. The five main principles are evolution and human behaviour, the dispositional signature, characteristic adaptations, life narratives and the challenge of modern identity and the differential role of culture.

- Critics of the integrative model of personality suggest that the authors over-emphasise the importance of evolution, the five-factor model and life narratives in their analysis and are somewhat vague about characteristic adaptations.

- Self-determination theory (SDT) is a human motivation theory focusing on the extent to which people's thinking, feeling and behaviour are the result of the choices they make, of their own free will, without any influence from external forces. The main distinction is between intrinsic, extrinsic and amotivational motivations.

- Four theories underpin SDT. These are basic needs theory, cognitive evaluation theory, organismic integration theory and causality orientation theory.

- The usefulness of SDT and the concepts contained within the four mini-theories have been tested in a number of domains, including exercise, work, health, education, well-being and psychotherapeutic practice.

Connecting up

A lot of this chapter requires some basic knowledge of the five-factor theory of personality and evolutionary and biological approaches to personality. If you need more information on these areas, read Chapters 7, 8 and 9. Also, a cursory understanding of some of the ideas discussed in Chapter 2 (psychoanalysis), Chapter 4 (learning) and Chapter 6 (humanistic approach) in regard to basic needs or drives and social learning principles is perhaps needed.

Critical thinking

Discussion questions

- Pick three major theorists/theories from an earlier discussion (Chapter 2 to Chapter 7).
  - Which is your favourite theory of personality and why?
  - Which two of the three theorists are most similar and why?
  - Which two of the three theorists are most different and why?
  - Compile a list of their most similar and most different aspects. Don't get sidetracked into describing aspects of their theories, just concentrate on identifying central themes and ideas.
- Discuss the main aspects of theories in culture and personality studies. Include in your discussion the main ideas, the main mechanisms and the main results/findings of these studies.

Essay questions

- Critically examine how culture and personality are interrelated.
- Critically examine the way that culture interacts with personality traits.
- What are the personality dimensions along which human cultures vary?
- Critically discuss the role of self-determination theory in understanding personality.
- Critically compare the main theoretical approaches within the domain of psychological anthropology.

Going further

Books

- McAdams, D. P. (2006). *The redemptive self: Stories Americans live by*. New York: Cambridge University Press.
- O' Boyle, C. G. (2006). *History of psychology: A cultural perspective*. Hove, UK: Psychology Press.

Journals

- *American Psychologist*. This journal has a number of articles relating to culture and personality. Published by the American Psychological Association. Available online via PsycARTICLES.
- *Integrative Psychological and Behavioral Science*. This journal explores the cultural nature of human conduct and its evolutionary history, anthropology, ethology, and the communication processes between people and within societies. It is published by Springer-Link. The homepage of the journal is here: **www.springerlink.com/content/1936-3567**.
- Two *Annual Review of Psychology* articles have covered culture and personality. Triandis, H. C. and Suh, E. M. (2002). Cultural influences on personality. *Annual Review of Psychology*, *53*, 133–160 looks at universal and culture-specific aspects of variation in personality. Heine, S. J. and Buchtel, E. E. (2009). Personality: The universal and the culturally specific. *Annual Review of Psychology*, *60*, 369–394 looks at both universal and culturally specific features to personality.
- Markus, H.R. (2004). Culture and personality: Brief for an arranged marriage. *Journal of Research in Personality*, *38*, 75–83 looks at the role of culture specificity in personality.

Web links

- We outlined some of the international research by Geert Hofstede. Summaries of his research about cultural difference plus details of the measures used are provided here: **http://geert-hofstede.com/national-culture.html**.

- There is a website detailing the major theoretical and empirical papers involved with self-determination theory as well as a number of measures: **www.psych .rochester.edu/SDT**.

Film and literature

- *Jerry Maguire* (1996, directed by Cameron Crowe). This is a story with a theme that looks at the motivations that underlie behaviours. In the story Jerry Maguire is a sports agent willing to do just about anything he can to get the biggest possible contracts for his sports clients. He then has second thoughts about what he's really doing. Another treatment of changing motivations is the book and film *Trainspotting* (book by Irvine Welsh; film (1996) directed by Danny Boyle). The movie follows a group of heroin addicts in early 1990s economically depressed Edinburgh and their passage through life.

- One film that plays off national stereotypes is *Dr. Strangelove or: How I Learned to Stop Worrying and Love the Bomb* (1964, directed by Stanley Kubrick). The film is based around the Cold War conflict and Peter Sellers plays a number of characters representing a number of different national stereotypes. Another analysis of culture and personality and how it can be (mis)understood in terms of national stereotypes is *Do the Right Thing* (1989, directed by Spike Lee), which looks at racial conflict in a multi-ethnic community in Brooklyn, New York.

Explore the website accompanying this text at **www.pearsoned.co.uk/maltby** for further resources to help you with your studies. These include multiple-choice questions, essay questions, web links and ideas for advanced reading.

PART 2
Intelligence

CHAPTER 11
An Introduction to Intelligence

Key themes

- Implicit theories of intelligence
- Expert and non-expert (laypersons') theories of intelligence
- Implicit theories of intelligence across the lifespan
- Implicit theories of intelligence across cultures
- The American Psychological Association Task Force on Intelligence

Learning outcomes

After studying this discussion you should:

- Be aware of laypersons' implicit theories of intelligence
- Understand how implicit theories of intelligence change across the lifespan
- Be familiar with how implicit theories of intelligence change across cultures
- Be aware of experts' implicit theories of intelligence

Introduction

Intelligence is part of our society. Each year, over 10,000 people take the Mensa Intelligence Test. Mensa is an organisation for people with high intelligence. Mensa was founded in England in 1946 by Roland Berrill, a barrister, and Dr Lance Ware, a scientist and lawyer. They had the idea of forming a society for bright people; the only qualification for membership was a high intelligence. The society's sole requirement for entry is that potential members must score within the top 2 per cent in any approved standardised intelligence test. Of the 10,000 people who take the Mensa Intelligence Test each year, around 2,500 pass to become members. Those who become members are now part of a forum for intellectual exchange, via lectures, journals and interest groups. In the summer of 2002, nine million people in the United Kingdom – to find out how intelligent they, and the rest of the country, were – took part in a national intelligence test broadcast via television. This programme is now repeated in the United Kingdom every year.

In 2003 a report from researchers in Russia expressed concern that lead poisoning can affect children's intelligence. Scientists at the Ural Regional Centre for Environmental Epidemiology at Ekaterinburg in Russia have found that lead is found naturally in soil and dust, and children who don't wash and who chew their nails are at greater risk of lead poisoning. These Russian scientists have suggested that lead poisoning is a concern because, apart from raising health concerns, it can affect children's intelligence.

These are examples. However, in this discussion we will show you how intelligence and conceptions of intelligence matter to humans. We will introduce you to the importance of everyday conceptions of intelligence and how conceptions of intelligence change over lifetimes, across cultures and around the world. We will also tell you why, in 1996, the American Psychological Association, the most powerful psychological association in

the world, decided to gather 11 leading psychological experts in intelligence together to write a defining paper on the subject. This discussion will provide you with a basic understanding of some of the issues and debates underlying the psychological study of intelligence.

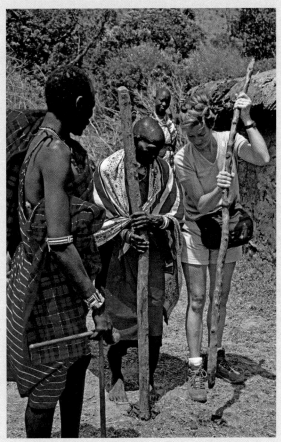

Source: Alamy Images/Danita Delimont

Why does intelligence matter?

Why does intelligence matter? Professor Robert J. Sternberg, who is a Professor of Psychology and Education at Yale University and a world authority on intelligence, suggests that our theories of intelligence are an important aspect of our everyday life. Our ideas of intelligence, and the way in which we perceive and evaluate our own and other people's intelligence, are at the heart of some of our everyday decisions as well as long-term decisions with regard to ourselves, our loved ones and even our children.

If you imagine your education so far, aside from your formal exam results, you and others have offered opinions about your and your friends' intelligence. For example, regardless of your previous examination results, you have some idea about how intelligent you *really* are. Your intelligence might be greater than your exam results suggest, or it might be less. Similarly, your parents have probably at some stage made comments about how intelligent you are. You also have some perception of your friends' intelligences. You will also have evaluated how you compare in terms of your friends' intelligence. You will know which of your friends are more intelligent, and which are less intelligent. You may even find that some of your conversations within the group focus or are oriented around each other's intelligence.

You can see, then, that even at this simple level among friends, intelligence is important. For Sternberg (1985b; 2001a), it is this perception and evaluation of intelligence that drives so many things in society. From birth, parents are concerned with their children's intelligence. Ideas of what intelligence is will drive parents to make decisions about when to correct children if they make an error in their speech. In love, intelligence matters. Most people want their long-term partners to be intelligent, so they can be with someone who will make proper and accurate decisions and act intelligently throughout the partnership (though for some short-term relationships, intelligence might be actively discouraged). In work, perceptions of intelligence are crucial. A candidate perceived as intelligent in a job interview situation will always be more likely to get the job than a candidate who is perceived as unintelligent. Throughout life your intelligence, and that of others, forms a crucial aspect of the decisions you make. It is this recognition, by academics such as Sternberg, of the importance of intelligence to everyone in everyday life that leads us to our first area of study in introducing the topic of intelligence: implicit theories of intelligence.

Implicit theories of intelligence

Implicit theories are people's everyday ideas that surround a particular topic area. Therefore, implicit theories of intelligence are our everyday ideas that surround intelligence. Sternberg (2001a) suggests four reasons that implicit theories of intelligence are important.

First, implicit theories of intelligence are important for the reasons just discussed above: they are important to everyday life. Implicit theories of intelligence drive the way in which people perceive and evaluate their own intelligence and that of others. Subsequently, people use such perceptions and evaluations to draw conclusions about themselves and others and make judgements about everyday life. It is easy to imagine how perceptions and evaluations of intelligence would inform job selection, parenting styles and approaches to friends and partners.

Secondly, implicit theories of intelligence can give rise to more formal theories of intelligence that researchers can investigate. Imagine that an academic wants to understand intelligence in a particular area of the world; let us say, for example, Europe. Then one method this academic might consider is to go out into the world and discover what folk, layperson, everyday theories exist in Europe. The academic then can condense all these theories into one big descriptive work, which provides a framework for researchers in the field to understand intelligence.

Thirdly, implicit theories are useful because they may provide useful avenues to research when an investigator thinks explicit theories are wrong. Again, let us use our example of the academic who wants to understand intelligence in Europe and has gathered together a number of implicit theories about intelligence. The researcher might then set about testing which implicit theories are supported with evidence and which are not.

Fourthly, and finally, implicit theories of intelligence can inform theories around psychological constructs, such as the development of intelligence and cross-cultural aspects of intelligence. For example, researchers may have a good understanding of intelligence in their own country or their own part of the world. However, when it comes to studying other cultures, they may feel less confident. Consequently, collecting information on implicit theories of intelligence in a number of countries might help researchers understand how the perception and evaluation of intelligence changes across cultures.

So, what work has been done to explore implicit theories of intelligence?

Research into implicit theories of intelligence

In this section we are going to explore some of the research that has been conducted regarding implicit theories of intelligence. We are also going to show how research into implicit theories of intelligence has shown that changes in these theories depend on the sample or population examined, and particularly how these changes inform cultural and developmental aspects of intelligence.

Laypersons' implicit theories of intelligence

A **layperson** is a non-professional or non-expert in an area. As we shall see, researchers have found it useful to look at laypersons' theories of intelligence. We will give you two examples of studies among US individuals so you can see how such studies are conducted as well as see some of the results. Robert J. Sternberg and three colleagues (Sternberg, Conway, Ketron and Bernstein, 1981) investigated individuals' conceptions of intelligence in a series of experiments. In the first experiment, 61 people studying in a college library, 63 people entering a supermarket and 62 people waiting for a train in a railway station were asked to list behaviours that were characteristic of 'intelligence', 'academic intelligence', 'everyday intelligence' or 'unintelligence'. Then 122 other people were asked to rate how well each of the behaviours listed in the first experiment reflected aspects of intelligence. Using findings from both of these studies, Sternberg and his colleagues found three dimensions of intelligence among this sample:

Profile

Robert J. Sternberg

Robert J. Sternberg was born in December 1949 in Newark, and grew up in Maplewood, New Jersey, USA. Sternberg is a leading expert in a number of areas of psychology, but his foremost expertise is in intelligence, where his academic works and research dominate the literature.

There seems to be a huge amount of irony surrounding Sternberg's early academic career and his latest achievements. Sternberg says he first became interested in psychology because as a child he performed badly in an intelligence test and was put back an academic year. It was only later at school, thanks to a teacher who believed he was capable of doing better, that he started doing very well at school. Sternberg went on to study psychology at Yale University. At university, he was initially put off studying psychology because a course lecturer suggested, when Sternberg got a C grade in an introductory psychology course, that there was already a famous psychologist of the same name in psychology – and it was obvious from his work that there would not be another famous psychologist called Sternberg. Despite this discouragement, Sternberg eventually graduated

with honours with exceptional distinction in psychology. Sternberg studied for his PhD at Stanford University and has since received four honorary doctorates from universities in Spain, France, Belgium and Cyprus.

Professor Sternberg is presently an IBM Professor of Psychology and Education at Yale University. He has had a distinguished career. He has published nearly 1,000 academic papers and books and has attracted nearly $7 million in academic research grants. He is highly cited in academic journals and introductory psychology textbooks, and during his career he has been the editor of *Contemporary Psychology* and *Psychological Bulletin*. He has received a number of awards from prestigious psychological associations and societies, including an early career award from the American Psychological Association and the Cattell award from the American Psychological Society.

Not content with being a world-leading expert in intelligence, Sternberg has done extensive research work and made significant contributions to the understanding of creativity, wisdom, thinking styles, and love and hate.

- **Practical problem-solving** – Practical problem-solving is the ability to be practical and logical with regard to the problems we all face in various situations and relationships. Specifically, when someone has a problem, they may feel overwhelmed and cannot see a way out. People who are good at practical problem-solving show the ability to analyse situations well and engage in a decision-making process that involves reasons. They are able to think around a situation, creating viewpoints and possible solutions to the problem. They are then able to address the problem effectively. For example, a student may have a problem with a particular essay. Good practical problem-solving skills would be to explore the essay topic, perhaps by seeking advice from the lecturer, revisiting the lecture notes, spending some time researching key papers and brainstorming several different answers to the essay question. Evidence of poor practical problem-solving skills here would be to complain about the essay to one's housemates and then head out for a consolatory drink.
- **Verbal ability** – This is the ability to express yourself and converse with others confidently and with some eloquence. Someone with high verbal ability understands the correct meaning for a word, is able to use language confidently, would be able to show comprehension when reading written text, would be able to identify what a missing word in a sentence is and can talk to

others in a way that others understand. Verbal ability includes things like the use of antonyms and analogies. An **antonym** is a word that has a meaning opposite to that of another word. So, for example, 'unhappy' is an antonym of 'happy'. The ability to use **analogies** is the ability to see similarity between two things that are otherwise dissimilar. So, for example, we might ask you to complete the phrase 'Cat is to MEOW as dog is to_____'. If you answered BARK or WOOF, you would be completing the analogy. Your lecturers will often use analogies. When explaining a complicated topic, they might use an everyday example to explain the concept to you. Or (and you understand this is an analogy), you may use an analogy when describing an argument with someone to your friend, 'Sometimes, it's like talking to a brick wall!'
- **Social competence** – This ability refers to the skills necessary to be accepted and fulfilled socially. Someone who has high social competence demonstrates high levels of knowledge, understanding, competency, motivation and confidence in terms of themselves and others. Someone who has a high level of self-awareness, shows good interpersonal skills and a good balance between independence and interdependence (relying on relationships with others) would be socially competent. He or she would have good life skills, be able to cooperate with others and see other people as important, as well as themselves. Someone with good social competence

would display personal responsibility and show a positive regard for others. For example, if someone made an accusation and then found out they were mistaken, a socially competent person would admit their mistake and would apologise to the person involved. A person who is not socially competent would refuse to apologise.

Another classic experiment into laypersons' theories of intelligence was carried out by Sternberg (Sternberg, 1985b). In a series of experiments (though we will concentrate on just two of the studies here), Sternberg asked a total of 47 adults to think of behaviours that were characteristic of an ideally intelligent person. From this sample Sternberg was able to provide 40 *descriptors* of intelligent behaviours. Sternberg then got 40 Yale college students to sort these descriptors into those that were 'likely to be found together' in a person. From this sorting task Sternberg reported similar findings to his 1981 study, but this time he found six aspects to intelligence:

- **Practical problem-solving ability** – Descriptors in the study that fell within this aspect included 'tends to see attainable goals and accomplish them' and 'is good at distinguishing between correct and incorrect answers'.
- **Verbal ability** – Descriptors included 'can converse on almost any topic' and 'has demonstrated a good vocabulary'.
- **Intellectual balance and integration** – Descriptors included 'has the ability to recognise similarities and differences' and 'makes connections and distinctions between ideas and things'.
- **Goal orientation and attainment** – Descriptors included 'tends to obtain and use information for specific purposes' and 'possesses ability for high achievement'.
- **Contextual intelligence** – Descriptors included 'learns and remembers and gains information from past mistakes or successes' and 'has the ability to understand and interpret his or her environment'.
- **Fluid thought** – Descriptors included 'thinks quickly' and 'has a thorough grasp of mathematics'.

We're not looking for any particular cohesion here in the results across the studies, though there are similarities. We have purposely gone into some detail about each of the aspects, so you can see the sort of language that is used around intelligence constructs in intelligence theory and research. What we will show you next is how implicit theories of intelligence change, particularly when considered: (1) across cultures; (2) by experts; and (3) across the lifespan.

Laypersons' implicit theories across cultures

It is clear to intelligence researchers (for example, Sternberg, 2001a; Berry, 1984) that conceptions of intelligence change depending on what area of the world you are in.

In western cultures researchers suggest there is an emphasis on the speed of mental processing and the ability to gather, assimilate and sort information quickly and efficiently (Sternberg *et al.*, 1981). As we can see in western cultures, speed is of the essence. Someone who can see answers to problems quickly and then act on them, or who comes up with the solution first, is seen as highly intelligent. Someone who articulates these ideas verbally, clearly, fluently and in a precise manner is also seen as intelligent. Someone who ponders the answers to questions, and perhaps suggests there are many answers and takes time to answer a question, is seen as less intelligent.

However, in studies that have tried to compare western and non-western ideas of intelligence, researchers have found similarities and differences relating to this western idea of an intelligent person.

The main emphasis in these cultural differences in intelligence is on how intelligence is related to the self and the social world. For example, Cypriot psychologists Andreas Demetriou and Timothy Papadopoulous (2004) draw attention to the fact that, in western views of intelligence, good cognitive skills and good memory refer only to the individual; in eastern cultures, these ideas additionally extend to social, historical and spiritual aspects of everyday interactions, knowledge and problem-solving. For example, in non-western cultures the ability to show skills in problem-solving includes not only the individual's own ability to solve the problem but also consideration of:

- their family and friends (perhaps through seeking advice);
- their knowledge of history (knowing how wise people have approached this problem in the past);
- their own spiritual needs (what consequences do the actions around the problem have for the human soul?).

For example, Shih-Ying Yang and Robert Sternberg (1997a) looked at Chinese philosophical (enlightened and wise) ideas of intelligence through two main traditions in China, the Confucian and the Taoist tradition. The Confucian tradition in China comes from the teachings of Confucius (551–479 BC), a Chinese philosopher, whose moral and political teachings included the instruction to love others, to honour one's parents and to do what is right instead of what is of advantageous. Taoism is China's only indigenous higher religion. The classical roots of Taoism lie in the writings and practices of unknown men and women who tried to refine and transform themselves to attain full integration with life's deepest realities. In terms of intelligence, Yang and Sternberg suggest that Confucian philosophy emphasises intelligence through benevolence (an inclination to perform kind, charitable acts) and doing the right thing, while the Taoist tradition emphasises humility, freedom from more traditional or conventional dimensions of judgement, the ability to be perceptive and responsive to changes in circumstances and the ability to show full

Fingers on the buzzer: in western cultures, researchers suggest that there is an emphasis on the speed of mental processing.
Source: The Kobal Collection/Workin' Man Films/Film Four

knowledge and understanding, not only of oneself but of the world around oneself.

Similarly, US psychologists Bibhu Baral and J. P. Das looked at Indian culture and examined how perceptions of intelligence in India differ from perception in western cultures (Baral and Das, 2004). In Indian culture high levels of thinking, judgement and decision-making are all important in intelligence. However, it is the way in which these different aspects of intelligence *gel* that is seen as crucial in defining intelligence. This gelling is achieved through a harmony of thought resulting from self-awareness and consciousness. Furthermore, intelligence in India is also thought to show an appreciation of others, politeness, interest in others and modesty.

Specific research examples allow us to examine some of these speculations. Yang and Sternberg (1997b) followed up their analysis of Chinese philosophy. In a methodology similar to that employed in Sternberg's earlier work, Yang and Sternberg looked for descriptors of intelligence among 68 Taiwanese Chinese people (government administrators, French-major college students, preschool teachers, soldiers, factory workers, businesspeople and high school teachers). The researchers then asked 434 individuals (about half were undergraduate students; about half were non-student adults) to rate each of these descriptors based on their importance in showing intelligent behaviour. You will remember that Sternberg's previous research had found practical problem-solving, verbal ability and social competence (as well as goals, context and fluidity of thought) to be important. Among Taiwanese Chinese people, five factors of intelligence emerged:

- **A general cognitive factor of intelligence**, which is like the western idea of practical problem-solving and understanding. In this study this included descriptors such as 'makes quick responses', 'has strong learning responses; learns things faster than others' and 'has strong intellectual ability, especially for some abstract disciplines like maths and physics'.
- **Interpersonal intelligence** refers to relating with others harmoniously and efficiently. Descriptors included 'is good at understanding and empathising with others' feelings', 'is kind and compassionate: treats others with politeness, warmth and understanding' and 'knows the appropriate ways to treat others and deal with daily matters'.
- **Intrapersonal intelligence** refers to knowledge about the self and the ability to view oneself objectively. Descriptors included 'knows the meaning and purpose of his/her life and has his/her own philosophy of life', 'has good self-control over the desire to show off: is a high achiever but does not flaunt achievements' and 'accepts different opinions and does not insist on his/her own ideas'.
- **Intellectual self-assertion** refers to a process for individuals who are confident and aware of their intellect and derive self-worth from it. Descriptors included 'puts his/her interests first', 'thinks him/herself very intelligent and is arrogant and proud', 'occasionally draws excessive attention to self' and 'claims others' affection easily and is well-liked'.
- **Intellectual self-effacement** refers to modesty or humility surrounding the person's intellect. Descriptors included 'is lonesome', 'is sensitive', 'likes to think quietly, day-dream, or be lost in thinking' and 'is often quiet in conversation, but talks at length about the topics which interest him/her'.

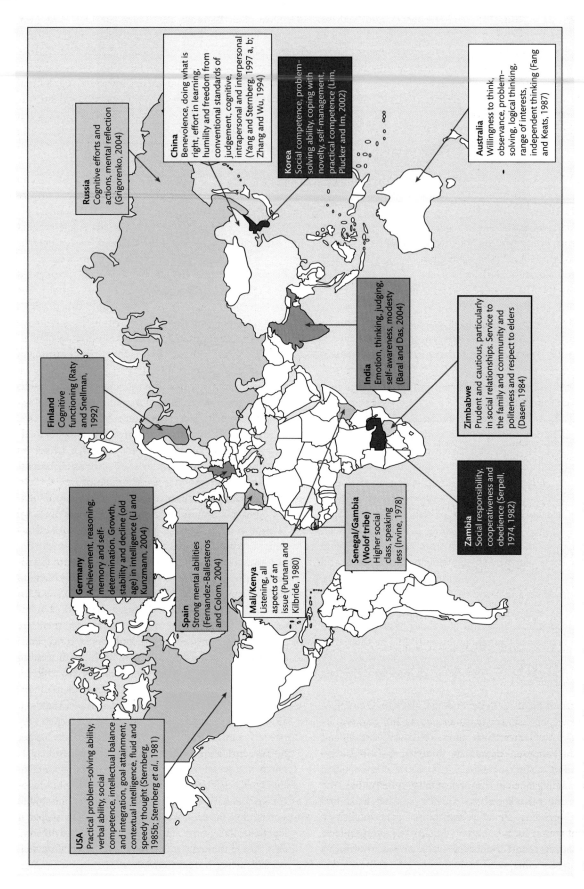

Russia
Cognitive efforts and actions, mental reflection (Grigorenko, 2004)

China
Benevolence, doing what is right, effort in learning, humility and freedom from conventional standards of judgement, cognitive, intrapersonal and interpersonal (Yang and Sternberg, 1997 a, b; Zhang and Wu, 1994)

Korea
Social competence, problem-solving ability, coping with novelty, self-management, practical competence (Lim, Plucker and Im, 2002)

Australia
Willingness to think, observance, problem-solving, logical thinking, range of interests, independent thinking (Fang and Keats, 1987)

Finland
Cognitive functioning (Raty and Snellman, 1992)

India
Emotion, thinking, judging, self-awareness, modesty (Baral and Das, 2004)

Zimbabwe
Prudent and cautious, particularly in social relationships. Service to the family and community and politeness and respect to elders (Dasen, 1984)

Germany
Achievement, reasoning, memory and self-determination. Growth, stability and decline (old age) in intelligence (Li and Kunzmann, 2004)

Spain
Strong mental abilities (Fernandez-Ballesteros and Colom, 2004)

Mali/Kenya
Listening, all aspects of an issue (Putnam and Kilbride, 1980)

Senegal/Gambia (Wolof tribe)
Higher social class, speaking less (Irvine, 1978)

Zambia
Social responsibility, cooperativeness and obedience (Serpell, 1974, 1982)

USA
Practical problem-solving ability, verbal ability, social competence, intellectual balance and integration, goal attainment, contextual intelligence, fluid and speedy thought (Sternberg, 1985b; Sternberg et al., 1981)

Figure 11.1 Implicit theories of intelligence by countries around the world.

As we can see from Yang and Sternberg's results, these factors reflect some of the emphasis within the Chinese philosophy of humility, the ability to be perceptive and show full knowledge and understanding of not only oneself but also the world that surrounds the individual.

Other authors looking at implicit theories of intelligence (including historical views) suggest that, although constructs such as good thinking skills always appear in western and non-western cultures, there are some stark differences between conceptions of intelligence across the world. We have collected a list of findings from studies of implicit theories of intelligence around the world (see Figure 11.1).

As you can see, the map largely supports the view that intelligence in the west is thought to comprise good individual cognitive skills, while in eastern cultures these ideas extend to social, historical and spiritual aspects of everyday interactions, knowledge and problem-solving.

However, one interesting study to note on the map is the study in Korea by US psychologists Woong Lim and Jonathan A. Plucker and Korean psychologist Kyuhyeok Im (Lim, Plucker and Im, 2002). Interestingly, findings in Korea are not very different from western ideas of intelligence. In their study, which employed a methodology very similar to the methodology used by Sternberg in his studies, Lim *et al.* found five factors among 384 Korean adults:

- **Social competence** – Descriptors in this study included 'befriends people easily', 'is modest and sets an example to others' and 'has a quick wit'.
- **Problem-solving ability** – Descriptors included 'has an ability to connect and generalise different academic themes', 'talks logically' and 'comes up with new ideas'.
- **Coping with novelty** – Statements in this study included 'solves puzzles well', 'is good at computer games' and 'is sensitive to new information'.
- **Self-management ability** – Statements in this study included 'thinks before acting', 'controls one's feelings well' and 'keeps his personal life and professional life separate'.
- **Practical competence** – Statements in this study included 'makes a record of things in a systematic way' and 'carries out the plan and is confident about it'.

On the face of it, Korean adults' implicit theories of intelligence look similar to studies of western samples by including problem-solving and social competence and intelligence centred around the individual. This finding might point to similarities in Korean and western conceptions of intelligence, suggesting that the differences between western and eastern cultures are not as different as first thought. However, Lim *et al.* suggest that there might be a different reason for this. Lim *et al.* asked their respondents which aspects of intelligence they valued most. They found that Koreans value social competence and responsibility

the most, and the other aspects less so. Lim *et al.* have described how the presence of other aspects may influence implicit theories of intelligence. Western intelligence tests have been used in Korea and other Asian countries and have had the unintended effect of reshaping cultural definitions and introducing different aspects of intelligence. The researchers present no evidence for this finding, but suggest an important aspect for us to consider. That is, in the modern age, western and eastern conceptions of intelligence might be converging.

Finally, clearly one way of comparing western and eastern conceptions of intelligence is to directly compare implicit theories of intelligence in samples at the same time. Two examples of these types of studies have suggested that there is a crossover between western and eastern perceptions of intelligence, and there are some differences.

Research conducted by Fang and Keats (1987) compared the conceptions of intelligence in China and Australia. The researchers found that both Australian and Chinese adults believe that willingness to think, observation, a wide range of interests and independent thinking are indicators of intelligence. However, the two samples differed in that Australian adults thought problem-solving and logical reasoning were also important to intelligence, while Chinese adults thought ability to learn, analytical ability, sharp thinking and displaying confidence were indicative of intelligence. Chen and Chen (1988) compared implicit theories of intelligence among students from Chinese-language schools as opposed to English-language schools. Both sets of students found non-verbal reasoning, verbal reasoning, social skills, numeracy and memory to be important descriptors of intelligence. However, students from the Chinese-language schools rated verbal skills as less important than did students from the English-language schools.

The various research studies show cross-cultural similarities and differences in intelligence. It is important to remember that differences between western and eastern implicit theories of intelligence do not suggest distinct differences, but rather emphasis in cultures. That is, there are many similarities between western and eastern conceptions of intelligence, but the emphasis is different, with western cultures emphasising the individual and eastern cultures emphasising the individual and how this extends to others, history and spiritual needs. Furthermore, Lim *et al.*'s research into Korean implicit theories of intelligence, in which they suggest that western and eastern conceptions of intelligence might be converging over time, clearly highlights the role that both culture and year of study play in everyday conceptions of intelligence. In our map of the world of implicit theories of intelligence (Figure 11.1), you can see that the studies are spread over 20 years. We must ask what might happen if we compared these countries today – would we find different results? Would we begin to see the convergence of implicit theories of intelligence across cultures?

Implicit theories of intelligence across the lifespan

We have looked at how perceptions of intelligence change across cultures. However, perceptions of intelligence change within cultures. This is particularly true for how perceptions of intelligence change across the lifespan. The strongest findings in this area have been among children, as we are now living in a time when individuals' perceptions and knowledge of the world change dramatically, and researchers can easily compare implicit theories among different age groups. We will begin by looking at implicit theories of intelligence among children. We will look at the theories in two ways. The first is to consider how people perceive intelligence at different stages of the lifespan. For example, do people expect intelligent behaviour in a 15-year-old to be the same as intelligent behaviour in a 35-year-old? The second is to look at how individuals at different ages perceive intelligent behaviour. For example, do 15-year-olds report different perceptions of what intelligence is than do 35-year-olds?

Stop and think

Different concepts of intelligence in different countries

Here is a table of studies or papers that have emphasised different concepts of intelligence in different countries. Rate on a scale of 0 (very uncharacteristic) to 10 (very characteristic) how relevant each dimension of intelligence is to the ideal intelligent person in your country.

Country	Dimension of intelligence	Out of 10
United States (Sternberg, 1985b; Sternberg *et al.*, 1981)	Practical problem-solving ability	
	Verbal ability	
	Social competence	
	Intellectual balance and integration	
	Goal attainment	
	Contextual intelligence	
	Fluid and speedy thought	
China (Yang and Sternberg, 1997b)	Benevolence (an inclination to perform kind, charitable acts)	
	Wanting to do what is right	
	Spends much effort in learning	
	Humility (the quality or condition of being humble)	
	Freedom from conventional standards of judgement	
	Full knowledge of oneself and external conditions	
Africa (Irvine, 1978; Putnam and Kilbride, 1980)	Higher social class	
	Someone who speaks less	
	Listening, all aspects of an issue	
India (Baral and Das, 2004)	Emotion	
	Thinking	
	Judging	
	Self-awareness	
	Modesty	

Do people perceive intelligence differently for different stages of the lifespan?
(Do people expect intelligent behaviour in a 15-year-old to be the same as intelligent behaviour in a 35-year-old?)

There is clear evidence that conceptions of intelligence differ for different ages. A clear example of how conceptions of intelligence change is in early child development. US psychologists Robert S. Siegler and D. Richards (1982) compared implicit theories of intelligence among US adults for four different stages of the lifespan. Siegler and Richard asked respondents to describe ideal intelligent persons at 6 months of age, 2 years of age, 10 years of age and as adults. At 6 months old, the ideal intelligent baby was thought to be able to recognise people and objects, show signs of motor coordination, show levels of awareness and make some verbalisation. Intelligence at 2 years was thought to comprise verbal ability, evidence of an ability to learn, awareness of people and the environment, motor coordination and curiosity. At 10 years, intelligence is thought to consist of verbal ability, learning, problem-solving, reasoning and creativity. Among adults, these familiar concepts of implicit theories of intelligence emerge: problem-solving, verbal ability, reasoning, learning and creativity.

Canadian psychologist Prem Fry (Fry, 1984) compared implicit theories of intelligence at three stages of educational development: primary school (5- to 11-year-olds), secondary school (11- to 18-year-olds), and tertiary (college and university) levels (18+-year-olds). In this study, Fry asked teachers to rate the ideal intelligent person. At primary levels, social variables such as popularity, friendliness, respect for rules and order and an interest in the environment were seen as important. At secondary levels, energy and verbal fluency were seen as most important, while at tertiary levels of education (e.g. college and university), logical thinking, broad knowledge, reasoning and the ability to deal maturely and effectively with problems were seen as evidence of intelligence.

Cynthia Berg and Robert Sternberg (1992) examined whether young (30 years), middle-aged (50 years) and older (70 years) adults view the concept of an intelligent person as similar or different during adulthood. In a similar methodology to that used in Sternberg's other studies, where a number of descriptors were generated by one sample and then rated by another sample, 140 adults (aged between 22 and 85 years) were used to characterise both 'average' and 'exceptional' intelligent behaviour of 30-, 50- and 70-year-olds. Average intelligence was defined in all three age groups as interest and ability to deal with novelty, everyday competence and verbal competence. However, when it came to exceptional intelligence, the trait of interest and ability to deal with novelty was emphasised as important for describing the exceptionally intelligent 30-year-old. Everyday competence and verbal competence were emphasised as important for describing exceptionally intelligent 50- and 70-year-olds.

Do individuals perceive intelligent behaviour differently at different ages?
(Do 15-year-olds report different perceptions of what intelligence is than do 35-year-olds?)

The question of whether individuals at different ages perceive intelligent behaviour differently has been examined in the intelligence literature. Children do hold different concepts about intelligence at different ages. US psychologists Steven R. Yussen and Paul Kane (1985) interviewed 71 high school children of differing ages (11–16 years) regarding their beliefs about intelligence. The researchers asked the children about their different views of intelligence (the sort of personal qualities and attributes that accompany intelligent behaviour), the nature of intelligence (i.e. how it comes about with the individual) and how it develops through life.

One of Yussen and Kane's first findings applied to how children view intelligence. The researchers found that older students categorise intelligence into different aspects – academic intelligence, social intelligence and physical intelligence – whereas younger students do not differentiate between these aspects and generally think of intelligence as one-dimensional. Therefore, among older students, a person can be academically intelligent but not socially intelligent; younger students do not make these distinctions and tend to see people as either intelligent or not. Yussen and Kane, however, found that all the students considered knowledge to be central to intelligence, but older students reported that academic skills were much more important to intelligence than social skills. Another important finding from this study was in response to questions about the nature of intelligence. Younger children held a stronger belief that intelligence is the result of nature, that it is inborn (i.e. either individuals are intelligent or not). However, older children believe more strongly in the joint influence of nature and nurture on intelligence.

So why is there this change in young people's perceptions of intelligence? Two Hong Kong researchers, Zi-juan Cheng and Kit-Tai Hau (2003), have suggested there are two reasons for this shift. The first reason for the differences between younger and older students is that older students are thought to have matured cognitively. That is, as children go through school they have a number of cumulative experiences regarding their own intelligence. They may succeed at certain things (e.g. they may pass an examination) and they may fail at others (they may do badly or struggle in a particular subject). Consequently, their experience and understanding of what constitutes intelligence will become more and more complex as they understand that several different factors determine intelligence.

Do our perceptions of intelligence differ for different generations?
Source: Getty Images/Photodisc

The second reason for the differences between younger and older students is that older students have undergone a process of socialisation. While students have been schooled, they have also been socialised by teachers, friends and family. Teachers, friends and family will influence students' ideas of what intelligence is. Teachers will indicate in class what is expected from an intelligent individual (working hard, showing good problem-solving skills), while friends will emphasise that different elements of intelligence (communication, coming up with ideas) are important to the friendship group. Meanwhile, parents may spend time extending children's education out of school by encouraging them to work harder and expecting their children to demonstrate other aspects of intelligence (respecting one's elders, being interested in out-of-school activities such as sports or social clubs).

To summarise the last two sections, we can see from the various studies that our views of intelligence and the emphasis we give to certain behaviours as characterising intelligence change throughout the lifespan. Evidence suggests this occurs from very young to very old, both in terms of how we perceive intelligence as being different for different stages of the lifespan and how at different stages of the lifespan we perceive intelligence differently.

Expert conceptions of intelligence

So far we have concentrated on research that has used non-experts for its definitions of intelligence. However, what do the experts of intelligence say about what comprises intelligence? Attempts to do this research started in 1921, when the editors of the *Journal of Educational Psychology* convened a special issue of the journal in which prominent psychological theorists of the day were asked to describe what they imagined intelligence to be. These experts included Edward L. Thorndike (a major figure in several fields of psychology: learning theory, applied psychology and mental measurement), Lewis M. Terman (a pioneer in mental measurement) and Louis Leon Thurstone (an intelligence theorist and psychometrician). Their definitions of intelligence were diverse:

- the power of good responses from the viewpoint of truth or facts (E. L. Thorndike);
- the ability to carry on abstract thinking (L. M. Terman);
- the capacity to inhibit an instinctive adjustment, the capacity to redefine the inhibited instinctive adjustment in the light of imaginably experienced trial and error and the capacity to realise the modified instinctive adjustment in overt behaviour to the advantage of the individual as a social animal (L. L. Thurstone).

In all, 14 different opinions were offered. Some of the opinions referred to perceived intelligent behaviours like those just listed; some referred to the measurement of intelligence. Sixty-five years later, in the form of a book entitled *What Is Intelligence?* (1986), Robert Sternberg and Douglas Detterman repeated the 1921 exercise by asking 24 experts (some of whom we will mention in this text) for their definition of intelligence. The researchers received many different definitions, including adaptability to new problems in life, ability in abstract thinking, adjustment to the environment, and capacity for knowledge, independence and originality.

Opinion differs in how much these publications told us about the nature of intelligence. Some authors interpret these findings as showing there was no consensus as to the meaning, definition or measurement of intelligence (e.g. Jensen, 1998), with 38 different experts in intelligence emphasising 38 different types of intelligence. However, an analysis by Sternberg (2000) suggests that the two publications (Jensen, 1998; Sternberg and Detterman, 1986) told us two things. First, certain themes and consensus did emerge between experts. Intelligence qualities such as adaptation to the environment, basic mental processes and aspects of higher-order thinking such as reasoning, problem-solving and decision-making are evident in both listings. Second, these differences between experts emphasise an argument about whether intelligence represents just one thing or a multitude of different abilities and behaviours.

One study emphasises this last point that intelligence represents a multitude of different abilities and behaviours. Sternberg (1985b), using the same methodology as in his other studies, asked 25 art, 26 business, 20 philosophy and 26 physics professors at US universities to list descriptors of an ideally intelligent person in their respective academic fields. Then, Sternberg asked 200 professors in the academic areas of art, business, philosophy and physics to rate the descriptors obtained from the first study for an ideally intelligent person in their area of study. Perhaps not unexpectedly, Sternberg found that professors from the different disciplines differed in their perceptions of the ideal intelligent person (see Figure 11.2):

- Art professors emphasised knowledge, the ability to use that knowledge to weigh up possible alternatives and the ability to see analogies.
- Business professors emphasised the ability to think logically, to focus on essential aspects of a problem and to follow others' arguments and see where they lead.

- Philosophy professors emphasised critical and logical abilities, the ability to follow complex arguments and the ability to find errors in arguments and generate new arguments.
- Physics professors emphasised precise mathematical thinking, ability to relate physical phenomena to the concepts of physics and the ability to grasp the laws of nature quickly.

These findings suggest that there is diversity among experts on what constitutes intelligence. As in studies of implicit theories of intelligence among general populations, although there is sometimes agreement on some constructs, there can be a huge diversity of conceptions of intelligence.

A task force in intelligence

However, the need for an expert view on intelligence was never more obvious than in 1994 when two US intelligence authors, Richard J. Herrnstein and Charles Murray, published a book called *The Bell Curve: Intelligence and Class Structure in American Life*. The book caused huge debate. It reported many things about intelligence, including the extent to which intelligence is genetically inherited. The authors claimed the rise of a 'cognitive elite' – a social group of persons with high intelligence, with an increasingly high chance of succeeding in life. They noted a number

Figure 11.2 Similarities and differences between expert implicit theories of intelligence across academic disciplines.
Source: Based on Sternberg (1985b).

Stop and think

Experts and lecturers

1   Nicholas Butler (1862–1947), an American education-alist, said of experts that 'an expert is one who knows more and more about less and less'. It is well accepted in academic circles that the more a person knows, the more they know they don't know. How appropriate are these sayings to attempts made by experts within the last 100 years to define intelligence?

2   Sternberg's research among art, business, philosophy and physics professors suggests that there are different conceptions of intelligence across different subjects at university. Think about the psychology discipline. What characteristics do you think your lecturers would say an ideal intelligent student of psychology has?

of cultural differences in intelligence, but also made some suggestions regarding the intellectual inferiority of certain cultural groups. Such work was perceived by many as difficult for US society because such findings were seen as having implications for social and public policy. For example, if academics presented evidence for one cultural group as intellectually inferior due to their genes, that might affect how a government treated that group, particularly in terms of funding educational and social enhancement. An unkind government might withdraw support for that group because they felt no amount of support would help its members because they were just naturally intellectually inferior. Such concerns were raised by this book, with the authors presenting data from US society on a number of aspects of intelligence and readers of the book debating the implications for US society.

We will go into some of the findings of and responses to *The Bell Curve* later (Chapter 13). But what is important about this book is that it caused a very public reaction and debate, particularly over its claims regarding intelligence and race. The book received a great deal of positive publicity, including cover stories in *Newsweek* and articles in *Time*, the *New York Times* and the *Wall Street Journal*. However, there was a large amount of negative response, particularly in the scientific community, suggesting the book was oversimplified and contained flawed analysis. This controversy surrounding *The Bell Curve* prompted the American Psychological Association (the largest and most influential psychological society in the world) to establish a special task force to publish an investigative report on the research presented in the book and to include an analysis of what is known and unknown about intelligence.

This task force was headed by Ulric Neisser (see Profile box), then at Emory University in the United States. After an extended consultative process, Neisser chose a range of academics representing a broad spectrum of expertise and opinion in the literature on intelligence: Gwyneth Boodoo, Thomas J. Bouchard Jr, A. Wade Boykin, Nathan Brody,

Stephen J. Ceci, Diane F. Halpern, John C. Loehlin, Robert Perloff, Robert J. Sternberg and Susana Urbina (some of whose work we outline in this text). The task force then set out to discuss a number of issues relating to intelligence and met twice in 1995. Between and after these meetings, sections of a report were circulated and revised and disputes were resolved by discussion. As a result, the task force presented a report that had the unanimous support of its members.

Formally, the task force set out to ask what is known and not known about intelligence and what questions need to be answered in the area of intelligence:

- major theories and concepts of intelligence;
- the role of intelligence tests and their scores;
- the relative importance and role of genes and the environment in determining intelligence.

However, what is also important for you to note is that, although the task force was able to agree on a number of knowns about intelligence, it also outlined a number of unknowns about intelligence. The challenges set out by the task force included understanding:

- the exact nature of the influence of genetics on intelligence;
- the exact nature of the influence of the environment on intelligence;
- how nutrition (the nourishment from food) affects intelligence;
- why there are differences in scores of intelligence tests between various groups.

The focus of this part of the text

The theory and research we have described shows you that everyone has an idea about what constitutes intelligence. More important, you now know that many people have

Profile

Ulric Neisser

Ulric Neisser was born in Kiel, North Germany, in 1928; he went, with his parents, to the United States at the age of 3. He studied at Harvard for both his bachelor's degree and PhD. He switched from physics to psychology and received his bachelor's degree in 1950. He studied behaviourism for his PhD, which he received in 1956. He then taught at Brandeis University, where he had the opportunity to pursue his interest in cognitive psychology. He has also taught at Cornell and Emory Universities in the United States.

Neisser is thought to be one of the forefathers of cognitive psychology, and the modern growth of cognitive psychology was thought to be led by the publication of his book, *Cognitive Psychology*, in 1967. His publications are in cognitive psychology, and his main research interests include memory (especially recall of life events) and intelligence (especially IQ tests and their social significance). In his later writings, he became critical of the methodology of much cognitive psychology, faulting it for being 'ecologically invalid'. Neisser emphasised the study of memory in natural surroundings.

He argued that laboratory experiments on memory did not reveal how a person's memory worked in everyday life. Gradually, people began trying to develop methods of improving memory in everyday life in these real-world settings. In 1995, Neisser headed an American Psychological Association task force that reviewed controversial issues in the study of intelligence. He is best known for his books *Cognitive Psychology* (Appleton-Century-Crofts), *Cognition and Reality* (Freeman), *Memory Observed* (Freeman), *The School Achievement of Minority Children* (Erlbaum) and *The Perceived Self* (Cambridge University Press), as well as for his studies of memory in natural settings.

---

many different ideas about intelligence and that these ideas change as we get older and as we move from culture to culture. However, you will have also noticed how similar themes and ideas do occur throughout these differing research studies.

So, what has psychology formally contributed to our understanding of intelligence? Well, in the rest of Part 2 (Chapters 12–16), we are looking at how psychology has formally measured intelligence and how intelligence is related to a number of variables, ranging from the sex and genetic makeup of a person, through culture, to numerous variables such as nutrition, education, child-rearing practices and work.

The focus for Part 2 of the book takes its lead from the 1995 task force report. The following chapters will deal with these topics:

- theories of intelligence (Chapters 12 and 13);
- measurement of intelligence (Chapters 12 and 13);
- problems, methodological issues and alternative approaches surrounding the measurement of intelligence (Chapter 13);
- how nutrition (the nourishment from food) affects intelligence (Chapter 13);
- intelligence and the nature–nurture debate: the exact nature of the influence of genetics and the environment on intelligence (Chapter 13; mostly Chapters 14 and 15);
- group differences (sex and race) in intelligence (Chapters 14 and 15).

We do, of course, elaborate on some of the issues discussed by the task force and cover some of the areas in greater depth. Furthermore, we dedicate large sections to concepts that were not covered at the time of the task force, notably emotional intelligence (Chapter 15) and how intelligence and personality ideas extend to education and the workplace (Chapter 16).

We have deliberately spread some of this material over two chapters. This is because many of the central issues relating to intelligence are considered in different contexts. We also hope you remember that this is a controversial but well-researched area. There is some challenging material, and you may do well to look over some supplementary material later on in this text and on the accompanying website, especially regarding academic argument (particularly fallacies in the online chapter on Academic Argument), statistics (particularly factor analysis and meta-analysis in the online chapter on statistics, Chapter 27), and psychometric testing (particularly notions of reliability and validity in Chapter 25).

One last point – often you will find intelligence referred to in the literature as either *intelligence* or *cognitive ability*. Don't let this put you off. Throughout this text, we will use the term 'intelligence'. However, in your further reading you may come across papers or studies that use the term 'cognitive ability'. Much more often than not, the authors will be referring to what we know as intelligence.

Final comments

We have used this discussion to introduce you to some of the ideas that you will come across in the next section (Chapters 12–16) on intelligence. We have covered implicit theories of intelligence and shown you how implicit theories of intelligence change across the lifespan, between experts and non-experts and around the world.

Summary

- Intelligence is seen as central to human life in the present day.
- Implicit theories are folk theories, layperson, everyday ideas that surround a particular topic area.
- Implicit theories of intelligence drive the way in which people perceive and evaluate their own intelligence and that of others. Implicit theories of intelligence can give rise to more formal theories of intelligence that researchers can investigate. Implicit theories are useful when an investigator thinks existing explicit theories are wrong and may provide useful avenues for research. Implicit theories of intelligence can elucidate theories around psychological constructs, such as the development of intelligence and cross-cultural aspects of intelligence.
- Sternberg and his colleagues found three dimensions of intelligence: practical problem-solving, verbal ability and social competence.
- In western cultures, researchers suggest, there is an emphasis on the speed of mental processing and the ability to gather, assimilate and sort information quickly and efficiently. In eastern cultures these ideas extend to social, historical and spiritual aspects of everyday interactions, knowledge and problem-solving. In non-western cultures, the ability to show skills in problem-solving, verbal ability and social

competence would not just extend to the individual, but rather to their ability to solve a problem within the context of their family and friends.
- There is evidence from Korea to suggest that western and eastern conceptions of intelligence might be converging.
- One way of comparing eastern and western conceptions of intelligence is to compare implicit theories of intelligence in samples at the same time.
- Perceptions of intelligence change across the lifespan. There are two ways of looking at this: (1) to look at how people perceive intelligence at different stages of life; and (2) to examine how individuals at different ages perceive intelligent behaviour.
- Other research has asked intelligence experts for their definition of intelligence. Intelligence qualities such as adaptation to the environment, basic mental processes and aspects of higher-order thinking like reasoning, problem-solving and decision-making, emerge from such research. However, professors in different academic disciplines differed in their conceptions of intelligence.
- The American Psychological Association established a special task force to publish an investigative report on the research presented in the book *The Bell Curve* and to conduct an analysis of what is known and not known about intelligence.

Connecting up

This is an introductory chapter to Chapters 12–16.

Critical thinking

Discussion questions

- Do you think that there are differences between western and eastern conceptions of intelligence?
- Studies on implicit theories of intelligence give us a wealth of characteristics that define intelligence around the world. Which characteristics best describe the ideal intelligent person in your country?
- Pick a country from another continent. Which characteristics best describe the ideal intelligent person in that country?

- What are characteristics of the ideal intelligent person in your country at 20 years of age, 40 years of age and 60 years of age?

Essay questions

- Critically compare western and eastern conceptions of intelligence.

- Critically discuss laypersons' versus experts' implicit theories of intelligence.
- Critically discuss how culture, between and within countries, influences implicit theories of intelligence.
- Critically examine what implicit theories of intelligence tell us about intelligence.

Going further

Books

- Sternberg, R. J. (ed.). (2000). *Handbook of intelligence.* Cambridge: Cambridge University Press.
- Deary, I. J. (2001). *Intelligence: A very short introduction.* Oxford: Oxford University Press.
- Mackintosh, N. J. (1998). *IQ and human intelligence.* Oxford: Oxford University Press.
- Sternberg, R. J. (ed.) (2004). *International handbook of intelligence.* Cambridge: Cambridge University Press.

Journals

- One article that will help you with a good overview of intelligence theory and research, not just for this, but for later discussions, is Sternberg, R. J. and Kaufman, J. C. (1998). Human abilities. *Annual Review of Psychology,* 49, 479–502. *Annual Review of Psychology* is published by Annual Reviews, Palo Alto, California. Available online via Business Source Premier.
- *Intelligence: A Multidisciplinary Journal.* This is one journal that you should start using. This psychology journal is devoted to publishing original research and

theoretical studies and review papers that substantially contribute to the understanding of intelligence. It provides a new source of significant papers in psychometrics, tests and measurement as well as all other empirical and theoretical studies in intelligence and mental retardation. Published by Elsevier Science. Available online via Science Direct.

- *American Psychologist.* This is another journal that might be worth checking whether you have access to at your university. This journal also contains regular debates about intelligence. Published by American Psychological Association. Available online via PsycARTICLES.

Web links

- A copy of the report prepared by the 1995 American Psychological Association Task Force on Intelligence is available at: **www.gifted.uconn.edu/siegle/research/ correlation/intelligence.pdf**.
- A full intelligence resource overseen by J. A. Plucker. This website covers historical influences, current controversies, teaching resources, debates and research in intelligence (**www.intelltheory.com**).

Film and literature

- The issues and pressures that can surround intelligence, and the perceptions of intelligence, are depicted in the film *Quiz Show* (1994, directed by Robert Redford). The film is based on a true story of an investigation into a TV quiz show that may be being fixed and his focus on two contestants on the show *Twenty-One*.
- *Being John Malkovich* (1999, directed by Spike Jonze). A puppeteer (John Cusack) discovers a door

in his office that allows him to enter the mind and life of John Malkovich (playing himself), though only for 15 minutes. The puppeteer then tries to turn the portal into a small business. This film explores the themes of what it is like to be inside someone else's head (albeit a famous actor). Would such experiences change our understanding and knowledge of the world around us?

Explore the website accompanying this text at **www.pearsoned.co.uk/maltby** for further resources to help you with your studies. These include multiple-choice questions, essay questions, web links and ideas for advanced reading.

CHAPTER 12
Theories and Measurement of Intelligence

Key themes

- Early theorists in intelligence: Galton, Binet, Terman and Yerkes
- General intelligence and its measurement: Spearman's 'g', the Wechsler and Raven's Matrices Intelligence tests
- Multifactor theorists: Thurstone, Cattell and Guilford
- Hierarchical theorists: Vernon and Carroll
- Gardner's multiple intelligences and Sternberg's triarchic model of intelligence

Learning outcomes

After studying this discussion you should:

- Be able to describe the birth of intelligence and IQ testing
- Be able to describe the theory of 'g' and some alternative models
- Be aware of some well-known measures of intelligence
- Know about multifactor and hierarchical theories of intelligence
- Be familiar with the theories of multiple intelligences and the triarchic model of intelligence

Introduction

In the last discussion we introduced you to the concept of intelligence, particularly through implicit theories of intelligence. Now we will introduce you to explicit, more formal, theories of intelligence. Furthermore, we will see how the development of theories of intelligence in psychology is intertwined from the very beginning, from the first attempts to conceptualise and measure intelligence. We will take you through the theories and measurement of intelligence from a historical perspective. Although the history of intelligence research in psychology goes back more than 200 years, throughout history the nature of intelligence has fascinated thinkers and scholars. Plato (428/427–348/347 BCE), a Greek philosopher, wrote that knowledge was not 'given' by the senses but acquired through them, and it was intelligence through reason that organised and made sense out of what was perceived. Aristotle (384–323 BCE), also a Greek philosopher and, by some, credited as the first psychologist, wrote about intelligence. He suggested that

intellect takes the form of the psyche, that it is essential to man, it is part of nature (and therefore biological) but it is what separates man from the animals. He suggested that intellect comprises two parts: passive intellect and active intellect. Similarly to Plato, Aristotle suggested that active intellect, the psyche, takes information that is gained through the senses (passive intellect) and organises it, makes sense of it and uses it. Therefore, for Plato and Aristotle, the active intellect explained intellectual activities such as thinking and intuition.

In this discussion we will show you how theories of intelligence and its measurement in psychology started and how they developed. We will show you why, in the late 1990s, a leading intelligence test developer, the leading proponent of intelligence theory and one of the pre-eminent educational psychologists and scholars, sat in meeting and were finally able to combine much that had been thought and learnt about intelligence into a single theory.

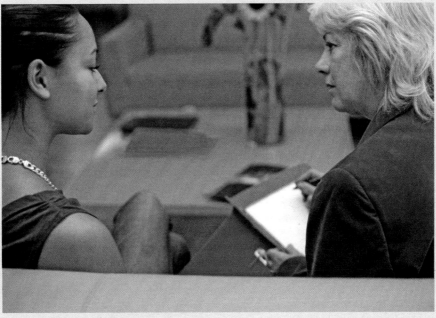

Source: Rex Features/Nick Kane/Arcaid

The birth of the psychology of intelligence: Galton and Binet

The modern foundations of intelligence theory and tests were formed just before the end of the nineteenth century through the work of two men: an Englishman, Francis Galton, and a Frenchman, Alfred Binet.

Galton

In 1865 Sir Francis Galton began to study heredity, after reading his cousin's (Charles Darwin) publication, *The Origin of Species*. You may remember (from Chapter 9) that Charles Darwin was the British naturalist (someone who studies natural history) who became famous for his theories of evolution and natural selection, which emphasised variations across species in nature. Following this work, Galton became interested in studying variations in human ability, and particularly intelligence. In particular, in his book *Hereditary Genius* (1869), Galton was convinced that higher intelligence was caused by superior qualities passed down to children by heredity. Much of this work was concerned with the hereditary nature of intelligence, and we will return to this topic later (Chapter 14). What is important to theories and measurement of intelligence is that Galton was the first to be interested in showing that human beings did differ in intelligence.

Galton is the forefather of intelligence tests. His central hypothesis was that there were differences in intelligence, and he set out to explore this hypothesis. Galton maintained that it is possible to measure intelligence directly, and he used a variety of methods to provide such measures. His choices of measurements are based clearly on a biological background and on the thoughts of some of the early philosophers mentioned previously. Galton felt that intelligent people show the ability to respond to the large range of information experienced through the senses. However, he said that 'idiotic' people demonstrate problems dealing with information gained through the senses. Galton felt that people of low intelligence will show less response to sensory information, such as being unable to distinguish between heat and cold and being unable to recognise pain. Galton suggested several methods, such as reaction time, keenness of sight and hearing, the ability to distinguish between colours, eye judgement and strength, as a way to determine intelligence through responsiveness to stimuli. Therefore, he claimed that someone who has a slow reaction time, has poor sight and hearing, is unable to distinguish between colours and shows poor eye judgement can be considered unintelligent. Galton tested people at his Anthropometric Laboratory that was set up in the International Health Exhibition in 1884, where visitors to the exhibition could take the tests.

Perhaps it is easy to scoff at the reliability and validity of some of these measures. Clearly, poor eyesight does not determine poor intelligence, but is the result of a problem with the eyes. However, some of the measures that Galton developed, such as reaction time, are still used today. Galton's work presented the first attempt to measure intelligence directly.

Binet

Alfred Binet created the first intelligence test. In 1904, the French Ministry of Public Instruction commissioned him to provide techniques for identifying children at a primary age whose lack of success or ability might lead them to require special education. In 1905, with Theodore Simon, Binet produced the Binet–Simon scale, the first intelligence

test, which Simon later described as 'practical, convenient, and rapid', that went on to be used with around 50 children.

To develop their test, Binet and Simon chose a series of 30 short tasks related to everyday life. This intelligence test included these tasks:

- following a lighted match with your eyes;
- shaking hands;
- naming parts of the body;
- counting coins;
- naming objects in a picture;
- recalling a number of digits after being shown a long list;
- word definitions;
- filling in missing words in a sentence.

The test questions were arranged in an increasing degree of difficulty to indicate levels of intelligence. The easiest of the tasks were tasks such as whether a child could follow a lighted match with their eyes; these tasks were expected to be completed by all children. Slightly harder tasks included asking children to name certain body parts or repeat simple sentences. More difficult tasks involved asking children to reproduce a drawing or construct a sentence that included certain words. The hardest tasks required children to repeat

Early IQ tests involved elementary tasks.
Source: Pearson Education Ltd. Lisa Payne Photography

seven random digits and to find rhymes for difficult words. Each level of test was designed to match a specific developmental level for children based on ages ranging from 3 to 10 years old. The Binet–Simon test could be used to determine a child's 'mental age' and whether a child was advanced or backward for their age. A child of 7 who passed the tests designed for a 7-year-old but failed the tests for an 8-year-old would be assigned a mental age of 7.

This use of age in psychological testing is one of Binet's lasting contributions to psychology. Within Binet's system, age among children could be used as a criterion of intelligence. That is, the Binet–Simon test could determine what level in an intelligence test children should be attaining at any given age. You will certainly have come across this idea at school with the idea of reading age, in which children are judged on their ability in reading in relation to where they should be at a certain age (this is applied to the sales of books; for example, the Harry Potter series is determined as having a reading age of 9–11 years).

Binet and Simon's intelligence test was a turning point in psychology. Not only did they devise a test, but they devised a test in which the performance of the child was compared to the performance of children of the same age. The final publication of tests was in 1911 (Binet and Simon, 1911), with not only tests for 3- to 10-year-olds, but some further tests for 12- and 15-year-olds and adults.

The search for measurement continues: the birth of 'IQ' and standardised testing

The search for the measurement of intelligence then shifted to the United States. It is here that we see the growth of the measurement of intelligence, the birth of the intelligence quotient (IQ), standardised testing, cultural considerations and time limits on taking an intelligence test.

Terman

The first notable development was made when Lewis Terman of Stanford University in the United States decided to use the Binet–Simon test among California schoolchildren. He found that the age norms that Binet and Simon had devised for children in France didn't work very well for schoolchildren in California. So Terman revised the test, adapting some of the items and writing 40 new items. In 1916 Terman introduced the Stanford–Binet test, which was applicable for use with children aged from 4 to 14 years.

Items on the test were similar to Binet and Simon's test. At 4 years, children would be asked to do things such as: (1) compare two horizontal lines and say which is longer;

Profiles

Francis Galton and Alfred Binet

Francis Galton

Francis Galton was born in 1822. At university he started out to study medicine but took time out to travel abroad. When he returned, he took a degree in mathematics from Trinity College in Cambridge. Outside his research and writing in psychology and intelligence, Galton was an explorer in Africa and the Middle East and created the first weather maps. He discovered that fingerprints were an index of personal identity and persuaded Scotland Yard to adopt a finger-printing system.

During his later career, Galton coined the term 'nature versus nurture', developed statistical concepts of correlation and regression to the mean and was the first to utilise the survey as a method for data collection.

Galton produced over 300 papers and books throughout his lifetime; they included *Hereditary Genius: An Inquiry into its Laws and Consequences* (1869) and *Inquiries into Human Faculty and its Development* (1883). He was knighted in 1909.

Alfred Binet

Alfred Binet received his law degree in 1878 and later studied natural sciences at the prestigious Sorbonne

University, Paris. Binet began to teach himself psychology and became interested in the ideas of British philosopher John Stuart Mill, who believed that intelligence could be explained by the laws of associationism, a theory that suggests that consciousness results from the combination of information derived from sense experiences.

Between 1883 and 1889, Binet worked as a researcher in a neurological clinic at the Salpêtrière Hospital, Paris. In 1891, Binet worked at the Sorbonne's Laboratory of Experimental Psychology and was appointed Director of the laboratory in 1894. That year he co-founded *L'Année Psychologique*, a major psychology journal. In 1904 Binet was called upon by the French government to appoint a commission on the education of retarded children; its purpose was to identify students in need of alternative education.

Binet published more than 200 books and articles in experimental, developmental, educational, social and differential psychology; but today he is most widely known for his contributions to intelligence, particularly his 1905 work *New Methods for the Diagnosis of the Intellectual Level of Subnormals* and (with T. Simon) *The Development of Intelligence in Children* (1916).

(2) copy a square; and (3) find a shape that matches a target shape. At 9 years, a child would be asked to do things such as: (1) show awareness of dates, including what day of the week it is and what year; (2) arrange weights from highest to lowest; and (3) be able to do some mental arithmetic.

Terman went on to use the test with over 1,000 children aged from 4 to 14, which was a much larger group than the 50 children used by Binet. Terman was able to gain far more accurate information on how children typically scored on intelligence tasks because he had a much more representative sample of children. This issue of researchers using representative samples to determine accurate and representative scores was the beginning of recognising the need for 'standardised testing'. That is, to assess one child by comparing them with other children, researchers need to ensure that data they have on other children is representative so the assessment of the one child is fair.

One of the main advances towards standardised testing was made at this time. In 1912 a German psychologist, William Stern, developed the idea of the intelligence quotient, or, as it is more popularly known today, IQ. Stern had been using Binet's intelligence test in Germany. While studying scores on Binet's test, Stern noticed that 'mental' age varied among children proportionally to their real age. So, for example, if a child who at the age of 6 years scores 1 year below their age on the test and has a mental age of 5, then when they are 10 years of age, they will have a mental age of 8 – two years below their real age. Stern discovered that if the mental age were divided by the chronological age, the ratio was fairly constant (as shown in the following example). He named the ratio of the mental age divided by the chronological age the intelligence quotient (IQ).

In its fullest sense, the definition of IQ is (mental age ÷ chronological age) × 100.

This calculation set an IQ of 100 as an average intelligence. That is, if a child of 8 takes an intelligence test and receives a score that indicates a mental age of 8, they would have an IQ of 100 (8 divided by 8 = 1, and 1 multiplied by 100 = 100). An IQ score of 100 indicates that a child is performing at the expected age, and 100 sets the standard by which children are then compared. This allows children to be compared not only across a particular age group but also across ages. A child who is 8 and has the mental age of a child of 10 will have an IQ of 125 (10 divided by 8 = 1.25; 1.25 multiplied by 100 = 125). A child who is 10 years old and has a mental age of 6 will have an IQ of 60 (6 divided by 10 = 0.60; 0.60 multiplied by 100 = 60).

Let us use the imaginary scores given in Table 12.1 to show how IQ is calculated. As we can see from our example table, the child who scored the mental age scores at the following ages based on Stern's findings (mental age of 5 at 6 years, mental age of 8 at 10 years and mental age of 11 at 14 years) would score an IQ of around 80 over their childhood (between 79 and 83).

Table 12.1 Example of Stern's ratio of real age to mental age, used to develop his concept of intelligence quotient (IQ)

Mental age	Chronological age	Ratio (mental age ÷ chronological age)
5	6	0.83
8	10	0.80
11	14	0.79

Terman adopted this procedure for calculating IQ based on his test. Using this procedure, together with the items of the Stanford–Binet test and the need to obtain large and representative samples to develop age 'norms' for the test, the Stanford–Binet had developed into an intelligence test against which all other tests were compared.

Yerkes

The demand for intelligence tests quickly increased. In 1917 the United States entered the First World War, and a committee was appointed by the American Psychological Association to consider ways in which psychology could help the war effort. Head of this committee was Robert Yerkes, then President of the American Psychological Association (although the committee included Terman) and also a US Army major. The committee was quick to realise that psychology could help the Army because assessing the intelligence of recruits would enable the Army to classify and assign soldiers to suitable tasks. However, it was also realised that such an exercise would involve a huge number of people and that the sorts of tests developed by Binet and Terman were not suitable as they were time-intensive. That is, an experimenter had to sit down with the subject and take them through five or six tasks. The committee decided that what was needed was a test that could be completed simultaneously by a number of people, administered by one examiner. Yerkes' aim was to develop group intelligence testing.

Yerkes, alongside a staff of 40 psychologists (including Terman), developed two group intelligence tests, known as the Army Alpha and Army Beta tests. The Army Alpha was designed for literate groups and the Army Beta was designed for illiterates, low literates or non-English-speaking groups.

The Army Alpha test

The Alpha test battery for literates included the testing of a variety of cognitive abilities by examining the person's knowledge base in both oral language and written language. The Alpha test included eight tests of an individual's ability to:

- follow oral directions, involving the comprehension of simple and complex oral language directions;
- solve arithmetical problems, showing knowledge of arithmetic and the ability to perform simple computations;

- show practical judgement, involving the ability to make the 'correct' choice on a scenario presented to the individual;
- use synonyms and antonyms, knowledge of the 'same' and 'opposite' of words;
- rearrange disarranged sentences, such as 'I back it and door ran to the opened';
- complete an uncompleted series of numbers (1, 2, 4, 8, 16, . . .);
- see analogies, which requires the ability to see a similarity between two things that are otherwise dissimilar;
- demonstrate information, an examination of the person's everyday knowledge base.

The administration of each of the eight subtests was designed to be completed within a certain time.

The Army Beta test

The Beta test was an intelligence test comparable to the Alpha but freed of the influences of literacy and the English language. People who were non-English speakers or poor at speaking English, or those who typically had less than 6 years of experience in speaking the English language, were sent to Beta testing. Furthermore, those who had tried the Alpha test but were later judged to be poor readers, were retested using the Beta test.

The Beta test instructions were given by the tester and their aides by making hand signals. The examiners recorded responses. The Beta test included seven tests of ability in which the participants had to:

- complete a maze task, by finding the best route to be taken on a picture of a maze;
- complete a cube analysis, by counting cubes in a graphic representation;
- read an X–O series of graphic displays in left-to-right sequences;
- complete a test using digit symbols, requiring scanning and matching of numbers to symbols;
- complete a test using number symbols, requiring scanning and matching of symbols to numbers;
- complete a picture by looking at an uncompleted picture and using given objects to complete the picture (a little like a jigsaw);
- undertake geometrical construction, which involved working with graphics information and mentally rearranging it to construct a figure.

Again, like the Alpha test, the administration of each Beta subtest was completed within a certain time.

For each test, to determine each person's intelligence level, scores for all subtests were combined into one total score. Based on the total score, each individual was assigned a category based on a letter grade. A letter grade of A suggested superior intelligence; B, C+, C meant average

intelligence, and C–, D, D– were considered as signifying inferior intelligence. The letter grade indicated the person's mental intelligence and was taken as a general indicator of the person's native intelligence.

In the end, Yerkes and his colleagues tested over 1.75 million people. This work was not completed until late in the war, and the work actually had little effect on the war effort; however, it did a lot to raise the status of psychology and the profile and potential usefulness of intelligence testing. For example, after the war, Yerkes received requests from the general public, business, industry and education for the intelligence test. In 1919 the National Intelligence Test was published and sold over half a million copies in its first year.

You can see that a growth in intelligence tests occurred from the work of Terman and Yerkes. Growth occurred not only in terms of what is measured and who can be measured but also: (1) in the number of people who can be measured at one time; (2) in developing an official way of scoring intelligence through IQ; and (3) in the consideration of culture and time limits on taking an intelligence test. These elements remain central to modern intelligence tests.

General intelligence (g): the theory and the measurement

Up to this point in the history of intelligence testing, approaches to intelligence had been very practical. Tests were developed for particular needs; that is, in response to French or American government demands. However, between 1904 and 1927, an English psychologist, Charles Spearman, introduced another way of conceptualising intelligence. He based his approach on the factor analysis of data (a technique for simplifying the relationships between a number of variables; see Chapter 25 for more details on this technique) that had already been collected. We will outline Spearman's research and theory of general intelligence and then introduce you to two measures of intelligence: the Wechsler and Raven's intelligence tests, which are designed to measure 'g'.

'g'

Charles Spearman (1904a; 1927), over the course of two publications – a journal article '"General Intelligence": Objectively determined and measured' and *The Abilities of Man*, introduced one of the most influential ideas in psychology, **general intelligence** or 'g'.

In 1904 Spearman set out to estimate the intelligence of 24 children in the village school. Initially, Spearman used intelligence tests of memory, light, weight and sound in which participants were asked to identify changes in the illumination, weight and pitch of Spearman's instruments and perform memory tasks.

Spearman's first 24 participants were the oldest pupils of a village school in Berkshire. Spearman claimed that this sample was most favourable as it was within 100 yards of his own house, and all the families of the children resided in the immediate neighbourhood (perhaps the most convenient sample of what is known these days as 'convenience' sampling). Like other intelligence tests, the test was done on a one-to-one basis.

After this first experiment Spearman moved on to the next 36 oldest children in the school, and then to a local school which sent a lot of its pupils to Harrow (a well-known public school in the United Kingdom). Over a period of time, further data collections were taken among individuals who lived further from Spearman's home. Between 1904 and 1921, Spearman analysed the relationships between the data collected using a variety of intelligence tests and subjected them to factor analysis.

He found that his data indicated a trend towards positive correlations between intelligence tests. That is, a person who does well on one intelligence test will perform equally well on a variety of *intellectual* tests, be they tests concerned with vocabulary, mathematical or spatial (awareness of space and movement around oneself) abilities. Equally, if a person did poorly on one intelligence test, then they will also tend to perform poorly on other intellectual tasks. He called this positive correlation between tests the 'positive manifold'. Spearman used this idea of a positive manifold between intelligence tests to propose a two-factor theory of intelligence.

The first factor of intelligence was **specific abilities**, or 's'. This was the name given to each type of intelligence needed for performing well on each different intelligence task that Spearman had observed. Therefore, vocabulary intelligence is a specific ability, mathematical intelligence is a specific ability and spatial intelligence is a specific ability.

The second factor was what Spearman thought was underlying all the positive correlations, and this was perhaps his most important and notable contribution to psychology: general intelligence, or 'g'. He argued that 'g' was underlying all the positive correlations: 'g' was the intelligence required for performance of intelligence tests of all types. Spearman envisaged 'g' as a kind of mental energy that underlies specific factors of intelligence. He saw it as a deeper fundamental mechanism which informed a number of intelligence abilities but was an intelligence also able to see relationships between objects, events and information and draw inferences from those relationships.

Spearman saw a person's ability in one specific ability test – for example, mathematical ability – as not only affected by one's specific ability to perform mathematical tasks but also as largely determined by that person's general intelligence.

The main point of Spearman's findings was the idea of 'g', and this became a major theory that informs many subsequent approaches to intelligence. Proponents of general intelligence, or 'g', still exist amongst prominent psychologists.

Measuring 'g': the Wechsler and Raven's Matrices

After Charles Spearman's introduction of his theory of intelligence, a central interest to intelligence developers was to develop a good measure of general intelligence, particularly among adults. Spearman's theory and research, together with the work of Terman and Yerkes, led to the development of more rigorous intelligence tests that could be used across the population to assess intelligence. However, there was some further work to be done. Both the Binet tests were primarily concerned with testing among children, and any testing done with adult samples involved relatively small samples. The Yerkes test was subject to a similar criticism. Although this test had been used with nearly one and a half million adults, they were all people who had applied to join the US Army. It was left for psychologists to devise intelligence tests that could be used to determine intelligence among the general population, and be used to assess a person's intelligence accurately in comparison to other people.

Two intelligence tests stand out in present psychology that show a historical move to standardised intelligence testing: the Wechsler test of intelligence and the Raven Matrices.

The Wechsler tests

David Wechsler was a US psychologist at Columbia University. In 1917 he had originally worked under the American Psychological Association/Yerkes' Army initiative and administered and interpreted intelligence tests that were used to assign army recruits to military jobs. During that time, the Army sent Wechsler to England and the University of London to work with Charles Spearman and Karl Pearson.

The history of what have now become known as the Wechsler tests spans the period from 1939 to the present day. Although Wechsler did not always agree with Spearman's view of intelligence, Wechsler's first tests were modelled on Spearman's two-factor model and Spearman's central position that intelligence covers a huge range of specific abilities that correlate within one another to form an overall measure of general intelligence (or 'g').

In 1939 Wechsler published the first of the Wechsler tests, the Wechsler–Bellevue Scale. The Wechsler–Bellevue Scale, unlike some former intelligence tests, was designed and standardised among a sample of 1,500 adults. However, in 1955 Wechsler introduced two tests:

Profile

Charles Edward Spearman

Charles Edward Spearman was born in London in 1863 to eminent parents. He joined the British Army and became an officer, serving in the Burmese and Boer Wars. After 15 years, he resigned his army post to study psychology. At the time, British psychology was more a branch of philosophy; and so, in 1897, Spearman chose to study in Leipzig, Germany. Spearman was accepted at university although he had no conventional qualifications, partly due to his officer and army training. There he studied under Wilhelm Max Wundt (a German physiologist and psychologist who is generally acknowledged as one of the founders of experimental psychology and cognitive psychology). He served in the army during the South African War again but, in 1906, Spearman gained his PhD when he was 41, having already published his 1904 paper on the factor analysis of intelligence.

Spearman then took a position in psychology at University College, London. He had impressed William McDougall, an English psychologist who studied the theory of instinct and of social psychology. McDougall arranged for Spearman to replace him when he left his position at the university. Initially, Spearman was head of the small psychological laboratory, but in 1911 he was promoted to a professorship of the Philosophy of Mind and Logic. He was elected to the Royal Society (the oldest learned society concerned with the improvement of natural knowledge) in 1924. His title changed to Professor of Psychology in 1928 and he stayed at University College until he retired in 1931. During his time at the university, Spearman and a colleague, Karl Pearson, developed separately the two most well-known correlation techniques in psychology. Above all, Spearman is renowned for: (1) determining the concept of general intelligence; and (2) his work on factor analysis.

Spearman's most famous works are '"General intelligence": objectivity determined and measured' (1904a) and 'Proof and measurement of association between two things' (1904b), which were both published in the *American Journal of Psychology*, and his book, *The Abilities of Man: Their Nature and Measurement* (Macmillan, 1927).

- the Wechsler Adult Intelligence Scale (WAIS) that had been standardised among 2,000 adults aged between 16 and 75;
- the Wechsler Scale for Children (WISC) for children aged between 5 and 16 years.

As with the Binet tests, the Wechsler tests were administered on a one-to-one basis. Both Wechsler scales contained a number of subtests to measure several different aspects of intelligence, including verbal and performance tests such as:

- **Arithmetic (verbal)** – This subtest involves solving problems using mental arithmetic.
- **Block design (performance)** – In this subtest, the participant is presented with nine coloured blocks, each with two red, two white and two diagonally red and white sides. In this task the participant is asked to arrange the blocks to form certain patterns.
- **Comprehension (verbal)** – This subtest involves the participant demonstrating an understanding of the meaning of words and sayings, and the appropriate response to a number of scenarios (e.g. two trains are travelling in opposite directions 100 miles apart; one train is travelling at 40 miles an hour while the other is travelling at 60 miles an hour. How long before the two trains meet?).
- **Digit span (verbal)** – In this subtest the participant is asked to repeat a series of digits in exact or reverse order.

- **Digit symbol (performance)** – This subtest requires the participant to change symbols to numbers.
- **Information (verbal)** – This subtest requires the participant to show general knowledge of areas such as science, politics, geography, literature and history.
- **Object assembly (performance)** – This subtest requires a number of simple jigsaws to be completed within a particular time limit.
- **Picture arrangement (performance)** – In this subtest, participants are presented with a series of cards with a number of pictures. They must arrange the cards to tell a simple story.
- **Picture completion (performance)** – In this subtest, the participant has to complete line drawings of objects or scenes in which one or two lines are missing.
- **Similarities (verbal)** – This subtest involves the participant comparing two things that are alike.
- **Vocabulary (verbal)** – This subtest involves asking the participant for definitions of words.

Some examples from the Wechsler Adult Intelligence Scale are given in Figure 12.1.

These scales are well-known tests that are still used today, although they have been revised. The Wechsler tests departed from previous intelligence tests in two important ways. First, the Wechsler scales were different from previous tests in that they were designed so that all people of all ages could take them. This was unlike Binet's

(a)

(b)

(c)

Item	Response
Q-3	3-Q
T-9-1	1-9-T
M-3-P-6	3-6-M-P
F-7-K-2-8	2-7-8-F-K
5-J-4-A-1-S	1-4-5-A-J-S
C-6-4-W-O-7-D	4-6-7-C-D-O-W

(d)

(e)

Figure 12.1 *(Continues)*

(f)   **Paraphrased Wechsler-like Questions**

Information

1   How many wings does a bird have?

2   How many nickels make a dime?

3   What is steam made of?

4   Who wrote *Tom Sawyer*?

5   What is pepper?

Comprehension

1   What should you do if you see someone forget his book when he leaves a restaurant?

2   What is the advantage of keeping money in a bank?

3   Why is copper often used in electrical wires?

Arithmetic

1   Sam had three pieces of candy and Joe gave him four more. How many pieces of candy did Sam have altogether?

2   Three women divided eighteen golf balls equally among themselves. How many golf balls did each person receive?

3   If two buttons cost $.15, what will be the cost of a dozen buttons?

Similarities

1   In what way are a lion and a tiger alike?

2   In what way are a saw and a hammer alike?

3   In what way are an hour and a week alike?

4   In what way are a circle and a triangle alike?

Vocabulary

This test consists simply of asking, 'What is a _____?' or 'What does _____ mean?' The words cover a wide range of difficulty.

Figure 12.1 Simulated items similar to those in the *Wechsler Adult Intelligence Scale*: picture arrangement (a), block design (b), letter-number sequencing (c), matrix reasoning (d), picture completion (e) and object assembly and Wechsler-like questions (f).

test, which primarily required a 7-year-old to take tests designed for 7-year-olds, and 10-year-olds to take tests designed for 10-year-olds. Clearly, it would not have been useful or productive to design intelligence tests for all the years from early childhood to late adulthood. The Wechsler intelligence test includes a number of subtests for different aspects of intelligence, and within each subtest there are a variety of items with a wide range of difficulty. However, all participants are tested on the same items.

The second way in which the Wechsler tests differed from previous tests was the introduction of the concept of 'deviation IQ'. You will remember that Terman used the concept of IQ based on the mental age and the real age of the participant [(mental age ÷ chronological age) × 100]. However, Wechsler was primarily concerned with applying intelligence testing to adults, and the calculation that Terman used was not wholly applicable to adults. For example, let us apply Terman's method for calculating an average intelligence test score to adults. A 20-year-old and a 40-year-old take the same intelligence test and score in a way that indicates they are of the same mental age, thus the 40-year-old would appear to be half as intelligent as the 20-year-old (solely based on age). This problem stems from the fact that there is a huge range of years in adulthood as compared to childhood and that intelligence increases rapidly in childhood yet starts to level out in adulthood.

Therefore, the challenge faced by Wechsler was to arrive at a fairer system of assessing IQ.

Wechsler's solution was not to define and score IQ based on mental and chronological age, but in terms of an individual's actual score on the intelligence test relative to the average scores obtained by others of the same age on the same intelligence test. The new formula for interpreting test scores in terms of deviation IQ was (actual test score ÷ expected score for that age) × 100.

However, this calculation involved two further steps to allow the standardisation in using the Wechsler IQ test: (1) determining the expected score for any particular age so all people could be compared; and (2) transforming the wide range of scores and variations among the population to a standardised form.

1 **Determining the expected score for a particular age.** Wechsler had to determine the average score on the intelligence test for all possible ages, so that it could be used effectively as a basis of comparison. To ensure that he had a reliable comparison, Wechsler collected data through stratified sampling, whereby sampling is based on randomly sampling individuals from mutually exclusive subgroups or strata of population (e.g. a certain number of 20-year-olds, 30-year-olds and so on). Wechsler ensured that he sampled people from various demographics, including social class, sex and region of the country. From this sampling Wechsler was able to establish intelligence norms for all ages.
2 **Transforming the wide range of scores and variations among the population to a standardised form.**

You will remember that the original calculation of IQ was based on an observation by German intelligence tester William Stern that 'mental' age varies among children proportionally with their real age. It was this growth of mental age against chronological age that allowed Stern to make certain assumptions in calculating IQ. However, Wechsler could not make these assumptions. First, Wechsler was not surprised to find that mental age and chronological age do not grow or change proportionally. Rather, he found that mental age fluctuates (goes up, goes down, stays stable) compared with chronological age. He could not assume the proportional growth that Stern used in calculations.

Wechsler developed a measure that used a comparison of the person scores to means, rather than age. To do this, he still used the idea of average IQ as being 100. The choice of 100 was fairly arbitrary, but was based on the original IQ calculations suggested by Stern and used by Terman. Therefore, all ranges of intelligence tests score for all ages were transformed so they had a middle score of 100. If 35-year-olds had a mean score of 80.1 IQ points on the intelligence test, then their average would be transformed to 100, and all scores would be shifted around this average. Final IQ scores for each individual were based on how much they deviated from the average. **Deviation IQ** was calculated as how much someone deviated from the average IQ of 100.

If you want to read more on how IQ scores are calculated, go to Stop and think: IQ scores and the normal distribution.

Stop and think

IQ scores and the normal distribution

The introduction of mean scores to calculating IQ led to a complication of how IQ was calculated. Overall, researchers found that they were dealing with much more information by introducing numerous mean scores across a huge age range on an intelligence test (for example, 103.2 average IQ test score for 32-year-olds, 102.2 average IQ test scores for 33-year-olds and so on), rather than equally increasing absolute age over a limited time period (5–16 years). This result led to issues for allowing comparisons.

For example, if a company was interested in obtaining IQ scores in recruiting for jobs, then the present scoring system would be complicated. Suppose, for example, a recruiter has two candidates:

- Person A, aged 20 years, who scored 105 on the intelligence test; this was 10 points below the average for

20-year-olds (115 being the average intelligence test score among 20-year-olds).
- Person B, aged 25 years, who scored 100 on the intelligence test; this was 5 points below the average for 25-year-olds (105 being the average intelligence test score among 25-year-olds).

Who should the recruiter hire – the person with the highest IQ (Person A) or the person who scores nearest to the average for their age (Person B)?

Wechsler realised that he had to standardise the scoring of IQ. He had to find a way of comparing all these different scores and still provide a standardised scoring system. To do this, Wechsler used the normal distribution curve. You may remember from your statistics classes that a normal distribution curve (see Figure 12.2) is the symmetrical distribution of scores in a curve, with most of the scores situated in the centre and then spreading out, showing progressively lower frequency of scores for the higher and lower values.

What is particularly notable about this approach is that researchers have found that many of the variables measuring human attitudes and behaviour follow a normal distribution curve. This finding is one of statistics' more interesting elements. Statisticians and researchers are often not certain why many variables fall into a normal distribution; they have just found that many attitudes and behaviours do, including intelligence.

However, statisticians have noted that, if scores on a variable show a normal distribution, this is potentially a powerful statistical tool because we can then begin to be certain about how scores will be distributed in a variable (i.e. that many people's scores will be concentrated in the middle and few will be concentrated at either end). This certainty has given statisticians the impetus to develop ideas about statistical testing, including most notably probability and significance testing, but also intelligence.

Normal distribution and the certainty that surrounds the ability to calculate where people fall under different points of the curve allow the calculation of how much

people deviate from the IQ score. Because of what we know about a normal distribution, and because Wechsler decided to use 100 as an average IQ (based on the original IQ calculations), we know that:

- 68 per cent of scores lie within 1 standard deviation of the mean (plus/minus), so 68 per cent of the population will score between 85 and 115.
- 95 per cent of scores will fall within 2 standard deviations of the mean, therefore 95 per cent of the population will score between 70 and 130. The average IQ score is 100. The standard deviation of IQ scores is 15.

It is then within these aspects that these scores are interpreted and classified. A score that is no more than 1 standard deviation (85–115) away from 100 can be interpreted as a normal score. A score that is between 1 and 2 standard deviations away from 100 can be interpreted as low (70–85) or high (115–130). A score that is more than 2 standard deviations away from 100 (lower than 70 or higher than 130) can be interpreted as very low (lower than 70) or very high (higher than 130). Therefore, Wechsler had provided a benchmark by which all people of all ages could be compared in IQ by using standard deviations.

Figure 12.2 A normal distribution curve of intelligence scores.

IQ scores have been traditionally categorised to provide some understanding of level of general intelligence. Some labels that have been used to describe low, high and average scores are provided in Figure 12.3.

Raven's Progressive Matrices

Scottish psychologist John Carlyle Raven first published his Progressive Matrices in 1938. In comparison to the Wechsler tests, the Raven Progressive Matrices seem dramatically different. However, like the Wechsler test, their rationale is based on the theory of Spearman.

In his writing, Spearman had emphasised 'g' as the abstract ability (theoretical thought, not applied or practical) to see

relationships between objects, events and information and draw inferences from those relationships. Raven thought the best way to test this abstract ability was to develop a test that was free of cultural influences, particularly language. As you have seen with the Wechsler tests, there was some reliance on culture and language (e.g. tests of general knowledge and vocabulary). Although this reliance on language is not always true of the Wechsler tests (e.g. block design, object assembly), Raven's Progressive Matrices were designed to minimise the influence of culture and language by relying on non-verbal problems that require abstract reasoning and do not require knowledge of a particular culture.

Examples of the items in Raven's Progressive Matrices are given in Figure 12.4. The participant is shown a matrix

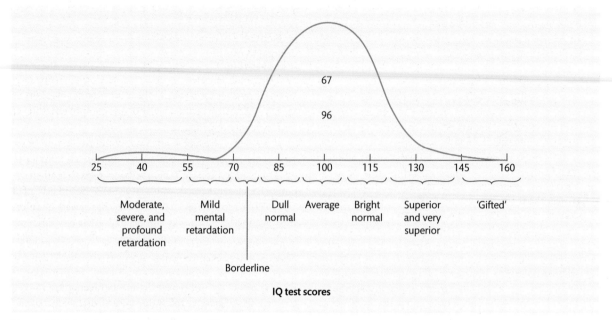

Figure 12.3 Labels traditionally given to IQ scores.

of patterns in which one pattern is missing. The aim of each item is to test a person's ability to form perceptual relations and to reason by analogy (seeing similarity between two subjects, and transferring information about one subject to another) independent of language. Put simply, the patterns within the matrix form certain rules, and the participant shows higher intelligence by being able to work out the rules that govern the patterns and then use these rules to select an item that best fits the missing pattern.

Raven's Progressive Matrices can be used with persons ranging from 6 years to adult. The overall test comprises 60 items, arranged into five sets of items, with each set of items arranged in increasing order of difficulty. Typically, like Wechsler's test and Spearman's theory of 'g', for the Progressive Matrices respondents are given an overall score. As in the Wechsler test, the overall IQ score is based on an individual's deviation from standardised norms. With the Matrices' emphasis on abstract (theoretical thought, not applied or practical) ability to see relationships among

Figure 12.4 *(Continues)*

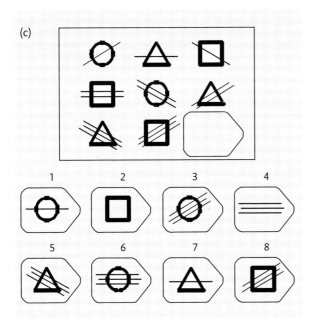

Figure 12.4 Simulated items similar to those in the Raven's Progressive Matrices: Raven's Colored Progressive Matrices (CPM) (a), Raven's Standard Progressive Matrices (b) and Raven's Advanced Progressive Matrices (APM) (c).

Source: Raven's Progressive Matrices *(Coloured, Parallel, Sets A, AB, B).* Copyright © 1998 NCS Pearson, Inc. Raven's Progressive Matrices *(Standard, Sets A-E).* Copyright © 1976, 1958, 1938 NCS Pearson, Inc. Raven's Progressive Matrices *(Advanced).* Copyright © 1976, 1947, 1943 NCS Pearson, Inc. Reproduced with permission. All rights reserved. 'Wechsler Adult Intelligence Scale', 'WAIS' and 'Raven's Progressive Matrices and Vocabulary Scales' are trademarks, in the US and/or other countries, of Pearson Education, Inc. or its affiliate(s).

objects, events and information and draw inferences from those relationships and its non-dependence on language, the Matrices are often favoured as a good measure of 'g'. Arthur Jensen, a prominent IQ researcher, wrote that, when compared to other measures of general intelligence, Raven's Progressive Matrices are probably the best measure of a general intelligence factor (Jensen, 1998).

Multifactor theorists: Thurstone, Cattell and Guilford

Both Wechsler's and Raven's intelligence tests were developments in the history of intelligence based on Spearman's theory, and these tests are used in present-day research. However, other developments from Spearman's theory sought to develop its theoretical elements. The next section outlines three such developments via the research of three academics: Louis L. Thurstone, Raymond B. Cattell and J. P. Guilford. A common thread running through all these academics' work was that they used the factor analysis approach, which Spearman developed, to understand intelligence. However, you will see that each of these academics produced rather different perspectives on the nature of 'g'.

Thurstone: 'g' results from seven primary mental abilities

L. L. Thurstone was a US psychologist and psychometrician who originally studied engineering at Cornell University under Thomas Edison (one of the most prolific inventors of the late nineteenth century). Thurstone completed a PhD at the University of Chicago.

Thurstone used factor analysis to inform his findings. That is, he explored the relationships between a number of intelligences and looked for underlying patterns and structures. Thurstone agreed with Spearman's hypothesis of a general factor of intelligence; however, he viewed 'g' differently from Spearman. Spearman defined 'g' as a central factor of intelligence, underlying and informing all aspects of intelligence, including specific abilities. Thurstone disagreed. He couldn't see how, from Spearman's studies, he had shown that a general factor of intelligence was influencing all single aspects of intelligence. Thurstone argued that all Spearman had shown was that intelligence tests correlate positively, and he maintained that there was no evidence for Spearman's description of 'g'. Thurstone agued that 'g' results from, rather than lies behind, these seven primary mental abilities:

- **associative memory** – ability for rote (learning through routine or repetition) memory;
- **number** – ability to carry out mathematical operations accurately;
- **perceptual speed** – ability to perceive details, anomalies, similarities in visual stimuli;
- **reasoning** – ability in inductive and deductive reasoning;
- **space (spatial visualisations)** – ability to transform spatial figures mentally;
- **verbal comprehension** – ability in reading, comprehension, verbal analogies;
- **word fluency** – ability to generate and use effectively a large number of words or letters (i.e. in anagrams).

Within Thurstone's theory of intelligence, general intelligence was the result of these seven different aspects of intelligence, which formed parts of 'g'. Thurstone's approach to intelligence was the first real *multi*factor approach to intelligence. That is, he suggested there were a number of factors to intelligence, rather than just one or two.

Cattell: fluid and crystallised intelligence

Raymond B. Cattell was born, studied and lectured in the United Kingdom. He later moved to the United States, where he become a Research Associate of E. L. Thorndike at Columbia University in New York.

Cattell also used factor analysis in his studies of intelligence. He acknowledged Spearman's work in accepting that there was general intelligence, but he suggested that 'g' comprises two related but distinct components: crystallised intelligence and fluid intelligence.

Cattell described **crystallised intelligence** as acquired knowledge and skills, such as factual knowledge. It is generally related to a person's stored information and to their cultural influences. Knowledge of vocabulary, comprehension and general knowledge would all be tests of an individual's crystallised intelligence. Following Spearman's lead (who termed general intelligence 'g'), Cattell abbreviated this component as 'Gc' (the *c* standing for crystallised).

Cattell described **fluid intelligence** as a primary reasoning ability; the ability to solve abstract relational problems, free of cultural influences. This component is defined by intelligence abilities such as acquisition of new information, understanding new relationships, patterns and analogies in stimuli. Cattell abbreviated this component as 'Gf' (the *f* standing for fluid).

Cattell saw a dynamic relationship between these two intelligence components. Crystallised intelligence (for example, knowledge) is intelligence that increases throughout life and is a reflection of one's cumulative learning experience. Fluid intelligence is thought to be present from birth and then is meant to stabilise in adulthood. An example of how crystallised and fluid intelligence may work in society is seen in the way these different components inform certain types of thinking. It is often found that the great mathematicians do some of their best work when they are in younger adulthood. This is because mathematics is based on abstract thinking, and achievement in this area reflects fluid intelligence. However, in other disciplines, such as history and literature, some of the best work is produced by academics in later adulthood as they have accumulated more knowledge; achievement in this area reflects crystallised intelligence.

One interesting aspect of Cattell's work is the distinction between fluid and crystallised intelligence in relation to developments in IQ testing. The Wechsler tests are, to some extent, measuring crystallised intelligence, containing measures such as comprehension, knowledge and vocabulary. Raven's Progressive Matrices, which reflect abstract thinking, are often used as a measure of general fluid intelligence.

Guilford: many different intelligences and many different combinations

J. P. Guilford was a US psychologist who studied at the University of Nebraska and Cornell University. He also conducted research at the University of Southern California and Santa Ana Army Air Base.

Guilford disagreed with the stance of Spearman and, to some extent, with Thurstone and Cattell. He didn't acknowledge the existence of 'g'; instead, Guilford (1977) eventually proposed that intelligence was the result of 150 independent abilities (though originally he suggested 120 independent abilities [Guilford, 1959]). His theory was named the Structure of Intellect (SI) theory.

Guilford argued that these elementary abilities fall into three groups: operations, contents and products.

Operations are types of mental processing, for example, what a person does. There are five types of operations:

- **evaluation** – ability to examine and judge carefully and appraise;
- **convergent production** – ability to bring together information into a single theme (e.g. a list comprising 'cats, dogs, mice' would be converged into 'type of animals');
- **divergent production** – ability to produce ideas from a common point (e.g. if a person was asked to list animals, divergent production would be to list 'cats', 'dogs', 'mice', etc.);
- **memory** – mental faculty of retaining and recalling past experience and information;
- **cognition** – mental process of knowing, including aspects such as awareness, perception, reasoning and judgement.

Contents comprise the mental material we possess *on* which operations are performed. There are five types of contents:

- **visual** – material relating to or gained by the sense of sight;
- **auditory** – material relating to or gained by the sense of hearing;
- **symbolic** – material relating to or expressed by means of symbols or a symbol;
- **semantic** – material relating to meaning, especially meaning in language;
- **behavioural** – material relating to our own behaviour.

Products consist of the form in which the information is stored, processed and used by the person to make associations or connections. There are six types of products:

- **units** – comprises the ability to use information relating to something being classed as a unit. It may be an individual, group, structure or other entity regarded as part of a whole (e.g. a 1-euro note [€1] is a *unit* of money);
- **classes** – comprises the ability to use information relating to a set, collection, group or configuration containing members regarded as having certain attributes or traits in common (e.g. the monetary units of euros – (€, €1, 50 cent, 20 cent, 10 cent, 5 cent, 2 cent and 1 cent – are a *class* of money);
- **relations** – comprises the ability to use information relating to seeing a logical or natural association between two or more things (e.g. there are 100 cents to €1; the association between these two units is a *relation*);
- **systems** – comprises the ability to use information relating to seeing a group of interacting, interrelated or interdependent elements forming a complex whole

(e.g. the euro, sterling, US dollars, Chinese yen and all the other currencies in the world form a *system*);

- **transformation** – comprises the ability to understand the changing nature, function or condition of any information (e.g. exchange rates between currencies);
- **implication** – comprises the ability to use a variety of information and apply logic to it or further understand suggestions, meaning and significance relating to that information (e.g. If I had all the money in the world, that would mean I would be rich).

A popular way of illustrating Guilford's Structure of Intellect (SI) theory is given in Figure 12.5.

Guilford argued that, theoretically, 150 different components of intelligence emerge from the combinations of these different skills. So, for example, the ability to remember seeing a dog would use all of the following components:

- visual (content; the act of visualising the dog – remember *seeing* the dog);
- unit (product; the object itself – the dog – remember seeing the *dog*);
- memory (operation; the remembering part – *remember* seeing the dog).

Guilford suggested that the model could be simplified and that further groups of intelligence could be recognised by taking each of the five intelligence operations and applying them to the products and contents aspects (see Figure 12.5). Guilford recognised a further set of abilities:

- Reasoning and problem-solving intelligence could be fully understood by taking convergent and divergent operations and subdividing them into the 30 distinct abilities for the six products and five contents.
- Memory intelligence could be fully understood by subdividing the memory into the 30 distinct abilities for the six products and five contents.
- Decision-making skills could be fully understood by subdividing evaluation into the 30 distinct abilities for the six products and five contents.
- Language-related skills could be fully understood by subdividing cognition into the 30 distinct abilities for the six products and five contents.

Guilford's model of intelligence really opens up the possibilities of intelligence. It clearly broadens the view of intelligence, while detailing how different aspects of intelligence intertwine to form specific abilities. However, it may be too complex to provide a definitive theory. Guilford researched and developed a wide variety of psychometric tests to measure the specific abilities predicted by SI theory. He largely based this work on groups of intelligence that could be found among the 150 different components. Although these tests may be useful on their own, when research has conducted factor analysis to examine whether these intelligences gather together in the way that Guilford suggests, there has been little support for his overall theory (Guilford and Hoepfner, 1971).

Intelligence and factor analysis – a third way: the hierarchical approach

So far we have considered theories of intelligence where 'g' is central (Spearman), apparent but not the most important (Thurstone and Cattell) or rejected (Guilford). Figure 12.6a shows how the theorists tend to be split between general theories of intelligence and specific abilities. However, there is a set of factor analysis theorists whose work fills the gap between the work of Spearman and Thurstone (see Figure 12.6b). These theorists developed hierarchical theories of intelligence, and we will now outline the work of Philip E. Vernon, John B. Carroll and John Horn.

Vernon

Philip E. Vernon was an English psychologist educated at Cambridge University. He was a Professor of Psychology and Educational Psychology at the Institute of Education, University of London.

Vernon (1950) described several different levels of intelligence. He proposed that neither Spearman nor Thurstone had considered the existence of group factors that linked 'g' to specific intelligence abilities. Vernon argued that intelligence comprises various sets of abilities that can be described

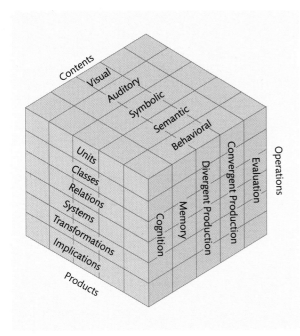

Figure 12.5 Guilford's Structure of Intellect (SI) theory.

Source: The Analysis of Intelligence, New York: McGraw-Hill (Guilford, J.P. and Hoepfner, R. 1971), copyright © 1971. Reproduced with permission of The McGraw-Hill Companies.

Figure 12.6 (a) Overview of theories by general intelligences and specific abilities. (b) How the hierarchical theories fit into this overview.

at various levels (i.e. from specific to grouped to general). Vernon's theory was the elaboration of 'g' to a series of group factors *in between* 'g' and 's' factors (see Figure 12.7).

Within Vernon's hierarchical theory, the highest intelligence level is 'g'. Like Spearman, Vernon thought 'g' was the most important factor underlying intelligence in human beings. The next level in Vernon's hierarchy comprises two *major group factors*, verbal/educational (v:ed) and spatial/mechanical abilities (k:m).

- The 'v:ed' factor represents largely verbal/educational intelligence, including verbal–numerical–educational abilities.
- The 'k:m' factor comprises spatial/mechanical intelligence, including practical–mechanical–spatial–physical abilities.

The next level of Vernon's hierarchy contains *minor group factors*, divided from the major group factors. That is, from the major group factor, 'v:ed', verbal, numerical and educational abilities are minor group factors. Similarly, from the major group factor, 'k:m', practical, mechanical, spatial and physical abilities are minor group factors.

At the bottom of the hierarchy are the specific intelligence factors. These are divided from the minor group factors.

That is, from the 'v:ed' major group factor family, and the educational abilities minor group factors, there would be specific abilities such as reading, spelling, use of grammar and punctuation. Similarly, from the 'k:m' major group factor family, and the spatial abilities minor group factors, there would be specific spatial abilities such as recognising an object when it is seen from different locations, the ability to imagine movement of an object and ability to think about spatial relations when the body of the observer is central.

Carroll: from the Three-Stratum Model of Human Cognitive Abilities to CHC

John B. Carroll, an American educational psychologist, proposed a hierarchical model of intelligence officially named the Three-Stratum Model of Human Cognitive Abilities.

Carroll (1993) proposed this hierarchical model of intelligence based on the factor analysis of 461 data sets obtained between 1927 and 1987. These data sets were important because they included a number of intelligence data sets from class intelligence studies reported during the past 50–60 years. Based on this analysis, Carroll proposed three

Figure 12.7 Vernon's hierarchical theory of intelligence.

hierarchical levels to intelligence, which he termed stratums:

- Stratum I comprises specific levels of intelligence. Overall, Carroll identified 69 different cognitive abilities/intelligences.
- Stratum II is made up of eight broad factors arising from these specific abilities:
  - fluid intelligence, abbreviated to (in a similar way to Cattell) Gf;
  - crystallised intelligence, abbreviated to Gc;
  - general memory and learning, abbreviated to Gy;
  - broad visual perception, abbreviated to Gv;
  - broad auditory perception, abbreviated to Gu;
  - broad retrieval ability, abbreviated to Gr;
  - broad cognitive speediness, abbreviated to Gs;
  - processing speed, abbreviated to Gt.
- Stratum III is the general level of intelligence representing general intellectual ability, similar to 'g'.

Carroll's work perhaps provided a much-needed systematic organisation and integration of over 50 years of research on the structure of human cognitive abilities. As you can see, it brings together a number of themes, including Spearman's 'g' and specific factors, Cattell's 'Gc' and 'Gf', Thurstone's specific factors and Vernon's hierarchical approach.

Cattell, Horn and Carroll (CHC): theory, research and practice together

Our story of factor-analytic studies and theories would be expected to stop with Carroll's 1993 work. However, it continues with recent convergence between Cattell's original work and Carroll's factor-analytic work.

US psychologist John Leonard Horn (Department of Psychology at the University of South Carolina), along with his advisor, Raymond B. Cattell, had been developing Cattell's original theory of intelligence that specifies two broad factors, fluid and crystallised intelligence. The main thrust of Horn's work had been to look for numerous specific factors that support the general ones. However, by the middle 1980s, John Horn had begun to conclude that the available research supported the presence of seven additional broad 'g' abilities beyond that of Gf and Gc and had abandoned the notion of a general 'g' factor. Although Horn retained the title 'Gf–Gc' (known as Cattell–Horn 'Gf–Gc') to describe the theory, there were actually nine dimensions to the intelligence theory, with an abbreviation accompanying each intelligence:

- fluid reasoning (Gf);
- acculturation knowledge intelligence (Gc);
- short-term apprehension and retrieval abilities (SAR);
- visual processing (Gv);
- auditory processing (Ga);
- tertiary storage and retrieval (TSR/Glm);

- processing speed (Gs);
- correct decision speed (CDS);
- quantitative knowledge (Gq).

Together, Carroll's and Cattell and Horn's work had dramatically informed people who were developing and using psychometric tests. One such person was Richard W. Woodcock (a US psychologist who has a wide background in education and psychology). With his colleague, M. B. Johnson, Woodcock developed a series of intelligence tests called the Woodcock–Johnson Psychoeducational Battery, of which the latest, Woodcock–Johnson Psychoeducational Battery – Revised: Tests of Cognitive Ability, is used for measuring cognitive ability for people aged 2 years and older. The test battery contains 21 different subtests and measures seven broad intellectual abilities, including auditory processing, comprehension knowledge, processing speed, visual process, short-term memory, long-term retrieval and fluid reasoning.

Woodcock had noticed that researchers and testers in the educational and applied psychometric testing field have struggled with the subtle differences between Horn's and Carroll's theories. Woodcock felt, as you may have noticed, that some amalgamation could be made between the two theories.

For example, although Cattell–Horn's model of intelligence didn't acknowledge a general 'g' factor, Carroll's did. Cattell–Horn's model emphasised a factor of quantitative knowledge that was not matched by Carroll, and both recognised similar factors such as:

- fluid intelligence (be it reasoning [Cattell–Horn, CH] or intelligence [Cattell, C]);
- crystallised intelligence (be it acculturation knowledge [CH] or crystallised intelligence [C]);
- general memory and learning abilities (be it short-term apprehension and retrieval abilities [CH] or general memory and learning [C]);
- visual perception (be it visual processing [CH] or broad visual perception [C]);
- auditory perception (be it auditory processing [CH] or broad auditory perception [C]).

So, in 1999, Woodcock met with Horn and Carroll at Chapel Hill, North Carolina, to seek a more comprehensive model that would incorporate the similarities between their respective theoretical models, yet also acknowledge and incorporate their differences. Woodcock engaged Horn and Carroll in a sequence of conversations and private communications, and, as a result of those meetings, the Cattell–Horn–Carroll (CHC) theory of cognitive abilities was developed.

The CHC theory represents both the Cattell–Horn and Carroll models of intelligence and was first described in the psychological literature by Flanagan *et al.* (2000) and Lohman (2001).

There are two main strata in the CHC theory of cognitive abilities: a broad stratum (stratum II) and a narrow stratum (stratum I), with the abandonment of a general intelligence factor. Overall there are 16 intelligences in the broad stratum, with each of these being divided into a number of abilities that make up the narrow stratum (see Table 12.2).

The CHC model of intelligence shows an attempt to build a synthesis of several intelligence theories and measurements.

However, we might here see some of the difficulties in combining the theoretical approach to intelligence with the practical use of intelligence tests. Clearly, the expectations of individual factor analysis academics working in a research setting and of those working in the applied setting might differ slightly. While individual factor analysis academic researchers might ultimately be looking for a

Table 12.2 Cattell–Horn–Carroll (CHC) theory of cognitive abilities: a broad stratum (stratum II) and narrow stratum (stratum I)

Broad stratum (stratum II)	Narrow stratum (stratum I)
Fluid intelligence/Reasoning (Gf) – The use of mental operations to solve novel and abstract problems	General sequential (deductive) reasoning, inductive reasoning, quantitative reasoning, logical thinking and speed of reasoning
Crystallised intelligence/Knowledge (Gc) – Intelligence that is incorporated by individuals through a process of culture	Language development, lexical knowledge, listening ability, general (verbal) information, information about culture, communication ability, oral production and fluency, grammatical sensitivity, foreign language proficiency and foreign language aptitude
General (domain-specific) knowledge (Gkn) – Breadth and depth of acquired knowledge in specialised (not general) domains	Knowledge of English as a second language, knowledge of singing, skill in lip-reading, geography achievement, general science information, mechanical knowledge and knowledge of behavioural content
Visual-spatial abilities (Gv) – The ability to invent, remember, retrieve and transform visual images	Visualisation, spatial relations, closure speed, flexibility of closure, visual memory, spatial scanning, serial perceptual integration, length estimation, perceptual illusions, perceptual alternations and imagery
Auditory processing (Ga) – Abilities around hearing	Phonetic coding, speech sound discrimination, resistance to auditory stimulus, distortion memory for sound patterns, general sound discrimination, temporal tracking, musical discrimination and judgement, maintaining and judging rhythm, sound-intensity/duration discrimination, sound-frequency discrimination, hearing and speech threshold factors, absolute pitch and sound localisation
Short-term memory (Gsm) – The ability to encode, be aware of information in the short-term memory	Memory span and working memory
Long-term storage and retrieval (Glr) – The ability to store information in long-term memory	Associative memory, meaningful memory, free recall memory, ideational fluency, associational fluency, expressional fluency, naming facility, word fluency, figural fluency, figural flexibility, sensitivity to problems, originality/creativity and learning abilities
Cognitive processing speed (Gs) – The ability to perform cognitive tasks automatically and fluently	Perceptual speed, rate of test-taking, number facility, speed of reasoning, reading speed and writing speed
Decision/Reaction time or speed (Gt) – The ability to react and make decisions quickly in response to simple stimuli	Simple reaction time, choice reaction time, semantic processing speed, mental comparison speed and inspection time
Psychomotor speed (Gps) – The ability to perform body motor movements rapidly and fluently	Speed of limb movement, writing speed, speed of articulation and movement time
Quantitative knowledge (Gq) – A personal breadth and depth of other abilities gained primarily during formal educational experiences of mathematics	Mathematical knowledge and mathematical achievement
Reading/Writing (Grw) – Abilities relating to reading and writing skills and knowledge	Reading decoding, reading comprehension, printed language comprehension, cloze ability, spelling ability, writing ability, English usage knowledge, reading speed and writing speed
Psychomotor abilities (Gp) – Ability to perform body motor movements with precision and coordination	Static strength, multilimb coordination, finger dexterity, manual dexterity, arm–hand steadiness, control precision, aiming and gross body equilibrium
Olfactory abilities (Go) – Abilities relating to the sense of smell	Olfactory memory and olfactory sensitivity
Tactile abilities (Gh) – Abilities that depend on the sense of touch	Tactile sensitivity
Kinaesthetic abilities (Gk) – Abilities that depend on the sense that detects bodily position, weight or movement of the muscles, tendons and joints	Kinaesthetic sensitivity

definitive model of intelligence, those individuals working in the psychometric test area might be looking not only for a definitive model of intelligence but also to develop an intelligence test that measures many aspects of intelligence (even those that are less popular) so they can produce a strong product that is of most use.

We can see that with the transfer of Carroll's work into applied test situations, his model of intelligence does not come through as strongly as it once seemed. Carroll's work seems to have led intelligence testing to a pinnacle by providing all sorts of definitive answers, with over 460 data sets on intelligence. However, following the meeting with educational test publishers, there seems to be a deviation from Carroll's concise eight-factor model to a more convoluted fifteen-factor model, which seems to satisfy the need of covering a number of possible dimensions in applied testing, but leaves us with the finding that some aspects of intelligence in this model (e.g. fluid intelligence and crystallised intelligence) are valid, comprehensive and more developed and understood than are other aspects (e.g. olfactory and tactile abilities).

Other theories of intelligence: Gardner and Sternberg

The CHC model shows a development of theory and measurement right up to the present day. However, there are two more theorists whose theories of intelligence are crucial in modern-day psychology: Howard Gardner and his theory of multiple intelligences and Robert Sternberg and his triarchic theory of human intelligence.

Howard Gardner: multiple intelligences

Howard Gardner is a Professor in Cognition and Education at the Harvard Graduate School of Education. His first concern is educational psychology. A lot of his work in this area favours and informs educational theory and practice, and to some extent is wary of the crossover between scientific study and educational practice (Gardner, 1983).

Gardner feels that there are difficulties with transferring scientific findings in intelligence to educational settings. He suggests that any findings in science may not be compatible with educational settings, as science demands objectivity, quantifiable data and direct measurement, while in education, researchers are dealing with children and applied settings and need more versatile methods. You can see how the more scientific aspects of intelligence testing do not translate easily into the classroom, where teachers are wrestling with improving the intelligence of children within all sorts of constraints, including the child's interest, their interactions with other children and their family background.

Gardner feels that there are some myths in traditional intelligence theory. One is that many intelligence theorists see intelligence as a sensory system. Gardner's view is that intelligence does not depend on an individual's sensory system; rather, intelligence is the sum of the processes that can take place, no matter what the sensory system. So, for example, linguistic intelligence can be demonstrated with all the senses, via being able to express oneself intelligently about what one sees, hears, tastes, touches and smells. Similarly, Gardner disagrees with theories of intelligence that suggest intelligence is the same as a learning mechanism, or a way of working. Rather, he describes intelligence as a computer that works more or less well.

Gardner's background is to challenge some of the assumptions of intelligence theory and IQ testing, particularly in education. He says that western educational systems tend to tailor their system of teaching around the logical-mathematical and the linguistic intelligences rather than other intelligences, such as interpersonal intelligences. He argues that this approach leads to bias in the education system, as teaching favours those children who are strong in specific intelligences (logical-mathematical and linguistic intelligences) over those who are not strong in those intelligences but are strong in other intelligences (such as interpersonal skills). In all, Gardner identifies nine intelligences (Gardner, 1983; 1998; Gardner *et al.*, 1996).

In 1983 Gardner first suggested that there were seven distinct intelligences. The first three are recognisable from conventional intelligence theory and IQ tests:

- linguistic (language skills);
- logical-mathematical (numerical skills);
- spatial (understanding relationships in space).

However, Gardner also included these four intelligences:

- musical (skills such as playing an instrument);
- bodily kinaesthetic (using the body);
- interpersonal (understanding and relating to others);
- intrapersonal (understanding oneself).

After 1996, Gardner suggested there are two other intelligences:

- **naturalist** – ability to interact with nature; people who are high in this intelligence might also excel at meteorology and biology;
- **existentialist** – ability to understand one's surroundings and place in the grand scheme of things. This intelligence might be linked to spiritual thinking.

Gardner explained that, within his theory, each intelligence resides in separate sections of the brain; they are independent of each other and exist as single entities without control from any other intelligence or central function of the brain. However, Gardner felt that they do interact and work together when needed. For example, being able to dance and

Is this a form of intelligence?
Source: Alamy Images/BananaStock

sing at the same time requires the interaction of musical and bodily kinaesthetic intelligences; solving a mathematical puzzle with a group may require logical-mathematical and interpersonal intelligence. He also argued that each individual has a separate set of intelligences, unlike those of others. Two people might have musical intelligence, but one might be able to sing while another can play the piano. Similarly, two people might have logical-mathematical intelligence, but one might be good with theoretical mathematics while another might be good with the real world of mathematics and applied statistics.

Gardner's theory of multiple intelligences challenges the 'general intelligence' theory; that is, that intelligence can be understood as one factor. Gardner argues that each intelligence is a separate dimension that is independent of the others. For example, whether someone has a high level of musical intelligence has no bearing on his linguistic intelligence. Theoretically, Gardner says each intelligence can be measured, but not through traditional general intelligence/IQ tests. Rather, it should be assessed through the activities engaged in by children at school (Gardner *et al.*, 1996). He also suggests that a precise measurement of all these different intelligences would require an extremely long test to be devised.

Although some authors (Sternberg, 2000) have suggested that Gardner's theory needs wider examination and testing before it can be accepted as a valid theory, it represents an interesting approach. It attempts to explore a number of intelligences not commonly identified in intelligence testing.

Profile

Howard Gardner

Howard Gardner was born in Philadelphia, Pennsylvania, in 1943. His parents were refugees from Nazi Germany. His favourite childhood pastime was playing the piano, and he cites music as being important in his life. He studied at Harvard University, originally as a developmental psychologist and then later as a neuropsychologist.

Howard Gardner is now Professor of Cognition and Education at the Harvard Graduate School of Education. He also holds positions at Harvard University and is Senior Director of Harvard Project Zero, a research group in human cognition that has a focus on the arts to achieve more personalised curriculum, instruction and assessment in educational settings.

Gardner is the author of over 20 books, the best known being *Frames of Minds* (1983), *The Art and Science of Changing Our Own and Other People's Minds* (Harvard Business School Press, 2004) and *Making Good: How Young People Cope with Moral Dilemmas at Work* (Harvard University Press, 2004).

Gardner has received numerous prizes for his work. He also has received honorary degrees from 20 colleges and universities, including institutions in Ireland, Italy and Israel.

Robert Sternberg

You have already been introduced to Robert Sternberg and his work on implicit theories of intelligence (Chapter 11). However, Sternberg himself (1985b; 1988) has developed a theory called the triarchic theory of intelligence. In this theory Sternberg identifies three different types of intelligence in terms of subtheories (however, these theories sometimes go by different names, depending on the audience):

- **Componential subtheory** – this subtheory refers to the mental mechanisms that underlie intelligent behaviour.
- **Contextual subtheory** – this subtheory describes how mental mechanisms interact with the external world to demonstrate intelligent behaviour.
- **Experiential subtheory** – this subtheory describes how experience interacts with the internal and the external world to form intelligence behaviours.

The componential subtheory

This subtheory of intelligence is sometimes referred to as *internal* aspects of intelligence and was described as *analytic* intelligence by the APA Task Force (see Chapter 11). The componential subtheory refers to the internal mechanisms that underlie intelligent behaviour. Sternberg described three sets of components (hence the name 'componential') that reflect these internal mechanisms of intelligent functioning.

- **Metacomponents** – these are mental mechanisms used by the individual to recognise a problem, to determine the exact nature of the problem and to develop strategies to solve the problem, allocating mental resources for solving the problem, monitoring the success of the strategy and evaluating the success of the efforts to solve the problem.
- **Performance components** – these are the processes actually involved in solving the problem. While the metacomponents form a type of executor that oversees the processing, the performance components are the processes that operate according to the plans laid down by the metacomponents. So, performance components are the processes involved in perceiving the problem, mentally generating a number of available solutions and comparing them.
- **Knowledge-acquisition components** – these include processes involved in acquiring and learning new material and using processes such as sifting out relevant from irrelevant information (Sternberg called this selective encoding), putting together new information into a whole (Sternberg called this selective combination) and comparing the new information with old information (Sternberg called this selective comparison).

These components are perhaps the hardest part of the triarchic theory of intelligence to distinguish between. So, we will give you a simplified example to illustrate how the componential subtheory might work. In this example, we are stepping a little outside of the model because much of it is to do with internal working of the mind. However, imagine doing an essay for one of your academic modules. You have started, but you are beginning to wonder whether you are getting it right.

Your *metacomponents* would do these things:

- start you to think about whether you are getting the essay right;
- start you to assess to what extent you are sure you are getting the essay right;
- suggest the development of strategies to ensure (reassure yourself) that you're getting the essay right;
- suggest that you check that any strategy adopted is successful.

Your *performance components* would do these things:
- determine whether you think you need any extra help with the essay;
- identify the possible different sources of help; that is, seeking advice from a lecturer, seeking advice from other students on the course, doing more reading or doing some more planning;
- determine which might be more effective strategies to be employed first; for example, talking to a lecturer;
- determine whether talking to the lecturer has been a successful strategy. (Did the lecturer tell you what you had already written, or did they give you more ideas?)

Your *knowledge-acquisition components* would (after you had spoken to the lecturer) do these things:

- sift out the information that is important to your essay (new ideas and new theories), separating it from irrelevant information (material that the lecturer may have used to illustrate an example but that shouldn't be used in an academic essay);
- combine the different pieces of information that were given to you by the lecturer so it all fits together and can be added to your essay;
- determine how this material can be integrated into the current content of your essay.

Remember that all these actions would have occurred in your mind when working through the problem of determining whether you were on the right lines in your essay. As such, this is all intelligence behaviour. The componential subtheory represents a mental analysis of a potential problem through general strategic thinking processes (metacomponents), specific problem-solving thinking processes (performance components) and information-processing processes (knowledge-acquisition components).

As we indicated earlier, Sternberg described the metacomponents as comprising higher-level processes, while the performance and knowledge-acquisition components are lower-level processes. For Sternberg, it is the metacomponents that represent what we know as 'g' (general intelligence), which is measured by the more traditional intelligence tests.

The contextual subtheory

This subtheory of intelligence is sometimes referred to as *external* aspects of intelligence and was described as *practical* by the APA Task Force. The second part of the triarchic theory involves the application of the componential subtheory (metacomponents, performance components and knowledge-acquisition components) in the real world; that is, their practical application.

Whereas the componential subtheory addresses internal mechanisms, the contextual subtheory sees what drives these components in the real world. That is, our internal dimensions of intelligence are forever interacting with the external world, and the context of the external world also determines our intelligence behaviour. Sternberg sees intelligence as forming within the context of three external dimensions: adaptation, shaping and selection.

- **Adaptation** – this dimension sees the individual's intelligence behaviour as adapting to the world around the individual. So, for example, people at university have learnt (adapted to) what constitutes intelligent behaviour in writing essays, performing well in exams, solving problems, presenting and talking to others.

The other two external world contexts arise when the individual is not satisfied with their ability to adapt their present and existing external world.

- **Shaping** – this dimension involves the individual adapting the environment to the individual, rather than the other way round. Sternberg thought this an important aspect of intelligence thought and behaviour, because it explained original thought and behaviour such as that of the great scientists who identified scientific theories and models rather than simply following them.
- **Selection** – this dimension involves choosing one environment over another. Often, individuals have choices about the external world in which they exist. For example, you may have a choice of doing two psychology projects: one involves developing questionnaires, collecting quantitative data and using statistical analysis techniques; the other involves collecting interview data by talking to people and assessing their responses. You may feel that your intelligence abilities are best based around using quantitative data and mathematical techniques, and consequently you would select the first project.

Unlike some aspects of componential subtheory that were measurable via traditional general intelligence tests, Sternberg needed to measure contextual subtheory (practical intelligence). To do so, he used a concept called tacit knowledge.

Sternberg *et al.*, (1995) defined tacit knowledge as 'action-oriented knowledge', usually learned without the help of others, or as direct instruction that allows people to achieve goals they personally value. Tacit knowledge is based on understanding procedures rather than facts; that is, knowledge about how to do something rather than knowledge about it. Largely, measures of tacit knowledge have been used in applied settings, particularly in a business setting to assess job performance. However, an example more suited to you involves the findings of research carried out by Nancy Leonard and Gary Insch (Leonard and Insch, 2005). This study looked at students' use of tacit knowledge in higher education; that is, procedures and processes (tacit knowledge) that led to success as a student rather than simple knowledge of facts. Leonard and Insch found, among 428 undergraduate students, that the following six aspects of tacit knowledge were important in education:

- cognitive self-motivation skills (e.g. attending class regularly and making time to study);
- cognitive self-organisation skills (e.g. showing self-control and staying on task);
- individual technical skills (e.g. speaking with lecturer after class and asking the lecturer questions);
- institutional technical skills (e.g. setting regular study times and meeting regularly with lecturers and advisers);
- task-related interaction skills (e.g. participating in student-organised study groups and getting to know other students in a class);
- social interaction skills (e.g. participating actively in different activities on campus and getting involved in campus clubs and societies).

The tests that measure tacit knowledge are domain-specific tests. That is, they are designed for particular areas of intelligence such as intelligence in business and intelligence in the army rather than as a measure of general intelligence across the population, which is the case with more traditional general intelligence tests.

The experiential subtheory

This subtheory of intelligence relates to aspects of experience and was referred to as *creative* intelligence by the APA Task Force. The experiential subtheory examines how experience interacts with intelligence in terms of the individual's internal world and the external world. Sternberg recognised that information-processing components are always applied to tasks and situations where the person has some level of previous experience of those tasks and situations. Sternberg identified two aspects of the experiential subtheory.

- **Novelty** – the ability to deal with relative novelty is a good way of assessing intelligence. People who are good at managing a novel situation can often solve it, and most people would not notice. For example, you may be given

Stop and think

Applying for a job

Imagine you are applying for the following job. This was a real job advertised in 2004.

Title: Part-time Research Assistant (.3 for 6 months)

Grade: R & AIA (Grade 6)

Department: Psychology

Main purpose of post

The appointee will take a role in an evaluation study, funded by the Learning and Teaching Support Network in Psychology, examining the usefulness of using mathematical puzzles to aid the learning of statistical concepts. The evaluation work is taking part on two university sites.

The main role of the appointee is to collect and analyse interview data with undergraduate students to enable evaluation of the usefulness of mathematical puzzles in aiding the learning of statistical concepts. The appointee will be expected to collect data on both of the aforementioned university sites. The post is a .3 post, which comprises 1 and a half days a week. There is a small travel budget available for travelling between the Leicester and Sheffield university sites.

Duties and responsibilities

- To assist the main researcher in undertaking the work supported by the Learning and Teaching Support Network in Psychology
- To interview 1st-year undergraduate students regarding learning experiences
- To provide a preliminary analysis of interview data

Personal specifications

Essential criteria:

- Have a relevant first degree
- Some experience of collecting data, particularly within university settings
- The ability to communicate effectively with research participants
- Some experience of computers, mainly word processing

Desirable criteria:

- Some experience of introductory statistics

Consider the Cattell–Horn–Carroll and Gardner's and Sternberg's theories of intelligence. Think about how, if you were to apply for the job, you might use each theory and the terms of the theory to show the prospective interview panel that you were an intelligent individual suitable for the job.

---

an exam in a particular topic and, although you may not have taken an exam in that academic area before, you may use your experience of other exams (how to revise, plan and how to present ideas) to do well at this new exam. Consequently, intelligent thinking and behaviour can emerge from an individual taking advantage or learning from one's experiences to solve new problems.

- **Automation** – the ability to automatise information is a key aspect of intelligence. Automation is an ability that has been performed many times and can now be done with little or no extra thought. Once a process is automatised, it can be run in parallel with the same or other processes. An example of this is reading. Remember your development from reading out loud in a deliberate fashion, concentrating on every syllable (and … the … stu … dent … said … to … the … lec … tu … rer) to reading silently and quickly. Now you can read the subtitles of a foreign film without it spoiling your appreciation of the visuals of the film.

Sternberg's theory is very influential in psychology, and we will see more of his work later (Chapter 16) when discussing

giftedness, wisdom and creativity. However, a lot of Sternberg's work remains relatively unexamined empirically. For example, although he has developed the Sternberg Triarchic Abilities Test, it is still an unpublished research instrument.

Final comments

Overall, in this discussion we have taken you from the earliest conceptions of intelligence in psychology (Galton, Binet), through many of the major theorists (Spearman, Cattell, Carroll), major measures of intelligence and its estimation (the Wechsler and Raven's Matrices IQ tests, IQ and deviation IQ), multifactoral and hierarchical model (Guilford and Carroll) and modern-day theorists (Gardner and Sternberg). Taken together, you should now have an understanding of how intelligence, both the concept and its measurement, has developed for over a century. In the next three discussions (Chapters 13–15) we aim to develop some of the ideas and look at many of the debates and controversies that surround intelligence.

Summary

- Galton is the forefather of intelligence tests. His central hypothesis was that there are differences in intelligence, and he set out to explore this hypothesis.
- Alfred Binet created the first intelligence test. In 1905, with Theodore Simon, Binet produced the Binet–Simon scale, the first intelligence test, which Simon later described as 'practical, convenient, and rapid'.
- Terman began to recognise the need for 'standardised testing'.
- William Stern developed the idea of the intelligence quotient or, as it is more popularly known today, IQ.
- Yerkes developed a group intelligence test, resulting in the Army Alpha and Army Beta tests.
- Charles Spearman introduced a two-factor theory of intelligence. The first factor of intelligence was specific abilities, 's'. The second factor was what Spearman thought was underlying all the positive correlations between intelligence tests – general ability, 'g'.
- In 1939 Wechsler published the first of the Wechsler tests, the Wechsler–Bellevue Scale. Later he introduced two tests that are still used today: the Wechsler Adult Intelligence Scale (WAIS) and the Wechsler Intelligence Scale for Children (WISC). Alongside these tests, he published a new way of calculating IQ through the use of standard deviations.
- Scottish psychologist John Carlyle Raven first published his Progressive Matrices in 1938. His test was a non-verbal measure of 'g'.
- Thurstone agreed with Spearman's hypothesis of a general factor of intelligence. However, he viewed 'g' differently from Spearman. Thurstone argued that 'g' results from, rather than lies behind, seven primary mental abilities.
- Cattell acknowledged Spearman's work in accepting that there was general intelligence, but he suggested that 'g' comprises two related but distinct components: crystallised intelligence and fluid intelligence.
- Guilford disagreed with the stance of Spearman and, to some extent, with Thurstone and Cattell; he did not acknowledge the existence of 'g'. Instead, Guilford (1977) eventually proposed that intelligence was the result of 150 independent abilities. His theory was named the Structure of Intellect (SI) theory.
- Vernon described intelligence as a hierarchy. Vernon thought that 'g' accounts for the largest amount of variability among humans. The next level in Vernon's hierarchy comprises two major group factors, then minor group factors and then specific factors.
- Carroll (1993) proposed a hierarchical model of intelligence, the Three-Stratum Model of Human Cognitive Abilities. Stratum I comprises specific levels of intelligence, stratum II is made up of eight broad factors arising from these specific abilities and stratum III is the general level of intelligence representing general intellectual ability, similar to 'g'.
- Gardner suggested there are nine distinct intelligences, resulting in his multiple intelligence theory.
- Sternberg developed the triarchic theory of intelligence, with intelligence comprising componential, contextual and experiential subtheories.

Connecting up

This chapter is a forerunner for Chapters 13 and 14 in this section. You may need to access (online) Chapter 27 of this book, which explains statistical techniques and particularly factor analysis.

We saw in this chapter the issues that occur between theory and research and practice in trying to arrive at a good theoretical definition and measurement of intelligence. We will see these issues repeated when we explore emotional intelligence (Chapter 15) and the difficulties of applying personality and intelligence constructs to education and the workplace (Chapter 16).

Critical thinking

Discussion questions

- When discussing intelligence, you really need to think about how all these different intelligence theories fit together. Should you reject 'g' as a valid theory as some theorists have done, or is it a simple and influential idea of intelligence that has helped researchers define and refine ideas about intelligence?

- What are your views on whether 'g' exists?
- Discuss and explain the advantages of culture-free intelligence tests over traditional intelligence tests. Are culture-free intelligence tests problem-free?
- What is your view of how many 'intelligences' there are?
- Which of the theories of intelligence do you think are strongest?
- Should the measurement of intelligence combine verbal and non-verbal problems?
- Gardner identified musical skills as a form of intelligence. Why do you think Gardner chose music and not other arts like painting or acting?
- Can we consider particular forms of body movement (such as gymnastics, sport and dance) as forms of intelligence?
- Without intelligence tests, there would be no intelligence theory. Without intelligence theory, there would be no intelligence tests. Discuss.

Essay questions

- Critically discuss the view that there is a single factor of intelligence.
- Critically compare Spearman's theory of 'g' with alternative theories of intelligence.
- Critically discuss the concept of intelligence and comment on psychologists' attempts to define and measure it.
- Critically discuss Gardner's theory of intelligence.
- Critically compare classical theories of intelligence against modern theories of intelligence in the way these theories describe the existence of 'g'.
- Critically discuss the role that factor analysis has had in informing theories of intelligence.
- Critically discuss how hierarchical theories of intelligence inform the debate about the nature of intelligence.
- Critically examine the role of intelligence tests in the development of intelligence theory.

Going further

Books

- Robert J. Sternberg (ed.) (2000). *Handbook of intelligence*. Cambridge: Cambridge University Press.
- N. J. Mackintosh (1998). *IQ and human intelligence*. Oxford: Oxford University Press.
- Gardner, H. (1983). *Frames of mind: The theory of multiple intelligences*. New York: Basic Books.

Journals

- Sternberg, R. J. and Kaufman, J. C. (1998). Human abilities. *Annual Review of Psychology, 49*, 479–502. *Annual Review of Psychology* is published by Annual Reviews, Palo Alto, California. Available online via Business Source Premier.
- Gottfredson, L. S. (1997). Why g matters: The complexity of everyday life. *Intelligence, 24*, 79–132. Published by Elsevier Science. Available online via Science Direct.
- *Intelligence: A Multidisciplinary Journal.* This journal in psychology is devoted to publishing original research and theoretical studies and review papers that substantially contribute to the understanding of intelligence. It provides a new source of significant papers in psychometrics, tests and measurement as well as all other empirical and theoretical studies in intelligence and mental retardation. Published by Elsevier Science. Available online via Science Direct.

- An article on Charles Spearman appeared in *The Psychologist*, Perks, J. (2006). Spearman and the importance of archives. *The Psychologist, 10*, 722–725. This article is freely available online via the archive at **www.thepsychologist.org.uk**.

Web links

There are some classic intelligence papers that you can access on the web, including Spearman, Binet and Terman.

- Spearman, C. (1904). 'General intelligence', objectively determined and measured. *American Journal of Psychology, 15*, 201–293 (at **http://psychclassics.yorku.ca/Spearman**).
- Binet, A. (1905/1916). New methods for the diagnosis of the intellectual level of subnormals. In E. S. Kite (Trans.), *The Development of Intelligence in Children*. Vineland, NJ: Publications of the Training School at Vineland. (Originally published 1905 in *L'Année Psychologique, 12*, 191–244.) Available online (**http://psychclassics.yorku.ca/Binet/binet1.htm**).
- Terman, L. M. (1916). The uses of intelligence tests. From *The Measurement of Intelligence* (Chapter 1). Boston: Houghton Mifflin. Available online (**http://psychclassics.yorku.ca/Terman/terman1.htm**).
- You can find out more about Cattell, Horn and Carroll's integration of work here on IQ tests; available online (**http://www.2h.com/Tests/iqtrad.phtml**).

Film and literature

- If you are looking for an example of someone who shows a great deal of intelligence by his reasoning ability, then the complete series of Sherlock Holmes by Arthur Conan Doyle (containing four novels and 56 short stories) is an excellent example. However, you may feel that these stories, like the portrayal of intelligence, are dated. In that case the Morse series by Colin Dexter, the Rebus series by Ian Rankin and the Banks series by Peter Robinson are excellent alternatives. They also display more modern examples of reasoning ability.
- *A Beautiful Mind* (2001, directed by Ron Howard). If you would like to see a film about someone with a great intelligence, see this film about the life of John Forbes Nash Jr, a maths prodigy able to solve problems that baffled the greatest of minds.
- We outline Gardner's theory of multiple intelligences, one of which is bodily kinaesthetic – using the body. You may not be convinced that using the body constitutes intelligence. However, consider this view in light of Asian films such as *Hero* (2002, directed by Yimou Zhang) and *Crouching Tiger, Hidden Dragon* (2000; directed by Ang Lee), which emphasise intelligence as part of the movement of the body.

Explore the website accompanying this text at **www.pearsoned.co.uk/maltby** for further resources to help you with your studies. These include multiple-choice questions, essay questions, web links and ideas for advanced reading.

CHAPTER 13
The Use of Intelligence Tests:
What Questions Emerge from the Measurement of Intelligence?

Key themes

- Psychometric intelligence tests
- Cognitive, biological and physiological measures of intelligence
- Uses of intelligence tests
- Criticism of intelligence tests
- Flynn effect
- Cognitive stimulation
- Nutrition

Learning outcomes

After studying this discussion you should:

- Be familiar with modern themes in intelligence tests
- Understand the features and uses of popularly used intelligence tests
- Know about the general criticisms of or concerns with intelligence tests
- Be able to discuss advantages of the continued use of intelligence tests
- Understand what the Flynn effect is and the discussions that emerge from this phenomenon
- Be able to outline the cognitive stimulation and nutritional hypotheses of intelligence

Introduction

Intelligence matters in the modern world. In 1999 the UK government gathered together a group of education experts to: (1) advise education ministers on how best to make sure that children fulfil their potential; and (2) tackle what they saw as an ethos of underachievement in schools. As part of this effort, the government set up the Excellence in Cities scheme, aimed to help children living in the inner cities break out of poverty. Furthermore, in 2002 a National Academy for Gifted and Talented Youth was set up to provide special provision for those children thought to be in the top 5 per cent of intelligence. The European Union has introduced initiatives like REACH (which involves the proper Registration, Evaluation and Authorisation of Chemicals) because of the effect that chemicals can have on, among other things, our intelligence. Intelligence tests are used in government departments, in selecting for the civil service and in the Armed Forces. You can see from examples like these that even at the highest levels of society, with those who govern us, intelligence matters.

What we are going to do in this discussion is to begin to examine the role that intelligence and the measurement of intelligence plays in society. We have already discussed several ways that intelligence has been conceptualised and measured over much of the twentieth century (Chapter 12). Now we are going to start looking at intelligence tests in modern use and outlining the uses and the criticisms of these intelligence tests. We are going to expand our consideration of intelligence tests to include measures that emphasise cognitive, physiological and biological processes. We are also going to examine a particular finding in the intelligence literature, the Flynn effect. This effect, which details a rise in IQ scores across generations leads to an interesting debate in the intelligence literature and the emergence of two hypotheses about increases in IQ: the cognitive stimulation hypothesis and the nutrition hypothesis.

Source: Corbis/John Henley

Types of intelligence tests

In the previous discussion (Chapter 12) we outlined the theory and gave you examples of the types of intelligence tests used to measure intelligence. We discussed earlier intelligence researchers such as Galton and Binet, who suggested that we could measure intelligence. Galton suggested that we could measure variability in intelligence, and he began to show that this was true through tests of

sensory discrimination and motor coordination. Binet, meanwhile, was developing intelligence tests among children. His test, the Binet–Simon scale, used many of the techniques that we see in modern-day intelligence tests – items presented in an order of difficulty, varying techniques to assess intelligence and standardised scorings to determine IQ. Later we see work by Terman and Yerkes among US adults; this research introduced the idea of mass testing, deviation IQ and consideration of culture and culture-free specific tests. Later, Spearman's introduction of the notion of general intelligence ('g') led to the introduction of the Wechsler tests and Raven's Progressive Matrices. With the theoretical work of Cattell, Horn and Carroll we see the development of the Woodcock–Johnson Psychoeducational Battery–Revised: Tests of Cognitive Ability.

There are many intelligence tests in use today that reflect this theoretical and empirical growth in the understanding of intelligence and IQ. The Stanford–Binet test described previously (Chapter 12) is now in its fifth edition (Roid, 2003), and is used among people aged from 2 to 90+ years. It can still be used not only to compute an overall measure of IQ but also to assess fluid reasoning, knowledge, quantitative reasoning, visual-spatial processing and working memory as well as the ability to compare verbal and non-verbal performance. The Wechsler tests are still in use today, and comprise the Wechsler Preschool and Primary Scale of Intelligence (WPPSI) for use among 3- to 7-year-olds, the Wechsler Intelligence Scale for Children (WISC) for use among 7- to 16-year-olds and the Wechsler Adult Intelligence Scale (WAIS) for use among people who are 16 years and over. The scale contains measures of verbal and performance intelligence. The Woodcock–Johnson III Tests of Cognitive Abilities are used among people aged from 2 to 90+ years and also give an overall score of general intelligence (IQ score), as well as looking at working memory and executive function skills.

The distinction between the psychometric and the cognitive psychology approaches to intelligence testing

The aforementioned tests (and those covered in Chapter 12) have become known to represent the **psychometric** approach towards intelligence. This is because they are based on the findings of factor-analytic studies that have looked at the various psychometric properties of intelligence scales.

However, there is another set of intelligence tests that reflect a slightly different approach in intelligence testing, called the **cognitive psychology** approach. One notable feature of intelligence tests that fall within the cognitive psychology approach is that they highlight biological and physiological processes and aspects to intelligence. We are going to introduce you to some of these cognitive tests; first, however, we need to give you a historical context to such tests, notably the history of measuring biological and physiological aspects to intelligence.

Simple biological and physiological measures of intelligence

Our story of biological and physiological measures of intelligence begins with the observations that intelligence can be linked to biological and physiological factors. There is evidence that relatively simple biological and physiological measures of intelligence might be very good indicators of intelligence. We will illustrate two areas: brain size and a series of tests called elementary cognitive tasks (ECTs), evoked potentials (EPs) and response times (RTs).

Brain size and intelligence

One area of research is the idea that intelligent people have bigger brains. As far back as 1836, German anatomist and physiologist Frederick Tiedmann (Tiedmann, 1836) suggested that there is an indisputable connection between the size of a person's brain and their mental energy. Modern studies that have used magnetic resonance imaging (MRI) have allowed such an idea to be examined. MRI is a method of creating images of the inside of organs in living organisms, such as the brain. Researchers have been able to take images of the size of participants' brains and compare them to their overall intelligence score. Studies have shown that there is a relationship between brain size and IQ. Willerman *et al.* (1991) examined brain size and IQ among 40 US university students and reported a correlation of $r = 0.35$. Raz *et al.* (1993) reported a correlation of $r = 0.43$ between brain size and general intelligence among 29 adults aged between 18 and 78 years of age. In a meta-analysis of 37 samples across 1,530 people (McDaniel, 2005), US psychologist Michael McDaniel estimated the correlation between brain size and overall intelligence was 0.33. The correlation was higher for females than males and higher for adults than children. However, in all age and sex groups, brain volume is positively correlated with intelligence.

Elementary cognitive tasks and intelligence

One of the main advocates of more biological examination is Arthur Jensen, an American educational psychologist. In his book, *The g Factor: The Science of Mental Ability* (Jensen, 1998), he argues the case for using biological measures of intelligence. He calls these measures elementary cognitive tasks.

Elementary cognitive tasks (ECTs) are simple tasks used to measure different cognitive processes such as understanding stimuli, stimuli discrimination, choice, visual search and retrieval of information from both the short-term and long-term memory. All ECTs are designed to be simple, so that every person in the study can perform them easily, and performance must be measured in terms of response time. Consequently, an individual's intelligence, as measured through ECTs, is based on their response times to different tasks that involve understanding and identifying a stimulus, being able to discriminate between stimuli, searching visual stimuli and being able to memorise things. You will see researchers who use ECTs measuring response time in different ways, including these:

- **Reaction time** – this is a participant's median reaction time, representing the average response time over a number of trials.
- **Standard deviation of reaction time (RTSD)** – this task is a measure of variability; that is, to what extent do a participant's responses vary over a number of trials? For example, are response times all roughly the same (low standard deviation), or do the subject's response times vary enormously (high standard deviation)? Because of the variability of response times, the RTSD is sometimes recorded so that researchers can present a fuller consideration as to how much each individual varies in elementary cognitive skills.
- **Inspection time (IT)/evoked potential (EP)** – these response time measures indicate the sheer speed of perceptual discrimination (visual or auditory) and the time people take to process information. Participants are linked to an electroencephalogram (EEG) machine, which measures brain waves. The participant is then presented with either visual (a flash) or auditory (a loud click) stimuli. On the EEG machine, after the participant receives this stimulus, a spike appears in the brain waves. This spike is what has been 'evoked' by the stimulus. The time between the stimulus and the spike is thought to be a measure of intelligence, with a shorter gap between stimulus and response representing higher intelligence.

Measures of response times to ECTs are correlated with more traditional measures of intelligence. There is some debate about to what extent these tasks are related to intelligence tests. Jensen himself suggests that the correlations range from about $r = 0.10$ to $r = 0.50$, with the correlations averaging about $r = 0.35$. However, overall scores based on the use of various ECTs with different measures of response times typically are found to correlate with scores on general intelligence tests of between $r = 0.50$ and $r = 0.70$.

Jensen argues that ECTs can be used to measure general intelligence more accurately and analytically than conventional intelligence tests. This, he claims, is because many of the items in those intelligence tests are based on knowledge, reasoning and problem-solving – all of which combine several relatively complex cognitive processes. For Jensen, ECTs are useful because they involve no past learned information, or, if they do, the content is so well known that it is familiar to all people doing the ECT (e.g. responding to pictures of a cat or a dog). Jensen concedes that the physiological properties of the brain that might account for the speed-of-processing aspects of intelligence are not yet known completely; he suggests that this way of measuring intelligence taps into several different cognitive functions that compare differences in neurological intelligence among individuals.

Alexander Romanovich Luria

The inspiration for cognitive measures of intelligence begins with the work of Soviet psychologist Alexander Romanovich Luria, who is best known for his work in neuropsychology but who also contributed to cross-cultural psychology. He gained his degree in 1921 at the age of 19, after entering university at the age of 16.

Luria's earliest research involved devising methods for assessing Freudian ideas about abnormalities of thought and mental processes. A lot of Luria's work was concerned with measuring thought processes, but he was also concerned with making diagnoses based on them. For example, one of the first tests that Luria developed was a 'combined motor method' (Luria, 1932). This method was used for diagnosing the thought processes of individual subjects who were asked to carry out three tasks simultaneously. Participants were asked to hold one hand steady while using the other to repeatedly press a key or squeeze a rubber ball and to respond verbally to experimenters' questions.

However, Luria's major contributions started in 1924, when he worked with Lev Semyonovich Vygotsky and Alexei Nikolaevitch Leontiev. Vygotsky was a Russian psychologist who had already made a huge contribution to conceptualising intelligence. Vygotsky influenced modern constructivist thinking, which is an area of psychology that emphasises knowledge as a value-laden, subjective construction rather than a passive acquisition of objective facts and features. That is, social meaning is an important influence on human thought and intelligence. Vygotsky also argued that, unlike animals, who react only to their environment, human beings are able to alter the environment extensively for their own purposes. Vygotsky's approach to intelligence emphasises it as a process of activity rather than a solid aspect that never changes. Within this work Luria, Vygotsky and Leontiev developed a psychological approach that accounted for how physical development and sensory mechanisms intertwine with culture to produce psychological processes and function in adults, including intelligence. The approach of Vygotsky and his colleagues encompassed aspects of 'cultural', 'historical' and 'instrumental' psychology. These researchers emphasised that these three aspects are important in understanding psychological functioning and intelligence; they also greatly emphasised the role of culture, the social environment and particularly language in influencing human thoughts, feelings and action.

From this work Luria sought to elaborate this cultural–historical–instrumental psychology. Luria was particularly interested in developing a comprehensive theory of brain and behaviour and focused on neurological connections. One of Luria's main contributions to psychology was to question the early assumption that all the processing of visual information, perception and visual imagery occurred within the right cerebral hemisphere of the brain and that the processing of auditory information, verbal expression and propositional thinking occurred in the left hemisphere of the brain (see Figure 13.1 for a breakdown of the processes of the brain).

Luria (1973) was one of the first academics who questioned this distinction and thought it too simplistic. He suggested that the left hemisphere of the brain contains greater cognitive power and viewed it as a source of conscious control of behaviour, with the right hemisphere of the brain responsible for automatic and subconscious aspects of behaviour not under the conscious control of the brain. Luria also distinguished between simultaneous (processing that happens all at once) and successive (characterised by a series or sequence of events) cognitive processing. **Simultaneous processing** is cognitive processing that allows individuals to explore and discover relationships between components of information and to integrate this information, leading to spatial awareness. For example, this is the sort of thinking that would allow you to gather information for an essay from several texts and then put it together into a new essay. **Successive processing** enables individuals to put information into a serial order. For example, to learn how to perform a statistical test on a computer, you must do it in a particular order to get the result. Luria thought successive processing occurred in the frontotemporal regions of the brain and simultaneous processing occurred in the occipital–parietal region of the brain.

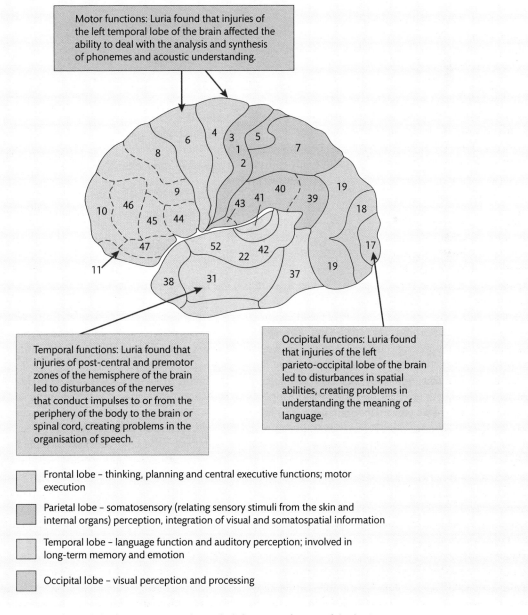

Figure 13.1 Summary of Luria's findings using Brodmann's definitions of areas of the brain.

During the 1930s Luria investigated perception, problem-solving and memory and specialised in the study of injuries to the higher cortical parts of the brain (those areas of the brain that deal with complex functions such as language or reading). With this approach, he compared and examined patients with brain injuries, using the results to understand how brain functions and higher functions such as language were intrinsically linked together. By studying these results, Luria was able to single out basic neuropsychological factors underlying speech. He was able to identify the following links:

- Injuries of the left temporal lobe of the brain affect the ability to deal with the analysis and synthesis of phonemes (the smallest sounds in a language capable of conveying a distinction in meaning, i.e. the 'm' in 'mum') and acoustic understanding (indicated by the pink motor functions box in Figure 13.1).
- Injuries of post-central and premotor zones of the left hemisphere of the brain lead to disturbances of the nerves that conduct impulses to or from the periphery of the body to the brain or spinal cord and create problems in the organisation of speech (indicated by the green temporal functions box in Figure 13.1).
- Injuries of the left parieto-occipital lobe of the brain lead to disturbances in spatial abilities, creating problems in understanding the meaning of language (indicated by the mauve occipital functions box in Figure 13.1).

If all these aspects of intelligence can be affected by neurological functions, you can then see why it must be acknowledged that these functions and their development are important to intelligence.

What was significant in Luria's work was that he didn't seek just to diagnose these neurological malfunctions, but to remedy them. Luria produced a variety of methodological approaches; but he never produced a test, because he believed that each patient was different, and the tests he used would need to be adapted for each patient. Luria published two case studies, both published a few years before his death. One study describes a man with an excellent but idiosyncratic (temperamental) memory, and the other describes a man with a traumatic brain injury (Luria, 1968; 1972). In both cases, Luria showed how it was possible to combine classical diagnostic methods with methods that sought to remedy neurological problems to improve the consequences of the brain injury.

It is Luria's emphasis on neurological functioning, his distinction between simultaneous and sequential processing and his emphasis on using tests to both diagnose the problem and improve performance, centred on the individual, that have influenced the work of current-day researchers, who have developed cognitive psychology intelligence tests. We will now outline two modern-day cognitive psychology intelligence tests that have been influenced by the biological and physiological work of Luria:

- J. P. Das and Jack Naglieri's cognitive assessment system;
- Alan and Naneen Kaufman's ability tests.

Das and Naglieri's cognitive assessment system and the Kaufmans' ability tests

Both Das and Naglieri and the Kaufmans have developed models and tests of IQ. These tests are based on biological and psychophysiological models of intelligence.

Das and Naglieri's Cognitive Assessment System (CAS)

In 1979, J. P. Das and colleagues (Das *et al.,* 1979) developed a successive-simultaneous test based on Luria's theory and validated the model with several studies of children. Within this test, Das used the simultaneous-sequential distinction made by Luria. It was this distinction, and this test, that became the basis of the cognitive assessment system (Naglieri and Das, 1997).

The **cognitive assessment system (CAS)** is an IQ test designed to measure cognitive processing, integrating theoretical and applied areas of psychological knowledge, thereby assessing how knowledge is organised and accessed in the memory system as well as assessing how various intellectual tasks are achieved. The model that Naglieri and Das devised to measure IQ is the PASS system (PASS stands for planning, attention, simultaneous and successive).

Naglieri and Das define each aspect of the PASS model as follows:

- **Planning** – this is a set of decisions or strategies that an individual not only uses but adapts to solve a problem and/or reach a goal. Within the CAS, planning is measured by presenting the participant with a task and asking them to develop some approach to complete the task efficiently and effectively.
- **Attention** – in the CAS, this refers to alertness or awareness of stimuli and is seen as important and a prerequisite for learning and memory. Attention tasks in the CAS require the individual to select one aspect and ignore the other aspect of a two-dimensional stimulus.
- **Simultaneous processes** – in Luria's theory, simultaneous processes reflect a person's ability or facility to see associations and integrate single and separate pieces of information. Simultaneous tasks in the CAS require the individual to put together different parts of a particular item in a meaningful way (i.e. complete a pattern) to arrive at the correct answer.
- **Successive processes** – in Luria's theory, successive processes represent the ability to place and maintain things in a particular order. Successive tasks in the CAS require the participants to order or reproduce a particular

sequence of events or answer some questions that require correct interpretation of the order of the events.

The CAS is used among children and adolescents between the ages of 5 and 17 years. The test not only predicts achievement and looks for discrepancies between ability and achievement, but uses the measures of planning and attention employed in the evaluation of attention deficits and hyperactivity disorders, learning disabilities, giftedness and brain injuries. The CAS helps practitioners and teachers to choose interventions for children with learning problems and to work with them to address those problems.

The Kaufmans' ability tests

Alan and Naneen Kaufman have developed a number of ability tests, including the Kaufman Assessment Battery for Children (K-ABC), Kaufman Brief Intelligence Test (K-BIT) and the Kaufman Adolescent and Adult Intelligence Test (KAIT). These tests are based again on research and theory in cognition and neuropsychology, although the Kaufmans draw not only on Luria's neuropsychological model but also on the Cattell–Horn–Carroll (CHC) approach (discussed in Chapter 12). One major aim of the Kaufmans' work is to address the number of children who are referred for evaluation with learning problems. The Kaufmans suggest that one reason for this increase is that a lot of school-based tasks are measures of verbal intelligence (vocabulary, general knowledge, oral arithmetic), and a lot of the children who are referred for help for learning problems are bilingual or bicultural. Using their test approach, the authors believe they can make meaningful school-based recommendations for children based on cognitive processes rather than cultural knowledge.

Profile

Alan S. Kaufman

Alan S. Kaufman, PhD, is Professor of Psychology at the Yale University School of Medicine, Child Study Center. Dr Kaufman was born in Brooklyn, New York, in April 1944. He earned his undergraduate degree from the University of Pennsylvania in 1965, his MA in Educational Psychology from Columbia University in 1967 and his PhD from Columbia University in 1970, where he studied under Robert L. Thorndike.

In 1968, Kaufman went to work as Assistant Director at The Psychological Corporation. There, he worked with David Wechsler on a revision of the Wechsler Intelligence Scale for Children. He worked at the University of Georgia in 1974 and at the University of Alabama starting in 1984 before taking his current position at Yale in 1995.

Kaufman is best known for his development of the Kaufman Assessment Battery for Children, which has been translated, adapted for and standardised in more than 15 countries. He has also developed a variety of other psychological and educational tests, including the Kaufman Brief Intelligence Test (K-BIT), the Kaufman Adolescent and Adult Intelligence Test (KAIT), the Kaufman Short Neuropsychological Assessment Procedure (K-SNAP) and the Kaufman Functional Academic Skills Test (K-FAST).

During his career he has published around 20 books and more than 200 journal articles. His books include the well-cited *Assessing Adolescent and Adult Intelligence* (1990), which is now into its third edition, with Liz Lichtenberger, published in 2005. He was a co-editor of the journal *Research in the Schools* from 1992 to 2004 and has been on the editorial board of five professional journals.

Stop and think

The British ability scales

Also worth noting alongside the IQ tests are the British Ability Scales. The British Ability Scales, now in their second edition, were developed by Colin Elliot (Elliot, 1983; 1996). The British Ability Scales are an individually administered cognitive battery for children, combining both the psychometric and cognitive approaches that we have outlined so far. The British Ability Scales are organised as follows:

- **Core and achievement scales** – block building; verbal comprehension; picture similarities; naming vocabulary, early number concepts; copying; block design; recall of designs; word definitions; matrices; similarities; quantitative reasoning, basic number skills; spelling and word reading.
- **Diagnostic scales** – matching letter-like forms; recall of digits; digits backwards; recall of objects; recognition of pictures; speed of information processing.

Sequential processing/short-term memory
'Say the numbers just as I do.'

2 – 9
6 – 4 – 3 – 1
8 – 10 – 5 – 2 – 6 – 4 – 3 – 9 – 1

(a) Number recall: The child says a series of numbers in the same sequence as the examiner recites them. The length of sequence increases from two to nine digits.

(b) Hand movements: The responses to this test are non-verbal. The child performs a series of hand movements in the same sequence as the examiners shows him or her.

(c) Word order: This subtest asks each child to respond by touching silhouettes of common objects after the examiner repeats their names in sequence.

Simultaneous/visual processing

(d) Conceptual thinking: This test for children ages 3–6 requires the examinee to look at a group of 4–5 pictures and identify the one that is not like the others.

(e) Triangles: Children are asked to copy or build designs using coloured triangles or plastic shapes of different sizes of colours.

Figure 13.2 *(Continues)*

(f) Rover: This subtest asks children to move a dog towards a bone through a checkerboard-like grid that includes obstacles. It requires the child to picture different possible routes and then select the shortest.

(g) Block counting: Shown a picture of a stack of blocks (some of which are hidden), the child must visualise the unseen blocks and determine how many there are in the stack.

(h) Gestalt closure: This subtest uses incomplete pictures to measure a child's ability to fill in gaps to identify an image.

Figure 13.2 Examples of the Kaufman's tests, including items measuring simultaneous and sequential processing. Both the Kaufman and cognitive assessment system have been influenced by the biological and physiological work of Luria and measure simultaneous and successive/sequential processing.

The Kaufman tests (see Figure 13.2) typically measure three aspects of intelligence:

- **Achievement** – this test measures acquired knowledge, including reading and arithmetic skills.
- **Simultaneous processing** – this test involves spatial or analogic tasks that ask the participant to simultaneously integrate and synthesise information.
- **Sequential processing scale** – in this test, the participant typically solves tasks by arranging the stimuli in sequential or serial order.

Features, uses and problems surrounding intelligence tests

In the last section we described different types of intelligence tests. In the following sections we are going to consider the features, uses and problems found in intelligence tests.

Typical features of intelligence tests

Let us establish some of the important aspects that are essential to good intelligence tests. Sattler (2002) establishes three main aspects that tend to be typical in all good intelligence tests.

A variety of tasks are involved in intelligence tests

To assess a full range of abilities, a good intelligence test needs to contain a number of tasks. For example, tests such as the Wechsler Adult Intelligence Scale will contain various measures, including ability tests of general knowledge, digit span, vocabulary, arithmetic, comprehension, similarities, picture completion, picture arrangement, block design, digit symbol and object assembly. Such 'subtests' used together provide a fuller understanding of the overall intelligence of the person as well as their particular strengths.

Standardisation of administration

The aim of standardising administration is to provide a controlled environment in which the test is taken to allow comparisons among children (although note that different test authors differ in the emphasis they place on the importance of making comparisons *among* children). For example, if conditions differed during the test administration, such as the wording of questions or the exact time given for the test, then differences in intelligence between children might be (at least partly) attributed to the differences in administration conditions rather than to differences in their intelligence. The administration of any intelligence test is standardised, from instructions for completing the test, to the location of the test, to which and how many people should be present. Two further important aspects to this standardisation are the length of administration of the test and the conditions under which it is taken.

- As typically intelligence tests are administered to school-children, the length of time children can take on a task will vary with the age of the child. For example, younger children will tend to be able to concentrate less over longer periods of time than older children will, and they will want to spend less time on more complicated tasks. Researchers will seek to standardise the length of time of the test depending on the age of the child.
- There is a need for the actual test to be done in comfortable conditions and to be administered by a qualified test administrator. If you have ever taken an intelligence test at school, you will probably recall that it was administered by a trained staff member. This qualified person ensures the quality of administration of the test. This person ensures that test-takers are comfortable, and, particularly where children are concerned, the administrator might seek to develop a rapport with the students, responding to needs as they arise (i.e. when a student is in distress, making sure respondents aren't rushed into starting the test). You can see that without being provided with this type of approach, individuals might feel that their performance on the test wasn't only due to their intelligence, but to the conditions in which it was taken.

Norm referencing

This is another form of standardisation. The aim of making an intelligence test norm-referenced is to allow comparisons to be made with other children. There is no point in determining the IQ score of a person as being 140, unless you have something with which to compare it. As we saw in the previous discussion with the work of Terman (Chapter 12), all tests will have to be administered to a large group of people of around the same age (or at the same age among children) and of similar demographics (sex, race, area of residence, occupational status) to allow accurate comparisons to be made. The standard example is to use 100 to describe an average score and then compare all scores around that number. Some authors of intelligence tests play down the need to make comparisons on this basis among children because the tests are designed for individual assessment. However, even these intelligence tests will provide some norm-referenced material, so that the person using the intelligence test may have a context for understanding individual scores.

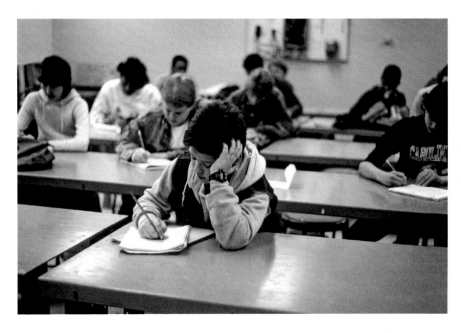

How do you think IQ tests have changed since the First World War?
Source: Alamy Images/Tina Manley

The uses of intelligence tests

Intelligence tests are used for all sorts of purposes, but mainly for the following three: selection, diagnosis and evaluation.

You may first come across intelligence tests in schools. Here, intelligence tests might be used for selection purposes, streaming children into high-ability and low-ability classes, or conceivably might be used by school selectors to ensure they only take on high-ability children. Intelligence tests might be used for diagnostic purposes, to help teachers determine whether there are problems in children with low ability and specifically where these problems might exist so children might be helped. They would also be used for evaluating the child's ability and could help teachers to decide which students might be capable of performing better in national examinations.

Similar ideas apply to intelligence tests when they are used in higher education and the workplace, with colleges, universities and employers using them to select candidates. You can easily see how an applicant who scores well in general knowledge, vocabulary, arithmetic and comprehension (all specific intelligence abilities) might be more likely to get a vacancy over someone who does not achieve a high score in these abilities.

This application of tests is not without good reason. People who suggest and support the use of intelligence tests would argue that IQ tests are valid and useful as they show a positive correlation with school achievement and job performance.

As regards school achievement, research has looked at various indices, including examination ability, specific abilities in a particular topic (for example, mathematics, English) and whether students stay on in school. There are a number of reviews by psychologists. Jencks (1979) reported correlations between generally intelligence and academic achievement ranging from $r = 0.40$ to $r = 0.63$ for six longitudinal studies in the USA. US psychologists Alan Kaufman and Elizabeth Lichtenberger (Kaufman, 1990; Kaufman and Lichtenberger, 2005) provide a review of key papers that have looked at the correlation between general intelligence and school attainment and achievement. The authors conclude that the average correlation between IQ scores and a number of school indicators is around $r = 0.50$. Mackintosh (1998) estimates the correlation between general intelligence and achievement at school to be between $r = 0.4$ and $r = 0.7$.

A study in 2007 by Ian Deary, Steve Strand, Pauline Smith and Cres Fernandes (Deary *et al.*, 2007) reported on a 5-year prospective longitudinal study of 70,000 + English children and examined the association between psychometric intelligence at age 11 years (as measured by the cognitive ability test which gives an overall assessment of general intelligence, 'g') and educational achievement in national examinations in 25 academic subjects at age 16. In this study the authors used General Certificate of Secondary Education (GCSE) scores to measure educational attainment, which is the academic qualification awarded in a number of subjects (e.g. mathematics, English, history, etc.) by students in secondary education in the United Kingdom. Table 13.1 shows some of the correlations between general intelligence and GCSE scores across a number of subject areas.

Clearly, all these studies considered together suggest that intelligence does unambiguously predict academic achievement.

Two strong examples of this predictive power of intelligence tests can also be found in the workplace. In 1984 two US psychologists, John E. Hunter and R. F. Hunter (Hunter and Hunter, 1984), did a meta-analysis (a **meta-analysis** is a technique that combines the results of several studies) and put together the results of studies that examined various predictors at the start of a job with eventual job performance. In all, the authors looked at results for over 32,000 workers. They found that the correlation between general intelligence (IQ) and job performance was $r = 0.54$ (a medium-sized correlation) and had a much larger association with job performance than with the curriculum vitae of the candidate ($r = 0.37$), previous experience of the candidate ($r = 0.18$), job interviews ($r = 0.14$) and education of the candidate ($r = 0.10$).

The first ever meta-analysis of this type was repeated in the United Kingdom by UK psychologist Cristina Bertua, Dutch psychologist Neil Anderson and Spanish psychologist Jesús F. Salgado, who looked at over 280 samples, comparing 13,262 people's scores on different intelligence

Table 13.1 Correlations between general intelligence and GCSE scores (based on Deary *et al.*, 2007)

Subject	Correlation with general intelligence ($r =$)
GCSE total points	0.69
GCSE best 8	0.72
Mathematics	0.77
Biology	0.51
Chemistry	0.46
Physics	0.50
English	0.67
English literature	0.59
History	0.63
Geography	0.65
French	0.64
German	0.61
Spanish	0.62
Drama	0.47
Art and design	0.43
Music	0.54

tests and their later job performance (Bertua *et al.*, 2005). In this study the researchers examined several different types of jobs, including clerical, engineering, professional, management and sales and ranging from low-skilled jobs to higher-skilled professional jobs. Bertua and her colleagues found that both general intelligence and specific ability tests were good predictors of job performance, with correlations being similar to those reported by Hunter and Hunter (1984) of between $r = 0.5$ and $r = 0.6$.

However, the potential usefulness of intelligence tests does not stop there. Some psychologists have shown that general intelligence in childhood can predict variables across the lifespan. In 1931 the Mental Survey Committee in Scotland met and decided (because there was no reliable way of getting a representative sample) to measure general intelligence and obtain IQ scores for everyone in Scotland. So on Wednesday, 1 June 1932, nearly every child attending school in Scotland who was born in 1921 took the same intelligence test ($n = 89,498$). This exercise was repeated in 1947, testing almost all people born in 1936 ($n = 70,805$).

A group of psychologists from Scotland – Ian Deary, Martha Whiteman, John Starr, Lawrence Whalley and Helen Fox (2004) – have pointed out that, in intelligence testing history, this sample is very unusual. Scotland remains the only nation with mental test data for an entire birth cohort, never mind two. In their study, the authors look at a number of factors in old age and their relationship to the test-takers' IQ scores from the 1932 and 1947 cohorts. Some of their main findings are summarised in Table 13.2. In this table we have taken some of the information from Deary *et al.*'s paper regarding the 1947 cohort in terms of those who were found to have died, those who had been diagnosed with cancer and those who had been diagnosed with a cardiovascular (involving the heart and the blood vessels) disease by the time of Deary *et al.*'s study.

What you can see from Table 13.2 is that people who were reported to have died and those having been diagnosed with cardiovascular disease had scored significantly lower on IQ in 1947 than those who had neither died nor been diagnosed with cardiovascular disease. However, note that no significant difference was found in the IQs of

people who were later diagnosed with cancer. This finding suggests, at the very least, that IQ has some level of predictive strength very much later in life.

This type of study, exploring the relationship between intelligence at a young age and health in later life, is named cognitive epidemiology, a term introduced by Deary and Der (2005). One of the largest studies ever to explore the relationship between intelligence at an early age and health in later life was carried out by David Batty, who is at University College London, UK with several colleagues (Batty *et al.*, 2009). Up to 2010, in Sweden for the past 100 years all men in early adulthood have had to undertake conscription into either the military or the civil service. For many decades, on entering conscription individuals have been given intelligence tests and been given a particular unique identifier code (like a national insurance number or passport number) that can be revisited at a later date to match up each person with information (such as health outcomes) that are collected later or as part of public databases or surveys. Therefore, in Sweden, there is a database linking intelligence at an early age (at the time of conscription) to health outcomes at a number of stages in later life across a number of decades. Batty *et al.* studied mortality rate, a measure of the number of deaths. They found that, among nearly 1 million men (994,242) studied across an average of 20 years, there were nearly 15,000 deaths (14,498). When age, year of birth and where they were tested were controlled for, lower IQ score was associated with an increased risk of *all-cause mortality* (that is, total mortality rate for the population across all causes of death). Furthermore, this association was not mediated (mediation being a mechanism that explains the association) by blood pressure, body mass index or cigarette smoking, these being variables associated with both intelligence and health. However, when the authors controlled for education level (which, as we've noticed above, is clearly closely correlated with intelligence), they found that the association between IQ and mortality diminished markedly. When it came to the relationship between intelligence and specific causes of mortality, IQ was associated with deaths from accidents, coronary heart disease and suicide, but not cancer.

Table 13.2 The relationship between general intelligence (IQ) scores and a number of health outcomes in later life

Outcome	Number of people suffering from the outcome	Number of people not suffering from the outcome	Mean IQ of people suffering from the outcome	Mean IQ of people not suffering from the outcome	Significance
People dying	125	783	97.7	104.6	P < 0.001
People being diagnosed with cancer	78	830	101.3	103.9	P > 0.05
People being diagnosed with cardiovascular disease	98	810	100.1	104.1	P < 0.05

Source: Statistics from Deary *et al.* (2004).

Stop and think

What are the mechanisms that underpin the relationship between IQ and mortality?

In the section on intelligence and health we saw that researchers like Batty *et al.* examined possible mediating factors (such as blood pressure, body mass index or cigarette smoking) that explain the relationship between intelligence and health. Batty *et al.* (2007) and Calvin *et al.* (2011) have tried to summarise, in terms of areas, the possible mechanisms that might explain this relationship between IQ and mortality. Remember that these studies are looking at the measurement of IQ, usually at a relatively early age in people's lives (and that IQ tests are taken a long time before the person dies), and linking it to mortality rates.

Batty *et al.* (2007) have argued that it is important to realise that aspects such as parental intelligence, socioeconomic environment, nutrition and somatic and psychiatric illness all influence IQ (and we cover influence of parental intelligence, socioeconomic environment and nutrition on IQ here and later [Chapter 14]). However, from this point on, Batty and his colleagues have suggested four possible domains that help us to understand the relationship between IQ before death (premorbid IQ) and mortality (see Figure 13.3). These are:

- **disease and injury prevention**: the extent to which one seeks to avoid developing disease or injuries;
- **disease and injury management**: the extent to which one seeks to manage and handle disease or injuries when they happen or emerge;
- **high socioeconomic position**: the extent to which individuals are living and working in healthier environments;

- **psychiatric illness**: many psychiatric illnesses (depression, schizophrenia) are lasting and permanent and are related to a number of factors or health behaviours related to mortality; for example, suicide, smoking or drinking alcohol.

It is better to see these relationships as a chain in this part of the lifespan, with IQ leading to one of these four domains, which in turn leads to different levels of mortality. For example, Calvin *et al.* describe how higher IQ leads to better education and work successes. People will therefore have better jobs and be able to access not only safer living areas, but also better health services. Therefore those with a high socioeconomic position will spend their time in safer and healthier environments and therefore be less at risk of death.

Of course some of these relationships are complicated, because, as noted earlier, social and economic status might not only influence the relationship between IQ and mortality, but the socioeconomic environment also predicts IQ from an early age (and also before birth; see this deicussion and Chapter 14), and therefore it may be a constant variable to account for. However, in this instance, look at the four domains and speculate for each domain how someone with a high IQ and someone with a low IQ might differ in terms of how they approach disease and injury prevention, disease and injury management, high socioeconomic position and psychiatric illness, and how this approach might eventually have an effect on mortality.

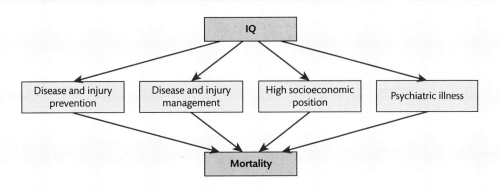

Figure 13.3 Possible mechanisms that explain the relationship between IQ at an early age and mortality (Batty *et al.*, 2007).

This high level approach to understanding the relationship between intelligence and health has also been carried out in other studies. Catherine Calvin and colleagues (Calvin *et al.*, 2011) carried out a meta-analysis of the 16 studies (encompassing longitudinal studies ranging from 17 to 69 years) that examined the relationship between intelligence in young people and all-cause mortality. In summarising these findings an increase of one standard deviation in the distribution of IQ scores led to a 24 per cent lower risk of death.

The relationship between general intelligence and other factors is the focus of debate in the next two discussion (Chapters 14 and 15). However, it is worth noting that, like the health variables just discussed, it is proposed that general intelligence predicts poverty, the likelihood of being in prison, being divorced or unemployed (Gottfredson, 1997). All in all, the evidence suggests that general intelligence – particularly IQ test scores – is not only related to, but may be a relatively important predictor of, many aspects of our lives.

Problems and issues with intelligence tests

However, intelligence tests are not without their criticisms. There are three main considerations of IQ tests that you will commonly find in the intelligence literature. These considerations are based on:

- the reliability of intelligence tests;
- the validity of intelligence tests;
- whether the usefulness of intelligence tests is overemphasised.

Reliability of intelligence tests

The reliability of any test refers to two aspects:

- **Internal reliability** – any measure of intelligence with good internal reliability will have a number of items that correlate positively with one another; this suggests they are measuring the same construct.
- **Test–retest reliability (reliability of the test over time)** – a good intelligence test will show a good level of reliability over time. Your general intelligence is thought to be relatively stable over time. Therefore you would expect that if you took an intelligence test on one occasion (and got an IQ score) and you took the same intelligence test 3 months later (and got an IQ score), you would expect your IQ scores to be very similar.

If you want to read more about reliability, you can refer to the supplementary material at the end of the text (Chapter 25).

The internal reliability of intelligence scales is often well established in the research programmes that accompany the development of intelligence tests. Tests such as the Stanford–Binet Intelligence Scales and the Wechsler Intelligence Scales will provide information in their test manuals that shows the items that make up the different subscales, and the subscales that are used to compute an overall IQ score are positively related to one another.

However, as established intelligence items and intelligence scales have largely been developed on the basis that they should be correlated with one another (i.e. if one item or subscale is not correlated, then test developers omit it from the test), the concern surrounding the internal reliability of established intelligence tests is not a major issue in intelligence. The issues surrounding the stability of intelligence test scores over time present a much more important consideration.

People who question whether intelligence tests are reliable over time point to the fact that general intelligence (IQ) scores fluctuate. That is, if you took an intelligence test today and took the same one a week later, your IQ score computed from taking that test would probably be different. Some researchers have estimated that this fluctuation may be as much as 15 IQ points (Benson, 2003). Furthermore, individual performances on intelligence tests may fluctuate between administrations because the individual may perform differently while taking the test (they may be having a particularly good day or a particularly bad day). This fluctuation is further compounded because test-takers are not meant to take the same intelligence test twice, as they will have learnt some of the answers or the techniques involved in the test and consequently would be expected to perform better. The point is that, once you have taken one general intelligence test, you will be assigned an IQ score. It is not possible to take the test again, because your later scores will be influenced by having taken the test before. Furthermore, given that IQ test scores fluctuate between administrations, how can you be sure that your first (and only) IQ score is not just a fluctuation from your real intelligence? You can see that if we are to assign people IQ scores and compare people's IQ scores based on their performance on a single administration of an intelligence test, these fluctuations of IQ scores may present a concern about the accuracy of IQ tests.

This concern of IQ scores fluctuating has been a long-term consideration of intelligence researchers, and it has spawned a whole area of research to consider these fluctuations over time. Findings suggest that, although intelligence test scores do fluctuate, they do remain relatively stable over time. We will now outline some of this research.

US developmental psychologists Harold E. Jones and Nancy Bayley (1941) set up what is now known as the Berkeley Growth Study. This study was started in the late 1920s and represents data from people born in Berkeley, California, between 1928 and 1929. These researchers tested a sample of children annually throughout childhood and adolescence on a number of measures, including intelligence, and calculated their IQ scores. Jones and Bayley found that IQ scores of children at 18 years were positively correlated with their IQ scores at 12 years ($r = 0.89$) and 6 years ($r = 0.77$).

It is important to remember here what is meant by stable IQ in childhood (Neisser *et al.*, 1996). You will remember that IQ scores are based around a mean of 100 and are calculated by comparing the individual's score with other individuals at that age. An average IQ score for a typical 7-year-old would be stable if the same person, at age 18, showed the same average IQ score. A lack of variation in IQ score between age 7 and age 18 does not mean that their IQ has stayed the same, because individual knowledge, critical thinking, vocabulary and ability to reason will increase with age. Rather, it means that their score stays the same to relative to other people. A 7-year-old with an IQ score of 100 is at the mean IQ of 7-year-olds, while an 18-year-old with an IQ score of 100 is at the mean of 18-year-olds.

The findings of Jones and Bayley are supported by more recent studies. The longest follow-up study of intelligence and relationship between IQ scores used the Mental Survey Committee in Scotland that had measured intelligence in Scottish children born in 1921 and attending school on 1 June, 1932 ($n = 87,498$). Scottish psychologists Ian Deary, Lawrence Whalley, Helen Lemmon, J. R. Crawford and John Starr (2000) followed up 101 people at the age of 77 years. They found that the correlation between the two occasions was $r = 0.63$ (which was adjusted to $r = 0.73$ when corrected for fine details regarding ability range within the 77-year-olds). In a follow-up study (Gow *et al.*, 2011) reported correlations of $r = 0.67$ between the ages

of 11 and 70 years, $r = 0.66$ for between the ages of 11 and 77 years, and $r = 0.51$ between the ages of 11 and 87 years. These findings show substantial stability from childhood to late life of IQ scores on tests.

The correlations between intelligence scores across these age ranges are impressive. However, they are not perfect; and, although we would not expect them to show perfect correlations, if there are fluctuations between IQ scores on administrations, you can see why people might be concerned or cautious when assigning a child a particular IQ score.

Validity of intelligence tests

Validity of tests refers to the question of whether the test measures what it claims to measure (for more information, see Chapter 25). In the context of intelligence tests we can ask, do intelligence tests measure intelligence?

Well, within one context they do; if we answer the question, 'Do intelligence tests measure what they *claim* to measure?' If you consider an intelligence test, like the Wechsler Adult Intelligence Scale, for example, then there is little doubt that the subtests of this intelligence test are measuring the different specific intelligence abilities that they have been designed to measure. Again, intelligence test developers set about establishing

Profile

Nancy Bayley

Nancy Bayley was born in Oregon in 1899. As a child she was rather ill, and this prevented her from attending school until the age of 8. Not deterred by this late start in her education, she went to the University of Washington with the intention of becoming an English teacher. However, Bayley quickly changed to psychology and earned her undergraduate degree in 1922 and her master's degree in 1924. During the study of her master's degree, she worked as a research assistant for the Gatzert Foundation for Child Welfare and devised performance tests for children under the age of 5. She gained her doctoral degree in 1926 from the State University of Iowa; for her thesis, she measured electrical skin responses to fear in children.

This type of research was to remain a focus of Bayley's research for the rest of her career. In 1928, she went to the Institute of Child Welfare at the University of California at Berkeley. She resided there for most of her career while holding research positions in psychology and anatomy at Stanford University at the same time.

At the Institute of Child Welfare, Bayley began a major study of normal and handicapped infant development. This became the now famous Berkeley Growth Study, which represents data from people born in Berkeley, Cali-

fornia, between 1928 and 1929. Her first publications – *The California First-year Mental Scale* (1933), *Mental Growth During the First Three Years* (1933) and *The California Infant Scale of Motor Development* (1936) – introduced new methodologies for assessing developments in infants and are seen as significant milestones in developmental psychology. Bayley published over 200 publications while also helping to design the National Collaborative Perinatal Project for the study of cerebral palsy, mental retardation and other neurological and psychological disorders.

Bayley was a fellow of the APA and of the American Association for the Advancement of Science. Her work was recognised by her contemporaries: she earned the G. Stanley Hall Award of the APA's Division of Developmental Psychology in 1971. She received the Gold Medal Award of the American Psychological Foundation in 1982. She earned the distinguished contribution award from the Society for Research in Child Development.

During her career, Nancy Bayley came to be recognised as a pioneer in the field of human development. Her career was dedicated to measuring and researching intellectual abilities in infants, children and adults. Bayley died of respiratory failure in 1994.

validity for all aspects of their intelligence test when developing them. If an intelligence test, or a particular intelligence subtest, did not show validity in development, then test developers would seek to improve that measure of intelligence. You can also see that, on the face of it (sometimes called **face validity**), an intelligence test that involves solving problems using mental arithmetic probably measures, to a greater degree, mental arithmetic intelligence. Similarly, a subtest that requires a number of simple jigsaws to be completed probably measures intelligence in object assembly.

Furthermore, intelligence tests show **concurrent validity** due to their relationship with other measures of intelligence. Neisser and the rest of the Intelligence Task Force (Neisser *et al.*, 1996) argue that it is generally accepted that individuals perform equally as well or poorly on different intelligence tests, suggesting that intelligence tests tend to correlate with other intelligence tests – although there is evidence to suggest that, when IQ is calculated from different intelligence tests, scores can also fluctuate by up to 15 IQ points (Benson, 2003). Also, as we have just seen, intelligence tests have been used to predict 'real-world' measures of intelligence or achievement; for example, school achievement and job performance (this is known as **predictive validity**). All these findings suggest evidence for the general validity of intelligence tests measuring what they claim to measure – general intelligence (as defined by an IQ score) that is worked out by adding together the performance on several subtests of specific abilities (e.g. arithmetic, object assembly, comprehension).

However, the discussion takes a turn when we consider the general question of validity in a slightly different way: 'Do intelligence tests measure *intelligence*?'

Some critics argue that the main problem with intelligence tests is that they assume, particularly when they produce an overall IQ score, that there is an idea of general intelligence when in fact there is no agreement on whether such a global mental capacity exists (Benson, 2003). We saw previously (Chapter 12) that, although some theorists and researchers suggest there is a general factor of intelligence (e.g. Spearman), other theorists and researchers have questioned the idea of general intelligence. For example, psychologists such as Howard Gardner identified nine intelligences that comprise his multiple intelligence theory (Gardner, 1993; 1995), and Robert Sternberg devised the triarchic theory of intelligence (Sternberg, 1985b; 1988) that comprises three aspects of intelligence (componential, contextual and experiential). In the current discussion we saw that cognitive intelligence tests (such as the Kaufmans') emphasise sequential and simultaneous cognitive processes as well as more traditional achievement abilities.

What is crucial about these different approaches is that some critics of intelligence tests emphasise that intelligence is probably much more than what can be measured by intelligence tests; rather, intelligence is the result of the individual engaging in a variety of skills and information within their cultural context. For example, previously we have seen (Chapter 11) how everyday theories that surround intelligence differ between eastern and western cultures, and how those theories change within cultures owing to changing perceptions of intelligence with age or across different disciplines (for example, business and philosophy).

Consequently, the concern is that many intelligence tests cannot be valid, as no single intelligence test covers the many different theoretical interpretations and cultural considerations that need to be made when accurately measuring intelligence.

Modern-day intelligence researchers continually wrestle with these types of considerations and distinctions. However, it is timely to remember that early intelligence researchers strived to develop intelligence tests that allowed and considered cultural differences. Both Yerkes' Army Beta test and Raven's Progressive Matrices were developed around theories of intelligence that emphasised general intelligence and IQ scores but sought to make their tests free of influences of literacy and the English language. The Wechsler Intelligence Scale for Children (WISC) and the Stanford–Binet Intelligence Scale have recently been changed so they better reflect the abilities of test-takers from diverse cultural and linguistic backgrounds.

None the less, one of the big distinctions regarding the validity of intelligence tests is the exact question we ask when questioning their validity. If we ask whether intelligence tests measure what they claim to measure, then they probably do. If we ask whether intelligence tests measure intelligence, then the answer is much less certain; it depends on what your definition of intelligence is.

Is the usefulness of intelligence tests over-emphasised?

Another criticism of intelligence tests is that their capacity to predict intellectual performance in different walks of life is overplayed, overstated or over-emphasised (Benson, 2003). We have seen how intelligence tests have been known to predict, quite strongly, both academic achievement and job performance. In the latter case of job performance, the predictive strength of intelligence tests is greater than that of interviews, curriculum vitae and previous experience. You can see why people would put emphasis on intelligence testing as it is such a strong predictor of job performance.

However, critics of intelligence testing note that there are fluctuations in the predictive strength of intelligence tests. For instance, time has a great effect on the ability of the intelligence test to predict performance. That is, the longer the time between the administration of the test and the measurement of the performance, the weaker the relationship. Furthermore, the predictive strength of intelligence tests fluctuates when other variables are considered; for example, when different demographics are considered (such as age, race, sex) or situations or tasks change.

Benson (2003) notes that one area where these concerns are apparent is that of special education, which is concerned with people with learning disabilities. This concern arises from the use of IQ tests to classify learning disabilities using the 'IQ-achievement discrepancy model'. The IQ-achievement discrepancy model was based on comparing children's achievement to their IQ score. Where children's achievement scores are a standard deviation or more below their IQ scores, they are identified as learning disabled. Benson (2003) suggests that identifying students using the IQ-achievement discrepancy model does little to help teachers understand what they need to do practically to help the student to learn, and it holds no clue to the educational programme that that child may need to undertake to improve. Therefore, other assessments of children's needs (for example, the child's behaviour at school and home) might be a better indicator. Indeed, problems with the use of intelligence tests in this area have been recognised by the US government. On 3 October 2001, the then President George Bush established a Commission on Excellence in Special Education to collect evidence on federal, state and local special education programmes. The reason for this was to develop policies for improving the education performance of students with disabilities. The President's Commission on Excellence in Special Education (PCESE) delivered its report to President Bush on 1 July 2002. One recommendation of this report was to suggest that the use of intelligence tests to diagnose learning disabilities should be discontinued.

Benson suggests that supporters of intelligence tests would readily accept the possible flaws in this application of intelligence testing within an IQ-achievement discrepancy model. Researchers in the area of intelligence have been thinking about such problems for a long time. For example, Kaufman and Kaufman (2001) were suggesting, before the President's Commission on Excellence in Special Education, that intelligence tests should not be administered by anonymous research scientists in schools, but by specially trained educational practitioners or teachers with an expertise in child learning. These administrators wouldn't just total an IQ score, but look at the child, work with the child more and make special recommendations. Kaufman and Kaufman (2001) suggest that in this context there is no reason to dispense with intelligence tests altogether. Rather, intelligence testing should be used with a number of educational tools to arrive at as good an assessment as possible of the child.

The intelligent use of intelligence tests

All this debate and concern about intelligence tests has led to one recommendation. If intelligence tests are to be used, they should be used intelligently (Benson, 2003).

A point made by Kaufman (Benson, 2003; Kaufman and Kaufman, 2001) is that there is a huge difference today in the way that intelligence tests are used and viewed – and in the theories and tests that have been developed around them. He suggests that critics of intelligence tests are generally using evidence and arguments that may have been accurate 20 or more years ago, but are less so today.

However, Kaufman argues that this misconception may be the result of some practitioners using the tests in more traditional ways. Kaufman and Kaufman have insisted that, while academic researchers and theorists are using more and more advanced methods of design and interpretation, if intelligence tests are still being administered en masse and IQ test scores are simply churned out to make comparisons today, then such an application is a long way behind modern-day thinking measurement and application.

Moreover, authors such as Naglieri suggest that, rather than abandoning intelligence testing, given its firm basis, it needs to be pushed further (Benson, 2003; Naglieri, 1998). Naglieri has suggested that, today, intelligence practitioners want not only to test children's intelligence but also to follow it up with interventions designed to improve the child's learning in the areas where they have shown weakness. These authors suggest that such a dynamic approach will not only more accurately determine a child's intelligence but also automatically consider the differing abilities of children from different linguistic and cultural backgrounds.

Stop and think

Alternatives to intelligence testing

Former APA President Dr Diane F. Halpern of Claremont McKenna College once said, 'Critics of intelligence testing often fail to consider that most of the alternatives are even more prone to problems of fairness and validity than the measures that are currently used.'

- What argument do you think Dr Halpern is trying to put forward?
- What alternatives do you think there are to intelligence testing?

Some concluding comments

It would be rash to simply dismiss intelligence tests. There is a lot of evidence for their reliability, their validity and their usefulness. However, the shortcomings of intelligence tests should not be ignored or under-emphasised. Fluctuations within and between intelligence tests are hard to ignore simply because the application of intelligence tests, particularly IQ scores, represents high stakes for individuals. When you are a child, intelligence tests can be used to classify your future at school. When you are an adult, they can be used to classify your access to the workplace.

That said, intelligence testing has begun to move on from a more traditional view. Intelligence test developers and researchers are the most aware of such shortcomings. Consequently, test developers are always working on new, more sophisticated, ways of creating items for intelligence tests, administering intelligence tests and interpreting the scores obtained on intelligence tests. This is why you see continually updated versions of the Stanford–Binet Scales, the Wechsler Intelligence Scales, the Raven's Matrices and the Woodcock–Johnson Psychoeducational Battery–Revised, along with papers in the psychological literature comparing and establishing both the reliability and validity of intelligence tests.

The Flynn effect

In the last section we talked about the features, uses and problems surrounding the use of intelligence tests. One thing we noted was that scores on intelligence tests, and particularly IQ scores, have a tendency to fluctuate. However, we have dedicated the second half of this discussion to a consideration of one of the most well-known fluctuations in intelligence testing history, the discovery of a continued year-on-year rise of intelligence test scores in all parts of the world. This rise, known as the **Flynn effect**, was named after the person who discovered it – James R. Flynn, now an Emeritus Professor of Political Studies at the University of Otago in Dunedin, New Zealand.

How was the Flynn effect discovered?

In 1981 Flynn had begun to survey the test manuals of well-known tests, such as the Wechsler and Stanford–Binet manuals (Flynn, 1999). Whenever a new IQ test had been published, one thing that was done to help establish the validity of the new test was to compare scores of the same people on the old version and the new version. Part of this process involves restandardising the norms for the test, so that subjects are not scored against norms that were established with the old version of the test, which might cause problems when comparing scores between different samples and populations. As hoped for by the test publishers, norms were established, and there was always a high correlation between both versions of the test, suggesting validity for the new test.

However, Flynn noted something else in the manuals. He noticed that whenever a sample of test-takers was given both the new test and an older test, they always got higher scores on the newer test. To illustrate, Flynn has looked at the Wechsler Intelligence Scale for Children, for which norms among a representative sample of white US residents had been established between 1947 and 1948, and its revision, the Wechsler Intelligence Scale for Children – Revised, for which norms were established in 1972. Flynn found that, if a group of participants averaged an IQ of 100 on the Wechsler Intelligence Scale for Children – Revised (1972), they averaged 108 on the Wechsler Intelligence Scale for Children (1947/1948). This meant that these samples were setting higher standards for average IQ scores over time. That is, you had to be more intelligent to score an average IQ of 100 on the new Wechsler Intelligence Scale for Children – Revised than you did to score an average IQ of 100 on the previous version of the Wechsler Intelligence Scale for Children. Flynn suggested from this finding that between 1948 and 1972 (a period of 24 years – a generation), among a sample representative of US residents, Americans had gained 8 IQ points.

Spurred on by this finding, Flynn (Flynn, 1984) looked at 73 studies (covering 7,500 US white participants aged between 2 and 48 years) in which each group of participants had taken two (or more) versions of either the Wechsler or Stanford–Binet IQ tests between 1932 and 1978. His analyses showed that during this time, white Americans had gained 14 IQ points, an average of 0.30 IQ points per year.

Then Flynn became interested in discovering whether this was a phenomenon only in the United States, or whether it could be found in other cultures. Also at that time, Flynn engaged in several personal communications with Arthur Jensen. Jensen noted to Flynn that Wechsler and Stanford–Binet tests may measure intelligence partially through items taught at school (e.g. vocabulary, general knowledge) and therefore rises in IQ that Flynn had noted might reflect better schooling (Flynn, 1999). Jensen suggested that it would be important to look not only at intelligence tests like the Wechsler and Stanford–Binet tests but also at tests like the Raven's Matrices, because these were purely non-verbal tests purporting to be a measure of general intelligence, and they would not be as open to cultural effects such as school. It is also important to note that this distinction between verbal and non-verbal intelligence tests is sometimes best represented by Cattell's theoretical distinction between fluid (primary reasoning ability, including the ability to solve abstract relational problems free of cultural influences) and crystallised intelligence (acquired knowledge and skills, such as factual knowledge, generally related to a person's stored information and their cultural influences; see Chapter 12 for more details).

Stop and think

Mozart and the rats

Listening to Mozart boosts your intelligence . . . or does it? In 1993 physicist Gordon Shaw and Frances Rauscher, a former concert cellist and an expert on cognitive development from the University of California, studied the effects on college students of listening to the first 10 minutes of the Mozart *Sonata for Two Pianos in D Major* (Rauscher *et al.*, 1993). The researchers found a temporary enhancement of spatial-temporal reasoning (ordering objects in space and time) by 8 or 9 points, lasting for 10–15 minutes, as measured by the Stanford–Binet IQ test. Writing later on the topic, Dr Alfred A. Tomatis coined the term 'Mozart effect', which is the suggested increase in brain development that occurs in children when they listen to the music of Wolfgang Amadeus Mozart. The original 'Mozart effect' researchers based their rationale on earlier findings by Leng and Shaw (1991) that neural firing patterns occur in the cerebral cortex (a part of the brain that helps with motor control, speech, memory and auditory reception) when subjects are listening to music and performing spatial tasks. The cerebral cortex is a part of the brain that helps with, among other things, motor control, speech, memory and auditory reception. Rauscher and Shaw (1998) argued that listening to certain types of complex music may 'warm up' neural transmitters inside the cerebral cortex and consequently improve spatial performance. This finding caused a great amount of media attention, and the 'Mozart effect' has been put forward as an educational tool (for example, some schools suggested playing Mozart during lesson times). Shaw (2001) reports that the 'Mozart effect' has been seen to be useful in enhancing the visual-spatial task performance of Alzheimer's disease/dementia patients and for reducing seizures in epileptic patients.

Clearly this finding attracted a lot of attention from the media as discussions of how music could raise intelligence in early childhood took hold. This interest also led to Shaw and Rauscher creating their own institute: The Music Intelligence Neural Development (MIND) Institute.

However, no sooner had such findings been reported and caused an interest than researchers were questioning their findings. In 1999, Christopher Chabris of Harvard University in the United States presented a meta-analysis of 17 studies. Chabris (1999) noted that the first 'Mozart effect' publication showed participants' spatial intelligence scores improved by 8–9 points, by far the largest increase reported in the literature. Across the other studies that measured changes in spatial intelligence, these studies showed a less dramatic increase of 2.1 IQ points. The change could not be considered significant, and Chabris concluded that the 'Mozart effect' is less

than what would arise by chance. Some authors, like US psychologist Kenneth M. Steele (2000), have suggested that the 'Mozart effect' might just be a phenomenon in testing in which the music arouses the participant or changes their mood to make them ready for doing well at the task, particularly if the person likes Mozart.

Rauscher and Shaw (1998) had already suggested that failures in replicating their findings were caused by inappropriate procedures or inappropriate spatial reasoning measures. Rauscher and Shaw have defended such criticisms by continuing their research and emphasising that they only noted a brief shift in spatial IQ performance in their original study. They argue that what they have shown, rather than that listening to Mozart passively raises your intelligence, is that patterns of neurons in pre-existing sites in the brain fire in sequences that respond to certain frequencies. Rauscher and Shaw have suggested that researchers should instead concentrate on the idea that the major transfer effects of music are likely to come from active involvement and playing of music and in continual music education experiences. For example, Rauscher, Shaw and their colleagues (Rauscher *et al.*, 1997) conducted an experiment with three groups of under 5-year-olds. One group received private piano lessons, a second group received private computer lessons and a third group received no additional lessons over a period of 6 months. Those children who received piano/keyboard training performed 34 per cent higher on tests of spatial-temporal ability than the others did. These findings indicate that music enhances preschool children's spatial-temporal reasoning.

One interesting finding also put forward as evidence of the 'Mozart effect' was a study by Rauscher and colleagues (Rauscher *et al.*, 1998). In these experiments rats were exposed in utero (before birth in the uterus), plus 60 days post-partum (the period shortly after childbirth) to either complex music (a Mozart sonata), a minimalist music composition (by Philip Glass; your parents will know who he is) or white noise or silence. The rats were tested for 5 days, three trials per day, in a multiple T-maze. On day 3, the experimenters reported that rats exposed to the Mozart completed the maze more rapidly and with fewer errors than the rats assigned to the other groups. The experimenters also found that this difference increased in magnitude through day 5. The authors suggested that this repeated exposure to complex music leads to improved spatial-temporal learning in rats, supporting those results found in human beings.

Kenneth M. Steele (2003) has, however, thrown doubts on these findings. First, Steele makes the point that the music in the uterus would have been ineffective in the experiment because rats are born deaf. Secondly, Steele points out that human beings and rats hear at different frequencies and that the range of hearing for rats is at a higher frequency than that of human beings. In his analysis of Mozart's sonata, Steele suggests that rats were deaf to much of the hypothesised effects of the music because more than half of the notes in the sonata were not in the frequency range of rats, and therefore they wouldn't have heard them.

Whatever the effect of Mozart on human beings and rats, the findings of Rauscher and Shaw provide both intrigue and controversy in equal amounts.

Flynn published what has become a seminal paper in the intelligence literature (Flynn, 1987). He published data from 14 countries (he later updated this to 20 in 1994; Flynn, 1994). We have adapted the table from his 1987 data to show the country, the test and type of test (verbal or non-verbal or both) administered, the growth in IQ points across many of the samples and a figure of average growth in IQ per year (see Table 13.3).

Table 13.3 Country, the test and type of test (verbal or non-verbal or both) administered, the growth in IQ points across many of the samples and a figure of average growth in IQ per year

Location	Test	Type of IQ test (verbal or non-verbal)	Period of study	Rise in IQ points over the period	Rate
Leipzig, East Germany	Raven's	non-verbal	1968–1978	10.00–15.00	1.250
France	Raven's	non-verbal	1949–1974	25.12	1.005
Japan	Wechsler	non-verbal/verbal	1951–1975	20.03	0.835
Vienna, Austria	Wechsler	non-verbal/verbal	1962–1979	12.00–16.00	0.824
Belgium	Raven's	non-verbal	1958–1967	7.15	0.794
West Germany	Wechsler	non-verbal/verbal	1954–1981	20.00	0.741
Belgium	Shapes	non-verbal	1958–1967	6.45	0.716
Netherlands	Raven's	non-verbal	1952–1982	20.00	0.667
Zurich, Switzerland	Wechsler	non-verbal/verbal	1954–1977	10.00–20.00	0.652
Norway	Matrices	non-verbal	1954–1968	8.80	0.629
Saskatchewan, Canada	Otis	verbal	1958–1978	12.55	0.628
West Germany	Horn–Raven's	non-verbal	1961–1978	10.00	0.588
Norway	Verbal–math test	verbal	1954–1968	8.15	0.582
Edmonton, Alberta, Canada	California Test of Mental Maturity	non-verbal/verbal	1956–1977	11.03	0.525
Australia	Jenkins	non-verbal	1949–1981	15.67	0.490
Belgium	Verbal–math test	verbal	1958–1967	3.67	0.408
Edmonton, Alberta, Canada	Raven's	non-verbal	1956–1977	8.44	0.402
France	Wechsler	non-verbal/verbal	1955–1979	9.12	0.380
France	Verbal–math	verbal	1949–1974	9.35	0.374
Saskatchewan, Canada	Otis	verbal	1958–1978	6.95	0.348
Australia	Raven's	non-verbal	1950–1976	8.76	0.337
United States	Wechsler–Binet	non-verbal/verbal	1932–1972	12.00	0.300
United States	Wechsler	non-verbal/verbal	1954–1978	5.95	0.243
New Zealand	Otis	verbal	1936–1968	7.73	0.242
Norway	Matrices	non-verbal	1968–1980	2.60	0.217
United Kingdom	Raven's	non-verbal	1938–1979	7.75	0.189
Solothurn, Switzerland	Wechsler	non-verbal/verbal	1977–1984	1.30	0.186
United Kingdom	Raven's	non-verbal	1940–1979	7.07	0.181
Norway	Verbal–math	verbal	1968–1980	–1.60	–0.133

Source: Statistics from Flynn (1987).

Flynn had some reservations about some of the data. For example, he noted that some of the data sets, particularly from Germany and Japan, may have been more unreliable or speculative. He also warned that the data covered different time periods. He suggested caution in comparing nations using this data. However, he did come to the conclusion that IQ scores were rising yearly across a number of nations.

Moreover, Flynn found the highest rises in IQ occurred in the non-verbal tests (fluid intelligence) and the lowest gains were in verbal tests (crystallised intelligence). Medium gains were seen in mixed verbal and non-verbal tests, such as the Wechsler tests.

Following his finding, the so-called Flynn effect was confirmed by numerous studies. In 1994, Flynn presented more evidence and considered this growth of IQ within generations (30 years) of populations across 20 countries for which data were available. He concluded that non-verbal tests (IQ tests of fluid intelligence) on average tended to show an increase of about 15 points per generation (ranging from 5 to 25 points), while verbal tests (IQ tests of crystallised intelligence) have been more moderate, with an average of about 9 points per generation.

What is particularly intriguing about this finding for the two different intelligences is that this is not what was suggested by Flynn and Jensen's discussion after Flynn's earlier findings – that rises in IQ scores on the Wechsler and Stanford–Binet tests might simply be the result of better schooling. If this was the case, then it would be the verbal/crystallised intelligence tests of IQ that would rise, rather than the non-verbal/fluid intelligence tests. Consequently, the reasons for, or the explanations of, the rise in IQ test scores over generations became Flynn's next concern.

Explanations of the Flynn effect

There are a number of explanations for the Flynn effect. These range from Flynn's first considerations of the reasons for the effect to a series of questions about the possible genetic and cultural effects. We will concentrate on some initial explanations of the Flynn effect, which we will see have themselves spawned areas of research. We will then show you how these areas have developed into a major division in the intelligence research literature – the nutrition versus the cognitive stimulation hypotheses.

Flynn began by considering some hypotheses (Flynn, 1987; 1994). The first was that generations are getting more and more intelligent. However, the idea that later generations are more intelligent than previous generations is one element that Flynn rules out. For this to be true, we would expect to find a lot more geniuses in the world (Flynn estimated 20 times as many, based on his statistics), and we would be undergoing some sort of intelligence revolution. Instead, he proposed that the results suggested that intelligence tests

do not measure intelligence but rather correlate with intelligence. He suggested that what had risen through generations was not intelligence itself, but some kind of 'abstract problem-solving ability'. Flynn (1994; 1999) favoured environmental explanations for the increase in these test scores. This was because these gains are far too rapid to result from genetic changes. The possible environmental influences were best summarised in a book edited by Ulrich Neisser in 1998 (Neisser, 1998a) to which a number of academics, including James Flynn, contributed (Flynn, 1998; Greenfield, 1998; Lynn, 1998; Neisser, 1998b; Schooler, 1998; Williams, 1998). Remember, the Flynn effect does not only concentrate on rises in IQ scores but also notes a greater rise for fluid (non-verbal) intelligence than for crystallised (verbal) intelligence. The Neisser book puts forward five main environmental areas to explain the Flynn effect:

- schooling;
- test-taking sophistication;
- parental rearing styles;
- visual and technical environment;
- nutrition.

Length of schooling

Intelligence test scores might be rising because people are attending school for more years than their parents and their grandparents did (Flynn, 1998; Neisser, 1998b; Williams, 1998). Two academics at the Hebrew University in Jerusalem, Sorel Cahan and Nora Cohen (1989), compared the effects of a year of school (controlling for age) with those of a year of age on a number of verbal (e.g. verbal and numerical skills) and non-verbal (abstract and reasoning tests, including the Raven's Matrices) IQ tests. Length of schooling was important in predicting the scores for all the verbal tests, and mattered more than age. Length of schooling, however, made a contribution (although a smaller contribution) to some of the non-verbal tests, including the items from the Raven's Matrices.

Although the findings suggest that length of schooling influences intelligence score, Flynn notes that this trend (schooling predicts larger rises in verbal tests and lower rises in non-verbal tests) is very different from the trend established by Flynn's data (generations have larger rises in non-verbal tests and lower rises in verbal tests). You will also note that this observation is consistent with Jensen's original proposal as outlined earlier. Both Flynn and Williams note that schooling is not a good explanation of the secular rise in IQ test scores through the generations.

Test-taking sophistication

Is there just a culture, or knowledge of taking IQ tests in modern life, that wasn't around when intelligence tests were first introduced? (Flynn, 1998; Williams, 1998). It would be true today that, before you even did this course or did psychology, you knew what an intelligence test was. If at school you were given an intelligence test, a great amount of time would be taken by the school to explain to you and your parents what the IQ tests were for. Both Flynn and Williams suggest that teaching today is increasingly geared to, or at least combines, certain kinds of achievement tests. If you think about it, even though verbal ability and mathematical ability contributed to schooling at the start of the twentieth century, advanced ideas about spatial reasoning contribute to classroom teaching today. Such ideas might not have been recognised, or even thought of, in the early twentieth century.

Certainly, then, it is likely that knowledge of intelligence tests by those taking them, and by parents and schools, might be related to increases in intelligence. However, would such knowledge explain the Flynn effect's emphasis on non-verbal rather than verbal aspects of intelligence? Furthermore, Williams notes that children who take the very same test twice usually only gain 5 or 6 IQ points, so increased familiarity with tests cannot fully explain the Flynn effect.

Child-rearing practices and Head Start

Let us go down to *Sesame Street*, a multi-award-winning programme whose principal purpose was to provide early mental stimulation to raise children's awareness and intelligence. *Sesame Street* is now recognised as historically changing children's educational television, particularly in encouraging the development of children's understanding and abilities (Palmer, 2003).

Flynn (1998) and Williams (1998) raise the issue that all parents today are more interested in their children's intellectual development and are probably doing more and more to develop it.

One example of such early interventions has not been shown to have 'lasting' effects on intelligence. A well-cited example is the Head Start programme in the United States. Established in the 1960s by President Lyndon Johnson, Head Start was designed to give America's poorest children a head start in preparing them for school to break the cycle of poverty. The programme, which still runs today, aims to narrow the gap between disadvantaged children and all other children in vocabulary, numeracy and writing skills. Here are some statistics regarding children in the Head Start programme today:

- Almost half of Head Start parents make less than $12,000 a year.
- About one in five children are reported to have been exposed to community or domestic violence in their lives.
- Almost one in every six Head Start children have one or more disabilities – generally a speech or language impairment, and half of all children's disabilities are identified after the child enters Head Start.

Very quickly, evidence was provided to assess the usefulness of such a programme. US Individual Differences psychologist Charles Locurta (Locurta, 1991) provides a review of this evidence. In 1969 Arthur Jensen suggested that Head Start had failed. The reason for Jensen's pronouncement was that, although children attending the programme had shown an initial increase in IQ points (sometimes as much as 7–8 points on IQ tests), after 2 or 3 years, these higher IQ points were lost (Locurta, 1991). There has been a lot of debate about the effectiveness of Head Start (see Stop and think: What other issues and evidence surround Head Start?). In terms of IQ gains, however, perhaps a final word goes to the Advisory Committee on Head Start Quality and Expansion, which published a final report in 1999. In 1981, the Advisory Committee undertook to synthesise all the early published and unpublished research on Head Start. More than 200 reports were studied, and 76 of these became part of the meta-analysis by McKey *et al.* (1985), who reported on

Stop and think

What other issues and evidence surround Head Start?

Despite a lack of evidence for a permanent rise of IQ test scores among children attending the Head Start scheme, debate still exists around its usefulness. Professor Michael J. A. Howe, writing an article in the British Psychological Society magazine *The Psychologist* (Howe, 1998) on whether an individual's IQ score is fixed, draws attention to a number of studies noting that there have been large gains in IQ scores as a result of the Head Start programme. Howe's point is that it may be foolish to disregard these findings simply because they are not long-term changes. Howe suggests that lots of abilities would decline if not given further opportunity to develop. For example now, you may have learnt a musical instrument as a child but given it up after a few years. If you tried to play the same musical instrument now, you wouldn't be as good as you once were. Therefore, in the case of Head Start, Howe suggests that the very conditions that led to the children being in Head Start – poverty, unemployment, poor housing – are still there when the children leave the programme, and therefore the children return to these conditions and the advantages fade.

Furthermore, the people who run Head Start stress that IQ test scores are not the only thing measured in the programme, and they can show that Head Start has obtained lasting educational benefits (McKey *et al.*, 1985). In McKey's meta-analysis of Head Start schemes, the evidence is clear that Head Start produces immediate gains for children and families by linking families with services available in the community. Furthermore, children in Head Start make substantial progress in word knowledge, letter recognition, writing skills and mathematics skills when compared to national averages. These findings suggest that children receive a much-needed boost and that, in terms of education achievement, compared to similar disadvantaged peers, Head Start children are less likely to repeat a year of study, more likely to graduate from high school and less likely to need special education services.

the IQ effects of the Head Start programme on children. In regard to scores on intelligence tests, McKey *et al.* (1985) reported that children enrolled in Head Start enjoy significant immediate gains in IQ test scores; however, in the longer term (3–4 years), the IQ scores of Head Start students do not remain superior to disadvantaged children who did not attend Head Start.

With such evidence, both Flynn and Williams suggest that early childhood experience and intellectual promotion in early childhood cannot explain the Flynn effect.

The cultural and technological age

Flynn (1998), Greenfield (1998) and Schooler (1998) suggest that we have to look at the cultural, visual and technical environment that surrounds us today. The most obvious change in the late twentieth century was our increasing use of and exposure to visual media. During the twentieth century, we have seen the growth of movies, video and then DVD; televisions in almost all homes; and the use of home computers. Because of such growth we may have become much more visually aware. Even with something as simple as television adverts, we are asked to extract meaning from many in which the message is obscured. Adverts have changed compared with many years ago, when their messages were more straightforward.

Children spend more time now learning through this medium, rather than just simply concentrating on material in a classroom setting presented by the teacher. At the same time, we adults are more used to processing complicated visual information.

It is this visual revolution that leads Greenfield and Schooler to suggest that this might account for growth in fluid intelligence. Remember that tests like the Raven's Matrices rely on only visual material. Therefore, recent generations' exposure to complex visual media has produced genuine increases in a significant form of intelligence, which these authors call visual analysis. Non-verbal intelligence tests such as Raven's Matrices may show the larger Flynn effect gains because they measure this visual analysis directly. Schooler, however, notes that little direct evidence exists for the visual-analysis hypothesis.

Nutrition and IQ

Nutrition is the study of food, and specifically the relationship between diet and states of health and disease. Richard Lynn, Professor at the University of Ulster, has proposed that nutrition and healthcare improvements are among the main causal factors of the Flynn effect (Lynn, 1990; 1998).

Lynn starts by drawing attention to gains in human height over the past century (approximately 1.2 cm per decade). These gains are being attributed to nutrition, such as growth in the consumption of milk and dairy products (300 per cent), fruit (100 per cent), vegetables (50 per cent) and fish (20 per cent). Lynn poses the question: if this is true of height, why not of something also biological, the brain and its functioning (i.e. intelligence), particularly as nutrition has been linked to larger brain sizes, and malnutrition has been linked to poor brain development? Lynn's hypothesis is that better nourished brains would allow subjects to perform better on IQ tests as well as in everyday activities.

The conclusion that nutritional sources can aid aspects of IQ as measured by intelligence tests is a common finding. Australian nutritionist Wendy H. Oddy and her colleagues (Oddy *et al.*, 2004) examined over 2,000 Australian children and followed them from before birth until the age of 8 years. Oddy and her colleagues found that stopping breast feeding early (at 6 months or less) was associated with reduced verbal intelligence, while children who were fully breast fed for more than 6 months scored between 3 and 6 points higher on a vocabulary test than did those who were never breast fed.

Similarly, another study conducted by US health psychologist Melanie Smith and her colleagues (Smith *et al.*, 2003) examined 439 school-age, low birth-weight children born in the United States. These authors found differences in intelligence test scores between breast-fed children and those who did not receive any breast milk. The researchers found that breast-fed children scored 3.6 IQ points higher for overall intellectual functioning and 2.3 IQ points higher for verbal ability than children who were not breast fed.

The argument that breast feeding leads to higher IQ is not always supported by research evidence when other variables are taken into account. Der *et al.* (2006) analysed data from more than 5,000 US children and their mothers. They found that children who had been breast fed did tend to score higher on IQ tests, but the authors found that the mothers of these children were also more intelligent. Der *et al.* found that, when mother's intelligence was taken into account, most of the relationship between breast feeding and the child's intelligence disappeared.

Chinese nutritionist Ming Qian and his colleagues (Qian *et al.*, 2005) looked at the effects of iodine on intelligence in children. Iodine was one of the first minerals to be recognised as crucial for good health. It is still considered one of the most important minerals. In the human body, it forms an essential component of the main hormone produced by the thyroid gland, which controls the basic metabolism and oxygen consumption of tissues, regulates the rate of energy production and body weight and promotes proper growth. It is also thought to improve mental ability. Qian *et al.* (2005), as part of a meta-analysis of 37 reported studies (for a total of 12,291 children), compared those children living in severely iodine-deficient areas who received iodine supplements during their mothers' pregnancy and after their birth as part of a health programme with those children living in severely iodine-deficient areas who received no supplements. Each group was matched on a number of social and economic demographic variables, and each group was compared and matched with a control group of children living in iodine-sufficient areas. Those children receiving iodine supplementation before and after birth scored 8.7 IQ points higher than the group who didn't receive supplements. The IQ score rose to between 12 IQ points on a non-verbal measure of intelligence (the Raven's Matrices) and 17.25 IQ points on a non-verbal and verbal measure of intelligence (the Stanford–Binet) 3½ years after the iodine supplementation health programme was introduced.

So, there is some data supporting a general hypothesis that nutrition increases intelligence. But what about the idea that nutrition accounts for the Flynn effect (more dramatic rises in fluid/non-verbal intelligence than in crystallised/verbal intelligence)? Testing Lynn's hypothesis is hard because he has formulated his ideas by looking at trends and changes in IQ scores over several decades, and today any studies will be of relatively well-nourished children, particularly in the western cultures where the effect was observed. However, researchers have tried to test Lynn's theory in relation to the Flynn effect.

A well-known study in this area was carried out by two Welsh psychologists, David Benton and Gwilym Roberts (Benton and Roberts, 1988), who published a study in the British medical journal, *The Lancet*. Benton and Roberts had completed an experiment on 90 children. Thirty of the children were given a supplement containing a number of vitamins and minerals, including riboflavin, vitamins A, B[12], C, D, E and K, magnesium and iron. Thirty children were given a placebo. The last group of 30 took no capsules. After 8 months, there was no significant difference between the groups on verbal intelligence scores. However, only the supplemented group increased in non-verbal (fluid) intelligence – from 111 to 120 IQ points – while the placebo group scores remained relatively unchanged, with these groups gaining no more than 4 IQ points. This sort of finding is consistent with Lynn's hypothesis.

This study caused great interest and controversy. In England the findings were reported in a special television programme, and by the following week, health shops had sold out of vitamin and mineral supplements for children. The findings generated commentary among the medical and nutritional communities, including criticisms of the study's methodology. *The Lancet*, where the study report originally appeared, published seven letters from a total of 11 nutritional scientists, two statisticians and three others who were all deeply critical of the study.

Benton and Roberts' study also led to further studies trying to replicate the findings. However, these studies have confused rather than clarified the situation. Some authors have replicated the findings but only with certain children and certain supplements. For example, US psychologist Stephen J. Schoenthaler, Professor of Criminal Justice at California State University, and his colleagues conducted randomised trials in which children were given placebos or low-dose vitamin–mineral tablets designed to raise nutrient intake to the equivalent of a well-balanced diet (Schoenthaler *et al.*, 2000). The authors reported significantly greater gains

Stop and think

Nutrition advertising

The Observer, on Sunday 18 September 2005 (Briffa, 2005), carried a report of the UK Advertising Standards Authority's decision regarding the claims of a particular breakfast cereal by its makers. The advert, like some others for breakfast cereal, suggested that eating a bowl of cereal in the morning can help children's concentration in school. Following these adverts, the Advertising Standards Authority (ASA) in the United Kingdom received complaints that

Cereal Partners UK had claimed in one of their adverts, for the breakfast cereal Shreddies, that 'studies show a breakfast like Shreddies helps give kids the mental energy they need to stay involved at school'. When the ASA asked the company to substantiate such claims, it could offer evidence from one small study that tested the effects of its cereal in this respect. However, some of this evidence involved a comparison between eating any breakfast and eating nothing at all; therefore, any effect could not be the result of eating Shreddies, but of eating breakfast. Consequently, the ASA judged that the advert made potentially misleading claims for the effects of Shreddies on children's concentration at school and banned the advert.

Imagine you were employed by Cereal Partners UK to help relaunch the campaign. Given the evidence just described, what recommendations would you make to them regarding the claims and the approach they could take in any advert?

in non-verbal intelligence (around 2–3 points) among some groups of children who were given vitamin–mineral tablets, but these were children who were poorly nourished. The authors suggest that lack of a greater rise was due to the fact that most western schoolchildren were already adequately nourished. However, other studies, such as that carried out by Ian K. Crombie and his colleagues (Crombie *et al.*, 1990), reported a small, non-significant difference between the control and supplementation groups in non-verbal intelligence; this finding thus provided no support of Benton and Roberts' findings.

Overviews of these types of studies (e.g. Benton, 1991) have drawn the following conclusion: in the majority of studies there is a positive effect on IQ as a result of vitamin-mineral supplements, in at least some of the children, on non-verbal measures of intelligence. Benton, like many commentators, suggests that more work needs to be done in this area – concentrating on a wide range of ages, dietary styles and different economic and social backgrounds – and that more work needs to be done in looking at what supplements affect what children, on what intelligence tests.

Lynn's hypothesis holds some weight. As Neisser (1998b) has pointed out, it is difficult to demonstrate a relationship between diet and intelligence because malnutrition or vitamin and mineral deficiency in childhood almost certainly produces negative cognitive effects. However, this also happens with other forms of deprivation, such as aspects of poverty, schooling, parenting styles and visual and technological environment (all mentioned earlier). That makes those effects difficult to analyse.

The nutrition hypothesis versus the cognitive stimulation hypothesis

However, the debate doesn't stop with the Neisser book commentaries. The arguments put forward by the Neisser book can be broken down into two general hypotheses that can be used to explain the Flynn effect. Lynn (1990) originally set up two opposing hypotheses that have been developed by the Neisser book and Flynn (2003). This

Reasons given for the Flynn effect include that we are becoming more technology minded.
Source: Pearson Education Ltd./Image Source

comparison is based on comparing a nutrition hypothesis with a cognitive stimulation hypothesis.

The nutrition hypothesis, as noted before, sees nutrition as part of a package in which increased intelligence is part of a nurturing environment that includes increased height and lifespan, improved health, decreased rate of infant disease and better vitamin and mineral nutrition.

The cognitive stimulation hypothesis now largely draws on the type of contributions made to the Neisser book that were mentioned earlier (Flynn, 1998; Greenfield, 1998; Neisser, 1998b; Schooler, 1998; Williams, 1998). It suggests that higher intelligence scores are derived from improvements in cognitive stimulation. This concept arises not only from 'visual analysis' intelligence but also from ideas about improved schooling, about different parental rearing styles, that parents are better educated, that families are smaller (so parents spend more time with each child) and about the greater availability of educational toys.

Researchers have used this distinction in trying to build some understanding for the Flynn effect. The suggestion has been that, if the cognitive stimulation hypothesis holds true, we should see a rise of intelligence test scores across generations at all levels of IQ (Flynn, 2003; Lynn, 1990). On the other hand, if the nutrition hypothesis holds true, intelligence gains will predominantly occur at the lower end of the distribution of IQ test scores where nutritional deprivation is most severe (Flynn, 2003). You can see an illustration of this in Figure 13.4 with the dotted lines representing the change to the distribution of scores and the corresponding effect that this has on the mean IQ score.

In 2005, Spanish psychologists Roberto Colom, Josep M. Luis-Font and Antonio Andrés-Pueyo (Colom *et al.*, 2005) presented data supporting the nutrition hypothesis. Two large samples of Spanish children (459 boys tested in 1970 and 275 boys tested in 1999) were assessed with a 30-year gap in a measure of fluid/non-verbal intelligence. Comparison of the IQ scores distribution indicated that the mean IQ had increased by 9.7 IQ points, suggesting the Flynn effect; however, the gains, which were concentrated in the lower half of the distribution, gradually but steadily decreased from low to high IQ. At the lowest level of IQ scores (lowest percentile) the difference was greatest, with the change in raw scores (not IQ points, but scores on the measure) on the fluid/non-verbal IQ test being around 9 IQ points. With average scores in IQ the increase in scores was 4–5 IQ points; and at the high level of IQ scores, the top percentile, the increase in scores was only around 1 IQ point. The authors claim their findings suggest that intelligence gains are mainly (although not exclusively) concentrated among lower intelligence levels and would support the nutritional hypothesis.

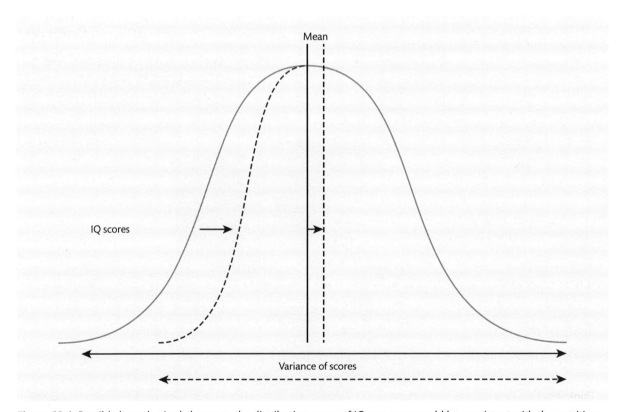

Figure 13.4 Possible hypothesised change to the distribution curve of IQ scores as would be consistent with the nutrition hypothesis.

Stop and think

Dickens/Flynn model

In 2001 William Dickens and James Flynn (Dickens and Flynn, 2001) developed the cognitive stimulation hypothesis into the Dickens Flynn model. Part of the Dickens/Flynn model explains that the rise in IQ scores results from an interaction between genetics and environments produced by the cultural and technological age. Dickens and Flynn argue that those people with higher intelligence from birth will seek out cultural and technological stimulating environments, thereby even further increasing their intelligence. Therefore they argue this interaction has an additional, even multiplying, effect on intelligence across a generation, the sort of dramatic effect that would result in high IQ rises across generations (e.g. the Flynn effect). We cover more on the relationship between genetic and environment influences on intelligence later (Chapter 14). However, try to think of a couple of examples of how certain individuals with a high intelligence from an early age to early adulthood might seek out stimulating environments that might further contribute to their intelligence. Also try to think of a couple of examples of how individuals with a low intelligence may not from an early age to early adulthood seek out stimulating environments and therefore restrict potential growth in their intelligence.

Colom and his colleagues point to two previous studies that also support their conclusions. First, Teasdale and Owen (1989) studied a Danish representative sample of 30,804 males. The gains in fluid/non-verbal intelligence were observed among lower IQ test score levels, with the authors finding no evidence of IQ gains in the top half of the distribution of IQ scores. Secondly, Lynn and Hampson (1986) – in a study of US, Japanese and British IQ test scores across several generations – reported a greater rise in the lower half of individuals' IQ scores on measures of fluid/non-verbal intelligence than in the top half of individuals' IQ scores among a British sample.

However, James Flynn provided a review of current evidence in 2007 that directly addressed this issue (Flynn, 2007). Flynn points out that there are only six countries in which psychologists have access to a full distribution of data (from top to bottom): France (1949–1974), Netherlands (1952–1982), Denmark (1958–1987), USA (1948–1989), Spain (1970–1999) and Norway (1957–2002). From these studies, Flynn notes that only in only three of these populations (Denmark, Spain and Norway) have researchers observed larger gains at the lower end of the distribution, consistent with the nutrition hypothesis. Therefore Flynn is keen to emphasise that we have only seen this change in three countries. Flynn also suggests that we can look at other data to see if the nutrition hypothesis is correct. He argues that if the lower half of any distribution rises then, regardless of whether we have all the data for the full population we should see the variance of scores (i.e. the range or spread of scores) lessen. This change is also indicated at the bottom of Figure 13.4. Flynn also reports that, in a number of data sets collected in Argentina, Belgium, Canada, Estonia, New Zealand and Sweden, there has been no evidence for the variance of scores decreasing.

Clearly this debate is in need of further examination through evidence. An important point to remember regarding research like this is that, by looking closely at trends in intelligence test scores, by revisiting and developing ideas, researchers are being inventive in examining whether rises in intelligence (whether in fluid/non-verbal or crystallised/verbal intelligences) can be attributed largely to one set of factors over another.

An end to the Flynn effect?

A number of recent studies in Europe have speculated that the Flynn effect may be at an end, or in reverse. In 2004, Norwegians Jon Martin Sundet, Dag G. Barlaug and Tore M. Torjussen (Sundet et al., 2004) published a

Stop and think

Think about the different environments you experienced as a child: at home, at school, with family, with friends.

Which of those environments were the most 'cognitively stimulating' and why?

study reporting trends for scores on a language and mathematics intelligence test (verbal/crystallised intelligence) and a Raven-like IQ (non-verbal/fluid intelligence) test among Norwegian male conscripts tested from the mid-1950s to 2002. Sundet and his colleagues, similarly to the findings of Flynn, found that IQ on a non-verbal measure of intelligence increased from the mid-1950s to the late 1990s by about 16–17 IQ points, and smaller gains were found for the two verbal tests measuring crystallised intelligence. However, the authors report that, for the non-verbal intelligence test, IQ ceased to increase after the mid to late 1990s. The authors suggest that this finding indicates the Flynn effect may have come to an end in Norway.

A year later, Danish psychologist Thomas W. Teasdale and US psychologist David R. Owen replicated Sundet et al.'s findings. Teasdale and Owen (2005) analysed the data for over 500,000 younger Danish men, tested between 1959 and 2004, and found that performance on intelligence tests peaked in the late 1990s and has since declined moderately to pre-1991 levels, suggesting the Flynn effect might be in decline.

Both groups of authors note a trend in these Scandinavian countries, but suggest that the gains seem to be caused mainly by a decreasing prevalence of low scorers. That is, the rise in IQ scores was a result of there being fewer and fewer low scorers who were dragging the average IQ score down. Eventually, in the 1990s, the prevalence of low scorers perhaps levelled out, and this has led to the levelling out of IQ test scores. As with the Flynn effect, no one knows the reason. However, it is tempting to attribute it to some factors that have been previously suggested. For example, if low nutrition among a number of people was a factor in the mid-1950s contributing to low IQ scores, then improving nutrition during the following decades would have slowly removed the number of people with low scores on IQ tests. What psychologists like Sundet are suggesting is that poor nutrition may no longer be a problem in the 1990s, and therefore the slow removal of people with low IQ scores on intelligence tests caused by poor nutrition has ceased.

Flynn (2009) looked at data for the Raven's Standard Progressive Matrices for schoolchildren in the UK between 1938 and 2008. Flynn found that the Raven's data show that, over this period, taking the ages of 5–15 together, UK schoolchildren have gained 14 IQ points at a rate of 0.216 points per year. However, since 1979, gains have declined with age and, between the ages of 12–13 years and 14–15 years, small gains turn into small losses. Similarly, among 6–11-year-olds in Australia, intelligence (IQ) measured by the Colored Progressive Matrices (a version of Raven's Progressive Matrices) has shown no increase from 1975 to 2003 (Cotton et al., 2005).

Flynn (2009) argues that many of the factors we discuss in this section, such as education, parental rearing, test-taking sophistication, technology and nutrition, can be seen to be important in explaining any levelling out of the Flynn effect. He argues that a much more subtle analysis of these factors could explain the levelling out of IQ gains. For example, we mentioned above that gains among UK schoolchildren have, since 1979, declined with age, and that between the ages of 12–13 years and 14–15 years the small gains in IQ turn into small losses. One hypothesis offered by Flynn is that, although parenting styles and education have since 1979 become much more cognitively stimulating (use of computers and educationally focused parenting styles), the gains in these developments are focused at the ages of 9–11 when children tend to spend more time with their parents and at school and spend more time being influenced by these factors. However, between the ages of 12 and 15 years, children become more independent and tend to spend more time with their friends. Flynn suggests that these activities with friends are less focused around being cognitively stimulated (e.g. seeing each other, listening to music, generally just 'hanging' out, chatting and gossiping). Therefore the gains seen in IQ since 1979 for 9-to 11-year-olds result from children being predominantly in situations where the environmental influences have become increasingly cognitively stimulating. However, these gains do not occur from the age of 12 onwards because there are other environmental influences present that have not developed in terms of how much cognitive stimulation they provide. That is, 'hanging out' with your friends for a teenager in 2008 comprises pretty much the same activities that it did for a teenager in 1979.

Final comments

Our last word on the topic perhaps goes to the comments of French psychologist France Bellisle, writing in the *British Journal of Nutrition* (Bellisle, 2004). As we have seen in this discussion, Bellisle writes that nutrition can affect intelligence, but the secret is that good regular dietary habits are the best way to ensure optimal mental performance at all times. These sentiments can be carried to other dimensions discussed here. Underlying each dimension are attempts to understand, to measure more effectively and to attain the optimal outcome for all people. From the uses of IQ tests to the problems and attempts to address these criticisms, to attempts to understand the Flynn effect, there is always an effort to imaginatively and thoroughly advance our understanding of intelligence. We would like you to leave this discussion on a positive note, particularly as there are some much darker debates to come.

Summary

- Many intelligence tests in use today reflect theoretical and empirical growth in the understanding of intelligence.
- There is a distinction between psychometric and cognitive intelligence tests.
- Psychometric intelligence tests are based on factor-analytic studies.
- Cognitive psychology tests of intelligence are based on biological and psychophysiological models of intelligence.
- There is a history of biological and psychophysiological theory and research in intelligence testing. Areas of research include brain size, ECTs (elementary cognitive tasks), EPs (evoked potentials) and RTs (response times).
- The inspiration for some modern cognitive measures of intelligence was the work of Luria. It is Luria's emphasis on neurological functioning, his distinction between simultaneous and sequential processing and his emphasis on using tests to both diagnose and improve performance centred on the individual that influences Das and Naglieri's cognitive assessment system (CAS) and the Kaufmans' ability tests.
- Sattler (2002) establishes three main aspects in all good intelligence tests: the variety of tasks involved, standardisation of administration and norm referencing. Intelligence tests are used for all sorts of purposes, but mainly for these three: selection, diagnosis and evaluation.
- IQ test scores are important in predicting school and work performance. The average correlation between intelligence and a number of school indicators is around $r = 0.50$, suggesting that intelligence does predict performance at school. The correlation between intelligence (cognitive ability) and job performance is also around $r = 0.50$.
- Some psychologists have shown that intelligence in childhood can predict variables across the lifespan; these include death by a certain age and people being diagnosed with certain illnesses, but not all health-related matters.
- At one level the criticisms of and issues with intelligence tests are rather easy to identify. The issues are of reliability, validity and whether the importance of intelligence tests is over-emphasised.
- There is a huge difference between the way that intelligence tests are used and viewed and the modern-day theories and intelligence tests that have been developed in the past 20 years. Naglieri has suggested that, today, intelligence practitioners want not only to test children's intelligence, but to follow it up with interventions that are designed to improve the child's learning in the areas where they have shown weakness.
- The Flynn effect is the continued year-on-year rise of intelligence test scores in all parts of the world, with these rises being larger with fluid/non-verbal intelligence than with crystallised/verbal intelligence.
- Explanations for the Flynn effect include schooling, test-taking sophistication, parental rearing styles, the visual and technical environment and nutrition. Later theorists have suggested that these explanations subsume two hypotheses: the nutrition hypothesis and the cognitive stimulation hypothesis.
- There is evidence to suggest that the generational IQ gains as detailed by the Flynn effect might be slowing down or coming to an end.

Connecting up

This chapter should be read after Chapter 12 (Theories and Measurement of Intelligence) in this part of the book. Many of the issues surrounding the cognitive stimulation hypothesis and the nutritional hypothesis are expanded on in Chapter 14.

Critical thinking

When discussing intelligence, you really need to think not only about how all these ideas fit around the idea of the 'usefulness' of intelligence tests but also about the issues they raise and the role they play in society.

Discussion questions

- How do the biological and psychophysiological measures of intelligence outlined in this discussion compare to those intelligence tests based on factor analytical studies described previously (Chapter 12)?
- Are intelligence tests valid measures of intelligence?
- What are some of the best uses of intelligence tests?
- The nutrition hypothesis suggests that each generation is generally getting better nutrition. Is this still true in modern society? Discuss how differences in nutrition levels within a society might help us to examine the Flynn effect.
- Discuss the relative merits of the nutrition and cognitive stimulation hypotheses.
- What do you think is the cause of the Flynn effect?
- Are people increasing in their intelligence?

Essay questions

- Critically examine the uses, advantages and problems that surround intelligence testing.
- Critically examine the role of physiological and biological factors in intelligence testing.
- Critically examine the view that rises in intelligence over a number of generations are due to:

  – nutrition
  – cognitive stimulation.

- Critically discuss how the nutrition hypothesis and the cognitive stimulation hypothesis contribute to our understanding of the Flynn effect.

Going further

Books

- Flynn, J. R. (1984). *The mean IQ of Americans: Massive gains from 1932 to 1978*. New York: Harper & Row.
- Flynn, J. R. (2009). *What is intelligence? Beyond the Flynn effect*. Cambridge: Cambridge University Press.
- Neisser, U. (ed.) (1998). *The rising curve*. Washington, DC: American Psychological Association.

Journals

These articles are recommended reading regarding modern uses of intelligence tests and evidences and issues around the Flynn effect.

- Flynn, J. R. (1987). Massive IQ gains in 14 nations: What IQ tests really measure. *Psychological Bulletin, 101*, 171–191. *Psychological Bulletin* is published by the American Psychological Association. Available online via PsycARTICLES.
- Deary, I. J. (2012). Intelligence. *Annual Review of Psychology, 63*, 443–48. *Annual Review of Psychology* is published by Annual Reviews, Palo Alto, California. Available online via Business Source Premier.
- Flynn, J. R. (1999). Searching for justice: The discovery of IQ gains over time. *American Psychologist, 54*, 5–20. *American Psychologist* is published by the American Psychological Association. Available online via PsycARTICLES.

- Naglieri, J. A. (1998). A closer look at new kinds of intelligence tests. *American Psychologist, 53*, 1158–1159. Published by the American Psychological Association. Available online via PsycARTICLES.
- In this discussion we looked at the notion of whether IQ and intelligence can change. A good article that summarises the main issues is Howe, J. A. (1998). Can IQ change? *The Psychologist, 11*, 69–72. This article is freely available online. You can find *The Psychologist* on the British Psychological Society website (**www.bps.org.uk**).

Articles on the main intelligence issues discussed here are often found in these journals.

- *Intelligence: A Multidisciplinary Journal*. Published by Elsevier Science. Available online via Science Direct.
- *Personality and Individual Differences*. Published by Elsevier Science. Available online via Science Direct.
- *American Psychologist*. Published by the American Psychological Society. Available online via PsycARTICLES.

Web link

- **Head Start** is an information and publication centre that supports the innovative early childhood development programme, and is sponsored by the US federal government (**www.acf.hhs.gov/programs/ohs**).

Film and literature

- *Good Will Hunting* (1997, directed by Gus Van Sant). A janitor at a prestigious university, Will Hunting is gifted in mathematics that can take him beyond his blue-collar job and roots. The film provides you with an analysis of how natural intelligence can come into conflict with socioeconomic variables.
- *Dangerous Minds* (1996, directed by John N. Smith). This is another film that shows how natural intelligence can come into conflict with socioeconomic variables. In this film, a US high school teacher starts teaching a class and slowly realises that the students in her class are highly intelligent but have social problems.
- *Discovering Psychology video* (1990, Educational Resource Film). Topics on intelligence, creativity and the self, limitations of testing and measuring the brain. WGBH/Annenberg-PCB-Project/CS.

Explore the website accompanying this text at **www.pearsoned.co.uk/maltby** for further resources to help you with your studies. These include multiple-choice questions, essay questions, web links and ideas for advanced reading.

CHAPTER 14
Heritability and Socially Defined Race Differences in Intelligence

Key themes

- Genetic heritability of intelligence
- Genetic and environmental influences on intelligence
- The bell curve
- Socially defined race differences in intelligence
- Eugenics in intelligence research

Learning outcomes

By the end of this discussion you should:

- Understand what is meant by genetic heritability in intelligence
- Be able to outline the different dimensions of genetic and environmental influences that are thought to affect intelligence
- Be familiar with the main points of Herrnstein and Murray's bell curve analysis
- Be aware of some criticisms of Herrnstein and Murray's bell curve analysis

Introduction

In 1994 Arthur Jensen, a prominent IQ psychologist, wrote:

> **Consideration of the book's actual content is being displaced by the rhetoric of denial: name calling ('neo-Nazi', 'pseudo-scientific,' 'racism'), sidetracks ('but does IQ really measure intelligence?'), non sequiturs ('specific genes for IQ have not been identified, so we can claim nothing about its heritability'), red herrings ('Hitler misused genetics'), falsehoods ('all the tests are biased'), hyperbole ('throwing gasoline on a fire'), and insults ('creepy', 'indecent', 'ugly').**

(Jensen, 1994, p. 48)

What book created these descriptions, and why did Jensen feel it necessary to defend such a book? In this discussion we address the history, theory and debate that surround the examination of race differences in intelligence, and explore the debates and consequences of some of the conclusions that are drawn from this research. It is not a pretty side of psychology. Assertions and evidence presented are not always palatable to many. Group differences in intelligence are an interesting area of debate, but it is not without its dark side. And as part of this discussion, we are going to explore the actual content of the aforementioned book.

This section is slightly longer than many others in the text. We deal with some controversial and sensitive issues in the psychology of intelligence. We argue that many areas need to be explained and fully explored. Additionally, we introduce a number of concepts that you have come across in previous discussions, so, rather than suggest you spend your time going backwards and forwards through the text, we have spent a little time restating the main issues and findings from other discussions, to make it clear how these issues apply to the debates put forward here. Consequently, you should find some of this material easier going because you have been introduced to a lot of the arguments previously.

We realise that there is slightly more material here, so we have split the discussion into two main sections. Please remember, however, that these two areas are intrinsically linked.

- **Section A – The heritability of intelligence** – in this section we will outline what has become known as the nature versus nurture debate, in which we compare and consider genetic versus environmental effects on intelligence. Key themes in this debate include heritability of intelligence and genetic and environmental influences on intelligence.

- **Section B – The bell curve: race differences in intelligence** – in this section we will outline what has become known as the bell curve debate. We consider evidence and arguments regarding race differences in intelligence. Key themes in this debate include an outline and consideration of a bell curve, group differences, most notably race differences in intelligence, and the role of eugenics in intelligence research.

Source: Getty Images/Tim Platt

Section A – the heritability of intelligence

Intelligence: the nature versus nurture debate

Here we will outline what has become known as the nature versus nurture debate. We will compare and consider genetic versus environmental effects on intelligence.

Galton

In 1865, Sir Francis Galton began to study the heritability of intelligence, following his reading of his cousin Charles Darwin's publication *The Origin of Species*, which dealt with the idea that all species gradually evolve through the process of natural selection. In following this work, Galton soon became interested in studying the variations in human ability, and particularly intelligence. In his book *Hereditary Genius* (Galton, 1869), he began investigating why higher intelligence seemed to run in families. He suggested that man's natural abilities are inherited under the same conditions as physical features of the animal world described by Darwin. Galton suggested that children inherit their intelligence from their parents.

To support such an assertion, Galton started analysing the obituaries of *The Times* newspaper so that he could identify the ancestry of eminent men. What Galton did was to compare different degrees of relationship between individuals in terms of being biological relatives (i.e. parents, siblings, cousins) and the eminence of each of these individuals. First-degree relatives are relatives with whom an individual shares an estimated average of 50 per cent (half) of their genes (though note this is an estimated average percentage; you will learn more about why this is an estimated average later in this discussion). First-degree relatives include your parents, brothers and sisters and children. A second-degree relative is a relative with whom an individual shares an estimated average of 25 per cent (a quarter) of their genes; that is, grandparents, grandchildren, aunts, uncles, nephews, nieces. A third-degree relative is a relative with whom an individual shares an estimated average of 12.5 per cent (one-eighth) of their genes. Third-degree relatives include your great-grandparents, great-aunts, great-uncles and first cousins. Galton found that the number of eminent relatives of an eminent person was greater for first-degree relatives than for second-degree relatives; and again, the number was greater for second-degree relatives than for third-degree relatives. This result suggested to Galton that there is evidence for the heritability of intelligence.

However, Galton quickly became concerned with whether intelligence was simply heritable or whether it was also influenced by the environment. It was here that Galton was the first psychologist to make the distinction between 'nature' and 'nurture' (and he was the first to use this now-common phrase). To examine this idea, he surveyed 190 Fellows of the Royal Society, of which Galton was a member (Galton, 1874). The Royal Society is a highly prestigious scientific society dedicated to establishing the truth of scientific matters through experiment. It has had several famous scientists as members, including Robert Boyle, Sir Christopher Wren and Isaac Newton. Galton asked his fellow members of the Society several questions regarding their birth order and the occupation and race of their parents. He wanted to find out whether members of the Society's achievements and interest in science were caused by their natural makeup (nature) or their environment; for example, the encouragement of their talents by others (nurture).

You have to remember that many of Galton's speculations arose before we knew as much about genetics as we do today. That is why many recognise him as a truly great scientist. Galton himself recognised the inherent problems of such studies (Galton, 1875). For example, he speculated about the confounding effects of the environment and realised that eminent people might not have arisen to their current status alone, but with the help of relatives. Galton believed that the question of whether nature or nurture influences intelligence could be examined more carefully by comparing twins. He suggested that comparisons of twins who were similar at birth but had grown up in different environments, and comparisons of dissimilar twins who had grown up in similar environments, might hold the key to examining the nature–nurture debate surrounding intelligence. He also proposed that adoption studies might be useful to analyse the different effects of heredity and environment. His speculations about twins and adoption studies laid the groundwork for modern attempts to examine the nature–nurture debate in intelligence.

Heritability of intelligence

Within the nature versus nurture consideration of intelligence, we find ourselves concentrating on behavioural genetic principles (you will have come across many of these ideas if you have read Chapter 8). One area of behavioural genetics concentrates on the relationships between genes and environment, to compare the similarities and differences between individuals within a particular population and assess the relative influence of genes and the environment on any behaviour. In this case, the behaviour we are looking at is intelligence.

Galton felt that there was some value in studying eminent families as an indicator of the heritability of intelligence. How well would such an approach work today?
Source: Shutterstock.com/Featureflash/Simon Burchell

What do we mean by heritability of intelligence?

Behavioural geneticists such as Robert Plomin have written extensively about behavioural genetics (Plomin 2004; Plomin *et al.*, 2000). Heritability of intelligence begins with the fact that genes are biologically transmitted from biological parents to the child. Children inherit 50 per cent of their father's genes and 50 per cent of their mother's genes. We can use this information as a starting point to explore how genes influence intelligence.

The assessment of the extent to which any phenotype (any outward manifestation of the individual – physical attractiveness, behaviour, intelligence) is passed on from parents to children, from the results of their genes, is termed **genetic heritability**. The genetic heritability of any phenotype is assessed in terms of variability (i.e. how much they differ) between the parents and the child. This variability is often assessed within the *proportion of shared variance* of that behaviour between the parent and child. Proportion of shared variance is presented as a percentage (i.e. out of 100 per cent). When a parent and child are very similar in a particular characteristic, there is thought to be a low variability between parent and child, and the proportion of shared variance of that behaviour is high (nearer 100 per cent). In other words, the parent and child are not very different in this characteristic. Conversely, when a parent and child are quite different in a particular characteristic, there is thought to be a high variability

between parent and child, and the proportion of shared variance of that behaviour is low (nearer 0 per cent).

The heritability of a human physical characteristic, such as having a nose, is entirely genetic and not in any way influenced by factors such as the environment. In fact, the environment is seen as having zero variability, or a proportion of shared variance of 100 per cent. However, some aspects of human behaviour (including intelligence), in which the environment is thought to have an influence, have greater amounts of heritable variability and lower shared variance. For example, choosing which football team to support would be heavily determined by environmental factors such as where you are born, your parents' football team, your friends and the first football team you see. Choosing a favourite football team has high variability between parent and child, but the proportion of shared variance of favourite football team caused by genetic heritability would be zero (0 per cent).

In behavioural genetics of intelligence, researchers are primarily interested in *estimating* the extent of genetic heritability of intelligence across a population, and stating the genetic heritability of that behaviour in terms of shared variance. This estimated average of genetic heritability is known as h^2. Therefore, h^2 is the *average estimate* of the proportion of variance for intelligence thought to be accounted for by genetic factors across a population.

You may have noticed that we emphasised *estimating*, *estimate* ('estimate' meaning to calculate approximately) and *average*. This is because, for a long time in psychology, for any phenotype (characteristic or behaviour) the estimates of the strength of genetics factors were done and interpreted within a process called *additive assumption*. Additive assumption suggests that there are only two dimensions that determine heritability of any behaviour (in our case, intelligence): (1) the genetic part, which we've just outlined; and (2) the environment. Consequently, overall, heritability of intelligence is estimated in terms of the relative strength of both (e.g. nature versus nurture). Therefore, the influence of genetic (G) and environmental (E) components, in this theory, will always add together to account for 100 per cent of the variance of intelligence. On the basis of this assumption, the heritability coefficient (h^2) can be subtracted from 100 per cent to calculate the environmental contribution to intelligence. If researchers computed, for example, that genetics accounted for an average of 25 per cent of the variance for intelligence, we would estimate that the environmental factors account for an average of 75 per cent of the variance of intelligence. However, it is important to note that the additive assumption is now considered a starting point for calculating heritability of intelligence and for estimating the number of genes that people are expected to share (e.g. brothers and sisters are expected to share 50 per cent). We will see later in this discussion that this view of assessing heritability has changed a lot. The idea of determining the relative strength of genetics and environmental factors by simply adding together genetic and environmental factors is more complicated than once thought, and psychologists really do emphasise the words 'estimate' and 'average' when referring to heritability.

Methods for assessing genetic heritability of intelligence

So, how might we assess genetic influences on intelligence? Well, as Galton himself mentioned, the relationship between genes and intelligence has traditionally been studied by concentrating on the similarities and differences between populations of individuals to assess the relative influence of their shared genes in intelligence.

Plomin (2004) identifies three main types of studies that use this technique: family studies, twin studies and adoption studies. As children share an estimated average of 50 per cent of their genes with each of their parents, and they also share genes with their brothers and sisters, it is of interest to behavioural genetics researchers to examine possible associations between parents' and children's behaviours within a family. This leads to the first type of study, family studies. However, these studies on their own potentially tell us very little because all children share an estimated average of 50 per cent of their genes with each of their parents and with their brothers and sisters. As well as

this, using observation, interview or questionnaire measures also presents a problem because similarities between personalities might be caused by environmental influence (i.e. an intelligent daughter might be like her extraverted mother because she copies her behaviour). These are real concerns until we consider the occasions when families don't typically share genes in this way. There are two main examples: twin studies and adoption studies.

Twin studies provide an interesting area of research, as there is a possibility of comparing different types of genetic makeup to compare genetic influences. The term 'twin' refers to two individuals who have shared the same uterus (the uterus or womb is the major female reproductive organ). Identical (or monozygotic, MZ) twins occur when a single egg is fertilised to form one zygote, but the zygote then divides into two separate embryos. The two embryos develop into fetuses sharing the same womb. Identical twins are always of the same sex and have the same arrangement of genes and chromosomes (which contain the hereditary information necessary for cell life). These twins share 100 per cent of genes with each other. Fraternal twins (non-identical, or dizygotic, DZ, twins) usually occur when two fertilised eggs are implanted in the uterine wall at the same time. The two eggs form two zygotes (hence they are dizygotic). These twins share an estimated average of 50 per cent of their genetic makeup. Consequently, some researchers compare behaviours across non-twins, identical and fraternal twins to examine the relative influence of genetics.

The influence of the environment and genetics is often compared in adoption studies. Intelligence can be compared between parents and adopted children, as there is no genetic heritability. Variables are often compared between siblings, or twins, reared apart to examine the extent of genetic and environmental effects. For example, if two twins show similar behaviours, despite being raised in different environments, this suggests that genes may be important in that behaviour.

Once you consider all these types of studies together, in which intelligence is compared between parents and children, and siblings that share 0–100 per cent genetic similarity, you can begin to make assessments of the extent of genetic heritability across a population.

It is important to remember that there is no physiological procedure in these sorts of studies. Behaviour geneticists do not have the ability to assess the genetic heritability of intelligence using advanced biological measures or a complex scientific genetic analysis (well, not yet). Rather, researchers look for similarities and differences in intelligence among individual people by using observation, interview or questionnaire measures. They look for similarities between parents' and children's intelligence (using intelligence measures) to determine the extent of genetic influence on intelligence. It is also important to remember that, when we deal with heritability estimates, we don't talk about heritability estimates for particular individuals; rather, researchers estimate the average heritability among certain populations of people – MZ (identical) twins, DZ (fraternal) twins, family members, parents and children. So, heritability estimate of 50 per cent for intelligence does not mean that we all inherit 50 per cent of that intelligence trait from our genes; it means that, across the population, the genetic heritability of intelligence has been estimated at an average of 50 per cent.

Heritability estimates of intelligence

What is the heritability of intelligence from these types of studies? Well, some studies have estimated the heritability of intelligence based on family, twin and adoption studies.

For example, there have been a number of findings from Bouchard's Minnesota Study of Twins Reared Apart (overseen by US behavioural geneticist Thomas Bouchard). This research involves not only the medical and psychological assessment of identical (MZ) and fraternal (DZ) twins separated early in life and reared apart, on which figures are given, but also their intelligence. A well-cited documentation of these studies was recently provided by behavioural

geneticist journalist Matt Ridley (Ridley, 1999). Ridley put together all the modern family, twin and adoption studies, which mainly included the findings of Bouchard and McGue's meta-analysis of 111 studies (Bouchard and McGue, 1981). The following analysis by Ridley is the concordance rate of IQ (the presence of the same intelligence level between two individuals) from all these studies (in parentheses are concordance rates given by Bouchard and McGue's meta-analysis; see also Figure 14.1):

- 100%: Perfect concordance rate;
- 87%: Same person tested twice;
- 86%: Identical twins reared together (86%);
- 76%: Identical twins reared apart (72%);
- 55%: Fraternal twins reared together (60%);
- 47%: Biological siblings reared together (47%);
- 40%: Parents and children living together (42%);
- 31%: Parents and children living apart (22%);
- 24%: Biological siblings reared apart (24%);
- 15%: Cousins (Bouchard and McGue only);
- 0%: Adopted children living together;
- 0%: Unrelated people living apart.

Evidence such as this, coming from studies throughout the century, was consistent, and researchers were able to make estimates on the level of genetic heritability of intelligence. You can see from evidence like this how people would tend to estimate the influence of genetics on intelligence

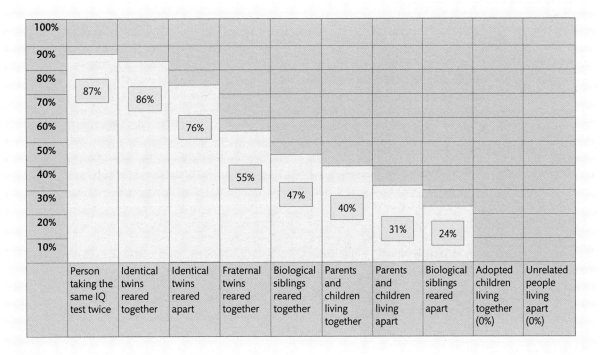

Figure 14.1 Concordance rates of intelligence.
Source: Based on data from Ridley, M. (1999). *Genome: the autobiography of a species in 23 chapters.* London: Fourth Estate. HarperCollins Publishers Ltd. © M. Ridley 1999.

as in some instances relatively high, because the evidence for heritability, in some instances, is over 80 per cent. For example, Professor Hans Eysenck (Eysenck, 1979) used this sort of evidence to suggest that the estimation of heritability of intelligence was around 69 per cent in the general population. Later, Herrnstein and Murray (1994), whose work we will discuss at greater length later, estimated heritability in the general population at 74 per cent.

Recent research suggests that previous figures quoted by Eysenck and Herrnstein and Murray may be a little high, but the view that genetics accounts for a weighty part of intelligence should not be ignored. In 2012 Ian Deary and a number of colleagues (Deary *et al.*, 2012) provided an estimate of the genetic contribution to stability of intelligence across most of the human lifetime. Deary compared the results of just under 2,000 unrelated individuals ($n = 1,940$) whose intelligence was measured first in childhood (age 11 years) and then again in old age (at age 65, 70 or 79 years). What was unique about this study was that the authors combined DNA analysis, a new statistical analysis, with data from the people in the study. They examined more than half a million genetic markers in this cohort to work out how genetically similar they were even though they were not related. What is important about this is that this method uses the same type of approach as that used in twin studies, looking for genetic similarity, and that the researchers are able to make, through the use of DNA analysis, more concise comparisons in terms of genetic similarity. Deary *et al.* found that the stability of cognitive ability from childhood to old age has a genetic contribution estimated at 38% of the variance.

However, in 2011, Deary (Deary, 2012) carried out a review on studies looking at the genetic contribution to stability of intelligence. An important point made by Deary is that the heritability of intelligence varies at different ages or across culture. In terms of age, Oliver Davis and colleagues (Davis *et al.*, 2009), using data in the Twins Early Development Study in the United Kingdom, found (from measures of verbal and non-verbal intelligence tests administered at ages 2, 3 and 4 years) that, for general intelligence, the heritability estimates were 23% in early childhood, and that this increased to 62% by middle childhood (from measuring intelligence from four mental ability tests at ages 7, 9 and 10 years). In terms of culture, studies among twin family studies in the Netherlands suggest the percentage of variance accounted for by genetic effects rises to over 80% for verbal IQ and just below 70% for performance IQ (Posthuma *et al.*, 2001). However, in Vietnam, findings suggest that genetic factors account for 49% of the variation in young adults and 57% in middle age (Lyons *et al.*, 2009).

Deary's research and reviews show that we are able to consider a lot more about the influences of genetics on intelligence today than previous work, and can provide a better consideration, though never perfect, of the relative influence of genetics and environment on intelligence. We have outlined some of these influences previously (Chapter 8), but we are going to outline them fully here so that you can see their relevance to the literature on intelligence as well as how estimates of the genetic influence on intelligence might be lower than previously estimated.

Considerations within behavioural genetics and intelligence

The idea of how genes and the environment are viewed, and used, to predict the heritability of intelligence has changed over recent years.

Authors such as US psychologists E. E. Maccoby (2000) and Robert Plomin (2004) suggest the additive principle of determining heritability of intelligence (or any phenotype) is not applicable any more. The validity of the additive assumption in computing the relative strength of genetics and environment in determining behaviour has been widely challenged. The first problem is that estimating the environment is usually done without utilising any direct measures of environmental factors. For example, researchers often compute genetic heritability and then subtract that from 100 per cent. Obviously, if the estimates of heritability are indeterminate, or prone to error, so are the estimates of E derived by subtracting heritability from 100 per cent. A further problem with the additive assumption of computing heritability is that, when genetic heritability is large, it assumes that all environmental factors associated with that behaviour must be small. Therefore, it is better to see human intelligence as a joint result of an interaction between a person's genes and environmental factors. Intelligence should not be seen as the result of 'genetics + environment' but rather of 'genetics × environment'. For example, it is better to view the relative influences of genes and environment on intelligence as the result of a long-term interaction, with environmental factors triggering certain genetic behaviours and the effects of the environment differing between individuals because of their genetic makeup.

What is important for you to note is that these changes and developments in research and thinking have been suggested, encouraged and developed by both theorists and researchers, many of whom we have already mentioned, who support and criticise the idea of genetic heritability in intelligence. So, what has brought about, and resulted from, such a general shift in thinking, from the additive principle of 'genetics + environment' to the later, more integrative, idea of 'genetics × environment'? Well, four considerations surrounding modern-day thinking in behavioural genetics are important when considering any phenotype, particularly intelligence (see Figure 14.2):

- conceptions of heritability and the environment;
- different types of genetic variance;
- the representativeness of twin and adoption studies;
- assortative mating.

Conceptions of genetic heritability and the environment

Gregory Carey (2002) suggests that there are two important contexts within which to consider heritability and environmental influences on intelligence:

- **Abstract concepts** – these are generally theoretical (not applied or practical) concepts. As Carey explains, whatever the numerical estimates of either genetic or environmental influences, they provide us with little information about the specific genes, or specific environmental variables, that influence intelligence.
- **Population concepts** – all of these estimates refer to any group of people considered as a population, but they tell us very little about any single individual. For example, just because intelligence may have a genetic heritability of around 60 per cent, it does not mean, for any one individual, that 60 per cent of their intelligence is due to genes and 40 per cent of their intelligence is due to the environment. Rather, it is estimated across the population that genetic heritability of intelligence is an average of around 40 per cent, and individuals will vary around that estimate.

Different types of genetic variance

So far in this discussion, we have treated genetic influence on intelligence only as a single entity, namely, the influence of your genes on your intelligence. However, behavioural genetics researchers such as Thomas Bouchard and M. McGue (Bouchard and McGue, 1981) note that genetic influence does not simply comprise one aspect, but in fact three aspects: (1) additive genetic variance; (2) dominant genetic variance; and (3) epistatic genetic variance.

Additive genetic variation is the genetic variance that we have described previously in this discussion; that is, genetic variation in behaviour that is the total of the individual's genes inherited from their parents.

However, the two other types of genetic variation are known as non-additive genetic variance.

First, **dominant genetic variance** is part of a process by which certain genes are expressed (dominant genes) and other genes are not expressed (recessive genes). Every one of us has two copies of every gene, one inherited from our mother and one from our father. Sometimes the two genes that determine a particular trait (for example, eye colour) will actually code for two types of characteristics (for example, blue eyes and brown eyes). If one of these genes is dominant, then only its character is expressed and not that of the other gene. For example, if blue eyes were a dominant gene, and your mother had brown eyes and your father had blue eyes, you would be likely to inherit blue eyes.

Secondly, **epistatic genetic variance** (known as interactive genetic variance) refers to a process by which genes interact. It is now known that several different genes not only influence physical characteristics and behaviour on their own, but work and interact together. Unlike dominant genetic variance, which just applies to one gene replacing another, epistatic genetic variance is the result of the way certain genes that we inherit determine whether other genes we inherit will be expressed or suppressed (this process is called **epistasis**).

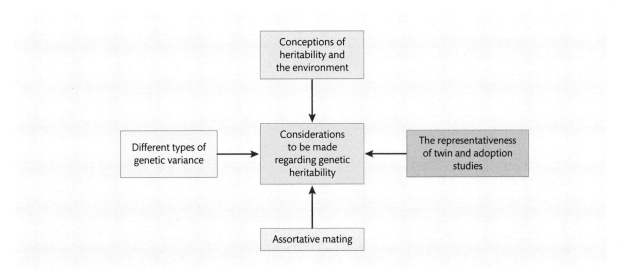

Figure 14.2 Considerations to be made regarding genetic heritability.

It is difficult to measure dominant genetic variance and epistatic genetic variance when it comes to intelligence. However, it is now accepted that these three aspects – additive genetic variance, dominant genetic variance and epistatic genetic variance – are thought to make up **total genetic variance** of intelligence.

You can see that the genetic side of things is a lot more complicated than just viewing genes as a single entity, as genes interact and suppress other genes. You will see, in the literature, behavioural geneticists referring to terms such as 'narrow heritability' and 'broad heritability'. Narrow heritability is just additive genetic variance. Broad heritability is all three aspects of genetic heritability (additive genetic variance + dominant genetic variance + epistatic genetic variance).

Consequently, authors such as Thomas Bouchard and M. McGue (1981) and US psychologists Heather Chipeur, Michael Rovine and Robert Plomin (1990) have suggested that original estimates of the average percentage of parental genes that children inherit, and siblings share, may have previously been oversimplified. For example, these authors suggest that genetic variations in heritability of any phenotype (including intelligence) should be made in the following terms:

- identical (MZ) twins = additive genetic variance = non-additive genetic variance (where previously it was presumed to be solely additive genetic variance);
- fraternal (DZ) twins = 0.5 of additive genetic variance + 0.25 of non-additive genetic variance (rather than just 0.5 of additive genetic variance).

As you can see, computing the level of genetic variance may be more complicated than previously thought. Today, behavioural geneticists take these factors into account when suggesting the strength of heritability estimates of intelligence.

Problems with the representativeness of twin and adoption studies

One of the considerations put forward by psychologists such as Maccoby and by Leon Kamin and Arthur Goldberger (2002) concerns adoption and twin studies. A significant portion of studies examining heritability effects is devoted to twin and adoption studies. Twin studies are important because they allow the comparison of different types of twins to compare genetic influences; MZ twins who share 100 per cent of their genes and DZ twins who share 50 per cent of their genes. Adoption studies are important because they include two sets of factors that may account for differences in behaviour: biological parents and environmental parents. Therefore, it is argued that these families aren't necessarily representative of the normal populations. This natural

bias in sampling may under- or over-estimate heritability estimates across the general population because genetic influences in these samples may not be representative of the whole population.

This issue is particularly important when considering research that assesses heritability of intelligence using twin and adoption studies. Leon Kamin and Arthur Goldberger (2002) estimate that twin studies might over-estimate the role of genetics, particularly because identical twins have more similar environments than do same-sex fraternal twins. Also, research shows that identical twins are treated more similarly by their parents, spend more time together and more often have the same friends. Their environmental experience comprises a greater proportion of each other's social environment than does that of fraternal siblings. Consequently, if genetic heritability estimates are usually larger in twin studies than in adoption studies, then some of the estimated similarity that is attributed to genetic influence might not be correct. Stoolmiller (1998) has also suggested that adoption studies lead to a similar restriction of the measurement of environmental factors. Stoolmiller argues that the placement strategies of adoption agencies might influence heritability estimates. For example, adoption agencies might always place children in affluent or middle- to high-income families; thus the effects of economic status are never fully explored in these studies, because an adopted child would rarely be placed into a household suffering from poverty.

Assortative mating

Nicholas Mackintosh (Mackintosh, 1998), animal-learning theorist at the University of Cambridge, raises the issue that assortative mating can have an effect on genetic variance and, therefore, on estimates of genetic heritability of intelligence. **Assortative mating** is a complicated name for the simple concept that, when couples mate, they either have several traits in common or contrast wildly in their traits. A lot of the understanding of genetic variation is based on the assumption that two individuals mate quite randomly with random people and, therefore, that any genetic similarity between them is by chance. But we know that this is not true. We know that people mate with people who they perceive to be similar to themselves. For example, we tend to see people mating with people who are of a similar size, or similar in their 'good-lookingness'. This is called positive assortative mating. Equally, we find people mating who are completely the opposite. This is called negative assortative mating. Therefore, in much the same way, the assortative mating principle can be applied to intelligence. That is, individuals may seek to mate with people who are of a similar intelligence. Think about your parents; do they have a similar educational background to each other?

Modern estimates of the genetic heritability of intelligence

In the light of the considerations just outlined, different researchers have tried to estimate the overall heritability of intelligence across the general population. These estimates tend to be broad estimates of genetic variance (additive and non-additive genetic variance) in intelligence. They break down by what percentage of intelligence is determined by genetics and what percentage can be attributed to the environment. As we have already mentioned, higher estimates of heritability have come from authors like Hans Eysenck (1971; 1991), who once estimated it at 69 per cent. There is no evidence to suggest that this is wrong; however, modern-day commentators, given the preceding issues relating to heritability estimates, are more conservative; they suggest that heritability falls into a range. The American Psychological Association Task Force (mentioned in Chapter 11), headed by Ulric Neisser, estimates that the heritability of intelligence ranges from 40 to 80 per cent (Neisser *et al.*, 1996), while Nicholas Mackintosh (1998) suggests a range of 30 to 75 per cent. If you are looking for a more exact figure, Chipeur *et al.* (1990) have suggested the genetic heritability of intelligence at 50 per cent which is a commonly – but not always – accepted viewpoint.

All this discussion, and we haven't even considered the extent of environmental effects on intelligence yet!

Environmental influences on intelligence

The list of possible environmental effects on intelligence could be endless. It could range from the effects on intelligence of long-term poverty (for example, never getting the opportunities to develop skills at home, at school and consequently in a career), through to one conversation with one teacher who suggests that the person will never amount to much. Thomas Bouchard and Nancy Segal (1985) list 21 factors that are related to intelligence, including malnutrition, weight at birth, height, years in school, father's economic status, father's and mother's education and influence, average TV viewing, self-confidence, criminality and emotional adaptation. However, the American Psychological Association Task Force (Neisser *et al.*, 1996) identified four main areas of environmental effects on intelligence that can be deemed as the most important. This information allows us to concentrate the debate. Some of these environmental effects you will have come across before (for example, nutrition, schooling and occupation) in the previous discussion (Chapter 13), but we will revisit them so that you can see how they apply directly to the issues of the nature versus nurture debate on intelligence. These four areas are: (1) biological variables; (2) family; (3) school and education; and (4) culture (see Figure 14.3).

Biological variables and maternal effects
Nutrition
Lead
Prenatal factors

School and education

Family environment
Shared and non-shared environments within- and outside-family factors
Social class and socioeconomic status
Birth order and family size

Culture
Decontextualisation
Quantification
Biologisation

Figure 14.3 Environmental effects on intelligence.

Stop and think

Cyril L. Burt

For many lecturers and students across the psychology discipline, Cyril Burt is psychology's equivalent of the bogeyman. Like parents who tell children who are naughty that the bogeyman will come and get them, lecturers inform students who are naughty and make up their data that they will be branded with the Cyril Burt label. No one knows the truth about Cyril Burt; however, stories of acts done a long time ago, are told through generations of lecturers. Your lecturers were told by their lecturers about Cyril Burt and, although many stories about him may be untrue, academics today still argue and swap conspiracy, and counterconspiracy, stories surrounding Cyril Burt.

Cyril L. Burt was born on 3 March 1893 and died on 10 October 1971. He was a British educational psychologist. He studied at Oxford in the United Kingdom, and in Germany. Between 1908 and 1971, he worked at the University of Liverpool and had a chair of Psychology at University College, London. He also worked as Chief Psychologist at London County Council. He was President of the British Psychological Society (in 1942), was editor and co-editor of the *British Journal of Statistical Psychology* (between 1947 and 1963) and was the first psychologist to be knighted (in 1946). He founded the field of educational psychology in the United Kingdom and helped to establish eleven-plus testing in Great Britain.

In his academic work, Burt published nine books and more than 300 articles, lectures and book chapters. Much of his work investigated differences in intelligence among social classes, gender and race, and examined heritability among intelligence of identical twins reared apart. It was this work that was to create the controversy.

During the 1970s Leon Kamin, who was opposed to the idea of genetic heritability, and Arthur Jensen, who was in favour of genetic heritability, both spotted something in Burt's reports on correlations for IQ test scores of identical twins (Jensen, 1973; Kamin, 1974). Burt's original results were published in 1943 for 15 pairs of twins. In 1955 he had results for 21 pairs of twins (including the 15 original pairs of twins), and by 1966 he reported the results for a total of 53 pairs of twins. What Kamin and Jensen noted was that the correlation coefficients between the IQ scores were similar across the samples. In his studies, Burt reported the following coefficients: $r = 0.770$ (1943); $r = 0.771$ (1955); and $r = 0.771$ (1966). Kamin and Jensen suggested that they would expect to see greater variability among the correlations when more sets of twins were added, and that it was very unusual that the correlations had stayed the same.

On 24 October 1976, an article, 'Crucial data was faked by eminent psychologist', was published by Dr Oliver Gillies in the UK newspaper *The Sunday Times*. In this article, Gillies not only pointed to the problems with the cor-

relational data but also claimed that Burt had invented his co-authors, Miss Margaret Howard and Miss J. Conway (who Burt claimed helped him to update the twin data), as they could not be traced. Gillies also pointed out that Howard and Conway did appear to have written book reviews praising Burt's work for the *Journal of Statistical Psychology* – but only during the time that Burt was editor. Later, US psychologist William H. Tucker picked up on accusations that Burt would have been unlikely to find so many sets of monozygotic twins reared apart. Tucker (1997) examined the numbers of participants involved in twin studies with similar criteria used by Burt between 1922 and 1990 and found that the combination of all the twins together did not total the number of participants that Burt had obtained.

With this, Cyril Burt seemed to be forever denounced as a fraud. However, people have reviewed this evidence. For example, UK psychologist Ronald Fletcher (1991) set out to locate the missing research assistants. He found proof of their existence. One of the assistants, Miss J. Conway, worked in childcare for London County Council. Miss M. A. Howard is listed as a member of the British Psychological Society in 1924. In addition, Fletcher reported that other individuals stepped forward and said they remembered Burt's assistants. Fletcher suggests that this repeated accusation against Burt may be the result of poor investigatory journalism rather than imagined helpers.

This is not the only accusation against the media. Some authors, such as Fletcher, Robert Joynson (1989) and J. Phillipe Rushton (1994), have suggested that Burt's reported correlation coefficients indicated a strong relationship between genetics and intelligence – and they point out that this was not, and still isn't, a popular finding. This is because such findings have strong implications where differences in intelligence are sexually or racially based. Often, there is the inference that certain groups of people (based on sex or race differences) are genetically inferior in intelligence. We will explore such ideas in full later in the discussion. However, these ideas are surrounded by controversy, and Fletcher and Rushton point out that, if Burt's findings can be discredited, then it seems to some that the case for the genetic heritability of intelligence is discredited. Therefore, Fletcher and Rushton argue that people who disagree with the genetic heritability of intelligence will be more likely to conspire in the media and in academia to discredit Burt's work.

Rushton points to possible conspiratorial behaviour. He suggests that not only the media sought to discredit Burt's findings too quickly, but that other academics did, too. He cites the example of Burt's papers being destroyed by his housekeeper immediately after his death – on the advice of Professor Liam Hudson, an educational psychologist at Edinburgh University, an ardent opponent of Burt who had rushed to Burt's flat after learning he had died.

Rushton also points out that new evidence from studies of twins raised apart (as we see from the summary of Ridley earlier) indicates results similar to Burt's high heritability estimate. Therefore, the accusations that he simply made up all the data to exaggerate the effects of genetics are somewhat weakened.

Authors like Ronald Fletcher and Robert Joynson suggest that the case of fraud by Burt is not proven. Whatever the truth, and the lessons to be learnt from Cyril Burt, we hope that whatever judgements you make, you understand the importance of giving the full facts before you pass on the story ... and *never* make up your data.

Biological variables and maternal effects

It is well acknowledged by the APA Task Force (Neisser *et al.*, 1996) that a number of biological factors influence intelligence. These include nutrition, before- and after-birth factors and substances like alcohol and lead poisoning.

Nutrition

We introduced much of the nutrition hypothesis in the last discussion (Chapter 13). Nutrition is the study of food; specifically, the relationship between diet and states of health and disease. You will remember from the last chapter that Lynn (1990) has proposed that nutrition and healthcare improvements are among the main reasons for the Flynn effect. However, outside Lynn's hypothesis there are findings that nutritional sources can aid aspects of intelligence.

Australian nutritionist Wendy H. Oddy and her colleagues (Oddy *et al.*, 2004) examined over 2,000 Australian children and followed them from birth until the age of 8 years. Oddy and her colleagues found that stopping breast feeding early (at 6 months or less) was associated with reduced verbal intelligence, while children who were fully breast fed for more than 6 months scored between 3 and 6 IQ points higher on a vocabulary intelligence test than did those children who were never breast fed. Similarly, another study conducted by US health psychologist Melanie Smith and her colleagues (Smith *et al.*, 2003) examined 439 school-age, low birthweight children born in the United States. These authors found differences in IQ test scores between breast-fed children and those who did not receive any breast milk. These were 3.6 IQ points for overall intellectual functioning and 2.3 IQ points for verbal ability. You will also remember the debate (in Chapter 13) surrounding the study carried out by two Welsh psychologists, David Benton and Gwilym Roberts (Benton and Roberts, 1988), who found that children given a vitamin–mineral supplement containing several vitamins and minerals were found to show increased IQ scores.

Regardless of the controversy surrounding this work, findings do suggest that nutrition has a positive effect on intelligence. It is important to remember, though, that a number of socioeconomic conditions are often associated with nutrition. You may also remember the words of Lynn (1990) (discussed in Chapter 13): the nutrition hypothesis sees nutrition as a package (or nurturing environment) in which increased intelligence is part of a nurturing environment that includes increased height and lifespan, improved health, decreased rate of infant disease and better vitamin and mineral nutrition. Where those things do not occur – where there is poverty, malnutrition and few economic and social opportunities – there might be lower intelligence scores.

Lead

However, while nutrition is seen as having a positive effect, there are occasions when other biological factors can have a negative effect on IQ. Neisser *et al.* (1996) highlight research concentrating on the effect that exposure to lead can have on intelligence.

The most comprehensive study was carried out in a place called Port Pirie in Australia. In 1986, Australian psychologist Anthony J. McMichael and four colleagues (McMichael *et al.*, 1986) examined the possible relationship between body lead burden and pregnancy outcome among 749 pregnant women in, and around, the largest lead smelting facilities in Australia. Among these women, premature deliveries were statistically significantly associated with higher levels of maternal blood lead concentration at delivery. What followed the initial findings was a series of studies in Port Pirie, which looked at the association between environmental exposure to lead and children's intelligence at 2 years (McMichael *et al.*, 1988), 4 years and 7 years (Baghurst *et al.*, 1992) and 11 and 13 years (Tong *et al.*, 1996). The Port Pirie cohort study started in 1979 and involved 723 children, although only 375 took part in the final study. IQ scores were made on the Bailey IQ scales at 2 years of age, the McCarthy IQ scale at 4 years of age and the Wechsler IQ scale for children at 7 years, 11 years and 13 years of age. At all these ages, IQ scores were significantly associated with lead concentration in people's bodies, even when socioeconomic status, home environment and maternal intelligence were controlled for. This study suggests that there is an association between early exposure to environmental lead and intelligence, and it persists into later childhood.

Prenatal factors

Finally, there are prenatal factors. You are well aware that pregnant women are expected to stop drinking and smoking. According to many health councils, avoiding smoking and alcohol consumption in pregnancy is crucial. Smoking nearly doubles a woman's risk of having a premature or low birth-weight baby who faces an increased risk of serious health problems. Further, many conditions can arise from the mother's alcohol consumption when she is pregnant; the most common condition is fetal alcohol syndrome (FAS), which is characterised by a pattern of facial abnormalities, growth retardation and brain damage.

Neisser *et al.* (1996) point to these types of consumption by mothers during pregnancy as having an effect on intelligence. Low birth-weight babies, as well as babies suffering from FAS, show reduced intelligence. Danish scientist Erik Lykke Mortensen and colleagues at the University of Copenhagen (Mortensen *et al.*, 2005) examined maternal smoking and subsequent IQ scores among 3,044 males aged between 18 and 19 years. The study found that, regardless of factors such as parental social status and education, single-mother status, mother's height and age, number of pregnancies, the women who smoked 20 or more cigarettes daily late in their pregnancy were likely to have sons who performed less well on standardised IQ tests at age 18 or 19. Evidence also suggests that FAS is related to a number of cognitive functions. US psychologist Sarah Mattson and colleagues at San Diego State University (Mattson and Riley, 1998; Mattson *et al.*, 1996) have found that children prenatally exposed to alcohol exhibit a variety of problems with memory (they found that children with FAS aged 5 years to 16 years had learned fewer words than children of comparable ages) and demonstrate attention problems. Uecker and Nadel (1996) found that children of mothers who drank heavily during pregnancy performed badly in learning spatial relationships among objects. Furthermore, South African psychologist Piyadasa Kodituwakku and her colleagues (Kodituwakku *et al.*, 1995) have shown that children with FAS show deficits in activities that require abstract thinking, such as planning and organising information.

However, research is by no means conclusive. Other research suggests that the links between factors such as smoking, or alcohol consumption, in pregnancy and intelligence might be moderated, disappear or be highlighted by other factors. US psychologists S. W. Jacobson, J. L. Jacobson, R. J. Sokol, L. M. Chiodo and R. Corobana (2004) found, among 337 inner-city African–American children, that prenatal alcohol exposure was not related to IQ scores on the Wechsler Intelligence Test. However, they found that among children who had older mothers, prenatal alcohol was related to IQ scores on the Wechsler Intelligence Test. Bailey *et al.* (2004) examined alcohol use among mothers at a prenatal visit, and then IQ among children at 7 years, among 500 black children. Again, no relationship was found between prenatal alcohol exposure and intelligence, although mothers who binge-drink when pregnant were 1.7 times more likely to have children who had IQ scores in the mentally retarded range.

These findings suggest that age and excess drinking are further factors in the relationship between prenatal drinking and offspring intelligence. But overall, the findings suggest that smoking and alcohol consumption are factors that, to a greater or lesser extent, are connected with IQ.

Maternal effects model

Today, factors such as prenatal nutrition and alcohol consumption are combined into the maternal effects model. US psychiatrist Dr Bernie Devlin and US statistician Michael Daniels (Devlin *et al.*, 1997) showed that prenatal conditions may have substantial effects on the concordance of subsequent scores on IQ for identical twins. Previously, maternal effects had usually been assumed to be small, or non-existent, in terms of affecting genetic variance of intelligence between twins. However, a meta-analysis of 212 studies suggests 20 per cent of genetic variance between twins and 5 per cent between siblings. These authors suggest that broad heritability estimates when including maternal effect (additive and non-additive genetic variance) might have to be reduced from about 60 to 48 per cent. This suggestion indicates that the environmental effects on intelligence may extend to interactions with biological factors.

Family environment

The second environmental factor identified by Neisser *et al.* (1996) is the family environment. There are three sources of related research and evidence that we will concentrate on in this discussion:

- shared and non-shared environments – within- and outside-family factors;
- the social and economic status of the family and the intelligence of the child;
- birth order, family size and child intelligence.

Shared and non-shared environments

We saw in the last discussion that the conception of genetics as a single dimension has developed over time. The same could be said of environmental factors. Within behavioural genetics, the conception of how the environment influences intelligence is through two sets of experiences: shared and non-shared. When growing up, siblings (brothers and sisters) are thought to experience both shared and unique environments. **Shared environments** are environments that are shared between two individuals, while **non-shared environments** are environments that are *not* shared between two individuals who share genes.

Siblings growing up within the same family will share many environments. These environments may range from minor experiences to more significant ones. Therefore, two siblings having the same parents, living within the same house, going to the same school and experiencing particular times together (e.g. same family relatives, home environment, chaotic mornings before school, dad's awful jokes) have shared environments. A unique environment is an environment that has not been shared by siblings. Again, these environments may range from minor experiences to significant ones. Examples of unique environments might be when two siblings have been raised by different families. However, siblings raised in the same family might also have unique environments from each other. Siblings may have different sets of friends, may go to different schools, may have different types of relationships with their parents and have different interactions with teachers.

What is important in this area is that the theory and research around the differences between environment influences on intelligence has grown in complexity. To begin with, researchers tend to concentrate on comparing how shared and non-shared environmental factors influence intelligence. Early consideration by reviewers such as Bouchard (1994) and Eysenck (1990b) suggested that the environmental influences shared by siblings or twins contribute only marginally to intelligence differences. However, one interesting point to emerge from the literature, carried out by such researchers as US behaviour geneticists Braungart et al. (1992a), is that those environmental factors that are unique (non-shared) to family members are influential over *shared* environmental factors. Therefore, non-shared environmental factors, such as different peer friendships, are important mechanisms that explain why members of the same family may differ in their intelligence. This idea is supported by two pieces of research suggesting that the extent of differences in the experiences during childhood among siblings have been found to be related to intelligence differences in adulthood (Baker and Daniels, 1990; Plomin and Daniels, 1987).

Such a finding has led to the development of whole areas of research that have emphasised how important non-shared environmental factors are to intelligence. Most of the research in this area considers how non-shared environmental factors develop: (1) within the family; and (2) outside the family.

Within-family factors

US behavioural geneticist David Reiss (1997) identifies three ways in which inherited genes form phenotypes (behaviours) based on the family environment (see Figure 14.4):

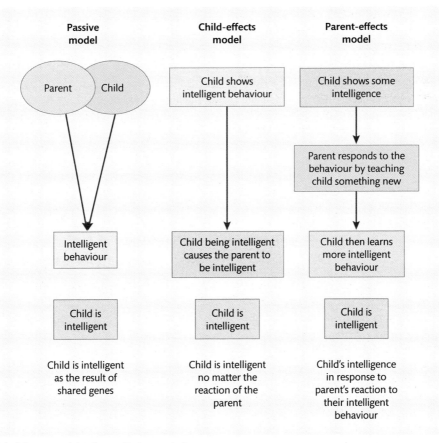

Figure 14.4 Reiss' three models of genetic transmission.

- the passive model
- the child-effects model
- the parent-effects model.

First is the **passive model**. This model suggests that intelligence is generally explained by the 50 per cent overlap between a child and their parent. Therefore, intelligence may occur in the child because the child and parent share the same genes that influence a particular type of behaviour. For example, if a child is highly intelligent owing to genetic influences, they are so because one of their biological parents had the genes that cause this high intelligence. The model, very much, just assumes a general genetic overlap and inheritance of behaviour without considering other possible factors and interactions within the family. This is why it is called the passive model. The other two models very much emphasise other dynamic occurrences.

In the **child-effects model**, the genes cause intelligence in the child, which in turn causes the same or similar behaviour in the parent. Within this model, the parent does not matter in the development of the behaviour, as the child's development of intelligence is the result of genes. An example of this is that the shared genes cause the child to be intelligent (because of their genetic makeup), which in turn causes the parent to act intelligently back to the child (because of their genetic makeup). The parent's own intelligence does not matter in the development of the behaviour, as the child's intelligence is a consequence of the genetic makeup of the child rather than the parent.

US psychologist Judith Harris (1995) has expanded this viewpoint to **child-driven effects**, which influence family circumstances that in turn influence the child's intelligence. Harris documents studies showing that adults do not behave in the same way to a child who shows different tendencies. They will treat an attractive child differently to one of their children who is less attractive; they will react differently to the child who shows bad behaviour than to the one who is well behaved. This behaviour will also apply to intelligence. For example, imagine a family with twin children, one of them intelligent and the other not as intelligent. These differences in the children will cause different reactions in the parents. The parents will begin to treat their children differently. The intelligent one may be encouraged to engage in more intelligent activities, while the one perceived to be less intelligent might not be encouraged to do these activities. Harris suggests that these reactions by parents to their children's natural intelligence tendencies can be viewed in two ways: *positive feedback loops* and *negative feedback loops*. Positive feedback loops arise from parents reinforcing children's natural tendencies, as in the example described earlier, where children's natural intelligence abilities are encouraged and any differences between children in their intelligence are developed (the intelligent child is encouraged to be intelligent, while the 'unintelligent' child

is encouraged and allowed to engage in other activities). Negative feedback loops occur when children are stopped from behaving in ways consistent with their natural tendencies. Therefore, an intelligent child might be encouraged to stop engaging in merely intelligence-stimulating activities, and an 'unintelligent' child might be encouraged to spend more time engaging in such activities.

In the **parent-effects model**, the behaviour of the child is responded to by the parent, which in turn brings out that behaviour in the child (see Figure 14.4). Within this model, how the parent responds does affect the development of the child's behaviour. For example, a child may begin showing intelligence; this then leads the parent to show intelligence with the child (as it is part of their genetic makeup). This in turn causes the child to become even more intelligent (as it is part of their genetic makeup). Within this model, the parent's behaviour leads to the development of intelligence, which then leads to the development of intelligent behaviour in the child.

Again, Harris extends this idea to within-family situations. In these situations, children might be treated in a particular way by parents, not because of that child's own characteristics, but because of the parents' own beliefs or the characteristics of a child's siblings (brothers or sisters). Let us first look at the example of how the parents' own beliefs shape natural tendencies of children. Again, take our family with the one intelligent twin and the one 'less-intelligent' twin. Our parents of the family may have certain beliefs about behaviour, such as 'children should know the limits of their knowledge and never contradict their parents'. Therefore, the children will be encouraged and directed to behave in such ways. So, in our example of the intelligent and less-intelligent twin, the intelligent child who is likely to contradict their parents will be encouraged not to show their intelligence, and the unintelligent child will be encouraged to gain some knowledge up to their 'limits'. Both children will have had their new behaviour (knowing their limits and not contradicting their parents) driven by their parents' behaviour. Secondly, let us look at how parents might influence children's behaviours in terms of a child's siblings. Harris notes research suggesting that parents who consider their first child to be 'difficult' tend to label their second-born as 'easy'. We can also see how less-intelligent children might be asked, or encouraged, to be more like their intelligent sibling. Equally, the intelligent sibling might be encouraged to spend less time in intelligence-promoting activities and play more like their brother or sister.

What Reiss' and Harris' commentaries do is to suggest that *within-family effects* pose problems when considering genetic heritability. That is, child effects and parent effects can lead to over- and under-estimations of heritability. Remember, behavioural geneticists looking at intelligence are only looking at the concordance between sets of children based on their scores on an intelligence test at some point. However, let us return to our family with one intelligent twin and one less-intelligent twin. Let us imagine that the parents of these twin children have been engaged in a negative feedback loop. They have been trying to encourage both children to be similar; that is, somewhat intelligent. Therefore, the intelligent child has been discouraged from being intelligent all the time, and the less-intelligent child is being discouraged from being too unintelligent. If we then compared these two children, we would find that these twin children have similar intelligence; but this is, in fact, not because of genetic tendencies at all. It is simply because the parents are trying to encourage similar behaviour in both children (i.e. not too active or not too quiet). Therefore, any estimation of similarities in intelligence being caused by genetic heritability of the twins would be an overestimation. However, if the same pair of twins had been reared differently and both had been in a positive feedback loop – the intelligent child had been encouraged to be more and more intelligent and the less-intelligent child had been encouraged to be more and more unintelligent – then any estimation of the similarities in intelligence being caused by genetic heritability would be an under-estimation because the differences have been exaggerated owing to the parents encouraging the twins to be more and more like themselves. Therefore, as Harris concludes, children's within-family situations not only play an important role in shaping their intelligence but are also an important consideration in estimating the genetic heritability of intelligence.

Outside-family factors

However, Harris (1995) has suggested that non-shared factors outside the family may in fact be more important in developing people's intelligence. Harris presents the group socialisation theory to explain the importance of non-shared environmental factors in determining intelligence.

Group socialisation theory is based largely on the ideas surrounding social identity theory and social categorisation (Tajfel and Turner, 1986). Social psychologists have provided a lot of theoretical and empirical research work that has looked at how individuals perceive their social world as comprising in-groups and out-groups and suggesting that these groups help us form our social identity. Social psychologists argue that one mechanism humans use for understanding the complex social world is social categorisation. In social categorisation, individuals are thought to place other individuals into social groups on the basis of their similarities and differences to the individual. Put simply, individuals who are viewed as similar to the person tend to be placed within their in-group. Individuals who are viewed as different to the person tend to be placed within an out-group. This is a process by which we come to understand our world. As a consequence, the individual's identity (social identity) is based on and derived from the groups they feel they belong to and their understanding of their similarities and differences to different social groups. Social groups can be anything, but common groups could be sex group, ethnic group, your religion, your peers, your interests, your educational status and so on. As such, your identity is based, to a greater or lesser extent, on how much you identify with different social groups. What is also important to our identity is that, when we attach ourselves to certain groups, we also try to fit in with those groups; therefore, our intelligence might begin to reflect the characteristics of a certain group (i.e., you might make friends with people who are highly intelligent; you may then do more intellectual activities than you used to, and you may become more intelligent).

Harris uses this theoretical basis to show how social groups can influence people's intelligence and points out how these non-shared environments that occur in children of the same family can have a huge effect on intelligence. As part of this theory, Harris lists five aspects that are important to consider in how non-shared characteristics might influence our intelligence (we go into greater depth on each of these issues earlier in the text [in Chapter 8] if you want to read more).

- **Context-specific socialisation** – this aspect refers to the fact that children learn intelligence abilities not only at home but also outside the home. As children get older, they become less influenced by their family life and more influenced by their life outside the family home.
- **Outside-the-home socialisation** – in this aspect Harris makes the point that children may identify with a number of social groups, based on people's age, gender, ethnicity, abilities, interests, personality, intelligence, etc. In other words, we have a range of groups that we identify with and share norms with (attitudes, interests, intelligence), and these groups have different influences on our intelligence.
- **Transmission of culture via group processes** – in this aspect Harris makes two points about the transmission of culture via group processes, which establish norms in our social world that influence our intelligence. First, the shared norms that might influence a child's intelligence aren't necessarily the result of parents sharing them with their children; they are really the result of shared norms among the parents' peers and social groups being passed on to the children. That is, your parents' values, abilities, personality and intelligence are not the result of their parents' norms, but rather of their own social identity, their identification with their own social groups. The second point considers that individual norms, which we have developed from our family, are shared with other people only if they are accepted. For example, an individual might be intelligent and like reading books. However, unless their friends

approve of this behaviour, they may be unlikely to carry on this pastime.

- **Group processes that widen differences between social groups** – it is important to note that with your intelligence, norms are based not just on how you identify with your in-group but also on whether you identify with or reject the out-groups. For example, consider sex roles; your intelligence as a male or female isn't just based on your identification with people of your own sex, but on your rejection of characteristics of the opposite sex. For example, some young women at school believe that subjects such as science and mathematics are men's subjects; consequently, these women become interested in what they perceive to be women's subjects, such as English. This behaviour might have an effect on intelligence.

- **Group processes that widen differences among individuals within the group** – so far, we have assumed that all the groups that we are involved in basically share the same structure. However, we know that within all our social circles we play different roles that might influence, or bring out, different aspects of our intelligence. In our family, as a child, we take a less-senior role; with our friends we might be allowed to be more like ourselves. However, the opposite may be true, and we might not feel we lead a group of friends, but tend to do what others say. It may even be possible that among one group of friends you feel more comfortable than others. Harris' point is that our position in groups changes, and that our intelligence – and influences on our intelligence – change due to the hierarchies within a group. For example, if you are in a group of friends and they all look up to you, your intelligence will be influenced because you might think there is an expectation to come up with ideas for things to do or to solve problems within the group.

What is important to consider in both within-family and outside-family factors is that these aspects can influence intelligence of children to a much greater extent than previously thought. It is not Harris' point that behavioural genetics is wrong and that environmental factors are more important, but rather that behavioural geneticists may sometimes have oversimplified family influences. By ignoring these variables, behavioural geneticists might be under- or over-estimating heritability effects of either genetics or the environment on intelligence.

Socioeconomic status of the family

A family's socioeconomic status is based on its income, parental education level, parental occupation and status in the community. Socioeconomic status is related to various factors, including number of children in the family, opportunities for success in employment, health and area of residence. These factors all might influence intelligence.

Often socioeconomic status is ranked in many countries. For example, in the United Kingdom, one way in which socioeconomic status is measured is by the grading of parents' occupations into five categories:

- Class I: professional occupations;
- Class II: managerial and technical occupations;
- Class III: skilled occupations: manual (M) and unmanual (U);
- Class IV: partly skilled occupations;
- Class V: unskilled occupations.

Socioeconomic status is related to intelligence. Authors such as Linda Gottfredson (Gottfredson, 1986), Arthur Jensen (Jensen, 1993a), Richard Herrnstein and Charles Murray (Herrnstein and Murray, 1994) and J. Phillipe Rushton and C. D. Ankney (Rushton and Ankney, 1996) estimate that in Europe, North America and Japan, socioeconomic status is significantly correlated with scores on standard IQ between $r = 0.3$ and $r = 0.4$, and that there are 45 IQ points between members of the professional occupations (Class I) and those of unskilled occupations (Class V).

In addition, Nicholas Mackintosh (1998) and Nicholas Mascie-Taylor (1984) presented evidence linking socioeconomic status to intelligence using the British National Child Development Study (NCDS) data. The NCDS examined social and obstetric (care of women during and after pregnancy) factors associated with stillbirth and infant mortality among over 17,000 babies born in Britain in 1958. Surviving members of this birth cohort have been surveyed on five further occasions to monitor their changing health, education, social and economic circumstances, including IQ, in 1965 (age 7), 1969 (age 11), 1974 (age 16), 1981 (age 23) and 1991 (age 33). Mackintosh (1998) and Mascie-Taylor (1984) present evidence that, even when aspects such as financial hardship, birth-weight, size of family, overcrowding, type of accommodation and residence area are taken into account, children who had fathers in Class I (professional occupations) scored 10 IQ points higher than did children who had fathers in Class V (unskilled occupations).

Research also suggests that improved socioeconomic status can improve intelligence. Canadian behavioural geneticist Douglas Wahlsten (Wahlsten, 1997) points to a series of adoption studies in France, in which an infant is moved from a family having low socioeconomic status to a home where parents have high socioeconomic status, and the child's IQ score improves by 12–16 points. Wahlsten also points to studies in the United States that have demonstrated improvements in children's IQ by the same margin, achieved by improving the lives of infants in families with low educational and financial resources and providing them with additional educational day care outside the home, every weekday from the age of 3 months to the start of school.

These types of findings turn our attention to the research that has examined the conditions arising in certain families

Often evidence of high levels of ability can be found in unexpected places.
Source: Getty Images/Daniel Berehulak

and how those conditions have influenced intelligence. One interesting and extensive debate has arisen from studies examining the influence on intelligence of birth order and family size.

Birth order, family size and intelligence

In 1973 Dutch psychologists Lillian Belmont and Francis Marolla (Belmont and Marolla, 1973) published a study looking at the birth order of the child, the size of family to which the child belonged and the child's overall IQ score on the Raven Progressive Matrices, among 386 19-year-old Dutch men. What Belmont and Marolla (1973) found was that, even when social class was controlled for, children from larger families had a lower IQ. Furthermore, the authors found that, within each family size, the first-born child always had a better IQ; and to some extent there were declining scores with rising birth order, so that the first-born children scored better than second-born children, second-born children scored better than third-born children and so on. These authors also found that these two factors interacted, and, as family size increased and birth order position increased, IQ scores became lower. So, for example, a second-born child from a family with three children would score higher than would a second-born child from a family containing four children.

Clearly, birth order, family size and intelligence are of interest to parents, politicians and researchers. Furthermore, if such findings are correct, they would have implications for optimum family size and parental choice regarding children's education. Since then, hundreds of research articles

have addressed the relationship between family size, birth order and intelligence, and the proposed relationships between family size, birth order and IQ have been found among many cross-section studies. For example, Russian psychologist T. A. Dumitrashku (Dumitrashku, 1996) found that family size and birth order affected intelligence among Russian schoolchildren.

However, this wouldn't be a section about intelligence if debate didn't fiercely surround these findings. The debate, today, on family size, birth order and intelligence centres on the explanation of why, and whether, such effects occur.

Family size and intelligence

In the research area of family size and intelligence, Joseph Lee Rodgers and his colleagues (Rodgers *et al.*, 2000) published a seminal paper that looked at data from the United States. The National Longitudinal Survey of Youth (NLSY) followed 11,406 young people at yearly intervals from ages 14–22 years, and then children born to the original female respondents were surveyed every other year. Rodgers *et al.* found no direct relationship between family size and intelligence. They suggested that previous research has been inaccurate because it combined 'across-family' measures (family size) with 'within-family' (birth order) measures and treated them in the same way. That, is previous authors had treated family size as a within-family effect.

Let us explain what the authors mean. What the authors are highlighting here is a statistical fallacy (see Chapter 26 on academic argument) that occurs when comparing populations of people.

Say, for example, that a statistical agency released figures for death rates of the UK Army during the recent Iraq War and for death rates in London (the capital of the United Kingdom). The agency found that, among the army, death rates were 13 per thousand, while deaths in London were 26 per thousand. You perhaps would also not be surprised to find that the announcement of these figures by the statistical agency caught the attention of the media. You might even find a national newspaper running a headline story suggesting that people were safer in the army in Iraq than they were living in London. However, the problem with this sort of statement is that you are comparing two different populations. In the army population you have men and women who are healthy, and most of them are young. In the second population, London, you have a full age range of people – including those people with high mortality rates, such as old people, and people who are terminally ill. The issue is that you are comparing two populations for which a number of different factors determine death rates.

This fallacy applies to the current debate. Rodgers *et al.* illustrate the fallacy with this example. They suggest comparing the intelligence of three children, but these children are:

- a first-born child in a large middle-class white family in Michigan;
- a second-born child in a medium-sized affluent black family in Atlanta;
- a third-born child in a small low-income Hispanic family in California.

If differences are observed in these children's intelligence, Rodgers *et al.* suggest it is impossible to tell whether the differences are down to birth order, family size, socioeconomic status, region of the country or any other variables related to these dimensions.

Birth order and intelligence

In the area of birth order and intelligence, research still generally supports Belmont and Marolla's findings. However, other authors have sought to explain that this relationship may be an artefact of another relationship rather than a real relationship. There are three models explaining why birth order may be linked to intelligence: the admixture hypothesis, the confluence model and the resource dilution model.

The first is the **admixture hypothesis**. E. P. Page and G. Grandon (1979) and, more recently, Joseph Rodgers (2001) suggested an 'admixture hypothesis' that explains the relationship between birth order and IQ. What this hypothesis suggests is that parental intelligence, or socioeconomic status, are additional factors to consider in the relationship between birth order and IQ scores, coupled with the fact that parents with lower IQ scores tend to have more children. This has made findings in previous studies look as if higher birth order causes lower intel-

ligence, when in fact lower intelligence results because parents with lower socioeconomic status and IQ scores tend to have more children. For example, a parent with five children is likely to have a lower IQ score and a lower socioeconomic status. Parents with higher IQ scores and higher socioeconomic status tend to have fewer children. Consequently, any calculation of the relationship between birth order and intelligence is problematic because parents with higher IQ scores and higher socioeconomic status do not tend to have as many children. Thus there cannot be equal measurement of the number of children across the population.

The second model is the **resource dilution model**. This model was proposed by Judith Blake (Blake, 1981) and elaborated by Douglas Downey (Downey, 2001), but its ideas were first presented by Galton (1874). The resource dilution model of birth order and intelligence test scores suggests that parental resources (time, energy and financial resources) are finite (i.e. *not* endless) and that, as the number of children in the family increases, the resources (time, energy and financial) that can be gained by any single child decreases. Therefore, the first child will get 100 per cent of available resources from their parents, the second child will only ever get 50 per cent, the third child will only ever get 33 per cent and a fourth child will only ever get 25 per cent. This model also feeds into the idea that children in larger families have lower intelligence test scores because, as that family grows, the resources that can be accessed also diminish.

Third is the **confluence model**, which was originally proposed by US psychologist Robert B. Zajonc (Zajonc, 1976; Zajonc and Markus, 1975) – though, again, Galton (1874) proposed some of these ideas. The confluence model suggests that intellectual development, and therefore intelligence, must be understood within the context of the family, and there is an ever-changing intellectual environment within the family. Zajonc suggests the following factors might influence the relationship between birth order and intelligence:

- First-borns have the advantage of some time in which they do not have to share their parents' attention with any of their siblings.
- Any additional birth automatically limits the amount of attention any of the siblings get, including the first-born.
- First-borns and older siblings have to look after and care for younger siblings to some degree. This means that they undertake some amount of responsibility and may have to explain things to their younger siblings. Zajonc believed that this sort of tutoring helps the older children to develop intelligence abilities, as they have to explain ideas and processes to other people.
- First-born children are exposed to a greater proportion of adult language and ideas from their parents. Those

children born later are exposed to less mature speech and ideas because they listen not only to their parents, but to their other siblings. This means they spend a lower proportion of their time listening to adult language and ideas and a greater proportion of time listening to other children's language and ideas.

These last two findings also feed into the idea that children in larger families have lower IQ scores because, as that family grows, the agenda and the context of the family focuses more and more on the children.

Education and intelligence

We mentioned education and its relationship to intelligence in the previous dicussion (Chapter 13). However, we will remind you of some of the findings and extend your view on this area here.

Neisser *et al.* (1996) found that education is both an independent and dependent variable in terms of its relationship to intelligence. Going to school is likely to increase your abilities, particularly those that comprise intelligence (intelligence is a dependent variable), and intelligence is likely to influence your attendance at school and your length of schooling (i.e. whether you end up going to university) and the quality of school you attend (intelligence is an independent variable here). Consequently, intelligence and education are intrinsically linked.

You will remember evidence from the last discussion (Chapter 13). Overall, reviews by US psychologists Alan Kaufman and Elizabeth Lichtenberger (Kaufman, 1990; Kaufman and Lichtenberger, 2005) provide a review of key papers that have looked at the correlation between general intelligence and school attainment and achievement. They conclude that the average correlation between IQ scores and a number of school indicators is around $r = 0.50$, suggesting that intelligence does predict performance at school. Also, two academics of the Hebrew University in Jerusalem, Sorel Cahan and Nora Cohen (1989), compared the effects of a year of school (controlling for age) with those of a year of age on a number of verbal (e.g. verbal and numerical skills) and non-verbal (abstract and reasoning tests, including the Raven's Matrices) intelligence tests. Length of schooling was important in predicting performance, and mattered more than age for all the verbal tests. Length of schooling, however, made a contribution – but a smaller contribution – to performance on some of the non-verbal tests, including the items from the Raven's Matrices.

Other key evidence you need to know when considering education as an environmental factor on intelligence is found in the well-cited papers of US child development psychologist Stephen Ceci (1990; 1991). Ceci did a meta-analysis of studies, and his findings suggest that there are many effects of education on intelligence test scores.

The data presented by Ceci includes the overall finding that children who attend school regularly score higher on intelligence tests than do those who attend less regularly, intelligence test scores among pupils decrease over the long summer holidays and there is a rise of 2.7 IQ points for each year of schooling (see also Winship and Korenman, 1997). Douglas Wahlsten (1997) notes that studies have shown that delays in starting school cause intelligence test scores to drop by 5 IQ points a year (i.e. Winship and Korenman, 1997).

Also, it is worth reminding you of Head Start and other similar programmes that have explored the relationship between education and intelligence. You remember that Head Start, which we mentioned in the last discussion (Chapter 13), was started in the 1960s by President Lyndon Johnson and was designed to give America's poorest children a head start in preparing them for school and to start to break the cycle of poverty. Evidence was provided to assess the usefulness of such a programme. US individual differences psychologist Charles Locurta (Locurta, 1991) provides a review of this evidence. In 1969, Arthur Jensen suggested that Head Start had failed. The reason for Jensen's pronouncement was that, although children attending the programme showed an initial increase in IQ points – sometimes as much 7–8 points on IQ tests – after 2 or 3 years these higher IQ points were lost (Locurta, 1991). There has been a lot of debate about the effectiveness of Head Start, but in terms of IQ gains, McKey *et al.* (1985) reported that children enrolled in Head Start had significant immediate gains in IQ scores. However, in the longer term (3–4 years), the IQ test scores of Head Start students did not remain higher than those of disadvantaged children who did not attend Head Start.

Finally, there is evidence to suggest that ideas covered in the last discussion regarding socioeconomic status are related to education variables, which, together, are related to intelligence. Socioeconomic status might influence aspects of education, and then intelligence, in a number of ways:

- Families with a high socioeconomic status are often able to prepare their children for school because they have access to resources (e.g. childcare, books and toys) and information (What are the best schools? What aspects are taught to children?) that enhance children's social, emotional and cognitive development and help parents to better prepare their young children for school (Demarest *et al.*, 1993).
- Families of a low economic status face hard challenges when it comes to providing the best care and education for their children. When basic necessities such as money and time are missing, food, housing, clothing and healthcare come first. Educational toys and books, and time searching out the best schools, are luxuries

that parents may not have the time or money to pursue (Ramey and Ramey, 1994).

- Parents from poor socioeconomic backgrounds often grew up in poor socioeconomic conditions themselves. Consequently, parents may have inadequate reading skills or may lack knowledge about childhood nutrition (or not be able to afford it), and these benefits aren't passed on to the children before school (Zill *et al.*, 1995).

Culture and intelligence

The final environmental area that Neisser *et al.* (1996) suggest is important to influencing intelligence is the cultural environment in which people live. 'Culture' refers to people's individual values, and the values of their society. Neisser *et al.* suggest culture can have an effect not only on intelligence but also on the type of intelligence that might develop.

You remember that earlier (in Chapter 11) we outlined implicit theories of intelligence. Those theories showed how the definition of what constitutes intelligence shifts across cultures, particularly when you compare western and eastern cultures, and how conceptions of intelligence shift across age and through different disciplines. Well, clearly that discussion of implicit theories of intelligence is relevant here (you may want to re-read some of that chapter).

However, in addition to implicit theories of intelligence, Serpell (2001) identifies three concepts that explain how intelligence in western societies is set apart from other cultures in the world. These three concepts are decontextualisation, quantification and biologisation.

Decontextualisation

A lot of western thinking is inherited from 3,000 years of classical Greek philosophy. Socrates, Plato and Aristotle were all Greek philosophers who have had a profound impact on the way we think in our culture. In western culture there is a tendency to emphasise mathematics, the scientific method and language. We make clear distinctions between what is right and wrong, what constitutes justice, the need to follow a logical progression and the idea that there are higher and lower planes of ideas and activities – and perhaps a universal truth.

Decontextualisation is the ability to disconnect, or detach oneself, from a particular situation and think abstractly, and then generalise about it. Serpell (2001) argues that the ability to think abstractly and generalise about things has gained importance in western society because of industrialisation. With the growth of capitalism there is a need for efficiency, some level of bureaucracy and functionality (the ability to come up with abstract

principles) to help govern western life, including the markets (financial, housing, consumer), industry and education. These needs become increasingly important. Serpell questions the need to always view decontextualisation as a sign of intelligence, and a failure to decontextualise as a sign of unintelligence.

Quantification

Quantification is the act of discovering, or expressing, the quantity of something. Serpell suggests that the study of intelligence is surrounded by quantification in three ways:

- First is the way that intelligence theory and research is designed to quantify intelligence. That is, when we ask 'what is intelligence?' we are trying to encapsulate a number of meanings and ideas into one word, 'intelligence'.
- Second is a concept called reification (see also Gould, 1981). Reification is the tendency to regard an abstract idea as if it had concrete or material existence. We see intelligence as something that is located in the brain, but we do not know where it is located. Intelligence isn't just about certain processes; but it encapsulates things that are not measurable, such as beauty or sophistication. For many, the invention of the steam engine, or the wheel, are highly intelligent acts; however, they are also acts of beauty to some, and they are certainly of sophistication to many.
- Third is a tendency to quantify intelligence in terms of numbers. We give people intelligence tests, which contain an optimum number of items that should be completed within a certain amount of time. These items have been selected in accordance with studies that have used statistical procedures to determine what aspects of intelligence are out there. The test that is given is determined by the person's age. When participants have finished, they are given scores for their performance, and these scores are then transformed into IQ scores. These IQ scores can then be compared against standardised scores for the tests of people of the same age.

Serpell suggests that consideration of these three points indicates that our understanding of intelligence is surrounded by quantification. All this is not to say that quantification is not a good process to understand intelligence. To produce meaning and conceptual understanding of words; to try to define, measure and locate concepts; and to use numbers as objective criteria are excellent methods by which to ensure the progress and understanding of intelligence. However, Serpell suggests that when we are dealing with something like intelligence, we must be sure that we do not seek to over-quantify this concept.

Biologisation

Serpell (2001) raises our awareness that biological and evolutionary theories have grown in prominence in late twentieth century and early twenty-first century thinking (**biologisation**). You will be aware that, in our psychophysiological and evolutionary chapters (Chapters 8 and 9), we outlined the dramatic developments in the understanding of genes, and that evolutionary psychologists are able to link the evolution of the human species to animals who lived billions of years ago. Many of the arguments put forward by biological and evolutionary psychology are convincing, and inspiring, in the understanding of why we behave the way we do. However, Serpell suggests some caution in over-emphasising these models. It must be remembered that many of these models talk about developments over millions of years, and our advanced study of ourselves is relatively new. Therefore, we must be careful to ensure that our understanding of genetics, evolutions over a long course of history, and genetic variation are not used to explain intelligence within a relatively short period of history.

Final comments on genetic heritability and environmental influences on intelligence

Perhaps the last word in this section goes to Bouchard and Loehlin (2001), who suggest a framework for observing sources of population variance in psychological traits (see Figure 14.5). We presented this framework earlier (Chapter 8) and think that it is applicable to intelligence.

To assess population variations in intelligence, Bouchard and Loehlin's framework is not only a good overview of the debate but also sets some prudent criteria in terms of assessing elements such as genetic effects and environmental effects on intelligence. So, in all, we must consider:

- **Genetic influences** – including questions about what gene is involved and what type of genetic variation (for example, additive or non-additive). Is there a sex limitation (e.g. brain size)?
- **Environmental influences** – including to what extent does environment influence the genes, what types of environments are involved (e.g. education, culture) and are there gender effects?
- **Interaction between genetic and environmental influence** – including what type are the interactions between genes and the environment (e.g. nutrition, prenatal causes)?
- **Developmental influences** – including do different genes influence during development, and do different environmental factors influence during development?
- **Assortative mating** – including is assortative mating present in intelligence, and are there sex differences in mating preference for intelligence?
- **Evolution** – including what sort of selective factors were at work during the original evolution of intelligence (e.g. different need for intelligences across different areas of the world)? Are there current selective factors at work?

Genetic
1 To what extent is the trait influenced by genes?
2 What type of gene is involved?
3 How many loci are involved?
4 Is there a sex limitation or sex linkage?
5 Are chromosomal effects involved?

Environmental
1 To what extent is intelligence influenced by the environment?
2 What type of environment is involved?
3 Are there gender effects?
4 Is transmission horizontal, or is it vertical?

Genetic and environmental influence
1 Are there any genetic x environmental interactions on intelligence?
2 What type are the interactions between genes and the environment?

Intelligence

Developmental
1 Do different genes influence during development?
2 Do different environmental factors influence during development?

Assortative mating
1 Is assortative mating present in intelligence?
2 Are there sex differences in mate preference for intelligence?

Evolution
1 What sort of selective factors were at work during the original evolution of intelligence?
2 Are there current selective factors at work?
3 Is intelligence an adaptation?

Figure 14.5 Framework and questions regarding sources of population variance in intelligence.
Source: Based on Bouchard and Loehlin (2001).

Clearly, when it comes to intelligence, some of these areas are easier to identify or consider than others. For example, no one has discovered whether there is a gene for intelligence; nor can we be certain about what the different evolutionary demands on intelligence are. However, many of the areas – assessing the level of genetic influence, the types of environmental influence and the possible interactions between genes and the environment – are known, or at least provide sources of evidence that provide evidence for a debate. Applying Bouchard and Loehlin's model to intelligence provides a focus to an area that debates the relative influences of: (1) genes; (2) the environment; and (3) the interactions between genes and the environment on intelligence.

Section B – the bell curve: race differences in intelligence

In this section we will outline what has become known as the bell curve debate. Here, we consider evidence and arguments concerning race differences in intelligence.

Figure 14.6 The distribution of IQ scores: a bell curve.

The bell curve

We have deliberately held back on discussing this material until now, although it covers some of the topics we have looked at in this and other discussions, because we wanted you to be prepared for this discussion. In psychology, the discussion of differences in intelligence, particularly race differences, raises a lot of emotions and debate. We will, later in this discussion, highlight this area of psychology further, in the area of eugenics. We would like to think that your reading of this material also raises emotions, not only as a psychologist but also as a human being. However, we would also like to think that you can see past some of your emotions, pick out the arguments and debates that exist here, and use argument, rather than emotion, to decide on the relative merits that are put forward (if you're worried about seeing this distinction, read more about academic argument and fallacies in online Chapter 26).

The bell curve: intelligence and class structure in American life

In 1994 two authors from the United States, Richard J. Herrnstein and Charles Murray, published a book called *The Bell Curve: Intelligence and Class Structure in American Life* (Herrnstein and Murray, 1994). The book is an analysis of IQ test scores in the United States. The term 'bell curve' refers to the shape of the distribution of a large number of IQ scores in the United States – it looks like a bell (see Figure 14.6).

The book caused huge debate because it reported many things about intelligence, particularly the extent to which intelligence is genetically inherited. It claimed to describe the rise of a 'cognitive elite' in the United States – a social group of persons with high intelligence, with an increasingly

Profiles

Richard Herrnstein and Charles Murray

Richard Herrnstein (1930-1994) was a prominent researcher in comparative psychology. He was Charles Sanders Pierce Professor of Psychology at Harvard University. During his career, he worked with B. F. Skinner (advocate of behaviourism, which seeks to understand behaviour as a function of environmental histories of reinforcement) in the Harvard pigeon lab, where he did research on choice and other topics in behavioural psychology.

In the 1960s, as part of this work on pigeon intelligence, Herrnstein formulated the 'matching law', which outlined how reinforcement and behaviour are linked. The matching law addresses the idea of choice. It views choice not as a single event or an internal process of the person, but as a rate of observable external events over time. Some have suggested that the matching law is an important explanatory account of choice behaviour, and

its applications spread from psychology into other fields, notably economics.

Charles Murray was born in 1943 in Newton, Iowa, in the United States. He studied for his undergraduate degree in history at Harvard. In 1965 he joined the Peace Corps for 5 years in rural Thailand (Peace Corps volunteers travel overseas and work with people there). By 1974 Murray had returned to the United States, where he completed his PhD in political science at the Massachusetts Institute of Technology. He has written extensively on economics, crime and poverty and has become one of the nation's most influential thinkers. His book *Losing Ground: American Social Policy, 1950-1980* (Murray, 1984) was used by President Ronald Reagan in developing his domestic policy. Murray has been the subject of articles in *Newsweek*, *The New York Times Magazine* and *The Los Angeles Times Magazine*.

---

good chance of succeeding in life. This book noted several cultural differences in intelligence, but its authors also made some suggestions regarding the intellectual inferiority of certain cultural groups. Such work was perceived by many as difficult for US society. The authors' findings were seen as having implications for social and public policy as well as pointing to potential sources of inequality in the United States. We will now briefly describe the main arguments put forward by Herrnstein and Murray.

Herrnstein and Murray's main arguments are built on six premises (or, as they present them, conclusions) about intelligence. We have used Herrnstein and Murray's original words here, but have put simpler wording in parentheses:

1. 'There is such a thing as a general *factor* of cognitive ability on which human beings differ.' (*There exists a general factor of intelligence, and individuals differ in their intelligence, i.e. high, low, average intelligence.*)

2. 'All standardised tests of *academic* aptitude, or achievement, measure this general factor to some degree, but *IQ* tests, expressly designed for that purpose, measure it most accurately.' (*There are many tests of academic aptitude or achievement, but IQ tests, which are specifically designed to measure intelligence, measure intelligence most accurately*).

3. 'IQ scores match, to a first degree, whatever it is that people mean when they use the word *intelligent or smart* in ordinary language.' (*IQ scores reflect whatever most people mean by the word intelligent.*)

4. 'IQ scores are stable, although not perfectly so, over much of a person's life.' (*Throughout an individual's life, their IQ score remains relatively stable.*)

5. 'Properly administered IQ tests are not demonstrably biased against social, economic, ethnic, or racial groups.' (*IQ tests, when they are properly administered, are not biased against any social, economic, ethnic or racial groups.*)

6. 'Cognitive ability is substantially heritable, apparently no less than 40 per cent and no more than 80 per cent.' (*Genetic heritability of intelligence is between 40 and 80 per cent.*)

Herrnstein and Murray then go on to discuss four main ideas in their book: (1) the cognitive elite; (2) socioeconomic variables and IQ scores; (3) the relationship between race and intelligence; and (4) the implications for social policy.

The cognitive elite: looking at the higher end of the bell curve

In their book, Herrnstein and Murray begin by looking at the high end of the bell curve – that is, at those who score higher on intelligence tests – and examine the relationship between intelligence and education. Herrnstein and Murray analysed IQ scores and admissions to universities and colleges over 50 years, and they found that the most important factor in college attendance was the intelligence of the students, not social class or wealth. It is this fact, Herrnstein and Murray maintain, that places the most intelligent people in US society in the same place – university and colleges.

Herrnstein and Murray argue that the next stage of this process is the relationship between university and colleges and the workplace. University and college graduates are often placed within a select few occupations, reserved for those obtaining college and university degrees, including teaching, engineering, law, research, medicine and accounting.

The authors then draw on studies showing that intelligence is related to efficient and proficient (advanced degree of competence) employees. You may remember the finding of two US psychologists, John E. Hunter and R. F. Hunter (1984), who did a meta-analysis (a meta-analysis is a technique that combines the results of several studies) that put together the results of studies examining various predictors at the start of a job with eventual job performance. They found that the correlation between intelligence and job performance was much larger than job performance and the individual's curriculum vitae, their previous experience, the job interview and education ($r = 0.10$). With findings like this, Herrnstein and Murray conclude that intelligence is the single most powerful predictor of job success and workplace productivity.

Herrnstein and Murray suggest that there is the emergence in the United States of the cognitive elite, based on a separation of society through education (university and colleges) and the workplace (certain professions such as teaching, research, law and medicine), in which the central factor is intelligence. Consequently, Herrnstein and Murray predict that intelligence will soon become the basis of the American class system, and people with higher intelligence will be at the top of this class system.

IQ scores and social and economic problems: looking at the lower end of the bell curve

Next, Herrnstein and Murray turn their attention to the lower end of the bell curve – that is, people with low scores on intelligence tests. What Herrnstein and Murray do is to look at several factors in the context of IQ scores; these factors include poverty, schooling, unemployment, family life, welfare dependency and crime.

An example of the type of analysis they performed is given in Table 14.1. This table is adapted from Linda Gottfredson (1997), who summarised Herrnstein and Murray's (1994) analysis, and we have picked out just a few of their findings to illustrate their analysis. The first row of the table shows the percentage of people who fall within the range of standardised IQ scores (remember that IQ scores are transformed to a mean of 100). This standardisation into a normal distribution is consistent with the practice of standardising scores into a mean of 100 and a standard deviation of 15 (there is more on this process in Chapter 12 if you need to refresh your memory). Therefore, the greater percentages of people are concentrated in the middle, with lower percentages at either end of the curve. As shown in the first row of numbers in Table 14.1, 50 per cent of people fall within the middle category of 90–110 IQ points range, with 20 per cent of individuals falling within the 75–90 and 110–125 IQ points range, and 5 per cent of people scoring less than 75 and greater than 125 IQ points.

Herrnstein and Murray examined each sample (i.e. number of people in poverty, number of people in prison) in terms of their IQ scores distribution and expressed this as a percentage of the overall population (i.e. less than 75; between 90 and 110 points). As you can see, larger percentages of people (expressed in terms of the overall population) in each of the social and economic subsamples are concentrated towards the lower end of the IQ curve; that is, less than 75 IQ points and 75–90 IQ points.

Table 14.1 Social and economic indicators broken down by sample, and divided in terms of IQ score category and expressed as a percentage of the overall population

Social and economic indicators	IQ				
	Less than 75	75–90	90–110	110–125	Greater than 125
US population distribution	5%	20%	50%	20%	5%
Men who are unemployed for more than 1 month out of year	12%	10%	7%	7%	2%
People who are divorced within 5 years of marriage	21%	22%	23%	15%	9%
Mothers with children with IQ less than 75	39%	17%	6%	7%	0%
Lives in poverty	30%	16%	6%	3%	2%
Ever been in prison	7%	7%	3%	1%	0%
Mothers in receipt of long-term welfare support	31%	17%	8%	2%	0%
Dropping out from high school (secondary education)	55%	35%	6%	0.4%	0%

Source: Reprinted from Gottfredson, L. S. (1997). Why *g* matters: the complexity of everyday life. *Intelligence*, Vol. 24, pp. 79–132. Copyright © 1997, reproduced with permission from Elsevier.

Herrnstein and Murray used these statistics to develop their argument. For Herrnstein and Murray the statistics on poverty, schooling, unemployment and crime clearly show that intelligence underlies many of these social and economic problems. They suggest that low IQ scores are a strong precursor to poverty, more so than any socioeconomic conditions. With schooling, low IQ scores predict whether people are likely to drop out of high school (secondary education) and decrease the likelihood of a person gaining a degree. The authors point out that the figures suggest that a person with a high IQ score is likely to finish high school regardless of their social or economic circumstances. Herrnstein and Murray find that low IQ scores are related to unemployment and are seen in people who are injured more often or who have given up work. They find that the best predictor of unemployment among men is not socioeconomic status or education, but IQ scores. The authors conclude that low IQ scores are associated with higher rates of divorce, lower rates of marriage and higher rates of illegitimate births. They also find that IQ scores are related to family structure, with families comprising a nuclear or traditional structure (two parents, two children) scoring higher on intelligence tests than did families with extended members living in the family home. They suggest that the disappearance of the traditional nuclear family in the United States was a result of low intelligence. Additionally, Herrnstein and Murray point to the fact that the average US criminal has an IQ score about 8 IQ points lower than that of the average US citizen, suggesting intelligence is linked to a propensity for crime in the United States.

In other areas, Herrnstein and Murray are less certain, but also suggest that long-term welfare dependency and parenting are related to IQ scores. They argue that low intelligence is the primary factor in predicting people's first use of welfare, but then a culture of dependency (learnt from childhood experiences of parents and relatives being on welfare) may emerge that leads to individuals using welfare in the long term. Finally, Herrnstein and Murray point out that low IQ scores among mothers correlate with their children's poor motor skills and with social development and behavioural problems from 4 years and upwards. Herrnstein and Murray point out that, although being of lower intelligence does not prevent individuals from being good parents, family environments where damage is done to a child's intellectual development occur when parents are on the lower end of the intelligence distribution.

In considering the relationships between these factors and intelligence, Herrnstein and Murray build an argument where they suggest that an individual's intelligence is more important than their socioeconomic status in predicting their eventual economic and social welfare.

The relationship between race and IQ: implications for social policy

Herrnstein and Murray next turn their attention to the differences that occur between various ethnic groups. They examine the different fertility patterns of groups on the intelligence distribution, but generally they adopt the position that intelligence is largely genetically heritable.

Herrnstein and Murray compared IQ test scores by ethnicity. For example, they found that individuals of Asian and Asian American ethnic origin scored on average around 5 IQ points higher than white Americans, particularly on measures of crystallised (verbal) intelligence. However, it is in the comparison between white Americans and black Americans that larger differences emerge.

On the Wechsler Intelligence test (remember that this is a measure of verbal and non-verbal [crystallised/fluid] intelligence), Herrnstein and Murray reported that white Americans score 15 IQ points higher than black Americans. On the Stanford–Binet test (remember this is also a measure of verbal/non-verbal intelligence), Herrnstein and Murray reported that white Americans scored 18 IQ points higher than black Americans. Therefore, on both intelligence tests, the gap between the two races is almost 1 standard deviation (15 IQ points). In terms of normed IQ scores, white Americans averaged 102 IQ points, while black Americans averaged 87 IQ points. Herrnstein and Murray also note that the average IQ score of immigrants coming into the United States was 95 IQ points, lower than the national IQ average (see Figure 14.7).

It is here that Herrnstein and Murray move towards the most controversial part of the book. They say the evidence suggests that certain social factors in the United States are pushing down its citizens' intelligence. These

Figure 14.7 Distribution of IQ scores for white Americans (average 102) and black Americans (average 87 IQ points).

Source: Adapted with the permission of The Free Press, a Division of Simon & Schuster, Inc., from *The Bell Curve: Intelligence and Class Structure in American Life* by Richard J. Herrnstein and Charles Murray. Copyright © 1994 by Richard J. Herrnstein and Charles Murray. All rights reserved.

factors include the number of children produced, which is greater for women who have lower IQ scores than for those with higher IQ scores; consequently, the United States is producing more and more children born into lower intelligence environments. They suggest that, as more and more immigrants come into the country, they show lower levels of intelligence. They suggest, then, that these factors are causing a downward pressure on intelligence in the United States; as the average intelligence of the nation falls, social problems such as poverty, unemployment and crime will increase as these social problems are associated with people with low intelligence scores. Additionally inherent in Herrnstein and Murray's argument is that, at least by implication, those groups of people in the country with lower intelligence (for example, immigrants, African–Americans), are potentially part of these social problems.

Moreover, Herrnstein and Murray suggest that the way forward is not to address social problems by trying to compensate for individual differences in intelligence through supporting and increasing these people's intelligence. They point to previous attempts to raise intelligence, such as nutrition (as mentioned earlier and in the previous discussion [Chapter 13]) or preschool programmes (such as Head Start) that have not been successful in permanently raising intelligence. They also suggest that, as intelligence has a 40–80 per cent genetic heritability, there should be little expectation that intelligence should rise in these situations.

Furthermore, they argue against affirmative action programmes in the United States. Affirmative action (or positive discrimination) is a policy providing advantages for people of a minority group who are seen to have traditionally been discriminated against. The aim of affirmative action is to create a more equal society. Herrnstein and Murray suggest that preferential access to education or employment for African–Americans and immigrant groups (where institutions increase the selection and promotion of candidates from these ethnic minority groups in the United States) has also failed. The authors argue that such approaches have not only led to a decrease of intelligence in education and the workplace (leading to further downward pressure on intelligence in US society and, therefore, increasing the potential of social problems), but have also caused racial tension in education and the workplace. This tension arises from resentment between ethnic groups owing to lower levels of student attainment – or more dropping out in education – and poorer job performance in the workplace as a result of people with lower intelligence undertaking study or jobs to which they are not suited.

Herrnstein and Murray's position is that American education and the workplace have been 'dumbed down' as they take on people with lower intelligence. The authors suggest that, while US education and work institutions have been good in helping the underprivileged, this success has been at the expense of gifted students. Thus, by being ignored, gifted students have not been able to develop their true potential. Herrnstein and Murray argue that their aim is to point to places of inequality; they observe that pretending inequality does not exist has not been sensible. Instead, they suggest, we should try living with inequality; doing so is preferable because it is reality.

Herrnstein and Murray suggest that the money for education should be shifted from supporting disadvantaged programmes for those with a low intelligence (where there is a predominance of African–Americans and other ethnic minorities) to programmes that support those with a high intelligence (where there is a predominance of white Americans and Asians). They argue that it is in promoting and further valuing the gifted, and in raising the intelligence of the nation, that the future of the United States lies. An educational system that aids the gifted will value and raise intelligence throughout society, particularly the workplace; and social problems such as poverty, unemployment and crime will be reduced.

Criticisms of *The Bell Curve: Intelligence and Class Structure in American Life*

When first published, the *The Bell Curve* received a great deal of positive publicity, including cover stories in *Newsweek* and articles in *Time*, *The New York Times* and the *Wall Street Journal*. However, there was a large amount of negative response, particularly in the scientific community, suggesting that the book was oversimplified and had flawed analysis. Much of this commentary was in response to the authors' discussion of race differences in intelligence. In reaction to this publicity and controversy surrounding *The Bell Curve*, the American Psychological Association established a special task force to publish an investigative report on the research presented in the book as well as an analysis of what is known and unknown about intelligence. This task force was headed by Ulric Neisser, then at Emory University in the United States. After an extended consultative process, Neisser chose a range of academics representing a broad range of expertise and opinion in the literature of intelligence, including Thomas J. Bouchard Jr, Stephen J. Ceci, Diane F. Halpern, John C. Loehlin and Robert J. Sternberg (who are all mentioned in these discussion). After analysing Herrnstein and Murray's conclusions regarding race and intelligence, the task force agreed that, while large differences exist between the average IQ scores of African Americans and white Americans, there is no definite evidence suggesting that these differences are genetic; they may, in fact, be cultural.

More extensive critical considerations of Herrnstein and Murray's book can be found in the literature. However, in the following discussion, we are going to highlight some of the critiques that appeared at the time of *The Bell Curve* so that you can develop a critical analysis of the arguments contained within Herrnstein and Murray's analysis.

There are three main areas of criticism of Herrnstein and Murray's book that we will now outline:

- analysis of the assumptions used by Herrnstein and Murray in their analysis (led by comments by Stephen Jay Gould);
- statistical and evidence-based problems in Herrnstein and Murray's analysis (led by comments by Leon J. Kamin);
- a darker side of psychology related to Herrnstein and Murray's analysis (led by comments by Stephen Jay Gould and Leon J. Kamin).

Analysis of the assumptions used by Herrnstein and Murray

Stephen Jay Gould (Gould, 1995), an academic at Harvard, starts to dismantle some of the premises within Herrnstein and Murray's book to attack their arguments regarding what should happen in the United States (for example, that money for education be shifted from supporting disadvantaged programmes for those with a low intelligence to programmes that support those with a high intelligence).

Premises are the foundation of any argument. There are more details on the importance of premises in arguments (although Gould used the term 'assumption', in this example they can be treated to mean the same thing) later in the text (online Chapter 26). For example, imagine that you criticise a particular person as useless (your argument about them) because they haven't done a job you asked them to, and you assume they have not done the job because they are lazy (your premise). If you find out later that they haven't done the job because they had hurt themselves, then this makes your

argument invalid (that they are useless) because the premise that forms your argument (that the person is lazy) is wrong.

In the same way, Gould begins to dismantle some of the premises informing the arguments that Herrnstein and Murray develop in their book about what should happen in the United States. We will now look at each of the premises that Herrnstein and Murray use – and Gould seeks to attack (although we have supplemented them with evidence and argument from more recent considerations to bring the debate up to date).

Assumption 1: 'There is such a thing as a general *factor* of cognitive ability on which human beings differ.'

In an earlier discussion (Chapter 12) we outlined Spearman's theory of a general factor of intelligence ('g'). However, we know from our earlier discussion of intelligence (Chapters 12 and 13) that there are difficulties in assuming that there is a general factor of intelligence (g). These difficulties reflect the work of theorists and researchers who:

- Use factor analysis to identify general factors of intelligence and suggest that intelligence is better understood as comprised in a hierarchy of intelligence abilities. For example, see Carroll (intelligence in three strata) or Cattell (intelligence comprised of two related but distinct components – crystallised intelligence and fluid intelligence) (Chapter 12).
- Challenge, entirely, the notion of a general intelligence, and suggest it is best represented by a number of different, and separate, intelligences. For example, see Sternberg's triarchic theory and Gardner's multiple intelligence theory (Chapter 12).
- Emphasise cognitive psychology processes and argue that intelligence is about not only general factors of abilities but also cognitive processes. For example, see the Kaufman's ability tests and Das and Naglieri's cognitive assessment system (Chapter 13).

Profile

Stephen Jay Gould

Stephen Jay Gould (1941–2002) was born and raised in New York. He obtained his PhD at Columbia and served as a member of the faculty at Harvard beginning in 1967. Gould's expertise was varied; he was a palaeontologist (a person who studies the forms of life existing in prehistoric or geologic times), evolutionary biologist and historian of science. At the end of his career he was the Alexander Agassiz Professor of Zoology at Harvard.

In 1972 he worked with Niles Eldridge to develop the evolutionary theory of punctuated equilibrium. In this theory, Eldridge and Gould suggested that evolution does not always represent long, drawn-out processes; instead, evolutionary change may sometimes work in fits and starts and can happen relatively rapidly, particularly in times of environmental stress.

As we can see, the assumption that there is a general factor of cognitive ability (intelligence) on which human beings differ is open to debate.

Assumption 2: 'All standardised tests of *academic* aptitude, or achievement, measure this general factor to some degree, but *IQ* tests expressly designed for that purpose measure it most accurately.'

If we accept the previous counterargument, that a general factor of cognitive ability (intelligence) on which human beings differ is 'open to debate', then the assumption that the intelligence tests expressly designed for measuring IQ can measure intelligence most accurately is also open to debate, as such tests cannot measure the many different definitions of intelligence proposed by the different theorists.

We have seen that, even with established general intelligence (IQ) tests (described in Chapters 12 and 13), there are distinctions between psychometric-based intelligence tests that measure verbal and non-verbal general intelligence (e.g. the Wechsler tests and the Stanford–Binet IQ), psychometric-based non-verbal intelligence (e.g. the Raven's Matrices) and cognitive-based intelligence tests that measure intelligence abilities and intelligence processes (Kaufman's abilities tests and the cognitive assessment system). Therefore, we can see that this assumption is open to debate, and may be particularly important because Herrnstein and Murray rely heavily on psychometric IQ test scores to build their arguments.

Assumption 3: 'IQ scores match, to a first degree, whatever it is that people mean when they use the word *intelligent* or *smart* in ordinary language.'

There is a problem with this assumption if we consider implicit (or everyday) theories of intelligence (which we covered in Chapter 11). Implicit theories of intelligence specifically address what people mean when they use the word 'intelligent' in ordinary language.

The first point to emerge from studies looking at implicit theories of intelligence is the difference between western and eastern cultures of intelligence. You will remember that intelligence in western cultures suggests an emphasis on the speed of mental processing and the ability to gather, assimilate and sort information quickly and efficiently. In eastern cultures, these ideas do not fully apply; instead, intelligence extends to social, historical and spiritual aspects of everyday interactions, knowledge and problem-solving. It would be unfair to extend this observation to debate Herrnstein and Murray's *Bell Curve* assumption as they were talking about only one western culture, the United States. None the less, they did build some of their arguments on the fact that immigrants coming into the United States are scoring lower than the national IQ score average and exerting a downward pressure on the intelligence of the United States. Might it be that these immigrants are coming from other countries where different types of intelligence are emphasised?

Other findings with studies of implicit theories of intelligence do extend directly to Herrnstein and Murray's argument. For example, our conceptions of intelligence do change across the age range, or across academic disciplines, in western cultures. Remember the study mentioned earlier (in Chapter 13) by Canadian psychologist Prem Fry (Fry, 1984), who found that intelligence at the three main stages of educational development – primary school (5- to 11-year-olds), secondary school (11- to 18-year-olds), and tertiary (college and university) levels (18+-year-olds) – differed strongly. Also remember Sternberg's study examining implicit theories of intelligence among art, business, philosophy and physics professors (Sternberg, 1986b). He found that conceptions of intelligence differed greatly across these experts.

Therefore, Herrnstein and Murray's assumption that intelligence test scores match, to a first degree, whatever it is that people mean when they use the word 'intelligent' in ordinary language, is widely open to debate.

Assumption 4: 'IQ (intelligence test) scores are stable, although not perfectly so, over much of a person's life.'

The assumption rests on whether intelligence can substantially change over a person's life. This is still a major debate; in the intelligence literature, it is referred to as the fixed versus malleable intelligence debate. There are two areas to consider in examining this assumption.

First is the view that intelligence does not substantially change during one's lifetime (that is, it remains fixed). As you will remember from earlier (Chapter 13), some authors have reported that IQ scores remain stable over long periods of time; these findings support the view that intelligence is generally fixed. Jones and Bayley (Jones and Bayley, 1941) found that IQ scores of children at 18 years were positively correlated with their IQ scores at 12 years ($r = 0.89$) and 6 years ($r = 0.77$). Deary *et al.* (2000) found that, over a period of 60 years, IQ scores had a high correlation (at least $r = 0.63$). Also, evidence that educational schemes such as Head Start among disadvantaged children (outlined in this chapter and in Chapter 13), in which initial gains in IQ scores were *not* sustained, supports the view that intelligence is fixed.

However, the second area to consider points to evidence suggesting that intelligence is malleable (does or can change). We described earlier Ceci's (1990; 1991) meta-analysis of hundreds of studies. His results suggest that there are many effects of schooling and education on IQ scores, including the findings that children who attend school regularly score higher on IQ tests (a rise of 2.7 IQ points) and that delays in starting school cause intelligence scores to drop (by 5 IQ points per year missed). We also described Wahlsten's (1997) mention of adoption studies in France: an infant is moved from a family with a low socioeconomic status to a family with a high socioeconomic status, and the child's IQ score improves by 12–16 points. Finally, you will remember our discussion of the role of nutrition in intelligence, particularly the role of vitamin supplements on IQ scores among children. Reviews of these studies suggest that, in the majority of cases, there is a positive effect on intelligence as the result of vitamin and mineral supplements in at least some of the children on non-verbal (fluid) measures of intelligence (Benton, 1991).

The question of whether intelligence is fixed or malleable is open to debate. Consequently, there is some evidence in this area to question the assumption that IQ scores are stable, although not perfectly so, over much of a person's life.

Assumption 5: 'Properly administered intelligence (IQ) tests are not demonstrably biased against social, economic, ethnic, or racial groups.'

The first thing to acknowledge in this area is that it was agreed by the APA Task Force (Neisser *et al.*, 1996) that properly administered intelligence tests are not demonstrably biased against social, economic, ethnic or racial groups. The argument that they are biased is often put forward by opponents, but this view that intelligence tests, themselves, are biased against such groups may be misguided. Rather, a more sensible position to adopt at this stage is not that intelligence tests are biased against such groups, but that the theory from which they are developed may be biased. For example, there is a general factor of intelligence, or the view that intelligence comprises *only* speed of mental processing and the ability to gather, assimilate and sort information quickly and efficiently, that is strongly emphasised in western culture.

Assumption 6: 'Cognitive ability is substantially heritable, apparently no less than 40 per cent and no more than 80 per cent.'

As we noted earlier in this discussion, a number of sources, including the APA Task Force (Neisser *et al.*, 1996), agree that cognitive ability is substantially heritable – apparently no less than 40 per cent and no more than 80 per cent. As you already know, there is some convincing evidence

that intelligence, to some extent, is genetically inherited. However, it is worth noting that this margin, of 40–80 per cent, is quite large.

Gould's issue with this assumption is that heritability can then be used to explain differences for intelligence scores between ethnic groups. You remember that earlier we outlined a fallacy in comparing populations and gave the example of comparing death rates among a population of army recruits and the death rates for the population of a capital city from the same general population. We noted that you have to be aware of several different factors determining death rates between these two different populations. Well, this fallacy also exists in Herrnstein and Murray's application of genetic heritability to explain differences between black and white Americans (though Herrnstein and Murray do acknowledge this problem in their work). However, Gould argues that substantial heritability of intelligence within a population group (e.g. white or black Americans) cannot be used to explain average differences between groups (white Americans versus black Americans).

To extend this argument, evidence from geneticists could even ask whether race is a valid distinction to make between populations. In terms of understanding differences in intelligence between populations, such as race, one important context to consider in genetic influence is the amount of variance that is accounted for by race in the first place. We all know the saying that the colour of one's skin is only skin deep. Well, as we also know, this is a scientific fact. Typically, people looking at race differences make those distinctions based on what they can see; this is called **socially defined race**. As R. S. Cooper and his colleagues note, researchers tend to define race within broad concepts of white, African, Asian, Chinese or Hispanic (Cooper *et al.*, 2000). However, these distinctions generalise across a huge number of different cultures and languages. For example, are white Americans the same as white individuals from the United Kingdom, Italy and Australia?

Because of advanced techniques in understanding our physiology, our understanding of race differences have changed dramatically. Authors such as US evolutionary biologists Masatosi Nei and Arun Roychoudhury (Nei and Roychoudhury, 1982; 1993) and Joseph Graves (Graves, 2001) note that the genetic variance within a population is around 10 times greater than genetic variance between races. In fact, two people who are closely related in terms of their 'race' may differ many more times in their genetic makeup than will two people of two separate 'races'. Today, biologists suggest the criterion by which we determine race, which is mainly based on skin colour, does not make sense in genetic terms. There are virtually no expressed genes (where the gene's information is converted into a living cell) that can be found in all the members of one race.

Stop and think

The arguments of Herrnstein and Murray and Gould

Let us take you through the two major arguments presented around Herrnstein and Murray's theories. Also remember that when we use the term 'true' here, we actually mean that 'a majority of evidence suggests', because in psychology we deal with probability estimates of findings. We cannot ever say anything is completely true, proved or disproved (see Chapter 26 if you want a full explanation of academic argument).

Argument 1: Herrnstein and Murray's argument

Major premises

- If it is true that there is such a thing as a general factor of cognitive ability on which human beings differ;
- and it is true that all standardised tests of academic aptitude or achievement measure this general factor to some degree, but IQ tests expressly designed for that purpose measure it most accurately;
- and it is true that IQ scores match, to a first degree, whatever it is that people mean when they use the word;
- and it is true that IQ scores are stable, although not perfectly so, over much of a person's life;
- and it is true that properly administered IQ tests are not demonstrably biased against social, economic, ethnic or racial groups;
- and it is true that cognitive ability is substantially heritable, apparently no less than 40 per cent and no more than 80 per cent;

Minor premises

- and if it is also true that one population group identified by their ethnicity had an average IQ score lower than another population group identified by their ethnicity;

Conclusion

- therefore, it must be true that the population group who had the lower average IQ score must be less intelligent than the population group who had the higher average IQ score.

Argument 2: The counterargument based on Gould's analysis

Major premises

- *it is not necessarily true* that there is such a thing as a general factor of cognitive ability on which human beings differ (because of multifactor theories of intelligence);
- *it is not necessarily true* that all standardised tests of academic aptitude or achievement measure this general factor to some degree, but IQ tests expressly designed for that purpose measure it most accurately (because general intelligence tests are very different today and there is a real distinction between psychometric and cognitive ability tests);
- *it is not necessarily true* that IQ scores match, to a first degree, whatever it is that people mean when they use the word (because implicit theories of intelligence suggest that conceptions of intelligence vary between and within cultures);
- *it is not necessarily true* that IQ scores are stable, although not perfectly so, over much of a person's life (because there is evidence that suggests intelligence does or can change substantially);
- it is true that properly administered IQ tests are not demonstrably biased against social, economic, ethnic or racial groups (mainly due to the conclusion drawn by the APA Task Force);
- it is true that cognitive ability is substantially heritable, apparently no less than 40 per cent and no more than 80 per cent:

Minor premises

- and if it is also true that one population group identified by their ethnicity had an average IQ score lower than another population group identified by their ethnicity;

Conclusion

- therefore, it can't be necessarily true (due to faults with four of the major premises) that the population group who had the lower IQ score must be less intelligent than the population group who had the higher IQ score.

Which argument would you support?

In fact Mei also suggests that within genetic research, most of the genes that influence appearance are not known. However, biologists have used the similarities between our common proteins to map human populations. Proteins are essential to the structure and function of all living cells and viruses, and play structural and mechanical roles in our genetic makeup. When scientists do this mapping, they get a different genetic picture of the world to socially defined race. For example, when geneticists have mapped the human population in terms of our blood types (remember, there are A, B, AB and O blood types), they find that the English, Spaniards, Eskimos and Norwegians cluster together; the Australians, Aborigines and Sicilians cluster together; the Icelanders and Japanese cluster together; and the Swedes and the Ethiopians cluster together.

In all, these considerations suggest that the validity of the arguments that Herrnstein and Murray develop from intelligence having some genetic heritability, and from race differences in IQ scores, is seriously questionable.

Gould's analysis, in which we are asked to consider the strength of Herrnstein and Murray's premises, begins to undermine some of their arguments. Although none of the assumptions are entirely wrong, there clearly exists debate around four or five of them. This suggests that the premises on which Herrnstein and Murray base their arguments and recommendations are less secure than originally presented.

If you want to see the two arguments presented in the final form, go to Stop and think: The arguments of Herrnstein and Murray and Gould. (It will help you to read Chapter 26, Academic Argument and Thinking, which can be found online.)

Statistical and evidence-based problems in *The Bell Curve* arguments

Leon J. Kamin (a Professor of Psychology at Northeastern University in the United States) questions some of the statistical thinking and research evidence used by Herrnstein and Murray (Kamin, 1995).

You may remember this statement from your first statistics classes in psychology: 'Correlation does not mean causation'. It is important to remember, when reporting any sort of correlation, not to infer immediately that one variable *causes* another. Therefore, if we found a relationship between optimism and depression, it would usually be the case that we would not infer causation. Often you will hear it is likely that the two variables influence each other (you can read more on this in Chapter 26). It is this criterion that Kamin applies to much of the evidence used by Herrnstein and Murray. Kamin suggests that Herrnstein and Murray, in a lot of their work, ignore this principle in interpreting correlations.

He also suggests that, in Herrnstein and Murray's pursuit of determining what factors may cause differences in intelligence and what factors are caused by differences in intelligence, they begin to blur the fact that they are just using correlational data. They end up ignoring the 'correlation, not causation' rule. Kamin uses as an example Herrnstein and Murray's analysis of the relationship between socioeconomic status and intelligence, which is central to many of their arguments. In exploring this relationship, Herrnstein and Murray use data from the National Longitudinal Survey of Labor Market Experience of Youth, in which over 12,000 children provided data on a number of variables, including their socioeconomic status and their intelligence. As part of their analysis, Herrnstein and Murray conclude that the intelligence of a person is more important than their socioeconomic status in predicting their eventual economic and social welfare. However, as we know from discussions here and previously (Chapter 13), socioeconomic status is bound up in a number of factors – including nutrition, educational success and poverty – that are related to intelligence. Kamin's problem with Herrnstein and Murray's analysis is that they force causal relationships on the variables when this approach is not appropriate. They do so by treating both IQ test scores and socioeconomic status as causal variables of eventual economic and social welfare. They then remove socioeconomic status as a factor, as it is not as powerful as intelligence in predicting eventual economic and social welfare. This hides the fact that intelligence and socioeconomic status are intrinsically linked not only with each other, but with economic and social welfare success. Kamin argues that this type of analysis is not valid.

Kamin also raises some questions regarding the research basis of Herrnstein and Murray's arguments. His first concern is with the validity of some of the measures used by Herrnstein and Murray to assess key variables. One of these is the variable mentioned earlier – socioeconomic status data from the National Longitudinal Survey of Labor Market Experience of Youth. The measurement of socioeconomic status was achieved by getting students' self-report of their socioeconomic status. No check was made in this study on whether students were accurate in their reporting of socioeconomic status (for example, by asking their parents). Kamin suggests that, while such reports are not completely unreliable, they do cast doubts on the reliability of Herrnstein and Murray's building of arguments and analyses based on this data.

Kamin also suggests that there are problems with some of the research studies used to support some of Herrnstein and Murray's arguments. Kamin suggests that Herrnstein and Murray rely too heavily on the work of certain academics in the world of intelligence, particularly that of Arthur Jensen and Richard Lynn. Kamin argues that there are problems with Jensen's and Lynn's work. One such piece of work is Herrnstein and Murray's reliance on a review paper by Lynn in which he examines the evidence for the evolution of race differences in intelligence and discusses the genetic components of intelligence as explaining differences between ethnic groups (Lynn, 1991). In his review paper, Lynn describes a publication by Ken Owen (who is with the Human Sciences Research Council, Pretoria, in South Africa) as the best single study of racial differences in intelligence (Owen, 1989). The study compared white, Indian and black pupils (including pupils from a Zulu tribe) on an intelligence measure called the Junior Aptitude Tests. In this study Owen did not assign IQ scores to any of the groups he tested; he merely reported test-score differences between groups. Owen also noted that the lower scores of black children (which there were) would be caused by the poor knowledge of English among the black participants. Also, Owen reported that the tests used figures of items such as electrical appliances and microscopes, which were unknown to Zulus. However, Kamin notes that, despite these reservations by Owen about his data, Lynn constructed IQ scores from the data and based many of his conclusions in this review on apparent differences between white, Indian and black children in the study.

Kamin points to other questions that surround Lynn's (1991) review paper and are then reported by Herrnstein and Murray. Lynn also refers to a finding by A. L. Pons, who tested 1,011 Zambian copper miners on the Raven's Matrices (Pons, 1974). Pons presented his data orally at the 1974 26th Congress of the South African Psychological Association. However, later, D. H. Crawford-Nutt reported this finding alongside some other data, when reporting on test and item bias in the use of the Junior Aptitude Test as a suitable measure of IQ among white, Indian and black pupils (Crawford-Nutt, 1976). Pons had found that the copper miners performed poorly on the Raven's Matrices, and Lynn used this finding in his review paper to support racial differences in intelligence. Yet, Kamin points out that in his paper, Crawford-Nutt also presented data among 228 black high school students in Soweto, South Africa, who had scored slightly higher on the Raven's Matrices when compared to the norms for the test for white students of the same age in the country. Yet, Lynn ignores this finding in his review paper.

Kamin also points to problems owing to Herrnstein and Murray's citing some of Jensen's work (Jensen, 1993b) regarding race differences in reaction time (an indicator of IQ). In this work, Jensen had tested black and white reaction responses to stimuli. As you may remember, there are different ways of measuring reaction time. Simply, reaction time measures how quickly a participant responds to any particular stimulus. However, Jensen had also developed a measure of 'choice reaction time', a more complex task, which required participants to react to various stimuli presented in a random order. Jensen found that black participants did better than white participants (suggesting they have higher intelligence), but the result was reported as an inconsistency.

For Kamin, the fact that Herrnstein and Murray have used problematic research evidence, as well as faulty statistical thinking, to build their arguments, casts doubts on the validity of their final arguments.

A darker side of psychology related to Herrnstein and Murray's analysis

Gould referred to the 'ghosts' of *The Bell Curve*. We noted at the beginning of this discussion that Jensen referred to a number of comments about Herrnstein and Murray's book, including it being described as 'neo-Nazi'. What are these authors referring to? Why did *The Bell Curve* book attract such comments? The answer is that many thought *The Bell Curve* was raising issues regarding eugenics.

Eugenics

To say that the role of eugenics in psychology is a controversial one is an understatement. It is something that is rarely talked about in psychology undergraduate classes, but psychology has a dark history.

Eugenics refers to a selection process within human reproduction with the intent to create children with desirable traits. Generally, eugenics policies are divided into two aspects: positive and negative eugenics. *Positive eugenics* refers to the practice of encouraging increased reproduction in those who are seen as having superior traits (for example, higher intelligence). *Negative eugenics* refers to the practice of discouraging or eliminating reproduction in those perceived to have poor hereditary traits (for example, lower intelligence).

To look at one of the first developments of eugenics, we must go back to where we first began in this discussion – Francis Galton. Galton, you will remember, became interested in studying the variations in intelligence after reading Charles Darwin's *The Origin of Species*, which described how all species evolve through a process of natural selection and survival of the fittest. In 1865, Galton outlined eugenics principles (Galton, 1865). He felt that human society sought to protect the weak, and that these principles were at odds with the process of natural selection that suggested the survival of the fittest.

As Galton felt that intelligence was something that was inherited through the genes, he argued that one could use artificial selection to increase intelligence among humans. He argued that such selection was needed as the less intelligent people were reproducing more than the intelligent people, and this was causing the human race to become weaker.

Galton's theories were adopted by other psychologists. One notable supporter was Lewis Terman (whom we mention in Chapter 12), at one time a president of the American Psychological Association, who had used the Binet–Simon test among California schoolchildren and later adapted it into the Stanford–Binet test. However, Terman continued Galton's ideas. In *Genetic Studies of Genius* (Terman, 1925; Terman and Oden, 1947; 1959), he argued that low intelligence was often found in Spanish–Indian, African–American and Mexican families, and that such low intelligence was inherited. He argued that such groups should be segregated into special classes and could only ever be trained to be efficient workers. He also expressed concerns that these families seemed to breed more than white Americans did and, from a eugenics point of view (the selection of certain traits), this presented a problem as it was necessary to protect the United States from low intelligence.

By then, eugenics views had made their way into social policy, politics and the law. By 1922 the process by which human selection was to be initiated was being made abundantly clear: sterilisation (the act of making a person infertile, unable to reproduce). A member of the US House of Representatives Committee on Immigration and Naturalization, H. H. Laughlin, published the Model Eugenical Sterilization Law. This bill formed the basis of state sterilisation laws, and in it Laughlin listed the types of people who were to be subjected to mandatory sterilisation. He included the feeble-minded (low intelligence), the insane, the criminal, the epileptic, the blind, deformed and the dependent (e.g. orphans, homeless).

In 1927, the US Supreme Court ruled in the case of *Buck v. Bell* and supported a new legislative law in the state of Virginia. The law concerned a 17-year-old woman named Carrie Buck, who was a resident at the Virginia Colony for the Epileptic and Feebleminded – an asylum home for epileptics, the mentally retarded and the severely disabled. Carrie had the IQ score of a 9-year-old, and her mother, who also resided at the colony, had a mental age of less than 8. Carrie Buck had given birth to a daughter who, at 1 year old, was given an infant IQ test and was found to be less than normal. In response to this, the state of Virginia wanted to have the child sterilised against her will. The US Supreme Court ruled in favour of the enforced sterilisation; in writing up the decision, Justice Oliver Wendell Holmes wrote, 'three generations of imbeciles are enough'. By that part of the twentieth century, 29 US states had laws allowing the compulsory sterilisation of individuals thought to be mentally retarded, alcoholic or 'having a criminal nature'. In 1945, information from the *Journal of the American Medical Association* suggested that over 42,000 people were sterilised in the United States between 1941 and 1943.

However, the United States was not alone. During the twentieth century, Canada, Sweden, Australia, Norway, Finland, Denmark and Switzerland all had various types of eugenics programmes. These included promoting different birth rates among populations, compulsory sterilisation, marriage restrictions, birth control and immigration control. However, it was in Germany that eugenics became a central focus, with Hitler, the Nazi Socialist Party and the Second World War.

In 1925, Adolf Hitler had published *Mein Kampf* (the book outlines Hitler's major ideas, including violent anti-Semitism), in which he identified the 'mentally unworthy' among the African race and suggested that they mustn't be allowed to perpetuate their race. In 1933, Adolf Hitler and the Nazi Socialist Party set up the sterilisation law, which was directly based on the Model Eugenical Sterilization Law introduced by H. H. Laughlin in 1922. In Germany, before the Second World War and between 1933 and 1939, over 20,000 people were sterilised for being feeble-minded. Then the Holocaust occurred. The Holocaust was the attempt to eradicate entirely particular target groups. By that time, sterilisation of target groups such as the mentally retarded had extended to the extermination of whole groups of people and races, including the Jews, the Poles, Russians, Communists, homosexuals, the mentally ill, the disabled,

Stop and think

To tell the truth, the whole truth and nothing but the truth

Consider the following story. It is part of an obituary written about Richard Herrnstein in 1994, after his death, by Charles Murray (Murray, 1994). Think about this statement with regard to reporting group differences in intelligence.

> About four years ago, shortly after Dick (Richard Herrnstein) and I had begun to collaborate on a new book about intelligence and social policy (*The Bell Curve*), we were talking over a late-evening Scotch at his home in Belmont, Mass(achusetts). We had been musing about the warning shots the prospective book had already drawn and the heavy fire that was sure to come. The conversation began to depress me, and I said, 'Why the hell are we doing this, anyway?' Dick recalled the day when, as a young man, he had been awarded tenure. It was his dream fulfilled – a place in the university he so loved, the chance to follow his research wherever it took him, economic security. For Dick, being a tenured professor at Harvard was not just the perfect job, but also the perfect way to live his life. It was too good to be true; there had to be a catch. What's my part of the bargain? he had asked himself. 'And I figured it out,' he said, looking at me with that benign, gentle half-smile of his. 'You have to tell the truth.'

(Murray, 1994, p. 22)

intelligentsia and political activists, Catholic and Protestant clergy, some Africans and common criminals. During the Second World War, Germany occupied a number of countries, including France and part of the Soviet Union. In 1939, 7 million Jews were killed in central and eastern Europe, 3 million in Poland and over 1 million in the Soviet Union.

Following the Second World War, and the experience of Nazi Germany and Hitler with his aspirations for the perfect race, eugenics fell into disrepute. The Nuremberg Trials were trials of Nazis involved in the Second World War and the Holocaust, and these trials revealed to the world the Nazis' genocidal practices. Clearly, governments couldn't condone those policies that had been advocated by Hitler, and many re-examined their eugenics-based policies. In 1948, and in response to this gross abuse, the United Nations affirmed that men and women of full age, without any limitation due to race, nationality or religion, have the right to marry and to found a family.

Eugenics and *The Bell Curve*

However, what has eugenics got to do with *The Bell Curve*? Well, critics of the book, such as Gould, felt that some of the issues raised by Herrnstein and Murray echoed eugenics thoughts and practices. Their emphasis on singling out people with low intelligence and segregating aspects of society, their emphasis on genetic influence on intelligence and their concerns about immigration brought up some issues that surround eugenics. These sorts of concerns about Herrnstein and Murray's work were not helped, as Kamin points out, by the fact that one main advocate of eugenics in modern intelligence research is an academic on whose evidence Herrnstein and Murray largely relied – Richard Lynn.

Richard Lynn, known for his work on race and a firm supporter of the genetic heritability of intelligence, wrote a book on dysgenics (the biological study of the factors producing degeneration of genes in offspring, especially of a particular race or species), which argued that eugenicists were right in their belief that modern populations have been deteriorating genetically in respect to their

intelligence (Lynn, 1996). In a second book (Lynn, 2001), he considers what measures could be taken to rectify the effects of dysgenics and argues that genetic improvement is likely to evolve when women use in vitro fertilisation (IVF; fertilisation of an egg in the laboratory) to grow a number of embryos, then have them genetically assessed before selecting those with genetically desirable qualities. However, it is important to note that Lynn does not condone Hitler's actions of genocide. Instead, he sees eugenics as purely a scientific pursuit to establish what is known about genetic inheritance and that the aims and objectives of eugenics should be open to scientific scrutiny.

It is also crucial to note that at no point do Herrnstein and Murray discuss eugenics research or policy. However, it is the discussion of a number of issues in Herrnstein and Murray's work that have been previously linked to eugenics (low intelligence, genetic inheritability of intelligence, race differences, their concerns about immigration past) that Gould is pointing to when he mentions the ghosts of *The Bell Curve*'s past.

Final comments

Phew! What a debate! That certainly may have got your blood boiling, but please remember when discussing such things in class and in essays that the arguments arising from the discussion must generally be academically based, not personally based (to read more on fallacies, go to the online chapter, Chapter 26, Academic Argument and Thinking). Notwithstanding the discussion, you should now be able to outline:

- what is meant by genetic heritability in intelligence;
- the different dimensions of genetic and environmental influences that are thought to impact on intelligence;
- the main points of Herrnstein and Murray's *Bell Curve* analysis;
- some criticisms of Herrnstein and Murray's *Bell Curve* analysis.

Summary

- Sir Francis Galton suggested that man's natural abilities are inherited under the same conditions as physical features of the animal world that had been described by Darwin. Galton suggested that intelligence is passed down to children through heredity.
- Heritability of intelligence is the estimated assessment of the extent to which intelligence is passed down from parents to children through their genes on average across the population.

- There are largely three types of study that you will regularly see in the heritability of intelligence: family studies, twin studies and adoption studies.
- Heritability estimates of intelligence vary greatly, ranging from an average of 40 per cent to an average of 80 per cent.
- There are four general issues surrounding genetic heritability estimates: conceptions of heritability and the environment, different types of genetic variance,

- the representativeness of twin and adoption studies and assortative mating.
- We identify five main areas in which to consider environmental effects on intelligence.
- The first area is biological variables (nutrition, lead and prenatal factors) and the maternal effects model.
- The second area is the consideration of family environment and shared and non-shared factors. Non-shared environments consider within-family factors and outside-family factors, including context-specific socialisation, outside-the-home socialisation, transmission of culture via group processes, group processes that widen differences between social groups and group processes that widen differences among individuals within the group.
- The third area is socioeconomic status variables that also include consideration of birth order, family size and intelligence.
- The fourth and fifth areas are education and culture, respectively, the latter comprising consideration of factors such as decontextualisation, quantification and biologisation.

- In 1994 two US authors, Richard J. Herrnstein and Charles Murray, published a book called *The Bell Curve: Intelligence and Class Structure in American Life* (Herrnstein and Murray, 1994). The term 'bell curve' refers to the distribution of a large number of IQ test results in the United States.
- Herrnstein and Murray analyse the distribution of scores, comparing the high end and low end of the distribution of IQ scores and discussing the emergence of the cognitive elite, social and economic problems and the relationship between race and IQ.
- There are huge criticisms of the arguments presented by Herrnstein and Murray. First, these criticisms centre on analysing some of the premises used in the argument, including whether: (1) there is such a thing as a general factor of intelligence; (2) all standardised tests of IQ measure intelligence accurately; (3) IQ scores match what people mean by intelligence; and (4) IQ scores are stable, although not perfectly so, over much of a person's life.
- Other criticisms of *The Bell Curve* focus on the consideration of the use of statistics and research ethics and its perceived link with eugenics ideas.

Connecting up

This chapter should be read after Chapters 12 and 13.

There are also some links to Chapter 8 (Biological Basis of Personality I: Genetic Heritability of Personality and Biological and Physiological Models of Personality), which outlines to a greater extent some of the issues surrounding heritability estimates.

Also Chapter 26, the supplementary chapter that we have provided online, may need to be read to gain better insight into some of the elements of academic argument.

Critical thinking

Discussion questions

- Discuss the relative importance of genes and the environment in determining IQ.
- Do differences in average IQ scores have any relationship to, or infer anything about, the race of an individual?
- Discuss the view that without Herrnstein and Murray's work, the public today would know a lot less about what factors influence intelligence.
- Critically examine the implications for schooling and work, assuming that intelligence consists of one general ability and is inherited.
- The second part of this discussion outlines a discussion around a book written by Herrnstein and Murray in 1994. In 2007, a researcher in intelligence found himself

at the centre of a controversy when he made comments about differences in intelligence between different parts of the world. As Hawkes (2007) notes, this controversy seems to occur once a decade. There are some online newspaper articles detailing this 2007 controversy (the web locations of these articles are given below). Read these articles. What are the main issues emerging from these articles? Why do you think this controversy keep reoccurring?

- **www.guardian.co.uk/science/2007/oct/20/genetics**
- **www.guardian.co.uk/international/story/0,,2193899,00.html**
- **http://news.bbc.co.uk/1/hi/sci/tech/7052416.stm**

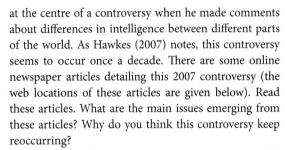

Essay questions

- Critically discuss the view that intelligence is largely genetically inherited.
- Critically assess the view that genetics is more important than the environment in determining intelligence.
- Critically discuss the view that there is a 'cognitive elite'.
- How important are socioeconomic status and variables in assessing the heritability estimates of intelligence?

- How do narrow and broad definitions of IQ heritability differ? How has our understanding of genetics informed the nature versus nurture debate on intelligence?
- To what extent do racial group differences in intelligence exist? Identify some important considerations relating to these findings.
- The main problem with Herrnstein and Murray's *Bell Curve* is that there are major flaws in the premises of the argument they present. Critically discuss.

Going further

Books

- Herrnstein, R. J. and Murray, C. (1994). *The bell curve.* New York: Free Press.
- Jacoby, R. and Glauberman, N. (eds). *The bell curve debate.* New York: Times/Random House.
- Plomin, R. (2004). *Nature and nurture: An introduction to human behavioral genetics.* London: Wadsworth.
- Plomin, R., DeFries, J. C., McClearn, G. E. and McGuffin, P. (2000). *Behavioral genetics: A primer.* London: Freeman.

Journals

- Zyphur, M. J. (2006). On the complexity of race. *American Psychologist, 61,* 179–180. In this discussion we explained that the analyses of race within mainstream psychology usually relies on simple social categories, but we also argued that there are problems with this method as it bears little resemblance to those methods used in the genetic analysis of race. If you want to read more about this issue, then a good short starting point is this article. *American Psychologist* is published by the American Psychological Association. Available online via PsycARTICLES.
- In this discussion and the last (Chapter 13), we looked at the notion of whether IQ and intelligence can change. A good article summarising the main issues is Howe, J. A. (1998). Can IQ change? *The Psychologist, 11,* 69–72. This is freely available online. You can find *The Psychologist* on the British Psychological Society Website (**www.bps.org.uk**).
- Maccoby, E. E. (2000). Parenting and its effects on children: On reading and misreading behavior genetics. *Annual Review of Psychology, 51,* 1–27. *Annual Review of Psychology* is published by Annual Reviews, Palo Alto, California. Available online via Business Source Premier.
- Deary, I. J. (2012). Intelligence. *Annual Review of Psychology, 63,* 443–48. *Annual Review of Psychology* is published by Annual Reviews, Palo Alto, California. Available online via Business Source Premier.

- Baker, L. D. and Daniels, D. (1990). Nonshared environmental influences and personality differences in adult twins. *Journal of Personality and Social Psychology, 58,* 103–110. Published by the American Psychological Association. Available online via PsycARTICLES.
- Bouchard, T. J. Jr and Loehlin, J. C. (2001). Genes, personality, and evolution. *Behavioural Genetics, 31,* 243–273. Published by Kluwer Academic Publishers. Available online via Kluwer or SwetsWise.
- Harris, J. R. (1995). Where is the child's environment? A group socialization theory of development. *Psychological Review, 102,* 458–489. Published by the American Psychological Association. Available online via PsycARTICLES.
- If you are interested in looking deeper into the genetics of brain structure and intelligence, then a possible article to read is Toga, A. W. and Thompson, P. M. (2005). Genetics of brain structure and intelligence. *Annual Review of Neuroscience, 28,* 1–23.

Articles on the intelligence issues discussed are often found in these journals:

- ***Intelligence: A Multidisciplinary Journal.*** Published by Elsevier Science. Available online via Science Direct.
- ***American Psychologist.*** This journal has a number of articles relating to the heritability of intelligence. Published by the American Psychological Association. Available online via PsycARTICLES.

Web link

- In this discussion we have covered a number of topics, including heritability of intelligence, *The Bell Curve* and birth order. Some of these topics are controversial and evoke a lot of emotions, and therefore there are a lot of websites that discuss these issues, but the evidence they use is not always appropriate. We would suggest that, when it comes to topics like these, it is best to adhere to academic books and journals. However, if you want to search the web, then the place to start is the Hot Topics section of the Human Intelligence website (**www.intelltheory.com**).

Film and literature

- *David Copperfield*, by Charles Dickens (1869) and *Under the Greenwood Tree*, by Thomas Hardy (1872). Our first discussion of intelligence was to do with Galton's view of intelligence and the reasons underlying it at the beginning of the twentieth century. Galton looked to members of the Royal Society and saw eminence as an indicator of intelligence. However, the argument of what surrounds intelligence was demonstrated in many novels of the time. The writing of Charles Dickens (for example, *David Copperfield*) and Thomas Hardy (*Under the Greenwood Tree*) used intelligence to distinguish the main characters. In both books, there is a contrast made between the small village family, whose members are intelligent in terms of the countryside around them and have inherited wisdom passed through generations of their family, and the city family, whose members are eminent, rich and own businesses but are actually portrayed as incredibly unwise compared to the village families. This treatment contrasts greatly with Galton's assumptions about the study of eminent people living in London as reflecting intelligence.

- *Gattaca* (1997, directed by Andrew Niccol). Vincent (played by Ethan Hawke) is one of the last 'natural' babies born into a sterile, genetically enhanced world, where a person's life expectancy and the likelihood of disease are ascertained at birth. Born with a heart defect and due to die at 30, Vincent has no chance of a career in a society that now discriminates against your genes, instead of your gender, race or religion. This film suggests a natural progression of eugenics, and raises some issues about what happens to those who fall foul of the perfect genetic world.

- *The Intelligent Man* (1984, Educational Resources Film). This video looks at the sometimes controversial work of Sir Cyril Burt and his work with intelligence tests and theory. The film-maker looks at the experiments and findings of the work carried out by Cyril Burt and contrasts intelligence theories. BBC Videos for Education and Training.

Explore the website accompanying this text at **www.pearsoned.co.uk/maltby** for further resources to help you with your studies. These include multiple-choice questions, essay questions, web links and ideas for advanced reading.

CHAPTER 15
Further Discussions and Debates in Intelligence:
Sex Differences in Intelligence and Emotional Intelligence

Key themes

- Sex differences in intelligence
- General intelligence
- Spatial intelligence
- Emotional intelligence

Learning outcomes

By the end of this discussion you should:

- Understand the extent of sex differences between men and women on general intelligence and specific aspects of intelligence
- Be able to describe possible biological and environmental variables that may explain sex differences in intelligence
- Be familiar with the major models of emotional intelligence
- Be able to provide a critical consideration of theory and research in emotional intelligence

Introduction

In June 2005, Tomás Chamorro-Premuzic and Adrian Furnham wrote an article in the British Psychological Society magazine, *The Psychologist* (Chamorro-Premuzic and Furnham, 2005). The article looked at individual differences in achievement. As part of this article, there was a 'Discuss and Debate' section in which the article asked, 'Do you think there are sex differences in intelligence?' In response to this question, Professor Richard Lynn of the University of Ulster wrote a letter to the magazine (Lynn, 2005). He argued that, although the historical view that men are on average more intelligent than women had been dismissed by many leading figures in the world of intelligence, including Terman, Spearman, Cattell and Jensen, recent evidence might suggest the historical view may have always been correct. Lynn cited his work and that of his colleague, UK psychologist Paul Irwing, which had reported on sex differences on the Raven's Progressive Matrices, and found that men scored on average 5 IQ points higher than women did (Lynn and Irwing, 2004; Irwing and Lynn, 2005).

These findings caused a huge reaction. Much of the reaction was among the UK press, including the *Observer*, *The Times*, the *Independent* and the *Guardian*, and raised early claims that women needed more 'manpower'. Quickly, experts were asked to comment on the work. Some claimed the methodology was flawed, while others accused the authors of being sexist. We would also suggest that these findings have probably already raised your interest, and you probably already have a view on the accuracy of the findings. Furthermore, we would guess that, depending on whether you are a man or a woman, your view on the accuracy of the findings might differ. We will return to discuss the importance of this research later.

In this discussion we are going to examine some further debates in intelligence. The first debate is in sex differences in intelligence. Much of this evidence draws from themes discussed previously, including genetic and environmental effects on intelligence. However, we are not going to seek to go over old material; rather, we are going to introduce you to new ideas in the intelligence literature, and in particular demonstrate the use of a technique called meta-analysis, and the importance of spatial intelligence, in this consideration. We are then going to introduce the concept of emotional intelligence, outlining the different models of emotional intelligence and the subsequent arguments and research that examine whether it is a useful concept to psychologists.

Source: Getty Images/Erik Dreyer

Sex differences in intelligence

Within this section we are going to look at sex differences in intelligence. We will consider:

- whether, and what, differences occur between the sexes on different measures of intelligence;
- biological factors that have been considered in explaining sex differences in intelligence;
- environmental factors that have been considered in explaining sex differences in intelligence.

In this section we are first going to examine whether there are sex differences for measures of:

- general intelligence;
- specific aspects of intelligence.

Sex differences on measures of general intelligence

In the first instance we are going to look at whether men and women score differently on general measures of intelligence, such as IQ scores, or on intelligence tests such as the Wechsler tests and the Raven's Progressive Matrices.

Throughout the past century, intelligence researchers concluded that there are no sex differences on measures of general intelligence. Louis Terman (1916) was the academic who decided to use the Binet–Simon test among Californian schoolchildren and, consequently, developed the Stanford–Binet test. Terman reported that when comparing nearly 1,000 4- to 16-year-olds, girls had a slightly higher score than boys did for overall IQ scores on the Stanford–Binet test. Charles Spearman (1927), the English psychologist who introduced the way of conceptualising intelligence as a single factor ('g'), argued that there were no sex differences in intelligence. Raymond B. Cattell, who theorised about the differences between fluid intelligence (primary reasoning ability, the ability to solve abstract relational problems; being free of cultural influences) and crystallised intelligence (acquired knowledge and skills, such as factual knowledge), suggested that a number of studies showed no significant differences between men and women on these two dimensions of intelligence (of all ages, including children).

A first systematic review of evidence on sex differences in intelligence was presented by J. H. Court (1983). In his writing on general intelligence ('g'), Spearman had emphasised that general intelligence was the abstract ability to see relationships between objects and events information, and to draw inferences from those relationships. The Raven's Progressive Matrices are designed to measure this type of intelligence, and this test is sometimes favoured as a good measure of general intelligence owing to its non-reliance on language. In his review, Court considered nearly 120 studies that had provided information on sex differences on the Raven's Progressive Matrices. He found that some studies suggested that women scored higher than men; in other studies, men scored higher than women; and, in the majority of studies, there was no difference. Overall, Court suggested that a review of studies suggested no difference between men and women in intelligence. Both evidence and similar sentiments were repeated by Jensen (1998) and Mackintosh (1998) in their analysis of the research literature on sex differences on the Raven's Progressive Matrices. For example, Mackintosh argued that the sex differences are generally small, amounting to no more than 1–2 IQ points in favour of males or females. More recently, Anderson (2004) reviewed the literature and concluded that, on the Wechsler intelligence tests and the Raven's Progressive Matrices, no significant differences occurred between males and females.

However, Richard Lynn and Paul Irwing, over the course of two studies (Irwing and Lynn, 2005; Lynn and Irwing, 2004), argued that there had been no actual statistical meta-analysis of sex differences in general intelligence. **Meta-analysis** is a technique that sums the size of statistical findings across a number of studies (see online Chapter 27 for more information). They pointed out that reports such as the one made by Court are known as narrative analyses. **Narrative analysis** is where the researcher weighs up the evidence presented across a number of studies; however, the sample sizes used in these studies vary, evidence can be taken from several different samples and results are analysed only in terms of whether the study does or doesn't support the main hypothesis. For example, in our case the results will show whether men, or women, or neither group, scored higher on general intelligence. Moreover, the samples used by Court, and those used to support the conclusions by Jensen and Mackintosh, were convenience samples – sizes were relatively small (i.e. much less than $n = 500$).

To remedy this situation, Lynn and Irwing set about collecting data on sex differences for scores on the Raven's Progressive Matrices. In all, Lynn and Irwing collected the data for large population samples (i.e. greater than $n = 500$) from 1939 to 2002. In all, Lynn and Irwing collected data for 57 studies from 30 countries and covering 195 samples, in total numbering more than 80,000 people. The authors found that, over the course of these two papers, among children there were no sex differences up to the age of 15. They found a slight difference among children at ages 15–19 years, with men scoring around 2 IQ points more than women. However, undergraduate student men scored on average about 3–5 IQ points more than women did; and among adults, men scored on average 5 IQ points more than women did.

However, to understand some of the implications of these findings fully, we need to provide you with some particular information. We are going to give you a statistic that is commonly reported within meta-analyses in sex differences in intelligence. This statistic is known as the effect size of the difference, commonly reported as d. What the effect size does is allow us to determine the importance of the findings (there is more information on this topic in online Chapter 27). The importance of the effect size is determined within the following criteria (Cohen, 1988):

- If $d = 0.2$, then the effect size is small, which means that the important difference is considered to be small.
- If $d = 0.5$, then the effect size is medium, which means that the important difference is considered to be medium.
- If $d = 0.8$, then the effect size is large, which means that the important difference is considered to be large.

Based on the effect size of Lynn and Irwing's findings, the effect size of the sex differences were as follows (see Table 15.1). As you can see, where there are the biggest differences between men and women on general intelligence (men scoring on average 5 IQ points more than women in adulthood), the effect size is small (near the $d = 0.2$ criteria).

We are going to comment further on Lynn and Irwing's findings later in this discussion. However, first, we need to introduce you to other research findings in the intelligence literature. These are considerations of sex differences on specific aspects of intelligence.

Table 15.1 Effect size of Lynn and Irwing's findings regarding sex differences in intelligence

General finding	Effect size (d)
There was no difference among children up to the age of 15	+0.02
There is a slight difference among children from the ages 15-19 years, with men scoring around 2 IQ points more than women	+0.16
Among undergraduate students, men scored on average about 3-5 IQ points more than women	+0.22–0.33
Among adults, men scored on average 5 IQ points more than women	+0.30

Note: *d* can be positive or negative; here, men scoring higher is represented by a positive number. If women were to score higher, then *d* would be a negative number. As you can see, the effect size of the difference between men and women in the last two categories is small.

Sex differences in specific intelligences

One common theme to comparing sex differences in intelligence is the finding that men and women score differently on specific aspects of intelligence.

In what is considered as a seminal study of the literature on sex differences, Eleanor Maccoby and C. N. Jacklin (Maccoby and Jacklin, 1974) concluded that men, on average, perform better on tests of spatial ability than women do. **Spatial ability** is the ability to visualise spatial relationships and to manipulate objects mentally. It is a mental process associated with the brain's attempts to interpret incoming information accurately. On the other hand, the researchers argued that women, on average, do better on verbal abilities, such as comprehension (the act of understanding the meaning, nature or importance of things) and language vocabulary (a knowledge of words in a particular language).

We are lucky to have a series of meta-analyses that report the effect sizes of sex differences in specific intelligences to see whether Maccoby and Jacklin's original conclusion is correct. Five main studies of meta-analyses have explored sex differences in specific aspects of intelligence, and two of these meta-analyses have been among adolescents:

- Alan Feingold at Yale University in the United States (Feingold, 1988) examined sex differences for spelling, language, verbal reasoning, abstract reasoning, numerical ability, perceptual speed, mechanical reasons and spatial relationships among five national samples of US adolescents.
- Larry Hedges and Amy Nowell at the University of Chicago (Hedges and Nowell, 1995) examined sex differences for reading comprehension (among five national samples), vocabulary (among four national samples), mathematics (among six national samples), perceptual speed (among four national samples), science (among four national samples) and spatial ability (among two national samples).

Three of these meta-analyses have been among samples of all ages:

- Marcia C. Linn at the University of California (United States) and her colleague A. C. Petersen (Linn and Petersen, 1985) examined sex differences for spatial perception (62 studies), mental rotation (29 studies) and spatial visualisation (81 studies) across all ages.
- Janet Shibley Hyde at the University of Wisconsin – Madison (United States) and Marcia Linn (Hyde and Linn, 1988) examined sex differences for vocabulary (40 studies), reading comprehension (18 studies) and speech production (12 studies) across all ages.

Stop and think

Sex differences in variability in IQ scores

Lynn and Irwing's paper also reported on variability of sex differences in IQ scores. This is an old question in the IQ literature – as old as the question 'do men and women, on average, score differently?' What this question asks is whether there is any difference in the way that men's and women's IQ scores spread out. Lynn and Irwing's paper suggest that there is – that is, men's scores are much more spread out than women's. Irwing and Lynn report that there are twice as many men with IQ scores of 125, and at scores of 155, associated with genius, there were 5.5 men for every woman. However, other commentators, such as Nicholas Mackintosh (2000), suggest evidence is varied. For example, Terman (1916) and Herrnstein and Murray (1994) found no differences in the variability of IQ scores for men and women. However, for the revised version of the Wechsler intelligence tests, men showed a 5 per cent greater variability in their scores than women did. Again, to some extent, Lynn and Irwing's findings are contrary to many, but not all, previous reports and findings.

Stop and think

What is spatial ability?

Because the term 'spatial ability' may be new to you, we present five examples of spatial intelligence here.

Spatial perception requires participants to identify the horizontal or the vertical object (usually a line) in a display while ignoring distracting information. One example of this task is Piaget's water-level task, which requires participants to draw in the water level in a picture of a tilted glass that is half filled with water (see below). The correct solution is to draw the water line parallel to the ground.

Spatial visualisation refers to analysing spatial information. Examples of tests that tap spatial visualisation are the embedded figures test (see figure below), in which a target figure is 'hidden' in the contours of a larger figure and the participant is expected to find it. Another example is a paper-folding task, in which participants have to imagine what the result is of folding a piece of paper in several ways.

Here is a simple form which we have labelled 'X':

This simple form, named 'X', is hidden within the more complex figure below:

Mental rotation involves being able to visualise objects from different angles and different positions. Examples of this sort of test include tasks where participants are presented pairs of drawings and asked whether the objects were the same, only rotated or mirror images of each other (see figure).

Test object

Spatiotemporal ability involves the participants making judgements about moving visual stimuli. Often respondents are asked to guess when certain objects will arrive at a certain point (see figure below).

Arrival point

Mechanical reasoning measures are the ability to understand basic mechanical principles of machinery, tools and motion. These tasks comprise principles that involve reasoning rather than specialised knowledge or training. The task illustrated below is an example of mechanical reasoning. Participants would be asked to indicate which direction vehicle A would go if it collided with vehicle B at point X.

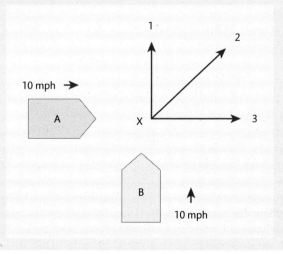

- Canadian psychologists Daniel Voyer and Susan Voyer at St Francis Xavier University and M. P. Bryden (Voyer *et al.*, 1995) at the University of Waterloo examined sex differences for spatial perception (92 studies), mental rotation (78 studies) and spatial visualisation (116 studies) across all ages.

Table 15.2 shows a summary of the findings from these five meta-analyses. Remember the criteria: $d = 0.2$ is a small effect size, $d = 0.5$ is a medium effect size and $d = 0.8$ is a large effect size.

In terms of men scoring higher on spatial abilities, we can see that across all ages, men score higher on measures of spatial perception, although it is a small to medium effect size. There is a larger effect size (medium to large) for mental rotation. Among adolescents, the greatest effect for men scoring higher than women is for mechanical reasoning (see Stop and think: What is spatial ability? if you need to be reminded of what these intelligence tasks involve).

In terms of women scoring higher than men in verbal ability, the only effect size of above 0.2 is for verbal production (i.e. 0.33). However, among adolescents, there is evidence for girls doing better than boys (effect size >0.2) on verbal abilities for spelling, language and perceptual speed. As Hyde and Linn (1988) suggest, the magnitude of the gender difference in verbal ability is so small that it can effectively be considered not to exist, particularly in adulthood. They also note that speech production does not refer to the amount of speech, but the quality of speech (before we get carried away with any stereotypes!).

Looking for explanations of sex differences in measures of intelligence

To generalise from the previous findings, research suggests that if we consider men and women on general and specific intelligences across all ages:

- there is a small effect for men over women on measures of general intelligence (IQ scores) – based on Lynn and Irwing's findings;
- there is a medium effect for men over women on measures of spatial intelligence;
- there is no evidence for a general effect of women over men for verbal intelligence abilities.

Consequently, it is of interest to consider why these two sex differences occur in general intelligence and spatial intelligence. Of course, any debate comparing two biological groups brings up the heritability of intelligence argument (the material covered in the first section of the previous discussion [Chapter 14], looking at the genetic and environmental influences on intelligence, is relevant here). However, it would be silly to retread arguments in this area,

Table 15.2 Summary of the findings from five meta-analyses examining sex differences on specific intelligences

Type of intelligence	d
Adolescents	
Feingold (1988)	
Mechanical reasoning	+0.76
Spelling	−0.45
Language	−0.40
Perceptual speed	−0.34
Spatial relationships	+0.15
Numerical ability	−0.10
Abstract reasoning	−0.04
Verbal reasoning	−0.02
Hedges and Nowell (1995)	
Science	+0.32
Perceptual speed	−0.28
Spatial ability	+0.19
Mathematics	+0.16
Reading comprehension	−0.09
Vocabulary	+0.06
All ages (children and adults)	
Linn and Petersen (1985)	
Mental rotation	+0.73
Spatial perception	+0.44
Spatial visualisation	+0.15
Hyde and Linn (1988)	
Speech production (quality of speech)	−0.33
Reading comprehension	−0.03
Vocabulary	−0.02
Voyer, Voyer and Bryden (1995)	
Mental rotation	+0.56
Spatial perception	+0.44
Spatial visualisation	+0.19

Note: *d* can be positive or negative. Here, men scoring higher is represented by a positive number; where women score higher, it would be a negative number.

particularly as we now know that there is an intrinsic link between biological and environmental factors on intelligence. Instead, we are going to outline theory and research that has explicitly examined sex differences in intelligence. We are going to break down this outline into two parts:

- biological explanations for sex differences in measures of intelligence (IQ scores);
- environmental explanations for sex differences in measures of intelligence.

Biological explanations for sex differences in intelligence

In this section we are going to outline a number of biological explanations for sex differences in intelligence. We are going to divide this discussion into two main considerations:

- biological reasons for sex differences on measures of *general* intelligence;
- biological reasons for sex differences on measures of *spatial* intelligence.

Biological variables for sex differences in measures of general intelligence

What is important to note about considering biological variables for sex differences in measures of *general* intelligence is that theory and explanation are limited. This is because, for a long time, it was generally considered that there were no sex differences in intelligence – until Lynn and Irwing's recent findings. However, Lynn has provided an explanation as to why there are sex differences in general intelligence that are worth considering. This explanation focuses on brain size and maturity rates.

The effect of brain size and maturity rates on general intelligence

Lynn's theory of the effects of brain size and maturity rates on general intelligence seeks to explain why there are differences in measures of general intelligence (IQ scores) between men and women in adulthood, but not in adolescence.

You may remember that earlier (Chapter 13) we discussed the relationship between brain size and intelligence. To summarise that discussion, studies have shown that there is a relationship between brain size and intelligence; Willerman *et al.* (1991) examined brain size and IQ scores among 40 US university students and reported a correlation of $r = 0.35$.

Raz *et al.* (1993) reported a correlation of $r = 0.43$ between brain size and IQ scores among 29 adults aged between 18 and 78 years of age. In a meta-analysis of 37 samples across 1,530 people (McDaniel, 2005), US psychologist Michael McDaniel estimated that the correlation between brain size and IQ was 0.33. The correlation was higher for females than males and higher for adults than children. However, across both sexes and all ages, it was clear that brain volume is positively correlated with intelligence.

Lynn (1994a) points out that, on average, men have 10 per cent larger brains than women do, and larger brains suggest larger brain power. This explains the difference between men and women on measures of general intelligence (IQ scores).

However, why no differences among adolescents? Well, Lynn (1994a) has proposed a developmental theory of sex differences in intelligence. He suggests that, as boys and girls mature physically and mentally at different rates, these events impact on general intelligence scores. Lynn suggests that boys and girls mature at the same rate up to the age of 7 years. However, at crucial times during development, girls mature faster than boys. This growth spurt starts at 8 years and slows down at 14 and 15 years; therefore, girls' brain size may be similar to that for boys around the start of adolescence (12–13 years). This leads to girls evening up with boys in intelligence scores for adolescents. Then, at the age of 16 onwards into adulthood, while growth rates continue, boys start to develop larger average brain sizes. These differences in general intelligence, which last into adulthood, start to develop.

Lynn formulated this hypothesis as early as 1994. In their 2004 paper (Lynn and Irwing, 2004), he and

---

Stop and think

It is not only about means!

Researchers into sex differences in intelligence have not only looked at mean differences in intelligence, but also at how males and females vary in their scores on IQ tests. Generally, analysis of large samples suggests that males vary in their scores more than females (e.g. Feingold, 1992; Hedges and Nowell, 1995), although this is not always the case (Irwing and Lynn, 2005) and not across all cultures (Feingold, 1994). In 2003, Deary *et al.* published data from the Scottish Mental Survey 1932 that contains data for a general population sample at the age of 11. Deary *et al.* found that, although there was no sex difference in the mean IQ, there was a larger standard deviation (an indicator of variability) among males and an excess of males at both the low (50 to

less than 60 IQ points) and high (130 to 140 IQ points) extremes, with a ratio of 1.4 boys to every 1 girl. Arden and Plomin (2006) examined sex differences in general IQ scores from several tests of verbal and non-verbal ability for a large sample of UK schoolchildren at ages 2, 3, 4, 7, 9 and 10 years. These authors found a greater variability among boys at every age except 2 despite the girls having a higher mean. They also found that girls were over-represented at the high end of IQ scores at ages 2, 3 and 4, while boys were over-represented at the low end of IQ scores at these ages. However, by the age of 10, boys were found to have a higher mean, greater variability and were over-represented at the high end of IQ scores.

Irwing tested this theory by looking at the effect sizes of differences between men and women at different ages (see Table 15.3). They suggest that they found a trend of IQ scores that supports this finding, but reported no significant differences between boys and girls in IQ scores at particular ages to support this hypothesis. Remember, a small effect size is 0.2, and these are very close to 0. As you can see from Table 15.3, although the hypothesis is interesting – and there may seem to be a trend – the effect sizes are very small to non-existent, suggesting little support for Lynn's hypothesis.

Lynn and Irwing's findings are relatively new, and consequently theorising is limited. However, it is important to remember that their general findings of sex differences in general intelligence can, at best, be considered as representing a small effect size in adulthood. Thus it may be better to turn to a theory that discusses findings with a medium effect size – biological explanations for sex differences in spatial intelligence.

Table 15.3 Summary of effect sizes of sex differences on intelligence from Lynn and Irwing across the age range

Age (years)	d
6	0.10
7	0.03
8	0.01
9	0.01
10	−0.03
11	0.05
12	−0.06
13	−0.02
14	0.07
15	0.10
16	0.21
17	0.15
18	0.16
19	0.16
20–29	0.30

Note: Boys scoring higher are represented by a positive number; girls scoring higher are represented by a negative number. Remember that an effect size of 0.2 is small.

Source: Based on Lynn and Irwing (2004).

Biological variables for sex differences in spatial intelligence

So, what biologically based explanations exist for men scoring higher on spatial intelligence measures than women do? We are going to outline three main explanations:

- evolutionary perspectives;
- brain functioning;
- testosterone.

Evolutionary perspectives and sex differences in spatial ability

University of Edinburgh evolutionary psychologists Catherine Jones, Victoria Braithwaite and Susan Healy summarised three evolutionary hypotheses that might explain why men might be better at spatial abilities: foraging, range size and warfare (Jones *et al.*, 2003).

- **Foraging** (see also Silverman and Eals, 1992). Foraging is the act of looking or searching for food or provisions. The male foraging hypothesis for sex differences in spatial ability is based on the premise that among humans men took the lead in foraging and had to develop particular spatial skills. For example, man needed spatial abilities in skills such as finding their way around the countryside, demonstrating awareness of the physical environment to be able to hunt and intercept animals and throwing weapons to kill animals.
- **Range** (see also Gaulin, 1995; Gray and Buffery, 1971). The range hypothesis focuses on the view of mating roles in evolutionary theory, and the theory that, while females seek out single relationships (monogamous), males seek

out multiple relationships (polygamous). To pursue and maintain multiple relationships, polygamous males need to cover a larger area of land to father offspring with several females and maximise their reproductive success. An area that an individual covers is known as **range size**. It is the development and experience of a larger range size and the experiences in a number of different environments that may explain why men develop better spatial abilities than women.

- **Warfare** (see also Geary, 1995; Sherry and Hampson, 1997). To some extent this theory is a combination of the first two points. Sex differences in human spatial ability are as a result of direct male-to-male, small-scale warfare. Within this hypothesis it is argued that men travel long distances to ambush other men, compete for resources and also compete for females. In fighting other men, men will have had to develop their spatial abilities so that they can effectively challenge and fight in new environments and changing environments.

As Jones *et al.* (2003) conclude, from an evolutionary perspective, those males with good spatial abilities would be able to forage effectively, develop a number of relationships over a long range and win in warfare. Consequently, they would be the individuals who would be more attractive to females. It is these male individuals who would be more likely to reproduce and their genes, including those leading to good spatial abilities, would be carried forward in the surviving population.

Brain functioning and sex differences in spatial intelligence

Some studies suggest that men and women differ in scores on spatial intelligence because of the way the brain is organised and functions.

US cognitive psychologists Stacy L. Rilea, Beverly Roskos-Ewoldsen and David Boles looked at the lateralisation of the brain (Rilea *et al.*, 2004). The popular notion that there is a left and right division of the brain, dealing with separate functions such as artistic tendencies or intuition, is thought these days to be oversimplified. However, there is evidence that some basic language processes are predominantly controlled by the left hemisphere and that mental rotation and spatial perception are coordinated by the right hemisphere. Both hemispheres of the brain are thought to work together on tasks, but tasks are thought to be solved more efficiently by the brain when they are carried out in one aspect of the brain (i.e. left *or* right) rather than across both sides of the brain (i.e. left *and* right).

Rilea *et al.* (2004) found that there was a sex difference between men and women in terms of solving a mental

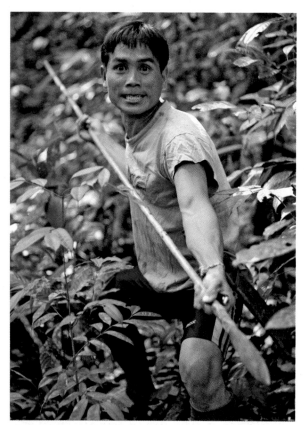

Evolutionary theory suggests that men have developed better spatial ability owing to being involved in hunting. However, men may have ended up in the hunter role because they naturally had better spatial ability and therefore were better at hunting.
Source: Alamy Images/Mark Eveleigh

rotation task. This difference wasn't in terms of successfully solving the task. Rather, the researchers found that, while women use both sides of the brain to solve the task, men use only the right-hand side of their brain. The authors concluded that men process this type of spatial information more efficiently in the right hemisphere. They concluded that the extent to which there is a male advantage in spatial abilities is determined by the extent to which the task is right-hemisphere-dependent. This finding suggests that sex differences in spatial intelligence are due to which portions and combinations of the brain each sex uses when engaged in spatial tasks.

A study in 2005 threw up another interesting finding regarding sex differences in spatial intelligence. Richard J. Haier, Professor of Psychology in the Department of Pediatrics at the University of California, presented findings suggesting that men and women achieve intelligence through different areas of the brain (Haier *et al.*, 2005). The researchers used magnetic resonance imaging (MRI) to find out where intelligence was in the brain. MRI is a fairly new technique that has been used since the beginning of the 1980s. An MRI scan is able to provide clear pictures of parts of the body that are surrounded by bone tissue, so the technique is useful when examining the brain and spinal cord. Haier *et al.* used a particular technique called **voxel-based morphometry** (VBM) that looks for grey and white matter around the brain. **Grey matter** can be understood as the parts of the brain responsible for information processing, whereas **white matter** is responsible for information transmission. Haier and his colleagues examined two samples of volunteers: 14 women and 9 men (with a mean age of 27) and 13 men and 12 women (with a mean age of 59). Participants were given the Wechsler Adult Intelligence Scale battery and underwent an MRI scan. The analysis (VBM) was used to examine whether IQ scores were related to brain areas where grey matter and white matter occurred. Haier *et al.* reported two interesting findings.

The first finding (illustrated in Figure 15.1) summarised which areas of the brain IQ scores are related to occurrences of grey matter (information processing):

- In men, grey matter volume was correlated to IQ most strongly in bilateral frontal lobes (areas 8 and 9 on the figure) and in the left parietal lobe (areas 39 and 40), also known as Wernicke's area. Wernicke's area is named after Carl Wernicke (1848–1905), a German neurologist and psychiatrist who, at the end of the nineteenth century, linked this part of the brain to language comprehension and speech that has a natural-sounding rhythm.

- In women, grey matter volume was correlated to the right frontal lobe (area 10), and the largest cluster was in Broca's area of the brain (areas 44 and 45). Broca's areas of

- Yellow – frontal lobe: thinking, planning and central executive function; motor execution
- Green – parietal lobe: somatosensory (relating sensory stimuli from the skin and internal organs) perception, integration of visual and somatospatial information
- Brown – temporal lobe: language function and auditory perception involved in long-term memory and emotion
- Blue – occipital lobe: visual perception and processing

Figure 15.1 Summary of the Haier *et al*. (2005) finding using Brodmann's definitions of areas of the brain.
Source: Haier *et al*. (2005).

the brain are named after the French physician, anatomist and anthropologist Paul Pierre Broca (1824–1880). These parts of the brain are thought to support the interpretation of stimuli, verbal processes and the coordination of the speech organs for the actual production of language that enable individuals to understand or create grammatically complex sentences.

The second finding was that women have more white matter and fewer grey matter areas related to IQ scores as compared to men. This finding suggests that intelligence is related to white matter in women and to grey matter in men. Haier *et al*.'s findings suggest that, among men, IQ score is related to those areas of the brain responsible for information processing (grey matter), whereas, for women, intelligence is generally related to those areas responsible for information transmission (white matter). This finding suggests that intelligence in men is related to information processing. Consequently, this might explain men's superior abilities in spatial intelligence.

Clearly, the links found in this study (between sex, IQ scores and parts of the brain) are reported for two small samples. To try to translate the findings to sex differences in intelligence outside the brain in the general population would be speculative. This study provides no direct evidence to support these links (for example, sex differences

in IQ scores were not found in the Haier *et al*. study). None the less, Haier's MRI analysis reveals that male and female brains may be anatomically different with respect to intelligence, and the findings suggest that different brain structures and processes in men and women might explain sex differences in intelligence.

Testosterone and sex differences in spatial intelligence

There is evidence that the male hormone testosterone is related to spatial intelligence, and this may explain the sex differences in spatial intelligence.

Hormones are the substances that travel around the human body to effect physiological activity, such as growth or metabolism. **Gonadal hormones** are those substances that create physiological growth in the organs of animals that produce sex cells; for example, ovaries in females (part of the female reproductive system) and testes in males (part of the male reproductive system). **Testosterone** (a gonadal hormone) is the male sex hormone that is necessary in the fetus for the development of male genitalia. Additionally, increased levels of testosterone at puberty are responsible for the further growth of male genitalia and for the development and maintenance of what are known as male secondary sex characteristics, such as voice changes and facial hair. **Estradiol** (also a gonadal hormone) is the most potent naturally occurring oestrogen. Oestrogen is produced chiefly by the ovaries and is responsible for promoting oestrus and the development and maintenance of female secondary sex characteristics, such as pubic hair and breasts. Males and females have both hormones, but greater concentrates of testosterone are found in men and greater concentrates of estradiol are found in women.

Canadian neuroscientists Jean Choi and Irwin Silverman have carried out a study of gonadal hormones (testosterone and estradiol) and spatial ability (Choi and Silverman, 2002). Choi and Silverman's work starts from a general finding in the literature that male and female humans and non-humans use different strategies to learn routes. Routes through the environment require individuals to use spatial ability. However, there is a sex difference in the way that men and women use routes (Choi and Silverman, 1996). Women tend to use relative directions (left, right, front and back) and landmarks (buildings, bridges, traffic lights, etc.) to learn routes (for example, 'you turn left at the bridge and then right at the next traffic light'). Men use distance (mileage, metres) and cardinal (the four principal compass points – north, south, east and west) directions (for example, 'you head down there for about 100 metres and then head west until you get to the next turning 50 metres down that road, and then head north'). C. L. Williams and W. H. Meck (Williams and Meck, 1991) found that, among rats, differing concentrations of testosterone and estradiol have different effects on the male and female organisation of the brain, particularly in their perception of the environmental cues that can be used to solve spatial problems. Choi and Silverman (1996) then examined this idea among humans.

The authors gave 46 male and 60 female undergraduate students a route-learning task, which comprised a map depicting a fictional town, with various landmarks and streets, and a compass indicator and distance scale. Participants were asked to learn the shortest route from one point to another on the map in 2 minutes, and then they were asked to recall the route back to the experimenter. The experimenter then coded the number of times that participants made a reference in their route to landmarks, relative direction, cardinal directions and distance. Respondents' testosterone and estradiol levels were measured by taking some of their saliva.

Choi and Silverman found that estradiol is not related to strategies for route learning. However, they found among men – but not among women – that the testosterone level is positively related to the use of male-biased route-learning strategies (the use of distance and cardinal rules).

Later, US Harvard University anthropologist Carole Hooven and her psychology colleagues Christopher Chabris, Peter Ellison and Stephen Kosslyn found that higher levels of testosterone in males are significantly related to faster responses and lower error rates on a mental rotation task (Hooven *et al.*, 2004).

This emphasis on testosterone being related to the use of distance and cardinal route strategies and responses to mental rotation tasks might explain, in part, why men, on average, score higher on measures of spatial intelligence than women do.

Summary of biological factors in sex differences in intelligence

Brain size, evolutionary forces, brain lateralisation, brain structure and testosterone have been used to explain sex differences in general intelligence and spatial intelligence.

Evidence for Lynn's theory of sex differences in brain size and maturity, used to explain sex differences in general intelligence across adolescence and adulthood, is not supported by his own data.

In terms of spatial ability, biologically based explanations such as evolutionary factors, brain lateralisation and structure and testosterone all provide evidence as to why men might score higher on measures of spatial ability.

However, let us move to the next stage of discussion. Having established some biological explanations for sex differences in intelligence, we are now going to concentrate on environmental influences on intelligence.

Stop and think

Women and white matter

Haier *et al.* (2005) found that, among women, IQ scores are related to those parts of the brain thought to support the interpretation of stimuli, verbal processes and the coordination of the speech organs for the actual production of language. Women were also found to have significantly more white matter than men. White matter is responsible for information transmission. Although meta-analysis of studies suggests that women and men do not differ greatly on verbal abilities, does the finding by these researchers provide evidence for the original speculations that women are more verbally intelligent than men?

Environmental explanations for sex differences in intelligence

In this section we are going to concentrate on theory and research that has identified how environmental influences on intelligence impact differently on men and women. A core central theme throughout this section is the role of stereotypes around intelligence and how they might be related to sex differences in intelligence.

In a review of sex differences in intelligence, Diane Halpern and Mary LaMay (Halpern and LaMay, 2000) suggest that the central variable in environmental influence on intelligence is the role of gender stereotypes. A stereotype stems from the use of schemas. **Schemas** are the mental pictures or general understandings of social occurrences. For example, we all develop schemas for:

- **People** – for example, the way people look; why people look and dress the way they do for certain occasions.
- **Roles** – for example, the roles we have in society, such as the way parents and children are expected to act and the way a student should generally act as opposed to a lecturer.
- **Events** – for example, what we expect to happen in certain situations. We develop schemas of how we act at social occasions (such as being out with friends) and at formal occasions (such as job interviews).

From the uses of schemas, stereotypes are thought to develop in the minds of individuals. Over time, stereotypes grow and operate in the minds of individuals to help them make sense of the social world. When we use stereotypes, we apply them to all sorts of people, roles and events; thus we come to expect certain things to happen within certain situations (for example, you would expect job interviewers to ask you questions about your qualifications, not tell you about their personal lives). Stereotypes operate quite automatically and unconsciously, and to a large extent quite harmlessly, as we use them to make sense of everyday situations in the world.

We find that the relationship occurs between stereotypes and intelligence in a number of situations, including preschool, school and everyday understanding of intelligence. Many of these influences may cover all aspects of intelligence; however, we will highlight particular influences on spatial ability because this is where much of the evidence suggests the largest sex difference occurs – and where, as a consequence, much of the theory and research is concentrated. We are going to consider these three areas in this section (see Figure 15.2):

- the influence of stereotypes on sex differences in intelligence outside of education;
- the influence of stereotypes on sex differences in intelligence within education;
- the interactions between technology and socioeconomic status and their influence on intelligence in the classroom.

Stereotypes and sex differences in intelligence outside of education

One area of the research that shows stereotypes are related to intelligence is in children's toy choice. US developmental psychologist Susan Levine and colleagues (Levine *et al.*, 2005) suggest that, although not a lot is known about what type of toys can be used to increase spatial skills, playing with building blocks, puzzles and video games is related to spatial skills, and boys spend more time with these toys than girls do (see also Dorval and Pepin, 1986; Subrahmanyam and Greenfield, 1994). Evidence among infants suggests there are differences in the toy choices of boys and girls that may affect their intelligence, particularly spatial intelligence. UK psychologist Anne Campbell and her colleagues (Campbell *et al.*, 2000) found that sex differences in preferences for toys started to appear as young as 9 months. Girls were found to want to play with dolls, while boys preferred trucks. Campbell

Figure 15.2 An illustration of the three aspects to consider when considering environmental influences on sex differences in (spatial) intelligence.

et al. (2000) suggest that there is already a potential among boys for preferring movement at that age. Research among monkeys supports this finding. US psychologists Gerianne Alexander and UK psychologist Melissa Hines found that monkeys showed sex differences in toy preferences that are similar to those for human children (Alexander and Hines, 2002). Young male monkeys preferred balls and cars, while female monkeys preferred dolls and a pot. Alexander and Hines conclude that these findings can be interpreted within an evolutionary framework (we discussed this approach earlier); they suggest a male preference for toys that involve the use of spatial abilities.

The role of stereotypes can also be assessed by observing the extent to which children refuse to play with certain toys. For example, Canadian developmental psychologists Eileen Wood, Serge Desmarais and Sara Gugula (Wood *et al.*, 2002) found that, although girls are as happy with action figures, chemistry sets and video games as they are with playing with cuddly toys, boys are quicker to reject a toy they consider to be a 'girl's toy'. This finding suggests that sex stereotypes quickly occur in childhood, whether they arise from the influence of parents or other children. Overall, there is evidence that girls tend to play with toys such as dolls and household objects that may encourage verbal and social skills while boys play with video games, building blocks, cars and other toys that encourage spatial visualisation (see, for example, Servin *et al.*, 1999).

Furthermore, you may remember our earlier evolutionary accounts of sex differences in spatial abilities being due to men spending more time in the environment hunting and gathering, thereby getting used to movement and being aware of their environment. However, US sociologist Doris Entwisle and her colleagues provided a more simplistic explanation (Entwisle *et al.*, 1994). They found

that boys are given more freedom to explore the neighbourhood around their home, and this observation is correlated with the male–female discrepancy in spatial ability. This suggests that we may not need to use an evolutionary explanation to explain sex differences in spatial ability, but a more modern-day explanation that boys rather than girls spend more time outside exploring new environments.

Finally, parents have stereotypical views about their own intelligence, and this might influence stereotypes of their sons and daughters about their own abilities. UK psychologist Adrian Furnham has carried out a series of studies looking at estimates by parents of their own, and their children's, intelligence. Men seem to see their own general intelligence as higher than that of women, though men feel that their strengths are in logical and spatial ability and women see their strengths in language and personal intelligences (Furnham, 2001; Furnham and Bunclark, 2006; Furnham and Petrides, 2004). If parents have these views about their own abilities, then they may have expectations about where the strengths of their own children's specific intelligences lie. Furthermore, if sons want to be like their fathers, and daughters like their mothers, they may seek to develop certain specific intelligence abilities to be more like their same-sex parents. These expectations or aspirations within the family regarding specific intelligences may lead to children developing particular beliefs about their strengths and weaknesses in their own specific intelligence abilities.

Stereotypes and sex differences in intelligence within education

The relationship between sex, stereotyping and intelligence continues in school. Research shows that there are two

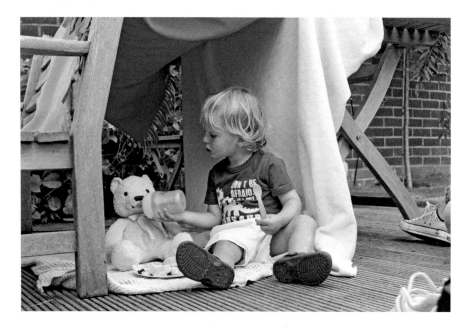

Breaking the stereotype?: little boy feeding teddy.
Source: Pearson Education Ltd. Jules Selmes

main stereotype factors that may influence intelligence at school. These are subject choice and stereotype interactions within the classroom.

Subject choice

Halpern and LaMay (2000) suggest that, while men and women nowadays reach similar levels of intelligence and achievement at school, their choice of subjects at school tends to follow a pattern based on their sex. At school, there is a large distinction in sex choices in science subjects (and to some extent aspects of mathematics that involve spatial reasoning). This can comprise positive subject choice, as in selecting particular subjects, or negative subject choice, as in avoiding particular subjects. The motivation around positive subject choice is outlined by Halpern and LaMay; they suggest that talented children will receive encouragement and/or rewards to develop certain talents. This will give them an incentive to develop in that area, in turn increasing their self-esteem. In the case of science subjects that involve spatial abilities (laws of movement, understanding how a formula comes together, understanding physical properties of objects and the environment), it is males, more than females, who look for mathematical or science-related experiences. Then, if they excel at these subjects, the males would receive more encouragement and rewards and may go on to study the subject more. Within this process, males are improving their spatial abilities more and more.

In a similar way, there is a negative subject choice in education. Girls may not favour mathematics and science classes, because sciences are stereotyped as masculine subjects. This rejection of science subjects leads to female students being absent from learning situations that involve the development of spatial abilities (Halpern and LaMay, 2000; Jonsson, 1999).

Interactions in the classroom

Plucker (1996) notes that one key idea on how sex differences may occur in intelligence is that **self-fulfilling prophecies** occur in the classroom. This is where positive or negative feedback influences a pupil's ideas about their own abilities and, regardless of their real potential regarding a particular ability, their ideas (not their potential) determine their attainment in that ability. So, for example, a self-fulfilling prophecy would occur when a person is told they will never do well in mathematics; they then begin to believe they are going to perform poorly in mathematics, and eventually they do perform poorly in mathematics because of this belief. This child has stereotyped him or herself because of a negative comment regarding a particular ability. There are all sorts of opportunities for stereotypes to arise that lead to self-fulfilling prophecies.

One issue is that teachers may have a role in self-fulfilling prophecies, and a single positive or negative comment (or a series of them) may spark off, or reinforce, a self-fulfilling prophecy (Plucker, 1996). Recent evidence from US psychol-

ogists Lee Jussim and Kent D. Harber (Jussim and Harber, 2005) suggests that self-fulfilling prophecies in the classroom do occur, but they tend to be small and do not develop over time. The most long-lasting self-fulfilling prophecies (positive and negative) occur among social groups that are held in low regard by other social groups. Jussim and Harber suggest that the evidence remains unclear on whether self-fulfilling prophecies affect intelligence and whether they can affect intelligence in a positive or negative way.

Some research has extended this idea of self-fulfilling prophecy to another variable that has been shown to have an effect on aspects of intelligence through the use of stereotypes. This variable is called **stereotype threat**. Stereotype threat has been used to explain why certain groups may perform poorly in test situations, particularly in tests of intelligence. Claude Steele, a social psychologist at Stanford University in the United States, coined the term 'stereotype threat' (Steele, 1997). Steele described stereotype threat as the feeling by someone that they are being viewed through a lens, or something in the air, that is looking to confirm a negative stereotype about them. When this stereotype is activated by a threat, the person worries about the threat, and this sometimes makes them do worse on whatever task they are going to complete. Steele found that this threat could have an effect on people's intelligence scores when taking a test. For example, Steele and his colleagues, Steven Spencer and Diane Quinn, examined the stereotype that women perform poorly in mathematics (Spencer et al., 1999). They carried out two studies involving a test of mathematical ability. In the first study the experimenters just gave the participants a test and compared results between men and women. However, before administering the test in the second study, the experimenters wanted to evoke the stereotype about women's mathematical ability. Participants were told that the mathematics test they were being given had shown sex differences in the past. The experimenters assumed that telling participants about the gender differences would lead them to believe that men did better than women (and participants confirmed later that this was their interpretation of the statement). The experimenters found that, in this experiment, the use of the stereotype threat led to poorer performance among women. This type of finding suggests that stereotypes about the social group you belong to (e.g. sex), and the abilities of the group as a whole, can have a real effect on your test performance when you are informed or reminded of that stereotype.

Interactions between technology and socioeconomic status and their influence on intelligence in the classroom

You may remember that (in Chapter 13) we noted Neisser (1998a) suggests that the visual and technical environment that surrounds us today (DVDs, video, the Internet and home computers) has a positive effect on intelligence. Sex differences in spatial abilities may become more apparent as teaching relies more on learning techniques that use visual and technical environments (e.g. computers and the Internet). Consquently, individuals who are strong in spatial abilities may be further advantaged by these visual and technical environments.

Canadian educational psychologists John Kirby and D. R. Boulter compared two groups of students on a new spatial ability task (Kirby and Boulter, 1999). One group was given the task via pen and paper, and the other was given the task via visual stimuli. Kirby and Boulter found that one factor in predicting success at the visual stimuli task was spatial ability before the task. Kirby and Boulter suggest that people who are weak at spatial ability before the task may be disadvantaged by the use of complex visual stimuli used as a teaching method, and this will further exacerbate their problems with spatial ability. Kirby and Boulter's findings suggest that, if females are weaker in spatial abilities, the differences between boys and girls in their spatial abilities will increase if teaching strategies rely on teaching methods that involve spatial intelligence.

However, these factors in the classroom might be further influenced by other factors outside the classroom, namely socioeconomic status. You may also remember from earlier discussions (in Chapters 13 and 14) that social class is related to intelligence. As a reminder, Richard Herrnstein and Charles Murray (Herrnstein and Murray, 1994) and J. Philippe Rushton and C. D. Ankney (Rushton and Ankney, 1996) estimate that, in Europe, North America and Japan, social class/socioeconomic status is significantly correlated with scores on standard IQ of between $r = 0.3$ and $r = 0.4$ and that there are 45 IQ points between members of the professional occupations (Class I) and those of unskilled occupations (Class V).

US psychologist Susan Levine and her colleagues at the University of Chicago found that socioeconomic variables might influence the sex differences in spatial skills in the classroom (Levine *et al.*, 2005). In a longitudinal study, children were administered two spatial tasks requiring mental transformations and a task of verbal comprehension. As with previous studies mentioned earlier, no sex difference was found between boys and girls in their verbal ability. However, on the two tasks, boys from the middle and high socioeconomic class did better than girls did on both spatial tasks, whereas boys and girls from the low socioeconomic group did not differ in their performance on the spatial task. It is important to note that the individuals from the low socioeconomic classes didn't find the test any harder. Susan Levine suggests as the main reason for this finding that children from lower socioeconomic backgrounds spend less time engaged in activities that promote spatial intelligence outside the classroom. This gives such children disadvantages in the modern-day classroom, which emphasises the use of spatial abilities. Levine suggests there are two activities that children from lower socioeconomic backgrounds spend less time doing outside the classroom that can influence spatial intelligence:

- **Using computers** – if using computers enhances spatial intelligence, then it may be that children from lower socioeconomic backgrounds spend less time with computers because they are relatively expensive and not readily available at home.
- **Being out in the neighbourhood** – you may remember the finding, mentioned earlier, that boys spend more time exploring the neighbourhood than girls do, and this activity was found to be related to better spatial ability. Levine *et al.* (2005) suggest that boys from lower socioeconomic backgrounds may spend less time out in their neighbourhood due to the perception, by themselves and parents, that there is more danger in poorer residential areas.

Levine *et al.* (2005) suggest that boys from medium and high socioeconomic backgrounds spend more time on activities that promote spatial abilities (i.e. using computers) and

Stop and think

How well do parents estimate their children's intelligence?

Findings of studies differ in regard to sex differences in parents' rating of their children's intelligence. Some studies suggest that parents give their sons higher overall intelligence estimations (Furnham, 2000; Furnham *et al.*, 2002), while Furnham and Bunclark (2006) suggest daughters are given significantly higher intelligence estimations by their parents (however, in this latter sample, Furnham and Bunclark found that women scored higher on measures of intelligence than men did). However, a crucial finding is that Furnham and Bunclark found that

the correlation between parents' estimation of their children's intelligence and their score on a measure of intelligence was $r = 0.44$. This is not a small correlation; however, as Furnham and Bunclark point out, it is around the same size relationship to when individuals have provided estimations of a stranger's intelligence ($r = 0.43$; Borkenau and Liebler, 1993). How might this finding be used to understand how self-fulfilling prophecies or stereotypes can threaten to emerge from parental expectations?

more time on exploring the environment (owing to living in less dangerous residential areas) and that these socio-economic factors are important in explaining differences in spatial ability. Although this research doesn't impact directly on sex differences on intelligence, as it is concentrated on boys, it does suggest that socioeconomic factors impact the classroom and are another further important factor to consider when looking at environmental influences on spatial intelligence.

A final consideration of sex differences in measures of intelligence

By now your mind might be spinning. Clearly, a number of biological and environmental factors (particularly stereotypes) are not only influencing sex differences in intelligence (particularly spatial intelligence) but are also interacting. As Halpern and LaMay (2000) point out, it is perhaps futile to try to separate out these biological and environmental effects. Rather, in terms of a critical consideration, Halpern and LaMay ask us to consider two main points:

- stereotype emphasis;
- placing the extent of the sex differences in intelligence within its proper context.

Stereotype emphasis

One crucial question that occurs in our consideration is, do real differences in intelligence influence the stereotypes that surround sex differences in intelligence? Or, do stereotypes influence the sex differences that are found on measures of intelligence?

A good example of an attempt to untangle this complicated relationship was provided by US psychologist Janet K. Swim. In her study, Swim (1994) assessed to what extent stereotypes reflect real sex differences across a number of characteristics, and one of these included intelligence. To do this, she looked at the size of differences between men and women for real scores on a number of variables as compared with the size of differences between sexes for stereotype ratings for each of the same variables. Swim then categorised these stereotypes as follows:

- **Over-emphasised stereotypes** (i.e. the estimated size of the sex difference for the variable was greater than the real difference between men and women on that variable) – this comparison might provide evidence that stereotypes might be overly attributed to difference between the sexes. For example, Swim found that we *over-emphasise* how aggressive men are.

- **Under-emphasised stereotypes** (i.e. the estimated size of the sex difference for the variable was smaller than the real difference between men and women on that variable) – this comparison may provide evidence that real sex differences are being under-estimated in our stereotypes. For example, Swim found we might *under-emphasise* men's helping behaviour in an emergency.
- **Accurate stereotypes** (i.e. the estimated size for the sex difference for the variable is the same as the real difference between men and women on that variable) – for example, we may be accurate in terms of viewing men as being more restless.

In terms of intelligence, Swim's study suggested that we are accurate in our perceptions of men being better in their mathematical abilities; however, subjects tended to over-estimate women's verbal abilities (a finding that is consistent with our earlier discussion regarding research suggesting that there are no sex differences in verbal abilities).

Placing the extent of sex differences in intelligence within its proper context

A second consideration is to place some of the sex differences in intelligence within a proper context. The final context to understand sex differences in intelligence is to consider how meaningful comparisons by sex are, and how they are best understood. US psychologists Janice Yoder and Arnie Kahn have suggested that there are two ways in which sex differences are treated in the literature (Yoder and Kahn, 2003). The first is an alpha bias, in which it is assumed that there are large differences; the second is beta bias, in which it is assumed there are minimal differences (also known as the gender similarity hypothesis). Although research on sex differences in intelligence does tend to speculate on reasons for differences, we must consider to what extent sex differences in intelligence are important.

Two points are important to such a consideration. First, it is important to note that, where sex differences in intelligence exist, they represent average differences between men and women as groups, not individuals. Knowing whether an individual is female or male reveals little about an individual's actual intellectual abilities. For example, we must remember that the variability between men and women for IQ scores is, at the most, 5 IQ points (Lynn and Irwing, 2004). However, there is a huge amount of variability in IQ scores within both population groups of men and women. That means that most men and women score within a full range of possible IQ scores from low (e.g. 75 IQ points) to high (e.g. 145 IQ points). Consequently, we will find that many women will score higher than many men on measures of IQ, despite the average finding across the populations. Within this context of huge variability of scores obtained by men and women on IQ tests, the

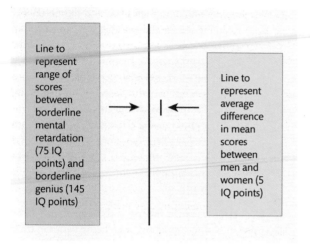

Line to represent range of scores between borderline mental retardation (75 IQ points) and borderline genius (145 IQ points)

Line to represent average difference in mean scores between men and women (5 IQ points)

Figure 15.3 Two comparison lines of difference. Comparing the range of variability in IQ scores within population groups of men and women with average difference between men and women (drawn to scale).

smaller difference of 5 IQ points seems less important. To see the extent of this comparison, look at Figure 15.3, which is drawn to scale.

Second, the effect sizes for sex differences in intelligence are relatively small when compared to other variables. When we consider all aspects of intelligence (general, verbal, non-verbal, spatial, language), many of the effect sizes range from small to non-existent for the large majority of intelligence variables. There is a small effect size of around 0.3 for general intelligence scores, and a medium to high effect size of between 0.5 and 0.7 for two aspects of spatial ability

(mental rotation and mechanical reasoning among adolescents). However, US psychologist Janet Shibley Hyde (2005) notes that when the ranges of these effect sizes for sex differences in intelligence scores are compared against the effect sizes for sex differences for other variables, their importance diminishes. In Table 15.4 we provide some effect sizes for sex differences for a number of other variables, including aggression, sexuality and personality. Again note that a + effect size means that, for example, effect sizes for physical and verbal aggression range from 0.09 to an effect size of 0.84, sexuality variables range from 0.29 to 0.81 and personality variables range from −0.01 to −0.91. Within this context, particularly in terms of some of the larger effects size (i.e. $d > 0.84$), the effect sizes reported for sex differences between men and women in intelligence seem relatively less important.

Interim summary for sex differences in intelligence

The literature on sex differences in intelligence throws up evidence of differences in general intelligence, in particular sex differences in spatial intelligence. There are also a number of biological factors (brain lateralisation, brain structure and testosterone) and environmental factors (stereotypes and their relationship to a number of factors) that are thought to influence sex differences in intelligence.

However, one aspect of this literature does not seem to be fully resolved. Despite no evidence that men and women score differently on measures of verbal intelligence, we have reviewed evidence that suggests the following:

Table 15.4 Summary of effect sizes of sex differences for a number of personality and social variables from Hyde (2005)

Trait	Effect size (d)	Study
Physical aggression	+ 0.60	Hyde, 1984; 1986
Physical aggression	+ 0.59	Knight et al. 2002
Physical aggression	+ 0.33 – + 0.84	Archer, 2004
Verbal aggression	+ 0.43	Hyde, 1984; 1986
Verbal aggression	+ 0.09 – + 0.84	Archer, 2004
Sexuality: attitudes about casual sex	+ 0.81	Oliver and Hyde, 1993
Sexuality: attitudes about extramarital sex	+ 0.29	Oliver and Hyde, 1993
Sexuality: arousal to sexual stimuli	+ 0.31	Murnen and Stockton, 1997
Neuroticism: anxiety	− 0.32	Feingold, 1994
Neuroticism: impulsiveness	− 0.01	Feingold, 1994
Extraversion: gregariousness	− 0.07	Feingold, 1994
Extraversion: assertiveness	+ 0.51	Feingold, 1994
Extraversion: activity	+ 0.08	Feingold, 1994
Openness	+ 0.19	Feingold, 1994
Agreeableness: trust	− 0.35	Feingold, 1994
Agreeableness: tender-mindedness	− 0.91	Feingold, 1994
Conscientiousness	− 0.18	Feingold, 1994

Note: Males scoring higher are represented by a positive number; females scoring higher are represented by a negative number.

Source: Based on Hyde (2005).

- Women see their strengths in language and personal intelligences.
- Girls tend to play with toys such as dolls and household objects that enhance verbal and social skills.
- Intelligence is related to white matter in women, and white matter is responsible for information transmission.

Might it be that there has been a mismatch between what traditional measures of verbal intelligence measure and where men and women's real differences lie in language and personal intelligence? It has been suggested that there is one concept that might, more accurately, reflect language and personal intelligences – that concept is emotional intelligence.

Emotional intelligence

In March 2000 Daniel Goleman published an article, 'Leadership that gets results', in the *Harvard Business Review* (a well-respected business management theory journal). When the chief executive officer (the highest-ranking officer of a company) of the leading worldwide pharmaceutical company read the article, he sent copies of it to the 400 top executives in the company. The article described the theory of emotional intelligence.

Generally, emotional intelligence is the ability to understand your own emotions and those of people around you. In this section we are going to take you through the major theories of emotional intelligence. To some extent the history and the development of theories of emotional intelligence are fragmented; none the less, the literature on emotional intelligence spans a number of perspectives, which certain authors have tried to link together. We will then go on and explore different psychological perspectives on emotional intelligence as well as some of the issues that surround the topic, particularly whether it is a useful concept for psychologists to consider. Finally, we will assess whether women are more 'emotionally intelligent' than men.

Salovey and Mayer's four-branch model of emotional intelligence

In 1990 US psychologists Peter Salovey at Yale University and John D. Mayer at the University of New Hampshire presented the first clear theory of emotional intelligence (Salovey and Mayer, 1990).

In defining emotional intelligence, Salovey and Mayer concentrated on the two words 'emotional' and 'intelligence'. We know it sounds obvious, but it is important that you

Stop and think

Science interests split the sexes

On Monday 13 of March, 2006, BBC News Online (**http://news.bbc.co.uk/1/hi/education/4800882.stm**) ran a story of a sex split in science interests. Professor Edgar Jenkins from the University of Leeds reported on the survey of 1,200 UK pupils who had taken part in a global study, based at Oslo University, looking at the relevance of science education. In this survey pupils were asked what their favourite topics were in science. Favourite topics in science were split down by boys and girls as follows.

Boys	Girls
• Explosive chemicals	• Why we dream and what it means
• How it feels to be weightless in space	• What we know about cancer and how to treat it
• How the atom bomb functions	• How to perform first aid
• Biological and chemical weapons	• How to exercise to keep fit
• Black holes and supernovae	• Sexually transmitted diseases and how to protect against them
• How meteors, comets or asteroids cause disasters on Earth	• What we know about HIV/AIDS and how to control it
• The possibility of life outside Earth	• Life and death and the human soul
• How computers work	• Biological and human aspects of abortion
• Effect of strong electric shocks and lightning on the body	• Eating disorders
• Dangerous animals	• How alcohol and tobacco might affect the body

Source: The Relevance of Science Education Project (ROSE) in England: A summary of findings, CSSME (Jenkins, E. W. and Pell, R. G. 2006).

How do the findings of the survey fit in with the theory and research evidence that surrounds sex differences in intelligence?

give equal weight to both words. For these authors emotion is important, as it comprises feelings that encompass physiological responses (for example, sadness, happiness, crying, fear) and cognitions (for example, assessments of the meaning of emotion, learning about ourselves from our emotions). Similarly, intelligence is important because it refers to capacities to think and reason about information. Salovey and Mayer brought these two areas together into one: emotional intelligence.

In their original paper, Salovey and Mayer divided the concept of emotional intelligence into four capacities:

- accurately perceiving emotions;
- using emotions to facilitate thinking;
- understanding emotional meanings;
- managing emotions.

By 1997 Mayer and Salovey had expanded on their model (Mayer and Salovey, 1997). In this more detailed model, they expanded the four branches as follows:

- **Perceiving branch: perception, appraisal and expression of emotion** – if you were high in this aspect of emotional intelligence, you would be able to recognise emotions in other people, particularly through their use of language (for example, if it is emotionally charged), sound (for example, when the tone of voice changes when they are upset) and behaviour (for example, if they are behaving differently or seem anxious). However, within this branch of emotional intelligence, you would be able to identify accurately your own emotions in relation to your own thoughts and feelings. You would also be able to express emotions properly in accordance with your feelings and thoughts.
- **Facilitating branch: emotional facilitation of thinking** – if you were high in this aspect of emotional intelligence, you would be able to use your emotions as an aid for your memory and to make judgements about certain feelings to prioritise your thinking. You would be able to use emotions to encourage the consideration of multiple viewpoints (for example, not focusing on one emotion, such as being unhappy) and to understand that particular emotions can be used in problem-solving (for example, being happy leads to creativity).
- **Understanding branch: understanding and analysing emotions; employing emotional knowledge** – if you were high in this aspect of emotional intelligence, you would be able to label emotions accurately and recognise the relationships between the emotions (for example, the similarities and differences between dislike and hate). You would also be able to understand the meaning behind emotions and know that some emotions are linked together in a process (for example, to do well in an exam would be accompanied by happiness). You would also understand that there are transitions among

emotions (for example, you may have told someone off because you were angry, but later regret it and think you did the wrong thing and feel remorse).

- **Managing branch: reflective regulation of emotion to promote emotional and intellectual growth** – if you were high on this aspect of emotional intelligence, you would have the ability to stay open to feelings that are both pleasant (for example, praise) and unpleasant (for example, criticism). You would have the ability to reflect or detach from a specific emotion to be able to see whether it is informative to you (for example, you may be upset about something, but can you detach yourself from being upset and note that your reaction might have been unreasonable?). You would be able to monitor emotions in yourself and others, and assess whether the emotion expressed is *typical* (for example, asking yourself whether your emotions are a normal reaction to something), is *influencing* you (for example, asking if the emotion is ruling your decision-making) or is *unreasonable* (you might be angry about someone, but realise you are being unfair). Finally, you would show the ability to manage emotion in yourself and others by monitoring emotions and, on some occasions, using them for personal, intellectual or emotional growth (for example, you can do something constructive with your anger).

Furthermore, the authors have further broken these four branches into two main areas:

- **Experiential (relating to, or derived from, experience)** – this area comprises the perceiving branch and the facilitating branch.
- **Strategic (related to intended objective, or plan of action)** – this area comprises the understanding branch and the managing branch.

This model of emotional intelligence is known as an *ability* model because it involves abilities in having and dealing with emotion, using emotion to enhance thought and to reflect and engage with a variety of emotions. Mayer and Salovey arranged the four aspects of emotional intelligence in an order of sophistication of ability. The order of sophistication, ranging from lowest to highest, is presented in Figure 15.4.

How do Mayer and Salovey measure intelligence? Now in its second edition, The Mayer–Salovey–Caruso Emotional Intelligence Test V2.0 (MSCEIT V2.0; Mayer *et al.*, 2002; 2003) is a 141-item scale used to measure the emotional intelligence abilities described earlier: perception, integration (facilitation), understanding and management.

In this test, the test-taker performs a series of tasks that are designed to assess their ability to perceive, identify, understand and work with emotion. For example, here are some typical items.

- **Ability to identify emotion** – the participant would be shown a picture of a face and asked to assess to what extent

Figure 15.4 Mayer and Salovey's model of emotional intelligence, including the order of sophistication.
Source: From Mayer, J.D., Salovey, P. and Caruso, D.R. (2000). Models of emotional intelligence. In R.J. Sternberg (ed), *The handbook of intelligence* (pp. 398, 404, 415). Cambridge: Cambridge University Press. Reprinted with permission from Cambridge University Press.

different emotions are shown in the face (i.e. happiness, anger, fear, excitement and surprise) (see Figure 15.5a).

- **Ability to use (facilitate) emotion** – the participant would rate on a 5-point scale to what extent a number of moods (i.e. tension, surprise, joy) might be helpful when meeting a partner's family for the very first time (see Figure 15.5b).

- **Ability to understand emotion** – the participant would imagine someone who is stressed about their work and whose boss gave them an additional project. The participant would then be asked to identify which of five emotions (overwhelmed, depressed, ashamed, self-conscious or jittery) they think the person would feel (see Figure 15.5c).

- **Ability to manage emotions** – the participant would be asked to imagine someone coming back from vacation feeling peaceful and content. The test-taker would then be asked to identify the effectiveness of a number of actions for maintaining the feelings of peacefulness and contentment (i.e. making a list of things to do, thinking about where and when to go for the next vacation or deciding whether it is best to ignore the feelings of being peaceful and content as it won't last anyway) (see Figure 15.5d).

Respondents can get overall emotional intelligence scores on the MSCEIT V2.0, as well as subscale scores for the perceiving branch, facilitating branch, understanding branch and managing branch.

Goleman's model of emotional intelligence

Goleman's development of emotional intelligence (Goleman, 1995), came after Salovey and Mayer's (1990)

theory, but is probably the most widely known model of emotional intelligence. Goleman drew on Salovey and Mayer's (1990) work, including an emphasis on physiological and cognitive terms, but he also introduced a number of new ideas.

One of these ideas was that Goleman linked emotional intelligence to a part of the brain called the amygdala. The amygdala is located in the brain's medial temporal lobe and is part of the limbic system of the brain. The **limbic system** is a group of brain structures that are involved in various emotions, including pleasure, fear and aggression as well as in the formation of memories. The amygdala (the part Goleman was interested in) is involved in aggression and fear, two basic responses that are related to responses to threat. You may recognise this as the 'fight-or-flight' response.

The flight-or-fight response was first described by Walter Cannon, a US physiologist (Cannon, 1929). His theory stated that when animals are faced by threats or danger they have physiological reactions, including the 'firing' of neurons through the sensory cortex of the brain, that are accompanied by increased levels of hormones and neurotransmitters such as epinephrine (adrenaline) and norepinephrine (noradrenaline). These hormones and neurotransmitters are pumped into the body, causing immediate physical reactions such as an increase in heart rate, tensing of muscles and quicker breathing, thereby making the animal alert and attentive to the environment and aware of the danger. This is known as a stress response. The animal is then faced with two choices. It can either face the threat ('fight') or avoid the threat ('flight').

Goleman uses the processes of the amygdala in his model of emotional intelligence. He argues that the fight-or-flight

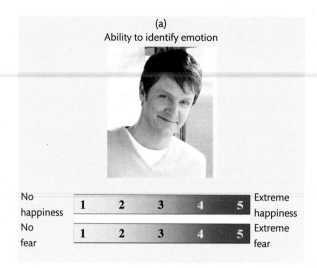

(a)
Ability to identify emotion

| No happiness | 1 | 2 | 3 | 4 | 5 | Extreme happiness |
| No fear | 1 | 2 | 3 | 4 | 5 | Extreme fear |

(b)
Ability to use (facilitate) emotion

1. What mood(s) might be helpful to feel when meeting in-laws for the very first time?

	Not useful				Useful
a. Tension	1	2	3	4	5
b. Surprise	1	2	3	4	5
c. Joy	1	2	3	4	5

(c)
Ability to understand emotion

Tom felt anxious, and became a bit stressed when he thought about all the work he needed to do. When his supervisor brought him an additional project, he felt_____.
a. overwhelmed
b. depressed
c. ashamed
d. self-conscious
e. jittery

(d)

Debbie just came back from vacation. She was feeling peaceful and content. How well would each action preserve her mood?
Action 1: She started to make a list of things at home that she needed to do.

(a) Very effective   (b) Somewhat effective   (c) Neutral
(d) Somewhat ineffective   (e) Very ineffective

Action 2: She began thinking about where and when she should go on her next vacation.

(a) Very effective   (b) Somewhat effective   (c) Neutral
(d) Somewhat ineffective   (e) Very ineffective

Action 3: She decided it was best ignore the feeling since it wouldn't last anyway.

(a) Very effective   (b) Somewhat effective   (c) Neutral
(d) Somewhat ineffective   (e) Very ineffective

Figure 15.5 Simulated Emotional Intelligence Items from the Mayer–Salovey–Caruso Emotional Intelligence Test 2.0.
(MSCEIT V2.0; Mayer *et al.*, 2002). Copyright © 1999, 2000, 2002, Multi-Health Systems, Inc. All rights reserved. In the USA: PO Box 950, North Tonawanda, NY 14120-0950, (800) 456-3003. In Canada: 3770 Victoria Park Ave., Toronto, ON M2H 3M6, (800) 268-6011. International Tel: +1-416-492-2627, Fax: 1-800-540-4484 or +1-416-492-3343.

Stop and think

Emotional intelligence qualities

Using Mayer and Salovey's model of emotional intelligence, where do you think your strengths of emotional intelligence lie? Perceiving, facilitating, understanding or managing?

response is central to emotional intelligence and that, as we develop, we learn to control these two basic emotions. For example, when we were very young and knew we would be told off by our parents, we might have tried to run away to avoid the trouble, or tried to fight (or least have a tantrum) with our parents. As we got older, we would have changed our strategy, and probably have just listened to being told off by our parents and accepted whatever punishment was coming our way. As we got older still, we might have tried to reason with our parents, tried to apologise and reassure our parents that it would never happen again. Goleman suggests that our emotional intelligence reflects a similar process. That is, over time, we learn to control our basic emotional responses (such as fight and flight) to varying degrees. The extent to which we are able to develop, control and use our basic emotional responses is the basis of Goleman's model of emotional intelligence.

Originally in Goleman's (1995) theory, there are five emotional intelligences:

- ability to identify one's emotional states and to understand that there is a connection between emotions, thought and action (for example, you are likely to laugh when you have a happy thought);
- ability to manage and control one's emotions, and to shift undesirable emotions to more adequate ones (for example, to shift the feeling of crying to a feeling of sadness);

- ability to have emotional states that are related with a drive for achievement and be successful (for example, the ability to be happy and for this to drive you on in your work, or in trying to achieve something to make you happy);
- ability to assess, be sensitive and influence other people's emotions (for example, to recognise someone's sadness and cheer them up);
- ability to enter and then sustain good interpersonal relationships (for example, to have good friends and maintain your relationship with them).

Within Goleman's theory, these emotional intelligences form a hierarchy (see Figure 15.6).

For example, to be able to manage your emotions (second aspect of emotional intelligence), you must be able to identify them (first aspect of emotional intelligence). To use your emotions in a drive for achievement (third aspect of emotional intelligence), you must be able to identify (first aspect) and manage (second aspect) them. To be able to assess and influence other people's emotions effectively (fourth aspect), you must be able to identify, manage and use them (all the first three aspects). Having all the first four aspects of emotional intelligence leads individuals to enter, and be able to sustain, good interpersonal relationships.

Little do we know it, but this is actually an 'Emotional Intelligence' seminar.
Source: Alamy Images/Ace Stock Ltd.

Figure 15.6 Goleman's model of emotional intelligence, arranged in the hierarchy.

Source: From Goleman, D. (2001). An EI-based theory of performance. In C. Cherniss and D. Goleman (eds), *The Emotionally Intelligent Workplace.* New York: Jossey Bass Wiley. Reprinted with permission of John Wiley & Sons Inc.

Over the years Goleman refined this model, not only in terms of its theory but also in its application. Goleman's theory and application became popular in the business world, and the development of Goleman's theory centres around the language used in the workplace.

By 2002 (Goleman, 2001; Goleman *et al.*, 2002), Goleman had revised his theory to there being four domains of emotional intelligence. To a great extent he had dropped the third aspect (using your emotions in a drive for achievement) and subsumed it into other aspects. Today, Goleman's theory of emotional intelligence comprises four aspects, which he termed emotional competencies:

- **self-awareness** – which was the old first aspect, the ability to identify one's own emotional states;
- **self-regulation/management** – which was the old second aspect, the ability to manage one's own emotional states;
- **social awareness** – which was the old third aspect, the ability to assess and influence others' emotions;
- **social skills/management** – which was the old fourth aspect, the ability to sustain good interpersonal relationships.

Goleman made two sets of distinctions between these four emotional competencies. The first distinction is between *personal* and *social* competencies. The first two aspects, *self-awareness* and *self-regulation*, are personal competencies, while *social awareness* and *social skills* are social competencies.

The second distinction is between *recognition* and *regulation*. *Self-awareness* and *social awareness* are emotional intelligences that are defined by recognition (identifying one's own emotional state and those of others), and *self-regulation* and *social skills* are emotional intelligences that are defined by regulation (managing one's own emotional states and sustaining good personal relationships).

Additionally, Goleman has identified up to 25 abilities that make up emotional intelligence, though this number changes based on the context of the situation in which emotional intelligence is being applied. For example, some of the abilities are very businesslike because of the model's application to relationships in work. It is difficult to produce a definitive model because Goleman has revised these ideas.

However, Table 15.5 shows how Goleman's emotional intelligence model can be broken down by personal and social competencies and by recognition and regulation competencies, with specific abilities used to illustrate each of the combinations of these competencies.

Goleman's model of emotional intelligence is known as a mixed model of emotional intelligence. The reason for the name 'mixed' is that these models of emotional intelligence combine (mix) central ideas of emotional intelligence with a variety of other personality or behavioural traits. For example, if we look at the abilities listed in Table 15.5, Goleman's model mixes ideas of emotional intelligence (for example, emotional states) with personality and behaviour traits (for example, conscientiousness, adaptability, trustworthiness).

Goleman's model of emotional intelligence is measured by the Emotional Competence Inventory (Goleman and Boyatzis, 2005), which is designed for use in the workplace, and the University Edition, which is designed for use in schools or universities. The Emotional Competence Inventory is a 360-degree instrument. This means that other people evaluate the individuals on their emotional intelligence. The assessor is asked to rate the person in terms of how characteristic they are of the abilities listed in Goleman's model.

Table 15.5 Goleman's model of emotional intelligence

	Personal competencies	Social competencies
Recognition	**Self-awareness** • Emotional awareness: recognising one's emotions and their possible effects. • Accurate self-assessment: knowing one's strengths and limitations. • Self-confidence: confidence about one's self-worth and capabilities.	**Social awareness** • Empathy: sensing others' feelings and perspective, and taking an active interest in their feelings and concerns. • Service orientation: anticipating, recognising and meeting people's needs. • Developing others: sensing what others need to develop and improve their abilities. • Leveraging diversity: creating and cultivating opportunities through diverse people. • Political awareness: reading a group's emotional state and understanding power relationships in the group.
Regulation/management	**Self-regulation/management** • Self-control: managing disruptive emotions and impulses. • Trustworthiness: maintaining standards of honesty and integrity. • Conscientiousness: taking responsibility for personal performance. • Adaptability: flexibility in handling change. • Achievement drive: self-motivation for achieving excellence. • Innovativeness/initative: being comfortable with and open to novel ideas and new information.	**Social skills/management** • Developing others: ability to help and improve others. • Influence: having effective tactics for persuasion. • Communication: sending clear and convincing messages. • Leadership: inspiring and guiding people and groups. • Change catalyst: initiating or managing change. • Conflict management: negotiating and resolving disagreements. • Building bonds: nurturing instrumental relationships. • Collaboration and cooperation: working with others towards shared goals. • Teamwork capabilities: creating group energy and synergy in pursuing collective goals.

Sources: Goleman (2001); Goleman *et al.* (2002).

Example items in the Emotional Competence Inventory include the assessor determining whether the person:

• presents themselves in an assured, forceful, impressive and unhesitating manner;
• respects, treats with courtesy and relates well to people of diverse backgrounds;
• accurately reads people's moods, feelings or non-verbal cues.

Bar-On's model of emotional intelligence

The third well-recognised model of emotional intelligence was put forward by US psychologist Reuven Bar-On. He names it the emotional–social intelligence model (Bar-On, 1997; 2005).

Like the models of Mayer and Salovey and Goleman, Bar-On's model of emotional intelligence has biological origins. However, rather than emphasising physiological reactions, or part of the brain, Bar-On draws on the evolutionary theory of Darwin. In his book *The Expression of the Emotions in Man and Animals*, Darwin wrote of how animals and humans express and signal to each other with their emotions (Darwin, 1872/1965). Darwin wondered whether human facial expressions are innate, and he set out to show

that animals have many of the same ways of physically expressing emotions as humans do. Darwin suggested that the importance of emotional expression was for adaptation and survival. The ability of humans and animals to express emotion (happiness, interest, sadness, fear, anger, surprise) helps animals bond with each other (happiness), is an important process in meeting a mate (interest) and may also act as a protective factor (showing anger to scare people away) or warn others of potential danger (fear). Within this context, Bar-On introduced his model of emotional–social intelligence, which addresses emotionally and socially intelligent behaviour within Darwin's theory of effective adaptation.

Overall, Bar-On saw emotional–social intelligence as a range of interrelated emotional and social competence abilities that allowed individuals to understand and express themselves effectively, understand and relate to others, and cope with environmental demands and pressures. Bar-On based his final model of emotional intelligence on key ideas that had appeared in previous descriptions, definitions and conceptualisations of emotional–social intelligence. In all, he identified five major domains and 15 aspects.

• **Intrapersonal skills** – the ability to recognise, understand and express emotions and feelings. The aspects of intrapersonal skills in this model are emotional self-awareness, assertiveness, self-regard, self-actualisation and independence.

- **Interpersonal skills** – the ability to understand how others feel and relate to them. The aspects of interpersonal skills in this model are interpersonal relationships, social responsibility and empathy.
- **Adaptability scales** – the ability to manage and control emotions. The aspects of adaptability skills in this model are problem-solving, reality testing and flexibility.
- **Stress-management scales** – the ability to manage change, adapt and solve problems of a personal and interpersonal nature. The aspects of stress management skills in this model are stress tolerance and impulse control.
- **General mood** – the ability to generate positive affect and be self-motivated. The aspects of general mood in this model are happiness and optimism.

Bar-On's model of emotional–social intelligence is also known as a mixed model of emotional intelligence. For example, Bar-On mixes ideas of emotional intelligence (i.e. emotional states) and behavioural traits (optimism and flexibility).

Despite developing the theory later, Bar-On was the first of the theorists to develop an emotional intelligence measure, the Emotional Quotient Inventory (EQ-i; Bar-On, 1997). The EQ-i is an estimate of emotional–social intelligence that contains 133 items and employs a five-point response scale format, ranging from 'very seldom or not true of me' (1) to 'very often true of me or true of me' (5). Three things can be computed from the EQ-i: one overall emotional–social intelligence score, five scales representing the main five domains and 15 subscales that make up the five domains.

The five main domains (with the 15 subscales in brackets) are as follows:

- intrapersonal (comprising the self-regard, emotional self-awareness, assertiveness, independence and self-actualisation subscales);
- interpersonal (comprising empathy, social responsibility and interpersonal relationship subscales);
- adaptability (comprising reality-testing, flexibility and problem-solving subscales);
- stress management (comprising stress tolerance and impulse control subscales);
- general mood (comprising optimism and happiness subscales).

However, Bar-On reserves something special for overall scores on the Emotional Quotient Inventory. Those scores can be converted into standard scores based on a mean of 100 and standard deviation of 15, leading to an emotional quotient (EQ) score. This is deliberately meant to resemble IQ (intelligence quotient) scores. High EQ scores suggest that an individual has effective emotional and social functioning in meeting daily demands and challenges. Low EQ scores suggest that an individual has an inability to be effective in meeting daily demands and challenges and suggests the possible existence of emotional and/or social problems.

Providing contexts for understanding the three models of emotional intelligence

So, in considering emotional intelligence, we are presented with three different theories and three different measures of emotional intelligence. One of the major concerns in the emotional intelligence literature is that the theory is not cohesive. However, certain people have set about integrating the theory. This has been done in two ways, by comparing:

- ability and mixed models of emotional intelligence;
- theories of emotional intelligence within a systems of personality approach.

Comparing ability and mixed models of emotional intelligence

The first way in which we can simplify the study of emotional intelligence is to make the distinction between ability models of emotional intelligence and mixed models of emotional intelligence. You may remember a distinction we made earlier (Chapter 13) between psychometric measures of intelligence (that we based on trying to define intelligence) and cognitive measures of intelligence (which additionally look at some of the cognitive processes that surrounded intelligence; for example, simultaneous and sequential processing). Well, a similar distinction can be made between the models of emotional intelligence.

Authors such as John Mayer, Peter Salovey and David Caruso (Mayer *et al*, 2000) and Robert Emmerling and Daniel Goleman (Emmerling and Goleman, 2003) point out that the model of emotional intelligence that is the most useful depends on what it is trying to achieve. These authors suggest that ability models of emotional intelligence follow the psychometric/measurement tradition by trying to define what the construct is (in this case, what is emotional intelligence). This theory and research are built around trying to identify and define a single theoretical framework that leads to a 'correct' or accurate understanding of what comprises emotional intelligence. Mayer and Salovey's four-branch definition focuses on defining a set of emotional intelligence abilities that are considered unique to emotional intelligence, and it does not include personality or behavioural characteristics that belong to other psychological models (as with the mixed models of emotional intelligence). Mayer *et al.* suggest that following this strategy leads to clear definitions of emotional intelligence. This strategy has a number of advantages:

Profiles

Four (emotionally) wise men: Peter Salovey, John Mayer, Daniel Goleman and Reuven Bar-On

Peter Salovey

Peter Salovey studied for a series of undergraduate and postgraduate degrees at Stanford University between 1980 and 1986. In 1986 he became an Assistant Professor at Yale University, and has been a full Professor since 1995.

Currently he is the director of the Health, Emotion and Behavior Laboratory at Yale University. He is also Assistant Director at Yale Center for Interdisciplinary Research on AIDS, and works with the Yale Cancer Center. Under these centres his work has examined how educational and public health messages can best be used to promote prevention and early detection of behaviours relevant to cancer and HIV/AIDS.

Salovey has authored more than 200 articles. He has been the editor or associate editor for three scientific journals: *Psychological Bulletin*, *Review of General Psychology* and *Emotion*. He has been awarded the William Clyde DeVane Medal for Distinguished Scholarship and Teaching in Yale College in 2000 and the Lex Hixon Prize for Teaching in the Social Sciences at Yale in 2002.

John D. Mayer

John D. Mayer is a psychologist at the University of New Hampshire. He received his BA at the University of Michigan, his PhD from Case Western Reserve University, and was a postdoctoral fellow at Stanford University.

He has served on the editorial boards of *Psychological Bulletin*, the *Journal of Personality* and the *Journal of Personality and Social Psychology*.

As well as his work on emotional intelligence, Mayer adopts a systems approach to personality psychology.

This systems framework joins together many different aspects of personality.

Daniel Goleman

Daniel Goleman was born in 1946 in Stockton, California. After graduating with an undergraduate degree from Amherst College, he studied for his MA and PhD in clinical psychology and personality development at Harvard (where he sometimes lectures).

Goleman wrote for the *New York Times*, editing its science page, specialising in psychology and brain sciences. He has received many journalistic awards for his writing, including two nominations for the Pulitzer Prize for his articles.

Goleman was a co-founder of the Collaborative for Academic, Social and Emotional Learning, which is now situated at the University of Illinois at Chicago. The mission of this collaborative is to introduce emotional literacy courses into schools.

Reuven Bar-On

Reuven Bar-On earned his doctorate at Rhodes University in South Africa and is currently at the University of Texas Medical Branch, in the Department of Psychiatry and Behavioral Sciences. He has worked as a clinical psychologist since 1972.

He is currently involved in a 25-year longitudinal study conducted by Human Resources Development Canada. The study is following the development of 23,000 young people, to determine the relationship between emotional intelligence and biomedical, cognitive, developmental, social and educational factors.

- Psychologists can clearly identify and communicate what emotional intelligence is.
- Psychologists can understand what emotional intelligence is and how it is related to similar psychological theories by examining the relationship between emotional intelligence and other measures of psychological thinking and feelings (for example, other measures of intelligence and emotion).
- Psychologists can then examine the real applied value of emotional intelligence by looking at its relationship to other variables such as mental health, work and school achievement.

Mayer *et al.* also suggest that, by using such an approach, you can clearly let people know exactly what emotional intelligence is and what it is not, and assure other psychologists that it is not part of some other variable that already exists (for example, personality).

However, Emmerling and Goleman (2003) have made the case for the usefulness of the mixed models of emotional intelligence. It has to be remembered that Goleman's theory and research have been largely developed within the context of applying emotional intelligence to the workplace. Bar-On's model emphasises emotional intelligence as being able to deal best with the demands and stress of the environment. Therefore, with Goleman's and Bar-On's models of emotional intelligence, attention shifts from a focus on defining emotional intelligence to defining the successful 'emotionally intelligent' person. This is done by investigating those abilities that successful emotionally intelligent people have. For example, Goleman's model of emotional intelligence seeks to develop a theory and research around work performance based on social and emotional competencies. He examines how a collection of abilities and behaviour come together in high achievers, or people who do excellently in the workplace (for example, company directors, work leaders), to define emotional intelligence. Emmerling and Goleman argue that this approach is well established in occupational psychology. They suggest that, by following this strategy, mixed ability models of emotional intelligence are able to provide a deeper understanding of people who succeed and of how emotional intelligence, as a sum of a number of new and existing behaviours, is a central part of that success.

Emotional intelligence in the context of a personality system framework

Despite the differences between the various models of emotional intelligence, there has been an attempt to integrate our view of emotional intelligence. John D. Mayer, Peter Salovey and David Caruso (2000) presented the three models of emotional intelligence within a personality systems framework (see Table 15.6).

We will now talk you through Table 15.6. A personality systems framework was introduced by Mayer (1995; 1998; 2005a, b); the framework suggests that there are two dimensions to consider in any set of behaviours:

- **The purpose of a psychological system** – this dimension reflects the contrast between responses to internal needs and experience and responses to the external world.
- **The level of the psychological subsystem** – this dimension reflects the distinction between low, middle and high functions. Mayer defines '**low functions**' as reflecting biological factors (for example, basic biological needs such as eating or physiological factors), '**middle functions**' as reflecting interactive factors (for example, the relationship between personality, cognitive variables and environmental variables) and '**high functions**' as reflecting learned factors (for example, culture).

Table 15.6 An overview of personality and its major subsystems with three models of emotional intelligence embedded within it

		Purpose of subsystem		
		Responding to internal needs	**Responding to the external world**	
Level of subsystem	**High function** Learned models culture	***Intrapersonal* qualities** *(understanding oneself, having good self-concept and self-esteem)* (1) Intrapersonal skills (2) Motivating oneself	***Interpersonal skills*** *(knowing how to socialise, being comfortable with other people)* (1) Interpersonal skills (2) Handling relationships	
	Middle function Interactive functions	**Motivational and emotional interactions** *(e.g., frustration with something leads to anger)*	**Emotional and cognitive interactions** *(e.g., understanding and perceiving emotions)*	
	Personality, cognitive functions interacting with the environment	(1) Stress management skills	(3) Perception/expression of emotion	(2) Knowing one's emotions
			(3) Facilitating emotion in thought	(2) Recognising emotions in others
			(3) Understanding emotion	(2) Managing emotion
			(3) Regulating emotion	
	Low function Biologically related mechanisms	**Motivational directions** *(satisfying basic needs such as eating)*	**Emotional qualities** *(being emotionally expressive, being happy and calm)*	**Cognitive abilities** *(ability to perceive patterns, being analytical)*
	Physiological and neuropsychological functions		(1) General mood	(1) Adaptability skills

Notes:

1 R. Bar-On, *The Emotional Quotient Inventory (EQ-i): A test of emotional intelligence* (Toronto, Canada: Multi-Health Systems, 1997).

2 D. P. Goleman, *Emotional intelligence: Why it can matter more than IQ for character, health and lifelong achievement* (New York: Bantam, 1995).

3 J. D. Mayer and P. Salovey, What is emotional intelligence? In P. Salovey and D. Sluyter (eds), *Emotional development and emotional intelligence: Implications for educators* (New York: Basic Books, 1997), pp. 3–31.

Source: Based on Mayer *et al.* (2000).

Mayer drew up a diagram of this system, as outlined in Table 15.6. What Mayer, Salovey and Caruso then did was to divide the different models of emotional intelligence within this framework. As you can see, using this framework emphasises where the different emotional intelligence models are distinct and where they overlap. In terms of each model of emotional intelligence, you can see that:

- Bar-On's model (labelled 1) is divided among the three levels of the personality subsystem: low in terms of adaptability and mood, middle in terms of stress management and high in terms of intrapersonal and interpersonal skills. This reflects Bar-On's intention that emotional intelligence represents successful adaptation to a stressful environment in Darwinian terms, thus involving biological factors combined with learned models of behaviours, involving oneself and others to cope with the stressful environment.
- Goleman's model (labelled 2) is split between the middle and high levels, emphasising intrapersonal and interpersonal skills combined with emotional and cognitive interactions, representing his mixed model of abilities in the social world (e.g. the workplace).
- Mayer and Salovey's model (labelled 3) is located entirely within the area of emotional–cognitive interactions, representing the authors' emphasis on emotional intelligence being a set of emotional and cognitive abilities separate from any other aspect of personality.

So, from these two considerations (comparing ability versus mixed models of emotional intelligence, and comparing models of emotional intelligence within a personality subsystems approach), we have a better understanding of how these three different models of emotional intelligence fit together.

The application of emotional intelligence in psychology

So, of what use to psychologists is the concept of emotional intelligence? Well, across a number of psychological domains, emotional intelligence has been found to have mainly positive outcomes, but does it sometimes have a dark side?

One area in which emotional intelligence has been found to be relevant is in health and psychological health. Schutte *et al.* (2007), in a meta-analysis of 44 effect sizes based on the responses of 7,898 participants, found that higher emotional intelligence was associated with better health and psychological health. Emotional intelligence had an average correlation of $r = 0.22$ with physical health, $r = 0.29$ with mental health and $r = 0.31$ with psychosomatic health. In a related area, Mikolajczak and Luminet (2008) examined the relationship between emotional intelligence and self-efficacy and challenge and threat primary appraisals. Self-efficacy is an individual's belief that they can perform some behaviour that will get them a desired positive outcome. Primary appraisals are concerned with how individuals evaluate the nature and meaning of a particular stressful event or situation. A challenge primary appraisal represents the degree to which a stressful event or situation is perceived as allowing for personal growth and development. A threat primary appraisal represents the degree to which a stressful event or situation is perceived as threatening to the person. Mikolajczak and Luminet found that individuals high in emotional intelligence exhibit greater self-efficacy in coping situations (i.e. they can perform some behaviour that will help them cope well with the situation) and appraise a stressful event as a challenge rather than a threat. Also, Externera and Fernandez-Berrocal (2005) found that emotional intelligence was related to life satisfaction and Chamorro-Premuzic *et al.* (2007) found that it was related to higher levels of happiness. Trait emotional intelligence is able to predict a number of successful outcomes, e.g. life satisfaction, lower levels of rumination and better coping, after controlling for personality factors (Petrides *et al.*, 2007).

Emotional intelligence has been found to have a positive benefit in education and the workplace. As we noted above, Goleman's model of emotional intelligence is based around achievement and leadership in the workplace and we

Stop and think

Another emotional intelligence: trait emotional intelligence

Another notable contribution to the emotional intelligence literature is the work of Konstantin Vasily Petrides and colleagues on the concept of trait emotional intelligence. Trait emotional intelligence is different from Salovey and Mayer's ability and Goleman's mixed-models of emotional intelligence and instead conceptualises emotional intelligence as comprising 'emotional self-perceptions' (Petrides and Furnham, 2001). Consequently, trait emotional intelligence centres around one's self-perceived emotional abilities and is sometimes referred to as emotional self-efficacy (belief in our ability to be successful in emotional situations).

consider this in more detail later (Chapter 16). In terms of other evidence, Downey *et al.* (2008) found that emotional intelligence was significantly associated with higher levels of academic achievement across a range of subjects (mathematics, science, art and geography) among 209 Australian secondary school students, suggesting the usefulness of emotional intelligence in education. Mavroveli *et al.* (2008) found emotional intelligence to correlate positively with teacher-rated positive behaviour and negatively with negative behaviour (e.g. emotional symptoms, conduct problems, peer problems and hyperactivity) among schoolchildren. Rozell *et al.* (2006) examined the relationship between emotional intelligence and individuals working in sales. These authors found that emotional intelligence was positively related to higher levels of performance in a number of sales tasks (e.g. meeting, managing and communicating with customers), which suggests the usefulness of emotional intelligence in the workplace. However, reviews of studies (e.g. Cote and Miners, 2006; Landy, 2005; Zafra *et al.*, 2008) have suggested that there are mixed results, with some studies finding a positive relationship and some studies finding no relationship between emotional intelligence and achievement in education and in the workplace (e.g. Charbonneau and Nicol, 2002; van der Zee *et al.*, 2002). In response to these mixed findings, two studies have suggested that there may be an interesting dynamic between emotional intelligence, general intelligence and academic and workplace achievement. Petrides *et al.* (2004) and, later, Cote and Miners (2006) have presented a 'compensatory' model of emotional intelligence and general intelligence to explain how emotional intelligence may influence achievement. This model suggests that the relationship between emotional intelligence and achievement becomes positive as general intelligence decreases. Together these authors found that, in education (Petrides *et al.*, 2004) and in the workplace (Cote and Miners, 2006), individuals with lower general intelligence demonstrated increased levels of achievement as they demonstrated increased levels of emotional intelligence.

But what about this dark side of emotional intelligence that we mentioned earlier? Well, in 2007, Elizabeth Austin and her colleagues looked at the association between Machiavellianism and emotional intelligence (Austin *et al.*, 2007). Machiavellianism is from the political doctrine of the philosopher Machiavelli, and denies any relevance of morality in political affairs. In psychology, Machiavellianism is generally viewed as a trait which reflects the tendency to be cunning and deceptive in everyday behaviour and interactions with others, particularly in terms of trying to gain advantage for oneself. Austin and her colleagues suggested that, as emotional intelligence comprises traits that enable the individual to manage the emotions of others (such as calming a colleague's angry mood or making someone feel better about oneself), then perhaps the emotional manipulation

capability of emotional intelligence might not always be used positively. That is, would someone who was able to manipulate people emotionally, manipulate emotions in other people in a negative way? To examine this idea, Austin *et al.* constructed an emotional manipulation scale and used it to examine the relationship between Machiavellianism and emotional intelligence. Austin *et al.* found that Machiavellianism was found to share a significant negative correlation with emotional intelligence, and emotional manipulation shared a significant positive relationship with Machiavellianism but was unrelated to emotional intelligence. Austin *et al.* concluded that, although people high in Machiavellianism endorse emotionally manipulative behaviour, the evidence did not support the view that such people were successful in emotionally manipulating people owing to the negative relationship between Machiavellianism and emotional intelligence. Furthermore, they found that emotional manipulation was unrelated to emotional intelligence, suggesting that there is no dark side to emotional intelligence.

Sex differences in emotional intelligence

In the light of our discussion earlier regarding sex differences in intelligence, the question arises: 'Do women and men differ in their emotional intelligence?' Well, theoretically, Goleman thinks they do. Goleman (1995) provided separate descriptors of an emotionally intelligent man and woman. Table 15.7 lists these descriptions.

However, the distinctions are not so easy to make when we consider whether women score higher than men do on measures of emotional intelligence. The evidence examining sex differences in emotional intelligence among the samples in the population suggests results are mixed, or that the effect size of any significant difference is small. Remember that we defined an effect size of 0.2 as small, 0.5 as medium and 0.8 as large.

For Mayer and Salovey's ability model of emotional intelligence (and their scores on their Mayer–Salovey–Caruso Emotional Intelligence Test), women are found to score significantly higher than men across the four aspects of emotional intelligence: perception, integration (facilitation), understanding and management. Canadian psychologists Arla L. Day and Sarah A. Carroll found, among 246 undergraduate students (70 men, 176 women), that the effect size for emotional intelligence was higher in women and ranged from 0.18 to 0.30 (Day and Carroll, 2004). Furthermore, US individual difference psychologists Melanie Schulte, Malcolm James Ree and Thomas R. Carretta found an effect size of 0.30 in favour of women scoring higher for overall scores on the MSCEIT than men did (Schulte *et al.*, 2004).

However, findings with Bar-On's Emotional Quotient Inventory (EQ-i) among a US sample of over 3,000 individuals (Bar-On, 1997) suggest a different picture. Bar-On found no significant difference between men and women

Table 15.7 Goleman's emotional intelligence against IQ and comparing sex differences

	Emotional intelligence
Men	• Outgoing and cheerful • Not prone to fearfulness or worry • Ability to show commitment to people or causes • Takes responsibility • Has an ethical outlook • Sympathetic and caring in relationships • Comfortable with oneself and others
Women	• Assertive and expresses feelings directly • Feels positive about oneself • Life holds meaning • Outgoing • Seeks and enjoys the company of others • Expresses feelings appropriately • Adapts well to stress • Spontaneous • Rarely feels guilty or ruminates

Source: Based on Goleman (1995).

for overall emotional intelligence scores. However, across the five aspects of emotional intelligence (intrapersonal, interpersonal, adaptability, stress management and general mood) and the 15 subscales that make up the EQ-i, sex differences on emotional intelligence are mixed. Bar-On reports that women score significantly higher on all three aspects of interpersonal skills (empathy, social responsibility and interpersonal relationships) and are more aware of their own emotions than men are. On the other hand, men seem to hold themselves in better self-regard, cope better with stress, are more independent, solve problems better, are more flexible and are more optimistic. These differences are very small, with all but one of the effects being below 0.16; the exception is empathy, where women score higher and the effect size is just under 0.45 (just under medium).

Critical consideration of emotional intelligence theory and research

There are a number of concerns regarding emotional intelligence. One of the first concerns is aimed directly at the mixed models of emotional intelligence. Eysenck (2000) described some of the tendency to mix aspects of intelligence with personality factors as an unscientific approach. Say, for example, that a mixed model of emotional intelligence is found to predict an aspect of work performance. Eysenck suggests that when it comes to understanding this finding, we will be unclear about what is predicting the job performance; that is, is it an aspect of emotional intelligence or is it a personality factor? Eysenck finds it hard to see how this

way forward is fruitful for psychology. However, Emmerling and Goleman (2003) argue that such an approach is fruitful. For these authors, mixed models of emotional intelligence allow the researcher to understand how a collection of behaviours come together to define high achievement in people in the workplace. He readily admits that this contrasts with Eysenck's scientific approach, but his method reflects a tradition in occupational psychology of trying to identify competencies that are found in people who achieve highly.

Findings by Melanie Schulte and her colleagues (Schulte *et al.*, 2004) provide evidence that supports Eysenck's view. To define overall ability and competence, the authors looked at the relationships between several measures of intelligence (general intelligence and verbal, quantitative and spatial abilities), the five-factor model of personality (neuroticism, extraversion, openness to experience, agreeableness and conscientiousness), overall scores on the Mayer–Salovey–Caruso Emotional Intelligence Test (a measure of ability-based emotional intelligence) and sex among 102 US college students. In defining human ability, they found that a very large amount of the variance of what can be described as ability was accounted for by general intelligence, personality factors and sex, and that the emotional intelligence measure added very little to our understanding of overall ability and competence. These findings suggest that there is some speculation about the usefulness of emotional intelligence for enhancing the understanding of human ability over and above what is already available, such as general intelligence, the five-factor model of personality and sex.

A second concern voiced by Eysenck is the problem that emotional intelligence has no benchmark by which to assess

Stop and think

Successful university students

The following is a list of 22 different intelligence skills (IQ related and emotional intelligences). On the scale of 1–10 (1 being 'not at all' and 10 being 'most definitely'), rate which intelligence you need most for being a successful university student.

Intelligence		Intelligence	
● Abstract reasoning		● Perceptual speed	
● Adaptability		● Reading comprehension	
● Emotional facilitation of thinking		● Emotional management	
● General mood		● Science knowledge	
● Interpersonal skills		● Space relations	
● Intrapersonal skills		● Spatial ability	
● Language		● Spelling	
● Mathematics		● Stress management	
● Mechanical reasoning		● Understanding and analysing emotions; employing emotional knowledge	
● Numerical ability		● Verbal reasoning	
● Perception, appraisal and expression of emotion		● Vocabulary	

In the box below, write in your seven top-scoring intelligences. Do you think this list of abilities defines a successful university student? How much are you like this student?

it. He suggests that, while intelligence has benchmarks of school grades and educational achievement, emotional intelligence has none. However, Goleman would point out that there are several benchmarks by which emotional intelligence could be judged, one of these being success in the world of work.

A third concern arises from the lack of empirical research to confirm some of the biological theories that were proposed alongside the models of emotional intelligence. Commentators such as individual difference psychologists Gerald Matthews, Moshe Zeidner and Richard Roberts have suggested that, while Goleman and Bar-On link their theories to biological aspects, there is no empirical research to support such assertions (Matthews *et al.*, 2004). Goleman has not sought to link the amygdala and the fight-or-flight response to emotional intelligence. Bar-On proposed that emotional intelligence represents a successful evolutionary adaptation to environmental stress. However, there is no evidence that supports the biological theoretical contexts into which Goleman and Bar-On place their models of emotional intelligence.

Final comments

You should now be able to outline the extent of sex differences between men and women on general intelligence and specific aspects of intelligence, particularly spatial and verbal intelligence. You should be able to describe possible biological and environmental variables that may explain sex differences in intelligence. You should also now be able to outline the major models of emotional intelligence and provide a critical consideration of theory and research in emotional intelligence.

Summary

- On measures of general intelligence (IQ), Court reviewed nearly 120 studies that had provided information on sex differences on the Raven's Progressive Matrices. He found some studies suggesting that women scored higher than men and other studies reporting that men scored higher than women. In the majority of studies, Court found there was no difference. Lynn and Irwing, however, using a meta-analysis of intelligence data taken from 57 studies in 30 countries, found that among adults, men scored on average 5 IQ points more than women.

- On measures of specific intelligence, meta-analytical studies suggest that men are better at spatial intelligence across all ages and, among adolescents, the only large effect is for mechanical reasoning. Women are better only in verbal abilities for speech quality across all ages, and they are better in spelling and language during adolescence only.

- Consideration of biological factors that may influence sex differences in intelligence include brain size, evolutionary forces, brain functioning and testosterone.

- Considerations of environmental factors that may influence sex differences in intelligence include the central role of stereotypes (in toy choice, education, subject choice, classroom interactions) and technological and socioeconomic factors.

- There are three main theories of emotional intelligence: an ability model devised by Mayer and Salovey, called the four-branch model of emotional intelligence; and two mixed ability models, Goleman's model of emotional intelligence and Bar-On's model of emotional–social intelligence.

- Together these three different theories offer two different types of models (ability versus mixed) and three different ways of measuring emotional intelligence. Two contexts can be provided to compare these three models: (1) comparing ability versus mixed models of emotional intelligence; and (2) understanding emotional intelligence in the context of a personality systems approach.

- Research evidence suggests that emotional intelligence is associated with better health, mental health, life satisfaction, happiness and sometimes with achievement in education and in the workplace.

- For sex differences in emotional intelligence based on emotional intelligence ability models, there may be a small effect size in favour of women scoring higher on emotional intelligence. However, findings for mixed models of emotional intelligence suggest no difference between men and women on general emotional intelligence; for specific aspects of emotional intelligence, each sex sometimes scores higher than the other sex – although effect sizes are usually small, except perhaps those for empathy.

- Problems with emotional intelligence theory and research include criticism that some of the approaches adopted are unscientific, there is no benchmark to be considered against and there is a lack of empirical research to support much of the theorising.

Connecting up

In this chapter we looked at some of the factors that might influence sex differences in intelligence. You may want to look back at the last chapter (Chapter 14, Heritability and Socially Defined Race Differences in Intelligence) to remind you of some of the other environmental variables that are considered to influence intelligence.

We explore the application of emotional intelligence to learning and the workplace in the next chapter.

Critical thinking

Discussion questions

- Do you think that men and women believe that they are intelligent in different ways?
- Which biological and environmental factors do you think play an important role in sex differences in intelligence?

- The ability model and the mixed models of emotional intelligence employ different strategies for defining emotional intelligence. Which do you think is best?
- Which do you think is the most useful concept – IQ or emotional intelligence?

Essay questions

- Critically examine the view that there are sex differences in intelligence.
- Discuss that view that sex differences in intelligence and emotional intelligence are over-emphasised in the literature.
- Critically examine the view that sex differences in intelligence are the result of stereotypical behaviour.
- Critically compare and contrast ability and mixed models of emotional intelligence.
- Critically compare three theoretical models of emotional intelligence.
- Critically examine how 'useful' the construct of emotional intelligence is to psychology.

Going further

Books

- Goleman, D. P. (2005). *Emotional intelligence: Why it can matter more than IQ for character, health and lifelong achievement.* New York: Bantam Books. As a general read, you might want to look at this book for a positive view of

emotional intelligence. However, it may sometimes lack a critical edge that will be needed for your academic work.
- Matthews, G., Zeidner, M. and Roberts, R. D. (2004). *Emotional intelligence: Science and myth.* London: MIT Press. This book gives a much more critical and comprehensive account of the emotional intelligence literature.

Stop and think

Discussion question: science interests split the sexes

Let us return to the BBC News Online story we discussed earlier of a sex split in science interests (**http://news.bbc .co.uk/1/hi/education/4800882.stm**, 16 March 2006). Professor Edgar Jenkins from the University of Leeds reported on the survey of 1,200 UK pupils who had taken part in a global study, based at Oslo University, looking at the relevance of science education. In this survey, pupils were asked what their favourite topics were in science. Favourite topics in science were split down by boys and girls, as shown in the table.

Report author Professor Edgar Jenkins said that the differences between the sexes could not be ignored, and

added, 'We have had a generation or more now of promoting gender equality but the differences exist and I raise the question as to whether we should teach the two sexes separately for some of the time.'

- Consider Professor Jenkins' idea for discussion; should boys and girls be taught separately in science for some of the time?
- What other strategies could be considered in the classroom to address the sex division in interests when teaching science?

Boys	Girls
• Explosive chemicals	• Why we dream and what it means
• How it feels to be weightless in space	• What we know about cancer and how to treat it
• How the atom bomb functions	• How to perform first aid
• Biological and chemical weapons	• How to exercise to keep fit
• Black holes and supernovae	• Sexually transmitted diseases and how to protect against them
• How meteors, comets or asteroids cause disasters on Earth	
• The possibility of life outside Earth	• What we know about HIV/AIDS and how to control it
• How computers work	• Life and death and the human soul
• Effect of strong electric shocks and lightning on the body	• Biological and human aspects of abortion
• Dangerous animals	• Eating disorders
	• How alcohol and tobacco might affect the body

Source: The Relevance of Science Education Project (ROSE) in England: A summary of findings, CSSME (Jenkins, E. W. and Pell, R. G. 2006).

Journals

- Mayer, J. D., Roberts, R. D. and Barsade, S. G. (2008). Human abilities: Emotional intelligence. *Annual Review of Psychology, 59,* 507–536. The *Annual Review of Psychology* is published by Annual Reviews, Palo Alto, California. Available online via Business Source Premier and PsycARTICLES.
- Landy, F. J. (2005). Some historical and scientific issues related to research on emotional intelligence. *Journal of Organizational Behavior, 26,* 411–424. The *Journal of Organizational Behavior* is published and available online via Wiley Interscience.
- Petrides, K. V., Furnham, A. and Frederickson, N. (2004). Emotional intelligence. *The Psychologist, 17,* 574–577. This article is freely available online. You can find *The Psychologist* on the British Psychological Society website (**www.bps.org.uk**).
- The journal *Emotion* ran a special issue on emotional intelligence, Issue 3 in 2001. *Emotion* is published by the American Psychological Association and is available online via PsycARTICLES.
- Now that we are coming to the end of a series of discussions about intelligence, you may want to read some conclusions on intelligence by two well-known UK individual difference researchers, Ian Deary and Adrian Furnham. The first article is Furnham, A. (2000). Thinking about intelligence. *The Psychologist, 13,* 510–515. The second is Deary, I. J. (2003). Ten things I hated about intelligence research. *The Psychologist, 16,* 534–537. They are both freely available online. You can find *The Psychologist* on the British Psychological Society website (**www.bps.org.uk**).

Articles on the intelligence issues discussed in these sections of the text are often found in these journals. Use 'intelligence' and 'emotional intelligence' as your search terms on library databases such as Web of Science and PsycINFO.

- *American Psychologist.* Published by the American Psychological Association. Available online via PsycARTICLES.
- *British Journal of Developmental Psychology.* Published by the British Psychological Society. Available online via IngentaConnect; SwetsWise.
- *Developmental Psychology.* Published by the American Psychological Association. Available online via PsycARTICLES.
- *Intelligence: A multidisciplinary journal.* Published by Elsevier. Available online via Science Direct.
- *Sex Roles: A journal of research.* Published by Kluwer. Available online via SwetsWise, or Expanded Academic ASAP.

Web links

- Emotional Intelligence Consortium (**www.eiconsortium.org**). The mission of the EI Consortium is to aid the advancement of research and practice related to emotional intelligence in organisations. The consortium has a number of articles discussing the nature of emotional intelligence.
- **John D. Mayer's Emotional Intelligence Information.** A site dedicated to communicating scientific information about emotional intelligence, including relevant aspects of emotions, cognition and personality (**www.unh.edu/emotional_intelligence**).

Film and literature

- *Pride and Prejudice* (1813, Jane Austen). This is a classic tale of love and values unfolding in the class-conscious England of the late eighteenth century. The five Bennet sisters – including strong-willed Elizabeth – have all been raised by their mother (Mrs Bennet) with one purpose in life, finding a husband. When a wealthy bachelor (Mr Darcy) takes up residence in a nearby mansion, Mrs Bennet stresses to her daughters that the only intelligent behaviour to ensure happiness and security is behaviour that leads to them making good marriages to this wealthy bachelor's friends. Adoption of this approach by Mrs Bennet and four of her daughters leads to some very silly behaviour. Mr Bennet, in contrast, is wise in his adoption of a cynical and detached ironic manner; and Elizabeth rejects the

intelligence used by her mother, preferring the intelligence of her father. Elizabeth and Mr Darcy are attracted to each other, but when Elizabeth first meets Mr Darcy she adopts her father's cynical and detached ironic manner, which causes Mr Darcy to withdraw. It is only when Elizabeth adopts both her mother's and father's intelligent approaches to life that she and Mr Darcy get together. We can see from this work that, as early as 1813, themes of what constitutes intelligent behaviour on the part of the sexes were being observed and analysed, with the suggestion that both approaches might work well together. The classic text has been made into a series of films. Recent films include

- *Pride & Prejudice* (2005, directed by Joe Wright and starring Keira Knightley) and *Bride & Prejudice* (2004, directed by Gurinder Chadha and starring Aishwarya Rai). (Watching *Bridget Jones' Diary I* and *II* does not count, as they bear no resemblance to *Pride and Prejudice* apart from Colin Firth playing a Mr Darcy in both films.)

- *Artificial Intelligence (AI)* (2001, directed by Steven Spielberg). In this futuristic fairy tale, 'David', a highly advanced robotic boy, hopes to become a real boy so that he can win back the affection of the human mother who abandoned him. The story contains themes of what attitudes and behaviour are seen as intelligent, and you might consider how emotions play a part in intelligence when watching this film.

- *Constructing the Future* (1988, Educational Resources Film, Brighton Polytechnic). Outlines the use of constructional toys in a primary school where they are used for fostering visuospatial experience, language development, social and personal development and play opportunities, early maths and design skills. Concord Video and Film Council, United Kingdom.

- *Sex Role Development* (1974, Educational Resources Film; McGraw-Hill). Questions sex roles and stereotypes in upbringing. Concord Video and Film Council, United Kingdom.

Explore the website accompanying this text at **www.pearsoned.co.uk/maltby** for further resources to help you with your studies. These include multiple-choice questions, essay questions, web links and ideas for advanced reading.

CHAPTER 16

The Application of Personality and Intelligence in Education and the Workplace: The Introduction of Other Intelligences

Key themes

- Personality and individual difference in education and work
- Learning styles
- Emotional intelligence
- Creativity
- Wisdom
- Giftedness
- Learning disabilities

Learning outcomes

At the end of this discussion you should:

- Be able to present a general overview of how a number of personality and intelligence ideas have informed our understanding of education and work
- Understand the role and values that commonly known personality and intelligence tests have in predicting education and work achievement
- Be aware of Kolb's theory of learning styles and some of its criticisms
- Know how emotional intelligence theory informs our understanding of learning
- Know how emotional intelligence theory informs our understanding of leadership
- Be familiar with theoretical descriptions and models of creativity
- Be familiar with theoretical descriptions and models of wisdom
- Be able to outline a series of models that describe giftedness
- Be able to outline a theory and programme of Structural Cognitive Modifiability

Introduction

In 1998, *Time* magazine sought to identify the greatest people of the twentieth century. In a special issue they considered great leaders, greater innovators, thinkers, scientists, artists and entertainers.

Were those who had achieved the most the greatest leaders? Or were they those who had defined and changed the political and social fabric of the world? Among those listed were Mohandas Gandhi, a political leader of India who led the struggle for Indian independence from the British Empire; Mikhail Gorbachev, leader of the Soviet Union from 1985 until 1991, whose attempts at reform led to the end of the Cold War; Franklin Delano Roosevelt, who led the United States through the Great Depression; and the Reverend Martin Luther King, the most famous leader of the American civil rights movement.

However, others were named by *Time* magazine: 'the Unknown Rebel', the anonymous man who, in a single act, became internationally famous when he was photographed standing in front of a line of tanks during the 1989 Tiananmen Square protests in China; Emmeline Pankhurst, the Victorian Englishwoman associated with her struggle for women's rights; Pablo Picasso, one of the most recognised figures in twentieth-century art; Bill Gates, successful businessman and chairman of the Microsoft Corporation; Albert Einstein, who proposed the theory of relativity and made major contributions to the development of quantum and statistical mechanics.

In the end, *Time* suggested that the person of the last century was Albert Einstein, followed by Franklin Delano Roosevelt and Mohandas Gandhi.

Of course, achieving such greatness is beyond most people's wildest dreams. But how might we achieve greatly in our lives? How might we achieve our greatest potential and show leadership qualities where they are needed?

We are going to look at some of the personality, intelligence and individual differences theories that surround education and work. We are going to take a wide view of education as it pertains not only to schools, but to the workplace – and to the environment in which you are most likely reading this book, university. We are going to draw on many of the preceding discussions, not only

the intelligence sections, and we will explore some ideas about personality and individual differences at work. However, our main focus is to concentrate on theories that suggest how to create and build success in education and the workplace. We will cover:

- Personality and intelligence predictors of achievement in education and the workplace
- How a concept called learning style has helped us to understand the way we learn
- How the concept of emotional intelligence is used in the workplace
- How psychologists have defined creativity and wisdom
- How giftedness is conceptualised by psychologists
- How individuals show leadership in education when working with those with learning disabilities.

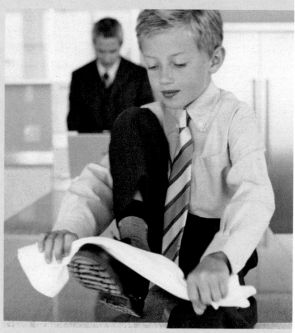

Source: Corbis/Grace/Zefa

Personality and intelligence predictors of achievement in education and the workplace

You may remember that we discussed the case of Robert Yerkes and the Alpha and Beta intelligence tests (Chapter 12). At that time, the American Psychological Association worked with the US Army to assess individuals' intelligence, thus enabling the army to classify and assign soldiers to suitable tasks. Since then, this approach – psychologically assessing people to predict not only what roles they should do but also whether they should be selected for a role – has been of interest to psychologists as well as employers, educators and governments.

Established measures of personality and intelligence: predictors of achievement in education and work

In terms of the relationship between intelligence and academic achievement, evidence suggests that general intelligence shows a strong relationship with academic achievement. Remember that, when it comes to size of correlations, a correlation of $r = 0.1$ is a small effect size, $r = 0.3$ is a medium effect size and $r = 0.5$ is a large effect size. (Go to the online statistics chapter, Chapter 27, that accompanies this book if you want to read more on effect sizes.)

There are a number of reviews by psychologists. Jencks (1979) reported correlations between general intelligence and academic achievement ranging from $r = 0.40$ to $r = 0.63$ for six longitudinal studies in the USA. American psychologists Alan Kaufman and Elizabeth Lichtenberger (Kaufman, 1990; Kaufman and Lichtenberger, 2005) provide a review of key papers that have looked at the correlation between general intelligence and school attainment and achievement. The authors conclude that the average correlation between IQ scores and a number of school indicators is around $r = 0.50$. Mackintosh (1998) estimates the correlation between general intelligence and achievement at school to be between $r = 0.4$ and $r = 0.7$.

In 2007, Ian Deary, Steve Strand, Pauline Smith and Cres Fernandes (Deary *et al.*, 2007) reported on a 5-year longitudinal study of over 70,000 English children which examined the association between general intelligence at age 11 years (as measured by the cognitive ability test) and educational achievement in national examinations in 25 academic subjects at age 16. In this study the authors used GCSE scores to measure educational attainment (this is the General Certificate of Secondary Education and is an academic qualification awarded in a specified subject and taken in a number of subjects, e.g. mathematics, English, history, by students in secondary education). Table 16.1 shows some of the correlations between general intelligence and GCSE scores across a number of subject areas.

However, authors such as Chamorro-Premuzic and Furnham (2006) have suggested that intelligence factors are not the only factors that predict academic success. Denis Bratko, Tomas Chamorro-Premuzic and Zrnka Saks' overview of the literature suggests that conscientiousness is the most consistent predictor of academic achievement (Bratko *et al.*, 2006). These researchers suggest that conscientiousness personality traits lead students to be organised, disciplined and motivated to succeed. This in turn has a positive effect on their ability to study and on the effort and commitment they put into their work. Bratko and colleagues also suggest that the relationship between the other factors of personality and achievement are less clear and less consistent. For example, Bratko *et al.* suggest

Table 16.1 Correlations between general intelligence and GCSE scores (based on Deary *et al.*, 2007)

Subject	Correlation with general intelligence ($r =$)
GCSE total points	0.69
GCSE best 8	0.72
Mathematics	0.77
Biology	0.51
Chemistry	0.46
Physics	0.50
English	0.67
English literature	0.59
History	0.63
Geography	0.65
French	0.64
German	0.61
Spanish	0.62
Drama	0.47
Art and design	0.43
Music	0.54

that, while neuroticism might cause people to perform badly in examinations because of their tendency to worry and be anxious before and during the examination, this worry and anxiety might make people work harder in the run up to the exam and therefore do much better. In a similar way, extraversion is inconsistently associated with academic achievement because extraverted people may be less worried and optimistic about examinations and therefore perform better in high-pressure situations such as examinations, or they may spend less time studying and more time doing other non-academic activities. Regardless of these speculations, it seems that conscientiousness, over the other personality factors, consistently predicts academic achievement.

Melissa O'Connor and Sampo Paunonen (O'Connor and Paunonen, 2007) carried out a meta-analysis (a technique that combines the results of several studies) of empirical studies that looked at the relationship between the five-factor model of personality and academic achievement. You will remember that the five-factor model comprises five personality dimensions (Costa and McCrae, 1992):

- openness (perceptive, sophisticated, knowledgeable, cultured, artistic, curious, analytical, liberal traits);
- conscientiousness (practical, cautious, serious, reliable, organised, careful, dependable, hardworking, ambitious traits);
- extraversion (sociable, talkative, active, spontaneous, adventurous, enthusiastic, person-oriented, assertive traits);
- agreeableness (warm, trustful, courteous, agreeable, co-operative traits);
- neuroticism (emotional, anxious, depressive, self-conscious, worrying traits).

O'Connor and Paunonen found that conscientiousness was consistently associated with academic success. The overall correlation across the studies was $r = 0.22$, with the highest correlation being reported by Furnham *et al.* (2003) as being between conscientiousness and grade point average ($r = 0.40$). They found that openness to experience was sometimes positively associated with scholastic achievement, with the highest relationship being reported by Dollinger and Orf (1991), with a correlation of $r = 0.30$ between openness and exam grade; however, the average correlation of the studies was low ($r = 0.05$). Extraversion was also sometimes negatively related to academic success, with Furnham *et al.* (2003) reporting a significant negative correlation between extraversion and grade point average, although the overall average correlation was also low ($r = -0.05$). O' Connor and Paunonen also found that very few significant relationships between academic performance and agreeableness (average correlation, $r = 0.06$) and neuroticism (average correlation, $r = 0.03$), leading to the suggestion that these personality dimensions may not be as relevant as predictors of academic achievement.

More recently, Poropat (2009) presented a meta-analysis of studies that examined the relationship between the five-factor model of personality and academic performance across studies totalling over 70,000 individuals. Poropat found that, although agreeableness, conscientiousness and openness were found to correlate significantly with academic performance, it was only conscientiousness that predicted academic performance independently of intelligence (when this was measured). Poropat (2009) also found that, when looking at individuals in tertiary education (i.e. universities), when individuals' secondary-level performance (i.e. results from secondary school) was controlled for, conscientiousness was able to predict tertiary academic performance as much as intelligence did.

In addition to these findings, some authors have found that the narrow personality traits or facets (those traits in brackets in the list of the five factors above) were sometimes stronger predictors of academic performance than the five main personality factors. For example, O'Connor and Paunonen found that facets of conscientiousness, being achievement-oriented, self-disciplined and diligent, were the best predictors of academic success. This finding suggests that the five-factor personality factors are too broad and the facets are more useful in understanding the relationship between personality and academic achievement. So, for example, compare these two statements:

- 'Conscientiousness predicts academic achievement.'
- 'Being achievement-oriented, self-disciplined and diligent predicts academic achievement.'

The second statement seems more meaningful and insightful when trying to understand why conscientiousness traits predict academic achievement.

Regarding job performance, research also suggests that intelligence is an important factor. Job performance can mean various things, but generally, US work psychologist Leaetta Hough, who served as president of the American Psychological Association Society for Industrial and Organizational Psychology, has defined several areas that indicate job performance (Hough, 1992). These include overall job performance (for example, ratings by employers, managers, the number of promotions the person has gained), poor behaviour (for example, lack of attendance at work through absence), competence, effectiveness, teamwork, creativity and effort.

In researching the area of intelligence and job performance, US psychologists John E. Hunter and R. F. Hunter (1984) provided a meta-analysis of studies that examined various predictors at the time of an interview for a job with eventual job performance. In all, the authors looked at results for over 32,000 workers. They found that the correlation between intelligence and job performance was $r = 0.54$ (a medium-sized correlation), and it shared a lot larger association with job performance than with curriculum vitae ($r = 0.37$), previous experience ($r = 0.18$) and education ($r = 0.10$). The first ever meta-analysis of this type in the United Kingdom was carried out by Cristina Bertua, Neil Anderson and Jesus F. Salgado, who looked at over 280 samples, comprising 13,262 people, and compared the scores on different intelligence measures with their job performance (Bertua *et al.*, 2005). In this study, the researchers examined several different types of jobs, including clerical, engineering, professional, managers and sales; the requirements ranged from low-skilled jobs to higher-skilled professional jobs. Bertua and her colleagues found that both general intelligence and specific ability tests were good predictors of job performance, with correlations being similar to those reported by Hunter and Hunter (between $r = 0.5$ and $r = 0.6$).

With personality measures and job performance, findings are also relatively consistent. Of the various personality measures, research suggests that the five-factor model is the most useful in understanding the relationship between personality and job performance (Hough and Oswald, 2000; Salgado, 2003). Researchers have conducted several meta-analytical studies of the relationship between personality and job performance (Hough, 1992; Robertson, 2001; Salgado, 2003). Overall, findings suggest the following three things:

- Of the five factors, conscientiousness and low neuroticism are consistently related to a number of indicators of job performance.
- Of these two factors, conscientiousness and neuroticism, conscientiousness is a better predictor of job performance.
- In meta-analyses, openness, agreeableness and extraversion are not related to job performance. They have

occasionally been related to job performance, but much less often – and not consistently (for example, extraversion is sometimes related to people in marketing).

On this last point Barrick and Mount (1991) reviewed 117 studies involving nearly 24,000 participants. These authors found that conscientiousness showed consistent positive relationships with work performance across a number of occupations, that extraversion was a good predictor for jobs involving social interaction (e.g. management and sales), and that extraversion and openness to experience were good predictors of individuals showing training proficiency.

You can see in Table 16.2 a comparison of those personality traits that consistently predict job performance and those that do not. Imagine that the traits in each column describe a different person that you are interviewing for a job. Which person would you be more likely to employ?

However, perhaps the best way to understand the relative importance of personality and intelligence is to compare the strength of different personality variables in predicting eventual job performance at the point of selection. Table 16.3 is a summary of such comparisons, based on findings from Anderson and Shackleton (1993) and Hunter and Hunter (1984). As you can see, personality and intelligence fare relatively well against various predictors of job performance.

One study that challenges the single importance of IQ on occupational status and success considers the relationship between intelligence and occupational success amongst those who are self-employed. This hypothesis is of interest because people who are self-employed will not have the same restrictions on their activities as those employed by others, and therefore the relationship between intelligence and occupational success will not be confounded by constraints of employer's practices or promotion policies (Hauser, 2010). In 2007 Robert M. Hauser (Hauser, 2007) looked at data from the Wisconsin

Table 16.3 Comparison of the strength of different variables in predicting eventual job performance at the point of selection

Assessment methods at selection	Correlation
Astrology (the study of positions and aspects of the planets and stars in the belief that they can influence the course of natural events and behaviour)	0.0
Graphology (the study of handwriting, employed as a means of analysing character)	0.0
Character references	0.13
Previous experience	0.18
Unstructured interviews	0.31
Curriculum vitae	0.37
Personality assessments	**0.38**
Intelligence	**0.54**
Samples of people's work	0.55
Structured interviews	0.62

Longitudinal Study (a long-term study of a random sample of 10,317 men and women who graduated from Wisconsin, USA high schools in 1957) and compared the effect of IQ scores and the income of self-employed women and men at the ages of 35–36 years and 53–54 years (remember, a longitudinal study will only look at a sample every few years). Hauser found that, among men at both ages and among women aged between 53 and 54 years (but not the younger age group), for each 1 point increase in IQ there was a 1.5 per cent increase in earnings. However, Hauser also found that, when educational attainment was controlled for, this relationship disappeared, suggesting that educational attainment was a key variable to income levels. Hauser's findings therefore suggest that, within this context of self-employment, there is no relationship between IQ and occupational status (as measured by income).

The difficulties with using established measures of personality and intelligence in education and work

Our European modern-day educational and workplace settings are not alight with a world of personality and intelligence theory and testing. The use of personality and intelligence in education and the workplace seems to be of limited interest to educators and employers. On one hand, they seem to be good, and relatively consistent, predictors of eventual education and job performance. However, using measures of personality and intelligence in the selection and assessment of individuals and their performance has not been enthusiastically received by people working in education and the workplace. There may be a simple explanation for this. Are intelligence tests and personality tests

Table 16.2 A comparison of those personality traits that consistently predict job performance and those that do not

Personality traits that consistently predict job performance	Personality traits that do not consistently predict job performance
Practical, cautious, serious, reliable, organised, careful, dependable, hardworking, ambitious, unemotional, not anxious, not depressive, not self-conscious, doesn't worry	Sociable, talkative, active, spontaneous, adventurous, enthusiastic, person-oriented, assertive, warm, trustful, courteous, agreeable, cooperative, perceptive, sophisticated, knowledgeable, cultured, artistic, curious, analytical, liberal

How similar are workplaces to school environments today?

expensive and time-consuming to use? Does personality and intelligence testing have a 'bad press'? For example, what would your view of intelligence testing be if you were a headteacher in a school and you knew about all the controversy over intelligence, and intelligence tests, that we have covered in the past three discussions? Or maybe intelligence and personality tests haven't had enough press. We would imagine that few employers know of the Hunter and Hunter findings of intelligence predicting job performance quite as well as they do. There are two other main, more detailed and research-based reasons for the seeming lack of enthusiasm by those working in education and the workplace:

- The relationships between personality, intelligence, education and workplace variables are not as straightforward as they first seem.
- Established measures of personality and intelligence are not a first consideration by educators and employers.

We will now consider these two points.

The relationships between personality, intelligence, education and workplace variables are not as straightforward as they first seem

There are many dimensions to both education and work. There are different subjects to be taught in school, different ways of assessing achievement, many different types of jobs in the workplace and many different types of responsibility.

Therefore, perhaps intelligence and personality variables do not provide very adaptable constructs within which to assess educational and workplace factors. Take, for example, the finding of Leaetta Hough (Hough, 1997; 1998) and UK work psychologist Ivan Robertson (Robertson, 2001), that conscientiousness (practical, cautious, serious, reliable, organised, careful, dependable, hardworking, ambitious traits) is the strongest predictor of work performance. The finding is impressive, until we consider two points suggested by Hough and Robertson:

- A person with conscientiousness personality traits is cautious and careful. Therefore, would a person with conscientiousness personality traits be best suited to a job that requires creativity and innovation?
- The world of work is constantly and rapidly changing, requiring people to be adaptable and flexible. Is a person with conscientiousness personality traits best suited to being flexible and adaptable?

You can see that, even with the most important personality predictor of work performance (conscientiousness), there is debate about its applicability across all job roles that are important in the workplace, particularly those that involve flexibility and adaptability. Consequently, as Roberston (2001) suggests, although conscientiousness and neuroticism are the consistent factors in predicting job performance, there is reason to believe that they may be redundant when considering certain types of jobs and the ever-changing world of education and the workplace.

Intellectual competence

One key development in this resurgence in intelligence is to think about the role of intelligence within a number of models in creative ways. One excellent example is the identification of intellectual competence (IC). This idea has been forwarded and led by Tomas Chamorro-Premuzic (University of London) and Adrian Furnham (University College London) to elaborate on the conventional notion of intelligence to include other determinants of future academic achievement. Chamorro-Premuzic and Furnham (2006) have defined IC as an individual's capacity to obtain and consolidate knowledge throughout the lifespan, presenting a model that unites traditional estimates of abilities (e.g. intelligence), personality traits (e.g. five-factor model of personality) and self-assessed intelligence (SAI; self-estimates of mathematical, spatial, verbal and logical and general knowledge abilities).

Research has focused on how this model can be used to elucidate the relationship between intelligence and personality in terms of predicting real life achievements, such as academic performance. For example, Chamorro-Premuzic and Arteche (2008) have found some interesting interactions among intelligence and personality predictors of academic performance among university students. For example, those higher in fluid intelligence (show greater capacity to think logically and solve problems in *novel* situations) were lower in levels of conscientiousness (i.e. lower levels of self-discipline,

carefulness and thoroughness traits) and this contributed to lower academic performance. These authors found that those higher in fluid intelligence do better in their academic performance, partly because it is linked to higher self-estimates of intelligence and higher crystallised intelligence (ability to use acquired skills, knowledge and experience). These findings open up and extend discussions about our understanding of how intelligence interacts with personality and self-estimates of ability in one's academic performance. This consideration of the dynamics that surround the model of IC has extended to the longitudinal consideration of children's academic achievement. Among a sample of 3,220 girls and 2,737 boys from the UK Twins Early Development Study examined at two time points (age 9 and 12), Chamorro-Premuzic et al. (2010) found that the effects of prior academic achievement on subsequent self-estimates of intelligence were of a similar size to previous self-estimates of intelligence on later academic achievement, independent of intelligence. These findings present interesting accounts of the relationship between perceptions of intelligence and academic achievement, and that children's accounts of their previous performance and self-efficacy (capable of performing in a certain manner to attain a certain set of goals) result from their beliefs about their own ability and have an important effect on later academic achievement.

Established measures of personality and intelligence are not a first consideration by educators and employers

Personality and intelligence measures are not a first consideration in the minds of educators and employers; there are many more important non-personality and non-intelligence factors to be considered. For example, workplaces do not base their selection on personality characteristics, but rather on factors that employees will encounter within the job. Modern-day legislation on equal opportunities in the workplace makes it a legal requirement for clear job descriptions to be written when advertising for a job. Therefore, personality and intelligence variables will not be at the forefront of any job description. For example, 'must have good communication skills' will always appear on a job description before 'must be extraverted' because the former clearly relates to a job skill, whereas the latter relates to general disposition in life. Equally, asking for someone to show they are intelligent in a job description and then giving them an intelligence test is somewhat redundant given that people outline their qualifications

on their application. If someone has a university degree, this is already an indication of their level of intelligence across a number of skills, and perhaps a better one than a 1-hour test made at an assessment centre where the person is feeling anxious and nervous. Therefore, although often used in large selection processes, measures of personality and intelligence are not usually employers' first thought when devising a job role.

Equally, in schools, using personality and intelligence tests presents difficulties. Take, for example, intelligence tests. A child of 7 takes an intelligence test, but their IQ score is kept secret from the child. This is done so that, if they have done poorly, they are not unfairly labelled as 'unintelligent' and thus discouraged from further study. Other teachers and parents aren't made aware of a child's IQ score for similar reasons; except perhaps in special circumstances, when identifying children with learning difficulties, and then teachers and parents would be made aware of a low score – although not necessarily the actual score. So, we must consider to what extent an IQ score is important to pupils, teachers and parents, when the scores are mostly kept secret.

Given these two particular considerations, we can see that within education and the workplace, personality and intelligence scores may have predictive strength; however, in the context of modern education and workplaces, there is little opportunity for teachers or employers to use this information. Despite the strength of personality and intelligence tests in predicting aspects such as job performance, it is easy to see why employers and educators may not consider the tests as central to the process of education and work.

So, what role does personality and intelligence research play in the modern workplace? In the remainder of this discussion, we are going to look at some personality, intelligence and individual differences theories and practices that have been met with more enthusiasm and interest in places of education and the workplace. To some extent, in considering these theories, we are now asking you to see a direct link between education and work. In today's society, experiences in education (for example, school and university) and work are similar. Many skills that are learnt at school or university are designed to prepare you for adulthood and the workplace. Further, more and more workplaces encourage additional education of their staff members through staff development programmes.

The particular theories and practices that we are going to focus on concentrate on successful learning, leadership and self-development in education and work. You will see what we mean by each of these concepts as we go through the discussion, but here it is worth pointing out a couple of things:

- These theories tend to concentrate on developing skills among individuals once they are in education and the workplace, rather than on selecting and assessing people and their potential. Therefore, the emphasis is on improvement rather than assessment.
- When we use the term 'leadership', we mean it in a very wide sense. Today, leadership is not just considered in the context of leading a company, organisation or political party. Rather, modern ideas of leadership extend from these traditional ideas of leadership to everyday situations: for example, a teacher showing leadership quality to their class by demonstrating the importance of patience, a parent showing leadership qualities to their child by being responsible or an adolescent showing a leadership quality among their friends by displaying strength of character.

In the rest of the discussion we are going to introduce you to these topics:

- Kolb's learning styles model and experiential learning theory;
- emotional intelligence, self-directed learning and leadership;

- developing successful intelligences: creativity and wisdom;
- theories of giftedness;
- working with those with learning disabilities.

Learning styles and experiential learning theory

In the 1970s US educational psychologist David A. Kolb introduced the concept of learning styles within his experiential learning theory (Kolb and Fry, 1975; see also Kolb, 1984). Kolb's theory uses ideas from some theorists that we have already covered in this text, including Jung, Rogers, Guilford and Gardner. The important aspects to Kolb's theory are learning processes and learning styles.

Learning processes

In his **experiential learning theory** (ELT), which emphasises learning relating to or derived from experience, David Kolb (1981) suggests there are four main aspects in learning:

- **Concrete experience (also known as *feeling*)** – occurs when we learn through being involved in a new experience. For example, we might learn how to use a *new* word processing package on the computer by loading it up and playing around with it.
- **Reflective observation (also known as *watching*)** – occurs when we learn through thinking about our own experiences, or watching others, or learning from the experiences of others. For example, where we watch someone using the new word processing package and learn how to use the package by watching what they do.
- **Abstract conceptualisation (also known as *thinking*)** – occurs when we learn by creating theories to explain our observations and behaviours. For example, we might have been using the new word processing package for a little while, seeing what it can do, and come to realise it is pretty much like all the other word processing packages we have used. The idea that our new word processing package is pretty much like all the other word processing packages would be our theory.
- **Active experimentation (also known as *doing*)** – occurs when we learn by using theories to solve problems and make decisions. For example, we want to know how to do something on our new word processing package. We don't know how to do it, but our theory is that the new word processing package is pretty much like all the other word processing packages we have used. So, what we would do is hunt around until we find the operation or button that allows us to do what we want to do.

Kolb saw these four aspects of learning as a learning cycle (Figure 16.1). He suggested that the best learning experience occurs when you move from one aspect to another. Therefore, concrete experience is best followed by observation and reflection, which then leads to abstract conceptualisation, which then leads to active experimentation and then back to concrete experience to form a continuous cycle.

Learning styles

Using these four descriptions of learning processes, Kolb identified individual differences in the way we prefer to learn. Kolb identified four learning styles: diverging, assimilating, converging and accommodating. Each learning style was made up of a combination of two of the learning processes described earlier and is best illustrated by the following matrix (Figure 16.2).

Kolb suggested the following four learning styles:

- **Accommodating** – this learning style combines the concrete experience and active experimentation learning processes, or *feeling* and *doing*. People who use an accommodating learning style (accommodators) tend to prefer to take a practical, hands-on approach. They will take risks, enjoy new experiences and work well in a role requiring action and initiative. An accommodator would work well in sales or marketing, as they go out and actively sell other people's products or information.
- **Diverging** – this learning style combines the concrete experience and observations and reflection learning processes, or *feeling* and *watching*. Divergers (as they are known) are people who are able to examine things from several different perspectives. They work best when they are watching situations and gathering information; then they use this information to generate

ideas and suggest solutions to problems. They are emotional, creative and enjoy working with people. Divergers are best when working in groups and excel in brainstorming situations. A diverger would work well in counselling.

- **Converging** – this learning style combines the active experimentation and abstract conceptualisation learning processes, or *doing* and *thinking*. Convergers are problem-solvers who are interested in solving practical issues. Convergers do well at applying ideas and theories to practical situations and coming up with answers. They tend not to be emotional and prefer working with 'things' rather than other people. Convergers would work well in physics or areas using mathematics.
- **Assimilating** – this learning style combines the observation and reflection and abstract conceptualisation learning processes, or *watching* and *thinking*. Assimilators prefer a logical approach and prefer concepts over emotion. They are able to understand a lot of information and organise and integrate it into a logical format. They enjoy theorising rather than practical application. Assimilators work well in areas where things are planned, such as political or social policy.

Figure 16.3 shows Kolb's four learning processes, presented as a cycle with his learning styles displayed on the outside.

Application and measurement of learning processes and styles

Kolb suggested that successful learning comes from engaging in all four learning processes. He felt that this would help individuals to develop different learning styles.

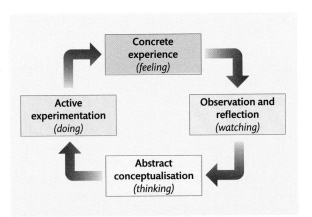

Figure 16.1 Kolb's four learning aspects, presented in a cycle.

	Active experimentation (doing)	Observation and reflection (watching)
Concrete experience (feeling)	Accommodating	Diverging
Abstract conceptualisation (thinking)	Converging	Assimilating

Figure 16.2 Four types of learning styles: diverging, assimilating, converging and accommodating - based on combinations of learning processes.

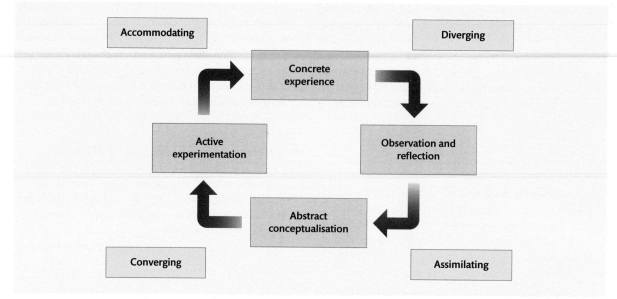

Figure 16.3 Kolb's four learning processes, presented as a cycle, with his learning styles displayed on the outside.

Kolb's work has been used extensively in schools and the workplace, because it clearly addresses the way that people learn and work together. It is suggested that the ideal teaching situation, such as a lecture at university, involves all the learning processes; the lecture not only visits the full learning cycle but also captures the whole audience through using all the learning processes. You can also see the advantage for employers in assessing people for their learning styles to see whether they fit the demands of the job. For example, there would be no use, according to Kolb's theory, in placing a person who has an assimilating learning style (someone who is logical and lacks emotion) into a counselling role.

Kolb argued that people sometimes rely too heavily on one learning style and don't look to develop their other learning processes or styles. Donna Smith and David Kolb (Smith and Kolb, 1986) have suggested that we might rely too heavily on a particular learning style for these reasons:

- **Personality** – a person who is high in extraversion may be drawn to those learning styles that emphasise action (accommodating) or working with people (diverging).
- **Schooling** – at school people learn to learn in different ways, and your learning styles may depend on the teaching approach used at that school.
- **Current job or task** – your current job demands may lead you towards a certain learning style. For example, if you are a physicist you may have to rely on the converging or assimilating learning style.

Profile

David A. Kolb

US educational theorist David A. Kolb was born in 1939. He received his BA from Knox College in 1961, his MA from Harvard in 1964 and his PhD in Social Psychology from Harvard in 1967. Since 1976 he has worked at Case Western Reserve University, where today he is in the Weatheread School of Management.

He has received four honorary degrees and several awards (including two by the Council for Adult and Experiential Learning), worked on the editorial board of five occupational and educational journals and has published nearly 100 books, book chapters and journal articles. Besides his work on experiential learning and learning styles Kolb writes on thinking around organisational behaviour, conversational learning and innovation in professional education.

Kolb's 12-item Learning Style Inventory (Smith and Kolb, 1986) is used to measure learning style, and is now in its third version (Kolb Learning Style Inventory – Version 3.1 [LSI3.1]). This scale quite simply asks people for their preferred way of learning. Respondents are asked to answer very simple forced-choice questions. For example, here is an item from the Learning Style Inventory. Respondents are asked to choose the description that best suits them.

When I learn:

As you can see, these questions measure Kolb's learning processes. Then, individuals' scores on each learning dimension are used to categorise them into a particular learning style (either diverging, assimilating, converging or accommodating).

Critical consideration of Kolb's theory

UK educationalist James Atherton (Atherton, 2002) suggests that Kolb's theory has produced one of the most useful models of learning because it gives tutors a way to ensure that teaching and learning are effective. Other commentators, such as UK educationalist Peter Jarvis (Jarvis, 1995), have suggested that Kolb's theory has had an important impact on educational and work theory and practice because it emphasises the learner, not just the instructor, as important in the learning process.

However, there are some criticisms of Kolb's theory and approach. For example, educationalist Alan Rogers (Rogers, 1996) suggests that the theory is too narrow. It does not account for many factors in an individual's learning, such as their goals, their purpose for learning, their intentions and whether they are in fact learning. Jarvis also suggests that Kolb's theory suffers because it doesn't take account of culture or particular conditions that surround teaching. Furthermore, empirical support, by way of research studies supporting the model, is weak (Jarvis, 1995; Tennant, 1997).

Emotional intelligence in education and the workplace

Earlier in the text (Chapter 15) we mentioned Daniel Goleman's theory of emotional intelligence. As you may not have studied this, or may need a reminder on it, we will briefly summarise the main elements of the theory here and then discuss the application of emotional intelligence to education and the workplace. (However, if you want more detail, we suggest you go back to Chapter 15. Please note that we detail a number of studies looking at the relationship between emotional intelligence and achievement in education and workplace in that chapter as well.)

Goleman's theory of emotional intelligence

Goleman's theory of emotional intelligence (Goleman, 2001; Goleman *et al.*, 2002) comprises four elements:

- **Self-awareness** – the ability to identify one's own emotional states.
- **Self-regulation/management** – the ability to manage one's own emotional states.
- **Social awareness** – the ability to assess and influence others' emotions.
- **Social skills/management** – the ability to sustain good interpersonal relationships.

Goleman made two distinctions between these four emotional intelligences.

- The first distinction is between *personal* and *social* competencies. The first two aspects, self-awareness and self-regulation, are personal competencies, while social awareness and social skills are social competencies.
- The second distinction is between *recognition* and *regulation*. Self-awareness and social awareness are emotional intelligences that are defined by recognition (the ability to identify one's own emotional state and those of others). Self-regulation and social skills are emotional intelligences that are defined by regulation (the ability to manage one's own emotional states and good personal relationships).

In this section we are going to give you two examples of how this model has been used in education and the workplace. The first is in leadership; the second is in self-learning.

Emotional intelligence and leadership

Goleman *et al.* (2002) used Goleman's model of emotional intelligence and the distinctions between personal/social and recognition/regulation competencies to show how the model could be shown in leadership skills. In all, Goleman *et al.* suggested that a good leader in the workplace would show the emotional intelligences listed in Table 16.4.

Table 16.4   Emotional intelligence in leadership

	Personal competencies	Social competencies
Recognition	**Self-awareness** ● Assessing and recognising one's own emotions ● Accurately knowing one's strengths and limitations ● Having self-confidence	**Social awareness** ● Understanding and taking an interest in others ● Recognising and meeting people's needs ● Showing an awareness of relationships within the workplace
Regulation/management	**Self-regulation/management** ● Adaptability and flexibility in dealing with situations that change ● Ability to control emotions when working with people ● Active, emphasises achievement, strives to do better, is trustworthy, has integrity and is optimistic in the workplace	**Social skills/management** ● Able to provide guidance to people ● Helps others improve their performance ● Inspiring to others ● Initiates change ● Able to resolve conflict ● Builds relationships within the organisation ● Encourages teamwork

Source: Based on Goleman *et al.* (2002).

Much of Goleman's research is making the world of work aware of the importance of emotional intelligence. One particular area that Goleman emphasises is in developing and encouraging the heads of organisations to develop emotional intelligence competencies.

Emotional intelligence and self-learning

However, Goleman's theory of emotional intelligence does not just lend itself to leadership of companies. Recently, theory and practice suggests that emotional intelligence ideas can be extended throughout the workplace and used to encourage us all to adopt leadership qualities.

A central figure in this development is US psychologist Richard E. Boyatzis, who, alongside others, including Daniel Goleman and the aforementioned David Kolb, developed a programme that guides individuals in the workplace through a process of self-discovery. This process is called self-directed learning (Boyatzis, 1994; Boyatzis *et al.*, 1995; Goleman *et al.*, 2002).

There are five aspects to Boyatzis' theory of self-directed learning (outlined in Figure 16.4):

● a consideration of an 'ideal self';
● a consideration of the real self and how this relates to the ideal self;

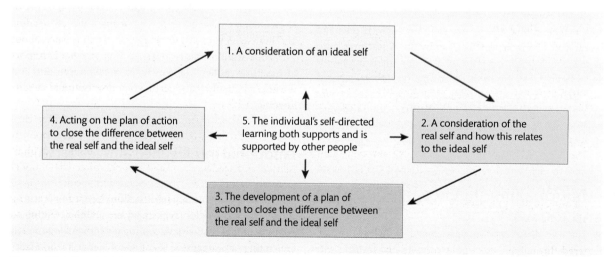

Figure 16.4   Boyatzis' theory of self-directed learning.

- the development of a learning plan designed to close the difference between the real self and the ideal self;
- acting on the learning plan to close the difference between the real self and the ideal self;
- the individual's self-directed learning both supports and is supported by other people.

Boyatzis and his colleague Ellen Van Oosten (2002) suggest that you can build emotionally intelligent workplaces based on this theory, and suggest that the five aspects of the self-learning theory represent five 'discoveries'. We will now outline these five discoveries so you can see how self-learning theory could be used.

- The first discovery is the discovery of the employee's 'ideal self'. The employee would consider who they want to be and what they want from work and life – for example, what their aspirations are.
- The second discovery is the discovery of one's 'real self'. Here, the individual would use Goleman's measure of emotional intelligence, the Emotional Competence Inventory. The Emotional Competence Inventory is a 360-degree instrument with which other people (for example, a manager or a colleague) evaluate the individuals within an organisation. The evaluator is asked to rate the person based on how characteristic the person is of the abilities listed in the emotional intelligence model. Example statements for rating the individual would include 'Presents self in an assured, forceful, impressive, and unhesitating manner'; 'Respects, treats with courtesy, and relates well to people of diverse backgrounds'; 'Accurately reads people's moods, feelings or nonverbal cues'. Then the individual, with the evaluator, examines differences and overlaps between the person's concept of their ideal self (who they want to be) and their real self (what they have achieved).
- The third discovery is the development of a learning plan. This plan sets out the focus for the person's development. Each plan is centred on all of the individual's needs, including their job, their learning style preferences, their flexibility, their aspirations and the structure of their work and lifestyle. In all, this plan focuses on building on the person's strengths so they can close the gap between the real self and the ideal self.
- The fourth discovery is the discovery of new behaviour, new thoughts and new feelings when carrying out the learning plan. By acting on the learning plan and experimenting in new practices, the individual will learn more about their self.
- The fifth discovery is the process of discovery encountered throughout the whole exercise. In working with someone else in the workplace, by engaging in reflection

and in new behaviours, the employees are engaging in a process that will lead to the workplace becoming a better place.

Consideration of emotional intelligence in education and the workplace

Using emotional intelligence in understanding leadership and the self-directed model has had some success in education and workplace settings. Goleman (1998) argued that numerous studies have shown that successful and effective leaders use emotional intelligence more than others in leadership positions (Goleman, 1998). Goleman et al. (2002) have shown how promoting emotional intelligence using the self-directed learning model has been useful among postgraduate business and management students.

We have already covered many of the criticisms of emotional intelligence (Chapter 15). The criticisms of emotional intelligence models in education and the workplace discussed here echo much of what has already been discussed.

The first concern is directed at the fact that Goleman's model of emotional intelligence is a mixed model of emotional intelligence (those models that mix emotional intelligence and personality variables). Eysenck (2000) described the tendency to mix aspects of intelligence with personality factors as an unscientific approach. That is, if a mixed model of emotional intelligence is being applied to work and learning situations, we will never be sure whether the key variables in the development of leadership and self-learning are personality or emotional intelligence. Without such a distinction, this approach can be considered as rather unscientific. However, Goleman points out that there is a priority in work and occupational psychology to identify, and encourage, the sort of competencies that are found in people who are leaders and high achievers without being overly concerned about the true nature of these variables. That is, what is important is knowing that these concepts work, not finding out whether they are truly personality or emotional intelligence variables.

A second concern arises from the lack of empirical research or comparison surrounding these self-development programmes. While it is true that the emotional intelligence and leadership – and the self-directed – model have had some success, there has been little comparison of these models with other emotional intelligence or learning models. For example, reviewing your abilities, talking to someone about that review, coming up with an action plan and acting on it occurs in most education and workplaces today. What is different about Goleman's and Boyatzis' work

Stop and think

Learning processes, learning strategies and emotional intelligences

Here are three brief descriptions of three different job advertisements. Assess which learning processes, learning strategies and emotional intelligences are required for each job.

Vacancy 1: Project manager in a multinational organisation

The External Relations team requires an experienced and enthusiastic professional to develop and implement communications projects. With a minimum of 2 years' communications experience, you will be a highly effective project manager with the ability to forge strong links internally and externally. You will be an excellent written and verbal communicator and have the ability to work to tight deadlines.

Vacancy 2: Data archivist in a physics lab

We are looking for an outstanding individual to manage the extensive data acquisition, storage and archiving systems on our computer system and to ensure that

they are maintained and upgraded to meet the growing demands of this world-class science facility. Job requirements:

- Take responsibility for the operation, use, access and security of online data store and upgrade the system as required.
- Predict computational and hardware requirements to capture, process and analyse data arising from future enhancements for the evolution of the data acquisition and storage systems.

Vacancy 3: Psychometric tester

Your major role in this post is to undertake the psychometric testing of children. You will also be providing sessional nursing support in each of the participating centres. You will be highly organised and have excellent communication skills. Previous experience in using developmental psychological tests and research experience is an advantage.

is that they emphasise emotional intelligence. However, the extent to which emotional intelligence provides a better framework over other development programmes that use a similar methodology but emphasise different abilities has not been examined. For example, would a self-directed learning model that emphasises extraversion traits, rather than emotional intelligence, work just as well? Such an examination is hard to test because businesses and

teaching establishments do not have the time or the inclination to test and compare the success of different models amongst their workforce and students. Rather, they want something that improves their workforce. On the face of it, programmes using Goleman's emotional intelligence models and Boyatzis' theory of self-directed learning suggest that emotional intelligence programmes seem to do this (Goleman, 1998; Goleman *et al.*, 2002).

Career focus: Working in occupational psychology

According to the British Psychological Society website, occupational psychologists are primarily concerned with how individuals, groups at work and organisations behave and perform. One of the key aims of an occupational psychologist is to improve individuals' satisfaction at work and organisations' effectiveness. The roles of the occupational psychologist can differ. In some cases they may be resident in an organisation, working

with that organisation's employees in a number of capacities such as personnel selection, appraisals, personal development and training. Often you find occupational psychologists working in a consultancy role, where they come into an organisation and work on a particular area of organisational development; for example, advising on new training programmes or changes to the organisation.

Professor Ivan Robertson, Managing Director of Robertson Cooper Ltd and Professor of Organisational Psychology, Leeds University Business School

1. **How/why did you choose to pursue the area of occupational psychology?**

   After I completed my bachelor's degree in psychology (the late 1960s . . . and, yes, I can remember them), it was very easy to get employment so I sampled a range of occupational areas for a few years. This experience got me interested in understanding how psychology could contribute to improving people's experience of work, so I returned to university to study for a PhD.

2. **In what way do the skills and/or knowledge you learned when studying personality and individual differences apply to your work/research today?**

   People's behaviour at work is heavily influenced by their personality, and understanding how personality can be described and assessed is an essential part of an occupational psychologist's skill set. My current research and the commercial work of the company relies heavily on personality measurement and theory. We have developed a five-factor model personality questionnaire and use this to generate one of our key products – leadership impact. This provides a report to managers on the likely impact that their personal approach could have on the performance and well-being of their work group.

For further advice on becoming an occupational psychologist, including guidance on the necessary qualifications and experience, visit the British Psychological Society website at **http://www.bps.org.uk/careers-education-training/ how-become-psychologist/types-psychologists/becoming-occupational-psychol**.

Successful intelligence and leadership: creativity, intelligence and wisdom

In the last section we began to look at emotional intelligence and the concept of leadership. Much of this work has occurred in the workplace and some in universities. However, other intelligence theorists have emphasised the notion of encouraging leadership qualities throughout education.

Robert Sternberg (Sternberg, 2003; 2005) introduced a model of positive leadership called wisdom, intelligence and creativity, synthesised (WICS). In the WICS model, Sternberg argues that positive leadership can be developed from a set of attributes that we can all consciously develop. This means that they don't simply reflect some sort of natural ability or disposition, but rather that we control them and can learn them.

We will introduce you to wisdom and creativity synthesised in a moment. However, the second part of the WICS model, intelligence, has already been discussed extensively as part of Sternberg's triarchic theory of intelligence (Chapter 12). To summarise, you will remember that in his model of intelligence Sternberg suggested three elements:

- The componential subtheory, sometimes referred to as internal aspects of intelligence. This subtheory refers to the mental mechanisms that underlie intelligent behaviour.
- The contextual subtheory, sometimes referred to as external aspects of intelligence. This subtheory describes how mental mechanisms interact with the external world to demonstrate intelligent behaviour.
- The experiential subtheory relates to aspects of experience and was referred to as creative intelligence. This subtheory describes how experience interacts with the internal and the external world to form intelligence behaviours.

We are now going to concentrate on the other two elements of the WICS – creativity and wisdom.

Creativity

Psychologists have studied creativity from a number of psychological perspectives. Although not directly linked to education or the workplace, we feel it is worth digressing a little and spending some time outlining some of the main theories of creativity, before outlining a theory of creativity that is directly focused on leadership, because it: (1) provides you with some of the main theory and findings in

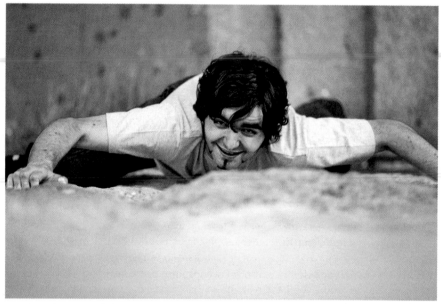

Sometimes creative behaviour comes from a willingness to surmount difficult obstacles.
Source: Alamy Images/Christoph & Friends/Das Fotoarchiv

the creativity literature; and (2) shows you some examples about how creativity is linked to intelligence theory.

The most worthwhile distinctions in individual differences were made by Rhodes (1961/1987) and were later used in a review of the area by Runco (2004), who suggested four different approaches in the study of creativity: namely the 4 Ps: person, process, press and product. The use of person, process, press and product by Rhodes is a way of conceptualising all studies on creativity. We will now briefly describe each category and give you examples of theory and research which fall under each category.

Person

The *person* category of creativity includes theory and research that concentrates on the personal characteristics of the person; for example, a theory or research that looked at the motivation or particular traits as core characteristics of creative persons.

In terms of motivations that underlie creativity, good examples would be psychoanalytic theory or the work of Maslow. Within psychoanalytic thought it is suggested that creativity results from successful sublimation (a defence mechanism [see Chapters 2 and 3] which converts unconscious desires into constructive behaviours) of instinctual demands (Freud, A., 1966). Also, Maslow, whose hierarchy of needs we covered previously (Chapter 6 previously), defined two aspects of creativity (Maslow, 1967): **primary creativity**, creativity involved in the person finding self-fulfilment (for example, painting a picture); and **secondary creativity**, those aspects of creativity that allow the person to be recognised in their chosen field (for example, putting on an art exhibition). So, for example, Maslow's primary

creativity, in which the person finds self-fulfilment, would fall under the person category as a motivation.

In terms of personality, research has looked at the personality traits that creative individuals typically possess by looking at a number of creative domains, such as art, literature and music. This has led to the development of traits measures such as the composite creative personality scale (Harrington, 1972; 1975). In measures like these a number of traits would be listed that defined creativity, such as: active, artistic, assertive, clear thinking, clever, curious, demanding, enthusiastic, idealistic, imaginative, independent, insightful, inventive, original. Today the measurement of creativity can be found on the International Personality Item Pool (IPIP; Goldberg *et al.*, 2006; **http://ipip.ori.org/ipip/**). One scale on the site that measures creativity contains the following items:

- have a vivid imagination;
- am full of ideas;
- love to think up new ways of doing things;
- have excellent ideas.

Process

The *process* category focuses on the thought, actions and behaviours that underpin the creative process. For example, how does an individual come up with ideas? Theory and research in the process category typically look at cognitive processes.

In terms of formal theories of creativity that describe the process of creativity, one of the first to be published was by Graham Wallas (Wallas, 1926). In this model Wallas described creativity as a process comprising five stages arising when a problem is presented.

1 *Preparation*: here the individual focuses first on the problem, explores the parameters of the problem and prepares to work on the problem.
2 *Incubation*: here the individual internalises the problem into their unconscious.
3 *Intimation*: here the person begins to 'feel' a solution to the problem.
4 *Illumination or insight*: here the creativity emerges from the unconscious into conscious awareness.
5 *Verification*: this is where the idea is present in the person's consciousness, and they start thinking about the creative idea and apply it.

Another theory that describes the process to creativity is perhaps one of the most influential in the literature on creativity. Guilford (1967), an intelligence theorist discussed earlier (Chapter 12), worked in the area of creativity and made the distinction between convergent and divergent production, which has been later recognised as convergent and divergent thinking. Convergent thinking is when an individual tries to develop a single and correct solution to a problem. Divergent thinking is a thought process that involves the generation of ideas to a problem. So examples of divergent thinking include being able to brainstorm, breaking problems into parts, showing great thinking, understanding causality, identifying importance with topics and being able to appreciate known and unknown qualities. For many psychologists, divergent thinking is the best example of creativity (Glazer, 2009).

Other more recent models include Finke *et al.*'s (1992) 'Geneplore' model, in which creativity comprises two phases:

- a *generative phase*: this is where the individual constructs mental representations regarding being creative that are called preinventive structures; and
- an *exploratory phase*, where the preinventive structures are used to come up with creative ideas.

Press

The *press* category focuses on the relationship between the creative individual and their environment. Press refers to the *pressures* on the creative process or on creative persons. Therefore this category considers environmental influences such as cultural, organisational or family or peer pressures. For example, are the individual's friends creative and influence the person to be creative? Or does being creative result from the state of interpersonal relationships, e.g. being in love or a relationship breaking up? (Runco, 2004). This category originates from the work of Murray *et al.* (1938), who distinguished between alpha and beta pressures. Alpha pressures are pressures that are obvious and measurable to all and are therefore objective (it might be time allowed to be creative, e.g. 1 week to create something). Beta pressures are the individual's own interpretation of the pressure (i.e. some people might feel that 1 week is not enough time to be creative, while others will see 1 week as ample time to be creative).

A list of situational influences has been developed by a number of authors (Amabile and Gryskiewicz, 1989; Witt and Beorkrem, 1989; Runco, 2004). This list is usually broken down into those situational influences that promote creativity and those situational influences that inhibit (restrict) creativity.

Those situational influences that promote creativity include:

- freedom
- autonomy
- good role models and resources (e.g. funding, time)
- encouragement that specifically focuses on creativity
- freedom from criticism
- environments in which creativity is rewarded and failure at being creative is not fatal.

Those situational influences that inhibit creativity include:

- lack of respect (specifically when related to creativity)
- red tape (excessive regulation or rigid conformity to formal rules within the environment)
- lack of freedom, autonomy and resources
- environments in which creativity is not rewarded or discouraged
- negative feedback
- time pressures
- competition
- unrealistic expectations.

One interesting series of studies highlighted by Runco is the work of Mednick (1962) and Gruber (1981; 1988). Mednick highlighted the importance of time to creativity. He argued that original ideas are often very distant and apart from the original problems or an initial creative idea, and that to arrive at an idea took time as the person moves from a first idea to the final creative idea. Research confirms this view of the influence of time on creativity. Rather than creativity comprising a 'lightbulb' moment when the idea suddenly emerges, the person needs to devote time to thinking and coming up with ideas, and even spending time away from thinking about the problem is important to creativity (Gruber, 1981; 1988).

Product

The *product* category focuses on outcomes or results of the creative process. So this might be studies of decisions made or ideas by the creative person or it may be publications, art or writing of the creative person. Often the study of eminent persons (e.g. great artists or thinkers) is a large feature within this category.

There is a wealth of literature that looks at the study of eminent persons and creativity. In the book *Genius and the Mind*, Andrew Steptoe examines the lives and works of several eminent individuals and examines how their creativity emerged (Steptoe, 1998). In this book Steptoe explores Mozart's precocity (early development or maturity), Byron's mania (excessively intense enthusiasm) and Shakespeare's literary brilliance and examines them as explanations of creativity. Another example of the study of eminent persons was carried out by Diamond *et al.* (1985), who examined the brain of Albert Einstein (German-born theoretical physicist who made many contributions to physics, including his special theory of relativity). Diamond and his colleagues examined the brain of Albert Einstein and found there was a significantly smaller ratio of neuron cells (nerve cells that transmit nerve signals to and from the brain) to glial cells (cells that provide support, nutrition and protection for neurons, known as the glue of the nervous system) compared to other 'control' scientists. Diamond *et al.* argued that this implied that Einstein's cortex (the structure within the brain that plays a key role in memory, attention, perceptual awareness, thought, language and consciousness) may have had a different 'metabolic need' (a higher need for chemical reactions that occur in living organisms to maintain life) and that this produced greater levels of creativity from associative thinking and the development of new concepts.

A more recent example of this type of study was carried out by Caroline Murphy (2009), who looked at the link between artistic creativity and psychopathology in the work of Salvador Dalí (a surrealist artist who was renowned for his outlandish art and persona). Murphy looked at Dalí's behaviour and art from various sources, including his autobiography, published interviews with himself, friends and family and information on his family history. Using such data, Murphy used two psychiatric assessment procedures: a computer program investigating the presence of psychotic disorder and a personality disorder questionnaire. On these assessment criteria Murphy found that Dalí met the diagnostic criteria for several personality disorders (personality styles which deviate from expectations of one's own society), as well as for psychotic illnesses. For more on the creativity and psychopathology debate, see the Stop and think box later in this discussion (Creativity, giftedness and 'psychopathology').

Clearly the extent to which these different theories of creativity are associated with education and the workplace varies. In the next section we are going to go into the detail of Sternberg's model of creativity because he sets creative leadership within the modern context of intelligence theory and education and the workplace.

Sternberg's creative leadership theory: what constitutes creativity?

Sternberg argues that creativity is not limited only to great thinkers and artists, but is an ability anyone can have, develop and use. Sternberg (2005) defines creative leadership as being any of the following (see Figure 16.5):

Figure 16.5 Sternberg's examples of different types of creativity.
Source: Based on Sternberg (2005).

- **Redefining problems** – this is the ability to take a problem and not just look at it from all angles but also to 'turn it on its head'. Poetry and art are good examples of this. For example, in poetry, people use meaning and what they know to create new situations and descriptions; phrases such as 'falling snow bouncing on the ground' and 'lions gathering to speak about economics' are creative. Snow doesn't bounce, nor do lions speak about economics, but these phrases inject imagery to help us describe what is happening as well as how it is occurring. Perhaps it was a particularly strong flurry of snow, or the lions that gathered did so in a particularly organised and intense way.

- **Questioning and analysing assumptions** – creativity can emerge from individuals questioning assumptions and then leading others to question those assumptions. Sternberg uses the example of Nicolaus Copernicus, an astrologer, astronomer and mathematician, who went against the thinking that the Earth was at the centre of the universe and discovered that in fact it is the Earth, as well as other planets, that go around the sun.

- **Realising that creative ideas do not sell themselves** – it is perhaps not good enough to be creative with your ideas; you also need to sell them. You may be a talented songwriter or politically brilliant, but you must also convince others that your ideas are good. If you are a songwriter, you must try selling yourself, touring, working on your self-image and approaching people in the industry. Equally, you may have great political ideas; however, if you confine your views to the pub or dinner parties, then you are not going to become known for your political thinking.

- **Realising that knowledge is a double-edged sword** – all creativity is built on knowledge. For example, you cannot come up with the theory about the Earth revolving around the sun (as opposed to the other way round) unless you understand the laws of astrology, astronomy and mathematics. However, Sternberg also notes that having a lot of knowledge may blind you to certain ways of thinking, particularly creative ideas. Many experts in a field may prefer certain ideas because they are so used to them. However, this may cause them to reject new and creative ideas because they feel that they know all there is to know about the area. Therefore, creativity stems both from having knowledge and from not thinking you know it all.

- **Willingness to surmount obstacles** – Sternberg suggests that people who are creative often meet resistance to their ideas. Either they are ignored or laughed at. Creative leadership, then, is the ability to continue believing in your ideas, even when others ignore or laugh at them.

- **Willingness to take sensible risks** – often in this world, the tendency is to do whatever everyone else is doing to succeed; for example, to do what one is told to do. However, eventually, creative leadership demands that the person comes up with new ideas. Creative ideas needn't have a large amount of risk or be outlandish, but to some extent they must have a degree of risk that other people admire and respect, constructively building on what is known or thought.

- **Tolerance of ambiguity** – we can all be uncomfortable with ambiguity, which occurs in situations where there is doubt or uncertainty. We like to know things for certain. We don't like to be faced with moral ambiguity; we like the idea that certain acts of crime will be punished appropriately and equally (we would not agree with the proposal that some people should be punished for a crime while others go unpunished). However, the world is full of ambiguity, and creative leaders are able to deal well with it.

- **Willingness to grow** – creative leadership is not just about having one or two good ideas; it is about continually coming up with new ideas and conquering new challenges over a lifetime.

- **Self-efficacy** – an individual's personal judgement of their own ability to succeed in reaching a specific goal is the trait of self-efficacy. Creative leadership requires the person to believe that they can be creative, and to believe in what they are creating.

- **Finding what one loves to do** – for a person to be a creative leader, they must find what they love to do. Sternberg suggests that the best creative leaders excel in what they do because it is what they enjoy most in the world.

- **Willingness to delay gratification** – being creative doesn't bring immediate rewards. There will often be a certain amount of time between someone coming up with a new idea, a new product or strategy and people eventually accepting it. Therefore, being creative does not bring immediate rewards; creativity demands some patience.

- **Courage** – finally, being creative means going against what is accepted and can be unpopular. Therefore, to be creative sometimes takes a certain amount of courage.

How does creativity occur? The 5 'r's and the 1 'f'

Sternberg suggests that it is important for teachers, educators and workplaces to allow creativity to encourage creative leadership. To do this, there is the need to recognise the different types of settings that allow the encouragement of creative leadership. Sternberg suggests there are three such settings: creative leadership that: (1) accepts current paradigms; (2) rejects current paradigms; and (3) integrates current paradigms.

Types of creative leadership that accept current paradigms

Types of creative leadership that accept current paradigms are those that accept current assumptions, concepts, values and practices. Sternberg suggests three types of creative leadership that accept current paradigms: **replication**, **redefinition** and **forward incrementation**.

- **Replication** – this is minimal creative leadership. It is where the person comes in and maintains the level of creativity. For example, a manager may come into an organisation and keep the same assumptions, concepts, values and practices of that organisation. Therefore, the person may still show a level of creative leadership, but it is no more or no less than that of their predecessor.
- **Redefinition (appearing to be different)** – this is where the person comes in and maintains the level of creativity, but may give the impression of changing things. Therefore, a manager may come into an organisation and keep the same assumptions, concepts, values and practices of that organisation, but may suggest different ways of doing things to look creative.
- **Forward incrementation** – this is where the creativity propels an area forward, but within the assumptions, concepts, values and practices that already exist. Therefore, a manager may come into an organisation and keep the same assumptions, concepts, values and practices of that organisation but propel the organisation forward through creative ideas or by speeding up creativity. An example of this may be a manager who starts work for an organisation selling a particular product through sales representatives. This manager suggests a policy to continue selling the product through their sales representatives, but they also add a website for the company to sell their product through.

Types of creative leadership that reject current paradigms

Types of creative leadership that reject the current paradigm are those that seek to undermine or change current assumptions, concepts, values and practices. These three types of creative leadership are **redirection**, **reconstruction/redirection** and **reinitiation**.

- **Redirection** – this is when the person takes an area in an entirely new direction. In an organisation this might be changes in their sales strategy; for example, moving from selling the product through their sales representatives on the road to making it entirely web-based.
- **Reconstruction/redirection** – this is where the person revisits a previous point in creative development and then starts again by taking the area in a new direction. An example of this is when you're writing an essay. You have your notes as a starting point, and then you start to write your essay. However, halfway through writing your essay, you find that the approach you have used is not working. So, you start the essay again from your notes, taking it in a new direction.
- **Reinitiation** – This is where the person moves an area in a new direction from a new starting point. So, for example, let us suggest that the current thought in an organisation is to expand a sales strategy from selling the product through their sales representatives in one country to hiring more salespeople across several countries to increase their market in those new countries. However, someone who was being creative through reinitiation might suggest moving all advertising onto the web to allow all the existing and new markets to come to them. Therefore, the person is not only taking the organisation in a new direction but is also starting from a new point.

Type of creative leadership that integrates current paradigms

The final type of creative leadership seeks to integrate two sets of assumptions, concepts, values and practices. This creative leadership neither accepts nor rejects current paradigms but aims to synthesise, unify and relate the paradigms to each other. So, for example, in a school where education of young people in terms of preparing them for their future is paramount, a creative leader might bring in a practice that is used in the world of work to improve young people's experiences of their future during education. This new idea doesn't reject the old idea that education of young people should prepare them for their future, but it brings together a number of ideas in a new setting.

Wisdom

The definition of wisdom is to judge what is true and right and have some unique insight. To some extent, wisdom represents common sense, good judgement and the insight of generations. Sternberg, however, has written a series of papers on wisdom (Sternberg, 2001b; 2003; 2005) and designed them to show what wisdom comprises as well as how it can be taught and developed so individuals can begin to show wise leadership.

Balance theory of wisdom

In Sternberg's theory of wisdom, the key term is 'balance'; hence the name, balance theory of wisdom. For Sternberg, wisdom is the need to achieve a common good while balancing several different factors (see Figure 16.6).

Therefore, in making a decision to achieve a common good, a wise person will:

- Balance the **intrapersonal** (self-interests such as money, ambition in one's work, the desire to educate oneself

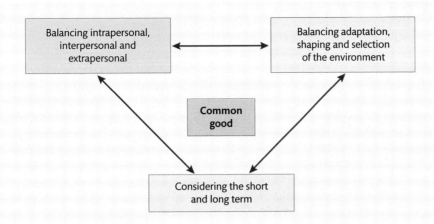

Figure 16.6 Sternberg's balance theory of wisdom.

more), the **interpersonal** (interests of others, such as their interest in money, their work ambitions, their need for good education) and the **extrapersonal** (the environment within which one lives, such as one's family, their community, one's country) when making a decision.

- Balance the short-term and the long-term consequences of any decision.
- Seek balance among existing environments when making the decision. To understand how the decision stands in the context of **adaptation** to existing environments (the individual being able to adapt to the world around them), **shaping** of existing environments (the individual also shaping the environment in some way) and the **selection** of new environments (being able to select one environment over another).

It is quite hard to see this process in operation, so let us use an example, perhaps the most classic and accepted case of wisdom, the act of King Solomon.

Two women bring a baby to Solomon. Each woman says that the baby is her child. As a test, Solomon decrees, 'Cut the baby in half and give half of the baby to each woman.' 'No!' screams the real mother. 'Give her the baby. Do not kill him.' Then Solomon knows who the real mother is because of the way she showed her love for the baby. He then gives the baby to the real mother.

Let us put this example within the terms of Sternberg's theory. First, there is the need to balance the intrapersonal, the interpersonal and the extrapersonal factors. Solomon has to balance his need to be seen as making a good and fair decision (intrapersonal) with the interests of each mother to keep the child (interpersonal) and the needs of his community and his kingdom for him to act like a king by providing a good and fair decision (extrapersonal).

Second is the need to consider both the short and long term. Here, Solomon considers the short-term outcome by coming to a quick decision because that is what the mothers are demanding (it would not be wise to say, 'let us wait until the child grows up and see who they look most like' before making the decision). He also considers the long-term outcome of making the correct decision so the child can be with its real mother.

Third is the need to find balance among existing environments. Clearly, Solomon balances these needs. He decides that he cannot simply *adapt* to the current situation and join in the argument; he has to somehow *shape* the current environment. In ordering that the child be cut in half, he thinks of new ways of reaching the truth; this allows him to arrive at a fair and just decision, thereby *shaping* the current environment.

Teaching and encouraging wisdom and wise leadership

Sternberg (2005) suggests that we can encourage and develop wisdom both in education and the workplace by encouraging wisdom in decisions, ideas and communications. In regard to developing and teaching wisdom, Sternberg suggests five issues that educators and employers need to be aware of:

- **Differences in the balancing of goals** – in Sternberg's model of wisdom, a central feature of the model is the desire to reach a common good. However, as individuals differ in their goals, they may differ in their desire to reach a common good or may believe in a different common good.
- **Differences in the balancing of responses to environmental contexts** – in this model of wisdom there are three ways in which we balance the environment: adaptation, shaping and selection. Of course, peo-

ple are different, and they differ in their balance of responses to the environment. Therefore, for some people a wise decision may involve adapting to the environment; for others, it involves shaping or selecting their environment.

- **Differences in the balancing of interests** – again, all people have different sets of interests. They themselves are balancing a series of interests when they have prioritised what is important to them. In the workplace, some people will work mainly to earn money so they can support their family, or way of life, while for others work will be an important part of who they are.
- **Differences in the balancing of the short term and the long term** – people differ in the priorities they give to the short term and the long term. For some people, the short term is most important ('you have to live for the moment'); for others, the long term has priority.
- **Differences in the balancing of procedure and values** – this aspect concentrates on something called tacit knowledge (knowledge based on understanding procedures rather than facts). The concern here is that people differ in the way they think decisions should be made. For example, some people may prefer a central individual to make the decision, while others may prefer to seek other's views first and discuss the issue openly.

In some ways you could consider these factors as suggesting a weakness in Sternberg's balance model of wisdom. These are fairly broad differences between people (goals, consideration for the long term, how people believe things should be carried out). However, you might also think that, on consideration, these factors pinpoint the issues surrounding wisdom, so that we might better understand how people can arrive at wise decisions. Why? Well, because if you balance all these different concepts and ideas, strengths and weaknesses, and still think it is important to teach wisdom, it is perhaps a wise thing to do!

Giftedness

We have so far discussed how people can develop abilities, be it in a learning style, emotional intelligence, creativity or wisdom. However, some people, from an early stage, show tremendous natural intelligence abilities, better known as **giftedness**. We are now going to outline how intelligence theorists have helped us to understand giftedness.

Giftedness, termites and IQ scores

You will remember that one of the first developments in intelligence testing was made by Lewis Terman of Stanford (see Chapter 12). Terman introduced the Stanford–Binet test and went on to use it with over 1,000 children. Terman also introduced Stern's idea of IQ in conjunction with the Stanford–Binet test.

Terman (Terman, 1925; Terman and Oden, 1947; 1959) is also known for one other development in the intelligence literature – his termites. From his PhD work, Terman wrote 'Genius and Stupidity: A Study of the Intellectual Processes of Seven Bright and Seven Stupid Boys.' Terman studied intelligence in a group of children from an early age into adulthood. This group of children became known as Terman's termites. Terman wanted to know whether children scoring higher on intelligence tests in childhood went on to achieve greatly in adulthood. He argued that special attention should be paid to those with high scores in intelligence tasks, and certainly to those falling within the top 1 per cent of IQ scores. Terman argued that gifted children should be identified as early as possible, be accelerated through school and be given a different curriculum and specially trained teachers. He also argued that such children should be viewed as a national resource, allowed to develop and direct their talents in any way that they emerge. Terman went on to study children and adults in their giftedness.

In later studies Terman went on to suggest that individuals scoring two standard deviations above the mean IQ score for their sample were found to be superior in physical, moral and behavioural dimensions (Terman and Oden, 1947; 1959). With these findings, Terman pushed for intelligence tests and estimates of IQ to be used among children so that US society could identify and stimulate the most gifted. US intelligence theorist and researcher Carolyn Callahan (2000) stresses that this 'IQ' definition of giftedness tends to be accepted by most schools and businesses today. Traditionally, individuals seen as high achievers are often deemed so because they fall into the top 3–5 per cent of students as measured by intelligence tests.

Overall, recent findings suggest that IQ scores might be a good indicator of giftedness. For example, gifted children score significantly higher than non-gifted children for measures of overall intelligence on the Wechsler Intelligence Scale for Children – Third Edition, Stanford–Binet Intelligence Scale – Fourth Edition (SB-IV) and the Woodcock–Johnson III tests of cognitive abilities (Rizza *et al.*, 2001; Simpson *et al.*, 2002).

Modern conceptions of giftedness: not just high IQ?

However, many psychologists, researchers and educationalists have revisited what is meant by giftedness and have tried to expand the view of giftedness. In modern times we have a sense of what we mean by gifted. Or do we? Some people refer to highly intelligent people, particularly children, as gifted. Normally, it is always assumed that something unique about the individual has led to their giftedness. However, research suggests that giftedness may be influenced by several factors.

In 2005, French psychologist J. Louis and colleagues (Louis *et al.*, 2005) looked at a number of factors in high intellectual potential in 412 French children aged from 8–11 years. The researchers split this sample into two groups, and 195 children were in a gifted group. These were children who had scored 130 IQ points or above on the Wechsler test. They placed another 217 children in a control group; these children were randomly selected from schools. Louis *et al.* found that some psychophysiological variables were related to giftedness. Those children falling into the gifted group tended *not* to be children of parents who had abnormal pregnancies or perinatal (5 months before and 1 month after birth) stress and presence of migraine. Furthermore, Louis *et al.* found a link between parents living together with a good and superior level of education and giftedness in children.

In 2001, US educational psychologist Spyros Konstantopoulos and his colleagues (Konstantopoulos *et al.*, 2001) used the National Education Longitudinal Study of 1988 to describe how gifted American students differ from their non-gifted counterparts. The National Education Longitudinal Study is a nationally representative sample of US eighth-graders (12–13 years old) who were first surveyed in the spring of 1988 and then resurveyed through four follow-up studies in 1990, 1992, 1994 and 2000. On the questionnaire, students reported on a range of topics, including school and home experiences; characteristics of their neighbourhood; educational support and resources; their perceived role of parents and peers in their education; educational and occupational aspirations; as well as a number of other attitudes and behaviours. Konstantopoulos *et al.*'s findings indicate that students who are self-reliant and spend more time on homework assignments and leisure reading per week are much more likely to be academically gifted than other students. In addition, high levels of parental educational aspiration (wanting their children to do well), as well as high levels of family socioeconomic status (high income, good professional occupations) are important predictors of academic giftedness.

Stop and think

If wisdom shows leadership, why are some leaders foolish?

Are all leaders necessarily wise? It would be wrong to assume that, just because wisdom reflects leadership qualities, it necessarily means that all leaders are wise. Sternberg (2002) notes that people who are placed in power – or gain positions of leadership – do not necessarily, or automatically, demonstrate wisdom. In fact, they can often be foolish. Sternberg suggests there are five reasons why, as leaders, we can show ourselves as foolish.

- **Unrealistic optimism** – leaders tend to use optimism to help people along. Optimism is a tendency to expect the best possible outcome in many, or all, situations. (You can read more about the different forms of optimism in Chapter 18.) You can see how instilling confidence in people in the future can be a leadership quality. However, although being optimistic is generally a good thing, being unrealistically optimistic is not a sign of wisdom. In being unrealistically optimistic, you begin to believe that, no matter what you do, things will always have the best possible outcome. People who are unrealistically optimistic in their attempt to be wise will always believe they can do no wrong; therefore, this doesn't lead to wisdom, as there will be times when things don't work out for the best.

- **Egocentrism** – egocentric individuals believe they are the centre, object and norm of all experience; they care only about themselves. Often great leaders see themselves at the centre of a particular world, and the people around them are followers. However, if you are egocentric, then you lose sight of all others' interests. You will thus be unable to balance other people's interests and the common good and undermine your attempts at wisdom.

- **Omniscience** – omniscience is having total knowledge, knowing everything. To some extent, we expect our leaders to have a certain level of knowledge above ours. But if, as a leader, you believe you know everything, you know you are always right, then how can you take account of everyone and everything and balance different factors? As a leader, you may be an expert in one area; however, believing that you are an expert in all areas is not a sign of wisdom, but foolishness.

- **Omnipotence** – omnipotence is having unlimited or universal power, authority or force. Many leaders have a great deal of power, be it as the president of a country or as a manager at work. However, leaders must be careful not to lose sight of the limitations of their power and not to abuse it. A company manager may believe they can order people around unfairly because in their job description they are given the power to reprimand staff members who do not do what they say. But if their staff complains to the company's managing director, then the manager may find themselves being reprimanded. As such, omnipotence does not lead to wise decisions, but to decisions that serve the interests of the individual over those of other people and those that represent your community (for example, an organisation or a country).

- **Invulnerability** – invulnerability is the tendency of a person to believe they are immune from hurt or attack, in this case against the position they currently

hold. People may believe they are too clever or too important – that if they do anything wrong, they will get away with it. History has many tales of politicians or important people resigning because they originally felt they could get away with an indiscretion or something illegal, but then didn't. Believing that you are invulnerable, believing that your thinking or actions are above those of other people, are not indicators of wisdom, because you are serving your own rather than others' interests (for example, an organisation or a country).

Findings of this sort have led commentators to spread their conceptions of giftedness more widely to encompass dimensions other than very high IQ scores. The Council on Exceptional Children in 1990 (using information from Russell *et al.* [1988] and Sisk [1990]) described the general characteristics of a gifted child. The Council for Exceptional Children based in Arlington, Virginia, in the United States is the largest international professional organisation dedicated to improving educational outcomes for individuals with exceptionalities, students with disabilities and/or the gifted. The council suggested that the following factors typically indicate giftedness, although no gifted child is expected to be outstanding in all of them (Council for Exceptional Children, 1990):

- shows superior reasoning powers and marked ability to handle ideas; can generalise readily from specific facts and can see subtle relationships; has outstanding problem-solving ability;
- shows persistent intellectual curiosity; asks searching questions; shows exceptional interest in the nature of man and the universe;
- has a wide range of interests, often of an intellectual kind; develops one or more interests to considerable depth;
- is markedly superior in quality and quantity of written and/or spoken vocabulary; is interested in the subtleties of words and their uses;
- reads avidly and absorbs books well beyond their years;
- learns quickly and easily and retains what is learned; recalls important details, concepts and principles; comprehends readily;
- shows insight into arithmetical problems that require careful reasoning and grasps mathematical concepts readily;
- shows creative ability or imaginative expression in such things as music, art, dance, drama; shows sensitivity and finesse in rhythm, movement and bodily control;
- sustains concentration for lengthy periods and shows outstanding responsibility and independence in classroom work;

- sets realistically high standards for self; is self-critical in evaluating and correcting his or her own efforts;
- shows initiative and originality in intellectual work; shows flexibility in thinking and considers problems from a number of viewpoints;
- observes keenly and is responsive to new ideas;
- shows social poise and an ability to communicate with adults in a mature way;
- gets excitement and pleasure from intellectual challenge; shows an alert and subtle sense of humour.

Although we would recognise many of the attributes listed here as behaviours that we see in intelligence tests, this view very much widens out the range of what comprises giftedness.

Psychological models of giftedness

Callahan (2000) suggests that there are five main psychological theories of conceptions of giftedness:

- Sternberg's triarchic model of giftedness.
- Gardner's model of multiple intelligences and giftedness.
- Renzulli's three-ring definition.
- Tannenbaum's psychosocial definition.
- Feldman's developmentalist position.

You will probably recognise two of the names – Sternberg and Gardner. We are not going into depth regarding these two theories of giftedness, because these models are largely extensions of their intelligence models (as presented in Chapter 12).

Sternberg's triarchic model of giftedness (Sternberg, 1997a) is based on his triarchic theory of intelligence (this we also mentioned briefly earlier, in considering his wisdom, intelligence and creativity, synthesised theory). Sternberg suggests there are three distinct types of giftedness:

- **Analytical giftedness** – this type of giftedness arises from mental mechanisms that underlie intelligent behaviour (componential intelligence); for example, a great scientist (such as Einstein), good at solving abstract problems and generating theories.

- **Practical giftedness** – this type of giftedness arises from mental mechanisms interacting with the external world (contextual intelligence); for example, a great practical problem-solver, such as a brilliant businessman).
- **Creative giftedness** – this type of giftedness arises from experience in interacting with the internal and the external world (experiential intelligence); for example, someone who has intuition and insight and works well with novelty, such as a great writer like Shakespeare.

Similarly, Gardner's model of giftedness (Gardner, 1983; 1993) is based on his theory of multiple intelligences and is based on excellence in any one of nine dimensions of intelligence (linguistic, logicomathematical, spatial, musical, bodily kinaesthetic, interpersonal, intrapersonal, naturalist and existentialist) being allowed to emerge and fully develop by encouragement from family, teachers and friends.

We are going to concentrate on these three conceptions of giftedness: three-ring definition, Tannenbaum's psychosocial definition and Feldman's developmentalist position.

Renzulli's three-ring definition

Joseph S. Renzulli, an American educational psychologist, suggested that giftedness can be conceptualised within three rings (Renzulli, 1978; Renzulli and Reis, 1997). Renzulli sought to promote a broadened conception of giftedness outside that which is usually determined by measures of intelligence and high IQ.

The important point to Renzulli's concept of giftedness is that giftedness comprises gifted behaviours rather than gifted individuals. These gifted behaviours are composed of three elements (rings):

- above-average ability;
- task commitment;
- creativity.

Within Renzulli's theory, **above-average ability**, at a general level, represents high levels of abstract thought, adaptation to novel situations and the ability to retrieve information rapidly and accurately. At a specific level, above-average ability comprises a high degree of applying general abilities to specific areas of knowledge, a capacity to sort out relevant from irrelevant information and a capacity to acquire and use advanced knowledge and strategies while pursuing a problem. **Task commitment** is the ability to show high levels of interest and enthusiasm for tasks, hard work and determination in a particular area, self-confidence and drive for achievement and setting high standards for one's own work. **Creativity** is the ability to show fluency, flexibility and originality of thought, to be open to new experiences and ideas and be curious and willing to take risks.

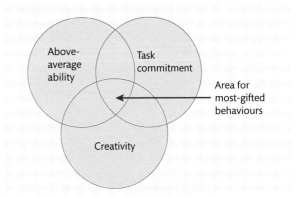

Figure 16.7 Renzulli's theory of giftedness.
Source: Reprinted from Renzulli, J. S. (1986). The three-ring conception of giftedness: a developmental model for promoting creative productivity. In R.J. Sternberg and J. Davidson (Eds.), *Conceptions of giftedness*. Cambridge: Cambridge University Press. Reproduced with permission from Cambridge University Press.

Renzulli conceptualises giftedness within these three categories by using a diagram (see Figure 16.7), with the area in the middle representing most-gifted behaviours.

Renzulli argues that giftedness represents a balance of all three areas. So, for example, someone who is creative and has above-average ability is not likely to succeed or produce unless there is task commitment. Take, for example, a songwriter. This person can write songs (creativity); when they write a song, it is considered a very good song that people enjoy (above-average ability). However, unless there is task commitment (the ability to produce many songs for successive albums), the songwriter is unlikely ever to be considered very gifted. For example, compare John Lennon and Paul McCartney of the Beatles with Hy Zaret and Alex North. 'Who', you say? Zaret and North wrote 'Unchained Melody', the most covered song of all time, which has been released 697 times and has been recorded by Bing Crosby, Elvis Presley – and the biggest-selling, Robson and Jerome(!). We can see how, in the case of Lennon and McCartney, all these three elements of giftedness came together; however, for Zaret and North, they did not.

Tannenbaum's psychosocial definition of giftedness

US psychologist Abraham Tannenbaum (Tannenbaum, 1986) took a similar position to Renzulli in suggesting that the key to giftedness is the ability to produce, rather than consume, information (Callahan, 2000). Tannenbaum suggests that developed talent exists only in adults, and that giftedness refers to a potential for becoming a great thinker, performer or producer of ideas that enhance many aspects of humanity (for example, physical, intellectual, emotional and social aspects of life). Tannenbaum referred to four types of talents:

- **Scarcity** – talents that allow people to make break-throughs in their field.
- **Surplus** – talents that allow people to add to the beauty of the environment.
- **Quota** – talents related to excellence in providing business, goods and services.
- **Anomalous** – practical talents.

Whereas Terman had previously linked giftedness to adulthood as an eventual development of giftedness, Tannenbaum defined the sorts of talents that gifted individuals possess. Tannenbaum also emphasised those factors that link childhood giftedness to the four dimensions of talent in adulthood, including superior general intelligence (this is 'g' as measured by IQ tests), exceptional special aptitudes, non-intellective facilitators (e.g. high motivation, high self-esteem), environmental influences and chance or luck.

Feldman's developmentalist view on giftedness: coincidence

US developmental psychologist David Feldman's view of giftedness rests on the concept of coincidence (Feldman, 1986; Feldman and Goldsmith, 1986). He argues that giftedness in adulthood is a coincidence of forces that have combined and worked together to produce the talented individual. He views these forces as:

- **Biological and psychological** – factors lying within the brain and the mind that predispose the individual to giftedness (e.g. good cognitive processing skills).
- **Social and environmental** – factors in the environment that are critical to the development of giftedness (good parents and good teachers).
- **Historical** – Reflects opportunities in the individual's lifespan to achieve this giftedness (for example, is the area of the child's giftedness in the education curriculum of their country?).
- **Evolutionary** – cultural and biological factors that support or hinder the development of giftedness.

Crucial to demonstrating Feldman's theory is the comparison of occasions when giftedness in adulthood emerges from childhood to other occasions when it does not. Morelock and Feldman (1991) use the example of many women who may not emerge as gifted in adulthood, though they have been identified as having the potential in childhood. These authors suggest that additional barriers are raised by stereotypes of female roles and behaviour in society, preventing the coincidence of forces to produce giftedness. For example, domestic and child-rearing responsibilities have historically interfered with women being able to express their ability in the arts and sciences. More recently, there are attitudes within society that may impede career and academic development among women,

such as a 'fear of success' or 'being viewed as unwomanly'. Morelock and Feldman have suggested that, for female children to become gifted in adulthood, it is important that parents become aware of the possibility that their daughters might be gifted, that the daughters have teachers who identify and value achievement in young women, and that their society facilitates and encourages female giftedness at all levels.

Summary of giftedness

The psychology of giftedness started with Terman's emphasis on excellent performance in measures of intelligence (i.e. high IQ). Later concepts of giftedness have expanded on this view, suggesting that biological, as well as family-, education- and society-based, factors all influence giftedness. Theorists such as Renzulli, Tannenbaum and Feldman have sought to expand on Terman's work by providing models of the key aspects of giftedness.

Working with those who have learning disabilities

So far in this discussion, we have talked about theories of excellence and improvement in education and the workplace, including learning styles, emotional intelligence, creativity, wisdom and giftedness. However, to this point we have neglected one core area. How do we translate some of the attempts to improve and reach our potential to teaching those who have learning difficulties?

To fully understand the context of present approaches to teaching those with learning disabilities, it is important, first, to outline the history to such approaches. In this section we are going to introduce you to two historical lines in the work with learning-disabled individuals: (1) the darker historical line; and (2) the positive historical line. We will then see how the positive history underlies the most dominant and well-recognised work in learning disabilities today, the work of Reuven Feuerstein.

Working with those who have learning disabilities: the darker historical line

Earlier in the text (Chapter 14) we spoke about a darker side of intelligence testing from the early part of the twentieth century to the Second World War. We noted that the consideration of people's intelligence, and intelligence testing, had been linked to the development of eugenics, first starting with Galton; we discussed how eugenics views had made their way into social policy, politics and the law.

During that time, people with learning disabilities were seen as mentally retarded. For example, in 1921, the American Association of Mental Retardation defined three levels of 'mental retardation': 'moron' (for those with an IQ score of 50–75), 'imbecile' (for those with IQ scores of 25–50) and 'idiot' (for those with an IQ score of less than 25) alongside strongly recommending using the Binet intelligence test as a method of assessing IQ.

In the United States, in 1922, a member of the US House of Representatives Committee on Immigration and Naturalization (H. H. Laughlin) published the Model Eugenical Sterilization Law. This formed the basis of state sterilisation laws; in it, Laughlin listed the types of people who were to be subjected to mandatory sterilisation (including those considered mentally retarded). In 1927, the US Supreme Court ruled in the case of *Buck* v *Bell* and supported a new legislative law in the state of Virginia. The law concerned a 17-year-old woman named Carrie Buck, who was a resident at the Virginia Colony for the Epileptic and Feebleminded – an asylum home for epileptics, the mentally retarded and the severely disabled. Carrie had the IQ score of a 9-year-old; her mother, also resident at the Colony, had a mental age of less than 8. Carrie Buck had given birth to a daughter who, at 1 year old, was given an infant IQ test and found to be less than normal. In response to this finding, the State of Virginia wanted to have the child sterilised against her will. The US Supreme Court ruled in favour of the enforced sterilisation. In writing up the decision, Justice Oliver Wendell Holmes wrote, 'three generations of imbeciles are enough'. By that part of the twentieth century, 29 US states had laws allowing the compulsory sterilisation of individuals thought to be mentally retarded, alcoholic or 'having a criminal nature'. In 1945, information from the *Journal of the American Medical Association* suggested that, between 1941 and 1943, over 42,000 people were sterilised in the United States.

Stop and think

Creativity, giftedness and 'psychopathology'

In the last few sections we have outlined theories of creativity and giftedness which give accounts of creativity in the context of both everyday thought and in high levels of creativity representing giftedness. Within psychology there is another side to creativity and other indicators of immense creativity such as giftedness. Aristotle, the Greek philosopher (384–322 BC), said 'No great genius was without a mixture of insanity', and since then it is well documented that great creative figures in history have shown signs of psychopathology. Vincent Willem van Gogh (1853–1890) was a Dutch post-impressionist artist and some of his paintings are now among the world's best known and most expensive works of art. Van Gogh cut off the lobe of his left ear in 1888 and it is recognised that he was affected by increasing mental problems, particularly in the last years of his life, but the causes are often debated. John Forbes Nash, an American mathematician, economist and Nobel laureate whose published key idea in game theory was recognised as genius, has struggled with schizophrenia all his life. Recently in the *Independent*, John Walsh (Walsh, 18 March 2007) looked at examples of madness and creativity in modern creative figures. He highlighted Stephen Fry (a British comedian) who, in a TV documentary, *The Secret Life of a Manic-Depressive*, talked about how many highly intelligent, creative people (e.g. Robbie Williams being one) have been diagnosed with manic-depression (a condition with mood swings from overly 'high' (manic) to overly 'low' (depressed) moods. In this documentary Fry said that many victims of the condition preferred to endure the aching chasms of depression without therapy or drugs because of the creative high they experienced in the manic stage.

Within psychology, the associations between high ability or higher levels of thinking (be it creativity or giftedness) and different forms of psychopathology are best examined within the creativity and psychopathology literature. Creativity has been long associated with different types of mood (high and low levels of anxiety and depression), neuroses (anxieties, compulsions, obsessions and phobias), mental rumination (reflection that may become persistently worrying), schizophrenia, psychosocial problems and suicide (Nettle, 2001).

In 2009, University of Oxford UK psychologist Emilie Glazer (Glazer, 2009) provided an excellent summary of modern psychological debates regarding the association between creativity and psychopathology. In this summary Glazer first highlights how researchers have conceptualised the causal relationship (which concept causes which concept) between creativity and psychopathology. First Glazer points to Richards and Kinney (2000), who have argued that there are five possible relationships:

- Psychopathology directly causes creativity
- Psychopathology indirectly causes creativity
- Creativity directly projects (being placed) onto the psychopathology

- Creativity indirectly projects onto the psychopathology
- A third factor influencing the relationship, such as a family disposition for the psychopathology.

Glazer also points to Ludwig (1995), who has argued that there are four ways to conceptualise the relationship between creativity and psychopathology:

- Psychopathology causes a decrease in creativity
- Psychopathology causes an increase in creativity
- Creativity enhances the psychopathology
- Creativity alleviates the psychopathology.

Glazer suggests that perhaps the best way to conceptualise the relationship between creativity and psychopathology is as complex and the relationship depends on the individual being studied, the type of psychopathology and the types of environmental factors involved. Glazer suggests three possible models for understanding creativity in terms of psychopathology as follows:

- The existence of different kinds of creativity, each associated with specific types of psychopathology
- Creativity operating as a continuum
- Creativity as a single entity.

1 **The existence of different kinds of creativity, each associated with specific types of psychopathology.** Glazer considers whether there are different types of creativity based on the type of psychopathology, drawing on the distinction between schizophrenia (a mental disorder characterised by abnormalities in the perception or expression of reality) versus affective disorder (mental disorder characterised by dramatic changes or extremes of mood). Here Glazer uses Sass' (2001) analysis to draw the distinction between different kinds of creativity in terms of 'normal' creativity and 'revolutionary' creativity. Sass argues that individuals with affective disorders are preoccupied with the cultural norms around them. Therefore in manic (highs) states in the affective disorder, individuals claim great grandiosity within a social hierarchy and, when depressed, they have a heightened sensitivity to social phenomena, feeling themselves overly attached to the world. Therefore Sass argues that affective disorder is related to creativity limited to the 'normal', observations around everyday life, concentrating on feelings. This may be why comedians with affective disorder, such as Stephen Fry, and notably Tony Hancock, produce comedy that is often concerned with the absurdity of everyday life. Moreover, Sass argues that the person with schizophrenia, who is suffering from altered states of perception or expressions of reality, is further detached from the world, works free of social boundaries and considers alternative views of the world, or perceives things differently and this predisposes them to 'revolutionary' creativity. In the art world, for example,

they distinguish between *depressive* art, which tends to focus on emotions and feelings, and *schizophrenic* art, which tends to be emotionally distant and sometimes surreal (bizarre or dreamlike). For researchers in creativity and psychopathology, such as Claridge (1998), the distinction between affective disorder and schizophrenia provides useful parameters for any researcher looking at the relationship between creativity and psychopathology.

2 **Creativity operating as a continuum.** The second way that Glazer suggests we examine creativity is as operating as a continuum. There are two parts to this model which are both illustrated in Figure 16.8. Axis A corresponds to the extremities of creativity, ranging from everyday creativity to the genius work of the eminent, and then outsider art and then unrecognisable creativity. Outsider art means 'raw art' or 'rough art' and was a description created by French artist Jean Dubuffet to describe art created outside the boundaries of official culture. Dubuffet argued that art created by insane-asylum inmates and that of the mentally ill are the best examples of outsider art (Glazer, 2009). Glazer notes that unrecognisable creativity comprises remote creative associations that extend past culturally recognisable work. Glazer argues that, as the axis extends from the everyday to the work of the eminent to outsider art and then to unrecognisable creativity, there is an increasingly

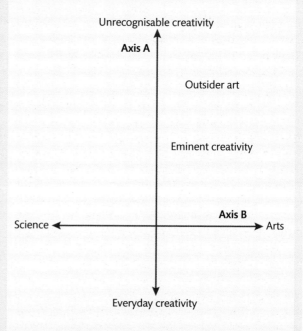

Figure 16.8 Creativity operating as a continuum.
Source: Based on Glazer (2009).

higher likelihood of psychopathology or psychopathological tendencies. That is not to say that all people on this axis are likely to have a psychopathology, but that there is a great probability that individuals higher up on this axis will have a psychopathology. Axis B represents creativity of the sciences to creativity harnessed in the arts and therefore creativity and psychopathology can be understood within the interaction of these two axes forming four quadrants.

3 **Creativity as a single construct.** The final model presented by Glazer is creativity as a single construct: divergent thinking. We talked about this earlier, under creativity as a process and Guilford's initial work. However, to remind you, divergent thinking is a thought process that involves the generation of ideas. So, an example of divergent thinking might be the ability to brainstorm, breaking problems into parts, showing great thinking, understanding causality, identifying importance with topics, being able to appreciate known and unknown qualities. Glazer maintains that divergent thinking is a feature of all the main theories of creativity. For examples of this see the models of creativity and giftedness outlined in this discussion, e.g. Sternberg, Gardner, Renzulli, Tannenbaum and Feldman. All these models describe thinking that could be described as divergent thinking. Glazer argues that the relationship between creativity and psychopathology may be best understood within a single construct of different levels of divergent thinking.

This is a commonly told story of the relationship between intelligence and people with learning disabilities. However, it would not be fair to assume all people working in intelligence worked within that perspective. Another historical line, which stretches as far back as the beginning of intelligence theory in psychology, has a much more positive side to it. That line leads us to modern-day thinking and practice in working with those who have learning disabilities.

Working with those who have learning disabilities: the positive historical line

The positive historical line of those working with learning disabilities starts with a French physician called Jean-Marc Gaspard Itard (1775–1838) and a young boy who became known as the 'wild boy of Aveyron' (Itard, 1801/1962).

In 1799, a young boy, thought to be around 11 or 12 years old, was found in a wood in Southern France. He was naked, filthy and didn't speak. Very quickly he was placed in care and was eventually taken to Paris where he could be studied. At that time, Jean-Marc Gaspard Itard was a chief physician with the National Institution for Deaf-Mutes in Paris. While other physicians declared that the boy was not wild, but rather had been abandoned by his parents because he was mentally deficient, Itard believed his mental deficiency was entirely caused by a lack of human interaction. Furthermore, Itard believed that, as the boy had survived alone in the woods for at least 7 years, he was not without intelligence. Itard named the boy 'Victor' and devoted the next 5 years to an intensive educational programme in which he tried to get Victor interested in the social world, improve his awareness of stimuli, extend his experiences (for example, culture, games, groups of people), teach him to communicate using pictures and words and teach him to speak. After 5 years Victor could read and speak a few words, but Itard was disappointed in this lack of progress. However, the key idea from this story is that Itard *tried* to make things better for Victor. This work is often cited as the beginning of modern special education.

Within this positive historical line, it is also useful to acknowledge how intelligence tests played a positive role. Although intelligence tests and IQ scores were used, by some, to advance eugenic ideas, US intelligence expert Douglas K. Detterman suggests that the IQ testing before the Second World War did have a positive impact (Detterman, 1987; Detterman et al., 2001). Detterman shows that, before intelligence testing at the start of the twentieth century, those individuals who had learning disabilities were treated no differently from those who were mentally ill – assuming that people with learning disabilities were simply uneducable, they were often institutionalised in mental asylums. Therefore, the introduction of intelligence testing, and the ability to identify those people who experienced learning disabilities, opened up new possibilities.

Detterman suggests that these possibilities came after the Second World War. After the war, the policies that had been born from eugenics fell into disrepute. Nazis involved in the Second World War and the Holocaust were tried at Nuremberg, revealing to the world the Nazis' genocidal practices. Clearly, governments couldn't condone those policies that had been advocated by Hitler, and many re-examined their eugenics-based policies. What then followed was a research agenda, particularly during the 1960s and 1970s, that sought to explore the nature of learning disabilities. Detterman et al. (2001) point to a body of research that looked at people with learning disabilities. Much of this research explored different aspects of memory, including short- and long-term aspects of rehearsal and their attention among individuals with learning difficulties. There was also research into autistic savants. Autism is characterised by extreme problems in communication and social interaction, displays of repetitive acts and excessive attachment to certain objects. Autistic savants are people who have autism; however, they also have one extraordinary mental ability, more often in numerical calculation but sometimes also in music or art. Examples of extraordinary abilities among autistic savants include being able to remember extensive lists of facts or statistics, re-creating in detail a particular scene from a painting or having exceptional musical ability but no musical education.

Detterman argues that all this research shows that people with learning disabilities are capable of learning and remembering complex materials and that those with learning disabilities have much more potential than previously thought. In the next section we are going to outline the work of one person who typifies the attempts to work with, rather than to exclude, those with learning disabilities. That person is Reuven Feuerstein.

Feuerstein and Structural Cognitive Modifiability

Reuven Feuerstein is an Israeli educational cognitive psychologist. He began his work in the period from 1945 to 1948, when he was a special education teacher and counsellor in youth villages in Israel; there, he worked with young survivors of the Holocaust, who were severely traumatised. Among the children that Feuerstein worked with, one common factor was that, before coming to Feuerstein's attention, the children were thought to be beyond psychological help of any kind. Over his career Feuerstein extended his work to other children with learning disabilities. The central idea in all of Feuerstein's work was that all children with learning disabilities – regardless of the nature, cause or severity of their disability – are capable of learning far more than is usually assumed. Over time, Feuerstein developed his theory and programme of Structural Cognitive Modifiability.

Theory and programme of Structural Cognitive Modifiability

There are three assumptions underlying Feuerstein's theory and programme of Structural Cognitive Modifiability (Feuerstein *et al.*, 2002; 2003a; 1979). The assumptions of this model are as follows:

- People's abilities and behaviours are dynamic and modifiable, not static or fixed. That is, we are able to change or alter their skills.
- Individuals have to want, or need, to modify.
- Cognitive abilities, particularly intelligence, play a central role in the ability to modify one's self.

The theory and programme of Structural Cognitive Modifiability includes three major elements:

- Mediated learning experience (MLE)
- The Learning Propensity Assessment Device (LPAD)
- Instrumental Enrichment (IE).

Mediated learning experiences

Feuerstein *et al.* (2002; 2003a) describe **mediated learning experience (MLE)**. For Feuerstein there are two types of learning: (1) direct learning and (2) mediated learning.

- **Direct learning** – this type of learning is a direct interaction between the learner and an environmental learning factor; for example, reading a book, using a computer or attending a lecture.
- **Mediated learning** – This is a different form of learning, where a mediator is placed in the middle of the learning process. Here, the mediator is able to interpret, change, emphasise and select the environmental learning factor to help the learner to learn. Therefore, using the direct learning examples, the mediator would help the learner with their reading when reading the book, they would work with them in using the computer or they would help them to understand the lecture.

Feuerstein focuses on using the second form of learning for individuals with learning disabilities (mediated learning experience). The mediator is there to help the learner interact more productively with the learning environment. At school you may have had classes where someone with a learning disability had a classroom assistant working directly with them while the class went on. This is an example of mediated learning.

For Feuerstein, mediated learning experience can be used for all people with learning disabilities. The dedicated and individualised attention from the mediator can be used to improve the cognitive skills, particularly intelligence, of the learner, leading them to be an independent learner. Feuerstein says that the absence of a mediator leads to underdevelopment of the child's abilities.

The Learning Propensity Assessment Device (LPAD)

The **Learning Propensity Assessment Device (LPAD)** is a type of intelligence test that adopts what Feuerstein terms an interactive or dynamic approach to assessing people's learning propensity – their natural potential or tendency for learning (Feuerstein *et al.*, 1998c).

The LPAD uses a set of instruments that identify the cognitive functions, learning processes and problem-solving strategies used by the learner. At first glance, the LPAD battery looks like any other intelligence test. It consists of 15 instruments aimed at assessing cognitive processes related to

Profile

Reuven Feuerstein

Professor Reuven Feuerstein was born in Israel. Between 1940 and 1944 Feuerstein attended Teachers College in Bucharest, Romania. From 1945 to 1948 he was a special education teacher and counsellor in youth villages in Israel, working with survivors of the Holocaust.

From 1950 to 1955 he studied in the University of Geneva, under Jean Piaget (a Swiss developmental psychologist, famous for his work with children and his theory of cognitive development). There, in 1952, he completed his degree in general and clinical psychology; in 1954, he gained his licence to practise in psychology. In 1970 Feuerstein obtained his PhD in developmental psychology at the Sorbonne, a prestigious university in Paris, France. From 1970 until the present day, Feuerstein

has worked as a professor in the School of Education at Bar Ilan University, Israel. He is also currently the director of the Centre for Development of Human Potential in Jerusalem, Israel.

Feuerstein's research and work have included Holocaust survivors, Down's syndrome children, brain-injured individuals and children with autism, among many others. He has received a number of honours and recognition, including the Canadian Variety Clubs International Humanitarian Award (1991) and the Distinguished Citizen of Jerusalem and Israel Prize in Education (1992). Feuerstein has published over 80 books, monographs, chapters and journal articles.

---

perception, attention, memory, problem-solving and logical reasoning, including the Raven's Progressive Matrices and Standard Progressive Matrices (Raven, 1938; 1962; 2004).

However, Feuerstein argues that, whereas traditional tests of ability, such as intelligence tests, seek to identify where a person is (for example, their IQ), the LPAD focuses on the person's potential for learning in the future. Unlike normal intelligence tests, which are administered over a relatively short period of time (1 or 2 hours), the LPAD is administered over a much longer period of time (over a number of sessions). The assessor uses the LPAD to investigate the learning-disabled person's cognitive skills, processes and learning strategies.

However, rather than simply seeing how well the person does on LPAD tasks, the test administrator looks for cognitive changes in the person while doing different tasks.

Overall, Feuerstein describes the LPAD as painting a picture, or creating a profile, of the person's learning

potential. When the profile is created, this leads to the Instrumental Enrichment programme.

Instrumental Enrichment

Instrumental Enrichment (IE) is a programme of cognitive learning that follows the Learning Propensity Assessment Device (LPAD) and is guided by mediated learning experiences (Feuerstein *et al.*, 1998a). Feuerstein states that Instrumental Enrichment enhances the skills that are needed for independent thinking and learning by the individual. The programme seeks to enhance the cognitive and intelligence skills of that person by:

- addressing deficiencies in the individual's learning skills;
- teaching them new operations and techniques for learning;
- increasing their motivation;
- developing student learning strategies and approaches.

Stop and think

Encouraging emotional intelligence, creativity and wisdom

Look over some of the theories discussed here, particularly the attributes listed in the discussion of emotional intelligence and Sternberg's descriptions of creativity and wisdom.

- What attributes described in these theories do you think you already have?

- What attributes described in these theories do you think you might do well to develop?
- How might you go about developing the attributes you identified in the previous question?

Each programme is tailored to the individual. Its implementation is directed by the mediator, who interprets, changes, emphasises and selects the environmental learning factors. The most important aspect of Instrumental Enrichment is the quality of the interaction between the learner and the mediator. Feuerstein estimates that an Instrumental Enrichment programme takes about 330 hours, comprising three 1-hour sessions a week, with a teaching time of over 18 months to 2 years.

Instrumental Enrichment has been used in over 60 countries through 2,000 projects. It is applied in several different ways, including programmes for children with special needs, children with disabilities and programmes for the rehabilitation of brain-injured individuals. There are also programmes for immigrant and cultural minority students, who may experience learning difficulties.

Final comments

In this discussion we have presented a general overview of how some common personality and intelligence ideas have informed our understanding of education and work. As a result, you should now understand the role and values of common personality and intelligence tests in predicting education and work achievement. However, it is also important to realise that personality and intelligence ideas in education and work extend beyond commonly known personality and intelligence measures. Therefore, we also described Kolb's theory, emotional intelligence, ideas around creativity and wisdom and work with people who have learning disabilities.

Summary

- Commonly known measures of personality and intelligence have been found to be good indicators of achievement in education and work. A series of findings suggest that IQ predicts performance at school and work. Of the five-factor model of personality, conscientiousness and neuroticism are consistently related to several indicators of job performance.
- Personality and intelligence fare relatively well against various predictors of job performance. However, there are two considerations: first, intelligence and personality variables don't provide very adaptable constructs within which to assess educational and work factors. Second, commonly known personality and intelligence variables aren't the first consideration in the minds of educators and employers, as there are many more important factors to be considered.
- In his experiential learning theory, which emphasises learning relating to, or derived from, experience, David Kolb (1981) suggests four main aspects in learning: concrete experience, reflective observation, abstract conceptualisation and active experimentation. Based on these four aspects of learning, Kolb identified four learning styles: diverging, assimilating, converging and accommodating.
- Emotional intelligence informs ideas of education as well as leadership in the workplace. Leadership is based on skills arising from self-awareness, self-regulation/ management, social awareness and social skills/management and from distinctions between personal and social competencies and recognition and regulation. Education is based on Boyatzis' theory of self-directed learning.
- Research on creativity is best understood within the 4 Ps: person, process, press and product.

- Sternberg considers two aspects of leadership: creativity and wisdom. Creative leadership can comprise various abilities, including redefining problems, questioning and analysing assumptions, realising that creative ideas do not sell themselves and willingness to take sensible risks. Creativity can be grouped into types of creative leadership that: (1) accept current paradigms (replication, redefinition and forward incrementation); (2) reject current paradigms (redirection, reconstruction/redirection and reinitiation); and (3) integrate current paradigms.
- Sternberg's balance theory of wisdom is the need to achieve a common good, whilst balancing several different factors: (1) intrapersonal, interpersonal and extrapersonal; (2) the short term and the long term; and (3) adaptation, shaping and selection.
- Giftedness is commonly used in referring to individuals who are thought to possess great natural intelligence. Findings suggest that IQ tests might be a good indicator of giftedness. However, there are other conceptions of giftedness, including Renzulli's three-ring definition, Tannenbaum's psychosocial definition and Feldman's developmentalist view.
- There are two interpretations of the history of working with those who have learning disabilities. The darker history emphasises eugenics, while the more positive history emphasises particular interventions with people who have learning disabilities. From the positive history, the theory and programme of Structural Cognitive Modifiability includes three major elements: mediated learning experience, the Learning Propensity Assessment Device and Instrumental Enrichment.

Connecting up

If you need more information on the theories of emotional intelligence, you can look back at the second part of Chapter 15, which is on the subject of emotional intelligence.

Critical thinking

Discussion questions

- We have looked here at several ideas of leadership. What qualities do you think makes a good leader in these roles?

  - Politician
  - Managing director of a company
  - Teacher
  - Parent.

- Do you think Kolb's theory of learning is a good explanation of how you learn? If not, why not?
- Think about situations when you are creative. How are these examples of creativity best understood within Runco's 4 Ps: person, process, press and product?
- Should gifted children be given as much support as children with learning disabilities?
- What is the best way of selecting the best people for jobs? Do personality and intelligence tests have a role in the selection process for jobs?

- Should we use personality and intelligence tests in education?

Essay questions

- Critically discuss the view that commonly known measures of personality and intelligence are not useful to the world of education and work.
- Critically compare Kolb's and Boyatzis' theories of how we might best learn.
- Critically discuss the main psychological models of creativity.
- Critically examine the view that wisdom and creativity can be considered alongside more traditional conceptions of intelligence.
- Critically compare models of giftedness.
- Critically examine theories of how we can best understand and work with children who have special needs in education.

Going further

Books

- Arnold, J. M. *et al.* (2004). *Work psychology* (4th edn). London: Pearson Education.
- Ormrod, J. (2005). *Educational psychology: Developing learners* (5th edn). London: Pearson Education.
- Subotnik, R. F. and Arnold, K. D. (1994). *Beyond Terman: Contemporary longitudinal studies of giftedness and talent (Creativity Research Series)*. New York: Ablex.

Journals

- Hough, L. M. and Oswald, F. L. (2000). Personnel selection: Looking toward the future – remembering the past. *Annual Review of Psychology, 51*, 631–664. In this article you will get an overall idea of the literature relating to

personnel selection in work. The *Annual Review of Psychology* is published by Annual Reviews, Palo Alto, California. Available online via Business Source Premier.
- Runco, M. A. (2004). Creativity. *Annual Review of Psychology, 55*, 657–687. Published by Annual Reviews, Palo Alto, California. Available online via Business Source Premier.
- Gersch, I. S. (2004). Educational psychology in an age of uncertainty. *The Psychologist, 17*, 142–145. In this article, Gersch looks at the factors that surround and are needed to inform present and future educational psychology practice. It is freely available online. You can find *The Psychologist* on the British Psychological Society website (**www.bps.org.uk**).
- Walsh, S. (1999). Shame in the workplace. *The Psychologist, 12*, 20–23. Sue Walsh presents the case that linking psychodynamic and organisational perspectives can

offer new insights into emotional experiences at work. It is freely available online at the British Psychological Society website (**www.bps.org.uk**).

- Sternberg, R. J. (2005). WICS: A model of positive educational leadership comprising wisdom, intelligence, and creativity synthesized. *Educational Psychology Review, 17*, 191–262. *Educational Psychology Review* is published by Kluwer Academic Publishers. Available online via Kluwer and Swets Wise.

Articles on personality and intelligence in education and work discussed here are often found in the following journals. Use 'personality', 'intelligence', 'emotional intelligence', 'special needs', 'learning difficulties', 'educational achievement' and 'work performance' as your search terms on library databases such as Web of Science and PsycINFO.

- *British Journal of Occupational and Organization Psychology.* Published by the British Psychological Society. Available online via IngentaConnect and Swetswise.
- *British Journal of Educational Psychology.* Published by the British Psychological Society. Available online via IngentaConnect and SwetsWise.

- *British Journal of Developmental Psychology.* Published by the British Psychological Society. Available online via IngentaConnect and SwetsWise.
- *Intelligence: A multidisciplinary journal.* Published by Elsevier Science. Available online via Science Direct.
- *Personality and Individual Differences.* Published by Elsevier Science. Available online via Science Direct.

Web links

- There are industrial-organisational psychology links (**www.socialpsychology.org/io.htm**) at the Social Psychology Network (**www.socialpsychology.org**).
- If you want to read more about some of the initiatives being undertaken within the European Union, then go to the link **http://europa.eu/index_en.htm**. Two areas that might interest you are 'Education, Training, Youth' and 'Employment and Social Affairs'. If you want to see what is being done today by the UK government's Department for Education and Skills resource to support the education profession, this is at **www.education .gov.uk/popularquestions/childrenandfamilies/special educationalneeds**.

Film and literature

- We have covered the theory of individual wisdom here. *The Wisdom of Crowds* (2005, James Surowiecki) is a book that challenges the notion of why the conventional wisdom of the individual expert is sometimes inferior to that of group wisdom. Don't treat this as an academic book for your work; you might have some fun reading this analysis of how wisdom arises, and doesn't arise, from group thinking together.
- In this discussion we spoke about working with people who have special needs, both in terms of giftedness and learning difficulties. The following two films deal with the issues surrounding special needs. *Little Man Tate* (1991, directed by Jodie Foster) is a film about Dede, a lone parent who's trying to bring up her son Fred. When she discovers that Fred is a genius, Dede is determined to ensure that he has all the

opportunities he needs and that he is not taken advantage of by people who forget that his extremely powerful intellect is harboured in the body and emotions of a child. *I am Sam* (2001, directed by Jessie Nelson) is a story of a man with learning disabilities who fights for custody of his 7-year-old daughter.

- *The Usual Suspects* (1995, directed by Bryan Singer) explores some of the themes outlined here, although we won't say exactly what themes, because it will give the ending away.
- *Miss Potter* (2006, directed by Chris Noonan). This is a film about the creativity of English author Beatrix Potter, who was able to combine scientific intellect and observation (she was a mycologist, which is a branch of biology) with an ability to write and illustrate best-selling children's books.

Explore the website accompanying this text at **www.pearsoned.co.uk/maltby** for further resources to help you with your studies. These include multiple-choice questions, essay questions, web links and ideas for advanced reading.

PART 3
Further Debates and Applications in Individual Differences

 The following additional material can be found
on the website (**www.pearsoned.co.uk/maltby**)

CHAPTER 17
Further Debates and Applications in Individual Differences: An Introduction

Key themes

- Ideas and approaches in individual differences
- Measuring individual differences
- Structural models
- Process models
- Clinical theories and armchair speculation
- Psychometric measurement
- Comparing and combining theories
- Further debates about and applications of individual differences

Learning outcomes

At the end of this discussion you should:

- Be familiar with how general ideas and approaches used in individual differences inform modern-day individual differences theory, methods and research
- Understand how individual differences can be applied to improve our understanding of psychological concepts
- Appreciate how individual differences can be applied to improve our understanding of competing or overlapping psychological concepts
- Understand how individual differences can be applied to much of the human experience

Introduction

In the introduction to this text we said that personality, individual differences and intelligence are about how people are similar and different in their behaviour, the way they think and their feelings. We have also outlined some personality, individual differences and intelligence theories that account for similarities and differences in behaviour, thoughts and feelings.

However, for many individual differences psychologists, this work does not even touch on a wealth of diverse theory and research that you would find if you opened any personality or individual differences journal today. Consequently, in the next eight chapters we are going to introduce you to a series of topics which cover further debates and applications within individual differences.

However, before introducing you to this theory and research, we need to present some ideas and approaches that underlie individual differences. Why is this? Well, you will see that, even with the handful of topics that we are going to discuss in this part of the book, there are a whole range of different theories and ideas within each topic. Therefore, considering many of these topic areas can be overwhelming, and you can quickly lose sight of the main individual differences issues. So, in this discussion we are going to introduce you to some ideas and approaches that are designed to help concentrate your mind on the main issues while exploring each of these topics.

We discuss three areas of ideas and approaches that are important to debates and applications in individual differences (see Figure 17.1):

- How individual differences can be applied to improve our understanding of psychological concepts
- How individual differences can be applied to improve our understanding of competing or overlapping concepts
- How individual differences theory is applied to demonstrate its usefulness within the psychology of human experience.

Source: Alamy Images/Image Source Pink

Individual differences can be applied to improve our understanding of psychological concepts

A common view of individual differences is that the approach considers an area, or perspective, in psychology and then incorporates the idea of individual differences within it. In other words, any psychological perspective, such as cognitive psychology, creates a theory of behaviour that describes how everyone acts. Individual differences approaches are then used to explain why an individual may not necessarily fit a particular theory exactly.

This type of individual differences approach is best described by Colin Cooper (1998). He argues that all other major perspectives and theories of psychology are not only based on generalisations about how people behave but also

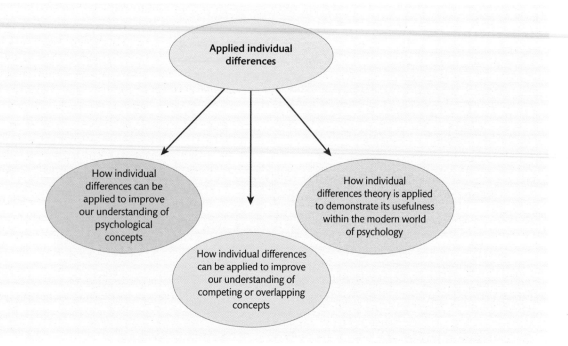

Figure 17.1 Three different individual differences approaches.

assume that people are all much the same. However, these assumptions do not take into account our everyday experiences that people are essentially different, or at least vary from one another. After all, most of us are proud of our individual idiosyncrasies, and we would not like to be thought of as exact replications of each other. However, within many psychology perspectives, individual theories are often generated to apply to everyone within a particular population.

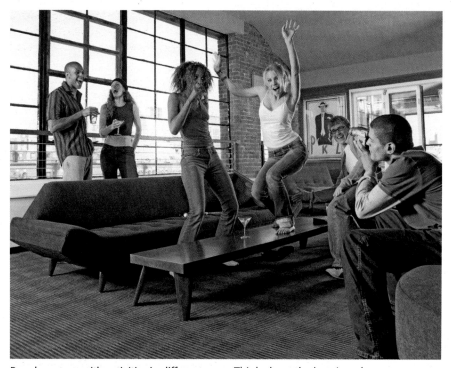

People engage with activities in different ways. Think about the last time that you were at a party. Did everyone act the same way?
Source: Getty Images/White Packert

Alcohol has different effects on people. Does the same drink have the same effect on people? Think about the last time you were at a party/social gathering.
Source: Alamy Images/Radius Images

Cooper gives us several examples; one is developmental psychology, in which theory describes how people are expected to develop and go through certain stages in their life in similar ways. However, in reality, some people never go through certain stages; if they do, they may go through them in different orders. For instance, some of us take longer to 'grow up', or mature, than others. Some of us choose not to settle down and get married until later in life, if at all; and, indeed, some of us choose not to have children. All these different life choices can have varying effects on how we develop as adults, and they refer to multiple, individual, stages of development. Likewise, Cooper uses examples within physiological psychology. Researchers show how the physiological aspects of the body and brain function in the same way; however, some people react differently to substances such as caffeine, nicotine or alcohol.

Equally, these ideas can be expanded to many areas of psychology. Within social psychology, authors may generalise to explain that people like each other mainly on the basis of physical attraction. However, some people end up in long-term relationships when they are not in the least attracted to their partner physically. Learning theories explains the way we all learn through rewards, punishments and positive and negative reinforcements; however, some people never learn. In cognitive psychology, authors generalise as to how we perceive, store and recall information. However, people perceive information in different ways; some people have better memories than others, and some people recall information differently.

Cooper suggests that it is important to note that individual differences approaches are not simply about people being different. Instead, they seek to establish psychological dimensions that apply to everyone but, at the same time, they allow for differences. Identifying and using individual differences thinking and approaches is crucial in facilitating a better understanding of the complexities of any behaviour or topic area.

The nature of individual differences

So how does individual difference theory and research contribute to these other psychological frameworks? This process is best conceptualised by Cooper (1998) and Lubinski (2000), who argue that, in attempting to understand the nature of individual differences, theorists must address two separate, but interrelated, sets of issues.

The first set of issues involves what Cooper calls the **structural model**, which considers the *nature* of individual differences. In other words, we need to ask ourselves 'how' individuals differ. The answer to this question could be influenced by a range of factors, such as our personality, our experiences and societal constructs or our cognitive processes. Many of these aspects are considered later in this text. For example, in the discussion on positive thinking (optimism – Chapter 18), we need to ask ourselves such questions as 'how do individuals differ in their positive thinking? Is it a learned trait, or are some people born to think positively?'

The second set of issues involves what Cooper calls **process models**, which consider the questions of 'why', 'where' and 'when' people differ, and give depth to understanding the 'how'. In other words, here researchers are interested in knowing the ways that people differ. What causes these differences? What are the consequences of these differences? Process models of individual differences might address questions such as these: Why do some people do better in relationships than others? Why do some people suffer from shyness? When do some people find it easier to forgive?

Profile

Colin Cooper

Colin Cooper grew up in Cornwall in England. After a year of studying at Exeter University for a chemistry degree, he started studying psychology. After graduating he worked as a psychologist on pilot selection for the government. Three years later he returned to Exeter University to do his PhD.

In 1986 Cooper moved to the University of Ulster, Northern Ireland, for his first lecturing post; in 2002 he moved to Queens University (Belfast, Northern Ireland) where today he is a Senior Lecturer in Psychology and researches and teaches the psychology of ability, personality, psychometrics and mood.

If you live in the United Kingdom, you may recognise Cooper's name because, in 2002 and 2003, he appeared on the BBC's TV programme *Test the Nation* where he devised the standardised intelligence tests used in these programmes.

Colin Cooper is a chartered psychologist and an associate editor of the international journal *Personality and Individual Differences*. He has published over 60 journal and chapter publications.

How are individual differences identified and measured?

A consideration that we need to address here is how individual differences are actually measured. Most of these methods have been looked at in depth earlier, but it is good to summarise them here as a reminder.

Many different techniques are involved in measuring individual differences. However, Cooper (1998) suggests that there are three main ways that individual differences are identified and measured.

The first way is through **clinical** ideas and approaches. These are best understood as theories that have grown from therapists' actual experiences of observing differences among their patients, or clients. In other words, within the therapy setting, the therapist is allowed access to the individual nature of their client and can see at first hand how that client either deviates or conforms to the generalisations of psychological theory. These observations then enable an enrichment of data for individual differences study. However, because of the small samples involved here, theories based on this technique can be flawed. Remember, the study of individual differences is not simply about how we all differ; researchers also need to identify certain psychological ideas that are applicable to everyone, but that at the same time allow for differences. Small sample sizes do not allow for this process, as it is harder to generalise to everyone when you have a smaller sample. Therefore, although these types of approaches enable an understanding of differences between people, they do not lend themselves for generalisation to larger samples.

Cooper calls the second main methodology **armchair speculation**, which refers to individuals, including psychologists, theorists and researchers, making unbiased observations of how people behave in certain situations and then generating and testing hypotheses about these behaviours.

For example, you may notice that some individuals tend to be more positive about life; they are pessimistic only in certain situations. You may notice that certain people tend to forgive more easily than others, and they may hold grudges only with specific people. These observed differences, then, are worthy of investigation. This type of data is valuable in the same ways that clinical ideas and approaches are valuable, but armchair speculation allows even deeper knowledge due to observations in different situations in life, as opposed to those only within clinical settings (for example, in a therapy session). Of course, like clinical theories, armchair speculation has some drawbacks. Observations like these may be wrong, or fail to take full account of the situation. However, Cooper suggests they are still worthy of investigation, especially if formulated into reliable and valid psychological measures.

The third main methodology described by Cooper is the scientific assessment of individuals using psychological and experimental tests. Individual differences researchers tend to see the scientific assessment of individuals as the least problematic and most used, particularly when reliable and valid measures of behaviour, thinking and feeling are used, because they facilitate the accurate measurement of psychological concepts. Because of this, most individual differences psychologists use this approach to study individual differences.

How individual differences can be applied to improve our understanding of competing or overlapping concepts or topic areas

In the last section we outlined the thinking and approaches that Cooper suggests are necessary in individual differences. He outlined the use of thinking and approaches that understand the structure (how) and processes (why, where and when) of concepts. He also emphasised the use of reliable observations and measurement as important aspects of individual differences.

However, we are going to expand on his viewpoint and examples. If you look at the individual differences literature, you will notice a common theme: individual differences psychologists regularly use a variety of psychological perspectives, methods and analysis techniques in trying to achieve a more holistic (emphasising the importance of the whole and the interdependence of its parts) and realistic understanding of concepts. It might sometimes be better to describe individual differences psychologists as psychology 'magpies'. They will 'borrow' and use *good* theories and methods from several disciplines to achieve a better understanding of any topic. So, for example, if they believe some findings from a set of clinical observations are strong and interesting, they may then try to test these observations in a wider setting using psychological or experimental measures and statistical techniques. Individual differences researchers are good at considering several different theories together. As you will have noticed throughout this book, individual differences theory is based around a number of biological, personality, social and cognitive explanations.

We can summarise this thinking and approach to individual differences study in two ways:

- **Comparing theories** – researchers compare different theories to find the best theories that account for individual differences in a concept.
- **Combining theories** – researchers combine theories to find better underlying theoretical explanations with existing theories.

We will now explain both of these approaches in depth.

Comparing theories

Modern individual differences researchers often *compare* different theories in psychology to find the best explanation of 'how' and 'why' individuals differ. For instance, if we wanted to better understand how and why some people suffer from extreme embarrassment when others feel only mild embarrassment – or indeed, none at all – then we could consider psychological theories from a variety of psychological perspectives to find the best explanations of embarrassment.

To illustrate this process, let us take you through a simple example. Imagine that, through armchair speculation, we have observed that some of our friends have a very poor body image, whereas other friends seem to be very confident with their bodies. By considering all the different perspectives of psychology, we can come up with many different psychological explanations and debates as to why and how these differences occur. For example:

- A social psychological explanation might be self-esteem. There are differences in people's general self-esteem, and those with high self-esteem (people who like, accept and respect themselves) may have better body image, whereas those with low self-esteem do not.
- Another social psychology explanation for poor body image could be because of the amount of the media the person engages with. For instance, your friends with low body image may read a lot of magazines that are full of beautiful, slim, fashionable people; these unrealistic images may profoundly affect how these friends see themselves. However, other people may lend more support to the belief that western society puts too much emphasis on appearance, and it is what's on the inside that counts. These differences in attitudes may explain differences in your friends' body images.
- We can also see that social learning or developmental factors may be factors to consider. For instance, those with low body image may have learned their dissatisfaction from their parents, perhaps by the parents continuously telling them they are overweight or by one or both of the parents passing down their own issues of body image onto the child. Children with good body image may not have learned to respond to their bodies in such a way, or they may have received a lot of positive reinforcement for their body shape from their parents.
- Another explanation of the differences of body image may be because of individual differences in personality. For example, those individuals who display high levels of neuroticism (nervous, worry and anxious traits) may be more nervous and worried about their body, while extraverted people (carefree and optimistic personality traits) may be less worried about their body.

Therefore, from identifying differences between people, we can actually come up with many different theories as to how, and why, differences occur in body image. However, individual differences researchers do not believe in relying on one debate or area of psychology – for example, adopting a social psychology position, or a cognitive explanation or suggesting it's all down to personality. They believe in looking at areas together and empirically comparing theories so they can form an accurate picture of what is going on.

Given the measurement and statistical knowledge we have today, we can compare these different theories by measuring variables that represent all the theories (i.e. self-esteem, learning factors, media use, personality) and then find out which theory or theories best explain differences in body image. This is one of the reasons that measurement, the reliability and validity of measures and statistical methods are so important to individual differences researchers – so that they can equally and accurately compare different theories. In other words, for our example of body images, individual differences researchers would seek to assess which of the theories described might best explain body image.

Let us take you through one research example to illustrate this technique. This was a study that tried to understand why some individuals believe in good luck, while others do not. There was very little theory in this area, so Day and Maltby (2003) engaged in a bit of armchair speculation and considered a variety of theories (and respective variables) that might explain belief in good luck. The variables chosen for the study were from a range of personality, cognitive and social psychology perspectives and included optimism (personality and cognitive), attribution style (social), neuroticism (personality), irrational beliefs (cognitive and social) and self-esteem (cognitive and social). (Don't worry if you don't know what some of these variables are; just follow the example.) The researchers then compared these theories using statistical analysis techniques to find out which of these variables were the best predictors of belief in good luck (if you are interested in reading more on how comparing theories can be achieved with statistical analysis, then refer to the 'Multiple regression' section in the online supplementary chapter on statistics [Chapter 27]).

After the analysis, it was found that optimism was the best predictor of good luck. The other variables were not, in comparison, good predictors of belief in good luck. Therefore optimism could be considered a major theoretical account over other major theories of attribution style, neuroticism, irrational beliefs and self-esteem in explaining belief in good luck (see Figure 17.2). This finding gave the literature on belief in good luck a focus for future research.

So, it can be seen here that comparing different theories is a practical approach to studying individual differences. However, this type of consideration is not only used in empirical examination. It can also be used at a theoretical level to enable a deeper understanding of individual differences variables. For example, you will see later (Chapter 18) how Seligman (a pioneer theorist and researcher on optimism) takes into account several variables and theories and tries to compare them to find the best explanations as to 'how' optimism helps the individual.

Combining theories

In the last section we described how individual differences psychologists emphasised comparing competing theoretical explanations. However, as well as *comparing* different theories, modern individual differences psychologists sometimes also *combine* different theories to discover new and underlying elements for understanding a topic area. This 'combining' of theories is particularly useful to better understand possible theoretical overlaps between theories. In other words, when comparing theories, researchers may find that some of the descriptions of the theories overlap and that simply treating them as separate, distinct theories might be incorrect. For example, would it be fair to say that a theory of neuroticism is distinct from a theory of worry, given that

Figure 17.2 Example of belief in good luck and other variables for comparing theories.

What variables best predict an election win?
Source: Rex Features/KeystoneUSA-Zuma

neuroticism comprises worrying personality traits? It may be better sometimes actually to view a theory as comprising a combination of variables. This combining of theories helps us to discover more complex psychological variables.

To illustrate what we mean, let us consider the concept of what makes us attracted to someone. Imagine that the psychology of attraction has suggested that physical and non-physical variables are important in attractiveness. We have a list: nice eyes, nice smile, nice bottom, nice legs, having a lot of money, having a good job, having a good sense of humour and kindness. We already have our two theories. There is the theory that physical variables are important (nice eyes, nice smile, nice bottom, nice legs). There is another theory that non-physical variables are important (having a lot of money, having a good job, a good sense of humour, kindness).

Imagine that we put all the variables together into an analysis, expecting to see two dimensions (physical and non-physical attractiveness) emerge from the analysis. However, instead of two dimensions emerging from the analysis, we get four! These four dimensions are:

- physical attributes of 'nice eyes' and 'nice smile' alongside non-physical attributes of 'kindness' and 'sense of humour';
- physical attributes of 'nice bottom' and 'nice legs';
- non-physical attributes of 'having a good job';
- non-physical attribute of 'having a lot of money'.

Therefore, looking closely at these dimensions has led to a different interpretation of our original variables. We can see that we have identified one particular dimension that combines both physical and non-physical variables: 'nice eyes' and 'nice smile' (physical), with 'kindness' and 'sense of humour' (non-physical). This is different to how we originally conceptualised the variables. We now have a new dimension of attraction, and this new dimension may give us a much deeper insight into attraction. From this analysis, we may theorise that not only do individuals actually look for physical and non-physical attributes in a potential partner, but there are links between people's perception of physical and non-physical attributes. For example, it could be that a nice smile and nice eyes are thought to reflect the personal qualities of kindness and sense of humour. Therefore we may have achieved a deeper psychological understanding of attraction by identifying attributes that may be overlapping or working together. So, by combining theories, we may get a deeper understanding within a topic area. (If you are interested in reading how this can be achieved statistically, then refer to the 'Factor analysis' section in the online supplementary chapter on statistics.)

Let us present you with a research example so that you can fully understand this approach. We have borrowed an approach used by Ferguson (2001), who looked for overlaps between personality theory and coping, but here we will apply only his general approach and use an entirely fictitious example. For this example we will use Eysenck's model of personality, which comprises:

- **neuroticism** – worry, nervous and anxious personality traits;
- **extraversion** – outgoing and optimistic personality traits;
- **psychoticism** – egocentric and antisocial personality traits.

(You can look back at Chapter 7 here to give you a better description of these concepts if you wish.)

You may be less familiar with coping. Coping is considered a cognitive variable that refers to the different ways in which people deal with stressful situations in their life. Coping is thought to comprise many dimensions, but one of the more useful distinctions has been the one between these strategies:

- **Problem-focused coping** – a strategy that involves dealing directly with stress and finding ways of addressing the source of the stress.
- **Emotion-focused coping** – a strategy that involves not tackling the stressful situation directly; instead, the person concentrates on the emotional responses to the stress.

You can read more about coping later (Chapter 18) when we discuss optimism.

Now, theories of personality and coping have been used to explain depression. Rather than compare these theories (as we did in the previous section), it may be useful to combine them because there are potential theoretical overlaps between personality and coping. For example, let us imagine that neuroticism overlapped with emotion-focused coping because people who tend to worry and be anxious (neuroticism) tend to focus on their emotions in times of stress (emotion-focused coping). Thus there is the opportunity to explore whether these overlaps help us to understand theoretical approaches to depression.

Figure 17.3 shows how this process is worked through. So far, we have identified two sets of variables: one of personality variables (psychoticism, neuroticism and extraversion) and one of coping variables (problem and emotion-focused coping). This is our first level of variables. From here, our combining of the variables (through statistical analysis) might show us that, when considered together, there is a second level of variables:

- a neuroticism/emotion-focused dimension (that is, people who worry and are anxious tend to focus on their emotions);
- an extraversion/problem-focused dimension (that is, people who are outgoing and optimistic tend to focus straight away on stress because they believe they can deal with the stress);

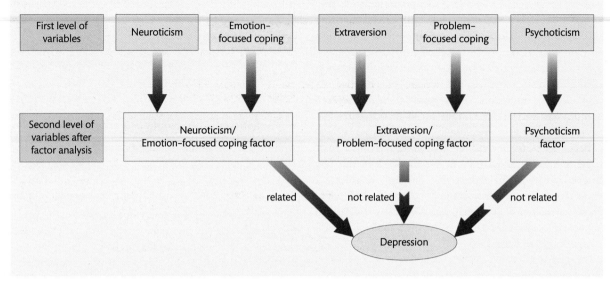

Figure 17.3 Example of personality and coping variables being combined to predict depression.

- a psychoticism dimension (that is, people who are ego-centric and antisocial do not adopt any particular coping style).

Once these new variables have emerged, the researcher would correlate them with depression to find out where significant relationships occurred between the variables. In this example, let us assume we have found that the neuroticism/emotion-focused factor is significantly related to depression (and that the other two dimensions are not related to depression). This means that, although we know (from previous research) that personality and coping factors are related to depression, we can show there are overlaps between personality and coping variables. This information would allow the individual differences psychologist to speculate about how neuroticism and emotion-focused coping might work together in explaining depression. This approach leads us to a deeper understanding of the relationship between the variables.

You can see again why issues of measurement and statistical analysis are so important to individual differences psychologists. This process of combining theories can be an important and powerful method for understanding overlaps between psychological concepts.

The following discussions in this section of the text present many examples of theory and research that seek to 'combine' concepts and topics.

How individual differences theory is debated and applied to demonstrate its usefulness within the psychology of human experience

So far, then, we have looked at a variety of ideas and approaches in individual differences that seek to provide holistic and realistic explanations of behaviour, feeling and thinking. However, we would like you to consider one last element: the modern contribution of individual differences research to psychology today.

Stop and think

The applications of individual differences theory and research

- Think about the different ways that individual differences ideas and approaches are used to inform theory and research. Do you think that other perspectives in psychology would benefit from such an approach?
- How likely is it that psychometric testing and statistical techniques can get to the root of individual differences? What are the possible drawbacks of these techniques?
- How can qualitative research methods be used to understand a number of competing or overlapping psychological concepts?

Individual differences are not just about the classical theories in personality and intelligence, armchair speculations, measurement, statistics, comparing and combining theories. This type of study has an *applied* purpose. It is this applied purpose that forms the focus of the rest of the topics covered. You have already seen how ideas of personality have been applied to clinical settings (for example, Chapters 5 and 6) and to education and the workplace (Chapter 16). However, there is a need to recognise that this application of individual differences can be seen throughout the modern literature in two ways.

The first is that individual differences ideas and approaches have applied value in understanding various concepts in psychology. If you were to look through some personality and individual differences journals, you might be surprised to see that they regularly feature topics such as optimism, irrational beliefs, social anxiety, shyness, embarrassment, love styles, attachment styles, forgiveness, attitudes, mental well-being, health and psychometrics. Indeed, these topics *are* commonly covered in the individual differences literature. We have gathered together eight of these topic areas:

- optimism
- irrational beliefs
- embarrassment, shyness and social anxiety
- personal relationship factors
- right-wing attitudes and religion
- well-being and personality disorders
- health
- psychometric testing.

The second way to consider the application of individual differences is that many of the aforementioned individual differences topics have been used to explain a range of positive and negative human experiences. They can be used to explain first and foremost our mental health; however, they also explain our physical health, our beliefs, our anxieties, our successes and failures in personal relationships and how we view the social world. Therefore, several individual differences topics are applied to several areas of human existence and experience, ranging from explaining our most intimate thoughts to describing our understanding of how society operates and is constructed. We will also consider how the central subject of each discussion has been used to understand aspects such as our mental health, our core beliefs, our feelings and our interaction with the social world.

Final comments

We have introduced you here to three main approaches in individual differences. We have considered how individual differences can be applied to better understand psychological concepts or topic areas, and particularly how distinctions between structural models ('how do people differ?') and process models ('why/when/where do people differ?') are crucial. We have also shown you how individual differences ideas and approaches can be applied to improve our understanding of competing or overlapping concepts or topic areas. Finally, we have considered how the application of individual differences now assists our understanding of several core areas of human experience.

An understanding of each of these elements is necessary for you to appreciate the following eight discussions within this text. We will constantly draw, and build, upon the points raised here.

Summary

- Cooper suggests that it is important to note that individual differences approaches are not simply about people being different; instead, they seek to establish psychological dimensions that apply to everyone, but at the same time allow for differences.
- To contribute fully to other psychological frameworks, individual differences researchers attempt to understand the nature of individual differences by addressing two separate but interrelated issues; to do so, they have developed structural and process models. Structural models consider the nature of individual differences, asking questions such as 'how' do individuals differ? Process models consider the questions of 'why', 'where' and 'when' do people differ, and give depth to understanding the 'how'.
- Clinical theories, armchair speculation, measurement and statistical analysis are all techniques for exploring concepts within individual differences; measurement and statistical techniques tend to have been emphasised in the discipline.
- Modern individual differences researchers compare different theories in psychology to find the best explanation for how and why individuals differ.
- Modern individual differences theorists also combine different theories to better understand possible theoretical overlaps and discover new underlying ideas.
- The application of individual differences now features in a variety of areas of human experience.

Connecting up

This chapter is a forerunner to Chapters 18–25. You may also want to read Chapter 1 again to remind yourself about getting a more extensive picture when evaluating theories and perspectives.

As we mentioned here, there are statistical techniques for comparing and combining variables. The statistical techniques of multiple regression and factor analysis are outlined in the online supplementary chapter on statistics.

Critical thinking

Discussion questions

- Discuss what value individual differences theory and research have to understanding other perspectives in psychology.
- Discuss the advantages and disadvantages of the different research techniques within individual differences.
- What do you think are the benefits of comparing and combining theories to understand behaviours?

Essay questions

- Critically outline the theoretical underpinnings of individual differences approaches and identify their implications for research.
- Critically discuss the major questions that individual differences theories aim to address.
- Critically examine the criteria that can be used to evaluate individual differences.

Going further

Books

- If you would like to read more on Cooper's description of approaches in individual differences, then refer to the first chapter of his book; Cooper, C. (2002). *Individual differences*. London: Hodder Arnold.

Journals

- Lubinski, D. (2000). Scientific and social significance of assessing individual differences: Sinking shafts at a few critical points. *Annual Review of Psychology, 51*, 405–444.

In the following journals, you will regularly find research articles relating to the individual differences theories described here.

- *American Psychologist*. Published by the American Psychological Association. Available online via PsycARTICLES.
- *Personality and Individual Differences*. Published by Pergamon Press. Available online via Science Direct.
- *European Journal of Personality*. Published by Wiley. Available online via Wiley InterScience.
- *Journal of Personality and Social Psychology*. Published by the American Psychological Association. Available online via PsycARTICLES.

- *Journal of Personality Assessment*. Published by the Society for Personality Assessment. Available online via Business Source Premier.
- *Journal of Personality*. Published by Blackwell Publishing. Available online via Blackwell Synergy, SwetsWise and Ingenta.
- *Journal of Research in Personality*. Published by Academic Press. Available online via IngentaJournals.
- *Personality and Social Psychology Bulletin*. Published by Sage Publications for the Society for Personality and Social Psychology. Available online via SwetsWise, Sage Online, Ingenta and Expanded Academic ASAP.
- *Personality and Social Psychology Review*. Published by the Society for Personality and Social Psychology, Inc. Available online via Business Source Premier.

Web links

- Visit the website that deals with scientific research programmes in individual difference psychology (**www.personalityresearch.org**).
- Also visit the site at **www.personality-project.org**. This site is a useful guide to the academic research literature in individual differences.

Film and literature

- *12 Angry Men* (1957, directed by Sidney Lumet). We suggest here that individual differences emphasise the process of looking at behaviour from several different perspectives. One film that represents such thinking is *12 Angry Men*. In this film a dissenting juror (Mr Davis) in a murder trial slowly manages to convince the others that the case is not as clear-cut as it seems in court. As the deliberations unfold, the story quickly becomes a study of the jurors' complex personalities, preconceptions, backgrounds and interactions. These provide the backdrop for Mr Davis' attempts to convince the other jurors that a not-guilty verdict might actually be appropriate.

- *Memento* (2000, directed by Christopher Nolan). We have emphasised here that individual differences involve bringing together pieces of information and interpreting them. This, like *12 Angry Men*, is a film that encourages this sort of thinking, not so much in its plot line (a man who is suffering from short-term memory loss uses notes and tattoos to find out what has happened to him) but in how the director puts the film together.

Explore the website accompanying this text at **www.pearsoned.co.uk/maltby** for further resources to help you with your studies. These include multiple-choice questions, essay questions, web links and ideas for advanced reading.

CHAPTER 18
Optimism

Learning outcomes

At the end of this discussion you should:

- Understand the main theories of optimism versus pessimism
- Be able to identify the differences between learned (explanatory style) optimism, dispositional optimism and situational optimism
- Be familiar with the theory of hope and identify its relationship with optimism
- For each theory, be able to show how theorists and researchers have applied these ideas to inform individual differences in coping, mental health and health
- Be able to identify some of the main debates that occur within each of the theories

Introduction

Source: Pearson Education Ltd.

In 2000, Dr Toshihiko Maruta of the Mayo Clinic in Minnesota, USA, reported that optimists have a longer lifespan than pessimists. Maruta found that people with a positive outlook on life live, on average, 19 per cent longer than those who are miserable. The study assessed optimism and pessimism traits in more than 1,100 patients between 1962 and 1965. While looking again at these patients 30 years later, the researchers discovered that those who had been classified as optimists had a 19 per cent higher chance of still being alive than the pessimists did.

So what are these concepts called optimism and pessimism? Well, a good way to illustrate what these two concepts are is outlined in Stop and think: Characteristics of optimism and pessimism.

Individual differences psychologists have looked closely at why some people are more optimistic than others and have proposed theories to explain exactly how and why optimism works. Consequently, the theory and application of optimism has been a widely researched and debated concept within psychology. It has resulted in psychologists understanding that optimism has a multitude of benefits for the individual. We will see that optimistic people have been shown to possess a more positive mood, have more effective problem-solving techniques, have greater success in life (such as academic and occupational success), have a

greater social popularity and possess good health and long life – and they do all this with less stress. Pessimism, on the other hand, has been shown for the most part to have the opposite, detrimental effects – particularly greater negative mood, such as depression and low self-esteem. For individual differences psychologists it is important to understand why, when and how some people are more prone to optimism than others are, whether there are ways to increase our own optimism in life and whether optimism is always a good thing.

During this discussion we are going to introduce you to the different theories of optimism (see Figure 18.1). We will first concentrate on the two main and influential theories: learned (or explanatory style) optimism (which emphasises optimism as a way of explaining setbacks in your life) and dispositional optimism (which emphasises optimism as a typical mood, temperament or quality). We will then show you that optimism, in its varying forms, is accompanied by research evidence suggesting that it is related to successful coping, better mental health and better physical health. We will then expand our consideration to look at other types of positive thinking. These will include situational optimism (which emphasises the use of positive statements to repress negative thoughts) and hope (hope being a belief that you can work towards and attain your goals). We will also consider alongside all these theories the concept of pessimism and its consequences for individuals.

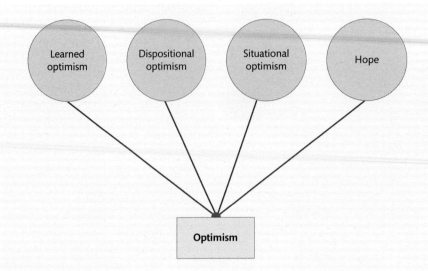

Figure 18.1 The main theories of optimism.

Stop and think

Characteristics of optimism and pessimism

The best way to explain the characteristics of optimism and pessimism is to remind you of those two wonderful childhood personalities of Tigger and Eeyore in the *Winnie the Pooh* stories. Here are some of their well-known sayings, illustrating clearly their optimistic (Tigger) and pessimistic (Eeyore) traits.

Tigger and his optimistic quotes	Eeyore and his pessimistic quotes
'Tigger: a Friendly Tigger, a Grand Tigger, a Large and Helpful Tigger, a Tigger who bounced, if he bounced at all, in just the beautiful way a Tigger ought to bounce.'	'Nobody minds. Nobody cares. Pathetic, that's what it is.' 'Even if you think you have nothing worth stealing . . . someone will come along and take your tail.'
'I love jumping' said Roo. 'Let's see who can jump farthest, you or me.' 'I can,' said Tigger. 'But we mustn't stop now, or we shall be late.' 'Late for what?' 'For whatever we want to be in time for,' said Tigger, hurrying on.	'You can give a donkey a happy ending . . . but the miserable beginning remains forever.'
'Can Tiggers swim?' 'Of course they can. Tiggers can do everything.'	'Life is a Box of Thistles . . . and I've been dealt all the really tough and prickly ones.'
'Can they climb trees better than Pooh?' asked Roo, stopping under the tallest Pine tree, and looking up at it. 'Climbing trees is what they do best,' said Tigger. 'Much better than Poohs.'	'Eeyore,' said Owl, 'Christopher Robin is giving a party.' 'Very interesting,' said Eeyore. 'I suppose they will be sending me down the odd bits which got trodden on. Kind and Thoughtful. Not at all, don't mention it.'
'It's a funny thing about Tiggers,' whispered Tigger to Roo. 'How come Tiggers never get lost?' 'Why don't they, Tigger?' 'They just don't,' explained Tigger. 'That's how it is.'	'Write down your worries. And then depress your companions by reading them out loud.'
'Tiggers never go on being Sad,' explained Rabbit. 'They get over it with Astonishing Rapidity.'	'Enjoy Boredom . . . It's all you've got to look forward to.' 'Visualise a Thunderstorm . . . . It's just what would happen!'

Source: A. A. Milne and E. H. Shepard (illustrator) from *Winnie the Pooh* (1926), *The House at Pooh Corner* (1928) and the poetry from *When We Were Very Young* (1924) and *Now We Are Six* (1927), now published in *Winnie the Pooh: Complete Collection of Stories and Poems* (London: Methuen, 2001).

Learned optimism – explanatory style

Learned optimism was formulated by Martin E. Seligman (a professor of psychology at the University of Pennsylvania in the United States) and his colleagues. They developed the theory from the 'attributional reformulation of the learned helplessness model' (Abramson *et al.*, 1978). In other words, Seligman had already presented a theory of how people could learn to be helpless (by way of attribution theory) and he used this to show how, by turning the theory on its head, you could actually learn to be optimistic (we will explain both attribution theory and helplessness in the following paragraphs). This new model was formed as a way of explaining individual differences in response to negative events (for example, stressful situations).

According to Seligman, helplessness occurs when people (or animals) find themselves in an uncontrollable situation; for instance, when a person cannot do anything about what is happening to them. Then the person learns to be helpless because they begin to expect events to be uncontrollable. Learned helplessness happens when a person has learnt to attribute their failures in situations to *internal* (to do with the person themselves), *stable* (will always be there) and *global* (will be there in every aspect of their life and in all situations) factors.

For example, if a person's romantic relationship breaks down, a person who has learned helplessness may attribute the breakdown to:

- **Internal factors** – for example, 'it's all my fault'; 'I'm not worthy of having someone love me'; 'no one could love such a terrible person as me'; and 'my personality is awful, I drove them away'.
- **Stable factors** – for example, 'it's always my fault'; 'I'll never be worthy'; 'I've always been a horrible person, and it will always be the same'.
- **Global factors** – for example, 'If I am so terrible, everyone must know it. This means that no one must like me, no one will ever want to have *any* sort of a relationship with me. Even my friends don't like me.'

From this rather extreme example, it is easy to see how these thoughts can lead to a feeling of helplessness and that a person may even give up trying for any type of relationship at all. We will look more closely at learned helplessness and how this theory was used to develop optimism shortly, but first let us look in more detail at the concept of an explanatory style.

Explanatory style, according to Seligman (1991), is the way that you explain your problems and setbacks to yourself and choose either a positive or negative way to solve them. For example, if a person lost their job, they may explain that event in two very different ways. First, that person may think that they lost their job because the economy is bad, and the company had to make people redundant – so they were just one of the unlucky ones. Secondly, that person may instead concentrate on the fact that not everyone was laid off, and begin to think that the company got rid of them because they did not work hard enough, or they weren't liked by their employers. These two different explanatory styles will have a different effect on how a person solves the problem, for example, of getting another job. Someone using the first explanatory style will probably have a positive way of solving it, as there are no negative thoughts attached to the explanation. Someone using the second explanatory style will have had negative thoughts, and this will probably have negative effects on them getting future jobs. Optimism and pessimism are thought of as habits of thinking that reveal your own personal explanatory style (Seligman, 1991). This style of thinking works on a continuum that goes from extreme pessimism right through to extreme optimism. In other words, individuals differ in where they are placed on this continuum, and a person can be either extremely optimistic or extremely pessimistic, or somewhere in between.

Learned helplessness versus learned optimism

According to Seligman's theory, people mostly have a tendency to be either pessimistic or optimistic. Although both sets of people have the same life experiences, it is how they handle and think about those experiences that set them apart from each other. Seligman (1998) goes further to argue that although being optimistic is better than being pessimistic, it is much easier to be pessimistic. In other words, it is much harder to remain confident and positive in the face of setbacks than it is to give in to the feeling that there is nothing you can do to help make the situation better. Seligman argues that it is easy to see that learned helplessness – a state of affairs where you feel there is nothing you can do to affect what happens to you, and life is uncontrollable – is at the centre of pessimism.

Seligman (1998) reports that he first identified learned helplessness in the late 1960s, as a graduate student, while working on another piece of research altogether. Seligman was working on a research project looking at how emotional behaviour can be learned (as part of conditional responses in behaviourism) and was looking at the phenomenon in dogs. In this research, the dogs were placed in a box and were repeatedly exposed to a tone that was then followed by a mild electric shock. The purpose of this research was to teach the dogs to learn to associate the tone with a shock, with the aim being that the dogs eventually learnt to be afraid of the tone, even when no shock was presented.

However, things did not happen as Seligman and the other researchers had expected (Overmier and Seligman, 1967; Seligman and Maier, 1967). Rather than learning to jump out of the box to avoid the shock, the experimenters found that the dogs became 'helpless', tending to just lie down, be somewhat passive, waiting for the electric shock to occur. Seligman concluded that the dogs had, over the course of the experiment, *learned to be helpless.* In other words, the dogs had learned that, no matter what they did, they would experience the electric shock; and they could not do anything to escape this negative event. For Seligman the dog had learnt something – they had learned to expect the shock – and this expectation resulted in a set of helpless behaviours.

Seligman (1998) reports that he carried on this research and found more evidence of learned helplesssness, but he discovered something else among other dogs. He found that dogs who learned initially, as puppies, that they could avoid the shock, didn't learn to be helpless like the other dogs. He found that this occurred even when they experienced other adverse stimuli in later experiments. Seligman concluded that these dogs had learned to expect that they could avoid any adverse stimulus (including the shock). Seligman also concluded that these dogs had learned to be optimistic; and, what is more, he found that the optimistic dogs never learned to show helpless behaviours. Therefore, Seligman suggested that the development of learned helplessness could be prevented.

Seligman continued his work and discovered something else (Seligman, 1998). He found that the dogs who had learned to be helpless could learn to stop being helpless by learning to avoid the shocks. However, Seligman also found that the dogs did not learn to overcome their helplessness automatically. He found they needed a lot of help from the experimenters.

Seligman later discovered similar effects when looking at humans (Seligman *et al.*, 1988). Seligman found, while doing an experiment that exposed people to extremely loud noises, that once people discovered that they were unable to find a way to avoid the noise, they became helpless. Seligman also found that on some occasions participants did not even try to escape the noise even when escaping was possible and relatively simple to achieve.

In reviewing this evidence, Seligman (1998) also reports that, as well as identifying learned helplessness whilst conducting these experiments, he also identified something different altogether – a learned optimism. He found that 33 per cent of both the dogs and the humans could not be taught to become helpless at all. In fact, they seemed resilient to the adverse situations and never became helpless; instead, they continued to find ways to avoid and escape.

Seligman found that there were individual differences between humans in the way they *explained* adverse and negative situations to themselves (explanatory style). For instance, people who explained their negative situations

Profile

Martin E. P. Seligman

Martin E. P. Seligman is Professor of Psychology at the University of Pennsylvania in Philadelphia, USA. He is Director of the Positive Psychology Centre, located within the university, where he conducts research on positive psychology, learned helplessness, depression and optimism and pessimism. He is renowned and respected worldwide for his contributions to these areas, as well as being a best-selling author. His theories on learned helplessness and learned optimism remain some of the most important theoretical contributions to the psychological literature on depression and optimism. Seligman presents real and easily achieved methods for clinical psychologists and individuals alike to enable psychological change.

Seligman has written over 200 articles and published at least 20 books, which are bought and read by the general public as well as academics. His best-known books are probably *Learned Optimism* (1991) and *What You Can Change and What You Can't* (1994), which teaches readers how to learn optimism and be optimistic.

Seligman is the recipient of two Distinguished Scientific Contribution awards from the American Psychological Association, the Laurel Award of the American Association for Applied Psychology and Prevention and the Lifetime Achievement Award of the Society for Research in Psychopathology. He has also received both the American Psychological Society's William James Fellow Award for his contributions to basic science and the James McKeen Cattell Fellow Award for the application of psychological knowledge (see Seligman's home page at **psych.upenn.edu/seligman/bio.htm**). Although he is best known for his conception of learned optimism, since 2000 Seligman has turned his attention to promoting the field of positive psychology, which includes research on positive emotion, positive character traits and positive institutions. He is also dedicated to training individuals to become positive psychologists, to 'make the world a happier place' (Seligman, 2003).

as **personal** (internal, e.g. 'The negative situation is all my fault'), **permanent** (stable, e.g. 'This negative situation will never get any better') and **pervasive** (global, e.g. 'My whole life is ruined because of this negative situation') became helpless. Seligman described these people as pessimistic. On the other hand, those people who explained their negative situation as **circumstantial** (external, e.g. 'This negative situation is just an unfortunate occurrence. It's not my fault'), **temporary** (unstable, e.g. 'This negative situation will end, and things will get better') and **specific** (explicit, e.g. 'This negative situation is bad but the rest of my life is really good') were active in trying to make their situations better. Seligman described these people as optimistic.

Seligman argued that pessimists believe the bad things that happen to you in life actually last longer and undermine anything you try to do (i.e. they are permanent and pervasive). As well as this, they believe it is usually their own fault that these bad things are happening (i.e. they are personal). Learned optimism seems to be the direct opposite. Optimists tend to use their 'optimism' to deal with situations that are stressful. They see bad things that happen in life as temporary setbacks that have no future bearing on their lives (i.e. they are temporary and specific). As well as this, these stressors are not a result of their own actions but rather explanations such as that bad luck, circumstances or other people have caused them (i.e. they are circumstantial). Here is an everyday example of these two views: Tony fails a psychology exam. If Tony is a pessimist (a person with learned helplessness), he blames himself for the failure and continually worries over the failed exam. However, if Tony is a learned optimist, he probably blames his failure on something other than himself; for example, the exam questions were unfair or too hard, or perhaps the teacher is an unreasonable marker. So, as you can see from this example, learned optimism is beneficial as it helps people to move on in their lives.

The ABC format

Of interest to individual differences psychologists is that Seligman believes you can learn optimism by assessing your ABCs. This view, the **ABC format**, is the basis of Seligman's theory of optimism (Seligman, 1991; 1998). Within Seligman's theory of optimism, the ABCs are adversity (A), forming beliefs about adversity (B) and the consequences those beliefs have (C).

Therefore, the key to learning optimism lies in the formation of belief (at B); in other words, how you may think and feel about bad things, or misfortunes (adversity – A) will actually determine the consequences (C) that you will face. For instance, if an individual is pessimistic about a certain bad event, that individual will probably experience either moderate or severe depression depending on the severity of the event. Let us use the earlier example of pessimistic Tony and the psychology exam: the psychology exam is the adversity (A). If Tony thinks he will fail his psychology exam no matter what he does (B), he will most probably fail or receive a low grade (C). However, if Tony learned to be more optimistic and felt he would pass the test if he studied hard enough (B), it is possible that he will not only pass the test, but probably get a high grade too (C).

Once Tony tackles his belief system and realises he can pass the test if he studies hard enough, then he will probably also be able to change the consequences of failing the test if he had remained pessimistic.

Distraction and disputation

As well as the ABC format just outlined, Seligman (1991) argues that there are two specific tactics to combat pessimism (or what he terms learned helplessness) and therefore stay optimistic.

Distraction is used to put adversities or problems aside for a while so that a person can re-evaluate the situation and adopt a fresh outlook. This tactic also allows the individual to negate the emotional issues of the situation. In other words, when a person faces a problem, if they are pessimistic, they will begin to fret about it, believing it is another problem that cannot be solved. Because of these thought processes, a lot of emotions are attached to the problem, which in turn makes the problem harder to solve. If, however, the person diverts attention away from the problem (distraction) by doing relaxation exercises, stopping any thoughts on the problem by going and thinking about something else for a while, then their emotions will calm down and they may be able to approach the problem better when they go back to it. Distraction, however, should be considered only as a short-term measure; the person must go back to the problem when they have calmed down, or else many other problems may occur because of it.

Disputation should be used after distraction, when the person has had time to calm down, to change their beliefs about the adversity. In other words, these beliefs should be challenged by the person. For example, they should ask themselves, 'Why am I thinking this about the situation?' rather than asking 'Why is this happening to me?'

Let us go back to our example about the psychology exam: Tony should ask himself why he feels he will fail. If he goes through this self-challenging process and comes up with a reason – for example, that he doesn't study hard enough – then he can deal with this reason more easily than with simply a belief that he will fail. In other words, Tony will realise that he will pass if he studies harder. If Tony uses this technique, then he will successfully change from pessimism to optimism on passing the psychology exam. However, he will have to use the same technique all the time to have a truly optimistic life.

Stop and think

Being optimistic daily?

- What do you think are the main weaknesses of Seligman's theory? Do you think the weakness may actually lie in assuming the ability to learn optimism? We could all easily follow Seligman's advice to become more optimistic in one instance or situation, but how painstaking would it be to go through this conscious effort each time to learn to be optimistic all the time?

- How successful do you think the transfer of the idea of learned helplessness to pessimism is? You may want to consider the definition issues here around learned helplessness and pessimism – do they mean the same thing?
- How probable is it that a person can learn to be optimistic via the ABC method? Consider in depth how the ABCs work. Are they too simplistic, or are they sufficient to enable change in a person?

Nevertheless, Seligman's theory allows individuals who are not optimistic to gain the benefits that an optimist has.

So far we have considered an influential theory of how individuals learn to be optimistic. In this theory it is easy to understand why individuals differ greatly on the continuum of optimism versus pessimism, as well as how optimism can be beneficial. However, are we to understand that individuals who are 'naturally' optimistic have simply learned the correct ABC techniques? The next main theory to be considered, that of dispositional optimism, may better explain this question.

Dispositional optimism

From 1981 onwards, two influential US psychologists, Charles Carver and Michael Scheier (Carver and Scheier, 1981; Scheier and Carver, 1985), explained individual differences in the theory of optimism and pessimism by identifying the concept of dispositional optimism. They defined dispositional optimism as a person's *general predisposition to be optimistic* in their mood or their temperament, and the reason for this view may be because of the individual's personality or a genetic disposition. In other words, genetic and personality factors may influence whether you are optimistic or pessimistic – instead of you learning to be optimistic or pessimistic. This predisposition leads a person to 'expect' either favourable or unfavourable outcomes depending on whether they are optimistic or pessimistic.

So, learned optimism is used by an individual to *explain* future events (i.e. they will explain events as positive because of their individual explanatory style), whereas individuals using **dispositional optimism** will *expect* good events (they don't explain things; they just expect them to be). A dispositional optimist will tend to continue to work towards attaining their goals, instead of simply giving up, because they will always expect outcomes to be favourable. A dispositional pessimist will always expect outcomes to be poor and may, as a result, give up on their goals (Scheier and Carver, 1985).

Scheier and Carver believe that these expectancies have an influence on an individual's 'affective experience' (a psychological term meaning arousal or emotion; in other words, whether a person usually has a negative or positive mood state), and they are considered to be stable characteristics that the individual will display consistently across time and across different contexts. For this reason, researchers consider dispositional optimism to be important in how well individuals deal with stress, and therefore it has been linked to coping and how people appraise stress (we will look at this topic later).

The Life Orientation Test: a measure of dispositional optimism

Scheier and Carver (1985) measure dispositional optimism versus pessimism with a brief self-report questionnaire called the Life Orientation Test (LOT), which originally contained four positively worded items and four negatively worded items. However, over time, there are now four 'filler' items (items that measure neither optimism and pessimism and are put in a questionnaire to stop the participant from guessing what the questionnaire is asking them about), three positively worded items and three negatively worded items, where respondents are asked to agree or disagree with the statements.

Here are the three positively worded items (measuring optimistic traits):

- In uncertain times, I usually expect the best.
- I'm always optimistic about my future.
- Overall, I expect more good things to happen to me than bad.

Profiles

Michael F. Scheier and Charles S. Carver

Michael F. Scheier

Michael F. Scheier is Professor of Psychology at the Carnegie Mellon University, Pittsburg, USA. His theory on dispositional optimism (along with Charles Carver) remains one of the most important theoretical contributions to the psychological literature of optimism. It also remains the only theory, so far, to explain why some people always expect positive outcomes. He has over 100 publications in the fields of behavioural self-regulation, personality and health psychology.

Charles S. Carver

Charles S. Carver is Professor of Psychology at the University of Miami, USA. He has published widely in the fields of emotion, health, personality and self-identity. However, again, he is perhaps best known for his partnership with M. F. Scheier and their work on the dimension of dispositional optimism versus pessimism. Like Michael Scheier, he is a prolific and influential theorist and researcher in a number of psychological fields, including behavioural self-regulation, personality and health psychology.

Here are the three negatively worded items (measuring pessimistic traits):

- If something can go wrong for me, it will.
- I hardly ever expect things to go my way.
- I rarely count on good things happening to me.

Optimism and well-being

In the following sections about optimism, we will be looking at exactly why optimism is important to well-being. We will consider how optimism is related to coping, appraisals of mental health (depression and self-esteem) and health.

However, although you can easily understand the concepts of depression, self-esteem and health, you probably have not come across the concepts of coping and appraisals. We will detour from optimism for a moment and use this next section to briefly explain coping and appraisals. This should allow you to read the rest of the discussion with complete confidence, knowing all the terms that will be presented to you.

Coping and appraisals

According to Lazarus (1966) and Lazarus and Folkman (1984), when we are faced with stressful situations in our lives, we make a sequence of choices when deciding how to deal with the stress. First, we assess whether the stress is harmful or useful to us. These assessments are known as primary or stress appraisals. Secondly, we decide on how best to deal with the stress depending on how we have assessed that stress. These decisions are known as secondary appraisals or coping strategies.

Primary appraisals

According to Ferguson *et al.* (1999), **primary appraisals** are judgements made by a person about what a stressful situation holds in store for them. Specifically, a primary appraisal is what a person perceives and assesses as the possible effects of demands and resources on their well-being of that stressful situation. For example, a demand might be the stressful situation's potential emotional impact. Primary appraisals have been found to comprise three dimensions:

- **Threat** – refers to seeing the stressful situation as having the potential to harm the individual.
- **Loss** – refers to seeing the stressful situation as comprising a potential loss for the person; for example, loss in friendships, health, self-esteem.
- **Challenge** – refers to seeing the stressful situation as having the potential for growth or benefits for the individual.

The individual then decides (appraises) whether the stressful situation represents the potential for threat or loss, or whether it has potential for some sort of challenge (they may gain or benefit).

According to Ferguson *et al.*, if a person decides the situation has the potential of a threat, or loss, then this appraisal triggers secondary appraisals, which are the processes of determining what coping options or behaviours are available to deal with the stressful situation. There are many situational factors that influence appraisals of threat or loss, including: their complexity; the individual's values, commitments and goals; novelty of the situation; social support; intensity of the situation; and the perceived controllability of the potential threat or loss (Ferguson

Stop and think

Optimistic bias

It is worth noting that naturally 'optimistic' people need to be careful of **optimistic bias** (ignoring or minimising risks). For example, a dispositional optimist could keep driving recklessly although very near the edge of a cliff because, in their eyes, the eventuality of falling over the edge just could not happen. Another example would be where an optimist keeps mindlessly and continuously pouring money into a failing business simply because they do not understand or 'recognise' the word 'failure'.

---

et al., 1999). When the stressful situation has been appraised as having the potential for threat or loss, and all these situational factors have been considered, this then leads to coping strategies.

Coping strategies (secondary appraisals)

People use a variety of coping strategies (or **coping styles**) in dealing with stressful situations. The most useful distinction made is between two specific forms: engaged and disengaged coping (Lazarus, 1966). Although these two forms are still considered today, two US psychologists, Lazarus and Folkman (Lazarus and Folkman, 1984), changed the name of these two forms of coping to problem-focused (engaged) and emotion-focused (disengaged) coping. According to Lazarus and Folkman, **problem-focused coping** strategies (sometimes called adaptive or direct coping) are coping strategies *directed at* the stress; they involve problem-solving by looking for logical and active ways to solve the stressful situations. These strategies may include efforts to understand and define the problem properly, weigh up the costs and benefits (advantages and disadvantages) of various actions, think of solutions, take actions to alter what is changeable and learn new skills. Problem-focused efforts can be directed outwards to change some aspect of the environment, or inward to change some aspect of the self.

On the other hand, **emotion-focused coping** involves coping attempts that are *not directed* at the stressful event and instead are directed at decreasing emotional distress caused by the stressful event (Rice, 2000). These tactics include such efforts as avoiding the problem, distancing themselves from the problem, developing selective attention, seeking blame for the problem, minimising the extent

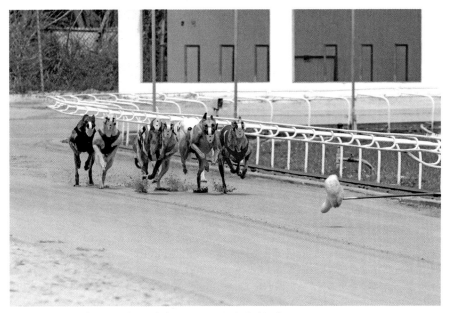

Would you say that greyhounds have an optimistic bias?
Source: Alamy Images/imac

of the problem, wishful thinking, venting and expressing emotions, and seeking social support (talking to others about the problem).

Both forms of coping do have advantages, depending on what the situation is. In general, research tends to support the view that it is always beneficial to use problem-focused coping and less beneficial to use emotion-focused coping (Folkman, 1997). However, it is worth noting that when a stressful situation is completely out of your control (for example, the death of a family member), then emotion-focused coping has been found to be useful.

Now that we have looked at the general themes within coping and appraisal, let us get back to the key themes of optimism and well-being.

Benefits of optimism and well-being

We will now show you some evidence regarding why optimism is beneficial. Extensive research has been done on the relationships between optimism and well-being variables. In this section we will briefly describe to you some of the areas in this literature: coping, depression, self-esteem and physical health.

Optimism, coping and appraisals

Since Scheier and Carver first identified dispositional optimism, a lot of research has been carried out into looking at what optimism and pessimism are related to. Much of this research was carried out not only by Scheier and Carver themselves but also by many other individual differences researchers (a relatively recent example is Edward C. Chang, 2000; 2002; Chang et al., 2009). Findings from early research suggested that optimism is associated with a general sense of confidence and persistence, particularly when confronting a challenge, whereas pessimism is associated with characteristics of doubt and hesitancy (Scheier and Carver, 1985). Particularly, research suggested that these different characteristics tend to be amplified when faced with a serious adversity or stressful event. Therefore, researchers quickly established that optimism may have important implications for the ways that people cope with stressful situations.

Considerations of this finding led to research that showed optimists are positively related to problem-focused (engaged) coping strategies and negatively related to emotion-focused (disengaged) coping strategies (Aspinwall and Taylor, 1992; Scheier et al., 1986; Carver and Connor-Smith, 2010). Other research has found that optimists tend to adopt problem-solving coping and actively seek social support coping strategies, whilst also emphasising the positive aspects of the stressful event. Pessimists were found to adopt denial and avoidance coping; they also pay too much attention to negative feelings and aspects of the

stressful event (Scheier et al., 1986). Chang (2002) carried out a study of optimism, pessimism and stress among a sample of young and middle-aged adults. Chang found that the relationship between appraised stress over a previous month and psychological symptoms was significantly more exacerbated for pessimists than it was for optimists across age groups. In other words, Chang found that, when pessimists perceived high levels of stress in their lives, they tended to experience greater psychological symptoms of stress than optimists. Other findings support the view that there are positive outcomes of being optimistic. Optimism is related to a better quality of life (Schou et al., 2005), to better psychological well-being (such as self-acceptance, positive relations with others, autonomy, environmental mastery, purpose in life and personal growth; Augusto-Landa et al., 2011), buffering against the harmful effects of body dissatisfaction (Brannan and Petrie, 2011), better exercise habits (Glazebrook and Brawley, 2011) and lower distress following surgery (David et al., 2006). Alongside this, optimists have often been found to use challenge appraisals over any other primary appraisal (threat or loss). For example, optimists see stressful situations as challenging, as ways for them to grow and learn from the situation (Carver and Scheier, 1999b; Scheier and Carver, 1985). In a meta-analysis (which combines the findings of many studies with similar research hypotheses), Carver and Connor-Smith (2010) found that optimism, extraversion, conscientiousness and openness together are related to more engagement coping; that neuroticism is related to more disengagement coping; and that optimism, conscientiousness and agreeableness together are related to less disengagement coping.

Because of findings like these, commentators suggest that optimists are better adjusted psychologically than are pessimists. Overall, it is argued that optimistic individuals have an 'optimistic advantage' over pessimistic individuals in life due to differences in their coping and appraisal strategies (Scheier et al., 1994).

A final important point is that optimism, coping and appraisals are often thought of as being intrinsically linked and lead to better mental and physical health. That is, optimistic individuals adopt problem-focused coping strategies and challenge appraisals, and it is the adoption of these processes that leads to better mental health and health outcomes (see Figure 18.2).

Therefore you should not be surprised when we now consider the relationship between optimism, mental health and physical health, to see terms that you associate with coping and appraisal.

Optimism and depression

What we think about affects our focus, our attitude and eventually our life. Seligman (1991) suggests that optimists

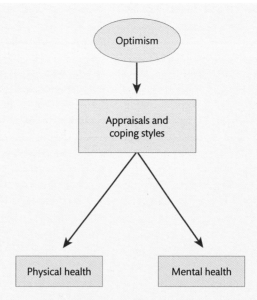

- Optimists' coping styles are suggested to enhance both mental and physical health
- They prefer problem-focused/active coping, and less emotion-focused/avoidant coping
- They use positive interpretation, acceptance, humour
- They use challenge appraisals
- They don't use denial and behavioural disengagement
- This leads to better physical and mental health

Figure 18.2 Optimism and well-being.

Stop and think

Optimism and personality

Although optimism is a very important construct in its own right, and is considered as either a learned construct around explanations of events (Seligman) or as a dispositional trait and expectancies (Scheier and Carver), authors such as Peterson (2000) have argued that we also need to consider how optimism is positioned alongside the larger concept of personality. An example of this type of research was carried out by Sharpe, Martin and Roth in 2011, who investigated optimism and its relationship to the Big Five factors of personality. They found that dispositional optimism was related to four of the five major personality factors, with optimism significantly positively correlated with extraversion, agreeableness and conscientiousness, and significantly negatively correlated with neuroticism. They further propose that optimism/pessimism should be considered through three major conceptual pathways to better describe the relationship of optimism with personality. These three pathways are:

- **The affective pathway** – this shows how optimism/pessimism is related to the negative affectivity of emotional stability/neuroticism and the positive affectivity of extraversion. This idea is widely accepted and supported within the literature.
- **The social pathway** – this shows how optimism/pessimism is related to extraversion and agreeableness, and considers the idea that optimists tend to have better relationships, find it easier to make friends and are generally more socially adept.
- **The persistence pathway** – this shows how optimism/pessimism is related to conscientiousness, and suggests that optimists don't only believe that they will experience more positive outcomes in life, but also that they vigorously pursue goals to achieve more positive outcomes.

Overall, these findings by Sharpe et al. in 2011 suggest that the relationship between optimism and personality may be a much more complex one than first thought.

and pessimists think differently and thus evaluate their life differently, which has an overall effect on their quality of life.

There has been extensive research on optimism and depression, particularly with learned optimism. The evidence suggests a strong negative relationship between the two variables (Conley *et al.*, 2001; Seligman, 1998). Basically, a pessimist looks at the downside of life and explains things in a pessimistic way. The result is often sadness and wanting to give up on things – even things that are achievable. Optimists, however, explain things by telling themselves that problems are not forever and that they can change things for the better. Numerous studies have shown that, as opposed to pessimists, optimists are less likely to become discouraged by problems and are less vulnerable to depression (Seligman, 1998; Ziegler and Hawley, 2001). Although there has been a multitude of research studies on depression with learned optimism, a lot of that research has looked at the relationship between dispositional optimism and depression. All studies show that higher levels of dispositional optimism are associated with lower levels of depression – and that dispositional pessimism is associated with higher levels of depression (Scheier *et al.*, 1994; Schweizer and Koch, 2001; Sing and Wong, 2011).

Indeed, there have also been studies looking at optimism and its relationship to suicidal behaviour. Rasmussen and Wingate (2011) found that optimism can moderate the effects of thwarted belongingness and perceived burdensomeness in the prediction of suicidal thoughts. This suggests that optimism may have an important role to play in alleviating suicidal thoughts, and needs to be considered for clinical applications.

Optimism and self-esteem

Self-esteem is a well established psychological term referring to how much a person likes, accepts and respects themselves overall as a person. High self-esteem suggests that a person likes, accepts and respects themselves a lot, whereas a person with low self-esteem does not. Research evidence shows that optimism and self-esteem are highly associated, suggesting that optimists have high self-esteem and pessimists do not (Brissette *et al.*, 2002; Makikangas *et al.*, 2004).

However, it is easy to see from this brief explanation why self-esteem could have a strong emotional impact on how an individual relates to the world and the self, as well as having a particular effect on mental health. Although self-esteem and optimism can be regarded as distinct constructs, it is also of interest to us how optimism and self-esteem may overlap to predict other mental health variables.

The overlaps between self-esteem and optimism have been studied in two ways: (1) to see which of the two variables has a larger effect on mental health; and (2) to sort out the effects of one of the variables when considering the other variable's relationship to mental health (in other words, to distinguish between what is optimism and what is self-esteem). Results suggest that optimism is still a good predictor of mental health when considered alongside self-esteem (Leung *et al.*, 2005).

An important point for us to consider has arisen from these types of studies. According to some researchers, an individual's favourable emotional understanding and assessment of themselves (i.e. self-esteem) and their favourable expectations of the future (i.e. optimism) are overlapping constructs in understanding one's mental health (Makikangas *et al.*, 2004; Wanberg and Banas, 2000). For example, according to Makikangas *et al.*, people with higher self-esteem and higher dispositional optimism will tend to enjoy greater mental and physical health than others do, most likely because they cope better with harmful perceived stress and are consequently more satisfied with life. Some researchers suggest that common to both optimism and self-esteem is an underlying construct of *resilience* (Wanberg and Banas, 2000). Resilience refers to individual differences in being able to react and cope to stressful situations (Rutter, 1990; Makikangas *et al.*, 2004). According to Makikangas *et al.*, individuals with resilience have a positive view of themselves, are optimistic about the future, as well as optimistic about their ability to appraise stress situations in a positive light and their potential ability to deal with a stressful situation. As you might recognise, this is the sort of self-confidence and positive thinking that would be expected in someone high in self-esteem and optimism.

However, Makikangas *et al.* suggest that, regardless of the issues with resilience, self-esteem and optimism can be considered as separate constructs. Self-esteem indicates the degree to which you experience yourself as worthy and capable (Rosenberg, 1979). Optimism, as we have seen here, is defined as generalised positive outcome expectancies and plays an important role in maintaining a person's goal-directed behaviour. So, in general, self-esteem refers to your emotional relationship and assessment of yourself, whereas optimism describes your relationship with the outside world and expectations of success (Makikangas *et al.*, 2004). Despite these definitional issues, in regard to whether optimism is good for us, what we generally discover from research into the relationship between optimism and self-esteem is that where you find a person who is optimistic, you will tend to also find a person who has high self-esteem.

Optimism and health

Although we have concentrated mostly on the benefits of coping and other mental health variables, it seems useful here to give an overview of how optimism affects dimensions of physical health. Scheier and Carver (1985) suggest that optimists develop fewer physical symptoms over time than their pessimistic counterparts do. However, it is also worth noting that there are some limitations to this conclusion, as physical symptoms tend to be self-reported. Thus, it could be proposed that optimists may actually be underreporting their physical symptoms (owing being optimistic; e.g. 'I don't feel so bad'), and pessimists may be overreporting their physical symptoms. Nevertheless, with this in mind, researchers have found four main ways in which optimism may influence health:

- by improving the immune system functioning (Segerstrom *et al.*, 2003);
- through use of adaptive coping strategies (Schroder *et al.*, 1998);
- through increased positive health habits (Kelloniemi *et al.*, 2005; Mulkana and Hailey, 2001; Ylostalo *et al.*, 2003);
- through absence of negative mood (Abele and Hermer, 1993; Carver *et al.*, 1994).

Indeed, a meta-analysis review carried out by researchers Rasmussen, Scheier and Greenhouse in 2009 found that optimism is a significant predictor of positive health outcomes. The studies focused on mortality, survival, cardiovascular outcomes and physiological markers, including immune function, cancer outcomes, outcomes related to pregnancy, physical symptoms and pain. In all studies optimism was found to be a significant beneficial predictor.

Optimism: a cloud in the silver lining?

A final word needs to be said here about optimism and its effects on well-being. Although we have substantially documented the positive effects on well-being, we have also noted that, according to Seligman (1991), optimism may not *always* be the preferred way of thinking, and this lends some hope to those of us who are hopelessly pessimistic. For instance, optimism may actually reflect an innate human tendency towards being unrealistic; therefore, it is easy to be positive if the world you live in is a self-generated illusion.

As well as this, there may also be a cautionary note about problem-focused coping; indeed, optimists may actually be at a disadvantage when stressful situations are not controllable or alterable. In other words, for some stressful events in our lives, there is no actual problem to be solved. Instead, the problem is unsolvable, and we just have to accept the situation (for example, the death of someone). It is at these times that emotion-focused coping (for example, talking to others or expressing your emotion) is the only coping strategy available to us (Peterson, 2000). However, Seligman (1991) suggests that optimists can actually use

a variety of coping strategies, including emotion-focused coping. In other words, they can adapt to the situation. So, when an optimist is faced with a stressful situation, they will always choose a problem-focused coping strategy. However, if this strategy doesn't work or is inappropriate, optimists have the ability to change their appraisals of the stressful situation and use an emotion-focused coping strategy.

Seligman has a further note of caution for us. He maintains that if your goal is to plan for a risky and uncertain future (for example, setting up a risky business venture), then optimism may not always be useful as it is foolish to ignore the negatives if your future livelihood is at stake. Another example where Seligman argues that optimism should never be used is in counselling, particularly when counselling patients with depression, as it may mask the real issues.

Situational optimism

We have talked extensively about the two main theories of optimism and how they are related to better well-being. However, one more theory on optimism has recently emerged and needs bringing to your attention. **Situational optimism** is the newest area of optimism research; so far, little evidential research has been carried out. However, the theory of situational optimism seems to expand on the theory of dispositional optimism; it refers to the expectations that an individual generates for a particular situation concerning whether good rather than bad things will happen (MacArthur and MacArthur, 2002; Segerstrom *et al.*, 1998). In other words, whereas dispositional optimists have much more generalised positive beliefs about the future – they expect good things to happen within *every* aspect of their lives – situational optimists tend to have specific positive beliefs about certain events – they expect good things to happen within *specific* areas of their lives. For example, a situational optimist may not be generally optimistic about things, but they may be very optimistic about their success at university or at their chosen career or at sports. As we have stated earlier, dispositional optimism is usually considered to be a stable and global trait that is always there. However, it is clear to individual differences psychologists that people can sometimes be optimistic in certain situations and yet not so optimistic in other situations. This behaviour has so far, to some extent, been explained by learned optimism; however, learned optimism only suggests how a person *explains* future good events – it does not suggest how a person *expects* future good events. Thus there seems to be some potential to explain this behaviour further within the context of situational optimism, where positive expectancy is focused on a specific situation. Because specific expectancies seem to be more effective in responses to specific events than dispositional beliefs are,

Stop and think

Big and little optimism

The term 'big and little optimism' is used by researchers to understand the differences between the two main theories of optimism outlined (Peterson, 2000). 'Big optimism' is dispositional optimism and 'little optimism' comprises explanatory style (see Figure 18.3). Big optimism is thought to be a biologically given tendency that is stable over time and that produces a state of general resilience to setbacks. Little optimism is thought to be the product of your own unique learning history and leads to specific actions that are adaptive in concrete situations.

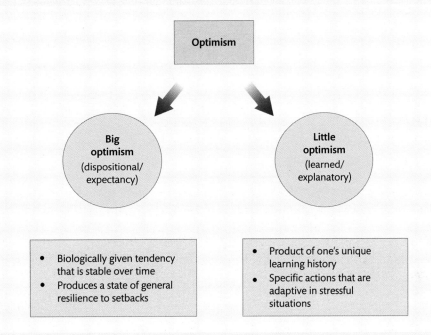

Figure 18.3 Big and little optimism.

they may be important predictors of psychological and biological well-being. US psychologist Suzanne Segerstrom and her colleagues (Segerstrom *et al.*, 1998) have found that, among a total of 140 law students, the situational optimists, rather than the dispositional optimists, seemed to demonstrate a more positive relationship with better mental health (for example, better mood and less stress).

So how is situational optimism measured? The answer is by assessing expectations about outcomes that are linked to particular contexts (or situations). Because of this, items

Stop and think

Dispositional optimism

- What do you think are the main weaknesses of the theory of dispositional optimism? If you are born optimistic, do you stay optimistic? If you are born pessimistic, do you stay pessimistic?
- In your view, is it always better to be optimistic, or does pessimism play a necessary role within our lives?

You may want to consider situations in life when it is better to be pessimistic, although you may also want to consider whether the benefits of pessimism outweigh the benefits of optimism.

to measure situational optimism vary from situation to situation; in other words, the researcher adjusts the questions asked in the items depending on the situation being measured. So, for example, instead of asking generalised questions about dispositional optimism, such as 'in uncertain times, I usually expect the best', researchers ask specific questions about the situation. So, as with the research done by Segerstrom *et al.* with 140 law students, questions may ask students to agree or disagree with specific statements such as 'it is unlikely that I will fail at law' or 'I feel confident when I think about law school' (Segerstrom *et al.*, 1998).

Generally, situational optimism is a way of explaining how people can expect good things to happen to them within a given situation. Dispositional optimism relates to how people expect good things to happen to them in all situations.

Hope

Although learned optimism and dispositional optimism are the main theories in optimism research, another area of positive thinking has emerged within psychology and is of interest to us. In 1994 Charles Richard Snyder, a US psychologist from the University of Michigan, tried to integrate aspects of these two approaches of optimism into a theory of hope (Snyder, 1994). Snyder has developed this thinking from earlier work by US psychologists Averill, Catlin and Kyum (1990) and Stotland (1969), who present **hope** in terms of an individual's expectations that goals can be achieved.

Snyder argues that these goal-directed expectations are composed of two measurable components. The first component is **agency**, which reflects an individual's determination that goals can be achieved. The second is identified as **pathways**, and it reflects the individual's beliefs that successful plans and strategies can be generated to reach goals. This second component, according to Peterson (2000), is Snyder's novel contribution and is not found in other formulations of optimism. In other words, the importance of Snyder's theory of hope is the realisation that people not only desire goals, and feel optimistic about them, but that they also make plans, or pathways, to enable them to achieve these goals. Therefore, hope is not just a 'dreamy' construct; instead, it is the thing that makes us plan towards achievement. There is also a third component in this theory – that of the goal itself.

So, let us explain Snyder's theory in more detail. As we have said already, the hope theory is based on three components: (1) the goal, (2) pathways and (3) agency (see Figure 18.4). This first component, the goal, refers to what we want to happen. Goals have pathways (second component) attached to them, such as 'how are we going to reach that goal?' and 'how good are we at devising, or producing, the routes to achieve that goal?' Last is the agency – that is, 'how much motivation do we have in going after that goal?' Agency, then, is the mental determination or belief to go after that specific goal.

Snyder (2002) argues that these goals represent mental targets to ourselves that we feel we have some probability

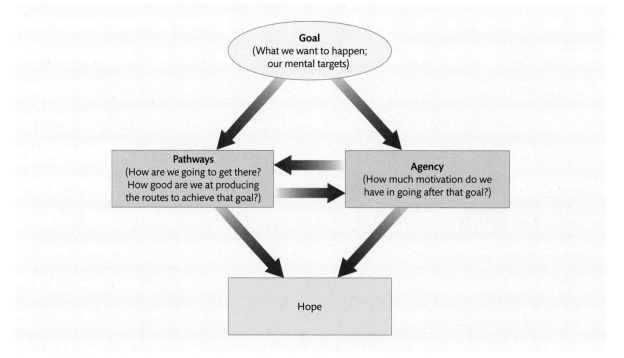

Figure 18.4 How goals, pathways and agency come together in Snyder's model.

of achieving. However, there is no absolute certainty that we will achieve these goals, or else we would not need hope! These goals can have differing degrees of importance (ranging from completing an essay set by our university tutors or simply arriving at an appointment on time right through to lifetime ambitions), and they can be short-term or long-term goals.

Snyder (2002) has also found evidence of 'low-hope' people and 'high-hope' people, for whom there are different consequences. People with low hope usually tend to have only one goal, and it is usually ambiguous in nature, whereas people with high hope typically tend to have lots of goals (Snyder estimates about six). These high-hope people seem to have more benefits, particularly as they are not putting all their efforts into just one goal. If one goal is not met, then they can go for another of their goals; in other words, they diversify. These people also tend to have more clarity about their goals; their hopes are clearer than those of low-hope people.

According to Snyder, benefits for high-hope people also occur within pathways. (Remember that pathways are basically the perceived ability to come up with plans, or routes, to achieve goals.) We usually have a preferred route to achieve our goals, but sometimes these routes can get blocked. Therefore, we need to come up with alternative pathways to achieve what we want to achieve. High-hope people seem to be better at finding these new routes. For example, if one of your goals is to become a psychotherapist, then some of your pathways will include getting to university by doing well at your A levels. The next pathway will be to achieve a high grade (i.e. a 2:1 or first) at university to get on a postgraduate course for psychotherapy, and so on. However, if one of these pathways becomes blocked (for example, you get a 2:2 at university instead of a 2:1), then it may be unlikely that you will get accepted on the postgraduate course. It would seem, then, that the goal is now unachievable; however, a high-hope person may start to look for a different pathway to achieve the same goal. They may get there by making new pathways via work experience in counselling, so that their work experience outweighs their academic success, which eventually might mean that they get accepted onto the postgraduate course. The potential benefits for high-hope people in being able to find many alternative pathways, or routes, to achieving their goals become clear.

The final component of hope, agency, also shows differences when considered among low-hope and high-hope people (Snyder, 2002). Agency is the mental determination, the ability to say 'I can'. In other words, it is the belief in one's ability to achieve the goal. Again, people with high hope seem to be better equipped for believing in themselves.

So, to summarise, a high-hope person has these characteristics:

- They have many goals, and the capacity to define these goals clearly.
- They have the ability to come up with routes to these goals, and this usually involves generating several different routes to achieve the goal (pathways).
- They have the ability to motivate themselves in the pursuit of those goals (agency).

Benefits of hope

It is not surprising that Snyder and other researchers have found evidence suggesting that high-hope people show better academic and athletic performance (e.g. for academic performance, McDermott and Snyder, 1999; Snyder *et al.*, 2002; Day *et al.*, 2010; Marques *et al.*, 2011, and, for athletic performance, Curry *et al.*, 1999). Research also suggests that there are no age or gender differences with hope; indeed, Merkas and Brajsa-Zganec (2011) showed that children also cluster into high-hope and low-hope groups. They also found that children with high hope are more satisfied with their life, have higher self-esteem, report better support from others and have better family cohesion as opposed to those children with low hope.

High hope is also related to optimism, through the agency component (e.g. motivation and positive belief), but it is not related to optimism through the pathways component (e.g. finding routes). In other words, this evidence seems to suggest that the more optimistic you are, the more motivated you seem to be in going for your goals; however, it doesn't seem to matter whether you are optimistic or not when identifying your routes to achieving those goals.

Finally, hope has been found to be related to mental health and physical health. High hope is related to high self-esteem, whereas low hope has been found to be related to depression (e.g. Snyder, 2000; 2002). As well as psychological benefits, researchers have found benefits with physical health. Particularly, high-hope people tend to show more knowledge about prevention of illness, they seem to recover more quickly and they show more healthy ways of dealing when they do get ill. For instance, they stick to regimens of treatment or medication much more easily (e.g. Snyder, 2000; 2002).

Therefore we can see that hope, like optimism, has a lot of benefits attached to it. But, why do some people have low hope where others have high hope? Well, this question is far from being answered. The debate is similar to that of optimism, in that people may be born with hope while others may learn to have hope. Hope theory is still in its early stages of research, and much more research is needed before any strong viewpoint explaining these individual differences can be proposed.

Profile

Charles Richard (Rick) Snyder

Charles Richard (Rick) Snyder was Professor of Psychology and Director of the Graduate Training Program in Clinical Psychology at the University of Kansas, Lawrence, USA.

He was born on 26 December 1944. He earned his BA degree from Southern Methodist University and MA and PhD degrees from Vanderbilt University. In 1972, he became an assistant professor of psychology at the University of Kansas.

Snyder's theory on hope remains the most important within the hope literature in terms of his contributions to how hope is conceptualised and, indeed, why hope is important for psychologists to understand, particularly with its effects on mental health. He spent more than 16 years investigating the research and clinical applications

of a cognitive and individual differences theory of hope. During that time, Snyder tried to identify and define hope and has compared it to many positive psychological concepts such as learned and dispositional optimism, self-efficacy and self-esteem. Among his in-depth research, he found hope to be related to health and coping, attachment issues, spirituality, meaning of life, depression and academic and athletic progression, to name just a few areas.

Snyder received 27 teaching awards at the university, state and national levels including the Outstanding Graduate Education award from the American Psychological Association. He has written or edited 23 books and 262 articles.

However, Snyder (2002) argues strongly that hope is a learned concept, and he has written much on how you can increase your hopes. He suggests that learning to be a better planner may help a great deal; in other words, planning many different types of routes or pathways might be the answer. He also suggests that using a 'goal checklist' may aid success, such as asking yourself, 'Is it a goal I really want?' Rank your goals from the most to the least important, and put aside enough time for important goals. From there, practise making different routes to achieve the same

goal; and, remember, if one route does not work, then use what you have learned from that experience to find a better route. Finally, Snyder suggests improving your agency by being positive and recalling your successes to remind you that 'you can' find a goal – or a goal that is more attractive and will be more fun – to enjoy the journey. Lastly, Snyder advises you to remember not to get tied up with the past – and don't let past failures affect future goals.

We have talked much about people having low or high hope. It is important to remember that, according

Even in situations of the most adversity, we can see evidence of optimism.
Source: Panos Pictures/Dieter Telemans

to Snyder, based on individual differences, there are also many different connotations to these two specific types of hope. There are many mixed types of hopers; some people have high motivation but no clear goals; others may have high motivation and strong goals, but no pathway. Snyder suggests that, if you can identify yourself as one of these mixed-hope people, you can also identify the issues that you need to work on. It is worth noting here, however, that, although these mixed types have been identified, there has been little substantial research in identifying their beneficial or detrimental effects on mental or physical health.

Measurement of hope

Snyder's theory of hope is measured with a brief self-report scale that asks individuals to agree or disagree with various statements (Lopez and Snyder, 2003; Snyder *et al.*, 1996). Snyder has developed two measures: the first measures hope among children, and it can be used among children from 7 to 14 years of age. This scale has six items; three of the items measure pathways and three measure agency. The second scale can be used to measure hope among adults and includes eight items: four for pathways and four for agency.

Here are two example items:

- I energetically pursue my goals (agency)
- There are lots of ways around any problem (pathways).

A consideration of false hope

Although we have looked in detail at the theory of hope, the beginnings of a debate are emerging within this arena as to the concept of false hope. Now, it is worth noting that, although the concept of false hope has been suggested, there is still no real evidence for its existence; indeed, Snyder himself has vehemently disputed the arguments set out so far. However, it is still worth commenting on the debate. To give you some idea of the debate over false hope, we will briefly present the case in terms of researchers who are for and against this concept. The argument for false hope has been put forward by two Canadian psychologists, Janet Polivy and C. P. Herman (2002). Snyder and his colleague K. L. Rand have put forth arguments against the Canadians' claim (Snyder and Rand, 2003).

Polivy and Herman argue that, despite repeated failure by some individuals to change aspects of their behaviour, these people continue to make frequent attempts at self-change. These researchers have described this cycle of failure and persistent effort as a **false hope syndrome**. The types of self-change they are talking about within this debate are behaviours such as dieting, giving up smoking and abstaining from alcohol. The researchers' argument for

this syndrome is that, although these people hope to make these changes in their life, their hopes are unrealistic.

Polivy and Herman sum up their ideas within a false hope model (see Figure 18.5). First, they suggest that these people produce *unrealistic expectations*, for example:

- how quickly these changes will take effect (speed);
- how easy these changes will be (ease);
- the amount of effort that will be needed to make the change (amount);
- rewards that they will receive from making these changes (reward).

Polivy and Herman do suggest that the decision to make these changes does, initially, make the individual feel more in control of their life and so the self-change effort begins well, with some success. However, Polivy and Herman suggest that, as time goes by, and the effort continues, these people

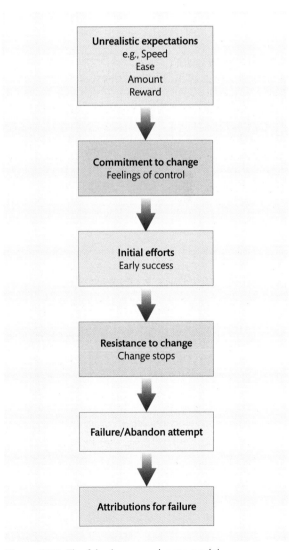

Figure 18.5 The false hope syndrome model.
Source: Based on Polivy and Herman (2002).

find it more difficult to sustain the effort (owing the unrealistic expectations in the first place) until no further progress is made. An example of this, given by Polivy and Herman, occurs when a person has set an unrealistic weight loss goal in an unrealistic period of time. They begin in earnest but soon find that the amount of dieting to achieve that certain weight loss is too difficult, and maybe they aren't losing the weight quickly enough. They then begin to stray from their goal and find that they are no longer losing weight. Polivy and Herman argue that, once one or more relapses have occurred, the person will abandon the effort. They will now deem themselves as a failure and probably feel worse than they did to start with. They may then try to soften the failure by making certain attributions to explain it away, perhaps shifting the blame away from the unrealistic goal altogether and maybe leading to starting the whole thing again. If, however, they had certain realistic goals and had not hoped for so much, they may actually have succeeded. Polivy and Herman suggest there are three forms of false hope:

- expectancies that are based on illusions instead of reality;
- inappropriate goals;
- poor strategies to reach the desired goals.

We have briefly presented the case for false hope; now let us consider Snyder and Rand's argument against Polivy and Herman's ideas. First, Snyder and Rand (2003) argue that there is no empirical support for Polivy and Herman's model. They argue that Polivy and Herman present no clear definitions for false hope, or indeed for hope itself – Snyder and Rand suggest that hope is more than simply self-change. Also, according to Snyder and Rand, Polivy and Herman do not consider individual differences, or permutations on their predictions, and so do not show possible different outcomes.

Snyder also worries about the suggestion in the false hope model that people would be healthier if they did not pursue their self-change goals; surely, when using examples of giving up smoking and alcohol, it is better to keep trying to quit than not to try at all.

Finally, Snyder and Rand argue against Polivy and Herman's ideas by referring to differences between low-hope and high-hope people. Snyder and Rand argue that there is evidence that it is low-hope people who fail to revise their expectations, not high-hope people. They argue that research has shown that high-hope people always have related to better outcomes in academics, athletics, well-being and psychotherapy.

Snyder and Rand debate the three forms of false hope put forward by Polivy and Herman (expectancies that are based on illusions instead of reality; inappropriate goals; poor strategies to reach the desired goals). Snyder argues that there is no existing evidence to support this model for high-hope people.

First, high-hopers show only a slight positive bias about their goals; this is not the same as illusion. In fact, Snyder and Rand suggest that extreme illusions suggest delusions through psychosis – not hope. For example, if a high-hope person is looking to achieve weight loss, then they will set a target of how much weight to lose within a given time frame. They may indeed set their weight-loss target a little high, but it will nevertheless be achievable. They would not, as Polivy and Herman suggest, set an unrealistic weight-loss target.

Secondly, Snyder and Rand argue that suggesting high-hopers have inappropriate goals is not evident in the research; in fact, people with lofty goals have been found to be no less likely to achieve them if they have strong pathways and agencies (Snyder and Rand, 2003). A good example of a goal that may seem rather lofty would be that of becoming an actor. Snyder and Rand argue that, if the person setting this goal is a high-hoper, then they will set achievable, or strong, routes and agencies. These may include, for example, going to drama school, learning the ropes and working up from the bottom so that the goal becomes achievable.

Thirdly, Snyder and Rand argue that the suggestion of poor strategies is unfounded. High-hopers have been found to generate much more effective routes, especially under impeding circumstances.

In summary, although Snyder and Rand present a good case against the idea of false hope, the concept of false hope may be a consideration that needs to be taken into account when considering hope.

Optimism versus 'positive thinking'

So far, all the theories concerning optimism that we have presented are psychological ones that have been commonly accepted in the psychology discipline (by way of being published in peer review journals). However, it seems apt here to mention the concept of **positive thinking** and its frequent use in the everyday world. You have probably heard the term 'positive thinking' before. Indeed, today positive thinking has been hailed in almost religious terms within society – and actually suggested as a crucial predictor of success in business, sports, politics and personal development. However, there is a note of caution within the academic world about this general use of the term 'positive thinking.'

Seligman (1991; 1998) has argued that to use the concept of positive thinking casually or frivolously as a general predictor of success in life is too simplistic for a complex world. According to Seligman, positive thinking is a 'childlike assumption that we can create our own destiny with the powers of the mind'. Although the concept is similar to the cognitive models of optimism and hope, it

Stop and think

The concept of realism, or unrealistic optimism

Although we have written at length about the benefits of optimism and the deficits of pessimism, many of you reading this will be thinking, 'I'm neither pessimistic nor optimistic; I'm a realist.' Well, there is a consideration about what realism is.

There is a debate centering on the question, is it better to be an optimist or a realist? Here, we will present to you a short summary of a debate laid down by Sandra Schneider (2001). She states that a realistic outlook on life improves the chances of negotiating life quite successfully, whereas optimism places priority on feeling good about life and the world. Nevertheless, are these two concepts so different from each other? Schneider suggests that the 'fuzzy' nature of the definition of realism places only loose boundaries on what it actually means to be realistic. On the other hand, many forms of optimism do not yield unrealistic outlooks. Nevertheless, research suggests that there are numerous 'optimistic biases' that involve self-deception, or convincing yourself that desired beliefs are achievable without any appropriate reality checks. For example, think about X Factor, the well-known reality television show in Europe and the United States. This show asks tens of thousands of 'wannabe' pop stars to audition through various rounds until there is one winner – the one with the 'X factor', who ultimately wins a recording contract. Consider those tens of thousands of contestants who attend the auditions in the first few weeks. Many of these contestants believe powerfully that they can sing; they are fully expecting to win, when in reality they can't sing a note in tune. This type of self-deception may be considered 'optimistic bias' at its worst.

Basically, then, until we consider 'realism', we are unsure whether optimism is actually *realistic* optimism (e.g. knowing you can sing well, and so there is a real chance of at least getting to the final 16 on *X Factor*) or whether pessimism is *realistic* pessimism (e.g. knowing you can't sing, and so don't even go to the *X Factor* auditions). Such analysis can also apply to unrealism as well, ranging from being *unrealistically* optimistic (about being able to sing when you can't in *X Factor*) through to being *unrealistically* pessimistic (e.g. not going to the *X Factor* auditions at all, because you believe nothing good ever happens to you, although you can sing wonderfully well). For more information on this article, go to: Sandra L. Schneider, In search of realistic optimism. *American Psychologist, 56,* 2001: 250–263.

Further research is now looking at how unrealistic optimism can actually be maintained whilst facing the realism of life. Sharot *et al.* (2011) examined this question and have suggested that optimism is facilitated by the brain's failure to code errors in estimation when it should call for pessimistic updates. This failure results in selective updating, which supports unrealistic optimism that is resistant to change. Therefore, Sharot *et al.* argue that dismissing undesirable errors in estimation makes us susceptible to view the future world through rose-coloured spectacles.

---

is too simplistic – and to some extent, potentially harmful. Seligman argues that, to consider a situation fully, individuals should allow themselves to explore their negative thoughts, not just deny them by thinking positively. Denial of negative thoughts can in fact lead to denial of important cognitions of the personality, and it could actually lead either to a splitting of character or to depression. Seligman suggests that there is a need to look closely at the psychological literature. For example, ideas surrounding learned optimism are embedded within reality (not to mention empirical research), and this approach does not attempt to simply repress negative thoughts. Instead, the approach

Stop and think

Snyder's theory of hope

- What do you think are the main strengths to Snyder's theory of hope? You may want to consider that this theory is flexible and very positive in suggesting ways that we all can hope and therefore realise our hopes and dreams – regardless how out of reach they seem.
- What do you think are the main weaknesses of the theory? Ironically, the weaknesses may actually lie in

the suggestion that all hopes are achievable, especially considering the theory of false hope.
- How probable is it that a person can learn to be a high-hoper? You might want to consider that if you put in the amount of hard work suggested by Snyder on planning and considering alternative routes, then you are motivated enough to actually achieve the goal.

seeks to reframe negative thought, in a systematic way, to better conform to reality and to be of more psychological use. Merely repeating positive statements, as one is expected to do by just thinking positively, does not raise mood or achievement (Seligman, 1991). Seligman stresses that it is important to know the difference between optimism and positive thinking.

Final comments

We have looked at different theories of optimism and hope and considered how these can inform individual differences by looking at why, where, when and how individual differences occur within optimism. We have outlined the main theories of optimism versus pessimism and identified the differences between two main theories of optimism: learned (explanatory style) and dispositional optimism. We have also outlined situational optimism and the theory of hope and have identified the relationship of each concept with optimism. For each of these theories, you should be able to show how theorists and researchers have applied these ideas to inform individual differences in areas of well-being, including coping, mental health and physical health. You should be able to identify some of the main debates that occur within the major theories.

Summary

- What drives much of the research within individual differences psychology are the findings that optimism, in its varying forms, has strong research evidence to suggest its relationship to better physical health and mental health.
- There are three different theories of optimism, but there are two main, or influential, theories: explanatory style optimism/learned optimism (Seligman) and dispositional optimism (Scheier and Carver).
- Learned optimism was developed from the attributional reformulation of the learned helplessness model as a way of explaining individual differences in response to negative events (stressful situations).
- Explanatory style is the way you explain your problems and setbacks to yourself and choose either a positive or negative way to solve them. Optimism and pessimism are thought of as habits of thinking that reveal your own personal explanatory style.
- Learned helplessness, a state of affairs where nothing you choose to do affects what happens to you, is at the centre of pessimism.
- Seligman believes you can learn optimism by assessing your ABCs: adversity (A), forming beliefs about adversity (B) and the consequences those beliefs have (C).
- There are two specific tactics to combat pessimism (learned helplessness) and therefore to stay optimistic:

distraction is used to put the adversities aside for a while to allow re-evaluation of the situation and a fresh outlook; disputation is used to change the individual's beliefs about the adversity.
- Dispositional optimism refers to a predisposition (e.g. personality trait/genetic disposition) towards expecting favourable outcomes; it describes individual differences in optimistic versus pessimistic expectancies.
- Dispositional optimism versus pessimism is measured with a brief self-report questionnaire called the Life Orientation Test (LOT).
- Situational optimism expands on the theory of dispositional optimism and refers to the expectations that an individual generates for a particular situation concerning whether good, rather than bad, things will happen.
- Hope theory relates to an individual's expectations that goals should be achieved. These goal-directed expectations are composed of three components: agency (determination that goals can be achieved), pathways (beliefs that successful plans can be generated to reach goals) and the goal itself.
- False hope syndrome refers to a cycle of failure in which individuals make persistent efforts to change aspects of their behaviour.

Connecting up

You may want to look back at the chapter on cognitive personality theories (Chapter 5), to read up on social-cognitive approaches and Ellis' rational-emotive behaviour therapy. Reading these chapters on Ellis will also give you a better understanding of the ABCs of Seligman's learned optimism theory mentioned here. You may also want to read Chapter 19 on irrational beliefs as an individual difference to get a wider view of positive thinking.

Critical thinking

Discussion questions

We have considered several theories necessary for you to understand optimism, and we have presented some considerations so you are able to appreciate the value of these theories. However, many issues remain unresolved in this topic area. We present those issues here in the form of discussion topics to allow you to think about them on your own, or within groups; your university seminars would also be a great place to discuss them. They are not for you to worry about; they are only presented as a way for you to appreciate the complexities of this topic.

- This first exercise is to get you generating some ideas about optimism. Let us consider some of the theoretical and empirical findings covered in this within an individual differences perspective (as outlined in Chapter 17).

    - Name five or six important theories and/or findings that emerge from this topic area.
    - If you were to present an overview of these five or six chosen theories and findings, what different areas of psychology would you be emphasising? For example, are they biological, physiological, personality, cognitive, social or clinical factors?
    - Of these five or six chosen theories and findings, which do you lend most weight to?
    - Are there any theoretical or empirical overlaps between the theories and findings and, if so, where do they occur?

- Although we have addressed why, when and where individuals are optimistic, individual differences theorists are still unsure of how optimism occurs. In other words, there is still confusion over where optimism actually comes from; its origins are unclear. It is believed that the genetic heritability of dispositional optimism is estimated at an average of 0.33 across the population (Scheier and Carver, 1985). In other words, an estimated average of 33 per cent of dispositional optimism across the population is thought to be accounted for by genetic influences. We can, of course, presume that the rest of the variance is accounted for by factors involving environmental influences. However, there are no clear theories as to what the factors are, other than that they are simply learned or they occur in situations. Can you identify certain environmental factors or processes that may influence optimism?

- Theories of optimism tend to suggest that optimism has the same positive effects on mental health because they are all related to the passivity or vigour with which individuals face the demands of life (Peterson, 2000). This leads to the questions 'which optimism is most beneficial?' and 'why have so many different theories?' What, then, is the point of having these different theories? Do they overlap, or should we view them as separate? Is one type of optimism more preferable to have than the others?

- Another issue, proposed by Peterson (2000), is that optimism should not just be considered as a cognitive characteristic; in fact, according to Carver and Scheier (1990), it has both emotional and motivational components. For example, optimism doesn't only mean that we 'think' optimistically; it also has an effect on how motivated we become, and this leads to feelings of happiness. On the whole, researchers seem to regard these motivations and emotions as outcomes that are separate from optimism. But we may need to consider such questions as 'how does optimism feel?' and 'is it a feeling of happiness, joy and contentment?' In terms of motivation, optimism is linked to perseverance but is specifically associated with a good choice of goals that lead to attainment (Peterson, 2000). However, not all individuals have the same goals or give the same merit to the same goals. Is optimism required for all goals? Are some goals not worth the 'optimistic' effort?

- One point that is also worthy of mentioning is an issue with dispositional optimism. This type of optimism has been extensively researched, but there have been problems with using the Life Orientation Test (LOT; a measure of dispositional optimism) as the measures of pessimism repeatedly showed positive correlations with neuroticism. Neuroticism is a personality trait that contains characteristics such as moodiness, being nervous, feeling easily fed up, being a worrier, being easily stressed and anxious. It is easy to see that neuroticism shares certain characteristics with pessimism. However, over the years, the Life Orientation Test has been revised by taking out items that were related to measuring neuroticism. Nevertheless, a question to discuss is whether pessimism is just another form of neuroticism.

- Another issue to consider is whether pessimism and optimism are different dimensions. Findings with optimism measures such as the Life Orientation Test suggest that pessimism and optimism may be independent of each other (Scheier and Carver, 1985). Peterson suggests that these two concepts are separate and should not actually be considered as extremes on one dimension (Peterson, 2000). How should we conceptualise optimism and pessimism? Is it worth considering not only that some individuals can use both optimism and pessimism in different situations but also that some individuals may actually expect both good *and* bad things within the same situation?

- Finally, why is optimism always welcomed and pessimism viewed suspiciously? We must not forget that the concept of pessimism may be valuable. For example, do pessimists sometimes provide us with a good dose of realism?

Essay questions

- Evaluate Seligman's theory of learned optimism and its relevance to an individual's well-being.

- Seligman argues that a person can learn to be optimistic. Discuss.
- Define the main concepts within the theory of dispositional optimism, and evaluate their relevance to individual differences.
- Compare and contrast the theories of learned, dispositional and situational optimism.
- Compare and contrast learned and dispositional optimism in relation to well-being.
- What are the main concepts within the theory of hope? Evaluate the uniqueness of the theory in relation to optimism.
- Critically discuss the concept of a false hope syndrome.

Going further

Books on learned optimism

These books give really good explanations of the theory of learned optimism to allow you to get an even deeper understanding. They also concentrate on explaining how you can actually learn to be optimistic, which we now know is nearly always a good thing.

- Seligman, M. E. P. (1990). *Learned optimism: How to change your mind and your life*. New York: Pocket Books.
- Seligman, M. E. P. (1991). *Learned optimism*. New York: Knopf.
- Seligman, M. E. P. (1994). *What you can change and what you can't*. New York: Knopf.

Books on hope

The following book explains in depth the theory of hope, as well as explaining the ways in which you can strengthen your agency and pathways.

- Snyder, C. R. (ed.). (2000). *Handbook of hope: Theory, measurement, and applications*. San Diego, CA: Academic Press.

Other useful books

The following book has been chosen to enable you to advance your knowledge in the areas of individual differences and the theory of coping. It is easy to read and useful to expand your knowledge.

- Rice, V. H. (ed.) (2000). *Handbook of stress, coping, and health: Implications for nursing, research, theory, and practice*. London: Sage.

Journals

- Peterson, C. (2000). The future of optimism. *American Psychologist, 55,* 44–55. *American Psychologist* is published by the American Psychological Association. Available online via PsycARTICLES.
- Folkman, S. and Moskowitz, J. T. (2004). Coping: Pitfalls and promise. *Annual Review of Psychology, 55,* 745–774. *Annual Review of Psychology* is published by Annual Reviews, Palo Alto, California. Available online via Business Source Premier.
- Positive psychology is one area that has grown from Seligman's work on optimism. You might be interested to read more about this area; if so, then you could access the special issue on positive psychology in *The Psychologist* (2003), Vol. 16, Part 3 (Guest editors: P. Alex Linley, Stephen Joseph and Ilona Boniwell). It is freely available online. You can find *The Psychologist* on the British Psychological Society website (**www .bps.org.uk**).

The following journals are available both online and accessible through your university library. These journals are full of published articles on research into optimism and hope, so use these terms in your searches when using an online library database (Web of Science; PsycINFO).

- *Journal of Personality and Social Psychology*. Published by the American Psychological Association. Available online via PsycARTICLES.
- *American Psychologist*. Published by the American Psychological Association. Available online via PsycARTICLES.
- *Personality and Individual Differences*. Published by Pergamon Press. Available online via Science Direct.

Web link

- Visit the Centre for Positive Psychology (**www.psych .upenn.edu/seligman**). This site contains all the recent research being done by authors such as Seligman and Snyder. It also presents information about each author. It is a useful source of information.

Film and literature

The following films and books are fun to watch or read and they will help you to consolidate the characteristics of optimism and hope.

- *The Shawshank Redemption* (1994, directed by Frank Darabont). This film is about a man, Andy Dufresne, who is sent to Shawshank Prison for the murder of his wife and her lover. At first he is very lonely and isolated, but he realises that there is something deep within him that other people can't touch – hope. The central theme of the film is how Andy's dreams and optimism rub off on his friend, and how his spirit and determination lead them into a world filled with courage and desire.
- *Chocolat* (2000, directed by Lasse Hallström). This film (from the book by Joanne Harris) is about a woman named Vianne Rocher, who arrives at a very small, set in its ways, French village, and opens up a confectionery shop. What evolves is an immense struggle between Vianne's optimism, positivism and reason and the village's mysticism and conservative morality.

- *Animal Farm* (1945, George Orwell). This classic book concentrates on the satire of dictatorship and the abuse of power, and involves the complex political ideas raised after the Russian Revolution. The animals on Manor Farm drive out their master and adopt new principles as commandments, such as 'All animals are equal'. However, the intelligent pigs soon adapt that principle to their own purpose of gaining greater control over others. The main themes within the novel are the good and evil aspects of society, and the plot moves full circle from hopelessness to optimism to hopelessness.
- *How to Be Happy* (1966, Educational Resources Film). This video looks at how to be happy. The BBC programme *QED* followed three unhappy people. The film shows how, under the guidance of a psychologist, their beliefs and attitudes are challenged and changed to produce a happier life. BBC Videos for Education and Training.

Explore the website accompanying this text at **www.pearsoned.co.uk/maltby** for further resources to help you with your studies. These include multiple-choice questions, essay questions, web links and ideas for advanced reading.

CHAPTER 19
Irrational Beliefs

Key themes

- Rational-emotive behaviour therapy
- The theory of rational and irrational beliefs
- The ABC model of human disturbance
- Must-urbatory thinking and disturbance
- Irrational beliefs and their effects on mental health
- Issues with irrational beliefs and rational-emotive behaviour therapy
- Irrational beliefs and religion, luck and superstitious beliefs

Learning outcomes

At the end of this discussion you should:

- Be able to outline the main concepts of rational-emotive behaviour therapy and identify the importance of irrational beliefs
- Understand the interactions of the ABC model and know how it affects individual differences in thoughts, emotions and behaviours
- Be familiar with the theories of religion, luck and superstitious beliefs and be able to understand these topics in the context of irrational beliefs
- Be aware of some of the main controversies that remain within rational-emotive behaviour therapy, and be able to describe ways forward for their development in order to assess the value of the theory for individual differences fully

Introduction

Do you have irrational beliefs? How often do you associate certain events with whether you are lucky or not? Do you believe in luck? For instance, while trying to win an important football or tennis match, might you wear a particular 'lucky' shirt? To succeed in exams, do you have various lucky charms and cuddly toys that you take into the exam with you? Indeed, while trying to meet your 'dream' partner one Friday or Saturday night, have you ever reverted to putting on your lucky 'pulling pants'?

Are you superstitious? For instance, the number 13 is considered unlucky because of the association of 13 disciples at Jesus Christ's Last Supper. Walking under a ladder is thought to be unlucky because the ladder, when leaning against a wall, forms a triangle, and moving inside this triangle would break the Holy Trinity that the triangle is thought to symbolise. Knocking on wood is thought to bring good luck because of ancient beliefs in kind tree gods. 'Superstitious rubbish!' you say? Well, one urban myth going round lecturer circles at the moment is the story of the lecturer who walks into a lecture class and asks the class whether any of them are superstitious. They all reply 'No'. He then asks the students to write the name of a loved one (their partner or a member of their close family) onto their lecture notes; however, before they do, he explains, they need to know that writing down that person's name will mean that the person will have a life-threatening accident in the next 24 hours. Not one of the students writes down a name. Would you?

The theory of irrational beliefs extends beyond beliefs such as luck and superstition and actually provides some deep psychological insight into some of the beliefs many of us hold dear. Irrational beliefs belong to the theory and therapy of rational-emotive behaviour therapy. The main aim of this discussion is to introduce you to the concepts behind rational-emotive behaviour therapy, identify common irrational beliefs and also show you evidence suggesting that irrational beliefs are thought to be detrimental to our mental health. We will also consider the theory's shortcomings and then introduce you to some theories and research that question whether having irrational beliefs is always *detrimental* to our mental health.

Source: Digital Vision

The basic theory of rational-emotive behaviour therapy (REBT)

From 1955, Dr Albert Ellis (Ellis, 1955) developed rational-emotive behaviour therapy (REBT). Ellis defines REBT as an action-oriented therapeutic approach that seeks to stimulate emotional growth in individuals by teaching them to replace their self-defeating (irrational) thoughts, feelings and actions with new and more effective beliefs. Overall, REBT teaches individuals to take responsibility for their own emotions and the therapy seeks to provide individuals with the power to change and overcome unhealthy behaviours, which Ellis believes interfere with an ability to function positively and to enjoy life.

According to REBT psychologists Russell Grieger and John Boyd, although REBT is a cognitive-behavioural therapy, it is essentially a humanistic approach (Grieger and Boyd, 1980). It is defined as the ability to enable and promote human dignity, and it allows for human fulfilment through reason and scientific method. According to Ellis (1955), REBT is also a simple theory of human disturbance, which takes account of the emotional and behavioural problems that we create by our faulty thinking.

Behind this simple theory are the two main concepts of *rational* thought and *irrational* (self-defeating) ideas. According to Grieger and Boyd, Ellis defines rational thought in the context that, in their lives, all people have fundamental goals, purposes and values that underlie their attempts to be happy and satisfied. If people choose to stay alive and be happy, then they act rationally – or self-helpfully – when they think, emote and behave in ways to achieve these goals. However, people act irrationally, or self-defeatingly, when they sabotage these goals (Ellis, 1957). Therefore, the whole purpose of REBT is to change people's irrational thinking into rational thinking. However, what types of 'irrational' thinking, or beliefs, are problematic for people?

Wayne Froggatt is a psychotherapist and member of the REBT organisation in New Zealand. Froggatt (2005) suggests that, to describe a belief as irrational is to say that:

- Irrational beliefs block the individual from achieving their goals and can create extreme emotions that persist over time, leading to distress and behaviours that harm themselves, others and their life in general.
- Irrational beliefs distort reality, as they are a misinterpretation of what is actually happening and are not supported by actual or available evidence.
- Irrational beliefs contain illogical ways of evaluating ourselves, others and the world.

Overall, then, irrational beliefs are beliefs we have that negatively affect our lives. The sole purpose of REBT is to identify these self-defeating or irrational beliefs and replace them with rational ones.

The ABCs of human disturbance

According to Grieger and Boyd (1980) and Wayne Froggatt (2005; 2006a; 2006b), the theory behind REBT is based on the fact that people never think, emote or behave in a singular, or rigid, way. In fact, when an individual emotes (experiences emotion), that individual also thinks and acts. Likewise, when an individual acts, they also think and emote. Finally, when an individual thinks, they also emote and act.

In other words, our thoughts influence our feelings, which in turn influence our actions. For instance, if you *think* people don't like you at work, you then *feel* disappointed and defensive, perhaps even resentful. The consequences of these thoughts and feelings may be that you *act* differently around them, perhaps becoming withdrawn and antisocial with your colleagues. You will certainly stop trying to get on with them.

For Ellis, REBT emerges from the concept that how we respond emotionally to something depends simply on our own interpretations, attitude, beliefs or thoughts of that

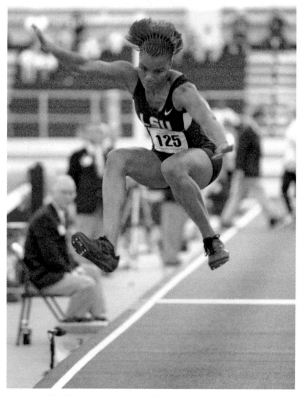

Irrational beliefs arise from self-defeating thoughts that everybody has. Some of us are able to deal with them more easily than others.

Source: Ingram Image Library – Diamond Edition, Vol. 1

situation. Put another way, how we view things, the things we say to ourselves, the way that *we*, not what actually happens to us, can cause our positive or negative emotions, which in turn influence the way we behave. Ellis (1962) argues that 'emotions' and feelings of 'emotional disturbance' are largely because of our direct beliefs, thoughts, ideas or constructs. In fact, Ellis (1987) goes so far as to suggest that people largely disturb themselves; it is their own unreasonable, or irrational, ideas that may make them feel depressed, anxious, angry or self-pitying about something.

It is from this simple theory that REBT has grown. It works on the premise that, if irrational beliefs and/ or thoughts cause most of our intense and unwanted emotional reactions, then the simple solution is to change our beliefs and thinking. This is largely done by challenging our ABCs.

Ellis uses an ABC format to illustrate the role of cognitions and behaviours within us; he particularly concentrates on how people become emotionally disturbed or self-defeating (see Figure 19.1). Within this framework, 'A' stands for our *activating* experiences that are of an unpleasant nature, such as what has happened to us to cause our unhappiness. 'B' stands for our *beliefs*, usually about what happened to us at A. These beliefs are usually irrational, or self-defeating, and they are considered to be the actual sources of our unhappiness. In other words, from the activating experiences, individuals bring their beliefs, values and purposes to these As. They then feel and act 'disturbedly' at point 'C' – their emotional and behavioural *consequences*. These Cs can include negative emotions, such as depression, anxiety and anger. Remember, these consequences (reactions at C) come about directly from our beliefs about what happened to us at point A.

Froggatt gives a good example of this: imagine that one of your friends passes you on the street without acknowledging you. This is the *activating* experience. Now, there may be a multitude of harmless reasons as to why this happened; it could be that your friend is preoccupied about something and didn't even see you. However, you may just as easily *believe* that your friend ignored you, and from this you may infer that your friend doesn't like you. From here it is a simple spiral downwards to believing that you are unacceptable as a friend and, therefore, must be worthless as a person. The *consequences* then lead to your emotional disturbance and, because of your belief that you are worthless, you may become withdrawn and depressed.

However, as well as these irrational beliefs, Ellis (1991b) believes that, mostly, people begin by having a set of rational beliefs. If, throughout their lives, they stayed with these rational ideas, then they would have only appropriate, or emotionally stable, consequences. This would mean that, after an unhappy activating experience, an individual could rationalise about what happened and not see it as an indication of wider or more serious issues. Instead, they would gain the determination to avoid having these upsetting consequences by going back to the *activating experience* and trying again. However, Ellis also argues that a person's belief system is seen to be the product of biological inheritance as well as our learning throughout life. The exact percentages of these two causes are unknown; however, Windy Dryden, an English psychotherapist (Dryden and Neenan, 1997), explains that the theory certainly suggests that our learned experiences hold the key. In other words, let us consider that an individual has initially rationalised the upsetting activating experience and, because of this, has no problem in revisiting the same experience because they

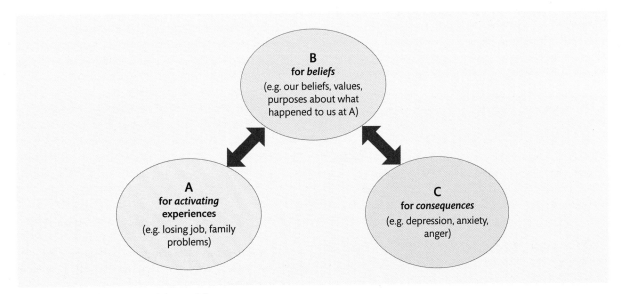

Figure 19.1 An illustration of the ABC format.

Profile

Albert Ellis

Albert Ellis was born in Pittsburgh in 1913 and grew up in New York. He had a difficult childhood but flourished by using his intelligence and becoming 'a stubborn and pronounced problem-solver' (Gregg, 2006). After attempts at varied careers, such as business administration, and novel and short stories writer, Ellis became a clinical psychotherapist in 1947. However, Ellis' faith in psychoanalysis declined. His main concern with psychoanalysis was the slow progress of the process when treating his clients. He found that when he saw his clients less frequently (i.e. only once a week, or every other week) they progressed in their therapy just as well as when he saw them daily. This prompted Ellis to begin to take a much more active role in sessions, where he would give advice and offer interpretations of behaviour (Gregg, 2006).

By 1955, Ellis concentrated his therapeutic approaches on changing people's behaviours by 'confronting' them with their irrational beliefs and then encouraging them to adopt more rational beliefs. He published his first book on rational-emotive therapy, entitled *How to Live with a Neurotic*, in 1957. Two years later he established the Institute for Rational Living, where he began to teach his therapeutic approaches and principles to other therapists; it was then that rational-emotive behaviour therapy (REBT) began to flourish (Gregg, 2006).

Albert Ellis was the founder of REBT and the president of the Albert Ellis Institute up until his death on 24 July 2007. The Albert Ellis Institute is a world centre of research, training and practice of REBT. He authored more than 70 books and 700 articles with the intention of helping people to overcome self-defeating and destructive emotions to improve their lives. Ellis received many awards – including distinguished psychological practitioner, scientific researcher and distinguished psychologist, from several associations, including the American Academy of Psychotherapists and the Academy of Psychologists in Marital and Family Therapy. He also earned one of the highest awards of the American Psychological Association: Distinguished Professional Contributions to Knowledge.

Visit **www.rebt.org** to find out more about Ellis, REBT and the Albert Ellis Institute. Also see Gregg, G. (2006). Also see a biography of Albert Ellis at **http://albertellis.org/about-albert-ellis-phd** (accessed 19 January 2013).

still hold emotionally stable thoughts about it. However, what seems to occur is that, if an inappropriate consequence occurs again, they will then begin to avoid the same *activating experience*; it is here that an irrational belief is established, which would be a learned behaviour.

A good example that we're going to use is based on a memorable one used by Myers (1997). Let us imagine that Chris loses his job (see Figure 19.2). Now, he may initially see this potentially damaging activating experience in a

positive, or rational, light. In doing this, he may think to himself that his boss was a complete idiot anyway and certainly was unpleasant to work for. He then feels that he actually deserves a much better job than this one. These beliefs or views lead to healthy consequences – he does not become depressed, and in fact may actually be happy about losing the job and go searching for a much better one elsewhere. Chris has then, very easily, put himself in the situation where it is possible that the same activating experience

Figure 19.2 Example of ABC format and the building on learned experiences.
Source: Based on Myers (1997).

may occur again (losing his job); however, he is certainly not worried or depressed about it. Now, let us imagine that the same activating experience does in fact happen again, and he loses this job. Chris may now begin to believe that the situation is hopeless, and that he must be worthless as a person if he can't even hold a job down. The consequences this time are emotional disturbance, which can easily lead to depression.

More recently Ellis (1991b) has added to this ABC format to include both D and E to show how these irrational beliefs can be altered to more rational ones. 'D' stands for the therapist, or individuals themselves, *disputing* the irrational beliefs, so that the client can appreciate the positive psychological *effects*, 'E', of rational beliefs. Later in this discussion, we will look more closely into how this process can alter our beliefs.

'Must-urbatory' thinking and disturbance

Grieger and Boyd (1980) describe how Ellis developed REBT to identify the most profound forms of 'crooked thinking' or 'cognitive slippage' that lead to self-defeating consequences; these are mostly absolutistic evaluations of *shoulds, oughts, musts, commands* and *demands* (see Figure 19.3). In other words, it is in our nature to *desire* goals to be fulfilled at point A; if we stick to these natural desires, then this behaviour should rarely cause us emotional

problems. However, it is also within our nature to insist that these goals *have to be* or *must be* fulfilled at A. If we use these must-urbations (or *core musts*), they will invariably lead to both emotional and behavioural problems (Dryden and Neenan, 1997; Ellis, 1991b; Froggatt, 2006a).

To explain this further, Ellis defines irrational beliefs as evaluative thoughts, beliefs and values that are presented in the form of rigid, dogmatic and absolute 'musts', 'shoulds' and 'have to's', and it is these forms of thinking that are at the heart of our emotional disturbances. Irrational beliefs, themselves, can neatly be grouped into three major demands, or musts: 'I must', 'you must' and 'the world must'. Because these thoughts are dogmatic in nature, when they are not met, irrational conclusions usually follow (Froggatt, 2005; Grieger and Boyd, 1980). These main must-urbations or irrational musts are known as '*awfulising*', '*low frustration tolerance*' and '*damnation*'.

In REBT, **awfulising** occurs when individuals believe that unpleasant or negative events are the worst that they could possibly be. In other words, they exaggerate the possible consequences of past, present or future situations or events, seeing them as the worst things that could possibly happen. Awfulising is characterised by words like 'terrible', 'horrible', 'horrendous' and 'awful'. Dryden and Neenan use the following examples to illustrate this thinking:

- 'I must do well and win approval from other people, or else I am a horrible person.'
- 'It's terrible to be thought of as selfish, as I *must* not be.'

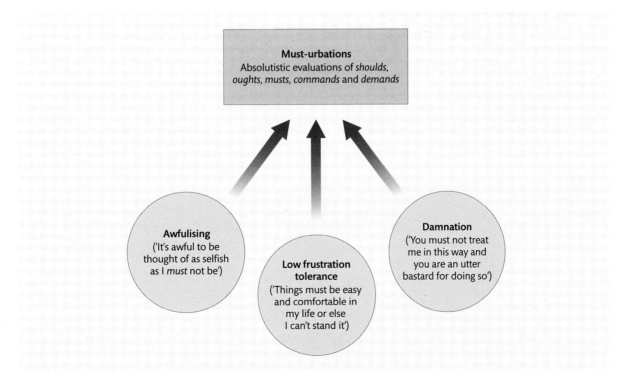

Figure 19.3 What are must-urbations?

Obviously, as you could actually be thought of as much worse than this, awfulising is a greatly exaggerated response to negative activating experiences. We are sure that you have all experienced awfulising thoughts in your everyday life, such as 'I must be liked by everyone; it would be just terrible if someone didn't like me', or 'the world should be different; it's an awful place to live'.

In REBT **low frustration tolerance** describes a person's perceived inability to put up with discomfort or frustration in their life; indeed, they may feel that happiness is impossible while such conditions exist (Dryden and Neenan, 1997; Ellis, 1991b; Froggatt, 2005). Froggatt and Dryden and Neenan suggest that examples of this type of thinking include:

- 'The conditions under which I currently live must get sorted out so that I get everything I want easily and quickly.'
- 'Things must be easy and comfortable in my life or else I can't stand it.'

We are sure that you have all experienced low frustration tolerance when having such thoughts as 'I can't bear it if my boyfriend/girlfriend left me; it must not happen', or 'I can't stand the way my boss treats me; it should not be allowed'. According to Dryden and Neenan and Froggatt, Ellis' REBT sees low frustration tolerance as possibly the most important reason that individuals perpetuate their psychological problems, as individuals with low frustration tolerance tend to avoid any discomfort and, instead, choose immediate gratification and comfort at the expense of longer term goals. In REBT, these low frustration tolerance beliefs are challenged and changed in order to experience and maintain 'high frustration tolerance'.

The third main must-urbation is **damnation**. Froggatt (2005) suggests that this term is used in REBT to explain a state of being that involves feeling either condemned or cursed; it reflects the tendency for individuals to damn or condemn themselves, others and/or the world if their demands are not met. Froggatt suggests examples of this type of thinking might be:

- 'Other people must treat me considerately and with kindness, in exactly the way I want them to treat me. If they don't, society and the universe should conspire and severely blame, damn and punish them for their ill treatment of me.'
- 'You must not treat me in this way and you are an utter *!@~!#*! for doing so.'

Again, we are sure that you have all thought these damnation ideas, such as 'nothing ever goes my way; someone up there must hate me', or 'I am a terrible person and I do not deserve anything'.

Froggatt also suggests that the rational alternative to damnation is to teach individuals these concepts:

- acceptance of self and others as fallible human beings;
- acceptance of the world as it is, but that it is OK not to like certain aspects of it.

Overall, Ellis (1991b) sums up must-urbations, or 'core musts', as taking the form of absolute statements. He suggests that instead of acknowledging a preference or a desire, we use this way of thinking to make unqualified demands on others and/or ourselves, or we convince ourselves that we have overwhelming needs. We have detailed these core musts in Figure 19.4.

We can see then, from the main core musts mentioned in Figure 19.4, that Ellis (Ellis, 1987; 1991b; Ellis and Harper, 1975) argues that most of these 'thinking errors' can be considered within the following three aspects:

- ignoring the positive;
- exaggerating the negative;
- overgeneralising.

We have given you the 12 common irrational ideas within these core musts, and these were developed within three aspects. However, Ellis has now identified that there are thousands of misery-causing false ideas; some of them are very obviously irrational, but many are much more subtle. Ellis (1994, 2006) has now refined these findings down to 12 irrational beliefs, which he believes to be at the root of most emotional disturbances. In the following list we present these 12 irrational beliefs, alongside suggested 'rational' interpretations that we have paraphrased from Ellis' own work so that you are presented with these rational interpretations within his words and terms (Ellis, 1994, 2006).

- **The irrational belief that it is a dire necessity for adults to be loved by significant others for almost everything they do.** Instead, Ellis suggests that 'rational' individuals concentrate on their own self-respect, on loving rather than on being loved and on winning approval for practical purposes.
- **The irrational belief that certain acts are awful or wicked and that people who perform such acts should be severely damned.** Instead, Ellis suggests that 'rational' individuals should believe that certain acts are self-defeating or antisocial and that people who perform such acts are behaving stupidly, ignorantly or neurotically. Essentially, they should realise that people's poor behaviours do not make them bad individuals.
- **The irrational belief that it is horrible when things are not the way we like them to be.** Instead, Ellis suggests that 'rational' individuals realise that when something is not the way they would like it to be, they try to change or control bad conditions so that they become more satisfactory, or, if that is not possible, temporarily accept their existence.
- **The irrational belief that human misery is invariably externally caused and is forced on us by outside people**

Here are some examples of the core musts, as set out by Ellis (1987):

- Everyone should love and approve of me (if they don't, I feel awful and unlovable).

- I should always be able, successful and 'on top of things' (if I'm not, I'm an inadequate, incompetent, hopeless failure).

- People who are evil and bad should be punished severely (and I have the right to get very upset if they aren't stopped and made to 'pay the price').

- When things do not go the way I wanted and planned, it is terrible and I am, of course, going to get very disturbed; I can't stand it!

- External events, such as other people, a screwed-up society or bad luck, cause most of my unhappiness. Furthermore, I don't have any control over these external factors, so I can't do anything about my depression or other misery.

- When the situation is scary or going badly, I should and can't keep from worrying all the time.

- It is easier for me to overlook or avoid thinking about tense situations than to face the problems and take the responsibility for correcting the situation.

- I need someone – often a specific person – to be with and lean on (I can't do everything by myself).

- Things have been this way so long, I can't do anything about these problems now.

- When my close friends and relatives have serious problems, it is only right and natural that I get very upset too.

- I don't like the way I'm feeling, but I can't help it. I just have to accept it and go with my feelings.

- I know there is an answer to every problem. I should find it (if I don't, it will be awful).

Figure 19.4 Core musts.
Source: Based on Ellis (1987).

and events. Instead, Ellis suggests that 'rational' individuals realise that neurosis is largely caused by a person's own views of unfortunate conditions.

- **The irrational belief that if something is, or may be, dangerous or fearsome, we should be terribly upset and endlessly obsess about it.** Instead, Ellis suggests that 'rational' individuals realise it is better to face some danger and cause it to become non-dangerous and, when that is not possible, to accept the inevitable.

- **The irrational belief that it is easier to avoid, than to face, life difficulties and self-responsibilities.** Instead, Ellis suggests that 'rational' individuals realise that the so-called easy way is usually much harder in the long run.

- **The irrational belief that we absolutely need something other, or stronger, or greater than ourselves on which to rely.** Instead, Ellis suggests that 'rational' individuals

realise it is better to take risks in thinking and to act less dependently.

- **The irrational belief that we should be thoroughly competent, intelligent and achieving in all possible respects.** Instead, Ellis suggests that 'rational' individuals realise it is better to *do*, rather than always need to *do well*, and they accept themselves as an imperfect creature who has general human limitations and specific fallibilities.

- **The irrational belief that because something once strongly affected our life, it should indefinitely affect it.** Instead, Ellis suggests that 'rational' individuals realise they can learn from their past experiences but not be overly attached to, or prejudiced by, them.

- **The irrational belief that we must have certain and perfect control over things.** Instead, Ellis suggests that 'rational' individuals realise the world is full of probability and chance, and they can still enjoy life despite this.

- **The irrational belief that human happiness can be achieved by inertia and inaction.** Instead, Ellis suggests that 'rational' individuals realise we all tend to be happiest when we are absorbed in creative pursuits, or when we are devoting ourselves to people or projects outside ourselves.
- **The irrational belief that we have virtually no control over our emotions and that we cannot help feeling disturbed about things.** Instead, Ellis suggests that 'rational' individuals realise we all have real control over our destructive emotions if we choose to work at changing the must-urbatory hypotheses that we often employ to create them.

Irrational beliefs and mental health

Now that we have identified what irrational beliefs are, we need to understand why these irrational beliefs are so detrimental to our mental health. We also need to understand how REBT can help. A multitude of research has considered mental health and irrational beliefs, especially regarding depression and anxiety. For example, Chang and D'Zurilla (1996) found that low frustration tolerance (one of the main must-urbations) is associated with depression and anxiety symptoms. Malouff *et al.* (1992) found that scores on measures of irrational beliefs were significantly associated with **state anxiety** scores, and they were found to predict increases in state anxiety in stressful situations. However, many other areas of mental health are affected by irrational beliefs. To give you an idea of how important these 'self-defeating' thoughts actually are, Froggatt (2005; 2006b) shows that researchers have found that irrational beliefs can lead to these situations:

- high levels of anxiety;
- high levels of depression;
- social dysfunction;
- isolation and withdrawal;
- phobias;
- anger, guilt and jealousy;
- relationship problems involving miscommunication;
- problems of dealing with criticism;
- lack of control over situations;
- low self-esteem.

As we can see from these examples of how irrational beliefs can affect our mental health, it is perhaps a necessity to find alternative ways of thinking. So how exactly does REBT work?

Dryden and Neenan (1997) describe REBT as a challenging form of therapy in which the therapist helps patients to identify when they are distressing themselves

with rigid and dogmatic beliefs. Then the therapist helps them to change their thinking and ultimately to replace these beliefs with rational alternatives. The authors outline this therapy as a practical, action-oriented approach, which places much of its focus on the present – that is, the currently held beliefs, attitudes, emotions, thought and maladaptive behaviours that can prevent a more complete and positive experience of life. In other words, instead of investigating the past – our childhood experiences – for how we came by these irrational thoughts, REBT focuses on changing how we think in the present and in the future. REBT also provides people with a set of techniques, specific to the individual, for helping them to solve their problems.

According to Dryden and Neenan, REBT practitioners work closely with people, exploring individual attitudes, thinking, expectations and personal rules, helping them to identify those beliefs that frequently lead to emotional distress. The therapist then provides the patient with a variety of methods to help reformulate those dysfunctional beliefs into more functional (sensible, realistic and helpful) ones by employing a technique called disputing. Dryden and Neenan explain that **disputing** is used to change the individual's beliefs; it involves highlighting the irrational thoughts and then contesting them. For example, let us use the irrational belief of 'everyone should love and approve of me; if they don't, I feel awful and unlovable'. The authors describe how the therapist may suggest to the individual that it is not possible for everyone to love and approve of any of us and that when we try too hard to please everyone, we are in danger of losing our identity; then we are not self-directed, secure or interesting. The therapist may continue to *dispute* that it is, in fact, better to love our own self, gain knowledge and understanding of our own values, beliefs, social skills and friendships rather than worry about pleasing everyone. This technique would allow the individual to become more self-accepting, as well as more accepting of other people who may not share the same beliefs and values (Dryden and Neenan, 1997).

Froggatt (2005) suggests that REBT enables individuals to develop a philosophy of life and approach and strategy to living that can increase their own effectiveness and happiness in all aspects of their life. This might include improving their own mental health, living productively with others, forging better relationships, being successful in education and/or work and seeking to make more positive contributions to their own community.

Now that we understand the basics of REBT, let us look at an example, following it through to how REBT could help a person. Let us imagine that Lynette is a 19-year-old student who goes to therapy because she cannot meet the high standards she has set herself. She is desperate to be the best in everything she does (her university work, her interests, her relationships), and her irrational belief is: 'I must

Stop and think

Irrational beliefs: how many do you have?

How many irrational beliefs do you think a person might hold? Write down as many as you can think of. (You might want to use those listed in Figure 19.5 as a memory prompt.) How many do you have? Now try and write down a rational alternative for each irrational belief you've listed.

do very well in everything I do, or I can't stand it.' In other words, Lynette is a perfectionist.

Lynette is so desperate about achieving highly that she's in danger of impeding herself completely; by spending so much time being desperate about achieving highly, she runs the risk of achieving nothing. This might sound silly, but Lynette is so disturbed with these thoughts that she has convinced herself that, if she can't be the best, then it is better to do nothing at all, rather than to come in second or third and confirm to herself (and others) that she is not the best.

An REBT therapist will help Lynette to see that the demands she makes of herself are illogical, inflexible and not grounded in reality. In time, REBT would help Lynette replace her illogical and dogmatic irrational beliefs with beliefs that are logical and flexible. At the end of the REBT, her beliefs ideally might centre on statements such as 'I would prefer to do very well and be the best; but if I don't, it's not the end of the world, and I could handle it.' This difference in attitude will take a lot of pressure off Lynette and will enable her to function much better than she did when she adopted 'the best or nothing' thinking.

REBT has been successfully used to help people with a range of clinical and non-clinical problems. Froggatt (2005) writes that these clinical applications include:

- depression;
- anxiety disorders;
- eating disorders;
- addictions;
- anger management and antisocial behaviours;
- general stress management;
- relationship and family problems;
- child or adolescent behaviour disorders.

Froggatt also describes typical clinical applications as including:

- **Personal growth** – REBT contains principles such as self-acceptance and risk-taking, which can be used to help people develop and act more fully with life.
- **Workplace effectiveness** – DiMattia (1991) has developed a variation of REBT, known as rational effectiveness training, that is designed for use in the workplace to improve the effectiveness of workers and managers.

Irrational beliefs and individual differences

We have now explained to you the basics of REBT and the central concepts behind irrational thinking. REBT is built around the concept that how we emotionally respond to something depends simply on our interpretations, views, beliefs or thoughts of the situation, which then produce a variety of responses, some of them self-defeating and some of them self-helpful. It is for these reasons that REBT lends itself well to individual differences. This theory is important as it shows in depth how individuals differ greatly from one another around a core variable: irrational beliefs. Irrational thoughts are also thought to be important because they can affect mental health variables, social relationships and social functioning.

Issues with irrational beliefs that need to be considered and addressed

For individual differences researchers, REBT lends itself well to individual differences considerations of individual emotions, behaviours and mental health. In other words, REBT allows us to understand how individuals differ in relation to a central set of (irrational) beliefs through their perceptions and thoughts about the world; REBT also shows differences in how people typically think, emote and act – all of which have different consequences on mental health outcomes. Therefore, this theory has been identified as an extremely important one for individual differences researchers as it shows in depth how individuals differ greatly from one another and how the irrational beliefs we have can affect the differences in mood, personality, social interactions and so on.

However, two issues need to be addressed:

- There are differences of opinion as to what Ellis considers as irrational.
- There may need to be subtlety and subjectivity when considering what constitutes irrationality for everyone, particularly when considered in view of mental health outcomes.

These two issues are largely intertwined, and we really need to understand the issues around the first point to fully understand the second. The first point is that there are differences in what Ellis calls irrational. The main issue here regards the ambiguities surrounding the classification of beliefs as 'irrational'. To explain this better, we are going to consider a few must-urbatory statements that Ellis (1987) classifies under the first major irrational belief. For example, 'I desperately need others to rely and depend upon; because I shall always remain weak'; 'I also need some supernatural power on which to rely, especially in times of crisis' and 'I must understand the nature or secret of the universe in order to live happily in it'. According to Ellis, these are irrational beliefs in supernatural forces and are detrimental to our well-being. We will consider whether beliefs based on must-urbatory statements are always detrimental to our well-being.

This leads us to the second point, that there may be a lack of subtlety and subjectivity in what constitutes irrationality for everyone, particularly when considered in view of mental health outcomes. Research in the areas of the psychology of religion, luck and superstitious beliefs (all beliefs that would be considered by Ellis as supernatural beliefs) suggests that these 'supernatural beliefs' are not always detrimental to our well-being, as would be predicted by the theory of irrational beliefs. To illustrate both points of consideration, we will look more closely at the theory and research that surrounds each of these supernatural beliefs (religion, luck and superstitious beliefs) in turn (see Figure 19.5).

The case for and against religion

So that you can better appreciate this debate, we will briefly present the 'case against religion', a phrase coined by Ellis himself (Ellis, 1980). We will then outline some theory and research that opposes, or presents counterarguments to, Ellis' 'case'.

Ellis starts out by explaining what the main aim of psychotherapy is. It is to help patients become less anxious and hostile; to this end, it is to help them to acquire the following six personality traits to help them develop into emotionally mature and healthy individuals:

- **Self-interest** – traits that reflect one's own true thoughts, feelings and ambitions and do not reflect a tendency masochistically (deriving some self-worth from being humiliated or mistreated) to sacrifice themself for others.
- **Self-direction** – traits that reflect a person taking responsibility for their own life and independently working out their own problems. Traits that reflect the ability to cooperate and seek help from others are considered healthy; however, traits that reflect a *need* to get the support of others for the person's own effectiveness and well-being are not.
- **Tolerance** – traits that allow and give other human beings the right to be wrong.
- **Acceptance of uncertainty** – traits that accept that we live in a world of chance, where there are never any absolute certainties.
- **Flexibility** – traits that reflect intellectual flexibility, openness to change at all times; these traits don't reflect

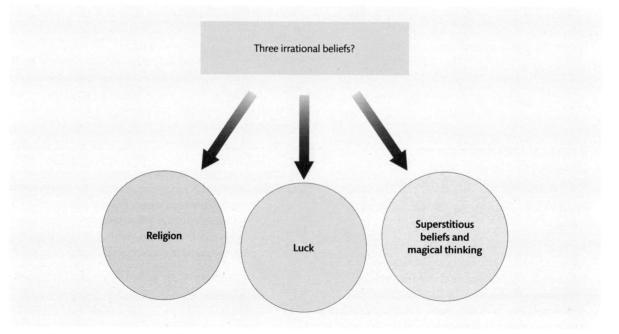

Figure 19.5 Three irrational beliefs?

bigotry and view the world of infinitely varied people, ideas and things as positive.

- **Self-acceptance** – traits that reflect a gladness to be alive, a person who accepts themselves, accepts their current existence and the power to enjoy themself and to create happiness in their life. These are *not* traits that assign worth or value to extrinsic achievements (achievements originating from factors outside or external to the person) or to what others think; they are traits that acknowledge the person's own existence and importance, their ability to feel, think and act and thereby create an interesting and absorbed life for themselves.

These, according to Ellis (1980), are the personality traits that psychotherapists are interested in helping their patients to develop.

Now let us turn to religion. Ellis (1980) begins his debate against religion by identifying the definitions of religion that are most acceptable to him and, indeed, what it is within religion that he deems 'irrational'. Therefore, here, we will do the same (see Stop and think: Definitions of religion).

For Ellis, a religion always includes a concept of a deity, which is any supernatural being that is worshipped for controlling some part of the world or some aspect of life. Ellis (1980) suggests that one of the main aims of psychotherapy is to argue against this 'dependence on a power above and beyond that which is human'.

However, Ellis believes that, instead of religion helping people to achieve healthy personality traits and thereby helping them to avoid becoming depressed, anxious and hostile, it actually does not help at all. He argues that, in most respects, religion seriously undermines mental health, as it does not encourage the six personality traits we have just outlined (self-interest, self-directedness, tolerance, acceptance of uncertainty, flexibility and self-acceptance).

First, Ellis questions how religion reflects **self-interest** traits. He suggests that religion, first and foremost, is not primarily interested in the person; it is 'god-interest'. In

other words, Ellis strongly believes that the truly religious person is expected to have no real views of their own; to have any would be presumptuous of the individual. Instead, the individual must primarily do the work of their god and the clergy (the body of people who are ordained for religious service; e.g. vicar, priests, clerics) of their religion. In this sense Ellis sees religiosity, to a large degree, essentially as masochism (deriving some self-worth from being humiliated or mistreated by others), a form of mental illness that works against self-interest.

In regard to **self-direction**, Ellis argues that it can easily be seen that the religious person is dependent on, and directed by, others rather than being independent and self-directed. Ellis argues that if a person is true to their religious beliefs, then they must follow and listen to the word of their god first, and of their clergy second. Religious individuals live according to their god's and their religion's rules while turning to god, the clergy and religious readings for inspiration, advice and guidance. Therefore, according to Ellis, religion requires and expects certain levels of **dependency**.

Ellis also argues that religion does not encourage **tolerance**. He states that tolerance is a trait that the firmly religious cannot possess or encourage, as the word of a god and the clergy is usually presented as the absolute truth, while other groups or viewpoints are considered false. As well as this, Ellis believes that religion tends not to accept an individual's wrongdoing or making mistakes, and this is where concepts such as sinning and punishment for sins occurs. Therefore, for Ellis, religion encourages *intolerance*.

Ellis also argues that religion doesn't encourage traits such as **acceptance of uncertainty**. He states that a primary purpose of religion is to encourage people to believe in **mystical certainties**; for example, that there is a god, this god is all-powerful, this god is all-seeing, there is life after death, there is heaven and hell.

Ellis also argues that religion does not encourage traits of **flexibility**. He argues that flexibility is also undermined

Stop and think

Definitions of religion, selected by Ellis

Ellis (1980) uses the following definitions of religion:

- '(1) Belief in a divine or superhuman power or powers to be obeyed and worshipped as the creator(s) and ruler(s) of the universe; (2) expression of this belief in conduct and ritual.' (*Webster's New World Dictionary*)
- 'A system of beliefs by means of which individuals or a community put themselves in relation to god or to a

supernatural world and often to each other, and from which the religious person derives a set of values by which to judge events in the natural world.' (*Comprehensive Dictionary of Psychological and Psychoanalytical Terms* [English and English, 1958])
- 'When a man becomes conscious of a power above and beyond the human, and recognizes a dependence of himself upon that power, religion has become a factor in his being.' (*The Columbia Encyclopaedia*)

by religious belief. For instance, Ellis raises the issue that the church states that 'thou shalt not covet thy neighbour's wife'; but, Ellis wonders, what is wrong about coveting someone as long as there is no intention to act? He says that religion is not tolerant of ambiguity, discussion or debate, but rather is presented as universal truths about the world (such as the Ten Commandments or religious doctrines).

Finally, in regard to **self-acceptance**, Ellis states that the religious person cannot possibly ever accept themselves fully and be satisfied and happy just because they are alive. Rather, Ellis sees that the religious person makes their self-acceptance dependent on the acceptance of their god, their church and their clergy. Ellis describes this belief as self-abasement, which is the lowering of oneself owing to feelings of guilt or inferiority and belief that the acceptance is achieved only through the praise of others. Therefore, in this case the self-abasement of the person in religion goes against the development of self-acceptance.

To summarise Ellis' views, so far, he clearly concludes that religion is directly opposed to the individual achieving emotional maturity and good mental health since it comprises elements of masochism, other-directedness, intolerance, refusal to accept uncertainty, inflexibility and self-abasement.

However, Ellis (1980) goes even further by suggesting that religion encourages five major irrational beliefs:

- **The idea that it is a dire necessity for an adult to be loved or approved of by all the significant figures in their life.** Ellis argues that this idea is encouraged by religion because, even if you cannot get people to love you, you can always rely on your god's love. However, Ellis maintains that the emotionally mature person understands that it is quite possible for you to live in the world whether or not other people accept you. He argues that religion doesn't encourage this viewpoint.
- **The idea that you must be thoroughly competent, adequate and achieving in all possible respects, otherwise you are worthless.** Ellis argues that religion also encourages this irrational belief. He accepts that religion encourages the belief that you need not be competent and achieving outside the church, because your god loves you and, as you are a good member of your church, such failures don't matter. However, Ellis argues that religion does encourage this irrational belief within the confines of religion because it sets down the condition that, as long as you are competent, adequate and achieving in all aspects of your religious life, you are a good person; however, if you are not competent, adequate and achieving in all aspects of your religious life, then you are worthless.
- **The notion that certain people are bad, wicked and villainous and that they should be severely blamed and punished for their sins.** Ellis argues that this belief is the basis of virtually all religions. The concepts of guilt, blame and sin are integral with religion. For example, the religious person is expected to feel guilt and accept blame if they sin against their religious teachings.
- **The belief that it is horrible, terrible and catastrophic when things are not going the way you would like them to go.** According to Ellis, this idea is central to religion. Ellis argues that the religious person believes that a god is there to supervise their thoughts and acts and protect them from the anxiety and frustrations of life. Therefore, when there is anxiety and frustration in the individual's life, the person may feel something must have either gone catastrophically wrong with their god's intentions for them, or that their god has abandoned them.
- **The idea that human unhappiness is externally caused and that people have little or no ability to control their sorrows or rid themselves of their negative feelings.** Once again, Ellis argues that this notion is central to religion, since religion invariably teaches religious individuals that only by trusting in and praying to your god will you be able to understand, control and deal with any unhappiness or negative emotions.

As you can see, Ellis certainly finds religion to be irrational in nature, and he even goes so far as to suggest that 'if we had time to review all the other major irrational ideas that lead humans to become and to remain emotionally disturbed, we could quickly find that they are coextensive with, or are strongly encouraged by, religious tenets' (Ellis, 1980, p. 27). In his final analysis Ellis believes that religion is neurosis, reflecting the basic irrational beliefs of human beings.

These arguments against religion, as set out by Ellis, are indeed stern. They paint a damning picture of the religious individual. However, the categorisation of religion as an irrational belief can be questioned by the findings of individual differences psychologists who theorise and research outside the realm of REBT.

Within religiosity, individual differences psychologists have identified three major orientations of religion: intrinsic religiosity, extrinsic religiosity and quest religiosity, all found to have differing effects on mental health for the individual. Later there is a section on religion that can give you expanded information on these three religious orientations and their relationship to mental health (Chapter 22), but we can briefly summarise the main points here.

First is **intrinsic religiosity**, which Allport and Ross (Allport, 1966; Allport and Ross, 1967) describe as individuals living their religious beliefs in such a way that the influence of their religion is evident in every aspect of their life. In other words, for those whose religion is intrinsic, religion is an end in itself; they take it very seriously and it is central to their lives. Allport argues that intrinsic religious individuals' central aims and needs in life are found within their religion; other aims and needs are regarded as less significant. Thus, having embraced a particular religion, the individual endeavours to internalise it and follow its philosophy and teachings fully. It is in this sense that the intrinsic individual *lives* their religion.

Now, it is this particular orientation towards religion that directly opposes Ellis' views of religion as irrational, as extensive research findings show that intrinsic religiosity can be beneficial to mental health (Park *et al.*, 1990; Genia, 1996; Genia and Shaw, 1991; Koenig, 1995; Nelson, 1989; Watson *et al.*, 1989). Research shows a multitude of benefits for this religious orientation, but the most important here are the findings that intrinsically religious individuals show lower levels of anxiety and depression as well as very high levels of self-esteem. Intrinsically religious individuals have also been shown to possess more positive ways of coping in times of stress (e.g. Maltby and Day, 2004). Therefore, we can suggest here that, in fact, intrinsically religious people definitely have *self-interest*, *self-direction* and *self-acceptance* and that some of these findings in relation to positive mental health outcomes might undermine Ellis' case against religion.

Second is an **extrinsic religiosity**, which Allport defines as the individual using religion to provide participation in a powerful in-group, seeking social status, protection and consolation in their religion. For example, within this dimension individuals look to religion for comfort, relief and protection and use religious practices, such as prayer, for peace and happiness. They also look to places of worship (such as a church) for making friends and feeling part of a social group.

Now, it is suggested that this particular orientation towards religion may support Ellis' views of religion. Indeed, extensive research findings show that extrinsic religiosity is associated with poorer mental health. For example, extrinsic religiosity is related to higher levels of neuroticism, anxiety and depression as well as to very low levels of self-esteem (e.g. Baker and Gorsuch, 1982; Bergin *et al.*, 1987; Sturgeon and Hamley, 1979). Extrinsically religious people are also shown to possess more negative ways of coping in times of stress (Pargament, 1997). Therefore, we can suggest that, by considering Allport's description of the extrinsically religious person and the research evidence relating extrinsic religiosity to poorer mental health, extrinsically religious people may be exposing themselves to aspects of religion that encourage **masochism, dependency, intolerance** and **self-debasement**.

The third religious orientation, **quest religiosity**, was conceptualised by Batson (1976) in response to religious dimensions that were missing in the intrinsic and extrinsic descriptions. These dimensions include religious complexity, religious completeness, religious flexibility and religious tentativeness (i.e. religious issues not fully worked out). According to Batson and Ventis (1982), the concept of quest represents the degree to which a person's religion involves 'an open-ended, responsive dialogue with existential questions raised by the contradictions and tragedies of life'. In other words, quest religiosity involves a person 'questioning' and seeking enlightenment within their religion. This orientation towards religion is less researched. However, research findings do show that, generally, individuals with quest religiosity were seen to have better mental health than those with extrinsic religiosity, but poorer than those with intrinsic religiosity. Therefore, although consideration of this orientation cannot fully go against Ellis' ideas of religion, there is some evidence to suggest that this type of religion encourages traits such as **flexibility** and **acceptance of uncertainty** and may lead to better mental health.

To summarise, Ellis believes that religion is a neurosis and that it goes hand in hand with the basic irrational beliefs of human beings. However, evidence suggests – particularly when considering intrinsic and quest orientations – that religion is not always neurotic or irrational and doesn't necessarily lead to poorer mental health.

We have seen that there are ambiguities surrounding the classification of what may be defined as irrational. In the psychology of religion literature, there are different findings as to whether religion actually *fails* to promote the traits of self-interest, self-directedness, tolerance, acceptance of uncertainty, flexibility and self-acceptance, all of which Ellis sees as important for emotional maturity and mental health. As we can see from the descriptions of intrinsic and quest religiosity, self-interest, self-directedness, acceptance of uncertainty, flexibility and self-acceptance are features of these aspects of religiosity.

You can also see how there may be a need for subtlety and subjectivity when considering what constitutes irrationality for everyone. In other words, instead of identifying irrational beliefs and stating that these beliefs are irrational for everyone, a more subtle and subjective approach may be needed to appreciate that there are individual differences and then to define these individual differences and summarise the extent to which they differ. For instance, in the case of religion, research suggests that it can sometimes be seen as irrational – as evidenced by the description of extrinsic religiosity and its relationship to poorer mental health. However, sometimes religion can be seen as comprising rational processes and having positive outcomes, as evidenced by the description of intrinsic religiosity or quest religiosity and their relationship with better mental health.

Therefore, religious beliefs can either be self-defeating (irrational) or self-helpful (rational) depending on the approach that the individual adopts towards religion. Let us further illustrate this particular distinction within the psychological literature on luck.

The case for and against luck: the importance of belief in good luck

Let us remember that the main issues are: (1) there may be ambiguities surrounding the classification and meaning of 'irrational'; (2) there are conflicting findings as to whether some 'irrational' beliefs are actually beneficial for our mental health; and (3) our understanding of irrational beliefs may require a more subtle and subjective approach. Remember also that we are presenting issues directly related to Ellis' concerns about the 'irrationality' of belief in the supernatural and this 'dependence on a power above and beyond the human'. We began to look at these issues in the case of religion. However, these issues are perhaps even better illustrated within the theory and research on luck.

Traditionally, belief in luck has been considered as either an external factor with no effect on health or, mostly, as an irrational belief as it relies on supernatural forces influencing our lives. Here, belief in luck is seen as detrimental to mental health.

However, two psychologists, Peter Darke and J. L. Freedman (Darke and Freedman, 1997), divided belief in luck into two parts: belief in *good* luck and belief in *bad* luck. It is from this division that interesting findings in respect to mental health have emerged.

In general, researchers have identified that there is a distinction between individuals who consider themselves as lucky (good luck) and those who consider themselves as unlucky (bad luck), with believers in good luck showing better mental health. Consequently, belief in good luck is considered to be a healthy, adaptive process, where the positive illusions surrounding luck, even in situations where the individual has little or no control over future expectations, can lead to feelings of confidence, control and optimism (Darke and Freedman, 1997). Believing in good luck has been found to be related to higher self-esteem and lower depression and anxiety (Day and Maltby, 2003). Maltby *et al.*, (2008) have also found belief in good luck to be related to higher optimism, high hope (both on pathways and agencies), external, stable and global attributes to positive events, high psychological well-being (particularly environmental mastery, positive relations with others and self-acceptance) and high subjective well-being (on satisfaction of life, positive affect and low negative affect). Therefore, individual researchers have so far concluded that a belief in good luck may provide a positive way of coping with perceptions that luck and chance play a role in everyday life. In other words, people who believe in good luck may use their belief to help them understand certain aspects of a world that seems to involve luck and chance, allowing them to stay optimistic when events in their lives seem to be out of their direct control.

In fact, UK psychologist Richard Wiseman, a researcher in the area of luck, has gone even further. He suggests that people who perceive themselves as lucky also meet their perfect partners, achieve their lifelong ambitions, find fulfilling careers and live happy and meaningful lives, as opposed to people who perceive themselves as unlucky (Wiseman, 2004).

Wiseman explains that this difference occurs because individuals perceive themselves as lucky or unlucky, and lucky people consequently encounter more chance opportunities than others. For example, in his book *The Luck Factor*, Wiseman (2004) carried out an experiment where he gave both lucky and unlucky people a newspaper to read; in the newspaper, he had placed a large advertisement that took up half a page and was printed in type more than two inches high. The message read, 'Tell the experimenter you have seen this and win £250'. Wiseman found it was only the self-assessed lucky people who noticed it. Wiseman has suggested that the reason for this is because of individuals' anxiety levels, and that unlucky people are generally more anxious than lucky people are. Wiseman argues that this anxiety disrupts unlucky people's ability to notice the unexpected; as a result, they miss opportunities because they are too focused on looking for something else. For instance, according to Wiseman, unlucky people may go to parties intent on finding their 'perfect partner' and, by doing so, miss the opportunities to make good friends. Likewise, they look through newspaper job listings determined to find the 'ideal' job and, because they only look for the ideal job, they miss other types of jobs that could also present them with opportunities for advancement in their careers.

Stop and think

Religion

How do you think religion should, overall, be perceived – as a rational belief or an irrational one? You may want to consider the arguments of Ellis and his suggestions that religion is neurosis and goes hand in hand with the basic irrational beliefs of human beings. You may also want to consider the research findings that surround intrinsic and extrinsic religiosity.

Profile

Richard Wiseman

Richard Wiseman is Professor of Psychology at the University of Hertfordshire, England, and is most well known for his research into the scientific examination of unusual areas within psychology, including the psychology of luck, deception and the paranormal.

Wiseman started his working life as a professional magician. He was one of the youngest members of The Magic Circle; it is perhaps these early experiences that have led him into the field of the paranormal.

Wiseman has written over 40 journal articles and published six books. However, he is perhaps best known for his many appearances on British television and radio presenting experiments on luck as well as on ghosts and hauntings.

Within his research on luck, Wiseman has concentrated on identifying the psychological differences between lucky and unlucky individuals. In early 2004, Wiseman published *The Luck Factor*, which was the comprehensive account of an 8-year research project investigating the *nature* of luck.

For the purposes of his 'unusual' psychological research, Wiseman has been funded by many organisations, including the Leverhulme Trust, the Wellcome Trust and the British Association for the Advancement of Science. Wiseman has become dedicated to training people in luck, and now runs a 'luck school' at Hertfordshire University, where he teaches unlucky people to become lucky. He estimates that he has been successful in around 80 per cent of cases.

Wiseman (2004) also argues that believing in good or bad luck may be caused by a self-fulfilling prophecy. In other words, those who believe in bad luck, due to anxiety and the missing of opportunities, may come to believe themselves to be unlucky because they realise that they are missing out on so many opportunities; thus, they perpetuate their bad luck. Likewise, because lucky people are more relaxed and open, they find many more 'lucky' or 'fortunate' opportunities, which, in turn, reinforces their lucky beliefs.

Therefore, Wiseman (2004) suggests that lucky people generate their good fortune through four main principles:

- They are skilled at creating and noticing opportunities.
- They make lucky decisions by listening to their intuition.
- They create self-fulfilling prophecies through their positive expectations.
- They adopt a resilient attitude that transforms bad luck into good.

In fact, Wiseman is so convinced by the benefits of luck, both in terms of people's mental health and their life opportunities, that he set up a 'luck school' at Hertfordshire University, where he teaches 'unlucky' people to become 'lucky'. He estimates that he has been successful in around 80 per cent of cases (Wiseman, 2004).

Therefore, you can see from this brief description of good luck that, although belief in luck may be 'irrational' by definition, it is by no means self-defeating when considered within the context of good luck. In fact, individual differences researchers have even found that there is a significant negative relationship between belief in good luck and irrational beliefs (Day and Maltby, 2003). In other words, people who believe in good luck tend to reject the types of thoughts usually associated with irrational beliefs. However,

findings from current research suggest that belief in bad luck is still considered as 'irrational' and self-defeating.

Thus, again, you can see that there are ambiguities surrounding the classification of what is irrational; indeed, within luck, there are conflicting findings as to whether some irrational beliefs are necessarily detrimental to our mental health. Also, regarding the debate around subtlety and subjectivity, research suggests that, when considering luck, as well as religion, sometimes belief is irrational (i.e. self-defeating, in the case of bad luck), but sometimes it is rational (i.e. self-helpful, as with good luck). Therefore, again, belief in luck can either be self-defeating or self-helpful depending on the individual themself. These findings support the argument that, instead of identifying irrational beliefs and stating that these beliefs are irrational for everyone, a more subtle and subjective approach may be needed.

We have now considered the debate within religion and luck. Let us bring this analysis to an end by considering superstitious beliefs.

Superstitious beliefs

To finalise this debate around Ellis' notion of 'irrationality' of belief in the supernatural, and a 'dependence on a power above and beyond the human', we will briefly consider research on superstitious beliefs.

Superstitions have been present in a range of different cultures for thousands of years, and they have sustained their influence today. Traditionally, superstition has been considered to result from a feeble mind or distorted thinking. Individuals believing in superstition have been found to suffer from poor psychological adjustment; they

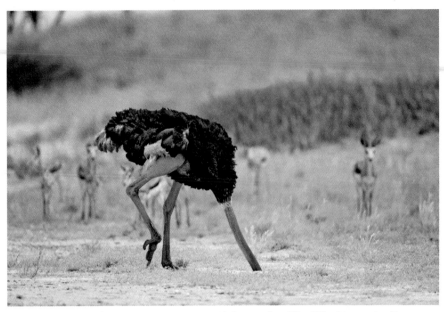

One irrational belief is that it is easier to avoid than to face life difficulties and self-responsibilities.
Source: Alamy Images/Steve Bloom Images.

have lower self-esteem, higher levels of anxiety and show more suggestibility (Roig *et al.,* 1998; Tobacyk and Shrader, 1991). It has been suggested by Dag (1999) that superstitious beliefs may develop in anxious individuals with a strong need for control, who attempt to overcome the uncertainties in their lives. Therefore, these findings and explanations support the view that superstitious beliefs are irrational in nature and have detrimental effects on mental health.

However, an alternative view is presented by Langer (1975) and Zusne and Jones (1982), who have argued that magical thinking, such as that seen in superstitious belief, can aid individuals in understanding circumstances that are beyond rational control and thus can have an adaptive function for the person (Subbotsky, 2004).

Wiseman and Watt (2005) point to measures of superstitious belief; for example, the superstition subscale of the Paranormal Beliefs Scale (Tobacyk, 1988) that has been used in a substantial amount of superstition research. Wiseman and Watt point out that the scale contains three items – 'the number 13 is unlucky', 'black cats can bring bad luck' and 'if you break a mirror, you will have bad luck' and that these have a suggestive association with unlucky and potentially harmful consequences. However, Wiseman and Watt point out that not all superstitious beliefs fall into the category of bad luck; indeed, superstitions such as carrying 'lucky' charms, touching wood and crossing fingers suggest a desire to bring about good luck. As we have already seen, these beliefs may actually be beneficial to mental health, rather than detrimental.

Although research evidence for these distinctions is limited, there is a suggestion that not all superstitions are bad for you. They may, in fact, help a person to feel lucky (Wiseman, 2004) and help them to cope with the diversity of life (Subbotsky, 2004; Zusne and Jones, 1982). Therefore, although there is a multitude of research supporting the irrationality of superstition, some further research may still be needed to examine this view fully.

Stop and think

Luck

- How do you think that luck should, overall, be perceived – as a rational belief or an irrational one? You may want to consider the distinctions between belief in good luck and belief in bad luck, and whether they should both be considered as 'irrational'.

- How probable is it that a person can learn to be 'lucky'?
- How probable is it that a person believes only in good luck or only in bad luck?

Stop and think

Superstition

- How do you think that superstition should, overall, be perceived – as a rational belief or an irrational one?
- How probable is it that a superstitious person can only believe in so-called healthy superstitions? Would

people who carry lucky charms worry about breaking a mirror?
- If you have them, consider you own superstitions. Can they make you feel better, particularly in times of worry?

Stop and think

Irrational beliefs and sport

An area where you can see irrational beliefs, luck, magical thinking and superstition coming together is within the sport and exercise world, particularly when focusing on superstitious and ritualistic behaviours. Are these behaviours detrimental or beneficial to mental health and performance in sport and exercise?

There is a prevalence of superstitious practice in today's sports. According to Schippers and Van Lange (2006) these practices and behaviours can range from abstention from sex before an event (Fischer, 1997), behaviours related to clothing (e.g. wearing the same shirt, clothes, underwear for a long series of matches) and food (e.g. eating the same food, eating at the same restaurant, etc.), pre- and post-competition rituals (e.g. coming onto the field first/last, touching/kissing the ground) and activities during competition (e.g. plucking at racket strings, eating so many bananas; Buhrmann et al., 1982). Schippers and Van Lange (2006) ask certain questions about these behaviours, such as why do people act in such unusual ways, do sportsmen and sportswomen need to do this for every match and does it matter whether the stakes are high or low?

These questions may be answered by considering the definition of superstitious rituals. Schippers and Van Lange (2006) argue that **superstitious rituals** are defined as unusual, repetitive and rigid behaviours that are perceived to have positive effects by the performer, whereas in reality there is no evidence to suggest that a causal link exists between the behaviour and the outcome of the event. These rituals differ from our normal routine in that the action is considered as having a special or magical significance. Another function of these rituals might be to enable the performer to prepare mentally for each performance; in this sense it could be considered rational as it has a useful purpose.

So, how does superstitious behaviour originate and why does it continue? Well, there are three particular suggestions that have been put forward to answer this question. The first is based on Ellis's cognitive behaviour

theory of irrational beliefs, that we have already looked at in detail here. However, Schippers and Van Lange (2006) also suggest another two areas:

- **Skinner's behavioural theory of operant conditioning** (Skinner, 1948; 1953): in one of Skinner's studies using the Skinner box (see Chapter 4), he gave pigeons food at irregular intervals. This meant that it was left to chance as to what kind of behaviour would be reinforced. Skinner found some very surprising results with this experiment; for instance, when a pigeon wanted food, it would perform the actions that it was doing the last time it got food, such as turning its head or walking around in the same direction. This behaviour couldn't be conditioned as the food was given at irregular times and not after each occasion that the pigeons performed these behaviours. Therefore, Skinner argued that this behaviour represented superstitious behaviour.
- **The illusion of control** (Langer, 1975): this theory concerns the idea that people will tend to overestimate their ability to control an event that is typically left to chance, and that their illusory control will produce a favourable outcome. So, for instance, illusion of control is common in gambling and beliefs in the paranormal; in other words, where chance as well as skill plays a role. Sport, although it involves skill, is also sometimes considered to contain chance (e.g. a 'lucky shot', a 'fortunate bounce'). Therefore, sport could be prone to the illusion of control and superstition.

Schippers and Van Lange (2006) researched superstitious rituals in 197 top sportspeople, including footballers, hockey players and volleyball players. They found that their superstitious behaviour became more pronounced when uncertainty on the outcome of the game was either high or moderate; for example, when there was high importance of success or success was seen as being dependent on external factors, rather than as being in their own control.

Schippers and Van Lange (2006) also argued that an important factor here was that superstition acted as a way to reduce psychological tension in the players. They also speculated that, when preparing for a match, the most important concern for players is to regulate their psychological and physical state. In other words, superstitious rituals, although irrational, may help a player, and these rituals work because the person believes in them and consequently expects beneficial effects on performance (known as the psychological placebo). However, other research findings (e.g. McCallum, 1992) show that superstitious sportspersons can be less self-confident and can experience a higher level of psychological tension before a match.

We have briefly looked at religion, luck and superstitious beliefs to consider the issues around classification of irrational beliefs, and, indeed, we have found that there are conflicting findings as to whether irrational beliefs have positive or negative mental health consequences. Also, regarding the debate around subtlety and subjectivity, research suggests that when considering religion and luck – and perhaps in some cases superstition – there is a distinction between irrational beliefs (bad luck, extrinsic religiosity and some superstitions warding off bad luck) and rational beliefs (good luck, intrinsic religiosity and superstitions related to encouraging good luck). Therefore, we can argue that irrational beliefs can be either self-defeating (irrational) or self-helpful (rational) depending on the individual. So, instead of identifying irrational beliefs and stating that these beliefs are irrational for everyone, a more subtle and subjective consideration may sometimes be needed.

Final comments

We have considered in detail the concepts of rational-emotive behaviour therapy (REBT) and irrational beliefs. We have indicated their importance to individual differences research, insofar as the considerations of individual emotions, behaviours and mental health are concerned. In other words, REBT allows us to understand not only how individuals differ in terms of their beliefs about themselves, others and the world but also how they typically think, emote and act. All of these behaviours have very different consequences on mental health outcomes. However, some issues need to be addressed in this area. First, although the theory surrounding REBT allows for individual differences, there are differences of opinion as to what Ellis considers as irrational. Secondly, there is a need for subtlety and subjectivity within the considerations of what constitutes irrationality for everyone, as evidenced by theory and research surrounding religion, luck and superstitions.

Summary

- What drives an area of theory and research within individual differences is the finding that the theory of irrational beliefs and the theory of rational-emotive behaviour therapy (REBT) have strong research evidence to suggest the detrimental effects of irrational beliefs on mental health, such as depression and anxiety, weak problem-solving techniques, relationship problems and low self-esteem.
- Although REBT is essentially a cognitive-behavioural theory, it lends itself well to individual differences considerations of mental health as it allows us to understand how individuals differ in terms of their approaches to things and through their perceptions and thoughts about the world.
- REBT is built around the concept that how we emotionally respond to something depends simply on our interpretations, views, beliefs or thoughts of the situation. In fact, when an individual emotes, they also think and act; when they act, they also think and emote; finally, when they think, they also emote and act.

- Within REBT theory there are two main concepts: of rational thought and of irrational (self-defeating) ideas.
  - Rationality is the sense that all people have fundamental goals, purposes and values in life that underlie their attempts to be happy and satisfied. If people choose to stay alive and be happy, then they act rationally, or self-helpfully.
  - Irrationality refers to self-defeating thoughts, which block the achievement of goals, distort reality and contain illogical ways of evaluating ourselves, others and the world; these ways include demandingness, awfulising and low frustration tolerance.
- Ellis' concepts of belief are fundamental to mental health in an ABC format: 'A' is for our activating experiences; 'B' stands for our beliefs, especially the irrational, and 'C' stands for the emotional and behavioural consequences of our beliefs.
- Must-urbations (or core musts) are absolutistic evaluations of shoulds, oughts, musts, commands and

demands. The main must-urbations are known as awfulising, low frustration tolerance and damnation.

- REBT is a challenging form of therapy used to change a client's thinking and ultimately to replace any irrational beliefs with rational alternatives.
- Ellis identifies that beliefs surrounding supernatural forces, or a higher being (e.g. religion, luck, superstitious beliefs), are irrational in nature and therefore detrimental to our mental health.
- However, religion has been identified as having three major, different orientations of intrinsic religiosity, extrinsic religiosity and quest religiosity. Intrinsic religiosity has been identified as actually being beneficial to mental health.

- The belief in luck has now been identified as two separate types of belief: a belief in good luck and a belief in bad luck. Belief in good luck has been found to include optimistic tendencies and is therefore beneficial to mental health. However, bad luck is still considered as irrational.
- Superstitious belief is still largely considered as irrational; however, recent research shows that this belief, too, may be divided into two categories having connotations of bad luck and good luck. Thus there are assumptions that not all superstitions are necessarily detrimental to mental health.
- There are considered to be issues for individual differences researchers as regards the lack of subjectivity of REBT, as well as the categorisations of irrational beliefs.

Connecting up

You may want to look back at the chapter on Cognitive Personality Theories (Chapter 5) to read more on Ellis' rational-emotive behaviour therapy and other social cognitive approaches.

You may want to read Chapter 22, Social Attitudes, to get a wider and more detailed view of individual differences in religion.

Critical thinking

Discussion questions

We have considered the central theory of irrational beliefs and their consequences for mental health, and we have included some considerations to help you evaluate this theory. However, there are some discussion points. We present them here in the form of discussion topics so that you can think about these issues either on your own or within groups; your university seminars would also be a great place to discuss them. They are not for you to worry about; they are presented only as a way for you to appreciate the complexities of this topic.

- This first exercise is to get you generating some ideas about the topic. Let us consider some of the theoretical and empirical findings covered here within an individual differences perspective (as outlined in Chapter 17).

  – Name five or six important theories and/or findings that emerge from this topic area.
  – If you were to present an overview of these five or six chosen theories and findings, what different areas of

psychology would you be emphasising? For example, are they biological, physiological, personality, cognitive, social or clinical factors?

  – Of these five or six chosen theories and findings, which do you lend most weight to?
  – Are there any theoretical or empirical overlaps between the theories and findings? If so, where do they occur?

- Of the three main must-urbations (awfulising, low frustration tolerance and damnation), which absolutistic demand do you think is the most damaging to people?
- Do you think that REBT is too simplistic to explain all mental health problems or does it allow for all eventualities?
- How common are irrational beliefs? How many can you identify in yourself and how easy do you think they may be to change to rational ones?
- Do you think that religiosity is fundamentally 'irrational' or does intrinsic religiosity point to a 'healthy' religion?
- How realistic is the consideration of luck and superstition as beneficial to mental health? What other factors,

other than those mentioned here, need to be taken into account?

Essay questions

- Critically outline the theory of irrational beliefs, and describe its usefulness for individual difference researchers.

- Compare and contrast the concepts of irrational thinking with two of the three following 'supernatural' beliefs:

  – religion
  – luck
  – superstition.

- Critically discuss the usefulness of REBT.
- Given Ellis' arguments against religion, do you think it is likely that a 'rational' religiosity exists? Discuss.

Going further

Books on irrational beliefs

These books give really good explanations of the theory of REBT and will give you an even deeper understanding. They also concentrate on explaining how you can actually change your irrational thoughts to rational ones.

- Dryden, W. (ed.). (2003). *Rational-emotive behaviour therapy: Theoretical developments*. London: Brunner-Routledge.
- Dryden, W. (1990). *What is rational-emotive behaviour therapy? A personal and practical guide*. London: Gale Centre Books.

Books on superstition and luck

The following books explain in depth the theories of superstition and luck; they also explain ways to make yourself a 'lucky' person.

- Vyse, S. A. (2000). *Believing in magic: The psychology of superstition*. New York: Oxford University Press.
- Wiseman, R. (2004). *The luck factor: Changing your luck, changing your life – the four essential principles*. New York: Hyperion.

Please note that, although these books are psychological, they present evidence and examples that are not suitable for inclusion in your academic work. None the less, they do give a good, structured overview of what it means to people to be superstitious and lucky.

Other useful books

The following books have been chosen to enable you to understand REBT and superstition at a glance, and are easy-to-read dictionaries.

- Dryden, W. and Neenan, M. (1997). *Dictionary of rational-emotive behaviour therapy*. London: Whurr.
- Opie, I. and Tatem, M. (1992). *A dictionary of superstitions*. New York: Oxford Paperbacks.

Journals

One article you may want to read to consider the research on religion, belief in good luck and superstitions is on magical thinking. This is Subbotsky, E. (2004). Magical thinking – Reality or illusion? *The Psychologist*, *17*, 336–339. Moreover, it is freely available online. You can find *The Psychologist* on the British Psychological Society website (**www.bps.org.uk**).

These journals are full of published articles on research into REBT, irrational beliefs, luck and superstition.

- ***Personality and Individual Differences***. Published by Elsevier. Available online via Science Direct.
- ***American Psychologist***. Published by the American Psychological Association. Available via PsycARTICLES.
- ***Journal of Rational-Emotive & Cognitive-Behaviour Therapy*** is a publication that has theory and research articles on REBT. It is published by Springer/Kluwer and available online via SwetsWise.

Web links

- Visit the Luck Project (**http://richardwiseman.wordpress.com/books/the-luck-factor**). This site contains all the recent research being done by Richard Wiseman on luck, and you can even take part in his studies.
- Visit the Albert Ellis Institute (**www.rebt.org**). This site contains all the research being done by Ellis and other psychotherapists, as well as much useful information on REBT. It is a useful source of information.

Film and literature

The following films and book are fun to watch or read and will help you to consolidate the characteristics of irrational beliefs.

- *It's a Wonderful Life* (1946, directed by Frank Capra). This film is about a man, George Bailey, who spends his life giving up his big dreams for the sake of everyone else in the town. His belief system could be described as irrational as he has set himself impossible standards to live by. He believes himself a failure and decides to kill himself. However, Clarence, an angel who hasn't yet earned his wings, is sent down to show George the error of his thinking and to convince him that he has, in fact, made something of his life.

- *Serendipity* (2001, directed by Peter Chelsom). This film illustrates how people put their trust in greater ('supernatural') powers. Jonathan Trager and Sara Thomas meet while Christmas shopping for their respective partners. The magic is right, and the night turns to romance.

Jonathan wishes to take their meeting further; however, Sara is unsure whether it is 'meant to be' and decides to leave it all up to fate. Many years later, both decide to try finding each other, resulting in many and twisted near misses and classic Shakespearean confusion. However, fate has the final word on their destiny.

- *Don Quixote*. For a classic example of someone who chases an irrational belief, *Don Quixote* is your book. This book has spawned the classic idea of 'chasing windmills'. Don Quixote, a middle-aged man from La Mancha, is obsessed with the chivalrous ideals touted in the books he has read. He decides to take up his lance and sword to defend the helpless and destroy the wicked. What ensues are ridiculous tales of adventure, misunderstandings, misguided principles and blind belief. In the end, the beaten and battered Don Quixote foreswears all the chivalric truths he followed so vehemently and dies of a fever.

Explore the website accompanying this text at **www.pearsoned.co.uk/maltby** for further resources to help you with your studies. These include multiple-choice questions, essay questions, web links and ideas for advanced reading.

CHAPTER 20
Embarrassment, Shyness and Social Anxiety

Key themes

- Social anxiety disorder
- Symptoms and causes of social anxiety disorder
- State and trait shyness
- Behavioural inhibition
- Fearful and self-conscious shyness
- Embarrassment
- The dramaturgic model
- The social evaluation model

Learning outcomes

At the end of this discussion you should:

- Understand the main theories, models and correlates of social anxiety and particularly social anxiety disorder
- Understand how the concept of social anxiety disorder provides a context for understanding individual differences in shyness and embarrassment
- Be familiar with the main theories, models and correlates of shyness
- Be familiar with the main theories, models and correlates of embarrassment

Introduction

Imagine if you had written the following in an examination paper: 'The Greeks were a highly sculptured people, and without them we wouldn't have history. The Greeks also had myths. A myth is a female moth.'

Or you could have been the Sky News reporter George Gavin, who asked a young actor, 'So, this movie you star in, *The Life Story of George Best*, could you tell us what it's about?'

What about Simon Fanshawe, a UK radio DJ, who on being told by a listener on a phone-in that their most embarrassing moment was when their artificial leg fell off at the altar on their wedding day, asked, 'How awful! Do you still have an artificial leg?'

Done or said worse? Think – what is your most embarrassing moment? What makes you shy? Being out on a date, out with some friends or when you have presented a piece of work in front of a few people? Probably, you rarely get embarrassed or shy. You may remember now with some fondness, or silent dread, the time when you were really embarrassed or overcome with shyness. To some extent you may even be able to look back and laugh. What, no? Still a little too raw? ... Well, let's move on.

Although everyone knows what shyness and embarrassment feels like, it can affect some people more than others. Think about the times when you have had a family get-together or a party; is there someone who is always missing from these occasions? Perhaps that person is your aunt, a reclusive neighbour, a work colleague, who always says they will make it, but never does. Well, that person may actually have declined your invitation because they are among the millions of sufferers of social anxiety disorder. For these people, seasonal celebrations and get-togethers can spark such intense feelings of anxiety that they avoid social gatherings altogether. Indeed, besides feeling an intense fear of groups of people, individuals suffering from these social anxieties can suffer physical symptoms such as blushing, sweating, shaking, nausea and difficulty talking, as well as feeling acute shyness or embarrassment.

It is clear from these examples that social anxiety, shyness and embarrassment are extremely important concepts to investigate within individual differences. Consequently, psychologists have looked closely at how these anxieties occur and have tried to understand better why we develop these intense feelings. In particular, they are trying to learn why some people suffer only mild shyness or embarrassment while others become completely debilitated by these feelings.

The aim of this discussion is to introduce you to two concepts that are widely acknowledged and commonly examined within the individual differences literature: shyness and embarrassment. However, though these concepts occur in many different aspects of the psychological literature, particularly the counselling literature, shyness and embarrassment can be considered within a wider context. A general context is known as social anxieties, and a specific context is a diagnostic mental health disorder called social anxiety disorder. Therefore we will first outline the theory and research surrounding social anxiety, and particularly social anxiety disorder, before outlining individual differences in shyness and embarrassment.

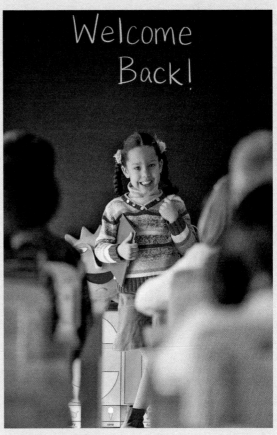

Source: Alamy Images/Blend Images

Introducing social anxieties and social anxiety disorder

In the social anxiety literature, shyness and embarrassment belong to a 'family' of social anxieties that also includes concepts such as shame and fearfulness. The theory, research and application that surround social anxieties have been widely researched and debated within individual differences psychology, which provides us with a useful context to understand shyness and embarrassment. It is important for individual differences psychologists to understand why, when and how some people are more prone to certain detrimental traits than others; and whether there are ways to overcome such tendencies. However, it is an extreme form of social anxiety, **social anxiety disorder**, that has particularly helped psychologists to understand how shyness and embarrassment can have a multitude of detrimental effects for the individual. Therefore we will look at social anxiety disorder first to provide you with a context for the main issues. We will then look at the concepts of shyness and embarrassment that have been more widely informed by individual differences psychologists.

What exactly is social anxiety disorder?

Before we begin looking at social anxiety disorder and learning exactly what it means, there is an issue around the terminology used within the psychological literature that needs addressing. Namely, it is worth noting that the general literature on social anxiety is often intertwined with the term 'social phobia', and a debate exists on whether these two terms mean the same thing. We are highlighting this issue because it can sometimes be confusing when reading the social anxiety and social phobia literature, as many authors use these terms interchangeably. So, rather than you getting confused, let us briefly outline the debate. It will also make clear in your mind what is meant by social anxiety disorder, and you can use this knowledge to guide your reading.

Some authors argue that social anxiety and social phobia are separate concepts. Australian psychologists Richard Mattick and Christopher Clarke (Mattick and Clarke, 1997) present psychometric evidence that these distinctions should be termed 'social phobia' and 'social interaction anxiety'. That is, social anxiety should emphasise the problems that occur in individuals' *interactions* with the social world. These authors refer to 'social phobia' as an individual feeling anxiety and fear at the prospect of being observed by other people, particularly when the individual experiences and expresses distress while undertaking certain activities in the presence of others. Mattick and Clarke suggest that such activities may include drinking, eating, writing, using public toilets or being looked at. On the other hand, they argue that 'social interaction anxiety' refers to distress that a person may feel when meeting and talking with other people, regardless of the status of those people, be it people of the opposite sex, strangers or friends. The central concern is over fears of being inarticulate, sounding stupid, or boring or being ignored, not knowing what to do or say or not knowing how to respond within social interactions. To summarise then, for psychologists who consider these two terms as separate, **social anxiety** is used to describe individuals who fear failing to do their best in front of others, in social situations and events; they mostly fear being negatively

judged by others. In contrast, **social phobia** is considered to include individuals who are insecure in unknown company; it is not a fear of failure or criticism, but rather one of feeling unsafe owing to having left their zone of comfort and safety.

On the other hand, other authors have argued that, within research and within the *Diagnostic and Statistical Manual of Mental Disorders* (*DSM-IV*, a definitive handbook by which psychiatric diagnoses are categorised; American Psychiatric Association, 1994), the two concepts are so similar in description that the terms 'social phobia' and 'social anxiety' can be considered as one and the same thing. In other words, if you look up these terms, the diagnostic criteria are very similar. However, Thomas Richards from the Social Anxiety Institute (Richards, 2006a; 2006b) goes even further within this debate; he puts forward strong arguments for using the term 'social anxiety' over and above the term of 'social phobia'. These arguments are outlined here:

- Most people, even professional organisations, have a difficult time understanding the definition of social phobia. For example, many professionals often misuse the term and, when discussing a person with social phobia, their discussion often turns into one about a person with **agoraphobia**, an entirely different anxiety disorder.
- Organisations, by lumping 'the phobias' together, are doing a disservice not only to individuals with social anxiety, but to individuals with 'true' phobias, such as phobias that involve the fear of snakes, flying or open spaces.
- Social anxiety influences and encompasses all aspects of a person's life. People with social anxiety *fear social situations and events*; they do *not* fear having panic attacks (which would be a phobia). They fear the high amount of anxiety and the negative self-appraisal experienced before, during and after a social event.
- Anxieties such as social anxiety and agoraphobia are entirely different in terms of operational definitions. *Social anxiety* is a fear of social events and activities, and the people associated with them; it results in high levels of anxiety and therefore leads the socially anxious person to avoid such events and activities. *Agoraphobia* is a reaction to panic attacks that occur frequently and in many places. People with agoraphobia feel unsafe when leaving a 'zone of safety'. The fear is of having a panic attack, not of being in social situations and associating with other people.
- The term 'social anxiety' (social anxiety disorder) is more precise, clear and understandable than 'social phobia'.

We are sure that such debates about definitions will continue. As to our needs for this discussion, for understanding the individual differences topics of shyness and embarrassment, a definition put forward by Mattick and Clarke (1997) is most useful. This is to consider social anxiety as social interaction anxiety, emphasising social anxiety that occurs when the individual has to deal with other people or social situations. It is this side of social anxiety, and its emergence as a disorder, that we will concentrate on here. However, to make it clear to you, we will first give you an example.

Imagine a university student, Paul, who has problems when interacting with others. He feels horribly anxious when expected to interact socially, often skipping lectures and seminars out of fear of being asked a question by the lecturer or being asked to contribute to the class. Even though Paul knows the subject well, the very thought of socially interacting while among so many people terrifies him. He has difficulty asking questions and talking to both the lecturer and his peers through fear that they may find him boring or uninteresting. He finds presentations in class impossible, and he has found that previous attempts have resulted in physical symptoms of anxiety, including a shortness of breath, dizziness and a trembling body and hands. Paul has always been shy. However, he feels that this anxiety is now taking over his life. He is worried about the ability to accomplish his life goals if these feelings carry on. Paul suffers from social anxiety disorder.

Authors such as Leitenberg (1990) and Hofman and Otto (2008) argue that it is important to remember that, although many people suffer from varying degrees of anxiety when relating to others, certain aspects of social interaction often incapacitate individuals with social anxiety disorder. Social anxiety disorder extends beyond just simple shyness; it may limit not only the social life of the individual who suffers from it, but their possible success at education and career choices. It can also be found to affect an individual's school life, through the person's interactions with peers, ability to function efficiently in the classroom, and success in making friends. For example, people with a social anxiety disorder will avoid taking classes where they may be at the centre of attention (for example, a presentation may be part of the assessment). In employment, social anxiety disorder may also affect a person's work success. They may not take on job responsibilities that may require chairing meetings, giving presentations or attending social functions, even if it means a promotion. In one's personal life, social anxiety disorder can decrease opportunities for meeting a future spouse. It has also been found to add stress to a marriage and is associated with an increased rate of divorce. So, social anxiety disorder can have serious effects on people's lives (Hofman and Otto, 2008).

Let us look more closely at the general symptoms, prevalence and conceptions of this disorder as it is presented in the psychological literature.

General symptoms, prevalence and conceptions of social anxiety disorder

US psychologists Leora R. Heckelman and Franklin R. Schneier outline the main symptoms and prevalence of social anxiety disorder (Heckelman and Schneier, 1995; Schneier, 2003). They note that the central aspect in social anxiety disorder is the fear of performing, or 'showing yourself up', in social situations and that consequently the individual will suffer humiliation, embarrassment or shame. These individuals' lives are made even more complicated by becoming fearful through the anticipation of a future social encounter. They will often experience an increase in physical symptoms such as increased heart rate or palpitations, sweating, trembling, changes in speech and blushing. Indeed, all these indicators of anxiety may form a vicious circle. For instance, when the individual experiences these physical symptoms, they then begin to feel concerned that their anxiety is obvious to other people. This, in turn, may lead to further feelings of humiliation, embarrassment or shame.

As you can see, social anxiety disorder has serious consequences, and it is perhaps shocking to realise that an estimated 16 per cent of the general population will suffer from it at some point during their life (Hidalgo et al., 2001). As Heckelman and Schneier note, many of us can relate to feelings of being nervous or shy in certain social situations, such as meeting someone for the first time, giving a presentation or walking into a social event (such as a party). However, Heckelman and Schneier remind us that those who suffer from social anxiety are often unable to function at all in these social settings. Interestingly, however, these authors also suggest that the appearance of social anxiety disorder can vary from individual to individual. Some people will report increasing shyness as they get older, while for others the onset of social anxiety disorder may occur because of specific life events. Typically, social anxiety disorder may appear in childhood or early adolescence and rarely develops after the age of 25. However, the recognition of social anxiety disorder is problematic, as it is difficult to identify where shyness ends and social anxiety begins.

In fact, some psychologists have suggested that social anxiety is a universal experience and may have important origins. In their review of population and family studies of social anxiety, US psychologists Tim Chapman, Salvatore Mannuzza and Abby Fyer noted that, in prehistoric times, social anxiety may have been necessary for our survival (Chapman et al., 1995). The authors argue that, at a time when people had to work together to hunt for food, confront their enemies and build shelters, social anxiety served the function of keeping people close and bonded to the wider group. This in turn ensured that they lowered their chances of death. In more modern times, however, we tend to belong, and want to belong, to social groups (be it friends or families). Therefore, a certain degree of social anxiety surrounding the thought of being alone could be considered normal, functional and beneficial. Having friends and families brings us many personal and social rewards, and a lack of anxiety about not having others around us might be of concern to us. Furthermore, we must all, to some extent, suffer some social anxiety.

If we never cared what others thought, or took on board their opinions, we might be considered as not very nice people to be around.

Many authors, including Leitenberg (1990) and Hofman and Otto (2008), have stressed that we have all felt embarrassment after spilling a drink; many of us get 'stage fright' before a big performance; it is common to feel awkwardness while talking to someone you don't know well or to experience nervousness during a job interview. In fact, these authors emphasise that these are common experiences that almost everyone has had at one particular time and this 'anxiety' has its use. For example, if you did not feel anxiety before an important job interview, then you perhaps would be less likely to take it seriously or be less alert during the process. However, since social anxiety is so universal, how do we know the difference between when it is useful and functional for a social interaction or occasion, and when this anxiety may reflect a problem? The answer may lie with the work of clinicians and therapists.

Definitions and diagnosis of social anxiety disorder

As Heckelman and Schneier (1995) note, therapists and clinicians use *The Diagnostic and Statistical Manual of Mental Disorders, Fourth Edition (DSM-IV)* to make diagnostic decisions. The *DSM-IV* (American Psychiatric Association, 1994) covers the diagnostic criteria for all mental health disorders for both children and adults. While Heckelman and Schneier note that the *DSM-IV* is not a perfect system, diagnoses of mental health disorders, such as social anxiety disorder, are important for defining research vital to understanding a problem and thus developing effective treatments for it. Otherwise, coordinated research programmes and practice will not and cannot take place. So, let us look at the specific criteria for the diagnosis of social anxiety disorder.

The *DSM-IV* says an individual with social anxiety disorder will:

- Show significant and persistent fear of social situations in which embarrassment or rejection may occur.
- Experience immediate anxiety-driven, physical reactions to feared social situations.
- Realise that their fears are greatly exaggerated, but feel powerless to do anything about them.
- Often avoid the dreaded social situation – at any cost.

Several US and European psychologists, such as Franklin R. Schneier (Schneier, 2003), Daniel W. McNeil (McNeil *et al.*, 2001), Stefan Hofman and Michael Otto (Hofman and Otto, 2008) and two people's work that we will discuss in detail later, Lynn Henderson and Philip Zimbardo (Henderson and Zimbardo, 2001), all identify three common ways in which social anxiety disorder can be defined.

- **Generalised social anxiety disorder** – this is indicated when an individual fears a wide range of social situations; for example, going to a party, being with friends, speaking to employers. A person with generalised anxiety will likely have dealt with issues of shyness for their entire life.
- **Non-generalised (performance) social anxiety disorder** – describes an anxiety response to one, or perhaps two or three, identified situations and affects individuals only when they are performing in front of others. An example would be active avoidance of, or severe anxiety in, speaking in public.
- **Avoidant personality disorder** – this disorder is considered by many specialists to be the most severe form of social anxiety. This disorder is considered to show a detached personality pattern, meaning that the person purposefully avoids people due to fears of humiliation and rejection. It usually starts at an early age and this disorder is much more common in males. Typical behaviours of someone with avoidant personality disorder include a reluctance to become involved with people, having no close friends, exaggerating potential difficulties and avoiding activities or occupations involving contact with others.

Finally, American psychologists Barbara and Gregory Markway have examined the diagnosis and treatment of social anxiety disorders (Markway *et al.*, 1992; Markway and Markway, 2003) and suggest that, once the basic criteria from the *DSM-IV* are met for a diagnosis of social anxiety disorder, the individual symptoms can vary. However, these symptoms fall into three specific categories (see Figure 20.1):

- *cognitive* or mental symptoms (what you think);
- *physical* reactions (how your body feels);
- *behavioural* avoidance (what you do).

Let us look at these three categories in more detail.

The cognitive symptoms

Markway and Markway (2003) describe the cognitive, or mental, symptoms as a way of identifying how people with

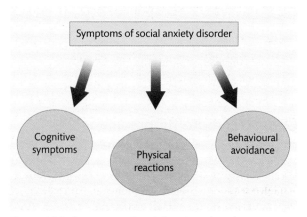

Figure 20.1 Symptoms of social anxiety disorder.

social anxiety disorder may think. For instance, the authors identify that social anxiety sufferers are more prone to negative thoughts and doubts about themselves and may have such thoughts as: 'Do I look all right?' 'Am I dressed in an appropriate manner?' 'What if other people don't like me?' and 'Will I sound stupid or boring?'. According to the authors, not only do social anxiety sufferers have these negative thoughts that focus on fear of rejection or disapproval, but they also spend time looking for the signs, or behaviours, from others that may affirm their negative thoughts about themselves. These negative thoughts, if left unchecked, can have severe consequences. They can lead to many other outcomes, including low self-esteem and feelings of inferiority.

The physical reactions

Markway and Markway (2003) describe the physical reactions as a way of identifying how people with social anxiety disorder may feel when they are anxious. The authors point out that many people do not realise the extent of these physical symptoms. For instance, an individual suffering from social anxiety can experience panic attacks, dizziness, shaking and sweating, shortness of breath, an increase in the beating of the heart, a tightness or pain in the chest, numbness in parts of the body and nausea.

Markway and Markway (2003) also emphasise an important distinction between social anxiety symptoms and individuals who suffer from panic attacks alone. In fact, the key to knowing whether an individual suffers from social anxiety or panic attacks lies in understanding the core fear. In panic disorder, the individual fears the panic attack itself and often feels as if they are actually dying during such an episode. In the case of social anxiety disorder, however, the fear is concentrated on the possibility that people might witness the panic attack and the resulting humiliation that would follow.

However, the authors remind us that not everyone with social anxiety experiences full-blown panic attacks; in fact, some people may not have them at all. Instead, their symptoms are focused on other particular physical aspects of the condition. For example, the most common symptoms include shaking, sweating and blushing. Nevertheless, regardless of any physical symptoms an individual might experience, the effects are never pleasant. Markway and Markway argue that having one's body in a state of constant alert takes its toll and can eventually lead to chronic fatigue, muscle tension and sleep disturbances.

Behavioural avoidance

Finally, Markway and Markway (2003) describe behavioural avoidance as a way of identifying what people with social anxiety disorder may do. Indeed, the Markways note that it is in our nature to avoid pain and suffering; in fact, evolutionary psychology suggests that individuals are programmed to either fight or flee from a dangerous or stressful situation. Consequently, people with social anxiety disorder tend to avoid (flee) potential situations that they believe will cause them harm. So this might mean never going out to social occasions (parties, restaurants, pubs, clubs); it may mean having few, if any, friends or intimate relationships; and it might mean being employed in a job beneath their potential.

These authors also argue that the behavioural consequences of avoidance, for those suffering with social anxiety disorder, will vary depending on the severity of their anxiety and on the individual. However, in all cases, people with social anxiety disorder will limit their choices out of fear and will make life decisions based on what they feel comfortable with rather than what they might really want to do.

As well as resorting to the outright avoidance of situations, social anxiety sufferers may engage in other, more subtle, avoidance behaviours (Markway and Markway, 2003). For instance, they may take alcohol to help them cope with anxiety (e.g. drinking before a party to get up the courage to go at all) or they may decide on certain parameters to allow them to get through social situations (e.g. staying at the party for only a short time). In summary, then, Markway and Markway argue that engaging in avoidance behaviours will, again, enhance the feelings of social anxiety. In other words, by avoiding threatening situations, individuals may never realise that they actually *can* manage their anxiety and cope with their fears.

What causes social anxiety disorder?

So, we have learned exactly what social anxiety disorder entails, but what are the causes of this disorder? Social anxiety disorder is a complex issue with many possible contributing factors. Therefore, so far, the exact cause of social anxiety disorder has been difficult to identify, and research still has a long way to go to clarify the primary influences. However, Richard Heimberg, Michael Liebowitz, Debra Hope and Franklin Schneier suggest that there are some basic theories as to the possible causes of social anxiety disorder (Heimberg *et al.*, 1995). We will introduce you to these causes, as they are important to understanding the context of some of the themes that will arise in the shyness and embarrassment literature further on within this discussion, and they reflect aspects of individual differences theories that we have covered so far in the text. The following are brief explanations of some of the theories regarding the possible causes of social anxiety disorder (see Figure 20.2).

Genetic and biological influences

Authors such as Tim Chapman *et al.* (1995) and P. V. Nickell and Thomas Uhde (1995) have suggested that there may be a genetic predisposition to social anxiety.

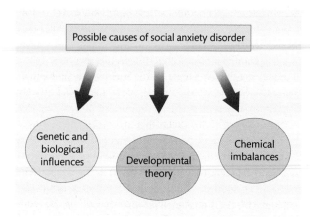

Figure 20.2 Possible causes of social anxiety disorder.

The best-known work in this area is by Jerome Kagan, who has explored the relative genetic and environmental influences on social anxiety (Kagan, 1994b; 1998). Kagan has focused on the development of inhibited (a tendency to restrain impulses or desires) and uninhibited (a tendency to be open and unrestrained) children from infancy through to adolescence and has found that biological influences may play a part in the development of social anxieties. He identified that around 10–15 per cent of babies were considered as irritable and that these babies then began to show signs of shyness and fearfulness and, overall, were behaviourally inhibited as toddlers. In turn, these children stayed quiet, introverted and cautious in their early school years. Later, as adolescents, they presented a rate of social anxiety disorder that was much higher than expected.

In addition, Kagan found that these children also possessed a higher-than-normal resting heart rate, and that this resting heart rate rose even higher in the presence of mild stresses or anxieties. Alongside this, when these children were exposed to new situations, they were behaviourally inhibited, becoming very quiet and restrained, avoiding interaction and even withdrawing from the situation (behavioural inhibition will be looked at more closely later, when considering shyness).

Interestingly, Kagan has found that a high percentage of the parents of these children also had social anxiety disorder or other related anxiety disorders. Kagan suggests that social anxiety may represent specific behaviour that expresses a genetically driven trait of social withdrawal, which may be related to an infantile inhibited temperament. This is known as Kagan's syndrome. So, in other words, sensitivity to criticism or social attention can be passed on from one generation of individuals to the next. Kagan suggests it is even possible that the child of one or two shy parents may inherit genes that amplify shyness into social anxiety disorder. Indeed, various studies have suggested that there is an increased risk of developing social anxiety disorder in individuals whose relatives also have the disorder. Moreover, twin and family studies show substantial genetic and environmental contributions

to social anxiety disorder (Fyer *et al.*, 1993; Kendler *et al.*, 1999). For example, a study of female identical twins suggests a 30 per cent heritability estimate for social anxiety disorder (Kendler *et al.*, 1992), although it must be made clear that this study looked at many phobias, not just social anxiety. However, whether these influences are genetic or environmental, or an interaction between the two, is always debatable (for a full review of the problems and the necessity of separating genetic and environmental effects, see earlier [Chapter 8]).

Developmental theory

Clearly, therefore, the development of the child is important in understanding how social anxiety grows, particularly as many think the onset of social anxiety disorder occurs in childhood or early adolescence. Researchers such as US psychologists Monroe Bruch and Jonathan Cheek (1995) and the aforementioned Kagan suggest that some individuals start life more prone to anxiety (an anxious temperament); as the individual gets older, this trait may be influenced by stressful life situations such as family, relationship problems or life events. Researchers have found that social anxiety emerges at different developmental stages within childhood (Kagan, 1994b; 1998). For instance, as early as age 7 months, babies can develop a fear of strangers. Likewise, separation anxiety is prominent in some children, and it is perhaps more obvious when children are first taken to day care, or nursery, or on their first days at a primary or infant school. In fact, being alone is very difficult for children right up to the age of 6 or 8 years. As children enter adolescence, solitude becomes a more important factor in a person's life as anxiety about physical appearance and performance in school increases (Crozier, 2002; Kagan, 1994b; 1998). Researchers have also found that traumatic or stressful life events occurring at an early developmental stage may increase the risk of social anxiety disorder (Bruch and Cheek, 1995; Crozier, 2002).

Chemical imbalances

Along with other theoretical explanations, some researchers such as US psychologists Nicholas Potts and Jonathan Davidson, and Michael R. Liebowitz and Randall Marshall (Liebowitz and Marshall, 1995; Potts and Davidson, 1995) have also identified that individuals with social anxiety disorder possess certain abnormalities in the functioning of some parts of their anxiety response system. Thus, often the symptoms of long-term social anxiety disorder are found to be the result of chemical imbalances within the brain.

This imbalance occurs with several neurotransmitters. **Neurotransmitters** are chemical substances that transmit nerve impulses across a synapse to neurons, muscle cells or the glands. These neurotransmitters are thought to be associated with social anxiety:

- **Serotonin** – a neurotransmitter that is involved in stimulation of the muscles and regulation of cyclic body processes.
- **Norepinephrine** – a hormone and neurotransmitter involved in the heart rate, blood pressure and sugar levels of the blood (also called noradrenaline).
- **Gamma-aminobutyric acid** – an amino acid that occurs in the central nervous system and is related to the transmission of nerve impulses.

With the mention of regulating body processes, heart rate, blood pressure and transmission through nerves, it is easy to see how these biological processes might be expected to relate to social anxiety disorder (for example, high heart rate, high blood pressure, suffering from 'nerves').

Alongside this, Nicholas Potts and Jonathan Davidson (1995) point out that four specific brain areas are critical to our anxiety-response system:

- **Brain stem** – the portion of the brain that connects the spinal cord to the forebrain and cerebrum and controls the cardiovascular and respiratory functions.
- **Limbic system** – a group of interconnected deep-brain structures involved in emotion, motivation and behaviour.
- **Prefrontal cortex** – the grey matter of the prefrontal lobe that is involved in a person's appraisals of risk and danger.
- **Motor cortex** – the area of the cerebral cortex where impulses from the nerve centres control the muscles.

It is these four structures within the brain where the serotonin, norepinephrine and gamma-aminobutyric acid neurotransmitters are found. Serotonin is found in neurons beginning in the midbrain, norepinephrine is found in neurons arising primarily from a part of the brain stem and gamma-aminobutyric acid is found in neurons that are widespread throughout the brain.

In terms of our emotional responses, this neurochemical process is crucial to sustaining a sense of emotional well-being within the individual. Physiological functions, such as regulation of blood flow as well as functioning of the nervous system and muscular system, all reflect our emotional well-being. Imagine yourself in a resting state, such as deep sleep; your muscles are relaxed and your heart is slowly pumping blood around the body. As you move to initial arousal, and then to extreme anxiety or panic, your muscles will become tighter, all tensed up; your nervous system is in overload, and your heart begins to pump blood more quickly around your body. If the neurological processes are linked to anxiety responses, you can easily imagine how an individual with social anxiety disorder might actually be suffering from chemical imbalances in the brain. Interestingly, an American neuropsychiatrist called Murray B. Stein and his colleagues (Stein *et al.*, 1998) found that three selective serotonin re-uptake inhibitors – paroxetine, sertraline and fluvoxamine (all antidepressants that enhance serotonin activity by inhibiting its uptake by neurons and, therefore, increasing the amount of serotonin in the neurotransmitter) – are the best drug treatments for social anxiety disorder.

Consideration of all the literature in this section suggests that there are different types, symptoms and possible explanations to the causes of social anxiety and social anxiety disorder. What is particularly important to note in this context is that individual differences researchers have become interested in particular aspects of social anxiety, namely, embarrassment and shyness. Although shyness and embarrassment are milder forms of social anxiety, particularly when compared to social anxiety disorder, it must be remembered that social anxiety, and particularly the work that has been carried out to describe and understand social anxiety disorder, must be considered as a context to shyness and embarrassment. Within our discussion of shyness and embarrassment, you will see similar themes to those that we have just discussed under social anxiety disorder. We will revisit some of these ideas, alongside other theories, when we discuss shyness and embarrassment. We will first turn to the concept of shyness.

Shyness

Clinicians have regarded 'shyness' with some caution, suspecting that it refers loosely to varying kinds and degrees of social fears. This contrasts with social anxiety, which is defined within clinical diagnostic criteria. Nevertheless, as US psychologist Daniel W. McNeil has noted (McNeil *et al.*, 2001), individual differences psychologists have begun to take shyness seriously and to consider its links with social anxiety.

As McNeil notes, shyness is often documented as a symptom of social anxiety disorder. We have briefly considered social anxiety disorder and understood that this level of anxiety is a clinical disorder. However, although social anxiety may not be apparent within a shy individual, the anxieties of shyness are not without their problems. Therefore, psychologists are keen to better understand how and why shyness occurs.

We will look closely here at some ways that shyness has been constructed and examined within individual differences. But first, the main drive of this research within psychology is the finding that shyness, in its varying forms, has strong research evidence to suggest a relationship to poorer physical and mental health. We will go into greater detail later; but, in short, to give you an idea of how important shyness is within general psychology, shyness has led to:

- self-consciousness;
- more negative thoughts about oneself;
- seeing oneself as awkward, unfriendly, incompetent;

Stop and think

Social anxiety

- Consider the three ways in which social anxiety develops (i.e. generalised, non-generalised and avoidant); do you understand the subtle differences between them? Think about the times when you have felt embarrassed or shy; can you place yourselves into one of these categories? If not, can you think of how else we could categorise social anxieties?
- Consider the debate around the discussion of social anxiety and social phobia. Think carefully about these two terms; do you think they are different, or do you think they explain the same symptoms?

- feeling less physically attractive (sometimes leading to sexual dysfunction);
- talking less, averting the eyes, fewer facial expressions, touching oneself self-consciously on parts of the body (for example, the face, arms and legs);
- remembering negative descriptions of oneself better than positive ones;
- dealing ineffectively with stress by worry;
- pessimism;
- loneliness and social isolation;
- abusing alcohol to relax.

Of course, it is important to note that not all shy people suffer from all of the detrimental effects just mentioned; in fact, McNeil has argued that many shy people see no need to overcome their shyness at all. Indeed, they actually think of their shyness as a positive personal quality, or see it as a personality trait that they have learned very well to deal with; in fact, it is part of who they are. Nevertheless, there is much research evidence to suggest that many more shy people see their shyness as a debilitating problem that they would choose to overcome if they could (e.g. Zimbardo, 1977).

US psychologist Philip G. Zimbardo (1977) was the first to carry out a substantial survey in the United States to identify the prevalence of shyness. This research is better known as the Stanford Shyness Survey. Zimbardo and his colleagues asked their respondents whether they regarded themselves as shy and went on to explore the respondents' thoughts and feelings of exactly what shyness entailed. The survey revealed that most shy people saw shyness as a quiet, inhibiting behaviour, including self-consciousness and apprehension about being negatively evaluated in social situations. Nearly all respondents reported feeling shy at one time or another. A surprising 40 per cent of people in the survey described themselves as chronically shy, while only 5 per cent believed they were never shy. In addition to these statistics, the reported 40 per cent has since increased by about 10 per cent in a partial replication of Zimbardo's work by

Bernard Carducci (Carducci, 1999) at Indiana University Southeast (USA), where 1642 students were surveyed between 1979 and 1991. Since this survey, many more cross-cultural studies have investigated whether the same prevalence is true in other countries. Harkins (1990) found evidence to suggest that in many countries across the world, people consistently describe shyness as an uncertainty about what to do or say and reflecting concerns about being evaluated by others.

What is shyness?

Before going on to examine the different theories of shyness, we must first consider what psychologists mean by the term 'shyness'. Lynn Henderson with Philip Zimbardo (founders and researchers of the Shyness Institute in the United States) suggest that shyness is best understood as the experience of discomfort and/or inhibition in interpersonal situations (situations that involve interaction with other people), and that this discomfort has an effect on our interpersonal or professional goals. **Shyness**, then, is considered to comprise excessive self-focus, a preoccupation with one's own thoughts, feelings and physical reactions.

According to Henderson and Zimbardo (1998), shyness may appear as chronic (long-lasting and experienced in many, or all, situations) and dispositional (part of our personality); it serves as a personality trait that is central in an individual's definition of their own identity, character, abilities and attitudes, especially in relation to other people or situations. However, shyness can also be considered as situational. Situational shyness involves the individual experiencing the symptoms of shyness in specific social performance situations, but it is not incorporated into a person's own self-concept (we will return to this distinction later in the discussion).

Alongside this, individual differences researchers (e.g. Crozier, 2001; 2002; Henderson and Zimbardo, 1998) have shown that shyness reactions can occur at any, or all, of the following levels:

- **cognitive** (e.g. fear of negative evaluation and looking foolish to others);
- **affective** (e.g. embarrassment and self-consciousness);
- **physiological** (e.g. blushing);
- **behavioural** (e.g. failing to respond appropriately to a situation).

Indeed, Henderson and Zimbardo (1998) have presented the following symptoms of shyness within these four levels (see also Figure 20.3).

Cognitive

- Negative thoughts about the self, the situation and others
- Worry and rumination, as well as perfectionism
- Fear of negative evaluation and looking foolish to others
- Self-blaming attributions
- Believing the self as weak (negative) and others as strong (powerful)
- Negative bias around self-concept (e.g. 'I am socially inadequate, unlovable, unattractive')
- A belief that there is a right way of doing something that the shy person doesn't know, or must guess.

Affective

- Embarrassment and self-consciousness
- Shame
- Low self-esteem
- Dejection and sadness
- Loneliness
- Depression
- Anxiety.

Physiological

- Racing heartbeat
- Dry mouth
- Trembling or shaking
- Sweating
- Feeling faint, dizzy, sick, nervous
- Blushing
- Feeling unreal or detached from everything
- Fear of losing control, of having a panic attack or heart attack.

Behavioural

- Inhibition or passivity
- Averting gaze
- Avoidance of fearful situations
- Speaking very quietly
- Little body movement, or over-the-top body movement with excessive nodding or smiling
- Speech faults (e.g. becoming tongue-tied, speaking too quickly)
- Nervous behaviour (e.g. touching your hair or face, tugging at clothes, rubbing hands).

Let us consider an example to explain this further. Imagine Helen is a very shy individual, and she is asked to do a presentation in one of her seminars at university. Cognitively, she may worry about looking foolish, believing that she is inadequate to perform the presentation successfully. Affectively she may become embarrassed, self-conscious or anxious. Before and during her presentation, she may experience a dry mouth, begin to shake and sweat or blush.

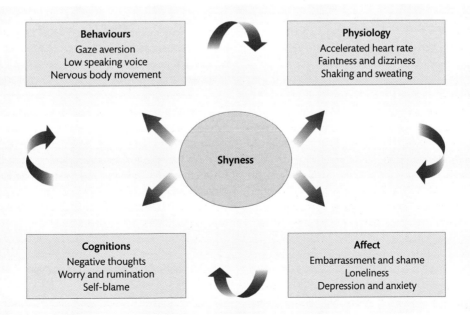

Figure 20.3 Symptoms and consequences of shyness.
Source: Reprinted from Henderson, L. and Zimbardo, P. G. (1998). Shyness. In H.S. Friedman (ed.), *The encyclopedia of mental health* (Vol. 7, pp. 497–509). San Diego, CA: Academic Press. Copyright © 1998 Elsevier Science, reprinted with permission.

Finally, her behaviour will seem inappropriate as she may overcompensate by speaking too fast and loud, by excessive body movements; alternatively, she may become very distant, averting her gaze, speaking low, getting tongue-tied and so on. As we can see, the experiences that shy people may go through are unpleasant and debilitating, not only in terms of their own negative biases about themselves but also in the other people's opinions of them.

Henderson and Zimbardo also point out that, as well as these unpleasant experiences, it is also worth remembering that these symptoms can be triggered by a wide variety of arousal cues (triggers). These cues may include speaking to or interacting with people in authority, one-to-one interactions, intimacy, talking to strangers, taking an active role in a group or initiating social interaction (Henderson and Zimbardo, 1998).

The consequences of shyness

Henderson and Zimbardo suggest the consequences of shyness are diverse; some shy individuals face only a few consequences, while others face many. Generally, shy individuals see their shyness as an ongoing problem, with them failing to take advantage of social situations, tending to be less expressive verbally and non-verbally, and showing less interest in other people. In addition, some shy individuals are painfully self-conscious, report many more negative thoughts about themselves and see themselves as awkward, socially incompetent (particularly with people to whom they are sexually attracted) and less physically attractive.

Researchers, such as Henderson and Zimbardo (1998), have also found that a small number of shy individuals tend to lack basic social skills. For instance, they may have difficulty in knowing what to say or do, how to behave and when best to respond in social situations. Alongside this, shy individuals tend to talk less, avert their gaze more often, show fewer facial expressions, touch themselves in a nervous manner and initiate fewer conversations. These poorer social skills, however, seem to be related to their lack of confidence in their ability to carry out the required behaviours, rather than not having the social skills.

Some research has been carried out on looking at sex differences in the consequences of shyness. There are differences between the sexes in this regard; however, they seem to relate to socially accepted gender behaviours rather than biological sex differences (e.g. Crozier, 2001; Henderson and Zimbardo, 1998). For example, shy men tend to look away when women meet their gaze, and they terminate their own gaze quickly; consequently, this behaviour leads to negative reactions in females. Shy women are also frequently unable to gaze at men; however, the women's behaviour does not seem to induce negative reactions in these men nor prevent the chance of a conversation taking place with them. According to Henderson and Zimbardo, this suggests that the cultural burden of shyness may rest more often on men, who are expected to take the initiative in heterosexual relationships.

Cheek (1996) suggests that, although shy individuals are generally considered as less assertive and less friendly than other people, they are not viewed as negatively as they fear they are. In fact, shy individuals tend to over-estimate the chances of unpleasantness in social interactions because of their tendency to remember negative feedback more than others do, as well as their tendency to remember negative self-descriptions better than positive ones. Interestingly, this type of thinking has been shown to interfere with social interaction more than does anxiety, and this behaviour has been found to be particularly influential in sexual encounters, such as a lowered pleasurable arousal and more sexual dysfunction (Crozier, 2001). In other words, these negative consequences tend to emerge because of shy individuals' preoccupation with how others see them rather than to their actual ability to function. Thus, shyness becomes a self-defeating strategy; it can even become an excuse, or a reason, for anticipated social failure that, over time, becomes a psychological crutch – for example, 'I can't do it because I am shy' (Henderson and Zimbardo, 1998).

There are many other less profound consequences of shyness that, nevertheless, affect a shy individual's quality of life. For instance, they may suffer with greater health problems owing a lack of social support networks and a failure to disclose personal or sensitive problems to their doctor. Alternatively, shy people tend to make less money in less suitable jobs because of less frequent requests for promotion, wage rises and performing less well at interviews; they also have limits on their job advancement in positions because usually promotions, which typically involve the management of other people, lead to taking on a role that requires greater verbal fluency and leadership skills (Jones et al., 1986).

Another consequence of shyness is that other people may perceive shy individuals as reticent (keeping their thoughts, feelings and personal affairs close to themselves). Therefore shy people are sometimes seen as unfriendly, arrogant or even hostile.

Now that we have considered the many consequences of shyness, we need to understand how individual differences researchers have conceptualised exactly *why* shyness occurs. One possible explanation of this is through the concepts of state versus trait shyness. We will then go on to consider *how* shyness occurs by looking at these two concepts.

State versus trait shyness

The shyness literature typically distinguishes between two categories of shyness: state (situational) shyness and trait (dispositional) shyness. **State shyness** (also called situational shyness) comprises immediate emotional and cognitive experience of shyness; for example, heightened self-consciousness in response to a social threat. This type of shyness may be experienced by virtually anyone from time to time, especially in certain social situations. For example, people are generally more shy in situations involving strangers than when interacting with friends or family.

In contrast, **trait shyness** refers to the long-lasting, or permanent, tendency to experience state shyness (heightened self-consciousness in many different and frequent situations); alternatively, it can refer to experiencing shyness in response to much lower levels of social threat than are usually needed to experience state shyness (A. Buss, 1980). In other words, for some people, state shyness diminishes when the circumstances responsible for the shyness either cease or change; trait shyness is considered a personality trait that remains stable over time and across situations (Russell *et al.*, 1986). Furthermore, the level of state shyness experienced by individuals who are high in trait shyness also varies from one situation to the next, but it is always higher than for persons low in trait shyness (Crozier, 2001). We will now outline in more detail how psychologists have described state and trait shyness.

State shyness

State shyness consists of an interplay of processes between the cognitive (e.g. self-focus, concern with one's performance), affective (e.g. anxiety), behavioural (e.g. nervous and excessive speech) and physiological (e.g. sweating, dry mouth) levels of experience. These experiences are so unpleasant that they usually lead to withdrawal from, or avoidance of, many social situations; however, they are also considered to compound the distress of shyness by distracting from skilled and self-confident social interactions (Henderson and Zimbardo, 1998).

There are thought to be two origins of state shyness. First, according to A. Buss (1980), where an individual is placed in a position of uncertainty or placed in situations that bring them under the attention of others, then the experience of shyness can emerge. For example, shyness may occur in situations involving some kind of evaluation or assessment, public performances, novelty, interaction with high-status or attractive people, formality such as weddings or funerals, self-presentations or being the centre of attention. The second contributing factor, according to A. Buss (1980), is the compounding variable of trait shyness. In other words, some people are predisposed to experience state shyness due to their personality or the way they typically and characteristically cope with social demands.

State shyness is also thought to be related to other social emotions such as shame, audience anxiety and embarrassment. All these social emotions involve some degree of social withdrawal. However, shyness is considered different to other aspects of social withdrawal because of its link to specific situations and the four specific components of experience (cognitive, affective, behavioural and physiological). For example, shame arises from the public detection of an immoral or undesirable behaviour, whereas shyness involves a lack of self-confidence and timidness in social situations (Izard, 1972).

Trait shyness

We have just introduced you to state shyness. The context for understanding state shyness is that most of us actually experience state shyness within our lives during specific situations that we may or will find ourselves in. However, the concept of trait shyness is much more complex. Therefore, we will look at this concept in much more depth, considering many different theories as to the origins of trait shyness – for instance, personality, genetic, environmental, attribution style and physiological theories.

As shyness is a relatively stable personality characteristic, one important issue is how it develops. Research and theory suggest two major sources of trait shyness (A. Buss, 1984). First, trait shyness may reflect a genetic predisposition towards inhibition and excessive anxiety. Several studies have found evidence for the genetic heritability of shyness (e.g. Plomin and Rowe, 1979). Alternatively, shyness may emerge as a trait because of problems in development, especially problems that revolve around the individual establishing a personal identity during adolescence (e.g. Asendorpf, 1989; A. Buss, 1984).

We will next consider theory and research surrounding the origins and development of trait shyness. This consideration will include both the theories of the origins of trait shyness, alongside various psychological theories (e.g. personality, biological factors and attribution style). You will also see how consideration of both these sets of theories leads to the introduction – and involves a further consideration of – two important theories of shyness: *behavioural inhibition and fearful* versus *self-conscious shyness*.

Shyness and personality

Zimbardo (1977) investigated shyness alongside the personality traits of extraversion and introversion. You will remember that extraversion comprises sociable, talkative, active, spontaneous, adventurous, enthusiastic, person-oriented, assertive traits, while introversion is at the opposite end of this personality dimension. (If you are still unsure, you need to look back at Chapter 7 of this book to remind yourself of these traits.) Zimbardo found that shyness and introversion are clearly distinguishable from each other. People generally consider introverts to be shy, or shy people to be introverts; however, this is not necessarily the case. Indeed, introverts do not fear social situations; they simply prefer their own company and solitary activities, whereas shy individuals would prefer to be with others but are restrained and reluctant to do so because of their shy nature. However, introverts may also be shy, according to many explanations, or theories, that we will look closely at in a moment.

Zimbardo reported another finding. Although we may generally consider extraverts not to be shy, some extraverts are, in fact, considered as such. Shy extraverts may be *privately* shy and *publicly* outgoing. Let us explain this further. Zimbardo and Henderson argue that extraverts may have the natural social skills to carry them through situations that are structured or familiar to them, where everyone knows their prescribed roles to play and there is little spontaneity (actions resulting from a natural impulse or tendency). However, the basic shyness of individuals may include anxieties about it being 'found out' that they are really personally inadequate, or about the fear that their 'real self' may be discovered. This may stop them from being intimate or make them withdraw from situations that are new or ambiguous to them. In other words, these people prefer to be in structured and familiar settings where they, the shy extravert, can play a role; however, they will falter when in one-to-one situations or in cases where their role is less certain (Henderson and Zimbardo, 1998).

Bernardo Carducci (1999) has also looked more closely at the relationship between shyness, introversion and extraversion and formulated some of these ideas further. Similarly to Zimbardo, he argues that introverts are often confused by others as being shy; they are not, as they possess the social skills and confidence to interact with others but simply choose not to. In contrast, shy individuals desire to be with others but lack the skills, thoughts, feelings and attitudes to allow good social interaction. Carducci goes on to argue that this desire to be with other people is classified as *sociability* (an extraversion personality trait) and states that, just because an individual is shy, it does not mean they are not sociable. It is here, according to Carducci, that the greatest pain for shy individuals exists – the conflict between the desire for social contact and their social inhibitions causes them the most difficulty. Your sociability may influence how much you want to be with others, but it does not affect how you handle that contact. Thus, individuals with the extraversion trait of sociability may just as easily be shy as having any other personality trait. In fact, Carducci (2000) has also found that shy people can use extraverted and social coping strategies. It is clear from this finding that, when it comes to considering trait shyness as the result of personality traits, shyness and the extraversion personality dimension are not related.

Shyness, genetics and behavioural inhibition

We have already introduced you to Jerome Kagan's ideas within the literature on social anxiety disorder; however, he is considered a useful contributor within the shyness literature as well. At Harvard University, Kagan began a wealth of literature looking at individual differences in temperament that appear at a very early age within babies. Kagan observed substantial variations in the emotional responses of children even as early as 1 month old; he called this temperament behavioural inhibition. Although not considered shyness as such, behavioural inhibition identifies children's reactions to all novel experiences. It can thus be used to identify those more inhibited children when they are confronted with experiences that elicit shyness. For example, behavioural inhibition occurs when children are observed with unfamiliar adults, when they are hesitant to make conversation and when they tend to hover at the edge of social gatherings – all these behaviours are indicators of shyness (Crozier, 2002).

Behavioural inhibition has been thought to originate from a child's reactions to a perceived threat and their consequential reactions of fear. Kagan (1994b) argues that this behaviour suggests a biological foundation to shyness, and it may be due to the action of the **amygdala** and the **hippocampus** within the brain. The amygdala is located in the brain's medial temporal lobe and is part of the limbic system of the brain. You may recall that the *limbic system* is a group of brain structures that are involved in various emotions, including pleasure, fear and aggression, as well as the formation of memories. Structures such as the hippocampus are involved in the formation of long-term memory, while the amygdala is involved in aggression and fear; thus, these are two basic biological reactions related to an individual's responses to threat. You may recognise this reaction more easily as the 'fight-or-flight' response.

The **fight-or-flight response** was first described by Walter Cannon, an American physiologist (Cannon, 1929). His theory (which has been widely used in a number of disciplines) stated that, when animals are faced by threats or danger, they have physiological reactions, including the 'firing' of neurons through the sensory cortex of the brain. These reactions are accompanied with increased levels of hormones and neurotransmitters such as epinephrine (adrenaline) and norepinephrine (noradrenaline) that are pumped throughout the body, causing immediate physical reactions, including an increase in heart rate, tensing of muscles and quicker breathing. These changes make the animal alert, attentive to the environment and aware of the danger; they comprise what is known as a stress response. The animal is then faced with two decisions. It can either face the threat ('fight') or it can avoid the threat ('flight').

The amygdala has been implicated in the association of specific stimuli with fear. Therefore, as Kagan argues, children with behavioural inhibition may in fact have overstimulated fear responses. There is some evidence for this suggestion. Davidson and Rickman (1999) found that shyness was related to heart-rate variability and to EEG activity in the frontal brain (EEG is the electroencephalogram, a measure of electrical activity produced by the brain).

Interestingly, there have been other biological findings within behavioural inhibitions, though they are less easily explained. For example, behavioural inhibition has been identified to be greater in children with blue eyes and fair hair and skin; it has also been found in children more susceptible to allergies like eczema and hay fever. Zimbardo and Henderson speculate that this may be related to levels of melatonin in the body. **Melatonin** is a hormone believed not only to lighten skin but also to play a role in the circadian rhythms of the body that regulate the body's functions (such as waking and sleeping) over the course of the day. As already noted earlier, Kagan (1994b) considers variations in the levels of norepinephrine and dopamine, neurotransmitters that play a key role in regulating sympathetic nervous system activity, that also explain behavioural inhibitions.

Perhaps more importantly, Kerr (2000) has identified that inhibition assessed at one age predicts inhibition and shyness at another, therefore indicating that behavioural inhibition may be a closely linked risk factor for the development of social anxiety such as shyness in adolescence. However, we must be cautious here. Inhibition in our childhood, although a predictor of shyness, does not necessarily lead to, or cause, shyness in adolescence. In fact, some children become less shy and others more so, suggesting that different social situations and experiences may also affect shyness (Crozier, 2002).

Henderson and Zimbardo (1998) argue that it is possible that behavioural inhibition may need to be aggravated by environmental triggers such as problematic parenting (such as the parents being inconsistent or unreliable), insecure attachments owing to difficult relationships with people when growing up (e.g. parents, family conflict, frequent criticism, a dominating older brother or sister) or a stressful school environment. In fact, these authors argue that, in studies where children have recalled their childhoods, parental factors such as criticism for not overcoming fears, having fewer parental friendships and having fewer family social activities have an impact on levels of shyness and social anxiety. Furthermore, Zimbardo and Henderson found that many children overcome shyness themselves, some through being altruistic (showing an unselfish concern for the welfare of others), some through an association with younger children that promotes leadership behaviours and some through contact with sociable peers. Finally, evidence shows that parents who are supportive of a child's temperament, but not overprotective, appear to help a child overcome their initial inhibition in new and challenging situations (Henderson and Zimbardo, 1998).

Fearful and self-conscious shyness

We have already mentioned that shyness in adults involves a preoccupation with being negatively evaluated by others, with the impression they feel they are making on others and with being embarrassed. However, Crozier (2002) argues

that, although young children can be obviously shy, such behaviour is unlikely to be because of self-presentation anxieties, as such anxieties require a certain level of cognitive, emotional and social awareness that is not developed by that age. Therefore, A. Buss (1986) suggests that there are in fact two distinct types of shyness: *fearful* shyness and *self-conscious* shyness. Fearful shyness appears early in life and may or may not influence future shyness behaviour (e.g. behavioural inhibition); self-conscious shyness emerges later within a person's development.

Buss argues that self-conscious shyness appears only when a child acquires a 'theory of mind'. A theory of mind is the ability of an individual to attribute mental states – beliefs, intentions, knowledge, etc. – to oneself and others and to understand that other people have beliefs, intentions, knowledge that are different from the individual. Therefore Buss argues that self-conscious shyness only occurs when individuals are able to reflect on their own behaviour from different people's perspectives. In other words, they learn to understand that other people have different beliefs, desires and intentions and that they can form theories and ideas about those beliefs, desires and intentions themselves. This process is thought to begin around the age of 5 years and onwards. However, it is important to note that fearful shyness is not superseded by self-conscious shyness; indeed, an individual can have one form of shyness without the other, or, in fact, may have both (Crozier, 2000).

Although Buss' concept of two types of shyness makes sense, research has a long way to go in this area. For instance, Crozier (2000) proposes that it is not yet known whether the distinction between fearful and self-conscious shyness means there are actually two different types of situations that bring forward shyness (for example, novel situations eliciting fearful shyness and evaluative situations eliciting self-conscious shyness). Alongside this, it is still not clear whether the emergence of self-conscious shyness suggests that there are children who become shy at this stage who were not previously considered as shy.

Self-conscious shyness and attribution style

Although not linked to Buss' two concepts of shyness, there are other theories that consider how self-conscious shyness may occur within adults. One such theory considers attribution style and shame-based concepts (Henderson and Zimbardo, 1998). Henderson and Zimbardo's research within student and clinical populations shows evidence to suggest that fearful and privately self-aware people tend to experience shame and blame themselves in social situations that have perceived negative outcomes. This tendency for shame and blame appears to be exacerbated by private self-awareness. Henderson and Zimbardo have found that shy individuals have been found to possess higher feelings of shame and blame in social situations with negative outcomes.

Henderson and Zimbardo argue that these findings point to the belief that shy people seem to act in an opposite way to something known as the self-enhancement bias. **Self-enhancement bias** is a social psychology term that refers to the process where individuals seek out and interpret situations to attain a positive view of themselves. Therefore, self-enhancers will tend to take credit for their successes, seeing the causes of the success as being internal (e.g. due to the person), stable (e.g. permanent and always there) and global (e.g. evident in every aspect of their life). On the other hand, they will tend to externalise the causes for their failures, seeing them as external (e.g. owing to unforeseen events or other people being to blame), unstable (e.g. only temporary, as things will get better) and specific (e.g. evident in only one aspect of their life). This attribution style can be seen to protect an individual's self-esteem and enable them to continue in their efforts towards interpersonal and professional goals.

Shy individuals have been found to reverse this bias in social situations by seeing failures as internal, stable and global (Henderson and Zimbardo, 1998). This attribution style fosters feelings of shame, a painful affective state that interferes with their cognitions and feelings about themselves as well as their behaviour, therefore contributing to their shyness.

Henderson and Zimbardo also suggest that the shy individual engages in **self-blaming** attributions. For instance, while self-blame among shy individuals is often confined to specific types of social situations, over a lifetime, self-blame can become a major factor for a shy person who is continually blaming themselves for all their failures. Consequently, these shy individuals may begin to experience loneliness, isolation and depression. In essence, frequent self-blaming owing to poor attribution styles can lead to negative biases about the self, which in turn enhance feelings of shyness (Henderson and Zimbardo, 1998).

Shyness and culture

Finally, there are interesting, but limited, findings for individual differences through looking at different cultures and shyness. Although the research is sparse, using adaptations of the Stanford Shyness Inventory (Zimbardo, 1977), researchers in eight different countries administered the inventory to groups of 18- to 21-year-olds. This research indicates that there may be a universality to shyness, with a large proportion of participants in all the cultures reported experiencing shyness to some degree (ranging from 31 per cent in Israel to 57 per cent in Japan). Henderson and Zimbardo (1998) report that, in Canada, Germany, India and Mexico, shyness was reported to be 40 per cent, a statistic similar to the results found for shyness for the United States.

Henderson and Zimbardo found that the cultural difference between Japanese and Israelis who reported having experienced shyness can be explained by how each culture attributes credit for success and blame for failure. In Japan, the credit for an individual's success is attributed externally (this might be to parents, grandparents, teachers, coaches and significant others), while failure is entirely blamed on the individual. As a result, shyness may develop by people overextending their own successes to other people and overblaming themselves for their failures; therefore, there may be reluctance to show initiative or take risks because they will get the blame if the initiative fails and no credit if the initiative succeeds. In Israel, however, the reverse is true. Failure is externally attributed to parents, teachers, coaches and friends, while success is credited to the individual. Consequently, in Israel, individuals are encouraged to show initiative or take risks and so to be less shy, because they receive credit for successes and are able to blame others for their failures (Henderson and Zimbardo, 1998).

Research also shows that the majority of the sample in each country perceived many more negative consequences than positive consequences of being shy. Around 60 per cent of people across different countries consider that shyness is a problem (except for Israel, where the figure is 42 per cent). There is no gender difference in reported shyness across the different cultures. However, Henderson and Zimbardo suggest that this may be because men have typically learned tactics and strategies for concealing their shyness, as it is often considered a more feminine trait in most countries.

Although these findings are intriguing, much more research is needed to appreciate the role of culture in shyness fully. It is also important to distinguish between cultural values that promote shyness as a desirable societal norm as opposed to personal values that make shyness an undesirable restriction on self-development.

Shyness and the Internet

There is one final area to consider when looking at shyness and its prevalence within society, and this includes social networking and Internet use. Although the research is relatively new in this area, there seems to be two contradictory ideas surrounding shyness and the Internet; first is the idea that the Internet attracts shy people but that it further debilitates, or enhances, shyness. The second idea, however, is that the Internet is empowering to shy individuals, allowing them the opportunity to experience social settings that they would not normally experience, and further allowing them to gain social competence and confidence (Saunders and Chester, 2008).

Carducci and Zimbardo (1995) suggested that the prevalence of shyness is on the increase, and that this increase is caused by a growing social isolation that many people experience today. There are many reasons for this isolation, such as moving far away from friends and loved ones due to work and there being a lack of community with our neighbours. However, Henderson and Zimbardo (1998) suggest that a main reason has been that more and more of our communications are occurring online and through mobile

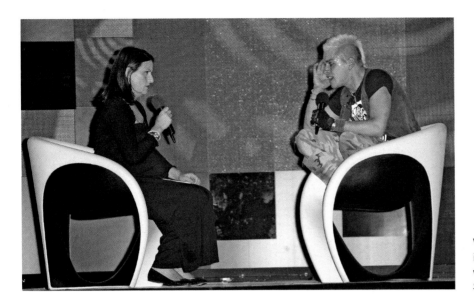

While some people revel in situations like this, many would be self-conscious.
Source: Rex Features/Stuart Atkins

telephones and texting (Henderson and Zimbardo, 1998). Indeed, how many of us prefer to text our friends rather than phone them and talk to them! According to Saunders and Chester (2008) and other authors such as Lee and Stapinski (2011), the main argument here is that the Internet has become a substitute for face-to-face connections and changed our interpersonal communications; therefore, we are losing the ability to interact socially with others and this has led to a shyness in face-to-face connections.

However, as mentioned earlier, there is also research that suggests that the Internet can influence shyness in a positive way. A theory called the social network theory (SNT), developed by Birnie and Horvath (2002), proposes that the Internet supplements and extends face-to-face social behaviours. In other words, it enhances communication by increasing ties between people. Other arguments suggest that the Internet can help to mask the physiological symptoms of shyness such as blushing, nervousness, etc., and that it therefore allows shy individuals to communicate with others and be more confident in their interactions (Stritzke *et al.*, 2004).

Embarrassment

US psychologist Roland S. Miller defines embarrassment as the self-conscious feeling individuals get after realising they have done something stupid, silly or dishonourable (Miller, 1995; 1996). Miller suggests that humans are social animals that are overly interested in what other people think of us. Miller argues that embarrassment surfaces when an individual feels they have done something that may lower themselves in terms of others' estimations, particularly when they wish to impress those individuals. You can be embarrassed by a whole host of people and situations; for example, by things you have done (e.g. got drunk when trying to impress someone, saying the 'wrong thing'), by people you know but wish you didn't (e.g. parents, friends), by things you don't know how to do (e.g. riding a bike, making an effective presentation), by personal or biological things (e.g. passing wind), or by money issues (e.g. lack of money). These are just a few examples, but we are sure the list is endless.

Profile

Philip Zimbardo

Philip Zimbardo is Professor of Psychology at Stanford University in California. He is chair of the Council of Scientific Society Presidents (CSSP), representing more than 60 science, mathematics and education societies.

Zimbardo is probably most known for his simulated prison experiment (he created a mock prison in a laboratory basement to study the psychology of imprisonment); however, curiously, it was from this study that Zimbardo became interested in the social and personal dynamics of shyness. Since 1972, he has been a leader in the research

into the causes, correlates and consequences of shyness in adults and children. Since then, Zimbardo has gone on to be a co-director, along with Lynne Henderson, at the Shyness Institute in California. Here, research has focused on treatment methods for shyness and social anxiety disorder/social phobia and the role of emotion in the phenomenon of shyness.

Visit the Shyness Institute at **www.shyness.com/ shyness-institute.html**.

Profile

Ray Crozier

Ray Crozier is Professor, and Reader, of Psychology at Cardiff University, Wales, and is a Fellow of the British Psychological Society. Crozier is probably best known for his research on shyness in childhood and adulthood, and on the nature and cause of blushing, although he also researches in the areas of artistic creativity and processes within decision-making. He has published many research articles on the topic of shyness, and he has written a number of books. In particular, his book *Understanding Shyness: Psychological Perspectives* is an essential read for all who are interested in this area.

Stop and think

Shyness

- Have you ever experienced shyness, or know someone who is really shy? How accurate are the main theories of shyness? Do you think children are born shy, or do they develop it later in life?

- How different do you think shyness is to social anxiety? Should they be distinct concepts, or do you think they are part of the same thing?

Embarrassment can range from minor blushing through to severe embarrassment, and we all experience it from time to time. However, as seen already within this discussion with shyness, embarrassment can become a debilitating problem that affects people in many different ways. Some people laugh off their embarrassment, whereas others may begin to avoid situations in which embarrassment can occur.

Until recently, embarrassment has generally been considered simply as a symptom of social anxiety or part of shyness. However, researchers have begun to treat embarrassment as an independent construct, with causes and consequences for the individual. Because of this relatively recent recognition, the research and theory are limited; however, it is worth looking more closely at what has been written so far in the literature.

Four theories of embarrassment

Generally, individual differences psychologists have generated four perspectives of why embarrassment occurs: the dramaturgic model, the social evaluation model, the situational self-esteem model and the personal standards model. However, Miller (1996) argues that there are two primary theoretical causes of embarrassment: the dramaturgic (or awkward interaction) and the social evaluation models (see Figure 20.4). Let us look at all these theories a little more closely.

The dramaturgic model

The **dramaturgic model** was proposed by psychologists Silver, Sabini and Parrott (1987), who suggest that

Figure 20.4 Four theories of embarrassment.

embarrassment is the flustered uncertainty that follows a poor public performance and leaves the individual at a loss about what to do or say next. In fact, it is the agitation and aversive arousal that triggers embarrassment after the realisation that the individual cannot calmly and gracefully continue that performance (Miller, 1996).

Therefore, according to Silver *et al.*, although embarrassed people are often worried about what others think of them, this concern for their public image only accompanies embarrassment and does not *cause* it. Instead, the flustering caused by the belief that the individual cannot perform is at the heart of embarrassment; in other words, it is because of the individual's inability to act a part.

Indeed, Miller (1996) argues that this model fits the feelings of embarrassment well, especially considering that most people feel awkward, stupid and immobilised when they experience embarrassment.

The social evaluation model

In contrast to Silver *et al.*'s model, the **social evaluation model** argues that it is the concern for what others are thinking of us that holds the key to embarrassment. Indeed, it is a failure to impress others that embarrassed individuals fear most (Edelmann, 1987).

In fact, supporters of this model acknowledge that embarrassing situations do leave individuals at a loss about what to do next, but these feelings are simply a *result* of embarrassment, not the cause. Instead, it is simply that individuals want to avoid evaluations from others indicating that the attempt to construct a desired image of himself or herself has failed.

According to Miller (1996), this model assumes that an individual must be concerned about others' opinions to feel embarrassed. Thus, if an individual does not care about how others see them, then that individual would not feel embarrassment. However, is this always the case? Although the social evaluation model is popular within psychology, many psychologists believe that there is more to embarrassment than just a preoccupation with the evaluation of others.

Situational self-esteem

According to the **situational self-esteem model** of embarrassment, negative self-evaluations (as outlined in the social evaluation model) simply set in motion the further events that actually cause embarrassment (Miller, 1996). Modigliani (1971), the creator of the Embarrassability Scale, believes that the root cause of embarrassment is a temporary loss of self-esteem that results from public failures. Therefore, negative self-evaluations do not cause embarrassment alone; instead, they are the trigger that allows individuals to judge *themselves* poorly.

This model suggests that it is our own opinions of ourselves and how we perform in faulty situations that are the cause of embarrassment. Presumably, it suggests that if individuals have a high opinion of themselves, which allows them to remain confident and sure when mistakes in performances occur, then these individuals should never feel embarrassed.

This assumption underlies the next and final model of embarrassment. But it goes further, to suggest that embarrassment stems from the negative arousal following violations of the individual's own personal standards (Miller, 1996).

The personal standards model

Babcock (1988) proposed, in the **personal standards model**, that embarrassment occurs when an individual realises they have failed in the standards of behaviour that they have set for themselves. However, you need to consider that it is not the situation that is embarrassing. In fact, regardless of how outrageously a person may behave in a social setting, if they are happy with the standards they set for themselves, then their behaviour should not be embarrassing for them. On the other hand, Rowland Miller proposes that this model could also suggest that these individuals may just as easily become embarrassed in their own company, when no one else is present, if they believe they have behaved in a less than satisfactory way according to their own standards.

Re-evaluation of the embarrassment models

So far we have considered four different models of embarrassment that suggest how and why embarrassment occurs. However, Miller (1996) evaluates these models further to propose that actually only two of them can be considered to possess primary causal possibilities of embarrassment. Miller suggests that, although the models propose different influences, there are overlaps within them. For example, many different situations can cause embarrassment that can result in the loss of what to say (dramaturgic model), that may also involve the fear of unwanted social evaluations (social evaluation model), that may affect your self-esteem (situational self-esteem model) and, finally, that may result in the painful realisation that you have let yourself down (personal standards model). Therefore, embarrassment may, in fact, contain all four models. However, is it possible that all four *cause* embarrassment, or is there one that is a more accurate model of embarrassment than the others?

Miller goes on to re-evaluate each model in turn, finally focusing upon two models that hold the most promise: the dramaturgic and social evaluation models. Let us outline Miller's process of development.

In re-evaluating the personal standards model, Rowland Miller observes that research (e.g. Parrott and Smith, 1991) findings suggest that individuals rarely experience embarrassment when they are alone. In addition, Miller (1992) has identified other problems with this model. For instance, a situation may occur when the individual has not let themselves down, via their own personal standards, but embarrassment still occurs owing to a poor audience reaction. Let us explain this further; a person may get embarrassed by unwarranted teasing, heckling or lack of attention, which has nothing to do with the person's own performance. Miller suggests that, although this model may be correct in considering the possibility that individuals dislike deviating from the guidelines they have set for themselves, there is a larger possibility that the guidelines they have set are linked to the impressions they will make on other people. Miller argues that the other three models of embarrassment already explain this aspect, and he suggests that these other models therefore do a better job of explaining embarrassment.

When considering the situational self-esteem model, Miller presents evidence that, although self-evaluations can play a role in creating embarrassment, self-esteem seems to play a more secondary role (Miller, 1995). In other words, individuals with low self-esteem do tend to become more embarrassed than do those with high self-esteem; however, susceptibility to embarrassment seems to depend more on the persistent concern of how others are thinking of us rather than how we think of ourselves. That is, people with high self-esteem may always want other people to hold them in the same high regard as they do themselves. Miller (1995) found that individuals who feel good about their performances (high self-esteem) actually become embarrassed if they learn that others have rated their performance poorly. Therefore, in essence, negative self-evaluations may intensify embarrassment, but they are not necessarily needed for embarrassment to occur.

Finally, Miller considers the dramaturgic and social evaluation models. After distinguishing that the personal standards and situational self-esteem models are less likely to be the root cause of embarrassment, Miller argues that the remaining two models are much more promising explanations of embarrassment. In fact, there is much research to suggest that awkward interactions, when an individual fails to perform well (dramaturgic), are a common explanation for embarrassment, and research by Miller suggests that individuals agree that they would feel embarrassed if such events occurred. However, Miller argues it is harder for a dramaturgic dilemma to cause embarrassment without simultaneously creating unwanted social evaluations (social evaluation model). Therefore, although there is much evidence to suggest that awkward interactions occur within embarrassment, it is the negative evaluation from others that seems to be of crucial importance.

To sum up, although there are four distinct theories to suggest that how embarrassment occurs, Miller suggests that the social evaluation model (followed by the dramaturgic model) seems to be more influential than the others. Nevertheless, it is important to remember that, because of individual differences in embarrassment, it is possible to experience embarrassment owing to all, or any, of the four models described.

Categorisation of embarrassing situations

From the models we have just examined, it seems acceptable to consider that different kinds of circumstances can produce, or cause, embarrassment. Therefore, in an attempt to clarify these causes, researchers such as Sabini *et al.*, (2000) have gone further by categorising types of embarrassing situations. These authors suggest that the two primary models (social evaluation and dramaturgic) can be

Some behaviours we do in private we would be embarrassed to do in public.
Source: Getty Images/Laurence Dutton

Profile

Rowland S. Miller

Rowland Miller is Professor of Psychology at Sam Houston State University in Huntsville, Alabama (USA). He received his degree in psychology from Cornell University in 1973 and his PhD from the University of Florida in 1978. He started to work at Sam Houston State University in 1978 and has been a visiting professor at Cornell University. He also possesses the Sam Houston State University excellence in research award.

Miller has been on the editorial board of the *Journal of Social and Clinical Psychology and Personal Relationships*. His research interests focus on social relationships, and he is perhaps best known for his groundbreaking research into embarrassment. That research is outlined in his book *Embarrassment: Poise and Peril in Everyday Life*. He has over 40 publications, including research articles, book chapters and books.

modified to include three kinds of embarrassment triggers: *faux pas*, sticky situations and being the centre of attention.

Faux pas

The *faux pas* type of embarrassment trigger emerges from the social evaluation model and is described as a situation in which an individual acts out a social failing. In other words, this type suggests that individuals become embarrassed because they create a social blunder (*faux pas*). Consequently, there is a concern for what others think of us because of the social blunder. As you can see, this trigger is easily understood within the social evaluation model explained earlier.

Sticky situations

On the other hand, sticky situations are considered to emerge from the dramaturgic model and include situations that challenge an individual's role. To explain further, these triggers would be present if an individual finds themselves in a 'sticky' social situation; for instance, where an individual must do or say something that may put another in a difficult or discreditable position. Sabini *et al.* suggest that asking someone to repay an overdue loan may be a useful example; this puts the other person in a discredited position and may trigger embarrassment in the individual asking for the repayment.

Interestingly, the sticky situations proposed here do not threaten the individual's self-esteem, or put them at the centre of attention or show some kind of social failing for which others may negatively evaluate them. However, because these situations actually involve a challenge to the role of the individual, these types of embarrassment are best placed within the dramaturgic model.

Centre of attention

The centre of attention type of embarrassment trigger is described by Sabini as 'an anomaly', as these situations

Stop and think

Empathetic or vicarious embarrassment

As we have seen, people usually get embarrassed through one of the four models mentioned above (the dramaturgic model, the social evaluation model, situational self-esteem or personal standards model). However, researchers such as Hawk *et al.* (2011), Krach *et al.* (2011) and Stocks *et al.* (2011) have argued that we also experience something called empathetic embarrassment or vicarious embarrassment.

Empathetic embarrassment or vicarious embarrassment is the tendency to get embarrassed on behalf of others. You may have experienced it yourself. When we are watching television programmes such as the *X Factor* or *The Apprentice* and people say silly or outrageous things, you may have felt embarrassed for them. Or, when we see a friend make a mis-

take or fall over in the street, you may have felt embarrassed or mortified for their potential humiliation.

Hawk *et al.* (2011) have argued that we feel this way because of **non-verbal mimicry** and/or **perspective-taking**. Non-verbal mimicry, according to researchers, occurs when we witness other people's emotional expressions and we then mimic these to produce and enhance empathy (Barsalou *et al.*, 2003; Dijksterhuis and Bargh, 2001). Perspective-taking, according to Hawk and colleagues, is a cognitive process where we imagine how we would feel in another person's situation. Therefore, the evidence suggests that we feel embarrassed for others because of mimicking the other person's emotional expressions and by imagining how we would feel in the same position.

cannot easily be explained by either of the two primary models. These types of triggers are best explained when the embarrassment is caused by the individual being the centre of attention although it is not because of some kind of failing. A good example here is the birthday party, or perhaps receiving praise in front of others.

Many previous researchers have not considered this type of trigger particularly important, mainly because the person is not seen as suffering because of these triggers. Nevertheless, many individuals feel at their most embarrassed when in these specific situations.

Embarrassment, measurement and personality

Most of the research carried out on embarrassment, and the theories mentioned, concentrate on situational embarrassment; in other words, considering how embarrassment occurs in a given specific situation. Situational embarrassment is measured using the Embarrassibility Scale compiled by Modigliani (1968). However, there are some drawbacks in using this measure. First, the scale mainly concentrates on measuring how embarrassed an individual may become in given situations and, although the scale can provide individual differences theorists with some insight into dispositional properties of embarrassment, the scale does not go far enough. In other words, it is unclear what dispositions (general temperament) an individual may possess that renders that individual susceptible to embarrassment. Secondly, according to Kelly and Jones (1997), asking respondents to rate how embarrassed they may feel within a situation has socially undesirable drawbacks. In essence, society considers embarrassment to be a negative emotion to be avoided at all costs; respondents who are asked to rate their degree of embarrassment may thus actually be less than truthful, as they would prefer to be looked at as socially desirable.

Therefore, Kelly and Jones (1997) created a new scale to address these drawbacks and to specifically measure whether an individual is actually prone to the trait of embarrassment; this scale is known as the Susceptibility

to Embarrassment Scale. The scale comprises 25 items, which are rated on a 7-point response format from 'not at all like me' through to 'very much like me'. Items focus on the characteristics of individuals who are easily embarrassed, measuring traits such as worrying about what others think of them as well as asking them to what extent they feel emotionally exposed and vulnerable. Examples of items include 'I feel clumsy in social situations', 'Sometimes I just feel exposed', 'I am concerned about what others think of me' and 'I feel mortified and humiliated over a minor embarrassment'.

Insofar as personality and embarrassment are concerned, researchers have identified that neuroticism (for example, worrying, anxious, nervous personality traits) is associated with being prone to embarrassment more than any other personality type. Kelly and Jones have looked at scores on the Susceptibility to Embarrassment Scale alongside a measure of the five-factor model of personality, and they have identified that the strongest relationships with embarrassment are two of the subscales of neuroticism: depression and self-consciousness. Researchers have also found that vulnerability and anxiety are related to embarrassment. Kelly and Jones have reported that embarrassment is *negatively* related to extraversion, particularly the subscales of assertiveness and positive emotions. In summary, then, individuals who are prone to embarrassment are *more likely* to be anxious, self-conscious and have feelings of vulnerability and depression; these individuals are also *less likely* to be assertive and have positive emotions.

Final comments

In this discussion we have considered the concepts of social anxiety and social anxiety disorder and used these as contexts to consider individual research into shyness and embarrassment. While research into shyness seems to be able to explain how and why these individual differences occur between people, there needs to be much more research to understand why individuals suffer embarrassment. You should now be able to outline the main theories, models and correlates of social anxiety disorder, shyness and embarrassment.

Stop and think

Embarrassment

- Do you think embarrassment may be a combination of all four models, or can embarrassment fit into one of the models? If so, which one?

- How well do the categorisations, or triggers, of embarrassment work? Are they sufficient to explain why someone may get embarrassed?

Summary

- The symptoms of social anxiety disorder generally fall within three specific categories: the cognitive or mental symptoms (what you think), the physical reactions (how your body feels) and the behavioural avoidance (what you do).
- The possible causes of social anxiety disorder are considered from the point of view of genetic and behavioural influences, developmental theory and chemical imbalances in the brain.
- Social anxiety disorder is believed to develop in three common ways: (1) generalised social anxiety disorder (e.g. an individual fears a wide range of different social situations); (2) non-generalised (performance) social anxiety disorder (e.g. an anxiety response to from one to three identified situations – affects individuals only when they are performing in front of others); and (3) avoidant personality disorder (e.g. the most severe form of social anxiety, which shows a detached personality pattern, meaning that the person purposefully avoids people due to fears of humiliation and rejection).
- Shyness reactions occur at any, or all, of the following levels: cognitive (e.g. fear of negative evaluation and looking foolish to others), affective (e.g. embarrassment and self-consciousness), physiological (e.g. blushing) and behavioural (e.g. failure to respond appropriately to the situation).
- Shyness is also categorised into two different forms: state (situational) shyness and trait (dispositional) shyness.
- Shyness is best understood as the experience of discomfort and/or inhibition in interpersonal situations and is considered to be a form of excessive self-focus, a preoccupation with one's own thoughts, feelings and physical reactions.
- There are considered to be four main causal models of embarrassment: the dramaturgic model (embarrassment is caused by the flustering caused by the belief that the individual cannot perform – that is, it is due to the individual's inability to act a part); the social evaluation model (embarrassment is due to the concern for what others are thinking of us); situational self-esteem model (embarrassment is caused by the temporary loss of self-esteem that results from public failure) and the personal standards model (embarrassment occurs when an individual realises that they have failed in the standards of behaviour that they have set for themselves).
- Embarrassment has also been categorised into three types of situation triggers: *faux pas* (the creation of a social blunder), sticky situations (situations that challenge an individual's role; i.e. where an individual must do or say something that may put another in a difficult, or discreditable, position) and being the centre of attention (the embarrassment is caused by the individual being the centre of attention when it is not because of some kind of failing).

Connecting up

If you want to read more on behavioural inhibition, we cover this topic within several biological theories of personality in Chapter 8.

Critical thinking

Discussion questions

- We have considered several theories necessary for you to understand social anxiety disorder, shyness and embarrassment and have presented some considerations so you may appreciate the value of these different theories. However, there are some discussion points. We present them here in the form of discussion topics to allow you to think about these issues on your own, or within groups; your university seminars would also be a great place to discuss them. They are not for you to worry about; we present

them only as a way for you to get an even deeper understanding of the complexities of this topic.
- This exercise is to get you generating some ideas about the topic. Let us consider some of the theoretical and empirical findings covered here within an individual differences perspective (as outlined in Chapter 17).
  - Name five or six important theories and/or findings that emerge from this topic area.
  - If you were to present an overview of these five or six chosen theories and findings, what different areas of psychology would you be emphasising? For example,

are they biological, physiological, personality, cognitive, social or clinical factors?

  – Of these five or six chosen theories and findings, to which do you lend most weight?

  – Are there any theoretical or empirical overlaps between the theories and findings? If so, where do they occur?

- Although this discussion has addressed many definitions of shyness and embarrassment, there are still problems in distinguishing one from the other. One way of distinguishing between them is presented by Rowland Miller (1996; 2001), who suggests that shyness can be considered as *anticipatory* (i.e. it is caused by a fear of encounters before judgements by others have even occurred), whereas embarrassment can be considered as *reactive* (i.e. that it pertains to the realisation that one has transgressed a social norm). Miller further argues that *embarrassment* can be socially helpful in repairing a *faux pas* and helping to restore order after an embarrassing encounter. However, he argues that *shyness* can only be detrimental as it prevents the individual from engaging in certain situations and denies possible opportunities with other people. Do you think there are other ways of distinguishing between shyness and embarrassment? What is the best way of distinguishing between shyness and embarrassment?

- Although some distinctions are useful in shyness and embarrassment, there are also problems in the ability to distinguish one from the other. This perhaps leads to the question, should the psychology of shyness and the psychology of embarrassment be separate psychologies or be integrated? What do you think is the best way of integrating or distinguishing shyness and embarrassment as psychological constructs?

- Crozier (2002) argues that there are many issues about the nature of shyness still to be resolved and suggests that longitudinal studies may be needed to document changes in shyness across childhood and adulthood. What areas do you think might be considered?

- So far, researchers do not know how the two forms of shyness (fearful and self-conscious shyness) relate to each other, or how inhibited children negotiate the self-presentation challenges they increasingly face as they grow older. How might we help children negotiate the self-presentation challenges?

- Theories of shyness and embarrassment raise fundamental questions about the self, social relationships and social interaction processes. Research continues to draw productively from a range of perspectives from personality theory and psychophysiology as well as social, clinical and developmental psychology. Discuss whether there are too many theories of shyness and embarrassment.

Essay questions

- Evaluate Kagan's theory of behavioural inhibition and its relevance to social anxiety and shyness for individual differences.

- Define the main concepts within the theory of shyness and evaluate their relevance to individual differences.

- Psychologists have argued that a person is born with social anxiety. Discuss.

- Compare and contrast the main theories of social anxiety and shyness in relation to individual differences.

- What are the main concepts within embarrassment? Evaluate the uniqueness of the theory in relation to shyness.

Going further

Books

The following books give really good explanations of some of the theories within social anxiety, embarrassment and shyness.

- Crozier, W. R. (2001). *Understanding shyness: Psychological perspectives*. London: Palgrave.
- McNeil, D. W., Lejeuz, C. W. and Sorrell, J. T. (2001). Behavioural theories of social phobia: Contributions of basic behavioural principles. In S. G. Hoffmann and P. M. DiBartolo (eds.), *Social phobia and social anxiety: An integration* (pp. 235–253). Needham Heights, MA: Allyn & Bacon.
- Miller, R. S. (1996). *Embarrassment: Poise and peril in everyday life*. New York: Guilford.

- Markway, B. G., Carmin, C., Pollard, C. A. and Flynn, T. (1992). *Dying of embarrassment: Help for social anxiety and phobia*. New York: New Harbinger Publications.
- Markway, B. G. and Markway, G. P. (2003). *Painfully shy: How to overcome social anxiety and reclaim your life*. New York: Thomas Dunne Books.

Please note that both the Markway books are clinically/counselling focused, so much of the evidence and examples presented may not be suitable for inclusion in your academic work. None the less, they do present a good structured overview of what it means to people to suffer from various forms of social anxiety.

Journals

An article on everyday ideas that surround shyness is Beer, J. S. (2002). Implicit self-theories of shyness. *Journal of Personality and Social Psychology, 83*(4), 1009–1024. Published by the American Psychological Association. Available online via PsycARTICLES.

The following journals are available online as well as accessible through your university library. These journals are full of published articles on research into social anxieties. You may also wish to search the following journals on an online library database (Web of Science; PsycINFO) with the search terms 'embarrassment', 'anxiety' and 'shyness'.

- **Journal of Social and Personal Relationships.** Published by Sage. Available via EBSCO Electronic Journals Service and SwetsWise.

- **Personality and Individual Differences.** Published by Elsevier Science. Available online via Science Direct.
- **Journal of Personality and Social Psychology.** Published by the American Psychological Association. Available online via PsycARTICLES.
- **Behaviour Research and Therapy.** Published by Elsevier Science. Available online via Science Direct.
- **Anxiety, Stress & Coping.** Deals with the assessment, experimental and field studies of anxiety, stress and coping. Published by Taylor & Francis. Available online via the Taylor and Francis website.

Web links

- Visit the Shyness Institute (**www.shyness.com**). This useful site contains all the recent research being done on shyness by Henderson and Zimbardo as well as some good information about shyness.

Film and literature

- *The King's Speech* (2010, directed by Tom Hooper). This is a film about King George VI's life and overcoming a stuttering condition which becomes most apparent when he has to make speeches in public.
- *Little Voice* (1998, directed by Mark Herman). We have discussed how people's shyness could cause isolation and loneliness. In this film, a shy girl known as Little Voice (LV) becomes a virtual recluse, never leaving the house and spending most of her time in her bedroom listening to music. The film shows how LV tries to battle and conquer her shyness.

- *Jane Eyre* (1847, novel by Charlotte Brontë). In this story Jane Eyre, an abused orphan, becomes a governess of a daughter in a Yorkshire mansion. Jane Eyre is shy and timid, but she has an inner strength that does not allow her to turn away from her moral beliefs. This is a classic piece of literature that shows you how shyness can be debilitating and how people can struggle to overcome it. But it also shows how shyness can mask a strength of character. You can read this story online (**www .literature.org/authors/bronte-charlotte/jane-eyre**). It has been made into a film a number of times; the most recent is *Jane Eyre* (2011; directed by Cary Fukunaga).

Explore the website accompanying this text at **www.pearsoned.co.uk/maltby** for further resources to help you with your studies. These include multiple-choice questions, essay questions, web links and ideas for advanced reading.

CHAPTER 21
Interpersonal Relationships

Key themes

- Interpersonal attraction
- Fatal attraction
- Love styles
- Adult attachments and interpersonal processes
- Relationship dissolution/break-up
- Dimensions of forgiveness

Learning outcomes

At the end of this discussion you should:

- Be familiar with the main theories and models of interpersonal attraction
- Be familiar with the main theories of love styles and be able to distinguish between Sternberg's and Lee's models of love
- Understand the role of attachment within relationships
- Be familiar with the main concepts behind relationship dissolution
- Be able to identify and distinguish between the two main models of forgiveness
- Understand the role of personality within forgiveness

Introduction

If you want to know where to go to get a single man in the United Kingdom, according to BBC News Online (14 February 2006), then the place to go is the Outer Hebrides, a small island just off the west coast of Scotland that has the highest ratio of single men to women. And before all you single ladies and single gay men head up to the Outer Hebrides in search of all these single men – and before all the rest of you single men go up there because you know that is where all the single ladies are going – let us introduce you to the individual differences of personal relationships.

It is unlikely that any other feeling can make you so deeply happy, and yet so full of despair, as the feeling of love. However, inevitably, while we search for love, there are just as many instances where our romantic relationships break down, leaving us with feelings just as intense and life-changing as when we were in love. Nearly everyone has been rejected by someone at some time in their life, and it hurts like hell.

The main aim of this discussion is to introduce you to many of the different theories of attraction, love styles and relationship break-up. A consideration of attachment and relationships will also be made, as well as how personality may have an impact on our relationship choices. In the second part we will concentrate on a related variable, forgiveness, and you will see how theory and evidence suggests that forgiving someone who has hurt you may be important to your mental health.

Source: The Kobal Collection/Film 4/Celador Films/Pathe International

Interpersonal attraction

As Hartz (1996) outlines, attractiveness theory and research has not only focused on describing characteristics that people find attractive in one another but also on understanding our responses to these characteristics. Hartz has emphasised that the general literature on interpersonal attraction concentrates on several characteristics – beauty, personality, wisdom, kindness, success, confidence, honesty and humour – that are all thought of as all crucial elements in attractiveness.

Individual differences psychologists are interested in why we are attracted to some people and not others. Individual differences in interpersonal attraction focus on a range of factors, from personality and cognitive variables to social psychological factors. Consideration of all these different psychological perspectives can help individual differences psychologists gain a wider understanding of the individual differences within interpersonal attraction. In the next section we are going to introduce you to five main theories – or, as they are termed, hypotheses – of interpersonal attraction.

Theories of interpersonal attraction

There are many different ideas surrounding the question of why people are attracted to some people and not to others. Krueger and Caspi (1993) attempted to summarise all these ideas, and they produced five distinct hypotheses relating to interpersonal attraction: the similarity hypothesis, ideal partner hypothesis, repulsion hypothesis, optimal dissimilarity hypothesis and optimal outbreeding hypothesis (see Figure 21.1). We will now outline each of these hypotheses in turn.

The similarity hypothesis

As Krueger and Caspi (1993) explain, this hypothesis suggests that we are more likely to be attracted to people who are similar to ourselves in both personality and attitude. The reason for this may be that we can better understand people who are more like us, as opposed to those who are dissimilar. People who are similar to us allow us to verify our own attitudes and behaviours, and there is greater opportunity for reciprocal rewards; in short, we like those people who like us back (Byrne, 1971). In addition to similarities in attitudes and personality, Rushton (1989) has suggested that we may be attracted to people who are 'genetically' similar to us, and that people might unconsciously detect signs of being genetically similar to certain people and so give these people preferential treatment.

The ideal partner hypothesis

Krueger and Caspi argue that this theory suggests we are more likely to be attracted to certain people who we believe possess certain specific traits or qualities that we think are ideal, such as stable emotions, sociability or intelligence (Buss and Barnes, 1986). It is argued that we all have an idea of what our 'ideal partner' should be like; and, generally, we tend to compare prospective partners to that ideal. The closer to the ideal that person is, the more attracted we are

to them. Kenrick and Keefe (1992) have found evidence to suggest that men are generally attracted to younger women as their ideal, while women are more attracted to older men as their ideal.

The repulsion hypothesis

The repulsion theory suggests that people are repulsed by people who are dissimilar to them. In other words, it is not that attitude similarity leads to attraction (similarity hypothesis), but rather that dissimilar attitudes lead to repulsion (repulsion hypothesis). The repulsion hypothesis is not simply the similarity hypothesis in reverse, which suggests that we choose people who are similar to us and feel nothing for other people. The repulsion hypothesis emphasises the point that we also actively avoid or dislike people with very different attitudes to our own. As Rosenbaum (1986) suggests, we first eliminate those people who are dissimilar to ourselves as potential partners, and then we begin to choose potential partners from those who are left.

The optimal dissimilarity hypothesis

According to Krueger and Caspi (1993), the optimal dissimilarity hypothesis suggests that individuals find people who are *slightly* different to themselves the most attractive. So, in other words, we are attracted by the novelty in someone slightly different, provided they are not too dissimilar for us to understand (Berlyne, 1967).

The optimal outbreeding hypothesis

Finally, Krueger and Caspi explain that the optimal outbreeding hypothesis expands on the optimal dissimilarity

Figure 21.1 The five hypotheses of interpersonal attraction.

hypothesis, and is based on findings that some animals show preference to breed with those that are somewhat, but not entirely different, to themselves (Bateson, 1982). Here the similarity variable has to do with genetic qualities rather than personality or attitude, qualities that are emphasised in the optimal dissimilarity hypothesis.

In an attempt to investigate the evidence for each of these five hypotheses, Krueger and Caspi (1993) showed a group of women computer-generated profiles of men who had personality traits similar to, and different from, their own. These women were then asked to describe what their emotional state might be like if they were on a date with these men, in order to investigate which of the hypotheses could be used to best explain their responses. Krueger and Caspi found a certain amount of support for some of these theories, but not all.

Overall, Krueger and Caspi reported the results as indicating that the women considered those men with similar personalities to themselves as most pleasurable and arousing (similarity hypothesis) and those who were dissimilar to themselves as unpleasant and unarousing (repulsion hypothesis). However, the results also showed that the women were also driven to seek males with the specific personality characteristics of sociability (extraversion), high activity levels and low levels of emotionality (neuroticism). In other words, it seems that the pursuit of partners who are similar is not sufficient alone; rather, the women moderated the importance of similar personality traits to consider also the extent to which the men possessed their ideal partner traits. So, the male personality best suited to a woman appears to be one that is an optimum trade-off between similarity to the woman's own personality traits and possession of their ideal characteristics for a partner. In summary, the results showed that similarity, difference (repulsion) and ideal personality traits are all important considerations by women when determining the attractiveness of a potential partner. Krueger and Caspi found no evidence for either the optimal dissimilarity or the optimal outbreeding hypotheses.

This research is interesting and shows support for some of the theories of attraction, as well as allowing us to gain insight into the individual differences of attraction. However, it is also important to remember that this research was carried out only on women. Research is still needed to investigate whether males show these processes when considering potential partners.

Fatal attraction

Interestingly, although we have considered the most popular theories on why individuals are attracted to some people and not others, Diane Felmlee (1995) has suggested that those characteristics we view as most important when choosing a partner may often be the very same characteristics that lead to the break-up of that relationship. Felmlee referred to this process as **fatal attraction** and suggests that individuals are initially attracted to a person because of a particular personality trait; however, at the end of the relationship, they report finding that trait annoying. Felmlee has found that there are many, and different, fatal attractions. She has identified five common themes in individual reports of these types of fatal attractions.

A first fatal attraction she identifies is 'nice to passive'. This fatal attraction, one of the most often reported by people, refers to individuals who have been attracted to their partner because they are nice, only to find at the end of the relationship that their 'niceness' is really annoying. For example, you may be attracted to someone because they are nice and considerate. However, you soon realise that, because they are being so nice, you can never really know what they are feeling as they never want to upset you. This then leads to you feeling frustrated with the person, that they are being 'too nice', and this eventually leads to you distancing yourself from them.

A second fatal attraction Felmlee identifies is 'strong to stubborn'. Felmlee describes individuals who have initially been attracted to the headstrong and independent nature of their partner. However, headstrong and independent people may be difficult to live with, because they are opinionated and do not share their worries or problems. At the end of the relationship, the 'strong' person is seen as stubborn and not actually revealing what has been happening in their life.

The third most common fatal attraction identified by Felmlee is that of 'funny to flaky', and it refers to individuals who have initially been attracted to someone who has a great sense of humour or the ability to have lots of fun. However, people going out with this sort of individual

Stop and think

Attraction

- How accurate are the five hypotheses of attraction, when considering individual differences? You might want to consider times when you have been attracted to someone; can you fit yourself into any of these categories?

- Have you ever experienced 'fatal attraction'? Do you think that these shifts in interpretation are sufficient to explain the break-up of a relationship?

found that these qualities annoyed them by the end of the relationship. After some time, the 'funny' person appeared immature, unable to take life seriously or, indeed, not always able take other people's feelings (including the partner's) seriously enough.

The fourth most common fatal attraction, 'outgoing to over the top', describes individuals who have found extraversion, being friendly and outgoing, as the most attractive quality in their partner. However, people who initially found themselves attracted to 'outgoing' individuals later complained that they talk too much, or they never relax.

Finally, Felmlee identifies the fifth most common fatal attraction reported by people as that of 'caring to clinging'. For example, women may find the quality of caring and sensitiveness in a man to be most attractive. However, as Felmlee found, individuals reported that by the end of the relationship this attraction was considered a major weakness, as during the relationship the caring person could become controlling and jealous, wanting to be in the person's company all the time and hating it when the person chose to be with their friends over them.

Felmlee suggests that fatal attraction might be caused by *too* many differences in partners (instead of similarities) and that those differences, although exciting and intriguing at first, soon begin to annoy and disturb the relationship. Felmlee suggests that her fatal attraction analysis demonstrates the shifting of meaning in particular personality attributes given to a partner during the relationship (i.e. from caring to clingy). In other words, this theory seems to suggest that, by the end of a relationship, we change our interpretation of our partner's qualities, rather than the partner experiencing a change in their personality.

Love styles

Another interesting area of research within interpersonal relationships is to understand what it is to be 'in love' for individuals. Although the concept of love is known and aspired to by all of us, there is still no agreed-upon definition of what it actually means – and, indeed, no consensus on whether we all experience love in the same way (Ireland, 1988).

Once again, various theories have attempted to conceptualise love, and many psychologists suggest that love is a multidimensional concept. For instance, Walster and Walster (1978) suggest that there are two kinds of love: *passionate love*, reflecting a short and intense relationship that is often accompanied by physiological arousal such as rapid heart rate and shortness of breath, and *compassionate love*, reflecting a close and enduring relationship that hinges on affection and feelings of intimacy outside physiological arousal. In contrast, Clark and Mills (1979) differentiate between **exchange relationships** (relationships based on costs and benefits) and **communal relationships** (relationships based on altruistic motives). In other words, exchange relationships involve the calculating of costs and benefits within the relationship (a cost might be having to spend a lot of your time with someone; a benefit might be doing the things you enjoy with someone); in contrast, communal relationships involve more self-sacrifices – you do not do something for your partner because you will get a reward (exchange), but rather because you choose to do so.

There are many more theories of love; however, two of the more common and comprehensive theories are the triangular theory of love developed by Robert Sternberg (Sternberg, 1986a; 1998) and the love styles theory developed by John Lee (Lee, 1973; 1988). We will look at these two theories in more detail.

The triangular theory of love

Sternberg (1986a; 1998) sees love as consisting of three basic components that sit, hypothetically speaking, at the three points on a triangle; these components are **intimacy, passion** and **commitment** (see Figure 21.2). The intimacy component deals with the emotions involved in a relationship and involves feelings of warmth, closeness, connection and the development of a strong bond, as well as the concern for each other's happiness and well-being. The passion component is concerned with romance and sexual attraction. Finally, the commitment component deals largely with our cognitive functioning (for example, thinking) and represents aspects of love involving both the short-term decision that one individual loves another and the longer term commitment to maintain that love (see also Regan, 2003).

Because these three basic components of love are positioned at the points of a triangle, each of the elements can be present within a relationship, and they can combine to produce seven relationship, or love, styles. These are outlined in Table 21.1.

Sternberg (1986a) describes these seven love styles as follows:

- **Liking/friendship** includes only one of the love components – intimacy. Liking refers to relationships that are essentially friendship. Intimate liking is characterised by intimacy, closeness, warmth and other positive emotional experiences but does not involve passion or commitment.
- **Infatuation** consists of passion alone and is described as the feeling of 'love at first sight'. However, without the intimacy and commitment components of love, infatuation is thought to disappear quickly.
- **Empty love** in which commitment is the only love component. This type of love is described as that seen at the end of many long-term relationships, where the two individuals are committed to each other and the

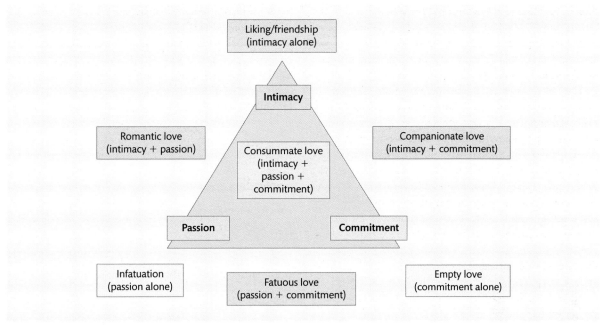

Figure 21.2 Sternberg's triangular theory of love.
Source: From Sternberg, R. J. (1998). Triangulating love. In R. J. Sternberg and M. L. Barnes (eds), *The psychology of love* (pp. 119–138), New Haven, CT: Yale University Press. Reproduced with permission.

relationship but have lost the intimate emotional connection and the passionate attraction.

- **Romantic love** is a combination of intimacy and passion and consists of partners who are bonded both emotionally, as in liking, and physically through passionate arousal and attraction.

- **Companionate love** consists of intimacy and commitment and is thought to typify the type of love found in marriages in which the passion has gone out of the relationship, but a deep intimacy and commitment remain (Sternberg, 1986a).

- **Fatuous love** comprises passion and commitment. This is where individuals' commitment to each other is based on passion rather than on deep emotional intimacy. In fact, these relationships are often called 'whirlwind' romances where the commitment is motivated by passion and lacks the stability of intimacy.

- **Consummate love**, according to Sternberg, is the only love style that includes all three components of intimacy, passion and commitment. This is the most complete love and represents the type of love that most of us are striving for; however, according to Sternberg, maintaining consummate love may be harder than actually achieving it.

As Sternberg (1986a) and Regan (2003) note, the triangular theory of love can be used to explain many individual differences that are seen in relationships. However, from the viewpoint of individual differences psychologists, not all individuals will fit neatly into one of these categories. These love styles can occur in varying degrees within a relationship, and they can change over time. Realistically, most people's relationships will reflect some combination of all these styles at some point during the relationship.

Table 21.1 Three basic components of Sternberg's love triangle combine to form seven different relationship, or love, styles

	Combinations of intimacy, passion and commitment		
Liking/friendship	Intimacy		
Infatuation		Passion	
Empty love			Commitment
Romantic love	Intimacy	Passion	
Companionate love	Intimacy		Commitment
Fatuous love		Passion	Commitment
Consummate love	Intimacy	Passion	Commitment

Love styles (or the colours of love)

The second major theory of love that we will look at was conceptualised by John Lee (1976) and has since enabled a widely used measure called the Love Attitude Scale (developed by Hendrick and Hendrick, 1986).

Within this theory, each style of love is likened to the way primary or secondary colours work; that is, there are three primary colours that mix together to form three secondary colours. In a similar way, Lee identified primary and secondary love styles, in which the secondary love styles are made up of a combination of two primary love styles (see Figure 21.3). Let us look at each of these love styles in turn (although note that Lee does not identify any love style with a particular colour).

Primary love styles

According to Lee (1976), there are three primary colours or styles of love. The first is called **eros** and describes passionate love. Eros lovers experience immediate and powerful attraction and are aroused by a particular physical type. They are prone to fall instantly and completely in love with a stranger (i.e. 'love at first sight'), and there is always a strong sexual component. Lee emphasises that the erotic lover is 'eager to get to know the beloved quickly, intensely – and undressed' (Lee, 1988, p. 50).

The second primary colour of love is **ludus** (or game-playing) love. Here, the 'ludic' lover enjoys love and sexual relationships, but they see them only as fun or diversion. They move from partner to partner and are more than happy to have several partners simultaneously. They view sexual activity as an opportunity for pleasure rather than for emotional bonding. According to Lee, the ludic lover is most easily recognised as the commitment-phobe, as they are not looking for commitment in their relationships,

avoid seeing the partner too often and believe that lies and deception are justified in a relationship.

Storge, the third primary love colour/style, is based on a solid foundation of friendship, trust and respect. According to Lee, the 'storgic' lover tends to see their partner as an 'old friend' and sees the relationship in terms of long-term commitment with little emphasis on passion, lust or sex. For this type of lover, love is an extension of friendship and is an important part of life but is not an essential goal in itself.

Secondary love styles

Like the primary colours of red, blue and yellow, the primary love styles can be mixed together to form secondary colours or love styles. Lee named the three secondary love styles pragma, mania and agape. These styles contain features of the primary love styles but comprise their own unique characteristics.

Lee describes pragma as a combination of storge and ludus; it is exemplified by a person with a practical and pragmatic outlook on love, seeking a compatible lover. According to Lee, the pragmatic lover produces a shopping list of attributes that they want or desire in a partner and selects a potential partner based on how well that individual fulfils the requirements. The person will end a relationship when the partner fails to 'measure up' to their expectations. Interestingly, this love style is reminiscent of the 'ideal partner' hypothesis mentioned earlier.

Lee considered the 'mania' love style as a combination of eros and ludus, but the person tends to lack the self-confidence associated with the passion of eros and the emotional self-control associated with ludus. This love style reflects the obsessive and jealous type of individual; the person with this love style has emotions that are

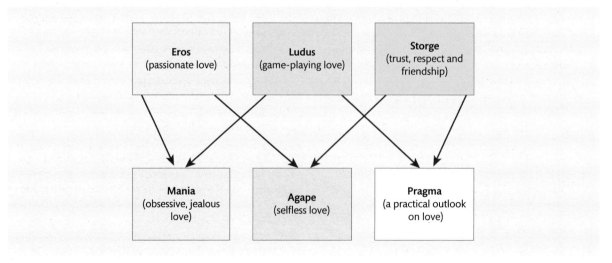

Figure 21.3 Lee's styles (colours) of love.

Stop and think

What's your love style?

Lee's love styles have been measured via numerous different scales; however, the most well known is that of the Love Attitude Scale (LAS) created by Hendrick and Hendrick (1986). This scale comprises 42 items and measures attitudes towards love on six different dimensions: passionate (eros), game-playing (ludus), friendship (storge), practical (pragma), dependent (mania) and selfless (agape). A shorter version, made up of 24 items, was made available by Hendrick, Hendrick and Dicke (1998). This short form contains the same six subscales – eros, storge, mania, pragma, ludus and agape – and each subscale has four items. We have presented the short form here so that you can identify your own love style.

Instructions

Answer the following items as honestly as possible, and try to answer the questions with your current partner in mind. If you are not currently dating anyone, answer the questions with your most recent partner in mind. If you have not been in love, answer in terms of what you think your responses would most likely be. For each statement, you should give a number indicating how much you agree or disagree with it in the following way:

> 1 = strongly disagree with the statement; 2 = moderately disagree with the statement; 3 = neutral – neither agree nor disagree with the statement; 4 = moderately agree with the statement; 5 = strongly agree with the statement.

Items

Eros

1 My partner and I were attracted to each other immediately after we first met.
2 My partner and I have the right physical 'chemistry' between us.
3 Our lovemaking is very intense and satisfying.
4 I feel that my partner and I were meant for each other.

Ludus

5 I try to keep my partner a little uncertain about my commitment to him/her.
6 I believe that what my partner doesn't know won't hurt him/her.
7 I have sometimes had to keep my partner from finding out about other partners.
8 I could get over my affair with my partner pretty easily and quickly.

Storge

9 It is hard for me to say exactly when our friendship turned into love.
10 To be genuine, our love first required caring for a while.
11 I expect to always be friends with my partner.
12 Our love is the best kind because it grew out of a long friendship.

Pragma

13 I considered what my partner was going to become in life before I committed myself to him/her.
14 I tried to plan my life carefully before choosing a partner.
15 In choosing my partner, I believed it was best to love someone with a similar background.
16 A main consideration in choosing my partner was how s/he would reflect on my family.

Mania

17 When things aren't right with my partner and me, my stomach gets upset.
18 If my partner and I break up, I would get so depressed that I would even think of suicide.
19 Sometimes I get so excited about being in love with my partner that I can't sleep.
20 When my partner doesn't pay attention to me, I feel sick all over.

Agape

21 I try to always help my partner through difficult times.
22 I would rather suffer myself than let my partner suffer.
23 I cannot be happy unless I place my partner's happiness before my own.
24 I am usually willing to sacrifice my own wishes to let my partner achieve his/hers.

To score your love styles, add up your ratings for each of the items in each subscale and then divide this total by four. You should then have your average scores for all the primary and secondary love styles. You can make a graph of your love profile by plotting all six of your mean scores, arranged from highest to lowest.

Source: Excerpts from Hendrick, C., Hendrick, S.S. and Dicke, A. (1998). The love attitude scale (short form). *Journal of Social and Personal Relationships*, Vol. 15 (2). Reprinted by permission of Sage.

self-defeating, makes desperate attempts to attract attention and affection from their partner and shows an inability to believe, or trust in, any affection their partner does display towards them. The manic lover is desperate to fall in love and to be loved by another. At the start of the relationship they immediately imagine a potential future with their partner and want to see the partner all of the time. According to Lee, manic lovers can be extremely jealous, obsessive, irrational, and, as a result, often unhappy.

Lee calls the final secondary love style '*agape*' which comprises eros and storge. Agape is characterised by altruism (the practice of placing others before oneself) and represents an all-giving, selfless love style that involves loving and caring for others with no expectation of reward.

If you haven't already identified yourself as having one of these love styles, you might like to see what love style you do have by trying out the Love Attitude Scale in Stop and think: What's your love style?

Individual and group differences in love styles

Researchers have used the Love Attitude Scale to look closely at the individual differences within Lee's love styles and have identified interesting differences between men and women (Regan, 2003). Hendrick and Hendrick (1995) found that men tend to identify themselves to be ludic and manic lovers, whereas women tend to identify themselves as storgic and pragmatic. There have also been many and varied research findings on cross-cultural differences; for instance, Americans tend to identify themselves as adopting more storgic and manic approaches to love, as compared to the French, who display higher levels of the agape love style (Murstein *et al.*, 1991).

In addition, individual differences theorists have found evidence relating the three-factor model of personality to love styles. To act as a reminder, extraversion comprises sociable and carefree personality traits, neuroticism comprises anxious and worrying personality traits and psychoticism comprises solitary and antisocial personality traits. Davies (1996) found that extraversion is positively associated with the ludus or eros love styles, reflecting the extraverts' sociability, emphasis on romance and game-playing. Neuroticism was positively associated with the mania lovestyle, while negatively associated with pragma, thus emphasising these individuals' needs for possessive relationships. Finally, psychoticism was positively associated with the ludus love style and negatively associated with storge and agape love styles. Therefore it would seem, not unsurprisingly, that people scoring high on psychoticism are not in favour of all-giving and selfless love (Davies, 1996).

However, it must be remembered that not all individuals possess one approach or style of loving. Individuals may adopt numerous love styles, and the particular love style an individual might adopt may change across relationships or over the lifetime of a relationship. For example, the obsession, preoccupation and intense need that is associated with a manic love style may occur more often at the beginning stages of a romantic relationship, when the partners are less certain as to how they feel, but are feeling the excitement of a new relationship. However, as the relationship progresses, these feelings may be replaced by storgic, erotic or agapic feelings (Furnham and Heaven, 1999; Heaven *et al.*, 2004). It may also be that your personality traits will lead you to a particular love style, but, because of experiences of love, your love style turns out to be very different. For example, at the start of your love life, you might find that you have adopted a manic love style as part of neuroticism traits, but, after finding that you are too intense and possessive in your relationships, you might try to change the way you behave in relationships.

Romantic love and attachment styles

We have considered in detail the influences of attraction and love styles on our personal relationships, and the extent

---

Stop and think

Sternberg's triangular theory of love

- What do you think are the strengths of Sternberg's triangular theory of love? Consider whether you have experienced any of these love styles, or whether you can actually experience one or more of these styles with the same partner.
- How different are Lee's love styles when compared to Sternberg's? You might want to consider why there are so many different concepts of love and whether

you can recognise your own love style. Does your style correspond to the scores you achieved on the Love Attitude Scale?
- How important is personality when considering love? You might want to consider why you are attracted to certain people and whether you love different people in the same way.

to which these theories can be considered within individual differences. However, within the literature on personal relationships, the theory of attachment is thought to play an integral role. Within this area, findings suggest that the close emotional bonds between parents and their children may influence the bonds that develop between adults in emotionally intimate relationships.

The theory of **attachment styles** was originally developed by UK psychoanalyst John Bowlby, who attempted to understand the distress experienced by infants when they are separated from their parents (Bowlby, 1969). Bowlby observed that, for infants to survive, they would develop a range of behaviours that enabled them to keep close to their mother or primary caregiver. These behaviours are called attachment behaviours and consist of certain gestures and signals recognised by their parent – such as crying or smiling – with later behaviours such as crawling toward their caregiver and becoming upset when they leave the room. Bowlby believed that how the parent responds determines the later child–parent bond.

Bowlby's work was expanded by Mary Ainsworth (Ainsworth *et al.*, 1978), who recognised that there were individual differences within attachment. She and her colleagues identified three different styles of attachment within babies: secure, anxious-resistant and anxious-avoidant.

Ainsworth found that a child with a **secure attachment** to its mother will become upset when the parent leaves the room, but on the return of the parent to the room, the child actively seeks out the parent and is easily comforted by them. These children are able to play and explore away from their parent, as they are secure in the knowledge that they have a safe and secure base to return to when they need to. Therefore, secure attachment is considered as the most adaptive and healthy of the attachment styles (Ainsworth *et al.*, 1978; Hazan and Shaver, 1987).

Children with an **anxious-resistant** insecure attachment show discomfort and, upon separation from the mother, become extremely distressed. Importantly, when reunited with their parent, these children have a difficult time being calmed down, exhibiting a conflicting set of behaviours suggesting they would like to be comforted, but also suggesting that they want to 'punish' the parent for leaving them in the first place (Ainsworth *et al.*, 1978; Hazan and Shaver, 1987).

Finally, a child with an **anxious-avoidant** insecure attachment will not appear too distressed when separated from their mother and, on being reunited with the parent, actively avoids seeking contact with their parent, sometimes turning their attention to other things such as playing with objects. In other words, they will ignore the mother, showing little emotion when they leave the room or return. In fact, Ainsworth noted that the anxious-avoidant child shows little emotion regardless of who is in the room, or if it is empty (Ainsworth *et al.*, 1978; Hazan and Shaver, 1987).

Ainsworth *et al.* (1978) also noted that these individual differences in attachment were correlated with the interactions between parent and infant in the home during the first year of life. In other words, children who are secure tend to have parents who respond to their needs. Children who appear insecure (anxious-resistant and/or -avoidant) often have parents who are insensitive to their child's needs, or such parents may be inconsistent or tend to reject the child in the care they provide.

Research into attachment theory is extensive across psychology, particularly in developmental psychology. However, one of the main findings of attachment research is the detection of similar patterns of behaviour in adult relations with romantic partners; in other words, the attachments formed in the partners' childhoods are mirrored in their adult relationships. These patterns were first conceptualised within romantic relationships by US psychologists Cindy Hazan and Phillip R. Shaver (Hazan and Shaver, 1987).

According to Hazan and Shaver, securely attached children are likely to become securely attached lovers. These are the individuals who find it easy to get close to their partners and are comfortable depending on them. They are not preoccupied by thoughts of being abandoned or being alone, nor do they worry about people getting, or being, too close to them. They are high on intimacy as well as passion and commitment. Interestingly, Feeney (1999) has also considered attachment styles with Lee's love styles and suggests that secure romantic attachments are related to the eros and agape love styles. Here are some other characteristics of the secure attached adult:

- more trusting;
- tend to have long-term relationships;
- high self-esteem and high regard for others;
- generous and supportive when lovers are under stress;
- positive, optimistic and constructive in interacting with others.

Hazan and Shaver describe anxious-resistant lovers as more eager to get close to their partners than the partners are eager to get close to them. While their major concern is that their partners are not as willing to get as close to them as they had hoped, the major worry faced by anxious-resistant lovers is abandonment. The word 'ambivalent' is sometimes used to describe anxious-resistant lovers as often their relationship is characterised by a mixture of opposite feelings or attitudes, such as a love–hate relationship. Anxious-resistant lovers are low on intimacy, passion and commitment, and this dimension has been found to relate to the manic love style (Feeney, 1999). Here are some other characteristics of anxious-resistant lovers:

- high break-up rate despite deep involvement;
- intense grieving following loss;
- unstable self-esteem with self-doubt;

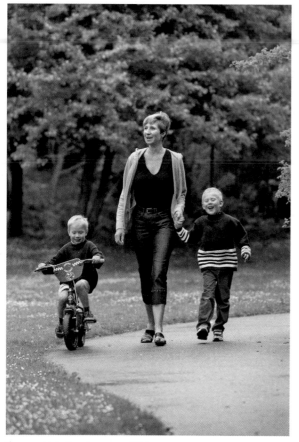

Do you think that these two children may grow up with different attachment styles?
Source: Alamy Images/Adrian Sherratt

- tend to be emotional, especially when under stress;
- jealous and untrusting.

Finally, Hazan and Shaver found that avoidant lovers do not feel comfortable being close to their partners, and they feel nervous when people get too close. They are low on intimacy, passion and commitment; this dimension has been positively related to the ludus love style (Feeney, 1999). Here are some characteristics of avoidant lovers:

- less investment in relationships;
- prefers to be alone;
- withdraws from partner when under stress;
- finds social interactions boring and irrelevant;
- doesn't like disclosure by self or others.

Researchers have also found that these aspects of attachment styles are related to the five-factor model of personality. As a reminder, the five factors of personality are neuroticism (e.g. anxious and worrying traits), extraversion (e.g. sociability and carefree traits), openness (e.g. curious and analytical traits), agreeableness (e.g. trustful and courteous traits) and conscientiousness (e.g. reliable and organised traits). Avoidant types tend to score higher

on neuroticism and lower on extraversion, agreeableness and conscientiousness. Anxious types tend to score higher on neuroticism and lower on agreeableness. Secure types tend to score higher on extraversion and agreeableness and lower on neuroticism (e.g. Baeckström and Holmes, 2001; Gallo *et al.*, 2003).

It is also finally worth noting that, owing to inconsistencies across research findings, there have been recent developments in research on the anxious-avoidant attachment style. For instance, Bartholomew and Horowitz (1991) found that some avoidant types have higher self-esteem than other avoidant types do, and they are less dependent. This type of attachment style has been relabelled as 'dismissing-avoidants'. The other type has been named 'fearful-avoidants' as they fail to bond with others because of a lack of self-esteem and fear of rejection (see Figure 21.4 for an overall view of the present-day model of attachment). It has been suggested by some researchers that several factors, including early sexual learning experiences with others, have influenced individuals' attachments in this way (Bartholomew and Horowitz, 1991).

Relationship dissolution

So far, we have looked closely at theories proposed by psychologists to help us understand better the individual differences of attraction and love styles. However, individual differences psychologists are also interested in the differences that occur when relationships come to an end. This event is known in the literature as relationship dissolution. We are going to look at a number of theories that explain *why* and *how* relationships end. The first theory, called the investment model, is the most important theory used to explain *why* relationships end.

The investment model

The most influential model describing relationship dissolution is a social psychological theory named the investment model. This model has been developed by US psychologist Caryl Rusbult (Rusbult, 1983; Rusbult and Martz, 1998; Rusbult and Zembrodt, 1983). According to Rusbult, the central variable in determining whether a relationship is sustained or ends is **commitment**. Commitment represents both a psychological attachment and a motivation to continue a relationship, even in times of trouble (Rusbult and Martz, 1998). According to the investment model, three elements work together to enable commitment in a relationship; these are satisfaction, quality of alternatives and investments. These three components are then thought to predict a fourth component, the individual's level of commitment to that relationship (see Figure 21.5).

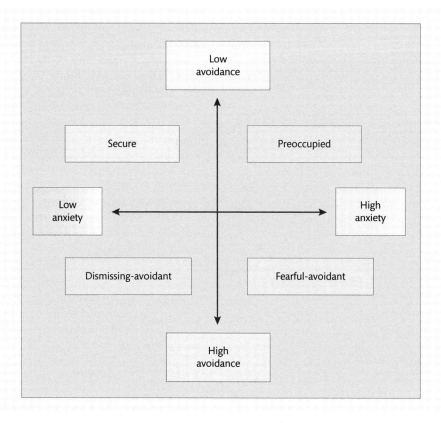

Figure 21.4 Individual differences in attachment styles.
Source: Based on Shaver and Fraley (2004).

First, **satisfaction** refers to the assessments that the individual makes about their relationship in terms of rewards and costs. Rewards can be anything that the person feels are positive aspects of the relationship, so they may be things like having somebody to share your life with, getting to go out to places with someone as a couple or getting gifts from this person. Costs are anything the person feels are negative aspects of the relationship. Cost might include the time it takes to sustain a relationship or the emotional turmoil that might be involved. Satisfaction with the relationship depends on a simple calculation: satisfaction = rewards − costs. If rewards outweigh costs, then the person is likely to be satisfied with the relationship. If costs outweigh rewards, then the person is likely to be unsatisfied with the relationship.

It is important to note that individuals differ on several aspects of satisfaction: individuals differ in what they

Figure 21.5 The investment model of relationships.

consider to be rewards and costs; for example, spending a lot of time with someone might be considered a reward, while for others it might be considered a cost. Individuals also differ in the emphasis they place on different rewards and costs. For example, for some people, receiving presents from their partner might be an important reward while, for others, receiving presents is not very important at all. Another central variable here is something called **comparison level**, which refers to the fact that people make comparisons within their life all the time (Do I feel better than I did yesterday? Do I think I am better than that person? Does that person like me more now than they did a year ago?). How satisfied you are with the relationship also depends on comparison level. In other words, through life you have amassed a history of relationships with other people, and this history has led you to have certain expectations as to what your current and future relationships should be like. People differ in their comparison level when it comes to satisfaction with relationships. Some individuals have a high comparison level; for example, they expect lots of rewards with few costs from a relationship, or they have had previous relationships with lots of rewards and few costs. Other people have a low comparison level; that is, they expect, or have had, few rewards and many costs in their relationships. Rusbult has found that, if the balance of your rewards and costs doesn't meet the comparison level, then you are likely to be dissatisfied with the relationship. For example, if you have a high comparison level (e.g. lots of rewards and few costs) and your current partner is not giving you lots of rewards and few costs, you are unlikely to be satisfied with the relationship. Satisfaction is positively related to commitment.

Second is the **quality of alternatives** to the current relationship. As Drigotas and Rusbult (1992) note, this element of the investment model represents the outcome of an assessment the person makes by assessing other possible relationships as an alternative to the current relationship they have – for instance, dating someone else or dating more than one person. Again, this dimension relates to the **comparison level**. The person compares their current relationships with possible other relationships. For example, the person might ask themselves, 'is there someone else I can be happier with?' Or, indeed, they may ask themselves, 'will I be happier on my own?' Some people will have an option(s) regarding an alternative relationship; some will have no alternatives. Individuals with no alternatives will look at that as a reason to stay in the relationship, while people with a quality alternative will look at that as a reason to leave the relationship (Rusbult et al., 1988). Overall, the quality of alternative is negatively related to commitment; for example, someone who has a high-quality alternative (someone else they want to be in a relationship with) is likely to be less committed to the relationship.

The third element is investment. **Investments** represent the things the individual has invested in the relationship and will potentially lose if the relationship were to end. These investments can be tangible (concrete or material assets) or intangible. Examples of tangible investments include shared possessions or financial benefits. Examples of intangible investments include 'shared history', companionship and emotional welfare of children. The greater amount of investment that the individual has in the relationship, the more likely they are to stay in that relationship – even sometimes if the satisfaction is low and there is a quality alternative to the current relationship (Rusbult and Martz, 1998). The level of investment in a relationship is positively related to commitment.

These three elements determine the level of commitment to a relationship, and commitment determines whether the person is likely to stay in the relationship. High commitment to a relationship (resulting from high satisfaction, low quality of an alternative and high investment) will mean that the person is likely to want to stay in the relationship. Low commitment to a relationship (resulting from low satisfaction, high quality of an alternative and low investment) will mean that the person is likely to want to leave the relationship.

There has been a huge amount of research considering the investment model as a predictor of relationship dissolution in relationships among college students, married couples of diverse ages, lesbian and gay couples, close non-sexual friends and for residents of the United States and Taiwan (Kurdek, 1992; Lin and Rusbult, 1995; Rusbult, 1983; Van Lange et al., 1997). Research suggests that the investment model is an excellent explanation of why relationships are sustained or end between two people.

Therefore, the investment model can be used to explain *why* people end a relationship, but it will also need to consider individual differences in *how* people end a relationship. Psychologists have divided the research into two specific areas:

- how individuals initiate the end of a relationship and what strategies are used;
- how individuals react when the other person initiates the end of the relationship, and how individuals differ in the way that they cope with the break-up.

We will now look briefly at each of these areas.

How individuals initiate the end of a relationship

Undeniably, relationships change over time. What might have been a highly satisfactory relationship may become unsatisfying for one or both parties. Rusbult et al. (1986) and Rusbult and Zembrodt (1983) have looked at how partners have dealt with these realisations that the relationship was coming to an end. These researchers then conceptualised the partners' behaviour and responses to these realisations into four basic response categories:

- **Exit strategy** – this strategy involves behaviours or responses that include ending the relationship by thinking about it or talking about it ending. It might also include acting in a potentially destructive way; for instance, threatening to end the relationship, move out of a shared home or separate or get a divorce (Rusbult and Zembrodt, 1983).
- **Voice strategy** – this strategy involves actively and constructively attempting to improve conditions, such as discussing problems, suggesting solutions, asking the partner what is bothering them about the relationship, seeking help through therapy and trying to change (Rusbult and Zembrodt, 1983).
- **Loyalty strategy** – this strategy involves waiting for things to get better, or hoping that they will sort themselves out in time. In other words, remaining passively loyal to the relationship (Rusbult and Zembrodt, 1983).
- **Neglect strategy** – this strategy suggests that individuals respond to the partner's dissatisfaction by doing nothing to improve things and letting the relationship fall apart. It may involve ignoring the partner, spending less time with them, criticising them for things unrelated to the problem and refusing to discuss the problems (Rusbult and Zembrodt, 1983).

These four responses, according to Rusbult *et al.* (1986), differ from one another along two dimensions: **constructiveness versus destructiveness and activity versus passivity**. The voice and loyalty strategies are relatively constructive responses as they involve the attempt to maintain or improve the relationship, whereas the exit and neglect strategies are considered to be more destructive to the relationship. As well as this, the exit and voice strategies are considered to be fairly active reactions as individuals can be seen to be doing something about the problems, whereas the loyalty and neglect strategies suggest a more passive approach to the problem.

Rusbult *et al.* suggest that these four strategies can also be linked to the investment model (see earlier). For instance, when there has been prior satisfaction within the relationship, then the individual is more likely to believe that it is desirable to restore the relationship to its former glory; they would therefore use the voice and loyalty strategies (constructive), not the exit and neglect (destructive) strategies (Rusbult *et al.*, 1982). The authors also suggest that high investment within the relationship should again promote these more constructive responses. However, according to Rusbult *et al.*, variations in the quality of the alternative will determine whether the individual's responses will be active or passive. For example, a high-quality alternative to the current relationship will probably invoke either an exit or voice strategy ('shape up or ship out') whereas, where there are low-quality alternatives, the

individual is more likely to show passive responses, such as passively waiting for things to improve (loyalty strategy) or passively allowing conditions to worsen (neglect strategy).

There has been some evidence to support these individual differences in ending relationships through the four responses (Rusbult *et al.*, 1982; 1986). However, there are other suggested theories that expand on these individual differences in how partners initiate the end of the relationship. For example, some evidence suggests that non-verbal signals might play a role in the relationship breaking up, as partners fail to respond to the non-verbal signals of the other person and appear less sensitive to their needs. This can lead to desires not being met and partners feeling hurt; consequently, the relationship dissolution has been initiated (Noller, 1985). Argyle and Henderson (1984) argue that factors such as the removal of trustworthiness or emotional support have the biggest impact on relationship dissolution; other researchers, such as Miller *et al.* (1986), suggest that lying or deception is at the root of the problems.

US psychologist Leslie Baxter (1986) considered different themes such as these and argued that the end of a long-term relationship is due to *expectations* not being met. In her research she identified eight major expectations that, if unfulfilled, can be important variables involved in the process of relationship dissolution.

- Partners expect a certain amount of autonomy, or independence
- Partners expect to find a good basis for similarity between them; for example, that the partners would empathise with each other, understand the other's social background and beliefs, aspirations and so on
- Partners expect support when upset or feeling down, or when self-esteem is low
- Partners expect loyalty and faithfulness
- Partners expect honesty and openness
- Partners expect to spend time together
- Partners expect to share, equally, effort and resources
- Partners expected some 'spark' to remain in the relationship.

Similarly to Rusbult, Baxter also believes that, once these expectations become constantly unmet, then individuals will initiate the end of the relationship. She highlights two distinct breaking-up strategies, called direct and indirect. Notice here that these two strategies are very much like the passive versus active strategies outlined by Rusbult. However, Baxter suggests that individuals specifically use these two strategies for ending the relationship once they have *made the decision* to break up.

Baxter argues that **direct strategies** include these behaviours and responses:

- 'fait accompli' – the instant dissolution of the relationship;

- discussions over the state of the relationship; for example, 'Do you think our relationship is working?';
- using arguments as a basis for the relationship to end;
- both people agreeing to end the relationship.

Indirect strategies include behaviours such as these:

- withdrawal – for example, 'I'm really busy with work at the moment';
- pseudo-de-escalation – for example, stating that the relationship should be less close and suggesting both people spend less time together;
- cost-escalation – exaggerating the cost of the relationship; for example, suggesting the other person is too demanding;
- passive aggressiveness – aggression expressed indirectly through negative attitudes and resistance to reasonable requests (usually in the hope that the other person gets fed up with them and ends it themselves);
- fading away – slowly disappearing from the relationship.

People give many other reasons that might help us to understand how partners initiate the end of a relationship. Many people try to rationalise and explain why the relationship ends. For example, they say there was a failure to distinguish between 'love' and 'infatuation' (Tennov, 1979) or that there was the loss of a 'novelty' factor in the relationship, which ceased to provide stimulation for both partners, and the relationship was seen as 'going nowhere' (Duck and Miell, 1986). Other factors identified by Duck and Miell can include the physical distance between partners as this can make relationships difficult to maintain (although it may not necessarily always be fatal to the relationship), social distance (for example, a person not getting on with their partner's friends), lack of effort by one or both partners, interference from others and a decline of affection (Duck and Miell, 1986). Rose and Serafica (1986) argue that reasons like those just outlined suggest that individuals tend to distance themselves from blame, and perhaps these reasons emphasise the tendency for people to adjust recollections of the relationship dissolution to rationalise and fit their emotional needs. This argument then might explain how people initiate the end of the relationship, particularly as people do not like to admit that a failure in a relationship was *all* their fault.

One last theory worth mentioning is the phase model, which was proposed by Steven Duck (1982). He identifies four phases or stages of break-up, where each phase is triggered by a threshold before moving on to the next. These phases are as follows:

- **Intrapsychic phase** – according to Duck, the relationship is fairly healthy at this stage. However, within this phase you begin to think about the negative aspects of your partner and of the relationship itself, but do not discuss these thoughts with your partner. Consequently, dissatisfaction builds up in the individual with feelings of 'there is something wrong'. Eventually, the 'I can't stand it any more' feelings build up to a point that pushes you into the stages of the relationship actually ending. Threshold: 'I can't stand this any more' (Duck, 1982).

- **Dyadic phase** – this phase involves confronting the partner with the negative thoughts from the intrapsychic stage and trying to sort out the various problems. The break-up is now in the open, with one person saying either 'I'm leaving' or 'I'm thinking of leaving'. Both partners must now face reality, and intensive discussions about the relationship may ensue. The focus here is on the partnership. Threshold: 'I'd be justified in withdrawing' (Duck, 1982).

- **Social phase** – this phase involves deciding what to do now that the relationship is effectively over; it includes thinking of face-saving accounts of what has happened. Eventually the pressure of 'I really mean it' breaks out, and the break-up becomes a public issue. Now the focus turns outwards to the perceptions of other people. Friends may be recruited to support either side, and issues of who is to blame and what should be done arise. Eventually, it becomes inevitable that the split will happen, and things move on to the next phase. Threshold: 'I mean it' (Duck, 1982).

- **Grave-dressing phase** – here, Duck argues that the relationship is now officially ended (buried), with all explanations for the relationship dissolution in place (true or otherwise). The phase focuses on communicating a socially acceptable account of the end of the relationship; it is an important phase in terms of preparing the people involved for future relationships. Threshold: 'It's now inevitable' (Duck, 1982).

There are some important differences between Duck's phase theory and some of the theories mentioned earlier. Most of the other theories focus on various strategies describing how relationships end, or begin to end. Duck's theory describes a whole process of relationship dissolution. Therefore, Duck's model may also have some useful practical applications as it can be used not only to identify, and therefore understand, the stages of breakdown a relationship may be going through but also to suggest appropriate ways that individuals can attempt to repair the relationship. The model also suggests, once a relationship ends, how couples can effectively deal with the end to start afresh in new relationships. For example, Duck suggests that couples in the intrapsychic phase should aim to re-establish a liking for their partner by concentrating and emphasising on the positive aspects of their relationship rather than giving in to the tendency in this phase to focus on the negative.

How individuals react when the other person initiates the end of the relationship

Inevitably, if one person initiates the end of a relationship, then the other partner has to handle the consequences. The second area within relationship dissolution focuses on how individuals respond and cope when the other person has initiated the end of the relationship.

Most of the research in this area focuses on the extent of distress and trauma that the individual will go through, rather than theoretically predicting self-specific emotional and behavioural reactions (i.e. Tashiro *et al.*, 2006). Overall, research suggests that the individual will suffer negative physical and self-specific emotional responses such as post-traumatic stress disorder, and responses can include mood swings, depression, feelings of rejection and loneliness (Chung *et al.*, 2002; 2003). However, this is perhaps hardly news to you; at the end of a relationship, particularly where the end has been initiated by the other partner, an individual reacts in negative rather than positive ways.

However, some researchers have investigated individual differences in how individuals cope with the end of a relationship; specifically, the consideration of coping and attachment theory. US psychologists Deborah Davis, Phillip Shaver and Michael Vernon (Davis *et al.*, 2003) have shown that individuals with anxiety attachments show greater preoccupation with the relationship dissolution, show more distress and anger and present dysfunctional coping strategies and disordered resolution with the loss of the relationship. Davis *et al.* suggest that people with this attachment style also find it most difficult to 'let go' and make frequent attempts to re-establish the relationship. It can be imagined, here, that alongside the trauma

and distress involved with the relationship dissolution, prolonging the distress can lead to further problems for the individual.

Alternatively, Davis *et al.* found that individuals with avoidant attachments show significantly fewer distress reactions, showing more avoidant tactics and self-reliant coping strategies at the end of a relationship. This attachment style may offer insights into why some people can very quickly move on to the next relationship, seemingly without a care in the world.

Finally, Davis *et al.* found that individuals with secure attachments tend to use their friends and family to help them cope with the end of the relationship. Davis *et al.* suggest that people with this attachment style still suffer unhappiness and distress at the end of a relationship but remain more optimistic about the future (Davis *et al.*, 2003).

Interestingly, some research has been carried out investigating the impact of personality and coping with the break-up of a relationship. Those scoring high on neuroticism, like those individuals with anxiety attachment styles, tend to take longer to get over the relationship, whereas those who score high on psychoticism take less time. As with individuals with secure attachments, individuals who score high on extraversion will tend to use family and friends; but again, they do feel negative emotions at the end of the relationship (Chung *et al.*, 2002; Furnham and Heaven, 1999; White *et al.*, 2004).

So far in this discussion we have considered love styles, attachment styles and relationship dissolution styles. However, there is another theory within psychology that can bring insights into this area: forgiveness. The theory of forgiveness is not only considered within personal relationships, it is considered wherever there has been a transgression (overstepping some boundary or limit) or offence against

Profile

Caryl E. Rusbult

Caryl E. Rusbult obtained a degree in sociology from UCLA in 1974, and received her PhD in psychology from the University of North Carolina at Chapel Hill in 1978. She then became a professor of psychology at the University of North Carolina. She has since moved from the University of North Carolina to the Free University in the Netherlands, where she is Professor and Chair of the Department of Social Psychology.

Rusbult has published over 90 journal articles, chapters and books. She is best known for her theory and research regarding commitment processes and relationship maintenance behaviours, but she also lists interests in these areas:

- tendencies by individuals to accommodate rather than retaliate when a partner behaves poorly;
- willingness to sacrifice for the good of a partner and relationship;
- forgiveness of partner for acts of betrayal;
- positive illusion, or tendencies to regard one's relationship as better than (and not as bad as) other relationships.

Rusbult received the 1991–1992 New Contribution Award from the International Society for the Study of Personal Relationships, as well as the 1991 Reuben Hill Award from the National Council on Family Relations.

Stop and think

Personal relationships

- What type of attachment style do you have? Do you think that your relationship with your parents mirrors how you interact with your partner?
- What do you think are the strengths of the investment model? You might want to consider how crucial commitment and investment are within relationships, and what the costs and benefits are.

- How useful is the phase model in understanding why relationships go wrong? Can you think of anything that might be missing in the model, or is it sufficient to explain the sequence of events leading to the end of the relationship?

---

someone; for instance, a falling out amongst work colleagues, where a friend betrays someone in some way, where a crime has been committed against someone – or even, sometimes, with natural disasters or illnesses. Think of times when you have needed to forgive someone; we are sure those instances may have been because of a variety of reasons.

However, regardless of the vast diversity of possible offences, the theory of forgiveness is applicable when we consider social and interpersonal relationships – particularly as it is likely that the biggest hurt you could ever experience occurs when your partner, or lover, wrongs or hurts you in some way. We will now look at the concept of forgiveness and examine some of the theories and research surrounding this concept.

Introducing forgiveness

There has been an increasing amount of theory and research within the field of forgiveness, with the growing awareness that forgiveness has a major impact on an individual's mental health. Indeed, some psychologists now suggest that forgiveness is one of the most important psychological and relational processes for promoting healing with individuals who have become alienated and estranged from one another (Hill, 2001). In fact, as some forgiveness theorists suggest, forgiveness is a positive method of coping with a hurt or offence that primarily benefits the victim through a reorientation of emotions, thoughts and/or actions toward the offender (Wade and Worthington, 2005).

Forgiveness, then, is a process that leads to the reduction of unforgiveness (which includes feelings of bitterness and anger) and the promotion of positive regard (such as love, compassion, sympathy, pity) for the offender. As Wade and Worthington state, forgiveness is not necessarily reconciliation with the offender, as an individual can forgive and at the same time decide to end a relationship with the person who has hurt them. Perhaps more important, forgiveness does not mean tolerating, condoning or excusing hurtful behaviour (Hill, 2001). Nevertheless, forgiveness itself has been

found to have extremely beneficial effects on an individual (Snyder and McCullough, 2000; Yamhure-Thompson and Snyder, 2003), whereas failing to forgive (unforgiveness) or thoughts of revenge have been found to lead to continued feelings of anger, hostility, fearfulness, depression, difficulty in maintaining future relationships and experiencing trust issues, to name just a few (Brown, 2003; Karremans *et al.*, 2003; Maltby *et al.*, and Day, 2001). For these reasons, individual differences theorists are particularly interested in understanding why some people find it easy to forgive when others do not, how individuals forgive and when forgiveness takes place.

What is forgiveness?

Hill (2001) writes that, for many forgiveness psychologists, forgiveness is a controversial term; they fear that many individuals see forgiveness as a weakness, suggesting a tolerance of abusive behaviour, condoning hurtful actions or overlooking painful experiences. However, Hill argues that these misunderstandings must be overcome, and researchers are concentrating on the extensive mental health benefits for individuals who do forgive.

One of the most difficult issues faced by psychologists in this area is the lack of consensus in defining forgiveness. However, most agree that forgiveness involves a willingness to abandon resentment, negative judgement and indifferent behaviour towards the person who has hurt them, while adopting qualities such as compassion, generosity and love towards that same person (Hill, 2001). McCullough *et al.* (2000) suggest that, although there are problems finding one specific definition, researchers have sought to differentiate it from concepts such as pardoning, condoning, forgetting, denying or even reconciling. Alongside this, many psychologists in the area seem to be in agreement that **forgiveness** is a positive method of coping with a hurt that involves complex cognitive, emotional and relational processes; this complexity suggests that forgiveness is not necessarily an act, but rather a process, of discovery (Wade and Worthington, 2005).

According to many researchers, such as Pargament *et al.* (2000), forgiveness is complex and involves both **intrapersonal** and **interpersonal** processes. Intrapersonal aspects of forgiveness involve processes to do with yourself – your individual thoughts and feelings about yourself. In other words, how you address aspects within yourself, how you feel about yourself, if you attribute blame for the hurt to yourself, whether you have low self-esteem and think you deserved to be treated that way, whether you are a forgiving person generally and how you generally cope when someone hurts you. In contrast, interpersonal aspects of forgiveness focus on how events and consequences in ongoing relationships between two people are assessed and acted upon (Exline and Baumeister, 2000; Gordon *et al.*, 2000). In other words, interpersonal aspects of forgiveness involve relationship management, which involves considering such things as whether you are still going to talk to that person, be kind to them or talk about the issue. Do you have empathy with that person? What is important for you to note about forgiveness is that it is not just about how you deal with the person who has hurt you, but how you yourself deal with the hurt. Pargament *et al.* (2000) have also stressed that perhaps, in order to forgive someone, you first have to deal with your own thoughts and emotions regarding the hurt (intrapersonal) before considering your interactions with the person who hurt you (interpersonal).

Hill (2001) has described forgiveness as similar to a grieving process, in which you must acknowledge the reality of the loss (or injustice/injury), experience pain, make needed adjustments and re-invest emotional energy. In fact, Hill and Mullen (2000) suggest that each task of the grieving process, or forgiveness process, needs to be carefully formulated, prudently articulated and critically processed. Unfortunately, as Hill notes, many individuals struggle to discover the forgiveness process. This happens because of individual differences in forgiveness. Individuals grow and learn in various contexts, and they have varied emotional and relationship experiences that set the stage for their ability to forgive. Different psychological variables (for example, personality traits) also can affect forgiveness.

However, there are contexts that can help us in understanding the process of forgiveness. We will now look in great detail at these processes of forgiveness as they have been formulated and set out within two major models of forgiveness: the Enright model of forgiveness and the Worthington pyramid model of forgiveness. We will then go on to consider how personality and attachment variables have been found to influence the forgiveness process.

Models of the forgiveness process

In a moment we will look closely at the two main models of forgiveness: the Enright model and the Worthington (pyramidal) model. However, it is important to remember that achieving a state of forgiveness is a complex process involving intrapersonal as well as interpersonal thoughts, feelings and behaviours. The process includes giving up feelings of hurt and ill-will towards the offender as well as no longer being preoccupied with the hurtful event (i.e. spending most of the time thinking about it). Forgiveness, then, is thought to have occurred when you can pick up the threads of your life and move forward in a healthy and constructive way – when you are no longer dwelling on it and bringing it to mind in similar situations, and when you have forgone vengeful behaviour (McCullough *et al.*, 2000; Wade and Worthington, 2005).

This is obviously an oversimplified summary, but it does indicate how complex the process is. Owing to this complexity, forgiveness seldom occurs quickly and needs to be worked on to be achieved. Many different thoughts, feelings and behaviours, as well as moods, emotions and attitudes, need to be considered. All these aspects are different from person to person; however, most forgiveness psychologists (e.g. Hebl and Enright, 1993; McCullough *et al.*, 2000; Wade and Worthington, 2005) agree that many of the following processes are felt and need to be considered within a process of forgiveness:

- feelings of shock, disbelief and/or a sense of unreality;
- attitudes and feelings of a relationship being violated;
- feelings of hurt, anger and hostility;
- a want to withdraw socially; feelings of isolation/or loneliness;
- feeling of depression.

With all these factors in mind, two well-known psychologists in the area of forgiveness, Robert Enright and Everett Worthington, have presented process models of forgiveness. We will look at these models in the following sections.

The Enright model of forgiveness

The Enright model of forgiveness was developed from the empirical research on forgiveness and was created specifically to promote forgiveness in individuals (Hebl and Enright, 1993). This is a process model of interpersonal forgiveness that originally involved an extensive 17 steps of forgiving that incorporate cognitive, affective and behavioural elements (Enright and The Human Development Study Group, 1991). This model describes many possible steps that an injured individual might go through before forgiving, and it has since been fully developed into a full 20-step model (Enright and Fitzgibbons, 2000). These 20 steps, or stages, are then organised into four distinct phases of uncovering, decision-making, work and outcome. The model, according to Enright, shows a general pathway that individuals follow when they forgive another. This process is not considered to be a rigid sequence; rather, individuals may experience all, or only a few, of these steps. In addition, some of the steps may loop backwards and forwards. Let us look in detail at these four phases (the model, stages and steps are shown in Figures 21.6 and 21.7).

Uncovering phase

The first part of the model includes steps 1 to 8. Enright and Fitzgibbons (2000) call this stage the uncovering phase and describe the importance of identifying psychological defences, confronting and releasing anger and realising the additional psychological hurt that the offence has caused, such as shame, unjust suffering and mental anguish from replaying the event over and over in the mind. Identifying and accepting the reality of the hurt, the negative consequences and the injustice of the situation are all parts of these initial steps (Wade and Worthington, 2005). In other words, this phase involves the individual exploring the fact that holding on to feelings of resentment, anger or hate can have a negative impact on their own life. It is here that the individual first becomes aware of the emotional pain that has been caused by the experience of deep or unjust hurt, as well as their feelings of anger and hatred toward the person who has hurt them.

For the process of forgiveness to begin, it is in the uncovering phase that all these negative emotions should be confronted, and the hurt itself should be understood. Enright suggests that this phase will probably cause the individual to experience extreme emotional distress; therefore, they must decide on the appropriate amount of energy to process this pain, yet still allow themselves to function effectively. While this may all seem extremely painful for the person, Enright suggests that it is only when the anger and all other negative emotions are brought out into the open and examined that healing can begin. In other words, the individual must confront their anger and negative emotions to release them, in order to prevent further damage to themselves. Indeed, the individual may also have to face the fact that they have been permanently changed by the hurtful event, but this realisation should give them a better chance of moving on (Enright and Fitzgibbons, 2000).

Decision phase

In Enright's model, the forgiveness process continues as the individual begins to make decisions about which of the affective, mental and behavioural changes can occur. The individual may experience 'a change of heart' towards the person who has hurt them, and makes a commitment to work towards forgiveness (see steps 9 to 11 in Figures 20.6 and 20.7). This next stage, called the decision phase, generally involves making a choice to try to forgive. Enright *et al.* (1998) and Enright and Fitzgibbons (2000) explain that the individual should now realise that to continue focusing on the hurt or on the person who has hurt them may, in fact, cause them more suffering in the long term. Therefore, the individual should begin to understand that a change must occur for them to go forward in the healing process. In other words, the individual should begin to see that forgiveness *can* be used as a healing strategy. This phase is an important first step; the individual, although still far from being able to forgive fully, should at least commit to the idea of forgiving as well as let go of any thoughts, feelings or intentions of revenge.

Work phase

According to Hebl and Enright (1993), to truly forgive, an individual must be able to see the person who has hurt them in their life context and develop compassion and empathy for the offender on the basis of situations that may have contributed to the offence (see steps 12 to 15). In other words, the commitment to forgive (established earlier, in the uncovering phase) should allow the individual to enter the work phase. It is here that the individual should begin looking at trying to forgive by reframing the incident, by accepting the hurt and by trying to find some empathetic (identification with the other person's situation, feelings and motives) understanding as to why the other person behaved in the way they did. This process, for instance, may involve developing new ways of thinking about the person who has hurt them, perhaps by considering that

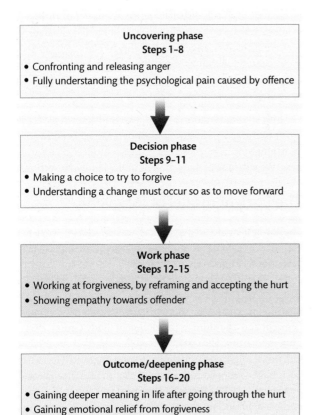

Figure 21.6 Enright's model of forgiveness – the four phases.

Uncovering phase

1 Examination of psychological defences
2 Confrontation of anger; the point is to release, not harbour, the anger
3 Admittance of shame, when this is appropriate
4 Awareness of cathexis
5 Awareness of cognitive rehearsal of the offence
6 Insight that the injured party may be comparing self with the injurer
7 Realisation that one may be permanently and adversely changed by the injury
8 Insight into possibly altered 'just world' view

Decision phase

9 A change of heart, conversion, new insights that old strategies are not working
10 Willingness to consider forgiveness as an option
11 Commitment to forgive the offender

Work phase

12 Reframing, through role taking, who the wrongdoer is by viewing them in context
13 Empathy towards the offender
14 Awareness of compassion, as it emerges, towards the offender
15 Acceptance and absorption of the pain

Outcome/deepening phase

16 Finding meaning for self and others in the suffering and in the forgiveness process
17 Realisation that self has needed others' forgiveness in the past
18 Insight that one is not alone
19 Realisation that self may have a new purpose in life because of the injury
20 Awareness of decreased negative affect, and perhaps increased positive affect, if this begins to emerge towards the injurer; awareness of internal, emotional release

Figure 21.7 Enright's 20-step model to forgiveness (Enright *et al.*, 1998).
Source: Based on Enright, Freedman and Rique (1998).

person's upbringing, or by looking at the offence within a different context considering the pressures or by considering feelings that the offender may have been experiencing themselves at the time of the offence. Enright argues that this work should not be done to excuse that person, but to better understand their reasons as another human being; in turn, this should bring a willingness to empathise and feel compassion towards them. For Enright this process presents 'a challenge of good will' for the person, but it will allow the individual to face the hurt. Enright maintains, however, that, although forgiveness and empathy have been undertaken, this does not necessarily mean that the individual should go through reconciliation with the other person. Indeed, there may be issues of trust and safety still to be considered (Enright and Fitzgibbons, 2000).

Outcome/deepening phase

The final stage, according to Enright and Fitzgibbons (2000), involves the individual finding meaning in the forgiveness process, gaining the awareness that they are not alone in the experience of being hurt and realising that the experience of the offence and hurt may produce a new purpose in their life (see steps 16 to 20). This final stage is that of the deepening, or outcome, phase that involves the individual trying to gain a deeper sense of meaning to their life as a result of going through the hurt. In general, the individual should gain emotional relief from going through the process of forgiveness, perhaps allowing themselves to find new meaning and enabling an increased compassion for themselves as well as others. Overall, forgiveness can

enable an individual to see new purpose and depth from their hurt, allowing them to see new and positive effects emerging from their emotional release.

Although these stages are set out in steps from 1 to 20, Enright reminds us that in reality, individuals may go back and forth between phases until forgiveness is finally achieved. Indeed, some studies have looked at individuals who have undergone treatment and gone through these phases. Compared to no-treatment control groups, the individuals who underwent treatment involving the Enright forgiveness model displayed decreased levels of anxiety and psychological depression as well as greater gains in forgiveness, self-esteem and hope (e.g. Enright and Fitzgibbons, 2000).

The Worthington (pyramidal) model

This second forgiveness model, again, focuses on a process to enable an individual to forgive. It was first developed by psychologists Michael McCullough and Everett Worthington (1995; McCullough *et al.*, 1997) and later refined into what is known as the pyramid model to REACH forgiveness (Worthington, 2001). Everett Worthington constructed the REACH model to consider five steps to facilitate and develop forgiveness for a specific hurt or offence, and each letter of the acronym REACH represents one step. These stand for (R) **R**ecall the hurt, (E) **E**mpathise with the one who hurt you, (A) **A**ltruistic gift of forgiveness, (C) **C**ommitment to forgive, and (H) **H**old on to forgiveness (see Figure 21.8).

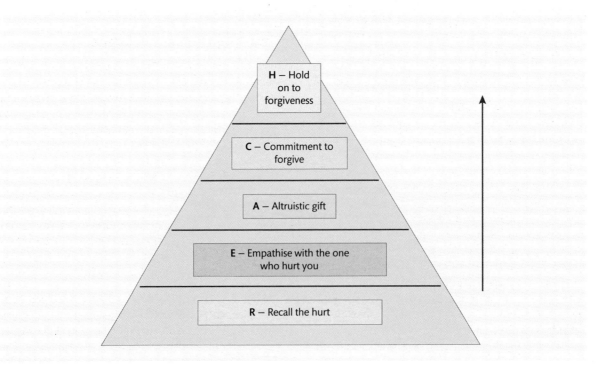

Figure 21.8 Worthington's pyramidal model of forgiveness.

This five-step model is considered to be a great facilitator to the processes of forgiveness. It is one of the most favoured techniques by counsellors who specialise in forgiveness and reconciliation (McCullough and Worthington, 1995; McCullough, *et al.*, 1997). Worthington suggests that the pyramid model helps the individual work through the process of forgiveness systematically, rather than remaining stuck in a type of limbo of wanting to forgive but not knowing where to begin. Let us now look a little closer at each of the steps of the Worthington (pyramidal) model in turn.

Step 1: Recall the hurt

In step one, Worthington (1998) describes how individuals are asked to recall the hurt in a supportive environment (e.g. a counselling or therapy session). It is here where the individual is encouraged to remember the hurt, the associated thoughts, feelings and behaviours as fully and clearly as possible. Again, as in the Enright model, this task may seem harsh. However, Worthington explains, when we are hurt we often try to protect ourselves by denying our hurt; this stops us from healing and moving on with our lives, as the thoughts and feelings threaten to intrude into our future relationships and happiness. Therefore, Worthington believes that we should recall the hurt as objectively as possible, stopping ourselves from thoughts and feelings that wish harm or misfortune on the person who hurt us, and not waste our time wishing or waiting for an apology that will never be offered or dwelling on our victimisation; instead, from recalling this hurt we should admit that a wrong was done to us and set our sights on healing. Interestingly, this step is similar to the beginning of the Enright model, which encourages an exploration of the consequences of the hurt (Wade and Worthington, 2005).

Step 2: Empathise with the one who hurt you

The next step of the model encourages individuals to build empathy towards the person who hurt them. Worthington (1998) suggests that this can be done by trying to imagine the thoughts and feelings of the offender before and during the time of the hurtful event. Again, this step should be taken while the individual is as relaxed as possible, enabling them to see the situational factors that led to the hurt. In other words, you should try to put yourself in the position of the offender, considering their thoughts, feelings and motives at that time. It may also help to remember positive things about the offender; for example, recalling good experiences that you had with them or complimentary things they have said about you. This step should allow you to better understand the offender's reasons and motives as well as to remember that they are also human and have faults. According to Worthington, this is the key step in the model; if done correctly and effectively, it should promote positive

thoughts, feelings and empathy and allow the individual to start addressing the negative feelings of fear and hurt.

Step 3: Altruistic gift

Ideas of empathy continue through the next step, giving an altruistic gift of forgiveness. Worthington (1998) suggests that, before fully considering the idea of giving a gift of forgiveness, the individual should remember times when they received forgiveness for hurts they caused to others. Individuals are asked to remember what it felt like to be forgiven. This step is intended to develop a healthy state of humility within the individual and to encourage them to remember what the emotion of gratitude felt like when they received forgiveness from other people (Worthington, 2001). In other words, this step comprises three experiences:

- **Guilt** – this occurs when the individual comes to realise that they too have wronged others in the past and are guilty of offending. This may also bring the realisation that the individual may, in fact, have hurt the offender in the past.
- **Gratitude** – this occurs when the individual imagines or remembers the gratitude they felt when receiving forgiveness in the past, and then imagines how the offender may feel if they too are granted forgiveness.
- **Gift** – this occurs when the individual consolidates the empathy, as well as the guilt and gratitude of humility, to create the motivation for them to forgive.

If these three experiences are successfully achieved, then, according to Worthington, the individual can proceed to the next step.

Step 4: Commitment to forgive

In the fourth step, Worthington suggests that individuals should begin 'publicly' to commit to the forgiveness that they are experiencing for the offender. He argues that this commitment may be a verbal or written commitment to forgive; however, it should be made public, perhaps in written form or by confiding in a close and trusted friend. In other words, although the individual may at this stage have forgiven the offender in their heart, it is only the act of making it public that makes it real. Worthington suggests that this is best done by talking about it openly to someone or by writing a letter to the person who has hurt you, although you may not send this letter to the person.

Step 5: Holding on to forgiveness

Committing to forgive is linked to the final step in the Worthington (pyramidal) model: holding on to forgiveness. This stage is designed to maintain the gains that have been achieved in the process of forgiveness. Worthington (1998) argues that it is hard to hold on to forgiveness, as the pain is remembered for a long time, and the individual may easily slip

People have different ways of dealing with people who have transgressed against them.
Source: Getty Images/Oppenheim Bernhard

back into a state of non-forgiveness. Indeed, it may be necessary to return to the previous steps a number of times before forgiveness is fully reached. However, by finally and fully committing to forgive verbally or in writing, and by realising the ways that they might doubt the forgiveness in the future, Worthington argues that the individual is more likely to maintain the changes they have achieved by following these steps.

So far then, we have looked at the models of forgiveness that attempt to explain how individuals might forgive; however, individual differences psychologists are also interested in understanding why some individuals find it easy to forgive and others do not. There are two variables that might give us some insight into this: attachment style and personality.

Attachment and forgiveness

One particular dimension, or context, that has an important impact on whether individuals forgive or not is that of early attachment styles (Hill and Mullen, 2000). As you may remember from before, early attachments with the mother may form the foundation for a child's social, cognitive and emotional development, which can influence how they act in personal relationships as an adult (Hazan and Shaver, 1987).

Hill (2001) argues that, from this perspective, an individual's early attachment experiences could certainly influence their ability to forgive in social and personal relationships. Hill and Mullen (2000) found that individuals with anxious

attachment styles experience levels of anxiety around personal relationships; as a result, they develop certain defence/coping mechanisms that allow them to protect themselves. Such protective mechanisms (such as denial or projection) become entrenched within these individuals to maintain their personal survival in the face of heightened anxiety. Hill and Mullen argue that, unfortunately, such protective mechanisms do not allow the development of close, intimate, empathic and anxiety-free relationships; thus, when it comes to forgiving people, anxiously attached individuals have learnt to protect themselves first and find it very hard to forgive.

Forgiveness and personality

Studies of the relationship between forgiveness and personality have generally been explored within the five-factor trait models of personality (Costa and McCrae, 1992). To help in our interpretation of findings, it is worth exploring the effect size of correlations reported between forgiveness and personality. (If you would like to know more about effect sizes, we discuss them in our online supplementary chapter on statistics, Chapter 27.) However, for now, it is useful for you to know that correlations of $r = 0.1$ are considered to be a small effect size, correlations of $r = 0.3$ are considered to be a medium effect size and correlations of $r = 0.5$ are considered to be a large effect size. Across a number of studies, the most consistent finding, that is often the most significant, is that higher levels

Profiles

Robert E. Enright and Everett L. Worthington Jr

Robert E. Enright

Robert E. Enright is a pioneer in the psychological study of forgiveness. Since 1978, he has been Professor of Educational Psychology at the University of Wisconsin – Madison. He teaches courses in adolescent development, social-cognitive development and identity development. His teaching has been recognised by the Chancellor's Distinguished Teaching Award and the Wisconsin Student Association Teaching Award.

Much of Enright's research work is on forgiveness and moral development and interventions designed to promote forgiveness. He is the author, or editor, of four books and over 80 publications in social development and the psychology of forgiveness. He is a licensed psychologist and has been on the editorial board of *Child Development*. He is currently on the editorial board of the *Journal of Early Adolescence*.

In 1997, after receiving a grant from the John Templeton Foundation, Enright became one of the founders of the International Forgiveness Institute, a non-profit organisation dedicated to the dissemination of knowledge about forgiveness.

Everett L. Worthington Jr

Everett L. Worthington Jr is another pioneer in the psychological study of forgiveness. He is Professor and Chair of the Department of Psychology at Virginia Commonwealth University in the United States, and he has been on the faculty since 1978. He received his doctorate from the University of Missouri.

Worthington has studied forgiveness since the 1980s. He has written 20 books and almost 200 articles, mostly on forgiveness, marriage and family issues. He is also a licensed clinical psychologist and is involved in psychological centres that concentrate on marital therapy. He directs 'A Campaign for Forgiveness Research' (**www.forgiving.org**), which seeks to support research into forgiving.

Stop and think

Self-forgiveness: the stepchild of forgiveness research

The term to describe self-forgiveness, the stepchild of forgiveness research, was a phrase coined by J. H. Hall and D. F. Fincham (Hall and Fincham, 2005). The reason for their description is that, throughout the earlier 2000s, research into interpersonal forgiveness and forgiveness of others grew, yet there was relatively little concept of empirical scholarship on self-forgiveness. In their paper, Hall and Fincham tried to define self-forgiveness and consider the ways it is different from interpersonal forgiveness.

Hall and Fincham suggest that forgiveness of self and forgiveness of others are similar in some ways. For example, both forms of forgiveness are intrapersonal processes, they are both processes that develop and unfold over time, and they both involve situations where the person who has committed the transgression is not entitled to forgiveness but is granted forgiveness.

However, Hall and Fincham describe some key ways in which forgiveness of others and forgiveness of self differ:

- While forgiveness of others is unconditional, self-forgiveness need not be. For example, one may set conditions for forgiveness, e.g. 'I will only allow myself to forgive myself for that transgression as long as I really make it up to the person'.

- With the forgiveness of others, there is no need for a reconciliation with the offender (i.e. you can choose to forgive the transgressor without ever seeing them again). However, for someone to forgive themself for a transgression against another, there is the need for the offender to make a reconciliation with themself over their actions.

- Forgiveness of others focuses upon the transgression towards a victim, whereas with forgiveness of oneself there are two dimensions; one may try to forgive oneself for a transgression against another person, or one may try to forgive oneself for some self-imposed harm. It may also be possible that one may have to forgive oneself for both these aspects for a particular transgression.

Finally, Hall and Fincham suggest that, to forgive oneself, one must publicly or privately acknowledge that the transgression was wrong and take responsibility for the behaviour.

In 2005, Yamhure-Thompson *et al.* (2005) introduced a measure of the self-forgiveness trait. Example items on this scale include:

- Positively worded items:

  - With time I can understand why I have made the mistakes that I have.

- Although I feel badly at first when I mess up, over time I can give myself some slack.

- Negatively worded items:

  - It is really hard for me to accept myself once I've messed up.
  - I don't stop criticising myself for the negative things I've felt, thought, said or done.

In terms of research into forgiveness and personality and well-being variables, trait self-forgiveness is positively associated with self-esteem and life satisfaction and negatively associated with neuroticism, depression, anxiety and hostility (Coates, 1997; Maltby *et al.*, 2001; Mauger *et al.*, 1992).

of forgiveness are statistically significantly predicted by lower levels of neuroticism (Berry *et al.*, 2001; Brose *et al.*, 2005; McCullough and Hoyt, 2002; McCullough *et al.*, 2001; Walker and Gorsuch, 2002), with the effect size of reported correlations ranging from small (e.g. $r = 0.21$; McCullough and Hoyt, 2002) to medium (e.g. $r = 0.52$; Brose *et al.*, 2005). Across studies, agreeableness seems also to show a fairly consistent relationship with many forgiveness measures, with the effect size of reported correlations ranging from small (e.g. $r = 0.21$; McCullough and Hoyt, 2002; $r = 0.33$; Berry *et al.* 2001) to small to medium (e.g. $r = 0.40$; Brose *et al.*, 2005; $r = 0.49$; McCullough *et al.*, 2001).

Additionally, higher levels of extraversion and conscientiousness have sometimes been found to share a statistically significant association with higher levels of forgiveness (e.g. Berry *et al.*, 2001; Brose *et al.*, 2005; McCullough *et al.*, 2000), with typically no statistically significant relationship found between forgiveness and these two personality domains, but, when there is, the effect size is at best small (e.g. extraversion, $r = 0.20$; Brose *et al.*, 2005; conscientiousness, $r = 0.24$; Berry *et al.*, 2001). It is important to note that, across all these studies, no statistically significant relationship and no correlation size of above $r = 0.20$ has been reported between any measure of forgiveness and the openness personality domain.

More specifically, research has also suggested that the facets of the five-factor personality model may be useful in examining forgiveness. This area is much less studied. Brose *et al.* (2005) examined the relationship between a series of dispositional and situational forgiveness measures (presence of positive forgiveness thoughts, feelings, absence of negative forgiveness thoughts, feelings and behaviour and forgiveness likelihood (Rye *et al.*, 2001)) and the broad and specific facet domains of the five-factor personality. Several facets of the five-factor domains were significantly correlated with forgiveness, but demonstrated inconsistent relationships. Forgiveness likelihood was negatively correlated with all neuroticism facets (correlation sizes ranging from $r = -0.28$ to $r = -0.47$), while presence of positive forgiveness was only negatively related to angry hostility and vulnerability facets of neuroticism, and showed, at best, small effect sizes ($r = <0.28$). All forgiveness measures were positively correlated with the positive emotions facet from the extraversion domain, but again show small effect sizes ($r < 0.29$) and were positively correlated with the trust facet from the agreeableness domain (r's ranging from 0.27 to 0.41).

However, although these personality traits are important to our understanding of why some people forgive and others do not, McCullough *et al.* (2000) argue that narcissism (an excessive love or admiration of oneself) may be a more important personality trait to consider. McCullough argues that the **narcissistic personality** is the antithesis (a direct contrast) of the forgiving personality and that narcissists not only have great difficulty in granting forgiveness but also have difficulty in seeking forgiveness.

Narcissism is an individual differences personality construct with the primary characteristic of an excessive love or admiration of oneself or grandiose and inflated sense of self (Campbell *et al.*, 2002). Because of this, the

Stop and think

Forgiveness

- Should we always forgive people who hurt us? Are there any circumstances when we shouldn't forgive?

- What do you feel about forgiveness? Do you think forgiving shows weakness, or do you think the benefits to our mental health are more important?

narcissist expects special or preferential treatment from others; if this treatment is not forthcoming, then they become easily offended. As well as this, they tend to externalise blame to other people, and, when offended against, they insist on being given retribution, whether through the other person seeking to make amends first or through revenge (Bishop and Lane, 2002). Research suggests that, if they are rejected or hurt in some way, narcissists are prone to attack those who have threatened their exaggerated sense of self-worth (e.g. Bushman and Baumeister, 1998). Therefore, it is easy to see why narcissism has a strong suggested link to unforgiveness, particularly as these individuals have great problems in empathising with others and expect the other person to make amends first. These problems would provide insurmountable obstacles to the narcissist in working towards forgiveness.

Final comments

We have considered the concept of personal relationships, with particular emphasis on theories of attraction, love styles, attachment, relationship dissolution and forgiveness. We have also considered how these theories can inform, and have been informed by, individual differences theory and research.

Summary

- Personality, social-psychological and cognitive factors seem to be important contributors to attraction, which all help individual differences theorists to gain a wider understanding of the individual differences within attraction.
- There are five distinct theories, or hypotheses, of interpersonal attraction: similarity, ideal partner, repulsion, optimal dissimilarity and optimal outbreeding.
- Fatal attraction suggests that those characteristics we view as most important when choosing a partner may often, in fact, be the very same characteristics that are instrumental in the break-up of the relationship.
- The triangular theory of love consists of three basic components: intimacy, passion and commitment. Because these three basic components of love are positioned at the points of a triangle, each of the elements can be present within a relationship, and they can produce seven different combinations, or love styles.
- Love styles consist of primary and secondary love styles, where the secondary styles are made up of a combination of two primary styles. Primary love styles include eros, ludus and storge. Secondary love styles include pragma, mania and agape.
- Attachment styles are considered to be a major component of personal relationships. Securely attached children are likely to become securely attached lovers; the anxious-resistant (ambivalent) lovers often find that they are more eager to get close to their partners than the partners are eager to get close to them; the avoidant lovers do not feel comfortable being close to their partners and feel nervous when people get too close.
- The investment model includes three elements that work together to enable the continuation of a relationship; these are satisfaction, alternative quality and investments. These three components are then thought to predict a fourth component, the individual's level of commitment to that relationship.

- Rusbult looked at how partners dealt with the realisation of the ending of their relationship; she conceptualised their behaviour and responses into four basic response categories: exit, voice, loyalty and neglect.
- The phase model identifies four phases or stages of break-up, where each phase is triggered by a threshold before moving onto the next. The four phases are intrapsychic, dyadic, social and grave-dressing.
- Early attachment styles can have an important impact on whether individuals forgive or not. The quality of early attachments forms the foundation for a child's social, cognitive and emotional development, which would have development implications for how individuals experience, or process, forgiveness.
- The Enright model of forgiveness was developed to promote forgiveness in individuals. It is a 20-step model of forgiving that incorporates cognitive, affective and behavioural elements. This model describes many possible steps that an injured individual might go through before forgiving. These series of 20 steps, or stages, are then organised into four distinct phases of uncovering, decision-making, work and outcome.
- The Worthington pyramid, or REACH, model, considers five steps to facilitate and develop forgiveness for a specific hurt or offence. Each letter of the acronym REACH represents one step: (R) Recall the hurt; (E) Empathise with the one who hurt you; (A) Altruistic gift of forgiveness; (C) offer Commitment to forgive; and (H) Hold on to forgiveness.
- When considering personality and forgiveness, individuals with the trait of extraversion tend to be more forgiving, whereas individuals with the trait of neuroticism tend to be less forgiving.
- However, because of a grandiose and inflated sense of self, the narcissistic personality is the antithesis of the forgiving personality. Not only that, but narcissists may have difficulty in seeking forgiveness.

Connecting up

You may want to look at the discussion of emotional intelligence in Chapters 15 and 16 because these theories describe several interpersonal skills. You may also want to look at the discussion in Chapter 9 on evolutionary psychology where we describe sex differences in mating strategies.

Critical thinking

Discussion questions

We have considered various theories regarding personal relationships (attraction, love styles, relationship dissolution and forgiveness) and presented some considerations so that you can appreciate the value of these different theories. However, there are some discussion points. We present them here in the form of discussion topics, so that you can think about these issues on your own or within groups; your university seminars would also be a great place to discuss them. They are not for you to worry about; they are presented only as a way for you to get an even deeper understanding of the complexities of this topic.

- This exercise is to get you generating some ideas about the topic. Let us consider some of the theoretical and empirical findings covered here within an individual differences perspective (as outlined in Chapter 17).

  - Name five or six important theories and/or findings that emerge from this topic area.
  - If you were to present an overview of these five or six chosen theories and findings, what different areas of psychology would you be emphasising? For example, are they biological or physiological, personality or cognitive, or social or clinical factors?
  - Of these five or six chosen theories and findings, which do you lend most weight to?
  - Are there any theoretical or empirical overlaps between the theories and findings? If so, where do they occur?

- We have covered two theories of love styles in depth. Consider your own love style: do you fit nicely into one style, do you engage in more than one or, in fact, can you fit in any of them? How important are these styles to understanding individual differences in love? Are there more important variables, and, if so, what are they?

- Continuing the consideration of love styles, we have introduced you to some information about gender

differences within Lee's styles. Do you think that males typically fit into the ludus and mania styles and females typically fit into storge and pragma styles? How might we explain these differences? How might genetic, evolutionary and environmental variables explain these differences?

- Can attachment styles account for individual differences in adult relationships?

- Can love be categorised by psychologists, or is it too abstract?

- How different do you think the models of how people end relationships are? What overlaps occur between the theories? What are the crucial differences between these theories?

- Consider the Enright and Worthington models of forgiveness. These models are extremely descriptive in their stages of forgiveness. Do you think any stages of these models are more important than other stages?

- Do you think the models of forgiveness are appropriate for all forms of forgiveness? Do you think forgiveness is important for any type of offence or hurt? How might forgiveness of an ex-partner differ from forgiveness of a work colleague you hardly know? Would it be easier to forgive an ex-partner or the work colleague you hardly know?

Essay questions

- Compare and contrast the love styles proposed by Sternberg and Lee.
- Critically discuss the role that personality has within the consideration of love styles and relationship dissolution.
- Critically discuss the role that attachment has in personal relationships.
- Critically compare the forgiveness models of Enright and Worthington.
- Personality and attachment variables play an influential role in forgiveness. Discuss.

Going further

Be careful with your reading. A lot of the books on relationships are written by non-academic psychologists or are popular self-help books, and they are not appropriate for your academic work. The following books give good explanations for some of the theories within relationships.

Books

- Bowlby, K. (2005). *Making and breaking of affectional bonds* (Routledge Classics Series). London: Routledge. If you would like to read some of Bowlby's original papers on attachment, then this is a book worth looking at.
- Cassidy, J. and Shaver, P. R. (2002). *Handbook of attachment: Theory, research and clinical applications.* New York: Guilford.
- Rhodes, W. S. and Simpson, J. A. (2004). *Adult attachment: Theory, research, and clinical implications.* New York: Guilford.
- Argyle, M. (1994). *The psychology of interpersonal behaviour* (Penguin Psychology Series). London: Penguin. This book provides theories and research surrounding non-verbal communication, social skills and happiness in interpersonal relationships.
- McCullough, M. E., Pargament, K. I. and Thoresen, C. E. (2000). *Forgiveness: Theory, research, and practice.* London: Guilford.
- Brehm, S. S., Miller, R. S., Perlman, D. and Miller-Campbell, S. (2006). *Intimate relationships* (3rd edn). New York: McGraw-Hill.

Journals

- Rusbult, C. E. and Martz, J. M. (1998). The Investment Model: Measuring commitment level, satisfaction level, quality of alternatives, and investment size. *Personal Relationships, 5,* 357–391.
- Finkel, E. J., Rusbult, C. E., Kumashiro, M. and Hannon, P. A. (2002). Dealing with betrayal in close relationships:

Does commitment promote forgiveness? *Journal of Personality and Social Psychology, 82,* 956–974. This work complements existing theory and the research discussed here by highlighting the role of commitment in motivating forgiveness. It may be a little hard going in places, but it is worth having a look through. *Journal of Personality and Social Psychology* is published by the American Psychological Association. Available online via PsycARTICLES.

The following journals are available online as well as accessible through your university library. These journals are full of published articles on research into relationships and forgiveness. Good keywords to use when searching an online database such as Web of Science and PsycINFO are 'attraction', 'attachment', 'personal relationships', 'relationship dissolution', 'love styles' and 'forgiveness'.

- *Journal of Personal and Social Relationships.* Published by Sage. Available via EBSCO Electronic Journals Service and SwetsWise.
- *Personal Relationships.* An international, interdisciplinary journal that promotes theory and research in the field of personal relationships. Published by Blackwells.
- *Personality and Individual Differences.* Published by Elsevier. Available online via Science Direct.
- *Journal of Personality and Social Psychology.* Published by the American Psychological Association. Available online via PsycARTICLES.

Web links

- One of the main topics at Social Psychology Network (**www.socialpsychology.org**) is interpersonal relations. This topic area includes information on romance and attraction, sexuality, divorce, family relationships and non-verbal communication.
- Check out the Adult Attachment Lab run by Phillip Shaver (**http://psychology.ucdavis.edu/labs/Shaver**).

Film and literature

The following books and films relate to some of the ideas explored here.

- *Pride and Prejudice* (1813, novel by Jane Austen). Relationships, love and love styles play a large role in *Pride and Prejudice*; some characters marry for security, some

marry for wealth and some marry for love. However, the two major themes of Jane Austen's *Pride and Prejudice* are summed up in the title. Pride is the character flaw that causes Elizabeth Bennet to dislike, and be prejudiced against, Fitzwilliam Darcy upon their first meeting. She perceives him as having a cold aloofness that she attributes to his own inflated opinion of himself. Yet Elizabeth herself also suffers from the same flaw; her pride in her own ability to analyse his character is such that she refuses to re-evaluate Darcy for the longest time, until eventually she realises she loves him. Does this show consideration of the similarity hypothesis, or maybe repulsion? The classic book has been made into a series of films. Recent films include *Pride & Prejudice* (2005, directed by Joe Wright and starring Keira Knightley) or *Bride & Prejudice* (2004, directed by Gurinder Chadha and starring Aishwarya Rai).

- *Kramer vs. Kramer* (1979, directed by Robert Benton). This film tells the story of a divorce and its impact on everyone involved, including the couple's young son. In the film, a man's wife leaves the family and the man adjusts to living alone and caring for his son; the woman then returns, leading to a battle over custody. This film is excellent in epitomising the trauma and distress of relationship dissolution.

- *Changing Lanes* (2002, Roger Michell). This film is a thriller that tells the story of two men: an attorney (played by Ben Affleck) who is in a rush to make a court appointment as part of his job, and a salesman (played by Samuel L. Jackson) who is also in a rush to make a court appointment in a custody battle over his children. They have a minor collision on a major road; however, the attorney leaves in a hurry, leaving the salesman to miss his court appearance. What ensues is a cat-and-mouse game that challenges the men (and the viewer) to consider choosing forgiveness over resentment and reconciliation over revenge. The film draws to a close when both men are at the point of requesting forgiveness as well as offering it.

Explore the website accompanying this text at **www.pearsoned.co.uk/maltby** for further resources to help you with your studies. These include multiple-choice questions, essay questions, web links and ideas for advanced reading.

CHAPTER 22
Social Attitudes

Key themes

- Right-wing attitudes
- Authoritarianism
- Conservatism
- Social dominance
- Religiosity
- Religious orientation
- Religious coping

Learning outcomes

At the end of this discussion you should:

- Be able to outline how psychologists define and measure right-wing attitudes and religiosity
- Understand, theoretically and empirically, how personality and individual difference variables are related to conservatism and religiosity
- Be able to present some evidence that either supports or detracts from each theory
- Appreciate some strengths and weaknesses of each of the research areas

Introduction

In 2002, a dramatic event occurred in France. For the first time ever in French politics, an extreme right-wing candidate – Jean-Marie Le Pen of the National Front – won through to the second round of the French presidential elections, with just over 20 per cent of the vote. In Italy, the National Alliance Party, an extremist right-wing party, received 12 per cent of the votes and entered the coalition government of Italian Prime Minister, Berlusconi. In February 2005 the European media was running headlines on the illness of the Pope, while preparing and speculating about his recovery and the possible implications of that. Between 2004 and 2005 Dan Brown's thriller, called *The Da Vinci Code*, dealing with religious meaning and themes in history and the modern world, became an international best-seller that was praised and criticised by the critics and was a major talking point among the public, media and academia.

Right-wing attitudes and religion are all-important aspects of modern-day life. Some people have strong political views, be they right-wing or left-wing. Most people would definitely be able to predict how they would vote at the next government election in their country. Some people would be able to predict how they would always vote in a government election in their country. Similarly, some people have, and will always have, deep religious attitudes. Some feel strongly about their religion, and may go to a place of worship and pray every day. Some may be less religious, and many people would claim not to be religious at all.

In the last few discussions, we have considered a variety of topic areas that take you from individual feelings of optimism and irrational beliefs through to social relationships. Now, we are going to take you a stage further and look at how personality and individual differences theory has informed how we understand the social world, specifically right-wing attitudes and religiosity. We are concerned here less with mental health consequences and more with social impacts on the individual.

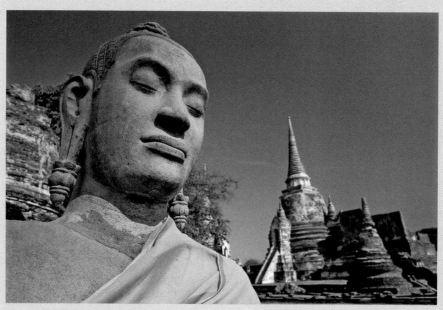

Source: Photodisc/Ingo Jezierski

Right-wing authoritarianism, conservatism and social dominance

On 25 April 1945, at the end of the Second World War, United States and Soviet troops met to divide Germany in two. Hitler had overseen the growth of economic and political fascism in Germany that culminated in the Second World War. There is a general agreement among commentators that the rise of fascism in Germany was not the result of a single factor. Rather, the growth of fascism was a result of Germany possessing a combination of a strong national identity, alongside a political system carefully manipulated by a party using persuasion and propaganda to influence the general population and attract voters, as well as a government that was weak and unable to resist social and economic crisis effectively.

It is perhaps no surprise, then, that psychological research into right-wing attitudes took hold in the 1950s following the Second World War, in particular looking at a concept called *authoritarianism*. However, a lot of key theory and research in right-wing attitudes, particularly around personality, was carried out in the 1970s and 1980s and focused on the concept of *conservatism*. Later, in the 1990s, we see further work on authoritarianism, and specific interest in the theory of right-wing attitudes re-emerged at the turn of the twenty-first century with *social dominance theory*. Here, we will deal with the theory, research and debate surrounding these three concepts of (right-wing) authoritarianism, conservatism and social dominance.

Authoritarianism

In 1950, US psychologist Theodore Adorno and his colleagues took part in the Berkeley School research project and introduced the term 'authoritarianism'. Adorno and his colleagues explained **authoritarianism** as a set of right-wing behaviours showing excessive conformity, intolerance of others and rigid and stereotyped patterns of thoughts (Adorno *et al.*, 1950). Adorno *et al.* argued that those who were authoritarian were so because of strict upbringing. These authors also linked this upbringing to the development of racist and fascist views. Their theory took a psychodynamic view, emphasising the interaction of various conscious and unconscious mental or emotional processes and particularly their effects on personality, behaviour and attitudes. Adorno used such a view to present authoritarianism as the identification of submissive behaviour towards authority, with the authoritarian person directing their aggression towards other social groups, often racial minorities, in an attempt to resolve feelings of personal weakness.

Adorno *et al.* (1950) depicted authoritarianism as a key personality variable and measured it by way of the California F(ascism) Scale. The F Scale includes items such as the following, and respondents are asked to indicate whether they agree or disagree with such statements.

- The businessman and the manufacturer are much more important to society than the artist and the professor.
- What the youth needs most is strict discipline, rugged determination and the will to work and fight for family and country.
- Nowadays, when so many different kinds of people move around and mix together so much, a person has to protect himself especially carefully against catching an infection or disease from them.

We can see how these descriptions are similar to the earlier descriptions of fascism; as such, Adorno's work became influential in psychology for providing a first psychological insight into right-wing attitudes such as fascism. However,

as early as the 1960s, the F Scale attracted a lot of criticism from academics. Gul and Ray (1989) summarise many of the problems and suggest that 'authoritarianism', as measured by the F Scale, reflects common myths and superstitions and has an old-fashioned orientation or outlook rather than any popular viewpoint. These academics were arguing that authoritarianism was not so much incorrect but outdated and that there were other emerging, more important right-wing, attitudes. Ideas such as 'the businessman and the manufacturer are much more important to society than the artist and the professor' may have been put forward previously by political thinkers or leaders, and many individuals in society may no longer believe them.

A psychologist from Canada named Robert Altemeyer, who is critical of the methods used by Adorno and the Berkeley team, suggested that authoritarianism is better defined as *right-wing* authoritarianism (Altemeyer, 1996; 1999) that comprises the following behaviours (see Figure 22.1):

- accept unfair abuse of power by government authorities;
- trust authorities too much;
- be prejudiced against people on racial, nationalistic, ethnic and sexual grounds;
- conform to the opinions of others;
- tend to see the world as dangerous;
- be self-righteous;
- hold contradictory ideas;
- uncritically accept insufficient evidence that supports their beliefs;
- trust people who tell them what they want to believe;
- tend to be hypocritical;
- may cause and inflame intergroup conflict;
- feel they have no personal failings;
- tend not to feel guilty for a long time after a misdeed;
- be dogmatic.

As you can see, these terms and ideas are simpler than those of Adorno *et al.* Consequently, Altemeyer (1996; 1999) introduced a 20-item measure of right-wing authoritarianism. This measure of right-wing authoritarianism contains statements such as these:

- I reason things out well. I seldom make the wrong inferences from facts. [item 3]
- Compared with most people, I am self-righteous and think I am morally better than most. [item 4]
- I tend to automatically trust people who tell me what I want to hear. [item 12]

Altemeyer (1996; 1999), using this scale, supplies a range of evidence to suggest that right-wing authoritarians do not have 'well-integrated' minds. Altemeyer found that right-wing authoritarians tend to agree vigorously with conclusions that closely match their own, even if the conclusion is false. So, for example, a right-wing authoritarian might believe that

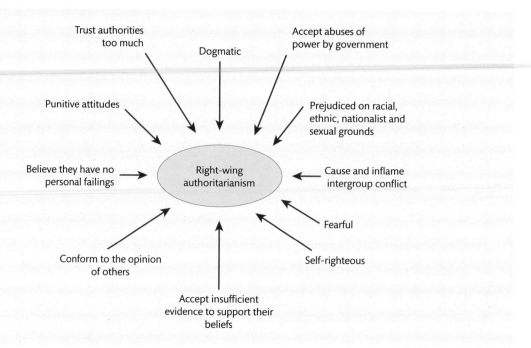

Figure 22.1 Altemeyer's model of right-wing authoritarianism.
Source: Based on Altemeyer (1996).

intellectuals are a detriment to society and that all universities should be abolished. He might then read a newspaper article, 'A day in the life of a student', in which a journalist claims that they met some university students who were rich and lazy and spent their time out socialising. Our right-wing authoritarian would then use that article as evidence to support his own beliefs and for his argument of abolishing universities. We (as people who work and study in universities) have a lot of evidence to show that students come from a variety of economic backgrounds – some rich, some poor – and that students do work very hard and have very little time to socialise. None the less, in our scenario, if we presented this evidence to a right-wing authoritarian, they would still put a lot of weight behind the journalist's original argument, because it fitted more readily with their existing view.

Altemeyer also found that right-wing authoritarians display double standards, or inconsistencies, in their thinking. They often insist on the rights of the majority when they are in the majority, and on minority rights when they are in the minority. For example, Altemeyer found that right-wing authoritarians insist on a Christian education in all schools across all religious denominations when they are in a majority, but insist on Christian specialist education when they find themselves in a minority; they will claim censorship when their own views are kept out of the curriculum, but will aim to censor any part of the curriculum that does not support their own.

What Altemeyer does with his work is to revitalise the approach to authoritarianism; however, he changes the emphasis from Adorno's psychodynamic approach, which sees authoritarianism as an interaction of various conscious and unconscious mental or emotional processes to highlight more cognitive processes (thoughts and thinking strategies) regarding how right-wing authoritarians perceive and deal with information.

Conservatism

A significant piece of the psychological literature on right-wing attitudes occurred between the 1950s and 1990s work on authoritarianism and was led by UK psychologist Glenn D. Wilson. Although Wilson's first work on **conservatism** was early in the 1970s, many of the ideas he introduced are still used in individual differences research today. He first set out to describe a typical conservative, something Wilson (1973b) calls the 'conservative type'. He viewed this conservative type as a collection of attitudes that, when identified together, comprise the 'ideal' conservative. Wilson argues that these conservative attitudes include religious fundamentalism, pro-establishment politics, advocacy of strict rules and punishment, militarism, intolerance of minority groups, conventional tastes in art or clothing, restrictions on sexual activity, opposition to scientific progression and the tendency to be superstitious.

Also at this time, Wilson introduced a way of measuring this 'ideal conservative' by way of a scale called the Wilson–Patterson Attitude Inventory (G. Wilson, 1975; Wilson and Patterson, 1968). The Wilson–Patterson Attitude

Stop and think

Left-wing authoritarianism: the Loch Ness monster of political psychology

One debate that occurs between researchers is whether the concept of authoritarianism occurs only with right-wing attitudes, or whether authoritarianism also occurs with left-wing attitudes. For example, we can look to history and find some historical figure who seemed to be very authoritarian and had left-wing views (such as Stalin). Some researchers accept the concept of left-wing authoritarianism as a valid idea, while some suggest it is an ideological myth.

One research study, which presents such a concept as a myth, is based on the findings of Robert Altemeyer (1996). Altemeyer suggests that left-wing authoritarianism is similar to right-wing authoritarianism as it comprises authoritarian submission, authoritarian aggression and conventionalism. However, a difference between the two concepts is that, while right-wing authoritarians are concerned with submission, aggression and conventionalism in regard to established authorities, left-wing authoritarians are concerned with submission (submission to those authorities who are dedicated to overthrowing the established authorities), aggression (aggressiveness against the established authorities) and conventionalism (adhering to the behavioural norms of a revolutionary movement) in regard to a left-wing revolutionary cause. Altemeyer then tried to measure left-wing authoritarianism by devising a scale that contained a number of questions designed to measure different aspects of left-wing authoritarianism. However, after investigating data of 2,544 Canadian participants, Altemeyer (1996) concluded that he could not identify a single left-wing authoritarian among the sample,

as no one scored high enough on the scale. Consequently, Altemeyer became sceptical of left-wing authoritarianism, calling it the 'Loch Ness monster of political psychology'.

However, Duriez et al. (2005) recently presented evidence amongst West European samples that supports the existence of the left-wing authoritarian. Reflecting on Altemeyer's findings, these authors suggest that there were two problems with Altemeyer's work. First, Altemeyer's failure to identify left-wing authoritarians was caused by the lack of appropriate samples; Altemeyer, in looking at left-wing authoritarianism among a general sample, would have missed left-wing political activist groups where left-wing authoritarianism exists. The second problem that Duriez et al. identified is Altemeyer's use of conventionalism to define left-wing authoritarianism. Duriez et al. argue that conventionalism is a belief system that essentially opposes ideologies promoting societal change. Subsequently, Duriez et al. developed Altemeyer's left-wing authoritarianism by excluding items that referred to conventionalism and using items that reflected aggressiveness (e.g. 'A revolutionary movement is justified in using violence because the Establishment will never give up its power peacefully') and submission (e.g. 'A revolutionary movement is justified in demanding obedience and conformity of its members'). Using this new scale, among a group of left-wing extremists, Duriez et al. reported that a high number of individuals showed levels of left-wing authoritarianism. Therefore, Duriez and his colleagues suggest that perhaps this new study goes some way to suggesting that left-wing authoritarianism does exist.

Inventory (WPAI) contains 50 questions, in which respondents are asked to indicate whether they agree or are in favour of things such as the 'death penalty' and 'abortion'.

Based on research using this scale, Wilson (1985) proposed a model of conservatism that identifies one main dimension (see Figure 22.2). This main dimension is a 'conservatism versus liberalism' factor. In addition to this first dimension, the WPAI contains four additional main dimensions of conservatism: ethnocentrism–intolerance, anti-hedonism, religion–puritanism and militarism–punitiveness.

Simply put, ethnocentrism–intolerance is a conservative belief in racial superiority and a preference for one's own social group; that is, someone who is very intolerant of ethnic groups other than their own. For example, this sort of conservative might be racist. Anti-hedonism is a type of social permissiveness, a tendency to view pleasure or pleasurable things in society as wrong. Someone who is opposed

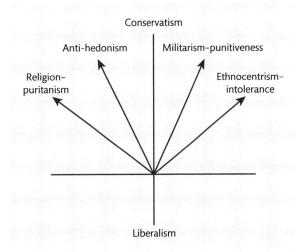

Figure 22.2 Glenn Wilson's model of conservatism.
Source: Based on Wilson (1985).

to sexual freedom of individuals or individuals drinking alcohol might be described as anti-hedonistic. Religion–puritanism refers to a particular approach to religion that emphasises a more traditional base to religiosity, such as a strict adherence for church authority and divine law or a belief in right-wing religious fundamentalism. Someone who believes that the church and the Bible are the only source of truth in the modern world would be showing the religion–puritanism dimension. Finally, militarism–punitiveness is a particularly hard-line political conservative dimension that centres on a willingness to protect the nation and its values. Someone who always believed in going to war at times of international disagreement would be showing militarism–punitiveness.

Profile

Glenn D. Wilson

Dr Glenn D. Wilson is a reader in Personality at the University of London's Institute of Psychiatry. His theory on conservatism remains one of the most important theoretical contributions to the psychological literature of right-wing attitudes, and he is still a widely cited author in the literature on conservatism.

Glenn Wilson was one of the first psychologists to bring psychology to the UK general population by talking about psychology on television in both discussion and factual programmes. He is a regular on TV programmes such as *Esther*, *The Time The Place*, *Vanessa* and *Trisha*. He has lectured widely abroad, having been a guest of the Italian Cultural Association and a visiting professor at California State University, Los Angeles; the University of Nevada; San Francisco State University and Stanford University. He was one of the forerunners of individual differences psychology in the United Kingdom as well as one of the foremost editors for the journal *Personality and Individual Differences*. He is an expert on individual differences, sexual behaviour and psychology applied to the performing arts; he has published more than 150 scientific articles and 25 books, including *The Psychology of Conservatism*, *The Experimental Study of Freudian Theories* (with H. J. Eysenck), *Love and Instinct*, *The Great Sex Divide* and *Psychology for Performing Artists*. He is the co-author of *Fame – The Psychology of Stardom*, *The Science of Love* and *CQ – Learn the Secret of Lasting Love*.

Stop and think

The dynamic theory of conservatism

Glenn Wilson (1973a) provides a very social-orientated explanation of how conservative attitudes develop; however, elsewhere in his 1973 book, he suggests another theory of conservatism that is more reminiscent of some of the psychodynamic theories of Adorno and the cognitive emphasis of Altemeyer. Wilson suggests that the conservative person is typified by those individuals who experience threat or anxiety in the face of uncertain stimuli (innovation, ambiguity, risk) and respond to uncertainty (freedom of choice, needs and desires). It is these ideas of uncertainty, and the feeling of vulnerability, that Wilson argues are fundamental to the attitude that forms the conservative person.

Wilson also suggests that it is the understanding of these two concepts that allows the syndrome to be traced down to a single underlying psychological factor. Fear of uncertainty may reveal itself as superstitious behaviour. Fear of anarchy manifests itself as right-wing politics. Fear of having to make decisions can be recognised as rigid morality. Wilson sees the conservative individual as typified by behaviours designed to avoid uncertain stimuli, an unwillingness to be placed in situations where novelty exists and a dislike for social disorganisation.

Wilson summarises the dynamic theory of conservatism. He argues that conservative attitudes and behaviours occur as the result of ego-defensive behaviour. Conservative attitudes allow the individual to control the external world, perceptual processes, stimuli preferences and inner feelings and desires. The individual imposes control on their needs by surrendering to external rules; this behaviour causes internal conflict. The major implication of this theory would seem to be that a cluster of conservative attitudes or behaviours cannot be explained by rational thought processes. Rather, there are motivational factors underlying the organisation of the personality of the conservative individual.

Empirical consideration of this theory is sparse and has mainly concentrated upon the theory of uncertainty that surrounds the conservative individual. Wilson, *el al.* (1973) found that conservatives tended to give negative ratings to complex pictures. Webster and Stewart (1973) found a need in conservatives for order, so as to avoid role conflict. Wilson (1973a) found conservatism to be positively correlated to fear of death. Some studies link dislike of uncertainty to conservatism, with conservatives tending to give negative ratings to complex stimuli and positive ratings to simple stimuli, such as giving positive ratings to traditional and classical art and negative ratings to abstract art (Gillies and Campbell, 1985; Maltby, 1997; Wilson *et al.*, 1973). However, no research has fully examined the dynamic theory of conservatism by testing these ideas, particularly the conflicts that may be essential to the development of these attitudes.

Theoretical perspectives on conservatism

So, what reasons does Wilson give for the existence of these conservative attitudes? You will remember that Adorno and his colleagues suggested that there were psychodynamic explanations for authoritarianism (i.e. interaction of various conscious and unconscious mental or emotional processes), while Altemeyer concentrated more on some of the thought processes surrounding right-wing authoritarianism. Primarily, Wilson concentrates on more social reasons for conservatism. Wilson (1973b) suggests four primary theoretical viewpoints of conservatism (see Figure 22.3).

- **Resistance to change** – a preference for traditional and existing institutions in society whereby social change, be it historical, scientific or technological, is resisted by the conservative. Institutions such as the church or the monarchy are traditional and existing institutions are usually preferred by the conservative.
- **Tendency to play safe** – Wilson suggests that conservative people will show 'a tendency to play safe' and reflect a disposition to be moderate, cautious and avoid risks.
- **Reflecting the distinction between generations** – Wilson views conservatism as a reflection of the distinction between the generations, evident from scores on conservatism measures that increase markedly with age. For example, Wilson would suggest this is why parents sometimes tend to be more conservative than their children.

- **Internalisation of parental values** – here, Wilson describes the individual who is thought to create a framework of attitudes and behaviours acceptable to society, passed on from their parents, peers and social institutions. Wilson suggests there is some consensus in society as to what behaviours are considered to be correct and respectable. Consequently, conservatism can be seen as the extent to which consensus can be absorbed.

Wilson sees the conservative person as influenced heavily by the social world around them, influenced by traditional institutions, tending not to want to take risks in the external world, undertaking their parents' values and becoming more conservative with age. This emphasis in Wilson's work at first contrasts with Adorno and Altemeyer's perspectives; however, you will remember (from Chapter 16) that individual differences researchers prefer to see contrasting viewpoints as complementary. As such, we would very much see these three viewpoints as providing a good theoretical basis to understanding right-wing attitudes.

Social dominance orientation

On 1 December 1955, Rosa Parks, a tailor's assistant, got on a bus in the racially segregated area of Montgomery, Alabama, in the United States. At the time, the first 10 rows of a bus were reserved for white passengers. Rosa, a black woman, sat down in these first 10 rows. As the bus travelled along its route, more people got on, and the 'white' section of the bus filled up. When another white man boarded, the driver ordered Rosa Parks and three other black people seated next to her to move. Parks refused to move and was arrested. This act of resistance is a seminal event in the civil rights movement. In December 1956, the US Supreme Court decided that bus segregation violated the Constitution. This energised the civil rights movement, and it led to the Civil Rights Act of 1964. However, many political commentators would note that, throughout the world, there are still huge differences in civil rights, whether it is based on race, gender or even religion. So how do such conventions come into existence, and how do some social groups maintain social dominance?

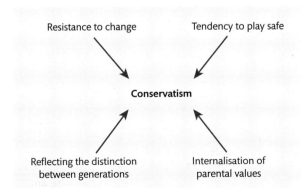

Figure 22.3 Glenn Wilson's four theoretical descriptions of conservatism.

To what extent do the criteria for what is socially acceptable frequently change?

Source: Alamy Images/Janine Wiedel Photolibrary

Theory of social dominance

So far, we have covered right-wing authoritarianism and conservatism, whose theoretical explanations range from psychodynamic to social orientation. However, one more area emerges with which to consider right-wing attitudes – **social dominance orientation**. Two US theorists, Jim Sidanius and Felicia Pratto, presented **social dominance theory** in 1999. For Sidanius and Pratto, social dominance theory would explain why ethnic minority couples are almost twice

as likely to be rejected for a home loan in the United States as white couples are and why a black man is more likely to be found guilty, and to receive a longer prison sentence, for committing the same crime as a white man.

This theory argues that humans are predisposed to form a social hierarchy. Within social dominance theory, most manifestations of oppression – be it sexism, racism or any other prejudice – are based on social hierarchy. Within this theory, attitudes in favour of social dominance are considered right wing.

Sidanius and Pratto (1999) suggest three basic concepts underlying social dominance theory that help psychologists to identify and understand the intrapersonal, interpersonal, intergroup and institutional processes that produce and maintain a group-based social hierarchy. You may need to be comfortable with the terms 'in-group' and 'out-group' before reading on; if so, see Stop and think: In-groups and out-groups.

Social dominance theory suggests that the production and maintenance of group-based social hierarchy is the result of three processes (see Figure 22.4):

- **Aggregated *individual* discrimination** – these are simple and sometimes unnoticeable individual acts of discrimination by one individual against another. This process might be seen in someone making a racist comment at work, or when an employer does not hire someone for a job on gender grounds. Aggregated individual discrimination refers to the total number of acts of individual discrimination occurring each day, every day, across a number of social situations.

- **Aggregated *institutional* discrimination** – group-based social hierarchy is also a result of the procedures and actions of social institutions, such as the political organisations, church, courts and schools. Procedures that cause institutional discrimination may be deliberate and overt, as in the case of political parties, or they may be subtle and unintended, as in schools that encourage group-based social hierarchy through numerous interactions between different teachers and different children. Imagine your typical American teen movie, in

Stop and think

In-groups and out-groups

In the section 'Social dominance orientation', you will notice that we have used the terms 'in-group' and 'out-group'. These two terms are often used by social psychologists to understand the complex social world. In the social psychology theory on groups, individuals are thought to place other individuals into social groups on the basis of their similarities and differences. Put simply,

individuals who are viewed as similar to the person tend to be placed within their in-group. Individuals who are viewed as different to the person tend to be placed within an out-group. Social psychologists, therefore, suggest that this 'social categorisation' of individuals into in- and out-groups helps individuals to understand their social world and forms the basis of intergroup contact and conflict.

Figure 22.4 Social dominance orientation.

which we can see that schools form certain social categories, with the popular kids at the top and the 'geeks' and the 'nerds' at the bottom. Although children decide much of this social hierarchy, schools help to form it by having sports teams, cheerleaders and class presidents. Sidanius and Pratto (1999) argue that *aggregated institutional discrimination* can also result in producing and maintaining social status hierarchy.

- **Behavioural asymmetry** – this process is based on the fact that members of dominant and subordinate groups will act differently in a wide variety of situations. These behavioural differences will both contribute to, and be reinforced by, the group-based hierarchical relationships within the social system. Often, members of subordinate groups *actively* participate in and contribute to their own subordination. For example, it is claimed that ethnic minority gangs in the United States often contribute to their own oppression by killing members of their own ethnic group through supplying drugs or through the use of guns. This fact then leads members of the US white majority to misconstrue all people of an ethnic minority group as dangerous and to feel legitimate in continuing with the subordination of that group. Consequently, political leaders of many ethnic minorities concentrate on promoting education and discouraging gun and drug use to stop the subordination of their own ethnic minority. These different forms of behavioural asymmetry are thought to be important because basic social hierarchies are not simply maintained by the oppressive activities of dominants, nor the compliance of subordinates; they are cooperative behaviours that *lead to* intergroup oppression and group-based social hierarchies.

The measurement of social dominance orientation

There is no simple way that researchers can measure the three aspects of the production and maintenance of group-based social hierarchy. For example, it would be impos-

sible for psychologists to measure or observe *aggregated individual* discrimination in a society, as these are unnoticeable individual acts of discrimination by one individual against another. Similarly, it would be impossible to measure *behavioural asymmetry*, as this would involve measuring numerous variables to assess the number of ways that dominant and subordinate groups act differently in a wide variety of situations.

Therefore, the measurement of social dominance has focused on measuring individual attitudes towards social dominance; this variable is called social dominance orientation. Someone who had a social dominance orientation would have a belief in group-based social hierarchy and a preference for inequality among social groups.

A variety of techniques have been used to measure social orientation dominance. The difference in these techniques often depends on how the scale is applied to the sample. So, for example, Pratto *et al.* (1994) presented a 4-item version because the study involved a general US sample, whereas Guimond *et al.* (2003) used a 10-item version because they were using the scale in a non-US sample. However, to illustrate how social dominance orientation is measured, we will use the 16-item measure presented by Sidanius *et al.* (1996). This measure of social dominance orientation contains statements such as:

- Some groups of people are more worthy than others. [item 1]
- To get ahead in life, it is sometimes necessary to step on other groups. [item 4]
- Inferior groups should stay in their place. [item 7]

Sidanius *et al.* (1996) tested social dominance orientation using European–American and African–American university students. They found that white European American students were more likely than students from ethnic minorities to support the social hierarchy in their sociopolitical beliefs. For example, they were more likely to agree with statements that reflect conservative beliefs or classical racism. They would see reasons for civil disturbance as a

Stop and think

Right-wing attitudes

- Consider the three theories of right-wing attitudes – right-wing authoritarianism, conservatism and social dominance. Which theory do you find most represents your own understanding of right-wing attitudes in your country? Write down the reasons for your choice.

- Within each of the theories of right-wing attitudes, theories based on psychodynamic, cognitive and social psychology approaches are provided to explain each right-wing attitude. To which perspective do you lend most credence?

reflection of criminal activity rather than an expression against oppression. Similarly, they would then be opposed to redistributing wealth to help the poor.

With this type of evidence, social dominance orientation has been used in individual differences research as a further indicator of right-wing attitudes.

Right-wing attitudes and personality

So, how is personality related to right-wing attitudes? Within the literature examining right–wing attitudes and personality, there is a general split depending on where in the world the study has been carried out. Generally, when studies are carried out in the United Kingdom, the examination of right-wing attitudes and personality tends to focus on the relationship between conservatism and Eysenck's model of personality. In the United States and Europe, researchers tend to look at the relationship between right-wing authoritarianism or social domination orientation and the five-factor model of personality.

Right-wing attitudes and Eysenck's theory of personality

Most of the research looking at conservatism and personality has considered how Glenn Wilson's measure and model of conservatism are thought to be related to personality. A lot of this analysis and work was done in the 1970s and 1980s; however, today it remains one of the more comprehensive theories of conservatism, particularly in its proposed relationship to personality.

Within Eysenckian theory, right-wing attitudes are linked to psychoticism. Hans Eysenck and Michael Eysenck (1985a) define the nature of psychoticism as comprising cruel, insensitive, unfriendly and antisocial traits. Furthermore, within Eysenck's theory, all attitudes are identified as either tender-minded or tough-minded. Tender-minded attitudes are thought to result from conditioning, whereas tough-minded

attitudes are thought to result from the lack of conditioning. Scores on the psychoticism dimensions are also thought to be related to conditioning; individuals scoring low on psychoticism show that they condition more easily. Consequently, it can be argued that attitudes can be readily linked to the psychoticism dimension (Eysenck, 1975; 1976b).

You will remember that, within Wilson's research on conservatism, one main factor emerges from the Wilson–Patterson Attitude Inventory; this is the conservatism versus liberalism factor (see Figure 22.5). In addition to this main factor, four other primary conservative dimensions emerge. These dimensions are ethnocentrism-intolerance (racial superiority; a preference for one's own social group), anti-hedonism (dislike of social permissiveness; a tendency to view pleasure as bad, or even to oppose sexual freedom), religion–puritanism (religious conservatism; right-wing religious fundamentalism, a concern for divine law and church authority) and militarism-punitiveness (political dimension; willingness to protect the nation and its values).

However, alongside this description of attitude structure, Wilson (1985) suggests that there is a tender-minded versus tough-minded factor that cuts across the main conservatism factor. Remember, tender-minded attitudes reflect low psychoticism and tough-minded attitudes reflect high psychoticism. The four different aspects of conservatism can be readily linked to psychoticism personality dimensions, but in different directions. Ethnocentrism-intolerance and militarism–punitiveness (that fall to the right of the main conservatism factor diagram) would be thought to be positively related to psychoticism, while anti-hedonism and religion–puritanism (that fall to the left of the diagram) would be thought to be negatively related to psychoticism.

Unfortunately, little evidence has been used to test this model by looking at the four dimensions of conservatism and its relationship to psychoticism. Pearson and Sheffield (1976) found no relationship between psychoticism and any of the dimensions of Wilson's model, and this research has left the accuracy of Wilson's theory unclear. Rather, researchers tend to concentrate on research into Eysenck's

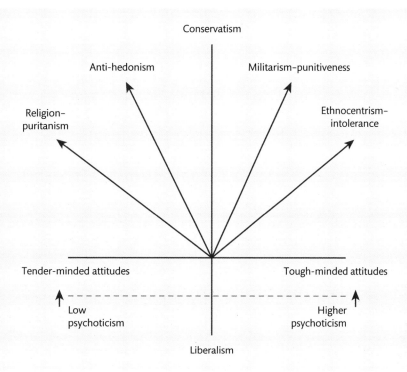

Figure 22.5 Glenn Wilson's model of conservatism incorporating Eysenck's psychoticism dimension.
Source: Based on Wilson (1985).

personality correlates of the main dimension of conservatism, but, again, results are inconsistent. Several studies in the United Kingdom by British psychologists have examined the relationship between general conservatism and psychoticism:

- Wilson and Brazendale (1973) found the main scale from conservatism correlates significantly with psychoticism.
- Kline and Cooper (1984) found that the conservatism scale was negatively related to psychoticism.
- Pearson and Sheffield (1976) found no relationship between general conservatism and psychoticism.

For the other aspects of right-wing attitudes and Eysenck's personality theory, there has been a lot less research. However, again findings are inconsistent in relation to psychoticism. Altemeyer (1998) found a significant positive association between the social dominance orientation and psychoticism, but not between right-wing authoritarianism and psychoticism.

Of course, Wilson's model of conservatism would predict such inconsistencies. Within Wilson's model it would be expected that tough-minded aspects of conservatism (ethnocentrism and militarism) would correlate positively with psychoticism, and tender-minded aspects of conservatism (anti-hedonism and religion–puritanism) would be negatively associated with psychoticism. Furthermore, it would be expected that general conservatism

(considered to be in the middle of these four conservative domains) would share no relationship with psychoticism. However, we get into dangerous territory if we start finding support for a model just because we find no relationship between two dimensions – we might as well have 'low to high custard-eating' running through the middle of the model where tender-minded and tough-minded attitudes are located (assuming that custard-eating is not related to conservatism). However, the fact that authors have sometimes reported a relationship between conservatism and psychoticism is of interest, and the fact that the five-factor model presents a two-factor version of psychoticism (agreeableness and conscientiousness) might help us further in this consideration.

Five-factor theory of personality and conservatism

The relationship between right-wing attitudes and the five-factor model of personality is more speculative than Wilson's model of conservatism, but more consistent. You will remember that the five-factor personality model comprises five personality types:

- openness (perceptive, sophisticated, knowledgeable, cultured, artistic, curious, analytical, liberal traits);

- conscientiousness (practical, cautious, serious, reliable, organised, careful, dependable, hardworking, ambitious traits);
- extraversion (sociable, talkative, active, spontaneous, adventurous, enthusiastic, person-oriented, assertive traits);
- agreeableness (warm, trustful, courteous, agreeable, co-operative traits);
- neuroticism (emotional, anxious, depressive, self-conscious, worrying traits).

What is important to remember before moving on to studies that have looked at right-wing attitudes and the five-factor model of personality is that there are clear overlaps between the three-factor and the five-factor models of personality. Apart from both models having measures of extraversion and neuroticism, you will remember that agreeableness and conscientious personality traits can be viewed as a two-dimensional view of psychoticism.

When considering right-wing authoritarianism, individual differences researchers such as US psychologists Robert Altemeyer (1996), J. Corey Butler (2000) and Gerard Saucier (2000), as well as Australian psychologists Patrick Heaven and Sandra Bucci (2001), have found right-wing authoritarianism to be negatively related to openness to experience. Additionally, Heaven and Bucci found that right-wing authoritarianism was positively related to conscientiousness. When considering conservatism, Belgian psychologists Alain Van Hiel and Ivan Mervielde (2004) and US psychologist Saucier (2000) have found conservatism to be negatively related to openness to experience.

Heaven and Bucci found social dominance orientation to be negatively related to openness to experience and agreeableness.

What is important to note is that one of the main findings across these studies is the relationship between right-wing attitudes and the two personality dimensions of agreeableness and conscientiousness. This finding is consistent with predictions, using the three-factor model of personality, that psychoticism is related to right-wing attitudes. Furthermore, the five-factor model of personality studies importantly adds to the findings of studies within the three-factor model in suggesting that people with right-wing attitudes are negatively related with openness.

Overall, despite the use of different measures of right-wing attitudes, and different personality theories, the collection of studies carried out using the major personality theories from 1970 to the present day suggests two things. The first is that right-wing attitudes are related to psychoticism (or agreeableness or conscientiousness) in some way. However, the direction of the relationship remains a tantalising proposition. Whether this relationship is positive or negative may depend on the dimension of right-wing attitudes used. For example, in Wilson's model, different dimensions of conservatism are expected to be associated with psychoticism in different ways. Second, contradictory findings are seen in the five-factor model of personality, with conscientiousness being positively associated with authoritarianism but negatively related to the social dominance orientation.

What does emerge from the research evidence with right-wing attitudes and personality is the importance of openness. The most consistent finding among studies is that people with right-wing attitudes tend not to have openness personality traits. These findings suggest that people who hold right-wing attitudes tend to be less perceptive, less sophisticated, less knowledgeable, less cultured, less artistic, less curious and less analytical; perhaps not surprisingly, they have fewer liberal traits. As such, openness, rather than psychoticism, might be seen as a consistent factor in right-wing attitudes.

Critical consideration of right-wing attitudes theory

Overall, the three theories present somewhat different views of right-wing attitudes. Further, each of the theories presents exciting explanations of these attitudes. The first

---

Stop and think

Conservatism

- Discuss Glenn Wilson's model of conservatism. Discuss whether researchers should find a statistical relationship between psychoticism and right-wing attitudes, and whether the occasional absence of any significant relationship between the two dimensions lends any support to the model.
- Research findings suggest that people who hold right-wing attitudes tend to have fewer openness

traits. That is, they tend to be less perceptive, less sophisticated, less knowledgeable, less cultured, less artistic, less curious and less analytical; perhaps not surprisingly, they have fewer liberal traits. How do these findings fit with Adorno's psychodynamic, Altemeyer's cognitive, and Wilson's and Pratto and Sidanius' social psychology explanations of right-wing attitudes?

two theories of (right-wing authoritarianism and conservatism) certainly provide dynamic explanations of right-wing attitudes, suggesting that difficult thought processes, or uncertainty, underpin these sets of attitudes. Clearly, Adorno's, Wilson's and Altemeyer's work has a inspired rich vein of research. Further, the social dominance orientation provides an exciting context to consider the development of right-wing attitudes.

The main obstacle in this area for the researcher is not only that right-wing attitudes may cover a range of different opinions across cultures but also that this area of study is vulnerable to changes over time. Clearly, different cultures will have different ideas of what is a right-wing attitude. For instance, asking people whether they adhere to church authority might still be a good indication of general conservatism in the west; however, in countries where the church is outlawed – as was the case in the former Soviet Union – adherence to church authority might be seen as a revolutionary attitude.

Such vulnerabilities also occur when measuring right-wing attitudes over time. We have already seen how Adorno's view of authoritarianism was considered old-fashioned. Also, if we consider some of the original items of the Wilson–Patterson Attitude Inventory (WPAI), we can see that this is still the case. In the 1970s individuals who didn't like nudist camps were considered as conservative, while today people might not like them as they're considered rather twee or old-fashioned. Furthermore, the item 'fluoridation' (which refers to fluoridation of water) within the 1970s WPAI stands out as rather innocuous in today's society. These problems, however, should not always be considered as serious as they seem. In simple terms, the changing nature of conservatism leads to continuous updating of conservatism measures, though it does mean that comparisons across time and cultures are difficult. Even social dominance theory, which is a recent development, may suffer from this problem in the future. Clearly, socially dominant groups and socially compliant groups will change over time. None the less, these are not compelling reasons for ignoring or criticising the work; rather, you should treat them as necessary considerations in a field of study. This is what several academics have done with the WPAI over the years, and recent studies in the United Kingdom by Lewis and Maltby (2000) and Maltby (1997) and in Australia by psychologists Truett et al. (1992) suggest that many of the items from the WPAI can still be used as a reliable and valid measure of conservative attitudes.

However, one question remains: how different are these different right-wing attitudes? Clearly, we have grouped these different theories under the same umbrella of right-wing attitudes, and we might consider that some of these ideas are reflecting similar processes. For example, when considered together, right-wing authoritarianism, conservatism and social dominance are considered side by side; they are usually significantly correlated and, more important, load on the same factor (Altemeyer, 1998; Kline and Cooper, 1984). Also, as we have seen, all these aspects are found to be negatively associated with openness to experience. Clearly, there are some overlaps between the concepts; however, some authors have argued that not only are the size of correlations not large enough to suggest that they are measuring the same thing, but there are distinctions that can be made between the concepts.

Altemeyer (1998) and Heaven and Bucci (2001) provide a breakdown of the differences between right-wing authoritarianism and social dominance orientation. Right-wing authoritarianism is thought to have rigid thought processes and lack cognitive complexity. The authors describe right-wing authoritarianism as describing people who lack imagination, have a need for structure and order and are orderly and accepting of traditional values. However, they contrast this rather passive character with a person who has a more socially aggressive social dominance orientation. Both these sets of authors go on to describe those who are high in social dominance orientations as tending to be uncooperative, lacking in sympathy, cold, aggressive and hostile. Clearly, Wilson's multidimensional model of conservatism crosses many of these boundaries, ranging from more tender-minded to more tough-minded attitudes. Therefore, certain aspects may overlap with both these dimensions; for example, social dominance orientation and the ethnocentrism–intolerance dimensions of Wilson's model of conservatism.

However, the possible differences and dynamics are also apparent when considering the relationship between right-wing attitudes and personality. When it comes to considering how psychoticism, from the three-factor personality model, and conscientiousness, from the five–factor model, are related to right-wing attitudes, researchers have sometimes found significant correlations – but in opposing directions. An explanation of these contrary findings could be provided by Wilson's model of conservatism and applied to all right-wing attitudes. Wilson draws the distinction between tender-minded versus tough-minded right-wing attitudes and their relationship with psychoticism (tender-minded attitudes will be negatively related to psychoticism, and tough-minded attitudes will be positively related to psychoticism). Different aspects of right-wing attitudes can be readily linked to the psychoticism personality dimension, but sometimes in different directions. Therefore, this might be a consideration of contrary findings for the future.

As the last paragraph shows, there might still be a lot more work to do. Despite these concerns, overall, there has been a lot of work trying to extract some psychological understanding about right-wing attitudes from a very difficult area of study. However, the theories of right-wing authoritarianism, conservatism and social dominance all provide interesting and dynamic explanations of why people adopt, or fail to adopt, right-wing attitudes in society. Figure 22.6 perhaps best summarises personality and individual differences approaches to understanding and explaining right-wing attitudes. As you can see we have identified three types of right-wing attitudes: right-wing authoritarianism, conservatism and social dominance orientation. Clearly, all these three approaches overlap. Surrounding these different theories are the explanations of these attitudes. While psychodynamic and cognitive theories were used very much to explain right-wing authoritarianism (and sometimes conservatism; see Wilson's dynamic theory of conservatism), social and cultural explanations are used to explain both conservatism and social dominance orientation. Finally, at the centre of all the attitudes, openness and sometimes psychoticism are personality traits that are seen as central to personality explanations of right-wing attitudes.

Figure 22.6 A summary of personality and individual differences approaches to understanding right-wing attitudes.

Religion

In 2003, French President Jacques Chirac proposed a law banning conspicuous religious symbols from schools and caused a debate about the wearing of religious head-scarves in schools. Also in 2003, Pope John Paul II visited the eastern border of Roman Catholic Croatia, which is near Serbia, and where there are still ethnic tensions after the conflicts in the 1990s. Here he called for reconciliation in this part of Eastern Europe. Again in 2003, while reality

television shows were attracting large audiences in some countries, in Italy, a spiritual offering on prime-time television (a series of films made for television based on the Bible or the lives of popes and saints) was drawing in 35 per cent of Italian households. Then, in 2005, a poll conducted by the Pew Forum on Religion and Public Life among US respondents found that 72 per cent agreed that the president of the United States should have strong religious beliefs.

Religion is still an important aspect of modern society; its role in people's lives has been of interest to personality and individual differences theorists and researchers. Religion is also an important aspect of many people's lives, so we can only scratch the surface; however, within this discussion, we will outline how religion has been usefully measured in psychology, how it relates to mental health and how we can understand the relationship between religion and mental health within a variety of personality and individual differences variables.

Dimensions of religiosity

However, before proceeding, we need to provide a clear understanding of how psychologists have defined religion. Clearly, religion takes on different meanings and consequences for a variety of people. There are thought to be about 10,000 religions in the world; the major religions are Hinduism, Buddhism, Jainism, Sikhism, Taoism, Confucianism, Shintoism, Zoroastrianism, Judaism, Christianity and Islam. It would be a really hard job to measure all these different approaches in the world; however, a stream of research that started in the late 1960s has concentrated on the measurement of religion. We are going to concentrate on two areas of religiosity that have been most useful to the psychology of religion.

Religious orientation

The first major area of consideration is religious orientation. Religious orientation is the *approach* that a person takes towards religion. Between 1966 and 1967, US psychologist Gordon Willard Allport published two papers (Allport, 1966; Allport and Ross, 1967) suggesting that there are two main religious orientations: an intrinsic orientation towards religion and an extrinsic orientation towards religion.

Allport described individuals that have an intrinsic orientation towards religion as wholly committed to their religious beliefs, and the influence of religion is evident in every aspect of their life. For this type of person, religion is deeply personal and is important in all areas of their life. Therefore, they would think about religion a lot, and they would see religion as being a part of their work, social and family life.

In measuring this aspect of religiosity, we will use examples from the Age Universal Religious Orientation Scale (Gorsuch and Venable, 1983), which was so called because its items were written to be applicable to both adults and children. Here are some questions on the scale that someone who has an intrinsic orientation towards religion would agree with:

1   My whole approach to life is based on my religion.
2   I have often had a strong sense of God's presence.
3   My religion is important because it answers many questions about the meaning of life.

On the other hand, those who demonstrate an extrinsic orientation towards religion have been described as using religion for these purposes:

● **Protection and consolation for the individual** – here the individual uses religion to make them feel that they are protected from all that is wrong in the world. Individuals, here, use religion as a protection from the harsh realities of the world, and believe religion can console them when things go wrong.
● **Participation in an in-group and social status for the individual** – religion allows the person who is a member of a religious group to feel they belong, and that they are part of a community; it enables them to establish friendships.

However, later researchers, such as US researcher Frederick T. L. Leong (e.g. Leong and Zachar, 1990), have shown that, among Australian and US samples, measurement of an extrinsic orientation towards religion may, indeed, be split into two areas: *extrinsic-personal* (where

aspects apply to the individual's protection and consolation) and *extrinsic-social* (where aspects apply to the individual's religious participation in an in-group and social status).

Again, we can illustrate the sort of questions used to measure these extrinsic dimensions from the Age Universal Religious Orientation Scale. Someone who has an extrinsic-personal orientation towards religion would agree with questions such as:

● I pray mainly to gain relief and protection.
● What religion offers me most is comfort in times of trouble and sorrow.

Someone who has an extrinsic-social orientation towards religion would agree with questions such as:

● I go to church mostly to spend time with my friends.
● I go to church because it helps me make friends.
● I go to church mainly because I enjoy seeing people I know there.

Although this psychological search for the main ways in which individuals approach religion spans 40 years, this distinction between intrinsic and extrinsic approaches to religion has been the most useful to the psychology of religion, particularly when considering aspects of religion and mental health and religion and personality. However, US psychologist Kenneth I. Pargament has something more to add to this picture.

Profile

Gordon Willard Allport

Gordon Willard Allport was born on 11 November 1897 in Montezuma, Indiana, USA. Between 1915 and 1919 he attended Harvard as an undergraduate with interests in psychology and social ethics, and between 1919 and 1920 he taught English and sociology in Constantinople (Istanbul). In 1920 he travelled to Vienna to meet with Sigmund Freud. When Allport arrived at the meeting, Freud simply sat and waited for him to begin. Allport later said that he was nervous in the presence of the great man, and so he blurted out an observation that he had made on his way to the meeting. He told Freud that he had seen a little boy on the bus who was upset at having to sit where an old and dirty man had sat previously. Allport speculated whether this behaviour was likely to be something the boy had learned from a neat and seemingly rather domineering mother. Freud instead took the experience to be an expression of a deep, unconscious process in Allport's mind, and said, 'And was that little boy you?' Apparently, for Allport, this was a turning point in his career. He began to think

that psychoanalytic psychology sometimes tries to overanalyse situations. Allport developed an approach that emphasised less psychological depth than Freud's, but looked for more meaning than was emphasised by approaches such as behaviourism. Between 1920 and 1967, Allport taught at several universities, including Cambridge and Harvard. Between 1936 and 1946 he held a Chair of the Psychology Department at Harvard. In the late 1930s and during the Second World War, Allport served the American Psychological Association as head of an Emergency Committee in Psychology to deal with refugee scholars from Europe. In 1939 he was President of the APA, and he served as editor of the *Journal of Abnormal and Social Psychology* from 1937 to 1948.

Allport's main academic works are *Personality: A Psychological Interpretation* (1937) and *The Nature of Prejudice* (1954). In 1964, he received the Distinguished Scientific Contribution Award to Psychology from the American Psychological Association.

Religious coping

The second main distinction in religion is in the realm of coping. The pioneer in this field was Kenneth I. Pargament, who is at Bowling Green State University in the United States. Pargament became interested in the way that researchers in religion had identified how different people use religion in different ways to deal with the harsh realities of the world. Pargament, as he notes in his book, *The Psychology of Religion and Coping* (1997), was particularly struck by interviews in *Life* magazine in 1989 from survivors of a recent air crash in the United States. He noticed that, in the interviews, many of the survivors reported showing feelings or beliefs about religion. For example, one passenger reported praying to God while another grasped tightly to their Bible.

Pargament noted that we all go through dramatic and traumatic events in our lives, and he became interested in examining how religion helps some people cope with such events. Specifically, Pargament went on to explore religious coping and the ways a religious person uses religion to deal with stressful events in their life. He argues that there are two main aspects to religious coping: *positive* and *negative* religious coping. Positive religious coping is a positive response to stress; it is deeply personal and involves some aspect of religious growth. An example of religious coping would be a religious couple's responses to losing a child during pregnancy. Positive religious coping would involve the parents accepting the loss of the child as part of God's plan, and that clearly God had a reason for not allowing the child to be born. Negative religious coping involves the person interpreting the stress as a punishment from God and may often lead to the person questioning God's power or love. In our example of the couple losing the child during pregnancy, if the couple's interpretation of losing the child were that it was a punishment from God for something they had done wrong, then this would be negative religious coping.

Pargament and his colleagues also developed a psychological test to measure these two types of religious coping: The *brief R(eligious)-COPE* (Pargament *et al.*, 1998a). In this measure, respondents are asked to think about the most stressful event they experienced in the last 3 years and to indicate on the questionnaire whether they felt some of the mentioned feelings. Someone who uses positive religious coping towards religion would agree with items such as:

1. tried to see how God might be trying to strengthen me in this situation;
2. focused on religion to stop worrying about my problems;
3. tried to put my plans into action together with God.

Someone who uses negative religious coping towards religion would agree with items such as:

1. wondered whether God had abandoned me;
2. wondered what I did for God to punish me;
3. wondered whether my church had abandoned me.

Pargament's work gives us two ways by which to understand religiosity. It is worth reminding you that we, in

The theory of religious coping suggests that acts such as prayer can help alleviate stress and worries. Try to think of religious attitudes and behaviours that may help and hinder mental health.

Source: Photodisc/Photolink/M. Freeman

no way, see these dimensions as the only approaches to religion and the only ways of dealing with stress; rather, the concepts of religious orientation and religious coping are essential ideas that have helped psychologists to understand the relationship between religion and mental health and between religion and personality.

Religion and mental health

You will remember that one of the main aims here is to explore the relationship between individual differences variables and mental health. There is no topic more worthy of this exploration than that of religiosity and its effects on mental health. So, how is religion related to mental health? You may be surprised to hear that religion is related to mental health; but why? Surely Jesus is reported in the Bible to have healed people by his touch. In 1905, Pope Pius IX requested 'to submit to a proper process' the most spectacular of the cures of Lourdes. Mention the name 'Lourdes' to anyone today and it is associated with famous religious pilgrimages in Southern France where miraculous cures happen. In 2000 and 2002, both CNN and *Time Magazine* ran segments on the power of prayer, particularly questioning whether patients can be helped by strangers praying for them without their knowledge. Within the psychology of religion, the suggestion of such relationships is not new. The relationship between religiosity and mental health dominates much of the psychology of religion literature, in which many researchers debate the issue of whether religion has beneficial or detrimental effects on the mental health of individuals.

Our insight into this area begins with the two approaches to religion just outlined: religious orientation and religious coping. With these two measures of religiosity, the story is relatively simple.

Generally, studies and reviews are consistent in finding a significant positive correlation between an intrinsic orientation towards religion and better mental health, and a significant positive correlation between extrinsic orientation towards religion (be it extrinsic-personal or extrinsic-social) and poorer mental health. Hundreds of studies have examined the relationship between religious orientation and mental health. However, consider these examples of the findings:

- a significant negative correlation between intrinsic orientation and anxiety and a significant positive correlation between extrinsic orientation and anxiety (Baker and Gorsuch, 1982; Bergin *et al.*, 1987; Sturgeon and Hamley, 1979);
- a significant negative correlation between intrinsic orientation and depression and a significant positive correlation between extrinsic orientation and depression (Genia, 1996; Genia and Shaw, 1991; Koenig, 1995; Nelson, 1989; 1990; Park *et al.*, 1990; Watson *et al.*, 1989).

A similar picture emerges when considering religious coping and mental health. In the United States, Pargament *et al.* (1998b) report that positive coping is associated with fewer symptoms of psychological distress, while negative religious coping was associated with higher levels of depression and reporting of psychological symptoms. In the United Kingdom, Maltby and Day (2004) found positive religious coping to be related to lower depression, anxiety, social dysfunction, somatic symptoms, stress and negative affect as well as to higher positive affect and life satisfaction. Furthermore, these authors found negative religious coping to be related to higher depression, anxiety, social dysfunction, somatic symptoms, stress and negative affect.

Figure 22.7 summarises these overall findings within the models of religiosity (religious orientation and religious

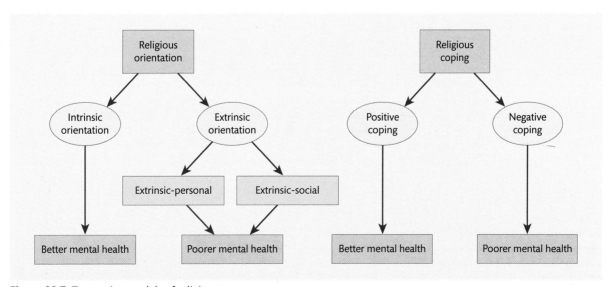

Figure 22.7 Two major models of religion.

coping) and mental health. But what are the reasons for these findings? Well, an overview of these findings depends on interpreting these two approaches to religion. This interpretation focuses on adaptive and maladaptive approaches to religion and religious coping, whereby adaptive approaches lead to better mental health, and maladaptive approaches lead to poorer mental heath. In the general coping literature, one way that this distinction between adaptive and maladaptive approaches is illustrated is by the distinction between problem- and emotion-focused coping. **Problem-focused coping** is where the individual experiences stress and tries to cope with it by recognising and addressing the problem (i.e. if a person is feeling stressed about an exam, they will do some more revision). **Emotion-focused coping** is where the individual experiences stress and reacts to the problem emotionally, and they may spend time talking about the problem rather than taking action to address it (i.e. if a person is feeling stressed about an exam, they will spend their time complaining to their friends about the exam). It is generally accepted that individuals who use problem-focused coping suffer from fewer mental health problems, while individuals who use emotion-focused coping suffer from more mental health problems.

We can apply this distinction of adaptive and maladaptive approaches to religiosity. We would suggest that intrinsic and positive religious coping represent an adaptive approach to religion. Intrinsic religiosity is a real and useful commitment to religion through which the person positively engages in religion and is able to understand life's hardships. Positive religious coping involves the individual responding positively, and actively making plans to deal with the stressor. It is, then, no surprise that someone for whom religion is very fulfilling, enabling them to deal with stress effectively, tends to suffer less from mental health worries. For example, someone who prays a lot has many opportunities to share their concerns with God, and when they feel stress, to make a plan with God to address that stress; it may be for these reasons that they can be expected to maintain good mental health. In sum, intrinsic religiosity and positive religious coping can be seen as adaptive approaches to coping. (For more information on the benefits of positive thinking, read Chapter 18.)

Meanwhile, if we contrast intrinsic and positive religious coping with an extrinsic orientation towards religion and negative religious coping, we can perhaps see why the opposite is true for these latter religious dimensions. First, those individuals who have extrinsic orientations towards religion are not seen as using their religion to its full potential. Rather, they use religion and their belief in God to provide themselves with protection and consolation, or to become part of a social circle. This, then, means that the person's

Stop and think

The power of prayer – praying for others?

In 1999 a group of US psychological researchers carried out what has turned out to be a controversial study of cardiac patients at St Luke's Hospital in Kansas City, Missouri. William Harris and seven other researchers examined the health outcomes of nearly 1,000 newly admitted heart patients at the hospital. The patients all had serious cardiac conditions, and were randomly assigned to one of two groups. Half of the patients received daily prayer for 4 weeks from five volunteers who believed in God and in the healing power of prayer. The other half of the patients received no prayers. All people involved in the study were Christians. The participants were blind to the study. The people praying were given only the first names of their patients and never visited the hospital. They were instructed to pray for these patients every day, and in their prayers to ask for 'a speedy recovery with no complications'. It was found that 18 of the 484 patients who received prayer got better within 24 hours, while only 5 of the 529 patients who did not receive prayer got better. Furthermore, using a list of events that could happen to cardiac patients (e.g. infection, chest pains and death), Harris concluded that the group receiving prayers fared better statistically in their health than the group that didn't receive prayers; the prayer group was reported as being 11 per cent better.

This study received media attention from CNN, and other academics were asked to comment on the study's findings and validity. Some criticisms of the study included people saying that adding up health events to judge a patient's outcome is subjective and open to bias, therefore questioning the validity of the finding. Another academic suggested that, although the prayers were for a 'speedy' recovery, no measure was made of how long individuals stayed in hospital; therefore, the predictions of a speedy recovery couldn't be supported. Indeed, given that only 23 of the 1,000 people recovered in 24 hours, this doesn't lend a lot of weight to the effect of the prayers, which asked for a speedy recovery. The last word goes to Harris, who in his original paper said that his results validated the need for more research. Rather than conclusively showing the power of prayer, the study provides some intriguing results that should encourage more studies to be done, independently and in different places, to get closer to the truth.

religious beliefs are not as fulfilling; consequently, they severely weaken their likelihood of accessing those aspects, considered for intrinsic orientations, that may help them in times of worry and stress. This effect is clearly echoed in the research on negative religious coping. As negative religious coping focuses on the person concentrating on feelings of abandonment and punishment, they are unlikely to engage positively with the problem. Rather, they may feel distressed and not come to terms with the problem. For example, someone who uses religion only for social purposes, and does not pray regularly, prevents themselves from being able to share their concerns with God and from making a plan with God to address that stress. Therefore, extrinsic religiosity and negative religious coping are seen as less adaptive approaches and coping strategies.

Religion and personality

Our second consideration is how religion is related to personality. Here we will concentrate on two major models of personality: the three-factor model and the five-factor model.

Three-factor model of personality and religion

There has been research within the last 20 years that centres on the application of the Eysenckian dimensional model of personality to understanding religious attitudes and behaviour. You will remember that, within Eysenck's theory, three personality dimensions are prevalent: psychoticism (solitary, troublesome, cruel, inhumane traits), neuroticism (anxious, worrying and moody traits) and extraversion (sociable, sensation-seeking, carefree and optimistic traits). Furthermore, you will remember from earlier in this discussion that Eysenck splits attitudes into tough-minded and tender-minded attitudes. Eysenck (1975; 1976b) argued that religiosity is a tender-minded social attitude, and tender-minded attitudes are thought to be a consequence of conditioning. Eysenck found that individuals who are more easily conditioned are found to score significantly lower on psychoticism measures. It is argued that psychoticism rather than other personality dimensions (such as neuroticism and extraversion) will be related to religiosity, and that religious people should score lower on psychoticism.

At present, there is a wealth of information suggesting that psychoticism is significantly negatively related to religiosity across a number of cultures. Over 100 published studies among children and adults in the United States, United Kingdom and Australia have employed different measures of religiosity – including measures of religious orientation and religious coping as well as measures of the frequency of religious behaviours (frequency of church attendance and personal prayer) – and the researchers have found that people who are religious score lower on psychoticism. At present then, there is little doubt that psychoticism shares a

significant negative correlation with many aspects of religiosity. This finding suggests that religiosity tends not to be accompanied by cruel, insensitive, unfriendly, antisocial traits; it suggests further that religious people are kind, sensitive, friendly and very social (Maltby and Day, 2004).

Five-factor model of personality and religion

Compared to the work done with the Eysenck theory of personality and religion, relatively few studies have looked at the relationship between religion and the five-factor model of personality.

You will remember that the five-factor personality comprises five personality types:

- Openness (perceptive, sophisticated, knowledgeable, cultured, artistic, curious, analytical, liberal traits).
- Conscientiousness (practical, cautious, serious, reliable, organised, careful, dependable, hardworking, ambitious traits).
- Extraversion (sociable, talkative, active, spontaneous, adventurous, enthusiastic, person-oriented, assertive traits).
- Agreeableness (warm, trustful, courteous, agreeable, co-operative traits).
- Neuroticism (emotional, anxious, depressive, self-conscious, worrying traits).

You will remember that agreeableness and conscientious personality traits can be viewed as a two-dimensional model of psychoticism.

French psychologist Vassilis Saroglou (2002) presents a meta-analytic review of studies (i.e. a statistical summary of all the results in the field) (for more information, see online Chapter 27) that have looked at the relationship between the five-factor model of personality and religiosity. Within this meta-analysis, Saroglou was able to identify the two main religious orientations, intrinsic and extrinsic orientation towards religion, within the studies. Saroglou found that intrinsic religious orientation shares a significant positive relationship with agreeableness and conscientiousness. The finding is consistent with research using Eysenck's three-dimensional model of personality, as low psychoticism is thought to be equivalent to higher levels of agreeableness and conscientiousness.

Furthermore, Saroglou found that extrinsic religiosity is positively related to neuroticism (emotional, anxious, depressive, self-conscious, worrying traits) and found to be related to higher neuroticism. This finding is interesting because it is consistent with the view that an extrinsic orientation towards religion reflects a maladaptive approach to religion. Luckily for us, the relationship between extrinsic religiosity and neurotic behaviours has been examined by other authors, who have used classical psychoanalytic theory to investigate extrinsic religiosity and neurotic behaviours.

Extrinsic religiosity and neuroticism: application of Freudian theory

Sigmund Freud, aside from speculating on the human condition as the result of a warring id and superego demands (see Chapter 2), also wrote some important papers about society, particularly religion. In 1907 Freud wrote the paper, 'Obsessive Actions and Religious Practices'. In it, Freud outlined parallels between obsessive actions and religious practices, describing how both neurotic and religious practice serve as defensive, self-protective measures involved in the repression of instinctual impulses. He notices how both obsessional behaviour and religion involve rituality (in terms of religion being considered as containing many different formats of religious services, or ceremonies, that are clearly laid out and repeated), the guilt involved if these practices are neglected (people who attend their place of worship weekly might feel guilty if they don't attend church one week) and the exclusivity with which these acts are carried out to other behaviours (going to a place of worship is usually done exclusively from other parts of life). UK and US psychologists Maltby et al. (1995) argued that the descriptions of extrinsic religiosity as being protective and social are reminiscent of Freud's descriptions of religion serving as a protective factor and involving social rituals. Freud's observations predict a relationship between extrinsic religiosity (social religiosity) dimensions and the neuroticism dimension. As we have seen, Saroglou's meta-analytic study, looking at a number of studies, found evidence to support this idea. Further, Maltby (1999), in British and Irish samples, and Maltby et al. (1995), in a US sample, found that extrinsic religiosity was related to neuroticism using Eysenck's measure of neuroticism.

Of course, none of this evidence supports Freud's view that religion is a repression of instinctual impulses. Nonetheless, his views provide a context within which to understand the relationship between extrinsic religiosity and neuroticism.

Religion, personality, coping and mental health

So far, we have considered the relationship between religiosity and mental health, and between religion and personality. We have tended to find evidence for the ideas that intrinsic approaches to religion, and positive religious coping, can be seen as adaptive (better mental health and lower psychoticism) and that extrinsic approaches to religion and negative religious coping can be seen as maladaptive (poorer mental health and higher neuroticism).

You may have noticed that we have reviewed two areas of work – religion and mental health, and religion and

personality – yet we have come to similar conclusions regarding the adaptiveness of these different religious approaches. You may also have been struck by the clear overlaps between the findings. The most striking is neuroticism (anxious, worrying and moody personality traits) and its relationship to extrinsic religiosity, which together lead to poorer mental health. As neuroticism underlies poor mental health, then, there is perhaps a need to examine some of these variables together.

This need to look at theories together is something we discussed earlier (Chapter 16). We introduced you to the individual differences approach of 'comparing' and 'combining' theoretical perspectives to best understand certain variables. Here, there is a clear need to examine religiosity, personality and mental health together by combining these elements.

One example of this combining of elements was to use factor analysis techniques (see Chapter 25 and online Chapter 27) to look for underlying factors between these variables to provide a better and simplified understanding of the correlates of these variables to mental health. In simple terms, this means looking for how personality, religiosity and coping variables overlap and then finding which combination of variables correlates to mental health.

This approach was used by Maltby and Day (2004) to produce a simplified account of the overlaps that occur between religiosity, personality and coping, and the resulting relationship these variables had with mental health. Maltby and Day used coping theory and personality theory to provide a context for the relationship between religion and mental health. It is important for you to note that, when you are putting variables together in this way, you must make sure to describe these relationships in accordance with our theoretical definition and understanding of the variables. For example, religiosity is viewed as part of a wider personality framework, because personality is thought to emerge from biologically based (e.g. genetic) and learned and established traits as a child, and religiosity is a learned social behaviour that *can* develop at any point in a person's life. Therefore it is likely, given these definitions, that personality can be considered as a much stronger general context for understanding religion (i.e. personality influences religion); religion cannot be considered as a strong general context for understanding personality (i.e. religion influences personality). Therefore we would ensure that any discussion of the combination of variables made these distinctions.

For the analysis, Maltby and Day used the findings of UK psychologist Eamon Ferguson (2001), who provided a factor analysis of Eysenck's personality dimensions (extraversion, neuroticism and psychoticism) and a measure of different coping strategies. In this analysis Ferguson has found that the personality and coping variables combined into four factors:

- **Problem-focused coping** – problem-focused coping is where the individual experiences stress and tries to cope with the stress by recognising and addressing the problem. Examples of this type of coping include active coping (actively dealing with the problem) and positive reinterpretation and growth (seeing the stress as an opportunity for growth).
- **Neuroticism and coping** – this factor combines neuroticism personality traits with coping styles such as denial, behavioural disengagement and mental disengagement, suggesting that neuroticism is associated with trying to deny the stress and using withdrawal coping strategies.
- **Psychoticism and coping** – this factor combines psychoticism personality traits with coping styles such as not using religion to cope, and using drugs and alcohol to deal with stress.
- **Extraversion and coping** – this factor combines extraversion personality traits with coping styles that emphasise emotional responses and seeking social support to help deal with the stress.

What these authors did next was to find out how measures of religiosity were related to these factors (see Figure 22.8). First, they found that intrinsic religiosity and positive religious coping were part of the psychoticism and coping factor, with both religious variables being negatively related to this factor (i.e. higher religiosity was related to lower psychoticism). Second, they found that extrinsic religiosity and negative religious coping were part of the neuroticism and coping factor. They found that low scores on the psychoticism and coping factor alongside intrinsic religious and positive religious coping were related to better mental health (e.g. lower depression, higher anxiety), and the neuroticism and coping factor with extrinsic religiosity and negative religious coping were related to poorer mental health (e.g. lower depression, higher anxiety).

You can see that this approach provides a simplified version of the relationship between two areas of religion (religious orientation, religious coping), personality, coping and mental health. Therefore these authors were able to conclude that, when it came to religion, personality and coping, there are two main factors (rather than a multitude of variables and relationships). The first factor sees intrinsic religious orientation and positive religious coping as part of a wider factor that comprises low psychoticism and a tendency not to use drugs and alcohol as a coping mechanism. The second factor sees extrinsic religious orientation and negative religious coping as part of a wider factor that comprises neuroticism and withdrawal coping strategies.

Identifying these two factors then allows us to understand the relationship between religion and mental health within the context of personality and coping variables. That is, we can see how an individual who is intrinsically religious will also tend to use positive religious coping,

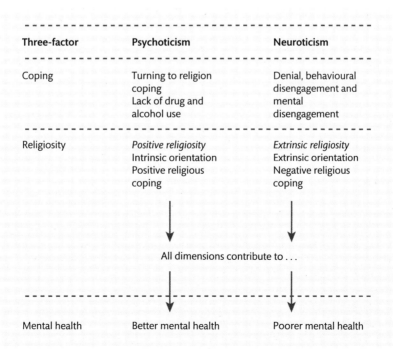

Three-factor	Psychoticism	Neuroticism
Coping	Turning to religion coping Lack of drug and alcohol use	Denial, behavioural disengagement and mental disengagement
Religiosity	*Positive religiosity* Intrinsic orientation Positive religious coping	*Extrinsic religiosity* Extrinsic orientation Negative religious coping

All dimensions contribute to . . .

| Mental health | Better mental health | Poorer mental health |

Figure 22.8 A summary overview of religiosity, personality, coping and mental health variables.

Stop and think

Religion and health

Researchers are interested in the idea that religion is beneficial to physical health. Religiosity is thought to significantly influence a variety of health outcomes, including heart disease, cancer, stroke and health-related behaviours such as smoking, drinking and drug use. Recent research in the United States confirms this observation. For example, Dedert et al. (2004) found that religiosity may have a protective effect on the physiological effects of stress among women with fibromyalgia. Benjamins (2004) found that more frequent religious attendance is associated with fewer functional limitations, whereas higher levels of salience are associated with more limitations. Van Ness et al. (2003) found that a lack of religiousness was associated with poor breast cancer survival among women. Koenig et al. (2004) found that religious activities, attitudes and spiritual experiences are prevalent in older hospitalised patients and are associated with greater social support and, to some extent, better physical health. Such research certainly is intriguing, and, if nothing else, should provide impetus for looking at the exact role that religion plays in health recovery.

---

which can be seen within the context of low psychoticism (a tendency to be sensitive, friendly and not cruel), alongside a tendency not to turn to alcohol and drugs when stressed. All these traits contribute to better mental health. We can also see that an individual who has an extrinsic orientation towards religion, who adopts negative religious coping, which is set within the context of neuroticism personality traits (anxious, worrying and emotional), alongside a tendency to withdraw from stressful situations, may consequently suffer from poorer mental health.

Most of all, you can see that the combination of different variables can be used to provide a simplified framework and understanding of the relationship between religiosity, personality and mental health.

Critical review

Clearly, personality and individual differences psychologists have spent a lot of time clarifying the main dimensions of religiosity and seeking to consider consistent religious correlates with mental health and personality. As such, this is a major strength of the area. However, there are some critical considerations to be made.

A first area of concern is that – as we have done here – other aspects of religiosity and related constructs are sometimes ignored. Critics would ask where aspects of spirituality and more expressive and reflective aspects of religiosity would fit in. This is a common accusation made of individual researchers in the psychology of religion; how can we define and capture all the possible elements of religious beliefs, particularly as some religious beliefs are ages old? The simple answer is that psychologists can only hope to answer some of these questions. All they can do is make inroads into a topic in the hope of gaining some understanding, rather than

being defeatist and seeing it as a lost cause. It would seem that the consistent findings regarding religion, personality and mental health are a good basis to start from.

The second important point is that the significant relationships between religion and mental health, and religion and personality variables, though consistent, are usually small. You may remember about effect sizes of correlations (see online supplementary chapter on statistics [Chapter 27]; correlations of $r = 0.1$ are considered small, correlations of $r = 0.3$ are considered medium and correlations of $r = 0.5$ are considered large). Usually, in this area, correlations are around 0.3 (medium effect size) at best, and usually around 0.2 (small effect size). We think this is worth pointing out for two reasons. First, this research suggests that a large amount of variance in religion is not accounted for by personality theory, nor does it have a great effect on mental health. Second, it's worth noting that explanations around this low correlation may focus not only on weak theoretical explanation but also on the fact that not all people are religious. There may be other aspects of social activity that may result from similar personality factors or may aid mental health in the same way as religious activity does. Consequently, the reasons that religion helps or hinders religious people in their mental health may be the same as those for people following their favourite football team (indeed, there are many parallels between supporting a football team and religion – group worship, intense feelings, iconic figures).

To summarise, in understanding individual differences in religion, research findings seem consistent and suggest that different aspects of religiosity are related in different areas of mental heath and personality. Consequently, researchers have built up a good understanding of the constructs that surround religiosity within a personality and individual differences perspective.

Stop and think

Religion

- Should psychology try to play a role in understanding the influence of religion on mental health?

- Does coping theory adequately explain the relationship between religion and mental health?

Final comments

The aim of this discussion was to introduce you to two areas of research that look at social behaviour and attitudes within individual differences. These were: (1) right-wing attitudes; and (2) religiosity. We have outlined the main principles of the theory and measurement surrounding each construct, and, where applicable, we have noted general research findings that relate each construct to mental health. Furthermore, we have looked at each of these areas alongside their relationship to the three- and five-factor models of personality. For each social attitude, we have provided an assessment of the strengths and weaknesses of the theory and research in that area.

Summary

- Research into right-wing attitudes encompasses right-wing authoritarianism, conservatism and social dominance theory.
- Authoritarianism was originally thought to comprise a set of right-wing behaviours showing excessive conformity, intolerance of others and rigid and stereotyped thought patterns.
- There are four primary theoretical viewpoints of conservatism: resistance to change, tendency to play safe, reflecting the distinction between generations and internalisation of parental values.
- The dynamic theory of conservatism suggests conservative attitudes can be more directly explained by the construct of uncertainty.
- Social dominance theory argues that humans are predisposed to form a social hierarchy. Social hierarchy is the result of three processes: aggregated individual discrimination, aggregated institutional discrimination and behavioural asymmetry.
- Right-wing attitudes are related to psychoticism (or agreeableness or conscientiousness) dimensions. However, whether this relationship is positive or negative may depend on the dimension of right-wing attitudes used. A more consistent finding is that people with right-wing attitudes tend not to show openness personality traits.
- Religion takes on different meanings and different consequences. However, a lot of research has been done on the measurement of religion, and two main aspects of religiosity emerge – religious orientation and religious coping. Religious orientation comprises intrinsic, extrinsic-personal and extrinsic-social religiosity. Religious coping comprises positive and negative religious coping.
- In regard to religiosity and mental health, an intrinsic religious orientation and positive religious coping are related to better mental health. Extrinsic religious orientation and negative religious coping are related to poorer mental health.
- In regard to religiosity and personality, religion – particularly personal and positive aspects – is negatively related to psychoticism. Extrinsic and negative coping aspects of religiosity are related to neuroticism.

Connecting up

You will want to look back at Chapter 7 for more information on the three-factor and five–factor models of personality.

To further consider how religiosity can have mental health consequences, you could look at Chapter 19.

Critical thinking

Discussion questions

We have considered a number of theories related to right-wing attitudes and religiosity and presented some considerations so you may appreciate the value of these different theories. However, there are some points to discuss. We present them here in the form of discussion topics to allow you to think about these issues on your own, or within groups; your university seminars would also be a great place to discuss them. They are not for you to worry about; they are presented only as a way for you to get an even deeper understanding of the complexities of this topic.

- This exercise is to get you generating some ideas about the topic. Let us consider some of the theoretical and empirical findings covered here within an individual differences perspective (as outlined in Chapter 17). For this exercise, you might want to separate right-wing attitudes and religiosity and choose to consider only one of them.

  - Name five or six important theories and/or findings that emerge from this topic area.
  - If we were to present an overview of these five or six chosen theories and findings, what different areas of psychology would you be emphasising? For example, are they biological, physiological, personality, cognitive, social or clinical factors?
  - Of these five or six chosen theories and findings, which do you lend most weight to?
  - Are there any theoretical or empirical overlaps between the theories and findings? If so, where do they occur?

- Of the three perspectives on right-wing attitudes (right-wing authoritarianism, conservatism and social dominance theory), which theoretical perspective do you think best explains:

  - racism in society;
  - political right-wing ideology;
  - sexism in society.

- Take each of the two following attitudes: banning smoking in public places and supporting the fight against terrorism. Can these attitudes be considered right wing? If so, under which theory of right-wing attitudes are these best considered? Are these attitudes best considered within the psychoticism or the openness personality dimensions?
- In his book, *The Future of an Illusion* (1927), Freud said that, when a man is freed of religion, he has a better chance to live a normal and wholesome life. Consider this view.
- Do you think right-wing attitudes are explained well by personality theory?
- Do you think religiosity is well explained by personality theory?

Essay questions

- Compare and contrast two of the three following perspectives on right-wing attitudes:

  - right-wing authoritarianism;
  - conservatism;
  - social dominance theory.

- Critically discuss how right-wing attitudes are related to personality.
- Critically examine whether religiosity has a positive or negative effect on your mental health.
- Critically discuss how religiosity is related to personality.
- Critically examine how personality and coping theory have been used to understand the relationship between religiosity and mental health.
- Does religion produce a positive psychological outcome? How do you think the research on religion, personality and mental health informs this viewpoint?

Going further

Books

- Altemeyer, R. (1996). *The authoritarian specter.* Cambridge, MA: Harvard University Press.
- Wilson, G. D. (1983). *The psychology of conservatism.* London: Academic Press.
- Beit-Hallahmi, B. and Argyle, M. (1997). *The psychology of religious behaviour, belief and experience.* London: Routledge.
- Pargament, K. I. (1997). *The psychology of religion and coping: Theory, research and practice.* London: Guilford.
- Wulff, D. M. (1997). *Religion: Classic and contemporary* (Vol. 2). London: Wiley.

Journals

- Emmons, R. A. and Paloutzian, R. F. (2003). The psychology of religion. *Annual Review of Psychology,*

54, 377–403. *Annual Review of Psychology* is published by Annual Reviews, Palo Alto, California. Available online via Business Source Premier.

- *The American Psychologist* (Vol. 58, 2003) has a special issue that covered issues of religion and spirituality. Published by the American Psychological Association. Available online via PsycARTICLES.

Articles on the personality and intelligence in education and work issues discussed are often found in the following journals. Use 'conservatism', 'authoritarianism', 'religiosity', 'religious orientation' and 'religious coping' as your search terms when using library databases such as Web of Science and PsycINFO.

- *Personality and Individual Differences*. Published by Elsevier. Available online via Science Direct.
- *Annual Review on Psychology*. Published by Annual Reviews, Palo Alto, California. Available online via Business Source Premier.

- *Journal of Personality and Social Psychology*. Published by the American Psychological Association. Available online via PsycARTICLES.

Web resources

- **Social Psychology Network**. Some of the main topics are prejudice, discrimination and diversity. This topic area includes information on racism and other race-related issues, diversity and multiculturalism, prejudice reduction, civil rights and affirmative action (**www.socialpsychology.org**).
- **Psychology of Religion Pages**. This is a general introduction to the psychology of religion; for example, as it is studied by scientists in Division 36 of the American Psychological Association. Here you will find a description of what psychologists have learned about how religion influences people's lives (**www.psychwww.com/psyrelig**).

Film and literature

- *Lord of the Flies* (1954, written by William Golding). The classic book about how a group of male children form a social hierarchy, and how authoritarianism and social dominance form in the group. This book was made into a film of the same name (1963, directed by Peter Brook).
- *A Time to Kill* (1989, written by John Grisham). The central theme of this book is a social hierarchy based on race. The story is set in Mississippi and concentrates on issues of race and white dominance. A lawyer and his assistant fight to save a father on trial for murder and are questioned about what they believe. This book was made into a film of the same name (1996, directed by Joel Schumacher).
- *Boyz n the Hood* (1991, directed by John Singleton). This film is about a group of teenage boys from Los Angeles' South Central District who come to terms with gang warfare and violent life on the streets. This film explores the theme *behavioural asymmetry*, particularly with issues surrounding members of subordinate groups who often *actively* participate in, and contribute to, their own subordination, while others try to break free of it.

- *Mean Girls* (2004, directed by Mark Waters). We have discussed the theory of social dominance and how many aspects of social dominance are in our everyday institutions. This film shows how social dominance works in school settings. A group of girls clearly have set themselves up as being at the top of the hierarchy. We also see how other individuals, who might be considered more 'nerdy', help to maintain that hierarchy. For other examples of these dynamics in schools, see a film called *Heathers* (1989, directed by Michael Lehman) and another called *The Breakfast Club* (1985, directed by John Hughes).
- *The Name of the Rose* (1980, written by Umberto Eco). We have looked at the distinction between intrinsic and extrinsic religiosity. This book tells the story of a priest who, at the time of the Inquisition, investigates a murder. A central theme in this book is examination of the differences between internal and organised religion and their consequences. The book was made into a film of the same name (1986, directed by Jean–Jacques Annaud and starring Sean Connery and Christian Slater).

Explore the website accompanying this text at **www.pearsoned.co.uk/maltby** for further resources to help you with your studies. These include multiple-choice questions, essay questions, web links and ideas for advanced reading.

CHAPTER 23
Well-being and Personality Disorders

Key themes

- Well-being
- The structure of mood
- Positive and negative affect
- Subjective psychological well-being and psychological well-being
- Personality disorders
- Genetic and environmental correlates of personality disorders

Learning outcomes

At the end of this discussion you should:

- Be able to describe the Circumplex Theory of Affect and the structure of mood
- Be able to describe the constructs of subjective well-being and psychological well-being and be able to explain how these two constructs differ
- Be able to describe how subjective and psychological well-being are related to personality
- Be able to outline and describe the main personality disorders as classified by the *Diagnostic and Statistical Manual of Mental Disorders (DSM)–IV*
- Be able to discuss the various genetic and environmental influences on personality disorders
- Be able to show an appreciation of the issues that surround the classification of, and overlaps between, personality disorders

Introduction

How are you feeling? But no, how are you really feeling? Happy? Sad? OK? Active, Frustrated? Fearful? How does that compare to how you felt this morning when you woke up, and how you think you will feel tomorrow? And how does this compare with how you feel about life most of the time? Also, what are your goals in life? Would you say you were essentially a happy person, or an unhappy person? How do you determine what your mood is on any one day and generally in life? In this discussion we are going to outline how individual differences psychologists have defined our well-being and moods, and how they've made the distinction between shorter term and longer term evaluations of our mood.

Also, we're going to look at extreme forms of well-being, particularly in terms of personality, and at personality disorders. During the nineteenth century, when dealing with persons under the United Kingdom Criminal Lunatics Act of 1800, there was a tendency for society to disown the mentally ill, treating their conditions as incurable, with individuals needing to be locked away to protect the rest of society. Are things very different today? On 4 February 2009, the BBC News website carried a story by Adrian Brown (Brown, 2009) entitled 'Prison "wrong" for mentally-ill inmates'. In this article the journalist finds that a lot of people with personality disorders are currently in prison. Have our attitudes, or at least treatment of people with such disorders, changed? We will not explore this issue here; rather we are going to outline the main personality disorders as recognised by the *Diagnostic and Statistical Manual of Mental Disorders (DSM)–IV* and discuss some of the genetic, environmental and other correlates of these personality disorders.

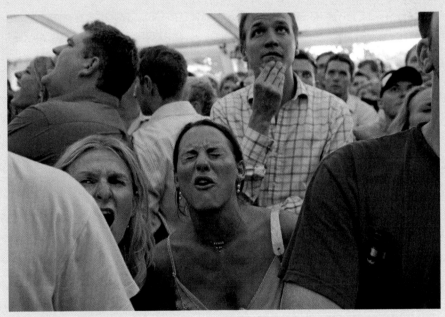

Source: Alamy Images/Network Photographers

The structure and measurement of well-being

In this first section we are going to look at how well-being is typically conceptualised in the individual differences literature. That is, how do individual difference theorists and researchers define and describe our well-being? First we are going to introduce you to the term 'mood', and explain how 'mood' is most commonly conceptualised within the individual difference literature, by the **Circumplex Theory of Affect**. We are then going to extend your view of well-being, beyond the Circumplex Theory of Affect, and introduce you to the terms **subjective well-being** and **psychological well-being**.

Circumplex Theory of Affect: the structure of mood

One of the most influential studies on affect was carried out by Professor David Watson at the University of Iowa, and his colleague Auke Tellegen (Watson and Tellegen,

1985). In 1985 these authors carried out a review of the research into mood and argued that mood comprised two main dimensions, *positive affect* and *negative affect*. Within psychology the term 'affect' refers to the adjective affective, and means the experience of feeling or emotion.

As a result of their research, Watson and Tellegen proposed the Circumplex Theory of Affect (see Figure 23.1). Circumplex theories have a tradition in psychology and the start of their development within psychology is attributed to US psychologist Timothy Leary. Leary (1957), who introduced the ordering of variables into a circumplex (a circle), concentrated on the interpersonal aspects of personality. Circumplex theories have been applied to many domains, but a feature of a circumplex, according to Leary, is thought to comprise three aspects:

- It provides a useful visual representation of a domain.
- It details how variables that are close together in visual representation are more related than variables that are far apart, with variables placed opposite to each other showing a negative relationship, and those at right angles to each other showing no relationship.
- It can be used to suggest how variables form a circumplex (circle) and therefore this model can be empirically examined to see whether the variables do in fact fit this model (e.g. do variables that are meant to be closely related correlate more highly than variables that are far apart and do variables that are meant to be negatively related show a negative correlation with each other?)

As you can see, Watson and Tellegen's Circumplex Theory of Affect model is set out in such a way that it comprises eight end points representing different mood states:

- High positive affect
- Low positive affect
- High negative affect
- Low negative affect
- Strong engagement
- Disengagement
- Pleasantness
- Unpleasantness.

Central to this are the bipolar dimensions (these are dimensions opposite to each other) of high and low positive affect and high and low negative affect:

- High positive affect is typified by feelings and emotions of being active, enthusiastic and excited.
- Low positive affect is typified by feelings and emotions of being dull, sleepy and sluggish.
- High negative affect is typified by feelings and emotions of being distressed, fearful and nervous.

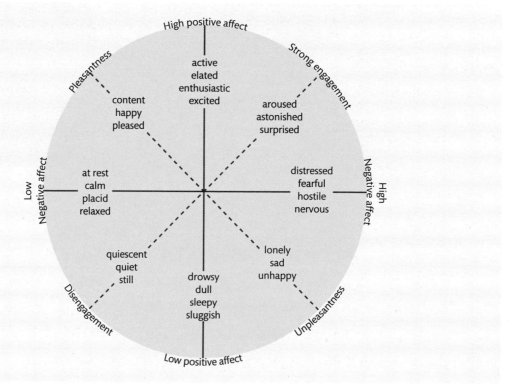

Figure 23.1 Watson and Tellegen's two-dimensional map of mood.
Source: Adapted from Watson and Tellegen (1985).

- Low negative affect is typified by feelings and emotions of being calm, relaxed and at rest.

However, it is also important to note that positive and negative affect is related to the four other end points of strong engagement, disengagement, pleasantness and unpleasantness:

- Strong engagement is typified by feelings and emotions of being aroused, astonished and surprised.
- Disengagement is typified by feelings and emotions of being quiet and still.
- Pleasantness is typified by feelings and emotions of being content, happy and satisfied.
- Unpleasantness is typified by feelings and emotions of being lonely, sad and unhappy.

Therefore it is useful to see our two main dimensions of positive affect and negative affect as comprising a combination of the other moods, such as:

- High positive affect is typified by a combination of *strong engagement and pleasantness*.
- Low positive affect is typified by a combination of *disengagement and unpleasantness*.
- High negative affect is typified by a combination of *strong engagement and unpleasantness*.
- Low negative affect is typified by a combination of *disengagement and pleasantness*.

In 1988, Watson, Tellegen and their colleague Lee Anna Clark (Watson *et al.*, 1988) developed the Positive and Negative Affect Schedule (more usually abbreviated to the PANAS) to measure positive and negative affect. In the PANAS there are 20 descriptors for measuring both positive and negative affect:

- Positive affect is measured by the 10 descriptors of attentive; interested; alert; excited; enthusiastic; inspired; proud; determined; strong; active.
- Negative affect is measured by the 10 descriptors of distressed; upset; hostile; irritable-angry; scared; afraid-fearful; ashamed; guilty; nervous; jittery.

Respondents are asked to indicate to what extent they feel each of these descriptors at the present moment and are then asked to mark one of five options ([1] very slightly or not at all, [2] a little, [3] moderately, [4] quite a bit or [5] extremely). Therefore, someone who was high in positive affect might respond 'quite a bit' or 'extremely' to the descriptors of 'excited' and 'interested'. However, someone who was high in negative affect might respond 'quite a bit' or 'extremely' to the descriptors 'upset' and 'nervous'.

Subjective and psychological well-being

Our modern understanding of well-being reaches far back into philosophy and is based on the distinction made between two types of philosophy. Our first example of how philosophy has influenced the way we think about well-being begins with the thoughts and writings of Aristippus. Aristippus was born in 435 BC, in Cyrene, a Greek colony in Northern Africa, and was a follower of Socrates and the founder of the Cyrenaic school of philosophy. It was Aristippus' belief that the ultimate aim of all human endeavours was pleasure, and that we should not refuse or defer pleasure for the sake of future pleasures. For Aristippus it was acceptable to break social conventions or rules, and behave in a shocking or undignified way, to gain pleasurable experiences. Therefore Aristippus' philosophy is associated with hedonism; the belief that pleasure is the most important pursuit.

Our second example of how philosophy has influenced how we conceptualise well-being is from the Greek philosopher Aristotle, who lived between 384 BC and 322 BC. He wrote on many subjects, including physics, music, logic, politics, government, ethics and biology, and is considered one of the most important founding figures in western philosophy. Aristotle's philosophy is different to the work of Aristippus in that, rather than emphasising 'pleasure' or 'hedonism', as Aristippus did, Aristotle emphasised eudaimonia. Eudaimonia in Greek means 'having a good guardian spirit', but in psychology it is understood as meaning to be successful and to flourish. There are then different interpretations of what eudaimonia means in psychological terms. Some take it to mean indicating a pleasant life, while others emphasise that it means a life of honour, or a life of wealth or a virtuous life. Regardless of these different meanings, eudaimonia is thought to represent some overall pleasant and successful life.

In terms of well-being, these two philosophical contexts have informed two different broad domains within the literature. This is **hedonic well-being** and **eudaimonic well-being**. Hedonic well-being is the relatively shorter term evaluation of well-being, representing a balance between feelings of positive and negative emotions, pleasure attainment and pain avoidance. Here, imagine someone who is always seeking out pleasurable experiences; these will tend to be short-term experiences, with the person moving from one experience to the next, always looking for their next pleasurable experience. Eudaimonic well-being is the longer term psychological well-being resulting from the engagement with individual development and challenges within life, with the individual looking for meaning and self-reflection in their life. Here, imagine a person who seeks to have a life that is well-lived. They are less concerned with seeking immediate pleasures, but are concerned with the longer term aspects of the meaning of life.

This distinction has created the background for modern thinking about well-being. In the current well-being literature there have been many authors who have discussed the validity and distinctions between these two ways of looking at well-being (Diener *et al.*, 1999; Kahneman *et al.*, 1999; Veenhoven, 1991). However, a key paper in the literature was presented by Keyes, Shmotkin and Ryff in 2002. In this paper Keyes *et al.* used the hedonic and eudaimonic well-being traditions to suggest that there are two types of well-being. In this paper the authors renamed these two well-being dimensions as **subjective well-being** and **psychological well-being**, with subjective well-being being hedonic well-being and psychological well-being being eudaimonic well-being (see Figure 23.2). They also suggested ways that psychologists could measure subjective well-being and psychological well-being.

The first way of understanding and measuring subjective well-being you've already read about; positive and negative affect. Subjective well-being is based on hedonic activity and therefore its measurement should assess the relatively shorter term evaluation of present-day feelings of positive and negative emotion, pleasure attainment and pain avoidance. The aforementioned Positive and Negative Affect Schedule (PANAS), which identifies feelings of positive and negative affect at the present moment, is a well used measure of subjective well-being. Another commonly used measure of subjective well-being is **life satisfaction**. This concept has been developed in the form of a scale, the Satisfaction with Life Scale (SWLS) developed by Ed Diener and colleagues

(Diener *et al.*, 1985). The SWLS consists of five items which ask respondents to indicate how they feel at the present moment, and examples of the items include 'I am satisfied with my life' and 'The conditions of my life are excellent'. Measurement of subjective well-being typically comprises positive affect, negative affect and life satisfaction.

However, the conceptualisation and measurement of psychological well-being means the introduction of an entirely new set of variables for you to consider. Psychological well-being, based on eudaimonia, is the engagement with individual development and the challenges within life, concentrating on issues of meaning and self-reflection. In Keyes *et al.* (2002) the authors argued that there are six aspects to psychological well-being:

- autonomy;
- environmental mastery;
- personal growth;
- purpose in life;
- positive relations with others;
- self-acceptance.

We will now briefly describe each of these dimensions in Table 23.1 by giving an example of the behaviours that illustrate these six dimensions of psychological well-being. The example items have been obtained from a set of measures developed by Carol Ryff in 1989 that are used

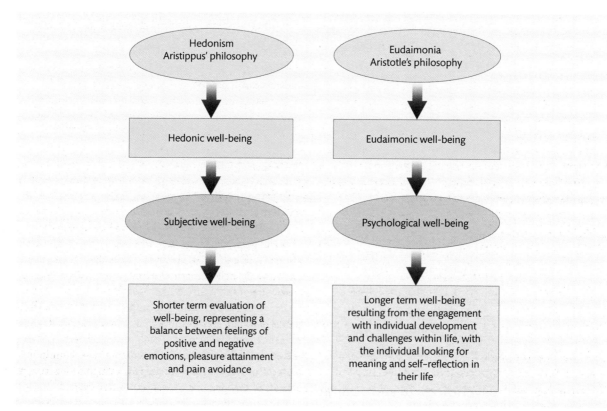

Figure 23.2 The two traditions of well-being.

Table 23.1 Examples of the behaviours that illustrate each of these six dimensions of psychological well-being

	High	Low	Example items would include
Autonomy	Self-determining and independent; tends to be able to resist social pressures to think and act in certain ways and regulates behaviour from within themselves and evaluates self by personal standards.	Is concerned about the expectations of others and conforms to social pressures. Relies on judgements of others.	'I have a sense of direction and purpose in life' and 'I enjoy making plans for the future and working to make them a reality.'
Environmental mastery	Has a sense of mastery and competence in managing the environment; controls complex array of external activities; makes effective use of surrounding opportunities; able to choose or create contexts suitable to personal needs and values.	Has difficulty managing everyday affairs; feels unable to change or improve surrounding context; is unaware of surrounding opportunities; lacks sense of control over external world.	'I am quite good at managing the many responsibilities of my daily life' and 'My daily life is busy, but I derive a sense of satisfaction from keeping up with everything.'
Personal growth	Has a feeling of continued development; sees self as growing and expanding; is open to new experiences; has sense of realising one's potential; sees improvement in self and behaviour over time; is changing in ways that reflect more self-knowledge and effectiveness.	Has a sense of personal stagnation; lacks sense of improvement or expansion over time; feels bored and uninterested with life; feels unable to develop new attitudes or behaviours.	'I think it is important to have new experiences that challenge how you think about yourself and the world' and 'For me, life has been a continuous process of learning, changing, and growth'.
Purpose in life	Has goals in life and a sense of directedness; feels there is meaning to present and past life; holds beliefs that give life purpose; has aims and objectives for living.	Lacks a sense of meaning in life; has few goals or aims, lacks sense of direction; does not see purpose of past life; has no outlook or beliefs that give life meaning.	'I have a sense of direction and purpose in life' and 'I enjoy making plans for the future and working to make them a reality.'
Positive relations with others	Has warm, satisfying, trusting relationships with others; is concerned about the welfare of others; capable of strong empathy, affection and intimacy; understands give and take of human relationships.	Has few close, trusting relationships with others; finds it difficult to be warm, open and concerned about others; is isolated and frustrated in interpersonal relationships; not willing to make compromises to sustain important ties with others.	'I enjoy personal and mutual conversations with family members or friends' and 'People would describe me as a giving person, willing to share my time with others'.
Self-acceptance	Possesses a positive attitude toward the self; acknowledges and accepts multiple aspects of self, including good and bad qualities; feels positive about past life.	Feels dissatisfied with self; is disappointed with what has occurred in past life; is troubled about certain personal qualities; wishes to be different than what one is.	'I like most aspects of my personality' and 'For the most part, I am proud of who I am and the life I lead'.

Source: Carol Ryff's 1989 Psychological Well-being Scales.

to measure these different psychological well-being dimensions (named Scales of Psychological Well-being).

Considering subjective and psychological well-being together, individual differences psychologists tend to view well-being as it is illustrated in Figure 23.3, with subjective well-being and psychological well-being representing two separate but related aspects of well-being, comprising a number of different specific aspects of well-being.

So, what is the research evidence to support the distinction between subjective and psychological well-being?

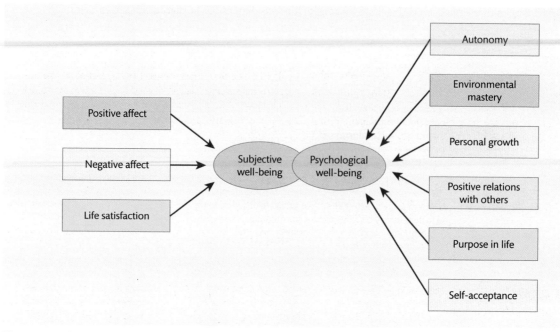

Figure 23.3 Components of subjective and psychological well-being.

Using factor analysis techniques to look for underlying themes among these measures (see online Chapter 27), Keyes *et al.*, (2002) assessed the relationship between these different concepts. Table 23.2 shows Keyes *et al.*'s finding of how many factors underpinned the well-being measures (i.e. two) and the factor loading of each of the scales from their study in the USA (with higher values representing a great importance of that variable to defining that factor, and a value of above 0.3 as a criterion for considering the variable as relevant to the study). In this study, a distinction emerges, with the first factor being a psychological well-being factor (as psychological well-being variables load highest on this factor) and the second factor being a subjective well-being factor (as the subjective well-being variables load highest on this factor).

This type of finding has supported the view that it is important to draw the distinction between subjective (or hedonic) and psychological (or eudaimonic) well-being, but that there are overlaps between the scales, and this leads to the debate over the definitions and concepts used to define the subjective and psychological well-being constructs, particularly psychological well-being. For example, Ryff (1989) proposed six dimensions of psychological well-being, developed from an extensive literature review, including self-acceptance, purpose in life, personal growth, environmental mastery, positive relations with others and autonomy. However, authors such as Kashdan *et al.* (2008) challenge these eudaimonic conceptions of well-being because authors are not consistent as regards the theory. For example, Ryff's overall description of psychological well-being could be criticised as it is very

different to Aristotle's seminal conception of eudaimonia, which was ultimately about the judgement of a life well lived and being successful and flourishing in relation to one's character. It is hard to see how the six scales of Ryff exactly relate to this philosophy, though it clearly has influenced these scales. Furthermore, Waterman (2008) argues that different interpretations can be made of eudaimonia and alternative approaches to the conceptualisation and measurement of psychological well-being can be proposed. For example, Samman (2007) has proposed that psychologists use self-determination theory, which emphasises concepts such as meaning, autonomy, competence and relatedness, to conceptualise psychological well-being. (You can read more about self-determination theory in Chapter 10.) None the less, the distinction between

Table 23.2 Factor loadings for US samples for subjective and psychological well-being measures

	USA adults ($n = 1,514$)	
	1	2
Positive affect	0.30	0.83
Negative affect	0.36	0.80
Satisfaction with life	0.29	0.74
Personal growth	0.76	0.36
Positive relationships	0.70	0.50
Self-acceptance	0.61	0.74
Autonomy	0.36	0.33
Purpose in life	0.79	0.24
Environmental mastery	0.47	0.75

Stop and think

Listed below are some example items from Ryff's 1989 Psychological Well-being Scales. Although these items do not represent the whole of the scale and therefore will not be an entirely accurate measurement, they are indicative of the scales. If you had to score yourself between 1 and 10 on each of these items, 1 being 'not at all like me', and 10 being 'very like me' and add up the two scores for each dimension, what would these scores tell you about your own psychological well-being?

	Score out of 10 0 = 'Not at all like me' 10 = 'Very like me'
Autonomy 'I am not afraid to voice my opinions, even when they are in opposition to the opinions of most people.' 'I am not the kind of person who gives in to social pressures to think or act in certain ways.'	
Environmental mastery 'I am quite good at managing the many responsibilities of my daily life.' 'My daily life is busy, but I derive a sense of satisfaction from keeping up with everything.'	
Personal growth 'I think it is important to have new experiences that challenge how you think about yourself and the world.' 'For me, life has been a continuous process of learning, changing and growth.'	
Positive relations with others 'I enjoy personal and mutual conversations with family members or friends.' 'People would describe me as a giving person, willing to share my time with others.'	
Purpose in life 'I have a sense of direction and purpose in life.' 'I enjoy making plans for the future and working to make them a reality.'	
Self-acceptance 'I like most aspects of my personality.' 'For the most part, I am proud of who I am and the life I lead.'	

psychological and subjective well-being is one of the most useful distinctions to make when considering well-being as a whole.

Personality, mood and well-being

So, how is well-being, in all its different forms (i.e. mood, subjective well-being, psychological well-being) related to other variables? Well, the best context in which to examine this question is the five-factor model of personality. You will remember (from Chapter 7) that the five-factor model comprises five personality dimensions (Costa and McCrae, 1992):

- openness (perceptive, sophisticated, knowledgeable, cultured, artistic, curious, analytical, liberal traits);
- conscientiousness (practical, cautious, serious, reliable, organised, careful, dependable, hardworking, ambitious traits);
- extraversion (sociable, talkative, active, spontaneous, adventurous, enthusiastic, person-oriented, assertive traits);
- agreeableness (warm, trustful, courteous, agreeable, cooperative traits);
- neuroticism (emotional, anxious, depressive, self-conscious, worrying traits).

In their introduction of the five-factor model, Costa and McCrae (Costa and McCrae, 1980; 1992; McCrae and Costa, 1991) have argued that, conceptually, positive

Sometimes well-being is represented by having positive relationships with others.
Source: Pearson Education Ltd./Jules Selmes

affect (attentive, interested, alert, excited feelings) is very like extraversion, and negative affect (distressed, upset, nervous) is very like neuroticism and therefore these concepts should be closely related. Also, McCrae and Costa (1991) have argued that conscientiousness, openness and agreeableness have an 'instrumental' relationship with well-being; that is, through having these personality traits, i.e. being organised, careful, dependable, hardworking, ambitious traits (conscientiousness), or being perceptive, sophisticated, knowledgeable, cultured, artistic, curious (openness), or being warm, trustful, courteous, agreeable, cooperative (agreeableness), will result in positive outcomes in terms of well-being (i.e. being higher in positive affect and lower in negative affect).

Generally, research supports this view that extraversion is related to positive affect and neuroticism is related to negative affect. In fact, the pattern for this relationship has been found across a number of samples (Costa and McCrae, 1980; 1992; McCrae and Costa, 1991; Watson and Tellegen, 1985). On average, the correlation between extraversion and positive affect, and neuroticism and negative affect, is thought to be around $r = 0.4$. In one study, Australian researchers Kay Wilson and Eleonora Gullone (Wilson and Gullone, 1999) looked at the factor structure of extraversion, neuroticism and positive and negative affect scales. Factor analysis simplifies the relationships between all the scales, and identifies to what underlying factors different variables are linked. (For a longer explanation of factor analysis go to Chapter 25, or the online supplementary chapter on statistics, Chapter 27.) Wilson and Gullone examined the underlying

factors compared to measures of neuroticism and extraversion and positive and negative affect among a sample of 533 participants: 228 children and early adolescents (8–15 years), 163 late adolescents and young adults (16–29 years) and 142 adults (30–68 years), thereby assessing personality and affect across different aspects of the lifespan. The authors found that positive affect loaded on an extraversion factor, while negative affect loaded on a neuroticism factor, suggesting that positive and negative affect represent two separate sets of relationships with personality.

What about conscientiousness, openness and agreeableness? Previous research is mixed, with relationships between conscientiousness, openness and agreeableness only sometimes being related to improved well-being (i.e. higher positive affect or lower negative affect). However, evidence does show support for the view that the relationship between positive and negative affect and these other aspects of personality is less definitive. A good illustration of this is the findings of Italian researcher Antonio Terracciano (Terracciano, 2003), who looked at the relationship between the five-factor domains and measures of positive and negative affect. In this case we are looking at the effect size of correlations. You will remember that the size of correlations helps researchers to understand how important the findings are, with correlations of $r = 0.1$ representing a small effect size $r = 0.3$ representing a medium effect size and $r = 0.5$ representing a large effect size, with larger correlations being considered as even more important. Terracciano found that neuroticism was significantly positively related with negative affect ($r = 0.69$; also finding that it was related $r = -0.34$ with positive affect) and extraversion was significantly positively related with positive affect ($r = 0.51$; also finding that it was related $r = -0.29$ with negative affect), suggesting that the effect size of the correlations between extraversion and positive affect, and neuroticism and negative affect is large. He also found that openness was significantly positively related to positive affect ($r = 0.34$), agreeableness was significantly negatively related to negative affect ($r = -0.20$), and conscientiousness shared a significant positive relationship with positive affect ($r = 0.38$) and a significant negative relationship with negative affect ($r = -0.27$). The effect sizes of these correlations are a lot smaller. This finding supports the aforementioned view of Costa and McCrae that extraversion and positive affect and neuroticism and negative affect are closely aligned, with the relationship between the other personality dimensions and well-being being more instrumental, sharing a vicarious (almost secondhand) relationship with well-being as people are receiving positive outcomes from people adopting certain personality traits.

In terms of psychological well-being, the relationship between personality and Ryff's Scales of Psychological Well-being is less explored. However, one study by Dutch psychologist Dirk van Dierendonck (2004) used factor analysis to see what personality factors underpinned autonomy, environmental mastery, personal growth, purpose in life, positive relations with others and self-acceptance. Dirk van Dierendonck found that neuroticism was negatively related with all aspects of psychological well-being (autonomy, environmental mastery, personal growth, purpose in life, positive relations with others and self-acceptance) and extraversion shared a positive relationship with positive relationships with others. Van Dierendonck also found that conscientiousness shares a positive relationship with purpose in life and personal growth, openness shares a positive relationship with autonomy, and agreeableness shares a significant positive relationship with a person's positive relations with others.

We have summarised our discussion above in Table 23.3. However, what these findings show is that, not only is personality related to well-being, but also that well-being can be better understood within some dimensions than others, and that certain elements of subjective and psychological well-being can be separated out from one another based on their relationship with different personality variables (i.e. extraversion is the best way to understand positive affect in personality terms, while neuroticism is the best way to understand negative affect in personality terms).

Personality disorders

We have explored many aspects of personality within the context of 'normal' functioning and well-being; for example, the five-factor model of personality (Chapter 7), the biological models of personality developed by Eysenck and Gray (Chapter 8) and the humanistic personality theory of Maslow (Chapter 6). However, we have also highlighted occasions when personality and individual difference theory has been used to understand less normal behaviours and inform treatment and therapy settings. For example, Rogers' person-centred therapy (Chapter 6), social anxiety disorder (Chapter 20) and irrational beliefs, emotions and thinking (Chapters 5 and 19). We are now going to introduce you to an area of individual differences and well-being that emerges from abnormal expressions of personality: personality disorders.

A personality disorder is an extreme or severe disturbance in the overall character and the behaviours shown by an individual that affects several aspects of the person's personality. A personality disorder will always involve a considerable amount of personal and social disruption, therefore not only affecting the individual him/herself, but

Table 23.3 Summary of the findings relating personality to subjective and psychological well-being

	Extraversion	Neuroticism	Conscientiousness	Openness	Agreeableness
Subjective well-being	Positive affect (smaller association with lower negative affect)	Negative affect (smaller association with higher positive affect)	Sometimes related with higher positive affect and lower negative affect with smaller effect size	Sometimes related with higher positive affect and lower negative affect with smaller effect size	Sometimes related with higher positive affect and lower negative affect with smaller effect size
Psychological well-being	Higher positive relationships with others	Low self-acceptance	Higher purpose in life	Higher positive relationships with others	
		Low positive relationships with others, low autonomy, low environment mastery, low purpose in life, low personal growth	Higher personal growth	Higher autonomy	

the people around the individual. According to psychologists, such as Paris (2003), personality disorders cause disturbances in behaviour, character and personality over the course of a person's life. Personality disorders tend to emerge early in an individual's life, with some symptoms of the disorder occurring in childhood. We are going to outline the general criteria for what is considered to be a personality disorder and then describe the main personality disorders.

General criteria for personality disorders: the *Diagnostic and Statistical Manual of Mental Disorders (DSM)–IV*

The American Psychiatric Association publishes the *Diagnostic and Statistical Manual of Mental Disorders (DSM)–IV* that provides the criteria for psychologists to diagnose mental disorders. Throughout the history of US psychiatry there have long been attempts to classify mental disorders. Since an 1840 census in the USA, agencies concerned with collecting statistical information have sought to make the distinction between different types of mental disorder, and in 1917 the 'Committee on Statistics', which was later to become the American Psychiatric Association, developed a manual, later to become known as the 'Standard' for mental hospitals, which contained diagnosis criteria for mental disorders (Grob, 1991; Houts, 2000). During the Second World War, the psychiatric profession was heavily involved in the assessment and treatment of soldiers and, from this involvement and subsequent discussion with American Psychiatric Association members, the *Diagnostic and Statistical Manual of Mental Disorders (DSM)* was first published in 1952, listing 106 mental disorders (Grob, 1991). Since then the American Psychiatric Association has produced three major revisions of the *DSM*; *DSM-II* in 1974, *DSM-III* in 1987 and the *DSM-IV* in 1994, with a text revision of the *DSM-IV* made in 2000, renaming it the *DSM-IV-R*. A *DSM-V* is scheduled for publication in 2013.

In all, the *DSM-IV* lists 297 disorders. When classifying disorders, the *DSM-IV* uses a multiaxial model. This model organises each diagnosis into five categories, each known as an Axis. These are:

- **Axis I** – this axis includes all clinical disorders, including all major mental, developmental and learning disorders.
- **Axis II** – this axis relates to underlying personality conditions or disorders.
- **Axis III** – this axis relates to acute (severe) medical conditions and physical disorders.
- **Axis IV** – this axis relates to environmental and psychosocial factors contributing to the mental disorder.
- **Axis V** – this axis relates to the assessment of functioning of the individual. It is the overall levels of psychological, social and occupational functioning.

As you can see, personality disorders are included on Axis II of the *DSM-IV*. (If you want to know how different axes are related to each other then have a look at the Stop and think: Organisation and interactions of Axis II (personality disorders) within the multiaxial model later in this discussion.)

The *DSM-IV* criteria explain that the first stage of identifying a personality disorder is the recognition of a *pattern* of behaviours and experience in the individual. This pattern of behaviour and experiences must deviate markedly from what is expected within that individual's culture. This deviation from what is expected would need to be manifested in two (or more) of the following ways:

(a) Cognitions (i.e. thoughts, perceptions) of the person. So, for example, it might be the way that they perceive themselves or others, or the way they interpret their own behaviours, or the behaviours of others or events.
(b) Affect (i.e. the emotions) of the individual. This might be the range of the affect, the intensity with which feelings and emotions are felt, the extent to which feelings and emotions are constantly changing (known as lability) and the appropriateness of these feelings.
(c) Interpersonal functioning of the individual. This is how the person interacts and relates to other people.
(d) Impulse control. The person feels influenced by a particular feeling or mental state that they are unable to control in some way.

On the identification of these patterns of behaviours based on the cognitions, affect, interpersonal and impulse control, the individual must additionally satisfy the following criteria:

- The pattern of behaviours and experiences must be enduring, inflexible and must be constant throughout a broad range of personal and social situations.
- The pattern of behaviours and experiences causes clinically significant impairment or distress that affects the individual's life in some way, be it personally, socially or in their work life.
- The pattern of behaviours and experiences must be stable over time and must be present over a long duration. In addition, the onset of the pattern of behaviours and experiences must have been tracked back to early adulthood or adolescence. As a result, people under the age of 18 years who show a pattern of behaviours and experiences are not usually diagnosed as having a personality disorder.
- The pattern of behaviours and experiences cannot be explained as part (i.e. a symptom) of another mental disorder.

- The pattern of behaviours and experiences is not the result of physiological effects of a particular substance (i.e. drug) or the result of a medical condition (e.g. head injury).

Within Axis II, the *DSM-IV* lists 10 different personality disorders. These 10 personality disorders are grouped into three Clusters:

- **Cluster A** comprises odd or eccentric disorders. The personality disorders in this cluster are paranoid personality disorder, schizoid personality disorder and schizotypal personality disorder.
- **Cluster B** comprises dramatic, emotional or erratic disorders. The personality disorders in this cluster are antisocial personality disorder, borderline personality disorder, histrionic personality disorder and narcissistic personality disorder.
- **Cluster C** comprises anxious or fearful disorders. The personality disorders in this cluster are avoidant personality disorder, dependent personality disorder and obsessive-compulsive personality disorder.

We will describe each of the 10 personality disorders by each of these clusters (see Figure 23.4). However, before we do this we must draw your attention to four things.

First, it must be remembered that, for a set of behaviours to become a personality disorder, it must meet all the requirements listed above (i.e. patterns of behaviour being enduring, inflexible, constant, clinically significant, stable over time and for a long duration, not explained as a symptom of another disorder and not being the result of a particular substance or medical condition).

Second, although you will see reference to terms such as 'schizotypal' and 'obsessive-compulsive' as personality disorders, these are not the same as abnormal psychological states such as schizophrenia and an obsessive-compulsive disorder. Although there are some clear overlaps between these two sets of disorders, both in terms of description and their relationship with each other and the causes and correlates of these sets of disorders, disorders such as schizophrenia and obsessive-compulsive disorder belong on Axis I of the *DSM-IV*, reflecting clinical and psychological diagnosis, while personality disorders exist on Axis II of the *DSM-IV*.

Third, we have not used the exact wording of the *DSM-IV* below. Instead we have simplified a lot of the technical and clinical language to aid your academic understanding of what behaviours, thoughts and feelings comprise each of the personality disorders.

Finally, and most importantly, we strongly advise a note of caution before we describe these personality disorders to you. The understanding of personality disorders is based on expert clinical diagnosis. The diagnostic labels in the *DSM-IV* are primarily for use by clinical professionals

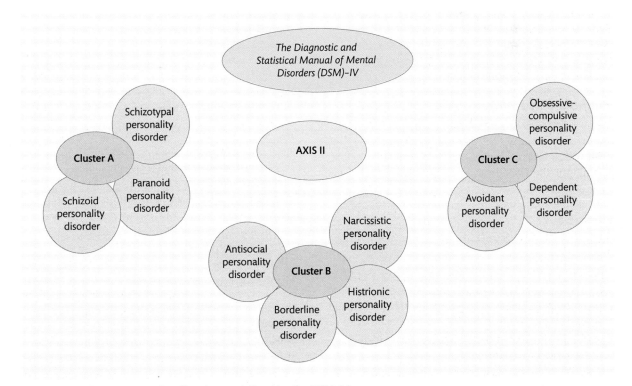

Figure 23.4 The 10 personality disorders as defined by the *DSM-IV*.

Stop and think

International Classification of Diseases and Related Health Problems (ICD)

There is another classification of personality disorders, which is outlined by the *International Classification of Diseases (ICD)*, the first version of which was published in 1893. Today the *ICD* is used by the World Health Organization member states and is in its tenth version. The difference between the *DSM* and the *ICD* is that the *ICD* covers many more health domains than the *DSM*, including a number of diseases, injuries and health com-plications, but the *ICD* also has diagnostic criteria for a number of personality disorders. However, it should not be seen as a rival diagnostic tool to the *DSM-IV*; since the 1990s the American Psychiatric Association and the World Health Organization have worked closely together to coordinate the diagnostic criteria and codes across both publications, although some differences between the two publications remain.

and the American Psychiatric Association advises non-clinical professionals only to use the criteria for informa-tion and not to make a diagnosis. Therefore you should most definitely not use these criteria to perform some self-diagnosis, or to diagnose others, using the information given here.

Personality disorders: Cluster A: paranoid, schizoid and schizotypal personality disorders

In Cluster A of Axis II of the *DSM-IV* are three personality disorders that represent odd or eccentric disorders. These are paranoid personality disorder, schizoid personality disorder and schizotypal personality disorder.

Paranoid personality disorder

According to the *DSM-IV* and academics in the field (e.g. Meissner, 1995), a paranoid personality disorder is characterised by a pattern of paranoia (e.g. delusions of persecution), extreme distrust or mistrust of other people and irrational suspicions of others. Therefore example behaviours of someone with a paranoid person-ality disorder might be that they are suspicious that others are deceiving them or they are not to be trusted (e.g. they may always be suspicious, without justification, that their spouse or partner is being unfaithful), and they tend to hold persistent grudges against certain people. They are hypersensitive, meaning they will tend to see simple and innocent statements made by others as attacks on them or threats against them. Meissner (1995) describes individuals with this disorder as needing to maintain a high degree of control over people around them. As a result of this high degree of control they tend to be critical and unable to cooperate or work with others, seeking out those who share

their beliefs. According to estimates in Europe, paranoid personality disorder is present in about 0.5–2.5 per cent of the general population (e.g. Torgersen *et al.*, 2001).

According to the *DSM-IV*, four or more of the following are required for a diagnosis of a paranoid personality disorder:

- Suspects, without any sufficient basis, that other people are exploiting, harming or deceiving them.
- The individual is preoccupied with unjustified doubts about the trustworthiness of friends or other people that are close to them.
- Shows reluctance to confide in others as they are fearful that the information they share will be used in a mali-cious way against them.
- Perceives innocent remarks or events as threatening or demeaning.
- Will consistently hold grudges against someone, and will not easily forgive other people when those people have insulted, injured or made a transgression against them.
- Will often perceive that others have made attacks on their character, though these attacks will not be appar-ent to other people, and will be quick to react angrily or to attack the person who they feel has made the initial attack.
- Will have recurring and unjustified suspicions regarding the fidelity of a sexual partner.

Schizoid personality disorder

According to the *DSM-IV* and academics in the field (e.g. Weismann, 1993; McGlashan *et al.*, 2000), a schizoid personality disorder is generally characterised by a pattern of detachment (disconnection) from interpersonal and social relationships and will tend to be demonstrated by a limited amount of emotion in social settings and rela-tionships. So, for example, an individual who has been diagnosed with a schizoid personality disorder will almost always choose to be solitary (be alone) and will neither search out nor enjoy being in close personal relationships, including family relationships. They will lack close friends, will appear indifferent when other people praise or criticise them, and show emotional coldness and a disconnection from other people. They will also have limited interest in a sexual encounter with another person. According to estimates in Europe, schizoid personality disorder is present in about 1.7 per cent of the general population (e.g. Torgersen *et al.*, 2001). According to the *DSM-IV*, four or more of the following are required for a diagnosis of a schizoid personality disorder:

- Will not enjoy or seek out close relationships, including being part of a family.
- Will almost always choose solitary activities.
- Has little or no interest in having sexual experiences with other people.
- Takes pleasure in few, if any, activities.
- Tends to lack close friends other than first-degree relatives.
- Will be indifferent to the praise or criticism of others.
- Will be emotionally cold, show low, or no, levels of attachment to others, or flattened emotions.

Schizotypal personality disorder

According to the *DSM-IV* and academics in the field (e.g. Berenbaum *et al.*, 2003), schizotypal personality disorder is evidenced by an extreme discomfort with, and a reduced tendency for, close relationships, as well as having distortions in thinking, feelings and perceptions and sometimes showing eccentric behaviour. According to estimates in Europe, schizoid personality disorder is present in about 0.6 per cent of the general population (e.g. Torgersen *et al.*, 2001). The symptoms of schizotypal personality disorder can be indicated by five (or more) of the following:

- Ideas of reference. These involve the person developing the belief that everyday events are referring to the individual when, in fact, they are not. So, for example, someone who has ideas of reference may believe that people on television or the radio are talking about them, or talking directly to them, or that headlines in newspapers are written about or for them. They may believe that strangers say things about them behind their back, or groups of people are plotting against them. They may see events or objects as being deliberately set up to have a particular meaning for them. Ideas of reference are not less firmly held or organised by the individual. However, people with schizotypal personality disorder do not have delusions of reference which represent similar symptoms as ideas of reference but have much more

strongly held beliefs which may cause impairment of functioning.
- Odd beliefs or magical thinking. Within psychology magical thinking is thinking that believes that the mind can affect the physical world or belief that everything is connected through forces and powers that exist in both the physical and spiritual world. These beliefs, however, exist outside cultural norms. Therefore they may be things like beliefs in telepathy, or a 'sixth sense' or bizarre fantasies or preoccupations.
- Unusual perceptual experiences, such as bodily illusions, which are like strange bodily feelings, phantom pains or distortions in how sensations in their body are perceived; for example, the sense of touch.
- Odd thinking and speech. For example, the individual may be vague about topics, use metaphors a lot (speech that directly compares seemingly unrelated subjects, e.g. 'life is a box of chocolates'), be circumstantial (incidental to the main facts) and over elaborate.
- Suspiciousness or paranoid ideas.
- Inappropriate, tense or constrained feelings or emotions.
- Lack of close friends or confidants, other than first-degree relatives, and feelings of extreme discomfort in interpersonal situations.
- General social anxiety related to paranoid fears about those people and events around them.

Personality disorders: Cluster B: antisocial, borderline, histrionic and narcissistic personality disorders

In Cluster B of Axis II of the *DSM-IV*, there are four personality disorders that represent dramatic, emotional or erratic disorders. These are antisocial personality disorder, borderline personality disorder, histrionic personality disorder and narcissistic personality disorder.

Antisocial personality disorder

According to the *DSM-IV*, an antisocial personality disorder is characterised by a general disregard for others. A person with an antisocial personality disorder may engage in persistent lying and stealing, have a lack of empathy for others, show recklessness and consistently fail to plan or keep to long-term goals, showing an inability to make or maintain friends or personal relationships; they may have recurring difficulties with the law, be unable to control their own anger and temper and show a tendency to violate the rights and boundaries of others. According to estimates in Europe, antisocial personality disorder affects between 0.7 and 3 per cent of the population (e.g. Torgersen *et al.*, 2001).

According to the *DSM-IV*, three or more of the following are required for a diagnosis of an antisocial personality disorder:

- Continued failure to conform to one's social norms in respect to law and repeatedly performing acts that the person could be arrested for.
- Continued deceitfulness; that is, repeatedly lying, using aliases or conning other people for one's own profit or pleasure.
- Show continued impulsivity (to act on impulse rather than thought) or repeated failures to plan ahead.
- Show consistent irritability and aggressiveness, such as repeatedly getting into physical fights or assaulting other people.
- Reckless disregard for safety for oneself or other people.
- Repeated acts of irresponsibility, such as failing to maintain consistent work behaviours or honour one's financial obligations.
- To show a continued lack of remorse; this might be characterised by being indifferent to or rationalising (to find reasons to justify or explain) hurting or mistreating other people.

Also, to be diagnosed as an antisocial personality disorder, the antisocial behaviour shown by the individual must not have occurred as the result of another disorder, e.g. schizophrenia.

Borderline personality disorder

According to the *DSM-IV*, someone with a borderline personality disorder tends to have unstable personal relationships, poor impulse control over things such as spending money, their sexual conduct and substance misuse or abuse. They also tend not to have a well-formed self-image of themselves or identity. They may make threats about committing suicide and engage in self-harm. They are also badly affected by stress, tending either to be anxious, depressed or show anger. According to estimates in Europe (e.g. Torgersen *et al.*, 2001), borderline personality disorder affects between 0.7 and 2 per cent of the population. The *DSM-IV* diagnosis of borderline personality disorder suggests that any five out of the following nine listed criteria need to be identified:

- Repeated attempts at suicidal behaviour, gestures, threats, or self-harming or self-mutilating behaviour such as cutting.
- Frantic efforts to avoid real or imagined abandonment (although this does not cover suicidal or self-mutilating behaviour listed above).
- Impulsivity (i.e. to act on impulse rather than thought) in at least two areas that are potentially self-damaging (e.g. in sexual behaviours, eating, substance misuse or abuse or dangerous driving, although this does not cover suicidal or self-mutilating behaviour listed above).
- Participates in intense and unstable personal relationships in which the individual changes the intensity of the relationship between idealisation (i.e. thinking the relationship is ideal and perfect) and devaluation (e.g. placing no value on the relationship).
- Identity disturbance, characterised by a persistent unstable self-image or sense of self.
- Instability in feelings, characterised by marked changes in mood, such as irritability or anxiety.

The borderline personality disorder is often portrayed in films.
Source: The Kobal Collection/Columbia Tristar

- Persistent and lasting feeling of emptiness or worthlessness.
- Shows great difficulty in controlling anger or displaying anger in inappropriate ways or situations. This may be having frequent displays of losing one's temper or continually having fights.
- When stressed, showing paranoid ideas or delusions or showing symptoms of dissociation (disruption of the normal way a person integrates their conscious or psychological functioning).

Histrionic personality disorder

According to the *DSM-IV*, histrionic personality disorder is characterised by a person who is always looking for attention and needs to be the centre of attention. They have an excessive need for approval, are overly dramatic with wild mood swings in minor situations. They get easily bored with normal routines and are always seeking new situations. In relationships they get over-involved with the other person very quickly, and they demand increased amounts of attention very quickly. They also tend to engage in provocative seductive sexual behaviour or appearance. According to estimates in Europe, histrionic personality disorder affects around 2 per cent of the population (e.g. Torgersen *et al.*, 2001). According to the *DSM-IV*, diagnosis of histrionic personality disorder suggests that any five or more of the following criteria need to be identified:

- Feels uncomfortable when placed in situations in which the person feels they are not the centre of everyone's attention.
- The individual interpersonal interaction with others is often sexually seductive or provocative.
- When displaying emotion this often changes and is often shallow.
- The individual uses their own physical appearance to draw attention to themselves.
- The individual will tend to speak in an impressionistic way (that their conversations are based on impressions as opposed to reason or fact) and they tend to lack detail when speaking.
- Tend to be over-dramatic about themselves and always expresses exaggerated emotion.
- Is very easily influenced by others or circumstances.
- Considers personal relationships to be much more intimate than they actually are in reality.

Narcissistic personality disorder

According to the *DSM-IV*, someone with a narcissistic personality disorder has an inflated self-importance (grandiosity), preoccupation with fantasies about their own achievement and success, tends to seek attention and admiration from others, and centres their interpersonal relations around themselves. According to estimates in Europe, narcissistic personality disorder affects around 0.8 per cent of the population (e.g. Torgersen *et al.*, 2001). According to the *DSM-IV*, diagnosis of narcissistic personality disorder suggests that any five or more of the following criteria need to be identified:

- The individual believes that they are 'special' and unique.
- Demands excessive admiration from others.
- Has an inflated (grandiose) sense of self-importance.
- Is preoccupied with fantasies of obtaining power, or showing brilliance, or achieving unlimited success, or finding ideal love.
- Has a belief that they are entitled to most things.
- Is exploitive (selfish or unethical) in their interpersonal relationships.
- Lacks empathy (i.e. lacks the capacity to understand other people's state of mind).
- Tends to be envious of other people or believes that other people are envious of them.
- Is arrogant in their behaviours and attitudes.

Personality disorders: Cluster C: avoidant, dependent and obsessive-compulsive personality disorders

In Cluster C of Axis II of the *DSM-IV*, there are three personality disorders that represent anxious or fearful disorders. These are avoidant personality disorder, dependent personality disorder and obsessive-compulsive personality disorder.

Avoidant personality disorder

An individual with an avoidant personality disorder tends to be socially inhibited (holds back socially) and socially withdrawn, avoiding social interactions. They have high levels of social discomfort, feelings of inadequacy and fear of being judged negatively by other people. They are extremely shy and timid and are sensitive to criticism or rejection. They tend to have low self-esteem. However, they have a desire for acceptance from other people, and will only form relationships when they feel that they won't be rejected. According to estimates in Europe, avoidant personality disorder affects around 5 per cent of the population (e.g. Torgersen *et al.*, 2001). According to the *DSM-IV*, diagnosis of avoidant personality disorder suggests that four or more of the following criteria need to be identified:

- The individual avoids activities within their occupation that would mean the person engaging in interpersonal contact, because they fear criticism or disapproval.

- They show an unwillingness to involve themselves with people unless they are sure they will be liked.
- Tend to be restrained in starting intimate relationships because of a fear of becoming embarrassed, shamed or rejected or having low self-worth.
- The individual is preoccupied with receiving criticism, disapproval or being rejected in social situations.
- In new interpersonal situations, the individual tends to be socially inhibited because they feel inferior or inadequate.
- Individuals view themselves as socially inept (without skill or aptitude, generally awkward or clumsy) or inferior or unappealing to others.
- Is reluctant to take personal risk or engage in new things or activities for fear of embarrassment.

Dependent personality disorder

According to the *DSM-IV*, an individual with a dependent personality disorder shows persistent psychological dependence on other people. They tend to allow others to take responsibility for major areas and aspects of their life because they feel they lack the confidence or the ability to undertake responsibility for these areas themselves. They only derive their self-worth through others. According to estimates in Europe, dependent personality disorder affects around 1.5 per cent of the population (e.g. Torgersen *et al.*, 2001). According to the *DSM-IV*, diagnosis of dependent personality disorder suggests that any five or more of the following criteria need to be identified:

- The individual will find it difficult to make normal everyday decisions without a large amount of advice from others and reassurance that they are doing the correct thing.
- Will need other people to take responsibility for major areas of their life.
- Will tend not to disagree with others because they are worried about losing the support or approval of others (does not include situations where the person may fear an act of retribution, e.g. some sort of punishment).
- Has difficulty doing things on his or her own owing to lack of self-confidence, motivation or confidence in his or her ability.
- The individual will go to excessive lengths to gain support from others, even if it means sometimes volunteering to do things that are unpleasant.
- Will feel uncomfortable when alone because of extreme concern of being unable to care for themselves.
- When a close relationship ends, will quickly seek out another relationship for support.
- Is unrealistically preoccupied with concerns and fears that they will be left alone to take care of themselves.

Obsessive-compulsive personality disorder

According to the *DSM-IV* and academics in the area (e.g. Samuels *et al.*, 2000), an individual with an obsessive-compulsive personality disorder is someone who shows great conformity to rules and moral codes. An individual with an obsessive-compulsive personality disorder will

Stop and think

Disordered personalities at work . . .

In 2005, United Kingdom psychologists Belinda Board and Katarina Fritzon compared personality disorder traits across forensic, psychiatric and 'normal' senior business manager samples. Board and Fritzon (2005) interviewed and gave the Minnesota Multiphasic Personality Inventory Scales, which are scales that contain *DSM* criteria for personality disorders, to high-level British executives and compared their profiles with those of criminal psychiatric patients at Broadmoor Hospital, a high-security psychiatric hospital, in the United Kingdom. They found that the profile of managers comprised significant aspects of three personality disorders:

- Histrionic personality disorder: including superficial charm, insincerity, egocentricity and manipulation.

- Narcissistic personality disorder: including grandiosity, self-focused lack of empathy for others, exploitativeness and independence.
- Obsessive-compulsive personality disorder: including perfectionism, excessive devotion to work, rigidity, stubbornness and dictatorial tendencies.

This was certainly an interesting finding. Board and Fritzon suggest that some traits that are associated with personality disorders might emerge in other individuals as successful characteristics in certain situations, e.g. being successful in business. That is, certain personality traits such as grandiosity, lack of empathy, independence, perfectionism, stubbornness, egocentricity and the ability to charm and manipulate might be useful traits to develop in business.

also tend to seek perfectionism in everything they do (everything must be just right and perfect) and they will have difficulty in doing anything unless it is done the way they want to do it. They will tend not to be flexible or open to others' ideas or be efficient in what they do. According to estimates in Europe, obsessive-compulsive personality disorder affects around 2.0 per cent of the population (e.g. Torgersen *et al.*, 2001). According to the *DSM-IV*, diagnosis of obsessive-compulsive personality disorder suggests that four or more of the following criteria need to be identified:

- The individual will be overly preoccupied with details, the organisation of things, rules, or order to a point where the purpose of the task or activity they are doing is lost.
- Shows a level of perfectionism that interferes with the completion of tasks (e.g. they will not complete a project they are doing because they spend too much time on trying to make it perfect).
- Is extremely and excessively devoted to work, so much so that leisure activities and friendships will suffer.
- Is inflexible and over-conscientious (overly meticulous and careful) about issues of morals, ethics and values (and these morals, ethics and values must not be able to be accounted for as part of the individual's cultural or religious background).
- Is unable to throw out worthless objects even when they have no sentimental value.
- Will not give people tasks and will not work with others unless the other people do the task or the work exactly how the person wants to do it.
- Tends to be miserly with money, both with themselves and others.
- Is rigid and stubborn in their attitudes and behaviours.

Genetic, biological and environmental influences on personality disorders

We are now going to look at heritability estimates in assessing personality disorders. We will outline some studies that have looked at genetic and environmental influences on personality disorders and outline heritability estimates, environmental influences (in the form of developmental and childhood experiences) and biological influences, including the relationship between some of the personality disorders and neuropsychology. However, we will not revisit details of the usefulness and issues that surround heritability estimates and what they mean here. (In Chapter 8 we discussed the role of heritability estimates in assessing *personality* and if you want to read up on the issues that surround heritability estimates you could read through the relevant sections of that chapter again.)

Heritability and personality disorders

In the first twin study that tried to investigate the heritability estimates of the whole range of personality disorders, Norwegian psychologists Svenn Torgersen and colleagues (Torgersen *et al.*, 2001) from the Department of Psychology, Oslo University, looked at possible genetic influences on personality disorder by looking at heritability estimates among twins. Using a twin sample from the Norwegian Twin Register (which includes several sets of populations and covers twin pairs born between 1895 and the present day) alongside the National Register for Mental Disorders, 92 monozygotic (MZ; identical) and 129 dizygotic (DZ; fraternal) twin pairs were compared to baseline data from 2,000 individuals. All twins were personally interviewed about their lifetime history of mental disorders using the Structured Clinical Interview for Personality Disorders.

Torgersen and his colleagues calculated heritability estimates for all personality disorders except for antisocial personality disorder, because of the low occurrence of antisocial personality disorder in the twin sample. The heritability estimates are provided in Table 23.4, with many of the estimates being substantial. These results lend support to the suggestion that personality disorders have a substantial genetic component. The authors noticed a large variation in the size heritability among the different personality disorders. However, Torgersen offers the explanation that this may be because of a moderate sample size and low prevalence of the specific disorders within the sample.

In 2001, Canadian psychologists Frederick Coolidge, Linda Thede and Kerry Jang (Coolidge *et al.*, 2001) looked at the heritability of personality disorders among 112

Table 23.4 Heritability estimates for personality disorders (except antisocial). Based on Torgersen *et al.* (2001)

	Heritability estimates h^2
Cluster A	0.37
Paranoid	0.28
Schizoid	0.29
Schizotypal	0.61
Cluster B	0.60
Antisocial	
Borderline	0.69
Histrionic	0.67
Narcissistic	0.79
Cluster C	0.62
Avoidant	0.28
Dependent	0.57
Obsessive-compulsive	0.78
Across all personality disorders	0.60

Stop and think

Comparing heritability estimates for normal personality and personality disorders

Find the heritability estimates for normal personality (Chapter 8). From these findings, do personality disorders seem to be more strongly or less strongly influenced by genetic effects than the broad personality dimensions? Or would you say they are about the same? What does your finding suggest?

children aged between 4 and 15 years. The sample included 70 MZ and 42 DZ pairs of twins. The authors used the Coolidge Personality and Neuropsychological Inventory for Children (CPNI; Coolidge, 1998) to measure 12 personality disorders according to the criteria in the *DSM-IV*. Coolidge *et al.* found that the average (median) heritability coefficient for the 12 scales was 0.75 (ranging from 0.81 for the dependent and schizotypal personality disorder scales to 0.50 for the paranoid and passive-aggressive personality disorder scales). These results lend further support to the suggestion that childhood personality disorders have a substantial genetic component and are similar to heritability estimates of personality disorder traits in adults.

There are very few other studies that have looked at heritability estimates on all the personality disorders at the same time. Other studies have tended to look at subsets of the disorders. Two recent studies have looked at specific personality disorders across European and Australian samples. Dutch psychologists M. A. Distel and colleagues (Distel *et al.*, 2008) examined twin samples for features of borderline personality disorder among 5,496 twins between the ages of 18 and 86 years from The Netherlands ($n = 3,918$), Belgium ($n = 904$) and Australia ($n = 674$). Distel and colleagues estimated that the additive genetic influences (genetic variation in behaviour that is the total of the individual's total genes inherited from their parents) (see Chapter 8) explain 42 per cent of the variation in borderline personality disorder features in both men and women, and that this heritability estimate was similar across The Netherlands, Belgium and Australia. In 2008, Norwegian psychologist, Ted Reichborn-Kjennerud and colleagues (Reichborn-Kjennerud *et al.*, 2008) looked at the Cluster C personality disorders, which include avoidant, dependent and obsessive-compulsive personality disorders. Some 1,386 young adult twin pairs from the Norwegian Institute of Public Health Twin Panel (NIPHTP) were assessed using the Structured Interview for *DSM-IV* Personality (SIDP-IV). Here, heritability ranged from 27 per cent for obsessive-compulsive personality disorder to 35 per cent for avoidant personality disorder.

Environmental influences on personality disorders: the result of developmental and childhood experiences

According to the *DSM-IV*, the assumption is that personality disorders tend to emerge early in a person's life, with some symptoms becoming evident in childhood. Therefore, one of the main focuses into research on the causes of personality disorders has centred on environmental influences on personality disorders, and particularly childhood experiences.

For those with antisocial personality disorder, research has suggested that childhood factors are important. Johnson *et al.* (2006) found that parenting behaviours, such as low levels of affection or nurturing by parents, were associated with a higher risk of antisocial personality disorder when children reached adulthood. Also Rettew *et al.* (2003), in a retrospective study of adults (that is, a study where researchers ask adult participants to report on their history and experiences at an earlier point in their life), found that 61 per cent of those individuals with antisocial personality reported high levels of childhood emotional abuse.

Similar findings occur for individuals with borderline personality disorder. Zanarini and Frankenburg (1997) found that individuals with borderline personality disorder also report a history of abuse and neglect in childhood. Furthermore, a number of researchers have found that sexual abuse in childhood is associated with the development of a borderline personality disorder (Brown and Anderson, 1991; Herman and Herman, 1992; Quadrio, 2005; Zanarini *et al.*, 1989). Also, those individuals with borderline personality disorder are likely to report that their parents often would not listen or ignore their thoughts and feelings, that they didn't feel protected by their parents, or that their parents withdrew from them (Dozier *et al.*, 1999; Zanarini *et al.*, 2000).

Helgeland and Torgersen (2004) reported on a study that compared a number of childhood factors between a group of 25 *DSM-IV*-diagnosed subjects with borderline personality disorder (who in their childhood had been

Stop and think

Retrospective studies

Some of the studies looking at childhood experiences and the development of personality disorders are retrospective studies which ask participants to look back over their lives and recount their experiences. What considerations (advantages and disadvantages) should be made of research that uses this methodology?

diagnosed at risk for borderline personality disorder) with a group of 107 non-borderline control subjects who were then followed up for 28 years. Helgeland and Torgersen found that the borderline personality disorder group showed higher levels of abuse, neglect, an unpredictable and unstable environment and that their parents showed higher levels of psychopathology (e.g. mental illness) than the control group. Helgeland and Torgersen (2004) also found that there were protective factors for the borderline personality disorder. They found that, among children thought to be at risk for borderline personality disorder, protective factors against developing a borderline personality disorder included possessing artistic talents, showing superior school performance or having above-average intellectual skills. Together, all these findings emphasise that childhood factors, such as abuse and neglect, environmental instability, as well as the absence of protective factors, may contribute to the development of borderline personality disorder.

There is also evidence that abuse in childhood may influence schizotypal personality disorder traits. Evidence suggests that problematic parenting styles (e.g. not talking much with the child, not supporting them), early separation of an individual's parents' marriage and early childhood neglect can lead to the development of schizotypal traits (Anglina et al., 2008; Berenbaum et al., 2003). These authors suggest that individuals with schizotypal personality disorder report childhood experiences being negative in nature. This in turn makes the individual, when a child, have difficulties in interacting with others, and therefore others see them as different and therefore they are treated differently throughout their childhood. Consequently, the individual begins to see other people as harmful and as treating them negatively. Anglina et al. and Berenbaum suggest that these developmental processes are the possible source of the 'ideas of reference' (developing the belief that everyday events are referring to the individual when, in fact, they are not) that are thought to be one of the characteristics of schizotypal personality disorder traits. This is because these individuals have experienced people being negative to them, and therefore they have learnt to expect people to continue to act negatively towards them and

believe all events will be related to them in a negative way (even though they are not).

Finally, one study has looked at all the personality disorders. In this study, Paul Miller and David Lisak (Miller and Lisak, 1999) studied 600 male college students and examined the relationship between childhood experiences of sexual and physical abuse and reported personality disorder symptoms. These authors found that childhood abuse histories were found to be significantly associated with greater levels of symptomatology across the Clusters A, B and C of personality disorders.

Biological and neuropsychological factors in personality disorders

Biological and neuropsychological factors may also be associated with personality disorders. L. J. Siever and K. L. Davis (1991) provide a biological and neurological model of psychopathology, which includes personality disorders, based on data gained from clinical phenomena and experience. This model is used to explain how neurotransmitters are related to personality disorders. Neurotransmitters are chemicals that are used to relay, amplify and modulate electrical signals in the brain. In terms of personality disorders, these authors suggest that neurotransmitters and personality disorders are associated in four aspects of psychological functioning and behaviour: (1) cognitive/perceptual, (2) impulsivity/aggression, (3) affect regulation and (4) anxiety/inhibition. We are now going to discuss these four aspects of psychological functioning and behaviour and have summarised the Siever and Davis model in Figure 23.5.

The first area to consider is **cognitive/perceptual** aspects in personality disorders. These aspects are based on the brain systems related to attention and response. The important neurotransmitter here is thought to be dopamine. Dopamine is crucial to the parts of the brain that control our movements and is commonly associated with the pleasure aspects of the brain, providing feelings of enjoyment and motivation to do things. In the frontal lobes of the brain, the part of the brain involved with planning, coordinating, controlling and executing behaviour, dopamine controls

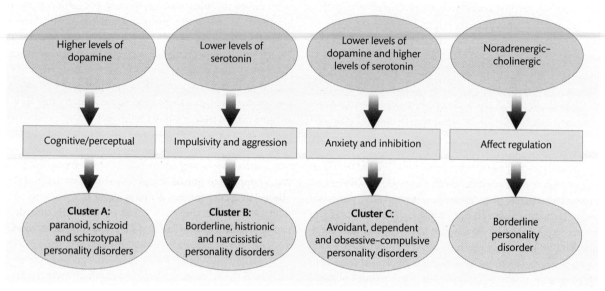

Figure 23.5 Siever and Davis' neuropsychological models of psychopathology applied to personality disorders.

the flow of information from other areas of the brain. With low levels of dopamine, concentration and focus are very difficult and also associated with an inability to concentrate on activities, or conversations. Increases in dopamine levels are associated with increased levels of excitement and energy, suspiciousness and paranoid behaviour and the tendency to misinterpret experiences in the environment, and feel overly stimulated by our environment. Therefore, Siever and Davis suggest that higher levels of dopamine activity are important in understanding Cluster A type personality disorders (paranoid, schizoid and schizotypal personality disorders). You will remember from earlier in this discussion that individuals with schizotypal personality disorder suffer from maintaining odd beliefs or magical thinking or have unusual perceptual experiences. Similarly, those with paranoid personality disorders believe that others are exploiting, harming or deceiving or have unjustified suspicions. These individuals have problems with the accuracy with which they are processing information about the world and therefore their information processing or perceptual experiences become distorted. According to Siever and Davis, this is the result of higher dopamine activity.

The second area to consider is impulsivity and aggression in personality disorders. This account is based on those brain systems that are associated with the capacity to inhibit behaviour. The central neurotransmitter here is thought to be serotonin (or 5-hydroxytryptamine, 5-HT). The serotonin neurotransmitter is known to modulate and regulate mood, emotion and sleep, and is involved in the control of numerous behavioural and physiological functions. As a consequence, serotonin is linked to the

inhibition of behaviours and emotions. It is understood that low serotonin levels result in emotions, pain and impulses being unregulated. That is, people with low serotonin levels do not tend to be uninhibited in their behaviours (i.e. they will tend to show emotion and act on their impulses). Conversely, higher levels of serotonin moderate and control these emotions and impulses. That is, people with high serotonin levels will tend to show inhibited behaviours (i.e. they will tend not to show emotion and act on their impulses). Siever and Davis suggest that decreased serotonin activity is important to understanding the Cluster B personality disorders (borderline personality disorder, histrionic personality disorder and narcissistic personality disorder). You will remember that antisocial personality disorder comprises behaviours such as continued failure to conform to one's social norms in respect to law and repeatedly performing acts that the person could be arrested for. Borderline personality disorder comprises behaviours such as poor impulse control over things such as spending money, sexual conduct and substance misuse or abuse. Finally, **histrionic personality disorder**, excessive need for approval, is overly dramatic with wild mood swings in minor situations. All these behaviours, show a failure to regulate/inhibit behaviour, suggesting low serotonin levels.

The third area to consider is **anxiety/inhibition** in personality disorders. In this, Siever and Davis combine the two neurotransmitters we have just mentioned; dopamine (aspects of the brain that control our movements and are commonly associated with the pleasure aspects of the brain) and serotonin (the neurotransmitter that is known to modulate mood, emotion and sleep).

However, on this occasion, Siever and David suggest that it is reduced dopamine activity (likened to a tendency to reduce pleasure-seeking or excitement and energy) and increased serotonin activity (where emotion and impulses are over-inhibited) that are related to Cluster C personality disorders (avoidant personality disorder, dependent personality disorder and obsessive-compulsive personality disorder). You will remember that individuals with avoidant personality disorder involve themselves in less interpersonal contact, because they fear criticism or disapproval. Dependent personality disorder is related to lack of self-confidence, or confidence in their ability. Obsessive-compulsive personality disorder reflects extremely and excessively inflexible and over-conscientious attitudes and behaviours. Therefore we can see how reduced dopamine activity (a tendency to reduce pleasure-seeking or seeking out new things) and increased serotonin activity (ability to be over-inhibited) can be related to avoidant or inhibited behaviour that is frequently associated with these personality disorders.

The final area to consider is **affect regulation** in personality disorders. You will remember that affect means emotional states. This area is based on those brain systems related to the stability of mood. The central mechanism here is thought to be noradrenergic-cholinergic neurotransmitter functioning. Norepinephrine (noradrenaline; relating to the first part of the word noradrenergic-cholinergic) is a stress hormone that affects parts of the human brain where attention and impulsivity are controlled. It is related to activation of the sympathetic nervous system, which regulates our responses to stress. Cholinergic (the second part of the word noradrenergic-cholinergic) is related to the neurotransmitter acetylcholine, which is believed to be involved in mood. Siever and Davis link these aspects to Cluster B

personality disorders but specifically borderline personality disorder. You will remember that borderline personality disorder is related to instability in feelings and is characterised by marked changes in mood, such as irritability or anxiety and repeated attempts at suicidal behaviour, gestures, threats, or self-harming or self-mutilating behaviour such as cutting. Therefore, Siever and Davis suggest increased noradrenergic-cholinergic activity is important in understanding borderline personality disorder. However, this final aspect is now considered to be not as important as the other three explanations, as it only applies to borderline personality disorder and the clinical evidence for this is much weaker.

As you can see, Cluster A, B and C personality disorders can be largely seen as a result of a combination of increased or decreased dopamine and serotonin levels.

Five-factor correlates of personality disorders

So how do personality disorders relate to normal personality? In 2004, Australians Lisa Saulsman and Andrew Page carried out a meta-analysis (a study that combines the results of several studies) of the relationship between the five-factor personality dimensions (neuroticism, extraversion, openness, agreeableness and conscientiousness) and each of the 10 personality disorders among 15 independent samples. We have outlined the relationships discovered by Saulsman and Page in Table 23.5. Remember it is useful here to note these relationships in terms of effect size, with 0.1 being small, 0.3 being medium and 0.5 being large. Saulsman and Page highlighted effect sizes of above 0.2 as noteworthy. In summary, they found that all personality disorders (with the exception

Table 23.5 Relationship between personality disorders and the five-factor model of personality

	Neuroticism	Extraversion	Openness	Agreeableness	Conscientiousness
Cluster A					
Paranoid	0.28	−0.12	−0.04	−0.34	−0.07
Schizoid	0.13	0.23	−0.12	−0.17	−0.03
Schizotypal	0.36	0.28	−0.01	−0.21	−0.13
Cluster B					
Antisocial	0.09	0.04	0.05	−0.35	−0.26
Borderline	0.49	−0.09	0.02	−0.23	−0.23
Histrionic	0.02	0.42	0.15	−0.06	−0.09
Narcissistic	0.04	0.20	0.11	−0.27	−0.05
Cluster C					
Avoidant	0.48	−0.44	−0.09	−0.11	−0.10
Dependent	0.41	−0.13	−0.11	0.05	−0.14
Obsessive-compulsive	0.08	−0.12	−0.07	−0.04	0.23

Stop and think

Schizotypal personality disorder: a combination of factors

We have been looking at how different explanations (i.e. genetic, biological, childhood experiences) are related to the development of personality disorders. You now know that it can be strongly argued that many individual differences in any behaviour or personality are a result of the combination and interaction between a number of genetic, biological and environmental factors. In 2006, Adrian Raine published a paper looking at diagnostic, developmental, demographic, psychosocial, genetic and neurodevelopmental factors relating to schizotypal personality disorder. As we have shown here, Raine noted that factors for schizotypal personality disorder, genetic and early environmental influences act to alter brain structure/function throughout development, resulting in disturbances to the basic cognitive (thinking/perceiving) and affective (emotional) processes of the individual in three ways: cognitive-perceptual, interpersonal and disorganised features. He argues that a distinction can be hypothesised in schizotypal personality disorder between: (a) neuro-developmental schizotypy, which has its roots in genetic, prenatal and early postnatal factors, and is relatively stable; and (b) pseudoschizotypy, which is influenced by psychosocial adversity, shows greater symptom fluctuations and may be more responsive to psychosocial intervention.

of dependent personality disorder) could be best understood with the dimensions of high neuroticism and lower agreeableness. Also, extraversion was found to be related to some personality disorders (e.g. positively related to histrionic personality disorder and negatively related to avoidant personality disorder). Consequently, these researchers have argued that neuroticism and agreeableness, and to some extent extraversion, may be used to understand personality disorders. That is to say, personality disorders, to some extent, can be understood within the five-factor model of personality, rather than seen as something separate from normal personality.

Issues with the conceptualisation and categorisation of personality disorders

There are a number of emerging issues with the conceptualisation and categorisation of personality disorders. These issues relate to something called comorbidity. Comorbidity, in areas such as personality disorders, means accounting for: (i) the presence of one or more personality disorders, in addition to a primary personality disorder; and (ii) the existence of additional clinical conditions alongside the initially diagnosed personality disorder. It is the presence of comorbidity that has led some psychologists to question how psychologists conceptualise and categorise personality disorders.

The first aspect of comorbidity is the presence of one or more personality disorders, in addition to a primary personality disorder. For example, the classification of personality disorders often raises concerns and interest among some

authors (e.g. Blagov *et al.*, 2007; Westen *et al.*, 2006) because the comorbidity rates among the personality disorders are high, meaning that there are huge overlaps between the personality disorders. This is a concern to clinicians, as well as researchers, in the field because it suggests that these 'definitive' categories, as defined by the *DSM-IV*, are not defined as precisely as they could be and this has implications for correctly identifying personality disorder. Imagine the time and resources you might spend with a patient treating one personality disorder, when, in fact, it may be that the symptoms you are treating are the result of another personality disorder. There are recent examples in the literature that look at this issue. One example is the work by Kenneth Critchfield *et al.* (2008), who explored which of the Cluster A, B and C personality disorders accompanied borderline personality disorder. Among 90 patients diagnosed with borderline personality disorder, Critchfield and his colleagues found that there were three subtypes based on the other Axis II personality disorder profiles:

- Borderline personality disorder with Cluster A reflecting elevated (raised and increased) paranoid and schizotypal features.
- Borderline personality disorder with Cluster B reflecting elevated narcissistic and histrionic features.
- Borderline personality disorder with Cluster C reflecting elevated avoidant and obsessive-compulsive features.

Similarly, Pavel Blagov and Drew Westen (Blagov and Westen, 2008) looked at histrionic personality disorder and its overlap with other personality disorders among adults and adolescents using around 1,000 clinicians' diagnoses of cases they had previously just seen. Blagov and Westen found evidence to question the *DSM-IV* classification of the histrionic personality disorder as a severe and distinct personality disorder. Rather, they suggest that the histrionic personality disorder might be a subtype of the more severe borderline and dependent personality pathologies.

The comorbidity issue with personality disorders also extends to the second area, the existence of additional clinical conditions alongside the initially diagnosed personality disorder. One example is the presence of other psychopathology occurring alongside personality disorders. You may remember from early parts of this discussion that personality disorders exist on Axis II of the *DSM-IV*. Well, on Axis I of the *DSM-IV* are clinical disorders, which are distinct from personality disorders as they refer to the major mental, developmental and learning disorders, including depression, anxiety disorders, bipolar disorder, attention-deficit/hyperactivity disorder (ADHD), phobias and schizophrenia. In 2008, Thomas Crawford and colleagues (Crawford *et al.*, 2008) reported on the comorbidity of personality disorders and Axis I disorders over a 20-year period in a community sample of the USA comprising 629 adolescents interviewed at a mean age of 13.8 years and again at a mean age of 33.2 years. What Crawford *et al.* found was that when Axis I and Axis II disorders presented together in a patient this led to the highest risk of negative outcomes, often providing several times the risk of negative outcomes than when symptoms from either axis were presented alone. Also, substance use disorders, also found on Axis I, have been found to have comorbidity with Axis II personality disorders. Andrew Skodol, John Oldham and Peggy Gallaher (Skodol *et al.*, 1999) looked at the the extent of comorbid substance use disorders in patients referred for treatment for personality disorders and interviewed for substance use and personality disorder. Skodol and his colleagues found that 60 per cent of subjects with substance use disorders had personality disorders. They also found that borderline personality disorder was significantly associated with substance use disorders (though not alcohol and cannabis), and that levels of alcohol, stimulant and other substance use disorders (excluding cannabis) were related with borderline personality disorder over one's lifetime. The authors also found that antisocial personality disorder was associated with substance use disorders (excluding alcohol, cannabis and stimulants) over the lifetime. (For an example of how different personality disorders are conceptualised alongside the other axes within the *DSM-IV*, look at the Stop and think: Organisation and interactions of Axis II (personality disorders) within the multiaxial model.)

Other evidence supports both these aspects of comorbidity. In 2008, Kenneth Kendler and his colleagues (Kendler *et al.*, 2008) looked at the structure of genetic and environmental risk factors for *DSM-IV* personality disorders. The important factor in this study is that this provides information on the pattern of comorbidity between personality disorders within the context of additional conditions (i.e. genetic and environmental risk factors). For example, if there are overlaps between heritability statistics or particular environmental factors for a specific personality disorder this tells us something about the extent of the possible overlaps between personality disorders. Kendler and his colleagues looked at a number of genetic and environmental factors in personality disorders among a total of 2,794 young adult members of the Norwegian Institute of Public Health Twin Panel. Kendler *et al.* found three genetic and three environmental general factors within the data. They found that a first genetic factor could be called negative emotionality, this was related to all the personality disorders, and Kendler *et al.* argued that this factor reflects a broad vulnerability to having a personality disorder. The second and third genetic factors reflected high levels of being impulsive, low agreeableness and introversion. They found that the second factor was related to borderline and antisocial personality disorders and that the third genetic factor was related to schizoid and avoidant personality disorders. This finding suggests that genetic risk factors for *DSM-IV* personality disorders do not reflect the Cluster A, B and C typology. However, the researchers found that, when it came to environmental factors, these reflected the Cluster A, B and C typology. Kendler *et al.* argue that environmental experiences may be responsible for the tendency for psychologists to separate personality disorders into Clusters A, B and C. What these authors are suggesting is that the classification of personality disorders into Clusters A, B and C is the result of psychologists noting only the environmental influences, because these are the only influences they can experience directly. However, genetic factors, such as negative emotionality, are factors that psychologists do not experience directly, because they are not in the environment, and it is these factors that are the basis for overlaps between the different personality disorders.

All this work on comorbidity has led many researchers and academics to question the usefulness of the categorical approach towards understanding personality disorders as outlined by the *DSM-IV*. Some authors have suggested that, rather than seeing personality disorders as separate psychological entities that fall outside standard personality measures in which clinicians can identify and treat individuals based on a diagnosis, as the levels of comorbidity are high with other personality disorders and other factors, there needs to be a different way of conceptualising and categorising personality disorders. Some researchers argue, for example, that there is evidence to suggest that personality disorders are nothing more than extremes of normal personality and that their conceptualisation should be understood with those models (for an example of this refer back to the section on Saulsman and Page's research on the five-factor correlates of personality disorders).

Final comments

In this discussion we have described the Circumplex Theory of Affect to explain the structure of mood. We have then widened out this consideration to describe the constructs of subjective and psychological well-being and explained how these two constructs differ conceptually, if not empirically, particularly in terms of their relationship to personality. We have also outlined and described the 10 personality disorders as classified by the *Diagnostic and Statistical Manual of Mental Disorders (DSM)-IV*, and discussed the various genetic and environmental influences on personality disorders as well as discussing a number of issues that surround the classification of, and overlaps between, personality disorders.

Stop and think

Organisation and interactions of Axis II (personality disorders) within the multiaxial model

We have noted that there are overlaps between the different axes of the *DSM-IV* and this presents an issue when understanding personality disorders. However, it is also important to note that the multiaxial model of the *DSM-IV* suggests that personality disorders (Axis II) are organised and interact with the other axes in particular ways. Theodore Millon and his colleagues have presented two ways to conceptualise the organisation and interaction of certain axes within the *DSM-IV* (Millon *et al.*, 2004). The first way to understand how personality disorders are ordered within the multiaxial model is through the level of organisation of the axes, particularly placing Axis II between Axis III and IV (see Figure 23.6). Axis IV relates to environmental and psychosocial factors influencing the individual's well-being (e.g. stress, family, peers, society) and Axis III relates to biological and genetic factors, including acute (severe) medical conditions and physical disorders influencing the individual's well-being (neurotransmitter profiles, genetic traits). Here, personality disorders (Axis II) are viewed as the interaction of the influences of social and biological axes.

Figure 23.6 Personality disorders and their levels of organisation and their relationship within the multiaxial model (based on Millon *et al.*, 2004).

The second way suggested by Millon *et al.* to conceptualise personality disorders within the multiaxial model of the *DSM-IV* is depicted in Figure 23.7. Here, personality disorders (Axis II) are seen in the middle of two of the other axes: Axis I, which relates to all clinical disorders, including all major mental, developmental and learning disorders (e.g. depression, eating disorders, phobias), and Axis IV, which relates to environmental and psychosocial factors influencing the individual's well-being (e.g. stress, family, peers, society). In this view Axis IV (psychosocial influences) and Axis II (personality disorders) interact to produce symptoms and disorders on Axis I.

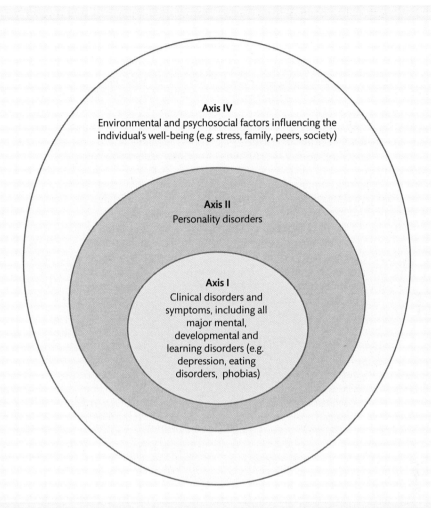

Figure 23.7 How personality disorders (Axis II) interact with psychosocial influences (Axis IV) to produce Axis I clinical disorders and symptoms (based on Millon *et al.*, 2004).

Summary

- Within psychology the term affect refers to the adjective affective, and is the experience of feeling or emotion.
- Watson and Tellegen argued that mood comprised two main dimensions – positive and negative affect. Watson and Tellegen suggested the Circumplex Theory of Affect which comprises eight end points representing different mood states: high and low positive affect, high and low negative affect, strong engagement, disengagement, pleasantness and unpleasantness. Watson *et al.* (1988) developed the Positive and Negative Affect Schedule (more usually abbreviated to the PANAS) to measure positive and negative affect.

- In terms of well-being, these two philosophical contexts have informed two different broad domains within the literature, these being the difference between hedonic well-being and eudaimonic well-being. Keyes *et al.* (2002) used the distinction between hedonic and eudaimonic well-being traditions to suggest two well-being dimensions: subjective well-being and psychological well-being.
- Subjective well-being, based on hedonic activity, is the relatively shorter term evaluation of present-day subjective well-being as a balance within positive and negative affect, pleasure attainment and pain avoidance where the measurement of subjective well-being

tries to assess an individual balance between positive and negative affect.

- Psychological well-being, based on eudaimonia, is the engagement with individual development and existential challenges within life, meaning and self-reflection. Keyes *et al.* argue that there are six aspects to the measurement of psychological well-being: autonomy, environmental mastery, personal growth, purpose in life, positive relations with others and self-acceptance.

- There is some evidence to support this conception of well-being in US and UK samples. However, this research suggests that, among samples more representative of the wider population, there is reason to believe these distinctions are less well defined.

- There is also debate over these definitions of the subjective and psychological well-being constructs. Kashdan *et al.* (2008) challenge the current eudaimonic conceptions of well-being because authors are not consistent as regards the theory. Waterman (2008) argues that different interpretations can be made of eudaimonia. The classification of psychological well-being as comprising six dimensions has been questioned by authors (e.g. Van Dierendonck, 2004).

- Generally, research looking at the relationship between the five-factor model of personality and well-being supports the view that extraversion is related to positive affect and neuroticism is related to negative affect. On average, correlations between extraversion and positive affect, and neuroticism and negative affect are thought to be around $r = 0.4$. Conscientiousness, openness and agreeableness are only sometimes related to improved subjective well-being (i.e. higher positive affect or lower negative affect).

- Neuroticism is negatively related with all aspects of psychological well-being (autonomy, environmental mastery, personal growth, purpose in life, positive relations with others and self-acceptance) and extraversion shared a positive relationship with positive relationships with others. Conscientiousness shares a positive relationship with purpose in life and personal growth, openness shares a positive relationship with autonomy and agreeableness shares a positive relationship with others.

- A personality disorder is an extreme or severe disturbance in both the character and the behaviours shown by an individual that affects several aspects of the person's personality. A personality disorder will always involve a considerable amount of personal and social disruption, not only to the individual, but to the people around the person.

- The American Psychiatric Association publishes the *Diagnostic and Statistical Manual of Mental Disorders (DSM)-IV*. The *DSM-IV* provides the criteria for psychologists to diagnose disorders. Personality disorders are included on Axis II of the *DSM-IV*.

- The *DSM-IV* suggests that the first stage of identifying a personality disorder is the recognition of a pattern of behaviours and experience. The pattern of behaviours and experiences must be enduring, cause clinically significant impairment or distress, must be stable over time, cannot be explained as part of another mental disorder and is not the result of physiological effects of a particular substance or the result of a medical condition.

- Within Axis II, the *DSM-IV* lists 10 different personality disorders. These 10 personality disorders are grouped into three clusters: Cluster A comprises odd or eccentric disorders. These are paranoid personality disorder, schizoid personality disorder and schizotypal personality disorder. Cluster B comprises dramatic, emotional or erratic disorders. These are antisocial personality disorder, borderline personality disorder, histrionic personality disorder and narcissistic personality disorder. Cluster C comprises anxious or fearful disorders. These are avoidant personality disorder, dependent personality disorder and obsessive-compulsive personality disorder.

- Studies suggest that personality disorders have a substantial genetic component and heritability estimates of personality disorder traits among children and adults are similar.

- Personality disorders tend to emerge early in a person's life, with some symptoms of this disorder occurring in childhood. One of the main focuses around environmental influence and association with personality disorders has tended to be on childhood experiences, and particularly a history of abuse and neglect in childhood is thought to be an important influence on the development of personality disorders.

- L. J. Siever and K. L. Davis (1991) provided a theoretical and largely empirical model to describe neurobiological dimensions, particular neurotransmitters, that underpin all categories of psychopathology, including personality disorders, relating to: (1) cognitive/perceptual; (2) impulsivity/aggression; (3) affect regulation; and (4) anxiety/inhibition. In this model, cognitive/perceptual and anxiety/inhibition aspects of personality disorders are related to dopamine; impulsivity and aggression aspects of personality disorders are related to serotonin (or 5-hydroxytryptamine, 5-HT); and affect regulation is related to noradrenergic-cholinergic neurotransmitter functioning.

- Findings suggest that personality disorders (with the exception of dependent personality disorder) could be best understood with the dimensions of high neuroticism and lower agreeableness. Also, extraversion was found to be related to some personality disorders (e.g. positively related to histrionic and negatively related to avoidant personality disorder).

- There are a number of emerging issues with the conceptualisation of personality disorders. One issue relates to comorbidity of other personality disorders and other factors. Comorbidity in areas such as personality disorders means: (i) the presence of one or more personality disorders, in addition to a primary personality disorder; or (ii) the existence of additional clinical conditions alongside the initially diagnosed personality disorder.

Connecting up

You will want to look back at Chapter 7 for more information on the five-factor model of personality.

If you want to read a little more about abnormal aspects of personality and behaviour revisit Freud (Chapter 2), the work of Ellis and rational-emotive behaviour theory (Chapters 5 and 19) and descriptions of social anxiety disorder (Chapter 20).

Critical thinking

Discussion questions

- Eudaimonia emphasises engaging in a pleasant and successful life. What do think represents a pleasant and successful life?
- What are the differences between people with 'bad personalities' and people with personality disorders?
- Do personality disorders exist? Or are they a way of describing people whose behaviour is difficult to categorise?

Essay questions

- Compare and contrast hedonic and eudaimonic descriptions of well-being.
- What is mood? How does it compare with subjective and psychological well-being?
- How do we diagnose personality disorders?
- Are personality disorders the outcomes of inherited traits?
- Critically discuss how childhood development can influence the development of personality disorders.
- Critically examine the different ways that well-being is associated with personality.

Going further

Books

- Millon, T., Grossman, S., Millon, C., Meagher, S. and Ramnath, R. (2004). *Personality disorders in modern life* (2nd edn). Hoboken, New Jersey: John Wiley & Sons.
- Magnavita, J. J. (2004). *Handbook of personality disorders: Theory and practice.* Hoboken, NJ: John Wiley & Sons.

Journals

- A 2006 report by the British Psychological Society authored by Nic Alwin, Ron Blackburn, Kate Davidson, Maggie Hilton, Caroline Logan and John Shine can be downloaded from here: **www.pdprogramme.org.uk/ assets/resources/52.pdf.**
- A 2006 article that accompanies the report by Christian Jarrett in *The Psychologist* on understanding personality disorder is presented here: **www.thepsychologist.org. uk/archive/archive_home.cfm/volumeID_19-editionID_ 137-ArticleID_1044.**
- A recent examination of behavioural genetics research and personality disorder is presented, Livesley, W. J. and Lang, K. L. (2008). The behavioral genetics of personality disorder. *The Annual Review of Clinical Psychology, 4,* 247–274.

Web links

- The Royal College of Psychiatrists' web page on personality disorders is here: **www.rcpsych.ac.uk/expertadvice/ problems/personalitydisorders.aspx.**
- Details of the National Personality Disorder Programme in England are provided here: **www.heacademy.ac.uk/ disciplines/psychology.**

Film and literature

- There are a number of films that depict a character with, or who portrays traits similar to, the following personality disorders:

  - **Paranoid personality disorder** – *Falling Down* (1994, directed by Joel Schumacher).
  - **Schizotypal personality disorder** – *Taxi Driver* (1976, directed by Martin Scorsese).
  - **Antisocial personality disorder** – *Fargo* (1996, directed by Joel Coen and Ethan Coen), *Primal Fear* (1996, directed by Gregory Hoblit).
  - **Borderline personality disorder** – *Basic Instinct* (1992, directed by Pail Verhoeven), *Girl Interrupted* (1999, directed by James Mangold), *Fatal Attraction* (1987, directed by Adrian Lyne) and *Single White Female* (1992, directed by Barbet Schroeder).
  - **Narcissistic personality disorder** – *To Die For* (1995, directed by Gus Van Sant).

- BBC Online has a programme on personality disorders as part of the *All in The Mind* series. Raj Persaud is joined by Dr Paul Moran, Clinical Senior Lecturer at the Institute of Psychiatry, to discuss the latest research into personality disorder and the current treatments available: **http://www .bbc.co.uk/radio4/science/allinthemind_20050315 .shtml**.

Explore the website accompanying this text at **www.pearsoned.co.uk/maltby** for further resources to help you with your studies. These include multiple-choice questions, essay questions, web links and ideas for advanced reading.

CHAPTER 24
Individual Differences in Health and Illness

Key themes

- Defining health
- Measuring individual differences in health
- Hypothesised relationships between personality and illness
- Type A/Type B personality and toxic components
- Hostility
- Type D personality
- Individual differences in response to illness
- *Negative emotions and health*: anxiety, depression, stress and burnout
- Locus of control
- Self-efficacy
- Intelligence and health
- *Positive emotions and health:* optimism, optimistic bias
- Positive psychology, health and happiness

Learning outcomes

At the end of this discussion you should:

- Appreciate and critically evaluate the relationships between individual differences in personality, health, illness and general well-being of individuals
- Appreciate the complexity of defining health and illness
- Understand the range of possible relationships between personality, health and illness
- Appreciate the impact of negative emotions on physical health and psychological well-being
- Be able to identify some of the major areas where links between personality and physical health have been made
- Appreciate the complexities involved in measuring well-being
- Understand the importance of positive emotions and well-being
- Conceptualise health and well-being within a positive psychology perspective

Introduction

There are many jokes about the ways that men and women respond to ill health. Women may refer to a man as having 'man flu' or a 'man cold' as opposed to simply flu or a cold. The implicit suggestion is that men appear to suffer more than women do when they have colds or flu. Similarly, there are jokes about women and their hormones, implying that women are emotionally more volatile than men are. These stereotypical responses convey an acknowledgement that individual differences do play a part in determining how we deal with illness or indeed how we approach our health. Otherwise, how do we account for one child, when diagnosed with asthma, immersing himself/herself in sport to improve his/her lung capacity and becoming an excellent athlete while another child uses the diagnosis of asthma as an excuse for not participating in sport and adopts more of an invalid role? How others treat the child will be important, but the child's personality will also be extremely influential in determining how she or he responds.

While in this discussion the focus is on health and illness, much of the material you have already covered is relevant to the topic and we encourage you to make these links. You will recall that many of the personality theories, such as the psychoanalytic theories, some of the learning and cognitive theories and humanistic theories are all clinically based theories designed to help explain individual differences in healthy and ill individuals. Indeed, most of these theories based their models on observations of clinical populations suffering from different degrees of mental illness. Individual differences do not only apply to mental illness but are also an important consideration in determining how individuals respond to physical conditions, as we shall see later.

There is now a separate discipline of health psychology, and the study of individual differences is a core part of the work of health psychologists as they seek to understand better the processes of health and illness, and also how we can better educate the public to take better care of their health. Individual differences are thus a core consideration in the development of campaigns for health education of the public and in the design of interventions to improve public health. Within health psychology, most research focuses on trait approaches to personality, particularly the Big Five, although some British work does use Eysenck's model of personality (Eysenck and Eysenck, 1985a). You may need to re-familiarise yourself with these models (which we covered in Chapters 7 and 8), although it is fair to say that, with the exception of the trait of neuroticism, most of the individual differences research focuses more on types and specific subtraits rather than adopting the superordinate trait approach.

The aim of this discussion is to give you an introduction to individual differences in health, in terms of how they

Source: Corbis

are conceptualised and some of the main areas where research is undertaken. We begin by defining what is meant by health, acknowledging the complexity of the topic and measurement issues, and this leads us nicely into a consideration of the possible links between personality, health and illness. Throughout we address issues of research design and evaluation whenever they arise to provide you with the ability to understand and then critically evaluate some of the research designs commonly used in different areas of health psychology. Next, one of the most researched areas of personality and health, cardiovascular disease (heart disease) is examined. Globally and in the UK cardiovascular disease is a major cause of death and disability, hence the research focus on it and its inclusion here. This research illustrates the importance of good methodology in research studies. We begin by reviewing the major clinically based studies undertaken largely by doctors and then go on to consider the studies focusing specifically on personality and conducted mainly by psychologists.

Much of the work of the health psychologist is in relation to patients with physical illnesses, so we look at individual differences in patients' reactions to physical illness next. This leads us to examine how illness is defined as a stressor that the individual has to cope with and we examine how individuals may cope with stress and the relationship between stress and illness. The commonest emotional reactions to serious physical illnesses are anxiety and depression, so we consider these next, beginning with depression as it occurs most commonly.

We have already introduced you to concepts that are applied fairly widely in health psychology. Now we bring these together to help you make the links with the previous work that you have studied. We bring together locus of control, self-efficacy, optimism and research on links between intelligence and health. The focus until this point is largely on illness, so finally we introduce you to positive psychology, a relatively new school of psychology that aims to promote health and well-being across the population, not just focusing on those with physical or psychological problems. Here we focus on happiness and well-being and examine some of the research linking it with health benefits. While we cover a lot of material, we hope that you find it interesting and as a result you understand more about the nature of health psychology and the importance of individual differences.

Defining health

We all feel that we know what health is and we commonly describe it as being about the absence of illness or disease. It is about not being sick, not having symptoms of any illness. However, these common sense definitions are problematical. Is someone who smokes heavily healthy? They may say that they feel well but their lungs are being damaged by heavy smoking of cigarettes. How about someone who is overweight and eats food high in saturated fats but feels fine? We commonly hear statements to the effect that it is unhealthy to be overweight and that fatty diets damage your arteries. These examples illustrate that health and ill health are not distinct categories but rather points on a continuum, with the super-healthy at one end and the very ill at the other. Most of us are probably somewhere in the middle where we may feel fine but know that if we took more exercise, for example, or paid more attention to our diet or controlled our alcohol intake we would be healthier.

Health is not simply about physical symptoms either, but needs also to encompass our mental health and social well-being. The most commonly cited definition of health is given by the World Health Organization (1948). It states that:

Health is a state of complete physical, mental and social well-being and not merely the absence of disease or infirmity.

(Official Records of the World Health Organization, no. 2, p. 100)

According to this definition, we need to have enough to eat, to feel secure and be relatively happy with our world with an absence of symptoms indicating psychological distress. Introducing mental health into the definition is important as many individuals living with chronic physical conditions like arthritis, for example, will claim to be very healthy for someone living with arthritis. They feel good; they manage their condition well and are satisfied with their lives. Yet compared to someone without arthritis, they may have restricted movement and suffer more pain and so on. We hope that these examples make it clear to you that

there is a subjective, evaluative element to assessments of health and illness. Health is not simply about the absence of physical or mental disease. Rather it is often about the attitude that the individual has towards their health and here individual differences are very important. You may get an individual fighting cancer who says, 'All things considered, I really feel pretty well' whereas someone with an irritating but certainly not life-threatening cold may act as if they are at death's door.

It is because of this complexity that care has to be taken in assessing individual differences in health. Measures like the General Health Questionnaire (Goldberg and Williams, 1988) are symptom checklists that summate the number of symptoms indicative of poor mental health that an individual has. While it includes both physical and mental symptoms and measures of how these symptoms have impacted on the individual's social life, it is designed as a measure of mental health. The physical and social life symptoms that are included in the General Health Questionnaire are those that have been shown by research to be associated with mental health. There are similar scales that only rate physical symptoms, such as those used by Hannay (1978) or Dunnell and Cartwright (1972), where a list of possible symptoms is presented and respondents rate their presence and/or severity and duration. However, these symptom-based measures do not assess how individuals actually feel about their health. To address this, a range of quality of life scales have been developed, such as the World Health Organization Quality of Life Scale (WHOQOL Group, 1995) and subjective well-being measures such as the Satisfaction with Life Scale (Diener et al., 1985) and the Flourishing and SPANE scales (Diener et al., 2010). There are also a number of illness-specific quality of life measures such as the Rotterdam Symptom checklist (De Haes et al., 1990) and various health status measures that assess the individual's perception of their level of health or illness. These various measures reflect this wider conceptualisation of health as being about perceived health status and quality of life, covering psychological, social, occupational and physical domains (Fallowfield, 1990). So, for example, some people may be diabetic but they control their diabetes well through diet, medication and a healthy

Stop and think

Your own responses to illness

If you are still not convinced about individual differences in response to illness, I suggest you conduct the following brief study. Think of the last time that you had a cold and try to answer the following questions about your behaviour in relation to that illness:

- How do you recognise that you have a cold?
- How do you cope?
- Do you take any medication?

- Anything else you do?
- How long do you expect it to last?
- Do you take any precautions against colds?
- Any other issues?

Once you have done this, compare your responses with others and you may be surprised at the individual differences you discover. We always are when we do it with our students.

---

lifestyle and they rate their quality of life as excellent and do not actually think of themselves as being ill although they have a medical condition. They are in control of their condition, whereas others with diabetes may not assume this level of control. They are careless about their medication and diet and do not lead a healthy life, drinking, smoking and failing to take exercise and consequently frequently need treatment for their diabetes, feeling weak, fainting and even going into diabetic comas. When asked about their condition, these individuals, by contrast, are likely to report symptoms which they attribute to their diabetes. They see themselves as having an illness that impacts negatively on their quality of life as they are frequently hospitalised and so on. While this example is about extremes, hopefully it gets across the importance of how the individuals themselves conceptualise their illness.

Personality, health and illness: how might they be linked?

Suls and Rittenhouse (1990) and Smith and Williams (1992) have suggested four possible ways in which personality and illness may be linked and we will deal with each one in turn.

1 There may be a direct link if personality traits are considered to be biologically based individual differences that play a *causal* role in health and illness and adjustment to illness. This mode, displayed in Figure 24.1, suggests that personality may directly influence biological activities that influence the development of physical disease and influence its course in individuals who are healthy. This approach is common in medicine, and McMahon (1976) outlines its history. He reports that it was the psychoanalysts who first described individuals with personality characteristics that were thought to put them more at risk of developing physical illness. Such individuals were described as having a disease-prone

personality (Alexander, 1950). It was thought that these individuals were more at risk of developing psychosomatic conditions. These are conditions where psychological factors are considered to play a major causal role in the development of the disorder. Examples of psychosomatic conditions include stomach ulcers and asthma. The traditional classification of ulcers as being purely psychosomatic is worth commenting on as it presents an interesting example of how psychology and medicine can get it wrong. Recent research has identified a bacterium, *Helicobacter pylori*, that plays a role in many cases in the causation of ulcers. However, individual differences in terms of stress proneness and how the individual copes with stress as well as genetic factors, also play a part in the formation and worsening of duodenal ulcers. Remember this approach is trying to identify a *causal role for personality* in the development of diseases. The research on ulcers usefully exemplifies the complexity of the process. There is research on individual differences in stress and emotion related to coronary heart disease that adopts this model and has resulted in identification of what is known as the Type A personality and we will return to this later.

2 Instead of a causal link, there may be a *correlational* link between personality and health or personality and illness, as pictured in Figure 24.1. The suggestion is that the same biological process might underpin personality traits and illness outcomes. Mathews *et al.* (2003) give the example of coronary heart disease. Here, it could be that an individual has a genetic susceptibility to develop heart disease and this same gene also results in a predisposition towards being a hostile person. Here there is a positive correlation or association between possessing high levels of hostility and having cardiac disease but the relationship is not causal. The cause of both the illness and the personality trait of hostility are thought to be an underlying gene. There is a great deal of correlational research in health psychology and we will examine some examples later.

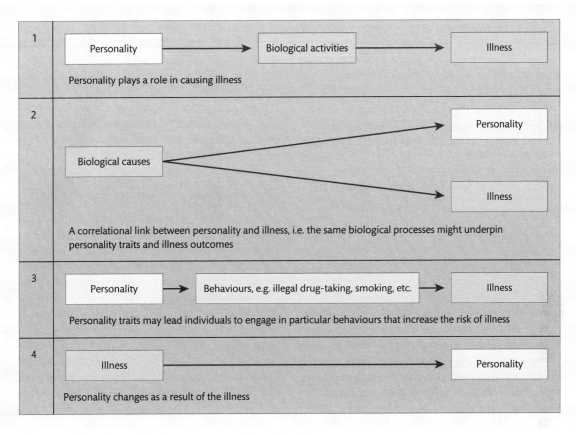

Figure 24.1 Possible relationships between personality and health.

3 The third possible link is more complex and is shown in Figure 24.1. Having certain *personality traits may lead individuals to engage in particular behaviours* that influence their health and/or increase the risk of illness. For example, an individual with a high need for novelty and exciting experiences, what psychologists have labelled 'sensation-seeking', may be more likely to engage in illegal drug-taking than an individual low in sensation-seeking. You are sure to be able to think of other examples. Indeed, you may recall (from Chapter 2) that Freud suggested that smokers had a high need for oral stimulation due to fixation at the oral stage of psychosexual development.

4 Finally, it could be that *having an illness, itself produces changes in personality,* as shown in Figure 24.1. For example, having a chronic condition like severe arthritis, which results in the individual having to live with pain all the time, may result in that individual going out less and feeling less sociable. They may also worry more about the future and about coping with their day-to-day activities. Because of these illness-induced changes, they are more likely to have lower scores on extraversion and higher scores on neuroticism on a personality test. When you then conduct a study to compare a group of individuals suffering from chronic arthritis

with a group of control participants without arthritis but matched with the arthritis groups in terms of their age, sex and income, any differences between the two groups could simply be revealing these illness-induced changes rather than original underlying differences in personality. Becoming physically ill and having to undergo treatment in hospital may have a significant psychological impact on individuals. Patients with brain tumours and other neurological conditions often report changes in mood and aspects of personality. Heckhausen and Schulz (1995) have looked at the effect of acute health crises like heart attacks and becoming chronically ill with long-term conditions and they conclude that such events can cause significant changes in some individuals. This is sometimes conceptualised as being a **psychosomatic** link; that is, where what has happened to the body is influencing the patient's mind.

This idea that the experience of illness and adversity can change an individual is widely acknowledged in sayings such as 'What does not kill you makes you stronger'. This type of model is more difficult to test as it requires what are called large prospective population studies. These involve taking personality and health measures from a large healthy population, and then following this up some years later in the hope that sufficient numbers of the population have become ill so that you can compare their scores with their baseline measures and the remaining healthy sample. This model tends to be explored mainly in qualitative studies where individuals are asked to reflect on whether their illness has changed them.

The main message from the four possible relationships described above is that a correlation between a health measure and a personality trait can be open to different interpretations. It is useful to recall Mischel's work on personality and situations here (Mischel, 1968; 2004) and which we covered earlier (Chapter 4). When measuring individual differences in health, studies need to be designed carefully. Finding a robust correlation between a personality variable and a health measure is only the first step in the process of understanding the relationship. Ideally, personality measures need to be taken before the onset of an illness and then measured after the onset of the illness and longer term in the case of chronic illnesses. Unfortunately, this is only possible in longitudinal studies but, as we shall see, this has been done for Type A personality and cardiac disease (Friedman and Rosenman, 1959; 1974; Rosenman *et al.*, 1975; Ragland and Brand, 1988). It is fair to say that most research has tended to focus on one aspect at a time and this may mean that relationships are over-simplified. Longitudinal studies that measure participants while they are still healthy are very expensive and thus relatively rare. Researchers sometimes try to compensate for these difficulties by getting individuals close to the patient who knew them before the onset of the illness to comment on any changes in the patient since the onset of the illness, and patients themselves can be asked if they are aware of being changed by the illness. While this does not solve the problem, as changes could be age-related, it does demonstrate sensitivity to the issue. Most of the research on personality and health has been in relation to cardiovascular disease and we will examine this in the next section.

Researching the links between personality, health and illness

We are going to outline the discussion that surrounds the identification and measurement of certain personality types and how this is linked to health and illness, and particularly cardiovascular disease.

Type A and Type B personality

Here the focus is on cardiovascular disease, which is an umbrella term for a group of conditions where there has been narrowing of the arteries that supply the heart resulting in heart attack or increased risk of heart attack. Globally,

heart disease is a major issue for humankind, resulting in 17.4 million deaths worldwide in 2005 according to the World Health Organization. That represents 30 per cent of the total deaths occurring in the world in 2005. Similarly, in the UK, heart disease and related circulatory disorders are the main cause of death, accounting for around 198,000 deaths each year, with one in five men and one in eight women dying from coronary heart disease (British Heart Foundation, 2010). As well as the costs related to mortality and lost years of life, coronary heart disease is also extremely costly in terms of treatment provision, days lost from work due to the illness and the development and support of health promotion initiatives to try to address it. This explains why the search for causal links has been supported, with governments investing large amounts of money in research in this area. Indeed, the inclusion of the topic here reflects its global importance in healthcare.

There is a long history linking heart disease to personality and looking for a causal link. For example, Osler (1910) described the angina sufferer 'as a man who is keen and ambitious and is always at full speed ahead'. Friedman and Rosenman (1959) fired the modern interest. They were physicians who wanted to try to predict who would develop cardiovascular disease. From physical factors alone, they could not predict accurately who would develop the condition and only after the addition of personality factors did their prediction rates improve. They identified a coronary-prone behaviour pattern which they labelled 'Type A' and

Type A personality is described as being driven to achieve, to meet goals, competitive and attracted to competition.
Source: Rex Features/OJO Images

contrasted this with non-coronary prone 'Type B' personality. The Type A personality is described as being driven to achieve, to meet goals, competitive and attracted to competition, quite hostile to competitors, with a persistent drive for recognition, advancement and power, works very hard and works to deadlines with high levels of mental and physical alertness. Such individuals dislike time-wasting, do things efficiently but can be easily roused to anger and hostility. They are commonly conceptualised as successful go-getting types. By contrast, the Type B personality is described as being very relaxed and unhurried in their approach. They may work hard on occasions but are rarely driven in the compulsive manner of the Type A. Type Bs are less interested in competition, achievement and power and are more likely to take life as it comes (Friedman and Rosenman, 1959). It is important to note that, although we talk of them as types, Type A and Type B, they are actually endpoints on a scale with individuals placed along the scale according to their degree of Type A or Type B. Individuals with scores towards the Type A end of the scale have been shown to be more likely to develop coronary heart disease than individuals lower down the scale towards the Type B end and this is a significant health risk.

Type B personality is described as being very relaxed and unhurried in their approach.
Source: Alamy Images/David Hancock

Measurement of Type A/B personality

Friedman and Rosenman (1959) used a structured interview (SI) to assess the tendency to Type A behaviour. It used two sources of data:

a   Participants' responses to questions in what was a challenging fast-paced interview where provocative questions were asked to see if they would become irritated by the interviewer.
b   Trained raters' assessments of the behaviour and speech patterns of the participant during the challenging interview.

While the interview process is a reliable method, it is labour-intensive and hence very expensive. To address these concerns, Jenkins *et al.* (1974) developed a self-report measure of Type A/B behaviour, called the Jenkins Activity Survey. It is easy to administer but behavioural observations are missing from this self-report measure. The Stop and think box, Measurement of Type A/B personality: Jenkins Activity Survey (1979), includes some example questions taken from the Jenkins Activity Survey (Jenkins *et al.*, 1979) and will give you a flavour of what is being measured in Type A/B behaviour.

Research on Type A/B personality

There are two strands to the research on Type A personality. The first involves very large studies carried out by doctors and the second more moderate studies by psychologists interested in personality. There are at least four major studies of personality and cardiovascular disease. The gold standard is for prospective, population-based, longitudinal studies. A large population is identified, their health is assessed and they are followed up regularly and those developing heart disease are identified. The advantage of this design is that you have actual measures of the individual's health before they become ill. Some of the major studies of this type are summarised below to give you a flavour of the research:

1   **Friedman and Rosenman's Western Collaborative Study Group.** In this study 3,524 men aged between 39 and 59 years were assessed in 1960–61 (Rosenman *et al.*, 1964). The sample was followed up 8½ years later and Type A men were found to have twice as much cardiovascular disease as Type B men (Rosenman *et al.*, 1975). However, a follow-up study of the same group after 22 years reported no effects of Type A personality on mortality but quite marked effects on mortality from blood pressure, cholesterol, smoking and age (Ragland and Brand, 1988).
2   **Framingham Study** (Haynes *et al.*, 1978a, 1978b). This study began between 1965 and 1967 and involved 5,127 men and women being assessed. In 1978, they followed

Stop and think

Measurement of Type A/B personality: Jenkins Activity Survey (1979)

Below are some example questions taken from the Jenkins Activity Survey (Jenkins et al., 1979). Which responses do you think indicate a Type A personality?

1 Do you ever have trouble finding time to get your hair cut or styled?

Never   Occasionally   Almost always

2 Ordinarily how rapidly do you eat?

- I'm usually the first one finished
- I eat a little faster than average
- I eat at about the same speed as most people
- I eat more slowly than most people do.

3 How often do you actually 'put words in the person's mouth' in order to speed things up?

Frequently   Occasionally   Almost never

4 How is your temper nowadays?

- Fiery and hard to control
- Strong but controllable
- No problem
- I almost never get angry

---

up those who had not died, a total of 3,102 individuals aged between 45 and 77 years. They found the incidence of cardiovascular disease to be significantly higher in Type As than Type Bs. However, in a follow-up study 8 years later their results were less clear-cut (Haynes et al., 1980). Women with cardiovascular disease scored more highly on Type A behaviour and suppressed hostility, tension and anxiety than men. Type A behaviour increased the risk of cardiovascular disease in men aged between 55 and 64 years but only if they were white-collar workers.

3 **Honolulu Heart Program** (Cohen and Reed, 1985). Here, 2,187 men were assessed over an 8-year period. No relationship was found between the subsequent incidence of cardiovascular disease and the baseline measures of Type A behaviour, as assessed by the Jenkins Activity Survey.

4 **British Regional Heart Study** (Johnston et al., 1987; Shaper et al., 1991; Wannamethee et al., 1997). In this British study, 6,177 men in 19 towns in the UK were assessed using a self-report measure of Type A behaviour. The researchers found no significant relationships between Type A personality and cardiovascular disease. This study continues and a link to their most recent publications is included in the web links at the end of the discussion.

Several reviews of the research literature have been undertaken to try to identify the reasons for the lack of consistent findings. A review panel on coronary-prone behaviour was set up in the USA in 1981. This panel concluded that there was a relationship between Type A personality and cardiovascular disease, but that improved measures were required as different studies used different measures, making comparisons difficult, and more attention needed to be paid to cultural and sex differences.

Mathews and Haynes (1986), in a literature review, concluded that Type A is associated with risk for cardiovascular disease and that the association may be causal, but again suggested that improved measures were required with more attention to potential sex differences. Booth-Kewley and Friedman (1987) carried out a meta-analysis of the literature. Meta-analysis is a statistical technique that allows the results of many studies to be entered into a communal data set to test hypotheses relevant to the topic area (you can read more about this in online Chapter 27). The meta-analysis found Type A to be reliably but modestly associated with cardiovascular disease. They also concluded that studies using interviews to assess Type A/B produced more reliable results than studies using self-report questionnaires. Miller et al. (1991) produced an excellent review of the area and concluded that the differences in findings were because of the differences in the ways of assessing Type A behaviour and the use of different outcome measures.

Further psychological research on Type A personality

The second strand of research in Type A behaviour has been undertaken mainly by personality theorists as opposed to clinicians, and this has been fruitful. Glass (1977) identified three separate components that made up the Type A personality. These were as follows:

1 Striving competitively for achievement in many areas of life.

2 A sense of urgency in everything they do.

3 High levels of hostility.

There have been several attempts to explain the sources of these differences. Glass (1977) suggests that one concept

Stop and think

Lessons learnt: Type A personality and health

Reading the brief outline of the history of research on Type A personality and health brings home certain lessons about the importance of accurate measurement in research. Very expensive research has been undertaken that has produced conflicting results owing to measurement issues. Researchers need to use reliable measures and also to be aware of the measures that are most commonly being used in the area in which they are working. It is only possible to compare studies accurately if the same measures are being used. There are

lessons here for when you conduct your own research later in your course. You need to ask yourself how reliable your measure is and also how other researchers in this area measure the concept in which you are interested. Some judgement may then be required so you are clear about what you are using and why. Also, when reading and evaluating research, remember that a study may have a large number of participants, a complex design and have been expensive to run but it is not necessarily a good study.

underlies all three components, namely a desire to exert control over the environment. The evidence for this claim comes from three research studies, although it is not very convincing. Rhodewalt and Davison (1983) reported that Type As are more likely to want something after being told that they cannot have it. Secondly, Yarnold *et al.* (1985) reported that Type As are more likely to be dominant in group discussions. Finally, Strube (1987) found that Type As have high levels of motivation and a high need for self-appraisal, indicative of a need for ongoing monitoring and/or control in a situation.

Other researchers have focused on trying to identify what they call the toxic components of Type A behaviour. By toxic component, they mean the behaviour that is causally linked to the development of cardiovascular disease. For example, Wright (1988) suggested that time urgency may be toxic. However, the majority of evidence relates to hostility being the toxic component. There have been several meta-analyses of all the published studies that examine hostility and cardiovascular disease (Dembroski and Costa, 1989; Ravaja *et al.*, 1996; Miller *et al.*, 1996). The results are shown to be heavily dependent on the measures the researchers had used to assess Type A personality, again emphasising the importance of methodology. Structured interviews produced the highest correlations, but all the results supported a relationship between hostility and cardiovascular disease. Since then, two further meta-analyses have been conducted, which reported some association between hostility and cardiovascular disease but suggested that there is inconsistency in the measures of hostility used, with some measures appearing to be more reliable than others (Rozanski *et al.*, 1999; Hemingway and Marmot, 1999). However, an excellent meta-analysis of 45 studies where the methodology was judged to be sound, concluded that hostility/anger was associated with a 20 per cent increased risk of coronary heart disease developing in people who

are originally healthy, and also led to poorer outcomes in patients with coronary heart disease (Chida and Steptoe, 2009). Research on Type A has tended to expand beyond coronary disease to examine its effect on other health risk behaviours, such as exercise (Yang *et al.*, 2012).

These latter studies report that individuals with high scores on the personality trait of hostility are more likely to suffer from cardiovascular disease than those with low hostility scores. While they are reporting correlations, they are assuming a causal link, in that the biological processes associated with hostile behaviour are associated with increased cardiovascular disease. For example, research has shown that very hostile men produce higher levels of a protein, C-reactive protein, in their immune system, and this is associated with an increased risk of cardiovascular disease compared with less hostile men matched for age, race, educational status and alcohol use (Suarez *et al.*, 2002).

Type D personality

One effect of the lack of consistent findings on Type A personality was that there was less emphasis on personality as a risk factor in studies of coronary heart disease and more emphasis on other individual differences. Researchers were interested in identifying what was different about patients who suffered from coronary heart disease and also, once diagnosed with coronary heart disease, were there individual differences in terms of how well patients did, how long they lived and whether they experienced further heart attacks? This research has resulted in depression, low levels of social support, high hostility and anger being seen as risk factors in coronary heart disease (Dickens *et al.*, 2007). This approach then assesses individual risk factors for the disease developing or having a poorer outcome once it is diagnosed and being treated.

However, a review of research on coronary heart disease by Rozanski *et al.* (1999) concluded that psychological risk factors tended to cluster together in some individuals and that those individuals with the clusters were more likely to experience cardiac problems when experiencing chronic stress. This led a Dutch health psychologist, Denollet (2000), to return to a personality type approach to explaining cardiac disease in some patients. He suggested that personality traits may influence the way that risk factors relating to heart disease come together in an individual, as described in the Type A research that we examined earlier. Denollet (2000) set out to identify patients at risk of experiencing this clustering of psychological risk factors.

From his review of previous research and his own studies he identified a personality type that was consistently associated with coronary heart disease and who demonstrated a particular pattern of clusters of psychological risk factors. He labelled this personality Type D, where 'D' stands for 'distressed'. The Type D personality is described as having a tendency towards what is termed negative affectivity; that is, they tend to think negatively and experience negative emotions as their typical style of thinking. They do this consistently and across many situations. It is the sort of person whose glass is always half empty, not half full, who worries a lot, and is irritable and fairly miserable in terms of their disposition. In addition, the Type D personality is described as being socially inhibited. This is the sort of individual who is not at ease in social situations and finds it difficult to express their feelings and open up to others. They display shyness, reticence and a lack of self-assurance when around other people (Denollet, 2000). Denollet developed a 14-item questionnaire which measures negative affectivity and social inhibition constituents of Type D. Research using this measure has found that individuals with coronary heart disease classified as being Type D on the questionnaire suffered from higher levels of emotional stress, anger and tension, and experienced low self-assessed feelings of well-being. These patients do less well during their treatment, being more likely to have further heart-related problems (Denollet, 2000; 2008; Denollet and Pederson, 2009). This is promising research that is growing fast and is beginning to examine possible causal links with unhealthy lifestyles in cardiac patients (Svansdottir *et al.* (2012). Now, however, we leave coronary heart disease to look at individual differences in reaction to illness more generally.

Individual differences in the reaction to physical illness

The Diagnostic and Statistical Manual of Mental Disorders (DSM-IV-TR), which is published by the American Psychiatric Association (2000), contains the official set of diagnostic criteria for mental disorders in the United States. At one time, physical illnesses that were considered to have a significant psychological component were termed psychosomatic disorders. These included conditions such as ulcers, migraine, hypertension, asthma and ulcerative colitis, for example. The *DSM-IV-TR* is revised periodically and is currently in its fourth edition. However, this most recent version of *DSM-IV-TR* does not include a list of psychosomatic disorders but instead physical illnesses are coded under *general medical conditions* and it has specified diagnostic criteria for psychological factors affecting medical conditions. These criteria are summarised as follows:

***DSM-IV-TR* as Diagnostic Criteria for Psychological Factors Affecting Medical Conditions (American Psychiatric Association, 2000).**

Criteria that must be present:

A. A general medical condition.

B. Psychological factors that adversely affect the general medical condition in at least one of the following ways:
   - **The factors can be shown to have influenced the course of the medical condition as shown by a close temporal association between the psychological factors and the development of the condition, or its exacerbation, or delayed recovery from the medical condition.**
   - **The psychological factors interfere with the treatment of the medical condition.**
   - **The psychological factors actually constitute additional health risks for the individual patient.**
   - **Physiological responses that are stress-related precipitate or exacerbate symptoms of the medical condition.**

Source: From the *Diagnostic and Statistical Manual of Mental Disorders.* Text Revision, Fourth Edition (Copyright 2000). American Psychiatric Association.

These criteria cover mental disorders like the presence of anxiety and depression but also include psychological symptoms, personality factors, maladaptive health behaviours and stress-related responses. From this you can see that individual differences both in terms of personality factors and responses to illness can adversely affect medical conditions in the ways outlined in *DSM-IV-TR*.

The commonest individual differences associated with physical illness are responses to **anxiety** and **depression**. Illnesses are usefully conceptualised as stressful life events and, before we look at depression and anxiety, we will consider how we deal with stress. Stress is a complex topic so here we only have space to cover the basics. Additional reading for those wishing to know more is included at the end of the discussion.

Conceptualising stress

Hans Seyle (1956), one of the early pioneers of stress research, suggested that stress was a non-specific response produced by the body to any kind of stimuli that the individual perceives as noxious and hence threatening. By non-specific, Seyle meant that the same pattern of responses could be produced by any number of different stressful stimuli, or stressors as they have come to be called. Seyle described the body's defensive activity in response to stress as the **General Adaptation Syndrome**. It consists of three stages which follow each other consecutively as follows:

1 **Alarm reaction** – this is where the nervous system becomes physically aroused to cope with the demand for action. This has come to be known as the **fight-or-flight response**; it is the body getting ready for extreme physical demands. Physically, hormonal changes occur, leading to an increase in the body's ability to cope with infection and repair damaged tissue, and glycogen, a type of sugar, is also released into the bloodstream to provide additional energy. Changes occur in the nervous system, with the heartbeat increasing in rate and strength, and blood is redirected from the skin and less vital organs such as the digestive system to the muscle system and the brain. Breathing deepens so that more oxygen can be processed by the body and sweating occurs to release the extra heat produced by the body. In this way the body is activated to fight or flee the stressor. However, the body cannot remain in this state of intense arousal for long. In laboratory studies with rats, Seyle (1976) found that prolonged, unremitting stress was extremely damaging, leading to premature death in some animals. If the stress continues but is not severe enough to cause death, the body tries to adapt to the stressor in the second stage – resistance.

2 **Resistance stage** – here the obvious physical arousal typical of the alarm reaction dies down but other processes are stimulated that allow the body to continue functioning despite continued physical demands. Physiological arousal is still higher than normal but the individual may not actually be showing any outward signs of stress. Seyle has shown that the ability to deal with any new stress may become impaired at this stage. He said that this damage to the system can result in what he called diseases of adaptation, such as high blood pressure, stomach ulcers, asthma and illnesses linked to impaired functioning of the immune system. In this way prolonged stress leads to damage to tissues and the experience of ill health and the exhaustion stage.

3 **Exhaustion stage** – here the body's capacity to resist stressors becomes exhausted. It results in physical and/or psychological illness. This is the stage that is sometimes described as **burnout** (Maslach and Jackson, 1982).

Individuals experience complete emotional and physical exhaustion. It has been studied, particularly in relation to individuals who work in caring professions such as social work and healthcare where high levels of stressors are likely to be encountered on a daily basis and there may be little sense of personal control in the situation.

The research here has shown us that repeated exposure to intense stressors is bad for our health. We also know that there are individual differences in the ability to deal with stress. While some situations, such as life-threatening illness, loss of a loved one or the impact of serious natural disasters, are stressful for everyone, many less dramatic experiences, like taking an exam, arguing with a loved one or getting stuck in traffic, are stressful for some people but not for others. Responses to stressful situations, even physiological responses to painful stimuli, can be powerfully influenced by psychological factors.

To understand stress we need to know how the person appraises a situation in terms of his/her particular motives and needs and resources to cope with the situation. We have already discussed coping and appraisal (in Chapter 18), but here we will further expand our knowledge of stress by locating primary and secondary appraisals within the transactional model of stress which is currently the model that is applied most widely. This model was developed by Lazarus and Folkman (1984) and is outlined in Figure 24.2. Within this model stress is viewed as neither a stimulus nor a response to a situation, but as a transaction or relationship between the person and the environment that taxes or exceeds the person's coping resources.

There is a heavy focus on how the individual personally perceives both the demands of the stressful situation and their own coping capabilities. This is known as a subjective perspective and it helps us to explain why there are individual differences in the classification of situations as stressful. Within this model, a demand occurs in the environment, causing the individual to undertake primary appraisal, resulting in her/his assessment of the perceived demands being made (i.e. their subjective appraisal = perceived demand). The demands being made on the individual require certain capabilities if they are to be undertaken and, again, the individual subjectively appraises her/his ability to deliver, resulting in the appraisal of their perceived capabilities. These are all termed cognitive appraisals occurring in the individual's thought processes. Basically, at the primary appraisal stage the individual is saying 'What does this mean to me? Am I fine or am I in trouble?' At the stage of secondary appraisal, the individual is asking, 'What can I do about it?' Finally, the perceived demands are compared to the perceived capabilities and, if there is a mismatch to the effect that the perceived demands are greater than the perceived capabilities, stress results.

Figure 24.2 The transactional model of stress.

Four components to the stress response are described in the model; these are all interrelated and together determine how the individual actually deals with the situation. Individuals experiencing stress generally describe a variety of negative emotions, such as anxiety, anger, hopelessness and so on. We have discussed the physiological fight-or-flight response that prepares the body for action. Fight or flight are obvious behavioural responses and we have discussed the range of coping responses that are possible (Chapter 18). For example, research has shown that high levels of absenteeism are associated with stressful work environments and stressful jobs (McCoy and Evans, 2005; Fitzgerald *et al.*, 2003; Hallsten *et al.*, 2011; Steptoe and Ayers, 2004).

While we have already seen how prolonged stress may result in physical illness through the physiological fight or flight response, being stressed also affects the ways that we

behave and may result in us taking less care of ourselves and becoming ill. For example, highly stressed individuals are more likely to eat less healthily, consume more fat and fewer vegetables and fruit, smoke cigarettes, drink more alcohol and be less likely to take exercise (Cartwright *et al.*, 2003). Individuals such as those living with and caring for their elderly partners or relatives have been shown over a 4-year period to have a significantly higher risk of dying than individuals in similar circumstances who are not undertaking a stressful healthcare role in their family (Schulz and Beach, 1999). All of this research suggests that we have a finite capacity to deal with stress, with the result that prolonged unremitting stress is bad for our health. One note of caution is necessary here. Many of the studies that examine stress and health and illness are correlational studies and, at best, may show an association between stress and ill health, but establishing causal links can be more difficult. There are many hypotheses, but collecting hard evidence is difficult and owing to the complexity of the processes involved. We will now look specifically at mental health although, as emphasised throughout, there are strong associations between physical and mental health, as evidenced in the research on health.

Depression

You have read about individual differences in coping with stressful events (in Chapter 18) and about individual differences in coping with illness. When you conceptualise illness as a stressor, as we discussed previously, physically ill patients may develop anxiety or depression as a reaction to their illness (Oltmans and Emery, 2006). Symptoms of anxiety and depression frequently occur together in individuals and this intuitively makes sense. If you are continually worrying, your outlook becomes gloomier over time as you are always anticipating the worst. When this continues unabated for some time, there is a high probability of individuals becoming depressed (Stein *et al.*, 2004). We will deal first with depression as it is such a common occurrence and has the greatest impact on health globally, and then we will examine anxiety and its relationship to health.

Lopez and Murray (1998), in an epidemiological study using statistical modelling, reported that depression was the single highest cause of disability worldwide as measured by years of life lived with a disability, affecting an estimated 50.8 million people at any one time. A distinction is made between depressed mood and clinical depression. An individual suffering from depressed mood experiences feelings of sadness, despair, feeling low or 'down' or 'blue'. It is unclear exactly when depressed mood becomes clinical depression; it appears to be a gradual decline. Solomon (2001), writing of his own depression, describes the depressed mood stage as being about experiencing dull, seemingly pointless, days, feeling tired, bored and self-obsessed but still able to keep going, although unhappy. He contrasts this with the onset of clinical depression, which he describes as the stage of collapse. Clinical depression involves emotional symptoms, cognitive symptoms, somatic symptoms and behavioural symptoms. Again, diagnostic criteria for clinical depression are specified in the *DSM-IV-TR* (American Psychiatric Association, 2000), which we mentioned previously. This ensures that we are clear about how we define depression. It is important to note that many measurement scales, such as the Hamilton Rating Scale for Depression (Hamilton, 1980) and the Beck Depression Inventory (Beck *et al.*, 1996), are referenced to the *DSM* criteria. This means that these scales have been constructed to ensure that they cover all the signs and symptoms of depression as specified in the *DSM*. Using measures related to *DSM-IV* diagnostic criteria is important in research studies to ensure that conditions are being appropriately identified and to allow comparisons with the wider research literature. The criteria in the *DSM-IV-TR* for depression are as follows:

DSM-IV-TR: Criteria for Major Depressive Episode.

A **Five or more of the following symptoms have been present during the same two-week period and represent a change from previous functioning: at least one of the symptoms is either (1) depressed mood or (2) loss of interest or pleasure.**

  (1) **Depressed mood most of the day, nearly every day, as indicated by either subjective report or observation made by others.**
  (2) **Markedly diminished interest or pleasure in all, or almost all, activities most of the day, nearly every day.**
  (3) **Significant weight loss when not dieting or weight gain.**
  (4) **Insomnia or hypersomnia nearly every day.**
  (5) **Psychomotor agitation or retardation nearly every day.**
  (6) **Fatigue or loss of energy nearly every day.**
  (7) **Feelings of worthlessness or excessive or inappropriate guilt nearly every day.**
  (8) **Diminished ability to think or concentrate, or indecisiveness, nearly every day.**
  (9) **Recurrent thoughts of death or suicide, or recurrent suicidal ideation without a plan, or a suicide attempt or plan.**

B **The symptoms do not meet criteria for a mixed episode.**

C **The symptoms cause clinically significant distress or impairment.**

Source: From the *Diagnostic and Statistical Manual of Mental Disorders*. Text Revision, Fourth Edition (Copyright 2000). American Psychiatric Association.

Stevens *et al.* (1995) review the literature on co-occurrence of physical disease and depression and report that depression is a common reaction to diagnosis and treatment of serious physical conditions. For example, depression is associated with a slower recovery from cardiac problems and an increased likelihood of a subsequent heart attack (Tennen *et al.*, 1999), and depressed patients have been shown to be less likely to comply with their treatment (Green, 1985; DiMatteo *et al.*, 2000). Individuals who are depressed have also been shown to cope less well with any pain associated with their condition (Tennen *et al.*, 2006). We will return to consider some individual differences factors that are also linked to depression later.

Anxiety defined

Anxiety can be adaptive in the context of health. It is anxiety that frequently motivates individuals to have their symptoms checked out. Worry about their health may motivate them to stop smoking, reduce their alcohol intake or exercise more. Conversely, it is also anxiety that may prevent other individuals going to have their symptoms checked out. Fear and anxiety are important motivators in our lives but they can be both adaptive and maladaptive. So, we have already identified a role for individual differences in terms of how quickly individuals seek medical advice about symptoms. A certain level of anxiety almost inevitably accompanies the diagnosis of an illness. This can be adaptive in that it can motivate the individual to comply with treatment and make healthy life changes. However, excessive worry is maladaptive and may become an anxiety disorder and there are large individual differences in the likelihood of this happening.

As with depression, a distinction is made in the literature between anxious mood and clinical level, anxiety-based disorders. *DSM-IV-TR* (American Psychiatric Association, 2000) recognises several subtypes of anxiety disorder. These include panic disorder, phobic disorders (which includes social phobias, agoraphobia and specific phobias), obsessive-compulsive disorder, generalised anxiety disorder, post-traumatic stress disorder and acute stress disorder. You may study some of these in clinical psychology modules,

Although anxiety is often thought of as a negative outcome, it sometimes can lead to positive outcomes as it motivates individuals to have their symptoms checked out.
Source: Alamy Images/Picture Partners

whereas here in relation to health we are generally discussing anxious mood. Anxiety, like depression, is defined in terms of negative emotional responses. Worry, guilt and anger often accompany anxiety. Many individuals who are anxious are also depressed and vice versa (Shankman and Klein, 2003).

Many patients experience significant levels of anxious mood related to their health, especially if it is likely to affect their future quality of life. Anxiety and fear are quite difficult to define and there is disagreement about how distinct the two are from each other. With fear, the source of the danger is usually obvious. With anxiety it is frequently difficult to specify exactly what the danger is; it is more a general level of worry. Barlow (2002) defines anxiety as an unpleasant inner state in which we are anticipating something dreadful happening that is not entirely predictable from our actual circumstances. It is a complex blend of physiological, behavioural and cognitive components. At the physiological level we are in a state of tension and chronic over-arousal, with increased heart rate and heavy breathing (Barlow, 2002). At the behavioural level we are likely to want to avoid situations where danger might be encountered. For example, we may keep ourselves busy in an attempt to ignore the symptoms of our illness (Lang, 1968; 1971). At the cognitive level, we will be experiencing negative mood, worry about possible future threats with thoughts (cognitions) such as: 'Am I going to recover?' or 'Will I be left dependent?' or even 'Will I survive?' This is often accompanied by a preoccupation with the self, paying greater attention to signs and symptoms and an accompanying sense of being unable to predict the future and a lack of ability to control it. Highly anxious individuals have a greater risk of developing a variety of physical illnesses (Contrada and Goyal, 2004; Smith and Gallo, 2001). Highly anxious patients recovering from heart attacks are at even greater risk of developing complications while in hospital (Moser *et al.*, 2007).

Excessive levels of anxiety about health can lead to what is known as hypochondria. Such individuals worry excessively about their health; they attend to every little change in their body state, such as minor aches or twinges, and constantly seek treatment, believing that they are ill despite what the medical profession tell them (American Psychiatric Association, 2000; Weck *et al.*, 2012). Both hypochondria and anxiety are associated with high levels of the personality trait of neuroticism (Costa and McCrae, 1985; 1989; 1997). Neuroticism is also associated with higher levels of somatic complaints, which, as we saw earlier, are conditions that are thought to have a significant psychological component, like ulcers and asthma (Costa and McCrae, 1997; Feldman *et al.*, 1999). Here then we have research evidence of correlational links between the personality trait of neuroticism, anxiety and both physical and psychosomatic conditions.

Stop and think

Health psychology and trait models of personality

Overall there is relatively little emphasis in health psychology on measuring personality traits, like the five-factor model of personality, for example. Why should this be?

Studying individual differences in health and illness provides health psychologists with very useful information that can help us to understand why some individuals are more vulnerable to some illness than others, but it can also be problematic. When we defined personality traits (in Chapter 7), we saw that traits are assumed to be the fundamental units of personality and that they are assumed to be consistent and fairly stable over time. If a health psychologist were to assess a patient's personality and discover, for example, that they score highly on neuroticism, how helpful is this? Neuroticism has been shown to have negative effects on many aspects of illness, yet as a personality trait it is fairly resistant to change. If you cannot change an individual's level of neuroticism, what can you do? Health psychologists would say that they would use the information to help them to understand the patient better and manage their care. However, this difficulty probably helps explain why health psychologists do not use personality assessments very much except as a research tool where it does provide additional information. In applying health psychology, personality testing is arguably a less useful tool.

Concepts especially relevant to health psychology covered previously

We are now going to explore how certain psychological concepts we have covered previously are linked to health.

Locus of control

Once individuals have become ill, their personality may influence how they then deal with their illness. Personality may influence how a disease develops, the individual's attitude towards his/her illness, his/her attitude to treatment, how well he/she adapts to the condition and, ultimately, the outcome. For example, hostile individuals, because of their hostility, may not benefit from appropriate social support to help them cope with their illness. Similarly, individuals with high levels of neurotic traits may become very focused on their condition and this may affect their ability to get on with their lives, as we have seen.

One personality factor that has shown to be influential here is Rotter's concept of locus of control (which we covered in some detail in Chapter 4 and which you may want to revisit now). Locus of control is one of the most heavily researched concepts in health psychology. We previously reviewed the relationships between locus of control and physical and mental health, concluding that, on balance, it appears that individuals with an internal locus of control become better informed about their conditions and cope better than those with an external locus of control. Internals are also more likely to try to do things to change their situation and take control (Rotter, 1966; 1982). While Rotter focused on the single dimension of internality/externality in his model, Hannah Levenson (1973) suggested that there are two additional factors as well as internality/externality that affect what you do in a particular situation: these are chance and the effect of powerful others, and they contribute to our locus of control. An example will help. Suppose you are worrying about a lump on your hand and you happen to find an article in a magazine when you are in the dentist's waiting room that describes what you seem to have and how easy it is to treat. This is a chance event, but it is likely to help you stop worrying and go to the doctor to seek treatment. If the article was written by a doctor and published in a reputable magazine you are more likely to believe it. While these are related concepts, the ratings of each are not necessarily the same. For example, in relation to getting treatment for your poor health, you might simultaneously believe that what you do makes a difference (making doctor's appointments, finding out about your condition, taking your medication, and so on) and that what powerful others such as the doctor do (recognising the problem, being willing to provide the treatment, etc.) influence outcomes, but that chance played no role.

Within the healthcare context, measures such as the Multidimensional Health Locus of Control Scale (Wallston et al., 1978) measure all three factors (internality, chance and powerful others), as this gives a better assessment of individual differences. Assessment is improved further by adding a measure of the value that individuals place on their health. These examples illustrate the complexity of assessing the impact of variables such as locus of control on health-related behaviours. Indeed, Norman and Bennett (1995), reviewing the research on locus of control, concluded that locus of control is best measured in relation to a specific situation or condition rather than as a generalised measure in the way initially described by Rotter (see Chapter 4).

A positive association between locus of control and health is more likely to be reported when such context-specific measures of locus of control are used (Lefcourt, 1992; Norman and Bennett, 1995). This is generally the current practice in research on locus of control. For example, there are locus of control measures for headaches (Martin *et al.*, 1990), diabetes (Bradley *et al.*, 1990), obesity (Saltzer, 1982), cancer (Watson *et al.*, 1990) and many others.

Self-efficacy

Continuing with the theme of making links to previous topics, we next revisit the influence of self-efficacy on health. You may recall that self-efficacy was an important concept in Bandura's theory of social learning (covered in Chapter 4). It is defined as an individual's belief that if he/she performs some behaviour it will get a desired positive outcome (Bandura, 1989; 1994). Self-efficacy influences the motivation that you have to undertake a task and the persistence that you display in working towards your desired goal and your likelihood of success (Bandura, 1997). As we saw previously (Chapter 4), self-efficacy is positively associated with a range of health behaviours, such as practising safe sex, stopping smoking, taking up exercising, dieting and so on. It is about the degree of confidence that the individual has in their ability to succeed at something and is therefore a relevant variable in many areas of health psychology. Self-efficacy makes us resilient and helps us to overcome adversity such as illness and resultant disability (Bandura, 2004).

Optimism

The final topic with relevance to health that we have already covered is optimism. (This is extensively covered in Chapter 18.) As we saw, the theory and application of optimism is a widely researched and debated concept within psychology, and has resulted in psychologists understanding that optimism has a multitude of benefits for the individual. In relation to health, optimistic people have been shown to be less susceptible to suffer anxiety and depression, experience better physical and mental health and quality of life and even to live longer (Seligman, 1998; Ziegler and Hawley, 2001; Leung *et al.*, 2005). Optimists also cope more effectively with stress, including the stress of illness. Indeed, Scheier and Carver (1987) suggest that optimists develop fewer physical symptoms over time than their pessimistic counterparts. However, as participants self-reported their symptoms in this study, it may be that optimists under-report their symptoms or pessimists over-report their symptoms. However, there is agreement that there are four main ways in which optimism may influence health. The first may be through the use of adaptive coping strategies when faced with stress (Schroder *et al.*, 1998). Secondly, it has been reported that these more effective ways of coping with stress

have a beneficial effect on the immune system, resulting in better experienced health (Segerstrom *et al.*, 2003). Thirdly, optimistic individuals are more likely to follow a healthy diet, take physical exercise and have satisfying interpersonal relationships, all of which bring significant health benefits (Kelloniemi *et al.*, 2005; Ylostalo *et al.*, 2003; Mulkana and Hailey, 2001). Finally, optimists experience more positive mood, which has a beneficial relationship with health (Carver *et al.*, 1994; Abele and Hermer, 1993).

Pessimism, on the other hand, has been shown mainly to have detrimental effects, particularly greater negative mood, such as depression and low self-esteem, as well as the experience of less good health generally. The overall picture is that optimism is good for health with one proviso regarding unrealistic optimism (covered in Chapter 18). This is known as optimistic bias or unrealistic optimism and is defined as the tendency to view oneself as invulnerable, or at least less likely than others to be susceptible to an illness. So, optimistic bias leads smokers to believe that, while the research suggests that smokers may get lung cancer, for some reason it does not apply to them. It can actually result in individuals indulging in risky behaviour such as unsafe sex. Somehow the risks happen to others and not to the individual with unrealistic optimism.

Intelligence

To conclude this section, we would like to draw your attention to some very interesting research that was undertaken in Scotland that reports relationships between intelligence and cardiovascular disease. We have already mentioned this research (in Chapter 13 in the section on questions emerging from the use of intelligence tests), but we repeat it here to allow you to make the link more specifically with health psychology. Intelligence is rarely considered as a variable in health research, so this study is fairly unique in this respect and the nature of the data also makes it a unique study. As you may recall, the intelligence of all of the children born in Scotland in 1921 and attending school on 1 June 1932 was measured, as was the intelligence of all children born in 1936 and attending school on 4 June 1947. This gave two data sets of the IQ scores for almost all the 11-year-old children in the population born in 1921 and 1936. Deary *et al.* (2004) followed up this data, linking it to public health records and following up participants who were still alive. These are very detailed complex studies but we will report some of the more interesting findings relevant to health here. Childhood intelligence was found to be associated with survival to age 76 at least. People with lower intelligence in childhood were more likely to die from lung and stomach cancers in adulthood, illnesses that are linked with cigarette smoking. Some of the data from the same programme using another similar sample tested in 1947, was presented previously (in Chapter 13). This suggested that lower intelligence in childhood was linked with cardiovascular disease in adulthood and also with earlier death. The authors suggest various explanations for their data which are beyond the scope of this discussion, but interested readers are referred to the paper which does make interesting reading.

Expanding definitions of health and well-being

So far, the emphasis of this discussion has mainly been on personality and illness even though the heading includes health. This is a common focus in health psychology where research is undertaken on various groups of patients. Consequently, most of this research looks at relationships with illness. Now we are going to change tack somewhat and look at research that includes health, well-being and personality. This is an increasingly important area as governments become more interested in trying to promote healthy lifestyles in the general population. The aims here are to reduce sickness levels and prevent the development of diseases, both of which are costly, and to promote the well-being of the general public.

There are now a large number of mainly correlational studies demonstrating links between personality and health. The majority of studies look at individual personality correlates and compare them with general health and well-being. Why are some individuals motivated to eat healthily, attend a gym regularly and avoid developing unhealthy habits like smoking or drinking too much? Other individuals seem driven towards unhealthy lifestyles, overeating, drinking to excess, smoking and indulging in risky behaviours like unprotected sex. Remember that one aim of personality theory is to explain human motivation (as we saw in Chapter 1). Within the health context, we are interested in explaining which personality factors motivate individuals to follow a healthy lifestyle while others are drawn to less healthy options. A lot of associations have been established, but identifying causal links has proved to be more difficult. One promising new school of psychology has emerged recently, with one of its stated aims being to promote health and well-being; this is 'positive psychology', which we will now briefly consider.

Personality and well-being: the positive psychology approach

Positive psychology is a relatively new development within psychology that has emerged this millennium. Martin Seligman, of learned helplessness fame, has played a major role in developing this approach. Basically, Seligman and Csikszentmihalyi (2000) describe the first 100 years of psychology as being focused largely on psychopathology. As psychologists we now know a lot about mental illness and

its treatment but we still do not know very much about how to improve the quality of the ordinary person's life. Imagine someone asks you, as a psychologist, how to bring up a child to maximise their chances of being happy in adulthood. Seligman points out that psychology can only put forward a few ideas about what might be psychologically unhelpful for the child's future happiness, like insecure attachments and so forth. They conclude that, overall, the area is under-researched.

One of the functions of personality theories is to look at what we, as a human species, want from life. What is our ultimate motivation? Personality theorists from quite diverse schools, for example, Rogers, Ellis and Jung, to name but a few, have shown a remarkable consistency here. They suggest that, as human beings, we aim to stay alive and to be happy above all. One of the main themes within positive psychology is happiness, and research is now emerging that suggests happiness may be one crucial factor determining our health. Research is also under way to try to understand the mechanisms underlying these links. Barak (2006) has examined the relationships between affective style, happiness, well-being and the functioning of the immune system. He reports that individuals with more negative affective styles (less happy individuals) have a weaker immune response and as a result may be at greater risk of illness compared with happier individuals.

Positive psychology has identified a range of character strengths that individuals possess and concepts like optimism, self-efficacy and happiness that we have examined here, as well as positive emotional states such as hope, wisdom, courage and spirituality, all fall within the scope of positive psychology. Peterson and Seligman (2004) have identified six main superordinate character strengths, with a number of subordinate strengths within each one, and these are summarised in Table 24.1.

Not everything about positive psychology is new and there is a much longer history of work on concepts such as optimism and also on positive concepts such as happiness. Psychologists often drop the term happiness in favour of the label 'subjective well-being' to define more clearly what is meant. The interest is in what constitutes happiness, in how individuals define 'the good life'. This last sentence identifies the crux of the issue, namely that the focus is on the subjective experience of well-being. There are an increasing number of measures available to assess subjective well-being. These include the Positive and Negative Affect Scale (Watson *et al.*, 1988), the Satisfaction with Life Scale (Diener *et al.*, 1985) and the Flourishing Scale (Diener *et al.*, 2010). While these measures are psychometrically sound, they do not give a particularly good measure of long-term satisfaction. They are subject to biases in responding such as the mood of the individual at the time of completion (Schwartz and Strack, 1999); however, they are heavily used to measure well-being in positive psychology research. Evidence is accumulating worldwide attesting to the importance of subjective well-being.

Table 24.1 Character strengths identified in positive psychology

1 Wisdom and knowledge.
   (a) Creativity: this includes artistic work but is wider than just that, covering all sorts of mental creativity and novelty.
   (b) Curiosity: this is about openness to experience.
   (c) Judgement and open-mindedness: this relates to the ability to think critically, to weigh evidence and make reasoned judgements.
   (d) Love of learning: really describes a thirst for knowledge.
   (e) Perspective: this relates to being wise and advises others wisely.
2 Courage: describes strengths in maintaining progress towards one's goals despite obstacles and so on.
   (a) Bravery: this includes, but is wider than, physical bravery, including standing up for one's views and so on.
   (b) Perseverance: this is about sticking power even when things are tough.
   (c) Honesty: about truthfulness in life.
   (d) Zest: being energetic, enthusiastic and full of life.
3 Humanity – strengths that involve caring and befriending others.
   (a) Capacity to love and be loved.
   (b) Kindness.
   (c) Social intelligence: this describes what we have called emotional intelligence (in Chapter 15).
4 Justice – this describes the skills and qualities necessary for healthy communities.
   (a) Teamwork.
   (b) Fairness.
   (c) Leadership.
5 Temperance – strengths that protect us against excesses in behaviour.
   (a) Forgiveness and mercy: giving people a second chance, not being vengeful.
   (b) Modesty and humility.
   (c) Prudence: taking care not to be rash and being considered about risk-taking.
   (d) Self-regulation: exercising self-control.
6 Transcendence – strengths that help individuals feel at one with the world and find meaning in their lives.
   (a) Appreciation of beauty and excellence.
   (b) Gratitude: expressing thanks and really feeling it.
   (c) Hope.
   (d) Humour.
   (e) Religiousness and spirituality.

Finucane *et al.* (2012), comparing happiness levels in healthy, chronic pain, depressed and PTSD individuals, found that the clinical groups experienced negative emotions much more frequently than did the healthy group, and the latter had the highest overall levels of happiness. Evans and Egerton (1992) found that people who are not happy are more likely to become ill and that mood has an effect on the immune system, with positive feelings boosting its function (Stone *et al.*, 1987; Barak, 2006). Clearly, some individuals are never going to be as happy as others, but happiness has clearly been established as beneficial for health and well-being (Argyle, 1997). While it is still early days for positive psychological approaches, the emerging evidence suggests that it may well help us to deepen our knowledge of how to improve health and well-being in the general population. If you want to read more about positive psychology and happiness, a good starting point is Martin Seligman's website and the address is provided at the end of this discussion.

Career focus: Working in health psychology

According to the British Psychological Society website, health psychologists work in the area of health and illness, and their particular focus is on promoting positive changes in individuals' attitudes, behaviour and thinking around health. Specific roles might include working on interventions to prevent problematic behaviour (such as drug abuse or poor diet), working with people with poor health or an illness (e.g. managing pain or managing the illness) and promoting good health practices around exercise, diet or monitoring one's own health and well-being. Health psychologists will work with a range of agencies, including hospitals, healthcare trusts and authorities, research units and universities.

Heather Buchanan, Registered Health Psychologist and Lecturer in Health Psychology at the University of Nottingham

1. How/why did you choose to pursue the area of psychology that you did?

I was lucky enough to take a module in health psychology when I was a psychology undergraduate. I loved it straight away! Health, illness and care are subjects that affect us all, and within health psychology there are so many different and exciting topics and questions to explore. I was mostly interested in the dental and medical areas of health psychology, so I chose to pursue these as a postgraduate and I am now a Registered Health Psychologist. I work with a variety of different health professionals, including anaesthetists, dentists and clinical psychologists.

2. In what way do the skills and/or knowledge you learned when studying personality and individual differences apply to your work/research today?

There are many aspects of personality and individual differences that apply to my work. For example, one of my research interests is the role of individual differences in preference for information in medical and dental settings. There is evidence to show that not all individuals want a lot of information preoperatively, and actually fare less well if given a lot of information. However, some patients need a lot of information to help them cope better. Therefore, my colleagues and I have explored informational coping styles in order to tailor information before, during and after invasive procedures to help patients fare better in terms of both physical and psychological outcomes.

You can read more on becoming a health psychologist at the British Psychological Society website at **http://www .bps.org.uk/careers-education-training/how-become-psychologist/types-psychologists/becoming-health-psychologis-0**.

Final comments

We began this discussion by posing the question of why we study personality in relation to health and illness. The conclusion has to be that an understanding of personality concepts greatly enriches our knowledge of what factors are likely to motivate individuals in particular situations and helps health psychologists to understand what individuals are experiencing and why they behave as they do. One clear message is emerging from research on personality and health with a positive psychology focus, namely that experiencing positive emotions is protective. Well-adjusted, socially stable individuals who are well integrated within their communities have a statistically significantly lower risk of developing disease and dying prematurely when compared with individuals who are more isolated, unstable, impulsive and alienated (Friedman, 2000). Such individuals are shown to experience more positive, subjective well-being and rate themselves as being happier with their lives (Diener *et al.*, 2008).

Personality theorists are focused on trying to explain human motivation, among other things. There is a fairly high level of consensus from personality theorists of different persuasions that the overarching life goals for human beings are about survival and achieving happiness. Illness is a threat to these fundamental goals, and an understanding of the different ways that individuals try to cope with illnesses that may threaten their goals is crucial as well as a knowledge of how to improve the health and well-being of the general population.

Summary

- Common sense definitions of health are problematical with their focus on absence of symptoms of illness.

Health is not simply about physical symptoms, so definitions need to encompass our mental health and social well-being. The World Health Organization definition from 1948 is still the most widely quoted one.

Health is a state of complete physical, mental and social well-being and not merely the absence of disease or infirmity.

(Official Records of the World Health Organization, no. 2, p. 100)

- It is hypothesised that there are four possible ways in which personality and illness may be linked. There may be a causal link (personality causes health); a correlational association between personality and health or personality and illness, with perhaps the same biological processes underpinning both, personality traits and illness outcomes; or it may be that having certain personality traits may lead individuals to engage in particular behaviours that influence their health and/or increase the risk of illness; finally, the experience of illness may actually change the individual's personality.

- The coronary-prone behaviour pattern associated with the Type A personality is well established and contrasts with the non-coronary prone Type B personality. Type As are driven to achieve while Type Bs are more laid back. The longitudinal studies on Type A exemplify the need for good measures of individual differences and sound methodologies. Hostility has been established as a toxic component in Type A personality and is associated with poorer health and cardiovascular problems. More recently, a Type D (distressed) personality has been identified. This describes a subgroup of patients suffering from coronary heart disease who are high in negative affectivity and social inhibition, the two constituents of Type D.

- There is an official diagnostic classification system for psychological factors affecting medical conditions within the *DSM-IV-TR* where they are coded under general medical conditions. This provides a useful tool for research purposes. The commonest psychological factors affecting medical conditions are anxiety and depression. There is a substantial body of research illustrating how anxiety and stress can exacerbate physical conditions.

- Illnesses are usefully conceptualised as stressful life events. The general adaptation syndrome describes the body's defensive activity in response to stress. It consists of three stages: the alarm reaction, the resistance stage and the exhaustion stage. The transactional model of stress is the most widely applied model and conceptualises stress as a transaction or relationship between the person and the environment that taxes or exceeds the person's coping resources.

- Individual differences that we have already discussed are also relevant to health and illness. These include locus of control, self-efficacy, optimism and intelligence. All of these have been shown to influence the likelihood of becoming ill, the way that illness is dealt with and even the individual's mortality.

- While much of the research in health psychology actually focuses on illness, recently more attention is being given to promoting well-being in the general population, and this is stimulated largely by the school of positive psychology. Positive personality traits and their influence on producing positive emotional states are increasingly being shown to foster health and well-being. This is exemplified by the research on happiness.

Connecting up

In this section we mention a number of concepts that we cover in detail in other chapters; locus of control and self-efficacy (Chapter 4), intelligence (Chapter 12, although we look specifically at intelligence and health in Chapter 13) and optimism (Chapter 18).

We mention trait models of personality here, and Chapter 7 contains more information on these models of personality.

Critical thinking

Discussion questions

- It is hypothesised that there are four possible ways in which personality and illness may be linked. There may be a causal link (personality causes health); a correlational

association between personality and health or personality and illness, with perhaps the same biological processes underpinning both, personality traits and illness outcomes; or it may be that having certain personality traits may lead individuals to engage in particular behaviours that influence their health and/or increase the risk of illness; finally, the experience of illness may actually change the individual's personality. Think about your own personality and your health behaviours. Which of the four possible ways can be used to help you understand the relationship between your personality and your health?

- The General Adaptation Syndrome describes the body's defensive activity in response to stress. It consists of three stages: the alarm reaction, the resistance stage and the exhaustion stage. Think about an event in which you felt stress and think about the process you went through. Describe the types of feelings you had at the time of this event in terms of:

  – alarm reaction

  – resistance stage

  – exhaustion stage

- The transactional model of stress is the most widely applied model and conceptualises stress as a transaction or relationship between the person and the environment that taxes or exceeds the person's coping resources. Think about an event in which you felt stress

and think about the process you went through. Describe the event in terms of: (a) the environment; and (b) you as a person.

  – What aspects of the environment were important in influencing levels of stress around the event?

  – What aspects of yourself were important in influencing levels of stress around the event?

Essay questions

- Examine the relationship between personality and health and illness.
- Discuss the impact of negative emotions on physical health and psychological well-being.
- Identify the major areas where links between personality and physical health have been made.
- Evaluate the importance of positive and negative emotions on health and well-being.
- Discuss how health and well-being have been examined within a positive psychology perspective. How does this compare with previous psychological perspectives?
- Identify the main complexities involved in measuring health and well-being.

Going further

Books

There are many health psychology textbooks that will cover the material we have discussed here and some references are given below.

- Morrison, V. and Bennett, P. (2009) *An introduction to health psychology* (2nd edn). Harlow: Pearson Education. Chapters 5 and 12. This is a British book and includes a lot of European research.
- Ogden, J. (2007) *Health psychology: A textbook* (4th edn). Berkshire: Open University Press. Chapter 2.
- Contrada, R. J. and Goyal, T. M. (2004). Individual differences, health and illness: the role of emotional traits and generalised expectancies. In S. Sutton, A. Baum and M. Johnston (eds), *The Sage handbook of health psychology*. London: Sage. This is a slightly more advanced chapter that assumes some knowledge of health psychology.
- Weinman, J., Wright, S. and Johnston, M. (1995). *Measures in health psychology: A user's portfolio*. London: NFER-Nelson. This provides a useful guide to measurement in health psychology and includes details of many scales that can be used to assess individual differences in health.
- Stevens, D. E., Merikangas, K. R. and Merikangas, J. R. (1995). Comorbidity of depression and other medical

conditions. In E. E. Beckham and W. R. Leber (eds), *Handbook of depression* (2nd edn). New York: Guilford. This provides an excellent review of the literature on co-occurrence of physical disease and depression and also some work on anxiety.

Journals

- Argyll, M. (1997). Is happiness a cause of health? *Psychology and Health, 12,* 769–781. This paper reviews the early research on happiness and health and comes to some interesting conclusions.
- Diener, E. (2000). Subjective well-being: The science of happiness and a proposal for a national index. *American Psychologist, 55,* 34–43. An interesting and thought-provoking article looking at the importance of well-being to nations.
- Löckenhoff, C. E., Terracciano, A., Ferrucci, L., Costa. P. T. (2012). Five-factor personality traits and age trajectories of self-rated health: The role of question framing. *Journal of Personality, 80,* 375–401. This is a good example of research examining the relationships between self-assessed health and personality.
- Iwanaga, M. (2004). Coping availability and stress reduction for optimistic and pessimistic individuals.

Personality and Individual Differences, 36, 11–22. This gives a good flavour of personality and health research.

- Research on individual differences in health is published in a wide range of journals: among the more specialist are *Health Psychology, Journal of Health Psychology* and the *British Journal of Health Psychology*.

Web links

- There are many good informative websites on depression and anxiety and this link is to one good site in the USA: **www.allaboutdepression.com/gen_01.html**.
- This brings you to Terman's website where you can find information about the longitudinal study of gifted individuals which has provided us with a great deal of health-related information: **www.stanfordalumni.org/news/magazine/2000/julaug/articles/terman.html**.
- This is the link to Seligman's authentic happiness website. Here you can assess your character strengths and read more about positive psychology: **www.authentichappiness.sas.upenn.edu/Default.aspx**.
- World Health Organization (WHO): this site provides useful statistics about health and provides a global perspective: **www.who.int/en**.
- This is the link to Ed Diener's site where you can find information about well-being and life satisfaction, including measures: **http://internal.psychology.illinois.edu/~ediener**.
- **British Regional Heart Study**, which is based at University College London: **www.ucl.ac.uk/pcph/research-groups-themes/brhs-pub**.

Film and literature

- ***Wall Street*** (1987, directed by Oliver Stone) depicts individuals with a Type A personality, where traits such as a drive to achieve, competitive needs, hostility to competitors and persistent drive for recognition, advancement and power are central to their character and behaviour.
- ***Super Size Me*** (2004, directed by Morgan Spurlock). The relationship between health and psychological concepts such as well-being, self-efficacy and anxiety is evident in this documentary. Spurlock's film documents a 30-day period during which he limits himself to only eat McDonald's food.

Explore the website accompanying this text at **www.pearsoned.co.uk/maltby** for further resources to help you with your studies. These include multiple-choice questions, essay questions, web links and ideas for advanced reading.

CHAPTER 25
An Introduction to Psychometric Testing

Key themes

- Psychometric testing
- Item writing
- Reliability
- Validity
- Exploratory factor analysis
- Confirmatory factor analysis
- Types and uses of psychometric tests

Learning outcomes

At the end of the discussion you should:

- Understand some of the ideas and criteria surrounding psychometric testing
- Know what is meant by reliability in psychometric testing
- Be able to explain what is meant by validity in psychometric testing
- Understand how factor analysis is used in psychometric testing
- Know the types and uses of different psychometric tests

Introduction

When you leave university, you may be attending a number of job interviews. You may be aware that, many employers use psychometric tests as part of the interview process for applicants. You may not be aware that, in the spring of 2004, it was announced that personality tests designed to weed out racist applicants to the police were introduced in all 43 police forces in England and Wales. This was in response to a BBC documentary, *The Secret Policeman,* which exposed racism in the Greater Manchester police force. You may also not be aware that, as the *Sunday Telegraph* reported in October 2003, even James Murdoch, son of media tycoon Rupert Murdoch, was reported to have to sit psychometric tests to find out if he was fit to head his father's company, satellite broadcaster BSkyB. In March 2003, the UK higher education minister Margaret Hodge pointed to the diverse ways that universities could develop different forms of assessment by which to improve decisions on students' admission to university, and she encouraged universities simply to look beyond candidates' exams. Margaret Hodge argued that, like employers, universities could use a whole range of techniques, including psychometric tests.

There is little doubt in our minds that measurement is a cornerstone of modern psychology. Even the government seems to be sanctioning measurement as an important aspect of education and work. Psychological tests are of fundamental importance to research in many areas of psychology. Probably the three areas in which that statement is most true are individual differences (including personality) and intelligence. However, psychological tests are also of immense value in developing areas such as health psychology (with its growing emphasis on quality of life), work psychology and educational psychology, as well as in more traditional areas such as social, cognitive and developmental psychology.

What we are going to do here, then, is to introduce you to what makes a good psychometric test. There are some very

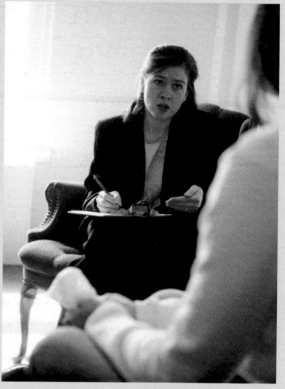

Source: Corbis/Tom Stewart

simple but elegant ideas behind a good test. Namely, a test should be both reliable (that is, those items within measures correlate and sometimes are consistent over time) and valid (that is, the test measures what it claims to measure).

You will already have been introduced to the terms 'reliability' and 'validity' in research methods classes. Here, you will see how these ideas are central to psychometric testing.

Types and uses of psychometric tests

In your career as a psychologist, you will come across a variety of psychometric tests. The main types of tests you will come across in the personality, intelligence and individual differences literature are measures of personality, ability, motivation, educational and psychological work, clinical assessment and attitude.

- Personality measures are designed to measure a set of psychological traits or characteristics of the person that remain relatively stable over time. An example of a personality measure might be a measure of the five-factor

model of personality that would include questions and response choices that look for underlying tendencies of the person's behaviour.

- Ability measures are designed to measure particular abilities. These tests often include intelligence tests (that measure an individual's ability at a number of cognitive processes, such as perceptual speed, comprehension or reasoning) and an aptitude test (measurement of particular, specific skills suited for a particular task). Therefore, ability tests could include measures of general intelligence or creative thinking or successful communication strategies in the workplace. Items from ability tests seek to test these thought processes; here is an example:

'Which of the following 5 makes the best comparison?'
'Son is to father as nephew is to . . .'

Respondents would then be given the following choices: (a) Niece, (b) Cousin, (c) Uncle, (d) Mother, (e) Sister.

- Motivation and attitude measures are usually concerned with measuring particular beliefs towards something, such as work. So, for example, respondents would usually be asked to respond to an item such as 'I am satisfied with the work I do'.
- Neuropsychological tests use measures of sensory, perceptual and motor performance to assess different parts of psychophysiological activity and neurological functioning within the brain.

So, how are these different psychometric tests used? For example, in educational psychology, ability tests are used in the study of educational success and may be used as a tool in school placement, in detecting possible learning disabilities, or in tracking intellectual development. Personality tests are widely used in occupational psychology, particularly in job selection. What employers do is create their job criteria and then go some way in trying to match applicants to these criteria via personality testing. For example, if an employer wanted someone to sell a product, they would want that person to be outgoing. Therefore, the employer might administer an extraversion test to all applicants to see which of the candidates was more outgoing. Clearly, intelligence and attitude tests (particularly around motivation to work) are also used in occupational settings. Psychometric tests are used in clinical psychology as a way of diagnosing clinical conditions and distinguishing between clinical groups. For example, a clinical psychologist might compare their current treatment group on a measure against a general population sample, as this might provide a useful insight into how they should treat the clinical group. Equally, they may use neuropsychological tests to assess consequences of medical illnesses or conditions. One example of such use might be among patients who have experienced brain damage; certain psychometric tests, particularly ability tests, might also be used to evaluate the extent of the damage and later to evaluate any improvement in a patient's condition.

Throughout the rest of the discussion we are going to introduce you to many of the aspects of psychometric testing by way of developing our own psychometric test.

Developing a psychometric test

For this exercise we are going to detail the development of a new measure of a concept – academic vindictiveness among students. As you might realise, there are many approaches that students might take in their study. We've seen earlier (from Chapter 16, The application of personality and intelligence in education and the workplace, which details personality, intelligence and education) that conscientiousness is a good predictor of educational performance. However, for the purpose of this discussion, we're wondering whether there might be another individual difference variable in the way that students approach their academic work – namely, academic vindictiveness.[1] This work was carried out in response to a finding that some students may make deliberate acts to sabotage others' work, and/or feel angry towards someone or act vengefully when they feel that somebody in their academic circle has wronged, misguided or surpassed them in some way (Crocker *et al.*, 2002; Crocker and Luhtanen, 2003). Therefore, in the next few sections we will be using this construct of academic vindictiveness and the development of a scale to measure academic vindictiveness to introduce you to a number of psychometric techniques.

Developing items for a psychometric test

Paul Kline (Kline, 1986), a United Kingdom psychometrician, points out that the secret to developing a very good scale is writing very good questions. For Kline, if you do not write good items, then you will never develop a good psychometric scale. Therefore, for Kline, developing the items is a crucial part of the process. There are a number of considerations you need to bear in mind when writing items for a scale, and in the next section we will introduce you to these considerations while developing items for our own scale of academic vindictiveness.

The first thing to consider is making the distinction between two different types of questions: open-format or closed-format questions. Open-format are questions that asked for some written detail but have no determined set of responses, e.g. 'Tell us about the occasions when you have been academically vindictive'. Therefore, any answer can be given to these questions. These types of questions lead to more qualitative data because there is a large number of possible responses. These are the problems with open-format questions in a psychometric test. Given that they produce a large number of possible answers, with each potentially different, open-format questions are also time-consuming for the researcher who has to analyse all the different answers.

As a consequence, in psychometric tests, researchers will tend to use closed-format questions. A closed-format question is a question where there is a short question or statement followed by a number of options. See, for example, Exhibit 25.1.

[1] This is a construct that was developed by a colleague, Rajvinder Lally, and we are very grateful to her for allowing us to use some of her initial work on this construct.

Exhibit 25.1

Indicate the extent to which you disagree or agree with the following statement, as it applies to you.

| 1 | I feel bitter towards those who do better than me on my course. | Disagree strongly | Disagree | Not certain | Agree | Agree strongly |

The main aim of closed-format questions is very simply to break down respondents' answers into data that can be quantified into answers that give you the information you want to know (i.e. to what extent do people agree or disagree with the statement as it applies to them).

However, the first stage of the process is to create the items. Kline suggests that the first place to start is to write as many items as possible. Now, this could be a matter of simply writing the items yourself, but this can be very laborious and you may also make mistakes or miss out important aspects. Therefore, in terms of initial item writing, you could also use the following sources:

- **Theoretical literature** – usually, scales are not developed from an entirely new construct. There will always be some theoretical perspective that underpins the development of a new scale, and the terms, phrases and ideas that appear in the theoretical literature should be used as the basis for writing items.
- **Experts** – you could recruit experts in the area to suggest particular items for your scale. This will enhance the quality.
- **Colleagues** – a colleague(s) or co-researcher(s) can help you to write items because, at the very least, this will generate more items than you could produce singly.

After you have written the initial set of items, you need to study them and rewrite them. Again, use experts or colleagues to examine the phrasing of each question and see if they can improve on them. It is also probably the case that you will have a large number of items.

It may then be a good idea to try to reduce the number of items you have written if you feel there are a huge number. It's difficult to determine what a huge number is, but in deciding on the final number you might like to keep a few points in mind:

- Kline suggests that the optimal length for any scale measuring one construct should be about 15–20 items. You may need many more items than this when initially constructing the scale to ensure that you end up with a scale of an appropriate length.
- When you administer the scale in the first instance the general rule is that you should have a certain number of participants for each item of the administration; guidelines change, but at least five participants to one item is acceptable. Ideally, most researchers aim for 10 participants to one item as a premium, with a minimum of 100 respondents. This is for statistical reasons because you need a good

number of responses to ensure that you have captured variation of responses across respondents. You might keep this in mind if you know how many participants you are likely to get to fill in your scale on a first occasion. For example, if you had 40 items, you would need 400 participants to answer the questionnaire. Therefore, if you were only likely to get 300 participants, you might wish to reduce the number of items, or lower the criteria to five to one.

- Who is the scale likely to be used with? It may be that, if the scale is designed for clinical settings, or with children, or where available administration time is short, you might actually look to reduce the number of items, even before you've developed the final scale.

It is difficult to say what the optimal number of items is. In most cases you need to make a judgement. One way to determine this is to get a group of participants, ideally experts, to rate the items in terms of potential effectiveness of measuring the construct. You could determine which items are considered the strongest and should be retained (i.e. those items rated highest by the participants) and which items are considered the weakest and could be excluded. This technique could be used to exclude items from the first administration of the scale if you felt you had too many items.

Writing items for a psychometric test

To illustrate the process and some of the techniques used in writing items we are going to talk about the development of a set of 23 items to measure vindictiveness. In developing this set of items we followed many of the procedures outlined above. A few lecturers and students wrote a list of 70 items. We then asked a group of five students to look at the items and suggest possible changes to the wording of the items. We then repeated the exercise with three lecturers.

For the purpose of the exercise we felt that 70 items was too many, so we decided to trim these down. We asked five students and five lecturers to rate the items in terms of their potential to measure academic vindictiveness, on a scale of 1 to 10 (1 = Not at all, 10 = Very much so). We then selected the top scoring items, those that scored an average rating score of 9 or over (although it is important to note that this was an arbitrary criterion). This amounted to 23 items, which we thought was a suitable number for the current exercise, and these are shown in Exhibit 25.2.

Exhibit 25.2

Potential items for our academic vindictiveness scale

1   I can be spiteful to my friends if they get a better mark than me.

2   In the past I have falsely told other students the wrong exam date, but only when they were too lazy to find out themselves, and only when I was in a bad mood, so they would miss the exam.

3   I would hate the student who got the best mark in one of my classes.

4   If I had the opportunity, resources and ability to change other students' exam grades so that mine were the best, I would do it.

5   I find myself wishing bad things on people that do better than me academically.

6   I always tell people I am happy for them when they do better than me in exams.

7   I have thought about spoiling someone's work because it is better than mine.

8   I wish bad things on people because they are smarter than me.

9   When other students on my course are praised for their excellent work, it makes me want to wish something bad on that person.

10   If my friend got a better mark than me, even if it was just 1 per cent, I would consider tampering with his/her work in some way.

11   I have mean thoughts towards people who score better than me in exams.

12   I resent people on my course who excel in their studies.

13   I feel bitter towards those who do better than me on my course.

14   I have lied to people on my course to try and hinder their progress so I can get the better mark.

15   If I came second best in a piece of work, because my friend got the top mark, I would still be happy.

16   I am a really bad person because I am academically vindictive.

17   I seek revenge on people who get better grades than me and take away my chance of success.

18   If I was Vice-Chancellor of a University I would ensure that students were not academically vindictive.

19   I have thought about spoiling someone's work because it is better than mine.

20   I would consider doing something nasty to somebody who threatened my chances of academic success.

21   My academic vindictiveness is a result of a mental illness.

22   When I find out I haven't got an excellent mark for a piece of work I get very upset with myself.

23   I work very hard so I am able to do the best I can at all academic activities.

Now, we have deliberately made some mistakes or errors in some of these items so we can demonstrate some of the skills in item writing: clarity, leading, embarrassing, hypothetical and reverse questions.

Clarity of questions

You have to ensure that there is clarity to the wording of your questions. Good practice suggests that questions must be clear, short and unambiguous. Look at the following questions, 4 and 10.

The main aim of writing a good psychometric test question is to make sure that the questions will not mean different things to different respondents. This is very important because it means that if your questions are ambiguous (the meaning can be interpreted differently) then your participants will, in fact, be answering different questions. This will muddy your results because you will never be sure what interpretation respondents have been answering. One of the main culprits of this is qualifying statements or trying too hard to capture all aspects of the situation. Question 4 is an example of an item trying to capture all the prerequisites that

---

4   If I had the opportunity, resources and ability to change other students' exam grades so that mine were the best, I would do it.

10   If my friend got a better mark than me, even if it was just 1 per cent, I would consider tampering with his/her work in some way.

might have to be in place that possibly underlie academic vindictiveness (opportunity, resources and ability). This means that respondents might concentrate on aspects of the question that focus on the opportunity, resources and ability before they were academically vindictive, rather than whether they have the tendency to be academically vindictive, therefore making the question ambiguous. Question 10 seeks to qualify the possible extremity of academic vindictiveness by highlighting issues about academic vindictiveness, even if the gap in scores was less than 1 per cent. Each of these questions can be simplified, as shown in Exhibit 25.3.

Exhibit 25.3

4   If I had the opportunity to change other students' exam grades so that mine was the best, I would do it.

10   If my friend got a better mark than me, I would consider tampering with his/her work in some way.

These questions are shorter and the meaning is much more clear. They may not seek to be as exact as the previous versions, through the use of qualifying statements, but they are unlikely to be ambiguous to respondents.

Leading questions

Leading questions are questions that try to steer the respondent to a particular answer, or in the direction of a particular answer.

However, leading questions can arise quite undeliberately and can occur because of the exact phrasing of the question. A brilliant example of the use of leading questions was demonstrated in one episode of the 1986 series *Yes, Prime Minister*, a fictional BBC comedy series set in the prime minister's office in 10 Downing Street that follows the prime ministerial career of Jim Hacker, who struggles to formulate and enact legislation or effect departmental changes, opposed by the will of the British Civil Service in the person of Sir Humphrey Appleby and his Principal Private Secretary Bernard Woolley. The interchange between Sir Humphrey and Bernard Woolley demonstrates how surveys can reach opposite conclusions about the introduction of national service (compulsory military service) for young people through the use of leading questions (see Exhibit 25.4).

Exhibit 25.4

Survey one

Sir Humphrey Appleby: Mr Woolley, are you worried about the rise in crime among teenagers?
Bernard Woolley: Yes.
Sir Humphrey Appleby: Do you think there is lack of discipline and vigorous training in our Comprehensive Schools?
Bernard Woolley: Yes.
Sir Humphrey Appleby: Do you think young people welcome some structure and leadership in their lives?
Bernard Woolley: Yes.
Sir Humphrey Appleby: Do they respond to a challenge?
Bernard Woolley: Yes.
Sir Humphrey Appleby: Might you be in favour of reintroducing National Service?
Bernard Woolley: Er, I might be.
Sir Humphrey Appleby: Yes or no?
Bernard Woolley: Yes.
Of course, after all you've said you can't say no to that. On the other hand, the surveys can reach opposite conclusions.

Survey two

Sir Humphrey Appleby: Mr Woolley, are you worried about the danger of war?
Bernard Woolley: Yes.
Sir Humphrey Appleby: Are you unhappy about the growth of armaments?
Bernard Woolley: Yes.
Sir Humphrey Appleby: Do you think there's a danger in giving young people guns and teaching them how to kill?
Bernard Woolley: Yes.
Sir Humphrey Appleby: Do you think it's wrong to force people to take arms against their will?
Bernard Woolley: Yes.
Sir Humphrey Appleby: Would you oppose the reintroduction of conscription?
Bernard Woolley: Yes.

As you can see, Sir Humphrey has been able to get Bernard Woolley to reach two opposing conclusions by using leading questions with which Bernard Woolley will tend to agree.

Our question 16 is a leading question: 'I am a really bad person because I am academically vindictive'. It is asking respondents to make a value judgement that they would find it difficult to disagree with, and therefore they would be led to answer because they feel they would be saying something about themselves and place themselves in a bad light. We would suggest removing this question.

Perhaps our question 2 is a less obvious example of a leading question; see Exhibit 25.5.

Exhibit 25.5

2   In the past I have falsely told other students the wrong exam date, but only when they were too lazy to find out themselves, and only when I was in a bad mood, so they would miss the exam.

Question 2 seeks to qualify the item asking about academic vindictiveness by closely defining the situation around the other student being lazy and whether the person was in a bad mood. This is clearly a situation in which academic vindictiveness may occur, but also seems to lead the respondent in a particular direction by potentially excusing the behaviour and almost suggesting that it could be acceptable under certain circumstances. Regardless of whether it encourages people to 'own up', it is leading the respondent by suggesting they could be justified in making the statement. We would suggest, in terms of directly assessing academic vindictiveness, a better item might be as shown in Exhibit 25.6.

Exhibit 25.6

2   In the past I have falsely told other students the wrong exam date, so they would miss the exam.

Embarrassing questions

Generally, questions dealing with personal matters should be avoided. This is because this may make your respondent feel embarrassed or uncomfortable, and doing research that causes this type of feeling in participants is not good practice; indeed, it is frowned upon. Equally, it is not good for the researcher because it may lead the participant to give incorrect or misleading information, or fail to complete the rest of the questionnaire. So, great care should be taken when asking personal or potentially embarrassing questions and you should spend a lot of time thinking about how best to ask these questions. Our question 21 ('My academic vindictiveness is a result of a mental illness') is a potentially embarrassing question and we should remove this item from our list.

Hypothetical questions

Hypothetical questions are questions that place the individual in a situation that they may never experience and ask them for their opinion on something. So, for example, you might ask 'If you were Prime Minister of the country, what would you do about psychology lecturers?' These types of questions might produce colourful answers, but are considered bad research practice because answers will be in response to a situation that the person may never have considered rather than their real view or feelings about something. Our question 18 ('If I was Vice-Chancellor of a University I would ensure that students were not academically vindictive') is a hypothetical question and therefore we should remove it from our list.

Questions with reverse wording

Researchers will often write items with some questions with *reverse wording*. This is usually done to force the person

Questions dealing with personal matters should be avoided, unless absolutely necessary, as they have the potential to cause embarrassment.
Source: Rex Features/Image Source

taking the psychometric test to read it carefully and not just to respond to all the items in the same way. Also, it is a good way to check for people who haven't taken answering the questionnaire seriously, as it will show up with contradictory answers. Ideally, you should try to maximise the number of reverse worded items in your scale, but we have just included reverse wording for two items, item 6 and item 15.

Therefore, taking all these changes into account, we have a final revised scale comprising 20 items, as shown in Exhibit 25.7.

Exhibit 25.7

1   I can be spiteful to my friends if they get a better mark than me.
2   I find myself wishing bad things on people who do better than me academically.
3   I would hate the student who got the best mark in one of my classes.
4   I feel bitter towards those who do better than me on my course.
5   In the past I have falsely told other students the wrong exam date, so they would miss the exam.
6   I always tell people I am happy for them when they do better than me in exams.
7   I have thought about spoiling someone's work because it is better than mine.
8   I seek revenge on people who got better grades than me and take away my chances of success.
9   When other students on my course are praised for their excellent work, it makes me want to wish something bad on that person.
10 If my friend got a better mark than me, I would consider tampering with his/her work in some way.
11 I have mean thoughts towards people who score better than me in exams.
12 I resent people on my course who excel in their studies.
13 If I had the opportunity to change other students' exam grades so that mine were the best, I would do it.
14 I have lied to people on my course to try and hinder their progress so I can get the better mark.
15 If I came second best in a piece of work, because my friend got the top mark, I would still be happy.
16 I wish bad things on people because they are smarter than me.
17 I do not like to help others with their work as it might result in them getting a better mark.
18 I would consider doing something nasty to somebody who threatened my chances of academic success.
19 When I find out I haven't got an excellent mark for a piece of work I get very upset with myself.
20 I work very hard so I am able to do the best I can at all academic activities.

Stop and think

Cultural considerations

There is other good practice in writing good questions. Try to consider language or culture and make sure that all questions can be understood by all people. Remember, people sometimes have a poor reading age so try to make the questions as simple as possible. Also, some questions may seem patronising to you, but people who have a high reading age will still be able to understand the question. Try to avoid jargon or technical language, particularly abbreviations.

Response formats

Another important area to consider is the response format of your scale. All closed-format questions give a series of choices, and there is even good practice in terms of response choices to use. Of course, the response formats generally vary.

There are a number of different formats that can be used. One of the response formats used with a lot of traditional personality tests is a 'yes–no' format or a 'true–false' format. For example, the Eysenck Personality Questionnaire (Eysenck and Eyseck, 1975) uses this sort of format (see Exhibit 25.8).

Exhibit 25.8

1	Does your mood often go up and down?	Yes	No
2	Do you often feel 'fed-up'?	Yes	No
3	Do you suffer from nerves?	Yes	No

Other scales measure the frequency of behaviour (i.e. how often it occurs). For example, the COPE scale (Carver et al., 1989), that measures individuals' various coping attempts to deal with stress, uses the response format shown in Exhibit 25.9 to measure the frequency to which people engage in various coping behaviours.

Exhibit 25.9

I try to grow as a person as a result of the experience	I usually don't do this at all	I usually do this a little bit	I usually do this a medium amount	I usually do this a lot
I turn to work or other substitute activities to take my mind off things	I usually don't do this at all	I usually do this a little bit	I usually do this a medium amount	I usually do this a lot
I get upset and let my emotions out	I usually don't do this at all	I usually do this a little bit	I usually do this a medium amount	I usually do this a lot

A common feature of many scales is the 'Strongly Agree' to 'Strongly Disagree' format. Traditionally, these were used with attitude scales, used to measure the extent of agreement with different attitudinal statements. However, you will see the 'agree–disagree' response format used in many different scales. For example, the Life Orientation Test-Revised (Scheier et al., 1994), which is used to measure optimism, uses a five-point 'Strongly Agree' to 'Strongly Disagree' scale to measure respondents' degree of agreement with statements in terms of how the statements describe them, as shown in Exhibit 25.10.

Exhibit 25.10

In uncertain times, I usually expect the best	Strongly disagree	Disagree	Not certain	Agree	Strongly agree
Overall, I expect more good things to happen to me than bad	Strongly disagree	Disagree	Not certain	Agree	Strongly agree

Sometimes some scales will ask respondents to indicate directly how much the statement describes them. For example, in the assessment of dispositional embarrassment (Kelly and Jones, 1997) respondents are asked to indicate to what extent the behaviour described in the statement is like them (see Exhibit 25.11).

Exhibit 25.11

	Not at all like me					Very much like me	
1 I feel unsure of myself	1	2	3	4	5	6	7
2 I don't feel uncomfortable in public unless my clothing, hair, etc. are just right	1	2	3	4	5	6	7

Finally, you will also see response formats that try to assess the extent of certain feelings or behaviours, and therefore the responses will assess the extent to which the respondent feels about something. So, for example, the PANAS scale (Watson *et al.*, 1988), which measures positive and negative affect, uses a scale that indicates the extent to which the participant feels about a particular emotion or feeling (see Exhibit 25.12).

Exhibit 25.12

Interested	Very slightly	A little	Moderately	Quite a bit	Extremely
Irritable	Very slightly	A little	Moderately	Quite a bit	Extremely
Distressed	Very slightly	A little	Moderately	Quite a bit	Extremely

There are fewer and fewer hard and fast rules about response formats these days. However, the main point is that your response format must make sense in terms of the questions you are asking. Therefore, discuss with colleagues and test carefully the response format that you intend to use. Also, a general guideline is to use simple rating scales or lists of choice and, where possible, minimise the number of choices. Five choices is thought to be the ideal number.

Instructions

Finally, the instructions that precede the scale are crucial. Usually there will be no need for a great number of instructions, and they can be rather simple. For example, the instructions for Eysenck and Eysenck's EPQ scale are as shown in Exhibit 25.13.

Exhibit 25.13

INSTRUCTIONS: Please answer each question by putting a circle around the 'YES' or 'NO' following the question. There are no right or wrong answers, and no trick questions. Work quickly, and do not think too long about the exact meaning of the questions.

However, you might look for more general traits reflecting more typical behaviours or attitudes. For example,

for Kelly and Jones' measure of dispositional embarrassment, the instructions are as shown in Exhibit 25.14.

Exhibit 25.14

We are interested in people's personality attributes. Listed below are a variety of statements. Please read each statement carefully and indicate to the left of each item the extent to which you feel it applies to you using the following scale.

However, you may want to specify a particular time period. For example, in completing Watson *et al.*'s Positive and Negative Affect Scales, respondents are given the following instructions, as shown in Exhibit 25.15.

Exhibit 25.15

This scale consists of a number of words that describe different feelings and emotions. Read each item and then mark the appropriate answer in the space next to that word. Indicate to what extent you feel this way right now; that is, at the present moment. Use the following scale to record your answers.

Finally, you might want the respondents to think very carefully about their responses. For example, you might want them to think about a specific instance, or a typical set of responses in a particular circumstance. For example, Carver *et al.*'s COPE scale, which measures reactions to stress, is preceded by the instructions shown in Exhibit 25.16.

Exhibit 25.16

We are interested in how people respond when they confront difficult or stressful events in their lives. There are lots of ways to try to deal with stress. This questionnaire asks you to indicate what you generally do and feel when you experience stressful events. Obviously, different events bring out somewhat different responses, but think about what you usually do when you are under a lot of stress.

Please try to respond to each item separately in your mind from each other item. Choose your answers thoughtfully, and make your answers as true FOR YOU as you can. Please answer every item. There are no 'right' or 'wrong' answers, so choose the most accurate answer for YOU–not what you think 'most people' would say or do. Indicate what YOU usually do when YOU experience a stressful event.

The main thing is that the researcher thinks carefully about the instructions, because this can be used not only to make the administration of the question easier but also to direct the respondent to look at the questions in a particular way, if so required.

Collecting the data

Following the advice from the preceding section we now have enough information for our scale. Our proposed scale is now shown in Exhibit 25.17.

Exhibit 25.17

Instructions: The following statements refer to your *own* beliefs and feelings about your own thoughts, feelings and behaviour. Read each statement and respond by circling the number that best represents your agreement with each statement.

[1 = Strongly disagree, 2 = Disagree, 3 = Not certain, 4 = Agree, 5 = Strongly agree]

1	I can be spiteful to my friends if they get a better mark than me.	1	2	3	4	5
2	In the past I have falsely told other students the wrong exam date, so they would miss the exam.	1	2	3	4	5
3	I would hate the student who got the best mark in one of my classes.	1	2	3	4	5
4	If I had the opportunity to change other students' exam grades so that mine was the best, I would do it.	1	2	3	4	5
5	I find myself wishing bad things on people who do better than me academically.	1	2	3	4	5
6	I always tell people I am happy for them when they do better than me in exams.	1	2	3	4	5
7	I have thought about spoiling someone's work because it is better than mine.	1	2	3	4	5
8	I wish bad things on people because they are smarter than me.	1	2	3	4	5
9	When other students on my course are praised for their excellent work, it makes me want to wish something bad on that person.	1	2	3	4	5
10	If my friend got a better mark than me, I would consider tampering with his/her work in some way.	1	2	3	4	5
11	I have mean thoughts towards people who score better than me on exams.	1	2	3	4	5
12	I resent people on my course who excel in their studies.	1	2	3	4	5
13	I feel bitter towards those who do better than me on my course.	1	2	3	4	5
14	I have lied to people on my course to try and hinder their progress so I can get the better mark.	1	2	3	4	5
15	If I came second best in a piece of work, because my friend got the top mark, I would still be happy.	1	2	3	4	5
16	I seek revenge on people who get better grades than me and take away my chances of success.	1	2	3	4	5
17	I do not like to help others with their work as it might result in them getting a better mark.	1	2	3	4	5
18	I would consider doing something nasty to somebody who threatened my chances of academic success.	1	2	3	4	5

19	When I find out I haven't got an excellent mark for a piece of work I get very upset with myself.	1	2	3	4	5
20	I work very hard so I am able to do the best I can at all academic activities.	1	2	3	4	5

The next step is to collect data to test these new items and assess whether you've got a good measure. Therefore, we need to administer the scale to some participants, with a minimum of 150 respondents. Of course, as a student you may not have access to that number of participants, but you should try to get at least two or three respondents for each item.

We administered our scale to 402 students, 161 males and 241 females, aged from 18 to 21 years, meaning that we had a ratio of 20 to 1 in terms of participants to items. Having collected the data we can now use this data to examine the scale.

We have included a copy of this data as part of the online resources with this book. Go to **www.pearsoned.co.uk/maltby** if you want to download the data.

Reliability

In psychometric testing, there are two forms of reliability: internal reliability and reliability over time (test–retest reliability). You may wish to read an extended version of some of the theory that lies behind reliability statistics in the 'Stop and think: Reliability: the role of error' box.

Internal reliability (internal consistency)

Internal reliability (or consistency) refers to whether all the aspects of the psychometric test are generally working together to measure the same thing. Therefore, we would expect to find that all these aspects would be positively correlated with each other. Commonly, these aspects would be a number of questions in a scale. Therefore, all the individual questions on our academic vindictiveness scale should correlate, suggesting they go together to form a single construct of academic vindictivenes.

A common statistical technique that you will see in the research literature, that is used to assess the internal reliability, is Cronbach's alpha (Cronbach, 1951). Cronbach's

Stop and think

Reliability: the role of error

Reliability in psychometric testing is a response to error in measurement. Error refers to a specific issue in research and that is, when you're measuring anything in research, it is almost certain that your measurement will contain error. Say, for example, I ask you the question, are you happy? I give you the option of 'Yes' or 'No'. Now what I'm hoping to do is measure your happiness. However, there are possible sources of error in this measurement. For example, you may say 'Yes', therefore you are happy. But you may not be totally happy, you may just be more happy than you are unhappy, but my measure just determines that you are happy. Therefore there is possible error in my measurement because I've not exactly assessed the correct level of happiness, so my assessment of your happiness is not wrong (you've said you're happy), but it has a degree of error to it. There are other potential sources of error in measurement. Perhaps I asked you two questions: are you happy in 'Work' and 'Life in general' to determine your happiness. If you answered 'Yes' to both then you are happy. But it is perfectly possible that you are not happy in other specific areas of your life, such as a relationship. Therefore, again, there is potential for

error here because our measure of happiness missed out a question on relationships that would have changed our assessment of your overall happiness. Also, if I asked you whether you were happy on a Monday, would you give the same answer on the following Friday?

There are many sources of possible error in measurement. It is important to note that these errors are mostly unknown quantities and are often not measurable. For example, it is impossible to know what real happiness is. Therefore, asking people are they happy and determining on that question alone whether they are happy or not has a huge possible amount of error, because the extent and depth of happiness is probably unknown and would probably make your head hurt just thinking about how to measure it. However, rather than simply giving up, researchers persevere. As a researcher it is almost impossible to eradicate all possible sources of error from research, but what researchers do is try to guard against possible error so they can establish confidence in their work. Reliability statistics are used in psychometric testing to assess the extent to which a psychometric test is free from error and provide confidence and evidence for its usefulness.

alpha, then, is used to assess the level of internal reliability that a set of items has. The figure that is produced to assess this level can range between -1 and $+1$, and its symbol is α. Usually, a Cronbach's alpha of $+0.7$ or above is seen as an acceptable level of internal reliability, although in some circumstances a much higher level is desired (i.e. $α > 0.8$) when a more exact measurement is wanted or required, i.e. in clinical assessments of patients.

You can work out the internal reliability of our items using SPSS for Windows. Load up the data, and in the data screen window, click on Analyse, Scale and select reliability analysis. Transfer the items (AV1 to AV20) into the items box (see Figure 25.1). Please note that for this analysis you

Figure 25.1 Reliability analysis window.

need to make sure you have recoded any reverse items. We have recoded the scores (using the RECODE statement in SPSS) for the reverse worded items, 6 and 15.

Then press OK. You should get the output shown in Table 25.1.

Here the Cronbach's alpha is $α = 0.866$ (or $α = 0.87$, as it is normally rounded up to two decimal places). The current Cronbach's alpha is good, above $α = 0.7$, and therefore is of acceptable internal reliability.

Using internal reliability to select items

However, we can look a little closer at our scale to see if the internal reliability of the scale can be improved. This is particularly useful if the reliability of your items has fallen below the criteria of $α = 0.7$. You should routinely do this anyway, because the procedures shown in Figure 25.2 allow you to identify items that are performing poorly.

Table 25.1 Reliability analysis output

Reliability statistics	
Cronbach's alpha	N of items
0.866	20

Stop and think

Other tests of internal reliability

There are other tests of internal reliability that are used less often in psychometric testing, but which, at some point, may prove useful to you.

In psychometrics, the **Kuder–Richardson Formula 20** (KR-20) is a measure of internal reliability for measures with dichotomous choices (i.e. two choices, Yes/No or Agree/Disagree). Many instruments have response formats that are dichotomous, and technically you should not perform a Cronbach's alpha on this. That said, many researchers do use Cronbach's alpha with measures with dichotomous choices. However, it may be useful for you to have an alternative. Values can range from 0.00 to 1.00, with higher values indicating a better level of internal reliability. The optimum level for internal reliability is within a KR-20 of 0.80–0.85 range. The Kuder–Richardson Formula 20 (KR-20), for example, calculates a reliability coefficient based on the number of test items:

$$r = \frac{k}{(k-1)} \left(1 - \frac{\Sigma pq}{\sigma^2} \right)$$

Where
  k = is the number of test items
  p = the proportion of the responses to an item that are correct or have been answered in one direction (i.e. yes or agree); i.e. the number of correct (or 'yes'/ 'agree') answers out of the total number of responses.
  q = the proportion of responses to an item that are incorrect or have been answered in the other direction (i.e. no or disagree); i.e. the number of incorrect (or 'no'/'disagree') answers out of the total number of responses.
  σ^2 = the variance, or the standard deviation squared.

Another form of internal reliability is *split-half reliability*. Here the research splits the items into two halves. This split might be made based on odd versus even numbered items, randomly selecting items for each half, or the first half versus the second half of the test. The researcher then correlates the total scores for each half. A common rule of thumb is 0.80 or high for adequate reliability, although practice does vary.

Figure 25.2 Reliability analysis: statistics window.

To perform this analysis in SPSS for Windows repeat the above analysis for the reliability but, before pressing the OK button, press the statistics button and tick the three boxes in the Descriptives for section (Item, Scale and Scale if item deleted (see Figure 25.2)). Then press Continue and then OK. You should then get an output that looks like that shown in Table 25.2.

Table 25.2 gives two pieces of information that are important to us, Corrected item-total correlation (column 4)

and the Cronbach's alpha if (the) item (was) deleted (column 5). The Corrected item-total correlation tells us how much each item is related to the overall score, and the Cronbach's alpha if item deleted tells us what the Cronbach's alpha of the scale would be if it was actually deleted. With these statistics we can see if any items are not contributing to the scale.

If we look at the corrected item-total correlation, good items should correlate above 0.3 with the total score, and not be below 0.20 (Kline, 1986). We can see here that items AV19 and AV20 are below these criteria (AV19 = -0.109; AV20 = -0.146). The Cronbach's alpha if item deleted column also suggests that, for both these items, the current alpha of $\alpha = 0.87$ would be improved, to $\alpha = 0.880$ (0.88) for AV19 and $\alpha = 0.882$ (0.88) for AV20. These statistics suggest the scale's Cronbach's alpha would be improved by removing these two items.

What you do in these circumstances is remove one item at a time, with the worst performing item (i.e. lowest correlation and most improved Cronbach's alpha) being the one that is removed first, and then seeing what effect it has on the results. You continue this until there is no more improvement.

In our example, the worst performing item is item AV20. Therefore we recompute the Cronbach's alpha with all the items except AV20. We then get an output that looks like Table 25.3.

We can see that the Cronbach's alpha coefficient has improved to $\alpha = 0.88$ (from 0.87) with the removal of

Table 25.2 Reliability statistics output

Item-total statistics

	Scale mean if item deleted	Scale variance if item deleted	Corrected item-total correlation	Cronbach's alpha if item deleted
AV1	46.8234	133.158	0.509	0.858
AV2	46.9353	133.632	0.611	0.854
AV3	47.3358	136.797	0.540	0.857
AV4	46.4453	132.402	0.535	0.857
AV5	46.9776	132.655	0.608	0.854
AV6	46.8632	134.158	0.532	0.857
AV7	46.7836	135.956	0.426	0.861
AV8	46.9602	133.320	0.546	0.856
AV9	47.1169	136.921	0.453	0.860
AV10	46.9080	136.747	0.435	0.860
AV11	46.8607	133.796	0.604	0.855
AV12	47.4303	136.814	0.595	0.856
AV13	46.8159	135.288	0.520	0.857
AV14	46.6418	133.831	0.516	0.857
AV15	46.7612	133.743	0.512	0.857
AV16	46.6741	132.978	0.644	0.853
AV17	46.8682	136.070	0.552	0.857
AV18	46.7264	132.947	0.508	0.858
AV19	45.4179	151.730	−0.109	0.880
AV20	45.4353	152.885	−0.146	0.882

Table 25.3 Reliability statistics output

Reliability statistics	
Cronbach's alpha	N of items
0.882	19

Item-total statistics

	Scale mean if item deleted	Scale variance if item deleted	Corrected item-total correlation	Cronbach's alpha if item deleted
AV1	43.0597	135.847	0.512	0.876
AV2	43.1716	136.402	0.611	0.873
AV3	43.5721	139.417	0.548	0.875
AV4	42.6816	135.145	0.535	0.875
AV5	43.2139	135.101	0.621	0.872
AV6	43.0995	136.748	0.539	0.875
AV7	43.0199	138.364	0.440	0.878
AV8	43.1965	135.819	0.557	0.874
AV9	43.3532	139.446	0.464	0.877
AV10	43.1443	139.371	0.442	0.878
AV11	43.0970	136.626	0.602	0.873
AV12	43.6667	139.455	0.604	0.874
AV13	43.0522	137.980	0.524	0.875
AV14	42.8781	136.471	0.521	0.875
AV15	42.9975	136.421	0.516	0.876
AV16	42.9104	135.658	0.648	0.872
AV17	43.1045	138.852	0.553	0.875
AV18	42.9627	135.742	0.507	0.876
AV19	41.6542	155.309	−0.130	0.897

AV20. However, if we look at the bottom of the table we can see that item AV19 shares a low negative correlation (−0.130) with the overall score, and that removal of the item will improve the Cronbach's alpha to $\alpha = 0.897$ (0.90 to two decimal places). Therefore, repeating the procedure and removing AV19 produces Table 25.4.

You can see now that all the corrected item-total correlations are satisfactory (all above 0.4) and our alpha coefficient of 0.90 can't really be improved upon if we look at the figures in the Cronbach's alpha if item deleted column. Consequently, we would use the first 18 items for our academic vindictiveness scale.

This type of analysis is useful for developing a scale, particularly when you first run the alpha coefficient and it falls below a satisfactory criterion. It may be that, by removing some items in this manner, one item at a time, you can improve the internal reliability of the scale.

Test–retest reliability (reliability over time)

Test–retest reliability assesses reliability over time. Researchers interested in constructs that are concerned with individuals being relatively *consistent* in their attitudes and behaviours over time are interested in test–retest reliability. In the personality, intelligence and individual differences literature, which is a literature interested in traits, you will see reference to the stability of tests over time.

Say, for example, that 402 respondents completed the newly developed academic vindictiveness questionnaire. We might be interested in finding out whether the test measured similar levels of academic vindictiveness in the respondents at another time. Researchers typically test people either a week, 2 weeks or a month apart from the first administration, although some researchers will also produce 6-month, 1-year and 2-year intervals between administrations. The ability of the academic vindictiveness test to find similar levels of academic vindictiveness across the 100 respondents would provide evidence of its stability, and therefore its test–retest reliability. A correlation statistic (i.e. the researcher would hope that there is a significant positive correlation between the two test administrations) is the most often used indicator of test–retest reliability and normally a value of the correlation of $r = > 0.7$ or above is considered as satisfactory.

For academic vindictiveness we would assume that this is a consistent trait and we could test our new academic

Table 25.4 Reliability statistics output

Reliability statistics	
Cronbach's alpha	**N of items**
0.897	18

Item-total statistics

	Scale mean if item deleted	Scale variance if item deleted	Corrected item-total correlation	Cronbach's alpha if item deleted
AV1	39.2786	138.012	0.516	0.892
AV2	39.3905	138.683	0.612	0.889
AV3	39.7910	141.617	0.554	0.891
AV4	38.9005	137.691	0.526	0.892
AV5	39.4328	137.104	0.632	0.889
AV6	39.3184	138.866	0.546	0.891
AV7	39.2388	140.696	0.440	0.895
AV8	39.4154	137.994	0.561	0.891
AV9	39.5721	141.517	0.474	0.893
AV10	39.3632	141.504	0.449	0.894
AV11	39.3159	138.895	0.603	0.890
AV12	39.8856	141.478	0.618	0.890
AV13	39.2711	139.974	0.536	0.892
AV14	39.0970	138.766	0.521	0.892
AV15	39.2164	138.709	0.517	0.892
AV16	39.1294	137.983	0.646	0.888
AV17	39.3234	141.162	0.553	0.891
AV18	39.1816	138.049	0.507	0.893

Stop and think

Mean scores and items

Another way of checking your items to see if the items are appropriate for your test is to look at the mean scores. This will give us some idea of the average scores. Why is this useful? Well, say, for example, that one of the mean scores for one of the items was particularly high. For example, for an item scored from 1 (Disagree strongly) to 5 (Agree strongly), a high mean (e.g. mean = 4.8) would mean that almost all people were just simply Agreeing strongly with an item. This would mean that the item produced little variance in responses, and would almost be redundant for your scale because it would not differentiate between respondents, i.e. almost all people answering that item would answer it in the same way.

We have, in the table below, listed the means and standard deviations of all our 18 items selected so far, as well as the minimum and maximum scores obtained from our sample for each item. As you can see we haven't got any extreme means (i.e. very high or low means), with most of the means being above 2. However, two items are worth further consideration; 'I would hate the student who got the best mark in own of my classes' (item 3) and 'I resent people on my course who excel in their studies' (item 12). Clearly the mean scores of these items are a little lower than the rest of the items and it is also worth noting that the maximum score obtained for item 12 is 4 (rather than 5), meaning that no one Strongly agreed with this item. The lower mean scores of these items might be because of the phrasing of the items. For item 3, 'hate' is a rather strong word to use and some people might not want to agree with an item that includes such a strong term. Similarly, for item 12, people might be concerned with using the phrase 'resenting people who excel in studies' and that might be problematic if you yourself excel in your studies because that may mean that you resent yourself. These reasons are speculative. There is no evidence that these items are problematic, and they may represent an accurate response to these statements. However, it would always be worth checking in future analyses how these two items perform, because you may pick up other clues that these items are not performing as well as other items and come to the conclusion that they could be dropped. Or, indeed, it might be worth considering rewording the item for future administrations. For example, with item 12 the clarity of the item might be improved by changing it to 'I resent *other* people on my course who excel in their studies'.

Item	Minimum	Maximum	Mean	Std deviation
1 I can be spiteful to my friends if they get a better mark than me.	1.00	5.00	2.3756	1.28901
2 In the past I have falsely told other students the wrong exam date, so they would miss the exam.	1.00	5.00	2.2637	1.07343
3 I would hate the student who got the best mark in one of my classes.	1.00	5.00	1.8632	0.96765
4 If I had the opportunity to change other students' exam grades so that mine were the best, I would do it.	1.00	5.00	2.7537	1.29127
5 I find myself wishing bad things on people who do better than me academically.	1.00	5.00	2.2214	1.14236
6 I always tell people I am happy for them when they do better than me in exams.	1.00	5.00	2.3358	1.17078
7 I have thought about spoiling someone's work because it is better than mine.	1.00	5.00	2.4154	1.25106
8 I wish bad things on people because they are smarter than me.	1.00	5.00	2.2388	1.20377
9 When other students on my course are praised for their excellent work, it makes me want to wish something bad on that person.	1.00	5.00	2.0821	1.11249
10 If my friend got a better mark than me, I would consider tampering with his/her work in some way.	1.00	5.00	2.2910	1.16575
11 I have mean thoughts towards people who score better than me in exams.	1.00	5.00	2.3383	1.07336
12 I resent people on my course who excel in their studies.	1.00	4.00	1.7687	0.88699
13 I feel bitter towards those who do better than me on my course.	1.00	5.00	2.3831	1.11105
14 I have lied to people on my course to try and hinder their progress so I can get the better mark.	1.00	5.00	2.5572	1.22442
15 If I came second best in a piece of work, because my friend got the top mark, I would still be happy.	1.00	5.00	2.4378	1.23836
16 I seek revenge on people who get better grades than me and take away my chances of success.	1.00	5.00	2.5249	1.06667
17 I do not like to help others with their work as it might result in them getting a better mark.	1.00	5.00	2.3308	1.00000
18 I would consider doing something nasty to somebody who threatened my chances of academic success.	1.00	5.00	2.4726	1.30623

vindictiveness scale for the scale's test–retest reliability. We asked all our respondents to fill in the scale again 4 weeks later. This data is provided in the data set and, by performing a Pearson Product moment correlation in SPSS (Analyse, Correlate, Bivariate and input our two variables ACADEMVIND [Time 1] and ACADEMVIND2 [Time 2] into the variables windows and press OK), we would get the output shown in Table 25.5. Here we can see that our academic vindictiveness scale shows acceptable test–retest reliability with a correlation of $r = 0.76$, larger than the criterion of $r = 0.7$.

Validity

Validity is concerned with whether a test is measuring what we claim it is measuring. Therefore, if we're proposing that the 18 items developed above measure academic vindictiveness, how can we show that this is indeed a measure of academic vindictiveness? There is no absolute way of showing that it is a measure of academic vindictiveness; rather, what we would have to do is try to collect evidence through a number of criteria to support the validity of our

Table 25.5 Correlation output

Correlations

		ACADEMVIND	ACADEMVIND2
ACADEMVIND	Pearson correlation	1	0.764(*)
	Sig. (2-tailed)		0.000
	N	402	
ACADEMVIND2	Pearson correlation	0.764(*)	1
	Sig. (2-tailed)	0.000	
	N	402	402

* Correlation is significant at the 0.01 level (2-tailed).

test as a measure of academic vindictiveness. Traditionally, a number of validity criteria can be applied to psychometric tests. These different types of validity include:

- **Convergent validity** – a psychometric test's convergent validity is assessed by the extent to which it shows associations with measures to which it should be related. So, for example, our new academic vindictiveness should be related to other aspects of vindictiveness; for example, a tendency to seek revenge, show spitefulness and vengefulness, particularly in academic settings.
- **Concurrent validity** – a psychometric test is thought to show concurrent validity when it shows acceptable correlations with known and accepted standard measures of that construct. Therefore, it is slightly different to convergent validity because it isn't against other related criteria, but

criteria that are reportedly measuring the same thing. So, we would expect our new academic vindictiveness to be related to other available measures of academic vindictiveness that already exist. However, sometimes this is difficult to assess if there are no other measures of the construct.

- **Discriminant validity** – something shows discriminant validity when it is *not* related to things that it shouldn't be related to. Sometimes this is difficult to assess because the finding needs to be useful. For example, there is little point suggesting that academic vindictiveness should not be related to cake-eating, because that tells us very little about the construct. Therefore, sometimes when examining the discriminate validity of a construct, researchers suggest that the new construct should *not* share high correlations with other constructs. For example, a measure of academic

Stop and think

What is a correlation?

As a test, the correlation coefficient can take values ranging from +1.00 through 0.00 to –1.00.

- A correlation of +1.00 would be a 'perfect' positive relationship.
- A correlation of 0.00 would indicate no relationship (no single straight line can sum up the almost random distribution of points).
- A correlation of –1.00 would be a 'perfect' negative relationship.

Commonly, then, correlation statistics range from +1 to –1, and the symbol of a correlation is r. Therefore, researchers will report the direction of correlation coefficients between variables. For example, the relationship between neuroticism (anxious and worrying personality traits) and depression would be expected to fall within the 0.00 to +1.00 range, while the relationship between extraversion (outgoing, optimistic personality traits) and depression would be expected to fall within the 0.00 to –1.00 range.

However, it is important to remember that the reporting of correlation statistics doesn't stop there. There are two ways of interpreting the strength of the correlation. The first is the significance level. You remember that a lot of statistics involves interpreting whether a statistical test result is significant at either the 0.05 or 0.01 level. Therefore, commonly, researchers report whether the correlation is significant, be it a positive or negative relationship.

However, it is also necessary to highlight the size of the correlation (the r statistic). Researchers often do this to consider the weight of their findings, and this is also known as effect size (Cohen, 1988). A correlation statistic of $r = 0.1$ and below is viewed as small, $r = 0.3$ as medium (or moderate) and $r = 0.5$ as large. These are used as indicators of the relative importance of findings. Therefore, if a researcher has predicted that there will be a relationship between two variables, a positive correlation of 0.5 would be a more important finding than a correlation of 0.2.

Stop and think

The difference between using a psychometric test as a diagnostic test and as a variable

Psychometric tests are used as a powerful assessment of clinical states. Here, we're going to give an outline of how these are and should be used. One example of a clinical assessment instrument is the Edinburgh Postnatal Depression Scale (EPDS)[2]. The 10-item scale was developed by Cox *et al.* (1987) as a way of assisting primary care health professionals to detect postnatal depression, thought to affect at least 10 per cent of women, among mothers who have recently had a baby. Before using the scale, researchers need to be aware of the following three things:

1   Care should be taken to avoid the possibility of the mother discussing her answers with others.
2   The mother should complete the scale herself, unless she has limited English or has difficulty with reading.
3   The EPDS may be used at 6–8 weeks to screen postnatal women. The child health clinic, postnatal check-up or a home visit may provide suitable opportunities for its completion.

The scale has 10 questions. Before going on to the questions, respondents are given the following instructions:

1   The mother is asked to underline the response which comes closest to how she has been feeling in the previous 7 days.
2   All 10 items must be completed.

Respondents will then be asked to complete the following scale.

As you have recently had a baby, we would like to know how you are feeling. Please UNDERLINE the answer which comes closest to how you have felt IN THE PAST 7 DAYS, not just how you feel today.

1   I have been able to laugh and see the funny side of things.

As much as I always could
Not quite so much now
Definitely not so much now
Not at all

2   I have looked forward with enjoyment to things.

As much as I ever did
Rather less than I used to
Definitely less than I used to
Hardly at all

3   *I have blamed myself unnecessarily when things went wrong.

Yes, most of the time
Yes, some of the time
Not very often
No, never

4   I have been anxious or worried for no good reason.

No, not at all
Hardly ever
Yes, sometimes
Yes, very often

5   *I have felt scared or panicky for no very good reason.

Yes, quite a lot
Yes, sometimes
No, not much
No, not at all

6   *Things have been getting on top of me.

Yes, most of the time I haven't been able to cope at all
Yes, sometimes I haven't been coping as well as usual
No, most of the time I have coped quite well
No, I have been coping as well as ever

7   *I have been so unhappy that I have had difficulty sleeping.

Yes, most of the time
Yes, sometimes
Not very often
No, not at all

8   *I have felt sad or miserable.

Yes, most of the time
Yes, quite often
Not very often
No, not at all

9   *I have been so unhappy that I have been crying.

Yes, most of the time
Yes, quite often
Only occasionally
No, never

10   *The thought of harming myself has occurred to me.

Yes, quite often
Sometimes
Hardly ever
Never

[2]*Source*: © 1987 The Royal College of Psychiatrists. The Edinburgh Postnatal Depression Scale may be photocopied by individual researchers or clinicians for their own use without seeking permission from the publishers. The scale must be copied in full and all copies must acknowledge the following source: Cox, J. L., Holden, J. M., and Sagovsky, R. (1987) Detection of postnatal depression. Development of the 10-item Edinburgh Postnatal Depression Scale. *British Journal of Psychiatry*, 150, 782–786. Written permission must be obtained from the Royal College of Psychiatrists for copying and distribution to others or for republication (in print, online or by any other medium). Translations of the scale, and guidance as to its use, may be found in Cox, J. L. and Holden, J. (2003) *Perinatal Mental Health: A Guide to the Edinburgh Postnatal Depression Scale*. London: Gaskell.

Answers are scored 0, 1, 2 and 3 according to increased severity of the symptoms. So for Item 1 'I have been able to laugh and see the funny side of things', 'As much as I always could' would be scored 0 and 'Not at all' would be scored 3. A higher score of '3' would mean that the respondent had not been able to laugh and see the funny side of things, indicating that they may be depressed. Items marked with an asterisk are reverse scored (though they would not be marked on the scale that is administered to participants). So, for example, for item 10, 'The thought of harming myself has occurred to me', 'Yes quite often' would be scored as 3 and 'Never' as 0. A total score for the scale is then computed by adding together the scores.

In research terms, researchers would use an overall score on the scale for use in correlational analysis. However, these scales can also be used to make an assessment. In terms of possible score, they could range from a minimum of 0 (not depressed at all) to 30 (very depressed) across the 10 items. It is unlikely that many people will score 30 on the scale. Indeed, Cox et al. (1987) suggest that anyone scoring 10 or greater may be suffering from possible depression. They also suggest that any assessment should look at item 10 closely for any possible suicidal thoughts.

This is the main thing about these sorts of questionnaires; they are a tool to make an initial assessment. Cox et al. emphasise that the scale should not be used over clinical judgement and is only a tool, and, where mothers score above 10, then a deeper clinical assessment should be performed to confirm the diagnosis. This is true of many of these types of tests; they are best used as potential indicators, but should never be used as a single indicator of anything.

There is one important distinction to make when using the test. Often, when using a psychometric test to measure any attitude or behaviour there is a temptation to try to categorise people as falling into a group having the attitude behaviour or falling into a group who do not demonstrate that behaviour. However, rarely in research do researchers make this distinction. They will most often just use scores on the test as a variable, and try not to categorise people (unless they have a very good reason to do so). This is because, as we have highlighted above, it is extremely difficult to make a diagnosis (i.e. group someone) just using a test alone. Indeed, for many tests it would be impossible to categorise someone for a behaviour. What are the criteria thresholds for deciding whether someone is intelligent or not, neurotic or not or optimistic or not? Consequently, in individual difference and intelligence research we tend to look at scores on scales, rather than splitting our samples into diagnostic groups, realising that clinical expertise is needed before making such distinctions.

vindictiveness should not share a high correlation with any of the main five personality dimensions (neuroticism, agreeableness, extraversion, openness and conscientiousness). However, we might expect the academic vindictiveness scale to share a small negative correlation with agreeableness, suggesting that the scale is largely independent of the five-factor model of personality.

- **Face validity** – this aspect of validity is concerned with what the measure *appears* to measure. Therefore, when a test has face validity, it means that it does look like a test that measures the concept it is designed to measure. As in the case of our new academic vindictiveness scale, the best way to consider this question would be to group together some experts in academic vindictiveness to judge whether they think the questionnaire represents a good measure of that construct.

- **Content validity** – refers to the extent to which a measure represents all facets of the phenomenon being measured. So, for example, in the case of academic vindictiveness we might have some ideas about different types of academic vindictiveness. For example, there might be academic vindictive behaviours, academic vindictive attitudes and academic vindictive feelings. Therefore, does our measure of academic vindictiveness cover all these domains, i.e. does the content of the test try to represent all aspects of academic vindictiveness (i.e. behaviours, attitudes and feelings)? If it doesn't, then it cannot be said to have content validity.

- **Predictive validity** – this type of validity assesses whether a measure can accurately predict something. For example, in the case of academic vindictiveness, it should be able to predict people acting in an academically vindictive way in the future. Therefore, our researcher might administer our new academic vindictiveness scale to a group of students at the beginning of the academic year and then measure the extent to which individuals reported a number of academically vindictive behaviours during the examination period at the end of the semester (for example, not sharing notes, not helping other people revise). If our new academic vindictiveness scale demonstrated predictive validity, it would be able to predict those students who didn't share notes or help other people revise during the examination period.

- **Third person rating of the individual** – getting other people to rate the individual on the items of the questionnaire is a very good way of potentially assessing the validity of the questionnaire because, ideally, the ratings given by the participants and the other person should be similar. Indeed, sometimes it is referred to as the gold standard of validity testing. Here, you might ask a person close to the individual filling in the questionnaire (e.g. a friend or member of the family) to rate that individual on each of the items of the questionnaire. Therefore, if the person's ratings of the individual for each question are similar to the person's actual answers, then this provides an independent assessment of the questionnaire and validity for the questionnaire. So, for example, for our academically vindictive questionnaire, we would expect scores for individuals to be correlated with their friends, and family's ratings of them.

However, psychometricians have developed some of these ideas into wider terms, and commonly in the modern psychometric literature you will see reference to two further ideas: *criterion-related validity* and *construct validity*. Both these forms of validity combine the different types of validity we have just mentioned to form new concepts of validity.

The first, criterion-related validity, assesses the value of the test by the respondents' responses on other measures, i.e. criteria. Two types of measure fall under criterion-related validity, **concurrent validity** (assesses whether the measure shows acceptable correlations with known and accepted standard measures of that construct) and **predictive validity** (assesses whether a measure can accurately predict something in the future).

The second is construct validity. Construct validity is a more general term and refers to validity that seeks to establish a clear relationship between the construct at a theoretical level and the measure that has been developed. Construct validity can be informed by the different types of validity previously mentioned, but in 1959 two authors, Donald Campbell and Donald Fiske (Campbell and Fiske, 1959), introduced two other types of validity – convergent validity (the measure shows associations with measures to which it should be related) and discriminant validity (the measure is *not* related to things that it should not be related to) – as the subcategories of construct validity and they developed a theory named the multitrait-multimethod which seeks to assess the construct validity of a measure by balancing the assessments between convergent validity and discriminant validity. You can read more about this method in the Stop and think box: Multitrait-multimethod matrix.

So let us test the validity of the academic vindictiveness scale using the following validity criteria. We will present a number of validity checks to see to what extent our new scale shows validity as a good measure of academic vindictiveness. What is important to note is that there is currently no other measure of academic vindictiveness so we cannot

carry out a concurrent validity check. We therefore need to look at the other forms of validity.

The first is convergent validity, which assesses the extent to which our scale shows associations with measures to which it should be related. In this case, we could look at some other measure of traits that a person who is academically vindictive should also score high on. For example, the International Personality Item Pool (see Stop and think: International Personality Item Pool) provides public domain (free to use) access to a number of personality and individual difference measures. For example, the site provides trait measures of *Morality* (e.g. 'I would never scheme against others'), *Integrity/Honesty* (e.g. 'I can be trusted to keep my promises') and *Machiavellianism* (a trait that suggests that deceit is justified in pursuing and maintaining power, e.g. 'I find it easy to manipulate others'). Therefore, we would expect a significant positive correlation between academic vindictiveness and Machiavellianism and a significant negative correlation between academic vindictiveness and morality and integrity/honesty.

In terms of discriminant validity, a good strategy would be to compare the academic vindictiveness scale to the five-factor personality measures of neuroticism, extraversion, agreeableness, conscientiousness and openness. Now, while we might expect academic vindictiveness to share a negative correlation with agreeableness (a tendency to be pleasant and accommodating), we can show discriminate validity for our measure by finding no significant relationship between our measure of academic vindictiveness and neuroticism, extraversion, conscientiousness and openness.

Our final attempt at validity is to examine third person ratings of the individual on the scale. Here, we asked a friend of the participant to rate the participant on the measure of academic vindictiveness. However, for this measure we asked the respondent to provide a friend who was also a classmate, so as to ensure that the friend had some knowledge of how the respondent was in an academic setting.

We now have a number of measures to establish the validity of our scale. All these measures are included in the data set we used earlier, and if you wish you can run

Stop and think

International Personality Item Pool

The International Personality Item Pool (IPIP) website (**http://ipip.ori.org/ipip/**) provides public domain access to a number of personality and individual difference measures. The main reason for the development of the site is that a lot of measures of personality (the MMPI,

16PF and NEO-PI) are copyrighted by the test authors and consequently cannot be used freely by other researchers, like you. The site provides freely available versions of all the main personality measures as well as over 200 measures of personality individual difference traits.

Table 25.6 Pearson product moment correlation coefficients between academic vindictiveness and morality, integrity/honesty and Machiavellianism

	Academic vindictiveness
Morality (IPIP)	−0.453**
Integrity/honesty (IPIP)	−0.410**
Machiavellianism (IPIP)	0.344**

** $P < 0.01$.

your own correlational analysis (remember we showed you how to run a correlation in the test–retest example, and remember our academic vindictiveness scale variable name in the data set is ACADEMVIND). Table 25.6 shows the correlations between our academic vindictiveness scale and of morality, integrity/honesty and Machiavellianism, the five-factor model of personality and the friend's rating of the respondent on the scale.

Our first set of results tries to establish convergent validity for our academic vindictiveness scale. In terms of our predictions, academic vindictiveness shares a significant negative correlation with morality and integrity/honesty and a significant positive correlation with Machiavellianism (see Table 25.6). What is also worth noting here is the size of the correlations. You remember that the effect size of a correlation statistic of $r = 0.1$ is viewed as small, $r = 0.3$ as medium (or moderate) and $r = 0.5$ as large. Here, the correlations are at least of a medium size.

We also sought to examine both the convergent but mainly the discriminate validity of our academic vindictiveness scale by looking at the relationship between the scale and the five-factor model of personality (see Table 25.7).

Stop and think

Multitrait-multimethod matrix

The multitrait-multimethod matrix establishes the construct validity of two or more constructs by two or more methods of assessment. What the multitrait-multimethod matrix does is establish the convergent and discriminant validity for a measure by comparing the level of correlations between the different constructs by the different methods. Usually this information is presented alongside reliability statistics to provide a rich assessment of the reliability and overall construct validity for a measure. Therefore we could demonstrate the multitrait-multimethod matrix with three different methods of measuring three different constructs in relation to our academic vindictiveness scale. For our current example, let us suggest that, in addition to academic vindictiveness, we could measure two potentially positively related constructs to academic vindictiveness: Machiavellianism and vengefulness. We would then seek to measure each of these constructs by three methods:

- Self-report psychometric test (Method 1)
- Peer-ratings of each of these constructs by a friend (Method 2)
- Behaviour measures in relation to an experimental task (Method 3).

We have outlined a traditional way in which the results of these measures would have then been examined using the multitrait-multimethod matrix. This matrix is presented in Figure 25.3 and provides us with information on convergent validity and discriminant validity.

The first thing to note in this analysis is the figures highlighted in parentheses. These would normally be the reliability statistics for each of the tests. This could be any indicator of reliability (Cronbach's or test–retest).

However, we are less concerned with these statistics at this stage; we would hope to see high reliability statistics in this presentation. The rest of the statistics presented in the matrix are correlational statistics. The next thing to note is those figures surrounded by a black line. These are the correlations between the different constructs as measured by the same method. When we are looking at similar constructs we would expect relatively a positive correlation between these constructs, particularly for our academic vindictiveness measures (as we hypothesised these constructs should show convergent validity). However, it is the other sets of figures we are most concerned with in terms of the multitrait-multimethod matrix and considering convergent validity and discriminant validity. Those correlations with a grey background and bold and underlined figures are the same construct as measured by three different measures. These correlations should be positive and strong (i.e. relatively large) and provide us with our evidence of convergent validity (i.e. the self-report measure of academic vindictiveness should share the strongest correlations with our peer-rating and experimental measures of academic vindictiveness). The constructs surrounded by the dotted line are different constructs as measured by different measures, and it is these correlations that should be the lowest of all within the matrix as they supply us with evidence of discriminant validity (i.e. an experimental measure of vengefulness should share one of the lowest correlations with the self-report measure of academic vindictiveness). Together these findings of convergent validity and discriminant validity provide one of the most eloquent and comprehensive ways of providing construct validity (convergent and discriminant validity) for a psychological test.

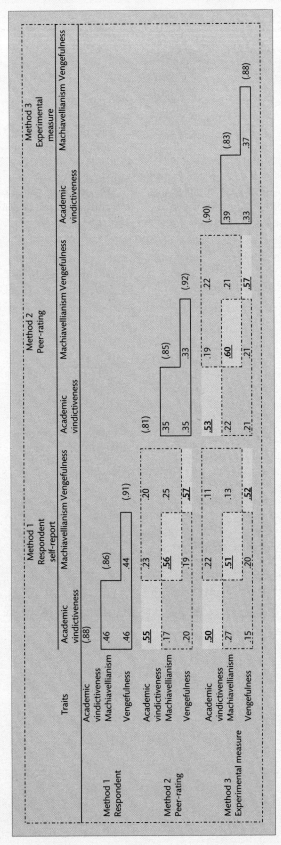

Figure 25.3 A multitrait-multimethod matrix of a self-report measure of academic vindictiveness, peer-rating of Machiavellianism and an experimental measure of vengefulness.

Table 25.7 Pearson product moment correlation coefficients between academic vindictiveness and the five-factor personality dimensions

Neuroticism	0.076
Extraversion	0.013
Openness	−0.074
Agreeableness	−0.320**
Conscientiousness	−0.097

** $P < 0.01$.

Table 25.8 Pearson product moment correlation coefficients between academic vindictiveness and peer rating

Peer rating	0.501**

** $P < 0.01$.

Again, the findings are consistent with our predictions. Academic vindictiveness shares a significant negative correlation with agreeableness (with a medium effect size), but our discriminate validity is demonstrated by its lack of any significant correlation with neuroticism, extraversion, openness and conscientiousness.

Finally, we had asked a friend to rate the person on the measure of academic vindictiveness (see Table 25.8). As we can see, there was a positive significant correlation between the respondent's answers and the friend's rating, with a large effect size.

Together we can see that there is some validity for our measure, particularly by the scales' expected relationships to measures of morality, integrity/honesty, agreeableness and Machiavellianism, as well as a clear association with a classmate and friend's rating.

This is the main point of establishing the validity of a test. You can never ascertain that it is perfectly valid, but you can carry out different studies and tests to develop more and more evidence to support the validity of your test. If you can replicate findings and find further ways of testing the validity of a scale you can build up the evidence base for assessing the validity of your test.

Profile

Paul Kline

Professor Paul Kline was born in 1937. He became an academic psychologist after training as an educational psychologist, which followed a period in which he taught classics before moving on to completing his PhD at Manchester University. In 1969, he undertook a position in the Exeter University psychology department, and he later became the first professor of psychometrics in the United Kingdom.

It has been noted by his colleagues that Kline, whose untimely death was in 1999, had two enthusiasms in psychology – psychometrics and Freudian theory. He wrote essential books on psychometrics. His 1986 *Handbook of Test Construction* provided an essential and clear introduction to a complex field. His 1999 book was fundamental in that it covered psychometric theory, the different kinds of psychological tests and applied psychological testing as well as evaluating the best published psychological tests. His 2000 book, *The New Psychometrics: Science, Psychology and Measurement*, sought to use his knowledge of psychological measurement to argue that truly scientific forms of measurement could be developed to create a new psychometrics that would transform psychology from a social science to a pure science. However, perhaps, in his most famous book, *Fact and Fantasy in Freudian Theory*, he was able to combine statistics and Freudian theory and brought forward many principles of reliability and validity to examine psychological studies of Freudian theory.

Stop and think

Self-assessment exercise

In our validity assessment of the academic vindictiveness scale we didn't examine the face validity and the predictive validity of our test. Can you think of an empirical study that would test the academic vindictiveness scale for both these sets of validity?

Advanced techniques in psychometric evaluation: factor analysis

We are going to introduce you to an advanced analysis technique that can be used to look at the psychometric properties of items. Factor analysis, in a psychometric test context, refers, in the first instance, to the area that we covered within the internal reliability of a test earlier in this discussion. We are very interested here in seeing whether a number of items correlate together to form a single scale. However, what happens if the scale that you have developed is designed to have more than one element to it? For example, personality measures have a number of factors; the five-factor personality scale has five factors. What happens if a number of elements exist to our academic vindictiveness measure, not just one? Well, one technique that is used to explore these issues is factor analysis. We will explain here two types of factor analysis: exploratory factor analysis and confirmatory factor analysis. Exploratory factor analysis is used to explore what elements (or, as they are known, factors) underlie sets of items. Confirmatory factor analysis is used to try to confirm what you may have found with exploratory factor analysis.

Sometimes things that are separate overlap.

Source: Rex Features/Brian Rasic

Factor analysis

Factor analysis is a multivariate (multiple variables) 'data reduction' statistical technique that allows us to simplify the correlational relationships between a number of variables.

Why would you wish to do so? Imagine if you wanted to look at the relationships between variables 1 to 20. This would imply having to interpret 190 relationships between variables. (For example, variable 1 can be correlated with variables 2 through 20. And, variable 2 can be separately associated with variables 3 through 20, variable 3 with variables 4 through 20 and so on.) Identifying real patterns is complicated further because the relationship between, for example, variables 1 and 12 may be affected by the separate relationships each of these variables has with variable 13, with variable 14 and so on. This complicated explanation of 190 relationships is a nightmare for researchers. The researcher will find it difficult to explain which variable is actually related to which other variables, as they may be uncertain whether the apparent relationship between two variables is genuine, or simply a facet of both variables' relationships with another, third, variable. Indeed, even writing an explanation of multiple correlations is difficult. What factor analysis does is to provide a reliable means of simplifying the relationships and identifying within them what *factors*, or common patterns of association between groups of variables, underlie the relationships.

Factor-analytic techniques are a solution to this type of problem, allowing us to look for simple patterns that underlie the correlations between many variables. Yet you may be surprised that you already use factor analysis regularly in your life. Imagine all musicians and music groups in the world. Now, think about the different definitions you can apply to sets of these groups. Some of these artists are very similar; some are very different. However, with the vast majority, you can categorise them as either pop music artists, rap artists or jazz, dance, R&B and so on. What you're doing through this categorising is simplifying a wealth of information regarding music to aid your understanding. So, when someone asks you what sort of music you like, rather than listing lots of groups – Destiny's Child, Justin Timberlake, Jennifer Lopez, Kanye West, Mary J. Blige, Kelis – you might simply say, 'R&B'. Well, factor analysis is very similar to this.

Let us take you through an example of factor analysis. Imagine the following 10 musical artists: Royksopp, BassHunter, Prodigy, 50 Cent, Snoop Dogg, Franz Ferdinand, Coldplay, Keane, Miles Davis and Charlie Parker. If we were to perform a factor analysis on these music artists, and the extent to which people like them, we might see something like Table 25.9.

What the factor analysis does is determine, first, the number of factors that exist. As you can see, our imaginary factor analysis has four factors. Then, what factor analysis

Table 25.9 Imaginary factor analysis of musical artists

	Factor 1	Factor 2	Factor 3	Factor 4
Royksopp	**0.73**	−0.21	0.09	0.21
BassHunter	**0.67**	−0.11	0.12	0.07
Prodigy	**0.55**	−0.05	0.03	0.02
50 Cent	0.10	**0.81**	0.18	0.03
Snoop Dogg	0.02	**0.85**	0.21	0.05
Franz Ferdinand	0.03	0.23	**0.74**	−0.01
Coldplay	0.14	0.06	**0.65**	0.02
Keane	0.12	0.10	**0.55**	−0.04
Miles Davis	0.25	0.05	0.01	**0.56**
Charlie Parker	0.20	0.02	−0.03	**0.78**

does is determine where on which factor each variable (i.e. each artist) falls by a number. This number, called a loading, can be positive or negative and can range from −1.00 through to +1.00. Regardless of whether the number is positive or negative, the higher the number is on the factor, the more important the variable is to the factor. Kline (1986) has suggested that you should ignore any number less than 0.3, and other authors have suggested that those numbers above 0.4 are important.

Using the imaginary factor analysis of music artists, we have shown the loadings above 0.4 in bold. From this analysis we would argue that the music artists broke down into four factors, the first factor being dance (Royksopp, BassHunter, Prodigy), the second being rap (50 Cent, Snoop Dogg), the third being indie (Franz Ferdinand, Coldplay, Keane) and the fourth being jazz (Miles Davis and Charlie Parker).

You will find reference to factor analysis throughout this text. However, there are two main ways you will see a reference to factor analysis: factor analysis that deals with: (1) simplifying relationships between single questions or items; and (2) simplifying relationships between variables. For (2), simplifying relationships between variables, turn to the previous discussion (Chapter 12) on intelligence and the theory of 'g' to see how factor analysis has been applied. However, here we are going to use exploratory factor analysis for (1) simplifying relationships between single questions or items. You will commonly see factor analysis used on items on a scale. All scales will have several items or questions, and factor analysis can be used to understand the relationships between these items. Therefore, you will see a factor analysis when researchers have devised a new psychological measure, or want to examine existing psychological measures and want to see how the

items on that scale break down into different factors, or, indeed, whether they form one factor. We are going to use a research example to show you how to carry out an exploratory factor analysis on a set of items to develop a psychometric scale.

Exploratory factor analysis

To illustrate exploratory factor analysis we are going to use the example of our academic vindictiveness scale and examine the factor structure of the scale. There are two main steps to exploratory factor analysis that we will outline here.

1 To determine how many factors underlie our data. This procedure is called extraction of factors.
2 To determine which items/variables load on each of the factors. This procedure is called rotation of factors.

Extraction

Extraction techniques allow you to determine the number of factors underlying the relationship between a number of variables. There are many extraction procedures, but the most common techniques, and the one we are going to use, is actually called principal components analysis ('factors', when using principal components analysis, are actually called components, but, for simplicity, we will continue to call them factors).[3]

Now, in terms of determining the number of factors, there are three methods. The first two methods we can obtain from SPSS for Windows. Load up the data set you used previously. Pull down the **Statistics** menu by clicking **Analyze** and then click on **Data Reduction** and then **Factor**. You should then get a screen that looks like Figure 25.4.

Figure 25.4 Factor analysis window.

---

[3]The difference between principal components analysis and factor analysis (although the procedures are the same) is that principal components analysis is used to simplify correlations between variables, while factor analysis is concerned with underlying factors to the correlations between variables. Here we have used principal components because it is commonly reported. It may be that your tutor suggests you use a different method. That will be fine because there will be a good reason why he or she has suggested it. All it will mean is a matter of choosing different options on SPSS; the output formats are the same (although the figures will differ), so you will still be able to follow our narrative. If you're really stuck, carry out the analysis as suggested here and then, at a later date, run it again, choosing the different options that have been suggested.

Figure 25.5 Factor analysis: extraction window.

Transfer your variables into the **Variables** box (remember to enter only variables AV1 to AV18) and then click on **Extraction**. You should then get a screen that looks like Figure 25.5.

Click on the box next to **Scree plot** and then press **Continue** and then **OK**. You should get an output as shown in Table 25.10 and Figure 25.6.

The first technique for deciding on the number of factors can be gained from Table 25.10. Here we are interested in the second column 'Total' under the initial eigenvalues. We can see a list here: 6.713, 1.538, 0.861, 0.814, etc. Here, the number of factors extracted are the number of values above 1, and in our case two eigenvalues, 6.713 and 1.538, are above 1. This is a traditional way of

deciding factors. SPSS calculates the number of factors, and assigns in descending order an eigenvalue. Traditionally, factors with eigenvalues above 1 are seen as significant factors, and SPSS will extract that number of factors. However, some statisticians claim that using eigenvalues can be unreliable and use something called the Scree test. What the Scree test does is to plot the eigenvalues so that a visual assessment is used to see how factors should be extracted (see Figure 25.6).

What the Scree plot does is to plot the eigenvalues, and we are meant to use a visual criterion to determine the number of factors. The Scree plot is named after the debris that collects at the bottom of a rocky slope on a mountain (a scree). This is important as we can see that the Scree plot looks like the side of a mountain. We determine the number of factors by selecting those eigenvalues that occur before the plot straightens outs (or rough straightens out). Another way is to imagine the plot as an arm with a bend in the elbow. You would select all points above the elbow. In this case the Scree plot flattens out (or the elbow occurs) at the third point, so we take all points before that, i.e. two points. This is the number of factors that we should extract.

So far, both techniques have suggested two factors be extracted. However, a third assessment, and one that is often seen as most accurate, is something called Parallel Analysis of Monte Carlo simulations (Horn, 1965). What this technique does is create a data set of random sets of

Table 25.10 Extraction output

Total variance explained

Component	Initial eigenvalues			Extraction sums of squared loadings			Rotation sums of squared loadings *
	Total	% of variance	Cumulative %	Total	% of variance	Cumulative %	Total
1	6.713	37.295	37.295	6.713	37.295	37.295	5.805
2	1.538	8.542	45.837	1.538	8.542	45.837	5.468
3	0.861	4.784	50.621				
4	0.814	4.520	55.141				
5	0.775	4.303	59.444				
6	0.756	4.200	63.644				
7	0.729	4.049	67.693				
8	0.697	3.870	71.563				
9	0.666	3.702	75.265				
10	0.621	3.449	78.713				
11	0.599	3.328	82.042				
12	0.545	3.029	85.071				
13	0.531	2.949	88.020				
14	0.505	2.807	90.827				
15	0.471	2.618	93.445				
16	0.412	2.288	95.733				
17	0.393	2.182	97.915				
18	0.375	2.085	100.000				

Extraction method: principal components analysis.
*When components are correlated, sums of squared loadings cannot be added to obtain a total variance.

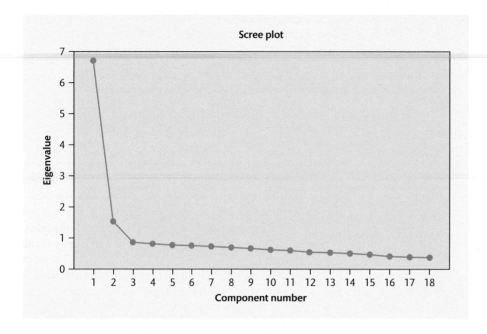

Figure 25.6 Scree plot.

eigenvalues that would be expected from purely random data with no structure. In simple terms, in this analysis you are comparing your data set against a data set that would happen completely by chance and therefore this analysis tells you what is important and what are just chance findings. In parallel analysis you compare the eigenvalues of your data set against the eigenvalues of the random data set to determine the number of factors to be extracted.

Now, the software for creating this data set is not in SPSS for Windows, but is a small simple program that is free and downloadable.[4] If you install it on your machine and run it, you'll get a simple interface, as in Figure 25.7 (although if you are running this in a university computer lab the computer might not let you run the software).

The program is simple, and all you need to input is **Number of Variables**, **Number of Subjects** and **Number of Replications**. For our data we have 18 variables and 402 respondents, so we input this into these boxes (see Table 25.11). We also enter 1000 into the number of replications; this is just a standard figure (however, if your computer has problems calculating this and freezes, lessen the number in this box to 100).

In the empty box of the application you should get the following (on the top of Figure 25.7). This is the criterion by which we will judge our own eigenvalues, and these are provided at the bottom of Table 25.11.

We then compare each of our eigenvalues against the random eigenvalues in turn. So, we compare the first of our eigenvalues against the first random eigenvalues, and then each one after that. At first, our eigenvalues exceed those in the random data set, but when they stop

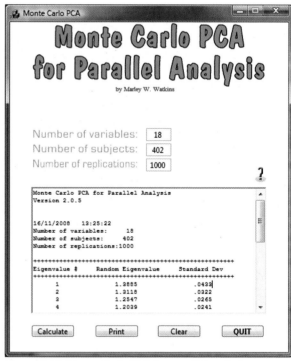

Figure 25.7 Monte Carlo PCA for parallel analysis.

exceeding the ones in the data set that's our criterion for determining the number of factors. For example, our first eigenvalue '6.713' exceeds the first eigenvalue in the random data set '1.3885'. Similarly, our second eigenvalue '1.538' exceeds the second eigenvalue in the random data set, '1.3118'. However, our third eigenvalue, '0.861' fails

---

[4]The program is available at **http://www.softpedia.com/get/Others/Home-Education/Monte-Carlo-PCA-for-Parallel-Analysis.shtml** or type 'Monte Carlo PCA for Parallel Analysis' into Google.

Table 25.11 Monte Carlo Analysis and the data set eigenvalues

Monte Carlo PCA for Parallel AnalysisVersion 2.0.5
16/11/2008 13:25:22
Number of variables: 18
Number of subjects: 402
Number of replications: 1000

Eigenvalue #	Random eigenvalue	Standard dev
1	1.3885	0.0433
2	1.3118	0.0322
3	1.2547	0.0265
4	1.2039	0.0241
5	1.1597	0.0223
6	1.1183	0.0197
7	1.0797	0.0191
8	1.0418	0.0183
9	1.0051	0.0182
10	0.9694	0.0178
11	0.9346	0.0174
12	0.9001	0.0182
13	0.8653	0.0185
14	0.8309	0.0196
15	0.7951	0.0196
16	0.7573	0.0207
17	0.7167	0.0222
18	0.6671	0.0275

Source: Monte Carlo PCA for Parallel Analysis ©2000 by Marley W. Watkins. All rights reserved.

Our eigenvalues . . .

	Total variance explained		
	Initial eigenvalues		
Component	Total	% of variance	Cumulative %
1	6.713	37.295	37.295
2	1.538	8.542	45.837
3	0.861	4.784	50.621
4	0.814	4.520	55.141
5	0.775	4.303	59.444

Extraction method: principal components analysis.

When components are correlated, sums of squared loadings cannot be added to obtain a total variance.

to exceed the third eigenvalue in the random data set, '1.2547'. This is our criterion for determining those factors; we only extract those factors that are greater in value than corresponding values in the data set. That is, because the generated data set is of purely random data, we are only sure that those eigenvalues that exceed the value in the random data set are not created by chance. Here, two of our eigenvalues exceed the values in the random data set, and therefore we would select two factors.

Among our data set all three criteria suggest that two factors be extracted from our data set.

Rotation

Rotation is necessary when extraction techniques suggest that there are two or more factors to extract. Simply put, the rotation of factors is designed to give us an idea of how the factors we extract are related, and provides a clear picture of which items load on which factor.

There are two sets of rotation techniques.

1 **Orthogonal rotations** – these are rotations that assume that each factor shares no association and is specifically unique. This is often used in psychology when applying a theoretical model to factor analysis and the model predicts that the factors are independent.

2 **Oblique rotations** – these tend to be used more often, as this procedure outlines the position of factors to one another, i.e. determines how they are usually related. The most specific procedure most often used for this is a technique called oblimin.

Each of these categories has a number of different types of rotation within them. However, the most specific procedure most often used for orthogonal rotations is a technique called varimax. The most specific procedure most often used for oblique rotations is a technique called oblimin. Usually, there are reasons for doing one or another. For example, researchers tend to prefer oblique rotations because they actually indicate how the different factors are related to one another. However, researchers will use orthogonal rotations when they feel the factors should be independent. Because of these differing views, and this would make sense when exploring factors, researchers tend to use both and report on those that produce the clearest results. We will now take you through an example that uses both these rotation techniques to illustrate rotation to you.

OK, we need to run our factor analysis procedure again as before, but this time in the Factor Analysis Window we press the **Rotation** button. You will then get a Window that looks like Figure 25.8. Click on **Direct Oblimin** and press **Continue** and then **OK**. Then run the whole procedure

Figure 25.8 Factor analysis: rotation window.

again, but this time click on **Varimax**. Then run the whole procedure again.

You should have two outputs that contain the values shown in Table 25.12. For the oblimin rotation the output you should look at is the pattern matrix (Table 25.12a). For the varimax rotation the output you should look at is the rotated component matrix (Table 25.12b). We have included the items so that you can see the item accurately. In the SPSS output you will just have the variable names.

First, we're going to look at Table 25.12a, the pattern matrix for the oblimin rotation. Each item loads on a factor. Loadings are the strength of the variable in defining the factor. Loadings on factors can be positive or negative, and when a number happens together this means very little to us at this stage. For instance, in the present example, the large majority of the loading on the first factor are positive and the large majority of the loadings on the second factor are negative. However, an item with a negative loading on a factor with a lot of items with a positive loading (or vice versa) would indicate that this variable has an inverse relationship with these other variables on the factor.

Now what we have to determine is what factor which item loads on. Opinions are fairly arbitrary about the point at which an item loads on a factor. However, Child (2006) suggests that anything above 0.44 could be thought of as important, with increased value of the loading becoming more vital in determining what the factor is. Kline (1986) suggests that you should not ignore any loading above 0.3. More commonly, a high loading (i.e. 0.40 or higher) on one factor and also a low loading (i.e. 0.20 or smaller) on all other factors is another suitable criterion to apply. However, what you need to remember is the higher the loading the more important that item is to that factor.

So, if we look at the rotated solution for our data, we can see that all the items, with the **exception** of AV1, AV2, AV3, AV4, AV6, AV7, AV14 and AV16 load on the first factor above 0.52. The items AV1, AV2, AV3, AV4, AV6, AV7, AV14 and AV16 load on the second factor above 0.56. So, we would suggest that we have two factors on which different items load.

But what about the orthogonal rotation? Well, this current analysis, and comparison of the two tables, raises an important point. From factor-analytic techniques you are always looking for a clear interpretation. What we mean by a clear interpretation is that all variables should load highly on one factor, and low on all other factors like our example. If you have a number of variables that load on a number of factors, or variables that load on none of the factors, then there is something wrong with your extraction techniques. Loading of a number of variables above the criteria of 0.44 and 0.3 across different factors might suggest you have not extracted enough factors, while, if a number of variables do not load on any factor, then you have extracted too many. (However,

Table 25.12 Pattern matrix (a) and rotated component matrix (b)

(a) Pattern matrix

	Component	
	1	2
AV1	−0.072	−0.745
AV2	−0.029	−0.799
AV3	−0.044	−0.753
AV4	−0.003	−0.677
AV5	0.645	−0.125
AV6	0.097	−0.601
AV7	0.017	−0.558
AV8	0.546	−0.146
AV9	0.542	−0.053
AV10	0.684	0.121
AV11	0.764	0.031
AV12	0.630	−0.124
AV13	0.672	0.010
AV14	0.183	−0.480
AV15	0.595	−0.048
AV16	0.081	−0.722
AV17	0.749	0.074
AV18	0.597	−0.031

Extraction method: principal components analysis.
Rotation method: oblimin with Kaiser normalisation.
Rotation converged in five iterations.

(b) Rotated component matrix

	Component	
	1	2
AV1	0.159	0.687
AV2	0.216	0.752
AV3	0.187	0.704
AV4	0.203	0.644
AV5	0.651	0.319
AV6	0.275	0.603
AV7	0.186	0.536
AV8	0.564	0.309
AV9	0.531	0.219
AV10	0.613	0.097
AV11	0.716	0.208
AV12	0.636	0.314
AV13	0.636	0.200
AV14	0.320	0.514
AV15	0.580	0.231
AV16	0.297	0.713
AV17	0.690	0.163
AV18	0.577	0.215

Extraction method: principal components analysis.
Rotation method: varimax with Kaiser normalisation.
Rotation converged in three iterations.

don't necessarily concern yourself if one variable loads on two factors. This is known as a cross-loading and may be due to a variable being ambiguous, a bad item (i.e. it should not be there) or genuinely being applicable to both factors.) Also, if you have an interpretation that is consistent with theory, or just makes common sense, then it is useful. However, most of all, you are looking for a clear interpretation with clear loadings.

If we look at Table 25.12b then we can see that this is a less clear solution. Items generally load in the same way, with the majority of items loading on factor 1 and the items AV1, AV2, AV3, AV4, AV6, AV7, AV14 and AV16 loading on factor 2. However, the items AV5, AV8 and AV12 load above 0.3 on both factors. This is a less clear interpretation than the previous one where the items are so clearly defined onto one factor (loading highest on one, and low on all other factors). Therefore we would most likely proceed with the oblimin solution, noting in the write-up that we had done both, and the oblimin rotation had produced the clearest solution.

We have a final job to do. We need to give our results some meaning. The next job is to define these factors. The reason we used the word 'define' is that factor analysis does not tell you the nature of the factor; you decide that for yourself. That is, you look at what variables load on a factor and then you give that factor a name. What you call the factor is up to you; it is usually a general term representing

the factor. However, the way in which you define the factor is by looking at the loading on the factor. To do this you have to return to the items. We have outlined the oblimin rotation again in Table 25.13.

If we look at the two factors and pick out some of the highest loading factors, you can see the following:

- Factor 1 comprises items such as:
  - I have mean thoughts towards people who score better than me on exams (item 11).
  - I do not like to help others with their work as it might result in them getting a better mark (item 17).
  - If my friend got a better mark than me, I would consider tampering with his/her work in some way (item 10).
  - I feel bitter towards those who do better than me on my course (item 13).
  - find myself wishing bad things on people who do better than me academically (item 5).
  - I would consider doing something nasty to somebody who threatened my chances of academic success (item 18).

- Factor 2 comprises items such as:
  - In the past I have falsely told other students the wrong exam date, so they would miss the exam (item 2).
  - I would hate the student who got the best mark in one of my classes (item 3).

Table 25.13 Factor analysis output

(a) Pattern matrix

		1	2
1	I can be spiteful to my friends if they get a better mark than me.	−0.072	−0.745
2	In the past I have falsely told other students the wrong exam date, so they would miss the exam.	−0.029	−0.799
3	I would hate the student who got the best mark in one of my classes.	−0.044	−0.753
4	If I had the opportunity to change other students' exam grades so that mine were the best, I would do it.	−0.003	−0.677
5	I find myself wishing bad things on people who do better than me academically.	0.645	−0.125
6	I always tell people I am happy for them when they do better than me in exams.	0.097	−0.601
7	I have thought about spoiling someone's work because it is better than mine.	0.017	−0.558
8	I wish bad things on people because they are smarter than me.	0.546	−0.146
9	When other students on my course are praised for their excellent work, it makes me want to wish something bad on that person.	0.542	−0.053
10	If my friend got a better mark than me, I would consider tampering with his/her work in some way.	0.634	0.121
11	I have mean thoughts towards people who score better than me in exams.	0.764	0.031
12	I resent people on my course who excel in their studies.	0.630	−0.124
13	I feel bitter towards those who do better than me on my course.	0.672	0.010
14	I have lied to people on my course to try and hinder their progress so I can get the better mark.	0.183	−0.480
15	If I came second best in a piece of work, because my friend got the top mark, I would still be happy.	0.595	−0.048
16	I seek revenge on people who get better grades than me and take away my chances of success.	0.081	−0.722
17	I do not like to help others with their work as it might result in them getting a better mark.	0.749	0.074
18	I would consider doing something nasty to somebody who threatened my chances of academic success.	0.597	−0.031

Extraction method: principal components analysis.
Rotation method: oblimin with Kaiser normalisation.

- I can be spiteful to my friends if they get a better mark than me (item 1).
- I seek revenge on people who get better grades than me and take away my chances of success (item 16).
- If I had the opportunity to change other students' exam grades so that mine were the best, I would do it (item 4).
- I have thought about spoiling someone's work because it is better than mine (item 7).

We can perhaps see a distinction between these two factors. Items on the second factor seem to represent active and direct vindictiveness towards people, actually being spiteful, seeking revenge, lying to other students, possibly changing their marks. The items on the first factor, however, seem to be more passive vindictiveness, or much less direct vindictiveness, thinking mean things, feeling resentful, wishing or considering doing something awful to another student. We would argue, and this may be open to debate, that the academic vindictiveness scale contains two factors: direct academic vindictiveness and passive academic vindictiveness. There are some useful things to remember regarding exploratory factor-analytic techniques. Factor analysis is a very descriptive procedure. It requires you to describe things, and it is not always a perfect science. This is a criticism of factor analysis as it can be very interpretative. Because of the interpretative nature of factor analysis, it is usually expected that you might perform a number of extractions and different rotation techniques to explore possible factors arising from your data fully. Revisiting extraction techniques, and trying to see whether extracting more or fewer factors and trying different rotation techniques is acceptable and useful.

However, we would suggest, from our results, that this distinction between 'direct' and 'passive' vindictiveness is possibly a good way of explaining the data. We would also recommend that, rather than computing an overall score, researchers should compute two separate scales' scores, one for direct academic vindictiveness and one for passive academic vindictiveness.

Confirmatory factor analysis

We will now introduce you to another factor analysis procedure that is used in the literature. We're not going to go into as much detail as exploratory factor analysis because: (1) it uses very advanced statistical techniques; and (2) demonstration of the procedure requires specialist software (e.g. programs called AMOS; LISREL). However, we're going to introduce you to some of the key terms and ideas because the technique is being used more and more within the psychometric literature. Therefore, this will enable you to read this literature and be able to understand and use it.

Confirmatory factor analysis is a technique that can be used to confirm any findings identified with exploratory factor analysis. So, for example, we can use confirmatory factor analysis to assess whether the two-factor model of academic vindictiveness we found in the above example can be replicated in other samples.

The underlying aim of confirmatory factor analysis is to assess whether any future data collected on the scale fits the explanation provided by the exploratory factor analysis, i.e. does other data collected fit our two-factor model? The key term you will see with confirmatory factor analysis is **goodness of fit**.

What you will see in many psychometric papers is an attempt to confirm previous models. In Figure 25.9 there is an illustration of the type of diagram you will see presented in a confirmatory factor analysis procedure which shows the suggested structure of the data. In our example you can see that we've connected our 18 academic vindictiveness items onto two main dimensions; direct and passive academic vindictiveness.

If we collected some more data on the scale, we could, within a suitable software package, test how well our new data fitted the suggested model outlined above.

We assess the goodness of fit of the data by the use of the goodness of fit statistics. As with any statistical procedure, there are several of these statistics, and what you will find is that authors report a number of these statistics to provide an overall assessment of the goodness of fit. The statistics

Stop and think

Study break

1 In the example above we called the academic vindictiveness direct and passive academic vindictiveness. Do you agree with this interpretation? Looking at these factors, and the item loading, can you think of better names for these factors?

2 Clearly, there would be further issues of validity here. What could you do to try to establish validity, not only for these two factors, but to support our distinction between the two types of academic vindictiveness: direct academic vindictiveness and passive academic vindictiveness?

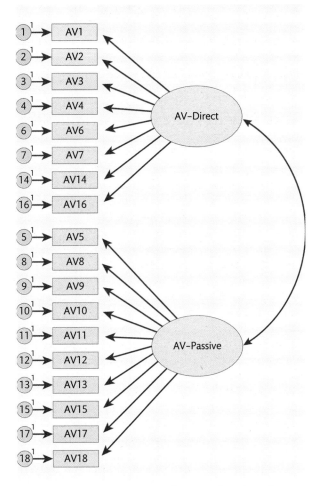

Figure 25.9 Our statistical two-factor explanation of academic vindictiveness.

you will usually see are as follows, and we have provided some suggested criteria by which goodness of fit is assessed.

- Chi-square (χ^2)
- The goodness of fit index (GFI)
- Normed fit index (NFI)
- Comparative fit index (CFI)
- Adjusted goodness of fit (AGFI)
- Index root mean square residual (SRMR)
- The root mean square error of approximation (RMSEA).

The figures produced by the analysis vary. The chi-square statistic usually provides quite a large number, i.e. around 1,000. Analysis for GFI, AGFI, NFI and CFI typically range from 0.00 to 1.00, with higher figures (i.e. those nearer to 1) indicating a better fit. The SRMR and RMSEA produce figures that centre around a low figure, e.g. working towards 0.01, with lower figures indicating better fit. As the chi-squared test is highly sensitive to sample size, it is usually just reported. Authors such as Hu and Bentler (1999) suggest that a good model fit is individually indicated with approximate values of GFI, NFI and CFI above 0.95, AGFI should also be at least

0.90, SRMR below 0.08, RMSEA below 0.06; these should be conventional values for accepting good models.

We subjected some new data we had collected among 300 adults to confirmatory factor analysis. We computed the following goodness of fit from the data:

- Chi-square, χ^2 = 931.4
- The goodness of fit index (GFI) = 0.957
- Normed fit index (NFI) = 0.950
- Comparative fit index (CFI) = 0.988
- Adjusted goodness of fit (AGFI) = 0.952
- Index root mean square residual (SRMR) = 0.038
- The root mean square error of approximation (RMSEA) = 0.013.

Using our criteria we can see that all our values exceed (in terms of the GFI, NFI, CFI and AGFI) and fall below (SRMR and RMSEA) the criteria, and, therefore, our current two-factor model presents a good explanation of the data.

One final use of confirmatory factor analysis is that it is very useful for comparing different explanations for data. So, for example, if there were two competing explanations for how a scale should be structured, then you could perform confirmatory factor analysis on both interpretations to see which presented the best fit. For example, with our academic vindictiveness scale, we could suggest an alternative idea that, given our earlier findings with the internal reliability analysis, the academic vindictiveness comprised one not two factors.

So, for example, our alternative model would look like Figure 25.10.

We ran a confirmatory analysis on this model and found the following statistics:

- Chi-square, χ^2 = 826.2
- The goodness of fit index (GFI) = 0.917
- Normed fit index (NFI) = 0.910
- Comparative fit index (CFI) = 0.928
- Adjusted goodness of fit (AGFI) = 0.882
- Index root mean square residual (SRMR) = 0.142
- The root mean square error of approximation (RMSEA) = 0.011.

These fit statistics for our data and model are quite good; in fact, you may see that many researchers would suggest, that although not a good fit, it is certainly reasonable. None the less, the statistics aren't as good as the statistics for a two-factor model, and therefore we would suggest that there is evidence that our academic vindictiveness scale comprises two factors. You will often see this technique in psychometric papers, with authors comparing different models using these statistics as a basis of comparison, based on either previous findings or on theoretical perspectives, to find out which models represent the best explanation of the data.

There is a lot more to confirmatory factor analysis but what we've outlined above has given you a brief introduction

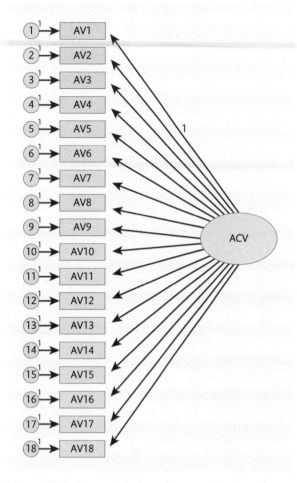

Figure 25.10 Our statistical one-factor explanation of academic vindictiveness.

and provided you with enough information to read some of the psychometric literature.

The International Personality Item Pool and the Higher Education Academy in Psychology practicals web page

One final point about psychometric tests is that in many instances there is already a measure available to use. We've already mentioned the International Personality Item Pool that contains main personality and individual difference measures (**http://ipip.ori.org/ipip**). There are other test bases online, but a recent one to appear is at the Higher Education Academy in Psychology practicals web page (**www.psychologypracticals.com**). This is a searchable library of over 1,500 psychometric tests that are in the public domain. Therefore, there is no need to develop new psychometric tests automatically, as there are already many available and these sites are worth checking out.

Final comments

As you can see, psychometric tests are useful in a number of areas of psychology. The main thing to remember about psychometric tests is that it is always important for them to show acceptable levels of reliability and validity. Clearly, if you are making decisions about people's education, their

---

Stop and think

Rasch analysis and item response theory

A different approach to analysis of psychometric scales was suggested by Georg Rasch in 1960. His original research was concerned with abilities but the theory behind it has now been applied to personality measures as well. The guiding principle behind Rasch analysis was clearly stated by him: 'a person having a greater ability than another person should have the greater probability of solving any item of the type in question, and similarly, one item being more difficult than another means that for any person the probability of solving the second item is the greater one' (Rasch 1960/1980, page 117). In other words, when participants complete a psychometric scale they provide us with two sources of information. They tell us how people respond to the items, which is used in reliability and factor analysis, but they also tell us how the participants score on the scale, that

information that is not much used in classical item analysis. Rasch suggests that we should use both pieces of information when we analyse scales.

The basics of the analysis are reasonably straightforward, although the mathematics behind it becomes more complicated. To take the item information first; it is easy to work out the difficulty of each item by using the percentage of the sample of participants who get the answer correct. This can be transformed into the probability of getting the item correct or the odds of getting an item correct. We can also calculate the ability of each participant by taking the percentage of items that they get correct and we can then turn this into a probability of that person answering an item correctly. Rasch's theory suggests that the probability of getting an individual item correct is

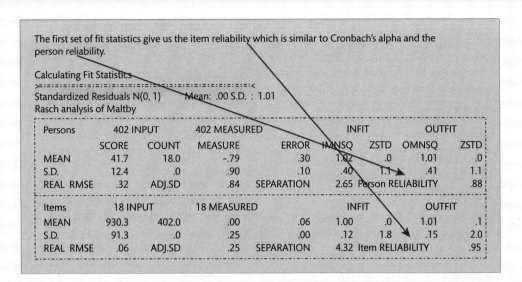

The first set of fit statistics give us the item reliability which is similar to Cronbach's alpha and the person reliability.

Calculating Fit Statistics
>=:<
Standardized Residuals N(0, 1)   Mean: .00 S.D. : 1.01
Rasch analysis of Maltby

Persons	402 INPUT		402 MEASURED		INFIT		OUTFIT	
	SCORE	COUNT	MEASURE	ERROR	MNSQ	ZSTD	OMNSQ	ZSTD
MEAN	41.7	18.0	-.79	.30	1.02	.0	1.01	.0
S.D.	12.4	.0	.90	.10	.40	1.1	.41	1.1
REAL RMSE	.32	ADJ.SD	.84	SEPARATION	2.65	Person RELIABILITY		.88

Items	18 INPUT		18 MEASURED		INFIT		OUTFIT	
MEAN	930.3	402.0	.00	.06	1.00	.0	1.01	.1
S.D.	91.3	.0	.25	.00	.12	1.8	.15	2.0
REAL RMSE	.06	ADJ.SD	.25	SEPARATION	4.32	Item RELIABILITY		.95

Figure 25.11

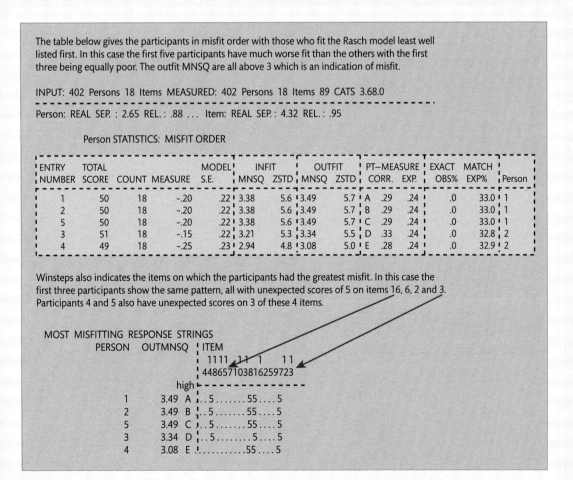

The table below gives the participants in misfit order with those who fit the Rasch model least well listed first. In this case the first five participants have much worse fit than the others with the first three being equally poor. The outfit MNSQ are all above 3 which is an indication of misfit.

INPUT: 402 Persons 18 Items MEASURED: 402 Persons 18 Items 89 CATS 3.68.0
- -
Person: REAL SEP. : 2.65 REL. : .88 ... Item: REAL SEP. : 4.32 REL. : .95

Person STATISTICS: MISFIT ORDER

ENTRY NUMBER	TOTAL SCORE	COUNT	MEASURE	MODEL S.E.	INFIT MNSQ	ZSTD	OUTFIT MNSQ	ZSTD	PT-MEASURE CORR.	EXP.	EXACT MATCH OBS%	EXP%	Person
1	50	18	-.20	.22	3.38	5.6	3.49	5.7	A .29	.24	.0	33.0	1
2	50	18	-.20	.22	3.38	5.6	3.49	5.7	B .29	.24	.0	33.0	1
5	50	18	-.20	.22	3.38	5.6	3.49	5.7	C .29	.24	.0	33.0	1
3	51	18	-.15	.22	3.21	5.3	3.34	5.5	D .33	.24	.0	32.8	2
4	49	18	-.25	.23	2.94	4.8	3.08	5.0	E .28	.24	.0	32.9	2

Winsteps also indicates the items on which the participants had the greatest misfit. In this case the first three participants show the same pattern, all with unexpected scores of 5 on items 16, 6, 2 and 3. Participants 4 and 5 also have unexpected scores on 3 of these 4 items.

MOST MISFITTING RESPONSE STRINGS
　　　PERSON　　OUTMNSQ ITEM
　　　　　　　　　　　　　　1111 11 1   11
　　　　　　　　　　　　　　448657103816259723
　　　　　　　　　　　　high

1	3.49 A	..5.......55....5
2	3.49 B	..5.......55....5
5	3.49 C	..5.......55....5
3	3.34 D	..5........5....5
4	3.08 E	...........55....5

Figure 25.12

caused by the difference in a person's ability and the item difficulty. To put it simply, if a person's ability is higher than a particular item's difficulty then the participant is more likely to get this correct than if it is lower than the item's difficulty. Using this information we can compare the data collected with what we would expect based on calculations of item difficulty and person ability. The closer the results are to the predicted results the better fit the data are to the Rasch model. Like many modern statistical procedures, however, Rasch analysis assumes that the model might be improved by iteration. That is, in this case we can modify our estimates of person and item difficulty so that they converge with the data, but still hold true to a Rasch model. This also allows us to identify which participants are not responding as the Rasch model predicts, and also which items do not fit the model. In both cases, there will be a larger disparity between the results in terms of correct responses and predicted results.

Rasch analysis is designed to produce unidimensional measures which, therefore, measure only one ability, personality trait or attitude at a time. It is also designed to produce measures in which the difference between participant scores is interval, which is better for statistical analysis.

In the example below, we have carried out a Rasch analysis on the data from the academic vindictiveness scale, which has two factors according to the factor analysis. The analysis was carried out on Winsteps (Linacre, 1999/2006) software, which is a program specifically designed for Rasch analysis. The first thing to note is that the Rasch solution and the data converged in nine iterations. This would indicate that the data is a reasonable fit to the one-dimensional model, given the number of participants and items. The item reliability of the 18-item scale is 0.95, which suggests that all of the items are measuring the same dimension. The person reliability, which tells us whether the participants are behaving in a similar way and is analogous to the item reliability, is 0.88. This suggests that there may be some participants who are not performing like the others (see Figure 25.11).

Factor analysis omitting the first five participants; please note the eigenvalue of the second factor.

Total variance explained

Component	Initial eigenvalues			Extraction sums of squared loadings		
	Total	% of variance	Cumulative %	Total	% of variance	Cumulative %
1	6.947	38.596	38.596	6.947	38.596	38.596
2	1.032	5.734	44.330	1.032	5.734	44.330
3	.893	4.963	49.293			

The Scree plot also suggests one factor (remember the number of points above the elbow).

Scree plot

Figure 25.13

We can investigate this by looking at person misfit; this indicates the participants who fit the Rasch model less well. In this case, there are five participants who have very poor fit and these are the first five on the SPSS file. Winsteps also indicates the items on which these participants are performing unusually. In this case they score unexpectedly high on items 2, 3, 6 and 16, which are all important in identifying factor 2 (see Figure 25.12).

It is, therefore, possible that the second factor might be attributable to the responses of five participants. If we carry out the factor analysis again, omitting these five participants, we find that the second factor now has an eigenvalue of 1.032, which is lower than the criterion for a second factor suggested by parallel analysis. In this case the second factor might be created by five participants who have an odd pattern of responding. It is perhaps important to note that some of the items that are aligned on different factors appear very similar; see, for example, items 3 and 12 (see Figure 25.13).

Increasingly, there is recognition that psychometric analysis should use more sources of information in its analysis, which has led to the development of a related set of techniques called item response theory (Embretson and Reise, 2000). Rasch/item response theory are often treated as relatively new developments in psychometric testing; however, the importance of Rasch's discovery was noted over 40 years ago by Loevinger (1965), who stated 'Rasch has derived a truly new approach to psychometric problems . . . Rasch must be credited with an outstanding contribution to one of the two central psychometric problems, the achievement of nonarbitrary measures'.

In conclusion, Rasch/item response theory is another statistical tool that can be used by a psychometrician in developing a reliable and valid psychometric tool.

Steven J. Muncer
Teesside University

livelihood, their treatment for a condition or their illness, you need to be quite confident of your diagnosis.

We have introduced you here to the main concepts of item writing, reliability, validity, exploratory factor analysis, confirmatory factor analysis and types and uses of psychometric tests. Therefore, you should now understand some of the ideas and criteria surrounding psychometric testing, know what is meant by reliability in psychometric testing, be able to explain what is meant by validity in psychometric testing, see how factor analysis is used in psychometric testing and the types and uses for different psychometric tests.

Summary

- The main types of tests you will come across in the personality, intelligence and individual differences literature are measures of personality, ability, motivation and attitude. Also, psychometric tests are used in clinical settings and great care must be taken with their use in assessing people.
- The key to a good psychometric test is writing very good questions. These include making sure the items are clear, not leading, not embarrassing, not posing hypothetical questions and including reverse wording items.
- The format of the response scale and instructions are also key to a good psychometric test.
- In psychometric testing, there are two forms of reliability: internal reliability and reliability over time (test–retest reliability). Internal reliability (or consistency) refers to whether all the aspects of the psychometric test are measuring the same thing. Test–retest reliability assesses reliability over time.
- Validity is concerned with whether a test is measuring what we claim it is measuring. Convergent validity is assessed by the extent to which it shows associations with measures to which that it should be related. Concurrent validity is when a test shows acceptable correlations with known and accepted standard measures of that construct. Discriminate validity is when the test is *not* related to things that it shouldn't be related to. Face validity is concerned with whether the measure measures what it claims to measure. Predictive validity assesses whether a measure can accurately predict something in the future.
- Getting other people to rate the individual on the items of the questionnaire is a good way of potentially assessing the validity of the questionnaire because, ideally, the ratings given by the participants and the other person should be similar.
- Factor analysis is a multivariate (multiple variables) 'data reduction' statistical technique that allows us to simplify the correlational relationships between a number of variables. There are two forms of factor analysis: exploratory factor analysis and confirmatory factor analysis.
- There are two procedures in exploratory factor analysis: (1) the extraction of factors, which determines how many factors underlie our data; and (2) rotation of factors to determine which items/variables load on each of the extracted factors.
- Confirmatory factor analysis is a technique that can be used to confirm any findings with exploratory factor analysis.

Connecting up

We have talked about factor analysis here. This technique was used extensively in determining the trait approach of personality, such as the five-factor model (see Chapter 7), and is crucial in the debate about the nature of intelligence and whether it forms a single factor or not (see Chapter 11). Also, throughout the text we have discussed different psychometric measures of the constructs we are outlining. In almost all cases many of these measures have established reliability and validity.

Critical thinking

Discussion questions

You might want to try the following two exercises to explore some of the issues that surround psychological testing.

- Researchers in America, such as Professor M. Groening, have developed a new measure of personality, the *Homer Simpson Personality Questionnaire*. Respondents are presented with five items and asked to indicate the extent to which they disagree or agree with each statement on a five-point scale (1 = Disagree strongly, 5 = Agree strongly). Here are the five items of the *Homer Simpson Personality Questionnaire*:

  1 'It takes two to lie. One to lie and one to listen.'
  2 'Weaselling out of things is important to learn. It's what separates us from the animals . . . except the weasel.'
  3 'If something is too hard, give up. The moral is to never try anything.'
  4 'Hmmmm. Donuts. . . . What can't they do?'
  5 'Just because I don't care doesn't mean I don't understand.'

  Consider, does this scale have good face validity? What studies could Professor Groening complete to establish or examine the scale's concurrent, discriminate, predictive and construct validity?

- In 2004 and 2005, BBC News reported a number of stories that centred on people's pessimism with the world. In June 2004, a survey by an international polling agency, GlobeScan, suggested that Nigerians and Zimbabweans were feeling especially pessimistic about their own countries. In Zimbabwe, just 3 per cent of those asked thought life was getting better. In Nigeria, 75 per cent of people asked thought that the country was heading in the wrong direction, with 66 per cent thinking it was more corrupt than a year ago. In December 2004, Romania's presidential and parliamentary elections on Sunday evoked a mood of pessimism in some of the country's newspapers. In January 2005, there was reported pessimism in France about public sector strikes. In Spain it was pessimism on peace in the Basque country. Also, in January 2005, those in the Arab world were thought to have a sense of foreboding as the elections in Iraq fast approached. Throughout 2008 and 2009, western economic systems were in crisis, with values of shares in stock markets falling, unemployment rising, industries and companies losing money, and most people being affected in some way by the 'credit crunch'. Given such a prevailing pessimism throughout the world's different continents, we are proposing the World Pessimism Trait Scale that measures an individual's pessimism about the world. The scale contains five items and asks the extent to which respondents disagree or agree with the statement on a 5-point scale (1 = Disagree strongly, 5 = Agree strongly). Here are the five items of the World Pessimism Scale:

  – I often think that things in the world are never going to get better.
  – I am often of the opinion that the human race is destined towards its own destruction.
  – I am certain that, year after year, the world will become a harder place for everyone to live in.
  – I often wonder what is so wrong with the world these days.
  – The world has so many problems that cannot be solved.

  Consider, does this scale have good face validity? What studies could the researchers do to establish the scale's validity?

- Imagine a health construct you might want to measure. How might you measure this construct? How could you establish reliability and validity (particularly validity) for this construct?

  Now, imagine that a questionnaire isn't suitable to measure this construct and that you have to choose two other methods, an interview and an experimental measure.

  – How could you establish reliability and validity of the interview measure?

– How could you establish reliability and validity of the experimental measure?

Now, think about rival ways of measuring the same variable that use different methods. What are the advantages and disadvantages of each measure, particularly in terms of reliability and validity?

Essay questions

● Discuss how a researcher establishes confidence in the use of a psychometric test.
● Outline the main types of reliability and validity.

Going further

Books

Paul Kline has written a series of readable books about psychometrics. The most recent is Kline, P. (2000). *Psychometrics Primer*. Free Association Books. However, other good books on psychological testing include: Gregory, R. J. (2007). *Psychological Testing: History, Principles and Applications* (5th edn), Harlow: Pearson Education; Anastasi, A. (1988). *Psychological Testing*, New York: Macmillan Publishing Company; and Rust, J. and Golombok, S. (2009). *Modern Psychometrics: The Science of Psychological Assessment* (3rd edn), London: Routledge.

Within the psychometric literature you will also see references to two other techniques used in psychometric testing: Rasch analysis and item response theory (see Stop and think box). Item response theory is a modern framework for psychometric test construction in which the investigator argues that there is a single underlying construct under which all the items reply and each respondent is assumed to have a certain amount of the construct being measured. The Rasch model is a mathematical framework that uses equations to predict the probability of respondents at different levels of skill answering test questions correctly. Like

confirmatory factor analysis both these techniques: (1) use very advanced statistical techniques; and (2) require specialist software to demonstrate these procedures. However, two good books that cover these topics are Wilson, M. (2005). *Constructing Measures; An Item Response Modeling Approach*, Hillsdale, NJ: Lawrence Erlbaum Associates; and Bond, T. G. and Fox, C. M. (2007). *Applying the Rasch Model: Fundamental Measurement in the Human Sciences* (2nd edn), New Jersey: Lawrence Erlbaum Associates.

Web links

A good library of psychological tests for public domain use is available at the International Personality Item Pool site (**http://ipip.ori.org/ipip**), and a searchable database is at the Higher Education Academy in Psychology practicals web page (**www.psychologypracticals.com**).

If you want to learn more about confirmatory factor analysis you need a copy of the computer programs AMOS/LISREL. Your department may have these, but they are advanced statistics programs. However, there are some good online guides; for example, at **www.indiana.edu/~statmath/stat/all/cfa/index.html**.

Film and literature

There are not many films that are clearly illustrative of and accurately portray psychometric testing. However, *The Recruit* (2003, directed by Roger Donaldson) gives a fictional insider's view into the CIA Agency: how trainees

are recruited, how they are prepared for the spy game and what they learn to survive. The film *Spy Game* (2001, directed by Tony Scott) is in a similar vein.

Explore the website accompanying this text at **www.pearsoned.co.uk/maltby** for further resources to help you with your studies. These include multiple-choice questions, essay questions, web links and ideas for advanced reading.

Don't forget the following additional material can be found on the website (www.pearsoned.co.uk/maltby)

CHAPTER 26
Academic Argument and Thinking

Key themes

- Structure and standard form of arguments
- Premises and conclusions
- Deductive and inductive arguments
- Fallacies

Learning outcomes

At the end of this discussion you should:

- Know how to put an argument into standard form
- Understand what major and minor premises are and how they relate to conclusions
- Appreciate the differences between deductive and inductive arguments
- Be able to outline a number of fallacies

Introduction

Throughout your life, within your academic life and career, you will be asked to consider arguments. Therefore, knowing how arguments are constructed and considered can be a powerful tool in advancing your academic work and understanding the work of others; and, frankly, it is the cornerstone of the critical analysis that your lecturers are so fond of mentioning. We are going to take you through the main theory that underlies arguments and show you some of the tricks and mistakes that people use in arguments.

The structure of arguments: premises and conclusions

First, we are going to introduce you to the idea of the components of argument. All arguments take what is known as a standard form; for example:

1 All university students are smart.
2 Sarah is a university student.
3 Therefore, Sarah is smart.

Each stage of this argument is given a name. Using the example just presented,

- Statement 1 is a major premise, a general rule.
- Statement 2 is a minor premise, a more specific statement, or case.
- Statement 3 is the conclusion.

This structure underlies much of our thinking and the way we construct arguments and debates across academia. However, what many people forget to do when discussing, writing and thinking about debates is to break down these arguments to help their work, or get to grips with the debate. This is the core skill that your lecturers are talking about when they keep mentioning critical analysis. Critical analysis is the ability to take a topic area, put together a number of arguments and then assess each argument in terms of the evidence (be it theoretical or empirical) that supports each premise of each argument. If you were to do that in an essay, then you would most certainly benefit from higher marks for your work, because you had provided a critical analysis of the topic area.

To show you how it could work for you, we will take you through an example. Let us take a debate regarding where children get their intelligence from. In this area, one argument that might emerge is from a social learning perspective (that we learn our behaviour).

A social learning perspective might produce the following argument:

- All children's thinking skills result from what they observe in others
- Intelligence is a thinking skill

- Therefore, children's intelligence results from what they observe in others.

However, with all areas there are always counterarguments. One possible counterargument could be that there is a genetic predisposition to children's intelligence. An argument from this area would be:

- All children's thinking is largely determined by genetics
- Intelligence is a thinking skill
- Therefore, children's intelligence is largely determined by genetics.

As you can see, these two standard forms can already give the core of an essay to enable debate. Is it the social learning argument, or is it the genetic predisposition argument?

At this stage, you may, of course, be thinking this is a simplistic way of showing the arguments. However, presenting the arguments in this way allows us to take a more sophisticated look at them and to begin fully exploring the debates.

The point of this type of analysis is that assessment of the arguments centres not on the conclusion, but on the major and minor premises.

Let us illustrate this. If the debate centres on the conclusions, you end up in a circular argument with one side arguing intelligence is largely determined by observed behaviour, while the other side argues it is largely determined by genetic predisposition. We have no critical insight into the debate. However, if we start to examine the premises, then we can gain an insight into the argument.

Let us take the social learning perspective as an example.

- All children's thinking skills result from what they observe in others
- Intelligence is a thinking skill
- Therefore, children's intelligence results from what they observe in others.

The first thing we can do, then, is to examine the major premise of this argument: 'All children's thinking skills result from what they observe in others.' We can look for ideas that either support, question or attack this premise, that, in turn, open this argument up to debate. We could, for example, ask the following questions:

- Do children only show thinking skills that they have observed?
- Can there be other influences on thinking skills?
- Is it true that all children's thinking skills result from observation, or might this be true for only some children?

We can also consider the minor premise in this way. Again, we can ask some questions:

- Is intelligence a thinking skill?
- Does intelligence represent other skills apart from thinking?

It is this structured consideration of these sorts of questions that is the key to developing critical analysis in your work.

How do we answer such questions? One crucial source of material to help you answer these questions is evidence from research studies or theoretical papers. This is where descriptions of studies or theories should fit into your essay. A descriptive essay (one that gets lower marks) will just list different studies in the area. An essay that includes critical analysis (and gets high marks) will use these studies to see if there is support for these types of questions or premises. For example, to consider the question of whether intelligence represents other skills apart from thinking, you might consider evidence indicating that intelligence is also an emotional skill.

Deductive versus inductive arguments

However, in terms of expanding such considerations from general discussion to your academic written work, you need to consider the following concepts: deductive versus inductive argument.

A **deductive argument** is an argument where the premises are guaranteed to provide a truthful conclusion. In a deductive argument, if the premises are true, it is *impossible* for the conclusion to be false. Therefore:

- *If it is true that* … All children's cognitive/thinking skills result from what they observe in others
- *And it is also true that* … Intelligence is a cognitive/thinking skill
- *Then it must be true that* … Children's intelligence results from what they observe in others.

An **inductive argument** is an argument in which the premises are probable; they support the probable truth of the conclusion. In an inductive argument, if the premises are probable, then it is unlikely that the conclusion is false. Therefore:

- *If it is probable that* … All children's cognitive/thinking skills result from what they observe in others

- *And it is probable that* … Intelligence is a cognitive/thinking skill
- *Then it is probable that* … Children's intelligence results from what they observe in others.

In psychology, we almost always rely on inductive methods. Because of the complexities of human nature, we are rarely sure of any premise to any argument. Therefore, when considering the arguments as well as the debates that surround the premise, you must consider the evidence supporting each premise. This strength of evidence determines to what extent the premises are probable.

Therefore, it is crucial for your essay writing (or your debates in class) for you to refer to the strength of evidence, be it theoretical papers or empirical research studies, to support the premises of your argument. To create an effective critical analysis, when considering the strength or debate of an argument, you need to ask the following questions about your premise:

- To what extent does theory/research support the major premise? That is, to what extent is this premise probable?
- To what extent does theory/research support the minor premise? That is, to what extent is this premise probable?

To illustrate this process, let us return to our discussion of social learning versus genetic predisposition explanations of children's cognitive/thinking skills. Let us consider that the social learning theory has a strong argument. This strong argument would result from the following statements:

- *The majority of evidence (or opinion) suggests that* … All children's cognitive/thinking skills result from what they observe in others
- *The majority of evidence (or opinion) suggests that* … Intelligence is a cognitive/thinking skill
- *Therefore, it is most probable that* … Children's intelligence results from what they observe in others.

Again, we are never certain owing to the complexities of human nature; therefore, in psychology, we would say that the evidence (opinion) strongly supports this argument. Let us consider that the genetic predisposition explanations comprise a strong argument. This would mean:

- *The majority of evidence (or opinion) suggests that* … All children's cognitive/thinking skills result from a genetic predisposition
- *The majority of evidence (or opinion) suggests that* … Intelligence is a cognitive/thinking skill
- *Therefore, it is most probable that* … Children's intelligence results from a genetic predisposition.

So, what is a weak argument? Let us imagine that the genetic predisposition is a weak argument. This would mean:

- *A **minority** of evidence (or opinion) suggests that ...* All children's cognitive/thinking is largely determined by genetics
- *A **majority** of evidence (or opinion) suggests that ...* Intelligence is a cognitive/thinking skill
- *Therefore, it is **unlikely** that ...* Children's intelligence is largely determined by genetics.

Furthermore, it is important to note that a weakness in the evidence used to support either of the premises would lead to the conclusion being weakened; so, for example:

- *Even if a majority of evidence suggests that ...* All children's cognitive/thinking is largely determined by genetics
- *But, a minority of evidence suggests that ...* Intelligence is a cognitive/thinking skill
- *Therefore, it is **unlikely** that ...* Children's intelligence is largely determined by genetics.

However, when this presents itself it is not time to panic. It is unlikely to be your argument that you are representing. Rather, you note that this argument is a weak one, caused by a lack of evidence (or support) for this perspective (i.e. your conclusion would be '*there is very little evidence that children's intelligence is largely determined by genetics*'). Of course, sometimes when you have mixed evidence or weak evidence you may wish to develop another argument.

Therefore you can see that you must be consistent in terms of the arguments and evidence you are putting forward. Try to see your written academic work as comprising a series of these sorts of considerations. That is, if you're talking about the strength of different arguments, try to assess to what extent there is agreement in regard to the major and minor premises that underpin these arguments, particularly in terms of the evidence.

Generally, trying to understand what arguments people are trying to put forward in all academic work, including your work, will always raise the standard of your work. By putting arguments into standard form, you will not only be able to examine what potential debates arise from arguments but also to realise what evidence is required to support the argument being made. This is a difficult task. Sometimes premises are hard to identify but, if you can identify them and accurately assess how well the evidence supports the premises and the final argument, this will raise the level of critical analysis in your work. If you find that you have difficulty following the argument that you have written in your own work then it is also likely that your tutor will. If you start thinking about these things when writing you will improve the structure and the critical analysis of your academic work.

Fallacies in arguments

When you are surrounded by arguments, particularly in contentious areas, you will find that a lot of people use a lot of different argument techniques. Many of them are straightforward and readily fit into the model of standard form we just outlined. However, sometimes people use little tricks, often quite unintentionally in their arguments. These are known as fallacies.

Fallacies in an argument are intended to lead to a false notion or be deceptive; a fallacy may be based on a false inference or incorrect reasoning. We are going to outline some fallacies in argument to help you to develop the correct arguments, and avoid incorrect arguments, in your work. Also, knowing common fallacies will help you to discuss and critically analyse other people's work and arguments.

Fallacies of the undistributed middle

Because it is based on the structure of arguments, a fallacy of the undistributed middle is a formal fallacy. It arises from a misuse or distortion of the type of standard form we described earlier. Here is a simple form of the fallacy of the undistributed middle:

- All horses have four legs
- All dogs have four legs
- Therefore, all horses are dogs.

This argument is based on association, and it leads to a false conclusion. All horses have four legs, and all dogs have four legs, but that does not mean that horses are dogs. Rather, there are other things that define both these animals that set them apart.

You will come across this sort of argument in previous sections of this text. One particular area is when we talk about the history of eugenics (social philosophy that advocates the improvement of human hereditary traits through social intervention) and its introduction and support by some intelligence researchers (Chapter 14). To a large extent, some of this discussion is worrying. However, we have to be careful that some of our criticisms of this work are not left open to the accusation of using the fallacy of the undistributed middle.

To use this example, recall that intelligence researchers such as Galton have lent some support to the notion of eugenics, as did Hitler and the Nazi Party. Therefore, a fallacy of the undistributed middle in this case would be:

- Nazis supported eugenics
- Galton supported eugenics
- Therefore, Galton was a Nazi.

The point is the same as we saw for the four-legged dogs and horses. Galton and the Nazis might be employing the idea of eugenics in different ways, and Galton and the Nazis had many different ideas that set them apart. Therefore, the conclusion is at fault. We are not saying there is anything wrong with Galton's work, or with eugenics; rather, if this is the argument against both these sets of ideas, then it is a fallacy, and alternative critiques need to be sought.

The fallacy of affirming the consequent

Another formal fallacy is known as the fallacy of affirming the consequent. Again, it is based on an argument structure:

- If P, then Q
- Q
- Therefore, P.

Here is a common example of this fallacy:

- If someone is human (P), then they are mortal (Q)
- John is mortal (Q)
- Therefore, John is human (P).

In fact, John may be a dog – which is also mortal, but not human. This perhaps may seem like a fairly straightforward problematic argument, but you can see how difficult this type of argument becomes with the following example, where we have simplified the debate to get across the argument.

What is important to note about this fallacy is that the conclusions sought may not always be wrong. For example, it is perfectly likely that John may indeed have been human. However, we must be careful, as such thinking can lead to a misrepresentation of the truth. In fact, sometimes this type of fallacy can even emerge within the psychology literature. A well-known example is based on a Freudian interpretation of repression.

- If someone has repressed a traumatic event (P), then they will have forgotten the event (Q)
- They have forgotten an event (Q)
- Therefore, they have repressed a traumatic event (P).

This argument can be considered as a fallacy as, simply put, it may be that the person never experienced a traumatic event in the first place.

However, there are many more complex, or less easily identified, fallacies within psychology. Indeed, this type of faulty argument, or fallacy, possibly occurs in more complicated forms within this text.

To use an example, we will look at an area we fully discussed earlier (Chapter 15), though we will provide an oversimplified version of this discussion here to illustrate

our point. In 2005, a research IQ psychologist, Richard Lynn, found that men scored higher than women in IQ in adulthood, but not in adolescence. Lynn presents the argument that sex differences in intelligence are the result of sex differences in brain size and maturity rates. There is evidence to suggest that brain size is related to intelligence. Adult men have bigger brains than women, and Lynn argues that this is why men are more intelligent. He presented a developmental theory of sex differences suggesting that, as boys and girls mature at different rates both physically and mentally during childhood, this affects their intelligence. Lynn suggests that, at crucial times during development, girls mature faster than boys. This growth spurt starts at 8 years and slows down at 14 and 15 years. Therefore, girls' brain size, and therefore intelligence, may be similar to that of boys around the start of adolescence at 12–13 years because of this growth spurt. It is only when men and women are both fully mature and boys start to develop larger average brain sizes that the differences in IQ, which last into adulthood, start to develop.

Therefore, Lynn's argument possibly may be a fallacy. Here is the argument:

- If brain size is related to IQ, and there are sex differences in brain size and maturity rates (P), then that would explain why men and women do not differ in intelligence in childhood but differ in adulthood (Q)
- Men and women do not differ in intelligence in childhood but differ in adulthood (Q)
- Therefore, sex differences in intelligence are explained by sex differences in brain size and maturity rates (P).

Therefore, as in the John the dog example, Lynn might be ignoring other issues. An equally plausible explanation is that something happens at the age of adolescence that separates the level of men's and women's intelligence in adulthood – perhaps owing to subject choice in school, conforming to stereotypes or sex differences in the advantages given to certain people at school.

An important point here is that we used this example to illustrate the fallacy. If these ideas were pursued at only a theoretical level, then we might consider this type of thinking or explanation as a possible fallacy. Other theories can be viewed in this way, and very often they need to be empirically investigated to test the argument (as, indeed, Lynn did). You will have been taught how to avoid this fallacy by considering other hypotheses and theories to your findings in your essay and report writing. However, these examples show that we must always be careful about alternative ideas and explanations and how we can avoid the fallacy of affirming the consequent, particularly when theorising.

Argument directed at the person (*argumentum ad hominem*, 'argument directed at the man')

An argument directed at the person is an informal fallacy. An informal fallacy is one that looks to attack an argument, but neither attacks the premise nor the conclusion; rather, it tries to deflect or undermine the issue by attacking the person who is making the argument.

For example, many people argue that one of the problems with Freud's theories (the structure of the mind, defence mechanisms) is that he was a cocaine user and prescribed this drug to his patients. Now, cocaine is a dangerous drug, and it should not be used; and it is true that Freud used cocaine. However, during Freud's time its use was not unlawful because no one was aware of its harmful effects. Indeed, when Freud used it, he was using it for its euphoric effects – something to help address his depression and achieve a sense of well-being – and he was particularly interested in cocaine as an anaesthetic to be used among his patients.

However, whatever the discussion about Freud's use of cocaine, the fact that he used it does not invalidate the theories he put forward. None of their premises or conclusions are based around him, nor around the use of cocaine.

Another example of this type of fallacy is *tu quoque* (Latin for 'You, too'). Imagine you are watching a television talk show, like *Oprah Winfrey*, *Jerry Springer* or *Ricki Lake* (in the United States), or *Trisha* (in the United Kingdom). Someone's behaviour is under discussion; they may have slept with their husband's father, or their best friend's married daughter. The host turns to the audience for questions. You can clearly imagine that someone in the audience may suggest that, whatever the behaviour the person has been undertaking, it might be incorrect. You can also imagine a time when that audience member's criticism has been met with 'You don't know me (what right have you to judge me)' or 'Talk to the hand (cuz the face ain't listening)'. This type of response is a fallacy, a strategy of undermining the argument by saying that the person has no right to judge or that they are not worth talking to about the issue. However, that response has nothing to do with the audience member's concern at the person's behaviour; rather, it is another attempt to deflect their argument.

Of course, we have to be careful, as not all arguments directed at the person are incorrect. For example, if Freud's claims of being aware of the unconscious came at a time when he was taking cocaine, then that might be a concern. If that is the case, then the debate has to shift to whether or not cocaine might have allowed Freud's insight into the unconscious, or whether it is an illusion created by the cocaine use. Whatever the reason, saying Freud's theories are incorrect because he took cocaine isn't sufficient; you need to explore that argument more thoroughly.

Appealing to ignorance or absence of fact (*argumentum ad ignorantiam*, 'argument to ignorance')

An argument appealing to ignorance is a fallacy because it tries to establish an argument by using the absence of evidence as a central or major premise. For example, we might argue, 'Of course there is a Santa Claus; no one has ever proved that there isn't'. It seems silly, of course, but it does apply to some psychological thinking. One area covered in this book is Freudian theory, and his reliance on unconscious and repressed ideas and thoughts. We could equally argue that 'Of course there is an Oedipal complex [a process by which the male child identifies with the father, through the repression and rejection of unconscious love for the mother] because no one has ever proved that there isn't.'

Appeal to popular beliefs (*argumentum ad populum*, 'argument to the people')

An appeal to popular beliefs is a fallacy that suggests an argument, or conclusion, is correct just because people believe it is. Technically, this argument uses the major premise that 'Anything that the majority of people believe must be correct or true.'

The problem with this line of argument is that, just because something is widely believed, that does not mean it is correct. For a long time, the major thinkers of the world believed that the Sun went round the Earth, and that the Earth was flat. These may seem extreme examples, but we do find such thought in psychology today. Some academics argue that genetic or personality influences on behaviour are incorrect because they go against a notion of our own free will. Some academics argue that intelligence testing is wrong because intelligence tests are biased. However, as you will see throughout this text, these arguments arise from popular beliefs rather than being based on fact. For example, you will see in the discussions on intelligence testing that the issues around intelligence testing do not come from intelligence tests themselves, but from issues with theories and interpretation of group differences or differences in what people consider to be intelligence.

Appeal to emotion (*argumentum ad misericordiam*, 'argument to pity')

An appeal to emotion is a fallacy through which someone does not address the premises of the argument, but rather uses a statement to excite the emotions of the people listening. For example, in a debate about the National Health Service, one person might suddenly claim, 'My grandfather believed in having a national health service, and he was a hero in the Second World War'. This fallacy attempts to back up the argument by appealing or manipulating people's emotions. Someone continuing arguing with this person might be met with the response, 'What, don't you agree with my grandfather, who was a national hero who fought for our freedom?' What the person is doing is trying to win the argument, and they are using their grandfather's heroics to try to stop people from disagreeing with the argument.

Again, we do also see this tactic used in psychology regarding statistics. A lot of people, especially those who are critical of the use of statistics in psychology, suggest that such analysis ignores subjective human existence and thought, and so is biased and misleading.

We have to be wary of this sort of argument because it begins to appeal to our emotions, particularly around the need for truth. It is true that statistics rely largely on numerical values and are open to abuse if statistical procedures are misused or misunderstood, but statisticians know this more than do the people who object to statistics. Statistics as a whole is not an entity that routinely abuses facts and figures; it is a method that has been developed and employed to apply objective criteria and make decisions about data that has been collected, mainly because in the past such objectivity wasn't available to scientists. Therefore, any data a researcher collects, be it quantitative or qualitative, must be analysed objectively or openly (e.g. statistically). To suggest that statistics is doing anything more – like deliberately misleading or distorting the truth – is an attempt to appeal to our emotions regarding our need for truth, rather than a reflection of a true understanding of statistics.

False dilemma

A false dilemma occurs when two choices are presented, and you are asked to choose between them when, in fact, there is a third option. For example, the statement 'You're either with us or against us' can present a false dilemma. In all likelihood you may actually not want to take either side, as you have your own views, but what a false dilemma does is to influence the person in the argument.

We can, again, see this fallacy in the practice of psychology. For example, the whole 'nurture versus nature' debate was presented as a false dilemma. Is behaviour the result of genetic influences or environmental influences? The false dilemma wasn't so much around the reasons for behaviours (as people argued they were both), but more or less around our explanations of behaviour. It was felt, originally, that the two were separate entities; divided at the birth of the person, with each separately explaining our behaviour development. However, you have seen (Chapters 8 and 14 on the heritability of behaviour and intelligence) that there are many ways in which genetics and the environment interact, with additive and non-additive genes and prenatal factors, all suggesting a third option to the nurture versus nature debate: 'nature **and** nurture'.

Comparing populations

A statistical fallacy can occur when comparing populations of people. Say, for example, that a statistical agency released figures examining death rates of the British Army during the recent Iran War as well as death rate figures in London (the capital of the United Kingdom). They found that, among the army, death rates were 13 per thousand, while death rates in London were 26 per thousand. You wouldn't be surprised to find, on the announcement of these figures, that a national newspaper ran a headline story concluding that people were safer in the army and being in Iran than they were living in London. However, the problem with this sort of statement is that you are comparing two completely different populations. In the army population you have men and women who are healthy, fit and mostly of a young age; however, in the London population you have a full age range of people, including those with high mortality rates, such as old people and people who are terminally ill and so on. Therefore, the issue is that you are comparing two populations in which several different factors determine death rates.

Again, you will see these issues arising in this text when we look at group differences. This is particularly so for birth order and race differences in intelligence (see Chapters 3 and 14), when people have compared two different populations.

To practise using the standard form of arguments, try your hand at the Stop and think: Reflective exercise.

Stop and think

Reflective exercise

1 Turn these arguments into standard form.
   a Personality and individual differences is an exciting topic in psychology because it considers a variety of psychology perspectives together.
   b People should be more optimistic in life because it is beneficial to their mental health.

2 Using the standard form for the 'optimism' statement, generate a list of possible issues surrounding each of the premises that would test the validity of the argument.

Answers to Stop and think: Reflective exercise

1a Personality and individual differences is an exciting topic in psychology because it considers a variety of psychology perspectives together.

   Major premise: Any topic that considers a variety of psychology perspectives together is exciting
   Minor premise: Personality and individual differences considers a variety of psychology perspectives together
   Conclusion: Therefore, personality and individual differences is an exciting topic.

1b People should be more optimistic in life because it is beneficial to their mental health.

   Major premise: Anything that is beneficial to their mental health people should engage in more
   Minor premise: Being optimistic in life is beneficial to mental health
   Conclusion: Therefore, people should be more optimistic in life.

Example issues might include:

Major premise: Is it necessarily true that anything that is beneficial to one's mental health should be engaged in more? For example:

a Can you have too much of something that is beneficial for mental health? For example, might there be an optimum level of positive thinking, i.e. not too much and not too little?
b Some attitudes might be good for one's own mental health. They may help the person make sense of the world and help them, but they might be considered detrimental in the long term for the individual or might cause difficulties for other people. For example, having an imaginary friend as an adult might help that individual to feel better, but in the long term maintaining a belief in an imaginary friend might not be effectively dealing with the cause of the original mental health difficulty.

Minor premise: Is it necessarily true that being optimistic in life is beneficial to mental health? For example:

a You might look at research data to examine whether optimism is always beneficial to mental health or whether sometimes there is no association and investigate whether sometimes it might be detrimental.
b You might look at research data to examine whether optimism is beneficial to different aspects of mental health (e.g. depression, anxiety, stress).
c You might look at the research data on different aspects of optimism and see how these aspects of optimism are related generally to mental health and different aspects of mental health.

Summary

We have covered some core ideas in academic argument here. We have shown how to put arguments into standard form, given that you have an understanding of what major and minor premises are, and explained how they are crucial to the conclusions we develop in arguments. We outlined the differences between deductive and inductive arguments and looked at some fallacies people use in their arguments.

Going further

Books

- Phelan, P. J. and Reynolds, P. J. (1995). *Argument and evidence: Critical thinking for the social sciences*. London: Routledge.
- Cottrell, S. (2005). *Critical thinking skills: Developing effective analysis and argument* (Palgrave Study Guides). London: Palgrave Macmillan.

- For a more satirical illustration of poor academic thinking and poor use of numbers have a look at Goldacre, B. (2008). *Bad science*. London: Fourth Estate Ltd, and Blastland, M. and Dilnot, A. (2008). *The tiger that isn't: Seeing through a world of numbers*. London: Profile Books.

Explore the website accompanying this text at **www.pearsoned.co.uk/maltby** for further resources to help you with your studies. These include multiple-choice questions, essay questions, web links and ideas for advanced reading.

CHAPTER 27
Statistical Terms

Key themes

- Statistical tests of association
- Statistical tests of difference
- Meta-analysis
- Effect size

Learning outcomes

At the end of this discussion you should be able to show some understanding of the ideas underlying:

- Correlation analysis, and how these statistics can be used to show associations between variables
- Factor analysis, and how this statistical procedure can be used to show primary variables within a number of associations between variables
- Multiple regression analysis, and how this statistical procedure can be used to find key variables within a number of associations between variables
- Test of differences, such as the t-tests and ANOVA, and how these statistics can be used to show differences between variables
- Meta-analysis, and how this procedure can be used to provide overviews of research data
- Effect sizes, and how these procedures can be used to help ascertain the importance of results

Introduction

You are probably aware of the role of statistics in our lives. For one, governments are always producing press releases that hinge on statistical information. For example, in Leicestershire, statistics for the last 3 months of 2004 showed that homelessness fell from 2,560 at the start of 2004 to 2,160 by the end of the year; and in the same area, unemployment was down 0.5 per cent, taking into account seasonal factors. As psychology students, you already know that statistics are powerful things and that you can ask further questions of these statistics. For example, homelessness fell from 2,560 at the start of 2004 to 2,160 by the end of the year, but was that a significant change? Is there a significant association between falls in unemployment and falls in homelessness?

We are aiming to refresh some of your knowledge of statistics here. We will also introduce you to some statistical terms that you haven't come across before, but that are regularly used in this text.

Of course, we realise that mentioning statistics will make you break into a cold sweat. However, now is the chance to put all your hard work in research methods and statistics classes into action. We are going to give you a brief review of statistical terms. We are doing this because we will use these terms at certain points within the book, and you will come across them many times within the research literature. You certainly will have come across some of these terms before.

The main aim of this discussion is to introduce you to some of the statistical methods that are commonly found in this text. By introducing, we mean that we are going to describe what the general test does; we will not be going into detail of how to calculate the test itself. The purpose here, then, is simply to give you a basic understanding of what the statistical test is and does. If you need a more comprehensive and technical breakdown, then we suggest you access a research methods book or a statistics book. You may want to dip in and out of this discussion as you deem necessary, rather than read it all in one go.

Tests of association

First we are going to examine tests of association. These tests are concerned with answering the question of what association occurs between variables. The three tests that we are going to introduce to you are correlation, factor analysis and multiple regression.

Correlation coefficients

A **correlation coefficient** is used to determine the strength of the relationship between two variables, and whether this relationship is positive or negative.

Imagine two variables, *amount of chocolate eaten* and *weight*. It is thought that chocolate contains a lot of fat, and that eating a lot of fat will increase your weight. Therefore, it could be expected that people who eat a lot of chocolate would also weigh a lot. If this were true, then the amount of chocolate you eat and your weight would be positively correlated. In other words, the more chocolate you eat, the more you should weigh.

Conversely, a negative correlation would represent a process by which scores on one variable rise while scores on the other variable fall. An example of this would be the amount of exercise taken and weight. It is thought that taking exercise will usually lead to a decrease in weight. If this were true, then the amount of exercise you take and your weight would be negatively correlated. In other words, the more exercise you take, the less you might weigh.

Finally, some variables might not be expected to show a correlation with each other – for example, the number of hot meals you have eaten and the number of times you have visited the zoo. Usually, we could expect that there would be no logical reason that eating hot meals and zoo visiting would be related, so eating more hot meals would mean you would visit the zoo more, or less (or vice versa). Therefore, you would expect the number of hot meals you have eaten and the number of times you have visited the zoo *not* to show any correlation. We use parametric and non-parametric tests and significance testing to determine whether a correlation occurs between two variables.

An easy way of illustrating this is through scatter plots. Scatter plots are graphs that plot scores for one variable against the scores on another variable. Consider the following three graphs showing scatter plots of scores against two variables, A and B (see Figure 27.1).

Figure 27.1a shows how scores will be when you have a 'positive relationship'. The low values on one variable tend to correspond with low values on the other variable, and high values on one variable correspond with high values on the other. A positive relationship is shown by points plotted moving from the lower left-hand corner up and across to the upper right-hand corner of the chart. You can also have 'negative relationships' between two variables, where the low values on one variable tend to go with high values on the other variable, and vice versa. A scatter plot

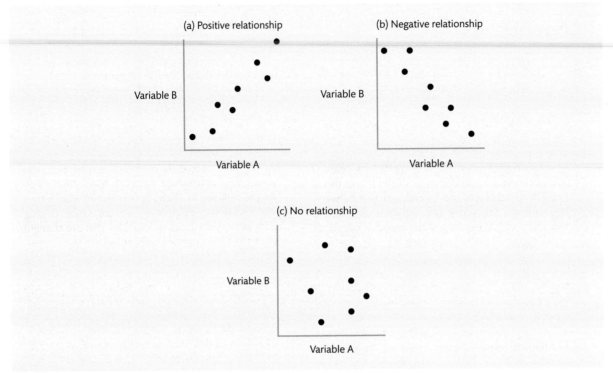

Figure 27.1 Examples of positive, negative and no relationship between two variables.

of a negative relationship would be similar to Figure 27.1b, with the plotted points moving from the upper left-hand corner down and across to the lower right-hand corner of the chart. Finally, Figure 27.1c depicts what scores might be like with no relationship; a more or less random scatter of scores showing no clear direction, going neither up nor down.

A correlation coefficient can be pictured as the single straight line that comes closest to all of the points plotted on a scatter plot of association between two continuous variables. However, using the correlation coefficient is more informative than this; it provides a statistic that tells you the direction, strength and significance of the relationship between two variables.

As a test, the correlation coefficient can take values ranging from +1.00 through 0.00 to −1.00.

- A correlation of +1.00 would be a 'perfect' positive relationship
- A correlation of 0.00 would be no relationship (no single straight line can sum up the almost random distribution of points)
- A correlation of −1.00 would be a 'perfect' negative relationship.

Commonly, then, correlation statistics range from +1 to −1 with researchers, and the symbol of a correlation is *r*. Therefore, researchers will report the direction of correlation coefficients between variables. For example, the

relationship between neuroticism (anxious and worrying personality traits) and depression would be expected to fall within the 0.00 to +1.00 range, while the relationship between extraversion (outgoing, optimistic personality traits) and depression would be expected to fall within the 0.00 to −1.00 range.

However, it is important to remember that the reporting of correlation statistics doesn't stop there. There are two ways of interpreting the strength of the correlation. The first is the significance level. You remember that a lot of statistics involves interpreting whether a statistical test result is significant at either the 0.05 or 0.01 level. Therefore, commonly, researchers report whether the correlation is significant, be it a positive or negative relationship.

Factor analysis

Factor analysis is a multivariate (multiple variables) 'data reduction' statistical technique that allows us to simplify the correlational relationships between a number of variables.

Why would you wish to do so? Imagine if you wanted to look at the relationships between variables 1 to 20. This would imply having to interpret *190* relationships between variables. (For example, variable 1 can be correlated with variables 2 through 20. And, variable 2 can be separately associated with variables 3 through 20, variable 3 with variables 4 through 20 and so on.) Identifying real patterns is

Stop and think

Some things to remember about correlations

1 **Types of correlation tests** You will commonly see two types of correlation tests: Pearson product-moment correlation coefficient and Spearman correlation. Both are reported in similar ways.

2 **Association** You will often find authors reporting the association between the two variables in a Pearson product-moment correlation coefficient, and this is thought to represent the shared variance between two variables. In theory, two variables can share a maximum of 100 per cent of the variance (identical) and a minimum of 0 per cent of variance (not related at all), and the association can be used to indicate the importance of a significant relationship between two variables. The association is found by squaring (multiplying by itself) the r value (r^2) and reporting it as a percentage. Therefore, a correlation of $r = 0.7$ is $0.7 \times 0.7 = 0.49$ and is reported as a percentage, 49 per cent. You often find researchers reporting the variance as part of their discussion, and it is sometimes used as an indicator of importance of the findings (or lack of importance of findings – as the smaller the percentage, the less important is any relationship between the two variables).

   You may think that this contrasts with what we've just mentioned about effect size and the reporting of r as an effect size to determine the importance of your correlation. You would be right, and opinion and practice differ. Some people use r, and some people use r^2. What is important for you to know is that both are used and that you need not be confused when you come across both techniques. You can work out one from the other if you prefer one technique. So, r^2 can be worked out from r by squaring r. And r can be worked out from r^2 by finding out the square root of r^2.

3 **Correlation does not represent causation** It is important to remember, when reporting any sort of correlation, not to immediately infer that one variable *causes* another. Therefore, if we found a relationship between optimism and depression, it would usually be the case that we would not infer causation. Often you will learn that two variables are likely to be influencing each other and/or certainly working together. Therefore, it is important to remember

in your wording always to talk about relationships, associations and correlations between two variables and not to infer that one variable causes another, unless you have a very good reason for thinking that one precedes another.

One good reason for this thinking often occurs in personality, intelligence and individual differences. As you will see in studying personality, intelligence and individual differences, we are often dealing with personality traits or variables that are thought either to have a genetic basis or to have been established in childhood. Therefore, you will often find that personality, intelligence and individual differences psychologists report correlational findings in a way that suggests a causal relationship in that it assumes the personality trait variables do have a stronger influence on another variable (i.e. neuroticism is a predictor of attitudes towards recycling). This is because personality traits (e.g. neuroticism) are thought to emerge from biologically based (e.g. genetic) and learned traits from childhood, and attitudes towards recycling are learned social behaviours that can develop at any point in a person's life.

Therefore it is likely, given these definitions and when these variables are considered together, that personality can be considered as a much stronger general context for understanding attitudes towards recycling (personality influences attitudes towards recycling) and that attitudes towards recycling cannot be considered as a strong general context for understanding personality (e.g. attitudes towards recycling influence personality). However, it is important to remember to watch the language you use when reporting correlations in this way. You should still never write in a way that infers causation, and you should still never say 'cause' (because it is conceivable that someone adopting positive attitudes towards recycling may, over time, change some of their personality behaviours as a result of adopting this attitude). Rather, you can just suggest that neuroticism is likely to be the stronger context to consider this type of relationship because of the theoretical and empirical distinction between the two variables.

---

complicated further because the relationship between, for example, variables 1 and 12 may be affected by the separate relationships each of these variables has with variable 13, with variable 14 and so on. This complicated explanation of 190 relationships is a nightmare for researchers. The

researcher will find it difficult to explain which variable is actually related to which other variables, as they may be uncertain whether the apparent relationship between two variables is genuine, or simply a facet of both variables' relationships with another, third, variable. Indeed, even writing an explanation of multiple correlations is difficult. What factor analysis does is provide a reliable means of simplifying the relationships and identifying within them what *factors*, or common patterns of association between groups of variables, underlie the relationships.

Factor-analytic techniques are a solution to this type of problem, allowing us to look for simple patterns that underlie the correlations between many variables. Yet you may be surprised that you already use factor analysis regularly in your life. Imagine all musicians and music groups in the world. Now, think about the different definitions you can apply to sets of these groups. Some of these artists are very similar; some are very different. However, with the vast majority, you can categorise them as either pop music artists, rap artists or jazz, dance, R&B and so on. What you're doing through this categorising is simplifying a wealth of information regarding music to aid your understanding. So, when someone asks you what sort of music you like, rather than listing lots of groups – Destiny's Child, Justin Timberlake, Jennifer Lopez, Kanye West, Mary J. Blige, Kelis – you might simply say, 'R&B'. Well, factor analysis is very similar to this.

Let us take you through an example of factor analysis. Imagine the following 10 musical artists: Chemical Brothers, Royksopp, Calvin Harris, 50 Cent, Snoop Dogg, Kasabian, Coldplay, Keane, Miles Davis and Charlie Parker. If we were to perform a factor analysis on these music artists, and the extent to which people like them, we might see something like Table 27.1.

What the factor analysis does is determine, first, the number of factors that exist. As you can see, our imaginary factor analysis has four factors. Then, what factor analysis does is determine where on which factor each variable (i.e. each artist) falls by a number. This number, called a loading, can be positive or negative and can range from −1.00 through to +1.00. Regardless of whether the number is positive or negative, the higher the number is on the factor, the more important the variable is to the factor. Kline (1986) has suggested that you should ignore

any number less than 0.3, and other authors have suggested that those numbers of above 0.4 are important.

Using the imaginary factor analysis of music artists, we have shown the loadings above 0.4 in bold. From this analysis we would argue that the music artists broke down into four factors, the first factor being dance (Chemical Brothers, Royksopp, Calvin Harris), the second being rap (50 Cent, Snoop Dogg), the third being indie (Kasabian, Coldplay, Keane) and the fourth being jazz (Miles Davis and Charlie Parker).

You will find reference to factor analysis throughout this text. However, there are two main ways you will see a reference to factor analysis: factor analysis that deals with: (1) simplifying relationships between single questions or items; and (2) simplifying relationships between variables.

Factor analysis of items

You will commonly see factor analysis used on items on a scale. All scales will have several items or questions, and factor analysis can be used to understand the relationships between these items. Therefore, you will see a factor analysis when researchers have devised a new psychological measure, or want to examine existing psychological measures and want to see how the items on that scale break down into different factors, or, indeed, whether they form one factor. So, for example, let us use some items from a popular personality questionnaire, the Eysenck Personality Questionnaire (Eysenck and Eysenck, 1975). You can read more about Eysenck's model of personality in earlier discussions (Chapters 7 and 8); however, for our purposes, let us take two of Eysenck's personality dimensions, neuroticism and extraversion. Neuroticism reflects behaviours such as being anxious, worrying a lot, being nervous and being moody. Extraversion reflects behaviours such as spending a lot of time with other people, being optimistic and generally being happy. These two personality factors are considered as separate. Eysenck has written items for these questionnaires. His neuroticism items include these:

- Do you often feel 'fed up'?
- Would you call yourself a nervous person?
- Are you a worrier?

For extraversion, Eysenck's items include these:

- Can you easily get some life into a rather dull party?
- Are you rather lively?
- Do other people think of you as being rather lively?

Therefore, individuals answering yes to these questions would be considered as showing either neuroticism or extraversion personality behaviours.

If we were to do a factor analysis of these items, we would expect to see something like Table 27.2, with neuroticism and extraversion items forming different factors.

Table 27.1 Imaginary factor analysis of musical artists

	Factor 1	Factor 2	Factor 3	Factor 4
Chemical Brothers	**0.73**	−0.21	0.09	0.21
Royksopp	**0.67**	−0.11	0.12	0.07
Calvin Harris	**0.55**	−0.05	0.03	0.02
50 Cent	0.10	**0.81**	0.18	0.03
Snoop Dogg	0.02	**0.85**	0.21	0.05
Kasabian	0.03	0.23	**0.74**	−0.01
Coldplay	0.14	0.06	**0.65**	0.02
Keane	0.12	0.10	**0.55**	−0.04
Miles Davis	0.25	0.05	0.01	**0.56**
Charlie Parker	0.20	0.02	−0.03	**0.78**

Table 27.2 Factor analysis of neuroticism and extraversion items

	Factor 1	Factor 2
Do you often feel 'fed up'?	0.76	0.14
Would you call yourself a nervous person?	0.82	0.09
Are you a worrier?	0.68	0.07
Can you easily get some life into a rather dull party?	0.01	0.89
Are you rather lively?	0.10	0.83
Do other people think of you as being rather lively?	0.14	0.78

Factor analysis of variables

Another factor analysis you may come across is the attempt to 'combine' different variables to discover new, underlying factors for understanding these differences. This analysis is used to better understand possible theoretical overlaps. It is achieved by using factor-analytic techniques to determine what is a higher-order factor amongst variables and to provide this most simplified account of the psychology surrounding that variable. (An example of this technique is one you will find in Part 2 of this book regarding the measurement of intelligence and something called 'g'.) Without going into too much detail, you will be aware that there are a number of ways in which people might be considered intelligent. People might be considered intelligent if they have good verbal skills, or good mathematical skills, or are flexible in their thinking or are able to think critically. Well, some intelligence theorists, particularly one called Spearman, argued that all these different aspects of intelligence correlated together and represented one underlying factor, 'g'. Therefore, a factor-analytic table of 'g' might look like that given in Table 27.3.

As you can see, factor analysis is an important technique for simplifying relationships between variables.

Table 27.3 Factor analysis of intelligence variables forming 'g'

	Factor 1
Verbal fluency	0.89
Mathematical ability	0.84
Flexible thinking	0.86
Critical thinking	0.83

Multiple regression

Multiple regression is a multivariate (multiple variables) statistical technique that allows researchers to determine which variable, or variables, emerge from a number of independent variables to best predict a dependent variable. As with factor analysis, you may be surprised to find that multiple regression techniques reflect everyday thinking.

Take, for example, a managing director of a toilet paper firm. Now, the director knows how much toilet paper the company sells, but he or she also knows that a number of factors influence the level of sales: TV advertising, customer satisfaction, performance of the sales team, price, product quality, product colour, packaging and so on. What the director wants to do is put some of the company's limited development money into the area that most influences sales. Therefore, what the director might want to do is, through the use of a multiple regression, find out which of the factors that influence levels of sales (independent variables) is the best predictor of toilet paper sales (dependent variable). You, yourself, use it. Every time you write an essay, or discuss in a seminar about different theories that surround a certain behaviour, you are performing a type of multiple regression. In these situations you are often asked to pick three or four variables that are important, and then you are asked to weigh up the available evidence and decide what the most important variables are.

You will see the use of multiple regression in *Personality, Individual Differences and Intelligence* many times. Throughout the text, you will see how modern personality and individual differences researchers compare different theories in psychology to best explain a variable. A researcher might want to find out what factors best predict a certain variable (e.g. depression). Therefore, researchers might compare several psychological variables (e.g. personality variables, coping variables and self-esteem variables) to see which one best predicts that variable.

Tests of difference

In this text, you will also see research that is concerned with comparing differences. These are tests that are concerned with answering the question of whether differences occur between sets of scores based on comparison of the average score (i.e. the mean). Now, the differences between these sets of scores might be based on groups, such as sex or social class, or number of occasions, such as administration of a drug. The two sets of tests we are going to introduce to you are tests of differences when there are *two* sets of scores, and tests of differences when there are *more than two* sets of scores.

Tests of difference for two sets of scores

The main distinction between these two types of statistical tests is that some are used when you are comparing two sets of groups (e.g. sex) and some are used when you are comparing two sets of time (e.g. before and after an exam). Overall, for each set of scores, be it a group or a time, a mean is computed for each set of scores, so that the researcher can see which set of scores, on average, is higher. Then the statistical test is used to determine whether an actual difference (significance) occurs between the two sets of scores.

Therefore, tests such as the independent-samples t-test or the Mann–Whitney U test are used to compare mean scores between two groups of scores. A common example would be to compare male and female scores on a personality scale to examine for sex differences in a personality construct, or to compare two social-class groups (working-class and middle-class people) for scores on an intelligence test. The researcher would then administer, to all respondents, a measure of intelligence or personality. Then they would split the group into two and examine whether a *significant* difference occurs for sex for either intelligence or personality.

Tests such as the related t-test (known as the dependent-groups t-test) or the Wilcoxon pairs tests are used to examine the differences between scores administered to the same sample on two occasions. The related t-test does this by comparing the average mean scores of the same subjects in two conditions, or at two points in time. For example, a researcher may wish to examine students' anxiety levels before and after an exam. The researcher will administer, to each student, a measure of anxiety before the exam (where the researcher might suspect anxiety levels might be high) and a measure of anxiety after the exam (where anxiety levels might be expected to be lower), to examine whether a *significant* difference occurs between anxiety levels before and after exams. However, tests like the related t-test are often used to examine for stability, rather than difference, of constructs over time. For example, as personality traits, or measures of trait behaviour, are expected to be stable over time, you will often see researchers testing for this stability and expecting not to see a difference. Therefore, a researcher who had established a measure of a personality trait, extraversion, would administer their scale to the same sample on two occasions, perhaps 1 year apart, and then use a test such as the related t-test and hope to see that no *significant* difference between scores occurs.

Tests of difference for more than two sets of scores

Tests of difference for more than two sets of scores are commonly known as analysis of variance (ANOVA). They are based on the same distinction as when you are comparing two sets of scores, such as groups or points of time, but are used when you have more than two sets of scores.

Therefore, statistical tests such as ANOVA – between subjects (and another one called the Kruskal – Wallis) are used to see whether a difference occurs between more than two sets of scores. Apart from that, these tests work in a similar way to a test such as the independent samples t-test, by comparing the average mean score between three groups or more. An example of this sort of test would be when a researcher is interested in comparing students from different academic disciplines (mathematics, nursing, psychology and history) on personality measures.

Statistical tests such as ANOVA – within subjects (and another one called the Friedman test) are tests you will see used when the same measure has been administered on three occasions or more. Again, this sort of test works in a similar way to the related t-test by comparing the same variable over a number of occasions. An example of this sort of test would be when a researcher is interested in comparing the same people, at several different times, on their intelligence. For example, a researcher would use a test such as ANOVA – within subjects to see whether a significant difference occurs for intelligence among individuals at the ages of 10 years, 20 years, 30 years and 40 years.

Meta-analysis

Imagine you are a researcher interested in a particular question in a particular area of psychology; say, for example, what is the effect of the personality variable agreeableness on depression? You do a literature search on a web library resource, and get 50 hits. The first study you read, published recently, among 100 US undergraduate students, says there is a small significant positive relationship between agreeableness and depression. The next paper, published around the same time, suggests a larger significant positive relationship among 200 UK adults. A third paper, published 5 years ago among 300 US undergraduate students, suggests there is a significant negative relationship between the two variables. As a researcher, what do you conclude? Do you argue that the evidence is mixed, or do you lend more weight to some findings, such as those studies with large numbers (i.e. more representative samples), or with more standardised samples (i.e. those among general populations rather than undergraduate students)? Well, there is another option: meta-analysis.

Meta-analysis can take many different forms, but today it is a statistical process that is carried out on a variety of studies to look for the overall relationship between the two variables across all the studies and, to a large extent, to average the statistic. We are being slightly cautious when we say this because meta-analysis doesn't simply average the results. All sorts of considerations can be made regarding variations between different studies, such as sample size or the reliability of the measures used.

Meta-analysis can be used for all sorts of statistics – correlations, multiple regressions, t-tests, ANOVA – and will provide an overall summary of the findings. Usually, the meta-analysis statistic representing the effect size is given as a *d*, but it is sometimes given as an *r* (most usually in correlational studies).

There are, however, three issues to remember with meta-analysis. These have been memorably defined by Sharpe (1997) as apples and oranges; file drawer; and garbage in, garbage out.

- **Apples and oranges** – this refers to the adage, often used in discussion, 'it's like comparing apples and oranges' (though you might be more familiar with the phrase 'chalk and cheese'). The phrase is generally understood to mean that apples and oranges cannot be compared. In the same way, Sharpe suggests that meta-analysis may suffer from this problem. For example, as a researcher, you may be looking at the relationship between personality and depression; therefore, you may gather together many studies that have measured depression. Of course, all these studies would have measured different aspects of depression: long-term depression, short-term depression, depressive thoughts, depressive symptoms and depressive scores on different measures of depression. In a meta-analysis, you would combine all these scores into a general construct of depression. However, a concern with such an approach is that you are combining many different aspects of depression (e.g. symptoms, long-term depression, depression scores) that may show different effects with personality. Therefore, in combining many different aspects of depression, you are potentially comparing things that are not the same (i.e. apples and oranges).
- **File drawer** – this concern arises from the finding that studies reporting statistically significant effects and relationships tend to be published, while those with non-significant findings tend not to be published, or remain left in the researchers' file drawers. Therefore, if only significant findings are published in a particular area, then this will distort the findings of the meta-analysis. This is why, when doing meta-analyses, researchers sometimes write to all the other published researchers in the field to ask if they have any unpublished data that can be used in their analysis.
- **Garbage in, garbage out** – this problem is that, if you collate all the data from all the studies that have ever been carried out, some of those studies will be poor-quality studies, while others are likely to be good-quality studies. Studies that are of poor quality will negatively affect the meta-analysis and distort the findings. Therefore, usually, researchers tend to exclude studies on the basis that they are of poorer quality. Many different criteria are used to exclude studies; however, a common one is to omit studies that are unlikely to be representative, or relevant, to the major aims. For example, a meta-analysis of the relationship between neuroticism and depression

might exclude a study that looks at the relationship between the two variables in a group of IT specialists because a study that has used a sample of IT specialists hasn't been derived from the general population.

Effect size

The consideration of the importance of findings is now common practice in statistics. This importance of findings has become what is known as **effect size**. The consideration of effect size is an important addition to statistical testing through significance. Why? Well, significance levels depend on sample size. The larger the sample size, the lower the criteria are for finding a significant result. For example, while a correlation of 0.2 is not significant among a sample of 50 participants, a correlation of 0.2 will be significant among a sample of 1,000 participants. This has led to an interesting dilemma for researchers. Imagine two drug trials, one with drug A and one with drug B, both designed to help one particular illness.

- In drug trial 1 with drug A, among 50 participants, the correlation between drug A and improvement of patients was $r = 0.32$. The probability value was $P = 0.10$, a non-significant result.
- In drug trial 2 with drug B, among 1,000 participants, the correlation between drug B and improvement with patients was $r = 0.22$. The probability value was $P = 0.01$, a significant result (although the correlation statistic is larger in the first study).

If we studied these two drug trials separately, we would come to different conclusions about the relationship between the two drugs and patient improvement. We would, based on significance testing, be likely to recommend drug B because there was a significant relationship between the drug and patient improvement, even though drug A had a stronger association with patient improvement.

This has led to a general rethink about reporting statistics, and about the notion of considering effect size when reporting statistics.

There are two sets of criteria that centre around effect size, one criterion for tests of difference and one for tests of correlation. For statistical tests of difference, that deal with differences in means (see independent groups *t*-test, etc.), effect size is often labelled as *d*. The criteria of 0.2 (small), 0.5 (medium) and 0.8 (large), introduced by US statistician Jacob Cohen (Cohen, 1988) to label the effect size *d* (or Cohen's *d* as it often referred to), are often computed and given alongside reports for differences between means in papers as a way of determining the strength of the finding. Even luckier for us at this stage, when it comes to correlation statistics, the *r* value is considered the indicator of effect size. So, with correlation, statistics of $r = 0.1$ and below are viewed as small, $r = 0.3$ as medium (or moderate) and $r = 0.7$ as large. Again, remember these values are used as indicators of your findings to help you in your consideration. If you have a significant correlation of 0.25, it is perhaps important not to conclude that this is a strong relationship. More important, if you have found a number of significant correlations or differences in your reading or study, you can judge the relative importance of the findings by the effect size statistic. Effect size criteria can be used to determine which correlations represent more important findings and which are less important.

Of course, things are not always that straightforward and often other symbols are used to indicate effect size. We

are now going to list the effect size statistic to be used for a variety of statistical tests. We are going to do this because you are going to come across it in the literature. You can recognise this statistic as an indicator of effect size, rather than be confused by it.

These effect size statistics are used for the following statistics:

- Correlations (Pearson and Spearman) – commonly r
- Multiple regression – r^2
- t-tests (including non-parametric versions) – d
- ANOVA – n^2 (eta squared)
- Meta-analysis – d, but sometimes r (when dealing with correlational statistics).

Summary

The preceding work outlines several statistical terms that you will come across in the text. Having read this discussion, you should now use it as a reference text, and you may want to refer to it again at certain stages.

Going further

Books

- Sometimes it good to see how mathematics relates to everyday life to help you feel more at ease with numbers. Two such books that might help you do this

are: Wyndham, J., Eastaway, R. and Rice, T. (2005). *Why do buses come in threes?: The hidden mathematics of everyday life*. London: Robson Books Ltd, and Eastaway, R. and Wyndham, J. (2003). *How long is a piece of string?* London: Robson Books Ltd.

Explore the website accompanying this text at **www.pearsoned.co.uk/maltby** for further resources to help you with your studies. These include multiple-choice questions, essay questions, web links and ideas for advanced reading.

CHAPTER 28
Research Ethics

Key themes

- What are research ethics?
- Why do we need ethical codes?
- Basic principles for ethical research
- Ethical principles for conducting research with human participants (The British Psychological Society research code of ethics)

Learning outcomes

At the end of this discussion you should:

- Understand the purpose of research ethics
- Be familiar with the basic principles underlying ethical research
- Be aware that there are special procedures for gaining ethical approval for NHS and Social Services research
- Know the principles underlying the British Psychological Society research code of ethics

Introduction

Research ethics, as in all areas of psychology, are important to personality, intelligence and individual differences. However, we think it is crucial to highlight ethics because some of these areas – particularly personality and intelligence testing, the use of psychometric tests, studies on animal behaviour and the examination of mental aspects of individuals – deal with potentially difficult and important topics. Therefore, it is important that you understand the ethical issues that surround the literature you are reading in *Personality, Individual Differences and Intelligence*.

What do we mean by research ethics?

The terms 'ethics' and 'morals' tend to be used interchangeably. Francis (1999) makes a useful distinction between the two. He suggests that morals generally refer to an unwritten set of values that provide a frame of reference that we use to help our decision-making and regulate our behaviour. Ethics generally refers to a written code of value principles that we use in a particular context. Research ethics are therefore the principles that we use to make decisions about what is acceptable practice in any research project.

Why do we need ethical codes?

Research participants have moral and legal rights, and it is important that, as researchers, we do not violate these rights. Individual researchers may not always share common moral values. This can result in very different judgements being made about what are acceptable and unacceptable ways to treat research participants. Sometimes enthusiasm for the research topic can lead researchers to pay less attention to the experience of the research participant as they are so focused on answering their research question. A code of research ethics is required to ensure that there are agreed standards of acceptable behaviour for researchers in order to protect participants' moral and legal rights.

In addition to protecting the individual participant, research ethics codes ensure that there is good scientific practice in research. They help to maintain scientific integrity. It is essential that the public be able to trust the results of research programmes, as these findings may significantly affect their lives. Having researchers conform to codes of research ethics protects against scientific dishonesty and fraudulent results. Most universities and professional bodies, such as the British Psychological Society, have research ethics policies and codes of conduct that all researchers have to comply with, so seriously do they take this issue.

Basic principles for ethical research

In this section we are going to outline the basic principles for ethical research.

Research studies have to comply with all legal requirements

Legal requirements for research studies include the data protection legislation and appropriate screening of researchers working with vulnerable groups of people. Undertaking research involving animals or biomedical research requires strict compliance with licensing requirements.

Research is required to comply with the commonly agreed international standards for good practice in research that are laid down in the Declaration of Helsinki in 1989. The World Medical Association developed the Declaration of Helsinki as a statement of ethical principles to provide guidance to researchers involving human subjects. Under this declaration it is seen as the duty of a researcher to promote and safeguard the health of the people they are using as research participants. These principles of the declaration can be categorised as:

- beneficence (do positive good)
- non-malfeasance (do no harm)
- informed consent
- confidentiality/anonymity.

While there are now a huge number of ethical codes in existence, most codes refer to the Declaration of Helsinki as encapsulating their core values. In the United Kingdom, for example, the National Health Service (NHS) has played a key role in developing ethical codes and regulatory practices for health service research, assisted by directives from the European Community Parliament. The NHS developments were in response to public concerns after well-publicised cases in which, for example, organs from deceased infants were used for medical research without the parents' knowledge or consent. Examples such as these get across the importance of complying with strict ethical codes. They protect participants and their families and ensure that the public has confidence in what researchers do.

Research participants

The welfare of all participants needs to be a prime concern of researchers, and all research needs to undergo ethical scrutiny. Research with individuals who are termed 'vulnerable' participants needs very careful consideration. Vulnerable participants can be defined as follows:

- Infants and children under the age of 18, or 16 if they are employed (Criminal Justice and Court Services Act, 2000)
- Vulnerable adults, defined as:
  - people with learning or communication difficulties;
  - patients in hospital or under the care of social services;
  - people with mental illness, including those with addictions to drugs and alcohol.

If you wish to recruit vulnerable participants as just defined, then you need to consider where you will be interacting with them. If you wish to undertake research with vulnerable populations that require you to be on your own with the individual in a private interview room or the like, then you will need to undergo Criminal Records Bureau Screening. Your university will be able to provide you with information about this screening. It will take some time, so you need to schedule this if it is necessary for your research. You may also be required to pay for the screening. It may be that you can arrange supervised access to your research participants. For example, you may interact with children in a public place such as the corner of a classroom or in the presence of a teaching assistant or some other public venue within the institution where you are not alone with the participant for significant amounts of time. These are

issues that you will have to discuss when arranging access to your research participants.

There are several other factors related to research ethics that you have to consider when designing your research project. These factors are summarised in Figure 28.1 and are listed below, and each will be discussed in turn.

Obtaining consent

Where possible, participants should be informed about the nature of the study. All aspects of the research that are likely to affect a person's willingness to participate in your study should be disclosed. This might include the time it is likely to take, particularly if you require significant amounts of their time. You are seeking to get informed consent from your participants, so they need to be adequately briefed. For research involving vulnerable participants, getting informed consent may involve briefing parents, teachers or caregivers about the study.

For some standard questionnaire studies, for example where the topic of the research is not a particularly sensitive issue, it may be sufficient to include a description of your study at the start of your questionnaire; completion of the questionnaire is generally accepted to imply consent. Your university will have rules here, and you must comply with them.

Observational research

Unless the participants give their consent to being observed, observational research must take place only where those observed could normally expect to be observed by strangers. Observational studies must not violate the individual's privacy and psychological well-being. You should also be sensitive to any cultural differences in definitions of public and private space.

Protection of participants

The Declaration of Helsinki that we discussed earlier provides the guiding principles here. As a researcher you must take care at all times to protect your participants from physical and mental harm. If potentially distressing questions may be asked, participants must have the right not to answer these questions, and this must be made clear to them at the start. If negative consequences might ensue, then the researcher has to detect and remove these effects. This might involve having telephone numbers of help lines or counselling services that participants could contact if they wanted to discuss the issues further. In research with children, you must not discuss the results you obtain from individual children with teachers and parents. In all cases, you can only report back your anonymised results.

Consent	Observational research
Protection of participants	Deception
Debriefing	Withdrawal from the research
Confidentiality	Data storage

Figure 28.1 Factors related to research ethics that you have to consider when designing your research project.

Deception

In most psychological research, deception should not be necessary. Sometimes, however, participants may modify their behaviour if they know what the researcher is looking for; in this case, by giving a full explanation to participants, you cannot collect reliable data. Deception should be used only when no other method can be found for collecting reliable data and when the seriousness of the question justifies it. A distinction is made between deliberately deceiving participants and withholding some information. Deliberate deception is rarely justifiable. Withholding of information does occur more frequently. This might mean, for example, giving your questionnaire a general title such as *An Exploration of Social Attitudes* rather than saying which attitudes in particular you are interested in. The guiding principle should be the likely and possible reactions of participants when the deception is revealed. If participants are likely to be angry or upset in some other way, then deception should not occur. If deception is involved, then you need to seek ethical approval for your study.

Debriefing

When deception has occurred, debriefing is particularly emphasised; however, it should be a part of all research to monitor the experience of the participants for any unanticipated negative effects. This may involve providing participants with written information describing the study and/or the contact details of help lines or counselling services or healthcare agencies that participants can contact if they want to discuss the issues further. Participants should also know how to contact you after the study. Generally, the inclusion of your university e-mail address is the best option; but again, here your university will have procedures.

Withdrawal from the research

Sometimes individuals may get distressed – during an interview, for example – and you must make it clear that they can withdraw from the study at any time without giving any reason. It may be that a participant decides after an interview that they have said things that they now regret. Participants should be able to withdraw their interview data in cases such as this. It is good practice in your participant information sheet, if you are interviewing on sensitive issues, to give a cut-off date up to which participant data can be withdrawn. This will normally be up to the time when you intend to start your data analysis. Remember that your participant information sheet and consent form comprise a contract between you, the researcher and your participants, so you must not make claims in it that you cannot deliver. A common instance of this is where consent forms unconditionally state that participants can withdraw their data. Once your data is analysed, withdrawal becomes more difficult; hence, it is a good idea to give a cut-off point for withdrawal.

Confidentiality

Here you must conform to data protection legislation, which means that information obtained from a research participant is confidential unless you have agreed in advance that this is not to be the case. So, you must take care to anonymise data that you obtain from participants, say, in interview studies. To do this you must not only change names but also change any details that might make the person easily identifiable. This should be done at the transcription stage, when interviews are recorded. You are required to assure your participants that they will have confidentiality. If you cannot successfully anonymise data, as in the case where you might be interviewing head teachers and there are only six in your area, then you have to make it clear to your participants that they may be identifiable. For example, in a qualitative study, their quotes may be recognisable, and here you need to come to an arrangement with the individual. They may not mind being recognised, although they may wish to see the quotes you intend to use before making your study publicly available to your university or to the general public in print.

Data storage

If the data you are collecting from participants is not confidential, then you must take special precautions to store the data appropriately to ensure the participants' anonymity. This means that tapes should be kept securely, and they should not be labelled with participants' real names. If it is necessary to be able to identify your participants' data, perhaps to match up data collected at a later time or at a second interview or the like, the key you use to match each participant to their data must be kept securely and separately from both the tapes and the transcripts. Interview tapes and other confidential material should be disposed of carefully when no longer required. You need to think carefully about where you transcribe such material, so that it is not overheard by others. The aim is keep the data confidential at all times.

NHS and social services/social care research

You need to be aware that NHS and social services and social care research that involves social services requires you, by law, to go through separate ethical approval and related processes. These procedures were developed, as mentioned earlier, to prevent some of the ethical issues arising in future that have brought adverse publicity to the NHS and to ensure that the research carried out conforms to sound ethical principles. The procedures are complex and time-consuming, but full details are available at the NHS web link given below.

Ethical principles for conducting research with human participants (The British Psychological Society)

We have discussed some general principles of research ethics, based on issues arising from the Declaration of Helsinki. However, a more detailed and definitive guide for psychologists was provided by The British Psychological Society in 1992 and updated in 2005 and 2009. The code can be found at the following link: **www.bps .org.uk/sites/default/files/documents/code_of_ethics _and_conduct.pdf**

Going further

Web links

All projects with NHS or Social Services involvement have to be presented for ethical review to an NHS or Social Care Research Ethics Committee. Applications for both are now handled through an online Integrated Research Application System (IRAS). Full details of the IRAS process and forms for doing this can be accessed at **www.myresearchproject.org.uk**. Under the NHS Research Governance Framework, approval to undertake the research must normally be obtained before the proforma is submitted. Details can be found at **www.dh.gov.uk/ en/Aboutus/Researchanddevelopment/index.htm**. This site also provides the definition of research used by the NHS and Social Care committees.

Explore the website accompanying this text at **www.pearsoned.co.uk/maltby** for further resources to help you with your studies. These include multiple-choice questions, essay questions, web links and ideas for advanced reading.

GLOSSARY

ABC format. Model used to illustrate the role of cognitions and behaviours within us; particularly concentrates on how people become emotionally disturbed or self-defeating. In other words, from the adversities (A), individuals bring their beliefs, values, purposes, etc. (B) to these As. They then feel and act 'disturbedly' at point (C) – their emotional and behavioural consequences. The key to learning optimism lies in the formation of belief (at B); in other words, how you may think and feel about bad things, or misfortunes (adversity – A) will actually determine the consequences (C) that you will face.

Ability traits. Traits that determine how well you deal with a particular situation and how well you reach whatever your goal is in that situation.

Above-average ability. Within Renzulli's three-ring theory of giftedness, above-average ability, at a general level, represents high levels of abstract thought, adaptation to novel situations and the ability to retrieve information rapidly and accurately.

Abreaction. The discharge of upsetting emotions relating to their conflicts, in a therapy session.

Abstract conceptualisation. Learning by creating theories to explain our observations and behaviours.

Abstract reasoning. To use the faculty of reason; think logically with abstract material.

Acceptance of uncertainty. Refers to individuals who completely accept the fact that we live in a world of probability and chance, where there are not – and probably never will be – any absolute certainties.

Accommodating. A learning style that is a combination of concrete experience and active experimentation.

Activating event. Within Ellis' ABC model, the activating event (A in the model) is usually an event of an unpleasant nature that causes some unhappiness.

Active experimentation. Learning by using theories to solve problems and make decisions.

Actual selves. A term to describe how individuals really state, how they really are (as opposed to ideal selves).

Adaptability. In the emotional intelligence literature, this is the ability to manage and control emotions.

Adaptation. A biological structure, process or behaviour of a member of the species that enabled members' species to survive in response to the (changed) environment, not only over other species but also over other members of the same species.

Additive genetic variance. Variation caused by the effects of numerous genes which combine in the defining of phenotypic behaviour.

Admixture hypothesis. A hypothesis used to explain the relationship between birth order and IQ. What this hypothesis suggests is that parental intelligence and socioeconomic status are additional factors to consider in the relationship between birth order and IQ scores, coupled with the fact that parents with lower IQ scores tend to have more children.

Adoption studies. Studies where comparisons are made between siblings, twins, reared apart, parents (both biological and non-biological) and adopted children to examine the extent of genetic and environmental effects on behaviour and personality.

Affect regulation. An area used by Siever and Davis to describe the association between neurotransmitters and personality disorders relating to levels of regulation of feelings and mood.

Agency. A component of hope; reflects an individual's determination that goals can be achieved; the mental determination or belief to go after that specific goal.

Aggregated individual discrimination. Part of social dominance theory; refers to the simple and sometimes unnoticeable individual acts of discrimination by one individual against another.

Aggregated institutional discrimination. Part of social dominance theory; explains social hierarchy as the result of the procedures and actions of social institutions, such as the political organisations, church, courts and schools.

Agoraphobia. An abnormal fear of open or public places.

Agreeableness. Warm, trustful, courteous, agreeable, cooperative personality traits.

Alarm reaction. Where the nervous system becomes physically aroused to cope with the demand for action.

Alpha range. A range within the wave signals provided by the brain. The alpha range is considered to reflect low states of arousal.

Altruism. Attitudes and behaviours that represent an unselfish concern for the welfare of others.

Amygdala. A neural structure that is part of the temporal lobe of the cerebrum; connected with the hypothalamus and the hippocampus. It is part of the limbic system and plays an important role in motivation and emotional behaviour.

Analogy. A comparison based on a similarity between two things that are otherwise dissimilar.

Analysis of variance (ANOVA) – between subjects. A parametric statistical test used to see whether a difference occurs between more than two groups of scores.

Analysis of variance – within subjects. A parametric statistical test used when the same measure has been administered on three occasions or more.

Anthropomorphic projections. Attribution of human motivation, characteristics or behaviour to inanimate objects, animals or natural phenomena.

Antisocial personality disorder. Engages in persistent lying and stealing, has a lack of empathy for others, shows recklessness and consistently fails to plan or keep to long-term goals, shows an inability to make or maintain friends or personal relationships, has recurring difficulties with the law, unable to control their own anger and temper and shows a tendency to violate the rights and boundaries of others.

Antonyms. A word having a meaning opposite to that of another word.

Anxiety. A psychological and physiological state characterised by feelings that are typically associated with uneasiness, fear or worry.

Anxiety/inhibition. An area used by Siever and Davis to describe the association between neurotransmitters and personality disorders relating to levels of anxiety and inhibition.

Anxious–avoidant. A type of attachment style. An insecure attachment where children do not appear too distressed when separated from a caregiver, and, upon reunion, actively avoid seeking contact with their parent.

Anxious–resistant. A type of attachment style. An insecure attachment style where children are ill at ease, and upon separation from a caregiver they become distressed. When reunited with their mother, these children have a difficult time being calmed down or soothed.

Apa. American Psychological Association.

Applied individual differences. Research that is not only interested in the general perspectives of psychology (such as social, developmental and cognitive, etc.), but is committed to understanding how these differences affect 'applied' settings, such as occupational, clinical and non-clinical, health and mental health and education.

Applied value. The usefulness of a theory as containing rules that can be applied to solve problems.

Approach–approach conflict. Describes the situation where there are two equally desirable goals, but they are incompatible.

Approach–avoidance conflict. Describes the situation where there is one goal; but, while an element of it is attractive, an aspect of it is equally unattractive.

Armchair speculation. A methodology that can be used by anyone; it involves making good, unbiased observations of how people behave in certain situations and then generating and testing hypotheses about these behaviours. This method allows deep knowledge due to observations in different situations in life, as opposed to only within the therapy room.

Ascending reticular activating system (ARAS). This system, which is located in the brain stem, manages the amount of information or stimulation that the brain receives.

Assimilating. A learning style that is a combination of observation, reflection and abstract conceptualisation.

Associational fluency. A highly specific ability to produce rapidly a series of words or phrases associated in meaning.

Associative memory. Ability to recall one part of a previously learned but unrelated pair of items.

Assortative mating. When individuals mate with individuals that are like themselves (positive assortative mating) or dissimilar (negative assortative mating). These two types of assortative mating are thought to have the effect of reducing and expanding the range of variation of heritable traits.

Asymmetrical in-group bias. An aspect of behavioural asymmetry. Dominant groups will tend to display higher levels of in-group favouritism or bias than subordinate groups will.

Attachment style. Considered to be a major component of relationships, and suggests that our childhood attachments influence our adult relationships.

Attitudes. One of three dynamic traits in Cattell's theory of personality. Attitudes represent a specific trait and help to predict how we will behave in a particular situation.

Attributes of the observer. Key characteristics of the person observing the behaviour.

Auditory processing. Abilities relating to the functions of hearing.

Authoritarianism (right wing). Thought to comprise a set of right-wing behaviours, showing excessive conformity, intolerance of others, rigid and stereotyped thought patterns.

Autonomy. Self-determining and independent

Avoidance–avoidance conflict. Describes the situation where the individual is faced with what they perceive to be two equally undesirable alternatives.

Avoidant personality disorder. Considered the most severe form of social anxiety; shows a detached personality pattern, meaning that the person purposefully avoids people due to fears of humiliation and rejection. Typical behaviours of someone with this disorder include a reluctance to become involved with people, having no close friends, exaggerating potential difficulties and avoiding activities or occupations involving contact with others.

Awfulising. Statements characterised by words like 'awful', 'terrible', 'horrible', etc. Awfulising occurs when individuals believe that unpleasant or negative events are the worst that they could possibly be. In other words, the person exaggerates the consequences of past, present or future events, seeing them as the worst that could happen.

Axis I. A classification within *The Diagnostic and Statistical Manual of Mental Disorders–IV (DSM-IV)*. This axis includes all clinical disorders, including all major mental, developmental and learning disorders.

Axis II. A classification within *The Diagnostic and Statistical Manual of Mental Disorders–IV (DSM-IV)*. This axis relates to underlying personality conditions or disorders.

Axis III. A classification within *The Diagnostic and Statistical Manual of Mental Disorders–IV (DSM-IV)*. This axis relates to acute (severe) medical conditions and physical disorders.

Axis IV. A classification within *The Diagnostic and Statistical Manual of Mental Disorders–IV (DSM-IV)*. This axis relates to environmental and psychosocial factors contributing to the mental disorder.

Axis V. A classification within *The Diagnostic and Statistical Manual of Mental Disorders–IV (DSM-IV)*. This axis relates to the assessment of functioning of the individual. It is the overall levels of psychological, social and occupational functioning.

Basic anxiety. Within Horney's theory of personality, basic anxiety is described as a feeling of being isolated and helpless in a potentially hostile world.

Basic needs theory. A subtheory of social determination theory that proposed three main universal, innate and psychological intrinsic needs that influence an individual's self-determination.

Basic personality structure approach. A psychological anthropology approach that compares the traits of the individuals of each society to achieve a basic personality for each culture.

Behaviour potential. The likelihood of a specific behaviour occurring in a particular situation.

Behavioural approach system (BAS). Comprises motivations to approach. This system causes the individual to be sensitive to potential rewards and to seek those rewards.

Behavioural asymmetry. Part of social dominance theory; refers to the fact that members of dominant and subordinate groups will act differently in a wide variety of situations.

Behavioural factors. Aspects of an individual's behaviour.

Behavioural genetics. The field of research that attempts to quantify the genetic contribution to behaviour and to locate specific genes, or groups of genes, associated with behavioural traits.

Behavioural inhibition. A tendency in babies to restrain their own impulses or desires.

Behavioural inhibition system (BIS). Comprises motivations to avoid. Within this system are those motivations that make the individual sensitive to punishment or potential and inclined to avoid those punishments.

Behavioural signature of personality. If … then … propositions that represent our characteristic reactions to situations.

Behaviourism. This describes a school of psychology, founded by J. B. Watson, where the focus is purely on observable aspects of behaviour. Within this approach individuals are understood in term of their learning history.

Being cognition (B-cognition). The different style of thinking adopted by self-actualisers. It is non-judgemental and involves feelings of being at one with the world. It is a transient state experienced at times of self-actualisation.

Being motives (B-motives). See growth motives.

Belief system. Beliefs, values and purposes (*B* in the model) of an individual, used specifically within Ellis' ABC model.

Beta range. A range within the wave signals provided by the brain. The beta range is considered to reflect activity.

Big optimism. Used by researchers to understand the differences between the two main theories of optimism. Big optimism is dispositional optimism.

Biologisation. An emphasis for arguments put forward by biological and evolutionary psychology.

Birth order. The order that children have been born into a family. Adler contributed significantly to the development of an individual's style of life.

B-love or Being-love. Involves being able to love others in a non-possessive, unconditional way. It is simply loving them for being. It is a growth need, and Maslow sees it as representing an emotionally mature type of love.

Borderline personality disorder. Characterised by unstable personal relationships, poor impulse control over things such as spending money, their sexual conduct and substance misuse or abuse.

Brain stem. The portion of the brain that connects the spinal cord to the forebrain and cerebrum and controls the cardiovascular and respiratory functions.

Broad heritability. A statistical estimate of the total genetic variation in a population; refers to both additive genetic variance and non-additive genetic variance.

Burnout. A state of emotional, mental and physical exhaustion caused by excessive and prolonged stress.

Cardinal traits. Single traits that may dominate an individual's personality and heavily influence their behaviour. These may be thought of as obsessions or ruling passions that produce a need that demands to be fulfilled.

Castration anxiety. When boys become aware that girls do not possess a penis, they respond by becoming anxious about the thought of losing their own penis. It has come to have a wider meaning in society, referring to a male's worry about losing his power, especially to a woman.

Catharsis. The physical expression of emotions associated with our earlier conflicts within the therapy session.

Cathexis. Refers to the way that libidinal energy becomes invested in the object or person that is providing satisfaction of the current instinctual need.

Causality orientation theory. A subtheory of social determination theory that looks at the role of individual differences in motivational orientations.

Central traits. The five to ten traits that Allport felt best describe an individual's personality. They are generally applicable to that person regardless of situational factors.

Characteristic adaptations. Individual motives, personal goals, self-image, schemas, significant life experiences that have been identified as influences on personality.

Characteristics of the model. Main features of the approach.

Child-driven effects. How differences between children within the same family will influence different reactions in the parents to how they treat the child.

Child-effects model. Describes genetic transmission of phenotypes; suggesting that the genes cause the behaviour, which in turn causes the same or similar behaviour in the parent.

Choice corollary. The process whereby people make judgements about their reality, choosing the alternative that in their view best fits the situation. Kelly saw individuals as free to choose and claimed that people generally make choices that increase their understanding of the world, and in this way they grow as individuals.

Choleric temperament. Describing an individual who has a tendency to be easily angered.

Circumplex Theory of Affect. A model of mood that comprises positive and negative affect.

Circumspection-pre-emption-control (CPC) cycle. Within Kelly's personal construct theory, this cycle describes the way that we behave when we are faced with a situation.

Circumstantial. Used by Seligman in optimism and helplessness theory; describes when a person has learned to attribute their failures in situations to do with factors outside or external to the individual (*compare to* Internal/Internal factors).

Classical conditioning. A form of associative learning that studies the relationship between a stimulus and the response to it.

Clinical theories. A methodology that involves observing differences among therapists' patients, or clients. In other words, within the therapy setting, the therapist is allowed access to the individual nature of their client and can see at first hand how that client either deviates from or conforms to the generalisations of psychological theory.

Cognitive-affective processing system (CAPS). Mischel and Shoda's model of personality; emphasises the individual's mental and emotional processes as essential components.

Cognitive-affective units (CAUs). Include the individual's representations of self, others, situations, expectations, beliefs, long-term goals, values, emotional states, competencies, self-regulatory systems and memories of people and past events.

Cognitive assessment system (CAS). An IQ test designed to measure cognitive processing, integrating theoretical and applied areas of psychological knowledge, thereby assessing how knowledge is organised and accessed in the memory system, as well as assessing how various intellectual tasks are achieved.

Cognitive evaluation theory (CET). A subtheory of social determination theory that describes how intrinsic motivations are affected by social context and specifically influenced by external events.

Cognitive/perceptual. An area used by Siever and Davis to describe the association between neurotransmitters and personality disorders relating to cognitive and perceptual functioning.

Cognitive processing speed (Gs). The ability to perform cognitive tasks automatically and fluently.

Cognitive psychology. An area of psychology that investigates internal mental processes such as problem-solving, perception, memory and language.

Cognitive stimulation hypothesis. Assumption suggesting that higher intelligence scores are derived from improvements in cognitive stimulation such as improved schooling, different parental rearing styles, better educated parents, smaller families and greater availability of educational toys.

Collective agency. Describes the situation where a group of individuals come together believing that they can make a difference to their own and/or others' life circumstances.

Combining theories. Research technique that involves combining different theories to discover new, underlying factors for understanding individual differences and is used to better understand possible theoretical overlaps. It is achieved by using factor-analytic techniques to examine higher-order factors amongst psychological theories and individual differences variables to provide a parsimonious account of the psychology surrounding that variable.

Commitment. A component of Sternberg's triangular theory of love, concerned with cognitive functioning; represents aspects of love that involve both the short-term decision that one individual loves another and the longer term commitment to maintain that love. In the investment model, commitment represents a psychological attachment to the relationship.

Common traits. Ways of classifying groups of individuals, with one group being classified as being more dominant, happier or whatever than another comparable group.

Communal relationships. Relationships based on altruistic motives.

Communality corollary. Refers to Kelly's view that individuals who share similar constructions of their experience are alike psychologically. This means that they will behave in similar ways.

Comparing theories. Research technique involves comparing different theories in psychology to find the best explanation for the 'how' and 'why' individuals differ. This is usually done by testing various theories and using multiple regression techniques to discover the best predictor of a particular behavioural difference.

Comparison level. Within theories of social and personal relationships, refers to the fact that people make comparisons within their lives all the time.

Componential subtheory. Subtheory of the triarchic theory of intelligence; refers to the mental mechanisms that underlie intelligent behaviour.

Comprehensiveness. Large in scope or content, to include much detail.

Compulsiveness. A person with behavioural patterns governed by a compulsion (e.g. repeated acts of behaviour).

Concordance. The rate of co-occurrence of a phenotype between individuals; for example, pairs of twins.

Concrete experience. Learning by being involved in a new experience.

Concurrent validity (or criterion validity). A type of validity that assesses a test's acceptable correlations with known and accepted standard measures of that construct.

Conditions of worth. The criteria we use to judge the adequacy of our own behaviour. They are based on other people's judgements about what is desirable behaviour.

Configurationalist approach. A school of thought in psychological anthropology that argues that the culture takes on the character of all its members' personalities.

Confluence model. A hypothesis used to explain the relationship between birth order and IQ. The model suggests that intellectual development, and thus intelligence, must be understood in the context of the family and an ever-changing intellectual environment within the family.

Conscientiousness. Practical, cautious, serious, reliable, organised, careful, dependable, hardworking, ambitious personality traits.

Conscious mind. Consists of the thoughts, memories, urges or fantasies that we are actively aware of at any given moment.

Consequence. What happens after a response; consequence is crucial, as it affects the probability of the response being repeated.

Consequences. In Ellis' ABC model, the Consequences (C in the model) are the emotional and behavioural reactions that occur as a result of the activating event (A in the model) and belief system (B in the model).

Consequences of imitating behaviour. The results or outcomes of reproducing or copying behaviour.

Conservatism. Conservative attitudes include religious fundamentalism, pro-establishment politics, advocacy of strict rules and punishment, militarism, intolerance of minority groups, conventional tastes in art or clothing, restrictions on sexual activity, opposition to scientific progression and the tendency to be superstitious.

Constellatory constructs. Refers to how we sometimes cluster information within our personal construct system so that membership of a particular construct implies that other constructs apply. Stereotypes are a good example of constellatory constructs.

Constitutional traits. The genetically determined personality traits in Cattell's system.

Construct validity. A type of validity that seeks to establish a clear relationship between a concept at a theoretical level and the measure that has been developed.

Construction corollary. Refers to the way we construct meaning for what is going on, and then we use this construction to help us understand and deal with future situations. Our constructions may be verbal or preverbal. Constructs represent the discriminations that we make when we perceive events.

Constructive alternativism. Refers to Kelly's assumption that we are all capable of altering our present interpretation of events or adopting entirely new interpretations.

Constructiveness versus destructiveness and activity versus passivity. The voice and loyalty strategies are relatively constructive responses as they involve the attempt to maintain or improve the relationship, whereas the exit and neglect strategies are considered to be more destructive to the relationship.

Contents. A term used in Guilford's Structure of Intellect (SI) theory that describes mental material that individuals possess.

Content validity. A type of validity that assesses the extent to which a psychometric test represents all of the content of the particular construct it is designed to measure.

Contextual subtheory. Subtheory of the triarchic theory of intelligence; describes how mental mechanisms interact with the external world to demonstrate intelligent behaviour.

Controlled elaboration. A process Kelly described in which clients are encouraged to think through their problems with the therapist and to reach a conclusion.

Convergent validity. A type of validity that assesses the extent to which a test shows associations with measures to which it should be related.

Converging. A learning style that is a combination of active experimentation and abstract conceptualisation.

Conversion reaction. Defence mechanism occurring when unacceptable thoughts or emotions are converted into physical symptoms, as with hysterical symptoms or psychosomatic symptoms of illness.

Coping styles. Cognitive strategies of coping with stressors. Also called secondary appraisals.

Core conditions of counselling. Within Rogers' theory of counselling, these are qualities and a psychological state that the client needs to have for a successful outcome of the treatment.

Corollary; corollaries. Within Kelly's personal construct theory, corollaries are the interpretative processes that operate to allow us to create our personal constructs.

Correlation coefficient. A statistical test that determines the strength of the relationship between two variables, and whether this relationship is positive or negative.

Counter-transference. Occurs when the analyst transfers some of his emotional reactions on to the patient. It is the reciprocal relationship to transference.

Craniology. The scientific study of the characteristics of the skull, such as size and shape, especially in humans.

Creativity. Within Renzulli's three-ring theory of giftedness, creativity is the ability to show fluency, flexibility and originality of thought; be open to new experiences and ideas; be curious and willing to take risks.

Criterion-related validity. Assesses the value of the test by the respondents' responses on other measures, i.e. criteria.

Cronbach's alpha. A statistical test used to assess the level of internal reliability.

Cross-species research. Research that looks for behaviour variation across species.

Crystallised intelligence. Acquired knowledge and skills, such as factual knowledge (abbreviated as Gc).

Damnation. Refers to a state of being that involves feeling either condemned or cursed; reflects the tendency for individuals to damn or condemn themselves, others and/or the world, if their demands are not met.

Decision phase. The second phase of Enright's model of forgiveness, where the process continues as the individual faces the decision points at which the affective, mental and behavioural change can occur. The individual may experience 'a change of heart' towards the person who has hurt them, and makes a commitment to work towards forgiveness (steps 9–11).

Decision/reaction time or speed. The ability to react and make decisions quickly in response to simple stimuli.

Decontextualisation. The ability to disconnect, or detach oneself, from a particular situation; to think abstractly and then generalise about it.

Deductive argument. Reasoning that starts with rules, premises or conditions leading to a solution.

Deepening phases. The final phase of Enright's model of forgiveness; involves the individual finding meaning in the forgiveness process, gaining the awareness that they are not alone in the experience of being hurt, and realising that the injury may produce a new purpose in their life (steps 16–20).

Defence mechanisms. The conflicting demands of the id, ego and superego create anxiety in the individual, who develops a defence mechanism to help protect them from that anxiety and help them to feel better about themself.

Defensive attitudes. According to Horney, these are protective devices that temporarily help alleviate pain and make individuals feel safer.

Deference or out-group favouritism. An aspect of behavioural asymmetry. A special case of asymmetrical in-group bias, said to occur when the degree of asymmetrical in-group favouritism is so strong that subordinates actually favour dominants over their own in-groups.

Deficiency cognition (D-cognition). The term Maslow used to describe the thoughts we have when we are making judgements about how well our experiences are meeting our deficiency needs.

Deficiency motives. Some basic needs that we lack and are motivated to get. They include drives like hunger, thirst, the need for safety and the need to be loved. They are the basic motives that ensure human survival. Deficiency motives create a negative motivational state that can only be changed by satisfying the need.

Delayed gratification. The ability to postpone the satisfaction of id impulses until some later, more suitable, time.

Denial. Occurs when we protect ourselves from upset by claiming that something upsetting has not happened when it actually has, or that something about ourselves is untrue.

Dependency. A state which relies on something for support to function properly; lack of independence or self-sufficiency.

Dependent personality disorder. Characterised by a person who shows persistent psychological dependence on other people. They tend to allow others to take responsibility for major areas and aspects of their life because they feel they lack the confidence or the ability to undertake responsibility for these areas themselves.

Depression. A psychological and physiological state that is characterised by a depressed mood, loss of interest or pleasure, feelings of guilt or low self-worth, and disturbed sleep.

Description. The act, process or technique of describing.

Deterministic view/Determinism. A philosophical approach suggesting that every aspect of humans' events, acts and decisions is the inevitable consequence of preceding events, independent of human free will.

Developmental theories. Area of theoretical thoughts, ideas and hypotheses relating to human development across the lifespan.

Deviation IQ. The ratio of tested IQ scores against a standardised IQ, usually expressed as a quotient in terms of a standard deviation.

Dichotomy corollary. Describes how all concepts are based on dichotomies. All our constructs are bipolar. This bipolarity allows for constructive alternativism; that is, the possibility of changing your mind about how you see things.

Direct strategies. In understanding how people end a personal relationship, direct strategies are thought to include direct behaviours and responses, such as discussions over the state of the relationship and both people agreeing to end the relationship.

Discomfort disturbance. Occurs when the person makes demands on self, others and the world which are related to dogmatic commands that life should be comfortable and things should not be too difficult to achieve. If these demands are not met, the person becomes disturbed.

Discriminant validity. A type of validity that assesses a test's correlations with constructs to which it should not be related.

Displacement. Defence mechanism occurring when we are too afraid to express our feelings directly to the person who provoked them, so we deflect them elsewhere (e.g. we kick the cat).

Dispositional optimism. A predisposition towards expecting favourable outcomes; describes individual differences in optimistic versus pessimistic expectancies.

Disputation. In Ellis' therapeutic process, clients are continually asked what the evidence for their beliefs is. Disputation occurs when the therapist undertakes to challenge the clients' irrational beliefs and discusses with them alternative beliefs that they could hold. Disputation, often referred to as *D*, is considered an extension of Ellis' ABC (or ABCDE) model.

Distraction. A way to combat pessimism. It is used to put adversity aside for a while to allow re-evaluation of the situation and allow a fresh outlook.

Diverging. A learning style that is a combination of concrete experience and observations and reflection.

Dizygotic (DZ) twins. Dizygotic twins arise when two eggs are released and fertilised separately. They are also known as fraternal or non-identical twins.

D-love or deficiency love. Defined by Maslow as consisting of individual yearning for affection, tenderness, feelings of elation and sexual arousal. It is a deficiency need and can result in selfish, manipulative behaviour.

Domain specificity. When an adaptive process is seen to solve a particular problem.

Dominant genetic variance. Part of a process by which certain genes are expressed (dominant) and other genes are not expressed (recessive).

Double approach–avoidance conflict. Describes the situation where there are multiple goals, some desirable and some undesirable.

Dramaturgic model. A model of embarrassment suggesting it is the flustered uncertainty that follows a bungled public performance and leaves the individual at a loss about what to do or say next. Thus, it is the agitation and aversive arousal that triggers embarrassment after the realisation that the individual cannot calmly and gracefully continue that performance.

Dyadic phase. One aspect of Duck's four phases or stages of personal relationship break-up; involves confronting the partner with the negative thoughts from the intrapsychic stage and trying to sort out the various problems.

Dynamic lattice. A term to describe Cattell's dynamic traits of attitudes, sentiments and ergs are organised in very complex and interrelated ways.

Dynamic theory of conservatism. Theory suggesting that conservative attitudes can be more directly explained by the construct of uncertainty.

Dynamic traits. The traits that motivate us and energise our behaviour.

Dysfunctional beliefs. Within Ellis' model of rational-emotive behaviour therapy, refers to attitudes held by the individual that are not helpful to their own well-being.

Ectomorphy. A term used by Sheldon to link the nervous system and the brain system of the body to a temperament of need for privacy, restraint and inhibition.

Education. Within Ellis' ABC (or ABCDE) model, refers to individuals learning about the therapeutic process.

Effect size. A statistical technique used to interpret the magnitude of a relationship between two variables.

Ego. The planning, thinking, organising part that develops within the personality. It operates according to the reality principle with related secondary process thinking. The ego becomes the mediator between the demands of the id and those of the outside world.

Ego disturbance. Occurs when the person makes demands on themselves, other individuals and the world, and when these demands are not met, the person becomes upset by what-else labels, damning themself.

Electroencephalogram (EEG). A measure of the electrical activity that is produced by the brain.

Electromodal measures (EDA). Measure the electrical activity of the skin.

Elementary cognitive tasks (ECTs). Simple tasks used to measure different cognitive processes such as understanding stimuli, stimuli discrimination, choice, visual search and retrieval of information from both the short-term and long-term memory.

Emic approach. A lexical approach to personality research using the personality terms that are found in the native language of the country.

Emotion-focused coping. A strategy involving coping attempts that are not directed at the stress.

Emotional stability. Describes objective, calm, peaceful, unemotional, even-tempered, secure, patient, uninhibited personality traits (also known as low neuroticism).

Empathic understanding. Within Rogers' theory of counselling, refers to the therapist understanding the client's internal frame of reference. This is about accepting that there is no external reality, but that we all have a subjective view of the world.

Empirical validity. Arguments, conclusions, reasons or intellectual processes that are persuasive because they are well founded due to evidence relying on or derived from observation or experiment.

Endomorphy. A term used by Sheldon to link the digestive system of the body to a temperament of love of relaxation and comfort.

Enduring. Lasting; continuing; durable.

Environment. The environment is taken to include everything that influences a person's phenotype, apart from their genotype.

Environmental factors. Aspects of the environment.

Environmental mastery. A sense of mastery and competence in managing the environment.

Environmental-mold traits. The environmentally induced traits in Cattell's system.

Epistasis. The masking or unmasking of the effects of one gene by the action of another.

Epistatic genetic variance. Refers to a process by which genes interact. Also known as interactive genetic variance.

EPs (evoked potentials). This response time measures sheer speed of perceptual discrimination (visual or auditory). Participants are linked to an electroencephalograph (EEG) machine that measures brain waves. On the EEG machine, after being presented with this stimulus, a spike appears in the participant's brain waves. This spike is what has been evoked by the stimulus. The time between the stimulus and the spike is thought to be a measure of intelligence.

Ergs. One of three dynamic traits in Cattell's theory of personality. Ergs are innate drives that cause us to recognise and attend to some stimuli more readily than others and to seek satisfaction of our drives.

Erogenous zone. The area of the body in which the libidinal energy is currently invested.

Eros. A term used to describe a love style, meaning a passionate physical and emotional love based on aesthetic enjoyment and a stereotype of romantic love.

Estradiol. The most potent naturally occurring oestrogen. Oestrogen is produced chiefly by the ovaries and is responsible for promoting oestrus and the development and maintenance of female secondary sex characteristics, such as pubic hair and breasts.

Etic approach. Uses personality questionnaires translated from another language, which in practice tends to be English.

Eudaimonic well-being. Longer term psychological well-being resulting from the engagement with individual development and challenges within life (see also Psychological well-being).

Eugenics. Literally means 'well born'. It refers to the doctrine that humanity can be improved by selective breeding.

Event-related potential (ERP). Corresponds to a measure of electrical activity produced by the brain stimuli.

Evolutionary personality psychology. Academic study of how evolutionary adaptation shapes human personality.

Exchange relationships. Relationships based on costs and benefits.

Excitatory mechanism. Relates to keeping the individual alert, active and aroused.

Exhaustion stage. This is the stage that is sometimes called burnout, where the body's capacity to resist stressors becomes exhausted. It results in physical and/or psychological illness.

Exit strategy. A strategy involved in initiating the end of a relationship; involves behaviours or responses that include ending the relationship by thinking about it or talking about it ending.

Expectancy. Our subjective estimate of the likely outcome of a course of behaviour.

Experience corollary. Describes how we are able to change the personal constructs we use in the light of our later experience.

Experiential learning theory. A theory of learning that emphasises learning relating to, or derived from, experience.

Experiential subtheory. Subtheory of the triarchic theory of intelligence; describes how experience interacts with the internal and external world to form intelligent behaviours.

Experimental neuroses. The symptoms of a neurotic condition, including anxiety, poor concentration and general distress, induced in a laboratory setting.

Explanation. The act or process of explaining.

Explanatory style. The way you explain your problems and setbacks to yourself and choose either a positive or negative way to solve it.

Expressional fluency. Ability to rapidly think of and organise words or phrases into meaningful complex ideas under general conditions.

Externalisation. Horney's terms for a set of mechanisms that are used for self-deception to protect the individual from their basic anxiety.

External perceived locus of causality. When the individual feels they are engaging in a behaviour as a result of external influence.

Externals. Individuals who believe that reinforcement depends on external forces such as powerful others in the person's world, luck, God, fate, the State and so on. Within Rotter's theory, refers to individuals who believe that reinforcement depends on external forces.

Extinction. A reduction in responding that occurs as a result of the behaviour no longer being reinforced.

Extrapersonal. Phenomena that occur outside of the individual.

Extraversion. Sociable, talkative, active, spontaneous, adventurous, enthusiastic, person-oriented, assertive personality traits.

Extraverts. This term describes individuals who are very sociable, energetic, optimistic, friendly and assertive.

Extrinsic religiosity. Religious orientation sometimes described as religious self-centredness. A person goes to their place of worship as a means to an end (i.e. for what they can get out of it). They might go to church to be seen, make friends or because it gives them respectability or social advancement.

Extrinsic-personal orientation towards religion. Participation in religion for protection and consolation.

Extrinsic-social orientation towards religion. Participation in religion to be part of an in-group and for social status.

Extroversion/Extraversion. 'Extraversion' is spelt as 'extroversion' within Jungian theory. Jung referred to this trait as a candid and accommodating nature that adapts easily to a given situation, is friendly, careless and confident. Formed the basis of later descriptions of extraversion comprising sociable, talkative, active, spontaneous, adventurous, enthusiastic, person-oriented, assertive personality traits.

Face validity. An aspect of validity that is concerned with what the measure appears to measure.

Facilitating branch (Mayer and Salovey [1997] model of emotional intelligence). In the emotional intelligence literature, this is the emotional facilitation of thinking.

Factor analysis. A multivariate data reduction statistical technique that allows us to simplify the correlational relationships between a number of variables.

Fallibility. The innate tendency of human beings to make errors and to get things wrong.

False hope syndrome. A cycle of failure and persistent effort at unrealistic goals.

Family studies. Families are studied according to genetic overlaps to consider the genetic heritability of behaviour and personality.

Fatal attraction. Theory suggesting that those characteristics we view as most important when choosing a partner may often, in fact, be the very same characteristics that led to the break-up of that relationship.

Feeling. Within Jungian theory, involves evaluating the desirability or worth of what has been presented.

Fight-or-flight response. First described by Walter Cannon in 1929. An animal has two options when faced with danger: they can either face the threat (fight) or they can avoid the threat (flight).

Figural fluency. Ability to draw or sketch many things rapidly.

Fixed-role therapy. A process in Kelly's therapy where the therapist interprets the sketch and then writes a role-play that the client has to re-enact.

Flexibility. Refers to individuals who remain intellectually flexible, open to change at all times; they view the infinitely varied people, ideas and things in the world around them without bigotry.

Fluid intelligence. Primary reasoning ability; the ability to solve abstract relational problems; free of cultural influences (abbreviated as Gf).

Flynn effect. The observed continued year-on-year rise of IQ test scores in all parts of the world. The highest rises in IQ occurred in the non-verbal tests (fluid intelligence) and the lowest gains were in verbal tests (crystallised intelligence).

Foraging. The act of looking or searching for food or provisions.

Forethought. Deliberation, consideration or planning beforehand.

Forgiveness. A willingness to abandon resentment, negative judgement and indifferent behaviour towards the person who has hurt you, while forming the qualities of compassion, generosity and love towards them. Forgiveness is considered a positive method of coping with a hurt, involving complex cognitive, emotional and relational processes; this complexity suggests that forgiveness is not necessarily an act, but rather a process, of discovery.

Forward incrementation. An element of creative leadership that accepts current paradigms; where the creativity propels an area forward within assumptions, concepts, values and practices that already exist.

Fragmentation corollary. Reflects the logical incoherence that may exist within the subsystems of an individual's construct system. It explains the inconsistencies that we can sometimes observe in an individual's behaviour.

Free association. A technique used in psychoanalysis and devised by Sigmund Freud. Via prompting, the individual is asked to relate anything that comes into their mind, regardless of how unimportant it may seem, and to repeat the process. It is thought that sooner or later the individual will stumble across a crucial memory. This term was mistranslated from the German *freier Einfall*, which actually means a 'sudden idea'. Free associations are thoughts that come spontaneously into one's mind.

Friedman test. A non-parametric statistical test used when the same measure has been administered on three occasions or more.

Frontal lobe. Part of the brain concerned with thinking, planning and central executive functions; controls motor execution.

Fully functioning person. The person who has achieved self-actualisation. Such individuals have few conditions of worth. They are high in self-acceptance and in touch with their organismic valuing processes.

Functional equivalence class of situations. Describes situations that individuals perceive as being very similar, resulting in their acting in characteristic ways in these situations.

Functionality. When an adaptive process is seen to serve a particular purpose.

Fundamental postulate. The concept at the core of Kelly's theory, which states that an individual's processes are psychologically channelled by the ways in which they anticipate events.

g (general intelligence). A common factor measured by different intelligence tests.

Gamma-aminobutyric acid. An amino acid that occurs in the central nervous system and is related to the transmission of nerve impulses.

Gene. The fundamental physical and functional unit of heredity, consisting of a sequence of DNA, occupying a specific position within the genome.

General Adaptation Syndrome. A description of the body's defensive activity in response to stress. It consists of three stages: the alarm reaction, resistance stage and exhaustion stage.

General (domain-specific) knowledge. Acquired knowledge in a specialised area.

General mood. In the emotional intelligence literature, this is the ability to generate positive affect and be self-motivated.

Generalise. Occurs when behaviour learned in one setting or context is transferred to other settings.

Generalised expectancies. Explains the process whereby individuals come to believe, based on their learning experiences, either that reinforcements are controlled by outside forces or that their behaviour controls reinforcements.

Generalised social anxiety disorder. Is indicated when an individual fears a wide range of social situations – for example, going to a party, being with friends, speaking to employers and so on. A person with generalised anxiety will likely have dealt with issues of shyness for their entire life.

Genetic. Of or relating to genetics or genes.

Genetic heritability. The extent to which genetic differences in individuals contribute to individual differences in a behaviour (e.g. personality or intelligence).

Genetic variation. The presence of different combinations of alleles in different individuals in a population.

Genotype. The internal genetic code or blueprint for constructing and maintaining a living individual. This genetic code is inherited, and it is found within all cells of the individual and involved with all aspects of the individual, from regulating the metabolism to influencing behaviour.

Giftedness. Refers to individuals who are thought to possess great natural intelligence.

Global attribution. Will be there in every aspect of an individual's life, in all situations.

Global/Global factors. The tendency to attribute the causes of successes or failures in certain situations as present in all aspects of their life. A term used by Seligman in optimism and helplessness theory and more generally used in describing an aspect of attribution style. The opposite construct to global is specific, where the person attributes their failures as not likely to be present in all aspects of their life (i.e. specific to that situation).

Goal. That which we want to happen.

Gonadal hormones. Substances that create physiological growth in organs in animals that produce sex cells; for example, ovaries in females (part of the female reproductive system) and testes in males (part of the male reproductive system).

Goodness of fit. A term used in confirmatory statistical analysis to indicate how well a set of data fits a theoretical or proposed model.

Grave-dressing phase. One aspect of Duck's four phases or stages of personal relationship break-up; involves preparing people involved for future relationships.

Grey matter. Brain matter that can be understood as the parts of the brain responsible for information processing.

Group socialisation theory. A term to describe how socialisation occurs from social group to social group.

Growth motives. Sometimes called being motives or B-motives, these needs are unique to each individual and are responsible for the development of the individual to their full potential. Growth motives represent a higher level of functioning. They differ from deficiency motives in that they create a positive motivational state that continues to develop.

Habit. The label describing the association between the stimulus and the response.

Habitual responses. A term used by Eysenck to describe the ways that individuals typically behave in a situation.

Hedonic well-being. Shorter-term evaluation of well-being, representing a balance between feelings of positive and negative emotions, pleasure attainment and pain avoidance (see also Subjective well-being)

Helplessness. Used by Seligman to describe what tends to occur when people (or animals) find themselves in an uncontrollable situation. For instance, when a person cannot do anything about what is happening to them, then they learn to be helpless because they begin to expect events to be uncontrollable.

Hereditary. Transmitted or capable of being transmitted genetically from parent to offspring.

Heritability. A statistical estimate of how much of the total variation in a population can be explained by genetic differences.

Heritability versus environment. A debate in psychology pertaining to whether personality development is determined more by genetic inheritance or environmental influences or by some sort of interactional effect.

Heuristic value. The usefulness of the theory as containing rules that can be used to understand many aspects of the human condition.

HEXACO model of personality. An extension of the 5-factor model of personality. The personality traits within this approach comprise Honesty–Humility (H), Emotionality (E; e.g. Neuroticism), eXtraversion (X), Agreeableness versus Anger (A), Conscientiousness (C), and Openness to Experience (O).

Hippocampus. Part of the brain; forms part of the limbic system that has a central role in the formation of memories.

Histrionic personality disorder. Characterised by a person who is always looking for attention and needs to be the centre of attention.

Hope. An individual's expectations that goals can be achieved.

Hormones. Substances that travel around the human body to effect physiological activity, such as growth or metabolism.

Hypothetical question. A question that places the individual in a situation that they may never experience and asks them for their opinion on something.

Id. The basic storehouse of raw, uninhibited, instinctual energy that we are born with and that energises our behaviour. Id instincts demand immediate gratification.

Ideal partner hypothesis. Theory suggesting that we are more likely to be attracted to certain people who possess certain specific traits or qualities, such as kindness and intelligence.

Ideal self. The image that individuals have of the person that they would like to be. Individuals use their concept of their ideal self to judge themselves.

Idealised selves/self. Within Horney's theory of personality, describes the ability to view oneself as a powerful and successful, perfect human being.

Ideational fluency. The ability to produce a series of ideas related to a specific condition.

Ideological asymmetry. An aspect of behavioural asymmetry. One's desire for group-based social hierarchy is related to one's social ideology and the wish that these factors are used by individuals to maintain social hierarchy.

Idiographic. An approach to personality that focuses on the individual and describes the personality variables within that individual. Theorists who adopt this approach in the main are interested only in studying individuals one at a time.

Impermeable constructs. Describes constructs that are rigid and do not allow change.

Implicit personality theories. Intuitively based theories of human behaviour that we all construct to help us to understand both others and ourselves.

Implicit theories. Common or everyday ideas around a subject. For example, implicit theories of intelligence are everyday ideas of intelligence.

Incentive factor. Something that provides the motivation to learn.

Independent-samples t-test. A parametric statistical test used to compare mean scores between two groups of scores.

Indirect strategies. In understanding how people end a personal relationship, direct strategies are thought to include indirect behaviours and responses, such as withdrawing or passive aggressiveness.

Indiscriminate. Not making careful distinctions or being unselective.

Indiscriminate usage. A phrase to describe how certain phenomena/behaviour might occur in a haphazard, non-select or thoughtless fashion. Horney argued that this is one of the ways neurotic needs can be distinguished from normal needs.

Individualism vs collectivism. A dimension within Hofstede's work on personality and national culture that looks at the extent that a society's social and cultural outlook emphasises independence and self-reliance or community and group values.

Individuality corollary. Embodies the observation that there are individual differences in behaviour. For Kelly there is no objective reality; rather, each individual has their own subjective view of events.

Inductive argument. Reasoning used to discover underlying solutions from specific cases.

Inferiority complex. Feelings that one is inferior to others in some way, but in an extreme form. An inferiority complex is an advanced state of discouragement, often resulting in the person withdrawing.

Inhibitory mechanism. Relates to the individual's inactivity and lethargy.

Inhibitory system. Reflects human temperament and governs the level of disinhibition/constraint in the two goal systems and the behaviour of the individual.

Inspection time. A measure of response time that indicates speed of perceptual discrimination (visual or auditory) and measures the time people take to process information.

Instinctoid tendencies. Maslow's description of human beings as having innate tendencies towards healthy growth and development.

Instrumental enrichment (IE). A cognitive educational programme that enhances the skills needed for independent thinking and learning.

Intellectual self-assertion. Refers to a process for individuals who are confident and aware of their intellect and derive self-worth from it.

Intellectual self-effacement. Refers to modesty or humility surrounding the person's intellect.

Internal attribution. Explanatory style to do with the person themselves.

Internal perceived locus of causality. When the individual feels they are engaging in a behaviour under their own free will.

Internal reliability (or consistency). Refers to whether all the items of a psychometric test are measuring the same thing.

Internal self-regulatory processes. Bandura describes these processes as being attempts at self-influence that include self-criticism, self-praise; valuation of own personal standards; re-evaluation of own personal standards if necessary; self-persuasion, evaluation of attainment, acceptance of challenges.

Internal/Internal factors. In helplessness theory (and in describing attribution style), describes when a person has learnt to attribute their failures in situations to do with the person themselves. The opposite construct to *internal* is *external*; where the person learns to attribute their failures in situations to do with factors external to themselves.

Internals. Within Rotter's theory, refers to individuals who believe that their behaviour does make a difference to an outcome.

Inter-observer agreement. The extent to which two or more observers agree in their personality rating across animals.

Interpersonal. Factors to do with relationships with other people.

Interpersonal forgiveness. Focuses on how events and consequences in ongoing relationships between two people are assessed and acted upon.

Interpersonal intelligence. Refers to relating with others harmoniously and efficiently.

Intimacy. A component of Sternberg's triangular theory of love; deals with the emotions involved in a relationship and involves feelings of warmth, closeness, connection and the development of a strong bond, as well as the concern for each other's happiness and well-being.

Intolerance. Unwillingness to recognise and respect differences in opinions or beliefs. Within Ellis' theory, intolerance is an unwillingness to grant equal freedom of expression to, or to accept, other beliefs or attitudes.

Intrapersonal. In Sternberg's balance theory of wisdom, an individual's decision-making around a common good may focus on the needs and interests of the individual.

Intrapersonal forgiveness. Involves processes to do with yourself; your individual thoughts and feelings about yourself.

Intrapersonal intelligence. Knowledge about the self and the ability to view oneself objectively.

Intrapsychic phase. One aspect of Duck's four stages of personal relationship break-up in which the individual begins to think about the negative aspects of their partner and of the relationship itself, but does not discuss these thoughts with the other partner.

Intrinsic religiosity. Refers to individuals who live their religious beliefs in such a way that the influence of their religion is evident in every aspect of their life.

Introversion. Within Jungian theory, reflects a hesitant, reflective, quiet and retiring nature.

Introverts. This term describes individuals who are reserved, independent rather than followers socially, even-paced rather than sluggish in terms of their pace of work.

Intuition. Within Jungian theory, refers to when we relate to the world with a minimum of interpretation and reasoning, instead forming hunches or having premonitions.

Investment model. Model that describes three elements working together to enable the continuation of a relationship: satisfaction, alternative quality and investments. These three components are then thought to predict a fourth component, the individual's level of commitment to that relationship.

Investments. Within the investment model, represents the things the individual has invested in the relationship and will potentially lose if the relationship were to end.

Iq. The ratio of tested mental age to chronological age, usually expressed as a quotient multiplied by 100.

Irrational behaviour. That which prevents people from achieving their basic goals.

Irrational belief. A belief that: (1) blocks a person from achieving their goals and creates extreme emotions that persist over time; (2) distorts reality; and (3) contains illogical ways of evaluating themselves, others and the world. Also, a term used by Ellis to describe a belief irrationally maintained in ignorance of the laws of nature or by faith in magic or chance.

Isolation. Defence mechanism occurring when the anxiety associated with an event or threat is dealt with by recalling the event unemotionally. All the feelings that would normally be associated with the events are separated and denied.

Kin altruism. Interactions between related individuals (be it a family or a species) that are designed to ensure, via competition and adaptation, that the species survives.

Kinaesthetic abilities. Abilities depending on the sense that detects bodily position, weight or movement of the muscles, tendons and joints.

Kruskal–Wallis test. A non-parametric statistical test used to see whether a difference occurs between more than two sets of scores.

Kuder–Richardson Formula 20. A measure of internal reliability for measures with dichotomous choices.

Latent dream content. The real meaning of the dream, it represents the contents of the individual's unconscious. The psychoanalyst uses skilled interpretation of the dream content and symbols to identify the latent content of the dream.

Layperson. A non-professional or non-expert in an area.

L-data. Short for 'life record data'. These are measurements of behaviour taken from the person's actual life or observations on the individual from individuals who know them well.

Leading question. A question that tries to steer the respondent to a particular answer, or in the direction of a particular answer.

Learned helplessness. A state of affairs where nothing you choose to do affects what happens to you; this behaviour is at the centre of pessimism.

Learned optimism. Explains individual differences in response to negative events (stressful situations).

Learning Propensity Assessment Device (LPAD). A measure of intelligence and ability that focuses on the person's potential for learning.

Left-wing authoritarianism. Left-wing authoritarians are concerned with submission (submission to authorities who are dedicated to overthrowing the established authorities), aggression (aggressiveness against the established authorities) and conventionalism (adherence to the norms of behaviour of a revolutionary movement) to a left-wing revolutionary cause.

Lexical knowledge. Extent of vocabulary.

Libido. The basic source of mental energy that originates in the id. It consists of largely sexual instincts in Freudian theory. During development it undergoes various transformations and results in the adult sex drive.

Life history. A schedule of reproduction and survival which maximises reproduction.

Life narrative. An approach that emphasises documenting an individual's life experiences to understand personality.

Life satisfaction. An individual's perceived level of well-being and happiness.

Life-process energy. Within Jungian theory, this energy results from the conflicts between the different forces within the psyche.

Limbic system. A group of interconnected deep-brain structures involved in emotion, motivation and behaviour.

Little optimism. Used by researchers to understand the differences between the two main theories of optimism. Little optimism comprises explanatory style.

Locus of control. Theory developed by Julian Rotter; describes how people tend to ascribe their chances of future successes or failures either to internal or external causes.

Long-term storage and retrieval. The ability to store information in long-term memory.

Long-term versus short-term orientation. A dimension within Hofstede's work on personality and national culture that describes the extent to which a culture refers to the importance attached by that culture to the future versus the past and present.

Love styles. Consist of primary and secondary love styles, where the secondary styles are made up of a combination of two primary styles. Primary styles include eros, ludus and storge. Secondary love styles include pragma, mania and agape.

Low frustration tolerance. Used by Ellis to explain a person's perceived inability to put up with discomfort or frustration in their life; indeed, they may feel that happiness is impossible while such conditions exist.

Low versus high power distance. A dimension within Hofstede's work on personality and national culture that describes the extent to which less powerful members of a culture, or institutions within that culture, accept and expect that power is distributed unequally throughout that culture.

Loyalty strategy. A strategy involved in initiating the end of a relationship; involves waiting for things to get better, or hoping that they will sort themselves out.

ludus. A term to describe a love style, meaning love that is played as a game or a conquest.

Managing branch. (Mayer and Salovey [1997] model of emotional intelligence). In the emotional intelligence literature, this is the reflective regulation of emotion to promote emotional and intellectual growth.

Manifest dream content. The description of the dream as recalled by the dreamer. It is not a true representation of the unconscious mind, as the dreamer unconsciously censors some of the true meaning of the dream or uses symbols to represent key elements so that they are not too disturbed by their recall of the dream.

Mann–Whitney *U*-test. A non-parametric statistical test used to compare mean scores between two groups of scores.

Masculine protests. Attitudes and behaviours associated with an individual's decision to reject the stereotypical female role of weakness associated with femininity.

Masculinity versus femininity. A dimension within Hofstede's work on personality and national culture that describes the extent to which a culture understands the culture in terms of masculinity and femininity.

Masochism. Pleasure in being subjected to pain or humiliation.

Mating effort. An evolutionary psychology term to describe the amount of energy put into mating by the animal/individual.

Meaningful memory. Ability to note, retain and recall information with meaning.

Measuring personality. Techniques used to describe and categorise personality.

Mechanical reasoning. A spatial ability that measures the ability to understand basic mechanical principles of machinery, tools and motion.

Mediated learning experience (MLE). A specialised form of learning interaction between a learner and a mediator.

Melancholic temperament. Associated with depressed mood and feelings of anxiety.

Melatonin. A hormone derived from serotonin that plays a role in sleep, ageing and reproduction in mammals.

Mental rotation. A spatial ability that involves being able to visualise objects from different angles and different positions.

Mesomorphy. A term used by Sheldon to link the musculature and the circulatory system of the body to a temperament of being physically assertive and competitive.

Meta-analysis. The process or technique of synthesising research results by using various statistical methods to retrieve, select and combine results from previous separate but related studies.

Metaneeds. The needs of self-actualising individuals. These are higher-level needs that are qualitatively different, being concerned with concepts such as beauty, truth, justice and ethics.

Method of amplification. A tool in dream analysis; involves the analyst and the patient identifying the significant symbols in the dream and focusing on them to explore their possible meaning in ever-greater depth.

Modal personality structure approach. A psychological anthropology approach that compares the most frequent traits of the individuals of each society to achieve a basic personality for each culture.

Modulation corollary. Refers to how fixed constructs are and how much change is possible within an individual's personal construct system. They contain permeable and impermeable constructs.

Monozygotic (MZ) twins. Identical twins. They occur when one fertilised egg splits early in the pregnancy (within 13 days of fertilisation).

Motivational basis. Underlying motivations for individuals doing things. For example, answering the question, 'Why do individuals behave as they do?'

Motor cortex. The area of the cerebral cortex where impulses from the nerve centres control the muscles.

MRI (magnetic resonance imaging). Procedure that is able to provide clear pictures of parts of the body that are surrounded by bone tissue.

Multiple abstract variance analysis (MAVA). A statistical technique developed by Cattell that allows the researcher to establish the relative contribution of genetics and environment to various personality traits.

Multiple intelligences. Gardner's theory of intelligence.

Multiple regression. A multivariate statistical technique that allows researchers to determine which variable or variables emerge from a number of independent variables in best predicting a dependent variable.

Multitrait-Multimethod Matrix. Establishes the construct validity of two or more constructs by two or more methods of assessment.

Must-urbatory thinking. Forms of 'crooked thinking' or 'cognitive slippage' that lead to self-defeating consequences and are mostly absolutistic evaluations of shoulds, oughts, musts, commands and demands.

Mystical certainty. To be sure of mystical forces. For example, in religion it may be to believe that there is a god, this god is all-powerful, this god is all-seeing, there is life after death and there is heaven and hell.

Narcissistic personality disorder. Characterised by an inflated self-importance (grandiosity), preoccupation with fantasies about their own self-achievement and success, tend to seek attention and admiration from others, and centre their interpersonal relations around themselves.

Narrative analysis. An approach that focuses on the ways in which people make and use stories to interpret the world.

Narrow heritability. A statistical estimate of the total genetic variation in a population; refers only to additive genetic variance.

National character. A psychological anthropology approach that describes the personality of more complex societies.

Negative affect. Indicating overall negative mood, e.g. distressed, upset; distressed hostile, irritable-angry; scared, afraid-fearful; ashamed, guilty; nervous, and jittery.

Negative reinforcements. Consequences that discourage repetition of the behaviour.

Negative religious coping. Involves the person interpreting stress as a punishment from God; often leads to the person questioning God's power or love.

Neglect strategy. A strategy involved in initiating the end of a relationship that involves individuals responding to the partner's dissatisfaction by doing nothing to improve things and letting the relationship fall apart.

Neuroticism. Tense, anxious, emotional, moody traits.

Neurotransmitter. A chemical substance, such as acetylcholine or dopamine, that transmits nerve impulses across a synapse.

Nomothetic. An approach to personality based on the assumption that a finite set of variables exists that can be used to describe human personality. The aim is to identify these personality variables or traits that occur consistently across groups of people.

Non-additive genetic variance. Variation caused by the effects of numerous genes that combine to have an effect in a dominant or interactive fashion.

Non-generalised (performance) social anxiety disorder. Describes an anxiety response to one, or perhaps two or three, identified situations and affects individuals only when they are performing in front of others. An example would be severe anxiety or active avoidance of speaking in public.

Non-shared environment. Environmental influences that make family members different from each other.

Non-verbal mimicry. Includes facial expressions, gestures, body postures and speech characteristics. It occurs when we witness other people's emotional expressions and we then mimic these to produce and enhance empathy.

Norepinephrine. A hormone and neurotransmitter involved in the heart rate, blood pressure and the sugar levels of the blood (also called noradrenaline).

Norm-referenced. Another form of standardisation. The aim of making an IQ test norm-referenced is to allow comparisons between the individual and the population.

Norms. A standard, model or pattern regarded as typical.

Numerous. When an adaptive process is seen to comprise numerous adaptive mechanisms.

Nutrition hypothesis. Proposal that increased intelligence is part of a nurturing environment that includes increased height and lifespan, improved health, decreased rate of infant disease and better vitamin and mineral nutrition.

Observable. A property (e.g. in psychology, a behaviour) that can be observed or measured directly.

Observational learning. Learning by watching and analysing the behaviour of another.

Obsessive-compulsive personality disorder. Characterised by someone who shows great conformity to rules and moral codes. An individual with an obsessive-compulsive personality disorder will also tend to seek perfectionism in everything they do (everything must be just right and perfect) and they will have difficulty in doing anything unless it is done the way they want to do it.

Occipital lobe. Part of the brain concerned with visual perception and processing.

OCEAN. This is an acronym that refers to the factors of the Big Five trait theory of personality factors. The letters refer to the super traits of Openness, Conscientiousness, Extraversion, Agreeableness and Neuroticism.

Oedipal complex. The anxiety said to be experienced by boys as they desire their mothers but are afraid of the power that their father has over them, ultimately the power to castrate them. The boy is thus trapped between his desire for his mother and his fear of his father. He resolves his anxiety by identifying with his father.

Olfactory abilities. Abilities relating to the sense of smell.

Openness. Perceptive, sophisticated, knowledgeable, cultured, artistic, curious, analytical, liberal personality traits.

Operant conditioning. Associative learning that stresses that what happened after the response to the stimulus, namely the reinforcement available, is a crucial aspect of learning.

Operations. Within Guilford's theory of intelligence, operations are types of mental processing.

Optimal dissimilarity hypothesis. Suggests that individuals find people who are only slightly (but not totally) different to themselves as most attractive. In other words, we are aroused, or attracted, by the novel and different, provided it is not too dissimilar for us to understand.

Optimal outbreeding hypothesis. Expands on the optimal dissimilarity hypothesis; based on findings that some animals show a preference to breed with those who are somewhat, but not entirely, different from themselves.

Optimistic bias. Ignoring or minimising risks.

Oral aggressive personality. Personality type in Freudian theory that reflects hostile and verbal abusive traits using mouth-based aggression.

Oral receptive personality/character. Refers to one of the outcomes of oral fixation. This personality type is overly dependent on other people for gratification of their needs; traits include being trusting, accepting and gullible.

Organisation corollary. Refers to the way that each individual's construct system is organised hierarchically. Some constructs may be prioritised over others to help us make decisions.

Organismic integration theory. A subtheory of social determination theory that looks at how when behaviours or motivations are endorsed by significant others then these too can be internalised by the individual.

Organismic valuing/organismic valuing process. An ongoing process whereby experiences are symbolised and valued according to optimal enhancement of the organism and self.

Paranoid personality disorder. Characterised by a pattern of paranoia (e.g. delusions of persecution), extreme distrust or mistrust of other people and irrational suspicions of others.

Parapraxes. Unintentional errors that are regarded as revealing our unconscious feelings; sometimes called Freudian slips.

Parent-effects model. Describes genetic transmission of phenotypes, suggesting that the behaviour of the child is responded to by the parent, which in turn brings out another behaviour in the child.

Parental investment. An evolutionary psychology term to describe the amount of energy put into offspring by a parent to ensure their survival.

Parietal lobe. Part of the brain concerned with somatosensory (relating sensory stimuli from the skin and internal organs) perception, integration of visual and somatospatial information.

Parsimony. Refers to the adoption of the *simplest* assumption in the formulation of a theory or in the interpretation of data.

Participant modelling. Occurs when the low self-efficacy person shadows a high-efficacy person in a new or dreaded task.

Passion. A component of Sternberg's triangular theory of love; concerned with romance and sexual attraction.

Passive model. Describes genetic transmission of phenotypes, suggesting that the effects of genetics are explained by the 50 per cent overlap between a child and their parent.

pathways. A component of hope; reflects the individual's beliefs that successful plans can be generated to reach goals.

Peak experiences. The term Maslow used for times when individuals experience self-actualisation.

Penis envy. Occurs when girls become aware that, while boys have penises, they do not. According to Freud, this leads to feelings of deficiency in girls.

Perceived locus of causality. Within self-determination theory this term refers to whether an individual feels they are engaging in a behaviour for either internal or external reasons.

Perceiving branch. (Mayer and Salovey [1997] model of emotional intelligence): in the emotional intelligence literature, this is the perception, appraisal and expression of emotion.

Perception of competence. The extent to which the individual believes they have the ability to carry out a behaviour.

Perceptual speed. Ability to search and compare visual stimuli rapidly and accurately.

Performance phase. In Dollard and Miller's two phases of treatment, occurs when the patient is encouraged to learn more adaptive habits and apply them in their life.

Permanent. Used by Seligman in optimism and helplessness theory; describes when a person has learnt to attribute that failures in situations will always be present (*compare to* Stable/Stable factors).

Permeable constructs. Describes constructs that allow additions to be made easily.

Personal. Used by Seligman in optimism and helplessness theory; describes when a person has learnt to attribute their failures in situations to do with the person themselves (*compare to* Internal/Internal factors).

Personal agency. The belief that you can change things to make them better for yourself or others.

Personal constructs. The criteria that we each use to perceive and interpret events.

Personal dispositions. Represent the unique characteristics of the individual. This approach emphasises the uniqueness of each person.

Personal factors. Include the individual's cognitions, emotions and biological variables that contribute to their inner state.

Personal growth. A feeling of continued development.

Personal standards model. A model of embarrassment that suggests embarrassment occurs when an individual realises they have failed in the standards of behaviour that they have set for themselves.

Personality coefficient. The correlation between trait measures and behaviour. Mischel reports this coefficient as being 0.2 and 0.3.

Personality type. A term used by Eysenck to describe a collection of traits.

Perspective-taking. A cognitive process where we imagine how we would feel in another person's situation.

Pervasive. Describes a process when a person has learnt to believe that their successes and failures in situations will be in all aspects of their life, primarily used by Seligman in describing optimism and helplessness theory (*compare to* Global/Global factors).

Phase model. Identifies four phases or stages of break-up, where each phase is triggered by a threshold before moving on to the next.

Phenotype. The outward manifestation of the individual, the sum of all the atoms, molecules, cells, tissues and organs. These traits range from appearance to behaviours.

Phlegmatic temperament. Describes an individual who is calm.

Phobic avoidance. Defence mechanism occurring when the anxiety we experience when we think about doing something is totally out of proportion with what would be reasonable in the situation. As a result of this anxiety, we try to avoid the situation at all costs.

Phonetic coding. Ability to code and process speech sounds.

Phrenology. Study of the shape and protuberances of the skull, based on the belief that they reveal information about the person's character and mental capacity.

Physiognomy. A theory linking facial features with character traits.

Pleasure principle. One of the basic principles governing our behaviour. It is not so much a desire to seek pleasure actively but rather an instinct to avoid displeasure, pain and upset and ensure that our needs are met. The pleasure principle is apparent in primary process thinking.

Population norms. A standard, model or pattern regarded as typical for particular populations.

Positive affect. Indicating overall positive mood, e.g. attentive, interested, alert, excited, enthusiastic, inspired, proud, determined, strong and active.

Positive reinforcement. Consequences that encourage the repetition of the behaviour.

Positive relations with others. Has warm satisfying, trusting relationships with others.

Positive religious coping. Positive personal and religious growth as a response to stress, leading to growing closeness with God.

Positive thinking. A general term to describe happy and optimistic thoughts, feelings and behaviour.

Practical problem-solving. The ability to be practical and logical with regard to the problems we all face in various situations and relationships.

Preconscious mind. Consists of the thoughts that are unconscious at this instant, but which can be readily brought into our conscious mind.

Predictive validity. A type of validity that assesses whether a measure can accurately predict something in the future.

Pre-emptive constructs. Very specialised constructs that contain only their own elements. Their operation is reflected in rigid thinking.

Prefrontal cortex. The grey matter of the prefrontal lobe that is involved in a person's appraisals of risk and danger.

Primary appraisals. How you assess the stressor; that is, its potential emotional impact.

Primary creativity. Creativity involved in the person finding self-fulfilment.

Primary drives. Innate physiological drives associated with ensuring survival for the individual. They include hunger, thirst, the need for sleep and the avoidance of pain.

Primary love styles. Encompasses the following three love styles: eros, ludus and storge.

Primary process thinking. Describes irrational mental activity best exemplified by our dreams, where the logically impossible becomes possible. Extreme contradiction is tolerated, and events are often oblivious to the categories of time and space. Freud considered it to be an inborn primitive instinct.

Primary reinforcer. This refers to something that is naturally reinforcing without any learning having to occur. It is sometimes called an unconditioned response.

Principle of entropy. A Jungian term to describe a drive to create balanced energies across the psyche so that we express more of ourselves in our behaviour.

Principle of equivalence. A Jungian term to describe how, if the activity in one part of the psyche increased, it would decrease correspondingly in another part of the psyche.

Principle of opposites. The system Jung described of creating life-process energy within the psyche.

Principle of synchronicity. When two events may occur at the same time without one causing the other.

Prisoner's Dilemma. A game theory situation. In this situation imagine there are two people who have been arrested because the police suspect they have committed a crime together. The dilemma represents what is the best strategy for both prisoners to reduce any possible prison sentence.

Private persona. Conceptualised as being the 'real' inner person.

Problem-focused coping. Sometimes called adaptive or direct coping; refers to strategies directed at the stress.

Process model. Considers the questions of 'why', 'where' and 'when' do people differ and gives depth to understanding the 'how'. In other words, it deals with the questions of what ways do people differ? What causes these differences? What are the consequences of these differences?

Products. A term used in Guilford's Structure of Intellect (SI) theory that describes how information is stored, processed and used by the person to make associations or connections.

Projection. Defence that occurs when we externalise our unacceptable feelings and attribute them to others. We are never at fault; rather, it is our flatmate, friend or whoever.

Propositional constructs. Represent flexible thinking, with every element of the construct open to change. Overuse of propositional thinking causes indecisiveness.

Proprium. A synonym for the self, used by Allport. The term represents all the constituent parts that go to make up the concept of self.

Proxy agency. Occurs when the individual enlists other people to help change some of the factors impacting on their life.

Psyche. Jungian term referring to the total personality.

Psychological anthropology. An approach that examines the origins, cultural development, social customs and beliefs of social groups.

Psychological construct. A mental concept that influences behaviour via the mind–body interaction.

Psychological well-being. Longer-term psychological well-being resulting from the engagement with individual development and challenges within life (see also Eudaimonic well-being).

Psychometric. A way of describing psychological measurement that is concerned with theory and technique.

Psychomotor abilities. Ability to perform body motor movements with precision and coordination.

Psychomotor speed. The ability to perform body motor movements rapidly and fluently.

Psychopaths. There are individuals that behave an antisocial manner and seem unable to appreciate the consequences of their actions despite any punishment meted out.

Psychosomatic. Pertaining to a physical disorder that is caused by or notably influenced by emotional factors.

Psychoticism. Impulsive, antisocial, egocentric personality traits.

Public persona. The way that an individual presents themselves to the outside world.

Purpose in life. Having goals in life and a sense of directedness.

Pyramid model. Worthington's model to REACH forgiveness, which considers five steps to facilitate and develop forgiveness for a specific hurt or offence. Each letter of the acrostic REACH represents one step: (R) Recall the hurt; (E) Empathise with the one who hurt you; (A) Altruistic gift of forgiveness; (C) offer Commitment to forgive; and (H) Hold on to forgiveness.

Q-data. Refers to pen-and-paper, self-assessed personality questionnaires.

Quality of alternatives. Within the investment model, refers to the outcome of an assessment the person makes by considering other possible relationships as an alternative to the current relationship they have.

Quantification. The act of discovering, or expressing, the quantity of something.

Quantitative knowledge. A personal breadth and depth of other abilities gained primarily during formal educational experiences of mathematics.

Quantitative reasoning. Reasoning involving mathematical principles.

Quest religiosity. Refers to a religious orientation characterised by complexity, incompleteness, flexibility and tentativeness. The concept of quest represents the degree to which a person's religion involves 'an open-ended, responsive dialogue with existential questions raised by the contradictions and tragedies of life'. In other words, quest involves a person's 'questioning' and seeking enlightenment within their religion.

Random or partial reinforcement schedules. Occur when reinforcements are applied to given responses occasionally in a pattern that is not predetermined.

Range (size). An area that an individual covers in distance.

Range of convenience corollary. Refers to how broadly a construct is applied. Some constructs are widely applied, while some others make sense only when applied more narrowly. There are large individual differences in terms of how broadly or narrowly individuals apply their personal constructs.

Rational behaviour. That which helps individuals to achieve their basic goals and purposes.

Rational belief. According to Ellis, all people have fundamental goals, purposes and values, in life, that underlie their attempts to be happy and satisfied. If people choose to stay alive and be happy, then they act rationally, or self-helpfully, when they think, emote and behave in ways to achieve these goals.

Rational-emotive behaviour therapy (REBT). An action-oriented therapeutic approach that stimulates emotional growth by teaching people to replace their self-defeating (irrational) thoughts, feelings and actions with new and more effective ones.

Rationalisation. Defence mechanism in which the justification of an event is given after it has occurred. The justification given also conceals the true motivation behind the event.

Reaction formation. Defence by which we overcome unacceptable impulses by exaggerating the opposing tendency.

Reaction time. Usually measured as an average response time to stimuli over a number of trials.

Real self. Horney's term for the unique potential that each individual has.

Reality principle. Refers to situations where our thinking is based on what is happening in the external world. It describes the thought processes governing conscious and preconscious mind. We learn it as we grow up. The reality principle governs secondary process thinking.

Reciprocal altruism. A form of altruism (practice of unselfish concern for, or devotion to, the welfare of others) in which an organism will make an altruistic act but will not expect any immediate benefit in return.

Reciprocal causation. A term introduced by Albert Bandura to refer to the mutual influence between sets of factors.

Reciprocal determinism. The belief that cognitive and environmental events interact to motivate behaviour.

Reconstruction/redirection. An element of creative leadership that rejects current paradigms; occurs when the person revisits a previous point in creative development and then starts again by going in a new direction.

Redefinition. An element of creative leadership that accepts current paradigms; occurs when the person comes in and maintains the level of creativity but may give the impression of changing things.

Redirection. An element of creative leadership that rejects current paradigms; occurs when the person takes an area in an entirely new direction.

Reflective observation. Learning by thinking about our own experiences or watching others.

Regression. Defence mechanism by which we try to avoid anxiety by returning to an earlier, generally simpler, stage of our life where we felt safe and things seemed simpler.

Reinforcement value. Refers to our preferences amongst the possible reinforcements available to us.

Reinitiation. An element of creative leadership that rejects current paradigms; occurs when the person moves an area in a new direction from a new starting point.

Related *t*-test. A parametric statistical test used to examine the differences between scores administered to the same sample on two occasions (also known as the dependent-groups *t*-test).

Relatively stable. In comparison to other aspects, generally resistant to change.

Reliability. There are two forms of reliability: internal reliability and reliability over time (test–retest reliability).

Renzulli's three-ring definition. Model of giftedness that comprises above-average ability, high levels of task commitment and high levels of creativity.

Replication. An element of creative leadership that accepts current paradigms; occurs when the person comes in and maintains the level of creativity.

Repression. The process of keeping material that we find unacceptable at some level, in our unconscious mind. It is conceptualised as an active, continuous process. Freud described repressed material as being dynamically unconscious to reflect this sense of activity. It is not material that has simply been forgotten.

Repulsion hypothesis. Theory suggesting that people are repulsed by dissimilar others. That is, attitude similarity does not lead to attraction (similarity hypothesis); rather, attitude dissimilarity leads to repulsion (repulsion hypothesis).

Resistance stage. Physical arousal when the alarm reaction dies down but other processes are stimulated which allow the body to continue functioning despite continued physical demands.

Resource dilution model. A hypothesis used to explain the relationship between birth order and IQ. This model suggests that parental resources (time, energy and financial resources) are finite and that, as the number of children in the family increases, the resources (time, energy and finance) that any one child can gain will decrease.

Response times (RTs). Speed of processing measures, including reaction time and standard deviation of reaction time.

Reticulo-cortical circuit. Controls the cortical arousal generated by incoming stimuli.

Reticulo-limbic circuit. Controls arousal to emotional stimuli.

Rigidity. An aspect of the personality characterised by resistance to change.

Sanguine temperament. Describes an individual who is confident and optimistic.

Satisfaction. Within the investment model, refers to the assessments that the individual makes about their relationship in terms of rewards and costs.

Schema. Mental pictures or general understandings of social occurrences.

Schizoid personality disorder. Characterised by a pattern of detachment (disconnection) from interpersonal and social relationships and will tend to be demonstrated by a limited amount of emotion in social settings and relationships.

Schizotypal personality disorder. Evidenced by an extreme discomfort with, and a reduced tendency for, close relationships, as well as having distortions in thinking, feelings and perceptions and sometimes showing eccentric behaviour.

Second creativity. Creativity that allows the person to be recognised in their chosen field.

Secondary drives. The drives learned initially to help us cope with our innate primary drives.

Secondary love styles. Encompasses the following three love styles: pragma, mania and agape.

Secondary process thinking. Rational thought, which is logical and organised and reflects the actual situation in the external world and the facts as we see them. It is characteristic of conscious and preconscious thought, and Freud suggested that we learn it as we are growing up.

Secondary reinforcers. Items or events that were originally neutral but have acquired a value as a reinforcer through being associated with primary drive reduction.

Secondary traits. Traits that are more concerned with an individual's preferences and are not a core constituent of their personality. Secondary traits may become apparent only in particular situations.

Secure. A type of attachment style considered the most adaptive and healthy. Children with this attachment style are able to play and explore away from their mother, secure in the knowledge that they have a safe and secure base to return to when needed.

Secure attachment. A form of attachment in which the child exhibits minimal distress when separated from caregivers and feels assured that the parent or caregiver will return.

Selection. In Sternberg's balance theory of wisdom, this relates to being able to select one environment over another.

Self-acceptance. Refers to individuals who are glad to be alive and like themselves just because they are alive, because they exist and because they (as a living being) invariably have some power to enjoy themselves, to create happiness and joy. Within a psychological well-being context it refers to having a positive attitude towards the self.

Self-actualisation. The sole motivator in Rogers' model. It is an innate, positive drive to develop and realise our potential.

Self-awareness. In the emotional intelligence literature, this is the ability to identify one's own emotional states.

Self-blaming. Tendency to blame oneself.

Self-characterisation sketches. A process in Kelly's therapy wherein clients are asked to write about themselves in the third person.

Self-concept. The term used to refer to our perception of who we are. It is based largely on the evaluations that other people have made of us during our development.

Self-debasement. To lower in character, quality or value; degrade oneself.

Self-debilitation. An aspect of behavioural asymmetry; occurs when subordinates show higher levels of self-destructive behaviours than dominants by maintaining certain stereotypes.

Self-defeating beliefs. A term used by Ellis, alongside the term 'irrational beliefs', to describe a fearful or miserable state of mind resulting from irrational beliefs.

Self-determination theory (SDT). A theory that focuses on the motivation of the individual and looks at the development of personality within the context of the social world.

Self-direction. Refers to individuals assuming responsibility for their own lives, being able to work out their own problems independently and not needing support from others for their effectiveness and well-being.

Self-efficacy. An individual's belief that they can perform some behaviour that will get them a desired positive outcome.

Self-enhancement bias. The process whereby individuals seek out and interpret situations to attain a positive view of themselves. Self-enhancers see successes as internal (due to them alone), stable (permanent and always there) and global (evident in every aspect of their lives). They see failures as external (caused by unforeseen events or other people and not their fault), unstable (temporary; things will get better) and specific (evident in only one aspect of their life).

Self-esteem. Pride in oneself; self-respect.

Self-fulfilling prophecy. Occurs when positive or negative feedback influences a person's ideas about their own abilities.

Self-interest. Refers to individuals primarily being true to themselves and not masochistically sacrificing themselves for others.

Self-realisation. A process that sees the individual continuously working towards achieving their potential, their own unique nature, and, in doing so, coming to accept themselves.

Self-regulation/management. In the emotional intelligence literature, this is the ability to manage one's own emotional states.

Self-reinforcement. Occurs when we evaluate our own behaviour; we may stop doing something we are getting no pleasure from, or that we judge as harming us in some way, while continuing to do things that bring positive reinforcement.

Sensing. Within Jungian theory, occurs when we experience stimuli without any evaluation.

Sentiments. One of three dynamic traits in Cattell's theory of personality. Sentiments are complex attitudes that include our opinions and interests that help determine how we feel about people or situations.

Serial perceptual integration. Ability to identify a visual pattern.

Serotonin. A neurotransmitter involved in stimulation of the smooth muscles and regulation of cyclic body processes.

Shaping. Occurs when approximations to the desired behaviour are reinforced to assist the learner to acquire new behaviour.

Shared environments. Environments that are shared between two individuals.

Short-term memory. The ability to encode and be aware of information in the short term.

Shyness. A tendency to be reserved by drawing back from contact or familiarity with others.

Similarity hypothesis. Suggests that individuals are more likely to be attracted to people who are similar to themselves in both personality and attitude.

Simultaneous processing. Reflects a person's ability or facility to see associations and integrate single and separate pieces of information.

Situational optimism. Refers to the expectations an individual generates for a particular situation concerning whether good rather than bad things will happen.

Situational self-esteem model. A model of embarrassment that suggests the root cause of embarrassment is a temporary loss of self-esteem that results from public failures. Therefore, it is the opinions that we hold of ourselves and how we perform in faulty situations that are the cause of embarrassment.

Social anxiety. Fear of being around, of having to interact with and of being watched, criticised or judged negatively by other human beings.

Social anxiety disorder. Fear of being around, of having to interact with and of being watched, criticised or judged negatively by other human beings. The term 'disorder' emphasises this as a clinical condition that affects the function of the mind and/or body.

Social awareness. In the emotional intelligence literature, this is the ability to assess and influence others' emotions.

Social competence. The skills necessary to be accepted and fulfilled socially.

Social context. Within Adlerian theory, this term is used to explain how the social world that we live in plays a crucial part in determining our personality.

Social dominance orientation. Tendency to endorse the view that humans are predisposed to form a social hierarchy.

Social dominance theory. Argues that humans are predisposed to form a social hierarchy.

Social evaluation model. A model of embarrassment that suggests it is the concern for what others are thinking of us that holds the key to embarrassment. Here, it is a failure to impress others that embarrassed individuals fear most.

Social interest. Variously translated as social feeling, community feeling, fellow feeling, community interest or social sense.

Social life. A term used by Adler to describe the social world comprising work, friendship and love.

Social phase. One aspect of Duck's four phases or stages of personal relationship break-up; involves deciding what to do now that the relationship is effectively over; including considerations of it as being a public issue.

Social phobia. Fear of being around, of having to interact with and of being watched, criticised or judged negatively by other human beings. The term 'phobia' emphasises these feelings as the anxiety is felt as persistent, abnormal and irrational fear.

Social skills/management. In the emotional intelligence literature, this is the ability to sustain good interpersonal relationships.

Sociality corollary. Explains the basis of social interaction. Some understanding of a person's construct system is necessary for us to be able to predict their behaviour and interact satisfactorily with them.

Socially defined race. Race identification based on social or visual differences completely independent of the other genetic aspects of their physical makeup.

Somatotypes. Descriptions of personality based on bodily type and temperament.

Source trait. The common trait revealed by factor analysing a collection of inter-correlated surface traits.

Spatial ability. A mental process associated with the brain's attempts to interpret certain types of incoming information.

Spatial perception. A spatial ability that requires participants to identify the horizontal or the vertical object (usually a line) in a display while ignoring distracting information.

Spatial scanning. Ability to survey visual images quickly and accurately.

Spatial visualisation. A spatial ability that refers to analysing visual information.

Spatiotemporal ability. A spatial ability that involves the participants making judgements about moving visual stimuli.

Specific. Describes when a person has learnt to believe that successes or failures in situations will only be confined to that situation. A term used by Seligman in optimism and helplessness theory and more generally used in describing an aspect of attribution style. An attribution theory is then seen as an opposing construct to global/global factors.

Specific abilities (s). Single aspects of intelligence.

Specific responses. A term used by Eysenck to describe observations of individual behaviour.

Stable attribution. Belief that the cause of the event will always be there.

Stable/Stable factors. The tendency to attribute the causes of successes or failures describes when a person has learnt to believe that failures in situations will always be present over time (i.e. in the past and in the future). A term used by Seligman in optimism and helplessness theory and more generally used in describing an aspect of attribution style. The opposite construct to *stable* is *unstable*, when the person believes the causes of successes and failures are not constrained by time (i.e. have not been there in the past or are not likely to be there in the future).

Standard deviation. Measure of variance of scores.

Standardisation of administration. Established procedures for providing a controlled environment in which a test is taken to allow comparisons across individuals.

Standardised testing. Psychological testing that conforms to a standard.

State anxiety. An unpleasant emotional arousal in the face of threatening demands or dangers, but placed within a particular situation or time.

State shyness. Shyness that is reactionary to situations and consists of an interplay of processes in the cognitive (e.g. self-focus, thoughts of escape, dread, preoccupation with the self, concern with one's performance), affective (e.g. anxiety, shame, embarrassment), behavioural (e.g. nervous gestures, inhibited speech, nervous and excessive speech) and physiological (e.g. sweating, heart palpitations, elevated blood pressure, dry mouth) levels of experience.

Stereotype. A set of beliefs about someone conforming to a set image or type.

Stereotype threat. The risk of confirming a negative stereotype about one's group as being self-characteristic.

Sternberg's triarchic model of giftedness. Model of giftedness that comprises analytical, practical and creative intelligence.

Storge. A term used to describe a love style, meaning an affectionate love that slowly develops from friendship.

Strategic pluralism. Evolutionary theory that suggests that multiple, sometimes even contradictory, behavioural strategies might be environmentally adaptive.

Stress-management scales. In the emotional intelligence literature, describes the ability to manage change, adapt and solve problems of a personal and interpersonal nature.

Structural model. Considers the *nature* of individual differences; in other words, it asks the question of 'how' do individuals differ?

Style of life. Adlerian term for a person's fundamental attitude towards life, the attitude that guides all their behaviour.

Subjective well-being. Shorter-term evaluation of well-being, representing a balance between feelings of positive and negative emotions, pleasure attainment and pain avoidance (see also hedonic well-being).

Sublimation. Defence mechanism outlined by Anna Freud (1936/2011) and occurring when we allow partial expression of our unconscious drives in a modified, socially acceptable and even desirable way. It is considered to be the most advanced and mature defence mechanism.

Subordinate construct. A construct that is included as an element in the context of another construct.

Successive processing. Represents a person's ability to place and maintain things in a particular order.

Superego. The third structure of personality that develops. It is composed of internalised parental attitudes and evaluations and acts as the child's conscience. The superego acts in opposition to the id, helping the ego to re-channel unacceptable id impulses.

Superordinate construct. A construct that is freely chosen, but it then determines subsequent choices. In this way, the initial exercise of free will determines subsequent behaviour. It demonstrates the way in which Kelly conceived the relationship between free will and determinism.

Superstitious rituals. Rigid behaviour that is considered repetitive and unusual, which takes on a somewhat magical significance for the individual; this then affects the individual in a positive way, although there is no evidence for a direct causal relationship between the behaviour and the outcome.

Supertrait. A term used by Eysenck to describe a collection of traits.

Surface traits. Collections of traits that cluster together in many individuals; that is, the scores on these traits are correlated with each other. Factor analysis uncovers a single underlying source trait common to the correlated group of surface traits.

Tactile abilities. Abilities that depend on the sense of touch.

Talking phase. In Dollard and Miller's two phases of treatment, this phase occurs when problem habits are identified, explored and labelled.

Tannenbaum's psychosocial definition of giftedness. Model of giftedness that comprises scarcity, surplus, quota and anomalous.

Task commitment. Within Renzulli's three-ring theory of giftedness, task commitment is the ability to show high levels of interest and enthusiasm for tasks, hard work and determination in a particular area, self-confidence and drive for achievement and setting high standards for one's own work.

T-data. Produced when participants are asked to complete tests where they do not know what the test is measuring so that they cannot fake or distort their answers.

Teleology. The study of purpose in natural phenomena; the belief that goals direct our current behaviour.

Temperament traits. The individual differences in the styles that people adopt when they are pursuing their goals.

Temporal lobe. Part of the brain concerned with language function and auditory perception; involved in long-term memory and emotion.

Temporary. The tendency to attribute the causes of successes or failures describes when a person has learnt to believe that failures in situations will always be present over time (i.e. in the past and in the future). Primarily used by Seligman in optimism and helplessness theory (*compare to* Stable/Stable factors).

Tender-minded attitudes. Part of Eysenck's theory of social attitudes. Tender-minded attitudes are thought to be a result of conditioning.

Testable concepts. Ideas that are able to undergo a procedure for determining the presence, quality or truth of something.

Testosterone. The male sex hormone, necessary for the development of male genitalia in the fetus. Increased levels of testosterone at puberty are responsible for further growth of male genitalia in the fetus and for the development and maintenance of what are known as male secondary sex characteristics, such as voice changes and facial hair.

Test–retest reliability. An assessment of reliability over time.

Thinking. Within Jungian theory, this describes a personality type that makes decisions and interprets stimuli using reason and logic.

Tolerance. Refers to the ability to fully give other human beings the right to be wrong.

Total genetic variance. The combination of additive genetic variance, dominance genetic variance and epistatic genetic variance.

Tough-minded attitude. State of mind thought to be caused by the lack of conditioning.

Trait. Generally, this term refers to a characteristic of behaviour. In psychology, it often refers to a part of personality. In biological psychology, traits refer to genetically inherited behaviours.

Trait shyness. Shyness that is dispositional; a relatively stable personality characteristic, suggesting a genetic predisposition towards inhibition and excessive anxiety.

Transference. Here the patient puts on to the analyst the feelings that were originally linked to previous figures in her or his life. It is a core element of psychoanalytic therapy.

Triangular theory of love. Consists of three basic components: intimacy, passion and commitment. These three basic components of love are positioned at the points of a triangle, and each element can be present within a relationship and can produce seven different combinations, or love styles.

Twin studies. Fraternal and identical twins are studied according to genetic overlaps to consider the genetic heritability of behaviour and personality.

Type A personality. A personality type typified by traits such as drive to achieve, competitiveness, hostility to competitors, persistent drive for recognition, advancement and power, working hard and working to deadlines with high levels of mental and physical alertness.

Type B personality. A personality type typified by traits such as being very relaxed and unhurried in their approach to life.

Tyranny of the shoulds. Compulsions originating in the idealised self.

Uncertainty avoidance. A dimension within Hofstede's work on personality and national culture that describes the extent to which members of culture develop social mechanisms or rules to attempt to deal with the anxiety that surrounds their lives.

Unconditional positive regard. Non-judgemental valuing of an individual. It is the term Rogers preferred over 'love', as he felt that most of what is termed love is not unconditional.

Unconditioned response. A response that occurs naturally.

Unconditioned stimulus/stimuli. Describes a stimulus that automatically elicits an unconditional response.

Unconscious. Consists of thoughts, memories, feelings, urges or fantasies of which we are unaware.

Unconscious mind. Consists of thoughts, memories, feelings, urges or fantasies that we are unaware of, because they are being actively kept in our unconscious, owing to their unacceptable nature.

Uncovering phase. The first part of Enright's model; includes steps 1–8 and describes the importance of identifying psychological defences, confronting and releasing anger and realising the additional psychological pain that the offence has caused. Identifying and accepting the reality of the hurt, the negative consequences and the injustice of the situation are all parts of these initial steps.

Understanding branch. In the emotional intelligence literature, this is understanding and analysing emotions; employing emotional knowledge (Mayer and Salovey [1997] model of emotional intelligence).

Undoing. Defence mechanism occurring when ritual behaviour is adopted that somehow magically cancels out the anxiety-provoking thoughts or actions that the person had earlier.

Unique traits. Rarer traits that tend to be unique to individuals.

Unlabelled. In learning theory, this term accounts for material being in the unconscious.

Unobservable. A property (e.g. in psychology, a behaviour) that cannot be observed or measured directly.

Validity. Describes researchers' concern with whether a test measures what they claim it is measuring.

Variability. The quality, state or degree of a variable varying.

Variety. In evolutionary theory, to be able to best adapt to the environment, the species must be prepared for that environment and any changes; therefore, the successful species will have a variety of behaviours within a generation, to ensure that at least some members of the species survive.

Verbal ability. The ability to express yourself and converse with others confidently and with some eloquence.

Verbal reasoning. To use the faculty of reason; think logically using verbal expression.

Vicarious experience. Occurs when the individual sees a person that they know shares the same fears as them actually performing the task they dread doing. This has a positive effect on the observer's self-efficacy.

Visual-spatial abilities. The ability to generate, retain, retrieve and transform visual images.

Voice strategy. A strategy involved in initiating the end of a relationship; involves actively and constructively attempting to improve conditions.

Voxel-based morphometry. Technique that seeks for grey and white matter around the brain.

Warfare. The waging of war against an enemy; armed conflict.

White matter. Brain matter that is responsible for information transmission.

Wilcoxon-pair test. A non-parametric statistical test used to examine the differences between scores administered to the same sample on two occasions.

Will to achieve. A term, within the five-factor model of personality, that refers to determined and organised traits of conscientiousness.

Within-family effects. Influences that occur within the family (e.g. with parents, children, siblings).

Within-species research. Research that looks for behaviour variation within a species.

Within-subject reliability. The extent to which two or more observers agree in their personality rating for one animal.

Work dimension. A term within the five-factor model of personality that refers to determined and organised traits of conscientiousness.

Work phase. Third phase of Enright's model of forgiveness. To truly forgive, an individual must be able to see the person who has hurt them in their life context and develop compassion and empathy for the offender based on situations that may have contributed to the offence (steps 12–15).

Working memory. Ability to store and perform a set of cognitive operations temporarily.

REFERENCES AND FURTHER READING

Aalto, A. M., Uutela, A. and Aro, A. R. (1997). Health-related quality of life among insulin dependent diabetics: Disease-related and psychosocial correlates. *Patient Education and Counseling, 30*, 215–225.

Abele, A. and Hermer, P. (1993). Mood influences on health-related judgements – appraisals of own health versus appraisal of unhealthy behaviours. *European Journal of Social Psychology, 23*, 613–625.

Abrahams, K. (1927). A short study on the development of the libido. In S. Freud (ed.), *Selected papers*. London: Hogarth Press.

Abramson, L. Y., Seligman, M. E. P. and Teasdale, J. D. (1978). Learned helplessness in humans: Critique and reformulation. *Journal of Abnormal Psychology, 87*(1), 49–74.

Adams, G. (2005). The cultural grounding of personal relationship: Enemyship in North American and West African worlds. *Journal of Personality and Social Psychology, 88*, 948–968.

Adler, A. (1917). *The neurotic constitution: Outline of a comparative individualistic psychology and psychotherapy*. New York: Moffat.

Adler, A. (1927). *Understanding human nature*. New York: Greenberg.

Adler, A. (1958). *What life should mean to you*. New York: Capricorn Books.

Adler, A. (1963). *The problem child: The life style of the problem child as analysed in specific cases*. New York: Moffat.

Adler, A. (1964). *Social interest: A challenge to mankind*. New York: Capricorn Books.

Adler, A. (1973). *The practice and theory of individual psychology*. Totowa, NJ: Littlefield, Adams & Co.

Adler, A. (1979). Advantages and disadvantages of the inferiority feeling. In H. L. Ansbacher and R. R. Ansbacher (eds), *Superiority and social interest: A collection of Alfred Adler's later writings*. New York: Norton.

Adorno, T. W., Frenkel-Brunswik, E., Levinson, D. J. and Sanford, R. N. (1950). *The authoritarian personality*. New York: Harper.

Advisory Committee on Head Start Research & Evaluation (1999). *Evaluating Head Start: A recommended framework for studying the impact of the Head Start Program*. Washington, DC: Administration for Children and Families.

Ainsworth, M. D. S., Blehar, M. C., Waters, E. and Wall, S. (1978). *Patterns of attachment: A psychological study of the strange situation*. Hillsdale, NJ: Erlbaum.

Alexander, F. (1950). *Psychosomatic medicine*. New York: Norton.

Alexander, G. and Hines, M. (2002). Sex differences in response to children's toys in nonhuman primates. *Evolution & Human Behavior, 23*, 467–479.

Allen, D. G., Weeks, K. P. and Moffat, K. R. (2005). Turnover intentions and voluntary turnover: The moderating roles of self-monitoring, locus of control, proactive personality, and risk aversion. *Journal of Applied Psychology, 90*, 980–990.

Allen, L. L., Haririfar, M., Cohen, J. and Henderson, M. J. (2000). Quality of life and locus of control of migraineurs. *Clinical Excellence in Nurse Practitioners, 4*, 41–49.

Allport, G. W. (1921). *Personality traits: Their classification and measurement*. New York: Holt.

Allport, G. W. (1937). *Personality: A psychological interpretation*. New York: Holt.

Allport, G. W. (1961). *Pattern and growth in personality*. New York: Holt, Rinehart & Winston.

Allport, G. W. (1966). Religious context of prejudice. *Journal for the Scientific Study of Religion, 5*, 447–457.

Allport, G. W. and Odbert, H. (1936). Trait names: A psycho-lexical study. *Psychological Monographs, 47*, 1–171.

Allport, G. W. and Ross, M. J. (1967). Personal religious orientation and prejudice. *Journal of Personality and Social Psychology, 5*, 432–443.

Almagor, M., Tellegen, A. and Waller, N. G. (1995). The Big Seven model: A cross-cultural replication and further exploration of the basic dimensions of natural language trait descriptors. *Journal of Personality and Social Psychology, 69*, 300–307.

Altemeyer, B. (1996). *The authoritarian specter*. Cambridge, MA: Harvard University Press.

Altemeyer, B. (1998). The other 'authoritarian personality'. In M. P. Zanna (ed.), *Advances in experimental social psychology*. Volume 30 (pp. 47–92). San Diego: Academic Press.

Altemeyer, B. (1999). To thine own self be untrue: Self-awareness in authoritarians. *North American Journal of Psychology, 1*, 157–164.

Amabile, T. M. and Gryskiewicz, N.D. (1989). The Creative Environment Work Scales: Work Environmental Inventory. *Creativity Research Journal, 2*, 231–254.

American Psychiatric Association (1994). *Diagnostic and statistical manual of mental disorders, fourth edition (DSM-IV)*. Washington, DC: American Psychiatric Association.

American Psychiatric Association (2000). *Diagnostic and statistical manual of mental disorders, fourth edition (DSM-IV-TR)*. Washington, DC: American Psychiatric Association.

Amir, M., Roziner, I., Knoll, A. and Neufield, M. Y. (1999). Self-efficacy and social support as mediators in the relation between disease severity and quality of life in patients with epilepsy. *Epilepsia, 40*, 41–49.

Amirkham, J. H., Risinger, R. T. and Swickert, R. J. (1995). Extraversion: A 'hidden' personality factor in coping. *Journal of Personality, 63*, 189–212.

Anderman, L. H. and Midgley, C. (1997). Motivation and middle school students. In J. L. Irvin (ed.), *What current research says to the middle level practitioner* (pp. 41–48). Columbus, OH: National Middle School Association.

Andersen, S. M. and Chen, S. (2002). The relational self: An interpersonal social-cognitive theory. *Psychological Review, 109*, 619–645.

Anderson, M. (2004). Sex differences in general intelligence. In R. L. Gregory (ed.), *The Oxford companion to the mind*. Oxford: Oxford University Press.

Anderson, N. and Shackleton, V. (1993). *Successful selection interviewing*. Blackwell: Oxford.

Angleitner, A. and Ostendorf, F. (1989). *Personality factors via self- and peer-ratings based on a representative sample of German trait descriptive terms.* Paper presented at the first European Congress of Psychology, Amsterdam, The Netherlands.

Anglina, D. M., Cohenab, P. R. and Chena, H. (2008) Duration of early maternal separation and prediction of schizotypal symptoms from early adolescence to midlife. *Schizophrenia Research, 103,* 143–150.

Ansbacher, H. L. and Ansbacher, R. R. (eds) (1956). *The individual psychology of Alfred Adler.* New York: Basic Books.

Archer, J. (2004). Sex differences in aggression in real-world setting: A meta-analytic review. *Review of General Psychology, 8,* 291–322.

Arden, R. and Plomin, R. (2006). Sex differences in variance of intelligence across childhood. *Personality and Individual Differences, 41,* 39–48.

Argyle, M. (1997). Is happiness a cause of health? *Psychology and Health, 12,* 769–781.

Argyle, M. and Henderson, M. (1984). The rules of friendship. *Journal of Personal Relationships, 1,* 211–237.

Arnett, P. and Newman, J. P. (2000). Gray's three-arousal model: An empirical investigation. *Personality and Individual Differences, 28,* 1171–1189.

Asendorpf, J. B. (1989). Shyness as a final common pathway for two different kinds of inhibition. *Journal of Personality and Social Psychology, 57,* 542–549.

Ashton, M. C. and Lee, K. (2001). A theoretical basis for the major dimensions of personality. *European Journal of Personality, 15,* 327–353.

Ashton, M. C. and Lee, K. (2007). Empirical, theoretical, and practical advantages of the HEXACO model of personality structure. *Personality and Social Psychology Review, 11,* 150–166.

Ashton, M. C., Lee, K. and Son, C. (2000). Honesty as the sixth factor of personality: Correlations with Machiavellianism, primary psychopathy and social adroitness. *European Journal of Personality, 14,* 359–368.

Aspinwall, L. G. and Taylor, S. E. (1992). Modeling cognitive adaptation: A longitudinal investigation of the impact of individual differences and coping on college adjustment and performance. *Journal of Personality and Social Psychology, 63,* 989–1003.

Atherton, J. S. (2002). *Learning and teaching: Learning from experience.* Available online at www.learningandteaching.info/learning/experience.htm; accessed 14 January 2005.

Augusto-Landa, J. M., Pulido-Martos, M. and Lopez-Zafra, E. (2011). Does emotional intelligence and optimism/pessimism predict psychological well-being? *Journal of Happiness Studies, 12,* 463–474.

Austin, E. J., Farrelly, D., Black, C. and Moore, H. (2007). Emotional intelligence, Machiavellianism and emotional manipulation: Does EI have a dark side? *Personality and Individual Differences, 43,* 179–189.

Averill, J. R., Catlin, G. and Kyum, K. C. (1990). *The rules of hope.* New York: Springer-Verlag.

Babcock, M. K. (1988). Embarrassment: A window on the self. *Journal for the Theory of Social Behaviour, 18,* 459–483.

Baeckström, M. and Holmes, B. M. (2001). Measuring adult attachment: A construct validation of two self-report instruments. *Scandinavian Journal of Psychology, 42,* 79–86.

Baghurst, P. A., McMichael, A. J., Wigg, N. R. *et al.* (1992). Environmental exposure to lead and children's intelligence at the age of seven years: The Port Pirie cohort study. *New England Journal of Medicine, 327,* 1279–1284.

Bailey, B. N., Delaney-Black, V., Covington, C. Y. *et al.* (2004). Prenatal exposure to binge drinking and cognitive and behavioral outcomes at age 7 years. *American Journal of Obstetrics and Gynecology, 191,* 1037–1043.

Bailey, M. B. and Bailey, R. E. (1993). 'Misbehaviour': A case history. *American Psychologist, 48,* 1157–1158.

Baker, L. D. and Daniels, D. (1990). Nonshared environmental influences and personality differences in adult twins. *Journal of Personality and Social Psychology, 58,* 103–110.

Baker, M. and Gorsuch, R. (1982). Trait anxiety and intrinsic-extrinsic religiousness. *Journal for the Scientific Study of Religion, 21,* 119–122.

Baldwin, J. M. (1913). *History of psychology.* London: Watts.

Bandura, A. (1977). *Social learning theory.* Englewood Cliffs, NJ: Prentice Hall.

Bandura, A. (1978). The self-system in reciprocal determinism. *American Psychologist, 33,* 344–358.

Bandura, A. (1989). Human agency in social cognition. *American Psychologist, 44,* 1175–1184.

Bandura, A. (1990). Some reflections on reflection. *Psychological Inquiry, 1,* 101–105.

Bandura, A. (1991). Self-efficacy. In R. Schwarzer and R. Wicklund (eds), *Anxiety and self-focussed attention.* New York: Harwood Academic.

Bandura, A. (1994). Self-efficacy. In V. S. Ramachandran (ed.), *Encyclopaedia of human behaviour.* New York: Academic Press.

Bandura, A. (1997). *Self-efficacy: The exercise of control.* New York: Freeman.

Bandura, A. (1998). Personal and collective efficacy in human adaptation and change. In J. G. Adair, D. Belanger and K. L. Dion (eds), *Advances in psychological science* (Vol. 1: *Personal, social and cultural aspects*). Hove, UK: Psychology Press.

Bandura, A. (1999). Social cognitive theory of personality. In L. Pervin and O. John (eds), *Handbook of Personality* (2nd edn). New York: Guilford.

Bandura, A. (2000). Exercise of human agency through collective efficacy. *Current Directions in Psychological Science, 9,* 75–78.

Bandura, A. (2001). Social cognitive theory: An agentic perspective. *Annual Review of Psychology, 52,* 1–26.

Bandura, A. (2002). Swimming against the mainstream: The early years from chilly tributary to transformative mainstream. *Behaviour Research & Therapy, 42,* 613–630.

Bandura, A. (2004). Self-efficacy. In W. E. Craighead and C. B. Nemeroff (eds), *The concise Corsini encyclopedia of psychology and behavioral science* (3rd edn). Hoboken, NJ: Wiley.

Bandura, A. (2006). Guide for creating self-efficacy scales. In F. Pajares and T. Urdan (eds), *Self-efficacy beliefs of adolescents.* Greenwich, CT: Information Age Publishing. Also available at www.des.emory.edu/mfp/self-efficacy.html.

Bandura, A. (ed.). (1995). *Self-efficacy in changing societies.* New York: Cambridge University Press.

Bandura, A. and Walters, R. H. (1963). *Social learning and personality development.* New York: Holt, Rinehart and Winston.

Bannister, D. (1985). *New perspectives on personal construct theory.* London: Academic Press.

Bannister, D. (ed.) (1977). *New perspectives in personal construct theory.* New York: Academic Press.

Bannister, D. and Fransella, F. (1966). A grid test of schizophrenic thought disorder. *British Journal of Social and Clinical Psychology, 5,* 95–102.

Bannister, D., Fransella, F. and Agnew, J. (1971). Characteristics and validity of the grid test of thought disorder. *British Journal of Social and Clinical Psychology, 10,* 144–151.

Barak, Y. (2006). The immune system and happiness. *Autoimmunity Reviews, 5,* 523–527.

Baral, B. and Das, J. P. (2004). Intelligence: What is indigenous to India and what is shared? In R. J. Sternberg (ed.), *International handbook of intelligence* (pp. 270–301). Cambridge: Cambridge University Press.

Barlow, D. H. (2002). *Anxiety and its disorders: The nature and treatment of anxiety and panic* (2nd edn). New York: Guilford.

Bar-On, R. (1997). *The Emotional Quotient Inventory (EQ-i): A test of emotional intelligence.* Toronto, Canada: Multi-Health Systems, Inc.

Bar-On, R. (2005). The Bar-On model of emotional-social intelligence. In P. Fernández-Berrocal and N. Extremera (guest eds), Special Issue on Emotional Intelligence. *Psicothema, 17.*

Baron-Cohen, S. (2002). The extreme male brain theory of autism. *Trends in Cognitive Sciences, 6*, 248–254.

Barrett, L., Dunbar, R. and Lycett, J. (2001). *Human evolutionary psychology.* London: Palgrave Macmillan.

Barrick, M. R. and Mount, M. K. (1991). The big five personality dimensions and job performance: A meta-analysis. *Personnel Psychology, 44*, 1–26.

Barron, F. (1953). An ego-strength scale which predicts response to psychotherapy. *Journal of Consulting Psychology, 17*, 327–333.

Barsalou, L. W., Simmons, W. K., Barbey, A. K., and Wilson, C. D. (2003). Grounding conceptual knowledge in the modality-specific systems. *Trends in Cognitive Sciences, 7*, 84–91.

Bartholomew, K. and Horowitz, L. M. (1991). Attachment styles among young adults: A test of a four-category model. *Journal of Personality and Social Psychology, 61*, 226–244.

Barton, K., Dielman, T. E. and Cattell, R. B. (1971). The prediction of school grades from personality and IQ measures. *Personality, 2*, 325–333.

Bateson, P. (1982). Preferences for cousins in Japanese quail. *Nature, 295*, 236–237.

Batson, C. D. (1976). Religion as prosocial: Agent or double agent? *Journal for the Scientific Study of Religion, 15*, 29–45.

Batson, C. D. and Ventis, W. L. (1982). *The religious experience: A social psychological perspective.* New York: Oxford University Press.

Batson, C. D., Schoenrade, P. and Ventis, W. L. (1993). *Religion and the individual: A social psychological perspective.* London: Oxford University Press.

Batty, G. D., Deary, I. J. and Gottfredson, L. S. (2007). Premorbid (early life) IQ and later mortality risk: Systematic review. *Annals of Epidemiology, 17*, 278–288.

Batty G.D., Wennerstad K.M., Davey Smith G. *et al.* (2009). IQ in late adolescence/early adulthood and mortality by middle age: cohort study of one million Swedish men. *Epidemiology, 20*, 100–9.

Baumeister, R. F. and Tice, D. M. (1988). Metatraits. *Journal of Personality, 56*, 571–598.

Baxter, L. A. (1986). Gender differences in the heterosexual relationship rules embedded in break-up accounts. *Journal of Social and Personal Relationships, 3*, 289–306.

BBC News Online. (14 February 2006). The UK Love Map. Available online at http://news.bbc.co.uk/1/hi/magazine/4712814.stm; accessed 26 March 2006.

Beck, A. (2005). The current state of cognitive therapy: A 40-year retrospective. *Archives of General Psychiatry, 62*, 953–959.

Beck, A. T., Steer, R. A. and Brown, G. K. (1996). *Manual for the Beck Depression Inventory-II.* San Antonio, TX: Psychological Corporation.

Beer, J. S. (2002). Implicit self-theories of shyness. *Journal of Personality and Social Psychology, 83*(4), 1009–1024.

Beit-Hallahmi, B. and Argyle, M. (1997). *The psychology of religious behaviour, belief and experience.* London: Routledge.

Bellisle, F. (2004). Effects of diet on behaviour and cognition in children. *British Journal of Nutrition, 92*, 227–232.

Belmont, L. and Marolla, F. A. (1973). Birth order, family size, and intelligence. *Science, 182*, 1096–1101.

Bem, D. J. and Allen, A. (1974). On predicting some of the people some of the time: The search for cross-situational consistencies in behaviour. *Psychological Review, 81*, 506–520.

Benassi, V. A., Sweeney, P. D. and Dufour, C. L. (1988). Is there a relationship between locus of control orientation and depression? *Journal of Abnormal Psychology, 97*, 357–367.

Bender, W. N. (1995). *Learning disabilities: Characteristics, identification and teaching strategies* (2nd edn). Needham Heights, MA: Allyn & Bacon.

Benedict, R. (1934). *Patterns of Culture.* Boston: Houghton Mifflin.

Benedict, R. (1946) *Chrysanthemum and the Sword.* Boston: Houghton Mifflin.

Benight, C. C. and Bandura, A. (2004). Social cognitive theory of posttraumatic recovery: The role of perceived self-efficacy. *Behaviour Research and Therapy, 42*, 1129–1148.

Benjamins, M. R. (2004). Religion and functional health among the elderly: Is there a relationship, and is it constant? *Journal of Aging and Health, 16*, 355–374.

Bennett, E. A. (1983). *What Jung really said.* New York: Schocken Books.

Benson, E. (2003). Intelligent intelligence testing. *APA Monitor on Psychology, 34.*

Benton, D. (1991). Vitamin and mineral supplements improve intelligence scores and concentration of six-year-old children. *Personality and Individual Differences, 12*, 1151–1158.

Benton, D. (2001). Dietary supplements and intelligence/academic performance. *Neuroscience and Biobehavior Review, 25*, 297–309.

Benton, D. and Roberts, G. (1988). Effect of vitamin and mineral supplementation on intelligence of a sample of schoolchildren. *Lancet, i*, 140–144.

Berenbaum, H., Valera, E. M. and Kerns, J. G. (2003). Psychological trauma and schizotypal symptoms. *Schizophrenia Bulletin, 29*, 143–152.

Berg, C. A. and Sternberg, R. J. (1992). Adults' conceptions of intelligence across the life span. *Psychology and Aging, 7*, 221–231.

Bergin, A. E. (1983). Religiosity and psychological well-being: A critical re-evaluation and meta-analysis. *Professional Psychology: Research and Practice, 14*, 170–184.

Bergin, A. E., Masters, K. S. and Richards, P. S. (1987). Religiousness and psychological well-being re-considered: A study of an intrinsically religious sample. *Journal of Counseling Psychiatry, 34*, 197–204.

Berlyne, D. E. (1967). Arousal and reinforcement. In D. Levine (ed.), *Nebraska Symposium on motivation* (pp. 1–10). Lincoln: University of Nebraska Press.

Berry, J. W. (1984). Towards a universal psychology of cognitive competence. In P. S. Fry (ed.), *Changing conceptions of intelligence and intellectual functioning* (pp. 35–61). Amsterdam: North Holland.

Berry, J. W., Worthington, E. L., Parrott, L., O'Conner, L. E. and Wade, N. G. (2001). Dispositional forgivingness: Development and construct validity of the Transgression Narrative Test of Forgivingness (TNTF). *Personality and Social Psychology Bulletin, 27*, 1277–1290.

Bertua, C., Anderson, N. and Salgado, J. F. (2005). The predictive validity of cognitive ability tests: A UK meta-analysis. *Journal of Occupational and Organizational Psychology, 78*, 387–409.

Biaobin, Y., Xue, Z. and Lin, Q. (2004). SWB and PWB: The distinction and integration of two well-being research orientations. *Psychological Science (China)*, *27*, 836–838.

Bieri, J. (1955). Cognitive complexity–simplicity and predictive behaviour. *Journal of Abnormal and Social Psychology*, *51*, 263–268.

Billingslea, F. Y. (1940). The relationship between emotionality, activity, curiosity, persistence and weight in the male rat. *Journal of Comparative Psychology*, *29*, 315–325.

Binet, A. (1916). New methods for the diagnosis of the intellectual level of subnormals. In E. S. Kite (trans.), *The development of intelligence in children*. Vineland, NJ: Publications of the Training School at Vineland. (Originally published 1905 in *L'Année Psychologique*, *12*, 191–244.)

Binet, A. and Simon, T. (1911). *La mesure du développement de l'intelligence chez les jeunes enfants*. Paris: A. Coneslant.

Binet, A. and Simon, T. (1916). *The development of intelligence in children*. Baltimore, MD: Williams & Wilkins. (Reprinted 1973, New York: Arno Press; reprinted 1983, Salem, NH: Ayer.) The 1973 volume includes reprints of many of Binet's articles on testing.

Birney, E. *et al.* [The ENCODE Project Consortium] (2007). Identification and analysis of functional elements in 1% of the human genome by the ENCODE pilot project. *Nature*, *447*, 799–816.

Birnie, S., and Horvath, P. (2002). Psychological predictors of internet social communication. *Journal of Computer-Mediated Communication*, *7*, 13–27.

Bishop, J. and Lane, R. C. (2002). The dynamics and dangers of entitlement. *Psychoanalytic Psychology*, *19*, 739–758.

Black, M. (1973). Some aversive responses to a would-be reinforcer. In H. Wheeler (ed.), *Beyond the punitive society*. San Francisco: Freeman.

Blagov, P. S. and Singer, J. A. (2004). Four dimensions of self-defining memories (specificity, meaning, content, and affect) and their relationships to self-restraint, distress, and repressive defensiveness. *Journal of Personality*, *72*, 481–511.

Blagov, P. S. and Westen, D. (2008). Questioning the coherence of histrionic personality disorder, borderline and hysterical personality subtypes in adults and adolescents. *Journal of Nervous and Mental Disease*, *196*, 785–797.

Blagov, P. S., Fowler, K. and Lilienfeld, S. (2007) Histrionic personality disorder. In W. O'Donohue, S. O. Lilienfeld and K. A. Fowler (eds), *Personality disorders: Toward DSM-V* (pp. 203–232). Thousand Oaks, CA: Sage.

Blake, J. (1981). Family size and the quality of children. *Demography*, *18*, 421–442.

Block, J. (1961). *The Q-sort methodology in personality assessment and psychiatric research*. Springfield, IL: Charles C. Thomas.

Block, J. (1977). Advancing the science of personality: Paradigmatic shift or improving the quality of research? In D. Magnusson and N. S. Emdler (eds), *Psychology at the crossroads: Current issues in interactional psychology* (pp. 37–63). Hillsdale, NJ: Erlbaum.

Block, J. (1993). Studying personality the long way. In D. C. Funder, R. D. Parke, C. Tomlinson-Keasey and K. Widaman (eds), *Studying lives through time* (pp. 9–41). Washington, DC: American Psychological Association.

Block, J. H. and Block, J. (1980). The role of ego control and ego resiliency in the organisation of behaviour. In W. A. Collins (ed.), *Development of cognitive, affect and social relations: The Minnesota symposium in child psychology* (pp. 39–101). Hillsdale, NJ: Erlbaum.

Block, J., and Block, J. H. (2006). Venturing a 30-year longitudinal study. *American Psychologist*, *61*, 315–327.

Blum, G. (1953). *Psychoanalytic theories of personality*. New York: McGraw-Hill.

Board, B. and Fritzon, K. (2005). Disordered personalities at work. *Psychology, Crime and Law*, *11*, 17–32.

Boies, K., Lee, K., Ashton, M. C., Pascal, S. and Nicol, A. A. M. (2001). The structure of the French personality lexicon. *European Journal of Personality*, *15*, 277–295.

Bonarius, J. (1965). Research in the personal construct theory of George A. Kelly: Role Construct Repertory Test and basic theory. In B. Maher (ed.), *Progress in experimental personality research*. New York: Academic Press.

Booth-Kewley, S. and Friedman, H. S. (1987). Psychological predictors of heart disease: A quantitative review. *Psychological Bulletin*, *101*, 343–362.

Borkenau, P. (1990). Traits as ideal-based and goal-derived social categories. *Journal of Personality and Social Psychology*, *58*, 381–396.

Borkenau, P. and Liebler, A. (1993). Convergence of stranger ratings of personality and intelligence with self-ratings, partner-ratings and measured intelligence. *Journal of Personality and Social Psychology*, *65*, 546–553.

Borkovec, T. D. and Lyonfields, J. D. (1993). Worry: Thought suppression of emotional processing. In H. W. Krohne (ed.), *Attention and avoidance*. Toronto: Hogrefe and Huber.

Botwin, M., Buss, D. M. and Shackelford, T. K. (1997). Personality and mate preferences: Five factors in mate selection and marital satisfaction. *Journal of Personality*, *65*, 107–136.

Bouchard, T. J. (1993). The genetic architecture of intelligence. In P. A. Vernon (ed.), *Biological approaches to the study of human intelligence*. Norwood, NJ: Ablex.

Bouchard, T. J. (1994). Genes, environment, and personality. *Science*, *264*, 1700–1701.

Bouchard, T. J. Jr and Loehlin, J. C. (2001). Genes, personality, and evolution. *Behavioural Genetics*, *31*, 243–273.

Bouchard, T. J. and McGue, M. (1981). Family studies of intelligence: A review. *Science*, *212*, 1055–1059.

Bouchard, T. J. and Segal, N. L. (1985). Environment and IQ. In B. B. Wolman (ed.), *Handbook of intelligence: Theories, measurements, and applications* (pp. 391–464). New York: Wiley.

Bower, G. H. (1981). Mood and memory. *American Psychologist*, *36*, 129–148.

Bowlby, J. (1969). *Attachment and loss* (Vol. 1: *Attachment*). New York: Basic Books.

Bowlby, J. (1988). Developmental psychiatry comes of age. *American Journal of Psychiatry*, *145*, 1–10.

Boyatzis, R. E. (1994). Stimulating self-directed learning through the Managerial Assessment and Development Course. *Journal of Management Education*, *18*, 304–323.

Boyatzis, R. E. and Van Oosten, E. (2002). Developing emotionally intelligent organizations. In R. Millar (ed.), *International executive development programmes* (7th edn). London: Kogan Page.

Boyatzis, R. E., Cowen, S. S. and Kolb, D. A. (1995). *Innovations in professional education: Steps on a journey from teaching to learning*. San Francisco: Jossey-Bass.

Boyle, G. J. (1989). Re-examination of the major personality factors in the Cattell, Comrey and Eysenck scales: Were the factor solutions by Noller *et al.* optimal? *Personality and Individual Differences*, *10*, 1289–1299.

Bradley, C., Lewis, K. S., Jennings, A. M. and Ward, J. D. (1990). Scales to measure perceived control developed specifically for people with tablet-treated diabetes. *Diabetes Medicine*, *7*, 685–94.

Brannan, M. E. and Petrie, T. A. (2011). Psychological well-being and the body dissatisfaction–bulimic symptomatology relationship: An examination of moderators. *Eating Behaviours, 12*, 233–241.

Bratko, D., Chamorro-Premuzic, T. and Saks, Z. (2006). Personality and school performance: Incremental validity of self- and peer-ratings over intelligence. *Personality and Individual Differences, 41*, 131–142.

Braungart, J. M., Plomin, R., DeFries, J. C. and Fulker, D. W. (1992a). Genetic influence on tester-rated infant temperament as assessed by Bayley's Infant Behavior Record: Nonadoptive and adoptive siblings and twins. *Developmental Psychology, 28*, 40–47.

Braungart, J. M., Plomin, R., DeFries, J. C. and Fulker, D. W. (1992b). Genetic mediation of the home environment during infancy: A sibling adoption study of the HOME. *Developmental Psychology, 28*, 1048–1055.

Brehm, S. (1992). *Intimate relationships*. New York: McGraw-Hill.

Brewin, C. R. and Andrews, B. (1998). Recovered memories of trauma: Phenomenological and cognitive mechanisms. *Clinical Psychology, 18*, 949–970.

Brewin, C. R. and Andrews, B. (2000). The example of repression. *The Psychologist, 13*, 615–617.

Briffa, J. (2005). Lovin' spoonful. *Observer*, Sunday, 18 September.

Briggs, S. R. (1989). Shyness: Introversion or neuroticism? *Journal of Research in Personality, 22*, 290–307.

Bringmann, M. W. (1992). Computer-based methods for the analysis and interpretation of personal construct systems. In R. A. Neimeyer and G. J. Neimeyer (eds), *Advances in personal construct psychology, 2*, 57–90. Greenwich, CT: JAI Press.

Brissette, I., Scheier, M. F. and Carver, C. S. (2002). The role of optimism in social network development, coping, and psychological adjustment during a life transition. *Journal of Personality and Social Psychology, 82*, 102–111.

British Heart Foundation (2010). *Coronary Heart Disease Statistics 2010*. British Heart Foundation. www.bhf.org.uk/research/statistics.aspx; accessed May 2012.

Britton, P. C., Williams, G. C. and Conner, K. R. (2008). Self-determination theory, motivational interviewing, and the treatment of clients with acute suicidal ideation. *Journal of Clinical Psychology, 64*, 52–66.

Brose, L. A., Rye, M. S., Lutz-Zois, C. and Ross, S. R. (2005). Forgiveness and personality traits. *Personality and Individual Differences, 39*, 35–46.

Brown, A. (2009). Prison 'wrong' for mentally-ill inmates. BBC News, Online, 4 February 2009, http://news.bbc.co.uk/1/hi/uk/7868330.stm; accessed 4 February 2009.

Brown, G. B., Have, T. T., Henriques, G. R. *et al.* (2005). Cognitive therapy for the prevention of suicide attempts: A randomized controlled trial. *Journal of the American Medical Association, 294*, 563–570.

Brown, G. R. and Anderson, B. (1991). Psychiatric morbidity in adult inpatients with childhood histories of sexual and physical abuse. *American Journal of Psychiatry, 148*, 55–61.

Brown, R. P. (2003). Measuring individual differences in the tendency to forgive: Construct validity and links with depression. *Personality and Social Psychology Bulletin, 29*, 759–771.

Brown, W. J. and Cody, M. J. (1991). Effects of a prosocial television soap opera in promoting women's status. *Human Communications Research, 18*, 114–142.

Bruch, M. A. and Cheek, J. M. (1995). Developmental factors in childhood and adolescent shyness. In R. R. G. Heimberg, M. Liebowitz, D. A. Hope and S. Scheier (eds), *Social phobia: Diagnosis, assessment and treatment* (pp. 163–184). New York: Guilford.

Bryant, R. A., Sackville, T., Dang, S. T., Moulds, M. and Guthrie, R. (1999). Treating acute stress disorder: An evaluation of cognitive behaviour therapy and supportive counselling techniques. *American Journal of Psychiatry, 156*, 1780–1786.

Buchanan, G. and Seligman, M. E. P. (eds). (1995). *Explanatory style*. Hillsdale, NJ: Erlbaum.

Buhrmann H. G., Brown, B. and Zaugg, M. K. (1982). Superstitious beliefs and behavior: A comparison of male and female basketball players. *Journal of Sport Behaviors, 5*, 75–185.

Buirski, P., Plutchik, R. and Kellerman, H. (1978). Sex differences, dominance, and personality in the chimpanzee. *Animal Behaviour, 26*, 123–129.

Bullock, W. A. and Gilliland, K. (1993). Eysenck's arousal theory of introversion–extraversion: A convergent measures investigation. *Journal of Personality and Social Psychology, 64*, 113–123.

Burger, J. M. (1995). Individual differences in preference for solitude. *Journal of Research in Personality, 29*, 85–108.

Burger, J. M. (1997). *Personality*. Pacific Grove, CA: Brooks/Cole.

Bushman, B. J. and Baumeister, R. F. (1998). Threatened egotism, narcissism, self-esteem, and direct and displaced aggression: Does self-love or self-hate lead to violence? *Journal of Personality and Social Psychology, 75*, 219–229.

Buss, A. H. (1980). *Self-consciousness and social anxiety*. San Francisco: Freeman.

Buss, A. H. (1984). A conception of shyness. In J. A. Daly and J. C. McCroskey (eds), *Avoiding communication: Shyness, reticence and communication apprehension* (pp. 39–50). Beverly Hills, CA: Sage.

Buss, A. H. (1986). A theory of shyness. In W. H. Jones, J. M. Cheek and S. R. Briggs (eds), *Shyness: Perspectives on research and treatment* (pp. 39–46). New York: Plenum.

Buss, A. H. (ed.). (1979). *Psychology in social context*. New York: Irvington.

Buss, D. M. (1991). Evolutionary personality psychology. *Annual Review of Psychology, 42*, 459–491.

Buss, D. M. (2011). Personality and the Adaptive Landscape: The role of individual differences in creating and solving social adaptive problems. In P. H. Hawley and D. M. Buss. *The evolution of personality and individual differences* (pp. 29–60). Oxford: Oxford University Press.

Buss, D. M. and Barnes, M. (1986). Preferences in human mate selection. *Journal of Personality and Social Psychology, 50*, 559–570.

Buss, D. M. and Schmitt, D. P. (1993). Sexual strategies theory: An evolutionary perspective on human mating. *Psychological Review, 100*, 204–232.

Buss, D. M., Abbott, M., Angleitner, A. *et al.* (1990). International preferences in selecting mates: A study of 37 societies. *Journal of Cross Cultural Psychology, 21*, 5–47.

Buss, D. M., Larsen, R. J., Westen, D. and Semmelroth, J. (1992). Sex differences in jealousy: Evolution, physiology, and psychology. *Psychological Science, 3*, 251–255.

Butler, J. C. (2000). Personality and emotional correlates of right-wing authoritarianism. *Social Behaviour and Personality, 28*, 1–14.

Byrne, D. (1961). Interpersonal attraction and attitude similarity. *Journal of Abnormal and Social Psychology, 62*, 604–623.

Byrne, D. (1971). *The attraction paradigm*. New York: Academic Press.

Cahan, S. and Cohen, N. (1989). Age versus schooling effects on intelligence development. *Child Development, 60*, 1239–1249.

Callahan, C. M. (2000). Intelligence and giftedness. In R. J. Sternberg (ed.), *Handbook of intelligence* (pp. 159–175). Cambridge: Cambridge University Press.

Calvin, C. M., Batty, G. D. and Deary, I. J. (2011). Cognitive epidemiology: Concepts, evidence and future directions. In T. Chamorro-Premuzic, S. von Stumm and A. A, Furnham, *The Wiley-Blackwell handboook of individual differences*. Chichester: Wiley/Blackwell.

Cameron, J. and Pierce, W. D. (1994). Reinforcement, reward, and intrinsic motivation: A meta-analysis. *Review of Educational Research, 64*, 363–423.

Campbell, A., Shirley, L., Heywood, C. and Crook, C. (2000). Infants' visual preference for sex-congruent babies, children, toys and activities: A longitudinal study. *British Journal of Developmental Psychology, 18*, 479–498.

Campbell, D. T. and Fiske, D. W. (1959) Convergent and discriminant validation by the multitrait-multimethod matrix. *Psychological Bulletin, 56*, 81–105.

Campbell, J. B. and Hawley, C. W. (1982). Study habits and Eysenck's theory of extraversion–introversion. *Journal of Research in Personality, 16*, 139–146.

Campbell, W. K., Rudich, E. and Sedikides, C. (2002). Narcissism, self-esteem, and the positivity of self-views: Two portraits of self-love. *Personality and Social Psychology Bulletin, 28*, 358–368.

Cannon, W. B. (1929). *Bodily changes in pain, hunger, fear and rage: An account of recent research into the function of emotional excitement* (2nd edn). New York: Appleton-Century-Crofts.

Capitanio, J. P. (1999). Personality dimensions in adult male rhesus macaques: Prediction of behaviors across time and situation. *American Journal of Primatology, 47*, 299–320.

Caplan, P. J. (1984). The myth of women's masochism. *American Psychologist, 39*, 130–139.

Carducci, B. J. (1999). *Shyness: A bold new approach*. New York: HarperCollins.

Carducci, B. J. (2000). What shy individuals do to cope with their shyness: A content analysis (Chapter 11). In W. R. Crozier (ed.), *Shyness: Development, consolidation and change*. London: Routledge.

Carducci, B. J. and Zimbardo, P. (1995). Are you shy? *Psychology Today, 64*, 34–40.

Carey, G. (2002). *Human genetics for the social scientists*. London: Sage.

Carifio, J. and Rhodes, L. (2002). Construct validities and the empirical relationships between optimism, hope, self-efficacy, and locus of control. *Work, 19*(2), 125–136.

Carlson, J. (1989). Brief therapy for health promotion. *Individual Psychology, 45*, 220–229.

Carlson, R. and Levy, N. (1973). Studies of Jungian typology: I. Memory, social perception, and personnel. *Journal of Personality, 41*, 559–576.

Carlstead, K., Mellen, J. and Kleiman, D. G. (1999). Black rhinoceros (*Diceros bicornis*) in U.S. zoos: I. Individual behavior profiles and their relationship to breeding success. *Zoo Biology, 18*, 17–34.

Carroll, J. B. (1982). The measurement of intelligence. In R. J. Sternberg (ed.), *Handbook of human intelligence* (pp. 29–120). Cambridge: Cambridge University Press.

Carroll, J. B. (1992). Cognitive abilities: The state of the art. *Psychological Science, 3*, 266–270.

Carroll, J. B. (1993). *Human cognitive abilities: A survey of factor-analytic studies*. New York: Press Syndicate of the University of Cambridge.

Carroll, J. B. (1997a). Psychometrics, intelligence, and public perception. *Intelligence, 24*, 25–52.

Carroll, J. B. (1997b). The three-stratum theory of cognitive abilities. In D. P. Flanagan, J. L. Genshaft and P. L. Harrison (eds), *Contemporary intellectual assessment: Theories, tests, and issues* (pp. 122–130). New York: Guilford.

Cartwright, M., Wardle, J., Steggles, N. *et al*. (2003). Stress and dietary practices in adolescents. *Health Psychology, 22*, 362–369.

Carver, C. S. (1998). Generalization, adverse events, and development of depressive symptoms. *Journal of Personality, 66*, 609–620.

Carver, C. S. and Connor-Smith, J. (2010). Personality and coping. *Annual Review of Psychology, 61*, 679–704.

Carver, C. S. and Scheier, M. F. (1981). *Attention and self-regulation: A control-theory approach to human behavior*. New York: Springer-Verlag.

Carver, C. S. and Scheier, M. F. (1990). Origins and functions of positive and negative affect: A control-process view. *Psychological Review, 97*, 19–35.

Carver, C. S. and Scheier, M. F. (1996). *Perspectives on personality* (3rd edn). Boston: Allyn & Bacon.

Carver, C. S. and Scheier, M. F. (1998). *On the self-regulation of behavior*. New York: Cambridge University Press.

Carver, C. S. and Scheier, M. F. (1999a). Optimism. In C. R. Snyder (ed.), *Coping: The psychology of what works* (pp. 182–204). New York: Oxford University Press.

Carver, C. S. and Scheier, M. F. (1999b). Stress, coping, and self-regulatory processes. In L. A. Pervin and O. P. John (eds), *Handbook of personality* (2nd edn, pp. 553–575). New York: Guilford.

Carver, C. S. and Scheier, M. F. (2000). *Perspectives on personality*. Boston: Allyn & Bacon.

Carver, C. S. and Scheier, M. F. (2001). Optimism, pessimism, and self-regulation. In E. C. Chang (ed.), *Optimism and pessimism: Implications for theory, research, and practice* (pp. 31–51). Washington, DC: American Psychological Association.

Carver, C. S. and Scheier, M. F. (2003). Self-regulatory perspectives on personality. In T. Millon and M. J. Lerner (eds), *Handbook of psychology: Personality and social psychology* (Vol. 5, pp. 185–208). New York: Wiley.

Carver, C. S. and White, T. L. (1994). Behavioral inhibition, behavioral activation, and affective responses to impending reward and punishment: The BIS/BAS Scales. *Journal of Personality and Social Psychology, 67*, 319–333.

Carver, C., Scheier, M. and Weintraub, J. (1989). Assessing coping strategies: A theoretically based approach. *Journal of Personality and Social Psychology, 56*, 260–283.

Carver, C. S., Kus, L. A. and Scheier, M. F. (1994). Effects of good versus bad mood and optimistic versus pessimistic outlook on social acceptance versus rejection. *Journal of Social and Clinical Psychology, 13*, 138–151.

Caspi, A. (1998). Personality development across the life course. In W. Damon (ser. ed.) and N. Eisenberg (vol. ed.), *Handbook of Child Psychology* (Vol. 3: *Social, emotional, and personality development*) (pp. 311–388). New York: Wiley.

Cattell, R. B. (1950). *Personality: A systematic, theoretical, and factual study*. New York: McGraw-Hill.

Cattell, R. B. (1957). *Personality and motivation: Structure and measurement*. New York: Harcourt, Brace & World.

Cattell, R. B. (1965). *The scientific analysis of personality*. Baltimore, MD: Penguin.

Cattell, R. B. (1971). *Abilities, their structure, growth, and action*. New York: Houghton Mifflin.

Cattell, R. B. (1973). *Personality and mood by questionnaire*. New York: Jossey-Bass.

Cattell, R. B. (1979). *Personality and learning theory (Vol. 1: A systems theory of maturation and structured learning)*. New York: Springer.

Cattell, R. B. (1980). *Personality and learning theory* (Vol. 2: *A systems theory of maturation and structured learning*). New York: Springer.

Cattell, R. B. (1982). *The inheritance of personality and ability*. New York: Academic Press.

Cattell, R. B. and Child, D. (1975). *Motivation and dynamic structure*. New York: Wiley.

Cattell, R. B. and Kline, P. (1977). *The scientific analysis of personality and motivation*. New York: Academic Press.

Cattell, R. B., Eber, H. W. and Tatsuoka, M. M. (1970). *Handbook for the Sixteen-Personality Factor questionnaire*. Champaign, IL: Institute for Personality and Ability Testing.

Cavanagh, K., Shapiro, D. A., Van Den Berg, S. *et al.* (2004). The effectiveness of computerized cognitive behavioural therapy in routine care. *British Journal of Clinical Psychology*, 45, 499–514.

Ceci, S. J. (1990). *On intelligence . . . more or less*. Englewood Cliffs, NJ: Prentice Hall.

Ceci, S. J. (1991). How much does schooling influence general intelligence and its cognitive components? A reassessment of the evidence. *Developmental Psychology*, 24, 703–722.

Cervone, D. (2004). The architecture of personality. *Psychological Review*, 111, 183–204.

Cervone, D. and Shoda, Y. (1999). Social cognitive theories and the coherence of personality. In D. Cervone and Y. Shoda (eds), *The coherence of personality: Social-cognitive bases of consistency, variability, and organisation* (pp. 155–181). New York: Guilford.

Chabris, C. F. (1999). Prelude or requiem for the 'Mozart effect'? *Nature*, 400, 826–827.

Chamorro-Premuzic, T. and Arteche, A. (2008). Intellectual competence and academic performance: Preliminary validation of a model. *Intelligence*, 36, 564–573.

Chamorro-Premuzic, T. and Furnham, A. (2005). Intellectual competence. *The Psychologist*, 18, 352–354.

Chamorro-Premuzic, T. and Furnham, A. (2006). Intellectual competence and the intelligent personality: A third way in differential psychology. *Review of General Psychology*, 10, 251–267.

Chamoro-Premuzic, T., Bennett, E. and Furnham, A. (2007). The happy personality: Mediational role of trait emotional intelligence. *Personality and Individual Differences*, 42, 1633–1639.

Chamorro-Premuzic, T., Harlaar, N., Greven, C. U. and Plomin, R. (2010). More than just IQ: A longitudinal examination of self-perceived abilities as predictors of academic performance in a large sample of UK twins. *Intelligence*, 38, 385–392.

Chang, E. C. (1997). Irrational beliefs and negative life stress: Testing a diathesis-stress model of depressive symptoms. *Personality and Individual Differences*, 22, 115–117.

Chang, E. C. (2002). Optimism-pessimism and stress appraisal: Testing a cognitive interactive model of psychological adjustment in adults. *Cognitive Therapy and Research*, 26, 675–690.

Chang, E. C. (ed.). (2000). *Optimism and pessimism: Implications for theory, research, and practice*. Washington, DC: American Psychological Association (APA).

Chang, E. C. and D'Zurilla, T. (1996). Irrational beliefs as predictors of anxiety and depression in a college population. *Personality and Individual Differences*, 20(2), 215–219.

Chang, E. C., Maydeu-Oliveras, A. and D'Zurilla, T. J. (1997). Optimism and pessimism as partially independent constructs: Relationship to positive and negative effectivity and psychological well-being. *Personality and Individual Differences*, 23, 433–440.

Chang, E. C., Chang, R. and Sanna, L. J. (2009). Optimism, pessimism, and motivation: Relations to adjustment. *Social and Personality Psychology Compass*, 3, 494–506.

Chapman, T. F., Mannuzza, S. and Fyer, A. J. (1995). Epidemiology and family studies of social phobia. In R. R. G. Heimberg, M. Liebowitz, D. A. Hope and S. Scheier (eds), *Social phobia: Diagnosis, assessment and treatment* (pp. 21–40). New York: Guilford.

Charbonneau, D. and Nicol, A. A. M. (2002). Emotional intelligence and leadership in adolescents. *Personality and Individual Differences*, 33, 1101–1113.

Cheek, J. and Buss, A. (1981). Shyness and sociability. *Journal of Personality and Social Psychology*, 25, 1700–1713.

Cheek, J. M. (1996). Shyness as a personality trait. *International Journal of Psychology*, 31, 23–52.

Chen, G., Gully, S. M. and Eden, D. (2001). Validation of a new general self-efficacy scale. *Organizational Research Methods*, 4, 62–83.

Chen, M. J. and Chen, H. C. (1988). Concepts of intelligence: A comparison of Chinese graduates from Chinese and English schools in Hong Kong. *International Journal of Psychology*, 223, 471–487.

Cheng, Z. J. and Hau, K. T. (2003). Are intelligence and personality changeable? Generality of Chinese students' beliefs across various personal attributes and age groups. *Personality and Individual Differences*, 34, 731–748.

Chida, Y. and Steptoe, A. (2009). The association of anger and hostility with future coronary heart disease: a meta-analytic review of prospective evidence. *Journal of the American College of Cardiology*, 53, 936–946.

Child, D. (1990). *The essentials of factor analysis* (2nd edn). New York: Continuum International Publishing Group Ltd.

Child, D. (2006). *The essentials of factor analysis* (3rd edn). New York: Continuum International Publishing Group Ltd.

Chipeur, H., Rovine, M. and Plomin, R. (1990). LISREL modelling: Genetic and environmental influences on IQ revisited. *Intelligence*, 14, 11–29.

Choi, J. and Silverman, I. (1996). Sexual dimorphism in spatial behaviors: Applications to route-learning. *Evolution and Cognition*, 2, 165–171.

Choi, J. and Silverman, I. (2002). The relationship between testosterone and route-learning strategies in humans. *Brain and Cognition*, 50, 116–120.

Chung, M. C., Farmer, S., Grant, K. *et al.* (2002). Gender difference in love styles and post-traumatic stress reactions following relationship dissolution. *European Journal of Personality*, 16, 210–220.

Chung, M. C., Farmer, S., Grant, K. *et al.* (2003). Coping with post-traumatic stress symptoms following relationship dissolution. *Stress and Health*, 19, 27–36.

Church, A. T. and Burke, P. J. (1994). Exploratory and confirmatory tests of the Big Five and Tellegen's three- and four-dimensional models. *Journal of Personality and Social Psychology*, 66, 93–114.

Claridge, G. (1998). Creativity and madness: Clues from modern psychiatric diagnosis. In A. Steptoe (ed.), *Genius and the mind. Studies of creativity and temperament* (pp. 227–250). Oxford: Oxford University Press.

Clark, M. and Mills, J. (1979). Interpersonal attraction in exchange and communal relationships. *Journal of Personality and Social Psychology*, 37, 12–24.

Cloninger, C. R. (1987). A systematic method for clinical description and classification of personality variants. *Archives of General Psychiatry*, 44, 573–578.

Cloninger, C. R., Svrakic, D. M. and Przybeck, T. R. (1993). A psychobiological model of temperament and character. *Archives of General Psychiatry*, 50, 975–990.

Coates, D. (1997). The correlations of forgiveness of self, forgiveness of others, and hostility, depression, anxiety, self-esteem, life adaptation, and religiosity among female victims of domestic abuse. *Dissertation Abstracts International, 58*(05), 2667B (UMI 9734479).

Cohen, J. (1988). *Statistical power analysis for the behavioral sciences* (2nd edn). Hillsdale, NJ: Erlbaum.

Cohen, J. B. and Reed, D. (1985). Type A behaviour and coronary heart disease among Japanese men in Hawaii. *Journal of Behavioural Medicine, 8*, 343–352.

Cohen, M. X., Young, J., Baek, J. M., Kessler, C. and Ranganath, C. (2005). Individual differences in extraversion and dopamine genetics predict neural reward responses. Brain research. *Cognitive Brain Research, 25*, 851–861.

Colom, R., Luis-Font, J. M. and Andrés-Pueyo, A. (2005). The generational intelligence gains are caused by decreasing variance in the lower half of the distribution: Supporting evidence for the nutrition hypothesis. *Intelligence, 33*, 83–91.

Columbia University Press (1935). *Columbia encyclopedia*. New York: Columbia University Press.

Concise Oxford Thesaurus. (1999). *Concise Oxford dictionary and thesaurus* (10th edn). Oxford: Oxford University Press.

Conley, C. S., Haines, B. A., Hilt, L. M. and Metalsky, G. I. (2001). The children's attributional style interview: Developmental tests of cognitive diathesis-stress theories of depression. *Journal of Abnormal Child Psychology, 29*(5), 445–463.

Conn, S. R. and Rieke, M. L. (1994). *The 16PF fifth edition technical manager*. Champaign, IL: Institute for Personality and Ability Testing.

Contrada, R. J. and Goyal, T. M. (2004). Individual differences, health and illness: The role of emotional traits and generalized expectancies. In S. Sutton, A. Baum and M. Johnston (eds), *The Sage handbook of health psychology*. London: Sage Publications Limited.

Conway, M. A. (1997). Past and present: Recovered memories and false memories. In M. A. Conway (ed.), *Recovered memories and false memories*. Oxford: Oxford University Press.

Coolidge, F. L. (1998). *Coolidge personality and neuropsychological inventory for children manual: CPNI*. Colorado Springs, CO: Author.

Coolidge, F. L., Thede, L. L. and Jang, K. L. (2001). Heritability of personality disorders in childhood: A preliminary investigation. *Journal of Personality Disorders, 15*, 33–40.

Cooper, C. (1998). *Individual differences*. London: Arnold.

Cooper, C. (2002). *Individual differences*. London: Hodder Arnold.

Cooper, C. and Rorison, B. N. (2001). The Apperceptive Personality Test located in personality space. *Personality and Individual Differences, 30*, 363–366.

Cooper, R. S., Guo, X., Rotimi, C. N. *et al.* (2000). Heritability of angiotensin-converting enzyme and angiotensinogen: A comparison of US blacks and Nigerians. *Hypertension, 35*, 1141–1147.

Cornelius, A. (2003). The struggles of organisational transitions. In F. Fransella (ed.), *International handbook of personal construct psychology*. London: Wiley.

Costa, P. T. Jr and McCrae, R. R. (1980). Influence of extraversion and neuroticism on subjective well-being: happy and unhappy people. *Journal of Personality and Social Psychology, 38*, 668–678.

Costa, P. T. Jr and McCrae, R. R. (1985). *The NEO Personality Inventory manual*. Odessa, FL: Psychological Assessment Resources.

Costa, P. T. Jr and McCrae, R. R. (1989). Personality continuity and the changes in adult life. In M. Storandt and G. R. Vanden Bos (eds), *The adult years: Continuity and change* (pp. 45–77). Washington, DC: American Psychological Association.

Costa, P. T. Jr and McCrae, R. R. (1992). *Revised NEO Personality Inventory (NEO-PI-R) and NEO Five-Factor Inventory (NEO-FFI) professional manual*. Odessa, FL: Psychological Assessment Resources.

Costa, P. T. Jr and McCrae, R. R. (1997). Stability and change in personality assessment: The revised NEO Personality Inventory in the year 2000. *Journal of Personality and Assessment, 68*, 86–94.

Cote, S. and Miners, C. T. H. (2006). Emotional intelligence, cognitive intelligence and job performance. *Administrative Science Quarterly, 51*, 1–28.

Cotton, S. M., Kiely, P. M., Crewther, D. P. *et al.* (2005). A normative and reliability study for the Raven's Colored Progressive Matrices for primary school aged children in Australia. *Personality and Individual Differences, 39*, 647–660.

Council for Exceptional Children (1990). Giftedness and the gifted: What's it all about? EC Digest # E476. *ERIC Document Reproduction Service*. ED 321 481.

Court, J. H. (1983). Sex differences in performance on Raven's Progressive Matrices: A review. *Alberta Journal of Educational Research, 29*, 54–74.

Cox, J. L., Holden, J. M. and Sagovsky, R. (1987). Detection of postnatal depression: Development of the 10-item Edinburgh postnatal depression scale. *British Journal of Psychiatry, 150*, 782–786.

Crabbe, J. C. (2002). Genetic contributions to addiction. *Annual Review of Psychology, 53*, 435–462.

Cramer, P. (1968). *Word association*. New York: Academic Press.

Crandall, J. E. (1975). A scale for social interest. *Journal of Individual Psychology, 31*, 187–195.

Crandall, J. E. (1980). Adler's concept of social interest: Theory, measurement, and implications for adjustment. *Journal of Personality and Social Psychology, 39*, 481–495.

Crawford, C. (1991). Psychology. In M. Maxwell (ed.), *The sociobiological imagination* (pp. 303–318). Albany: State University of New York Press.

Crawford, M. P. (1938). A behavior rating scale for young chimpanzees. *Journal of Comparative Psychology, 26*, 79–91.

Crawford, T. N., Cohen, P., First, M. B. *et al.* (2008). Comorbid Axis I and Axis II disorders in early adolescence. *Archives of General Psychiatry, 65*, 641–648.

Crawford-Nutt, D. H. (1976). Are black scores on Raven's standard Progressive Matrices test an artefact of the method of test presentation? *Psychologica African, 16*, 201–206.

Critchfield, K. L., Clarkin, J. F., Levy, K. N. and Kernberg, O. F. (2008). Organization of co-occurring Axis II features in borderline personality disorder. *British Journal of Clinical Psychology, 47*, 185–200.

Crnic, K. and Lamberty, G. (1994). Reconsidering school readiness: Conceptual and applied perspectives. *Early Education and Development, 5*(2), 99–105. Available online at http:// readyweb.crc.uiuc.edu/library/1994/crnicl.html; accessed 10 August 2006.

Crocker, J. and Luhtanen, R. K. (2003). Level of self-esteem and contingencies of self-worth: Unique effects on academic, social, and financial problems in college freshmen. *Personality and Social Psychology Bulletin, 29*, 701–712.

Crocker, J., Sommers, S. and Luhtanen, R. (2002). Hopes dashed and dreams fulfilled: Contingencies of self-worth in the graduate school admissions process. *Personality and Social Psychology Bulletin, 28*, 1275–1286.

Crombie, I. K., Todman, J., McNeill, G. *et al.* (1990). Effect of vitamin and mineral supplementation on verbal and non-verbal reasoning of schoolchildren. *Lancet, 335*, 1158–1160.

Cronbach, L. J. (1951). Coefficient alpha and the internal structure of tests. *Psychometrika*, 16, 297–334.

Cronbach, L. J. (1990). *The essentials of psychological testing*. New York: Longman.

Cronbach, L. J. and Meehl, P. E. (1955). Construct validity in psychological tests. *Psychological Bulletin*, 52, 281–302.

Crozier, W. R. (2000). *Shyness: Development, consolidation, and change*. London: Routledge.

Crozier, W. R. (2001). *Understanding shyness: Psychological perspectives*. London: Palgrave Macmillan.

Crozier, W. R. (2002). Shyness. *The Psychologist*, 15, 460–463.

Crumbaugh, J. and Maholick, L. (1969). *Manual of instructions for the Purpose in Life Test*. Munster, IN: Psychometric Affiliates.

Csikszentmihalyi, M. (1999). If we are so rich, why aren't we happy? *American Psychologist*, 54, 821–827.

Curry, L. A., Maniar, S. D., Sondag, K. A. and Sandstedt, S. (1999). An optimal performance academic course for university students and student-athletes. Unpublished manuscript, University of Montana, Missoula.

Cvengros, J. A., Christensen, A. J. and Lawton, W. J. (2005). Health locus of control and depression in chronic kidney disease: A dynamic perspective. *Journal of Health Psychology*, 10, 677–687.

Dag, I. (1999). The relationships among paranormal beliefs, locus of control, and psychopathology in a Turkish college sample. *Personality and Individual Differences*, 26, 723–737.

Dalbert, C. (1996). *Dealing with injustice: A psychological analysis*. Bern, Switzerland: Huber.

Dalbert, C. (1998). Belief in a just world, well-being, and coping with an unjust fate. In L. Montada and M. J. Lerner (eds), *Responses to victimizations and belief in a just world* (pp. 87–105). New York: Plenum.

Dalbert, C., Lipkus, I. M., Sallay, H. and Goch, I. (2001). A just and an unjust world: Structure and validity of different world beliefs. *Personality and Individual Differences*, 30, 561–577.

Dalgleish, T. and Power, M. (1999). *Handbook of cognition and emotion*. New York: Wiley.

Daly, M. and Wilson, M. (1982). *Sex, evolution and behaviour* (2nd edn). Belmont, CA: Wadsworth.

Danziger, K. (1990). *Constructing the subject: Historical origins of psychological research*. Cambridge: Cambridge University Press.

Danziger, K. (1997). *Naming the mind: How psychology discovered its language*. London: Sage.

Darke, P. and Freedman, J. (1997). Lucky events and beliefs in luck: Paradoxical effects on confidence and risk-taking. *Personality and Social Psychology Bulletin*, 23, 378–388.

Darwin, C. (1859). *On the origin of species*. London: Murray.

Darwin, C. (1872/1965). *The expression of the emotions in man and animals*. Chicago: University of Chicago Press.

Das, J. P., Kirby, J. and Jarman, R. F. (1979). *Simultaneous and successive cognitive processes*. New York: Academic Press.

Dasen, P. R. (1984). The cross-cultural study of intelligence: Piaget and the Baoulé. In P. S. Fry (ed.), *Changing conceptions of intelligence and intellectual functioning: Current theory and research* (pp. 107–134). New York: North-Holland.

David, D., Montgomery, G. H. and Bovbjerg, D. H. (2006). Relations between coping responses and optimism–pessimism in predicting anticipatory psychological distress in surgical breast cancer patients. *Personality and Individual Differences*, 40(2), 203–213.

Davidson, R. J. and Rickman, M. (1999). Behavioral inhibition and the emotional circuitry of the brain: Stability and plasticity during the early childhood years. In L. A. Schmidt and J. Schulkin (eds), *Extreme fear, shyness, and social phobia: Origins, biological mechanisms, and clinical outcomes* (pp. 67–87). New York: Oxford University Press.

Davies, D. R. and Parasuraman, R. (1992). *The psychology of vigilance*. London: Academic Press.

Davies, M. (1996). EPQ correlates of love styles. *Personality and Individual Differences*, 20, 605–607.

Davis, C. M. (1928). Self-selection of diet by newly weaned infants. *American Journal of Diseases of Children*, 36, 651–679.

Davis, D., Shaver, P. R. and Vernon, M. L. (2003). Physical, emotional, and behavioral reactions to breaking up: The roles of gender, age, emotional involvement, and attachment style. *Personality and Social Psychology Bulletin*, 29, 871–884.

Davis O. S., Haworth, C. M. and Plomin, R. (2009). Dramatic increase in heritability of cognitive development from early to middle childhood: an 8-year longitudinal study of 8700 pairs of twins. *Psychological Science*, 20, 1301–1308.

Day, A. L. and Carroll, S. A. (2004). Using an ability-based measure of emotional intelligence to predict individual performance, group performance, and group citizenship behaviours. *Personality and Individual Differences*, 36, 1443–1458.

Day, L. and Maltby, J. (2003). Belief in good luck and psychological well-being: The mediating role of optimism and irrational beliefs. *Journal of Psychology*, 137, 99–110.

Day, L. and Maltby, J. (2005). 'With good luck': Belief in good luck and cognitive planning. *Personality and Individual Differences*, 39, 1217–1226.

Day, L., Hanson, K., Maltby, J., Proctor, C. and Wood, A. (2010). Hope uniquely predicts objective academic achievement above intelligence, personality, and previous academic achievement. *Journal of Research in Personality*, 44, 550–553.

De Haes, J. C. J. M., Van Knippenberg, F. C. E. and Neijt, J. P. (1990). Measuring physical and psychological distress in cancer patients: structure and application of the Rotterdam Symptom Checklist. *British Journal of Cancer*, 62, 1034–1038.

De Mann, A., Leduc, C. and Labrèche-Gauthier, L. (1992). Parental control in child rearing and multidimensional locus of control. *Psychological Reports*, 70, 320–322.

De Pascalis, V., Fiore, A. D. and Sparita, A. (1996). Personality, event-related potential (ERP) and heart rate (HR): An investigation of Gray's theory. *Personality and Individual Differences*, 20, 733–746.

De Raad, B. (2000). *The Big Five personality factors: The psycholexical approach to personality*. Seattle, WA: Hogrefe and Huber.

Deary, I. J. (2012). Intelligence. *Annual Review of Psychology*, 63, 453–482.

Deary, I. J. and Der G. (2005). Reaction time explains IQ's association with death. *Psychological Science*, 16, 64–69.

Deary, I. J., Whalley, L. J., Lemmon, H., Crawford, H. and Starr, J. M. (2000). The stability of individual differences in mental ability from childhood to old age: Follow-up of the 1932 Scottish Mental Survey. *Intelligence*, 28, 49–55.

Deary, I. J., Thorpe, G., Wilson, V., Starr, J. M. and Whalley, L. J. (2003). Population sex differences in IQ at age 11: the Scottish mental survey 1932. *Intelligence*, 31, 533–542.

Deary, I. J., Whiteman, M. C., Starr, J. M., Whalley, L. J. and Fox, H. C. (2004). The impact of childhood intelligence on later life: Following up the Scottish Mental Surveys of 1932 and 1947. *Journal of Personality and Social Psychology*, 86, 130–147.

Deary, I. J., Strand, S., Smith, P. and Fernandes, C. (2007). Intelligence and educational achievement. *Intelligence*, 35, 13–21.

Deary, I. J, Yang, J., Davies, G. *et al.* (2012). Genetic contributions to stability and change in intelligence from childhood to old age. *Nature*, 482, 212–215.

Deci, E. L. (1976). Notes on the theory and metatheory of intrinsic motivation. *Organizational Behavior and Human Performance*, 15, 130–145.

Deci, E. L. and Ryan, R. M. (1985). *Intrinsic motivation and self-determination in human behavior*. New York: Plenum.

Deci, E. L. and Ryan, R. M. (1991). A motivational approach to self: Integration in personality. In R. Dienstbier (ed.), *Nebraska Symposium on Motivation:* (Vol. 38: *Perspectives on motivation*) (pp. 237–288). Lincoln: University of Nebraska Press.

Deci, E. L. and Ryan, R. M. (1995). Human autonomy: The basis for true self-esteem. In M. Kemis (ed.), *Efficacy, agency, and self-esteem* (pp. 31–49). New York: Plenum.

Deci, E. L. and Ryan, R. M. (2002). Self-determination research: Reflections and future directions. In E. L. Deci and R. M. Ryan (eds), *Handbook of self-determination research* (pp. 431–441). Rochester, NY: University of Rochester Press.

Deci, E. L., Koestner, R. and Ryan, R. M. (1999). A meta-analytic review of experiments examining the effects of extrinsic rewards on intrinsic motivation. *Psychological Bulletin, 125*, 627–668.

Dedert, E. A., Studts, J. L., Weissbecker, I. *et al.* (2004). Religiosity may help preserve the cortisol rhythm in women with stress-related illness. *International Journal of Psychiatry in Medicine, 34*, 61–77.

DeKay, W. T., Buss, D. M. and Stone, V. (unpublished manuscript). Coalitions, mates and friends: Toward an evolutionary psychology of relationship preferences. Department of Psychology, University of Texas, Austin, Texas.

Demarest, E. J., Reisner, E. R., Anderson, L. M. *et al.* (1993). *Review of research on achieving the nation's readiness goal.* Washington, DC: US Department of Education.

Dembroski, T. M. and Costa, P. T. (1989). Coronary-prone behaviour: Components of the Type A Pattern and hostility. *Journal of Personality, 55*, 211–235.

Demetriou, A. and Papadopoulous, T. (2004). Human intelligence: From local models to universal theory. In R. J. Sternberg (ed.), *International handbook of intelligence* (pp. 445–474). Cambridge: Cambridge University Press.

Denollet, J. (2000). Type D personality: A potential risk factor refined. *Journal of Psychosomatic Research, 49*, 255–266.

Denollet, J. (2008). Prognostic value of a Type D personality compared with depressive symptoms. *Archives of International Medicine, 168*, 431–432.

Denollet, J. and Pederson, S. S. (2009). Anger, depression and anxiety in cardiac patients: the complexity of individual differences in cardiac risk. *Journal of the American College of Cardiologists, 53*, 947–949.

Depue, R. A. and Collins, P. F. (1999). Neurobiology of the structure of personality: Dopamine, facilitation of incentive motivation, and extraversion. *Behavioral and Brain Sciences, 22*, 491–517.

Der, G., Batty, D. and Deary, I. J. (2006). Effect of breast feeding on intelligence in children: prospective study, sibling pairs analysis, and meta-analysis. *British Medical Journal, 33*, 945.

Detterman, D. K. (1987). Theoretical notions of intelligence and mental retardation. *American Journal of Mental Deficiency, 92*, 2–11.

Detterman, D. K., Gabriel, L. T. and Ruthsatz, J. M. (2001). Intelligence and mental retardation. In R. J. Sternberg (ed.), *Handbook of intelligence* (pp. 141–158). Cambridge: Cambridge University Press.

DeVito, A. J. (1985). Review of Myers–Briggs Type Indicator. In J. V. Mitchell (ed.), *The ninth mental measurement yearbook.* Lincoln, NE: Buros Institute of Mental Measurement.

Devlin, B., Daniels, M. and Roeder, K. (1997). Heritability of IQ. *Nature, 388*, 468–471.

DeYoung, C. G., Peterson, J. B. and Higgins, D. M. (2002). Higher-order factors of the Big Five predict conformity: Are there neuroses of health? *Personality and Individual Differences, 33*, 530–552.

Diagnostic and Statistical Manual of Mental Disorders (2000). Fourth Edition, Text Revision. New York: American Psychiatric Association.

Diamond, M., Scheibel, A., Murphy, G. and Harvey, T. (1985). On the brain of a scientist: Albert Einstein. *Experimental Neurology, 88*, 198–204.

Di Blas, L. and Forzi, M. (1998). An alternative taxonomic study of personality-descriptive adjectives in the Italian language. *European Journal of Personality, 12*, 75–101.

Di Blas, B., Perugini, M., Hrebickova, M. and Szarota, P. (1998). Lingua franca of personality: Taxonomies and structures based on the psycholexical approach. *Journal of Cross-Cultural Psychology, 29*, 212–232.

Dickens, C., McGowan, L., Perceival, C. *et al.* (2007). Depression is a risk factor for mortality after myocardial infarction: Fact or artefact? *Journal of the American College of Cardiologists, 49*, 1834–1840.

Dickens, W. T. and Flynn, J. R. (2001). Heritability estimates versus large environmental effects: The IQ paradox resolved. *Psychological Review, 108*, 346–369.

Diener, E. (2000). Subjective well-being: The science of happiness and a proposal for a national index. *American Psychologist, 55*, 34–43.

Diener, E. and Seligman, M. E. P. (2002). Very happy people. *Psychological Science, 13*, 81–84.

Diener, E., Emmons, R. A., Larson, R. J. and Griffin, S. (1985). The satisfaction with life scale. *Journal of Personality Assessment, 49*, 71–76.

Diener, E., Suh, M., Lucas, E. and Smith, H. (1999). Subjective well-being: Three decades of progress. *Psychological Bulletin, 125*, 276–302.

Diener, E., Kesebir, P. and Lucas, R. (2008). Benefits of accounts of well-being: For societies and for psychological science. *Applied Psychology: An International Review, 57*, 37–53.

Diener, E., Wirtz, D., Tov, W. *et al.* (2010). New well-being measures: Short scales to assess flourishing and positive and negative feelings. *Social Indicators Research, 97*, 143–156.

DiGiuseppe, R. A., Miller, N. J. and Trexler, L. D. (1979). A review of rational-emotive psychotherapy outcome studies. In A. Ellis and J. M. Whiteley (eds), *Theoretical and empirical foundations of rational-emotive therapy.* Monterey, CA: Brooks/Cole.

Digman, J. M. (1990). Personality structure: Emergence of the five-factor model. *Annual Review of Psychology, 41*, 417–440.

Digman, J. M. (1997). Higher-order factors of the Big Five. *Journal of Personality and Social Psychology, 73*, 1246–1256.

Digman, J. M. and Takemoto-Chock, N. K. (1981). Factors in the natural language of personality: Re-analysis, comparison, and interpretation of six major studies. *Multivariate Behavioral Research, 6*, 149–170.

Dijksterhuis, A. and Bargh, J. A. (2001). The perception-behavior expressway: Automatic effects of social perception on social behavior. In M. Zanna (ed.), *Advances in experimental social psychology, 33*, pp. 1–40.

DiMatteo, M. R., Lepper, H. S. and Croghan, T. W. (2000). Depression is a risk factor for non-compliance with medical treatment: meta-analysis of the effects of anxiety and depression on patient adherence. *Archives of Internal Medicine, 160*, 2102–2107.

DiMattia, D. (1991). Using RET effectively in the workplace. In M. E. Barnard (ed.), *Using rational-emotive therapy effectively: A practitioner's guide.* London: Plenum.

Dina, C., Zohar, A., Gritsenko, I. and Ebstein, R. P. (2004). Fine mapping of a region on chromosome 8P gives evidence for a QTL contributing to individual differences in an anxiety-related personality trait, TPQ harm avoidance. *American*

Journal of Medical Genetics, Part B: Neuropsychiatric Genetics, 130B, 51–52.

Dingemanse, N. J. and Wolf, M. (2010). Recent models for adoptive personality differences: A review. *Philosophical Transactions of the Royal Society of London, Series B, 365*, 3947–3958.

Dingemanse, N. J., Kazem, A. J. N., Réale, D. and Wright, J. (2010). Behavioural reaction norms: animal personality meets individual plasticity. *Trends in Ecology and Evolution, 25*, 81–89.

Dinkmeyer, D., McKay, G. D. and Dinkmeyer, D. Jr (1997). *The parent's handbook: Systematic training for effective parenting.* Circle Pines, MN: American Guidance Service.

Distel, M. A., Trull, T. J., Derom, C. A. *et al.* (2008). Heritability of borderline personality disorder features is similar across three countries. *Psychological Medicine, 38*, 1219–1229.

Dollard, J. and Miller, N. (1941). *Social learning and imitation.* New Haven, CT: Yale University Press.

Dollard, J. and Miller, N. (1950). *Personality and psychotherapy: An analysis in terms of learning, thinking, and culture.* New York: McGraw-Hill.

Dollinger, S. J. and Orf, L. A. (1991). Personality and performance in 'personality': Conscientiousness and openness. *Journal of Research in Personality, 25*, 276–284.

Dorval, M. and Pepin, M. (1986). Effect of playing a video game on measure of spatial visualization. *Perceptual Motor Skills, 62*, 159–162.

Dosamantes-Alperson, E. and Merrill, N. (1980). Growth effects of experiential movement psychotherapy. *Psychotherapy, Theory, Research, and Practice, 17*, 63–68.

Downey, D. B. (2001). Number of siblings and intellectual development: The resource dilution explanation. *American Psychologist, 56*, 497–504.

Downey, G., Feldman, S. and Ayduk, O. (2000). Rejection sensitivity and male violence in romantic relationships. *Personal Relationships, 7*, 45–61.

Downey, L. A., Mountstephen, J., Lloyd, J., Hansen, K. and Stough, C. (2008). Emotional intelligence and scholastic achievement in Australian adolescents. *Australian Journal of Psychology, 60*, 10–17.

Dozier, M., Stovall, K. C. *et al.* (1999). Attachment and psychopathology in adulthood. In J. Cassidy and P. Shaver (eds), *Handbook of attachment* (pp. 497–519). New York: Guilford Press.

Drigotas, S. M. and Rusbult, C. E. (1992). Should I stay or should I go: A dependence model of break-ups. *Journal of Personality and Social Psychology, 62*, 62–87.

Drigotas, S. M., Safstrom, C. A. and Gentilia, T. (1999). An investment model prediction of dating infidelity. *Journal of Personality and Social Psychology, 77*, 509–524.

Dryden, W. and Neenan, M. (1997). *Dictionary of rational-emotive behaviour therapy.* London: Whurr.

DuBois, C. (1960) *The People of Alor.* Cambridge, MA: Harvard University Press.

Duck, S. W. (1982). *Personal relationships 4: Dissolving personal relationships.* London and New York: Academic Press.

Duck, S. W. (1988). *Relating to others.* London: Open University Press.

Duck, S. W. and Miell, D. E. (1986). Charting the development of personal relationships. In R. Gilmour and S. W. Duck (eds), *The emerging field of personal relationships.* Hillsdale, NJ: Erlbaum.

Dumitrashku, T. A. (1996). Family structure and children's cognitive development. *Voprosy Psikhologii, 2*, 104–111.

Dunbar, R. I. M. (2004). Gossip in an evolutionary perspective. *Review of General Psychology, 8*, 100–110.

Dunnell, K. and Cartwright, A. (1972). *Medicine takers, prescribers and hoarders.* London: Routledge and Kegan Paul.

Duriez, B., Van Hiel, A. and Kossowska, M. (2005). Authoritarianism and social dominance in Western and Eastern Europe: The importance of the socio-political context and of political interest and involvement. *Political Psychology, 62*, 299–321.

Eaves L. J., Eysenck H. J. and Martin N. G. (1989). *Genes, culture and personality: An empirical approach.* London: Oxford University Press.

Edelmann, R. J. (1987). *The psychology of embarrassment.* Chichester, UK: Wiley.

Edelmann, R. J. and McCusker, G. (1986). Introversion, neuroticism, empathy, and embarrassibility. *Personality and Individual Differences, 7*, 133–140.

Einstein, D. A. and Menzies, R. G. (2004). The presence of magical thinking in obsessive-compulsive disorder. *Behaviour, Research and Therapy, 42*(5), 539–649.

Ellenberger, H. F. (1970). *The discovery of the unconscious.* New York: Basic Books.

Elliot, C. D. (1983). *British Ability Scales technical handbook.* Windsor: NFER-Nelson.

Elliot, C. D. (1996). *British Ability Scales II (BAS II).* Windsor: NFER-Nelson.

Ellis, A. (1951). *The Folklore of Sex.* New York: Charles Boni.

Ellis, A. (1954). *The American Sexual Tragedy.* New York: Twayne.

Ellis, A. (1955). New approaches to psychotherapy techniques. *Journal of Clinical Psychology Monograph Supplement,* Brandon, VT.

Ellis, A. (1957). *How to live with a 'neurotic'.* New York: Crown Publishers.

Ellis, A. (1958a). Rational psychotherapy. *General Psychology, 59*, 35–49.

Ellis, A. (1958b). *Sex without Guilt.* New York: Grove Press.

Ellis, A. (1962). *Reason and emotion in psychotherapy.* Secaucus, NJ: Citadel Press.

Ellis, A. (1976). The biological basis of human irrationality. *Journal of Individual Psychology, 32*, 145–168.

Ellis, A. (1978). Towards a theory of personality. In R. J. Corsini (ed.), *Readings in current personality theories.* Itasca, IL: Reacock.

Ellis, A. (1979). The theory of rational-emotive therapy. In A. Ellis and J. M. Whiteley (eds), *Theoretical and empirical foundations of rational-emotive therapy.* Monterey, CA: Brooks/Cole.

Ellis, A. (1980). *Case against religion: A psychotherapist's view and the case against religiosity.* Austin, TX: American Atheist Press.

Ellis, A. (1984). Rational-emotive therapy. In R. J. Corsini (ed.), *Current psychotherapies* (3rd edn, pp. 196–238). Itasca, IL: Peacock.

Ellis, A. (1985a). The essence of RET. *Journal of Rational-Emotive and Cognitive-Behavior Therapy, 2*(1), 19–25.

Ellis, A. (1985b). *Overcoming resistance: Rational-emotive therapy with difficult clients.* New York: Springer.

Ellis, A. (1987). Ask Dr. Ellis. *Journal of Rational-Emotive & Cognitive-Behavior Therapy, 5*, 135–137.

Ellis, A. (1991a). Counselling in the classroom: Interview with Albert Ellis. *Journal of Rational-Emotive & Cognitive-Behavior Therapy, 9*, 247–263.

Ellis, A. (1991b). The revised ABC's of rational-emotive therapy (RET). *Journal of Rational-Emotive & Cognitive-Behavior Therapy, 9*, 139–172.

Ellis, A. (1992). My early experiences in developing the practice of psychology. *Professional Psychology: Research and Practice, 23*(1), 7–10.

Ellis, A. (1994, 2006). *The essence of rational-emotive behaviour therapy: A comprehensive approach to treatment.* Available online at www.rebt.ws/albert_ellis_the_essence_of_rebt.htm; accessed 28 February 2006.

Ellis, A. (1996). Responses to criticisms of rational-emotive behavior therapy. *Journal of Rational-Emotive and Cognitive-Behavior Therapy, 14*, 97–121.

Ellis, A. (2001). *Feeling better, getting better, staying better*. Atascadero, CA: Impact.

Ellis, A. (2003). Reflections on rational-emotive therapy. *Journal of Consulting and Clinical Psychology, 61*(2), 199–201.

Ellis, A. and Harper, R. A. (1975). *A new guide to rational living*. Englewood Cliffs, NJ: Prentice Hall; Hollywood, CA: Wilshire Books.

Embretson, S. E. and Reise, S. P. (2000). *Item response theory for psychologists*. Hillsdale, NJ: Lawrence Erlbaum.

Emmerling, R. J. and Goleman, D. (2003). *Emotional intelligence: Issues and common misunderstandings*. Consortium for Research on Emotional Intelligence in Organizations. Available online at www.eiconsortium.org/research/ei_issues_and_common_misunderstandings_caruso_comment.htm; accessed 27 December 2005.

Endler, N. S. and Hunt, J. M. (1966). Sources of behavioural variance as measured by the S-R inventory of anxiousness. *Psychological Bulletin, 65*, 336–346.

Endler, N. S. and Hunt, J. M. (1968). S-R inventories of hostility and comparisons of the proportions of variance from persons, responses, and situations for hostility and anxiousness. *Journal of Personality and Social Psychology, 9*, 309–315.

English, H. B. and English, A. C. (1958). *A comprehensive dictionary of psychological and psychoanalytic terms: A guide to usage*. New York: David McKay.

Enright, R. D. and Fitzgibbons, R. P. (2000). *Helping clients forgive: An empirical guide for resolving anger and restoring hope*. Washington, DC: American Psychological Association.

Enright, R. D. and The Human Development Study Group. (1991). The moral development of forgiveness. In W. Kurtines and J. Gerwitz (eds), *Handbook of moral behaviour and development* (Vol. 1, pp. 123–152). Hillsdale, NJ: Erlbaum.

Enright, R. D., Freedman, S. and Rique, J. (1998). The psychology of interpersonal forgiveness. In R. D. Enright and J. North (eds), *Exploring forgiveness* (pp. 46–62). Madison: University of Wisconsin Press.

Entwisle, D. R., Alexander, K. L. and Olson, L. S. (1994). The gender gap in math: Its possible origins in neighborhood effects. *American Sociological Review, 59*, 822–838.

Epstein, S. (1979). The stability of behaviour (Vol. I: On predicting most of the people much of the time). *Journal of Personality and Social Psychology, 37*, 1097–1126.

Epstein, S. (1980). The stability of behaviour (Vol. II: Implications for psychological research). *American Psychologist, 35*, 790–806.

Erdelyi, M. H. (1984). *Psychoanalysis: Freud's cognitive psychology*. New York: Freeman.

Erdle, S., Irwing, P., Rushton, J. P. and Park, J. (2010). The general factor of personality and its relation to self-esteem in 628,640 internet respondents. *Personality and Individual Differences, 48*, 343–346.

ERIC Clearinghouse on Handicapped and Gifted Children. (1990). Giftedness and the gifted: What's it all about? Reston, VA: ERIC Identifier ED321481.

Evans, P. D. and Egerton, N. (1992). Mood states and minor illness. *British Journal of Medical Psychology, 65*, 177–186.

Exline, J. J. and Baumeister, R. F. (2000). Expressing forgiveness and repentance: Benefits and barriers. In M. E. McCullough, K. I. Pargament and C. E. Thoresen (eds), *Forgiveness: Theory, research, and practice* (pp. 133–155). London: Guilford.

Exline, J. J., Bushman, B. J., Baumeister, R. F. and Campbell, W. K. (2004). Too proud to let go: Narcissistic entitlement as a barrier to forgiveness. *Journal of Personality and Social Psychology, 87*, 894–912.

Externera, N. and Fernandez-Berrocal, P. (2005). Perceived emotional intelligence and life satisfaction: Predictive and incremental validity using the Trait Meta-Mood Scale. *Personality and Individual Differences, 39*, 937–948.

Eysenck, H. (1971). *Race, intelligence and education*. London: Maurice Temple Smith.

Eysenck, H. J. (1947). *Dimensions of personality*. London: Routledge and Kegan Paul.

Eysenck, H. J. (1952). The effects of psychotherapy: An evaluation. *Journal of Consulting Psychology, 16*, 319–324.

Eysenck, H. J. (1963). *Use and abuses of psychology*. Baltimore, MD: Penguin.

Eysenck, H. J. (1965a). The effects of psychotherapy. *International Journal of Psychiatry, 1*, 99–142.

Eysenck, H. J. (1965b). *Fact and fiction in psychology*. Baltimore, MD: Penguin.

Eysenck, H. J. (1967). *The biological basis of personality*. Springfield, IL: Charles C. Thomas.

Eysenck, H. J. (1970). *The structure of human personality* (3rd edn). London: Methuen.

Eysenck, H. J. (1975). The structure of social attitudes. *British Journal of Social and Clinical Psychology, 14*, 323–331.

Eysenck, H. J. (1976a). *The measurement of personality*. Lancaster: Medical and Technical Publishers.

Eysenck, H. J. (1976b). Structure of social attitudes. *Psychological Reports, 39*, 463–466.

Eysenck, H. J. (1979). *The structure and measurement of intelligence*. New York: Springer-Verlag.

Eysenck, H. J. (1982a). Development of a theory. In H. J. Eysenck (ed.), *Personality, genetics and behaviour*. New York: Praeger.

Eysenck, H. J. (1982b). Left-wing authoritarianism: Myth or reality? *Political Psychology, 3*, 234–238.

Eysenck, H. J. (1986). *Decline and fall of the Freudian empire*. London: Penguin.

Eysenck, H. J. (1990a). Biological dimensions of personality. In L. A. Pervin (ed.), *Handbook of personality: Theory and research* (pp. 244–276). New York: Guilford.

Eysenck, H. J. (1990b). Genetic and environmental contributions to individual differences: The three major dimensions of personality. *Journal of Personality, 58*, 245–261.

Eysenck, H. J. (1991). Dimensions of personality: 16, 5 or 3? Criteria for a taxonomic paradigm. *Personality and Individual Differences, 12*, 773–790.

Eysenck, H. J. (1992). The definition and measurement of psychoticism. *Personality and Individual Differences, 13*, 757–786.

Eysenck, H. J. (1993). Comment on Goldberg. *American Psychologist, 48*, 1299–1300.

Eysenck, H. J. (1994). Personality: Biological foundations. In P. A. Vernon (ed.), *The neuropsychology of individual differences*. London: Academic Press.

Eysenck, H. J. (1995). *Genius: The natural history of creativity*. New York: Cambridge University Press.

Eysenck, H. J. (2000). *Intelligence: A new look*. London: Transaction Publishers.

Eysenck, H. J. and Eysenck, M. W. (1985a). *Personality and individual differences: A natural science approach*. New York: Plenum.

Eysenck, H. J. and Eysenck, M. W. (1985b). The psychophysiology of personality. In *Personality and individual differences: A natural science approach* (pp. 217–236). New York: Plenum.

Eysenck, H. J. and Eysenck, S. B. G. (1975). *Manual of the Eysenck Personality Questionnaire*. London: Hodder & Stoughton.

Eysenck, H. J. and Eysenck, S. B. G. (1982). Recent advances in the cross-cultural study of personality. In C. D. Spielberger and J. N. Butcher (eds), *Advances in personality assessment*. Hillsdale, NJ: Erlbaum.

Eysenck, H. J. and Eysenck, S. B. G. (1991). *Manual for the EPQR-R*. Sevenoaks, England: Hodder & Stoughton.

Eysenck, S. B. G. (1965). *Manual of the junior Eysenck personality inventory*. London: Hodder & Stoughton.

Eysenck, S. B. G., Barrett, P. T. and Barnes, G. E. (1993). A cross-cultural study of personality: Canada and England. *Personality and Individual Differences, 14*, 1–10.

Eysenck, S. B. G., Makaremi, A. and Barrett, P. T. (1994). A cross-cultural study of personality: Iranian and English children. *Personality and Individual Differences, 16*, 203–210.

Fagen, R. and Fagen, J. M. (1996). Individual distinctiveness in brown bears, *Ursus arctos L. Ethology, 102*, 212–226.

Falbo, T. and Polit, D. (1986). Quantitative review of the only child literature. *Psychological Bulletin, 100*, 176–189.

Fallowfield, L. (1990). *The quality of life*. London: Souvenir Press.

Fang, F. and Keats, D. (1987). A cross-cultural study on the conception of intelligence. *Acta Psychologica Sinica, 19*, 255–262.

Feaver, J., Mendl, M. and Bateson, P. (1986). A method for rating the individual distinctiveness of domestic cats. *Animal Behaviour, 34*, 1016–1025.

Fechner, T. F. (1860). *Elemente der Psychophysik*. Leipzig: Breitkopf und Härtel.

Feeney, J. A. (1999). Adult romantic attachment and couple relationships. In J. Cassidy and P. R. Shaver (eds), *Handbook of attachment: Theory, research, and clinical applications* (pp. 355–377). New York: Guilford.

Feingold, A. (1988). Cognitive gender differences are disappearing. *American Psychologist, 43*, 95–103.

Feingold, A. (1992). Sex-differences in variability in intellectual abilities – a new look at an old controversy. *Review of Educational Research, 62*, 61–84.

Feingold, A. (1994). Gender differences in personality: A meta-analysis. *Psychological Bulletin, 116*, 429–456.

Feldman, D. H. (1980). *Beyond universals in cognitive development*. Norwood, NJ: Ablex.

Feldman, D. H. (1986). Giftedness as a developmentalist sees it. In R. Sternberg and J. Davidson (eds), *Conceptions of giftedness* (pp. 285–305). New York: Cambridge University Press.

Feldman, D. H. and Goldsmith, L. T. (1986). *Nature's gambit: Child prodigies and the development of human potential*. New York: Basic Books.

Feldman, P. I., Cihen, S., Doyle, E. J., Skoner, D. P. and Gwaltney, J. M. (1999). The impact of personality on the reporting of unfounded symptoms and illness. *Journal of Personality and Social Psychology, 77*, 370–378.

Felmlee, D. H. (1995). Fatal attractions: Affection and disaffection in intimate relationships. *Journal of Social and Personal Relationships, 12*, 295–311.

Felmlee, D. H. (1998). 'Be careful what you wish for . . .'. A quantitative and qualitative investigation of fatal attractions. *Personal Relationships, 5*, 235–253.

Felmlee, D. H. (2001). From appealing to appalling: Disenchantment with a romantic partner. *Social Perspectives, 44*, 263–280.

Fenichel, O. (1945). *The psychoanalytic theory of neurosis*. New York: Norton.

Ferguson, E. (2001). Personality and coping traits: A joint factor analysis. *British Journal of Health Psychology, 6*, 311–325.

Ferguson, E., Matthews, G. and Cox, T. (1999). The Appraisal of Life Events (ALE) scale: Reliability and validity. *British Journal of Health Psychology, 4*, 97–116.

Ferguson, E., Chamorro-Premuzic, T., Pickering, A. and Weiss, A. (2011). Five into one doesn't go: A critique of the general factor of personality. In T. Chamorro-Premuzic, S. von Stumm and A. Furnham (eds), *The Wiley-Blackwell Handbook of Individual Differences* (pp. 167–186). London: Wiley–Blackwell.

Fernandez-Ballesteros, R. and Colom, R. (2004). The psychology of human intelligence in Spain. In R. J. Sternberg (ed.), *International handbook of intelligence* (pp. 79–103). Cambridge: Cambridge University Press.

Feuerstein, R., Rand, Y. and Hoffman, M. B. (1979). *The dynamic assessment of retarded performers: Learning Potential Assessment Device, theory, instruments and techniques*. Baltimore, MD: University Park Press.

Feuerstein, R., Feuerstein, R. and Gross, S. (1997). The learning potential assessment device. In D. Flanagan, J. Genshaft and P. Harrison (eds), *Contemporary intellectual assessment*. New York: Guilford.

Feuerstein, R., Jackson, Y. and Lewis, J. (1998a). Feuerstein's IE and structural cognitive modifiability. In R. Samuda (ed.), *Advances in cross-cultural assessment*. Thousand Oaks, CA: Sage.

Feuerstein, R., Jackson, Y. and Lewis, J. (1998b). Feuerstein's LPAD. In R. Samuda (ed.), *Advances in cross-cultural assessment*. Thousand Oaks, CA: Sage.

Feuerstein, R., Falik, L. H. and Feuerstein, R. S. (1998c). The Learning Potential Assessment Device: An alternative approach to the assessment of learning potential. In R. Samuda, R. Feuerstein, B. Sternberg, A. S. Kaufman and J. Lewis (eds), *Advances in cross cultural assessment* (pp. 77–154). New York: Sage.

Feuerstein, R., Falik, L., Rand, Y. and Feuerstein, R. S. (2002). *The dynamic assessment of cognitive modifiability: The LPAD*. Jerusalem: ICELP Press.

Feuerstein, R., Falik, L., Rand, Y. and Rafi, S. (2003a). *Feuerstein's theory and applied systems: A reader*. Jerusalem: ICELP Press.

Feuerstein, R., Rand, Y. and Hoffman, M. (2003b). *The dynamic assessment of cognitive modifiability: The LPAD*. Jerusalem: ICELP Press.

Figueredo, A. J., Vasquez, G., Brumbach B. H. *et al.* (2005). The K-factor: Individual differences in life history strategy. *Personality and Individual Differences, 39*, 1349–1360.

Finke, R., Ward, T. B. and Smith, S. M. (1992). *Creative cognition: Theory, research, and applications*. Boston, MA: MIT Press.

Finkel, D., Pedersen, N. L., McGue, M. and McClearn, G. E. (1995). Heritability of cognitive abilities in adult twins: Comparison of the Minnesota and Swedish data. *Behavior Genetics, 25*, 421–431.

Finucane, A. M., Dima, A., Ferreira, N., Halvorsen, M. (2012). Basic emotion profiles in healthy, chronic pain, depressed and PTSD individuals. *Clinical Psychology and Psychotherapy, 19*, 14–24.

Fischer, G. (1997). Abstention from sex and other pre-game rituals used by college male varsity athletes. *Journal of Sport Behavior, 20*, 176–184.

Fisher, M. (1995, December 6). Freudian slip. *San Jose Mercury News*, p. 25A.

Fisher, M. and Greenberg, R. P. (1996). *Freud scientifically re-appraised: Testing the theories and the therapy*. New York: Wiley.

Fishman, I., Ng, R. and Bellugi, U. (2011). Do extraverts process social stimuli differently from introverts? *Cognitive Neuroscience, 2*, 67–73.

Fiske, D. W. (1949). Consistency of the factorial structures of personality ratings from different sources. *Journal of Abnormal and Social Psychology, 44*, 329–344.

Fitzgerald, S. T., Haythornwaite, I. A., Suchday, A. and Ewart, C. K. (2003). Anger in young black and white workers. Effects of job control dissatisfaction and support. *Journal of Behavioural Medicine, 26,* 283–296.

Flanagan, D. P., Genshaft, J. L. and Harrison, P. L. (eds) (1997). *Contemporary intellectual assessment: Theories, tests, and issues.* New York: Guilford.

Flanagan, D. P., McGrew, K. S. and Ortiz, S. (2000). *The Wechsler Intelligence Scales and Gf–Gc theory: A contemporary approach to interpretation.* Needham Heights, MA: Allyn & Bacon.

Fleeson, W. (2001). Toward a structure- and process-integrated view of personality: Traits as density distribution of states. *Journal of Personality and Social Psychology, 80,* 1011–1027.

Fletcher, R. (1991). *Science, ideology and the media: Cyril Burt scandal.* New Brunswick, NJ: Transaction Books.

Flora, S. R. (1990). Undermining intrinsic interest from the stand-point of a behaviorist. *The Psychological Record, 40,* 323–346.

Flynn, J. R. (1984). The mean IQ of Americans: Massive gains from 1932 to 1978. *Psychological Bulletin, 95,* 29–51.

Flynn, J. R. (1987). Massive IQ gains in 14 nations: What IQ tests really measure. *Psychological Bulletin, 101,* 171–191.

Flynn, J. R. (1994). IQ gains over time. In R. J. Sternberg (ed.), *Encyclopedia of human intelligence* (pp. 617–623). New York: Macmillan.

Flynn, J. R. (1998). IQ gains over time: Toward finding the causes. In U. Neisser (ed.), *The rising curve: Long-term gains in IQ and related measures.* (pp. 25–66). Washington, DC: American Psychological Association.

Flynn, J. R. (1999). Searching for justice: The discovery of IQ gains over time. *American Psychologist, 54,* 5–20.

Flynn, J. R. (2003). Movies about intelligence: The limitations of g. *Current Directions in Psychological Science, 12,* 95–103.

Flynn, J. R. (2007). *What is intelligence?* Cambridge: Cambridge University Press.

Flynn, J. R. (2009). Requiem for nutrition as the cause of IQ gains: Raven's gains in Britain 1938–2008. *Economics and Human Biology, 7,* 18–27.

Folkman, S. (1997). Positive psychological states and coping with severe stress. *Social Science Medicine, 45,* 647–654.

Folkman, S. and Lazarus, R. S. (1988). *Manual for the Ways of Coping questionnaire.* Palo Alto, CA: Consulting Psychologists Press. (Now published by Mind Garden.)

Folkman, S., Moskowitz, J. T., Ozer, E. M. and Park, C. L. (1997). Positive meaningful events and coping in the context of HIV/AIDS. In B. Gottlieb (ed.), *Coping with chronic stress* (pp. 293–314). New York: Plenum.

Fonagy, P., Kachele, H., Krause, R. *et al.* (1999). *An open door review of outcome studies in psycho-analysis.* London: International Psychoanalytical Association.

Ford, K. M. and Adams-Webber, J. R. (1991). The structure of personal construct systems and the logic of confirmation. *International Journal of Personal Construct Psychology, 4,* 15–41.

Fowles, D. C., Roberts, R. and Nagel, K. (1977). The influence of introversion–extraversion on the skin conductance response of stress and stimulus intensity. *Journal of Research in Personality, 11,* 129–146.

Francis, R. D. (1999). *Ethics for psychologists: A handbook.* London: BPS Books.

Fransella, F. (2003). *International handbook of personal construct psychology.* London: Wiley.

Fransella, F., Bell, R. and Bannister, D. (2004) *A manual for Repertory Grid Technique* (2nd edition). Chichester: John Wiley and Sons .

Freud, A. (1936/2011). *The ego and the mechanisms of defence.* London: Karnac Books.

Freud, A. (1966). *The ego and the mechanisms of defence.* New York: International Universities Press.

Freud, S. (1901/1953). *On dreams.* London: Hogarth Press.

Freud, S. (1901/1965). *The psychopathology of everyday life.* London: Hogarth Press.

Freud, S. (1907/1961). Obsessive actions and religious practices. In J. Strachey, (ed. and trans.), *The standard edition of the complete psychological works of Sigmund Freud* (Vol. 9, pp. 167–175). London: Hogarth Press & the Institute of Psychoanalysis. (Original work published 1907.)

Freud, S. (1913/1950). *Totem and Taboo.* London: Hogarth Press.

Freud, S. (1920/1977). *Beyond the pleasure principle.* New York: Norton.

Freud, S. (1923/1960). *The ego and the id.* New York: Norton.

Freud, S. (1924/1961). The economic problem of masochism. In J. Strachey (ed. and trans.), *The standard edition of the complete psychological works of Freud.* London: Hogarth Press.

Freud, S. (1927/1961). The future of an illusion. In J. Strachey (ed. and trans.), *The standard edition of the complete psychological works of Sigmund Freud* (Vol. 21, pp. 21–45). London: Hogarth Press & the Institute of Psychoanalysis.

Freud, S. (1940/1969). *An outline of psychoanalysis.* New York: Norton.

Freud, S. (1965). *The interpretation of dreams.* New York: Avon.

Freud, S. and Breuer, J. (1966). *Studies on hysteria* (Vol. II). London: Hogarth Press.

Friedman, H. S. (2000). Long-term relations of personality and health: Dynamisms, mechanisms, tropisms. *Journal of Personality, 68,* 1089–1107.

Friedman, M. and Rosenman, R. H. (1959). Association of specific overt behaviour pattern with blood and cardiovascular findings. *Journal of the American Medical Association, 169,* 1286–1296.

Friedman. M. and Rosenman, R. H. (1974). *Type A behaviour and your heart.* New York: Knopf.

Friedrich, J. (1824–1825). *Psychology as knowledge newly founded on experience, metaphysics and mathematics* (Vols. I & II).

Froggatt, W. (2005). *A brief introduction to rational-emotive behaviour therapy* (3rd edn). Available online at www.rational.org. nz/misc/about-REBT.htm; accessed 22 October 2012.

Froggatt, W. (2006a). *Taking Control: Manage stress to get the most out of your life.* Auckland: Harper Collins.

Froggatt, W. (2006b). *About REBT.* Available online at http://www. rational.org.nz/misc/about-REBT.htm; accessed 22 October 2012.

Fromm, E. (1941). *Escape from Freedom,* New York: Rinehart.

Fry, P. S. (ed.). (1984). *Changing conceptions of intelligence and intellectual functioning: Current theory and research.* Amsterdam: North Holland.

Fullerton, J., Cubin, M., Tiwari, H. *et al.* (2003). Linkage analysis of extremely discordant and concordant sibling pairs identifies quantitative-trait loci that influence variation in the human personality trait neuroticism. *American Journal of Human Genetics, 72,* 879–890.

Funder, D. C. (1999). *Personality judgement: A realistic approach to person perception.* San Diego, CA: Academic Press.

Funder, D. C. (2001). Personality. *Annual Review of psychology, 52,* 197–221.

Funder, D. C. (2002). Personality psychology: Current status and some issues for the future. *Journal of Research in Personality, 36,* 638–639.

Funder, D. C. and Block, J. (1989). The role of ego-control, ego-resiliency, and IQ in delay of gratification in adolescence. *Journal of Personality and Social Psychology, 57,* 1041–1050.

Furnham, A. (1985). Just world beliefs in an unjust society: A cross-cultural comparison. *European Journal of Social Psychology, 15*, 363–366.

Furnham, A. (2000). Parents' estimations of their own and children's multiple intelligences. *British Journal of Developmental Psychology, 18*, 583–594.

Furnham, A. (2001). Self-estimates of intelligence: Culture and gender difference in self and other estimates of both general (g) and multiple intelligences. *Personality and Individual Differences, 31*, 1381–1405.

Furnham, A. and Bunclark, K. (2006). Sex differences in parents' estimations of their own and their children's intelligence. *Intelligence, 34*, 1–14.

Furnham, A. and Heaven, P. (1999). *Personality and social behaviour.* New York: Oxford University Press.

Furnham, A. and Petrides, K. V. (2004) Parental estimates of five types of intelligence. *Australian Journal of Psychology, 56*, 1017.

Furnham, A. and Proctor, E. (1989). Belief in a just world: Review and critique of the individual difference literature. *British Journal of Social Psychology, 28*, 365–384.

Furnham, A., Hosoe, T. and Tang, T. (2002). Male hubris and female humility? A cross-cultural study of ratings of self, parental and sibling multiple intelligence in America, Britain and Japan. *Intelligence, 30*, 101–115.

Furnham, A., Chamorro-Premuzic, T. and McDougall, F. (2003). Personality, cognitive ability, and beliefs about intelligence as predictors of academic performance. *Learning and Individual Differences, 14*, 49–66.

Fyer, A. J., Mannuzza, S., Chapman, T. F., Leibowitz, M. R. and Klein, D. F. (1993). A direct interview family study of social phobia. *Archives of General Psychiatry, 50*, 286–293.

Gale, A. (1973). The psychophysiology of individual differences: Studies of extraversion and the EEG. In P. Kline (ed.), *New approaches in psychological measurement.* New York: Wiley.

Gale, A. (1983). Electroencephalographic studies of extraversion-introversion: A case study in the psychophysiology of individual differences. *Personality and Individual Differences, 4*, 371–380.

Gallo, L. C., Smith, T. W. and Ruiz, J. M. (2003). An interpersonal analysis of adult attachment style: Circumplex descriptions, recalled developmental experiences, self-representations and interpersonal functioning in adulthood. *Journal of Personality, 71*, 141–181.

Galton, F. (1865). Hereditary talent and character. *Macmillan's Magazine, 12*, 157–166, 318–327.

Galton, F. (1869). *Hereditary genius: An inquiry into its laws and consequences.* London: Macmillan.

Galton, F. (1874). *English men of science: Their nature and nurture.* New York: Appleton.

Galton, F. (1875). The history of twins, as a criterion of the relative powers of nature and nurture. *Fraser's Magazine, 92*, 566–576.

Galton, F. (1884). Measurement of character. *Fortnightly Review, 36*, 179–185.

Gangestad, S. W. and Simpson, J. A. (2000). The evolution of human mating: Trade-offs and strategic pluralism. *Behavioral and Brain Sciences, 23*, 573–644.

Garber, J., Weiss, B. and Shanley, N. (1993). Cognitions, depressive symptoms, and development in adolescents. *Journal of Abnormal Psychology, 102*, 47–57.

Garcia, J. (1993). Misrepresentations of my criticisms of Skinner. *American Psychologist, 48*, 1158.

Gardner, H. (1983). *Frames of mind: The theory of multiple intelligences.* New York: Basic Books.

Gardner, H. (1993). *Multiple intelligences: The theory in practice.* New York: Basic Books.

Gardner, H. (1995). Cracking open the IQ box. *The American Prospect, 20*, 71–80.

Gardner, H. (1998). Are there additional intelligences? The case for naturalist, spiritual and existential intelligences. In J. Kane (ed.), *Education, information, and transformation* (pp. 111–132). Englewood Cliffs, NJ: Prentice Hall.

Gardner, H., Kornhaber, M. and Wake, W. (1996). *Intelligence: Multiple perspectives.* Fort Worth, TX: Harcourt Brace.

Gaulin, S. J. C. (1995). Does evolutionary theory predict sex differences in the brain? In M. Gazzaniga (ed.), *The cognitive neurosciences* (pp. 1211–1225). Cambridge, MA: MIT Press.

Geary, D. C. (1995). Sexual selection and sex differences in spatial cognition. *Learning and Individual Differences, 7*, 289–301.

Geen, R. G. (1984). Preferred stimulation levels in introverts and extraverts: Effects on arousal and performance. *Journal of Personality and Social Psychology, 46*, 1303–1312.

Genia, V. (1996) I, E, Quest, and fundamentalism as predictors of psychological and spiritual well-being. *Journal for the Scientific Study of Religion, 35*, 56–64.

Genia, V. and Shaw, D. G. (1991). Religion, intrinsic-extrinsic orientation, and depression. *Review of Religious Research, 32*, 274–283.

Gilles, D. M., Turk, C. L. and Fresco, D. M. (2006). Social anxiety, alcohol expectancies, and self-efficacy as predictors of heavy drinking in college students. *Addictive Behaviours, 31*, 388–398.

Gillies, J. and Campbell, S. (1985). Conservatism and poetry preferences. *British Journal of Social Psychology, 24*, 223–227.

Gillies, O. (1976). Crucial data was faked by eminent psychologist, *The Sunday Times*, October 24.

Ginsburg, E., Livshits, G., Yakovenko, K. and Kobyliansky, E. (1998). Major gene control of human body height, weight and BMI in five ethnically different populations. *Annals of Human Genetics, 62*, 307–322.

Glasgow, M. R. and Cartier, A. M. (1985). Conservatism, sensation-seeking, and music preferences. *Personality and Individual Differences, 6*, 393–395.

Glass, D. C. (1977). *Behavior patterns: stress and coronary heart disease.* Hillsdale, NJ: Erlbaum.

Glass, D. C., Snyder, M. L. and Hollis, J. (1974). Time urgency and the Type A coronary-prone behaviour pattern. *Journal of Applied Social Psychology, 4*, 125–140.

Glazebrook, K. E. and Brawley, L. R. (2011). Thinking about maintaining exercise therapy: Does being positive or negative make a difference? *Journal of Health Psychology, 16*, 905–916.

Glazer, E. (2009). Rephrasing the madness and creativity debate: What is the nature of the creativity construct? *Personality and Individual Differences, 46*, 755–764.

Goddard, M. E. and Beilharz, R. G. (1983). Genetics of traits which determine the suitability of dogs as guide-dogs for the blind. *Applied Animal Ethology, 9*, 299–315.

Goldberg, D. P. and Williams, P. (1988). *The User's Guide to the General Health Questionnaire.* London: NFER-Nelson.

Goldberg, D. P. and Williams, P. (1991). *A user's guide to the general health questionnaire.* London: NFER-Nelson.

Goldberg, L. R. (1981). Language and individual differences: The search for universals in personality lexicons. In L. Wheeler (ed.), *Review of Personality and Social Psychology* (Vol. 2, pp. 141–165). Beverley Hills, CA: Sage.

Goldberg, L. R. (1990). An alternative 'description of personality': The Big Five factor structure. *Journal of Personality and Social Psychology, 59*, 1216–1229.

Goldberg, L. R. (1993). The structure of phenotypic personality traits. *American Psychologist, 48*, 26–34.

Goldberg, L. R. and Saucier, G. (1995). So what do you propose we use instead? A reply to Block. *Psychological Bulletin, 117,* 221–225.

Goldberg, L. R. and Somer, O. (2000). The hierarchical structure of common Turkish person-descriptive adjectives. *European Journal of Personality, 14,* 497–531.

Goldberg, L. R., Johnson, J. A., Eber, H. W. *et al,* (2006). The International Personality Item Pool and the future of public-domain personality measures. *Journal of Research in Personality, 40,* 84–96.

Goleman, D. and Boyatzis, R. (2005). *Emotional Competence Inventory (ECI).* Boston: Hay Resources Direct.

Goleman, D. P. (1995). *Emotional intelligence: Why it can matter more than IQ for character, health and lifelong achievement.* New York: Bantam.

Goleman, D. P. (1998). *Working with emotional intelligence.* London: Bloomsbury.

Goleman, D. P. (2001). An EI-based theory of performance. In C. Cherniss and D. Goleman, (eds), *The emotionally intelligent workplace* (pp. 27–44). New York: Jossey-Bass.

Goleman, D., Boyatzis, R. E. and McKee, A. (2002). *Primal leadership: Realizing the power of emotional intelligence.* Boston: Harvard Business School Press.

Gomez, R. and McLaren, S. (1997). The effects of reward and punishment on response disinhibition, moods, heart rate and skin conductance level during instrumental learning. *Personality and Individual Differences, 23,* 305–316.

Gordon, K. C., Baucom, D. H. and Snyder, D. K. (2000). The use of forgiveness in marital therapy. In M. E. McCullough, K. I. Pargament and C. E. Thoresen (eds), *Forgiveness: Theory, research, and practice* (pp. 203–227). London: Guilford.

Gorsuch, R. L. (1988). Psychology of religion. *Annual Review of Psychology, 39,* 201–221.

Gorsuch, R. L. and Venable, G. D. (1983). Development of an 'age universal' I-E scale. *Journal for the Scientific Study of Religion, 22,* 181–187.

Gosling, S. D. (1998). Personality dimensions in spotted hyenas (*Crocuta crocuta*). *Journal of Comparative Psychology, 112,* 107–118.

Gosling, S. D. (2001). From mice to men: What can we learn about personality from animal research? *Psychological Bulletin, 127,* 45–86.

Gosling, S. D. and John, O. P. (1999). Personality dimensions in non-human animals: A cross-species review. *Current Directions in Psychological Science, 8,* 69–75.

Gosling, S. D. and Vazire, S. (2002). Are we barking up the right tree? Evaluating a comparative approach to personality. *Journal of Research in Personality, 36,* 607–614.

Gosling, S. D., Kwan, V. S. Y. and John, O. P. (2003a). A dog's got personality: A cross-species comparative approach to evaluating personality judgments. *Journal of Personality and Social Psychology, 85,* 1161–1169.

Gosling, S. D., Rentrow, P. J. and Swann, W. B. Jr (2003b). A very brief measure of the Big-Five personality domains. *Journal of Research in Personality, 37,* 504–528.

Gottfredson, L. S. (1986). Societal consequences of the *g* factor in employment. *Journal of Vocational Behavior, 29,* 379–410.

Gottfredson, L. S. (1997). Why *g* matters: The complexity of everyday life. *Intelligence, 24,* 79–132.

Gough, H. G. (1987). *California Psychological Inventory administrator's guide.* Palo Alto, CA: Consulting Psychologists Press.

Gould, S. J. (1978). Morton's ranking of races by cranial capacity: Unconscious manipulation of data may be a scientific norm. *Science, 200,* 503–509.

Gould, S. J. (1981). *The mismeasurement of man.* New York: Norton.

Gould, S. J. (1995). Mismeasure by any measure. In R. Jacoby and N. Glauberman (eds), *The Bell Curve debate: History, documents, opinions* (pp. 3–13). New York: Random House. (This paper originally appeared in *The New Yorker* on 28 November 1994 and was entitled 'Curveball'.)

Gow A.J., Johnson W., Pattie A. *et al.* (2011). Stability and change in intelligence from age 11 to ages 70, 79, and 87: the Lothian Birth Cohorts of 1921 and 1936. *Psychology and Aging, 26,* 232–40.

Graves, J. (2001). *The emperor's new clothes: Biological theories of race at the millennium.* New Brunswick, NJ: Rutgers University Press.

Gray, J. A. (1970). The psychophysiological basis of intraversion-extraversion. *Behavior Research and Therapy, 8,* 249–266.

Gray, J. A. (1981). A critique of Eysenck's theory of personality. In H. J. Eysenck (ed.), *A model for personality* (pp. 246–276). New York: Springer.

Gray, J. A. (1987). *The psychology of fear and stress* (2nd edn). Cambridge: Cambridge University Press.

Gray, J. A. (1988). The neuropsychological basis of anxiety. In C. G. Last and M. Hersen (eds), *Handbook of anxiety disorders.* Oxford: Pergamon Press.

Gray, J. A. and Buffery, A. W. H. (1971). Sex differences in emotional and cognitive behaviour in mammals including man: Adaptive and neural bases. *Acta Psychologica, 35,* 89–111.

Graziano, W. G. and Eisenberg, N. H. (1990). Agreeableness: A dimension of personality. In S. Briggs, R. Hogan and W. Jones (eds), *Handbook of personality psychology.* New York: Academic Press.

Green, C. J. (1985). The use of psychodiagnostic questionnaires in predicting risk factors and health outcomes. In P. Karoly (ed.), *Measurement strategies in health psychology.* New York: Wiley.

Greenfield, P. M. (1998). The cultural evolution of IQ. In U. Neisser (ed.), *The rising curve: Long-term gains in IQ and related measures.* (pp. 81–124). Washington, DC: American Psychological Association.

Gregg, G. (2006). A sketch of Albert Ellis. Albert Ellis Institute. Available online at www.rebt.org; accessed 22 October 2012.

Gregory, R., Canning, S., Lee, T. and Wise, J. (2004). Cognitive bibliotherapy for depression: A meta-analysis. *Professional Psychology, 35*(3), 275–280.

Grieger, R. and Boyd, J. (1980). *Rational-emotive therapy: A skills-based approach.* New York: Van Nostrand Reinhold.

Grigorenko, R. L. (2004). Is it possible to study intelligence without using the concept of intelligence? An example from Soviet/Russian psychology. In R. J. Sternberg (ed.), *International handbook of intelligence* (pp. 170–211). Cambridge: Cambridge University Press.

Grob, G. N. (1991) Origins of *DSM-I*: A study in appearance and reality. *American Journal of Psychiatry, 148,* 421–431.

Gruber, H. E. (1981). *Darwin on man: A psychological study of scientific creativity* (2nd edn). Chicago: Chicago University Press.

Gruber, H. E. (1988). The evolving system approach to creative work. *Creativity Research Journal, 1,* 27–51.

Grünbaum, A. (1993). *Validation in the clinical theory of psychoanalysis: A study in the philosophy of psychoanalysis.* Madison, CT: International Universities Press.

Guidano, V. and Liotti, G. (1983). *Cognitive processes and emotional disorders.* New York: Guilford.

Guilford, J. P. (1950). Creativity. *American Psychologist, 5,* 444–454.

Guilford, J. P. (1959). Three faces of intellect. *American Psychologist*, *14*, 469–479.

Guilford, J. P. (1967). *The nature of human intelligence*. New York: McGraw-Hill.

Guilford, J. P. (1977). *Way beyond the IQ: Guide to improving intelligence and creativity*. Buffalo, NY: Creative Education Foundation.

Guilford, J. P. (1982). Cognitive psychology's ambiguities: Some suggested remedies. *Psychological Review*, *89*, 48–59.

Guilford, J. P. and Hoepfner, R. (1967, 1971). *The nature of human intelligence*. New York: McGraw-Hill.

Guilford, J. P. and Hoepfner, R. (1971). *The analysis of intelligence*. New York: McGraw-Hill.

Guimond, S., Dambrun, M., Michinov, N. and Duarte, S. (2003). Does social dominance generate prejudice? Integrating individual and contextual determinants of intergroup cognitions. *Journal of Personality and Social Psychology*, *84*, 697–721.

Gul, F. A. and Ray, J. J. (1989). Pitfalls in using the F scale to measure authoritarianism in accounting research. *Behavioural Research in Accounting*, *1*, 182–192.

Guralnik, B. (ed.) (1972). *Webster's new world dictionary of the American language* (2nd college edn). New York: World Publishing.

Haaga, D. A. F. and Davison, G. C. (1993). An appraisal of rational-emotive therapy. *Journal of Consulting and Clinical Psychology*, *61*(2), 215–220.

Hahn, D. W., Lee, K. and Ashton, M. C. (1999). A factor analysis of the most frequently used Korean personality trait adjectives. *European Journal of Personality*, *13*, 261–282.

Haier, R. J., Jung, R. E., Yeo, R. A. et al. (2005). The neuroanatomy of general intelligence: Sex matters. *NeuroImage*, *25*, 320–327.

Halkitis, P. N., Kutnick, A. H. and Slater, S. (2005). The social realities of adherence to protease inhibitor regimens: Substance use, health care and psychological states. *Journal of Health Psychology*, *10*, 545–558.

Hall, C. S. and Klein, S. J. (1942). Individual differences in aggressiveness in rats. *Journal of Comparative Psychology*, *33*, 371–383.

Hall, J. H. and Fincham, F. D. (2005). Self-forgiveness: The stepchild of forgiveness research. *Journal of Social and Clinical Psychology*, *24*, 621–637.

Hallsten, L., Voss, M., Stark, S. and Josephson, M. (2011). Job burnout and job worn-out as risk factors for long-term sickness absence. *Work*, *38*, 181–192.

Halpern, D. F. and LaMay, M. L. (2000). The smarter sex: A critical review of sex differences in intelligence. *Educational Psychology Review*, *12*, 170–189.

Hamilton, M. (1980). Rating depressive patients. *Journal of Clinical Psychiatry*, *41*, 21–24.

Hamilton, W. D. (1964a). The genetical evolution of social behavior: I. *Journal of Theoretical Biology*, *7*, 1–16.

Hamilton, W. D. (1964b). The genetical evolution of social behavior: II. *Journal of Theoretical Biology*, *7*, 17–52.

Hampson, S. E. (ed.) (2000). *Advances in personality psychology* (Vol. 1). London: Psychology Press.

Hampson, S. E. and Colman, A. M. (eds) (1995). *Individual Differences and Personality*. London and New York: Longman.

Hannay, D. R. (1978). Symptom prevalence in the community. *Journal of the Royal College of General Practitioners*, *28*, 492–499.

Hardoon, S.L., Whincup, P.H., Wannamethee, S.G. et al. (2010). Assessing the impact of medication use on trends in major coronary risk factors in older British men: a cohort study. *European Journal of Cardiovascular Preventive Rehabilitation*, *17*, 502–508.

Hare-Mustin, R. T. and Marecek, J. (1988). The meaning of difference: Gender theory, postmodernism, and psychology. *American Psychologist*, *43*, 455–464.

Harkins, J. (1990). Shame and shyness in the Aboriginal classroom: A case for 'practical semantics'. *Australian Journal of Linguistics*, *10*, 293–306.

Harrington, D. M. (1972). Effects of instructions to 'Be creative' on three tests of divergent thinking abilities. PhD thesis: University of California, Berkeley.

Harrington, D. M. (1975). Effect of explicit instructions to 'be creative' on the psychological meaning of divergent thinking test scores. *Journal of Personality*, *43*, 434–454.

Harrington, D. M., Block, H. J. and Block, J. (1987). Testing aspects of Carl Rogers' theory of creative environments and child-rearing antecedents of creative potential in young adolescents. *Journal of Personality and Social Psychology*, *52*, 851–856.

Harris, J. R. (1995). Where is the child's environment? A group socialization theory of development. *Psychological Review*, *102*, 458–489.

Hart, C. L., Taylor, M. D. and Smith, G. D. et al. (2003). Childhood IQ, social class, deprivation, and their relationships with mortality and morbidity risk in later life: Prospective observational study linking the Scottish Mental Survey 1932 and the Midspan studies. *Psychosomatic Medicine*, *65*, 877–883.

Hartz, A. J. (1996). Psycho-socionomics: Attractiveness research from a societal perspective. *Journal of Social Behavior and Personality*, *11*, 683–694.

Hasuo, C. (1935). Effect of milieu upon character. I. Experiments with young chickens. *Japanese Journal of Experimental Psychology*, *2*, 109–118.

Hauser, R. M. (2007). Will practitioners benefit from meta-analysis? *Academy of Management Perspectives*, *21*, 24–28.

Hauser, R. M. (2010). Causes and consequences of cognitive functioning across the life course. *Educational Researcher*, *39*, 95–109.

Hawk, S. T., Fischer, A. H. and Van Kleef, G. A. (2011). Taking your place or matching your face: Two paths to empathic embarrassment. *Emotion*, *11*, 502–513.

Hawkes, N. (2007). 'IQ differences are real, but do they matter?' *The Times*, 18 October.

Haynes, S. G., Feinleib, M., Levine, S., Scotch, N. et al. (1978a). The relationship of psychosocial factors to coronary heart disease in the Framington Study II. Prevalence of coronary heart disease. *American Journal of Epidemiology*, *107*, 384–402.

Haynes, S. G., Levine, S., Scotch, N. et al. (1978b). The relationship of psychosocial factors to coronary heart disease in the Framington Study I. Methods and risk factors. *American Journal of Epidemiology*, *107*, 362–383.

Haynes, S. G., Feinleib, M. and Kannel, W. B. (1980). The relationship of psychosocial factors to coronary heart disease in the Framington Study III. Eight year incidence of coronary heart disease. *American Journal of Epidemiology*, *111*, 37–58.

Hazan, C. and Shaver, P. (1987). Romantic love conceptualized as an attachment process. *Journal of Personality and Social Psychology*, *52*(3), 511–524.

Hearnshaw, L. (1979). *Cyril Burt: Psychologist*. Ithaca, NY: Cornell University Press.

Hearnshaw, L. S. (1987). *The shaping of modern psychology*. London: Routledge & Kegan Paul.

Heaven, P. and Bucci, S. (2001). Right-wing authoritarianism, social dominance orientation and personality: An analysis using the IPIP measure. *European Journal of Personality*, *15*, 49–56.

Heaven, P. C. L., Da Silva, T., Carey, C. and Holen, J. (2004). Loving styles: Relationships with personality and attachment styles. *European Journal of Personality, 18,* 103–113.

Hebb, D. O. (1949). *The organization of behavior: A neuropsychological theory.* New York: Wiley.

Hebl, J. H. and Enright, R. D. (1993). Forgiveness as a psychotherapeutic goal with elderly females. *Psychotherapy, 30,* 658–667.

Heckelman, L. R. and Schneier, F. R. (1995). Diagnostic issues. In R. R. G. Heimberg, M. Liebowitz, D. A. Hope and S. Scheier (eds), *Social phobia: Diagnosis, assessment and treatment* (pp. 3–20). New York: Guilford.

Heckhausen, J. and Schulz, R. (1995). A life-span theory of control. *Psychological Review, 102,* 284–304.

Hedges, L. V. and Nowell, A. (1995). Sex differences in mental test scores, variability, and numbers of high-scoring individuals. *Science, 269,* 41–45.

Heimberg, R. R. G., Liebowitz, M., Hope, D. A. and Schneier, F. R. (eds) (1995). *Social phobia: Diagnosis, assessment and treatment* (pp. 334–365). New York: Guilford.

Helgeland, M. I. and Torgersen, S. (2004). Developmental antecedents of borderline personality disorder. *Comprehensive Psychiatry, 45,* 138–147.

Hemingway, H. and Marmot, M. (1999). Evidence based cardiology: Psychosocial factors in the aetiology and prognosis of coronary heart disease. Systematic review of cohort studies. *British Medical Journal, 318,* 1460–1467.

Henderson, L. and Zimbardo, P. G. (1998). Shyness. *The encyclopedia of mental health, 3,* 497–509.

Henderson, L. and Zimbardo, P. G. (2001). Shyness, social anxiety and social phobia. In S. Hofmann and P. di Bartolo (eds), *From social anxiety to social phobia: Multiple perspectives* (pp. 46–64). New York: Allyn & Bacon.

Hendrick, C. and Hendrick, S. (1986). A theory and method of love. *Journal of Personality and Social Psychology, 50,* 392–402.

Hendrick, C. and Hendrick, S. S. (1990). A relationship-specific version of the Love Attitude Scale. *Journal of Social Behavior and Personality, 5,* 239–254.

Hendrick, C., Hendrick, S. S. and Dicke, A. (1998). The Love Attitudes Scale: Short form. *Journal of Social and Personal Relationships, 15,* 147–159.

Hendrick, S. and Hendrick, C. (1995). Gender differences and similarities in sex and love. *Personal Relationships, 2,* 55–65.

Heponiemi, T., Keltikangas-Järvinen, L., Puttonen, S. and Ravaja, N. (2003). BIS/BAS sensitivity and self-rated effects during experimentally induced stress. *Personality and Individual Differences, 34,* 943–957.

Herman, J. L. and Herman, M. D. (1992). *Trauma and recovery.* New York: BasicBooks.

Herrera, N. C., Zajonc, R. B., Wieczorkowska, G. and Cichomski, B. (2003). Beliefs about birth rank and their reflection in reality. *Journal of Personality and Social Psychology, 85,* 142–150.

Herrnstein, R. and Murray, C. (1994). *The bell curve: Intelligence and class structure in American life.* New York: Free Press.

Hershberger, S. L., Plomin, R. and Pedersen, N. L. (1995). Traits and meta-traits: Their reliability, stability, and shared genetic influence. *Journal of Personality and Social Psychology, 69,* 673–685.

Hidalgo, R. B., Barnett, S. D. and Davidson, J. R. T. (2001). Social anxiety disorder in review: Two decades of progress. *International Journal of Neuropsychopharmacology, 4,* 279–298.

Higgins, E. T. (1996). Ideals, oughts, and regulatory focus: Affect and motivation from distinct pains and pleasures. In E. P. Gollwitzer and J. A. Bargh (eds), *The psychology of action: Linking cognition and motivation to behaviour* (pp. 91–114). New York: Guilford.

Hill, E. W. (2001). Understanding forgiveness as discovery: Implications for marital and family therapy. *Contemporary Family Therapy, 23,* 369–384.

Hill, E. W. and Mullen, P. M. (2000). Contexts for understanding forgiveness and repentance as discovery. *Journal of Pastoral Care, 54,* 287–296.

Hobson, J. A. (1999). The new neuropsychology of sleep: Implications for psychoanalysis. *Neuro-Psychoanalysis, 1,* 157–224.

Hoffman, B. (1962). *The tyranny of testing.* New York: Collier Books.

Hoffman, C., Lau, I. and Johnson, D. R. (1986). The linguistic relativity of person cognition. *Journal of Personality and Social Psychology, 51,* 1097–1105.

Hofman, S. G. and Otto, M. W. (2008). *Cognitive-behavioral therapy of social anxiety disorder: Evidence-based and disorder-specific treatment techniques.* London: Routledge.

Hofstede, G. (1997). *Cultures and organizations: software of the mind.* London: McGraw Hill.

Hofstede, G. (2001). *Culture's consequences: Comparing values, behaviors, institutions and organizations across nations.* Thousand Oaks, CA: Sage.

Hofstede, G. and Hofstede, G. J. (2005). *Cultures and organizations: Software of the mind, revised and expanded* (2nd edn). New York: McGraw-Hill.

Hooven, C. K., Chabris, C. F., Ellison, P. T. and Kosslyn, S. M. (2004). The relationship of male testosterone to components of mental rotation. *Neuropsychologia, 42,* 782–790.

Horn, J. L. (1965). A rationale and test for the number of factors in factor analysis. *Psychometrika, 30,* 179–185.

Horn, J. L. and Cattell, R. B. (1967). Age differences in fluid and crystallized intelligence. *Acta Psychologica, 26,* 107–129.

Horney, K. (1945). *Our inner conflicts.* New York: Norton.

Horney, K. (1950). *Neurosis and human growth.* New York: Norton.

Horney, K. (1977). *The Neurotic Personality of our Time.* New York: Routledge and Kegan Paul.

Horney, K. (1993). *Feminine psychology.* New York: Norton.

Hough, L. M. (1992). The 'Big Five' personality variables–construct confusion: Descriptive versus predictive. *Human Performance, 5,* 139–155.

Hough, L. M. (1997). The millennium for personality psychology: New horizons or good old daze. *Applied Psychology International Review, 47,* 233–261.

Hough, L. M. (1998). Personality at work: Issues and evidence. In M. Hakel (ed.), *Beyond multiple choice: Evaluating alternatives and traditional testing for selection* (pp. 131–159). Hillsdale, NJ: Erlbaum.

Hough, L. M. and Oswald, F. L. (2000). Personal selection: Looking toward the future – remembering the past. *Annual Review of Psychology, 51,* 631–664.

Houston, J. M., Mcintire, S. M., Kinnie, J. and Terry. C. (2002). A factorial analysis of scales measurring competitiveness. *Educational and Psychological Measurement, 62,* 284–298.

Houts, A. C. (2000) Fifty years of psychiatric nomenclature: Reflections on the 1943 War Department Technical Bulletin, Medical 203. *Journal of Clinical Psychology, 56,* 935–967.

Howe, J. A. (1998). Can IQ change? *The Psychologist, 11,* 69–72.

Hoy, A. W. and Davis, H. A. (2006). Teacher self-efficacy and its influence on the achievement of adolescents. In F. Pajares and T. Urdan (eds), *Self-efficacy beliefs of adolescents.* Greenwich, CT: Information Age Publishing.

Hu, L. T. and Bentler, P. M. (1999). Cut off criteria for fit indices in covariance structure analysis: Conventional criteria versus new alternatives. *Structural Equation Modeling, 6,* 1–55.

Hull, J. G., Tedlie, J. C. and Lehn, D. A. (1995). Modelling the relation of personality variables to symptom complaints: The unique role of negative affectivity. In R. H. Hoyle (ed.), *Structural equation modelling: Concepts, issues, and applications* (pp. 217–235). London: Sage.

Hunt, J. M. (1979). Psychological development: Early experience. *Annual Review of Psychology, 30*, 103–143.

Hunter, J. E. and Hunter, R. F. (1984). Validity and utility of alternative predictors of job performance. *Psychological Bulletin, 96*, 72–98.

Huntingford, F. A. (1976). The relationship between anti-predator behaviour and aggression among conspecifics in the three-spined stickleback. *Animal Behaviour, 24*, 245–260.

Huusko, J. (2008). Again we ask: what is wrong with us? *Independent*, 24 September 2008. www.independent.co.uk/opinion/commentators/jukka-huusko-again-we-ask-what-is-wrong-with-us-940305.html; accessed 4 June 2009.

Hyde, J. S. (1984). How large are gender differences in aggression? A developmental meta-analysis. *Developmental Psychology, 20*, 722–736.

Hyde, J. S. (1986). Gender differences in aggression. In J. S. Hyde and M. C. Linn (eds), *The psychology of gender: Advances through meta-analysis* (pp. 51–66). Baltimore, MD: Johns Hopkins University Press.

Hyde, J. S. (2005). The gender similarities hypothesis. *American Psychologist, 60*, 581–592.

Hyde, J. S. and Linn, M. C. (1988). Gender differences in verbal ability: A meta-analysis. *Psychological Bulletin, 104*, 53–69.

Hyde, J. S., Fennema, E. and Lamon, S. (1990a). Gender differences in mathematics performance: A meta-analysis. *Psychological Bulletin, 107*, 139–155.

Hyde, J. S., Fennema, E., Ryan, M., Frost, L. A. and Hopp, C. (1990b). Gender comparisons of mathematics attitudes and affect: A meta-analysis. *Psychology of Women Quarterly, 14*, 299–324.

Ireland, W. (1988). Eros, agape, amor, libido: Concepts in the history of love. In J. Lasky and H. Silverman (eds), *Love: Psychoanalytic perspectives* (pp. 14–30). New York: New York University Press.

Irvine, J. T. (1978). 'Wolof magical thinking': Culture and conservation revisited. *Journal of Cross-cultural Psychology, 9*, 300–310.

Irwing, P. and Lynn, R. (2005). Sex differences in means and variability on the progressive matrices in university students: A meta-analysis. *British Journal of Psychology, 96*, 505–524.

Itard, J. M. G. (1962). *The wild boy of Aveyron.* (G. Humphrey and M. Humphrey, trans). New York: Appleton-Century-Crofts. (Original works published 1801 and 1806.)

Iwanaga, M. (2004). Coping availability and stress reduction for optimistic and pessimistic individuals. *Personality and Individual Difference, 36*, 11–22.

Izard, C. E. (1972). *Patterns of emotions: A new analysis of anxiety and depression.* New York: Academic Press.

Jacobi, J. (1962). *The psychology of C. G. Jung.* New Haven, CT: Yale University Press.

Jacobson, S. W., Jacobson, J. L., Sokol, R. J., Chiodo, L. M. and Corobana, R. (2004). Maternal age, alcohol abuse history, and quality of parenting as moderators of the effects of prenatal alcohol exposure on 7.5-year intellectual function. *Alcoholism: Clinical and Experimental Research, 28*, 1732–1745.

Jamison, C. and Scogin, F. (1995). The outcome of cognitive bibliotherapy with depressed adults. *Journal of Consulting & Clinical Psychology, 63*, 644–650.

Jang, K. L., Livesley, W. J. and Vernon, P. A. (1996). Heritability of the big five personality dimensions and their facets: A twin study. *Journal of Personality, 64*, 577–591.

Jarvis, P. (1995). *Adult and continuing education: Theory and practice* (2nd edn). London: Routledge.

Jencks, C. (1972). *Inequality.* New York: Basic Books.

Jencks, C. (1979). *Who gets ahead?: The determinants of economic success in America.* New York: Basic Books.

Jenkins, C. D., Rosenman, R. H. and Zyzanski, S. J. (1974). Prediction of coronary heart disease by a test for the coronary prone behaviour pattern. *New England Journal of Medicine, 23*, 1271–1275.

Jenkins, C. D., Zyzanski, S. J. and Rosenman, R. H. (1979). *Jenkins Activity Survey.* New York: Psychological Corporation.

Jensen, A. R. (1969). How much can we boost IQ and scholastic achievement? *Harvard Educational Review, 39*, 1–123.

Jensen, A. R. (1972). *Genetics and education.* London: Methuen.

Jensen, A. R. (1973). *Educability and group differences.* New York: Harper & Row.

Jensen, A. R. (1981). *Straight talk about mental testing.* New York: Free Press.

Jensen, A. R. (1982). The limited plasticity of human intelligence. *Eugenics Bulletin*, Fall.

Jensen, A. R. (1993a). Psychometric G and achievement. In B. R. Gifford (ed.), *Policy perspectives on educational testing* (pp. 117–227). Boston: Kluwer.

Jensen, A. R. (1993b). Why is reaction time correlated with psychometric g? *Current Directions in Psychological Science, 2*, 53–56.

Jensen, A. R. (1994). Paroxysms of denial. *National Review, 46*(23), 48.

Jensen, A. R. (1998). *The g factor: The science of mental ability.* Westport, CT: Praeger.

Johnson, D. L., Wiebe, J. S., Gold, S. M. and Andreasen, N. C. (1999). Cerebral blood flow and personality: A positron emission tomography study. *American Journal of Psychiatry, 156*, 252–257.

Johnson, J. G., Cohen, P., Chen, H., Kasen, S. and Brook, J. S. (2006). Parenting behaviors associated with risk for offspring personality disorder during adulthood. *Archives of General Psychiatry, 63*, 579–587.

Johnston, D. W., Cook, D. G. and Shaper, A. G. (1987). Type A behaviour and ischemic heart disease in middle aged British men. *British Medical Journal, 295*, 86–89.

Jokela, M., Kivimaki, M., Elovainio, M. and Keltikangas-Jarvinen, L. (2009). Personality and having children: A two way relationship. *Journal of Personality and Social Psychology, 96*, 218–230.

Jones, C. M., Braithwaite, V. A. and Healy, S. D. (2003). The evolution of sex differences in spatial ability. *Behavioral Neuroscience, 117*, 73–84.

Jones, H. E. and Bayley, N. (1941). The Berkeley Growth Study. *Child Development, 12*, 167–173.

Jones, W. H., Cheek, J. M. and Briggs, S. R. (eds) (1986). *Shyness: Perspectives on research and treatment.* New York: Plenum.

Jonsson, J. O. (1999). Explaining sex differences in educational choice: An empirical assessment of a rational choice model. *European Sociological Review, 15*, 391–404.

Joynson, R. B. (1989). *The Burt affair.* New York: Routledge.

Julian, D. G. and Cowan, J. C. (1992). *Cardiology.* London: Baillière Tindall.

Jung, C. G. (1954). *The development of personality.* New York: Pantheon.

Jung, C. G. (1959). *The archetypes and the collective unconscious.* Princeton, NJ: Princeton University Press.

Jung, C. G. (1964). *Man and his symbols.* New York: Dell.

Jung, C. G. (1965). *Memories, dreams, reflections.* Princeton, NJ: Princeton University Press.

Jung, C. G. (1968). *Analytical psychology: Its theory and practice.* New York: Pantheon.

Jung, C. G. (1971). *Psychological types*. Princeton, NJ: Princeton University Press.

Jussim, L. and Harber, K. D. (2005). Teacher expectations and self-fulfilling prophecies: Knowns and unknowns, resolved and unresolved controversies. *Personality and Social Psychology Review, 9*, 131–155.

Kagan, J. (1994a). *Galen's prophecy*. London: Free Association Books.

Kagan, J. (1994b). *The nature of the child* (10th anniversary edn). New York: Basic Books.

Kagan, J. (1998). *Three seductive ideas*. New York: Harvard University Press.

Kagan, J. (2001). Temperamental contributions to affective and behavioural profiles in childhood. In S. G. Hoffmann and P. M. DiBartolo (eds), *From social anxiety to social phobia: Multiple perspectives* (pp. 216–234). Boston: Allyn & Bacon.

Kahneman, D., Diener, E. and Schwarz, N. (eds) (1999). *Well-being: The foundations of hedonic psychology*. New York: Russell Sage Foundation.

Kamin, L. J. (1974). *The science and politics of IQ*. Potomac, MD: Erlbaum.

Kamin, L. J. (1995). Lies, damned lies, and statistics. In R. Jacoby and N. Glauberman (eds), *The Bell Curve debate: History, documents, opinions* (pp. 81–105). New York: Times/Random House.

Kamin, L. J. and Goldberger, A. S. (2002). Twin studies in behavioral research: A skeptical view. *Theoretical Population Biology, 61*, 83–95.

Kardiner, A. and Linton, R. (1939) *The individual and his society*. New York: Columbia University Press.

Karremans, J. C., Van Lange, P. A. M., Ouwerkerk, J. W. and Kluwer, E. S. (2003). When forgiving enhances psychological well-being: The role of interpersonal commitment. *Journal of Personality and Social Psychology, 84*, 1011–1026.

Kashdan, T. B., Biswas-Diener, R. and King, L. A. (2008). Reconsidering happiness: The costs of distinguishing between hedonics and eudaimonia. *Journal of Positive Psychology, 3*, 219–233.

Kassin, S. (2003). *Psychology*. New York: Prentice Hall.

Kassin, S. M., Ellsworth, P. C. and Smith, V. L. (1989). The 'general acceptance' of psychological research on eyewitness testimony. *American Psychologist, 44*, 1089–1098.

Kaufman, A. S. (1984). K-ABC and giftedness. *Roeper Review, 7*, 83–88.

Kaufman, A. S. (1990). *Assessing adolescent and adult intelligence*. Boston: Allyn & Bacon.

Kaufman, A. S. and Kaufman, N. L. (2001). *Specific learning disabilities and difficulties in children and adolescents: Psychological assessment and evaluation*. Cambridge: Cambridge University Press.

Kaufman, A. S. and Lichtenberger, E. O. (2005). *Assessing adolescent and adult intelligence* (3rd edn). Boston: Allyn & Bacon.

Kelley, H. H., Holmes, J. G., Kerr, N. L. *et al.* (2003). *An atlas of interpersonal situations*. New York: Cambridge University Press.

Kelloniemi, H., Ek, E. and Laitinen, J. (2005). Optimism, dietary habits, body mass index and smoking among young Finnish adults. *Appetite, 45*(2), 169–176.

Kelly, G. A. (1955). *The psychology of personal constructs* (Vols 1 & 2). New York: Norton.

Kelly, G. A. (1958). Man's construction of his alternatives. In G. Lindzey (ed.), *Assessment of human motives*. New York: Rinehart and Winston.

Kelly, G. A. (1963). *A theory of personality: The psychology of personal constructs*. New York: Norton.

Kelly, G. A. (1966). *The psychotherapeutic relationship*. Waltham, MA: Brandeis University.

Kelly, J. (2008). Sweet smell of success: Binge drinking in Britain is just a side-effect of an endearing national trait: unbridled enthusiasm. *Guardian*, 22 September 2008. Available online at www.guardian.co.uk/commentisfree/2008/sep/22/drugsandalcohol.britishidentity; accessed 4 June 2009.

Kelly, K. M. and Jones, W. H. (1997). Assessment of dispositional embarrassibility. *Anxiety, Stress, and Coping, 10*, 307–333.

Keltner, D. and Buswell, B. N. (1997). Embarrassment: Its distinct form and appeasement functions. *Psychological Bulletin, 122*, 250–270.

Kendler, K. S., Neale, M. C. and Kessier, R. C. (1992). The genetic epidemiology of phobias in women: The interrelationship of agoraphobia, social phobia, situational phobia, and simple phobia. *Archives of General Psychiatry, 49*, 273–281.

Kendler, K. S., Karkowski, L. M. and Prescott, C. A. (1999). Fears and phobias: Reliability and heritability. *Psychological Medicine, 29*, 539–553.

Kendler, K. S., Aggen, S. H., Czajkowski, N. *et al.* (2008). The structure of genetic and environmental risk factors for *DSM-IV* personality disorders: A multivariate twin study. *Archives of General Psychiatry, 65*, 1438–1446.

Kenrick, D. T. and Keefe, R. C. (1992). Age preferences in mates reflect sex differences in reproductive strategies. *Behavioral and Brain Sciences, 15*, 75–85.

Kern, C. W. and Watts, R. E. (1993). Adlerian counselling. Special issue: Counsellor educators' theories of counselling. *TCA Journal, 21*, 85–95.

Kern, M. L. and Friedman, H. S. (2008). Do conscientious individuals live longer? A quantitative review. *Health Psychology, 27*, 505–512.

Kerr, M. (2000). Childhood and adolescent shyness in long-term perspective: Does it matter? In W. R. Crozier (ed.), *Shyness: Development, consolidation and change* (pp. 64–87). London: Routledge.

Keyes, C. L. M., Shmotkin, D. and Ryff, C. D. (2002). Optimizing well-being: The empirical encounter of two traditions. *Journal of Personality and Social Psychology, 82*, 1007–1022.

Kihlstrom, J. F. (1999). The psychological unconscious. In L. A. Pervin (ed.), *Handbook of personality: Theory and research* (pp. 424–442). New York: Guilford.

Kilmann, R. H. and Taylor, V. A. (1974). A contingency approach to laboratory learning. *Human Relations, 27*, 891–909.

Kincheloe, J., Steinberg, S. and Gresson, A. (1996). *Measured lies*. New York: St. Martin's Press.

King, J. E. and Figueredo, A. J. (1997). The five-factor model plus dominance in chimpanzee personality. *Journal of Research in Personality, 31*, 257–271.

King, K. B. (1984). Coping with cardiac surgery. Unpublished doctoral dissertation, University of Rochester.

Kinkade, K. (1973). Commune: A Walden Two experiment. *Psychology Today, 6*, 35.

Kirby, J. R. and Boulter, D. R. (1999). Spatial ability and transformational geometry. *European Journal of Psychology of Education, 14*, 283–294.

Kitcher, P. (1987). Precis of vaulting ambition: Sociobiology and the quest for human nature. *Behavioral and Brain Sciences, 10*, 61–100.

Kline, P. (1981). *Fact and fantasy in Freudian theory* (2nd edn). London: Methuen.

Kline, P. (1986). *A handbook of test construction: Introduction to psychometric design*. London: Methuen.

Kline, P. (1999). *The handbook of psychological testing* (2nd edn). London: Routledge.

Kline, P. (2000a). *The new psychometrics: Science, psychology and measurement*. London: Routledge.

Kline, P. (2000b). *A psychometrics primer*. London: Free Association Books.

Kline, P. and Cooper, C. (1984). A factorial analysis of the authoritarian personality. *British Journal of Psychology, 75*, 171–176.

Knapp, R. R. (1976). *Handbook for the personal orientation inventory*. San Diego, CA: EDITS Publishers.

Knight, G. P., Guthrie, I. K., Page, M. C. and Fabes, R. A. (2002). Emotional arousal and gender differences in aggression: A meta-analysis. *Aggressive Behavior, 28*, 366–393.

Kodituwakku, P. W., Handmaker, N. S., Cutler, S. K., Weathersby, E. K. and Handmaker, S. D. (1995). Specific impairments in self-regulation in children exposed to alcohol prenatally. *Alcoholism: Clinical and Experimental Research, 19*, 1558–1564.

Koenig, H. G. (1995). Religion and older men in prison. *International Journal of Geriatric Psychiatry, 10*, 219–230.

Koenig, H. G., George, L. K., Titus, P. and Meador, K. G. (2004). Religion, spirituality, acute hospital and long-term care use by older patients. *Archives of Internal Medicine, 164*, 1579–1585.

Kolb, D. A. (1981). *The learning style inventory*. Boston: McBer.

Kolb, D. A. (1984). *Experiential learning: Experience as the source of learning and development*. Englewood Cliffs, NJ: Prentice Hall.

Kolb, D. A. and Fry, R. (1975). Toward an applied theory of experiential learning. In C. Cooper (ed.), *Theories of group process*. London: Wiley.

Konner, M. (1985, October 6). One gene at a time. *The New York Times Book Review*, 48.

Konstantopoulos, S., Modi, M. and Hedges, L. V. (2001). Who are America's gifted? *American Journal of Education, 109*, 344–382.

Krach, S., Cohrs, J. C., Cruz de Echeverría Loebell, N. *et al.* (2011). Your flaws are my pain: Linking empathy to vicarious embarrassment. *PLoS ONE, 6*(4), 1–9.

Kraus, S. J. (1995). Attitudes and the prediction of behaviour: A meta-analysis of the empirical literature. *Personality and Social Psychology Bulletin, 21*, 58–75.

Krebs, J. R. and Davies, N. B. (1993). *An introduction to behavioural ecology* (3rd edn). London: Blackwell.

Krueger, R. F. and Caspi, A. (1993). Personality, arousal, and pleasure: A test of competing models of interpersonal attraction. *Personality and Individual Differences, 14*, 105–111.

Kuipers, B. S., Higgs, M. J., Tolkacheva, N. V., de Witte, M. C. (2009). The influence of the Myers–Briggs Type Indicator profiles on team development processes: An empirical study in the manufacturing industry. *Small Group Research, 40*(4) 436–464.

Kurdek, L. A. (1992). Relationship stability and relationship satisfaction in cohabiting gay and lesbian couples: A prospective longitudinal test of the contextual and interdependence models. *Journal of Social and Personal Relationships, 9*, 125–142.

Lakatos, I. (1970). Falsification and the methodology of scientific research programmes. In I. Lakatos and A. Musgrave (eds), *Criticism and the growth of knowledge* (pp. 91–195). New York: Cambridge University Press.

Lam, D., Drewin, C., Woods, R. and Bebbington, P. (1987). Cognitive and social adversity in the depressed elderly. *Journal of Abnormal Psychology, 96*, 23–26.

Lamb, K. (1992). Biased tidings: The media and the Cyril Burt controversy. *Mankind Quarterly, 33*, 203.

Lamb, M. E., Thompson, R. A., Gardner, W. P., Charnov, E. L. and Estes, D. (1984). Security of infantile attachment as assessed in the 'strange situation': Its study and biological interpretation. *Behavioral and Brain Sciences, 7*, 127–171.

Landy, F. J. (2005). Some historical and scientific issues related to research on emotional intelligence. *Journal of Organizational Behavior, 26*, 411–424.

Lane, J. and Lane, A. M. (2001). Self-efficacy and academic performance. *Social Behaviour and Personality, 29*, 687–694.

Lang, P. D. (1971). Applications of psycho-physiological methods to the study of psychotherapy and behaviour modification. In A. E. Bergin and S. L. Garfield (eds), *Handbook of psychotherapy and behaviour change*. New York: Wiley.

Lang, P. J. (1968). Fear reduction and fear behaviour: problems in treating a construct. In J. M. Shlien (ed.), *Research in psychotherapy*. Washington, DC: APA.

Langer, E. J. (1975). The illusion of control. *Journal of Personality and Social Psychology, 32*, 311–328.

Langer, E. J. and Roth, J. (1975). Heads I win, tails it's chance: The illusion of control as a function of the sequence of outcomes in a purely chance task. *Journal of Personality and Social Psychology, 32*, 951–955.

Larsen, R. J. (1992). Neuroticism and selective encoding and recall of symptoms: Evidence from a combined concurrent-retrospective study. *Journal of Personality and Social Psychology, 62*, 480–488.

Larsen, R. J. and Buss, D. M. (2002). *Personality psychology: Domains of knowledge about human behaviour*. New York: McGraw-Hill.

Lasky, J. and Silverman, H. (1988). *Love: Psychoanalytic perspectives*. New York: New York University Press.

Laurett, J. and Stark, K. (1993). Testing the cognitive content-specificity hypothesis with anxious and depressed youngsters. *Journal of Abnormal Psychology, 102*, 226–237.

Lazarus, R. S. (1966). *Psychological stress and the coping process*. New York: McGraw-Hill.

Lazarus, R. S. (1985). The psychology of stress and coping. In C. D. Spielberger (ed.), *Stress and anxiety* (Vol. 10, pp. 399–418). Washington, DC: Hemisphere.

Lazarus, R. S. (1991). *Emotion and adaptation*. New York: Oxford University Press.

Lazarus, R. S. (1999). *Stress and emotion: A new synthesis*. New York: Springer.

Lazarus, R. S. and Folkman, S. (1984). *Stress, appraisal, and coping*. New York: Springer.

Leahey, T. H. (2000). *A history of psychology: Main currents in psychological thought* (4th edn). Englewood Cliffs, NJ: Prentice Hall.

Leak, G. K. and Gardner, L. E. (1990). Sexual attitudes, love attitudes, and social interest. *Individual Psychology, 46*, 55–60.

Leak, G. K. and Williams, D. E. (1989). Relationship between social interest, alienation and psychological hardiness. *Individual Psychology, 45*, 369–375.

Leak, G. K., Millard, R. J., Perry, N. W. and Williams, D. E. (1985). An investigation of the nomological network of social interest. *Journal of Research in Personality, 19*, 197–207.

Leary, T. (1957). *Interpersonal diagnosis of personality*. New York: Ronald.

Lee, B. W. and Stapinski, L. A. (2011). Seeking safety on the internet: Relationship between social anxiety and problematic internet use. *Journal of Anxiety Disorders, 26*, 197–205.

Lee, J. (1976). *The colors of love*. Englewood Cliffs, NJ: Prentice Hall.

Lee, J. A. (1973). *The colors of love: An exploration of the ways of loving*, Toronto: New Press.

Lee, J. A. (1988). Love-styles. In R. J. Sternberg and M. L. Barnes (eds), *The psychology of love* (pp. 38–67). New Haven, CT: Yale University Press.

Lee, K. and Ashton, M. C. (2008). The HEXACO personality factor in the indigenous personality lexicons of English and 11 other languages. *Journal of Personality, 76,* 1001–1054.

Lefcourt, H. (1992). Durability and impact of the locus of control construct. *Psychological Bulletin, 112,* 411–414.

Leiby, R. (1997). The magical mystery cure. *Esquire* (September), 99–103.

Leitenberg, H. (1990). *Handbook of social and evaluation anxiety.* New York: Springer.

Lemke, F., Clark, M. and Wilson, H. (2011). Customer experience quality: an exploration in business and consumer contexts using repertory grid technique. *Journal of the Academy of Marketing Science, 39,* 846–869.

Leng, X. and Shaw, G. L. (1991). Toward a neural theory of higher brain function using music as a window. *Concepts in Neuroscience, 2,* 229–258.

Leonard, N. and Insch, G. S. (2005). Tacit knowledge in academia: A proposed model and measurement scale. *Journal of Psychology, 139,* 512.

Leong, F. T. L. and Zachar, P. (1990). An evaluation of Allport's Religious Orientation Scale across one Australian and two United States samples. *Educational and Psychological Measurement, 50,* 359–368.

Lerner, M. J. (1977). The justice motive: Some hypotheses as to its origins and forms. *Journal of Personality, 45,* 1–32.

Lerner, M. J. (1980). *The belief in a just world: A fundamental delusion.* New York: Plenum.

Lerner, M. J. and Miller, D. T. (1978). Just world research and the attribution process: Looking back and looking ahead. *Psychological Bulletin, 85,* 1030–1051.

Lerner, Y., Kertes, J. and Zilber, N. (2005). Immigrants from the former Soviet Union, 5 years post-immigration to Israel: Adaptation and risk factors for psychological distress. *Journal of Psychological Medicine, 35,* 1805–1814.

Leung, B. W. C., Moneta, G. B. and McBride-Chang, C. (2005). Think positively and feel positively: Optimism and life satisfaction in late life. *International Journal of Aging and Human Development, 61,* 335–365.

Levenson, H. (1973). Multidimensional locus of control in psychiatric patients. *Journal of Consulting and Clinical Psychology, 41,* 397–404.

Levin, M. (1997). *Race matters.* Westport, CT: Praeger.

Levine, S. C., Vasilyeva, M., Lourenco, S. F., Newcombe, N. S. and Huttenlocher, J. (2005). Socioeconomic status modifies the sex difference in spatial skill. *Psychological Science, 16,* 841–845.

Lewis, C. A. and Maltby, J. (2000). Conservatism and religiosity. *Personality and Individual Differences, 29,* 793–798.

Lewontin, R. C. (1979). Sociobiology as an adaptationist program. *Behavioral Science, 24,* 5–14.

Lewontin, R. C. (1991a). *Biology as ideology: The doctrine of DNA.* New York: HarperCollins.

Lewontin, R. C. (1991b). Perspectives: 25 years ago in genetics: Electrophoresis in the development of evolutionary genetics: Milestone or millstone? *Genetics, 128,* 657–662.

Li, A. and Bagger, J. (2006). Using the BIDR to distinguish the effects of impression management and self-deception on the criterion validity of personality measures: A meta-analysis. *International Journal of Selection and Assessment, 14,* 131–141.

Li, S. and Kunzmann, U. (2004). Research on intelligence in German-speaking countries. In R. J. Sternberg (ed.), *Handbook of intelligence* (pp. 135–169). Cambridge: Cambridge University Press.

Lieb, R., Schreier, A., Pfister, H. and Wittchen, H. U. (2003). Maternal smoking and smoking in adolescents: A prospective community study of adolescents and their mothers. *European Addiction Research, 9,* 120–130.

Liebowitz, M. R. and Marshall, R. D. (1995). Pharmacological treatments: Clinical applications. In R. R. G. Heimberg, M. Liebowitz, D. A. Hope and S. Scheier (eds), *Social phobia: Diagnosis, assessment and treatment* (pp. 366–386). New York: Guilford.

Lim, W., Plucker, J. A. and Im, K. (2002). We are more alike than we think we are: Implicit theories of intelligence with a Korean sample. *Intelligence, 30,* 185–208.

Lin, Y. H. and Rusbult, C. E. (1995). Commitment of dating relationships and cross-sex friendships in America and China. *Journal of Social and Personal Relationships, 12,* 7–26.

Linacre, J. M. (2006). Winsteps (version 3.61.2). Chicago: Winsteps.com.

Linn, M. C. and Petersen, A. C. (1985). Emergence and characterization of sex differences in spatial ability: A meta-analysis. *Child Development, 56,* 1479–1498.

Linton, R. (1945) *The cultural background of personality.* New York: Appleton-Century-Crofts.

Lipsitt, L. P. (1977). Taste in human neonates: Its effects on sucking and heart rate. In J. M. Weiffenbach (ed.), *Taste and development: The genesis of sweet preference.* Washington, DC: US Government Printing Office.

Liu, X., Tein, J., Zhao, Z. and Sandler, I. N. (2005). Suicidality and correlates among rural adolescents of China. *Journal of Adolescent Health, 37,* 443–451.

Lizarraga, M. L. S. D. and Garcia Ganuza, J. M. (2003). Improvement of mental rotation in girls and boys. *Sex Roles, 49,* 277–286.

Locurta, C. (1991). *Sense and nonsense about IQ: The case for uniqueness.* New York: Praeger.

Loehlin, J. C. (1989). Partitioning environmental and genetic contributions to behavioral development. *American Psychologist, 44,* 1285–1292.

Loehlin, J. C. (1992). *Genes and environment in personality development.* Newberry Park, CA: Sage.

Loehlin, J. C. and Martin, N. G. (2001). Age changes in personality traits and their heritabilities during the adult years: Evidence from Australian Twin Registry samples. *Personality and Individual Differences, 30,* 1147–1160.

Loehlin, J. C., Willerman, L. and Horn, J. M. (1985). Personality resemblances in adoptive families when the children are late-adolescent or adult. *Journal of Personality and Social Psychology, 48,* 376–392.

Loevinger, J. (1965). Person and population as psychometric concepts. *Psychological Review, 72,* 143–155.

Loevinger, J. and Wessler, R. (1970). *Measuring ego development* (Vol. 1: *Construction and use of a sentence completion test*). San Francisco: Jossey-Bass.

Loftus, E. F. (1979). *Eyewitness testimony.* Cambridge, MA: Harvard University Press.

Lohman, D. F. (2001). Issues in the definition and measurement of abilities. In J. M. Collis and S. J. Messick (eds), *Intelligence and personality: Bridging the gap in theory and measurement* (pp. 79–98). Mahwah, NJ: Erlbaum.

Lopez, A. D. and Murray, J. L. (1998). The global burden of disease, 1990–2020. *Nature and Medicine, 2,* 1241–1243.

Lopez, S. and Snyder, C. R. (eds). (2003). *Positive psychological assessment: A handbook of models and measures.* Washington, DC: APA Press.

Louis, J., Revol, O., Nemoz, C., Dulac, R. M. and Fourneret, P. (2005). Psychophysiological factors in high intellectual potential: Comparative study in children aged from 8 to 11 years old. *Archives de Pédiatrie, 12,* 520–525.

Lubinski, D. (2000). Scientific and social significance of assessing individual differences: 'Sinking shafts at a few critical points.' *Annual Review of Psychology*, 51, 405–444.

Lubinski, D. and Dawis, R. V. (eds) (1995). *Assessing individual differences in human behaviour: New methods, concepts, and findings*. Palo Alto, CA: Consulting Psychologists Press.

Ludwig, A. M. (1995). *The price of greatness*. New York: Guilford.

Luria, A. R. (1932). *The nature of human conflicts*. New York: Liveright.

Luria, A. R. (1961). *The role of speech in the regulation of normal and abnormal behaviour* (J. Tizard, ed.). London: Pergamon.

Luria, A. R. (1966a). *Human brain and psychological processes*. New York: Harper & Row.

Luria, A. R. (1966b, reprint 1980). *Higher cortical functions in man* (B. Haigh, trans.). New York: Basic Books.

Luria, A. R. (1968). *Mind of a mnemonist: A little book about a vast memory*. New York: Cape.

Luria, A. R. (1970). *Traumatic aphasia: Its syndromes, psychology, and treatment* (D. Bowden, trans.). Berlin: Mouton de Gruyter.

Luria, A. R. (1972). *The man with a shattered world*. New York: Basic Books.

Luria, A. R. (1973). *The working brain: An introduction to neuropsychology* (B. Haigh, trans.). New York: Basic Books.

Luria, A. R. (1976). *Neuropsychology of memory* (B. Haigh, trans.). Washington, DC: Winston.

Luria, A. R. and Bruner, J. (1987). *The mind of a mnemonist: A little book about a vast memory*. Cambridge, MA: Harvard University Press.

Luria, A. R. and Solotaroff, L. (1987). *The man with a shattered world: The history of a brain wound*. Cambridge, MA: Harvard University Press.

Lynn, R. (1990). The role of nutrition in secular increases of intelligence. *Personality and Individual Differences*, 11, 273–286.

Lynn, R. (1991). The evolution of racial differences in intelligence. *Mankind Quarterly*, 32, 99–121.

Lynn, R. (1994a). Sex differences in brain size and intelligence: A paradox resolved. *Personality and Individual Differences*, 17, 257–271.

Lynn, R. (1994b). Some reinterpretations of the Minnesota transracial adoption study. *Intelligence*, 19, 21–28.

Lynn, R. (1996). *Dysgenics: Genetic deterioration in modern populations*. Westport, CT: Praeger.

Lynn, R. (1998). In support of the Nutrition Theory. In U. Neisser (ed.). *The rising curve: Long-term gains in IQ and related measures* (pp. 207–217). Washington, DC: American Psychological Association.

Lynn, R. (2001). *Eugenics: A reassessment*. Westport, CT: Praeger.

Lynn, R. (2005). Sex differences in IQ. *Psychologist*, 18, 471.

Lynn, R. and Hampson, S. (1986). The rise of national intelligence: Evidence from Britain, Japan, and the United States. *Personality and Individual Differences*, 7, 23–32.

Lynn, R. and Irwing, P. (2004). Sex differences on the progressive matrices: A meta-analysis. *Intelligence*, 32, 481–498.

Lyons M.J., York T.P., Franz C.E. *et al.* (2009). Genes determine stability and the environment determines change in cognitive ability during 35 years of adulthood. *Psychological Science*, 20, 1146–1152.

MacArthur, J. D. and MacArthur, C. T. (2002). *Optimism/Pessimism*. Available online at www.macses.ucsf.edu/research/Psychosocial/optimism.php; accessed 23 October 2012.

Macaskill, A. and Maltby, J. (2001). An exploration of social interest in English students post-Conservatism. *Journal of Individual Psychology*, 57, 388–400.

Macaskill, N. D. and Macaskill, A. (1997). Rational-emotive therapy plus pharmacotherapy versus pharmacotherapy alone in the treatment of high cognitive dysfunction depression. *Cognitive Therapy and Research*, 20, 575–592.

Maccoby, E. E. (2000). Parenting and its effects on children: On reading and misreading behavior genetics. *Annual Review of Psychology*, 51, 1–27.

Maccoby, E. E. and Jacklin, C. N. (1974). *The psychology of sex differences*. Stanford, CA: Stanford University Press.

MacDonald, D. A. (2000) Spirituality: description, measurement, and relation to the Five Factor Model of personality. *Journal of Personality*, 68, 153–197.

MacDonald, K. (1997). Life history theory and human reproductive behavior: Environmental/contextual influences and heritable variation. *Human Nature: An Interdisciplinary Biosocial Perspective*, 8, 327–359.

Mackintosh, N. J. (1998). *IQ and human intelligence*. Oxford: Oxford University Press.

Mackintosh, N. J. (2000). *IQ and human intelligence*. Oxford: Oxford University Press.

Madison, P. (1961). *Freud's concept of repression and defence: Its theoretical and observational language*. Minneapolis: University of Minnesota Press.

Magnusson, D. (2001). The holistic-interactionist paradigm: Some directions for empirical developmental research. *European Psychologist*, 6, 153–162.

Makikangas, A., Kinnunen, U. and Feldt, T. (2004). Self-esteem, dispositional optimism, and health: Evidence from crosslagged data on employees. *Journal of Research in Personality*, 38, 556–575.

Malouff, J. M., Schutte, N. S. and McClelland, T. (1992). Examination of the relationship between irrational beliefs and state anxiety. *Personality and Individual Differences*, 13, 451–456.

Maltby, J. (1997). The concurrent validity of a short measure of social conservatism among English students. *Personality and Individual Differences*, 23, 901–903.

Maltby, J. (1999). Personality dimension of religious orientation. *Journal of Psychology*, 133, 631–639.

Maltby, J. and Day, L. (2000). The reliability and validity of a susceptibility to embarrassment scale among adults. *Personality and Individual Differences*, 29, 749–756.

Maltby, J. and Day, L. (2004). Should never the twain meet? Integrating models of religious personality and religious mental health. *Personality and Individual Differences*, 36, 1275–1290.

Maltby, J., Talley, M., Cooper, C. and Leslie, J. C. (1995). Personality effects in personal and public orientations toward religion. *Personality and Individual Differences*, 19, 157–163.

Maltby, J., Macaskill, A. and Day, L. (2001). Failure to forgive self and others: A replication and extension of the relationship between forgiveness, personality, social desirability and general health. *Personality and Individual Differences*, 29, 1–6.

Maltby, J., Day, L. and Barber, L. (2004). Forgiveness and mental health variables: Interpreting the relationship using an adaptational-continuum model of personality and coping. *Personality and Individual Differences*, 37, 1629–1641.

Maltby, J., Day, L., Gill, P., Colley, A. and Wood, A. M. (2008). Beliefs around luck: Confirming the empirical conceptualization of beliefs around luck and the development of the Darke and Freedman beliefs around luck scale. *Personality and Individual Differences*, 45, 655–660.

Markway, B. G. and Markway, G. P. (2003). *Painfully shy: How to overcome social anxiety and reclaim your life*. New York: Thomas Dunne.

Markway, B. G., Carmin, C., Pollard, C. A. and Flynn, T. (1992). *Dying of embarrassment: Help for social anxiety and phobia.* New York: New Harbinger.

Marques, S. C., Pais-Ribeiro, J. L. and Lopez, S. J. (2011). The role of positive psychology constructs in predicting mental health and academic achievement in children and adolescents: A two year longitudinal study. *Journal of Happiness Studies, 12,* 1049–1062.

Martau, P. A., Caine, N. G. and Candland, D. K. (1985). Reliability of the Emotions Profile Index, primate form, with *Papio hamadryas, Macaca fuscata,* and two *Saimiri* species. *Primates, 26,* 501–505.

Martin, N. J., Holroyd, K. A. and Penzien, D. B. (1990). The headache-specific locus of control scale: adaptation to recurrent headaches. *Headache: The Journal of Head and Face Pain, 30,* 729–737.

Martinez, J. C. (1994). Perceived control and feedback in judgement and memory. *Journal of Research in Personality, 28,* 374–381.

Mascie-Taylor, C. G. N. (1984). Biosocial correlates of IQ. In C. J. Turner and H. B. Miles (eds), *The biology of human intelligence.* London: Proceedings of the 20th Annual Symposium of the Eugenics Society.

Maslach, C. and Jackson, S. E. (1982). Burnout in health professionals: A social psychological analysis. In G. S. Sanders and J. Suls (eds.), *Social Psychology of Health and Illness.* Hillside, NJ: Erlbaum.

Maslach, C., Schaufeli, W. B. and Leiter, M. P. (2001). Job burnout. *Annual Review of Psychology, 52,* 397–422.

Maslow, A. H. (1954). *Motivation and personality.* New York: Harper & Row.

Maslow, A. H. (1962). Lessons from the peak experience. *Journal of Humanistic Psychology, 2,* 9–18.

Maslow, A. H. (1964). *Religions, values and peak experiences.* Columbus: Ohio State University Press.

Maslow, A. H. (1965). *Eupsychian management: A journal.* Homewood, IL: Irwin-Dorsey.

Maslow, A. H. (1967). The creative attitude. In R. L. Mooney and T. A. Rasik (eds), *Explorations in creativity* (pp. 43–57). New York: Harper & Row.

Maslow, A. H. (1968). *Toward a psychology of being.* Princeton, NJ: Van Nostrand.

Maslow, A. H. (1970). *Motivation and personality* (2nd edn). New York: Harper & Row.

Mather, J. A. and Anderson, R. C. (1993). Personalities of octopuses *(Octopus rubescens). Journal of Comparative Psychology, 107,* 336–340.

Mathews, G., Deary, I. J. and Whiteman, M. C. (2003). *Personality traits.* Cambridge: Cambridge University Press.

Mathews, K. A. and Haynes, S. G. (1986). Type A behaviour pattern and coronary disease risk: Update and critical evaluation. *American Journal of Epidemiology, 123,* 923–960.

Matthews, G. and Amelang, M. (1993). Extraversion, arousal theory and performance: A study of individual differences in the EEG. *Personality and Individual Differences, 14,* 347-364.

Matthews, G. and Gilliland, K. (1999). The personality theories of H. J. Eysenck and J. A. Gray: A comparative review. *Personality and Individual Differences, 26,* 583–626.

Matthews, G., Zeidner, M. and Roberts, R. D. (2004). *Emotional intelligence: Science and myth.* London: MIT Press.

Mattick, R. P. and Clarke, J. C. (1997). Development and validation of measures of social phobia scrutiny fear and social interaction anxiety. *Behaviour Research and Therapy, 36,* 455–470.

Mattson, S. N. and Riley, E. P. (1998). A review of the neurobehavioral deficits in children with fetal alcohol syndrome or prenatal exposure to alcohol. *Alcoholism: Clinical and Experimental Research, 22,* 279–294.

Mattson, S. N., Riley, E. P., Delis, D. C., Stern, C. and Jones, K. L. (1996). Verbal learning and memory in children with fetal alcohol syndrome. *Alcoholism: Clinical and Experimental Research, 20,* 810–816.

Mauger, P. A., Perry, J. E., Freeman T. *et al.* (1992). The measurement of forgiveness: Preliminary research. *Journal of Psychology and Christianity, 11,* 170–180.

Mavroveli, S., Petrides, K.V., Shove, C. and Whitehead, A. (2008). Investigation of the construct of trait emotional intelligence in children. *European Child and Adolescent Psychiatry, 17,* 516–526.

Mayer, J. D. (1995). A framework of the classification of personality components. *Journal of Personality, 63,* 819–877.

Mayer, J. D. (1998). A systems framework for the field of personality psychology. *Psychological Inquiry, 9,* 118–144.

Mayer, J. D. (2005a). A tale of two visions: Can a new view of personality help integrate psychology? *American Psychologist, 60,* 294–307.

Mayer, J. D. (2005b). *Personality psychology: A systems approach* (3rd edn). Boston: Pearson Custom.

Mayer, J. D. and Salovey, P. (1997). What is emotional intelligence? In P. Salovey and D. Sluyter (eds), *Emotional development and emotional intelligence: Implications for educators* (pp. 3–31). New York: Basic Books.

Mayer, J. D., Salovey, P. and Caruso, D. R. (2000). Models of emotional intelligence. In R. J. Sternberg (ed.), *Handbook of intelligence* (pp. 396–420). Cambridge: Cambridge University Press.

Mayer, J. D., Salovey, P. and Caruso, D. R. (2002). *Mayer-Salovey-Caruso Emotional Intelligence Test (MSCEIT).* Toronto, Canada: Multi-Health Systems.

Mayer, J. D., Salovey, P., Caruso, D. R. and Sitarenios, G. (2003). Measuring emotional intelligence with the MSCEIT V2.0. *Emotion, 3,* 97–105.

McAdams, D. P. (1988). *Power, intimacy and the life story.* New York: Guilford Press.

McAdams, D. P. (1993). *The stories we live by: Personal myths and the making of the self.* New York: Guilford Press.

McAdams, D. P. (1995). What do we know when we know a person? *Journal of Personality, 63,* 365–396.

McAdams, D. P. (2006). *The redemptive self: Stories Americans live by.* New York: Cambridge University Press.

McAdams, D. P. and Pals, J. L. (2006). A new Big Five: Fundamental principles for an integrative science of personality. *American Psychologist, 61,* 204–217.

McCallum, J. (1992). Green cars, black cats, Lady Luck. In S. J. Hoffman (ed.), *Sports and religion* (pp. 191–202). Champaign, IL: Human Kinetics.

McCourt, K., Bouchard, T. J., Lykken, D. T., Tellegen, A. and Keyes, M. (1999). Authoritarianism revisited: Genetic and environmental influences examined in twins reared apart and together. *Personality and Individual Differences, 27,* 985–1014.

McCoy, I. M. and Evans, G. W. (2005). Physical work environment. In I. Barling, E. K. Kelloway and M. R. Frone (eds), *Handbook of work stress.* Thousand Oaks, CA: Sage.

McCrae, R. R. (1995). Positive and negative valence within the five-factor model. *Journal of Research in Personality, 29,* 443–460.

McCrae, R. R. and Costa, P. T. (1989). Reinterpreting the Myers-Briggs Type Indicator from the perspective of the five-factor model of personality. *Journal of Personality, 57,* 17–40.

McCrae, R. R. and Costa, P. T. Jr. (1991). Adding *Liebe und Arbeit*: the full Five-Factor Model and well-being. *Personality and Social Psychology Bulletin, 17*, 227–232.

McCrae, R. R. and Costa, P. T. Jr (1995). Trait explanations in personality psychology. *European Journal of Personality, 9*, 231–252.

McCrae, R. R. and Costa, P. T. Jr (1997). Personality trait structure as a human universal. *American Psychologist, 52*, 509–516.

McCrae, R. R. and Terracciano, A. (2006). National character and personality. *Current Directions in Psychological Science, 15*, 156–161.

McCrae, R. R., Costa, P. T., del Pilar, G. H., Rolland, J. P. and Parker, W. D. (1998). Cross-cultural assessment of the five-factor model: The Revised NEO Personality Inventory. *Journal of Cross-Cultural Psychology, 29*, 171–188.

McCrae, R. R., Costa, P. T., Ostendorf, F. *et al.* (2000). Nature over nurture: Temperament, personality, and life span development. *Journal of Personality and Social Psychology, 78*, 173–186.

McCullough, M. E. and Hoyt, W. T. (2002). Transgression-related motivational dispositions: Personality substrates of forgiveness and their links to the Big Five. *Personality and Social Psychology Bulletin, 28*, 1556–1573.

McCullough, M. E. and Worthington, E. L. Jr (1995). Promoting forgiveness: Psychoeducational group interventions with a wait-list control. *Counseling and Values, 40*, 55–69.

McCullough, M. E., Worthington, E. L. Jr and Rachal, K. C. (1997). Interpersonal forgiving in close relationships. *Journal of Personality and Social Psychology, 73*, 321–336.

McCullough, M. E., Pargament, K. I. and Thoresen, C. E. (2000). The psychology of forgiveness: History, conceptual issues, and overview. In M. E. McCullough, K. I. Pargament and C. E. Thoresen (eds), *Forgiveness: Theory, research, and practice* (pp. 1–14). New York: Guilford.

McCullough, M. E., Bellah, C. G., Kilpatrick, S. D. and Johnson, J. L. (2001). Vengefulness: Relationships with forgiveness, rumination, well-being and the big five. *Personality and Social Psychology Bulletin, 27*, 601–610.

McCurry, J. (2008). Japanese government measure fails to cut suicide rate. *Guardian*, 20 June 2008. Available online at www.guardian.co.uk/world/2008/jun/20/japan; accessed 4 June 2009.

McCutcheon, L. E. (2002). Are parasocial relationship styles reflected in love styles? *Current Research in Social Psychology, 7*, 82–94.

McDaniel, M. A. (2005). Big-brained people are smarter: A meta-analysis of the relationship between in vivo brain volume and intelligence. *Intelligence, 33*, 337–346.

McDermott, D. and Snyder, C. R. (1999). *Making hope happen: A workbook for turning possibilities into reality*. Oakland, CA: New Harbinger Publications.

McDermott, D. and Snyder, C. R. (2000). *The great big book of hope: Help your children achieve their dreams*. Oakland, CA: New Harbinger Publications.

McGlashan, T. H., Grilo, C. M., Skodol, A. E. *et al.* (2000). The collaborative longitudinal personality disorders study: Baseline axis I/II and II/II diagnostic co-occurrence. *Acta Psychiatrica Scandinavica, 102*, 256–264.

McGregor, B. A., Bowen, D. J., Ankerst, D. P. *et al.* (2004). Optimism, perceived risk of breast cancer, and cancer worry among a community-based sample of women. *Health Psychology, 23*, 339–344.

McInnes, D. (2004). The theories underpinning rational emotive behaviour therapy: Where's the supportive evidence? *International Journal of Nursing Studies, 41*, 685–695.

McKey, R. H., Condelli, L., Granson, H. *et al.* (1985). *The impact of Head Start on children, families, and communities*. Washington, DC: CSR.

McLean, K. C. (2008a). Narrative as the mechanism for personal continuity in late life: Relations to wellbeing. Paper presented at the Society for Personality and Social Psychology, Albuquerque, NM, February 6–9.

McLean, K. C. (2008b). The emergence of narrative identity. *Social and Personality Psychology Compass, 2*, 1685–1702.

McLean, K. C. and Thorne, A. (2003). Late adolescents' self-defining memories about relationships. *Developmental Psychology, 39*, 635–645.

McMahon, C. E. (1976). The role of imagination in the disease process: Pre-Cartesian medical history. *Psychosomatic Medicine, 6*, 179–184.

McMichael, A. J., Vimpani, G. V., Robertson, E. F., Baghurst, P. A. and Clark, P. D. (1986). The Port Pirie cohort study: Maternal blood lead and pregnancy outcome. *Journal of Epidemiology and Community Health, 40*, 18–25.

McMichael, A. J., Baghurst, P. A., Wigg, N. R. *et al.* (1988). Port Pirie cohort study: Environmental exposure to lead and children's abilities at the age of four years. *New England Journal of Medicine, 319*, 468–475.

McNeil, D. W., Lejuez, C. W. and Sorrell, J. T. (2001). Behavioral theories of social phobia: Contributions of basic behavioral principles. In S. G. Hofmann and P. M. DiBartolo (eds), *Social phobia and social anxiety: An integration* (pp. 235–253). Needham Heights, MA: Allyn & Bacon.

McPeek, R. W. (2008). The Pearson–Marr Archetype Indicator and psychological type. *Journal of Psychological Type, 68*(7), 52–67.

Mead, M. (1949) *Coming of age in Samoa*. New York: Mentor.

Mead, R. (1994). *International management: Cross-cultural dimensions*. Cambridge, MA: Blackwell.

Mednick, S. A. (1962). The associative basis for the creative process. *Psychological Review, 69*, 200–232.

Meehl, P. E. (1981). Ethical criticisms in value clarifications. *Rational Living, 16*, 3–9.

Meissner, W. W. (1995). Paranoid personality disorder. In G. O. Gabbard (ed.), *Treatment of psychiatric disorders for DSM-IV* (2nd edn, Vol. 2, pp. 2249–2259). Washington, DC: American Psychiatric Press.

Merkas, M. and Brajsa-Zganec, A. (2011). Children and different levels of hope: Are there differences in their self-esteem, life satisfaction, social support, and family cohesion? *Child indicators research, 4*(3), 499–514.

Meyer, G., Finn, S., Eyde, L. *et al.* (2001). Psychological testing and psychological assessment: A review of evidence and issues. *American Psychologist, 56*, 128–165.

Mikolajczak, M. and Luminet, O. (2008). Trait emotional intelligence and the cognitive appraisal of stressful events: An exploratory study. *Personality and Individual Differences, 44*, 1445–1453.

Miller, C. L. (1987). Qualitative differences among gender-stereotyped toys: Implications for cognitive and social development. *Sex Roles, 16*, 473–487.

Miller, E. M. (1995). Environmental variability selects for large families only in special circumstances: Another objection to differential *K* theory. *Personality and Individual Differences, 19*, 903–918.

Miller, G. R., Mogeau, P. A. and Sleight, C. (1986). Fudging with friends and lying to lovers: Deceptive communication in interpersonal relationships. *Journal of Social and Personal Relationships, 3*, 495–512.

Miller, P. M. and Lisak, D. (1999). Associations between childhood abuse and personality disorder symptoms in college males. *Journal of Interpersonal Violence*, 14, 642–656.

Miller, R. S. (1987). Empathic embarrassment: Situational and personal determinants of reactions to the embarrassment of another. *Journal of Personality and Social Psychology*, 53, 1061–1069.

Miller, R. S. (1992). The nature and severity of self-reported embarrassing circumstances. *Personality and Social Psychology Bulletin*, 18, 190–198.

Miller, R. S. (1995). On the nature of embarrassibility: Shyness, social evaluation, and social skill. *Journal of Personality*, 63, 315–339.

Miller, R. S. (1996). *Embarrassment: Poise and peril in everyday life.* New York: Guilford.

Miller, R. S. (2001). Embarrassment and social phobia: Distant cousins or close kin? In S. G. Hofmann and P. M. DiBartolo (eds), *From social anxiety to social phobia: Multiple perspectives* (pp. 65–85). Needham Heights, MA: Allyn & Bacon.

Miller, T. Q., Turner, C. W., Tindale, R. S., Posavac, E. J. and Dugoni, B. L. (1991). Reasons for the trend toward null findings in research on Type A behaviour. *Psychological Bulletin*, 110, 469–485.

Miller, T. Q., Smith, T. W., Turner, C. W., Guijarro, M. L. and Hallet, A. J. (1996). A meta-analytic review of research on hostility and physical health. *Psychological Bulletin*, 119, 322–348.

Millon, T., Grossman, S., Millon, C., Meagher, S. and Ramnath, R. (2004). *Personality Disorders in Modern Life* (2nd edn). Hoboken, NJ: John Wiley & Sons.

Mills, D. S. (1998). Personality and individual differences in the horse: Their significance, use and measurement. *Equine Veterinary Journal, Supplement 27: Equine Clinical Behaviour*, 10–13.

Minsky, R. (1996). *Psychoanalysis and gender.* London: Routledge.

Mischel, W. (1968). *Personality and assessment.* New York: Wiley.

Mischel, W. (1973). Toward a cognitive social learning reconceptualization of personality. *Psychological Review*, 80, 252–283.

Mischel, W. (1979). On the interface of cognition and personality: Beyond the person-situation debate. *American Psychologist*, 34, 740–754.

Mischel, W. (1983a). Alternatives in the pursuit of the predictability and consistency of persons: Stable data that yield unstable interpretations. *Journal of Personality*, 51, 578–604.

Mischel, W. (1983b). Delay of gratification as process and person variable in development. In D. Magnusson and V. P. Allen (eds), *The coherence of personality: Social-cognitive bases of consistency, variability, and organization* (pp. 37–61). New York: Guilford.

Mischel, W. (1990). Personality dispositions revisited and revised. In L. A. Pervin (ed.), *Handbook of personality: Theory and research* (pp. 111–134). New York: Guilford.

Mischel, W. (1999). Personality coherence and dispositions in a cognitive-affective personality (CAPS) approach. In D. Cervone and Y. Shoda (eds), *The coherence of personality: Social-cognitive bases of consistency, variability, and organisation* (pp. 37–60). New York: Guilford.

Mischel, W. (2004). Toward an integrative science of the person. *Annual Review of Psychology*, 55, 1–22.

Mischel, W. and Peake, P. K. (1982). In search of consistency: Measure for measure. In M. P. Zanna, E. T. Higgins and C. P. Herman (eds), *Consistency in human behaviour: The Ontario symposium* (pp. 187–207). Hillsdale, NJ: Erlbaum.

Mischel, W. and Shoda, Y. (1995). A cognitive-affective system theory of personality: Reconceptualising situations, dispositions, dynamics, and invariance in personality structure. *Annual Review of Psychology*, 49, 229–258.

Mischel, W. and Shoda, Y. (1998). Reconciling processing dynamics and personality dispositions. *Annual Review of Psychology*, 49, 229–258.

Mischel, W., Shoda, Y. and Mendoza-Denton, R. (2002). Situation-behaviour profiles as locus of consistency in personality. *Current Directions in Psychological Science*, 11, 54–50.

Mitchell, R. W. and Hamm, H. (1997). The interpretation of animal psychology: Anthropomorphism or behaviour reading? *Behaviour*, 134, 173–204.

Mittleman, W. (1991). Maslow's study of self-actualisation: A re-interpretation. *Journal of Humanistic Psychology*, 31, 114–135.

Modigliani, A. (1968). Embarrassment and embarrassibility. *Sociometry*, 31, 313–326.

Modigliani, A. (1971). Embarrassment, facework, and eye contact: Testing a theory of embarrassment. *Journal of Personality and Social Psychology*, 17, 15–24.

Molesky, R. and Tosi, D. (1976). Comparative psychotherapy: Rational-emotive therapy versus systematic desensitization in the treatment of stuttering. *Journal of Consulting and Clinical Psychology*, 44, 309–311.

Morelock, M. and Feldman, D. (1991). Extreme precocity. In N. Colangelo and G. A. Davis (eds), *Handbook of gifted education* (pp. 347–364). Boston: Allyn & Bacon.

Morf, C. C. and Rodewalt, F. (2001). Explaining the dynamic self-regulatory processing model of narcissism: Research directions for the future. *Psychological Inquiry*, 12, 243–251.

Morokoff, P. F. (1985). Effects of sex, guilt, repression, sexual 'arousability', and sexual erotica on female arousal during erotic fantasy. *Journal of Personality and Social Psychology*, 49, 177–187.

Morrison, V. and Bennett, P. (2006). *An introduction to health psychology.* Harlow: Pearson Education.

Mortensen, E. L., Michaelsen, K. F., Sanders, S. A. and Reinisch, J. M. (2005). A dose-response relationship between maternal smoking during late pregnancy and adult intelligence in male offspring. *Paediatric & Perinatal Epidemiology*, 19, 4.

Moser, D. K., Riegel, B., McKinley, S. *et al.,* (2007). Complications after myocardial infarction. *Psychosomatic Medicine*, 69, 10–16.

Moskowitz, D. S. (1994). Cross-situational generality and the interpersonal circumplex. *Journal of Personality and Social Psychology*, 66, 921–933.

Motley, M. T. (1985). Slips of the tongue. *Scientific American*, 253, 116–127.

Motley, M. T. (1987). What I mean to say. *Psychology Today* (February), 24–28.

Mount, M. K., Barrick, M. R., Scullen, S. M. and Rounds, J. (2005). Higher-order dimensions of the Big Five personality traits and the Big Six vocational interest types. *Personnel Psychology*, 58, 447–478.

Mulkana, S. S. and Hailey, B. J. (2001). The role of optimism in health-enhancing behavior. *American Journal of Health Behavior*, 25(4), 388–395.

Murnen, S. K. and Stockton, M. (1997). Gender and self-reported sexual arousal in response to sexual stimuli: A meta-analytic review. *Sex Roles*, 37, 135–154.

Murphy, C. (2009). The link between artistic creativity and psychopathology: Salvador Dalí. *Personality and Individual Differences*, 46, 765–774.

Murray, C. A. (1984). *Losing ground: American social policy, 1950–1980.* New York: Basic Books.

Murray, C. A. (1994). Richard J. Herrnstein, RIP. *National Review*, 46, 22.

Murray, H. A. (1938). *Explorations in personality.* New York: Oxford University Press.

Murstein, B. I., Merighi, J. R. and Vyse, S. A. (1991). Love styles in the United States and France: A cross-cultural comparison. *Journal of Social and Clinical Psychology, 10*, 37–46.

Musek, J. (2007). A general factor of personality: Evidence for the Big One in the five-factor model. *Journal of Research in Personality, 41*, 1213–1233.

Myers, D. G. (1992). *The pursuit of happiness: Who is happy – and why*. New York: Morrow.

Myers, D. G. (1997). *Psychology* (3rd edn). New York: Worth Publishers.

Myers, I. B. and McCaulley, M. H. (1985). *Manual: A guide to the development and use of the Myers–Briggs Type Indicator*. Palo Alto, CA: Consulting Psychologists Press.

Myers, L. B. (2000). Deceiving others or deceiving themselves? *The Psychologist, 13*, 400–403.

Myers, L. B. and Steed, L. (1999). The relationship between dispositional optimism, dispositional pessimism, repressive coping and trait anxiety. *Personality and Individual Differences, 27*, 1261–1272.

Nagel, T. (1980). What is it like to be a bat? In N. Block (ed.), *Readings in philosophy of psychology* (Vol. 1, pp. 159–168). Cambridge, MA: Harvard University Press.

Naglieri, J. A. (1998). A closer look at new kinds of intelligence tests. *American Psychologist, 53*, 1158–1159.

Naglieri, J. A. and Das, J. P. (1997). *Cognitive assessment system: Interpretive handbook*. Itasca, IL: Riverside.

Naveteur, J. and Roy, J. C. (1990). Electrodermal activity of low and high trait anxiety subjects during a frustrative video game. *Journal of Psychophysiology, 4*(3), 221–227.

Nei, M. and Roychoudhury, A. (1982). Genetic relationship and evolution of human races. *Evolutionary Biology, 14*, 1–59.

Nei, M. and Roychoudhury, A. (1993). Evolutionary relationships of human populations on a global scale. *Molecular Biology and Evolution, 10*, 927–943.

Neisser, U. (1998a). (ed.), *The rising curve: Long-term gains in IQ and related measures*. Washington, DC: American Psychological Association.

Neisser, U. (1998b). Introduction: rising test scores and what they mean. In U. Neisser (ed.), *The rising curve: Long-term gains in IQ and related measures.* (pp. 3–24). Washington, DC: American Psychological Association.

Neisser, U., Boodoo, O., Bouchard, T. J. *et al.* (1996). Intelligence: Knowns and unknowns. *American Psychologist, 51*, 77–101.

Nelson, P. B. (1989). Ethnic differences in intrinsic/extrinsic religious orientation and depression in the elderly. *Archives of Psychiatric Nursing, 3*, 199–204.

Nelson, P. B. (1990). Intrinsic/extrinsic religious orientation of the elderly: Relationship to depression and self-esteem. *Journal of Gerontological Nursing, 16*, 29–35.

Nettle, D. (2001). *Strong imagination: Madness, creativity, and human nature*. Oxford: Oxford University Press.

Newcombe, T. M. (1929). *Consistency of certain extrovert–introvert behaviour patterns in 51 problem boys*. New York: Columbia University, Teachers College, Bureau of Publications.

Newman, L. S., Duff, K. J. and Baumeister, R. F. (1997). A new look at defensive projection: Thought suppression, accessibility, and biased person perception. *Journal of Personality and Social Psychology, 72*, 980–1001.

Nickell, P. V. and Uhde, T. W. (1995). Neurobiology of social phobia. In R. G. Heimberg, M. R. Liebowitz, D. A. Hope and F. R. Schneier (eds), *Social phobia: Diagnosis, assessment, and treatment* (pp. 113–133). New York and London: Guilford.

Nikelly, A. G. (2005). Positive health outcomes of social interest. *The Journal of Social Interest, 61*(4), 329–342.

Nisbett, R. E. and Ross, L. D. (1980). *Human inference: Strategies and shortcomings of social judgement*. Englewood Cliffs, NJ: Prentice Hall.

Nissen, H. W. and Crawford, M. P. (1936). A preliminary study of food-sharing behavior in young chimpanzees. *Journal of Comparative Psychology, 22*, 383–419.

Noller, P. (1985). Negative communications in marriage. *Journal of Social and Personal Relationships, 2*, 289–301.

Norman, D. A. (1981). Categorisation of action slips. *Psychological Review, 88*, 1–15.

Norman, E. (2010). 'The unconscious' in current psychology. *European Psychologist, 15*(3), 193–201.

Norman, P. and Bennett, P. (1995). Health, locus of control. In M. Conner and P. Norman (eds), *Predicting Health Behaviour*. Buckingham: Open University Press.

Norman, W. T. (1963). Towards an adequate taxonomy of personality attributes: Replicated factor structure in peer nomination personality ratings. *Journal of Abnormal and Social Psychology, 66*, 574–583.

O'Connor, M. C. and Paunonen, S. V. (2007). Big Five personality predictors of post-secondary academic performance. *Personality and Individual Differences, 43*, 971–99.

Oddy, W. H., Sherriff, J. L., de Klerk, N. H. *et al.* (2004). The relation of breastfeeding and body mass index to asthma and atopy in children: A prospective cohort study to age 6 years. *American Journal of Public Health, 94*, 1531–1537.

Ogden, J. (2004). *Health psychology: A textbook* (3rd edn). Berkshire: Open University Press.

Olason, D. T. and Roger, D. (2001). Optimism, pessimism and 'fighting spirit': A new approach to assessing expectancy and adaptation. *Personality and Individual Differences, 31*, 755–768.

Oliver, M. B. and Hyde, J. S. (1993). Gender differences in sexuality: A meta-analysis. *Psychological Bulletin, 114*, 29–51.

Oltmans, T. F. and Emery, R. E. (2006). *Abnormal psychology* (5th edn). New York: Pearson Education.

Orlebeke, J. F. and Feij, J. A. (1979). The orienting reflex as a personality correlate. In E. H. Van Olst and J. F. Orlebeke (eds), *The orienting reflex in humans* (pp. 567–585). Hillsdale, NJ: Erlbaum.

Osler, W. (1910). The Lumleian Lectures on angina pectoris. *Lancet, i*, 696–700.

Ostendorf, F. (1990). *Sprache und Persoenlichkeitsstruktur: Zur Validitaet des Funf-Factoren-Modells der Persoenlichkeit*. Regensburg, Germany: S. Roderer Verlag.

Overmier, J. B. and Seligman, M. E. P. (1967). Effects of inescapable shock upon subsequent escape and avoidance responding. *Journal of Comparative and Physiological Psychology, 63*, 28–33.

Owen, K. (1989). *Test and item bias: The suitability of the Junior Aptitude Test as a common test battery for white, Indian and black pupils in Standard 7*. Pretoria: Human Sciences Research Council.

Page, E. B. and Grandon, G. (1979). Family configuration and mental ability: Two theories contrasted with US data. *American Educational Research Journal, 16*, 257–272.

Palmer, A. (2003). The 'street' that changed everything. *APA Monitor, 34*, 90.

Panksepp, J. (1999). *Affective neuroscience*. Oxford: Oxford University Press.

Pargament, K. I. (1997). *The psychology of religion and coping: Theory, research and practice*. London: Guilford.

Pargament, K. I., Smith, B. W., Koenig, H. G. and Perez, L. (1998a). Patterns of positive and negative religious coping with major life stressors. *Journal for the Scientific Study of Religion, 37*, 710–724.

Pargament, K. I., Zinnbauer, B. J., Scott, A. B. et al. (1998b). Red flags and religious coping: Identifying some religious warning signs among people in crisis. *Journal of Clinical Psychology, 54,* 77–89.

Pargament, K. I., Koenig, H. G. and Perez, L. M. (2000). The many methods of religious coping: Development and initial validation of the RCOPE. *Journal of Clinical Psychology, 56,* 519–543.

Paris, J. (2003). Personality disorders over time: Precursors, course and outcome. *Journal of Personality Disorders, 17,* 479–488.

Park, C., Cohen, L. and Herb, L. (1990). Intrinsic religiousness and religious coping as life stress moderators for Catholics versus Protestants. *Journal of Personality and Social Psychology, 59,* 562–574.

Parrott, W. G. and Smith, S. F. (1991). Embarrassment: Actual vs. typical cases, classical vs. prototypical representations. *Cognition and Emotion, 5,* 476–488.

Patton, C. J. (1992). Fear of abandonment and binge eating. *Journal of Nervous and Mental Disease, 180,* 484–490.

Paulhaus, D. L., Trapnell, P. D. and Chen, D. (1999). Birth order effects on personality and achievement within families. *Psychological Science, 10,* 482–488.

Paunonen, S. V. and Jackson, D. N. (2000). What is beyond the Big Five? Plenty! *Journal of Personality, 68,* 821–835.

Pavlov, I. P. (1906). The scientific investigations of the psychical faculties or processes in the higher animals. *Science, 24,* 613–619.

Pavlov, I. P. (1927). *Conditioned reflexes.* London: Oxford.

Pavlov, I. P. (1928). *Lectures on conditioned reflexes.* New York: International Publishers.

Peabody, D. and Goldberg, L. R. (1989). Some determinant of factor structures from personality trait descriptors. *Journal of Personality and Social Psychology, 57,* 552–567.

Pearson, P. R. and Sheffield, B. F. (1976). Is personality related to social attitudes? An attempt at replication. *Social Behaviour and Personality, 4,* 109–111.

Pedersen, N. L., Plomin, R., McClearn, G. E. and Friberg, L. (1988). Neuroticism, extraversion, and related traits in adult twins reared apart and reared together. *Journal of Personality and Social Psychology, 55,* 950–957.

Pedersen, N. L., McClearn, G. E., Plomin, R. et al. (1991). The Swedish adoption/twin study of aging: An update. *Acta Geneticae Medicae et Gemellologiae, 40,* 7–20.

Pelham, B. W. (1993). The idiographic nature of human personality: Examples of the idiographic self-concept. *Journal of Personality and Social Psychology, 64,* 665–667.

Pelletier, L. G., Tuson, K. M. and Haddad, N. K. (1997). Client motivation for therapy scale: A measure of intrinsic motivation, extrinsic motivation, and amotivation for therapy. *Journal of Personality Assessment, 68,* 414–435.

Perugini, M. and Di-Blas, L. (2002). The Big Five Marker Scales (BFMS) and the Italian ABC5 taxonomy: Analyses from an eticemic perspective. In B. De Raad and M. Perugini (eds), *Big Five assessment* (pp. 281–304). Seattle, WA: Hogrefe and Huber.

Pervin, L. (1996). *The science of personality.* New York: Wiley.

Pervin, L. A. (1994). A critical analysis of trait theory. *Psychological Inquiry, 5,* 103–113.

Peterson, C. (2000). The future of optimism. *American Psychologist, 55,* 44–55.

Peterson, C. and Seligman, M. E. P. (2004). *Character strengths and virtues: A handbook and classification.* Washington, DC: American Psychological Association.

Peterson, C., Lee, F. and Seligman, M. E. P. (2003). Assessment of optimism and hope. In R. Fernández Ballesteros (ed.), *Encyclopedia of psychological assessment* (pp. 646–649). London: Sage.

Petrides, K. V. and Furnham, A. (2001). Trait emotional intelligence: Psychometric investigation with reference to established trait taxonomies. *European Journal of Personality, 15,* 425–448.

Petrides, K. V., Frederickson, N. and Furnham, A. (2004). The role of trait emotional intelligence in academic performance and deviant behavior at school. *Personality and Individual Differences, 36,* 277–293.

Petrides, K.V., Pita, R. and Kokkinika, F. (2007). The location of trait emotional intelligence in personality factor space. *British Journal of Psychology, 98,* 273–289.

Petrill, S. A., Plomin, R., Berg, S. et al. (1998). The genetic and environmental relationship between general and specific cognitive abilities in twins age 80 and over. *Psychological Science, 9,* 183–189.

Plomin, R. (1986). Behavioral genetic methods. *Journal of Personality, 54,* 226–261.

Plomin, R. (2004). *Nature and nurture: An introduction to human behavioral genetics.* London: Wadsworth.

Plomin, R. and Daniels, D. (1987). Why are children in the same family so different from one another? *Behavioral Brain Sciences, 10,* 1–16.

Plomin, R. and Rowe, D. C. (1979). Genetic and environmental etiology of social behavior in infancy. *Developmental Psychology, 15,* 62–72.

Plomin, R., Chipuer, H. M. and Loehlin, J. C. (1990). Behavioral genetics and personality. In L. A. Pervin (ed.), *Handbook of personality: Theory and research* (pp. 225–243). New York: Guilford.

Plomin, R., DeFries, J. C., McClearn, G. E. and McGuffin, P. (2000). *Behavioral genetics: A primer.* London: Freeman.

Plucker, J. A. (1996). Secondary science and mathematics teachers and gender equity: Attitudes and attempted interventions. *Journal of Research in Science Teaching, 33,* 737–751.

Polivy, J. and Herman, C. P. (2002). If at first you don't succeed: False hopes of self-change. *American Psychologist, 57,* 677–689.

Pons, A. L. (1974). *Administration of tests outside the cultures of their origin.* 26th Congress South African Psychological Association.

Popper, K. (2002, 1969). *Conjectures and refutations: The growth of scientific knowledge.* London: Routledge.

Poropat, A. E. (2009). A meta-analysis of the Five-Factor Model of personality and academic performance. *Psychological Bulletin, 135,* 322–338.

Posthuma, D., de Geus, E.J.C. and Boomsma, D.I. (2001). Perceptual speed and IQ are associated through common genetic factors. *Behavioural Genetics, 31,* 593–602.

Potts, N. L. S. and Davidson, J. R. T. (1995). Neurobiology of social phobia. In R. R. G. Heimberg, M. Liebowitz, D. A. Hope and S. Scheier (eds), *Social phobia: Diagnosis, assessment and treatment* (pp. 113–133). New York: Guilford.

Powell, L. (1992). The cognitive underpinnings of coronary-prone behaviours. *Cognitive Therapy and Research, 16,* 123–142.

Power, M. (2000). Freud and the unconscious. *The Psychologist, 13,* 612–614.

Pratto, F., Sidanius, J., Stallworth, L. M. and Malle, B. F. (1994). Social dominance orientation: A personality variable predicting social and political attitudes. *Journal of Personality and Social Psychology, 67,* 741–763.

Préau, M. and the APROCO study group (2005). Health-related quality of life and health locus of control beliefs among HIV-infected treated patients. *Journal of Psychosomatic Research, 59,* 407–413.

Putnam, D. B. and Kilbride, P. L. (1980). *A relativistic understanding of social intelligence among the Songhay of Mali and Smaia of Kenya.* Presented at Meeting for Social and Cross-Cultural Research, Philadelphia, Pennsylvania.

Qian, M., Wang, D., Watkins, W. E. *et al.* (2005). The effects of iodine on intelligence in children: A meta-analysis of studies conducted in China. *Asia Pacific Journal of Clinical Nutrition, 14,* 32–42.

Quadrio, C. (2005). Axis One/Axis Two: A disordered borderline. *Australian & New Zealand Journal of Psychiatry, 39,* 141–156.

Quick, J. (1997). Idiographic research in organisational behaviour. In L. Cooper and S. Jackson (eds), *Creating tomorrow's organisations* (pp. 475–991). Chichester, UK: Wiley.

Ragland, D. R. and Brand, R. J. (1988). Coronary heart disease mortality in the Western Collaborative Group Study: Follow-up experience of twenty-two years. *American Journal of Epidemiology, 127,* 462–75.

Raine, A. (2006). Schizotypal personality. Neurodevelopmental and psychosocial trajectories *Annual Review of Clinical Psychology, 2,* 291–326.

Ramey, S. L. and Ramey, C. T. (1994). The transition to school: Why the first few years matter for a lifetime. *Phi Delta Kappan, 76,* 194–198.

Rands, S. A., Cowlishaw, G., Pettifor, R. A., Rowcliffe, J. M. and Johnstone, R. A. (2003). Spontaneous emergence of leaders and followers in foraging pairs. *Nature, 423,* 432–434.

Rapaport, D. (1960). *The structure of psychoanalytic theory: A systematising attempt.* (Psychological Issues, Monograph 6). New York: International Universities Press.

Rasch, G. (1960/1980). *Probabilistic models for some intelligence and attainment tests* (revised and expanded edition). Chicago: The University of Chicago Press. Original work published in 1960.

Rasmussen, H. N., Scheier, M. F. and Greenhouse, J. B. (2009). Optimism and physical health: A meta-analytic review, *Annals of Behavioral Medicine, 37*(3), 239–256.

Rasmussen, K. A. and Wingate, L. R. (2011). The role of optimism in the interpersonal-psychological theory of suicidal behaviour. *Suicide and Life-threatening Behaviour, 41,* 137–148.

Raty, H. and Snellman, L. (1992). Does gender make any difference? Commonsense conceptions of intelligence. *Social Behavior and Personality, 20,* 23–34.

Raty, H., Snellman, L. and Vainikainen, A. (1999). Parents' assessments of their children's abilities. *European Journal of Psychology of Education, 14,* 423–437.

Rauscher, F. H. and Shaw, G. L. (1998). Key components of the Mozart effect. *Perceptual and Motor Skills, 86,* 835–841.

Rauscher, F., Shaw, G. L. and Ky, K. (1993). Music and spatial task performance. *Nature, 365,* 611.

Rauscher, F. H., Shaw, G. L., Levine, L. J. *et al.* (1997). Music training causes long-term enhancement of preschool children's spatial-temporal reasoning. *Neurological Research, 19,* 2–8.

Rauscher, F. H., Robinson, K. D. and Jens, J. J. (1998). Improved maze learning through early music exposure in rats. *Neurological Research, 20,* 427–432.

Ravaja, N., Keltignagas-Jarvinen, L. and Keskivaara, P. (1996). Type A factors as predictors of changes in the metabolic syndrome precursors in adolescents and young adults: A three year follow up study. *Health Psychology, 15,* 18–29.

Raven, J. C. (1938). *Progressive Matrices.* London: Lewis.

Raven, J. C. (1962). *Standard Progressive Matrices.* London: Lewis.

Raven, J. C. (2004). *Standard Progressive Matrices.* San Antonio, TX: Harcourt Assessment.

Ravizza, K. (1977). Peak experiences in sport. *Journal of Humanistic Psychology, 17,* 35–40.

Raz, N., Torres, I. J., Spencer, W. D. *et al.,* (1993). Neuroanatomical correlates of age-sensitive and age-invariant cognitive abilities: An in vivo MRI investigation. *Intelligence, 17,* 407–422.

Read, S. J. and Miller, L. C. (2002). Virtual personalities: A neural network model of personality. *Personality and Social Psychology Review, 6,* 357–369.

Réale, D., Dingemanse, N.J., Kazem, A. J.N. and Wright, J. (2010). Evolutionary and ecological approaches to the study of personality. *Philosophical Transactions of the Royal Society B, 365,* 3937–3946.

Reason, J. (1979). Actions not as planned: The price of automatisation. In G. Underwood and R. Stevens (eds), *Aspects of consciousness* (Vol. 1: *Psychological issues).* London: Wiley.

Reason, J. (1990). *Human error.* New York: Cambridge University Press.

Reason, J. (2000).The Freudian slip revisited. *The Psychologist, 13,* 610–611.

Reason, J. and Lucas, D. A. (1984). Using cognitive diaries to investigate naturally occurring memory blocks. In J. Harris and P. Morris (eds), *Everyday memory: Actions and absent-mindedness.* London: Academic Press.

Rector, N. A. and Beck, A. T. (2001). Cognitive behavioural therapy for schizophrenia: An empirical review. *Journal of Nervous Disorders, 189,* 278–287.

Regan, P. (2003). *The mating game: A primer on love, sex and marriage.* Thousand Oaks, CA: Sage.

Reichborn-Kjennerud, T., Czajkowski, N., Neale, M. C. *et al.* (2008). Genetic and environmental influences on dimensional representations of DSM-IV cluster C personality disorders: a population-based multivariate twin study. *Psychological Medicine, 37,* 645–53.

Reif, A. and Lesch, K. P. (2003). Toward a molecular architecture of personality. *Behavioural Brain Research, 139,* 1–20.

Reiss, D. (1997). Mechanisms linking genetic and social influences in adolescent development: Beginning a collaborative search. *Current Directions in Psychological Science, 6,* 100–105.

Renzulli, J. S. (1978). What makes giftedness? Reexamining a definition. *Phi Delta Kappan, 60,* 180–184, 261.

Renzulli, J. S. (1986). *Systems and models for developing programs for the gifted and talented.* Mansfield Center, CT: Creative Learning Press.

Renzulli, J. S. (1986b). The three-ring conception of giftedness: A developmental model for promoting creative productivity. In R. J. Sternberg and J. Davidson (eds), *Conceptions of Giftedness.* Cambridge University Press.

Renzulli, J. S. (1998). The three-ring conception of giftedness. In S. M. Baum, S. M. Reis and L. R. Maxfield (eds), *Nurturing the gifts and talents of primary grade students.* Mansfield Center, CT: Creative Learning Press.

Renzulli, J. S. and Reis, S. M. (1997). *The schoolwide enrichment model: A how-to guide for educational excellence.* Mansfield Center, CT: Creative Learning Press.

Retherford, R. D. and Sewell, W. H. (1988). Intelligence and family size reconsidered. *Social Biology, 35,* 1–40.

Rettew, D. C., Zanarini, M. C., Yen, S. *et al.* (2003). Childhood antecedents of avoidant personality disorder: a retrospective study. *Journal of the American Academy of Child Adolescence and Psychiatry, 42,* 1122–1130.

Rhodes, M. (1961/1987). An analysis of creativity: The role of ability, cue consistency and active processing. *Creativity Research Journal, 9,* 9–23. (Research first published in 1961.)

Rhodewalt, F. and Davison, J. (1983). Reactance and the coronary prone behaviour pattern: the role of self-attribution in responses to reduced behavioural freedom. *Journal of Personality and Social Psychology, 44,* 220–228.

Rice, V. H. (ed.) (2000). *Handbook of stress, coping, and health: Implications for nursing, research, theory, and practice.* London: Sage.

Richards, G. (2002). *Putting psychology in its place: A critical overview.* London: Routledge.

Richards, M. and Eves, F. (1991). Personality, temperament and the cardiac defense response. *Personality and Individual Differences, 12,* 999–1004.

Richards, R. and Kinney, D. K. (2000). 'Creativity advantage', mood disorders, and what we all can learn. *Bulletin Psychology and the Arts, 1,* 44–46.

Richards, T. A. (2006a). *What is social anxiety?* Available online at www.socialanxietyinstitute.org/define.html; accessed 24 October 2012.

Richards, T. A. (2006b). *DSM-IV clinical definition of social anxiety disorder.* Available online at www.socialanxietyinstitute.org /define.html; accessed 24 October 2012.

Ridley, M. (1999). *Genome: The autobiography of a species in 23 chapters.* London: Fourth Estate.

Riemann, R. and De Raad, B. (1998). Editorial: Behaviour genetics and personality. *European Journal of Personality, 12,* 303–305.

Riemann, R., Grubich, C., Hempel, S., Mergl, S. and Richter, M. (1993). Personality and attitudes towards current political topics. *Personality and Individual Differences, 15,* 313–321.

Riemann, R., Angleitner, A. and Strelau, J. (1997). Genetic and environmental influences on personality: A study of twins reared together using the self- and peer report NEO-FFI scales. *Journal of Personality, 65,* 449–475.

Rilea, S. L., Roskos-Ewoldsen, B. and Boles, D. (2004). Sex differences in spatial ability: A lateralization of function approach. *Brain and Cognition, 56,* 332–343.

Rizza, M. G., McIntosh, D. E. and McCunn, A. (2001). Profile analysis of the Woodcock-Johnson III tests of cognitive abilities with gifted students. *Psychology in the Schools, 38,* 447–455.

Robertson, A. (2003). Making sense of the 'group mind'. In F. Fransella (ed.), *International handbook of personal construct psychology.* London: Wiley.

Robertson, I. T. (2001). Undue diligence. *People Management, 7* (22 November), 42–43.

Robinson, P. W., Robinson, M. P. W. and Dunn, T. W. (2003). STEP parenting: A review of the research. *Canadian Journal of Counselling, 37*(4), 270–278.

Robinson, R. (1983). Book reviews: Culture's consequences: International differences in work-related values. *Work and Occupations, 10,* 110–115.

Rodgers, J. L. (2001). What causes birth order-intelligence patterns? The admixture hypothesis, revived. *American Psychologist, 56,* 505–510.

Rodgers, J. L., Cleveland, H. H., van den Oord, E. and Rowe, D. C. (2000). Resolving the debate over birth order, family size, and intelligence. *American Psychologist, 55,* 599–612.

Rogers, A. (1996). *Teaching adults* (2nd edn). Buckingham: Open University Press.

Rogers, C. (1970). *Encounter Groups.* New York: Harper & Row.

Rogers, C. R. (1931). *Measuring personality adjustment in children.* Boston: Houghton Mifflin.

Rogers, C. R. (1939). *Clinical treatment of the problem child.* Boston: Houghton Mifflin.

Rogers, C. R. (1951). *Client-centered therapy: Its current practice, implications, and theory.* Boston: Houghton Mifflin.

Rogers, C. R. (1954). The case of Mrs. Oak: A research analysis. In C. R. Rogers and R. F. Dymond (eds), *Psychotherapy and personality change.* Chicago: University of Chicago Press.

Rogers, C. R. (1956). What it means to become a person. In C. E. Moustakas (ed.), *The self: Explorations in personal growth* (pp. 195–211). New York: Harper.

Rogers, C. R. (1959). A theory of therapy, personality and interpersonal relationships, as developed in the client-centred framework. In S. Koch (ed.), *Psychology: A study of a science* (Vol. 3). New York: McGraw-Hill.

Rogers, C. R. (1961). *On becoming a person: A therapist's view of psychotherapy.* Boston: Houghton Mifflin.

Rogers, C. R. (1965). *Client-centered therapy: Its current practice, implication, and theory.* Boston: Houghton Mifflin.

Rogers, C. R. (1969). *Freedom to learn.* Columbus, OH: Merrill.

Rogers, C. R. (1977). *Carl Rogers on personal power.* New York: Delacorte Press.

Rogers, C. R. (1980). *A way of being.* Boston: Houghton Mifflin.

Rogers, C. R. (1983). *Freedom to learn for the 80s.* Columbus, OH: Merrill.

Rogers, C. R. and Dymond, R. F. (eds). (1954). *Psychotherapy and personality change.* Chicago: University of Chicago Press.

Rogers, C. R. and Freiberg, H. J. (1993). *Freedom to learn* (3rd edn). New York: Merrill.

Rogers, C. R. and Stevens, B. (1967). *Person to person: The problem of being human.* New York: Simon & Schuster.

Roid, G. H. (2003). *Stanford–Binet Intelligence Scales (SB5)* (5th edn). Itasca, IL: Riverside.

Roig, M. K., Bridges, R., Hackett-Renner, C. and Jackson, C. R. (1998). Belief in the paranormal and its association with irrational thinking controlled for context effects. *Personality and Individual Differences, 24*(2), 229–236.

Rose, S. and Serafica, F. C. (1986). Keeping and ending casual, close and best friendships. *Journal of Social and Personal Relationships, 3,* 275–288.

Rosenbaum, M. E. (1986). The repulsion hypothesis: On the non-development of relationships. *Journal of Personality and Social Psychology, 50,* 729–736.

Rosenberg, M. (1979). *Conceiving the self.* New York: Basic Books.

Rosenman, R. H., Friedman, M., Straus, R. *et al.* (1964). A predictive study of coronary heart disease. *Journal of the American Medical Association, 189,* 103–110.

Rosenman, R. H., Brand, R. J., Jenkins, C. D. *et al.* (1975). Coronary heart disease in the WCGS: Final follow up experience of 8.5 years. *Journal of the American Medical Association, 233,* 872–877.

Ross, L. and Nisbett, L. D. (1991). *The person and the situation: Perspectives of social psychology.* New York: McGraw-Hill.

Rotter, J. B. (1966). Generalized expectancies for internal versus external control of reinforcement. *Psychological Monographs, 80* (whole no. 609).

Rotter, J. B. (1982). *The development and application of social learning theory: Selected papers.* New York: Praeger.

Rozanski, A., Blumenthal, J. A. and Kaplan, J. (1999). Impact of psychological factors on the pathogenesis of cardiovascular disease and implications for therapy. *Circulation, 99,* 2192–2217.

Rozell, E. J., Pettijohn, C. E. and Parker, S. R. (2006). Emotional intelligence and dispositional affectivity as predictors of performance in salespeople. *Journal of Marketing Theory and Practice, 14,* 113–124.

Rueggeberg, R., Wrosch, C. and Miller, G. E. (2012). The different roles of perceived stress in the association between older adults' physical activity and physical health. *Health Psychology, 31,* 164–171.

Rummel, A. and Feinberg, R. (1988). Cognitive evaluation theory: A meta-analytic review of the literature. *Social Behavior and Personality, 16,* 147–164.

Runco, M. A. (2004). Creativity. *Annual Review of Psychology, 55,* 657–687.

Rusbult, C. E. (1983). A longitudinal test of the investment model: The development (and deterioration) of satisfaction and commitment in heterosexual involvement. *Journal of Personality and Social Psychology, 45,* 101–117.

Rusbult, C. E. and Martz, J. M. (1998). The investment model: Measuring commitment level, satisfaction level, quality of alternatives, and investment size. *Personal Relationships, 5,* 357–391.

Rusbult, C. E. and Zembrodt, I. M. (1983). Responses to dissatisfaction in romantic involvements: A multidimensional scaling analysis. *Journal of Experimental Social Psychology, 19*, 274–293.

Rusbult, C. E., Zembrodt, I. M. and Gunn, L. K. (1982). Exit, voice, loyalty, and neglect: Responses to dissatisfaction in romantic involvements. *Journal of Personality and Social Psychology, 43*, 1230–1242.

Rusbult, C. E., Johnson, D. J. and Morrow, G. D. (1986). Determinants and consequences of exit, voice, loyalty, and neglect: Responses to dissatisfaction in adult romantic involvements. *Human Relations, 39*(1), 45–63.

Rusbult, C. E., Martz, J. M. and Agnew, C. R. (1998). The Investment Model Scale: Measuring commitment level, satisfaction level, quality of alternatives, and investment size. *Personal Relationships, 5*, 357–391.

Rushton, J. P. (1985). *Race, evolution, and behavior.* New Brunswick, NJ: Transaction.

Rushton, J. P. (1989). Genetic similarity, human altruism, and group selection. *Behavioral and Brain Sciences, 12*, 503–518.

Rushton, J. P. (1994). Victim of scientific hoax (Cyril Burt and the genetic IQ controversy). *Society, 31*, 40.

Rushton, J. P. and Ankney, C. D. (1996). Brain size and cognitive ability: Correlations with age, sex, social class, and race. *Psychonomic Bulletin and Review, 3*, 21–36.

Rushton, J. P. and Irwing, P. (2008). A general factor of personality (GFP) from two meta-analyses of the Big Five: Digman (1997) and Mount, Barrick, Scullen and Round; (2005). *Personality and Individual Differences, 45*, 679–683.

Rushton, J. P. and Irwing, P. (2009). A general factor of personality (GFP) from the Multidimensional Personality Questionnaire. *Personality and Individual Differences, 47*, 571–576.

Rushton, J. P. and Irwing, P. (2011). The general factor of personality: Normal and abnormal. In T. Chamorro-Premuzic, S. von Stumm and A. Furnham (eds). *The Wiley–Blackwell Handbook of Individual Differences* (pp. 132–166). London: Wiley–Blackwell.

Russell, B. T. (1949). *The scientific outlook.* London: Allen & Unwin.

Russell, D., Cutrona, C. E. and Jones, W. H. (1986). A trait-situational analysis of shyness. In W. H. Jones, J. M. Cheek and S. R. Briggs (eds), *A sourcebook on shyness: Research and treatment* (pp. 239–249). New York: Plenum.

Russell, D. W., Hayes, D. G. and Dockery, L. B. (1988). *My child is gifted! Now what do I do?* (2nd edn). Winston-Salem, NC: North Carolina Association for the Gifted and Talented.

Rutter, M. (1990). Psychosocial resilience and protective mechanisms. In J. Rolf, A. Masten, D. Cicchetti, K. Nuechterlein and S. Weintraub (eds), *Risk and protective factors in the development of psychopathology* (pp. 181–214). New York: Cambridge University Press.

Ryan, R. M. and Connell, J. P. (1989). Perceived locus of causality and internalization: Examining reasons for acting in two domains. *Journal of Personality and Social Psychology, 57*, 749–761.

Ryckman, R. M., Thornton, B. and Butler, J. C. (1994). Personality correlates of the Hypercompetitive Attitude Scale: Validity tests of Horney's theory of neurosis. *Journal of Personality Assessment, 62*, 84–94.

Ryckman, R. M., Libby, C. R., van den Borne, B., Gold, J. A. and Lindner, M. A. (1997). Values of hypercompetitive and personal development of competitive individuals. *Journal of Personality Assessment, 69*, 271–283.

Rye, M. S., Loiacono, D. M., Folck, C. D. *et al.* (2001). Evaluation of the psychometric properties of two forgiveness scales. *Current Psychology, 20*, 260–277.

Ryff, C. D. (1989). Happiness is everything, or is it? Explorations on the meaning of psychological well-being. *Journal of Personality and Social Psychology, 57*, 1069–1081.

Sabido, M. (1981). *Towards the social use of soap operas.* Mexico City: Institute for Communication Research.

Sabido, M. (2002). *El tono (The tone).* Mexico City: Universidad Nacional Autónoma de México.

Sabini, J., Siepmann, M., Stein, J. and Meyerowitz, M. (2000). Who is embarrassed by what? *Cognition and Emotion, 14*(2), 213–240.

Saggino, A., Cooper, C. and Kline, P. (2001). A confirmatory factor analysis of the Myers–Briggs type indicator. *Personality and Individual Differences, 30*, 3–9.

Salgado, J. F. (2003). Predicting job performance using FFM and non-FFM personality measures. *Journal of Occupational and Organizational Psychology, 76*, 323–346.

Salkovskis, P. M. (1985). Obsessional-compulsive problems: A cognitive-behavioural analysis. *Behaviour Research and Therapy, 23*, 571–583.

Salovey, P. and Mayer, J. D. (1990). Emotional intelligence. *Imagination, Cognition, and Personality, 9*, 185–211.

Saltzer, E. B. (1982). The Weight Locus of Control (WLOC) Scale: A specific measure for obesity research. *Journal of Personality Assessment, 46*, 620–628.

Samman, E. (2007). *Psychological and subjective well-being: A proposal for internationally comparable indicators.* OHPI Working Paper Series, University of Oxford.

Samuels, J. *et al.* (2000). Personality disorders and normal personality dimensions in obsessive-compulsive disorder. *British Journal of Psychiatry, 177*, 457–462.

Sapir, E. (1949) *Culture, Language, and Personality.* Berkeley: Language Behavior Research Laboratory.

Saroglou, V. (2002). Religion and the five factors of personality: A meta-analytic review. *Personality and Individual Differences, 32*, 15–25.

Sass, L. A. (2001). Schizophrenia, modernism, and the 'creative imagination': On creativity and psychopathology. *Creativity Research Journal, 13*, 55–74.

Sattler, J. M. (2002). *Assessment of children: Behavioral and clinical applications* (4th edn). San Diego, CA: Jerome M. Sattler.

Saucier, G. (1995). What has personality got to do with personality disorders? *Contemporary Psychology, 40*, 645–647.

Saucier, G. (2000). Isms and the structure of social attitudes. *Journal of Personality and Social Psychology, 78*, 366–385.

Saucier, G. (2002). Gone too far – or not far enough? Comments on the article by Ashton and Lee (2001). *European Journal of Personality, 16*, 55–62.

Saucier, G. and Goldberg, L. R. (1998). What is beyond the Big Five? *Journal of Personality, 66*, 495–524.

Saucier, G. and Goldberg, L. R. (2001). Lexical studies of indigenous personality factors: Premises, products and prospects. *Journal of Personality, 69*, 847–879.

Saucier, G. and Ostendorf, F. (1999). Hierarchical sub-components of the Big Five personality factors: A cross-language replication. *Journal of Personality and Social Psychology, 76*, 613–627.

Saucier, G., Hampson, S. E. and Goldberg, L. R. (2000). Cross-language studies of lexical personality factors. In S. E. Hampson (ed.), *Advances in personality psychology.* London: Psychology Press.

Saudino, K. J. and Plomin, R. (1996). Personality and behavioral genetics: Where have we been and where are we going? *Journal of Research in Personality, 30*, 335–347.

Saulsman, L. M. and Page, A. C. (2004). The Five-Factor Model and personality disorder empirical literature: A meta-analytic review. *Clinical Psychology Review, 23*, 1055–1085.

Saunders, P. L. and Chester, A. (2008). Shyness and the internet: Social problem or panacea? *Computers in Human Behavior, 24*, 2649–2658.

Scheier, M. F. and Carver, C. S. (1985). Optimism, coping, and health: Assessment and implications of generalized outcome expectancies. *Health Psychology, 4*, 219–247.

Scheier, M. F. and Carver, C. S. (1987). Dispositional optimism and physical well-being: The influence of generalized outcome expectancies. *Journal of Personality, 55*, 169–210.

Scheier, M. F., Weintraub, J. K. and Carver, C. S. (1986). Coping and stress: Divergent strategies of optimists and pessimists. *Journal of Personality and Social Psychology, 51*, 1257–1264.

Scheier, M. F., Carver, C. S. and Bridges, M. W. (1994). Distinguishing optimism from neuroticism (and trait anxiety, self-mastery, and self-esteem): A re-evaluation of the Life Orientation Test. *Journal of Personality and Social Psychology, 67*, 1063–1078.

Scheier, M. F., Carver, C. S. and Bridges, M. W. (2001). Optimism, pessimism, and psychological well-being. In E. C. Chang (ed.), *Optimism and pessimism: Implications for theory, research, and practice* (pp. 189–216). Washington, DC: American Psychological Association.

Schipper, M. C. and Van Lange, P. A. M. (2006). The psychological benefits of superstitious rituals in top sport: A study among top sportspersons. *Journal of Applied Social Psychology, 36*(10), 2532–2553.

Schmitt, D. P. and Buss, D. M. (2000). Sexual dimensions of person description: beyond or subsumed by the Big Five? *Journal of Research in Personality, 34*, 141–177.

Schneider, S. L. (2001). In search of realistic optimism: Meaning, knowledge, and warm fuzziness. *American Psychologist, 56*, 250–263.

Schneier, F. R. (2003). Social anxiety disorder. *British Medical Journal, 327*, 515–516.

Schoenthaler, S. J., Bier, I. D., Young, K., Nichols, D. and Jansenns, S. (2000). The effect of vitamin-mineral supplementation on the intelligence of American schoolchildren: A randomized, double-blind placebo-controlled trial. *Journal of Alternative and Complementary Medicine, 6*, 19–29.

Schooler, C. (1972). Birth order effects: Not here, not now! *Psychological Bulletin, 78*, 161–175.

Schooler, C. (1998). Environmental complexity and the Flynn Effect. In U. Neisser (ed.), *The rising curve: Long-term gains in IQ and related measures* (pp. 67–80). Washington, DC: American Psychological Association.

Schou, I., Ekeberg, O. and Ruland, C. M. (2005). The mediating role of the appraisal and coping in the relationship between optimism-pessimism and quality of life. *Psycho-oncology, 14*, 718–727.

Schroder, K., Schwarzer, R. and Konertz, W. (1998). Coping as a mediator in recovery for cardiac surgery. *Psychology and Health, 13*(1), 83–97.

Schulte, M. J., Ree, M. J. and Carretta, T. R. (2004). Emotional intelligence: Not much more than *g* and personality. *Personality and Individual Differences, 37*, 1059–1068.

Schultz, D. (1975). *A history of modern psychology.* New York: Academic Press.

Schulz, R. and Beach, S. R. (1999). Caregiving as a risk factor for mortality: The Caregiver Health Effects Study. *Journal of the American Medical Association, 282*, 2215–2219.

Schutte, N. S., Malouff, J. M., Thorsteinsson, E. B., Bhullar, N. and Rooke, S. E. (2007). A meta-analytic investigation of the relationship between emotional intelligence and health. *Personality and Individual Differences, 42*, 921–933.

Schwartz, N. and Strack, F. (1999). Reports of subjective well-being: Judgmental processes and their methodological implications. In D. Kahneman, E. Diener and N. Schwartz (eds) *Well-being: The foundation of hedonic psychology.* New York: Russell Sage Foundation.

Schwarzer, R. and Born, A. (1997). Optimistic self-beliefs: Assessment of general perceived self-efficacy in thirteen cultures. *World Psychology, 3*, 177–190.

Schwarzer, R. and Jerusalem, M. (1995). Generalized Self-Efficacy Scale. In J. Weinman, S. Wright and M. Johnson (eds), *Measures in health psychology: A user's portfolio, Causal and control beliefs* (pp. 35–37). Windsor, England: NFER-Nelson.

Schweizer, K. and Koch, W. (2001). The assessment of components of optimism by POSO-E. *Personality and Individual Differences, 31*, 563–574.

Scogin, F., Jamison, C. and Gochneaur, K. (1989). Comparative efficacy of cognitive and behavioral bibliotherapy for mildly and moderately depressed older adults. *Journal of Consulting & Clinical Psychology, 57*, 403–407.

Scott, W. E. (1975). The effects of extrinsic rewards on 'intrinsic motivation': A critique. *Organizational Behavior and Human Performance, 14*, 117–129.

Segan, C. J., Borland. R. and Greenwood, K. M. (2006). Can transtheoretical model measures predict relapse from the action stage of change among ex-smokers who quit after calling a quitline? *Addictive Behaviors, 31*, 414–428.

Segerstrom, S. C., Taylor, S. E., Kemeny, M. E. and Fahey, J. L. (1998). Optimism is associated with mood, coping, and immune change in response to stress. *Journal of Personality and Social Psychology, 74*, 1646–1655.

Segerstrom, S. C., Castaneda, J. O. and Spencer, T. E. (2003). Optimism effects on cellular immunity: Testing the affective and persistence models. *Personality and Individual Differences, 35*, 1615–1624.

Seligman, M. E. P. (1991). *Learned optimism.* New York: Knopf.

Seligman, M. E. P. (1994). *What you can change and what you can't.* New York: Knopf.

Seligman, M. E. P. (1998). *Learned optimism: How to change your mind and your life* (2nd edn). New York: Pocket Books.

Seligman, M. E. P. (2003). *The past and future of positive psychology.* In C. L. M. Keyes and J. Haidt (eds), *Flourishing: Positive psychology and the life well-lived* (pp. xi–xx). Washington, DC: American Psychological Association.

Seligman, M. E. P. and Csikszentmihalyi, M. (2000). Positive psychology: An introduction. *American Psychologist, 55*, 5–14.

Seligman, M. E. P. and Maier, S. F. (1967). Failure to escape traumatic shock. *Journal of Experimental Psychology, 74*, 1–9.

Seligman, M. E. P., Castellon, C., Cacciola, J. *et al.* (1988). Explanatory style change during cognitive therapy for unipolar depression. *Journal of Abnormal Psychology, 97*, 13–18.

Serpell, R. (1974). Aspects of intelligence in a developing country. *African Social Research, 17*, 576–596.

Serpell, R. (1982). Measures of perception, skills, and intelligence. In W. W. Hartup (ed.), *Review of child development research* (Vol. 6, pp. 392–440). Chicago: University of Chicago Press.

Serpell, R. (2001). Intelligence and culture. In R. J. Sternberg (ed.), *Handbook of intelligence* (pp. 549–577). Cambridge: Cambridge University Press.

Servin, A., Bohlin, G. and Berlin, L. (1999). Sex differences in 1-, 3-, and 5-year-olds' toy choice in a structured play situation. *Scandinavian Journal of Psychology, 40*, 43–48.

Seyle, H. (1956). *The stress of life.* New York: McGraw-Hill.

Seyle, H. (1976). *Stress in health and disease.* Reading, MA: Butterworth.

Shaklee, A. B. (1963). Comparative studies of temperament: Fear responses in different species of fish. *Journal of Genetic Psychology*, 102, 295–310.

Shankman, S. A. and Klein, D. N. (2003). The relation between depression and anxiety: An evaluation of the tripartite approach-withdrawal and valence-arousal models. *Clinical Psychology Review*, 23, 605–637.

Shaper, A. G., Wannamethee, G. and Weatherall, R. (1991). Physical activity and ischaemic heart disease in middle-aged British men. *British Heart Journal*, 66, 384–394.

Sharot, T., Korn, C. W. and Dolan, R. J. (2011). How unrealistic optimism is maintained in the face of reality. *Nature Neuroscience*, 14, 1475–U156.

Sharpe, D. (1997). Of apples and oranges, file drawers and garbage: Why validity issues in meta-analysis will not go away. *Clinical Psychology Review*, 17, 881–901.

Sharpe, J. P., Martin, N. R. and Roth, K. A. (2011). Optimism and the Big Five factors of personality: Beyond neuroticism and extraversion. *Personality and Individual Differences* 51(8), 946–951.

Shaver, P. R. and Fraley, R. C. (2004). *Self-report measures of adult attachment*. Available online at www.psych.uiuc.edu/~rcfraley/measures/measures.html; accessed 26 March 2006.

Shaw, G. L. (2001). The Mozart effect [Letter to the editor]. *Epilepsy & Behavior*, 2, 611–613.

Sheldon, K. M., Ryan, R. M. and Reis, H. T. (1996). What makes for a good day? Competence and autonomy in the day and in the person. *Personality and Social Psychology Bulletin*, 22, 1270–1279.

Sheldon, W. (1970). *Atlas of men*. New York: Macmillan.

Sherer, M., Maddux, J. E., Mercandante, B. *et al.* (1982). The Self-Efficacy Scale: Construction and validation. *Psychological Reports*, 51, 663–671.

Sherry, D. F. and Hampson, E. (1997). Evolution and the hormonal control of sexually dimorphic spatial abilities in humans. *Trends in Cognitive Sciences*, 1, 50–56.

Shoda, Y. and LeeTiernan, S. J. (2002). What remains invariant? Finding order within a person's thoughts, feelings, and behaviours across situations. In D. Cervone and W. Mischel (eds), *Advances in personality science* (pp. 241–247). New York: Guilford.

Shoda, Y. and Mischel, W. (1998). Personality as a stable cognitive-affective activation network: Characteristic patterns of behaviour variation emerge from a stable personality structure. In S. J. Read and L. C. Miller (eds), *Connectionist Models of Social Reasoning and Social Behavior*. Mahwah, NJ: Erlbaum.

Shoda, Y., Mischel, W. and Wright, J. C. (1993). The role of situational demands and cognitive competencies in behaviour organisation and personality coherence. *Journal of Personality and Social Psychology*, 65, 1023–1035.

Shoda, Y., Mischel, W. and Wright, J. C. (1994). Intra-individual stability in the organisation and patterning of behaviour: Incorporating psychological situations into the idiographic analysis of personality. *Journal of Personality and Social Psychology*, 67, 674–687.

Shoda., Y., LeeTiernan, S. J. and Mischel, W. (2002). Personality as a dynamical system: Emergence of stability and consistency in intra- and interpersonal interactions. *Personality and Social Psychology Review*, 6, 316–325.

Shostrum, E. L. (1966). *Manual for the personal orientation inventory*. San Diego, CA: Educational and Industrial Testing Service.

Shuey, A. (1966). *The testing of Negro intelligence*. New York: Social Science Press.

Sidanius, J. and Pratto, F. (1999). *Social dominance: An intergroup theory of social hierarchy and oppression*. New York: Cambridge University Press.

Sidanius, J., Levin, S. and Pratto, F. (1996). Consensual social dominance orientation and its correlates within the hierarchical structure of American society. *International Journal of Intercultural Relations*, 24, 385–408.

Siegler, R. S. and Richards, D. D. (1982). The development of intelligence. In R. J. Sternberg (ed.), *Handbook of intelligence* (pp. 896–971). New York: Cambridge University Press.

Siever, L. J. and Davis K. L. (1991). The pathogenesis of mood disorders. In K. L. Davis and H. Klar (eds), *Foundations of Psychiatry* (pp. 254–262). Philadelphia: Saunders and Company.

Silver, M., Sabini, J. and Parrott, W. G. (1987). Embarrassment: A dramaturgic account. *Journal for the Theory of Social Behaviour*, 17, 47–61.

Silverman, I. and Eals, M. (1992). Sex differences in spatial abilities: Evolutionary theory and data. In J. H. Barkow, L. Cosmides and J. Tooby (eds), *The adapted mind* (pp. 533–549). New York: Oxford University Press.

Silverman, I., Choi, J., Mackewn, A. *et al.* (2000). Evolved mechanisms underlying way finding: Further studies on the hunter-gatherer theory of spatial sex differences. *Evolution and Human Behavior*, 21, 201–213.

Silverman, L. H. (1976). Psychoanalytic theory: The reports of my death are greatly exaggerated. *American Psychologist*, 31, 621–637.

Simonton, D. K. (1994). *Greatness: Who makes history and why?* New York: Guilford.

Simpson, M., Carone, D. A., Burns, W. J. *et al.* (2002). Assessing giftedness with the WISC-III and the SB-IV. *Psychology in the Schools*, 39, 515–524.

Sing, C. Y. and Wong, W. S. (2011). The effect of optimism on depression: The mediating and moderating role of insomnia. *Journal of Health Psychology*, 16, 1251–1258.

Singhal, A. and Rogers, E. M. (1989). Pro-social television for development in India. In R. E. Rice and S. K. Atkin (eds), *Public communication campaigns* (2nd edn) (pp. 331–350). Newbury Park, CA: Sage.

Sisk, D. (1990). The state of gifted education: Toward a bright future. *Music Educators Journal* (March), 35–39.

Skinner, B. F. (1948). Superstition in the pigeon. *Journal of Experimental Psychology*, 38, 168–172.

Skinner, B. F. (1948). *Walden two*. New York: Macmillan.

Skinner, B. F. (1953). *Science and human behaviour*. New York: Macmillan.

Skinner, B. F. (1963). Behaviourism at fifty. *Science*, 140, 951–958.

Skinner, B. F. (1971). *Beyond freedom and dignity*. New York: Knopf.

Skinner, B. F. (1972). *Cumulative record: A selection of papers* (3rd edn). New York: Appleton-Century-Crofts.

Skinner, B. F. (1973). Answers for my critics. In H. Wheeler (ed.), *Beyond the punitive society*. San Francisco: Freeman.

Skinner, B. F. (1976). *About behaviourism*. New York: Vintage Books.

Skodol, A. E., Oldham, J. M. and Gallaher, P. E. (1999). Axis II comorbidity of substance use disorders among patients referred for treatment of personality disorders. *American Journal of Psychiatry*, 156, 733–738.

Skodol, A. E., Gunderson, J. G., Pfohl, B. *et al.* (2002) The borderline diagnosis I: Psychopathology, comorbidity and personality structure. *Biological Psychiatry*, 51, 936–950.

Smith, B. D. (1983). Extraversion and electrodermal activity: Arousability and the inverted U. *Personality and Individual Differences*, 4, 411–419.

Smith, D. M. and Kolb, D. A. (1986). *The user's guide for the Learning Style Inventory: A manual for teachers and trainers.* Boston: McBer & Company.

Smith, M. B. (1988). The wrong drummer: A reply to Blight. *Journal of Humanistic Psychology, 28,* 62–66.

Smith, M., Durkin, M. S., Hinton, V., Bellinger, D. and Kuhn, L. (2003). Influence of breastfeeding on cognitive outcomes at age 6–8 years: Follow-up of very low birth weight infants. *American Journal of Epidemiology, 158,* 1075–1082.

Smith, S. (1996). Dating-partner preferences among a group of inner-city African-American high-school students. *Adolescence, 131,* 79–90.

Smith, T. W. and Gallo, L. C. (2001). Personality traits as risk factors for physical illness. In A. Baum, T. A. Revenson and J. E. Singer (eds) *Handbook of Health Psychology.* Mahwah, NJ: Erlbaum.

Smith, T. W. and Williams, P. G. (1992). Personality and health: Advantages and limitations of the five-factor model. *Journal of Personality, 60,* 395–423.

Smith, T. W., Pope, M. K., Rhodewalt, F. and Poulton, J. L. (1989). Optimism, neuroticism, coping, and symptom reports: An alternative interpretation of the life orientation test. *Journal of Personality and Social Psychology, 56,* 640–648.

Snyder, C. R. (1994). *The psychology of hope: You can get there from here.* New York: Free Press.

Snyder, C. R. (1995). Conceptualizing, measuring, and nurturing hope. 'Current Trends', Focus Article in *Journal of Counseling and Development, 73,* 355–360.

Snyder, C. R. (1996). To hope, to lose, and hope again. *Journal of Personal and Interpersonal Loss, 1,* 1–16.

Snyder, C. R. (2002). Hope theory: Rainbows in the mind. *Psychological Inquiry, 13,* 249–275.

Snyder, C. R. (ed.). (2000). *Handbook of hope: Theory, measurement, and applications.* San Diego, CA: Academic Press.

Snyder, C. R. and McCullough, M. E. (2000). A positive psychology field of dreams: If you build it they will come. *Journal of Social and Clinical Psychology, 19*(1), 151–160.

Snyder, C. R. and Rand, K. L. (2003). The case against false hope. *American Psychologist, 4,* 820–822.

Snyder, C. R., Harris, C., Anderson, J. R. *et al.* (1991). The will and the ways: Development and validation of an individual differences measure of hope. *Journal of Personality and Social Psychology, 60,* 570–585.

Snyder, C. R., Sympson, S. C., Ybasco, F. C. *et al.* (1996). Development and validation of the State Hope Scale. *Journal of Personality and Social Psychology, 70,* 321–335.

Snyder, C. R., McDermott, D., Cook, W. and Rapoff, M. (2002). *Hope for the journey.* Clinton Corners, NY: Percheron.

Snyder, M. and Ickes, W. (1985). Personality and social behaviour. In G. Lindzey and E. Aronson (eds), *Handbook of social psychology* (Vol. 2, 3rd edn). Reading, MA: Addison-Wesley.

Solms, M. (1997). *The neuropsychology of dreams.* Mahwah, NJ: Erlbaum.

Solms, M. (2000). Freudian dream theory today. *The Psychologist, 13,* 618–619.

Solomon, A. (2001). *The noonday demon: An atlas of depression.* New York: Scribner.

Spearman, C. E. (1904a). 'General intelligence', objectively determined and measured. *American Journal of Psychology, 15,* 201–293.

Spearman, C. E. (1904b). Proof and measurement of association between two things. *American Journal of Psychology, 15,* 72–101.

Spearman, C. E. (1927). *The abilities of man: Their nature and measurement.* New York: Macmillan.

Spearman, C. E. and Jones, L. W. (1951). *Human abilities.* London: Macmillan.

Spencer, H. (1855). *The principles of psychology.* London: Williams & Norgate.

Spencer, S. J., Steele, C. M. and Quinn, D. M. (1999). Stereotype threat and women's math performance. *Journal of Experimental Social Psychology, 35,* 4–28.

Steele, C. M. (1997). A threat in the air: How stereotypes shape intellectual identity and performance. *American Psychologist, 52,* 613–629.

Steele, K. M. (2000). Arousal and mood factors in the 'Mozart effect'. *Perceptual and Motor Skills, 91,* 188–190.

Steele, K. M. (2003). Do rats show a Mozart effect? *Music Perception, 21,* 251–265.

Stein, M. B., Liebowitz, M. R., Lydiard, R. B. *et al.* (1998). Paroxetine treatment of generalized social phobia (social anxiety disorder): A randomised controlled trial. *Journal of the American Medical Association, 280,* 708–713.

Stein, M. B., Heimberg, R. G. and Stein, M. B. (2004). Well-being and life satisfaction in generalized anxiety disorder: Comparison to major depressive disorder in a community sample. *Journal of Affective Disorders, 79,* 161–166.

Steiner, J. F. (1966). *Treblinka.* New York: Simon & Schuster.

Stelmack, R. and Houlihan, M. (1995). Event-related potentials, personality, and intelligence: Concepts, issues, and evidence. In D. H. Saklofske and M. Zaidner (eds), *International handbook of personality and intelligence* (pp. 349–366). New York: Plenum.

Stelmack, R. M. and Stalikas, A. (1991). Galen and the humour theory of temperament. *Personality and Individual Differences, 12,* 255–263.

Stenberg, G. (1992). Personality and the EEG: Arousal and emotional arousability. *Personality and Individual Differences, 13,* 1097–1113.

Steptoe, A. (1998). *Genius and the mind: Studies of creativity and temperament.* Oxford: Oxford University Press.

Steptoe, A. and Ayers, S. (2004). Stress, health and illness. In S. Sutton, A. Baum and M. Johnston (eds), *The Sage Handbook of Health Psychology.* London: Sage.

Stern, P. J. C. (1977). *Jung: The haunted prophet.* New York: Delta Books.

Sternberg, R. J. (1985a). *Beyond IQ: A triarchic theory of human intelligence.* New York: Cambridge University Press.

Sternberg, R. J. (1985b). Implicit theories of intelligence, creativity, and wisdom. *Journal of Personality and Social Psychology, 49,* 607–627.

Sternberg, R. J. (1986a). A triangular theory of love. *Psychological Review, 93,* 119–135.

Sternberg, R. J. (1986b). A triarchic theory of intellectual giftedness. In R. J. Sternberg and J. E. Davidson (eds), *Conceptions of giftedness* (pp. 223–243). New York: Cambridge University Press.

Sternberg, R. J. (1988). *The triarchic mind: A new theory of human intelligence.* New York: Cambridge University Press.

Sternberg, R. J. (1997a). The concept of intelligence and its role in lifelong learning and success. *American Psychologist, 52,* 1030–1037.

Sternberg, R. J. (1997b). Still smarting. *Teacher Magazine, 8,* 40–41.

Sternberg, R. J. (1998). Abilities are forms of developing expertise. *Educational Researcher, 27*(3), 11–20.

Sternberg, R. J. (2001a). The concept of intelligence. In R. J. Sternberg (ed.), *Handbook of intelligence* (pp. 3–15). Cambridge: Cambridge University Press.

Sternberg, R. J. (2001b). Why schools should teach for wisdom: The balance theory of wisdom in educational settings. *Educational Psychology, 36,* 227–245.

Sternberg, R. J. (2002). Smart people are not stupid, but they sure can be foolish: The imbalance theory of foolishness. In R. J. Sternberg (ed.), *Why smart people can be so stupid* (pp. 232–242). New Haven, CT: Yale University Press.

Sternberg, R. J. (2003). *WICS: A theory of wisdom, intelligence, and creativity, synthesized*. New York: Cambridge University Press.

Sternberg, R. J. (2005). WICS: A model of positive educational leadership comprising wisdom, intelligence, and creativity synthesized. *Educational Psychology Review*, 17, 191–262.

Sternberg, R. J. (ed.). (2000). *Handbook of intelligence*. Cambridge: Cambridge University Press.

Sternberg. R. J. and Detterman, D. K. (1986). *What is intelligence?* Norwood, NJ: Ablex.

Sternberg, R. J., Conway, B. E., Ketron, J. L. and Bernstein, M. (1981). People's conceptions of intelligence. *Journal of Personality and Social Psychology*, 41, 37–55.

Sternberg, R. J., Wagner, R. K., Williams, W. M. and Horvath, J. A. (1995). Testing common sense. *American Psychologist*, 50, 912–927.

Stevens, D. E., Merikangas, K. R. and Merikangas, J. R. (1995). Comorbidity of depression and other medical conditions. In E. E. Beckham and W. R. Leber (eds), *Handbook of Depression* (2nd edn). New York: Guilford.

Stevenson-Hinde, J. (1983). Individual characteristics and the social situation. In R. A. Hinde (ed.), *Primate social relationships: An integrated approach* (pp. 28–35). Sunderland, MA: Sinauer.

Stevenson-Hinde, J. and Zunz, M. (1978). Subjective assessment of individual rhesus monkeys. *Primates*, 19, 473–482.

Stevenson-Hinde, J., Stillwell-Barnes, R. and Zunz, M. (1980a). Individual differences in young rhesus monkeys: Consistency and change. *Primates*, 21, 498–509.

Stevenson-Hinde, J., Stillwell-Barnes, R. and Zunz, M. (1980b). Subjective assessment of rhesus monkeys over four successive years. *Primates*, 2, 66–82.

Stevenson-Hinde, J., Zunz, M. and Stillwell-Barnes, R. (1980c). Behaviour of one-year-old rhesus monkeys in a strange situation. *Animal Behaviour*, 28, 266–277.

Stocks, E. L., Lishner, D. A., Waits, B. L. and Downum, E. M. (2011). I'm embarrassed for you: The effect of valuing and perspective taking on empathic embarrassment and empathic concern. *Journal of Applied Social Psychology*, 41, 1–26.

Stokes, D. (1986). Chance can play a key role in life, psychologist says. *Campus Report* (June 10), 1–4.

Stone, A. *et al.* (1987). Evidence that secretory IgA antibody is associated with daily mood. *Journal of Personality and Social Psychology*, 52, 988–993.

Stone, W. F. (1981). The myth of left-wing authoritarianism. *Political Psychology*, 2, 3–19.

Stoolmiller, M. (1998). Correcting estimates of shared environmental variance for range restriction in adoption studies using a truncated multivariate normal model. *Behaviour Genetics*, 28, 429, 441.

Storr, A. (1973). *Jung*. London: Fontana.

Storr, A. (1989). *Freud*. Oxford: Oxford University Press.

Storr, A. (1999). *The essential Jung: Selected writings*. Princeton, NJ: Princeton University Press.

Stotland, E. (1969). *The psychology of hope*. San Francisco: Jossey-Bass.

Strauss, J. and Ryan, R. M. (1987). Autonomy disturbances in subtypes of anorexia nervosa. *Journal of Abnormal Psychology*, 96, 254–258.

Stritzke, W. G. K., Nguyen, A. and Durkin, K. (2004). Shyness and computer-mediated communication: A self-presentational perspective. *Media Psychology*, 6, 1–22.

Strube, M. J. (1987). A self-appraisal model of the type A behaviour pattern. In R. Hogan and W. Jones (eds), *Perspectives in Personality Theory*, 2, 201–250.

Strube, M. J., Boland, S. M., Manfredo, P. A. and Al-Falaij, A. (1987). Type A behaviour pattern and the self-evaluation of abilities: Empirical tests of the self-appraisal model. *Journal of Personality and Social Psychology*, 52, 956–974.

Sturgeon, R. S. and Hamley, R. W. (1979). Religiosity and anxiety. *Journal of Social Psychology*, 108, 137–138.

Suarez, E. C., Lewis, J. G. and Kuhn, C. M. (2002). The relation of aggression, hostility, and anger to lipopolysaccharide-stimulated tumor necrosis factor (TNF)-α by blood monocytes of normal men. *Brain, Behavior and Immunity*, 16, 675–684.

Subbotsky, E. (2004). Magical thinking – reality or illusion? *The Psychologist*, 17, 336–339.

Subrahmanyam, K. and Greenfield, P. M. (1994). Effect of video game practice on spatial skills in girls and boys. *Journal of Applied Developmental Psychology*, 15, 13–32.

Sulloway, F. J. (1992). *Freud, biologist of the mind: Beyond the psychoanalytic legend*. Cambridge, MA: Harvard University Press.

Sulloway, F. J. (1997). *Born to rebel: Birth order, family dynamics, and creative lives*. New York: Vintage.

Sulloway, F. J. (2001). Birth order, sibling competition, and human behaviour. In H. R. Holcomb III (ed.), *Conceptual challenges in evolutionary psychology: Innovative research strategies* (pp. 39–83). Dordrecht and Boston: Kluwer Academic Publishers. Available online at www.sulloway.org/metaanalysis.html; accessed 8 July 2006.

Sulloway, F. J. (2002). Technical report on a vote-counting meta-analysis of the birth-order literature (1940–1999). Available online at www.sulloway.org/metaanalysis.html; accessed 10 August 2006.

Suls, J. and Rittenhouse, J. D. (1990). Models of linkages between personality and disease. In H. S. Friedman (ed.), *Personality and Disease*. New York: Wiley.

Sundet, J. M., Barlaug, D. G. and Torjussen, T. M. (2004). The end of the Flynn effect? A study of secular trends in mean intelligence test scores of Norwegian conscripts during half a century. *Intelligence*, 32, 349–362.

Svansdottir, E., van den Broek, K. C., Karisson, H. D., Gudnason, T. and Denollet, J. (2012). Type D personality is associated with impaired psychological status and unhealthy lifestyle in Icelandic cardiac patients: A cross-sectional study. *BMC Public Health*, 12, 42–44.

Swann, W. B. (1984). Quest for accuracy in person perception: A matter of pragmatics. *Psychological Review*, 91, 457–477.

Swann, W. B. and Seyle, C. (2005). Personality psychology's comeback and its emerging symbiosis with social psychology. *Personality and Social Psychology Bulletin*, 2, 155–165.

Swim, J. K. (1994). Perceived versus meta-analytic effect sizes: An assessment of the accuracy of gender stereotypes. *Journal of Personality and Social Psychology*, 66, 21–36.

Szirmak, Z. and De Raad, B. (1994). Taxonomy and structure of Hungarian personality traits. *European Journal of Personality*, 8, 95–117.

Tajfel, H. and Turner, J. C. (1986). The social identity theory of inter-group behavior. In S. Worchel and L. W. Austin (eds), *Psychology of intergroup relations*. Chicago: Nelson-Hall.

Tannenbaum, A. J. (1986). Giftedness: A psychosocial approach. In R. J. Sternberg and J. E. Davidson (eds), *Conception of giftedness* (pp. 221–252). New York: Cambridge University Press.

Tashiro, T., Frazier, P. and Berman, M. (2006). Stress-related growth following divorce and relationship dissolution. In

M. Fine and J. Harvey (eds), *Handbook of divorce and relationship dissolution*. Mahwah, NJ: Erlbaum.

Taubman, P. (1976). The determinants of earnings: Genetics, family and other environments; a study of male twins. *American Economic Review*, 66, 858–870.

Tayeb, M. H. (1996). Hofstede. In Warner, M. (ed.), *International Encyclopaedia of Business and Management* (Vol. 2, pp. 1771–1776). London: Thompson Press.

Taylor, S. E. (1989). *Positive illusions: Creative self-deception and the healthy mind*. New York: Basic Books.

Taylor, S. E. and Armor, D. A. (1996). Positive illusions and coping with adversity. *Journal of Personality*, 64, 874–898.

Teasdale, T. W. and Owen, D. R. (1989). Continuing secular increases in intelligence and a stable prevalence of high intelligence levels. *Intelligence*, 13, 255–262.

Teasdale, T. W. and Owen, D. R. (2005). A long-term rise and recent decline in intelligence test performance: The Flynn effect in reverse. *Personality and Individual Differences*, 39, 837–843.

Tehrani, J. and Mednick, S. (2000). Genetic factors and criminal behavior. *Federal Probation*, 64, 24–28.

Tellegen, A., Watson, D. and Clark, L.A. (1999). On the dimensional and hierarchical structure of affect. *Psychological Science*, 10, 297–303.

Tennant, M. (1997). *Psychology and adult learning* (2nd edn). London: Routledge.

Tennen, H., Eberhardt, T. L. and Affleck, G. (1999). Depression research methodologies at the social-clinical interface. Still hazy after all these years. *Journal of Social and Clinical Psychology*, 18, 121–159.

Tennen, H., Affleck, G. and Zautra, A. (2006). Depression history and coping with chronic pain: A daily process analysis. *Health Psychology*, 25, 370–379.

Tennov, D. (1979). *Love and limerence: The experience of being in love*. New York: Stein & Day.

Terman, L. M. (1916). *The measurement of intelligence*. Boston: Houghton Mifflin.

Terman, L. M. (1921). Intelligence and its measurement: A symposium (II). *Journal of Educational Psychology*, 12, 127–133.

Terman, L. M. (1925). *Genetic studies of genius* (Vol. 1: *Mental and physical traits of a thousand gifted children*). Stanford, CA: Stanford University Press.

Terman, L. M. and Oden, M. H. (1947). *Genetic studies of genius* (Vol. 4: *The gifted child grows up*). Stanford, CA: Stanford University Press.

Terman, L. M. and Oden, M. H. (1959). *Genetic studies of genius* (Vol. 5: *The gifted group at mid-life*). Stanford, CA: Stanford University Press.

Terracciano, A. (2003). The Italian version of the NEO PI-R: conceptual and empirical support for the use of targeted rotation. *Personality and Individual Differences*, 35, 1859–1872.

Thomas, D. R., Shea, J. D. and Rigby, R. G. (1971). Conservatism and response to sexual humour. *British Journal of Social and Clinical Psychology*, 10, 185–186.

Thorndike, E. *et al.* (1927). *The measurement of intelligence*. New York: Teachers College Press.

Thorne, A. and Gough, H. (1991). *Portraits of type: An MBTI Research Compendium*. Palo Alto, CA: Psychologists Press.

Thurstone, L. L. (1953). *Examiner Manual for Thurstone Temperament Schedule*. Chicago: Science Research Associates.

Tiedmann, F. (1836). *Sur l'encéphale du Nègre comparé à celui de l'Européen et celui de l'orangoutang*. Philosphical Transactions of London.

Tobacyk, J. (1988). *A revised Paranormal Belief Scale*. Unpublished manuscript, Louisiana Tech University, Rushton, LA.

Tobacyk, J. and Shrader, D. (1991). Superstition and self-efficacy. *Psychological Reports*, 68, 1387–1388.

Tong, S. L., Baghurst, P., McMichael, A., Sawyer, M. and Mudge, J. (1996). Lifetime exposure to environmental lead and children's intelligence at 11–13 years: The Port Pirie Cohort Study. *British Medical Journal*, 312, 1569–1575.

Torgersen, S., Kringlen, E. and Cramer, V. (2001). The prevalence of personality disorders in a community sample. *Archives of General Psychiatry*, 58, 590–596.

Trivers, R. L. (1971). The evolution of reciprocal altruism. *Quarterly Review of Biology*, 46, 35–57.

Truax, C. B. and Carkhuff, R. R. (1967). *Toward effective counseling and psychotherapy: Training and practice*. Chicago: Aldine.

Truett, K. R., Eaves, L. J., Meyer, J. M., Heath, A. C. and Martin, N. G. (1992). Religion and education as mediators of attitudes: A multivariate analysis. *Behavior Genetics*, 22, 43–62.

Trull, T. J. and Geary, D. C. (1997). Comparison of the big-five factor structure across samples of Chinese and American adults. *Journal of Personality Assessment*, 69, 324–341.

Tucker, W. H. (1997). Re-reconsidering Burt: Beyond a reasonable doubt. *Journal of the History of the Behavioral Sciences*, 33, 145–162.

Tupes, E. C. and Christal, R. E. (1961/1992). Recurrent personality factors based on trait ratings. Technical Report No. ASD-TR -61 -97, US Air Force, Lackland US Air Force Base, San Antonio, TX. Reprinted in *Journal of Personality*, 60, 225–251.

Tyrer, P. and Bateman, A. (2004) Drug treatment for personality disorders. *Advances in Psychiatric Treatment*, 10, 389–398.

Uecker, A. and Nadel, L. (1996). Spatial locations gone awry: Object and spatial memory deficits in children with fetal alcohol syndrome. *Neuropsychologia*, 34, 209–223.

Van Court, M. and Bean, F. D. (1985). Intelligence and fertility in the United States 1912–1982. *Intelligence*, 9, 23–32.

Van der Linden, D., te Nijenhuis, J. and Bakker, A. B. (2010). The general factor of personality: A meta-analysis of Big Five intercorrelations and a criterion-related validity study. *Journal of Research in Personality*, 44, 315–327.

van der Zee, K., Schakel, L. and Thijs, M. (2002). The relationship of emotional intelligence with academic intelligence and the big five. *European Journal of Personality*, 16, 103–125.

Van Dierendonck, D. (2004). The construct validity of Ryff's Scales of Psychological Well-being and its extension with spiritual well-being. *Personality and Individual Differences*, 36, 629–643; *Intelligence*, 9, 23–32.

Van Hiel, A. and Mervielde, I. (2004). Openness to experience and boundaries in the mind: Relationships with cultural and economic conservative beliefs. *Journal of Personality*, 72, 659–686.

Van Lange, P. A. M., Rusbult, C. E., Drigotas, S. M. *et al.* (1997). Willingness to sacrifice in close relationships. *Journal of Personality and Social Psychology*, 72, 1373–1395.

Van Ness, P. H., Kasl, S. V. and Jones, B. A. (2003). Religion, race, and breast cancer survival. *International Journal of Psychiatry in Medicine*, 33(4), 357–375.

Vansteelandt, K. and Van Mechelen, I. (1998). Individual differences in situation-behaviour profiles: A triple typology model. *Journal of Personality and Social Psychology*, 75, 751–765.

Vansteenkiste, M., Lens, W., Dewitte, S., De Witte, H. and Deci, E. L. (2004). The 'why' and 'why not' of job search behaviour: Their relation to searching, unemployment experience, and well-being. *European Journal of Social Psychology*, 34, 345–363.

Vaughan, P. W., Rogers, E. M. and Swalehe, R. M. A. (1995). The effects of 'Twende Na Wakati', an entertainment–education radio soap opera for family planning and HIV/AIDS prevention in Tanzania. Unpublished manuscript, University of New Mexico, Alberquerque.

Veenhoven, R. (1991). Is happiness relative? *Social Indicators Research, 24,* 1–34.

Veillette, S., Perron, M., Mathieu, J., Prevost, C. and Hebert, G. (1992). Sociocultural factors influencing the spread of myotonic dystrophy in the Saguenay-Lac-Saint-Jean region of the province of Quebec. In A. H. Bittles and D. F. Roberts (eds), *Minority populations: Genetics, demography and health.* London: Macmillan.

Vernon, P. E. (1950). *The structure of human abilities.* London: Methuen.

Vining, D. R. (1995). On the possibility of the re-emergence of a dysgenic trend: An update. *Personality and Individual Differences, 19,* 259–265.

Viswesvaran, C. and Ones, D. S. (1999). Meta-analyses of fakability estimates: Implications for personality measurement. *Educational and Psychological Measurement, 59,* 197–210.

Voyer, D., Voyer, S. and Bryden, M. P. (1995). Magnitude of sex differences in spatial abilities: A meta-analysis and consideration of critical variables. *Psychological Bulletin, 117,* 250–270.

Wade, N. G. and Worthington, E. L. Jr (2005). In search of a common core: A content analysis of interventions to promote forgiveness. *Psychotherapy Theory, Research, Practice, Training, 42,* 160–177.

Wahlsten, D. (1997). The malleability of intelligence is not constrained by heritability. In B. Devlin, S. E. Fienberg and K. Roeder (eds), *Intelligence, genes, and success: Scientists respond to The Bell Curve* (pp. 71–87). New York: Springer.

Waldman, I. D., Scarr, S. and Weinberg, R. A. (1992). The Minnesota Transracial Adoption Study: A follow-up of IQ test performance at adolescence. *Intelligence, 16,* 117–135.

Waldman, I. D., Weinberg, R. A. and Scarr, S. (1994). Racial-group differences in IQ in the Minnesota Transracial Adoption Study: A reply to Levin and Lynn. *Intelligence, 19,* 29–44.

Walker, D. F. and Gorsuch, R. L. (2002). Forgiveness within the Big-Five personality model. *Personality and Individual Differences, 32,* 1127–1137.

Wallas, G. (1926) *The art of thought.* New York: Harcourt Yovanovich Brace.

Waller, N. G. (1999). Evaluating the structure of personality. In C. R. Cloninger (ed.), *Personality and psychopathology* (pp. 155–197). Washington, DC: American Psychiatric Association.

Wallston, K. A., Wallston, B. S. and DeVellis, R. (1978). Development of Multidimensional Health Locus of Control (MHLC) Scales. *Health Education Monographs, 6*(2), 160–170.

Walsh, J. (18 March, 2007). Is there a link between madness and creativity? www.independent.co.uk/life-style/health-and-wellbeing/health-news/is-there-a-link-between-madness-and-creativity-440374.html; accessed 27 February 2009.

Walster, E. and Walster, G. (1978). *A new look at love.* Reading, MA: Addison-Wesley.

Wanberg, C. R. and Banas, J. T. (2000). Predictors and outcomes of openness to changes in a reorganising workplace. *Journal of Applied Psychology, 85,* 132–142.

Wannamethee, S. G., Shaper, A. G. and Perry, I. J. (1997). Serum creatinine concentration and risk of cardiovascular disease: A possible marker for increased risk of stroke. *Stroke, 28,* 557–563.

Waterman, A. S. (2008). Reconsidering happiness: A eudaimonist's perspective. *Journal of Positive Psychology, 3,* 234–252.

Watkins, C. E. (1992). Adlerian-oriented early memory research: What does it tell us? *Journal of Personality Assessment, 59,* 248–263.

Watson, D. and Clark, L. A. (1992). On traits and temperament: general and specific factors of emotional experience and their relation to the Five-Factor Model. *Journal of Personality, 60,* 441–476.

Watson, D. and Pennebaker, J. W. (1989). Health complaints, stress, and distress: Exploring the central role of negative affectivity. *Psychological Review, 96,* 234–254.

Watson, D. and Tellegen, A. (1985). Toward a consensual structure of mood. *Psychological Bulletin, 98,* 219–235.

Watson, D., Clark, L. A. and Tellegen, A. (1988). Development and validation of brief measures of Positive and Negative Affect: The PANAS Scales. *Journal of Personality and Social Psychology, 54,* 1063–1070.

Watson, J. B. (1913). Psychology as the behaviorists view it. *Psychological Review, 20,* 158–177.

Watson, J. B. (1919). *Psychology from the standpoint of a behaviorist.* Philadelphia: Lippincott.

Watson, J. B. (1924). *Behaviorism.* New York: Norton.

Watson, J. B. (1936). John Broadus Watson. In C. Murchison (ed.), *A history of psychology in autobiography* (Vol. 3, pp. 271–281). Worcester, MA: Clark University Press.

Watson, J. B. and Rayner, R. (1920). Conditioned emotional reactions. *Journal of Experimental Psychology, 3,* 1–14.

Watson, M., Pruyn, J., Greer, S. *et al.* (1990). Locus of control and adjustment to cancer. *Psychological Reports, 66,* 39–48.

Watson, P. J., Morris, R. J. and Hood, R. W. Jr (1989). Sin and self-functioning, Part 4: Depression, assertiveness, and religious commitments. *Journal of Psychology and Theology, 17,* 44–58.

Webster, A. C. and Stewart, R. A. C. (1973). Theological conservatism. In G. Wilson (ed.), *The psychology of conservatism* (pp. 129–147). London: Academic Press.

Weck, F., Neng, J. M. B., Richtberg, S. and Stangier, U. (2012). Dysfunctional beliefs about symptoms and illness in patients with hypochondriasis. *Psychosomatics, 53,* 148–154.

Weinberger, D. A. (1997). Distress and self-restraint as measures of adjustment across the life span: Confirmatory factor analyses in clinical and non-clinical samples. *Psychological Assessment, 9,* 132–135.

Weinberger, D. A. (1998). Defenses, personality structure, and development: Integrating psychodynamic theory into a typological approach to personality. *Journal of Personality, 66,* 1061–1080.

Weinberger, J. and Silverman, L. H. (1990). Testability and empirical verification of psychoanalytic dynamic propositions through subliminal psychodynamic activation. *Psychoanalytic Psychology, 7*(3), 299–339.

Weinman, J., Wright, S. and Johnston, M. (1995). *Measures in health psychology: A user's portfolio.* London: NFER-Nelson.

Weismann, M. M. (1993). The epidemiology of personality disorders. A 1990 update. *Journal of Personality Disorders* (Spring issue, Suppl.): 44–62.

Westen, D. and Shedler, J. (2000) A prototype matching approach to diagnosing personality disorders toward DSM-V. *Journal of Personality Disorders, 14,* 109–126.

Westen, D., Shedler, J. and Bradley, R. (2006) A prototype approach to personality disorder diagnosis. *Am J Psychiatry, 163,* 846–856.

Westkott, M. (1986). *The feminist legacy of Karen Horney.* New York: Yale Books.

Whalley, L. J., Fox, H. C., Deary, I. J. and Starr, J. M. (2005). Childhood IQ, smoking, and cognitive change from age 11 to 64 years. *Addictive Behaviors, 30,* 77–88.

Whitbeck, L. B. and Hoyt, D. R. (1994). Social prestige and assortive mating: A comparison of students from 1956 and 1988. *Journal of Social and Personal Relationships, 11,* 137–145.

White, J. K., Hendrick, S. S. and Hendrick, C. (2004). Big-five personality variables and relationship constructs. *Personality and Individual Differences, 37,* 1519–1530.

WHOQOL Group (1995). The World Health Organization Quality of Life Assessment (WHOQOL): Position paper from the World Health Organization. *Social Science and Medicine, 41*(10), 1403–1409.

Wielebnowski, N. C. (1999). Behavioral differences as predictors of breeding status in captive cheetahs. *Zoo Biology, 18*, 335–349.

Willerman, L., Schultz, R., Rutledge, J. N. and Bigler, E. (1991). In vivo brain size and intelligence. *Intelligence, 15*, 223–228.

Williams, C. L. and Meck, W. H. (1991). The organizational effects of gonadal steroids on sexually dimorphic spatial ability. *Psychoneuroendocrinology, 16*, 155–176.

Williams, G. C., Grow, V. M., Freedman, Z. R., Ryan, R. M. and Deci, E. L. (1996). Motivational predictors of weight loss and weight-loss maintenance. *Journal of Personality and Social Psychology, 70*, 115–126.

Williams, W. M. (1998). Are we raising smarter children today? School- and home-related influence on IQ. In U. Neisser (ed.), *The rising curve: Long-term gains in IQ and related measures.* (pp. 125–154). Washington, DC: American Psychological Association.

Wilson, E. O. (1975). *Sociobiology: The new synthesis.* Cambridge, MA: Harvard University Press.

Wilson, E. O. (1978). *On human nature.* Cambridge, MA: Harvard University Press.

Wilson, G. D. (1973a). A dynamic theory of conservatism. In G. D. Wilson (ed.), *The psychology of conservatism* (pp. 257–265). London: Academic Press.

Wilson, G. D. (1973b). The psychology of conservatism. In G. D. Wilson (ed.), *The psychology of conservatism* (pp. 1–23). London: Academic Press.

Wilson, G. D. (1975). *Manual for the Wilson-Patterson Attitude Inventory.* Windsor: NFER.

Wilson, G. D. (1985). The 'catchphrase' approach to attitude measurement. *Personality and Individual Differences, 6*, 31–37.

Wilson, G. D. and Brazendale, A. H. (1973). Social attitude correlates of Eysenck's personality dimensions. *Social Behaviour and Personality, 1*, 115–118.

Wilson, G. D. and Patterson, G. (1968). A new measure of conservatism. *British Journal of Social and Clinical Psychology, 7*, 264–269.

Wilson, G. D., Ausman, J. and Mathews, T. R. (1973). Conservatism and art preferences. *Journal of Personality and Social Psychology, 25*, 286–288.

Wilson, K. and Gullone, E. (1999). The relationship between personality and affect over the lifespan. *Personality and Individual Differences, 27*, 1141–1156.

Winship, C. and Korenman, S. (1997). Does staying in school make you smarter? The effect of education on IQ in *The Bell Curve.* In B. Devlin, S. E. Fienberg and K. Roeder (eds), *Intelligence, genes, and success: Scientists respond to* The Bell Curve (pp. 215–234). New York: Springer.

Wirth, H. and Luttinger, P. (1998). Assortive mating by class. Patterns of association between husband's and wife's class in 1970 and 1993. *Kolner Zeitschrift für Soziologie und Sozialpsychologie, 50*, 47–57.

Wiseman, R. (2004). *The Luck Factor: Changing your luck, changing your life – the four essential principles.* New York: Hyperion.

Wiseman, R. and Watt, C. (2005). Measuring superstitious belief: Why lucky charms matter. *Personality and Individual Differences, 37*, 1533–1541.

Witt, L. A. and Beorkrem, M. (1989). Climate for creative productivity as a predictor of research usefulness and organizational effectives in a research and development organization. *Creativity Research Journal, 2*, 30–40.

Wong, M. M. H. (2000). The relations among causality orientations, academic experience, academic performance, and academic commitment. *Personality and Social Psychology Bulletin, 26*, 315–326.

Wood, A. M. and Joseph, S. (2007). Grand theories of personality cannot be integrated. *American Psychologist, 62*, 57–58.

Wood, E., Desmarais, S. and Gugula, S. (2002). The impact of parenting on gender-stereotyped toy play of children. *Sex Roles, 47*, 39–49.

Woodcock, R. W. and Johnson, M. B. (1978). *Woodcock–Johnson Psycho-Educational Battery.* Hingham, MA: Teaching Resources.

Woodcock, R. W. and Johnson, M. B. (1989). *Woodcock–Johnson Psycho-Educational Battery – Revised.* Chicago: Riverside.

Woodcock, R. W., McGrew, K. S. and Mather, N. (2001). *Woodcock–Johnson III Tests of Cognitive Abilities.* Itasca, IL: Riverside.

World Health Organization (1948). Preamble to the Constitution of the World Health Organization as adopted by the International Health Conference, New York, 19–22 June, 1946; signed on 22 July 1946 by the representatives of 61 States (Official Records of the World Health Organization, no. 2, p. 100) and entered into force on 7 April 1948.

Worthington, E. L. Jr (1998). An empathy–humility–commitment model of forgiveness applied within family dyads. *Journal of Family Therapy, 20*, 59–76.

Worthington, E. L. Jr (2001). *Five steps to forgiveness: The art and science of forgiving.* New York: Crown.

Wright, L. (1988). Type A behaviour patterns and coronary artery disease. *American Psychologist, 43*, 2–14.

Wulff, D. M. (1997). *Religion: Classic and contemporary* (Vol. 2). London: Wiley.

Wundt, W. (1874). *Grundzüge der Physiologischen Psychologie.*

Wylie, R. (1979). *The self-concept: Theory and research on selected topics* (Vol. II; rev. edn). Lincoln: University of Nebraska Press.

Yamhure-Thompson, L. and Snyder, C.R. (2003). Measuring forgiveness. In S. J. Lopez and C. R. Snyder (eds), *Positive psychological assessment: A handbook of models and measure.* Washington, DC: American Psychological Association.

Yamhure-Thompson, L., Snyder, C. R., Hoffman, L. *et al.* (2005). Dispositional forgiveness of self, others, and situations. *Journal of Personality, 73*, 313–359.

Yang, S. and Sternberg, R. J. (1997a). Conceptions of intelligence in ancient Chinese philosophy. *Journal of Theoretical and Philosophical Psychology, 17*, 101–119.

Yang, S. and Sternberg, R. J. (1997b). Taiwanese Chinese people's conceptions of intelligence. *Intelligence, 25*, 21–36.

Yang, X., Telama, R., Hirvensalo, M. *et al.* (2012). Leadership component of Type A behaviour predicts physical activity in early midlife. *International Journal of Behavioral Medicine, 19*, 48–55.

Yarnold, P. R., Mueser, K. T. and Grimm, L. G. (1985). Interpersonal domination of Type As in group discussions. *Journal of Abnormal Psychology, 94*, 233–236.

Yerkes, R. M. (1921). *Psychological examining in the United States Army: Memoirs of the National Academy of Sciences* (Vol. XV). Washington, DC: US Government Printing Office.

Ylostalo, P. V., Ek, E., Laitinen, J. and Knuutila, M. L. (2003). Optimism and life satisfaction as determinants for dental and general health behaviour – oral health habits linked to cardiovascular risk factors. *Journal of Dental Research, 82*, 194–199.

Yoder, J. D. and Kahn, A. S. (2003). Making gender comparisons more meaningful: A call for more attention to social context. *Psychology of Women Quarterly, 27*, 281–290.

Yule, W., Gold, R. D. and Busch, C. (1982). Long-term predictive validity of the WPPSI: An 11-year follow-up study. *Personality and Individual Differences, 3*, 65–71.

Yussen, S. R. and Kane, P. T. (1985). Children's conceptions of intelligence. In S. R. Yussen (ed.), *The growth of reflection in children* (pp. 207–241). Orlando, FL: Academic Press.

Zafra, E. L., Jimenez, M. I. and Espartal, N. R. (2008). Emotional intelligence and academic performance: An overview. *International Journal of Psychology, 3-4*, 793.

Zajonc, R. B. (1976). Family configuration and intelligence: Variations in scholastic aptitude scores parallel trends in family size and the spacing of children. *Science, 192*, 227–236.

Zajonc, R. B. and Markus, H. (1975). Birth order and intellectual development. *Psychological Review, 82*, 74–88.

Zanarini, M. C. and Frankenburg, F. R. (1997). Pathways to the development of borderline personality disorder. *Journal of Personality Disorders, 11*, 93–104.

Zanarini, M. C., Gunderson, J. G., Marino, M. F., Schwartz, E. O. and Frankenburg F. R. (1989). Childhood experiences of borderline patients. *Comprehensive Psychiatry, 30*, 18–25.

Zanarini, M. C., Frankenburg, F. R., Reich, D. B. *et al.* (2000). Biparental failure in the childhood experiences of borderline patients. *Journal of Personality Disorders, 14*, 264–273.

Zebb, B. J. and Moore, M. C. (2003). Superstitiousness and perceived anxiety control as predictors of psychological distress. *Journal of Anxiety Disorders, 17*, 115–130.

Zhang, H. and Wu, Z. (1994). A survey of the Beijing public's views on intelligence. *Psychological Science, 17*, 65–81.

Ziegler, D. J. and Hawley, J. L. (2001). Relation of irrational thinking and the pessimistic explanatory style. *Psychological Reports, 88*, 483–488.

Zill, N., Collins, M., West, J. and Hausken, E. G. (1995, December). School readiness and children's developmental status. *ERIC Digest* [Online]. Available at http://ceep.crc.uiuc.edu/eecearchive/digests/1995/zill95.html; accessed 10 August 2006.

Zimbardo, P. G. (1977). *Shyness: What it is, what to do about it.* Sydney: Addison-Wesley Publishing Company.

Zuckerman, M. (1991). *Psychobiology of personality.* Cambridge: Cambridge University Press.

Zuckerman, M., Kuhlman, D. M., Joireman, J., Teta, P. and Kraft, M. (1993). A comparison of three structural models for personality: The Big Three, the Big Five, and the Alternative Five. *Journal of Personality and Social Psychology, 65*, 757–768.

Zusne, L. and Jones, W. H. (1982). *Anomalistic psychology: A study of extraordinary phenomena and experience.* Hillsdale, NJ: Erlbaum.

INDEX

Page numbers in colour denote items from the online chapters (chapters 26, 27 and 28 at www.pearsoned.co.uk/maltby). **Emboldened** words denote glossary terms.